The Small Commercial Garden

HOW TO MAKE $10,000 A YEAR IN YOUR BACKYARD

by Dan Haakenson
The Gourmet Gardener

The Small Commercial Garden

How to Make $10,000 a Year in Your Backyard

Drawings by Dan Haakenson
Photography by Dan, Becky, and Julie Haakenson
Cover Photo: Photography by George Masseth Jr, Mandan, North Dakota
Cover design by Doug Yellowbird
Illustrations and cartoons by Tim Bumb
Printed by Richtman's Printing, Bismarck, North Dakota

Publisher's Cataloging in Publication

Haakenson, Dan
    The small commercial garden / Dan Haakenson.
    p. cm.
    Includes index.
    ISBN 0-9642861-0-6

    1. Truck farming. 2. Vegetable gardening.   I. Title.

SB321.H33 1995   635
                                            QBI94-21157

Published by
PC-Services
PO Box 7294
Bismarck, North Dakota 58507-7294

Table of Contents

Foreward by Ms. Sarah Vogel, North Dakota Commissioner of Agriculture ..4
Dedication 5
Preface 7
Acknowledgments 8

Part I - Commercial Gardening
1. Introduction 9
2. Commercial Gardening 15
3. Marketing 23
4. Commercial Design 39
5. Planning 53
6. Growing Transplants 65
7. Growing 79
8. Harvesting 93

Part II - Crop Recommendations
9. Recommended Crops 99
10. Beans 104
11. Cabbage 111
12. Carrots 119
13. Cucumbers 129
14. Onions 147
15. Peas 154
16. Peppers 157
17. Tomatoes 163
18. Zucchini 173
19. Other Crops 176

Part III - This Business of Gardening
20. This Business of Gardening 184

Annexes
Annex A - Newsletters and Brochures 193
Annex B - Footnotes 199

Index 203
Order form 207

Foreward

By Ms. Sarah Vogel
North Dakota Commissioner of Agriculture

Success in agriculture lies in the details, like applying the right amount of fertilizer, or choosing the right variety of cabbage for North Dakota. Sometimes a seemingly insignificant decision, such as when to plant, can mean the difference between a successful crop and a mediocre one. Unfortunately, there are so many details to learn that we often make mistakes. Some of these mistakes are caused by a lack of information. Others, however, are based upon assumptions that perhaps are not always true. For example, you may have always assumed that a career in agriculture was impossible, because you were not raised on a farm, or because your family doesn't have a thousand acres of farmland.

But suppose that assumption was wrong. Let's assume for a minute, that you could start with as little as a half-acre. Would you be interested in becoming a part of the agricultural community? Would you be interested in becoming "a farmer"? It is an exciting possibility, isn't it?

The ideas presented in this book open agriculture to thousands of families who have never considered the possibilities before, because they assumed they needed hundreds of acres, or millions of dollars worth of machinery. Dan explodes that assumption with a success story that could be repeated thousands of times across the countryside.

As the Commissioner of Agriculture I spend most of my time working with large farmers, and their complicated problems. I do that because of the enormous impact their problems have on the economy in North Dakota. But that does not diminish my interest in a local farmers market in Dickinson, or a roadside stand in Dawson. Because therein lies the independent, pioneering, entrepreneurial spirit that makes this country great. I believe that state government must foster and support that spirit, and encourage more people to get involved in agriculture, regardless of size. I am confident you will find that agricultural agencies across the nation share this obsession with service to the small, beginning member of our marvelous profession.

For the past several years I have cosponsored an important event in North Dakota called "Marketplace". We invite our best entrepreneurs to share ideas and solutions with ambitious people who have the courage and perseverance to try something new. One of our mottos is "Think big, start small, stay solvent." This book provides the details on starting small. If enough readers start small and stay solvent, the fresh fruits and vegetables they produce will have a very big impact on the quality of life in America. I wish you the best of luck as you begin your new career. And, remember! Success is in the details.

Dedication

This book is dedicated to my father, Melvin J. Haakenson, a lifelong resident of Maxbass, North Dakota.

When my father died a few years ago, I reflected upon the impact he had on my life. In many ways he wasn't a traditional father. He didn't teach me how to hunt and fish and he wasn't always at my basketball games. But Dad had this pile of junk, two acres of rusting machinery, old car bodies, and weathering wood. His 'culch' pile was our playground. We could drill holes, saw, weld, and pound nails into any piece in the pile. We made some wonderful things, a motor bike powered with a gasoline clothes washer engine. And there were failures. We cracked the engine of a '38 Plymouth because we neglected to put antifreeze in it. But the one memory that will remain forever is the '42 Ford with a Case combine engine.

My brother and I bought the Ford without a motor because Dad said we could use the engine from the recently scrapped combine. But installing the engine wasn't easy and it didn't work the first time. The chassis was too short. So we lengthened it. Then the motor wasn't parallel with the drive train. So we added a universal joint from a McCormick swather. Now the chassis was once again too short. So we lengthened it again. Finally it worked! We spent many happy, dusty hours on the back roads of Hastings Township, in a Dad-modified Ford, powered by J.I. Case.

What I learned from that project is much more important than the ability to shoot a duck or catch a fish. Dad and that '42 Ford taught me the importance of perseverance and the rewards of tenacity. I learned that if success doesn't happen with the first try, don't give up, just attack from another angle, with another idea.

From those childhood experiences I developed the freedom from the fear of failure. We fear failure because there are sometimes painful consequences. But on that culch pile there were few restrictions on what we could use and no consequences whatsoever for failure. If our project didn't work, we simply placed it back on the pile, to weather and rust with the rest of the junk. To be free from the fear of failure is a marvelous gift.

But an even greater gift is the freedom from the fear of trying. There are so many reasons not to try, and the possibility of failure is only one of them. Trying requires imagination, a vision, a dream.

Trying requires confidence in our capabilities to create, and a passion for the probability of success. Trying requires taking risks, becoming vulnerable, and making mistakes. There was no compelling reason to experiment with that pile of junk, nor was there any necessity. But the pile was there, a wonderful opportunity to create, to learn, and to try.

We started the Gourmet Garden because the opportunity was there, not because we were experienced gardeners with a strong vision of where we were going. We soon became fascinated with the possibilities. We experimented with ingenious solutions to problems. We rejected the idea that 'we can't do it that way because we haven't done it like that before.' Some of our innovations worked. Others were placed back on the pile, to weather and rust with the rest of the junk.

I hope you enjoy the freedom to try something new, because small commercial gardening requires a leap of faith into a sometimes confusing but fascinating world. But it's worth the risk, and the mistakes are not only survivable, they are a large part of the fun. And who knows? In the process, you might discover your '42 Ford, and the freedom that can come from a Case combine engine, the freedom from the fear of trying.

Author's Preface

I read dozens of gardening books as I prepared for a career as a commercial gardener. Many of these books discussed proper soil preparation, fertilization, how to start seeds, when to water, and when to harvest. But I couldn't find a book that explained how to start a small commercial garden. So I made notes as we plunged into the unknown, and recorded our mistakes and successes. This book is about that journey. Consequently, a few cautions are required.

• This is not a finished script. There are so many possibilities that we have not yet tried, and so many fine mistakes waiting to be made, we would be remiss to portray this as gardening gospel. Every year we make changes and discover a better way of doing things. And yes, we still make some new mistakes.

• The ideas presented here are not universally true. We have a short season, and a market that lasts only a few months. What works for us may not work in your situation. However, we do guarantee that at least a few of these ideas will work for you. Picking the right ones is your job.

• The book is not based upon research of other successful, commercial gardens. It is based on how we grow and sell fresh vegetables. Consequently, we assume that there might be better ways of doing some of the tasks presented here.

We believe there are many home gardeners who would like to become commercially profitable, but have not had the information that would convince them it is possible. We wrote this book because we believe a small commercial hobby gardener can become profitable, and still thoroughly enjoy the work of gardening and selling.

For those already involved in commercial farming and gardening, we offer ideas that will increase production and profits. Sometimes it's interesting to hear how other growers are doing things. If you have a better idea, we would love to hear from you.

Most books don't have the audacity to reveal mistakes, they just document the final conclusions, the successes. This one breaks the mold, and with a healthy mix of courage and insanity, we share it all. Life isn't long enough to make every mistake yourself. So we offer these pages to save you the time, expense, and embarrassment. But having said that, we hope you make a few colossal mistakes on your own, just to experience the thrill of learning. And most mistakes can be corrected, if not this season, there is always next year.

Good luck!

Acknowledgments

A project of this size cannot be completed without the help of family and friends. A warm thank you goes to the many people who have been instrumental in making this book happen.

First, my gratitude to my wife, Caroline, for her patience and understanding in the development of the garden over the past few years. And for accepting the pecking of the computer at odd hours of the night.

To my two daughters, Becky and Julie, who have been an important part of the garden from the start. Planting onions wasn't always on their short list of neat things to do, but they did it anyway. Their gregarious personalities have been indispensable in the development of loyal customers.

To Justin, and Stephanie, and Amy, and Stessa who helped make commercial gardening enjoyable with their willingness to work hard at the mundane job of growing and preparing vegetables for the market.

To the members of the Bismarck Farmers Market for providing the market that made it all possible. To Jerry Hegstad, a member of that market and my first mentor, who encouraged me to try commercial gardening. To Dann Knudsen, my favorite gardener, for his enthusiastic help with the greenhouse and marketing. And to our many customers without whom there would be no Gourmet Garden, and no "Small Commercial Garden".

To my brother, Dave, who applied the "Case combine" concept to publishing, and made me his newspaper publisher, with no other qualification than a willingness to try. This experience in the early 1970's made self-publishing this book possible.

To Ms. Sarah Vogel, North Dakota Commissioner of Agriculture for graciously agreeing to write the foreward. She has been a champion of the small farmer and gardener and works very hard to increase our marketing possibilities.

To Tim Bumb for the illustrations and cartoons. It isn't easy to make vegetables funny, but Tim has that unique sense of humor that makes it possible. And enjoyable.

To Don Baglien, a superb 'detail' reader, for the final proofreading and editing. His experience with the Mouse River Farmers Press came in handy.

And finally, to my coworkers at the North Dakota Army National Guard who have tolerated tall tales of garden production, and shared the struggles of writing and publishing a book.

Part I - Commercial Gardening

Chapter One

Introduction

Gardening is the most popular hobby in America. This book will show you how to supplement your income with this hobby you enjoy. We will demonstrate how to grow large quantities of produce on a small plot, and how to market that produce at a profit.

One word of caution. If you do not enjoy hard physical labor, or if you think you will get rich quickly with a small commercial garden, then please put this book away, and look for something else to occupy your time. Any successful garden, hobby or commercial, requires a commitment to long hours of hard work. The ideas presented in this book do not reduce that requirement.

COMMONLY ASKED QUESTIONS

So if it is so much hard work, why did we start a commercial garden? When customers tour our garden, this question doesn't come up as often as it should. People often ask how we got started, but seldom wonder why. But as you read this book about how, you need to ask yourself why. I can't answer that for you. I can only suggest some possible answers to this question and answers to a few other questions that might concern you.

What is a commercial garden?

I suppose there are many home gardeners who have accepted money from a neighbor who insisted upon paying them something for their work. Accepting money does not make your hobby a commercial enterprise. You become a commercial gardener when you *expect* customers to pay for your produce. When you have done this, you have established a market. It's all wrapped up in this one word, marketing, regardless of how simple or complex your methods might be, you expect to be paid.

That's no small step. It involves a host of life-style changes. So why would we choose to make

Market gardening is undergoing a revival because it is profitable. Many growers today are making most, if not all, of their family's income from small acreages planted in high-dollar crops that can be sold directly to consumers in the cities.

Lynn Byczynski[1]

9

the traumatic transition from a comfortable hobby garden to a sometimes chaotic commercial venture?

WHY?

For me it was a hobby that got out of hand. Badly! I didn't start out with concise objectives, nor with a well-designed comprehensive plan. Instead, I just added a little at time, without thinking much about what would happen next. It was fun, and I enjoyed the journey. That's a horrible answer, but it is honest. There are, however, several legitimate reasons that you might consider.

I enjoy gardening. This is not a reason for a life-style change, but a prerequisite. There is no requirement to increase the size of your garden. You can continue to enjoy gardening on a small scale. To justify the transition to a large garden, there must be other reasons. However, if you do not enjoy planting, watering, harvesting, and the hundreds of other required tasks, commercial gardening becomes a job to be endured, a season that must be survived.

I want to be in business for myself. The entrepreneur thing. The independence thing. These forces are real. Don't underestimate the power of these motivational elements. I believe of all of the factors that drove me (and I use that word for good reason) to commercial gardening, these were probably the strongest.

I want to learn a skill, become an expert. Being labeled an expert happens automatically because you are expected to be an expert once you become a commercial gardener, even if you are in the early stages of production. This creates several problems. There are hundreds of book written about various aspects of gardening. It is a very large body of

knowledge. No one can be an expert in all of it. We are very good at what we do, but if you ask me about a shrub, I can't help you. We are delighted to share the expertise we have, but we are also very quick to admit to our limitations.

There is tremendous satisfaction in developing gardening skills and making them profitable. Experts claim that job satisfaction is more important to most people than the compensation they receive. In retrospect, this 'why' has been the most rewarding.

I need to make money. This is most likely the primary motivation for most of us. However, there is a big difference between the desire to make money and the need to make money. If commercial gardening is to be a large part of your livelihood, two adjustments are necessary. First, you need to look beyond your back yard. Several acres would be necessary to assure an adequate income. Second, you might need to consider multiple markets to be able to sell the quantities raised on several acres.

Can I finance expansion with my profits?

When the need for money is the primary objective, it is tempting to spend our profits rather than reinvesting them in the business. We were able to develop advanced growing systems because we did not need to live from the profits from the garden. For several years, we reinvested everything. Without that financial flexibility, we probably would not have been able to afford the many mistakes it took to design the techniques that finally worked for us.

You have an advantage, of course, in that you have the benefits of our mistakes. However, there is still considerable investment in-

Good ideas are common; the people who can implement them are rare. Passion, choice, and a deep knowledge are the key characteristics behind virtually every entrepre-neur's success.

Jon P. Goodman[2]

10

volved, and if you do not have the money to do everything at once, reinvestment of profits will be required over the first few years. Otherwise, maximum profits will never be achieved.

Is my yard large enough?

Our subtitle promises profits from your backyard. We believe the following backyards qualify:

• The home owner with an acre or more. These larger lots are available around most major cities. This is the ultimate arrangement, where the garden is large enough to enjoy the economies of scale required for profitable commercial gardening, and close enough to be an efficient use of leisure time.

• The home owner whose property lies adjacent to farmland. My brother lives on the edge of a small town in western Minnesota. His lot touches some of the richest farmland in the country. If he could arrange a long-range rental agreement with the local farmer, he could justify the time and money spent to develop his garden.

• The owner of an adjacent city lot. If you purchase a home with commercial gardening in mind, it might be possible to purchase two lots and use the extra space for the garden. Taxes and zoning restrictions might restrict the use of this option in some areas.

• Rental of farmland is a fourth option. It has the potential disadvantages of travel and security, but still might be viable under the right circumstances. A long-range lease would be required to justify the capital improvements made to the property.

DISCLAIMER

We guarantee nothing in this book except that the techniques work for us. To guarantee they will work for you is to ignore the dramatic differences in growing conditions and markets. We recommend you try those ideas that you think will work. If they do not work, discard them, and try something else.

THE IMPORTANCE OF LOCATION

This book is not based upon research from across America. It is a personal documentary about one garden in north Bismarck, North Dakota. We do not profess to publish universal truths. We are simply reporting what has worked for us. Consequently, there are four factors that must be considered as you adjust this information to your location.

What can you grow?

Most of the vegetables mentioned in this book can be grown anywhere. However, you will probably need to adjust the varieties for your climate and growing conditions.

When can you grow it?

A much larger adjustment will be required here. Our entire system is predicated upon being the first grower to the market with tomatoes and cucumbers. First to market in Zone 3 is too late in Zone 5.

Your market possibilities

Markets can vary from complete saturation to no competition at all. There are sections of the country that have a very mature fresh produce direct marketing system. Entering

If there's one thing we've learned at the National Gardening Association, it's that there is no one correct way to garden. There are as many ways to garden as there are varieties of seeds and gardeners to grow them. No one of them is best for every gardener in every location at all times.

Charles Scott[3]

these markets might be very difficult because most niche markets are already covered, and standard products are in adequate supply. There may already be growers that are successfully working the early tomato and cucumber markets.

On the other hand, there are also large sections of the country that have no direct marketing of produce at all. Customers rely solely on the supermarkets for fresh produce. This presents opportunities, but not without challenges. Creating new markets is sometimes difficult because you must change well entrenched purchasing habits.

Bismarck provided a market that was well-established, but not saturated. With aggressive marketing we were able to sell our produce within the existing farmers markets system. We believe this will be the most prevalent condition across the country in larger population centers. Markets have been established, but there is room for innovation and

quality marketing. If you enter this market, there are a two additional factors that must be considered.

Determine the nature of the competition. Competition among growers is usually a friendly affair. Prices are maintained until supplies reach an intolerable level. Only then are prices reduced to move produce. If severe price cutting is the norm, you might wish to consider looking for another market.

Determine the market attitude towards new growers. Customers have become accustomed to having many choices at the supermarkets. We believe that farmers market customer numbers will increase in direct proportion to the number of growers at the market. In other words, if we offer more choices, we attract more customers. There are those that disagree and discourage new growers from joining our market.

The Home Garden issue

North Dakota is a very rural community. Though fewer and fewer of us are involved in farming, many of us came from there. Consequently, there is a tremendous interest in gardening, probably because of these roots from the soil. Therefore, in North Dakota, home gardening is the primary factor in the length of the farmers market season.

When home gardens produce heavily, home gardeners give their extra produce away and our primary market is over by the end of August. We cannot compete with such philanthropy. Fortunately, most home gardeners need almost perfect weather to attain 'giveaway' production. In the past four years, only two seasons provided such weather, the other two were disasters. If home gardens do not produce, our market remains strong into October.

You may not be faced with this source of competition. There are sections of the country where home gardens are not a significant factor. If that is the case, your marketing strategy can be adjusted to a longer, more stable season and early production may not be as critical.

FOR THE HOME GARDENER

A special message to those who decide to remain hobby gardeners.

For most gardeners, this is the right decision, because the transition to commercial gardening requires a list of conditions that doesn't exist for most people. However, there are still many commercial techniques described in this book that can be used to great advantage by the home gardener. I list them here in the order I believe they will make your more productive.

Raised beds. This one baffles me. I do not understand why raised beds are not standard practice throughout the country. There are so many overwhelming advantages. And the only disadvantage is the few hours it takes to construct the bed.

Drip irrigation. This is the only irrigation method that will insure an adequate and consistent water supply.

Protective plastic. Most home gardeners relish the thought of being the first garden on the block to pick a ripe tomato or slicing cucumber. This can be done consistently with the use of protective plastic as described in this book.

Trellises. Growing vertically creates opportunities for increasing production in a limited space.

Plastic mulching. This conserves water, and warms the soil earlier in the spring.

Composting. We have developed methods of composting that can

THE VIDEO

Throughout the book you will encounter references to our video. Books have limitations that a video tape does not. We can write many pages trying to describe how to construct a cucumber trellis. We can add a few pictures, and you may get the general idea. But a five-minute video quickly answers all questions, and the procedure becomes absolutely clear. For that reason, we recommend that you purchase the video if you are serious about implementing the more complicated techniques presented in this book. The video can be ordered from PC-Services, PO Box 7294, Bismarck, ND 58507-7294 or by calling 1-800-871-4296. An order form is provided on page 207.

be used for grass clippings.

A greenhouse. For the serious home gardener, we provide details on how to build and operate a small greenhouse.

SOURCES

Annex B provides explanations for the numerous quotations and footnotes scattered throughout the book. The following list is intended as a great place to start your commercial gardening library.

Newsletters

Small-Scale Agriculture today. The Office For Small Scale Agriculture prints a quarterly newsletter that often contains new information on sources, meetings, laws and regulations, and research. To get on the mailing list, send your name and address to: Office for Small Scale

Agriculture, Aerospace Building Room 342, 14th and Independence Ave SW, Washington DC 20250-2200

Growing for Market. A monthly newsletter written for the small direct marketer. It is published by growers who are still actively engaged in the business of direct marketing fruits, flowers, and vegetables. Subscriptions are $26 per year and can be ordered from Fairplain Publications, PO Box 3747, Lawrence, KA 66046.

Books

These five references will provide you with the additional information you need to make your gardening decisions. All five are generally available at larger bookstores

High Yield Gardening. Written by Marjorie Hunt and Brenda Bortz and published in 1986 by Rodale Press. This book provides detailed information for growing large amounts of vegetables in a small area.

Gardening. Published in 1985 by Addison-Wesley and written by the staff of the National Gardening Association. This is one of the best in-depth books on individual vegetables.

The New Seed Starters Handbook. Written by Nancy Bubel and published by Rodale Press. It is an important reference for any greenhouse operations.

The New Organic Gardening Encyclopedia. Published by Rodale Press in 1992. It is a marvelous reference for introductory material on any topic related to gardening. However, it does not have the space to provide detailed information on any topic.

The ORTHO Home Gardener's Problem Solver. The book is based on the *Professional Problem Solver* you find at many fine hardware and garden stores. It is the most comprehensive pest control book on the market and can be found at most large bookstores.

Magazines

Magazines provide current information and ideas on improving production. Most of these are available at your local newsstand.

Back issues are made more useful by an index published by CompuDex Press, PO Box 27041, Kansas City, MO 64110. If you have a library of gardening magazines, this index is a tremendous help in locating articles of interest.

Gardening. Published by the National Gardening Association every other month. Its strength is the depth of its feature articles. The articles provide a fairly even split between flowers and vegetables.

Organic Gardening. Published nine times a year by Rodale Press, this magazine is devoted to all aspects of organic production with an emphasis on vegetables. It has a delightfully entertaining style while providing the latest organic growing information.

Fine Gardening. Published by Tauton Press six times a year with an emphasis on flowers. The articles are well researched and written.

Horticulture. Published ten times each year by Horticulture, Inc. This publication also leans towards flowers, but usually has at least one major article on vegetable or fruit production.

Flower and Garden. Published six times a year by KC Publishing. The best recommendation I can give you is to give it a try and see if you like it. Of all of the magazines, a subscription to this one is the least expensive. Well worth a try.

Chapter Two

Commercial Gardening

We begin our introduction to commercial gardening by exploding a few popular misconceptions.

GARDENING MYTHS

Myth #1. *A commercial gardener must farm many acres to be profitable.*

An acre contains 43,560 square feet. Our garden has 9246 square feet in actual production or less than 1/4 acre. Add space for paths and our garden is still smaller than 1/2 acre. And we are profitable. Next year we will achieve our gross income goal of $2 per square foot, or $18,492.

The garden model described in chapter four is 112' by 116', 12,992 square feet, or less then 3/10 of an acre. We project sales of $12,000, a net income of over $10,000, and an average return of $2.25 per square foot of growing space. This estimate is based upon actual recent returns from the crops suggested for this model.

Myth #2. *Home gardening experience is necessary.*

Experience certainly helps, but careful research, a willingness to take risks, and hard work quickly compensate for a lack of knowledge. Sometimes inexperience can be an advan-

tage because it eliminates the "we've never done it that way before" attitude. Consequently, we try something new because we don't know better, and learning occurs through this constant experimentation.

Our two previous attempts at gardening were failures; one on a sand pile west of Maxbass, North Dakota, and the other on a shaded city lot. In both cases we were frustrated because we made fundamental mistakes. We didn't take the time to research the problems or ask the right questions of the right people.

We started gardening in our present location in 1985 and sold our first produce four years later. This garden succeeded because we provided adequate time and money, and we were persistent in researching and solving problems.

Myth #3. *All experts agree on the best way to garden.*

Give me an expert that advises planting tomatoes horizontally and I will show you one that considers this technique a waste of time. Show me research that praises a particular tomato variety and I will provide data that suggests otherwise. The diversity of gardening environments and the interdependency among options

I disagree with those who say we have too many farmers. We have too many farmers trying to produce the same things in the same ways.
  Jim Hightower[1]

2-1. The Start. 1989. Is experience necessary? This is how we started at our first farmers market in 1989. And we sold it all! But who could resist the big smiles and red bandannas?

We must design gardening systems that compliment our climate, soil, and resources. We must experiment until we find techniques that work for our unique environment.

makes guaranteed gardening impossible.

If experts do not agree, if there are no guaranteed gardening practices, how should we garden? We must design gardening systems that compliment our climate, soil, and resources. We must experiment until we find techniques that work for our unique environment.

You may choose to start with the information presented in this book. But please do not stop there. You must continue to experiment and adjust to new information and experiences. For that reason, we include the process of experimentation throughout the book, so you can learn not only from the conclusions that we have drawn, but also from mistakes we made in the process.

Myth #4. *Commercial gardening is more difficult than hobby gardening.*

In many ways commercial gardening is easier, there is just more of it. The commercial gardener experiences tremendous economies of scale. We devote an entire raised bed to a single crop so we can adjust soil pH, fertilizer, and water to meet the specific needs of the crop. A home gardener grows crops with different growing requirements in a small area, providing challenges unknown to the commercial gardener.

STRATEGIES FOR SUCCESS

Most of us define success as the achievement of our goals. A home gardener may consider himself a success when produce is fresh, varied, abundant and early. That was his intent when he planted the garden, and he has achieved his objective. Defining success for a small commercial gardener is a bit more difficult because there are more options, more combinations of elements. When defining our objectives we must consider the following:

Time. How much time are we willing to devote to our commercial garden? A retired executive, for example, may consider commercial gardening as a productive use of time because he enjoys the work. A busy accountant, on the other hand, might have limited time, and define success as maximum profits from minimum time.

Capital. A shortage of money limits our options. We may not be able to purchase a greenhouse or install trellises. This grower with a shortage of cash may define success as maximum profits from minimum expenses, because capital is not available.

Space. A grower with 40 acres doesn't consider space a limiting factor. This grower may define success as maximum profits from a minimum of labor because time is short, but space is plentiful.

Profit. Some growers are unconcerned with profits because it is truly a hobby, and they enjoy the work. They may consider their endeavors as an important contribution to the community.

Once we have defined our objectives, we develop strategies to provide the details for our business plan. The plan provides direction and focus. To understand the remainder of this book, you must understand our strategy, our business plan. We define success as maximum profits from minimum space. We are willing to provide whatever capital and labor are necessary to assure this success. Lets look at each element of this strategy.

Maximum profits. This requires that we market to retail customers. This strategy drives our obsession with aggressive retail marketing, the focus on the early market, and the focus on profitable vegetables. If our objective was maximum production, we could sell to wholesale accounts.

Minimum space. This is the central concept for our strategy, driving the intensive gardening part of our operation. If space was not an issue, we could achieve maximum profits in many different ways. Interplanting and double-cropping would not be necessary. We could plant potatoes, corn, melons, and squash.

Provide capital and labor. We do not work at commercial gardening full time. However, our current jobs do allow sufficient time to garden. That could change. Then labor could become a problem. We might need to hire additional help, or change our objective, or change our business plan.

There are many possible combinations of the elements that make up a commercial garden business plan. You will most likely use selected pieces of the plan that follows. That is as it should be. Because this works for us does not mean it will work for you. But the discussion that follows provides a solid starting point.

MARKET AGGRESSIVELY

We believe customers want garden fresh fruits and vegetables, but they want the produce sold like a supermarket. Farmers market customers are sophisticated and sometimes very demanding. The vendor that satisfies these demands will sell quickly and profitably. The days of dirty vegetables and rickety sales tables are over.

Provide a professional marketing environment

We use a brightly painted, custom-built stand with three hanging scales for weighing vegetables. Prices are clearly marked, signs advertise our merchandise, and all produce is clean and attractively displayed. We use plastic bags conveniently located for self-serve operations. Please take another look at the picture on the front cover. Notice the striking color contrast between the vegetables and the yellow boxes. The hanging scale and the handy roll of plastic bags are clear indications of our focus on customer service.

During the rush season we have as many as five people working to provide quick service, to those customers who must return to work or wish to purchase other items at the market that we do not provide. We use battery-operated printing calculators so customers can be assured they are not overcharged.

Sell only your best quality produce

It is painful to throw out perfectly good, but slightly damaged produce. However, it is necessary. Nothing disturbs a customer more than damaged produce. They will remember where they bought it and will remain reluctant to return.

Farms in metropolitan areas, which comprise only 16 percent of U.S. land area, account for more than two-thirds of fruit and vegetable sales. Yet faced with urban development pressures, future small-scale farmers must become involved with specialized intensive production systems.

Bud Kerr, Jr.[2]

2-2. Raised Beds.
We use two types of raised beds. The beds in the foreground are unsupported beds with sloping sides. They are very economical to build but more space is lost to the pathway.
The beds in the background are supported beds, constructed with treated lumber. They are quite expensive but esthetically pleasing.

Both types of beds are seven feet apart. The difference is that the unsupported beds have about 38 inches in production, the supported beds have 48 inches.

Guarantee your produce

We bag all of our produce and include a written money-back guarantee. If a customer is dissatisfied in any way, they do not need to return the merchandise, just mention what was wrong, and we will replace it with fresh vegetables or return their money.

Develop an obsession with service

Customer service is such a simple concept. Find out what the customer wants and give it to them. The problem is that customers want different things. Some want mild onions, some strong. Some want low prices, others want to make a purchase as quickly as possible, regardless of price. We do our best to get to know our customers and cater to their individual needs.

This policy goes beyond friendliness and courtesy. If a customer comes to our stand with vegetables from other vendors, we offer them a large bag with handles to carry it all to their car. We try to give them a reason to come back.

GARDEN INTENSIVELY

Intensive gardening means growing maximum quantities in minimum space. This is particularly important to the urban gardener with limited space. Intensive gardening also means we attempt to control as much of the growing process as possible, to mitigate the effects of weather extremes.

Raised beds

There are many advantages to raised beds.

Good drainage. Most crops require well-drained soil for maximum production. This was demonstrated dramatically in 1993 as Bismarck was deluged with record rainfall during July. Many growers had crops standing in water, but our crops were dry due to the raised beds and the gentle slope of the garden.

Warms earlier in the spring. The spring sun shines on the side of the raised beds and warms them earlier than flat fields. This allows us a better chance at the critical early market.

Easier to work. You perhaps wouldn't think the 6-8 inch rise would make it easier to work the beds, but it is much easier on the back. It is even possible to sit at times while weeding.

Reduced compaction. Since we seldom have to walk on the bed, there is no compaction during the growing season, and we provide a healthier growing environment for our vegetables.

Esthetics. Properly constructed raised beds make an esthetically pleasing garden. This is important to growers who may have reluctant neighbors.

There are also disadvantages to raised beds.

Labor intensive to construct. This is a onetime requirement and well worth the trouble.

More difficult to cultivate. When cultivating a flat garden you can start at one end and cultivate the entire patch. With raised beds you must carefully cultivate each one.

More difficult to clean in the fall. On a large, flat garden, residue can be tilled into the soil. This is very difficult with raised beds because of the volume of residue that must be tilled into a very small area.

Use wide rows

Now that the hard work of raising our beds is finished, it would be wasteful to plant just a single or double row down the middle of the bed. Instead, we plant wall-to-wall. Again there are many advantages.

Increased production. We plant 14 rows of carrots, and 7-9 rows of onions on a single raised bed.

Less movement. This seems like a small thing, but when the garden is in full production, every saved step is energy we can use for something productive.

Easier weeding. Closely spaced plants create a natural shading which reduces weed growth. In addition, weeding nine rows at a time is much easier than moving between seven single rows.

Speeds harvesting. When we can dig 14 rows of carrots at once, it takes only a fraction of the time to chase down separate rows.

Simplifies watering. With a well mulched row and drip irrigation, we can water the entire bed with a single irrigation line.

Provides a living mulch. This reduces evaporation and assists in weed control.

Use drip irrigation

Drip irrigation is any system that allows the water to seep from a hose laying on the ground without getting the leaves wet. Advantages to drip irrigation are:

Saves water. Since we only water those parts of the garden in production, we do not waste water on paths and other non-producing areas.

Fertilization. A simple plumbing addition to the water system makes applying water soluble fertilizer possible.

Precise control of water volume. With a little practice it is possible to calculate water volumes accurately.

There are also disadvantages:

High initial costs. A system worth having is expensive. The better ones are guaranteed for ten years or more so the initial expense can be spread over many years.

Maintenance takes time. We pull the tubing each fall and set it out again in the spring. Emitters must be checked periodically for plugging.

Root development. If we over water, roots may not stretch out to find water, thereby reducing their ability to pull nutrients from the soil. This may cause stunted growth and decreased production.

Grow vertically

Cucumbers, peas and beans grow well on trellises. This saves precious horizontal space and increases total production.

Interplant

Again, the options are limited but worthwhile. We interplant dill with onions; pole beans with bush beans; and peas with cabbage and lettuce.

GROW THE RIGHT VEGETABLES IN THE RIGHT QUANTITIES

If we can produce for the early market, the optimum mix is one-third of the garden into tomatoes, one-third in cucumbers, and one-third in crops chosen to draw customers into the stand. Cucumbers and tomatoes are our profit crops. There are many

Successful entrepreneurs don't have failures. They do have learning experiences.

Jon P. Goodman[3]

19

This picture was taken two years before we started selling commercially. We were already experimenting and making mistakes. These trellises were made from treated 4x4s. I'm sure they could have survived a hurricane. They were also placed on the side of the bed instead of in the middle. That restricted our use to only one side of the trellis.

markets when tomatoes and cucumber draw customers into our stand. However, diversity is necessary because customers want other crops. When tomatoes and cukes are plentiful, we need other produce to draw customers to our stand to purchase those two profit crops. The following crops are listed in the order of their ability to draw customers to the stand.

Onions - Our niche crop. We grow Walla Walla onions, the mildest variety that can be grown in our area. We have developed a reputation for these onions, and enjoy a growing clientele that comes to our stand to purchase them.

Carrots - A tremendous draw because you cannot purchase carrots of this quality at the supermarket. However, carrots are profitable only if double-cropping or interplanting is possible.

Beans and peas- Excellent drawing power, particularly if beans are picked small and peas are picked for eating raw. They are profitable only when interplanted with other crops.

Peppers - Excellent profit per plant. Very solid early market, with consistent demand throughout the season, especially if the fruits are large and straight.

Zucchini - Consistent seller if small. Very profitable, almost as good as tomatoes but with a limited market.

Cabbage - A staple crop, sells consistently throughout the season. This crop does not have much drawing power. We grow it because it interplants well with the peas and beans.

We also grow cut flowers because we believe this niche crop will draw almost as well as onions and carrots.

There are two phases to commercial gardening that pertain to the selection of crops and varieties. The *development phase* must focus on learning how to grow and market the standard crops mentioned in the previous paragraphs. These crops represent most of the potential income for any market gardener regardless of experience or location. A beginner must concentrate on doing this phase properly.

The *diversification phase* involves adding varieties for the purpose of attracting customers. Diversity provides challenges that a beginning commercial gardener should not consider. However, as we become competent growers of basic produce, we must begin to attract customers that want more exotic vegetables and a greater variety of the standards.

The diversification phase is possible only after we have developed our production and marketing systems, and have the experience to manage harvesting small quantities of specialty items. This is no small task.

If we choose to grow twenty varieties of tomatoes or peppers, each variety must be kept separate at every stage of production, from sowing of the seed to selling of the fruit. Harvesting is the most challenging task because of the tremendous time constraints, and the need to prepare small quantities of each variety for market. Marketing is complicated because of the necessity to keep the varieties separate. We may also loose sales because customers expect a specific variety. If we have sold out of their usual choice, they may not purchase an alternate variety.

However, it is this capability that separates the beginners from the established, experienced market gardeners. The principle advantage is the development of long-range loyal customers that will return to your stand year after year because you grow those special items they want. The secret is to ask them what they want, and then give it to them. They will be yours forever.

FOCUS ON THE EARLY MARKET

'Early market' does not refer to the first few weeks of the season. It refers to being the first grower to bring tomatoes and cucumbers to the market. Early tomatoes bring $2 per pound as compared to 33¢ - 50¢ per pound for canners. Early cucumbers are worth 33¢ - 50¢ each versus 10¢ - 20¢ each later in the season. Our objective is to have two to three weeks of tomato and cucumber sales before quantities bring prices down. It is more difficult to produce for the early market, but well worth the effort. This part of our strategy requires more capital than any other element.

Grow transplants

We set out plants that are several weeks larger than those normally available. These larger plants provide a two to three week head start on the market. We also plant three times as many plants as we need, and select only the best.

Provide plant protection

Protective cloches on cucumbers pay off handsomely. We wrap our tomato and pepper cages in plastic and cover the top with spun fabric. This creates a small greenhouse for the cool spring weather.

We use black plastic mulch to warm the soil in the spring and provide extra warmth to those heat-loving plants.

DEVELOP A NICHE MARKET

A niche is something you do better than anyone else because you devote the time and effort to do it well. You focus on it, and draw attention to it. It becomes your primary draw.

We are currently working on two niche markets and, at present, only one is working. We stumbled into onions. We started growing Walla Walla onions from seed and soon discovered that no one in the market was doing that on any scale. They started to sell well, and we expanded production. The secret to a mild onion is plenty of water. Because of our drip irrigation system, we are able to provide the quantities of water required to keep the onion mild even during extreme heat.

Our second niche market is flowers. Although there are some flowers at the market, no grower specializes in sufficient varieties to

2-4. Early mistakes. We were convinced from the very beginning that early marketing was the secret to profits. However, some of our early attempts to achieve that goal were disasters. The frame at right was a complicated design that lost out to the power and persistence of the North Dakota wind.

2-5. The green-house. A greenhouse is critical for success at the early market. This simple lean-to design is very economical to construct. This one has a fiberglass roof and glass windows. However, plastic can be used to minimize cost.

Small acreage doesn't mean small profits. Well-run compact farms can generate surprising gross incomes. And net income can be a real eye-opener.

Gary Acuff [4]

---

create a niche. We have people coming to market just to purchase our onions. That is not true of flowers. Sales are erratic and unpredictable. However, information from other markets indicates that our perseverance will pay off.

In review, our garden is driven by these principles:

Focus on the early market. This principle drives our planning process and determines what we grow and when we plant.

Garden intensively. This principle determines the methods we use to achieve our minimum space objective.

Grow the right vegetables in the right quantities. This is the first of three principles directed towards marketing.

Develop a niche market. This principle acknowledges the necessity to attract customers and that we must compete with other growers.

Market aggressively. This principle drives our obsession with service and our extensive marketing program.

DEVELOPING STRATEGIES

These five principles define the strategy used to achieve our objectives. Your strategy, your business plan may look very different from ours because your situation is differ-

ent. We recommend, however, that you consider each element in our plan, compare it with your environment, and accept it or reject it based upon how it fits your objectives.

To develop your strategy, start with the answers to these basic questions. Then expand them into a comprehensive plan for your business.

• Define your objectives. What do you want the garden to do for you? Is profit important?

• Define the resources you are willing to commit to the business. What time, money, and space is available to you?

• Define your marketing method. Wholesale or retail? Farmers market, roadside stand, or other marketing alternative?

• Determine if you want to focus on the early market. This is critical because so many other decisions are based upon this one.

• Define your gardening methods. How will you irrigate? Will you use raised beds and trellises? Which crops you will grow?

Once these questions are answered, expand this into a complete plan that includes the following:

• A prioritized list of tasks that need to be accomplished.

• A list of materials and services that must be purchased.

• A time line of when tasks and purchases must be accomplished and who will do them. This is project management, and is the culmination of your planning process.

The remainder of the book will build upon the principles discussed in this chapter. We will share the mistakes and successes that led us to the conclusions we have drawn, so you can decide which of these principles belong in your "strategy for success."

Chapter Three
Marketing

We start with marketing because it is where you must start.

FINDING A MARKET

If you do not have a market, there is no reason to grow any more produce than you can use yourself. Find your market first, then design and build your garden. Finding a market may be easier than you think. Our experience indicates a large market for fresh vegetables remains unserviced. All you need is a small piece of the following possibilities:

Wholesale marketing

> Florists
> Grocery stores
> Restaurants

Direct marketing

> Retail
>> Farmers markets
>> On-farm sales
>> Roadside stand
>> Home delivery
>> Pick-your-own
>> Entertainment agriculture
>> Mail-order
> Subscriptions
>> Community Supported
>> Subscription services

Your market choice must be made early in the planning process because these decisions affect many other aspects of the plan.

The first decision is whether to sell produce directly to the customer, or sell it wholesale to restaurants, supermarkets, and florists. With the right products, wholesaling may be a viable option, particularly if you have no interest or patience for constant customer contact. Marketing costs are minimal and advertising is not required because name recognition is not an issue.

Wholesale marketing

In many ways wholesale marketing is much easier than direct marketing. You establish a relationship with the produce buyer, and you deliver according to his needs. However, you take a cut in price for this convenience.

We have not tried wholesaling because we enjoy direct marketing. However, for those who do not have the time or interest for retail marketing this is a very viable option. Wholesale prices are lower, but so are your marketing costs. We recommend the following:

3-1. Customer Service. We work at it! Here Julie helps a customer bag produce to make his trip to the market more enjoyable, even though most of it was purchased from other vendors.

• *Quality is still critical.* Produce buyers demand the same quality as retail customers. In your initial conversation, establish these standards, and then adhere to them religiously.

• *Delivery is even more important.* A restaurant or grocery store depends on your delivery schedule. Nothing will sour a relationship faster than missing delivery dates and quantities.

• *Don't try to compete with national markets.* If you grow the same onion that can be imported for 15¢ per pound, the buyer has no reason to pay you any more than that. Instead, grow a mild onion that cannot be purchased on the open market. The retail outlet can charge more because it is a better onion. In turn, you will get a better price.

• *Don't give your produce away.* Many buyers will attempt to get your produce as cheaply as possible because this increases their profits. Learn how to negotiate. If you have a quality product, they will be willing to adjust prices.

• *Lock in your market before you sow a single seed.* This principle should never be violated. I'm not talking about signed contracts, although that would be nice. I'm talking about solid commitments from buyers to purchase most of the produce you plan to sell. If you cannot arrange that, don't plant anything.

The secret to wholesale marketing is the relationships you develop with the produce buyers. They must learn to trust your ability to deliver produce as promised. If you cannot deliver, you must give them sufficient lead time so they can find another supplier. If you do not give them this time, you have lost your credibility as a dependable source of produce.

Constant communications is necessary. Talk to them, and they will be willing to work with you. They understand the hazards and tentative nature of vegetable production. They just require adequate notice of delivery problems.

Direct marketing

Direct marketing requires more time but is potentially more profitable. Onions that sell for 60¢ per pound retail, will only bring 15¢-30¢ at wholesale markets. However, direct marketing also requires more work and a broader range of marketing skills.

Direct marketing can be further divided into two categories, subscription sales and retail.

Subscription marketing also subdivides in two ways, by the degree of commitment from the customer, and who shares the risks. In subscription marketing, produce is sold prior to production. The two categories are:

Community Supported Agriculture (CSA). Customers join the CSA and for a set fee, often paid in advance, the farmer agrees to supply vegetables throughout the season. Families become partners and the risk is spread throughout the customer base. This provides some income protection for the grower and assures families delivery of the types and qualities of produce they want. Additional produce diversity is required in a CSA because customers have some control over what is planted. Delivery varies from farm pickup to home delivery. Some patrons may trade work for produce.

Subscription services. A subscription service differs from a CSA in that customers pay as they go. There may be a membership fee that is paid up-front as a commitment to the grower but there is no sharing of risks. If a hailstorm wipes out the crop, that loss is borne by the grower. Marketing plans vary from families filling out weekly orders, to automatic delivery of produce available on a given day. Delivery varies from farm backup to home delivery. Customers may pay upon delivery or be billed monthly.

Retail marketing

Retail sales options involve only two issues, location and who harvests the produce. In retail sales, produce is sold when it is delivered to market. Prices are usually close to supermarket prices.

On-farm sales. Customers come directly to the garden to purchase produce. Hours may be posted but often they are not and the garden is always open. Disruptions may be almost constant, and it may be difficult to get anything else done. City ordinances may place restrictions on selling from your yard.

A roadside stand. This differs from on-farm sales in that your produce is sold away from the garden in a high-traffic area. Produce is available only at scheduled times. This requires loading and hauling the produce to the stand, but eliminates zoning and distraction problems. Direct competition may be limited so higher prices may be possible.

Delivery. This varies from a roadside stand in that the stand is portable and brought to location on schedule. For example, a trailer loaded with produce may be brought to an apartment complex at a given time during the week. With a properly designed trailer, this could be a very efficient way to market fresh produce. Prices could be set at a slight premium because of the lack of competition and the convenience of delivery.

Pick-your-own. This differs from on-farm sales in that customers harvest their own produce. Pick-your-own operations reduce harvesting and marketing time and expense. However, amateurs plod through carefully manicured beds concerned only about getting the produce they want.

Farmers Markets. The farmers market differs from the roadside stand in that other growers are present. For that reason farmers markets are in some ways the most difficult direct marketing alternative. It has distinct advantages, though, in that many markets are well established with a stable customer base, and advertising costs are shared among the members. However, when customers are in short supply and produce abundant, price competition among growers can make some crops unprofitable.

Combination marketing. The approach involves two or three of the options listed above. One of the large growers in the state starts the season with a roadside stand. When production increases, he attends a local farmers market. Finally, he converts to pick-your-own late in the season when produce is plentiful and prices have fallen.

Entertainment agriculture. This marketing alternative is spreading rapidly in many sections of the country. Growers attract produce customers by offering entertainment ranging from simple hay rides to full blown Pow Wows. Admission is charged for the entertainment and many farmers are quickly discovering that this is more profitable than selling produce. It is necessary to have the right farm and the right location for this marketing method to work.

From a viewpoint of maximum profitability, my first choice in marketing systems would be a market garden with its own farm stand.
Andy Lee[2]

25

MARKET ANALYSIS

Market analysis must begin with a look at the competition. That is, what's already in place? This competition comes from three primary sources.

Existing direct marketers. Determine how well they are providing for their customer's needs. In many cases, the market is established, but the competition from other growers is manageable.

Supermarkets. The supermarkets present a more difficult type of competition. They are very good at marketing produce, and produce quality has improved substantially over the past decade. Older members of the market tell stories of selling tremendous quantities because the supermarkets could not deliver the same quality of fresh produce. That has changed for many items, but quality favors the direct markets for carrots, early potatoes, tomatoes, beans, peas, and cucumbers. We must focus on those items that provide a freshness advantage over the supermarkets.

Supermarkets have a second advantage that keeps thousands of shoppers away from the direct markets. They are convenient. Customers must go to the supermarkets to get meat, milk, cereal, and other daily necessities. It is convenient to purchase produce at the same time, even though it may not be as fresh as the produce available at the farmers market. We must address this issue as we choose our marketing strategy.

Home gardens. We discussed this issue in Chapter One. Don't ignore it. It is a primary marketing factor in many sections of the country.

Once we have surveyed the competition, we are ready to complete a comprehensive market analysis to add detail to the marketing strategy piece of our business plan. The procedures for this analysis vary significantly between subscription sales and direct marketing.

Subscription sales

You can observe local subscription growers, but you cannot steal their customers. You must find your own. Consequently, the market analysis for this strategy involves considerable personal contact to line up your customers and determine what they want you to grow. However, until those customers are committed, you do not have a market and cannot proceed with your plan.

Retail sales

A market analysis for retail sales is more complicated because of the larger number of possibilities, and the complexity of competition.

Develop an estimate of possible production based upon your garden plan. This identifies the quantities of specific crops you must sell at the market.

Observe local markets the season before you plan to enter the market. If you have more than one market, visit them all. For example, you may have three farmers markets, two pick-your-own markets, one on-farm sales, and twelve roadside stands. Visit them all, and often. Determine the following:

- Is there an unsatisfied niche?
- What produce is selling? Talk to the customers. Is there produce they cannot find? Are quantities and prices satisfactory?
- Are growers hitting the early market for cukes and tomatoes?
- Do markets encourage more growers?

The annals of business failures are filled with businesses that attempted to market what they thought would sell, instead of finding out first what will sell!

Bob Reynolds[3]

When anyone wants to join our market, I encourage them because I believe our market will become stronger. Customers like to have choices, and will patronize the larger markets.

Join a farmers market

The following factors must be considered before joining a farmers market:

Fees. Our market charges an annual fee of $50-$75 depending upon when you pay the fees. Other markets have a daily market fee charged to those members that sell on a given day. Other markets use a combination of the two. These fees must be reasonable for the small grower, or your profits will all go to the Farmers Market.

Restrictions on membership. Many markets have limited space which also limits the total number of members. This may require waiting until a space becomes available.

Operating hours. We do not consider a once-a-week farmers market as a complete marketing system. Three days a week is a minimum requirement. Otherwise, produce becomes too large or over-ripe to qualify as 'fresh'.

Pricing policies. Some markets are organized as marketing cooperatives and have the legal right to establish prices. Others allow prices to float freely while others use a market manager to enforce informal price cooperation.

Starting a farmers market

If you plan to start your own farmers market, begin by recruiting other growers. Customers expect variety and want choices. They will not have that without a good selection of vendors. We recommend the following:

Create a legal marketing cooperative. This allows you to establish an acceptable range of prices. Members of the market sign a agreement to abide by the pricing policies. Policies could be in effect only for the first two hours of the market and until a preset point in the season.

Establish standards for produce quality, and marketing procedures. Do not allow dirty produce or produce that is obviously several days old. Establish standards for the display of produce.

Set your fees high enough to provide for adequate advertising. Some advertising will be required to attract customers to your market.

Pay a market manager. Hire a market manager with the authority to enforce the prices and standards. Everything must be written in the bylaws, including the consequences for noncompliance.

Develop community support. Many markets are successful because they start here, by getting a local agency to sponsor the market.

MARKETING PRODUCE

Now that we have decided on a market, we must sell our produce. Marketing involves all aspects of selling to include public image, our selling techniques and environment, customer service policies, pricing, advertising, etc. There are thousands of variations on how this is all done. However, several universal principles apply regardless of how and where produce is marketed.

Focus on developing loyal customers. This core group of satisfied customers provides a base level of sales. When produce is plentiful, these customers continue to buy because relationships have been established. Cater to their specific needs. Make them feel wanted and appreciated. Learn their first names. Nothing develops loyalty quicker than this single act of recognition. Become an expert, talk to your customers. Many of them are still involved in gardening, perhaps with flowers, or with a limited number of vegetables.

Use signs. Post prices. Customer are accustomed to that, and expect it. It saves time because we are not required to constantly explain prices. Draw attention to sale items. Explain unusual items with a sign. After our first frost, we had 15-20 bushels of peppers for sale. We packaged them in large plastic bags, and priced them reasonably at 75¢ and $1.50 per bag. We had some of the only tomatoes at the market so our early crowd was excellent. But we had failed to display special signs drawing attention to the peppers. When the tomatoes were gone, many of the peppers remained.

Protect produce from the elements. Use a canopy or umbrella to reduce wilting. Spray down produce if necessary to keep it cool and looking fresh.

Review the display during the market. Stand back 20 feet and look at the overall visual impact of the display. Then sort through each box and throw out the uglies that detract from the in-close visual impact. If the market is strong enough, sell the uglies later at a slight discount.

What else can I get for you?" This question should be an obsession. Instead it is a very common mistake. A customer picks up a bag of onions, and a pound of carrots. Since we are in the middle of the rush, we announce, "That will be $2.25." WRONG! "What else can I get for you?" Push sale items, or produce in oversupply.

Make effective use of color. Take another look at our marketing stand on the front cover. Notice the striking contrast between the yellow boxes and the red and green vegetables. Flowers add spectacular color even if they are not always profitable. The burgundy aprons contrast nicely with the yellow shirt.

Be aggressive when the market is at it's best. On the surface, this seem wasteful and counterproductive. However, in produce marketing great markets do not always last very long. When the market has slowed, your customers will return because you treated them well through the busy time.

MARKET PHASES

There are three sometimes distinct phases in the market. Marketing techniques change during each phase. (Please remember that these phases are dependent upon a strong home garden environment. If you live in an area where home gardens are not a factor, the final phase will not be nearly as acute as what we face.)

Shortage phase

The early phase is characterized by a shortage of produce. Early tomatoes and cucumbers bring premium prices. If the market is well attended, sellout may take less than one hour. It is critical during this phase, to be capable of handling large numbers of people in a short time. Two or three scales and cash boxes are well worth the expense. Customers patronize a particular vendor because the produce they want is available. Marketing techniques are limited during this phase because there just isn't time for anything fancy.

Normal phase

The next phase is more humane to both the customer and the vendor. There are adequate supplies of most produce and customers chip away at the produce until it is all gone. Marketing takes on added significance because produce must now be prime, and additional service is expected.

During this phase customer loyalty is critical. Prices are fairly uniform throughout the market. Therefore, customers patronize a grower because they have established favorites, and they trust the vendor to provide consistent quality and service.

Oversupply phase

The final phase, late in the season, is when home gardens have arrived, and the market is plugged with produce. Available advertising dollars must be spent to increase the number of customers coming to the market. Loyal customers, so carefully cultivated throughout the season, pay off, because they will be back, but only if prices are comparable to the other growers. Many pounds of produce must be brought to market to match the gross sales made so easily a few weeks earlier.

During this final phase, alternative markets are sometimes necessary. Restaurant sales, sales to wholesale dealers or supermarkets, pick-your-own, or on-farm sales, may be considered. Pickling and canning markets might be expanded through advertising.

Weather and market phases

Weather can have a dramatic affect on these market phases. Rainfall is a factor only in the final phase. If moisture has been plentiful, par-ticularly in the spring, home gardens will come in with a vengeance, and the oversupply phase will be very pronounced. We will look at the three possible scenarios.

Cold. 1992 produced the third coldest July on record. This cool weather severely delayed warm weather crops like tomatoes and cucumbers, and the first two phases shifted by several weeks. The over-supply phase never arrived because home gardens never became a factor. 1993 was very similar, just more pronounced, as the overall season was one to two weeks later than 1992. Tomatoes were in very short supply and prices didn't go below $1.50 per pound. Melons never arrived. Cucum-bers were in oversupply only for a few markets. Home gardens were never a factor.

Moderate. This is the standard by which other seasons are measured. Phases arrive on time, and the sever-ity of the oversupply phase is deter-mined by the amount of rainfall. 1991 delivered perfect weather for home gardening and by mid-August the market was almost dead because of oversupply.

Hot. Crops mature quickly with consistent, warm weather and the phases arrive one to two weeks early. If the weather remains dry, home gardens are less of a factor because gardeners do not usually supply adequate water in a timely manner, so production is reduced. If rainfall is adequate to plentiful, the oversupply phase can be early and very devasta-ting to profits. Prices slide as demand diminishes.

PRICES

If we are to continue in busi-ness, we must receive a fair price for our produce. On the other hand, if we are to maintain a solid customer base,

Unless you can re-tail, you seldom get properly compen-sated for quality.
Wayne Weber[6]

29

we must also provide quality produce at competitive prices. Somewhere in the middle of this tap dance, lies the answer to intelligent pricing. Two factors should be considered in setting prices.

I believe that if we do not hear occasional complaints about prices, our prices aren't high enough.

Base price

There is a base price customers will pay regardless of oversupply. We assume that the average supermarket price is 'fair', because most people are willing to pay that price. We add an acceptable quality 'premium' and this becomes our base price. We do not match sale prices as they reflect spot overproduction in California and other areas of the globe.

Price resistance

Each product also has a price where customers walk away or buy very small amounts. We had some excellent large slicing cucumbers and some smaller grown-up pickles. We priced the pickles at 3 for $1 and the slicers at $.50 each. The pickles were gone within minutes, but the slicers remained, even though they were larger and of higher quality. As soon as we dropped the price to 3 for $1, they too were gone. People do not seem willing to pay 50 cents for a cucumber, regardless of how good they are. Cucumbers appear to have a base price of 3 for $1 and price resistance at 50¢ each.

Base prices and price resistance change with the market phases. Both will become lower as the amount of produce increases. Early produce usually draws a premium close to the resistance price.

So what is a fair price? Whatever the customer will pay and come back next week. I believe that if we do not hear occasional complaints about prices, our prices aren't high enough. I have been told that a few

years back, farmers markets attracted customers because they sold produce at prices far below the local supermarkets. Low prices sold produce. But as customers became concerned with freshness, growers started raising prices and started selling produce on quality, not price. We need to price our produce high enough to guarantee a profit, and just low enough to keep the customers coming to the market.

Pricing and profit

When demand is high and supply is low, we call that 'fun'. When the opposite is true, lowering prices will increase demand, but only to a point. When we drop prices beyond that point we only decrease our profits, doing little to increase the volume of our sales.

As the season wears on, people tire of specific items and smaller quantities will be sold regardless of price. Cucumbers provide a good example because they are often in oversupply late in the season. Customers have also eaten plenty of cukes giving us a second problem, less demand. It is difficult for me to believe that profit can be increased by selling cucumbers at 10 for $1 than you will at 5 for $1. More cucumbers will be sold, but for less money. Let's say we have 300 cucumbers. If we sold half of them at 5 for $1, or all of them at 10 for $1, total income is $30. A 50% decrease in price requires a 200% increase in sales to bring home the same gross income. What happens when we do that?

• We sell out at the expense of other growers since total demand at this point of the season is very steady.

• Other growers may follow our price drop. Then we won't sell more cucumbers, just get less for the ones we do sell.

By selling produce at a base price, gross income is higher, the customer still walks away happy, and comes back to the next market.

THE BISMARCK FARMERS MARKET

When we started growing commercially, Bismarck already had a well-established Farmers Market. They accepted anyone willing to pay the $50 annual fee. It has worked out well and we have sold almost all of our produce at these markets.

We have five markets each week; Sunday at noon, Tuesday at 11 AM, Thursday at 11 AM, and two markets on Saturday at 8 AM. The Saturday morning market has been and still is our most successful market. It is an upscale crowd, with little concern for prices if they are reasonable. It has good staying power, with some growers selling until noon. The Sunday and weekday markets go strong for about an hour, and die down to a slug-it-out scenario. In most cases we are able to eventually sell most of our produce, but late in the season, it is sometimes not worth the effort.

Four market days per week is optimum. We pick in the mornings for Sunday, Tuesday, and Thursday noon markets. We pick a little lighter on Thursday, because Friday evening we must pick for the Saturday morning market, our best market. Two of the markets are two days apart, and the other two are a day and one half apart. There is no better way to split a seven day week.

Farmers market principles

People want fresh produce, but they want it to look like the supermarket. The following marketing principles are unique to members of a farmers markets.

Have fun!! If you are having fun, customers will enjoy coming to your stand to purchase produce. Fun is contagious. It is worth working at.

Attract customers early. The more customers you have at your stand, the more you will have a few minutes later. Customers are curious, and when they see a crowd, they head in that direction to see what is happening. The best way to achieve this is with large quantities of vegetables attractively displayed. Offer samples. If you have too many zucchini, make some bread and offer customers free samples. Marvelous way to sell zucchini.

Be prepared for the rush. Sales during our first hour are often 1/2-2/3 of the total sales for the day. We use up to six people, three cash boxes, and three scales to keep customers flowing smoothly through our stand. Four people are selling while the other two are refilling boxes and providing customers with plastic bags.

Develop name recognition. A customers arrives at the farmers market for the first time. What are they looking for? Something familiar! If they have seen or heard your sign or name before, they are more likely to visit your stand first. Use a large sign to identify yourself. We purchased a $40 custom-made sign that mounts on the back of the pickup. As customers approach our stand, they can see our name in large letters behind the stand

Flaunt quantity. Customers want choices. If you have only ten cucumbers, few people will stop. If you have 500, let customers know that and they will be attracted by the abundant choices. Keep the boxes full, and when quantities diminish, reduce the size of your display so you still look well stocked.

You never have to worry about the competition, if you can beat them on quality.
Steve Hall[6]

Have plenty of plastic bags handy. Customers are accustomed to that convenience. Make sure they are accessible. Have some in your pockets to offer customers. "Would you like a bag?" As soon as they accept your offer, you have made a sale.

Offer smaller packaging. Many customers are purchasing for only one or two people. They know the market will be available next week, and they want only a few onions so they stay fresh. Three pounds is too much. Make up a few one pound or $1 bags for these customers.

Experiment with packaging options. There many possibilities for adding value to your produce simply with packaging. Use small paper bags with handles to package small portions of produce. Plastic containers sometimes show off produce in ways that make it attractive.

Try simple processing. A food processor can make short work of processing small quantities of vegetables for those customers who want the convenience and are willing to pay for it. This might require some simple refrigeration such as a large cooler. And, before you start, check local ordinances on regulations and required inspections.

THE MARKETING STAND

An elaborate stand is not required, but it certainly attracts people, and attraction is the first step to selling produce at a farmers market. We use bright yellow boxes that show off the green and red vegetables. The stand is a subdued mauve (We had a choice between mauve and country blue. In 1990 we tried country blue for the boxes. Then a friend of mine, a K-Mart manager in Oklahoma, explained that supermarkets use either green or yellow to accent the produce. So we changed the boxes to yellow, and made the stand mauve. It was great advice and the bright yellow boxes have become our trademark.)

We are very happy with the marketing stand so we will describe it in detail for those readers who may wish to duplicate the design. The capabilities are as follows:

• Can be setup in an L-shape or straight as demonstrated in figure 3-1 and 3-2.

• Has three sets of interior boards, 4', 6', and 8'. This allows us the flexibility to set up according to how much produce we have.

• Cash boxes fit into the stand for optimum accessibility.

• Hanging scales mount on the stand.

• Umbrellas mount on the stand to provide protection from the sun.

• The stand comes apart in sections and loads neatly into a

3-1, 3-2. The marketing stand. *These pictures illustrate the two possible configurations. When space is limited we set up in the 'L' shape. (Bottom picture) When we have plenty of space, we prefer an in-line setup. (Top picture)*

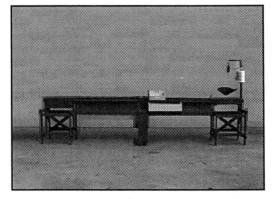

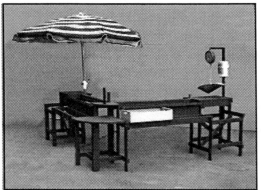

special rack on the pickup. When we arrive at the market, we can be ready for business in less than ten minutes.

FINE TUNING YOUR MARKETING

In the first part of this chapter we have discussed the basics of marketing your produce. Once these skills are mastered, there are still many things that can be done to improve your market share. Advertising falls into this category because it is not required in all markets or from all growers.

Building an image

Marketing is consummated at the market stand but starts much earlier than that. We attempt to distinguish our operation from other growers so new customers can pick us out from a crowd.

Name recognition

Customers want to know who they are buying produce from, and that means more than just a farm name. A politician friend of mine made that point very clear, and we added our last name to our sign. It now reads, "Haakenson's Gourmet Garden." It makes our presentation more personal, and that is very important to developing customer loyalty.

Your company name should provide a good indication of your special emphasis or niche. We used the word gourmet because our intention was to raise herbs and other hard-to-find crops. We haven't done that, but gourmet still describes our obsession with quality vegetables.

Media

The media has a fascination with farmer's markets. Every year the

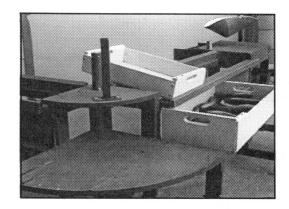

*3-3. **The corner stand.** This pie-shaped stand is used when we setup in an 'L' configuration. The small yellow boxes sit at a slight angle on the top boards. The large boxes rest securely in the bottom rack.*

*3-4. **Construction details.** The boards mount on joist hangers on the side of the stand.*
Cash box.
Umbrella mount.

*3-5. **Mounting the stand on the pickup.** The stands sit on a rack built at the front of the box. The boards lay in the racks over the wheel wells. The picture at the right illustrates the tie-down bar we designed to hold the stands in place.* 33

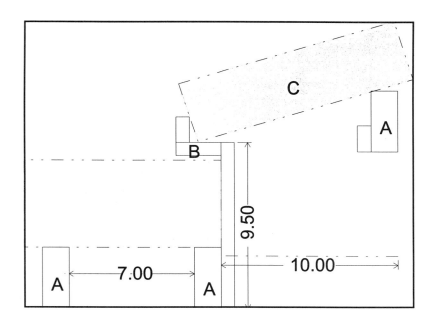

3-6. An end view of the interior boards for the marketing stand. *Refer to figure 3-3. If you were able to remove the corner stand and look to the left, this is what you would see. The strength for the boards is provided by the 2x4s (A). The center board is the only one that is complicated. The board on the right is a 1x10, (B) is a 1x3 and the small board above (B) is a 1x2. All three 2x4s are attached to the stand with standard joist hangers. We attach a small steel strap at the ends of the 2x4s that extends below the board by about one inch. This keeps the boards from slipping out of the hangers during set-up.*

Many marketers provide press releases for local news outlets. There are many rules for writing a good press release, but none are more important than writing something that would interest or be useful information for readers or listeners. Media outlets must compete for customers just as we do. They print information that is unusual, new, relevant to surrounding events, a triumph over adversity, and often information because it is unique and unreported. They do not print advertisements, they charge for them.

Garden tours

A few years ago we invited a second grade class to tour the garden. The response was invigorating. It was hard to keep their attention talking about gardening on a warm spring day. We handed out coupon calling cards with an offer for free carrots or onions when the market started. We got a number of them back from people who might not have otherwise been at the market. This one event exposed many parents to the market that might not have been interested without the tour.

Last year more than 50 members of the local garden club toured our garden. Many of them had never attended a farmers market because they have always grown their own. But most of the members grow only flowers, and by the end of the season, we had seen some of them at the market. During the tour we had our marketing stand set up, and lunch was served off the stand. When any of them arrived at the market, they could recognize our stand.

Public presentations

Surveys indicate that most people fear speaking in public more than they fear death. However, if you

television stations come out and shoot a segment on our market. Last year we were able to get a station to come out to our garden because we had some unique growing ideas. It dramatically helped sales for a week or so. The problem is they usually want to come early in the season when we have plenty of customers. Any publicity is great publicity, but it would be advisable to ask them to come late in the season when a shortage of customers exists. We have also had a large colored picture in the Bismarck Tribune for three of the past four years. This is certainly because of the bright colors of our display which show up well in the paper.

DAN HAAKENSON
The Gourmet Garden

can get past that fear, public presentations offer tremendous opportunities, including service clubs, garden clubs, and various women's groups. Use good graphics, 35mm color slides, or computer generated slides.

Educating your customer

This aspect of marketing is unique to the grower involved in direct marketing fruits and vegetables. It is also the easiest way to build customer loyalty. Many customers that purchase fresh vegetables do so because they know it is a healthier life choice. However, they do not always know the best way to use their purchases. The following paragraphs describe some ideas for customer education. We believe it will become one of your most important marketing skills.

Recipes. Customers seem to have an almost insatiable thirst for new recipes. Use recipes that require the produce currently in oversupply. If you have a bumper crop of beans, provide recipes that use beans. Recipes do not need to be complicated, just informative on slightly different ways to use a particular vegetable. Have the printer pad the recipes and place them on a special display so customers have access to them even during market rush times. The reverse side of the recipes can

contain promotional information. These recipes should be printed in February, long before they are needed.

Food preservation information. Canning and freezing is quickly becoming a lost art. Because of the availability of fresh, frozen, and canned vegetables, young families have quit storing produce for themselves. Some of that is due to the hectic life-styles we live, where canning might be too complicated or time consuming. However, much of the lack of interest is because of ignorance on exactly how to get the job done. If we take the time to educate our customers we will have the opportunity to provide the produce to them. We would recommend starting with salsa because of increased interest in this product.

Gardening information. A large percentage of our customers are gardeners or have been gardeners. They are very interested in how we grow our produce, how we ripen tomatoes so early. Providing solid information develops your image as an expert, and some customers prefer to purchase from someone they trust as a competent grower.

THE MARKETING BUDGET

We have proposed many ideas on marketing, but how much will all of this cost? This is where most small growers go wrong. They believe that marketing costs money, that advertising is an expense. It doesn't, and it isn't. Marketing pays off, it is an investment that improves profits. Experts suggest that 15-20% of gross income should be spent in marketing and about 60% of that should be spent on existing customers.

3-7. On Television! *You can't purchase advertising like this, a spot on the evening news. Some advice: When you have a camera in your face, take your time to answer the questions. The clip will be edited anyway, so the pause will be cut out. This gives you time to formulate an intelligent answer and deliver it properly.*

35

We want marketing to accomplish two tasks, to keep existing customers, and attract new ones. To keep our current customers we need to spend money, because other growers will be spending money trying to take them away from us. It is tempting to take these customers for granted, and focus our marketing on attracting new ones. In the long run, this is an expensive and ineffective use of marketing dollars.

Lets look at a proposed budget based upon our projected gross income of $12,000. If we use 15% of our gross for marketing, we would spend $1800. It doesn't take a mathematical genius to figure out that if we spend that much, we can never make the $10,000 promised in the first chapter. True, but then there are two ways of looking at this problem. First, marketing is an investment that will pay off in future years. Second, if we market properly, we may sell $14,000 this year and cover that marketing investment. Lets examine a possible marketing plan.

Keeping our current customers

Many of the things that we do to maintain a loyal clientele do not cost anything. However, there are some things that must be included in our advertising budget.

Brochures can accomplish many things for you. We recommend the following guidelines:

• Begin the differentiation process. Capitalize on who you are, because customers like to know something about the farmer that grows their food. Many have lost contact with rural life, and this is one small way to bring it back. Explain any special things you do to enhance the quality of your operation, how you are different from other growers.

• Personalize your operation. Include a picture of your family and a short biographical sketch.

• Provide your market schedule. We have a rather complicated schedule, so we include it in the brochure for permanent reference.

• Introduce prices. If your pricing will be fairly stable, include base prices for all major vegetables with a short discussion on pricing policies.

• Establish a guarantee with a strongly worded promise to replace any produce your customers find unacceptable.

Several ideas for a brochure are included in Annex A. The brochure is an introduction to who we are and how we bring produce to market. We draw attention to those things that distinguish us from other growers at the market.

Newsletters provide a different service to your customer, providing current information and ideas. We provide the following suggestions for those that might consider using a newsletter:

• Write the majority of the copy prior to the beginning of the season. It is time consuming to collect and compile the necessary information. It is impossible to get this all done during 'crazy season'.

• Supplement the prepared material with current information. Each season is unique and brings new challenges. A timely article will help bring credibility to your newsletter.

• Keep the copy light. Try to entertain as well as inform your customers.

Direct mail is used to announce our arrival at the market. The first mailing should coincide with full production when we have cucumbers and tomatoes in adequate supply to handle increased demand. The second mailing should occur later in the season when the entire market starts to suffer from an oversupply of produce. This mailing might include *coupons* to reward loyal customers with special discounts.

There was a time not long ago, when newsletters and brochures were a questionable option for the small grower because it was difficult to make the pages look professional. With the introduction of high-power word processors and laser printers, this is no longer true. We use Microsoft Word (Version 6) and a Hewlett Packard LaserJet. If you do not include pictures a quick-print shop can duplicate the publications for a reasonable cost. If you use pictures, you will need to use a commercial printer and your cost will be slightly higher. However, this may be worth the extra effort and cost for the brochure since you will have more copies printed, and a picture 'is worth a thousand words.'

This past year we were able to get only one newsletter printed. We received many positive comments about it, and people asked when the next one would be finished. However, the rush of the season postponed the publication, the market weakened, and we finally caved into fatigue. In retrospect, we learned one very important lesson, the need for a well-designed brochure. Newsletters contain current information and can be thrown after they are read. Brochures, on the other hand, focus on season-long issues and we would hope that our customers would keep them around for awhile.

Advertising

The Bismarck Farmers Market participated in a cooperative advertising program sponsored by the North Dakota Department of Agriculture. I was privileged to be the advertising coordinator and learned many things about advertising. This section is based upon that experience.

I include costs to serve as a reference. Your costs will vary considerably depending upon your location. However, the cost ratios between mediums should be close. For example, if I can purchase a Bismarck billboard for $550 or six 30 second TV spots, or 30 column inches in the newspaper, these price ratios should be similar where you live.

Radio

Radio is the best media for special events or sales, but keep your message simple. Use the best stations available that cater to your audience. Purchase the best times available. The ads cost more but for a good reason, they are reaching more listeners. For example, radio could be used to advertise your niche crop, Walla Walla onions. The ad would be for a specific market, Saturday morning. Don't confuse listeners by listing your entire schedule. They won't remember it anyway. Best times average around $20 per 30 second spot.

Television

Television provides spectacular visual impact because of the sharp contrast between the colors of fresh vegetables. We use television to increase the customer base late in the season. Purchase the best times on your best station. It works. Cost: One 30 second spot on the 10 PM news cost $95. Other decent times are about $50 each. Best available scheduling might be considered because of the visual impact and reasonable cost, about $20 each.

You do not make money from high-quality tomatoes. You make money from satisified customers.

Matty Matarazzo[8]

Newspapers.

Printed media is a great place to advertise your full schedule. Newspapers are too expensive for visual impact. However, they have the advantage of providing hard copy. Customers can clip the schedule and keep in handy.

Attracting new customers can be expensive so it must be done carefully. You must give your customers a compelling reason to purchase produce from you. When cucumbers first dropped in price last year, we ran a few radio spots to announce that to the world. The response was marvelous, and we saw many new customers at the market. We are confident that we easily paid for the cost of the advertising in additional sales. Some of these new customers continued to shop for produce at our stand for the remainder of the season. And this is our advertising objective, to develop a long-term relationship that will provide sales over several months. If we can break even on the advertising with additional sales, we are delighted.

SOURCES

There are many books on marketing that might be useful. We recommend these two.

Sell What You Sow. The Growers Guide to Successful Produce Marketing by Eric Gibson. This book has been meticulously researched and is extremely well organized. The resources section is the most comprehensive list you will find anywhere and is well worth the price of the book.

Backyard Market Gardening, The Entrepreneur's Guide to Selling What You Grow is written by Andrew W. Lee, a 20-year veteran of market gardening. The book includes numerous reprinted articles from The New Farm magazine. Consequently, the book is not always well organized, and rambles at times. However, there is a tremendous amount of solid information. Much can be learned from the numerous articles from growers who have successful operations. The strength of the book, however, lies in the marketing chapters.

AND FINALLY . . .

Marketing is pay day. Without a pay day there is no reason to consider commercial gardening. Once you have a marketing plan, it's time to design a garden to grow the produce you will sell next season.

Chapter Four

Commercial Design and Construction

Potential market gardeners face either a site selection decision, or the challenges of using an existing site. In this chapter, we provide guidelines for those readers that will use an existing site. However, most of the chapter will be devoted to the ideal commercial garden that can only be achieved with the right location.

Please remember that the suggested designs are based upon the principles outlined in the previous chapter. There are hundreds of ways to develop a profitable commercial garden. The designs presented here work well with the production methods we use.

SITE SELECTION

The garden site must provide water, sunshine, and the nutrients plants need to grow and produce fruit. Production and profits are directly influenced by how well we provide all three of these key elements. Well-watered tomatoes in rich soil will provide few fruits if grown in the shade. Conversely, full sunshine will not compensate for poor soil or inadequate water. All three elements must be present for maximum production.

Water

We begin with water because it is the most critical element, and the most difficult problem to solve. The growing methods used in our system require water quantities far above normal. For example, we use plastic mulch on the tomatoes and cucumbers. If rain comes in a downpour, most if it runs off, and must be replaced through irrigation. Intensive spacing of plants requires moisture that can seldom be met through normal rainfall. Consequently, we must irrigate almost all season.

Therefore, a reliable source of quality water is required for optimum production. The garden described later in this chapter requires a minimum of 3000 gallons per week, and during full production, probably twice that. Rainfall will provide some of the required moisture. However, we must plan for the worst case and have the capability to sustain the garden without rainfall. We must never permit the garden to become stressed because of a shortage of water.

4-1. The water truck. We used this old gasoline truck for the first few years. Hauling water is an option for solving water problems, but very expensive and time consuming. Rust in the tank was a constant problem.

Solving water shortage problems

If water is short, the best option is to select another site. Unfortunately, we do not always have this option, and must live with the restrictions of our current location.

A second option is to haul water. We hauled water for three years using a two-ton gasoline truck. (Figure 4-1) We mounted a jet-pump on the back to provide water pressure for the irrigation system. For two years the City of Bismarck installed a water meter on a fire hydrant just a few blocks away so our turnaround time was less than 15 minutes per load. This arrangement made hauling water a viable option.

However, there are less expensive ways to haul the water. License and insurance on the truck was $150 per year. Since we need a pickup to market our produce anyway, a heavy trailer with a 1500 gallon tank might be more economical than a truck dedicated to the task. A couple words of caution are necessary. Water is heavy. Fifteen hundred gallons weigh between 12,000 and 13,000 pounds. Add the weight of a trailer heavy enough to haul the water, and load restriction problems in the spring are possible. Secondly, moving 13,000 pounds requires a pickup with some horsepower and a strong power train. If you haul water we recommend the following:

Use a plastic 1500 gallon tank, available at most farm supply stores.

If your water source is a municipality, ensure that they will allow you to load even when water is rationed in the heat of the summer. Rationing is an option for a lawn, but not for a garden. If your source is a lake or stream, ensure you have the proper permits to draw water legally.

Consider the distance and the number of trips required. A two-ton truck hauling 1500 gallons per trip would require two to four trips per week. These trips take precious time during the peak season, time that should be used for other critical tasks.

A third option is to build a cistern and capture rain water. A one inch rain captured from a 3000 square feet roof would put 1875 gallons in the cistern. This method would work only in areas where rainfall is consistent. This could still be done in other areas, but an additional source of water would be required.

Solving water quality problems

Water quality is just as important as having sufficient water available. The most common water quality problems are:

• *High soluble salts.* Too much sodium will make your soil rock-hard after just a few years. Total salts should not be above 500 ppm (parts per million).

• *High or low pH.* Since this is the first time we have encountered the concept of pH, we need to explain that in some detail. pH is the acronym for potential hydrogen, or the number of positive ions in our water. It measures how acid (low pH) or alkaline (high pH) the water or soil is. pH ranges from 0-14 with 7 being neutral. pH is critical because it determines the ability of plants to absorb nutrients. For example, the ability of a plant to absorb nitrogen is reduced at pH levels below 6 and above 8. Phosphorus absorption is reduced below 6.5 and above 7.5. Most plants grow best in soil that is slightly acid, from a pH of 6-7. The pH of water is important because if we put high pH water on our garden, we will eventually raise the pH of the soil. Water with high or low pH can still be used but frequent soil pH monitoring would be required.

• *Chlorine* levels should not be above 142 ppm.

Soil

Soil is not a major factor in site selection because most soil problems can be corrected with organic material and time. However, since conditioning is time consuming and expensive, it is advantageous to start with quality soil if at all possible. Soil quality is determined by three factors, the condition of the soil, the nutrients that are present, and the soil pH.

Soil condition. Soil condition refers to the physical properties that encourage plant growth, the ability to retain water, sustain earthworms and microbes, and resist crusting. These are not major factors since these problems can all be corrected with the addition of organic matter. Organic matter provides nutrients, stores water for a more uniform supply, loosens soil structure for improved drainage and easier working soil. Weeds and root crops pull easier.

Nutrients. Although plants require 16 nutrients to survive, only nitrogen, phosphorous, and potassium are likely to be deficient. All of these deficiencies can be fixed with the application of the right fertilizer.

pH. If your pH is too low, raising it by applying lime is rela-tively easy. If pH is too high, things get a bit complicated. The pH can be lowered with the application of sulfur or nitrogen fertilizers. However, high sulfur soil is not always desirable, particularly if raising mild onions. Peat moss is an alternative because it has a pH of about 3.5. This option is expensive, but peat does a superb job in conditioning the soil and increases the water holding ability of the beds. Of all the things we have done to improve our soil, the addition of about four cubic feet of peat moss per 150 square feet of raised beds has been the most successful.

Healthy soil will increase production more than any other factor, provided that adequate water and full sun are provided. The key word here is balance. If the soil has too much nitrogen, tomatoes may have extensive vines but very few fruits. If the soil has too much fresh organic matter, the organism that break down the soils may use too much nitrogen, causing a deficiency. We recommend the following:

• Start with a professional soil analysis. We waited four years before we had one done. When we got the results we were surprised that our pH was too high and our nitrogen danger-ously low. When we discovered the nitrogen problem we added granular nitrogen in the fall, liquid nitrogen during the season, and enjoyed significant increases in production.

• Locate several sources of organic material and have them tested. We used 40 truckloads of old manure that had been in piles for 7-8 years. The nitrogen had leached out, so we had very high amounts of phosphorus and potassium, but our soil required supplemental nitrogen.

• Take all tests to a soils expert to determine the proper way to condition the soil.

- If possible, compost the organic matter before adding it to the soil. Because of the quantities involved, this would be no small task. However, it would pay for itself many times in increased production and fewer weed problems.

Sun

Full sun. That's it. No compromise. If you have shade problems, look for another location or remove the trees.

Drainage

A gentle slope of less than a 1% grade is optimum. This ensures that excess rainfall will drain away from the raised beds. A flat site allows water to stand and most plants do not grow well in standing water. Steeper slopes are workable, but encourage erosion and create unnecessary fatigue for gardeners.

GENERAL DESIGN CONSIDERATIONS

Once the site has been selected, it is time to design the garden. There are many issues that must be resolved, but the first is whether to grow produce organically.

What about organic?

Raising vegetables organically is not a simple issue. From a marketing perspective it isn't justifiable unless you live in an area with a well established market for organic produce. That isn't true in North Dakota, and probably won't be for some time. We occasionally field questions concerning organic practices but the question isn't raised frequent enough to justify the added work and expense. If you strip the mystery out of growing organically, these differences remain:

- Chemicals cannot be used to control pests. We abide by this restriction because it is the principle concern of many customers. In a University of Wisconsin study of 973 direct marketing customers, 87% expressed concern about chemical use. There are many organic pest control options, and healthy plants seem to survive all except the most extreme infestations.
- Chemicals cannot be used to control disease. This is not big problem because most diseases do not respond to chemicals anyway. Prevention through crop rotation, variety selection, and growing healthy plants does more for disease problems anyway.
- Synthetic fertilizers cannot be used. It has been proven many times that a nutrient deficiency problem can be solved organically over time. We use a tremendous amount of organic fertilizer, compost the residue, and return it to the soil. However, in isolated cases with cucumbers and peppers, we find it beneficial to apply supplemental synthetic fertilizers.
- Transplants must be grown organically. This is our greatest deviation from organic principles. The success of our system is predicated upon the early market. One of the primary requirements is strong, healthy transplants. The easiest way to accomplish that is with the use of synthetic fertilizers in the greenhouse. They can be grown organically, but with extra effort.

There are only two reasons to grow organically, ideology or economics. If you believe in the necessity of organic production, you are obviously willing to accept the extra time and effort required. If you plan to make the decision based upon economic returns, we recommend a thorough market analysis. Determine

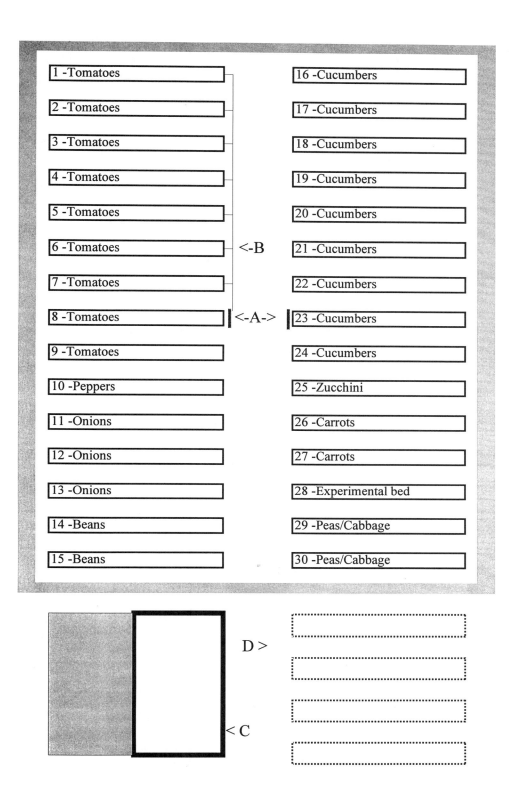

1 -Tomatoes	16 -Cucumbers
2 -Tomatoes	17 -Cucumbers
3 -Tomatoes	18 -Cucumbers
4 -Tomatoes	19 -Cucumbers
5 -Tomatoes	20 -Cucumbers
6 -Tomatoes <-B	21 -Cucumbers
7 -Tomatoes	22 -Cucumbers
8 -Tomatoes <-A->	23 -Cucumbers
9 -Tomatoes	24 -Cucumbers
10 -Peppers	25 -Zucchini
11 -Onions	26 -Carrots
12 -Onions	27 -Carrots
13 -Onions	28 -Experimental bed
14 -Beans	29 -Peas/Cabbage
15 -Beans	30 -Peas/Cabbage

D >

< C

4-2. The master garden layout plan. *This is not a scale drawing. (A) indicates the irrigation manifolds. (B) is a rough sketch of how the supply lines for each bed would be constructed. Please remember that each bed has its own line from the manifold even though this rough drawing doesn't indicate that. (C) is the greenhouse and storage area. This can also be used for preparation of produce and even a sales area. (D) could be used for future expansion based upon what vegetables are selling well.*

43

if there is a demand for organic produce, and whether a premium is paid. You will need that premium to cover additional costs and time required to raise the same amount of produce.

If you plan to certify, make that decision now, since many of your early actions will affect your ability to certify later.

Layout of the garden

The model garden design is illustrated at Figure 4-2. For the remainder of the book we will base our planning on that hypothetical garden. We would use ours, but it was put together a piece at a time so it is not very well designed.

Beds must run north and south to receive optimum sunshine in the morning and afternoon. We use trellises extensively, so if the beds ran east and west, shade would become a serious problem.

Build all the beds the same length. This simplifies planning, and provides flexibility for irrigation hoses and trellises. When we first started we had beds in three lengths, 70', 50', and 45'. We could not rotate cucumbers easily because our trellis mesh was 50' long. We had to mark the irrigation hoses in the fall to prevent confusion in the spring. Planning was complicated because each year we had to estimate quantities based on differing lengths of beds.

Leave space around the garden for a single pass with your cultivator. This will keep the weeds and grasses in the surrounding area from invading your garden.

Provide a 10-12' center walkway down the middle of the garden for composting residue, storing hail protection boards, tool storage, and many other tasks.

Construct your greenhouse and storage area at the end of this waterway. This minimizes the walking required to operate the garden.

Regardless of where you live, it is advisable to fence the garden. If resources are available, we strongly recommend a windbreak type board fence. Research indicates that a 50% fence will protect to a distance of 10 times the height. Therefore a six foot fence would protect the first sixty feet of garden. Such a windbreak would significantly reduce wind damage and increase yields.

Construction

Construct the garden one year prior to production to allow adequate time to do it right and eliminate weeds and grasses. We built ours during production years. We were always behind, and production sometimes took second priority. Consequently, we did not do as good a job of gardening as we could have.

Raised Beds

There are two types of raised beds, supported and unsupported. Supported beds have boards or timbers around the edge to confine the soil to the bed. We do not recommend using supported raised beds because of the extra cost and effort involved. Unsupported beds will produce very well with the system described in this book. To construct an unsupported bed:

1. Cultivate the garden as deeply as possible with a large tractor. We used spikes on an old Ford 8N cultivator. With a larger tractor you would be able to cultivate deeper which would be very beneficial. References on double-digging raised beds recommend digging to a depth of 24". We will raise the bed 6" above the average ground level. Therefore,

if the tractor can cultivate to a depth of 12", we will have tilled to 18" below the top of the finished bed.

2. Cultivate the entire garden several times with the tiller. This pulverizes the soil and makes it much easier to work with. From here on you will be working only with the top 6-8 inches. Therefore it would be possible to spread your organic material and work it into that topsoil with the cultivator. That would greatly reduce the hand labor required to spread manure.

3. If you are concerned with straight beds, mark the bed with a chalk line. Cultivate along the line to twice the width of the top of your bed. We use a 36" bed width, so we cultivate 6' from the chalk line. Move the chalk line to the next bed. We allow 7' between beds, although 6 1/2 feet might be adequate.

4. Dump manure on top of your first pass. The quantity should be based upon your soil and manure analysis. Spread the manure with a rake, and cultivate one more time with the tiller. Now comes the hard part.

5. Using a flat spade, start digging on the outside of the second pass, taking all of the earth that comes easily and throw it on the first pass. The deeper you dig, the higher your bed will be. We take only the soil that has been cultivated by the tiller. Continue down the bed taking only the outside width of the spade.

6. The remaining earth between the trench you have dug and the new bed, can be thrown up on the bed easily with a minimum of lifting, by using your knee against the spade and scooping rather than lifting.

7. Rake it out to flatten it a bit, and then make a pass with the cultivator, remaining careful to stay straight and in the center of the bed.

4-3. The bed before we started.

4-4. Adding organic material. This step is not required if you apply all of your organic material prior to bed construction.

4-5. Using the knee. The secret to constructing beds easily is to use the knee to scoop up the remaining soil.

8. Spread manure on the bed once more, and work it in with the cultivator.

Using this method, a 50' raised bed can be constructed in about an hour or two without too much fatigue. Our video provides a complete explanation of the construction of an unsupported raised bed.

IRRIGATION SYSTEM

Drip irrigation systems vary in construction from thin irrigation tape to heavy soaker hoses. However, the

45

4-6. Raising the bed. *Notice the two passes of the cultivator. Organic material has already been applied to the left side and it has been recultivated. We start on the right side by scooping out two widths of the flat spade. The remaining soil can be moved onto the bed easily using a scooping motion with the knee. Using this method, we can build a 50-foot bed in just over an hour.*

principle parts remain the same.

Supply lines carry the water from the source to the drip lines. If long distances are involved, hydrologic friction losses must be considered when selecting the size of pipe. Valves are required to regulate the flow to individual lines. At the end of the supply lines, irrigation tubing carries the water from the supply lines to the emitters which drip the water to the plants. Various fittings are required throughout the system. Filters, back-flow preventers, and pressure regulators are installed at the water source.

There are many drip system suppliers, but all systems fall into four categories.

Spaghetti tubes. Main lines are run throughout the garden and smaller spaghetti tubes are installed from these lines to the individual plants. An emitter is placed at each plant. This system works extremely well for tomatoes where each plant can have a dedicated emitter.

In-line emitters. Emitters are installed along the main lines at set intervals. This does not provide the precision of the spaghetti tubes, but is much more economical to install. It works well for closely spaced row crops such as peas, beans, onions, and carrots.

Dual-chambered hose. The design of this thin-walled hose provides equalized pressure along the length of the hose. Laser installed holes are spaced evenly along the hose. This system can be buried to protect it from the elements and from rodent damage.

Soaker hoses. Rubber soaker hoses are great improvements over canvas hoses. However, water pressure variations along the hose are still a problem. This is the most expensive system, but does not allow the flexibility of other systems. It is impossible for us to recommend soaker hoses for the commercial garden.

When choosing an irrigation system, reliability is the most important consideration. That is, will the system consistently supply water with a minimum of maintenance. We cannot afford to damage production because of irrigation system failure. The revenue lost would quickly pay for a more expensive but more

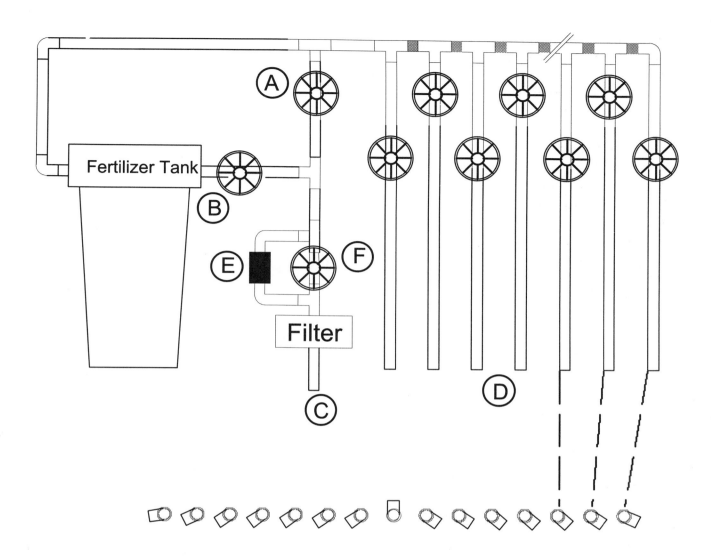

4-7. The irrigation manifold. *The water source is at C. The filter is first in the design to protect all elements from particles in the water. E is the pressure reducer. This is not needed if several valves are open. Therefore valve F is closed only when pressure reduction is necessary. If we are not fertilizing, valve B is closed and valve A is open. When we fertilize we start with both A and B open. This allows some water to filer through the fertilizer and agitates the top of the solution. If we close valve A, all of the water goes through the tank, and agitation will be sufficient to remove all fertilizer from the tank. The drawing on the bottom is looking at the individual pipes, D, from the top. It illustrates the angles needed to get the individual hoses in from the beds.*

reliable system.

We chose the Submatic in-line drip irrigation systems because of its reliability and durability over many years of use. We have not been disappointed. The only problem we have had is occasional plugging of emitters. This happens in any system even with a good filter system. Emitters require constant monitoring throughout the season.

Submatic has two emitters, 2 gallons per hour and 4 gallons per hour. In soil with adequate organic matter, the 4 gal/hr emitters will work. With less organic material, the soil cannot absorb water as

4-8. The end connection. This drawing depicts the connection on both ends of the pipes that are laid between the manifold and each bed (A). (B) is the adapter that goes from ¾" poly hose to 3/4 " pipe threads. (C) goes from ¾" pipe to ½" copper or CPVC. (D) is an elbow and (E) is either 1/2" copper or CPVC, whichever you choose. On the manifold end, this completes the hookup.

The connection on the bed end adds another adapter (C). (F) is an adapter that goes from ¾ pipe to a male garden hose fitting. Most fittings for drip irrigation are of the hose variety. The length of (E) is determined by how far the pipe is buried from the bed. (F) needs to be just outside the area of the bed that is cultivated, otherwise it will be in danger of being damaged.

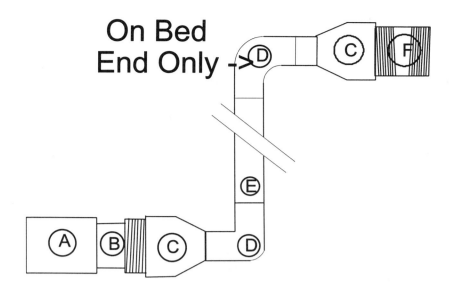

On Bed
End Only

quickly and 2 gal/hr emitters might be a better choice. We spaced our emitters at 1-½' spacing rather than the 2' recommended by Submatic because of our intensive spacing. We have some runoff with the 4 GPH emitters because not all of our beds have sufficient organic content to absorb the water at these increased flows.

Control of the irrigation system is accomplished with two 15-valve manifolds. One manifold also provides filters and fertilization capabilities. Each bed is fed with a ¾" poly pipe from the manifold, permanently buried in the center pathway.

Construction of the irrigation system

A rough sketch of the system (figure 4-2) indicates the location of the manifolds, and the installation of the supply lines to each bed. Figure 4-7 provides the detail for construction of the manifold, and figure 4-8 details how to connect the supply line at the bed and at the manifold.

The irrigation system consists of three components. The first is the irrigation hoses and emitters. Construction consists of cutting the hoses

to length, installing the emitters, and installing the fittings. We have found that emitter installation is simplified if a small hole is drilled in the hose first using a simple jig on a drill press.

The second component is the supply lines that lie between the beds and the water supply manifold. These are ¾" poly pipe available from lumberyards, hardware stores, and farm supply stores. The ends (figure 4-8) are very similar. The bed end adds the fittings to connect to the irrigation hoses.

The final component is the manifold. This one is a bit complicated.

Construction of the manifolds.

We recommend using ½" copper. It is more difficult to construct but provides flexibility for future construction and maintenance. If a CPVC valve quits working, it is impossible to replace it without cutting the pipes and using splices. Copper valves can be replaced with a torch and solder. Copper is also more forgiving during construction. Once CPVC glue is applied, you have only a few seconds to align the pieces.

48

Copper, on the other hand, can be reheated and adjusted as necessary.

The secret to soldering is to ensure that both surfaces are clean. Use a steel brush to clean inside joints and fine sandpaper for the outside of the pipe. Coat both surfaces with solder paste and slide the connection together. Hold the flame on one side, and the solder on the other. When the solder melts you know you have sufficient heat to bond the copper around the entire joint.

Cut all of the pieces. Prepare all joints for solder or cement. Construct subsections of the assembly, working on a flat surface to assure parallel construction where necessary.

Construct the manifold frame. Install the 4x4 posts, and screw the 3/4" plywood to the posts. Install the main subsection of the manifold, then add the filter and fertilizer assemblies. Finally, join the complete assembly to your water source.

Install the poly pipe to each bed. Dig the trenches down each side of the center path. These do not need to be more than a few inches deep as the water will be blown out before freezing becomes a problem. Lay out the poly pipe. Make the connection at the manifold, and then roll out the pipe towards the bed. When you get to the bed, you know the length is right because the manifold end is already connected. Install the poly to pipe adapter. Pipe clamps are not required because the system will rarely carry more then 10-20 pounds of pressure and a friction fit will be sufficient. When all connections are complete, fill in the trench.

ESTIMATED INVESTMENT

Most businesses require some investment and commercial gardening is no exception. The initial investment depends upon how much equipment you already have and whether you need to add a greenhouse and storage building

Equipment.

Basic tools for gardening and simple construction tasks are required. These include power saws, carpentry and plumbing tools, spades, rakes, etc. If these must be purchased, add $500-1000 to the initial investment estimate.

Cultivator. We recommend a good quality self-propelled rear-tine tiller with a seven or eight horse engine. These sell for $1500-$2000.

Shredder. Quick composting requires a shredder. The garden produces a tremendous amount of residue. The easiest way to compost it is to make a large pile and let nature do its thing. The fastest way is to shred it. These sell for $500 -$800.

Drip irrigation is essential for optimum production. There are many systems on the market. We use one of the most expensive initially, Submatic of Lubbock, TX. However, the system will last for many years. Major items are: 1500 feet of irrigation hose; 1000 emitters; 30 male ends with caps; 30 female ends; 60 ¾" poly to ¾" pipe adapters; 60 hose clamps; 33 ¾" CPVC valves; 30 plastic ¾" hose to garden hose adapters; 800 feet of ¾" poly hose; Screen; Water pressure reducer; Water filter body; 30 ¾" CPVC Ts; 10 ¾" CPVC Elbows; 100' ¾" CPVC pipe, cleaner and cement. Total estimated cost is $700-$900.

Possible Investment Costs		
Investment Item	**Low**	**High**
Irrigation equipment	$700	$900
Cages, trellises, and cloches	$1,200	$1,300
Garden and construction tools	$200	$1,000
Shredder	$500	$800
Tiller	$1,500	$2,000
Marketing equipment	$200	$500
Total operating equipment	$4,300	$6,500
Greenhouse equipment	$400	$600
Greenhouse construction	$750	$2,000
Total greenhouse cost	$1,150	$2,600
Storage shed	$4,000	$6,000
Total possible investment	$9,450	$15,100

4-9. Estimated investment costs. *These are very rough estimates but should get you somewhere in the ballpark.*

Marketing equipment. Your investment depends upon which marketing strategy you adopt. Don't skimp here. Money spent on marketing will pay off as much or more than any other investment. A good wash rack should be included in your budget. Costs depend entirely on how much you build yourself. Cost estimate: $200-$500.

Cages, trellises, and cloches. Your investment depends on how many tomatoes, peppers, peas, beans, and cucumbers you grow as these are the ones that use this equipment. Cages cost about 75¢ each, cloches about $1, and trellises $1 per running foot. The model garden requires 700' of trellis, 540 tomato cages, 180 cloches, and 6 pepper cages. Total cost is $1270.

Seed starting equipment. You will need germination equipment, light racks, hundreds of trays, large pots, etc. Estimated cost is $400-600

Buildings

Storage is necessary to protect the equipment from the weather during the off season. Since this equipment is outside during the growing season, this building could also serve as the vegetable processing area. If properly positioned, it could also be used as a marketing area for on-farm sales.

Our *preparation area* is 24' by 28'. Our storage area is 12' by 26'. Since our total production is slightly greater than the model garden from Chapter Four, a building 24' by 26' should be sufficient. Such a building would cost between $4000 - $6000 depending on how much of the work you did yourself.

Greenhouse

A greenhouse is necessary unless you find a supplier willing to provide larger than normal plants at reasonable prices. Greenhouses are not difficult to build if you have a building that you could add to on the south side. Optimum greenhouse width is 12'. If we put a 12' by 26' greenhouse on the south side of our storage building, we would add $500 - $1000 to our investment depending upon how we covered the greenhouse. Circulation fans would cost $150-$300. We found a used hanging heater for $100. Plastic covering is inexpensive but must be replaced each year. Fiberglass on the roof adds $? per square foot. Glass on the sides adds $5 per lineal foot of wall if the bottom of the wall is boarded up.

Total Cost Estimate (figure 4-9)

We begin with those items unique to commercial gardening as discussed earlier. The low figure represents used equipment or a previous purchase.

Greenhouse costs can actually go much higher than these estimates if a freestanding kit is purchased. This figure represents the cheapest lean-to construction. Restrictive building codes might push it somewhat higher.

Finally, we add the cost of a storage shed. If you have an area that can be used, you are well on your way to solving your investment in commercial gardening.

This brings your total cost to somewhere between $9450 and $15,100. Individual items may vary considerably, but we believe this initial investment estimate to be reasonable close for financial planning purposes. Much of your cost, of course, depends on the requirement to construct a storage building and greenhouse.

THE CONSTRUCTION PLAN

One year prior to the first market:

• Prepare the ground with a large farm tractor, cultivating as deeply as possible.

• Test the soil to determine what supplements are required. Test the source of organic matter. Consult a soils expert and develop an estimate of how much the garden requires.

• Till the garden, and add the organic material and fertilizer supplements.

• Construct the raised beds.

• Construct the water manifolds, lay the supply lines, and prepare the irrigation hoses.

• Construct the cages, cloches, and trellises.

• Construct the greenhouse and storage shed.

If all of this construction is completed prior to the first season, time will be available to make those final adjustments and repairs that always seem to appear at the most inopportune times.

PAST AND FUTURE HITS AND MISSES

The most significant problem we had throughout construction was the absence of a well designed master plan. Consequently, we redesigned and reinstalled our water system, incurring unnecessary and additional expenses. If you use the recommendations of this chapter you should not have these problems.

We are currently using watering zones with five to six beds per zone. This is far from ideal because different crops within the zone have different watering requirements. We recommend that you invest the money and do it right the first time with a valve for each bed.

I have often wondered if a small skid-steer loader could be used for bed construction. It would require some additional hand work to bring the bed to final form. It would also require cultivation of the loader tracks as beds were constructed from one end of the garden to the other. I think it could be done with a little practice, and might reduce construction time considerably.

THE HOME GARDENER

Two highlights from this chapter that should be considered by every serious hobby gardener. These are raised beds and drip irrigation. Since the specifics were discussed already, we will focus our attention on the changes required for the home garden.

The installation of a drip irrigation is not as difficult as you might think. Most manufacturers offer a starter's kit that would provide the pieces you need to experiment. Then you can order the additional hardware required for a full installation.

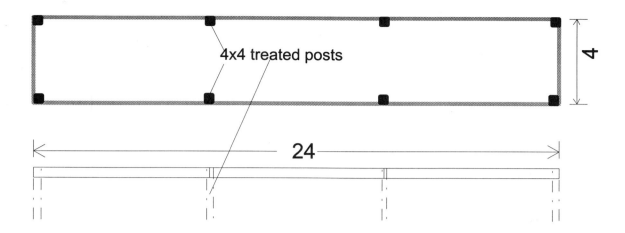

4-10. Supported bed construction. *These dimensions provide an efficient use of expensive resources. Posts can be from 24-32" in length. We use 2x6 side boards, and elevate them about two inches above the ground level for an 8" total rise. Four feet wide is about as wide as you can reach easily for working the beds. Bed should be fairly level. We have about a 2-3" slope over the 24 feet. If 24" posts are used, each bed requires seven 8' 2x6s and two 8' 4x4 posts.*

Raised beds can be constructed in many ways. If esthetics is an issue, we recommend a supported bed using treated lumber, cedar or redwood (Figure 4-10).

Cultivate the bed to the desired depth. Traditional double-digging recommends a depth of 24 inches. Since the bed will be eight inches above the ground, cultivation to sixteen inches would be sufficient. This will require that the top layers of soil be set aside while the bottom layers are cultivated.

Add conditioning material to the lower layers. If you have clay-based soil, you may wish to add some sand. If you have high pH, you might want to add some peat moss. In any case, you will want to use plenty of organic material.

Once the bottom layers are finished, install the posts. We use 32 inch posts, although 24 inches might be sufficient in those sec-

tions of the country where frost doesn't go too deep.

The posts should be tamped into place to facilitate construction. Replace the top soil and install the side boards. Finally, condition the top soil as required with sand, peat moss, and organic material.

If you plan to construct more than one bed, leave at least three feet in between beds for work space and garden equipment. The width of the bed should not be more than 48 inches. Anything wider than that is almost impossible to work without getting into the bed.

We have constructed 26 supported beds. Because of the large quantity involved, we cheated a bit and used the cultivator on the tractor rather than double-digging by hand. We installed the posts and side boards first and left one end off so we could back the cultivator into the bed. Since we were not cultivating to 24 inches, this worked quite well.

By the end of the chapter, you might feel a bit like this!

Chapter Five

Planning

When we started gardening commercially, we were overwhelmed with the complexity of planning. We grew many vegetables, each with different growing requirements, germination dates, planting dates, and transplant dates. Six years later, planning has become much easier for the following reasons:

• *Simplicity.* We grow a few vegetables well, rather than attempt to grow a large number of different crops.

• *Experience.* Planting dates have been tested and verified. We have an established range of dates that work for the techniques we use. One of the most frustrating aspects of our early planning efforts was the uncertainty of what we were doing. We were not confident things would work according to plan.

• *Better equipment.* We have built light and germination racks that provide a more uniform environment for young plants removing much of the guesswork from planning. We know when tomato seeds will germinate because we provide uniform

temperature and moisture.

Careful planning is critical to profitability so we will present the general concepts in this chapter. Then, in Part II, each crop chapter will provide planning details for that crop.

A complete planting plan requires the answers to the following questions:

• What crops will we grow?
• Which varieties will we grow?
• When will we plant them?
• When will we transplant them into the garden?
• Where will we plant them in the garden?

WHAT CROPS WILL WE GROW?

There are several ways to arrive at the answer to this question. The method you use will be determined by your overall strategy developed in chapter two. Our strategy is to grow those two crops which provide maximum profits, tomatoes and cucumbers. Since we want to rotate crops every three years, each of these crops commands 1/3 of the garden space.

The difference between a good garden and a great garden is often in the planning. Although there are no hard and fast rules for planning a garden, a few basic principles will steer you toward success: Plan your garden to fit your needs.

From Gardening[1]

53

What you grow is determined by your overall strategy. Crop selection decisions cannot be made without considering your marketing plan and your growing options. Decisions must fit together in a cohesive, coherent, integrated plan.

The final third is split between our niche crop, onions, and the most profitable popular crops that will draw customers to our marketing stand.

The success of this strategy is determined by our ability to produce tomatoes and cucumbers earlier than other growers. If we were to devote 1/3 of our garden to tomatoes and 1/3 to cucumbers without two to three weeks of limited competition, we would not be able to sell what we produced. On the other hand, we can sell 1/3 to 1/2 of our yearly gross during those two to three weeks, if we can achieve full production.

If, for some reason, you cannot focus on the early market, your planting decisions must be based upon how much you can sell, and the 1/3 rule will not apply. This is particularly true upon entry into a mature market where produce is generally available. It takes time, quality, and a diversity of produce to break into an established mature market.

Please read the next few sentences carefully as they will affect your profitability more than any of the other concepts in the book. *What you grow is determined by your overall strategy. Crop selection decisions cannot be made without considering your marketing plan and your growing options. Decisions must fit together in a cohesive, coherent, integrated plan.* You must not grow eggplant because you are good at it. You must decide to grow eggplant because you can sell all you grow. We use the 1/3 planting rule because it fits with our greenhouse, our intensive gardening, our early marketing, and because no one else is doing it.

Any plan must be adjusted from year to year based upon changes in marketing strategy, competition, and experience. For example, suppose a potential niche market develops in the pickle and salsa canning markets. If you want to satisfy this market need, garlic, jalepeno peppers, and storage onions must be added to the planting plan.

We are in our seventh year and we are still making substantial adjustments to our plan. We have discovered that careful adjustment of the garden plan increases profitability more than any other factor.

WHAT VARIETIES WILL WE GROW?

There are many varieties of each vegetable available. Variety selection is often a matter of compromise. That is, we cannot always find a variety that meets all our requirements. So we compromise and pick the variety that is strongest in the area that is the most important to us. We make our selection based upon the following factors.

Maturity dates. There are tremendous variations in available maturity dates. Cabbage, for example, will mature in a range from 56 days to 110 days. Since we focus on the early market we select varieties that will mature with our marketing plan without compromising the other factors.

Taste. Farmers markets are based on this factor more than any other. We sell fresh vegetables that taste better. Many magazine articles are written about comparative taste tests, and we consider these closely in our selection.

Disease tolerance. In localities with disease problems, this can become the most important factor. We have not had a disease problem so we consider this factor, but it does not dominate our selection.

Yield. Profitability is determined not only by market price, but total

	A	B	C	D	E	F	G	H	I	J
1	**The Planning Calendar**									
2	Dys	Date	Dys	Date	Dys	Date	Dys	Date	Dys	Date
3	110	29-Jan	78	1-Mar	46	2-Apr	14	4-May	18	5-Jun
4	109	30-Jan	77	2-Mar	45	3-Apr	13	5-May	19	6-Jun
5	108	31-Jan	76	3-Mar	44	4-Apr	12	6-May	20	7-Jun
6	107	1-Feb	75	4-Mar	43	5-Apr	11	7-May	21	8-Jun
7	106	2-Feb	74	5-Mar	42	6-Apr	10	8-May	22	9-Jun
8	105	3-Feb	73	6-Mar	41	7-Apr	9	9-May	23	10-Jun
9	104	4-Feb	72	7-Mar	40	8-Apr	8	10-May	24	11-Jun
10	103	5-Feb	71	8-Mar	39	9-Apr	7	11-May	25	12-Jun
11	102	6-Feb	70	9-Mar	38	10-Apr	6	12-May	26	13-Jun
12	101	7-Feb	69	10-Mar	37	11-Apr	5	13-May	27	14-Jun
13	100	8-Feb	68	11-Mar	36	12-Apr	4	14-May	28	15-Jun
14	99	9-Feb	67	12-Mar	35	13-Apr	3	15-May	29	16-Jun
15	98	10-Feb	66	13-Mar	34	14-Apr	2	16-May	30	17-Jun
16	97	11-Feb	65	14-Mar	33	15-Apr	1	17-May	31	18-Jun
17	96	12-Feb	64	15-Mar	32	16-Apr	0	18-May	32	19-Jun
18	95	13-Feb	63	16-Mar	31	17-Apr	1	19-May	33	20-Jun
19	94	14-Feb	62	17-Mar	30	18-Apr	2	20-May	34	21-Jun
20	93	15-Feb	61	18-Mar	29	19-Apr	3	21-May	35	22-Jun
21	92	16-Feb	60	19-Mar	28	20-Apr	4	22-May	36	23-Jun
22	91	17-Feb	59	20-Mar	27	21-Apr	5	23-May	37	24-Jun
23	90	18-Feb	58	21-Mar	26	22-Apr	6	24-May	38	25-Jun
24	89	19-Feb	57	22-Mar	25	23-Apr	7	25-May	39	26-Jun
25	88	20-Feb	56	23-Mar	24	24-Apr	8	26-May	40	27-Jun
26	87	21-Feb	55	24-Mar	23	25-Apr	9	27-May	41	28-Jun
27	86	22-Feb	54	25-Mar	22	26-Apr	10	28-May	42	29-Jun
28	85	23-Feb	53	26-Mar	21	27-Apr	11	29-May	43	30-Jun
29	84	24-Feb	52	27-Mar	20	28-Apr	12	30-May	44	1-Jul
30	83	25-Feb	51	28-Mar	19	29-Apr	13	31-May	45	2-Jul
31	82	26-Feb	50	29-Mar	18	30-Apr	14	1-Jun	46	3-Jul
32	81	27-Feb	49	30-Mar	17	1-May	15	2-Jun	47	4-Jul
33	80	28-Feb	48	31-Mar	16	2-May	16	3-Jun	48	5-Jul
34	79	29-Feb	47	1-Apr	15	3-May	17	4-Jun	49	6-Jul

5-1. The planning calendar for Bismarck, North Dakota.

quantities produced. Therefore, it is imperative that we select a variety that produces well.

Climate. Some varieties will not grow well in North Dakota. Regardless of their other redeeming virtues, this one fault eliminates them from serious consideration.

WHEN WILL WE PLANT THEM?

Profitable commercial gardening, like good humor, is a function of timing. If we plant at the right time, and transplant at the right time, the plant will produce at the right time when prices are high, and supply is limited.

To assist in this task we use the planning calendar, Figure 5-1. Notice that two dates are highlighted, the Frost Free Date (FFD) and the estimated first day of our market, FFD+45. This allows you to translates dates from this book into specific dates for your area. For example, if we plant a crop on FFD-65, you should be able to do the same. But since your FFD is different, your planting date will also be different. However, the relationship to FFD should be about the same.

Maturity and germination

Timing decisions start with the published maturity dates. These dates estimate the day of first harvest. For transplants, these dates are usually from the date they are transplanted not from the date they are planted. For direct sown products, the maturity dates are either from the date of sowing or from the date of germination. Germination is the time it takes for a seed to start growing after we plant it. Germination is affected by temperature and moisture.

Germination and maturity dates are estimates based upon breeder averages. Obviously, weather will affect these dates considerably. Our unique growing conditions may influence them as well. However, we don't have anything better so we start with them. Then we keep records and adjust our data for future seasons.

For transplants the size and health of the plant and the soil temperature at the time of transplanting will affect the maturity date. For example, a 10 week-old tomato plant transplanted into 65° soil will produce fruit much earlier than a 6 week-old plant in 55° soil.

Let me provide a dramatic example of actual versus seed catalog maturity dates. In 1993 we planted the first bed of Earlibird Nantees carrots the third week of April. We harvested this bed on the 17th and 18th of July, about 85 days after planting. Stokes advertises this as a 50-day variety. Our early planting and cool spring weather delayed the maturity date considerably. Use published maturity dates as guides, and adjust for your unique growing conditions.

Planting dates

There are five factors besides maturity and germination that determine planting or transplant dates.

The first is *plant hardiness*, that is, at what temperature will the plant survive. Cabbage will take a freeze and continue to thrive. Cucumbers will wilt the first time the temperature reaches 32°.

Opening market date. This does not refer to the local market's traditional opening date. This is the day our strategy says we should start marketing. For us, that is the day cucumbers and/or tomatoes become available. In 1993 we averaged less than $225 per week for the three weeks prior to the arrival of cukes

Use published maturity dates as guides, and adjust for your unique growing conditions.

Master Planting Plan

Date	Vegetable	Variety	Amount	Remarks
1-Feb	Onions	Walla Walla	6500	Plant in large trays
1-Mar	Peppers	Ace	300	Sow in flats - pick the best
15-Mar	Tomatoes	Oregon Spring	1100	Sow in flats - pick the best
28-Mar	Cabbage	Stonehead	250	Sow in 1204s
11-Apr	Cabbage	Stonehead	250	Sow in 1204s
18-Apr	Peas	Multistar	600	Direct seed
25-Apr	Cabbage	Stonehead	250	Sow in 1204s
25-Apr	Carrots	Earlibird Nantees	9000	Direct seed
1-May	Cucumbers	Calypso	500 hills	4 seeds per hill - sow in large trays
1-May	Bush beans	Strike	1200	Direct seed - 2-3", thin to 4-6"
10-May	Zucchini	Zucchini Select	33 hills	5 seeds per hill - direct seed

and tomatoes. In the first week after those crops arrived, we sold over $1200.

Maturity. The third factor is whether a crop must go to market when it is mature, or whether it can remain safely in the garden. If we plant peas too early, we may have to go to market with just peas, hardly a profitable use of time. However, if we plant carrots too early, they can wait until we are ready to take other produce to market.

The affect of weather on various crops. Tomatoes and cukes require warm weather, cabbages do not. Therefore, if spring weather is cool, the cabbage will be ready for market long before the cucumbers mature. Zucchini doesn't seem to care what the weather is, it will be ready for anything.

The optimum age of transplants. Crops vary in how long it takes to grow a plant capable of surviving outside. Cabbages are ready in 4-6 weeks while peppers take 10-12 weeks. However, survivability is not the issue when we are trying to hit the early market. We want to grow a transplant to optimum size, that is, so

it still transplants well, and gets us as close as possible to production at the opening of market.

Each crop brings a different combination of these factors to the planning process. And therein lies the planning challenge, to attempt to get these variables to converge at a point in the market with quantities that will prove profitable.

Beans must be picked when they are ready. They are a warm weather crop like cucumbers but differ in that they are direct seeded. However, they will react to the weather parallel to cukes and tomatoes. Earliest plant date is determined by soil temperature.

Because of their tolerance to cold weather, it is possible to grow cabbage that is too large when the cucumbers arrive. However, cabbage can remain in the garden for awhile unless excess moisture causes them to split. The planting of cabbage, then, is driven by the day we want to bring to market.

Carrots can remain in the ground for a limited time after reaching maturity. But carrots present a special problem. They are profitable

5-2. The Master Planting Plan. Until you get to this detail, you do not really have a complete planting plan. We do not include transplanting dates in this plan because there are too many variables; wind, temperature, status of plants, etc.

5-3. The Seed Plan. This appears to be a tremendous amount of work. However, if we do not take our planning to this point, we do not have a complete plan.

Seed Plan						
Vegetable	**Variety**	**Source**	**Amount**	**Cost**	**Ord**	**Rec**
Beans	Blue Lake FM-1	Jordans	1 pound	$1.90		
Beans	Strike	Jordans	1 pound	$2.29		
Cabbage	Stonehead	Stokes	1000	$2.13		
Carrots	Earlibird Nantees	Stokes	1/2 ounce	$7.80		
Cucumbers	Calypso	Stokes	3 ounces	$10.95		
Onions	Walla Walla	Jordans	1 ounce	$4.75		
Peas	Multistar	Johnnys	1 pound	$4.75		
Peppers	Ace	Stokes	1/16 ounc	$7.80		
Tomatoes	Oregon Spring	Nichols	1/8 ounce	$5.25		
Zucchini	Select	Stokes	1 ounce	$4.30		
			Total	$51.92		

only if we can double-crop or inter-plant them. If we choose to double-crop, carrots must be planted as early in the spring as possible, and harvested as soon as they are ready. Otherwise, the fall crop will come too late for the market. As in most planning projects, compromise is necessary. Carrots tolerate cool weather, but do not thrive as cabbages do. We plant carrots as early as possible, and if we get nice weather, they will mature about the same time as cukes and tomatoes. If not, we will bring them to market when they are ready because they sell so easily.

Onions are easy because they do better if left in the garden past opening market. They are a long season crop and the earlier we plant, the larger they will be when we want to go to market.

Peas are a very hardy short-season crop that must be picked when ready. Plant date is determined by when we want to bring them to market.

Peppers are tender plants that will not mature until mid-to-late summer. Since the fruits can remain on the vines, planting is determined by the earliest transplant date. Market arrival is largely a matter of variety.

Zucchini must be picked when they are ready. They grow very quickly so can easily beat tomatoes to the market. Plant date is determined by when we want to bring them to market.

Once we determine specific planning data for each crop, we enter it into the master planting plan, figure 5-2.

SEED PLAN

Once we know what crops we will plant, we develop a complete plan for our seed purchases.

Quantities Required

This is calculated by taking our spacing times the number of beds we plan to plant. We then calculate a safety factor for germination problems. Specific examples are included in each of the individual crop chapters.

Source

The seed plan, figure 5-3, provides a record for ordering seeds on time and in the right quantities. Consider the following in selecting sources.

Use fresh seed. If you plan carefully, you will be able to order about the right amount. Since the quality of the seed affects the health

Crop Rotation Plan			
Bed	1994	1995	1996
1	Tomatoes	Cucumbers	Onions
2	Tomatoes	Cucumbers	Onions
3	Tomatoes	Cucumbers	Onions
4	Tomatoes	Cucumbers	Beans
5	Tomatoes	Cucumbers	Beans
6	Tomatoes	Cucumbers	Carrots
7	Tomatoes	Cucumbers	Carrots
8	Tomatoes	Cucumbers	Experimental
9	Tomatoes	Cucumbers	Peas/Cabbage
10	Peppers	Zucchini	Peas/Cabbage
11	Onions	Tomatoes	Zucchini
12	Onions	Tomatoes	Cucumbers
13	Onions	Tomatoes	Cucumbers
14	Beans	Tomatoes	Cucumbers
15	Beans	Peppers	Cucumbers
16	Cucumbers	Onions	Tomatoes
17	Cucumbers	Onions	Tomatoes
18	Cucumbers	Onions	Tomatoes
19	Cucumbers	Carrots	Tomatoes
20	Cucumbers	Carrots	Tomatoes
21	Cucumbers	Beans	Tomatoes
22	Cucumbers	Beans	Tomatoes
23	Cucumbers	Experimental	Tomatoes
24	Cucumbers	Peas/Cabbage	Tomatoes
25	Zucchini	Peas/Cabbage	Peppers
26	Carrots	Tomatoes	Cucumbers
27	Carrots	Tomatoes	Cucumbers
28	Experimental	Tomatoes	Cucumbers
29	Peas/Cabbage	Tomatoes	Cucumbers
30	Peas/Cabbage	Tomatoes	Cucumbers

5-4. The Crop Rotation Plan. *This plan is critical for disease control. A rotation plan involves not only individual crops, but also crop families. That is, peppers and tomatoes are in the same family of plants and subject to similar diseases and pests. Consequently, we treat them as a single unit for rotation purposes. Related crops are:*

- *Nightshades: Tomatoes, peppers, potatoes, and eggplant.*
- *Cucurbits: Squash, cucumbers, and melons.*
- *Brassicas: Cabbage, Broccolli, cauliflower, brussel sprouts, kale, collards, mustard, and turnips.*
- *Umbelliferae: Carrots, parsley, parsnips, and dill.*
- *Goosefoot: Beets, spinach, and chard.*
- *Allium: Garlic, leeks, and onions are in the same family but are rarely bothered by pests or diseases.*

of your plant, it doesn't make sense to save seed from year to year. Why take the chance on weak seed?

Price. Prices vary considerably for the same variety. For example, Blue Lake beans, a standard variety, is $4.60 per pound from Stokes, and $1.90 per pound from Jordans. Oregon Spring tomatoes are $12 per ounce from Nichols, and $16 per 1/2 ounce at Garden City Seeds.

Quantities. Each company packages seeds differently. If you need ½ ounce, find the company that gets closest to that amount at a competitive price. Back to the tomatoes. We don't need an ounce of seed. We need about 1/4 ounce, which would cost $11 at Garden City. For another $1 we get a full ounce from Nichols, allowing us to plant more seeds and select the best of the bunch.

Shipping costs. Handling charges average $1.50 - $3.00 per order. Therefore, if you order from five firms you pay five handling charges. Sometimes money can be saved by buying higher priced seeds to eliminate shipping costs from an additional source. The optimum situation is to purchase all seeds from one source. However, the right varieties are generally not available in one place in the quantities we desire.

Where will we put each crop?

Crop placement is almost exclusively a matter of crop rotation, a key factor for successful control of pests and diseases. The rotation plan, figure 5-4, must include provisions for crop families.

The rotation plan for the model garden is very simple. If we use a clockwise rotation for the next year, tomatoes and peppers move to where the cucumbers are, cukes move to the bottom third, and our onions, peas, beans, cabbage and carrots move up to where the tomatoes and peppers are. This is easy because the garden splits nicely into three parts, and we have no previous garden history to consider. Our actual garden rotation is extremely complicated because we did not design the garden with rotation in mind, and our early planning was often haphazard. Compromises have been necessary and over the next few years, we will adjust the plot plan to allow for intelligent crop rotation.

We use a computer spreadsheet to develop the plot plan. This facilitates the many changes we make as we go through the planning process. It would be possible to complete the plan manually, but it would most likely be inefficient and messy.

The plot plan for the next season is developed as the current season progresses. Marketing changes, strategy adjustments, and production experiences are considered, and by the end of the current season, the plan for the next season is in rough draft.

Spacing

Spacing may not be critical to a large grower with many acres, but it is a very important planning factor for the intensive gardener working on limited space. Let's use beans as an example. Many sources recommend a 4-6" spacing. At 6 inches we have two plants per foot, at 4 inches we have three, or half again as many. That means we can get a 50% increase in production with the closer spacing.

Well, maybe! When plants are crowded, they produce less. Therefore, spacing is often variety specific. That is, if the bean variety has very large leaves, crowding may actually reduce production. On the other hand, if the leaves are smaller, crowding may increase production by that desired 50%.

Experimentation plan

The key to long range success in commercial garden is constant experimentation. However, it must be well designed and methodical to achieve optimum benefits. This requires meticulous records such as the example provided in figure 5-5.

Let me give you an example from a bean experiment that didn't work very well. In 1993 we planted three varieties. Provider is widely available, a dark brown seed early bean (50 days from germination) that is tolerant to cool soil. Strike (45 days from gemination) is an extra early bean available from Stokes. Based on an Organic Gardening article, we tried one packet of Harris Seeds Espada, a 56 day BLUE LAKE type. The Provider beans were planted on

60

Experimentation Plan		
Problem	**Experiment**	**Result**
Soil mix for cucumbers has had too much soil so the trays were extremely hard to water deeply. Need a soil mix that will facilitate watering but still hold together when planting.	April 1 - Fill a tray with 3 different mixes. 1. 1/2 potting soil, 1/2 peat; 2. 1/3 soil, 1/3 peat, 1/3 vermiculite; 3. 1/3 soil, 1/3 peat, 1/3 perlite. Plant 3 seeds per cell. April 15 - Repeat with another tray.	
Can we set out cukes that are beyond three weeks?	May 1 - Transplant to 5" pots to determine right soil mix. Set a few out to determine sensitivity to cold, and the protection provided by the cloches. May 15 - set out next tray to determine if we can use 4-week old plants.	
How profitable are slicers compared to pickles? How do the pounds picked vary? Theory says that if we have good pollination, the number of pounds should be about equal.	Document one row for at least a week during good slicer production. Document the same row about a week after it has been converted to pickle production. Document weather so adjustments can be made.	
How will purchased onion plants produce compared to those we raise ourselves.	Purchase 2000 from Piedmont.	No significant difference in maturity date.

May 2, Strike on May 17, and Espada on May 22.

I need to raise a critical point on variety experimentation. We tried three different varieties but we planted them on different dates. Therefore it is impossible to conclude that performance variance was because of the variety. Performance may have been adversely affected because of the cool soil conditions. In future variety trials, we will plant a portion of all varieties on the same dates.

Adjusting production

Refer to figures 5-6 and 5-7, our sales figures by date and product for July 1993 and July 1994. Please remember that 1993 was an unusually cool and wet season. A normal season would bring cukes and tomatoes to market 10 days to two weeks earlier. After a performance review of the early days at the market in 1993 we can conclude the following:

• Total sales were not significant until cucumbers and tomatoes arrived for market on the 24th and 27th of July. Our marketing strategy to this point assumed that all crops should be grown as early as possible. Based upon this experience, we changed our definition of early market to include only cukes and tomatoes.

• Most cabbage sales came too early. Cabbage can be left in the garden but probably not that long. Cabbage is not adversely affected by cool weather. Therefore, had we had warm weather, tomatoes and cukes would have arrived earlier and cabbage would have been available at the right time.

• Carrot sales demonstrate our staggered plantings very well. If we slip our planting just about a week, our carrots will arrive at about the right time.

• Onion sales can be postponed easily without changing anything we are doing. The onions we harvested at this point were small. Even though we received 75¢ per pound, we would

5-5. Experimentation Plan. Perhaps you have a better memory than I do, but if I don't write this information down, I won't remember what possible changes I wanted to research during the season.

5-6. Adjusting production from sales data. *After a careful analysis of this spreadsheet, we changed our production strategy. We now attempt to grow the earliest tomatoes and cucumbers at the market. The production of all other crops is planned to coincide with the arrival of these two crops.*

July 1993 Sales

Product	3	6	10	15	17	18	20	24	27	29	31	Totals
Beans							3	10	9	9	11	42
Brassicas	9	11	45	20	32	24	35	45	23	7	44	295
Carrots					87	22			13	21	50	193
Cucumbers					10			8	24	24	26	92
Onions	5	4	30	11	27	20	15	36	10	9	53	220
Peppers					31	5	9	21	6	4	31	107
Tomatoes									14	30	90	134
Zucchini			5	7	11	4	1	19	10	21	15	93
Totals	14	15	80	38	198	75	63	139	109	125	320	1176

still get more if we let them grow for another three weeks, and sell them for 60¢ per pound.

• Pepper sales indicate that peppers can be grown to arrive concurrently with cukes and tomatoes. Those few we sold early, could easily have been left on the vine. Therefore, we will duplicate our planting plan from last year.

• Zucchini reacts better to cool weather than cukes and tomatoes. If we were to have warm weather, zucchini would arrive a little earlier. Therefore, we will slip our plant date about two weeks.

• Beans were about right. Since beans like warm weather, it should be possible to consistently arrive with tomatoes and cukes. However, they must be picked when they are ready so timing is better late than early.

Now let's compare these conclusions with our performance in 1994.

We used pole beans so they came in very late and sales were lost. We will change that next year by planting both pole and bush beans.

Notice the relationship between cucumbers and tomatoes. In a cool year like 1993, they came in about the same time. In a normal year, cucumbers responded much more quickly to the warm weather, and arrived about two weeks earlier then the tomatoes. We will attempt to push tomatoes just a little earlier.

Timing on peas and carrots is largely irrelevant unless your market is over supplied. They will sell regardless of when you bring them. Peppers, beans, zucchini, and cabbage sell better if you have a larger customer base. That is, there is generally some oversupply and if you can attract customers with tomatoes and cukes, they sell very well. Our experience with onions is that they will sell well anytime, but are more profitable if sold later in the season when they are larger.

Planning is one of the most important skills that a new commercial gardener must learn. Unfortunately, it is also one of the most difficult. We hope these suggestions will help you.

FOR THE HOME GARDENER

Of the five planning factors introduced in this chapter, the problem we see most often with hobby gardeners is the "I'm going to plant my garden today" problem. Our family did that when I was growing up, usually on Memorial Day week-

Product	30	2	3	7	9	10	12	14	16	17	19	21	23	24	26	28	30	31	Totals
Peas												24	13		24	40	34	30	165
Beans																		9	9
Brassicas	3	3		4	10	11	12	5	18	4	5	5	14	6	6	5	12	6	129
Carrots													2		2		37		41
Cukes	22	109	69	92	16	48	129	177	185	256	203	254	210	157	158	163	163	120	2531
Pickles																		47	47
Onions	7	15	8	8	18	10	15	16	35	27	28	26	63	31	41	23	83	27	481
Peppers					17	3	16	5	17		12	8	32	8	12	13	40	10	193
Tomatoes				3	2		12	21	101	65	122	170	155	90	150	250	250	350	1741
Zucchini		3	3	4	15	4	12	7	22	20	22	15	13	20	20	16	17	17	230
Flowers-Dried					0	5	5	0	0						25	13	30	30	108
Flowers-Fresh		15	12	7	25	34	48	23	79	28			134	63	61	3	70	15	617
Garlic	6	5	1										14	19	21	25	38	30	159
Other							2						5	2	3	3	5	3	23
Totals	38	150	93	115	104	117	251	254	457	400	392	502	655	396	523	554	779	694	6474

July 1994 Sales

end. However, peas planted the end of May will not produce as well as peas planted the first of May. Each crop should be planted at the optimum time, not on a single day. Planting everything on Memorial Day is convenient, but not very smart.

The serious home gardener wants quality produce as early as possible (preferably the first on the block). Throughout the book we provide ideas on how this can be done. However, an important secondary planning consideration is the consequence of planting at the wrong time. With these factors in mind, let's adjust our planning. We'll use the Frost Free Date (FFD) as a reference.

Beans cannot be rushed because they need warmth to germinate and mature. Consider using cloches for earlier beans. If you want beans all season, succession plant or use a combination of bush and pole beans.

Cabbage can be set out very early, long before your last frost. If you want cabbage all season you can plant varieties with different maturity dates or succession plant.

Carrots can be planted about a month before the last frost, but germination might be delayed by cool soil. The best tasting carrots are grown in cool weather. Consequently, this early planting is highly recommended. Maturity dates for carrots do not vary much, so succession planting is necessary for a continuous crop.

Cucumbers can be pushed a little in the spring with transplants and cloches. However, without warm weather, production will be limited. This short-season crop will not tolerate frost. Planting shortly after your FFD might be about right.

Lettuce is very hardy and can be set out with cabbage and onions.

Onions can be set out very early, shortly after you can first work the garden.

Peas can be planted shortly after the onions. Peas will not tolerate hot weather so succession planting probably is not an option.

Peppers are extremely sensitive to cool weather so a week or so past the FFD is about right.

Tomatoes are tougher. They will tolerate cool weather but not frost. With the protection of plastic de-

5-7. July 1994 Sales. When these figures are compared with the previous year, figure 5-8, a clear idea of the effects of weather emerges.

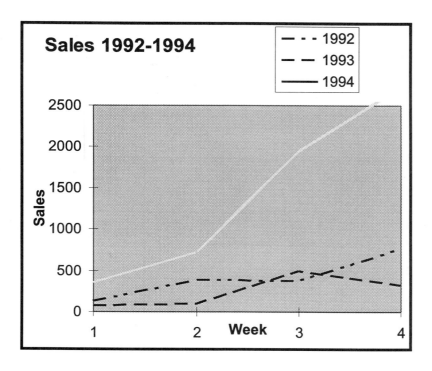

Sales 1992-1994

Legend: — - - 1992 — — 1993 —— 1994

Y-axis: Sales (0, 500, 1000, 1500, 2000, 2500)
X-axis: Week (1, 2, 3, 4)

5-8. Sales per week.
This chart illustrates the differences in July sales caused by the weather. During the third week of July we sold less than $500 in produce during the 1992 and 1993 seasons. However, because of warmer weather in 1994, we sold almost $2000 during that same week.

scribed later in this book, they can be set out on about your FFD, and with some supplemental heat or protection, perhaps a bit earlier.

Zucchini can be started as a transplant or direct seeded with some protection.

Another serious frustration is the severe limitation of available varieties. In many communities, greenhouses stock only the standard cultivars. If you want to experiment with more exotic options, you will need to consider raising your own transplants.

Crop rotation may have only limited use for disease prevention in a small garden. However, it is still worth the effort because planning the rotation is not difficult . The key is to recognize the vegetable families, and draw out a three year plan.

Constructing the spreadsheet

The planning calendar, figure 5-1, is the only spreadsheet that makes extensive use of formulas. We could enter all of the numbers manually, but the power of the spreadsheet is its ability to use formulas. For that reason, we included the column and row designations on figure 5-1 to guide us through this process. The formulas are from Microsoft Excel. You may have to adjust them for your spreadsheet formula syntax. Your spread sheet must be capable of formatting to dates.

Enter your FFD in cell H17 and zero at G17. Notice that I use the military format, because I find that more readable. There is no reason to include the year in the columns.

At H16 enter the formula, =H17-1. Copy the formula in all cells up to H4. The power of the modern spreadsheet will do that very easily and quickly.

G16 adds one day to G17 with the formula, =G17+1. Copy this formula to G4.

We want to pick up the figures from G4 and H4 at the bottom of columns E and F. We do that with the formulas at E34, =G4+1, and at F34, =H4-1. At E33 enter, =E34+, and at F33 enter, =F34-1. Copy those formulas over to A34 thru D34. Then copy the formulas in A34 through F34 up to row 3.

At G18 enter =G17+1 and at H18 enter =H17+1. Copy these forumlas to row 34. At I3 enter =G34+1 and at J3 enter +H34+1. At I4 enter =I3+1 and at J4 enter J4+1. Copy these last two formulas to row 34 and the spreadsheet is finished.

64

Growing Transplants

Growing healthy transplants is necessary for optimum production. Healthy transplants provide the foundation for the success of the season. Production ceilings are established in this critical phase. If transplants become stressed because of a lack of water or exposure to extreme temperatures, they become stunted and never fully recover.

The model garden plan, figure 4-2 on page 43, requires 540 tomatoes, 200 peppers, 297 hills of cucumbers, 4000 onions, and 400 cabbages. Only cucumbers could be direct seeded, the rest must be grown as transplants. We have three options.

First, we can purchase transplants from a national source, such as Piedmont[1] for about $150 plus air freight costs. This is the least expensive option, but limits variety selection to those varieties they sell. Cucumbers are not available but could be direct seeded. We know a very large, profitable, commercial gardener who has been in the business for over 20 years and still buys his plants this way.

A second option is to contract with a local greenhouse or another grower to provide the transplants from the seeds we supply. We have

not tried this but believe it to be a very viable option. Every community has numerous greenhouses. Certainly one would be willing to work with a wholesale account.

YOUR OWN GREENHOUSE

The last option is to build our own greenhouse. This provides optimum control for the grower. However, like so many decisions we make, this one is certainly not without problems.

Certified organic growers have fewer transplant choices as certifying agencies require organically grown transplants. There are organic greenhouses but plants are expensive and in limited supply. Consequently, a greenhouse is almost mandatory.

Advantages

• Growing transplants assures earlier harvests. Neither of the first two options will provide plants of optimum size. We use plants much larger than those normally provided by commercial greenhouses. The only way we can get those is to grow them ourselves.

• Gardening starts early in the spring. Greenhouse work is great fun

I suspect that I'd continue to raise my own seedlings even without a good excuse, because I enjoy the process, but when I stop to think about it I realize that there are all kinds of good reasons for nurturing one's own plants from seed.

Nancy Bubel[2]

65

6-1. Greenhouse construction. Nothing fancy here, just simple 2x4 framing on a 2x6 treated plate. If we were to do it again, we would insulate the floor on the first greenhouse to be used in the spring. The lean-to design makes the project economical and quick to build.

in late winter before the snow melts. For many, it is the most enjoyable aspect of gardening.

• Homegrown transplants are much healthier. Most seed is inexpensive so we plant 2-3 times what we need and choose only the best plants. We have fewer problems with pests and diseases that plague commercial greenhouses. When plants are purchased from a local nursery, those problems come home with you.

• Experimentation with varieties is possible. After perfecting the basics of commercial gardening, increased production and sales depends upon proper variety selection. Many of the best varieties for commercial use are not available at local nurseries. Oregon Spring tomatoes, for example, are only available from a few national seed houses, and no local nurseries grow them as plants.

Disadvantages

• Greenhouse production is demanding in that conditions must be just right most of the time or plants can be damaged. A greenhouse is not very forgiving. Transplants require constant and careful attention to small details.

• A greenhouse can be expensive to build. Initial investment in the greenhouse and equipment is not prohibitive with a simple design, but can be substantial if esthetics become an issue.

• Greenhouses are expensive to operate. In the long run you will not save money. Greenhouse operating costs are much higher than the cost of purchasing plants from a wholesaler because of the small quantities involved.

Considerations

Before you decide to build a greenhouse, consider the following:

• Do you have the time in the spring to devote to a greenhouse?

• Can you find a greenhouse that will grow the seeds you supply?

• Do you have the space for the greenhouse, and can it be built for a reasonable price? The easiest design is a lean-to added to an existing building.

• Do you have a source of supplemental heat for the greenhouse? If weather turns cold, heat will be required to keep the plants healthy and growing.

• Do you have good water immediately available? The source should be close by. An outside spigot and a hose would work well.

• Do you have a place to work your plants? Ideal germination requires a small heated area that can be kept at optimal temperature. Throughout the process repotting is necessary which requires a place to work.

Greenhouse construction

Greenhouses can be built in several ways:

Kits are available from many sources. They range from the very simple to very sophisticated and expensive.

A self-standing structure can be built with an economical 2x4 frame with plastic stretched across the framework.

A lean-to design saves money and is simple to construct.

Hoop houses are made from light metal pipe. Plastic is stretched over the hoops. Quite often there is a layer of air between double plastic sheets. A fan keeps the sheets apart providing some insulating value.

Our greenhouse consists of two lean-tos built on the south side of our garage and storage shed. The first section, in figure 6-2, is only 8 feet wide because we didn't have the space to make it wider. Eight feet is very inefficient because it provides a four-foot rack on one side and a two-foot rack on the other.

We use styrofoam sheets to divide this smaller greenhouse into two sections to save on the heating bill in early spring. We start by heating only one half, then when we need more room we remove the dividers. The larger greenhouse is twelve feet wide. This width appears to be the most cost effective arrangement. It gives us a little extra room in the center walkway.

Since our greenhouse is a permanent building, we used glass on the side windows and fiberglass on the roof. The glass added $400 to the cost but eliminated the need to fight with external plastic installation each spring. We do install plastic on the inside of the greenhouse to conserve heat. Racks are simple 2-by-4 frames

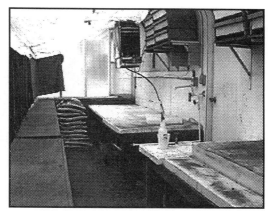

6-2. The greenhouse. The top picture is the eight-foot wide section. Notice the cramped walkway. The wider greenhouse in the bottom picture allows four 1020 trays end-to-end on the benches and still provides a spacious walkway. Both of the greenhouses are a simple lean-to construction.

covered with welded wire.

We may have made several mistakes in the design of the greenhouse. We chose to have windows only on the top half of the south wall and to enclose and insulate the bottom. This does not allow sunshine to warm the ground below. Consequently, the floor remains cool. Our second mistake was not to insulate the floor. If we were to do it again, we would lay a 4-6" styrofoam base with treated plywood over the top. To compensate for these errors we place styrofoam on top of the racks to keep the soil temperature close to the air temperature.

EQUIPMENT

Trays and pots

The *1020 tray* is an industry standard and measures 11" x 22". These trays serve many purposes. We use them as flats for initial planting of seeds. During initial transplanting, we use inserts for the 1020 trays. Finally,

67

Large trays
Center-rib 1020s
5½" pots
1204 inserts

cells per insert. A 1204 insert has 12
packs per insert and four cells per
pack for a total of 48 cells per insert.
Inserts cost less than 30¢ each so we
replace them every year to avoid
possible disease problems.

Several years ago we ordered
paper pots from Gardener's Supply
Co. The system consists of large
plastic trays, 16" W x 20" L x 4" H.
The paper dividers come separately
and fan out to provide individual cells
for the plants. When transplant time
arrives, the thin papers are stripped
away and the plant suffers very little
root damage.

We liked the system very well,
but there were two problems, the
plastic trays were not very strong, and
the paper pot inserts were very
expensive. So we modified the
system a bit and have been using it
ever since (figure 6-4). We built
supporting frames for the trays and
cut our own pots from strips of 90 lb
index card stock from a local printer.
Slots are spaced to provide 35 'pots'
per tray. Cutting slots in the paper is
done on a radial arm saw. The trick to
a clean cut is to C-clamp a scrap
board on both sides of the blade to
provide support during the cut. Other
growers use newspaper rolled around
a cylinder to form the individual pots.
The plastic trays are available from
Gardeners Supply at $3 each[3].

We will continue to use the large
trays for onions. However, we will
use a square plastic pot for intermediate potting of tomatoes and peppers.
We can justify the cost because we
need these pots for our cucumbers.

We want plants much larger
than those available at local greenhouses. Large plants need space for
the roots to grow so for our final
repotting we use 5½" pots. These fit
eight to a 1020 tray for ease in

we use them to transport the larger
5½ inch pots. For several years we
used the ones with a reinforcing rib
down the center for additional
strength. Then we found some heavy
duty flats from National Polymer.
They cost about 40¢ each but will last
for years and are much easier to work
with.

Inserts for the 1020 trays come
in many sizes. Most manufacturers
use a standard numbering system. An
806 insert has eight packs per insert
and six cells per pack for a total of 48

*These trays are an
expedient way to
provide additional
space for plants to
grow larger for
earlier harvest. The
peppers in the
bottom picture have
just been trans-
planted from the
1204s so this is their
third home. We do
not always need to
repot peppers a
fourth time into the
five inch pots.*

68

moving the pots. The pots cost about 13¢ each but are heavy enough to last for many years.

How much greenhouse is required?

To calculate maximum greenhouse space requirements, we begin with the worst case scenario and assume that all of the plants will be in the greenhouse at the same time at their largest configuration.

We grow tomatoes and peppers in 5½ inch pots which require about 30 square inches of space. 740 of these plants require 154 square feet. (740 x 30/144)

Cucumbers and cabbages require about 10 square inches each. These 697 plants require about 48 square feet. (697X10/144)

Onions require about one square inch to grow to optimum size or about 48 square feet. (7000/144)

The total requirement is 250 square feet of shelf space. If the greenhouse is 12' wide with a 3' aisle, it would need to be 28 feet long.

Let's look at a typical season

and adjust our space estimate. Compromises are necessary because of limited resources.

The season starts with onions. Since they are a long season crop we start them all at the same time. If we gave each onion the optimum 1" space, we would need 48 square feet of onions, or 22 of our large trays. That ties up these trays until the end of April when the onions are set out into the garden. We do not have that many trays nor is it advisable to grow all the onions the same size. If onions are crowded in the greenhouse, they will not grow as large. We want some small onions available throughout the season, so we will crowd some of them in the large trays. We estimate that 15 trays will be required, or 34 square feet.

About mid-March peppers and tomatoes are planted in flats. For the first two weeks space limitation are negligible since hundreds of seeds can be germinated in each tray. Then they are transplanted into 1204s. Each tray requires 1.7 square feet of greenhouse

6-5. Greenhouse space calculations. The numbers in the body of the chart indicate the number of square feet required by each crop at any given time. The totals on the second line up from the bottom indicate the required size of the greenhouse in rack space. The bottom row is the number of large trays required at any given time.

Product	Tray Size	Mar 1	Mar 8	Mar 15	Mar 22	Mar 29	Apr 5	Apr 12	Apr 19	Apr 26	May 3	May 10	May 17	May 24	May 31
Onions	Lg	34	34	34	34	34	34	34	34	34					
Tomatoes/Peppers	1204			9	9	37	37								
Tomatoes	Lg							41	41						
Tomatoes	5.5										121	121	121	121	
Cabbages	1204				20	20	20								
Cabbages	Lg							29	29	29					
Peppers	Lg								11	11	11				
Peppers	5.5											34	34	34	34
Cucumbers	Lg										37	37	37		
Total Square Feet		34	34	43	63	91	91	104	115	195	169	192	192	34	34
Large trays required		16	16	16	16	16	16	48	53	34	22	17	17	0	0

6-6. Mixing soils. *We found a cement mixer to be extremely helpful because of the volumes of soils that must be prepared, especially for the five inch pots. The plastic garbage cans are used for perlite and vermiculite.*

space. We need 690 plants to set out into the garden. Consequently, we will start with half again as many or 1035. There are 48 plants per tray so we will plant 22 flats which will require about 37 square feet.

Cabbages are next, planted directly into 1204s. We need 400 cabbage plants so will plant 576, 12 trays, to ensure 400 vigorous ones. This will take 20 square feet.

Tomatoes are repotted from the 1204s into the large trays. The larger trays hold 35 plants each. We need 540 tomato plants. At this point we have selected the best plants from the flats, and have over 800 plants available. We can get by with 10-15% extra since chances are good they will continue to grow well. Eighteen trays, 41 square feet, will provide us with 630 plants.

Cabbages will be repotted into the large trays next. We need 400 plants and will not require much of a safety factor. Consequently, we will plant 13 trays or 29 square feet.

Peppers are a bit slower maturing than tomatoes so will not be transplanted into large trays for another week or so. We need 150 plants. If we use the same safety factor we will use 5 trays, 175 plants, requiring 11 square feet.

Tomatoes will be repotted into 5½" pots. We will allow only a 5% safety factor or 568 plants. At eight per flat we will need space for 71 flats, or 121 square feet.

Cucumbers are planted the first week in May. We need 297 hills but have had problems with germination so will plant 17 large trays, 595 hills, or 37 square feet.

Finally, peppers are transplanted into 5½" pots. We need 150 plants so will plant 20 1020 trays of eight 5½" pots. That will give us 160 plants and will require 34 square feet.

A review of figure 6-5 reveals a maximum usage of 192 square feet of greenhouse space during the early part of May. This is fairly close to our initial estimate. The difference in the two estimating methods is that the first does not take into account the extra plants we grow to make sure we have enough strong healthy plants to set out into the garden. The second method does that, and then adjusts for the planting schedule. Consider the following when fine-tuning your greenhouse space requirements:

• Onions and cabbages are certain to be in the garden before the peppers are transplanted into the largest pots. This reduces the requirement by about 21 square feet.

• Cucumbers are only in the greenhouse for about three weeks. Onions and cabbages can most likely be left outside during this time unless weather is extreme.

• If you plan to work your plants in the greenhouse, an additional 20-30 square feet will be required.

Figure 6-5 can also be used to estimate required resources as demonstrated by the bottom entry. We do not worry about 1204s because they are inexpensive and we should have plenty available. However, large trays and 5½" pots are expensive and therefore in limited supply.

Greenhouse soils

Once we have our containers, our next requirement is a growing medium. We use one mix for germination and another for growing larger plants. Soils must perform four tasks.

• They must *supply water* to the root system. Salts that are applied as fertilizers, such as nitrogen, phosphates, calcium, and potash often accumulate in the soil and plants can become stunted, damaged, or even be killed. We prevent this buildup through leaching, applying more water than is necessary to wash the salts out of the soil through the holes in the bottom of the container. Therefore, the soils that we use must be capable of holding water, but must also allow water to pass through, that is, provide adequate drainage.

• The mix must *provide nutrients* for plant growth. Garden soil and compost are the best candidates for this job. Compost also provides some water holding capability.

• Soils must *provide oxygen* to the root system. Materials such as sand, vermiculite, or perlite provide excellent aeration of the soil.

• The mix must *provide for mechanical support and anchorage.* When the seedlings are small, this is not a major problem. However, as the plants get larger, soil must be added to the mix to provide adequate physical support.

The importance of each of these factors changes as the plant matures from germination to blossoming. Consequently, the ingredients must also change.

There are hundreds of possible soil mixing options. However, they start with these basic ingredients.

Vermiculite is a form of mica that has been exposed to heat, and popped like popcorn. It holds large amounts of water and absorbs nutrients from fertilizers and releases them slowly to plants. It can be used alone or with other ingredients. However, make sure you have the horticulture vermiculite and not construction material. Construction vermiculite is highly alkaline and may contain toxic substances. Masonry vermiculite may be coated with material to resist absorbing water which ruins its most endearing quality. Horticulture vermiculite is available from larger garden stores. Wholesale suppliers sell a 4 cubic foot bag for between $8 and $9.

Perlite is 'popped' from volcanic ash and promotes excellent drainage in the soil mixture because the granules are much larger, creating a looser, rougher-textured soil. It holds water but not quite as well as vermiculite. Wholesale suppliers sell a 4 cubic foot bag for about $7.

Peat is formed by the accumulation of plant material in swamps or bogs. Peat moss holds six to fifteen times its own weight in water, providing a uniform supply of water over several days. It holds nutrients well, and provides a roothold for seedlings. It is quite acidic which helps counteract the high alkaline water we use in the greenhouse. For germination we prefer the milled sphagnum because it has a finer texture. Peat is widely available in the spring with an average cost of $8-$10 for a compressed 4 cubic foot bale.

Compost is used later in the life of the plant to provide the nutrients necessary for vigorous growth.

Soil is also used in the 5" pots to provide the nutrients required by larger plants.

When we plant directly into 1204s we use a standard germination mix such as Fusions Mix #3.

Skill in raising vegetable plants from seed is the very cornerstone of gardening independence. Choice of seeds and careful handling can bring you not only earlier harvests, but better vegetables.

Nancy Bubel [4]

71

6-7. Light and germination racks. *The top picture provides an idea of how the racks are constructed. The lights are mounted in sections so they can be adjusted to accommodate different plant heights.*

As the plants grow, their nutrient requirements increase. We have two options, provide the nutrients from soil and compost, or use synthetic fertilizers. At this point the tender plants are still susceptible to disease, so most commercial greenhouses use a sterile mix of peat, perlite, and vermiculite. They provide the nutrients with water-soluble fertilizers applied during watering. We use this approach for the first repotting into 1204s.

Germination mix

During germination the seeds do not need much physical support because they are so small and remain in this mix for a very short period. The plant does not need nutrients because the seed contains the nutrients it needs for the early part of its life. However, constant moisture and oxygen are necessary for the seed to break dormancy and then to use the stored nutrients. Therefore, the growing medium we use for germination must create this environment. In addition, germination requires two unique conditions. The soil must permit the small cotyledons to push through to find the light they need to continue to grow. Any soil that forms a crust must not be used for germination. The soils must also be disease free because the seedlings are very sensitive to damping-off, a fungus that attacks and kills the plants. Most commercial growers use a sterile mix to alleviate this problem. Germination mix often includes vermiculite, sphagnum moss, and perlite.

Growing mix

Most of the plants purchased from commercial greenhouses are sold in packs of 4, 6, or 8. That is, they grow the plants hydroponically and never go beyond the 1204 stage. We go beyond that because we want larger, healthier plants. As the plants grow, nutrient requirements increase. Consequently, we add soil and compost to the mix to provide the trace elements and microorganism the plants need for optimum growth. Soil sterility is no longer required as the plants have the strength to fight off many of the diseases that are fatal to younger plants. We make our own potting soils because of the quantities required to fill the large trays and 5½ inch pots. The mix varies some but generally is 1/3 sphagnum moss, 1/3 garden soil and compost, and 1/3 vermiculite and perlite. The exact mix of these ingredients seems to be quite forgiving with plants growing well in many different combinations

6-8. Germination room. *This is the enclosure in the corner of the shop. This simple arrangement has dramatically increased our germination rate because we can control both the temperature and humidity.*

72

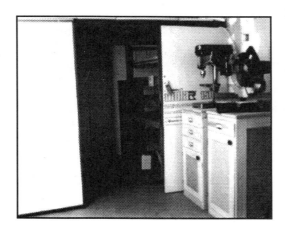

LIGHT AND GERMINATION RACKS

We start our onions on February 1st, one month before we put heat into the greenhouse. Consequently, we need light racks to keep the onions growing for that first month.

Our rack, figure 6-7, uses cheap shop lights available at discount stores from $7 - $10 each. We use three light fixtures across each level to provide optimum light. All three lights are attached to a cross bar, suspended from a chain. This chain allows for adjustment to inspect and water the plants. We use regular bulbs since grow lights are too expensive. The light racks double as germination racks. We often leave the newly germinated plants under lights for a few days to allow remaining seeds to germinate.

In the past few years we have experimented with different germination arrangements. We built a small box that would hold four trays and was heated with a 200 watt light bulb hooked to a thermostat. The tray at the bottom seemed to get too hot and the thermostat seemed to allow a much to wide temperature range. Electric thermostats are adjustable and adjustment helped some. The arrangement also didn't work for those flower that needed some light to germinate properly. I can't say that this arrangement worked very well. Germination was somewhat erratic.

We then built a larger germination rack that would hold 16 trays. We enclosed it with styrofoam and put four 200 watt light bulbs under the rack for heat. We added small circulation fans to move the heat throughout the rack. It worked much better than the small rack, but heat was still uneven and germination was erratic. We have since removed the fans and installed supplemental heat on the

6-9. Flats. *Tomatoes and peppers start their lives in flats like this. This gives us the opportunity to pick only the strongest ones for transplanting into the 1204s.*

bottom of each shelf. The product is used to heat bathroom floors and is available at many home improvement stores. It installs easily and does a great job in keeping the soil warm.

Then we built a simple eight foot by five foot enclosure in one corner of the shop, large enough for the germination rack and the light rack. This temporary shelter was constructed from styrofoam sheets and a simple 1x2 frame. We heat the enclosure with a small thermostatically controlled electric heater that blows across a pan of water to increase the humidity. We keep the room temperature at about 80° so the soil temperature stays at about 70°. This has worked out extremely well. We have had better germination and the small 'room' is large enough to work in to water the trays.

GREENHOUSE OPERATIONS

Now that we have our equipment and materials, we are ready to start our plants.

Sowing the seeds

At this point in the season, greenhouse space is plentiful so we spread the seeds out in the trays rather than crowding them. This requires more trays, but produces healthier plants because more soil remains with the roots, reducing transplant shock.

73

Gardening is no less an art than music. In the end the best gardens are the product of careful observation, experimentation, and a skilled hand. Nowhere is this more true than in raising tranplants.

Shepherd Ogden[5]

It makes the first transplanting easier because the roots are not tangled together. Planting is a rather simple task. Fill the tray with about an inch of germination mix, and pack it down a bit. Sprinkle the seeds thinly over the mix, and cover them with another half inch of mix, and pack lightly. Our experience has been that because of the properties of the mix, depth of planting is not critical. We plant the seeds deeper than the recommended depth because they break through the germination mix easily.

Germination

Germination is the most challenging of greenhouse tasks. Seeds require moisture and proper temperature for germination. Optimum germination temperatures are generally 10-15 degrees higher than optimum growing temperatures so supplemental heat is required. However, it is important to note that the critical temperature is soil temperature not room temperature. We monitor soil temperature with a standard thermometer used for cooking meat.

The secret to germination is consistent temperature and adequate moisture. We water the flats every day. As soon as the first seeds germinate, we turn on the lights. This is important as the first seeds that germinate are generally the strongest. These are the ones we want. However, the plants will be permanently stunted if they do not get light immediately.

Published average germination dates are just that, averages. We beat those dates consistently and record our unique germination data to adjust future plans.

Transplanting

When the first true leaves appear, we transplant the seedlings into 1204s. The most critical part of transplanting is the selection process. We want only the best plants. There is some evidence that suggests that the seeds that germinated first, will produce the strongest plants. Therefore, we select only the largest seedlings. I wish to make a point here that demonstrates the primary advantage of operating a greenhouse. If we need 540 tomato plants, and plant only that many, the law of averages dictates that a percentage of these plants will be weak and unproductive. If we plant twice as many, we have a much better chance of selecting plants that will remain healthy and productive. If we plant three times what we need, we are guaranteed to have enough plants to make successive selections during subsequent transplantings and still have plenty of high quality plants.

Transplanting is not difficult but does require considerable time. Prewet the soil you will use in the 1204s. Place a small amount of the mix in the bottom of the inserts.

Grasp the plant by the leaves. Use a pointed tool to prick the roots free of the growing medium. Leave as much soil as possible around the roots.

Immediately place the plant into the 1204 and cover with soil to just below the leaves. Immediately firm the soil around the plant. Even a few minutes of drying can damage the tender roots. This transplanting process goes much faster with two people. One person removes the plants and the other plants them into the 1204s.

Place the plants under lights to give them a day or so to acclimate to the new environment, then move them to the greenhouse.

Our second transplanting takes place when the plants just start crowding the 1204s. The procedures are similar to those explained above. However, the plants are now grasped by the stem as it is stronger. The plants are removed from the plastic inserts by pushing on the bottom. Dividers are placed in the large tray, and filled with about an inch of potting soil.

The third transplanting occurs when the plants appear to be crowded. Five inch pots are filled with an inch of potting soil. Removing the plants from the large trays is done with a small shovel. The plants are set into the pots and covered with potting soil.

Fertilizing

Peat moss, vermiculite, and perlite do not contain sufficient nutrients to feed the plants. Therefore, when we use these growing mediums, we are essentially involved in hydroponic culture. That is, we feed the plants by adding nutrients to the water.

Siphon systems are available to automatically inject the fertilizer into our watering system. However, since our greenhouse is only operational for a few months in the spring, the $260 investment might be difficult to justify. Therefore, we use a manual dilution system. We first prepare a concentrated solution. Then we dilute it for application on the plants. We have found the easiest way to do this is with gallon containers. There are 16 cups per gallon. If we mix one cup of concentrate to 15 cups of water we have a 15:1 dilution. So we start by mixing the concentrate. Fertilizer solutions are expressed in parts per million (ppm). Most references recommend a nitrogen concentration

of about 200 ppm for bedding plants that are fertilized periodically. Commercial fertilizers are expressed as nutrient percentages. That is, a 20-10-20 fertilizer has 20% nitrogen, 10% phosphorus, and 20% potash by weight. We use Peat-Lite Special, a 20-10-20 soluble fertilizer. To attain a 15:1 concentrate that will yield 200 ppm we must mix 2 ounces of the dry fertilizer to one gallon of water. This is printed on the back of the bag. If you need to calculate a mix, use the following formula:

Let's say we have some 15-16-17 fertilizer, and we want a final solution of 300 ppm We will use a 15:1 concentrate so we need 4500 ppm in the concentrate to get 300 ppm in each gallon. To get that concentration we multiply 4500 by .16 and then divide by 1205 times the percentage of nitrogen in the fertilizer.

$$\frac{16 \times 4500}{1205 \times .15} = \frac{720}{180.75} = 3.98 \text{ oz}$$

We round up to four ounces, ½ cup, of fertilizer and mix that with one gallon of water. Then we use this concentrate at a rate of one cup per gallon of water to make our final solution that is applied to the plants.

Watering

It is said that the profits from a commercial greenhouse are determined by the person who does the watering. Watering is that critical, and watering is tricky. Success is determined by our understanding of what overwatering means. Overwatering means watering too often, not applying too much water at a time. We are using an ideal growing medium, that drains all excess water out through the holes in the bottom of the containers. If by chance, we apply too much water that excess water will drain out within minutes. If, on the other hand,

Plants that are started too soon and have grown too large for their containers will be permanently set back and won't yield as well as those that are grown quickly.
Shepherd Ogden[6]

we water too often, the roots do not have to search for water and they are not stimulated to grow. We want maximum root structure because the plants will need those roots to thrive after we have placed them in the garden.

Water the entire root system, not just the top of the soil. It is usually impossible to get sufficient water to soak in on a single pass so multiple applications of smaller quantities of water are necessary. The important thing to remember is that you cannot over water in a single watering. Water until the excess drains through the holes in the bottom of the container. This will ensure that all of the root system has been watered.

We water 1204s every sunny day for two reasons. First there is very little growing medium, only a few cubic inches. Under bright sun, the black plastic heats up and dries out the soil very quickly. Second, there are no nutrients in the soil, the plants depend on the nutrients they get from the water. Sometimes if it is cloudy we skip a day.

Once we get to the large trays, conditions change. Each plant has over 25 cubic inches of soil. The interior plants are protected from the drying effects of the container edge. Soil and compost provide some of the necessary nutrients. We apply some water along the outside edges every day. Our experience indicates that the plants along the edge tend to be smaller than the interior plants. This is most likely due to the drying affect of the sun along the edge of the container.

We determine watering needs by weight. We water a tray well and weigh it. Then we let it stay unwatered until the first plants show signs of wilting. Then we weigh that tray again. This indicates the avail-

able water in the tray. From then on we water when 60-70% of the available water has been used. For example, if a tray weighs 15 pounds wet, and 10 pounds at the wilt stage, that means that five pounds of water are available. When 3-3.5 pounds (60-70% of 5 pounds) have been used we water again, when the tray weighs 11.5-12 pounds (15 pounds minus 3-3.5 pounds).

The key here is uniformity. Potting mixes will vary in their water holding capacity depending upon the types of materials used. Therefore, we must use the same potting mix and watering procedures on every tray. For example, we have twenty trays of cucumbers, all with the same potting mix. If we water each tray in the same manner, we can weigh one tray and accurately assume that the remaining trays have similar water conditions.

Of course, we do not weigh every tray every day. We know what a dry tray feels like when we lift it, and how much heavier a saturated tray is than a dry one. With a little practice we can determine approximate weight just by lifting the tray.

The 5½" pots contain over 100 cubic inches of soil. This is sufficient holding capacity to provide water for several days if watered properly.

Conditioning or Hardening Off

In the greenhouse the plants are protected from full sun and from the wind. If you move the plants from this protection to a hostile outside environment, they will get set back. Therefore, most references recommended that you harden them off by exposing them to full sun and wind for short periods for the first few days. We don't always get this done very well because of the volume of plants involved. Instead we provide protection for the transplants in the garden. Then we phase the removal of the protection to harden them off properly.

Temperature

Temperature has a dramatic affect on greenhouse plants. If it is too cool, plants will be stunted, too hot and they will be spindly and weak. Optimum temperature for most plants is 70-75° during the day and 60-65° at night. The closer we maintain those temperatures, the more successful we will be at producing healthy bedding plants.

Ventilation is also important. Growing plants need carbon monoxide so outside air must be supplied. We use two large fans to bring in outside air, and three regular attic fans to vent the hot air. These are all on a thermostat separate from the heat thermostat. We started using a combination thermostat but then someone had to switch it over in late morning. When this didn't get done the greenhouse sometimes got very warm before we changed from heat to cool. In 1993 we added a second thermostat and it worked much better. The cooling thermostat is set at 70.

By May we have too much sun and the fans cannot keep the greenhouse cool. We use a 30% shade stretched over the outside of the greenhouse. We ordered them from A.M. Leonard and had grommets placed every two feet to correspond with our rafters and studs. We used tie down straps to keep tension on the cloth so the wind didn't rip it apart. The affect was immediate and effective. The advantages to using the hooks and tie down straps is that in a period of cloudy weather, we can quickly remove the shade to give us the sunlight we need for optimum plant growth.

Plants placed too close to the side windows might burn simply because of inadequate ventilation. We keep them a few inches away and then there doesn't seem to be a problem.

Potential problems

Prevention is the best strategy for the solution of potential problems.

Temperature. If temperatures are too low, particularly at night, growth will slow considerably. If temperatures are too high, plants will grow too fast, and become spindly.

pH. Our water is quite alkaline. The fertilizers we use are acidic. When we mix the two, our pH remains within a tolerable range. If your water is not alkaline, you may encounter nutrient problems, not because they are absent, but because pH imbalance prohibits the plants from using the nutrients.

Accumulation of salts. If the top of the soil starts turning white, a salt accumulation has developed. It is time to drench the soil with pure water to flush the salts out. Excess salts can create many problems. Our well water is very salty, so we have a tremendous problem with salts, especially with onions that remain in the greenhouse for so many months.

Improper watering. This is probably the leading cause of problems. Work at watering. Analyze your procedures, test your soils, experiment.

Light. If it remains cloudy, there is nothing you can do. Artificial light is not economically feasible or practical. On the other hand, it is possible to shade the greenhouse to protect plants from too much sunlight in late spring.

If you are attempting to do everything right, and problems still remain, it is time to pinpoint the specific procedure that is creating the problem. Fortunately, plants with problems provide adequate clues to what is ailing them.

Leaf curl is most likely caused by overfertilization. Reduce fertilizer application and leach the soil with plain water. If that doesn't work, repot the plant into a larger container.

Discolored leaves indicate a nutrient deficiency. If leaves are a pale green, nitrogen is deficient. If the undersides are reddish purple, a phosphorus deficiency is indicated. If the leaf edges are brown, potassium may be deficient. If the lower leaves turn yellow, it may signal a magnesium deficiency.

PAST AND FUTURE HITS AND MISSES

Over the past five seasons, we have learned many things about growing healthy transplants. I highlight them here because they are likely the same problems you will encounter as you enter this fascinating facet of commercial gardening.

Soil temperature is critical. The greenhouse may be 60° at night but if the soil is 50° little growth will occur. If I were to design a greenhouse now, I would provide heat under the racks to keep the soil at optimum temperature.

Greenhouses must be kept cool. I always thought that heat would be good for young plants. Not so. If the temperature rises much above 80°, plants tend to grow leggy. We want strong stocky plants so it is critical that we keep it cool. Plants like sunshine and warmth but not extreme heat. With the proper fans and exterior shade cloth, this is possible.

Fertilize properly. There are few nutrients in the commercial greenhouse mixes so supplemental fertilization is required for optimum growth.

Track germination times. This is the only way to make adjustments to planting time based upon your specific growing environment.

FOR THE HOME GARDENER

There are two reasons a home gardener might want a greenhouse. The first is to increase the number of available varieties. The second is to grow strong and early transplants. For the seasoned gardener, these are the two biggest frustrations with purchased plants.

If you can't grow your own transplants there are still a few options. Perhaps you can work something out with a local greenhouse or a neighbor to plant the varieties you want and when you want them. If you are a member of a local garden club, perhaps a consolidated request would be acceptable to a greenhouse operator.

If all else fails, and you must purchase from available stock, it is critical that you know how to pick the right ones when you purchase your bedding plants.

Once you've mastered the basics, you can work with the relationships between heat, light, water, and nutrients the way a musician works with melody and counterpoint.
Shepherd Ogden[7]

"Wan'na pollinate?"

Chapter Seven

Growing

Several years ago I heard a brilliant Brigadier General from the 1st Cavalry Division explain his ideas on how to win a war. "We don't have time to be perfect," he said. "And fortunately, we don't need to be perfect to win, we just need to be *about right.* We need about the right number of troops, about the right amount of ammunition and fuel, and be in about the right spot at about the right time."

About right! That phrase has stuck in my mind for many years. It not only describes the proper way to win a war, but also applies to the winning combination for successful commercial gardening. We don't need the exact nutrients, or just the right amount of water. We don't need to destroy every harmful insect. We just need to be about right, because we don't have time to do it any other way.

We have selected the right varieties, grown healthy transplants, and now we must nurture the plants into optimum growth. The hard work is behind us as nature normally provides the water, nutrients, and sunshine that plants need to grow. Our job now is to supplement nature, to lend a helping hand only where necessary. As we walk through the garden during the growing season, we look for plants that look sick and insects that look healthy. We focus on these four things:

1. *Nutrient deficiencies.* If we have prepared our soil properly with plenty of organic material, deficiency problems will most likely be limited to inadequate nitrogen.

2. *Insects.* A constant problem that is best handled immediately. However, there is no need to panic, as nature many times handles the problem without our interference.

3. *Diseases.* If disease can be identified quickly, the plant can be removed to prevent spreading of the disease.

7-1. Spreading fertilizer. We start with a fairly uniform application of nitrogen in the spring. Then we supplement with liquid nitrogen throughout the season as required by each crop.

This is a great shot of Justin, a neighbor who has helped us for several years. Don't underestimate the young people who work for you. They want to be involved in the problem solving process and they have active and innovative minds. Some of the best solutions we are using were Justin's ideas.

4. *Water problems*. This requires constant vigilance to ensure plants never run short of water.

PREPARING THE GARDEN

As the transplants mature, we must prepare the garden for planting. First, start whenever the weather allows. There are no guarantees that the weather will provide you the leisure of starting when you want to. And if you delay, the weather may cause you to be extremely late. There are many things that can be done anytime in the spring:

• Fertilize and work the beds.
• Erect the trellises. This is very time consuming, and they need to be in place when it is time to plant.
• Put the tomato cages in place.
• Position the plastic and cloches.
• Test and install all irrigation hoses.

FERTILIZING

Long range commercial garden success happens right here. If we improve the fertility of the soil, properly and in balance, production will increase, and disease and pest problems will decrease because our plants will be healthier. Fortunately, the fertilizing process is relatively forgiving. We only need to be 'about right'.

We begin this section with a quick course on plant nutrition. Sixteen nutrients are known to be needed for plant growth. Plants require large amounts of carbon, hydrogen, and oxygen. These nutrients are readily supplied by air and water so deficiencies are rare. Plants also need large quantities of nitrogen (N), phosphorus (P), and potassium (K). Incidentally, commercial fertilizers are expressed in percentages of these three nutrients in this sequence. If you have a 20-10-20 fertilizer, it contains 20% nitrogen, 10 % phosphorus, and 20% potassium. Therefore, the application of five pounds of the fertilizer on the soil would apply one pound of nitrogen, ½ pound of phosphorus, and one pound of potassium.

Plants grow by photosynthesis, a complicated process involving sunlight and the green plant pigment in the plant leaves, chlorophyll. It is nitrogen that produces leaf growth and maintains healthy chlorophyll. Therefore, if plant leaves turn yellow because of a shortage of nitrogen, it means the plant has less chlorophyll to make photosynthesis work. The plant becomes stunted and unproductive. On the other hand, too much nitrogen is also destructive because the plant will have too many leaves, a small root system, and limited and less tasty fruit. Consequently, it is this vital nutrient that will occupy much of our fertilizing effort. Our task is complicated because nitrogen is a mobile nutrient, moving easily with water. Therefore, with excess rainfall or irrigation, nitrogen will leach down into the soil beyond the reach of the root system. It is for this reason that nitrogen must be replaced each year.

Phosphorus is required for strong root development, disease resistance, and fruit and seed development. It's not mobile and can generally be supplied with organic material, rock phosphate, or bone meal. It is often included in 'starter' fertilizers because of its ability to encourage root formation. Injection into a drip irrigation system is not recommended because of the danger of clogging emitters.

Potassium promotes strong growth and increases disease resistance. It is necessary for the formation of proteins, carbohydrates, and chlorophyll. Potassium is more likely to leach than phosphorus, so requires frequent replacement.

Calcium, magnesium, and sulfur are the remaining major nutrients required for plants growth. Problems with these and the micronutrients can best be prevented with periodic soil tests since deficiencies are quite unusual.

We use an integrated fertilizer approach similar to pest management. We provide the proper nutrients starting with the healthiest options. Then if that doesn't fulfill all of the plant requirements we supplement carefully. Our plan is as follows:

• Provide the nutrients organically if at all possible through an annual application of compost and manure. All of our research indicates that constant use of synthetic fertilizers will create soil problems. There-

fore, they should only be used as a supplement when time is the critical factor.

• Foliar feed once a week with Spray-and-Grow. It costs so little that any production improvement pays for the cost and time.

• Soil test once each year.

• Add synthetic supplemental nutrients only as necessary and in minimum amounts.

• Use the irrigation system to apply fertilizer. Fertilizer efficiency is improved because fewer nutrients are lost through leaching. Root damage is reduced because of the highly diluted fertilizer solution. It also provides greater flexibility.

Nitrogen

Nitrogen is normally the nutrient with supply problems because it leaches out easily. Normal rainfall and irrigation will drive this nutrient into the ground where roots cannot get to it. Therefore it must be replaced every year. However, we must be very careful in applying it because oversupply can be just as destructive at a shortage. Too much nitrogen creates an abundance of foliage and a shortage of fruit, particularly in tomatoes. Therefore, it is advisable to spread our nitrogen fertilization throughout the season.

I have read many books on raising vegetables, and I still haven't found one that states clearly how much nitrogen a cucumber plant needs. So let's try to develop an intelligent estimate. A bulletin from the University of Illinois recommends planting cucumbers 10-12 inches apart in rows five to six feet apart. Each plant occupies 4.16 to 6.00 square feet in the field from which it can draw nutrients. The bulletin also recommends the application of 75-100 pounds of nitrogen. An acre is

Fertilizer Estimates									
Crop	Plant Spacing Inches	Row Spacing Feet	Sq/ft per Plant	Plants per Acre	Rec N lbs/ac	Lbs of N per plant	Plants per bed	Lbs of N per bed	28-0-0 in cups	Lbs Fresh Chicken Manure
Cucumbers	11	5.5	5.04	8640	100	.0116	66	.764	1.876	38.19
Onions	2	3	0.50	87120	100	.0011	1250	1.435	3.523	71.74
Carrots	1	1.1	0.09	475200	80	.0002	3500	.589	1.447	29.46
Beans	2	2.5	0.42	104544	40	.0004	500	.191	0.47	9.57
Cabbage	12	2.5	2.50	17424	150	.0086	150	1.291	3.171	64.57
Peas	2	2.5	0.42	104544	75	.0007	400	.287	0.705	14.35
Peppers	21	3.5	6.13	7111.8	125	.0176	150	2.636	6.473	131.82
Squash	12	9	9.00	4840	100	.0207	33	.682	1.674	34.09
Tomatoes	30	5	12.50	3484.8	125	.0359	60	2.152	5.284	107.61

7-2. Wild guess fertilizer estimates. *The first five numerical columns were taken from current publications. From those we were able to calculate an estimated nitrogen requirement per plant. If we take that times the number of plants we have in each bed, we can calculate the nitrogen we need.*

acre we have applied about .0023 pounds per square foot. If we use the tightest spacing, 4.16 square feet per plant, we conclude that each plant requires about .01 pounds of nitrogen during the entire season. We grow 66 plants per bed, so we need to apply .66 pounds per bed per year. Dried poultry manure is about 5% nitrogen, so we would need just over 13 pounds of poultry manure per cucumber bed per year. That's easily done. Or we could apply 6½ pounds of poultry manure in the spring, and apply .33 pounds of nitrogen using liquid fertilizer throughout the season through the irrigation system. We have included other estimates in figure 7-2.

Caution!!!
These estimates have not been verified. However, it is the best fertilizer information we have and is based upon published estimates for growing these crops under normal field spacing. We include it here as a wild guess, a place to start. Then we recommend that you research thoroughly and experiment carefully. This does point out the problem with commercial intensive gardening. The research available for traditional growing methods is of limited use with intensive spacing.

I want to make a critical point here on the quality of organic fertilizers. I had always assumed that if I had plenty of organic matter in my soil, and that I followed a good composting program, that I would be able to satisfy all of the plant's nutrient requirements. This simply isn't true for nitrogen. If you want to remain organic, you will need to spend some effort to ensure that your organic fertilizers provide adequate nitrogen.

The liquid fertilizer we use is 28% nitrogen and weighs 11 pounds per gallon. If we need .33 pounds of actual nitrogen we must apply 1.18 pounds of liquid nitrogen over the season, or just over 1/10th of a gallon, or 1.7 cups of liquid fertilizer. Now we are getting useful information. Our model garden plan has nine cucumber beds which will collectively cucumber beds which will collectively require about 15½ cups of liquid fertilizer. They produce for about 8-10 weeks, or 1½-2 cups of liquid fertilizer per week, or 1 cup for the twice-per-week watering. That is the figure I have been looking for!

Take another look at figure 4-7. Our irrigation system is set up to allow fertilizer to be placed directly into the system. We use individual valves for each bed for two reason; to control the application of fertilizer, and supply just the right amount of water to each vegetable. If we need to apply one cup of fertilizer to the cucumbers, we throw open only those nine valves while applying the liquid fertilizer.

Each of the crop chapters in Part II discusses the nutrient requirements of that crop.

COMPOSTING

Our garden seems to have an insatiable thirst for compost. I believe you can never have enough since compost is critical for healthy soil, and healthy soil is necessary for maximum production in a small space.

Equipment

Bins. Materials compost better if they are piled up, so bins of some kind are required. We use concrete reinforcing wire, cut to 16 feet long and two feet high. This allows us short folks to fork the materials into the bin without straining.

Shredder. The more surface area you have on your material, the faster the composting process becomes. A shredder will accomplish that task, but it takes considerable time and effort. If you are short of space, you might not have much of a choice. However, if you can afford to store

Crop	Harvest Residue	End of Season Residue
Beans	none	moderate, shreds easily
Cabbage	moderate	none
Carrots	moderate	none
Cucumbers	rejects only	moderate, shredding difficult
Onions	moderate	none
Peppers	rejects only	heavy, stalks difficult to shred
Peas	none	moderate, not easily shredded
Tomatoes	rejects only	very heavy, shreds easily
Zucchini	rejects only	heavy, shreds easily
Flowers	limited	heavy, shredding varies

the compost for about a year, shredding is not required.

Materials

Regardless of source, sufficient volume is required each time so the pile can heat up. If the material is spread too thinly over the pile, it will just dry out.

Harvest residue. We harvest steadily for six to seven weeks, generating carrot tops, onion tops, damaged vegetables, and other residue. Three options are available:

Compost after each market. This is the best option. It keeps everything cleaned up, and none of the material gets ripe. However, there are times when this is impossible because of the small amount of material.

Compost twice a week, or after every other market. This provides sufficient depth to get the pile to reheat. If you choose this option, empty the plastic garbage cans next to the compost pile as soon as you are finished. Otherwise, the residue can get quite rank in the cans, especially during warm weather.

Haul out the residue. This can be quite expensive depending on the local dumping charges but if you do not have the space, you may not have the option.

7-3. Residue. All plants provide some residue, but fortunately not all at the same time. Shredding difficulty is also indicated. Sometimes it is easier to haul the residue to the landfill.

7-4. The shredder. *This has been modified a bit to handle the large volume of material generated by a commercial garden. The top chute was removed and replaced with a longer one. The chipper chute was removed because it was not required.*

Grass clippings are great, but some cautions are in order. We live only a few blocks from the residential area of Bismarck. On any given night we can pick up all the grass clippings we want. However, it is impossible to know if chemicals have been applied recently. Consequently, we have several people who call us when they have clippings, or bring them out in exchange for a few veggies. That way we can verify that no herbicide is present. So far, we have not had any trouble. Clippings mixed with normal garden residues heat up nicely, and provide a steady supply of compost.

Weeds make great composting materials. However, care must be taken if the seeds are mature.

We find *manure* to be almost indispensable for good composting. The manure is loaded with the organisms that create the composting process.

Water content

There is probably more danger from having the material too dry than too wet. It seems that even if most of the pile is too wet, somewhere conditions are right, and the heat from that place in the pile reduces the moisture gradually and eventually the remainder of the pile heats up. On the other hand, if the pile is too dry, it will never heat up.

There are tremendous differences in the water content of composting material. There are times when we have quantities of cucumbers and zucchini that cannot be sold. This high water content material must be mixed with something dryer. Grass clippings also vary considerably. Experimentation will determine how to mix the materials and when to add water.

The recipe

Composting is quite forgiving. If you have 'about' the right materials, and 'about' the right amount of water, your pile will heat up nicely. You can read all you want to about the right carbon-to-nitrogen ratio, but I have rarely had a pile that didn't heat up. When I did, I just ran it through the shredder one more time, mixed it with other materials, and it worked fine.

Our compost recipe for shredded material is simple. First, spread out a two to three inch layer of residue, then sprinkle manure over the top. Add a one to two inch layer of grass clippings and then more manure. If the material is dry, we spray each layer with water before applying the manure. It seems to stick a little better. Then we use a fork, and turn the layers together.

The recipe for material that is not shredded is even simpler. There are only three rules. First, make sure the water content is about right, otherwise, the pile will not decay at all. Second, mix your materials. Several different materials are usually available at any given time. Use layers of cabbage leaves, then carrot and onion tops, then grass clippings, then reject cucumbers, etc. Third, use plenty of manure as a catalyst.

MULCHING

The secret to mulching is not to do it too early. Soil temperature is important for many crops and mulching will cool the soil considerably.

We use plastic mulch for tomatoes, peppers, and cucumbers. We discovered the necessity to mulch cucumbers. When they are on trellises much of the plant surface is subjected to the constant wind. We thought we were providing sufficient water, but had not mulched the bed, so there was evaporation from the bed as well. The cukes quit producing during a hot spell, and never fully recovered.

IRRIGATION

Proper irrigation is complicated because there are so many factors that determine the amount of water required at any given time.

The *types of soil* and subsoil determine how much water is available. The water-holding capacity can be increased with the addition of organic matter to the soil.

Water evaporation from the soil increases with temperature and wind. These losses can be reduced with the application of organic or plastic mulch.

The amount of water required by a plant increases as the *temperature* increases because there is more evaporation from the leaves. Mulch will not mitigate these losses.

Stage of development. Water requirements increase as the plant grows and starts production.

Part of the water requirements may be supplied by *rainfall*. However, if the rain comes a downpour, most of the rain drains off and is of no use to the plants. Plastic mulch reduces the rainfall reaching the plants.

Intensive spacing challenges even the most accurate watering

7-5. The compost piles. We use cages of reinforcing wire to keep the piles reasonably attractive. Notice the pile of manure in the background. We find this ingredient essential to good compost production.

estimates. Most published data involves traditional row spacing that provides individual plants more area from which to draw water.

How do we manage this complicated task? Where do we start?

• Start with *conditioning* the soil by adding organic matter. Organic matter absorbs and holds water. It provides the water reserves for periods of high evaporation. It is the cushion that uncomplicates watering.

• Use drip irrigation. The advantages were discussed in Chapter One.

• Start with an irrigation schedule based upon published estimates and your experience. Adjust it for temperature, wind, and rainfall.

• Monitor with a moisture tester and constant observation. Learn to identify water stressed plants.

Calculating water needs

The amount of water required is determined by the growth stage of the plant, and the weather. A three-week old transplant needs less water than an 8-week plant in full-production.

85

tion. This picture demonstrates the advantages of drip irrigation. The plant is not getting wet because we apply the water where it can do the most good, directly on the roots. And we are not wasting water on non-productive garden space.

Windy, sunny, 90° days require more water than cloudy 65° days. Consequently, the intelligent use of water resources required a more sophisticated plan.

However, you will often see water requirements stated in weekly averages. For example, one reference states that beans require 1.5 inches of rain per week from flowering to harvest. For intensive gardening, this is an unworkable oversimplification. There too many variables that are not considered.

The weather is not the only complicating factor in planning irrigation. The bean reference mentioned above is based on rows spaced from 18-40 inches apart. We plant a row of beans among the carrots or cabbages. I doubt that 1.5 inches per week would satisfy the needs of all of the plants in the bed. It is possible to use an inches-per-week irrigation system. And over several seasons, it could be adjusted to be quite accurate. For example, if we calculate that the beans need 1.5 inches and the carrots 1.5 inches, we could supply 3 inches of water per week.

First we must convert inches into gallons. A gallon is 231 cubic inches of water. One square foot requires 144 cubic of water to provide 1" of water. Therefore, each gallon will provide 1" if depth over 1.6 square feet. Our beds are 50' long and 3' wide, or 150 square feet. If we divide that by 1.6 we determine that we need 93.75 gallons to provide 1" of water on the entire bed. If we want three inches, we must apply 281.25 gallons.

We know we have 33 4 gal/hr emitters on a 50' line, which will provide 132 gallons per hour at a constant pressure of 10 PSI. We have two hoses on this bed so we are providing 264 gallons per hour. If we divide 281.25 by 264 we determine we must water for 1.065 hours per week, or twice a week for 32 minutes.

Sometimes you find water requirements expressed as gallons per plant, or gallons per foot of row. Let's use the bean/cabbage bed in full production. Beans require 1 gal/ft/week, and cabbages about 1.5 gal/wk/plant. We have 100 feet of beans, and 50 cabbage plants in each bed. Once again, we have two hoses per bed. The 175 gallons per week can be supplied in two twenty-minute waterings.

There are two problems with this method of estimating water requirements. The first is the ability of the soil to accept water at this rate. The limiting factor here is the type of soil and the organic content of that soil. That is, can the bed absorb water that fast, or will it run off? We have a clay based soil with 6-7% organic content. It cannot absorb water at a rate of 264 gallons per hour.

The second problem is that only one or two beds could be irrigated at a time to maintain 10 PSI, or 4 gallons per hour per emitter. A water system can supply a limited amount of water. A home with a 3/4" service line and meter can supply only 12 gallons per minute at 50 PSI, or 720 gallons per hour. As the water moves through the system, it experiences friction losses from pressure regulators, filters, valves, and small pipes. If all of the valves in your house are closed, a water pressure gauge may well read 50 PSI because the system has had time to build up that pressure. What happens when you open a valve? The pressure drops because now the water is moving and is subjected to all of the frictional losses. What happens to the water pressure at the first valve when you open a second? The pressure drops considerably. You've been in the shower when someone flushed the toilet. Same thing.

We can easily reduce the pressure to 5 PSI by opening more valves, by watering more of the garden at one time. It is advisable to test actual application rates by placing a container under one emitter and timing how long it takes to drip a given amount of water. A cup would work perfect. There are 16 cups per gallon. Determine how long it takes for one emitter to fill one cup of water. Divide that figure into 60 minutes to determine cups per hour. Multiply that figure by 16 to determine gallons per hour per emitter.

With raised beds overwatering is not a serious problem because excess water will drain away from the bed. However, overwatering can adversely affect the taste of your produce. The calcuations in the previous paragraphs are a great place to start. Then adjust your watering based upon careful observations for water-stressed plants. The crop chapters address the consequences of irrigation mistakes.

INTEGRATED PEST MANAGEMENT

We use an integrated pest management system for all pests; insects, diseases, and weeds. This involves alternative approaches starting with the least toxic options.

Chemicals are not eliminated but are used as the last resort. Integrated pest management recognizes the concept of the natural survival of the fittest. There is a reason for insects and diseases in nature. Their job is to destroy the weak plants so only the best ones survive and reproduce. If you observe early insect populations you will find them on those plants that are the weakest, the runts of the crop. They won't do much damage there because those plants will not produce much anyway. So the key is to control the pests at that stage, where they are doing their jobs, but have not yet reached destructive numbers. (There are exceptions. Cutworms are indiscriminate destroyers, and should be squashed on site!)

Our first line of defense is prevention. There are many things that can be done to prevent pests from becoming a problem. Crop rotation, soil development, resistant cultivars, and garden cleanliness will solve many pest problems.

Our second line of defense is healthy plants. We accomplish this by providing the right nutrients and moisture, and by protecting the plants from the weather as best we can. Healthy plants are much less likely to be attacked, and will sustain some damage with little or no decrease in production. Healthy plants will defend themselves successfully against most diseases.

Our third defense is close monitoring to identify problem while they are small and manageable. If we find a few cucumber beetles, or flea beetles there is no need to panic and spray the entire garden with pesticides. They are simply doing their jobs, eliminating those weak plants. However, we start controlling them at that point with the least toxic options available. In most seasons, this will be

87

*7-7. **THE book on pest problems.** I wish this book had been available when I started gardening. Published in 1993, it is available at most fine book stores for $34.95. If it is not in stock, ask them to order ISBN 0-89721-255-X It is a superb reference for identification of pest problems. It also provides recommended chemical remedies. However, it is still useful for organic growers because even organic solutions start with proper identification of the problem.*

sufficient. Diseased plants are destroyed to prevent spreading of the disease.

Our fourth defense is organic controls. There are so many of these and new ones are being developed every year. These include predatory insects, traps, row covers, Bacillus Thuringiensis (Bt), pyrethrum, rotenone, copper, sabadilla, and insecticidal soap.

Our final defense is chemical controls. If all other defenses have been used in a timely and effective manner, we rarely need to use this toxic option. There are two problems with chemicals. First, they are indiscriminate, destroying beneficial organisms along with the destructive ones. We use ladybugs to control aphids. If we apply a pesticide, we destroy these beneficial insects along with the cucumber beetles. If we apply herbicides, we destroy the earthworms that build the healthy soil we need to develop plants capable of resisting diseases. Second, if we constantly apply insecticides, the only insects that remain are those that can

survive the chemical. Therefore, over a short period of time, a strain of insects emerges that is immune to the affects of the insecticide. Consequently, most experts now recommend using chemicals only as a final option. This insures maximum affects from application of the expensive insecticides.

Years of indiscriminate chemical use have taught us that there are no simple solutions. However, there are times when chemicals are our first option, such as with Morning Glory (bindweed). I know of no other effective way to control it. However, we apply the chemical carefully, and usually only to the paths, and seldom to the top of the bed.

We have not had any severe pest problems. The worst we had was aphids on peppers that was quickly solved with a half pound of Lady Bugs. Cabbage worms are always easily controlled with bT. And we lose a few transplants to cutworms each year so we grow a few extra and simply replace them rather than worry about collars.

We have plenty of grasshoppers around. So far they have not done much damage. We have an area of pasture that we do not cut and they seem to prefer that area to the garden. We spread grasshopper spore throughout the area, and if we catch it just right when the hoppers are small in the spring, we spray the pasture with Malathion.

The key to success is early identification. I walk the garden several times a day looking for the emergence of new pests or diseases. Identification is often difficult because so there are so many possibilities. We recommend that you find a local Master Gardener. You can call your local extension agent or contact the local garden club. Many of them are delighted to help. They know most of the pests that bother local gardens.

I believe the key to success is cleanliness. We keep our garden clean all year. Plant residue is picked up and composted religiously.

Insect control

I could provide many pages of specific information on the various types of insects that might plague your garden and a long list of controls available to you. Instead, I have chosen to limit our discussion to a few words of advice. There is a good reason for that. We worry too much about insects. The truth is that destructive levels of insects occur only when conditions are favorable. And there are many things we can to do disrupt that cycle, so insect populations remain manageable. Then, if they become a problem, effective controls are available. A few words of advice:

Know the insects that are most likely to present problems. Every section of the country is a bit different, and each season presents an ideal environment for different insects. Of the many insects in our garden, only a few have the potential to reach destructive numbers. If we know what these are, we can effectively monitor their presence and population.

Don't worry about a few bugs. In many cases nature will correct the problem through a natural predator. *But monitor very carefully.* Any IPM expert will tell you that monitoring is the most important part of the program. You cannot react intelligently to a potential problem unless you know it is present.

Think control, not elimination. We are not trying to eliminate every cucumber beetle in the garden. We are simply attempting to reduce their population to a point where damage does not affect production. There is a tremendous difference. There will always be destructive insects in our garden, but if they do not affect production, their numbers are irrelevant. The trick is to recognize the break point before it occurs. That is, at what point do we begin to apply controls. Every year we have problems with aphids on our peppers. We use ladybugs, a very effective predator control. However, if we apply them too early, the ladybugs will leave the garden. If we apply them too late, we have damaged our pepper crop. If our timing is right, the ladybugs will keep our garden free from aphids all season as they move from crop to crop.

Study insect life cycles. This provides the secrets to control through prevention. If we can disrupt this cycle, we will not have an insect problem. For example, we do not have a problem with cutworms because we do not allow any weeds to remain in the garden during the spring. Cutworms cannot begin feeding on the transplanted stems of tomatoes. They need something smaller. Their life cycle starts with small weeds. If the weeds are not present, they die.

Study your options. And there are so many if can be very confusing. There are no shortcuts here. It takes considerable effort to sift through the available information, but it needs to be done.

Read the labels. There is no organic or chemical insecticide that kills all insects. If there was we wouldn't want to use it. Make sure the control is approved for the plant you want to protect, and that it will control the specific pest that is present. Otherwise, you are subjecting your garden to substances that

7-8. Onion maggot damage. The secret to pest control is early identification and quick remedial action. Notice how this plant has lost its turgidity. It must be pulled immediately or the maggots will migrate to another plant.

might prove destructive and still not kill the insect you need to control.

Use the least toxic control that will handle the problem. By toxic we refer to the affect the control has on yourself as well as to beneficial insects. This is the heart of the IPM program. Don't spray your garden with malathion just because you have a few cabbage worms. Use BT instead and just on the cabbage.

Keep the garden clean, removing or composting all residue. Of all of the things we have done, I believe this one to be the most important. We had a problem with onion maggots this past year. In retrospect, it is easy to understand. We had not removed all of the onion plants the previous fall. Onion maggots overwinter as pupae in this residue so we had a destructive level of maggots instead of an acceptable level as we have had in previous years.

Disease control

Diseases are caused by four types of pathogens, fungi, viruses, bacteria, and nematodes. Only two of these can be controlled. All overwinter well and can be spread in many ways, by insects, water, wind and by gardeners. The bad news is that diseases are always present in your garden. The good news is that conditions must be right for the diseases to become destructive. Fortunately, there are many things we can do to prevent this from happening.

Plants have natural defenses against diseases just as humans do. If the plants are healthy, the defenses are usually sufficient. Therefore, our job is to ensure that the plants are as healthy as possible. This natural defense is also the basis for resistant cultivars. Plant breeders are able to develop and select natural defense attributes. If we use those varieties, we have increased our chances of winning the disease war.

Sometimes plants are physically damaged and become weakened, even though all other growing requirements have been met. Wind and hail are good examples of physical damage. Disease takes over the plant. Now we must be able to identify the problem. If we suspect disease we must remove that plant because the disease organisms are now reproducing and spreading to other plants. It becomes a numbers issue. If our healthy plants are attacked by 1000 organisms, they may be able to defend themselves. If they are attacked by three billion, odds of survival are diminished significantly. Do not place the plant on the compost pile. Throw it in the garbage, or better yet, burn it.

Many diseases live in the soil. They attack only certain crops, or families of crops. They need these plants to reproduce. If they are not available, the disease organism dies. This is the reason for crop rotation. If we plant the same crops in the same area every year, the diseases continue to multiply each year, and eventually they win the numbers battle, and overpower even the healthiest of plants. If we plant the same crops only every third year, the diseases are reduced to quantities healthy plants can resist.

Pest management is one facet of gardening where experience becomes an important factor. Let me give you an example. We were in our second season of gladiolas and had about 300 of them. The blossoms were not maturing properly, and turned brown shortly after they opened. The problem was not obvious through casual observation. However, an experienced greenhouse grower visited the garden and immediately explained we had a problem with thrips. It was too late in the season to correct the problem and the entire crop was lost. We suspected something was wrong but didn't know what to look for.

The chapters on individual crops will discuss diseases only if we have experienced a particular problem. Otherwise, the measures mentioned above have been sufficient to prevent disease problems.

Weeds

The best advice we can give you is to do it early and often. This takes considerable discipline when forty other tasks are screaming for attention. However, it must be done because small weeds kill easily. Once their roots are established it becomes much more time consuming.

Our original intention was to remain organic. However, because of nitrogen deficiency we found that impossible. And local produce is not drawing a premium as it does in larger metropolitan areas. Therefore, we started spraying the main paths rather than pulling or hoeing the weeds. We do not apply any chemical on the growing beds and we still hoe the paths in between the beds. We use a hoe with a small horizontal blade that 'rubs' back and forth rather than chops. In an hour one person can weed all of the paths.

7-9. Hail boards. We use these to protect our tomatoes. They work, of course, only if we can get them in place before the storm arrives.

We use chemicals on the beds only when we get an infestation of stubborn grasses or bindweed. Grasses in the beds pull easily whereas the paths are badly compacted and killing grasses is extremely time consuming. I would rather spend this time doing other more productive work.

Hail

I don't suppose hail is a pest, but it can certainly be as destructive. However, it is possible to mitigate some of the damage. Figure 7-9 illustrates the hail boards we use for protecting our tomato crop. Of course, we must be present and have sufficient warning to get them in place. Unfortunately, this was not the case last summer, and we lost much of our tomato crop.

PAST AND FUTURE HITS AND MISSES

I plan to get a hay chopper in to provide some chopped straw or hay made from these large round bales. This would provide the carbon rich material that could be mixed with the nitrogen rich grass clippings for optimum compost.

Our intent is to make our garden into a research center for commercial intensive gardening. There are a few things that need to happen to make this possible. The first is a reasonable interest in our annual newsletter. We would then be able to conduct research on water and fertilizer rates, and the affects on production and quality.

The problem with research is the inordinate amount of time required to measure the results. This requires additional time and labor and we cannot do that while operating under profits from selling our produce. Good research also requires that we test the limits of fertilizer and water. This will adversely affect production and profits on some of our beds. We must make up that lost revenue with sales of the annual newsletter.

If you are interested in supporting this research, please subscribe to the newsletter by calling 1-800-871-4296. An order blank is provided at the end of the book.

FOR THE HOME GARDENER

Most of the information in this chapter requires some adjustments for the hobby garden. Let's take them one at a time, from the top.

Fertilizing. If you have been adding compost or manure every year, your potassium and phosphorus levels are probably adequate.

You can certainly put down a base level of nitrogen in the spring. However, be careful. If you get too much, many plants will give you plenty of foliage, but not much fruit.

The use of liquid nitrogen through the irrigation system is probably not an option. You will need to sidedress instead, according to the specific needs of your individual crops.

Composting. The only material you have in abundance is grass clippings. That's satisfactory, but only if you use the right recipe. If you pile up grass clippings, the smell can strain even the healthiest neighborhood relationships. The secret is to add some well-rotted manure. We have done this many times, and have gotten the pile to heat to over 150°. Fork in a two to three inch layer of clippings, and then sprinkle some manure over it. After you have several layers, mix the entire pile up with a fork. Moisture levels are critical so add water if necessary.

Irrigation. The challenge you have is the requirement to provide different amounts of water to different plants. That can be done easier with drip irrigation than any other method. Drip rates can be varied with different emitters, and different emitter spacing. It can also be done with zones similar to what we are using, but with perhaps a more simple valve system.

Pest management. In a small garden, crop rotation probably won't do you much good. In larger home gardens, however, it is certainly work trying. The principles outlined in our planning chapter will work just fine.

The hands of harvest!

Chapter Eight

Harvesting

Harvesting is 'crazy season' at the Gourmet Gardens. We must pick vegetables for four markets each week. In between harvests we must water, weed, and do all the growing things that need to be done. But its payday, and there is nothing we enjoy more than selling quality vegetables at the market.

To introduce you to the complexities of commercial harvesting, we provide a description of a typical Sunday morning at full production. First an introduction to the cast. Justin is a young man from the neighborhood who works part-time for us during the season. Julie is our youngest daughter, currently a college student. Caroline is my wife.

Saturday evening: We pick the tomatoes, placing the best fruits in the marketing trays. Seconds are placed in flats for bagging the next morning. If we know we will be short of time the next morning, we prepare carrots for market an leave them in pails of water overnight.

Sunday, 7AM: I start on cucumbers, Caroline on peas, Justin on onions. Julie starts bagging tomatoes. As soon as the first cucumbers are picked, Julie washes and sorts them.

She weighs and bags peas as they are picked. She records produce count as each crop is finished.

8 AM. I am still on cucumbers, Caroline on beans, Justin on onions. Julie moves between crops as they become available, bagging beans and peas, and washing and sorting cucumbers.

9 AM. Caroline picks zucchini and peppers. Justin picks cabbage, prepares the heads for market, and starts on carrots. My time is now split between picking cucumbers, arranging the boxes on the racks, and helping Julie with the cleaning, weighing, and bagging of the produce.

10 AM. Caroline finishes peppers and starts on flowers. Justin completes carrots and starts helping me on cucumbers. As we complete our picking tasks, we help Julie wash peppers, wipe down the zucchini, bag the carrots, and wash and sort cucumbers.

11 AM. Final produce preparations are completed. The marketing stands and cash boxes are loaded on the pickup, and the pickup is backed up to the loading stand. We shower and dress for market. The produce

Once you've spent some time in a garden you begin to understand that "yield" is measured in terms far greater than the bushels of tomatoes harvested. There is a deep reserve of pleasure from which to draw, day after day, as you behold a garden that is pleasing to look at and a joy, not a drudgery, to tend. From High Yield Gardening[1]

8-1. Harvest Equipment
(From left to right)
Picking pails.
Caster table - *We use this table to move produce from the wash stand to other parts of the work area.*
Small marketing boxes -
Wheelbarrow
Large marketing boxes
Large cart
Large garbage can
Two-wheel cart

racks are rolled into the pickup and one final check is made to ensure all marketing equipment is loaded. We leave for market.

EQUIPMENT

Picking pails. We have a friend in the commercial painting business who sells us five gallon paint pails for 50¢ each. It takes some time to clean them, but it is worth the effort. We routinely use 10-15 of these every market, and when we are in full production, 20-25 are required.

Produce bags and twistees. We use two sizes of vented produce bags, three pound, and five pound.

Wheelbarrows. Three or four are required to move the produce from the garden to the preparation area.

Shears and knives. We have found a Joyce Chen scissor is perfect for harvesting. It is available at most fine kitchen stores.

Air compressor. We use a two-horse air compressor to remove the dirt and skins from onions to prepare them for market.

Large garbage cans. We use these for the plant residue. When they are full we empty them on the compost pile.

Scales. We use the same scales for harvesting and marketing. However we have found it necessary to purchase extra pans because they get a bit too tacky for market when we use them for harvesting.

Marketing boxes. We use these to organize and store produce as it becomes ready for market. We store them on carts with casters so we can place the boxes where we need them.

Carts. We have several sizes that we use to bring produce in from the garden. A two-wheel cart is a back saver in many ways. Purchase one early in your gardening career.

Figure 8-2. A Place to Work.
The wash rack in the top left of this drawing, is also at the top left of the picture at the top of this page.
The marketing boxes on this drawing are those on the two stands shown in Figure 8-1.
The exact arrangement is not important, only that you provide space for the work that must be done.

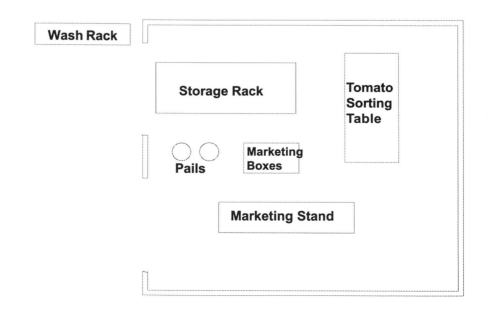

A PLACE TO WORK

It quickly becomes obvious from the previous discussion that you will need a place to process your vegetables once you get them picked. You must provide space for weighing, bagging, washing, sorting, and storing.

Weighing and bagging

We use the marketing stand for harvesting as well. Since I use the pickup to go to work each day, I must remove the stand after each market. I set the stand up in the garage, and hang the scales. This provides a convenient workplace for weighing and bagging produce. We also have three other places where scales can be set up quickly. One is in a special place for tomatoes because we must do that every market. The second is on the wash stand for vegetables that we can bag after they are washed. The third is the extra scale in case we run out of time and still have beans to weight and bag.

Washing

A wash rack is an absolute necessity, particularly for onions and carrots. We made ours eight feet long with an old kitchen sink in the middle. If we remodel it, we will take out the sink as it isn't needed and reduces the usable space. The water runs into a small tub where a sump pump pumps the water into the trees.

Sorting

The marketing stand can be use for sorting tomatoes and cucumbers. Cucumbers must be sorted by size during pickle production so we sort into a few of the marketing boxes. Then we weigh and bag them. By using the marketing stand it is very convenient to set up a scale for weighing.

We set up a special place for sorting tomatoes because we spend so much time at this task during full production. If you have the space it is worth the extra effort.

Storage

Once produce is prepared for market, we must have a place to store it until we are ready to leave. We do not want the produce sitting in the sun. We have built a special storage system that we believe is as unique as it is practical. It is derived from the design of the marketing stand. You may find it helpful to review this design from Chapter Three. These two systems, marketing and harvesting, were designed together to allow us to use the stand for both.

As we prepare produce for market, we store it in the boxes we will use for marketing. Four of these boxes are set on each metal rack. They can be stacked 3-4 boxes high if necessary. The racks have casters on them and sit on a special stand in the garage constructed at the height of the pickup tail gate. Just before market, we back the pickup up to the rack, and roll the produce into the pickup.

The advantage to this system is that once the produce is prepared it is moved out of our way, and we will

8-3. The Wash Stand. It would be impossible to harvest efficiently without this stand. The tarp in the background protects us from the wind on cool mornings. We have two hoses so more than one person can work at the stand. This model has an old kitchen sink in the middle. This is not necessary and we plan to remove it next season.

8-4. The Rack. Refer to the drawing in the right column. If you were standing on the far right, this is what you would see as you looked towards the pickup. As we harvest we place the produce in our marketing boxes. They are placed on these racks

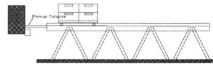

8-5. The Rack Drawing. If you were looking from the left side of the picture in the left column, you would see what is depicted in this drawing. Four saw horses support the platform. Three racks with casters provide places for the marketing boxes as we fill them. When we are ready for market, we back the pickup up to the platform and roll the racks into the pickup.

not need to handle it again until we arrive at the market. Once at the market, the produce is already in the boxes that will be used for display.

In figure 8-2, we have the storage rack shown on the top of the drawing. We moved that last year to the other garage door on the bottom of the drawing to alleviate conflicts with the wash rack and the normal collection of equipment that surrounds that work space.

HARVESTING SPECIFICS

Now that we have our preparation area designed, we are ready to meet the challenge of harvest. The chapters on vegetables provide more detailed harvesting techniques for each crop. We will limit our discussion here to the general harvesting environment to provide an estimate of the amount of work required to prepare for the market. Estimates are based upon the garden plan described in Chapter Three.

Beans and peas are picked in 5-gallon pails, brought to the garage, weighed into one pound bags, placed in boxes and loaded on the racks.

Cabbages are picked into a wheel barrow and brought to the wash stand. We strip the outer leaves and check closely for insect damage. The heads are washed, and loaded in boxes.

Carrots are picked into 5-gallon pails with the tops removed. The pail is filled with water and left for awhile to loosen the soil on the roots. They are dumped onto the wash rack and sprayed down. This takes some time because it is often necessary to pick off the remaining leaves. Carrots produce over a few weeks in the early market, and again in the fall if the double-cropping is successful. When they produce, considerable harvesting effort is required. However, carrots can be left for later markets if harvesting time is short. They can also be harvested early and stored in pails of water without any affect on freshness.

Cucumbers are harvested into five-gallon pails, and take them into the garage for sorting. It is usually faster to put them on the wash rack and spray them down. However, if there aren't too many, they can be wiped down with a rag. We pack the slicers into market boxes, 60-70 per box depending upon size. The pickles are separated into those used whole, and those that will be cut up. Experience will allow this to be done quickly. This process is critical since our reputation as a pickle grower hinges on not including too many large pickles in the canning boxes.

Onions are harvested into a wheel barrow and brought to the wash rack. If the tops are still green we trim off the tops, otherwise we cut them off completely. The important thing about onions is that they must be very clean. We use an air compressor later in the season when the outside skins have started to set. The outside layers blow off easily. We trim the roots, and remove the tops. A quick spray with water produces a very clean onion.

Peppers are easy. We pick them in five gallon pails, spray them off with water, and pack them directly into the marketing boxes.

We pick *tomatoes* into five gallon pails, being careful not to fill the pail too full. We have tables and beverage flats in the garage to store them till they ripen. Each market we go through the flats, placing ripe ones into the marketing boxes.

Zucchini - These are picked in five gallon pails, washed or wiped off depending on how dirty they are, and put directly into marketing boxes.

MANAGEMENT

As we approach each market we must determine the following:

1. How much produce must be picked? Cucumbers, peas, beans, and zucchini fall into this category. These crops cannot wait for the next market or they will be beyond their prime. Priority must be given to these crops.

2. How much discretionary produce can I sell? Cabbage, carrots, onions, peppers and tomatoes are in this category. These crops will keep

for another market, so harvest depends upon market and harvest conditions. For example, we know we can sell 100 pounds of carrots on Saturday morning. However, we only have time to harvest 40 pounds. We can live with that lower figure, or add help for the remaining 60 pounds. The carrots will keep until the next market without and degradation in quality.

3. How much labor is required? How much help is available? This determines how much discretionary produce is picked, and whether onions and carrots are picked early. Flowers can also be picked the day before, if refrigeration is available. Carrots can be picked the night before, and stored in water overnight. We do this only if we are short of help and know we will have difficulty making the market on time.

HARVEST RECORDS

We keep close records of what we bring to market. We have a clipboard hanging in the garage where we prepare for market. As we fill the boxes we record approximate quantities and gross sales figures. When we come home from the market we adjust for what we bring home and what discounts we might have made. We make our planting

8-6. Loading the pickup. Just before we go to market, we roll the loaded racks into the pickup. This keeps the produce out of the sun, and still provides us a convenient place to store the produce that has already been prepared for market.

Product	Price	Number	Value
Beans			
Brassicas			
Carrots			
Cucumbers			
Flowers-Dried			
Flowers-Fresh			
Garlic			
Onions			
Peas			
Peppers			
Tomatoes			
Zucchini			

8-7. Market records. *We use this simple form to record crop quantities as we prepare them for market. Then we adjust sales figures as required upon our return. This data enables us to fine tune future production.*

decisions for the coming year based upon these harvest and marketing records.

When we return from the market we count the money and return 20 $1 bills and four $5 bills to each of the cash boxes. Then we match this sales total with the tally sheet we prepared while preparing the produce for market.

A few examples might be helpful. Suppose we have $400 worth of produce with us and we return with $325 in sales. Some of the adjustments are easy. If we sold all but two bags of beans at $1.50 per bag, we subtract the $3 from the total.

Estimating sales accurately is complicated by two problems, discounting and weighing produce at the market. We 'think' we have 125 pounds of tomatoes, but as we sell them and estimate prices, we may not be exact each time. At the end of many markets, we discount produce so we don't have to put it on the compost pile. We attempt to keep track of the amounts, but . . .

Fortunately, we only need to be about right to get the information we need to make intelligent planting decision for the next year. And that's not that hard to do.

AND FINALLY. . .

Garden cleanup begins after each bed is completely harvested. Cleanup hits full speed after the first killing frost. It is no small task. Our recommendations are:

1. Do it quickly. Hire help if necessary.

2. Some of the plants are difficult to compost. Don't waste the time. Haul them out. We disconnect the cucumber vines and let them dry. Then we cut down the trellis mesh, and haul the vines and the mesh to the landfill.

I am working on a plan to convert a corn silage chopper to work with this final garden cleanup. Maybe next year cleanup will be easier.

Part II - Recommended Crops

In Part I we detailed our strategies for success. Growing the right vegetables was an important ingredient in that strategy. The chapters in Part II provide the information you need to grow these 'right' crops recommended for beginning commercial gardeners. Each chapter includes a snapshot analysis of the planning factors involved with that vegetable. This chapter provides an explanation for those entries. We also include some recommendations on how to adapt the information to your situation. Finally, we provide some background data on the seasons that will be discussed in Part II.

THE DATA BOX

Take a few minutes to review a few of the chapters that follow and familiarize yourself with the types of entries contained in the data box for each vegetable. Such a review will make this chapter easier to understand.

Propagation is the method used to start the plant. Direct seeding means the seeds are planted where they will grow in the garden. Transplants are indicated for those crops that must be started in the greenhouse.

Frost tolerance indicates when plants can be planted or transplanted. It ranges from very hardy to very tender. This designation is also an indication of the soil temperature needed for germination and growth. We have tried to include recommended soil temperatures when they apply.

Earliest plant or transplant date is directly related to frost tolerance. Very hardy plants can be set out four

Chapter Nine

Recommended Crops

to six weeks prior to the frost free date (FFD). Hardy plants should be set out two to three weeks prior to FFD, tender plants about FFD, and very tender plants one to two weeks after FFD. Onions are a very hardy crop and can take a hard frost. Therefore, they can be set out about a month prior to FFD. Peppers, on the other hand, are very tender, will die at 32° and should not be set out until after all danger of frost is past.

Maturity date is the expected day of first harvest. For transplants this is from the date of transplant. For direct seeded crops, it is usually from the date of germination. These are published averages and may vary considerably from your own experience and from season to season.

Seeds per ounce or pound is a critical planning factor for ordering the proper amount of seed.

Seed viability indicates how long the seed will keep if kept relatively cool and dry. We include this data in case you intend to keep your seed from year to year. Viability can be increased significantly if seeds are kept very dry and in a refrigerator.

Intensive spacing provides an acceptable range of minimum spacing for wide row planting. Plants may be stunted if spaced too close. Production will decrease if spacing is too

THE DATA BOX

Planning

Propagation ....

Frost tolerance ....

Earliest plant or transplant date ....

Maturity date ....

Seeds per ounce or pound ....

Seed viability ....

Intensive spacing ....

Planting depth ....

Germination temperature ....

Germination time ....

Weeks to transplant size ....

Growing temperature (Day/Night) ....

Growing

pH ....

Nutrient requirements ....

Pests ....

Diseases ....

Critical watering ....

Harvest

Harvest before ....

Yield ....

Average selling price ....

Average income per square foot ....

generous. The secret is to determine what works for your variety and growing conditions. This can only be done with experimentation.

Planting depth is most important for direct seeded crops. Germination may be reduced if seeds are planted outside this range. Transplants provide more flexibility as the germination mix allows a wider range of planting depths.

The next two factors are directly related to each other. *Germination temperature* lists the range of temperatures where germination will occur. If temperatures are outside this range, germination may not occur at all. The optimum temperature is in parenthesis.

Germination time is the number of days between planting and seed germination. The longest number of days corresponds to the coldest germination temperature, the shortest to the optimum temperature.

In the case of transplants, two more elements are necessary. *Weeks to transplant size* gives the approximate time it will take to grow transplants of normal size. If you want larger transplants, it may be necessary to give yourself more time.

Growing temperature is the optimum greenhouse temperature, given for both day and night growing.

pH lists the range wherein satisfactory growth will occur. Nutrient deficiencies may occur if soil pH is outside this range.

Nutrient requirements fall into three categories. Heavy feeder indicates the crop requires above average nitrogen. Light feeder indicates minimum nitrogen required. Soil builder indicates a legume that replaces nitrogen in the soil.

The *pest and disease* entries list the two or three problems that are most likely to inflict damage on the crop.

Critical watering indicates the times in the life of the plant when adequate watering is critical. If water is short during this period, production will be reduced.

The *harvest before* entry indicates the proper time for harvesting the crop. This timing may not produce maximum quantities, but will provide optimum taste and marketability. For example, carrots can be left until they reach two to three inches in diameter. However, customers prefer them smaller and they sell easier if picked at their peak flavor. Production, on the other hand, would be much greater at the larger sizes.

Yield is the anticipated harvest per square foot. It is not provided for all crops because of problems with estimating an accurate figure.

Average selling price indicates the high and low sales price for our area. Prices at markets around the country may vary considerably from this average.

Average income per square foot is based upon our growing system. This is the bottom line on whether or not the crop is profitable. It is based upon average yield times average selling price.

THE MODEL GARDEN PLAN

This plan provides a complete plan for our model garden. Entries in the crop chapters may vary slightly from this generic plan.

Quantity is the number of beds we plan to plant.

Spacing between plants determines the next two entries, the *seeds per running foot of row* and the *plants per row*. To calculate the number of seeds per row we divide 12 inches by the spacing in inches and multiply times the length of the bed. If we have a spacing of three inches, we have four seeds per running foot. If our beds are fifty feet long, we have 200 plants per row.

In the planning factors section, we included a range of acceptable intensive spacings. In this section we must decide exactly what spacing we want. Spacing for direct seeded plants must consider thinning. For example, if we desire a pole bean spacing of 4 inches, we may plant at 2 inches and thin to 4. For calculating our seed order, we must use the 2 inch spacing.

Spacing sometimes determines the number of *rows per bed*. We want a four inch spacing on onions. Our

---

THE MODEL GARDEN PLAN

The seed plan

Quantity ....
Spacing ....
Seeds per running foot of row ....
Plants per row ....
Rows per bed ....
Plants per bed ....
Total seeds required ....
Seeds per pound ....
Seed Order ....
Variety ....
Source ....
Cost ....

The planting plan

Planting date (Approximate) ....
Transplant date ....
Location ....

The marketing plan

Estimated yield ....
Selling price ....
Gross Income ....
Income per square foot ....

---

beds are about 36 inches across so nine to ten rows are mathematically possible. However, experience changes this figure. We know that without careful measuring, we average seven rows of onions because we do not want them too close to the edge of the bed.

Seeds per bed is determined by multiplying the number of rows per bed times the number of plants per row. We plant cabbages on nine inch spacing, or 67 cabbages per row. We can get four rows across the bed, or 268 cabbages per bed.

To calculate the total number of *seeds required* we multiply the number of seeds per bed times the number of beds we will plant.

We can then determine the quantity of *seed we need to order*, by dividing the *seeds per ounce*, or pound, by the number of seeds we need. Let's go back to cabbage. We plan for two beds for a total of 536 cabbages. Here's where the process gets a bit sloppy. We want Stonehead cabbages. Stokes sells them in a 200-250 seed packet for $1.15. We will need at least three packets, $3.45, because of possible germination problems, and because we want to select only the strongest plants. Stokes also sells Stoneheads for $2.13 per 1000 seeds. So we purchase 1000 seeds, not because we need them, but because they are cheaper.

The final entries in the seed plan explain which *varieties* we will plant, how many of each, where we will purchase the seeds, and how much they will cost. This is not complicated unless we plan to use several varieties. Then the detail is extremely important to our planning process. The second part of the plan determines when and where we will plant each variety. No plan is complete without this information.

The final part of the plan outlines the estimated yield, selling price, gross income, and income per square foot. These figures are presented to assist you in selecting the crops that will be the most profitable for your limited space. If we interplant, we calculate these figures using half of the bed space for each crop, even though crops on trellises might actually use less space than that.

CAUTION!

It is dangerous to make recommendations as we do in the following chapters. Therefore, we preface our thoughts with several cautionary notes. We ask that you consider the following as you make your decisions.

Research your market

Before you select from these crops, research your market, particularly if you plan to join a farmers market. In the next few years we plan to corner Walla Walla onion sales because it is our niche crop. We know how to grow them, and we work at selling them. If you were to join our market it would be difficult for you to break into that market on the scale presented on our model garden. Figure 4-2, the model plan, has three rows of onions. If you research your market and someone is already dominating onion sales, it will be necessary to adjust this plan.

Adjust crop selection to location

Bismarck, North Dakota is on the edge of zones three and four. Our weather is fairly typical, very changeable and unpredictable. Our spring weather just comes a bit later than most sections of the country. The recommended crops grow well here. You must select the crops for your section of the country and adjust growing techniques to your location and climate. You may have much greater opportunities for double cropping because of a longer growing season. Take advantage of those opportunities. We have never gardened in the South where heat is a constant danger. The cool weather crops may need to be dropped or protected in some way.

Observe weather patterns

We watch the Weather Channel and they sometimes provide insight into the predominate patterns. The National Weather Service issues 30 and 90 day extended forecasts based upon these weather patterns. I believe we can take limited chances if the weather patterns are favorable. In 1992 the predominate weather pattern changed in May and continued throughout the summer. We made some mistakes by not accepting this pattern and adjusting accordingly.

Experiment

The secret to improving profitability is constant experimentation. Unfortunately, the secret to experimentation is documentation. Articulate your objectives so you do not loose track of what you were trying to accomplish. Enter it into your master plan. Review your plan at least once a week and record results. If you do not stay focused on specific objectives, the experiments will be lost in the rush of the season.

Concentrate on what works

Please do not assume everything in this book or any other book to be gospel truth. We are still learning, and there are many techniques we have not tried. What works here may not work elsewhere. That is why you will find conflicting information in many books and articles. Truth is relative to experience. If we try pelletized carrot seed and it doesn't work, then that is true for us. Growers who have had success with the seed would report it differently.

PRODUCTION NOTES

In the following chapters we provide very specific information on nine crops. We recommend them because they represent the most popular crops and therefore the largest potential volume. They are also the most profitable crops to grow in a limited area. We recommend you start with these crops, then adjust to fit your weather, location, and market.

Each crop chapter has a final section that lists our experiences during the past few seasons. Weather is always a significant factor so we describe the seasons here rather than repeat the description in each chapter.

1991 was a perfect year for the home gardens. We had above average rainfall in May and June to get the gardens off to a healthy start. It turned very warm in July so crops ripened on time or ahead of schedule. About mid-August the home gardens arrived with a vengeance and the market weakened. 1992 was a frustrating season from the very start. The season was one of the coldest summers on record. Several areas of the state experienced killing frosts until the first week of June. Many days were cool and cloudy so production was almost a month late. Home gardens never became a factor. Consequently, we made more money because prices held up due to the shortage of produce and a longer lasting market.

1993 was almost a duplicate of 1992, just more pronounced. It was the third coolest summer on record and the wettest ever. Crops were extremely late because of the dominate cloudy weather pattern. Many home gardeners never picked a ripe tomato. Our early market focus paid off handsomely and for weeks we had the only tomatoes and cucumbers on the market. Production was limited, but prices held all season.

1994 provided another dramatic change. A late April snow storm and 10 days of high winds in May created later than normal planting and transplanting. When we did get the plants out, they were under considerable stress because of the warm May weather. If we had been able to get plants out earlier, it would have made a tremendous difference in our season. Rain was plentiful into July and then it became extremely dry for the remainder of the season. However, home gardens already had a healthy start and by mid-August, the best part of the market was over.

We are now ready to discuss individual crops in detail. We ask that you read with your environment in mind. That is, always ask the question, "How will this crop and these growing and marketing techniques work for me?"

Chapter Ten

Beans

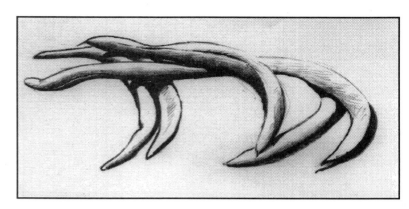

Beans are divided into two general categories, shell beans that are grown for their seeds, and snap beans that are grown for their pods. There are certainly niche markets for shell beans, but the primary market is for snap beans, and more specifically, green snap beans. Therefore, we will limit our discussion to this market crop. Once you are comfortable growing this bean, you may wish to expand into some of the niche markets.

Beans are a tender, warm-weather crop requiring air temperatures above 70° and soil temperatures above 60°. They require full sun, and a well-drained soil rich in organic material. Nitrogen-rich soil is not required because beans are a legume, fixing nitrogen from the air into the soil through bacteria that live on the roots. A reference we received from the University of Illinois indicates that beans have a narrow pH tolerance. If you have trouble growing beans, check your pH.

Green snap beans can be grown as pole beans or bush beans. Pole beans require support for vines that will grow five to seven feet high. Pole beans bear later in the summer, produce for a longer period, and produce more and better tasting beans.

Harvest begins 45-65 days after germination. Bush beans bear heavily for two weeks, pole beans until frost. If a continuous harvest of bush beans is desired, succession planting is required.

COMMERCIAL PLANNING

There are three viable marketing strategies for beans. The first is to concentrate on the early market with bush beans. This is possible because beans are a short season crop. The primary justification for this strategy is that the demand for beans drops off after the first few weeks of the market. We have used this strategy with moderate success. Our primary problem has been cool spring weather which delayed bean development and reduced production.

The second strategy is to focus on quality and sell beans all season. Most beans at the market are much too mature for optimum taste. There is a spectacular difference in taste between a bean with fully developed seeds, and a pencil sized bean picked young and tender. The secret is to develop a reputation for selling the

104

best beans at the market. This takes time but if quality is consistent, customer loyalty will be developed and sales will remain steady. The advantage of this approach is that beans can be used to draw customers to the stand throughout the season. They will buy the beans they want, but with good salesmanship, cucumber and tomatoes can also be sold. The disadvantage to this strategy is that it requires hiring additional labor as bean harvesting is very time consuming, particularly when picked small.

A third marketing option is to plant both bush and pole beans and sell them all summer. This is profitable only with a steady demand and price.

Varieties

Green snap beans are certainly the most popular market bean. The primary decision for snap beans involves the selection of bush beans or pole beans. Both have distinct advantages and should be selected based upon your marketing strategy as previously explained. If you want to concentrate on the early market, bush beans are your only choice. If you wish to use beans as a market draw throughout the season, use pole beans and pick them young and tender.

Green snap bush beans. Bush beans produce early and heavily for about two weeks. We have used Easypik, Contender, Strike, Provider, and Espada. Our earliest planting is usually Provider, a dark brown seed that tolerates cold soil better than other varieties.

Green snap pole beans. Blue Lake is the taste standard by which all green beans are measured, pole or bush. Pole beans should be considered by anyone with limited space.

BEAN DATA

Planning

Propagation	Direct Seed
Frost tolerance	Tender
Earliest plant date	Soil temperature greater than 60°
Maturity date	45-60 days
Seeds per pound	1600
Seed viability	3 years
Intensive spacing	3-4"
Planting depth	1"
Germination temperature	60-95° (85°)
Germination time	6-14 days

Growing

pH	6-7.5
Nutrient requirements	Soil builder
Pests	Bean beetles, cabbage looper, aphids, cucumber beetles
Diseases	Anthracnose, bacterial blight, mosaics, and rust
Critical watering	pollination and pod development

Harvest

Harvest before	Seeds get too large
Yield	1/4 lbs per plant
Average selling price	$1.25-1.50/lb
Average income per square foot	75-80¢

Yellow wax beans. We consider yellow beans a niche crop as there is a much smaller market. However, if no one is meeting this demand, a small planting could be profitable.

Filet beans. These are gourmet bush beans that might bring premium prices. Johnny's Select Seeds offers Fortex, a pole filet bean.

Choosing a variety varies with your marketing strategy. The early market strategy must consider maturity first as maturity dates vary from 43 days to almost 60. Tolerance to cold soil may be a factor if you chance an extra early planting. Dark beans will tolerate cold soil better than the white beans.

Taste is always a factor but less important in pole beans that are

105

Once beans have sprouted, temperature plays a big role in how soon you'll harvest your crop.

Diane Bilderback[2]

picked small. There is a tremendous difference in taste within any variety between an overripe bean and one picked young and tender. Picking at the right time is probably more important to good bean taste than choosing the right variety.

Disease tolerance includes tolerance to anthracnose, bean mosaic virus, downy mildew, and powdery mildew. This can become an overriding factor in areas with severe disease problems.

Appearance. Beans vary considerably in length, from 4" - 11". Longer beans mean more pounds picked per hour. If you plan to specialize in the filet bean market, a long, slender bean is required.

Higher *yields* mean higher production per square foot of space. Seed catalogs will identify those varieties that boast exceptional yields.

Successful *freezing* requires the right variety. Darker green types are better for freezing if you are concentrating on that market.

Quantities

Early demand is very strong, with only moderate and sometimes erratic demand for the remainder of the season. We recommend planting on the side of too many beans, because of the limited space involved when interplanted. Beans also supply the soil with nitrogen. If beans are not always sold, the plants are still providing benefits to the garden. If you overestimate demand, just pull the plants, and little is lost. On the other hand, if you underestimate demand, nothing can be done, and profits are lost.

The bean canning market is limited and accessible only with some discount in price. Early identification of potential canners is critical.

Our model garden, Figure 4-2, suggests 100 feet of pole beans grown on trellises interplanted with 200 feet of bush beans. Market research will pay off here because of the flexibility afforded by interplanting. If you wish to capture the early bean market, plant bush beans along the sides of the cabbage beds. Pole beans are best interplanted with carrots because they must be planted late. Cabbage is an early crop so the plants are quite large by the time beans can be planted. Spacing would need to be adjusted to interplant beans with cabbage. Peas can be substituted for beans in any of the four rows. The exact mix of bush beans, pole beans, peas, carrots and cabbage should be determined by market research.

Planting Plan

Timing for planting is also determined by the marketing strategy. The only way to hit the early market is to plant beans at the right time and get the right weather. If planted too early beans may suffer from 'inhibition' shock and never fully recover. If planted too late, the market may be too soft for profitable pricing. If the weather stays cool, beans may not be ready for opening day regardless of when they are planted.

Most references recommend planting beans after the FFD. However, soil temperature rather than the calendar seems to be the most critical factor. We plant when the soil temperature at three inches reaches 60° and the weather is promising for the next few days. If this happens before our FFD we take a chance because it works for us in a normal season. We have protective blankets in case the frost is light. If the beans freeze down, we replant them since seed is not expensive.

If you choose to focus on the early market with bush beans, succession planting will be necessary. Plant the next rows when the second level of leaves forms on the most recent planting.

Timing late market pole beans is easier. We plant them after the soil is close to 70° because taking chances isn't required to bring beans to market when tomatoes and cucumbers are in full production.

GROWING

Planting

In our production system, beans are always interplanted with other crops, such as carrots, cabbages, or lettuce. Since beans are a warm-weather crop, they are the last crop to be planted. This creates growing problems that can only be solved with careful planning, particularly if pole beans are to be interplanted with cabbages. It would be possible to have cabbages large enough to shade the beans during their early stages of growth. Experimentation with timing the planting might be necessary. Another option is to trim the cabbage leaves until the beans have grown up the trellis far enough to survive.

Optimum spacing can only be determined with careful experimentation. Production per plant is reduced as plants are crowded together, but because we have more plants, our yields may be greater. Optimum spacing may vary with different varieties.

Germination in cool soil is erratic even with adequate moisture. If you attempt to push the early market, plant the early beans closer together and thin them later. This will allow for germination problems. Protective cloches will encourage early production.

THE PLAN FOR BEANS

The seed plan

Quantity	2 beds bush, 2 beds pole
Spacing	2-3", thinned later to 4-6"
Seeds per running foot of row	4-6
Plants per row	200-300
Rows per bed	2
Plants per bed	400-600
Total pole bean seeds required	1200 each
Total bush bean seeds required	1200 each
Seeds per pound	1600
Seed order	1 pound each variety(1600 seeds)
Pole bean variety	Blue Lake FM-1
Pole bean source	Jordan seeds
Pole bean cost	$1.90 per pound
Bush bean variety	Strike
Bush bean source	Jordan seeds
Bush bean cost	$2.29 per pound

The planting plan

Bush bean planting date (Approximate)	(FFD-17) May 1
Pole bean planting date (Approximate)	(FFD) May 18
Location	Beds 14 & 15

The marketing plan

Estimated yield	200 pound per bed, 400 pounds total
Selling price	$1.50 per pound
Gross income	$600
Income per square foot	$2

Beans should not be planted until the soil temperature reaches 60° at a 2-3" depth at 8 AM. At 60°, germination may take two weeks or more. At 75 - 80° better then 90% of the seeds germinate in about a week. Soaking or pre-sprouting the seeds is not recommended. Uniform soil moisture after planting will ensure maximum germination.

Bush beans. Plant the seeds within 2-3 inches of the slope of the bed, 1 inch deep, and 2-3 inches apart in a single row. The irrigation system should already be in place. If it is not,

10-1. Interplanting beans with carrots. *Notice that the large bean leaves are shading the carrots. This got worse as the season progressed because we did not tie the pole beans back against the trellis. With a few adjustments, this interplanting arrangement could work quite well.*

dig a furrow one inch deep and two inches from the beans and lay the irrigation hose in the furrow. Repeat this procedure for the other side of the bed. This double irrigation hose provides the consistent watering required for good bean germination.

Pole beans. The trellis must already be in place as well as the companion crop. Suitable companion crops include carrots, cabbages, broccoli, and lettuce. Coat the seeds with inoculant. To be completely correct you must use *rhizobium phaseoli.*[3] Plant the seeds 1 inch deep, and 2-3 inches apart along one side of the trellis. A double irrigation hose should already be in place with the companion crop.

Germination. Moisture must be present in the top 2" of soil for optimum germination. For bush beans the irrigation hoses are placed adjacent to the bean rows so this is not a problem. However, with pole beans the irrigation hoses are several inches from the beans. In dry years, it may be necessary to spray the beans down with a hose to ensure adequate moisture. Beans germinate in about a week if average soil temperature is 77°. If the soil temperature is 60°, germination will require almost two weeks.

Caring for the plants

Thinning. Plant twice as many seeds as you want because of potential germination problems and early losses of tender plants. However, do not thin immediately but wait until the plants have become established, and then thin to 4-6 inches apart.

Mulching. If bush beans are planted on the sides of the beds, mulch with grass clippings when the bed warms up and the pods start forming. This will keep the pods clean and save washing time at harvest. Mulching for pole beans is not required because the companion crop provides a living mulch and most beans mature away from the ground.

Watering. Beans must be kept moist to germinate properly, which can be accomplished with frequent shallow waterings. Once germination has occurred, continued irrigation prior to flowering provides few benefits for production. Once the beans start flowering, they will require 1-1½ gallons per foot of row per week and a minimum soil moisture of 50%. We usually err on the side of overwatering because there is less potential damage than if we underwater. Water deficits will cause poor pod fill and pithy pods.

Pests and diseases. Beans are subject to many insects and diseases. Diseases include anthracnose, bacterial blight, mosaic, rust, and downy mildew. Pests include aphids, cabbage loopers, corn earworms, corn borers, Japanese beetles, Mexican bean beetles, leaf miners, striped cucumber beetles, and spider mites.

To reduce disease problems, do not harvest when the beans are wet. This requires some careful management as beans can normally be left for an additional day or so, but beyond that they start to get too large. If rain is forecast for your normal picking time, beans can be picked early and refrigerated.

Fertilization. Beans do not require additional nitrogen because they are legumes and fix nitrogen in the soil. They require only moderate amounts of phosphorus and potassium.

HARVESTING AND MARKETING

Harvesting

Pick beans while the seeds are small and undeveloped, when the first bean seeds just start showing on the pod. Pick them often and thoroughly to maintain production. However, take care to support the plant as you pull off the beans, or the plant may be permanently damaged. Throw overdeveloped beans rather than selling them. Beans should be picked in the morning. They can be refrigerated with very little loss in freshness. Since picking is time consuming, we often use refrigeration to spread out the work load by picking the beans the day before the market.

Harvesting bush beans is slow and backbreaking work and worthwhile only when the plants are in full production and beans are at full price. However, if demand remains strong, it pays to hire extra help to pick the beans. Otherwise, we recommend that you pull the plants and spend your time on higher profit crops. Pole beans produce a bit later in the season and are much easier to pick, but not much faster.

Marketing

Pre-bag beans into one pound bags. There is seldom time to weigh and bag them while at the market. Beans do not bag easily. It is easy to look clumsy and inefficient bagging beans while a customer waits. There are two ways to bag beans.

First option: Place the beans on the scale. When you have exactly a pound, stuff the beans into the bag. You will quickly discover that beans do not go into the bag willingly. You drop a few, and before long, you are no longer confident that a pound still remains in the bag.

Second option: Place the bag in the five-gallon pail and put about a pound in the bag. Then place the bag on the scale and add or subtract beans to make an even pound. After some practice only a few beans will be required for adjustment.

Beans do not sell themselves unless you need to place them in a conspicuous place in your display. We try to keep a few close to the scales so every customer can see that we have them.

We sell beans for $1.50 per pound and there is some price resistance there but early demand is usually greater than the available supply. We offer late season canners a discount for quantities over 5 pounds. We keep a list of canners for the following year. As this list grows we may consider increasing production.

PAST AND FUTURE HITS AND MISSES

In 1991 we tried pole beans for the first time. We used twine looped over the angle iron trellis we use for cucumbers. It took some training to get the beans up the twine but once they started, they continued to climb without assistance. Production was late but yields were good.

Even one forgotten pod can make a plant stop flowering, so remove all pods, including those you might have overlooked during an earlier harvest.

Betty Besal[4]

109

Beans should be considered for commercial gardens because of the demand for them. However, profitability is a function of interplanting and careful attention to growing them properly.

In 1992 we used Contender, a 52-day standard variety. We planted only 100' and sold $127 of beans for a $1.50 per square foot average. Germination was inconsistent because of shallow planting and inadequate moisture during germination. The spring was cool so our beans were late and we didn't sell any until three weeks after the market had opened.

In 1993 we planted six 50' rows of bush beans all at 2-3" spacing. All three beds were planted with a double row of cabbages down the center. The cabbage thrived in the cool spring weather and crowded the beans before the weather warmed up. We had to clip the outside cabbage leaves several times to provide space for the beans to grow which slowed cabbage growth. Because of the record setting cool summer weather, beans were extremely late. We didn't sell any beans until July 19th. We finished the season with $182 in sales for an average of $1.21 per square foot.

In 1994 we returned to pole beans because of a major shift in our marketing strategy. We had abandoned pole beans for bush varieties because we wanted to hit the early bean market. When we shifted to using beans as a draw, and concentrating on quality, pole beans were a natural choice. We interplanted them with carrots and made a few mistakes. First, we didn't thin out the beans. This made picking very difficult and time consuming. Then we didn't tie the bean plants back against the trellis so the large bean leaves shaded the carrots, causing stunted carrot production. Finally, we picked some of them a bit too small. It's hard to make money on beans regardless of how they are harvested, but it is much harder when they are picked too small. We sold $362 of beans from 225 square feet of bed for an average yield of $1.61 per square foot. We sold our first beans the last day of July, and by August 20th production was reduced to the unprofitable stage. We were able to sell all of our beans until the end of the season when the home gardens became a factor.

We will continue with the pole beans and interplanting. However, we will interplant with bush beans and use cloches to get the beans to harvest earlier. When the bush beans are about finished, the pole beans should be ready to harvest. We will plant 150 lineal feet in pole beans and 300 feet in bush beans. This will give us a steady supply of beans over the season but should not produce more than we can sell easily.

FOR THE HOME GARDENER

If you have never tried pole beans, you may be pleasantly surprised by their excellent taste. The trellis we describe in chapter 13 works very well for pole beans as well as for cucumbers and peas.

Beans are warm weather plants and should not be pushed in the spring unless you use a dark seeded bush bean such as Royalty Purple, Provider, and Kentucky Wonder. Otherwise, let the ground warm up first, and you will be rewarded with a bumper crop. Protective cloches might help if you are adamant about getting early beans.

If you want a continuous crop of beans, try the combination of pole and bush beans. Add varieties of different maturities and experiment with the one you like best.

Don't fertilize or fertilize lightly where your beans will be planted. Too much nitrogen will give you plenty of leaves but fewer pods to eat.

Chapter Eleven

Cabbage

A scarecrow in the cabbage patch? *We'll try anything to keep those pesky white butterflies from our cabbage!*

Drawing by Tim Bumb

Cabbage provides the opportunity to discuss succession planting, and gives us another opportunity for interplanting. Growing cabbage also provides the basic skills needed to grow other members of cole family, broccoli and cauliflower. We recommend that you start with cabbage and then add broccoli as soon as you are comfortable with growing cabbage. Growing all three crops provides diversity for your market, and makes marketing all three crops easier. We have included more information on lettuce and broccoli in chapter nineteen.

Cabbage is not our most profitable crop. There is a steady demand for cabbage throughout the season, but little premium for being early. However, recent changes in our production and marketing techniques make cabbage a more competitive option for our limited space. The secret to profitable cabbage is spacing. If we crowd the plants to nine inches, the heads remain small, at about two pounds. These small heads sell easily at 75¢ each, but still provide income of $1.33 per square foot. If we interplant peas on trellises in the same bed, we can easily reach our goal of $2 per square foot for those beds. And peas and cabbage are very compatible because they are both cool weather crops.

Cabbages must be started as transplants and can be set out in the garden several weeks prior to our FFD. They are a short-season, cool-weather crop but will withstand 95° temperatures if adequate moisture is provided. However, the best tasting cabbages are raised when the heads develop during cool weather. Therefore we grow cabbage as a spring crop and our heads are usually all sold by the end of July.

COMMERCIAL PLANNING

Planning for cabbages is complicated by the need to stagger planting. If we plant all of the cabbage on the same day, the entire cabbage crop may be ready for market at one time. Demand for cabbage is not sufficient to absorb large quantities in a single market without a drastic reduction in price.

CABBAGE DATA

Planning

Propagation	Transplants
Frost Tolerance	Very Hardy
Earliest transplant date	FFD - 28 days
Maturity date	67 days
Seeds per ounce	6000-8000
Seed viability	4 years
Intensive spacing	9"
Planting depth	1/2"
Germination temp	75°
Germination time	4-6 days
Days to transplant size	28-42 days
Growing temp (D/N)	60°-70°/50°-60°

Growing

pH	7-7.5
Nutrient requirements	Heavy feeder
Pests	Cabbage loopers and worms, cutworms, flea beetles
Diseases	Black rot, downy mildew
Critical watering	When heads are forming

Harvest

Harvest when	proper market size, 2-3lbs, and heads are solid
Yield	2-3 lbs per plant
Average selling price	75¢ each
Average income per square foot	$2.50 if interplanted

Quantities

Cabbage provides the opportunity to plan for limited quantities. Let's assume that our market research indicates early cabbage will sell at a rate of 70-80 cabbages per week. Consumption will slow considerably as other produce becomes available. Mid-season markets sell at about the same price but at about half the quantity.

We will start with 70-80 cabbages for the first two weeks of the market, then reduce that by 50% for the next eight weeks. This plan translates into 420-480 cabbages per season. We don't plan to sell more than that, and we want them at the right time. Our two beds will produce a maximum of 536 cabbages, so we will be about right for our first year.

This planning exercise illustrates the special problems associated with extracting maximum production from limited space. If we were not concerned with that, we could plant extra cabbage and hope for the best. But with a limited market for cabbage, we must plant only what we can sell easily.

Varieties

Maturity dates. Cabbage varieties are generally classified by growing season, early, main season, and late varieties. Maturity dates can vary dramatically from 56-110 days. Early varieties are notorious for splitting, but they are also the best tasting. Mid season varieties will stand longer in the garden without splitting, but have thicker leaves so they don't have quite the taste. Late season cabbages will store longest. Select a variety and then use it as it is intended. For example, do not direct seed an early variety late in the season. You will not get consistent results.

We can extend the season in two ways. We can plant cabbages with different maturity dates all at the same time or we can vary our planting dates for the same variety. The problem with the second option is that later plantings seem to 'catch up' with the early plantings as the weather warms in the spring. Since we plant only a small amount of cabbage, we have used this option successfully. However, it you plan larger plantings, you may wish to consider using differing maturities.

Unlike most other crops, one of the primary selection considerations is to choose varieties to spread out the season if we plan to sell cabbage all season. However, unless we plan to sell to the late season storage market, early or main season varieties would be our best choices.

Taste. Taste is an important consideration because taste is what distinguishes direct marketers from the supermarkets. Taste seems to be associated with thinner leaves. Since the early varieties have the thinnest leaves, they are generally the best tasting. In addition, short cored varieties provide more usable cabbage and tend to be better-flavored.

Hybrid versus Open Pollinated. Hybrids provide a much more uniform crop of cabbage. If you look down a row of hybrids standing next to a standard variety, the difference is striking. The hybrids are almost all the same size whereas open pollinated varieties vary considerably. There are arguments for both varieties. A lack of uniformity spreads out maturity giving us more time to sell the cabbages at the right size. On the other hand, quality may be more consistent with a hybrid cabbage.

Bolt resistance. Cabbage will go to seed if placed under stress, especially hot weather and insufficient moisture. This factor should be considered in warmer climates.

Resistance to splitting. When cabbages grow too quickly some varieties will split. This makes the produce unsalable at market price. Splitting is a critical factor especially in areas with considerable rainfall. In a normal year we do not have this problem and can control the growth of the cabbage with careful watering. Cabbage stores well with proper refrigeration so we could pick it at the right size and store it for later markets. However, that is not fresh produce, the all-important factor that distinguishes us from mass markets. Consequently, if cabbage can remain in the field without splitting, we will be able to pick just what we need for each market, and retain our fresh produce reputation.

Pest tolerance. A secondary consideration unless you have a specific disease history. There are varieties that are tolerant to yellows, black rot, thrips, and tip burn. If these are serious problems in your area, you may wish to favor one of these varieties.

Red Cabbage. There are several varieties of red cabbage. They tend to be mid-season, have thicker leaves, and are a bit hotter tasting. Consequently, it is a niche market that could be developed over time. As with most niche crops, we recommend starting small and working into the market slowly.

Chinese cabbage. There is perhaps a larger niche market for Chinese cabbage than red cabbage. Varieties include both heading and non-heading types. The advantage to the intensive gardener is that these cabbages grow upright so a 6" spacing is possible, allowing for four times as much cabbage to be grown per square foot. If you have a niche market, this crop is worth considering.

Planning Dates

Some crops that use transplants are driven by the earliest transplant date. That is, they will not survive freezing weather so cannot be transplanted until after the last frost. This is not true of cabbage. Cabbage planning is driven by the market date. It is possible to raise cabbage that will mature prior to the opening of the

Some varieties taste markedly better than others, which means that gardeners with inside information have a large measure of control over cabbage quality.

Jack Cook[1]

THE CABBAGE PLAN

The Seed Plan

Plant spacing .... 9"
Plants per row 67
Rows per bed 4
Plants per bed 268
Number of beds 2
Total number of plants 536
Seed required 750
Seeds per ounce 6000-8000
Seed ordered 1000
Variety .... Stonehead
Source .... Stokes ($2.13 per 1000 seeds)

The Planting Plan

Planting date .... (FFD-50) Last week in March, then each 2 wks
Transplant date .... (FFD-15) May 3
Location .... Beds 29 and 30 interplanted with peas

Marketing Plan

Est yield .... 500 heads @ 2 lbs avg
Selling price .... .75¢ per head
Gross income $375
Income per square foot ....$2.50 if interplanted

market. Our market opens about July 1st. However, crowds are small so we do not want too many at that time. Consequently, we use July 15th for our planning market date.

Cabbage can be set out about a month before your FFD. We have had cabbages survive temperature in the low twenties. We subtract the number of days to maturity, 67, from the market day and determine that we should set them out around the 3rd of May. Our FFD is about May 18th, so we are well within the range of survivable cabbage weather.

If we plan to set them out the first week of May, we must start them 4-5 week prior to that, or around the last week in March. Remember that we are not concerned with having large quantities of cabbage ready for the early market. We would rather have sufficient supplies arrive about the time tomatoes and cucumbers are in full production. If you wish to hit the early market with cabbages, you might want to push the planting date back 10-15 days. You may need to repot them one more time into 5" pots to get them past the 8th true leaf stage. There would be some danger in transplanting them into the garden before the 5th true leaf.

It is important to remember that late spring seeded cabbage will mature 10-14 days earlier because of the warmer growing conditions. We use succession plantings to replace cabbage harvested throughout the summer.

GROWING

Planting

We start the cabbages in 1204s since they grow quickly. They seem to germinate at close to 100% so we plant only one seed in each cell. They germinate in about 4 days and we move them immediately to the greenhouse because they like a cooler growing environment. When they develop their first true leaf, we repot them into large trays. We throw out any small plants or those with crooked stems, keeping only the best plants. The large trays provide ample room for the cabbages to grow to transplant size.

Young cabbage plants are very sensitive to stress and cold weather between the 5th and 8th true leaf stage. (A true leaf is any over 2 cm.) We try to have them set out prior to that as the younger plants survive adverse field conditions much easier than older plants.

Spacing. We transplant at 9" spacing to reduce head size. We do not want large heads as they are difficult to sell for the fresh cabbage market. The tighter spacing did not seem to slow normal growth as the cabbages matured about on schedule.

Interplanting. We have many options. We can plant two rows of cabbage down the center of the bush bean beds. If cool spring weather delays the beans, trimming of the cabbage leaves may be necessary to provide sunshine to the beans. However, this is not time intensive, so this planting arrangement is still a very viable option. Planting only one row down the center eliminates this requirement but reduces overall production.

We can also plant two rows down each side of trellised beans or peas. This is a more economical arrangement as it allows for four rows of cabbage in a bed, plus one double row of peas or beans. Interplanting with beans is complicated because beans are a warm weather crop and will not be up far enough for early spring cabbage transplants. The large cabbage leaves will shade the emerging bean plants and full production will not be possible.

The best arrangement is to interplant with peas. We can still get four full rows of cabbage across the 38 inch bed. If you need more cabbage than that, the next best option is to transplant cabbage after the beans are up. This will provide heads for mid-season sales.

Double-cropping. One of the advantages of cabbage is that it is possible to raise a late season crop because it is very frost tolerant. However, this is advisable only if you have a healthy late-season market. It would be possible to follow early season crops such as radishes, lettuce, and even early bush beans with cabbage transplants. It would not be advisable to follow early cabbage

with a late cabbage crop because of potential disease and pest problems.

Caring for the Plants

Insects. The most persistent problem with cabbage is cabbage worms. They can be easily controlled by spraying *Bacillus thuringiensis* as soon as the white moths appear and every week thereafter. We have very little damage from worms, except in those cases when we neglected to apply Bt on schedule.

Flea beetles can be a problem, particularly with young plants later in the season. However, when we set ours our early, the plants are too large for the beetles when they emerge in the spring and can survive without much damage. Flea beetles can be controlled with rotenone or pyrethrum. If you must transplant young cabbages during the height of the flea beetle season, cover with spun fabric row covers.

Watering. The amount of water applied, within reason, does not seem to be a major factor. The critical element is that watering must be even or the cabbages may crack. This can be a problem if a soaking rain occurs after you have irrigated. If splitting becomes a problem, twist the head a half turn to break off some of the root to slow growth.

PREPARING FOR MARKET

Harvesting.

Cabbages should be harvested when they are about two pounds. Small heads sell easily at 75¢. Cabbages beyond four pounds are more difficult to sell, When checking for harvestable cabbage, squeeze the head hard to determine if the head is solid. You will notice that many shoppers will do the same because

Early cabbages mature in about 60 days. They are the smallest, producing two- to three-pound heads, just right for those who garden in raised beds with close spacing.
Diane Bilderback [2]

115

they do not want a loose headed cabbage.

To harvest cabbage, push the outside leaves down and cut the head off with a long knife, leaving the plant in the bed. Haul the heads to the wash rack. Trim off all leaves that detract from the fresh appearance of the cabbage and remove all worm damage as customers seem to be sensitive about worms.

One of the commercial growers at our market leaves several of the outside leaves on, as this is the way wholesale grocery markets want the product. This provides protection for the head prior to arrival at the supermarket where they trim off the final leaves, and wrap the head in plastic. This grower has developed a large cabbage clientele over the years which proves there is more than one way to prepare cabbage for the market.

After the market we pull the plant, put it on the compost pile, and remove all residue from the bed to reduce disease and pest problems.

Marketing

Cabbages must be clean, and without insect damage. If you choose to sell by the pound use a small label to price the cabbage before you get to the market. This is particularly helpful in busy markets. Customers know how much the cabbage will cost them and we do not have to take the time to weigh the produce. One producer shrink-wraps his cabbage. This keeps the produce looking fresh and allows the grower to refrigerate those he does not sell without degradation in appearance.

Cabbage pricing runs contrary to our early market principle. Bringing the first cabbage to market does not bring premium prices for two reasons. First, it is easy to have cabbage ready for the early markets, and second, demand is limited. But the price doesn't dip much towards the end of the season either. The going price throughout the season is about 35¢ per pound. Even at that good income per square foot can be realized. We normally sell our small early cabbage for 75¢ each and move them easily.

An important point should be made here. You may be in an area with a much stronger cabbage market. If so, there are a few additional marketing considerations. We can increase sales by dropping the price. However, we loose 25-50¢ per head and per square foot. We are much smarter to manage our planting to mature at the proper time to maintain our prices because we have the right number of cabbages at any given market. One of the primary advantages to growing cabbage is that the crop can remain in the garden without any loss of quality. We can justify cutting prices only when the cabbage is threatened by splitting or disease.

In 1993 we started selling early cabbage for 39¢ per pound, the local supermarket price. However, there was some price resistance there, and another grower was selling larger cabbages for $1 per head. We matched that price for one Saturday market because of over supply and sold 35 heads. We checked the supermarket price, and it had increased to 59¢ per pound so we went back to 39¢ and sold at a rate of 15 heads per weekday market, and 35 on Saturday.

PAST AND FUTURE HITS AND MISSES

We will take a slightly different approach for this section, and highlight specific lessons learned over the past few seasons.

Don't direct seed cabbages.

Transplants are easy to grow, so it is of little advantage to direct seed. The season in most sections of the country is too short anyway for successful marketing of direct seeded cabbage. In addition, flea beetles and other insects can be very destructive to the young plants when direct seeded. A healthy transplant doesn't seem to attract the same attention from insects.

Adjust production to fit the market

Cabbages provide us with the opportunity to demonstrate the planning required for adjusting production. In 1992 we grew 140 cabbages and sold all of them in the first two weeks of the market. We watched other growers sell cabbage throughout the season, and it became obvious that demand remained steady. Before making the decision to expand production, we considered several factors.

Should we convert garden space currently planted to other crops to fill this demand for cabbage? Would it be more profitable? With double cropping, our return on cabbage would be over $2.00 per square foot. Carrots and flowers did not do that well in 1992 so we could convert some of that space.

Will double cropping work? All of these crops will take some frost. Normally we have a light frost or two in the fall, and then we may not go below freezing for another 3-4 weeks. But would the late cabbage market be sufficient to absorb a second crop?

Can we compete with our wholesale cabbage grower at our market. He knows how to grow great cabbage, and has a very loyal clientele. If we use our very best marketing skills, it will still take time to chip away at his market. We do not want to do it with a price drop. That doesn't help any of us. Consequently, we must increase production carefully and market aggressively.

We decided to increased production. We were not sure we could move 600 cabbages but thought it possible. We sold $437 in cabbage and broccoli for an average yield of 73¢ per square foot, which proved we could sell more cabbage but profitability was still a problem. However, these problems were in production, not in marketing. Our late cabbage heads were small, probably for the same reasons cited for broccoli and cauliflower. Customers do not want eight pound cabbages, but they do not want softball sized heads either. The small heads sold at a discount, 50-75¢ per head. One large grower overplanted broccoli, driving late prices to 50¢ per head, too low to make it a viable late crop.

Double cropping isn't easy.

And it may not be profitable. In 1993 we planted cabbage, broccoli, and cauliflower plants the end of May for our fall crop. We used the large trays to give the plants space as we knew they would be larger than normal before they would be transplanted. There were plenty of problems with this plan.

The plants were grown outside. We covered the trays with spun fabric to protect them from insects. When they were about a month old, the plants were a pale purplish-brown color, indicating the plants were under stress. The potting soil was a mix of peat and garden soil but probably didn't have the nutrients needed by the rapidly growing plants. The plants responded well to fertilization, but the damage had most likely already been done.

Cabbage has a longstanding reputation as king of the cole crops. Like its cousins—broccoli, cauliflower and kale— cabbage is loaded with flavor and nutrients, but is by far the most productive member of the family, giving you the most usable pounds of produce per square foot of growing space.
Vicki Mattern [3]

117

We never harvested a single head of late broccoli. They all bolted even though late summer temperatures were perfect for good production. We consulted a local expert who explained that the plants were too old when we transplanted them. Broccoli should be no more than five weeks old when transplanted into the garden.

We harvested only one cauliflower head. We believe there were three problems with the slow maturing heads. First, we stressed the plants while they were very small. It seems that plants that have been set back, do not fully recover the vigor they start with. Second, the plants were too mature when we transplanted them into the garden. Third, had we had the patience, we may have been able to harvest some more heads. Our early fall weather was spectacular. However, it is not worth our time to go to market with only a few cauliflower heads.

We threw out the last 100 cabbage heads because of *a severe thrips infestation.* We can find worms and remove them before market. Thrips are so small they invade the entire head, making them unmarketable.

Double-cropping is risky at best. Even if we can work out late season production problems, we may still experience a weak late cabbage market.

Cabbage varieties survive frost differently

Most varieties can take temperatures below 25, however, the earlier varieties seem more sensitive to frost damage. 1992 we had Stonehead and Early Copenhagen. We were after the early cabbage market, and subjected the plants to temperatures in the mid-20's. The Stoneheads seem unaffected, but damage to the Copenhagen cabbages was noticeable. The plants recovered nicely but it did set them back some.

FOR THE HOME GARDENER

Cabbages can be set out very early in the season. If you purchase plants at that time, you will most likely get much healthier plants. Most of the cabbage plants we see at greenhouses later in the spring are a sickly yellow, and may have already been set back because of a severe lack of root space.

Try crowding the cabbages a bit if you like the smaller heads, especially if you are short of space.

If you grow peas on trellises, interplant cabbages next to them. This will give you almost free space for your peas.

Chapter Twelve
Carrots

We grow carrots because they epitomize what direct marketing is all about. Supermarket carrots are not selected for taste. They are selected to survive mechanical handling and extended storage. We select varieties that taste best and we pick them by hand. Supermarkets cannot compete with the sweetness of our carrots. Consequently, they sell easily and at premium prices. Unfortunately, it is still difficult to make money growing carrots because of spacing and germination problems.

Soil texture plays an important role in carrot variety selection. Long, slender carrots can be grown only in loose, deeply cultivated beds. However, there are varieties for almost any soil condition. Stubby Royal Chantenay, for example, will grow well in clay soil. The important thing is to select a variety that grows well in your area of the country, and in your particular soil.

Regardless of the type soil you have, soil preparation is more critical than with any other vegetable. Carrots do not like stones, and will become forked and unmarketable in rocky soil. If you have a severe problem with stones, you may wish to pass on carrot production, and opt for other crops that won't mind a few rocks.

Germination is the next challenge to profitable carrot production. Carrots are notorious for less than 100% germination. Consequently they must be over planted and then thinned out for a maximum harvest.

Carrots prefer to grow in cool weather, so early planting provides the best tasting carrots. They can be direct seeded up to six weeks prior to FFD. They germinate slowly in cool soil so the first few frosts don't bother them. Small carrots are hardy and will take a frost, especially if covered with spun fabric.

Optimum harvest begins when 20% of the carrots are 1½" in diameter and lasts for about three weeks. If a longer harvest is desired, succession planting is recommended.

COMMERCIAL PLANNING

To start the planning process, we must return to our marketing strategy because marketing decisions determine our method of production. We receive less per square foot for carrots than any other vegetable we grow. Therefore, we use carrots as a draw to bring customers into our stand during peak production. If you choose to use carrots as a main crop, you will want to plant earlier, plant successive crops, and double crop whenever possible.

12-1. Seeding carrots. We use the cheese shaker to scatter the seeds. Then we cover the seeds with sawdust. Finally, we place spun fabric over the seedbed to keep the seeds in place. The spun fabric is held in place with 10' sections of 3/8" rebar. Notice the split bed because of the bean trellis.

CARROTS DATA

Planning

Propagation	Direct Seed
Frost tolerance	Hardy
Earliest transplant date	FFD - 28 days
Maturity date	70-80 days
Seeds per ounce	18,000 - 23,000
Seed viability	3 years
Intensive spacing	2-3"
Planting depth	1/4"
Germination temperature	40°-95° (80°)
Germination time	10-17 days

Growing

pH	6.5
Nutrient requirements	Light feeder
Pests	Aphids, carrot rust flies, cutworms, carrot weevils
Diseases	leaf blight, aster yellows, root knot nematodes
Critical Watering	Throughout season

Harvest

Harvest when	tops are 1-1½"
Average selling price	75¢-$1/lb
Average income per square foot	$1 - $1.50

Succession planting. Carrots are at their peak flavor for a relatively short time, so if we plan to sell over the season, it is necessary to plant every week or two to maintain quality. I'm talking peak flavor here. Some carrot varieties can be left in the soil until Thanksgiving but peak flavor for the carrot connoisseur is available only for a few weeks.

Interplant. Carrots will interplant well with crops grown on trellises, like peas and beans. The disadvantage to this approach is that they must be removed carefully, other wise the roots of the other crops might be damaged. The carrots must be pulled by hand which requires more time, and excellent soil conditioning.

Double-cropping might be possible in longer season areas. It would require changes in the marketing plan, that is, early sales and the development of a niche market.

Varieties.

Variety selection is more important with carrots than any other vegetable because the taste is determined almost entirely by the variety you select. In addition, quality of a particular variety may differ from one seed company to another. And to complicate the selection even more, a given variety from one vendor may react to varying weather from year to year, and your quality may vary some.

Published *maturity dates* vary from 50-70 days but actual maturity varies widely with weather conditions. This factor is important only if prices fall because of an oversupply of carrots. We do not have that problem so we can plant carrots with later maturity dates without economic consequences.

Taste is the primary factor for variety selection. Taste distinguishes farmers market carrots from those that are harvested mechanically for the supermarkets. Find one that grows well in your soil, and tastes better than others that you have grown. Taste is also affected by the weather. The best tasting carrot will be harvested when the weather is cool.

Disease tolerance is rarely mentioned except for some tolerance for various blights.

Yield is always important. We have found it advisable to talk to seed company representatives. They can generally give you good advice on which varieties will provide the best yields.

Soil type. If you have raised beds with ample organic matter, you can raise almost any carrot. However, if you have heavy soil, consider a Chantenay or Danvers type carrot.

Storage capabilities. The ability of a variety to store well is important only if you plan to sell into the storage market in late fall.

The *size of the carrot tops* may limit our ability to crowd them for greater production. Medium sized tops might work better than growing carrots with large, strong tops.

Heat tolerance is important in the south, where hot weather can make for frustrating carrot production.

Given this long list of considerations, final selection may take several years. Once you find the right variety for your soil and market, continue to experiment, but on a limited scale.

Spacing

Carrots illustrate the intensive spacing concept better than any other vegetable so we will spend some time explaining that. If you view a conventional carrot row from above it looks something like the top drawing on Figure 12-2. If the carrots are spaced too tightly, the tops can spread out to the sides, and the roots will develop by pushing their neighbors aside.

Intensively spaced carrots are illustrated in the bottom two drawings on Figure 12-2. If these are spaced too tightly, there is no place for the tops to spread out to get the sunlight they need. So they grow upward, getting weak and spindly. The roots cannot get the nutrients they need because the tops are not large enough, and because much of the growing energy is spent on even bigger tops.

Spacing, then, becomes a function of the carrot tops, which vary with variety. Consequently, we cannot tell you what your exact spacing should be, because this is

Conventional carrot planting

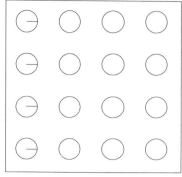
Wide rows - 3" spacing

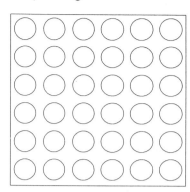
Wide rows - 2" spacing

determined by the variety you have chosen.

Profits from carrots are determined by three factors, spacing, germination and thinning. Spacing presents special challenges because if carrots are spaced too far apart, we cannot achieve maximum production. If they are too close, production can be reduced significantly because the plants cannot get the sunshine they need. Therefore, we must experiment to determine optimum spacing for the variety that we grow. Lets look at the potential profit between spacing options.

We will assume an average of eight carrots per pound and $1 per pound selling price. If we use a three inch spacing we will harvest a maximum of 16 carrots per square foot. At eight carrots per pound, we will receive $2 per square foot.

A 2" spacing increases the number of carrots to 36 per square foot. IF (and this is a gigantic IF) the carrots remain the same size, at 8 per pound, the increase in profit is substantial, to $4.50 per square foot.

However, it is very unlikely that crowded carrots will produce the same size roots. Suppose carrots size dropped to 16 carrots per pound. We

12-2. Carrot spacing. Three inch spacing on the left will provide 16 carrots per square foot. Two inch spacing on the right will yield 36 carrots per square foot.

121

THE CARROT PLAN

Seed plan

Quantity 2
Plant spacing .... 2½"
Plants per row 240
Rows per bed 14
Plants per bed 3360
Estimated germination rate 75%
Seeds required per bed 4480
Total seeds required 8960
Seeds per ounce 18,000
Seeds ordered .... ½ ounces
Variety .... Earlibird Nantes
Source .... Stokes
Cost $7.80

Planting plan

Planting date .... (FFD-23) April 25th
Location .... Beds 26 and 27

Marketing Plan

Estimated yield .... 1.5 lbs per square foot
Selling price .... $1 per pound
Gross income $450
Income per square foot $1.50
Sell only when carrots reach optimum size. Sell hard, bringing as many as we think we can sell to each market.

would still produce more at the 2" spacing, $2.25 per square foot. However, we must clean twice as many carrots for that extra 25¢. Somewhere in between two and three inch spacing lies optimum carrot size.

The conventional farmer in you objects. "Why go to all of this bother, when it would be easier just to plant plenty, in large fields measured in thousands of feet of carrot rows.

Because there is no free lunch. Certainly you would not need to spend as much time thinning, and experimenting with spacing. But you would have to water those rows, and

fertilize, and weed them. So we choose to spend our time thinning to optimum spacing to save weeding time, and walking, and wasted water and fertilizer.

Quantities

Demand for carrots is seldom satisfied. We have yet to bring any early carrots home. Planning, then, is not based upon how many can be sold, but by the garden space available after more profitable crops have been planted.

In ideal conditions 90% germination is possible in a wide temperature range, from 50° to 86°. Since our conditions are less than ideal, we assumed a 75-80% germination rate. Minimum wide row spacing is 2-3" in each direction. If we use a 2.5" average, we can grow 23 carrots per square foot, or about 3400 carrots per 3' by 50' raised bed. With a 75% germination rate, we must plant about 4500 seeds. There are about 18,000 carrots seeds per ounce, so we need 1/4 ounce per bed.

Planting Dates

One of the frustrations with carrots is though they prefer to mature in cool weather, they do not like cool soil for germination. Carrots germinate in about 10 days if the soil temperature is around 60°, and 17 days if soil temperature is closer to 50°. Consequently, planting them too early is counterproductive. We try to get ours into the ground by the end of April if the weather looks promising and the soil temperature is high enough for germination.

If you plant only a few carrots, you can plant them all at one time and sell them easily because there is usually a tremendous demand for quality carrots, regardless of timing. However, if carrots are a major crop, it would be advisable to plant over several weeks to ensure optimum taste because taste is what sells carrots.

The calendar doesn't mean much when timing succession plantings. If you space plantings by one or two weeks, the late plantings will likely catch up to the earlier ones because of rising soil temperatures which shorten germination time. That is, if you plant when soil temperature is 50° it will take 17 days to germinate. Two weeks later you plant again and the soil temperature has risen to 60°. This planting takes only 10 days to germinate and the two are now only one week apart instead of two. The best option is to wait until the first planting has germinated, and then sow the new beds.

GROWING

Sowing

Install a double irrigation hose, and water the bed well starting two weeks prior to planting. Lay aside the irrigation hoses and, if you are planting a dedicated carrot bed, cultivate one last time just before planting to thoroughly loosen the soil.

The secret to this sowing is to know how many seeds we need for each bed. Our final spacing objective is 2½" apart in each direction or 23 carrots per square foot. Our beds are each 150 square feet so we need 3450 seeds per bed. We assume a germination rate of 75%, so we must scatter 4600 seeds. Sow the seeds using one of two viable options, scattering the seed, or using a mechanical planter.

Scatter method.

There are 18,000 - 23,000 carrot seeds per ounce, depending on variety. That spread is large enough to affect our final production. If we assume 23,000 seeds per ounce, we would seed 2/10 ounce of seed. If we were wrong and there were only 18,000 seeds, we would have sown only 3600 seeds instead of the 4600 we needed. On the other hand if we made the mistake on the safe side and assumed 18,000 seeds per ounce, we would plant .26 ounce of seed. If we were wrong and there were 23,000 seeds per ounce we would have seeded 5878 seeds or 1278 extras that would need to be thinned out. Err on the safe side, and plant too many seeds. They can always be thinned out. Keep records and adjust the planting rate the following year.

One fourth ounce of seed isn't very much. We use a cheese shaker we purchased from a restaurant supply firm. Shake the seeds unto the bed as evenly as possible. Even with practice, this method does not provide very uniform distribution.

Mechanical Planter

We use a small Earthway planter, available at many hardware and farm supply stores for less than $100. It has no planter wheel fine enough to handle raw carrot seeds, so we purchase pelletized seeds. We use the smallest wheel in the planter and raise the planting depth adjustment all the way up so the seeds are not covered at all and plant rows about 2" apart. The planting wheel plants seeds about every three inches. This combination gives us about an average 2½" spacing or 23 carrots per square foot.

With pelletized seed it is very easy to get an exact count on the seeds we plant. They come in bags of 10,000 seeds. We weigh the contents, and then calculate what we need. Then we continue to plant on the bed until the seeds are gone. If thinning is required, reduce the number of seeds planted in subsequent years until you

Though there are thousands of varieties to choose from, breeders and seedsmen we talked to across the country agreed that only one type delivers the best flavor and quality —Nantes.

Kent Martin [1]

12-3. Keeping the germinating beds moist. This is the most important part of good germination. Because it requires constant movement of the water hose, we devised this T-bar system to keep the hose from damaging the seed beds. The T-bars are made from reinforcing rods.

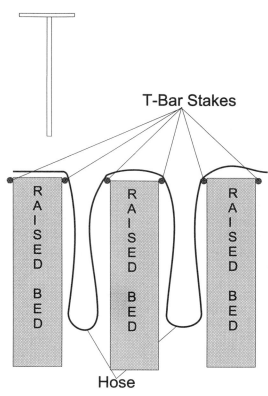

T-Bar Stakes

RAISED BED   RAISED BED   RAISED BED

Hose

have the desired result. Once again, documentation is necessary to adjust your production procedures.

Pelletized seed provides near perfect spacing, saves time, and requires less thinning. Stokes sells the pelletized seed for about 55¢ per 1000 seeds, or about $2.53 per bed. For that small cost, we recommend the investment in the planter as you will get a much more even distribution with this system as opposed to the scatter method.

Getting the seeds to grow

If I were to blame profitability problems on one factor, it would be germination. Carrots seeds are very small so they are difficult to space out properly. Once in the soil, germination can be erratic and translate into open, unproductive spots in the carrot bed. Profits plummet as the number of these spots increases.

Germination is not difficult, but requires special techniques. To get the germination we need, we must overplant, protect the seeds, and keep them moist. Then when we get good germination, we must thin the plants to optimum spacing. It doesn't make sense, but we have found no easy way to maximize production.

We do not cover the seeds with soil as germination can be reduced by crusted soil. Instead we use ½" of sawdust from a local cabinet shop. The sawdust holds the moisture required for good germination and protects the seeds.

Then we cover the beds with spun fabric. Spun fabric does many good things for carrots. It protects the seeds from winds that can make germination impossible. Early in the season it provides a little warmth on cool sunny days that permits the plants to grow faster. Finally, it protects the maturing plants from leaf hoppers that carry Aster Yellows disease. Wind can be severe in North Dakota so the fabric must be stretched tightly. We use 10' sections of 3/8" rebar rolled up into the extra fabric. Standard fabric width is about 64". With a 38" bed, it leaves us about 13" on each side to roll up into the rebar and tie with twine.

We interplant carrots with trellised peas or beans which divides the bed in half. The rebar is permanently tied to the spun fabric in ten foot sections, 32" wide. See figure 12-1. This system can easily be installed by one person, and removed for weeding and thinning.

After planting we water the beds daily with a sprinkler to keep the seeds wet for optimum germination. To keep the hose off the beds we use T-bars made from rebar as described in figure 12-3.

Thinning

Profits from carrots is determined by thinning, especially when using the scatter method. If the plants are not thinned properly, the carrots will be crowded and small. There will be more of them, but the number of pounds produced will be reduced significantly.

Don't thin until the carrots reach a survivable size and are well rooted. There will, of course, be bare spots. Carrots around these spots can be crowded closer than 2½" because their tops will still have space to grow. As thinning is accomplished, spread an inch of compost around the plants to protect them and conserve moisture. We use our best compost and run it through the shredder since the carrots are small and need a fine compost.

That's a lot of work you say! Will it pay off? It takes about two hours to thin one bed depending upon the success of our sowing effort. At minimum wage this will add $10-12 to our cost per bed which would require an extra 11-14 pounds of carrots at 90¢ per pound to make thinning pay off. There is no question in my mind that this is money well spent.

Watering

Adequate moisture during germination is critical. We use garden hoses to spray down the beds every day. After germination, the secret to watering carrots is to maintain an even, abundant supply. Uneven distribution may cause misshapen or cracked roots. Overwatering during root development can create bland tasting carrots, and may cause them to crack. We use a double irrigation hose on the carrot beds.

Fertilizing

Organic matter is critical to growing the long slender carrots our customers want. However, applying manures just prior to planting may result in forked roots. It is better to apply well rotted manure in the fall to eliminate this potential problem.

The best soil conditioner is peat moss. We added 12 cubic feet per 150 square foot bed. The results were dramatic. If the bed is moist, it is possible to bury a six inch shovel with only normal hand pressure. This makes pulling carrots by hand possible, which is necessary to minimize root disturbance of the interplanted crop.

Carrots need early nitrogen to grow tops that can support rapid growth. We apply about ½ pound granular nitrogen per bed each spring. When we take the spun fabric off, we work in a light layer of compost as a moisture conserving mulch and to keep the tops from turning green.

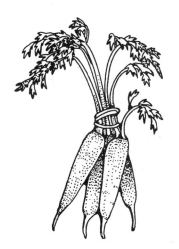

Diseases, insects, and weeds

Weeding is important early on, but then the carrot tops form a living mulch and only an occasional weed makes it through the canopy.

Carrots are remarkably pest and disease free. We have had some problems with Aster Yellows. Infected plants have pale yellow leaves and fine rootlets on the taproot. The carrots have a bitter taste so should be discarded. The disease is spread by the leafhopper and can be controlled by controlling the insect infestation.

Before we covered the beds with fabric we had trouble with the wind blowing off enough soil so the ants could get at the tender roots and they would chew off the tops. A light mulching kept that from happening.

HARVEST AND MARKETING

Harvest

Harvest carrots when they are at peak color and 20% of the carrots are 1½ inches in diameter. If you pick them too early you loose production and they will not have the sweet taste of a mature carrot. If you pick them too late they may become too large and difficult to sell.

As the carrots develop, start tasting them. Each variety is somewhat different, but you will soon develop the ability to determine when they taste best, and are therefore ready for harvest. Taste is the most important factor to determine when to harvest, with size running a reasonable second. Carrots remain sweet for about three weeks. When they are ready we harvest them all and have never had a problem selling them.

Harvesting carrots presents two problems, getting them clean and removing the tops. The tops often have small leaves that are difficult to remove and which detract considerably from the display. Cleanliness of any root crop is critical to marketing.

We do not harvest by thinning. It requires too much time and we want to clear the entire bed for replanting. There are many possible ways to harvest carrots. Here are two methods we use. You may find other combinations that work better for you.

Cut off the tops while the carrots are still in the ground, trimming off the smaller leaves. This leaves a longer top than individually topped carrots, however, customers do not seem to mind and it provides a little green color among the pile of orange carrots. Dig the carrots with a potato fork. If they are interplanted with peas or beans, only the outer carrots can be dug with a fork. Those close to the peas or beans must be pulled by hand to minimize root disturbance. Wash the carrots on the wash rack. This method saves time removing the tops, but it is more difficult to get the carrots completely clean.

If your bed is properly prepared, you can pick carrots by hand. We consider this easier and faster. Move them to the wash rack. Grab five or six at a time, and spray them down. By rolling them over with the tops, it is possible to clean them quickly and completely. Cut off the tops individually or remove several at a time with the help of a cutting board.

Throw out any deformed or hairy carrots that would detract from the display.

One of the advantages of carrots is that they will keep if you need to harvest them early for the market. For example, if you are short of help, you could harvest them the night before for a noon market. Store them in 5-gallon pails filled with water and bag them just prior to the market.

Marketing

There is tremendous demand for sweet carrots. This is one crop that defies the local supermarket price because of the substantial difference in taste. Supermarkets charge 25-33¢ per pound and we receive 75¢ to $1 per pound. That is only possible with a superior product.

We pre-bag most of the carrots into one and two pound bags. Customers are accustomed to this supermarket practice and many of them prefer this approach. However, we leave some in bulk for the discriminating buyers that want only one size.

Some growers sell by the bunch, usually $.50 and sometimes $.75 per bunch. This is quite common among the older growers, as it was quite acceptable years ago. However, customers are accustomed to purchasing supermarket carrots by the pound so it seems reasonable to match that practice at the farmers market. But if it works . . . . . .

Many of these growers also leave the tops on. We haven't been able to understand why this marketing practice still exists. Beet tops are edible so should be left for those customers that want them. But carrot tops are useless, and should be removed. We have seen customers purchase carrots with the tops, and then ask the vendor to remove them before they take them home.

PAST AND FUTURE HITS AND MISSES

The cool 1992 growing season was perfect for carrots and we grew the finest tasting carrots in our experience. We tried A+ hybrid because it is a high beta carotene variety. We also used Earlibird Nantees from Stokes. Then we made a classic mistake. We tried succession planting but planted the A+ first which is a 65 day carrot. Had we planted the Earlibird first, a 50 day variety, we may have had carrots for opening market. Our taste preference was for the Earlibird. We planted 5 50' beds and sold $386 at 75 cents a pound for an average return of about 51¢ per square foot. Much of the production problems were related to poor germination.

In 1993 we cut back to three beds of Earlibird Nantees. One of the other markets in the state charged $1 a pound for carrots, so we raised our price to 89¢ per pound. We sold all of our carrots at 89¢ per pound without any complaint. Customers returned for additional carrots and were disappointed that we had sold them all. We sold $363 for an average of 81¢ per square foot. Better germination was achieved through the use of row covers.

1993 was a cool year so sales started out slowly. We gave in to the temptation to pull carrots to boost sales. We probably sacrificed 25-35% of our potential production. It is much more profitable to delay carrot sales until they are large enough for optimum production and taste. They will sell well if picked at the proper stage, and the increased production will boost total sales.

For the past two years we have diluted the carrot seeds with a mixture of crushed vermiculite before shaking them on the bed with the cheese shaker. We thought we would get a more uniform distribution of seed. However, this methods makes it impossible to tell if you are spreading seeds or vermiculite. Consequently, you cannot return to an area that has too few seeds because you cannot identify those areas. Adequate vermiculite might be present, but that does not guarantee that carrot seeds are in the mixture. On the last bed we seeded this spring, we used only seed and got a much better distribution because we were able to replant areas that were short. The bed required a bit more thinning, but the additional production was well worth the extra effort.

In 1994 we interplanted carrots with peas and beans for the first time. Our first mistake was to plant the carrots too close to the trellis. Both peas and beans require some room to spread out before climbing the trellis. Consequently, some of the carrots were shaded and did not grow well. This also required the rods holding down the spun fabric to be closer to the trellis. It was impossible to

Although bunched carrots may be attractive, they must be marketed rapidly or the attached tops may cause the roots to shrink from loss of water.
Circular 1241 [3]

"You better get with the bunch if you wan'na get out'ta here!"

position the rod without covering carrots, peas or beans. Consequently, we removed the fabric early in the season. Our second mistake was to leave the bed flat rather than slope it to get more growing area. We did this because of previous problems with water running off the bed from the drip irrigation emitters. However, we did not fully understand the conditioning power of peat moss. We added 12 cubic feet of peat moss to each 150 square foot bed. The affect on water absorption was dramatic. With that soil supplement, a slightly sloped bed would not create any water runoff.

Interplanting increased our income per square foot because 1/2 of the bed was allocated to beans or peas with very little reduction in space for carrots. However, spotty seeding reduced the total yield and we lost space because of the flat bed. We sold $329 from 338 square feet for a return of 97¢ per square foot.

Next year we will go back to the mechanical planter and pelletized seed. We have discovered that it is sometimes difficult to get the thinning done on time because of the many tasks that must be done around that time. Therefore, if we can get good germination from pelletized

seed, this might be a better solution.

We will also plant carrots alone on wider beds. Carrots can be profitable if we can get adequate germination and get them to grow large enough. It doesn't appear that interplanting with trellis crops will permit them to grow to optimum size. We can still spread them out when interplanted, but a full bed may be more profitable. We have a few raised beds running east and west that are four feet wide. We can't use trellises on these beds so planting options are limited. We'll find out.

Another idea rolling around is to build a vacuum seeder similar to those used to seed plug trays. This would not be difficult to do except for getting the right sized holes. If the holes are too large, more than one seed is sucked up, and we get too many doubles. We would use a 2" spacing to cover germination losses. Then we will plant the carrots four to six inches away from the trellis wire, and slope the bed slightly to provide a wider planting area of about 15 inches.

FOR THE HOME GARDENER

If you are planting in a row, try a few wide rows. If your spacing is right you will get more carrots, and of proper size.

Raised beds are perfect for carrots since it allows the roots to grow longer. This would be especially helpful if you have heavy soil. Mix plenty of peat moss, sand, and organic material in a raised bed, and I'm sure you will be impressed with the harvest.

Plant earlier than normal and protect the plants with spun fabric.

If you have had germination problems, try our sawdust method.

Chapter Thirteen

Cucumbers

I believe that most cucumber breeders prefer to eat pick-lers rather than slicers fresh.
Todd C. Wehner [1]

When it comes to cucumbers, we are solidly in the minority. *"Cucumbers are difficult to transplant,"* experts claim. Not so! We transplant cucumbers that are too old according to conventional wisdom. That gives us the first cucumbers at the market when prices are most attractive.

"Pickles are pickles and slicers are slicers. Grow slicers for that market and pickle varieties for pickle customers." Not so! In fact, most cucumber breeders acknowledge that they prefer picklers over slicers for eating fresh.

Cucumbers are our second most profitable crop, because of high demand and prolific production. Careful marketing of pickles can extend profitable cucumber sales almost to the first frost. In cool seasons, the slicer market stays active, and every fruit can be sold at a fair price.

Fortunately cucumbers are not difficult to grow, provided you give them plenty of warmth and water. They require a well-drained, moderately rich soil. They are not heavy feeders but do benefit from several applications of nitrogen during the peak growing season.

Cucumbers are a short season crop. Many varieties produce their first fruits in less than 60 days when planted from seed. When transplants and protective cloches are used, production can begin even earlier. Weather, however, is still the deciding factor because sunshine and warmth are necessary for full cucumber production.

We will start this chapter in a different place to explain the use of trellises and cloches. These two growing techniques are critical to our cucumber production method so we begin with a discussion of how they are built.

GROWING TECHNIQUES

We use two growing techniques to improve cucumber production; trellises and cloches. Construction is time consuming so both must be constructed prior to the start of the season.

Trellises

Traditional cucumber production provides space for the vines to spread out horizontally. We do not have that space so we grow them vertically instead, on trellises. Cucumbers are natural climbers, with tendrils that wrap themselves around

129

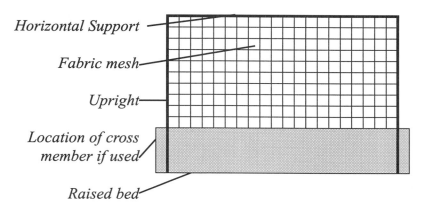

Horizontal Support

Fabric mesh

Upright

Location of cross
member if used

Raised bed

13-1. The Trellis. *We provide this drawing to define and illustrate the parts of the trellis discussed throughout the construction details.*

13-2. Installing the cross member. *Make a mark on the upright at two feet. Line the cross member up with the two foot mark. Hold*

Tri-square
2-foot mark
cross member

it loosely in place with a clamping pliers. Use a tri-square to square the cross member with the upright. Then clamp the pliers tightly for final welding.

almost anything. With minimum training, the vines will crawl to the top of our five foot trellis, providing maximum production in minimum space.

Our trellis has three parts: (Figure 13-1) an upright, a horizontal support, and the mesh. Our uprights have a cross member welded at ground level, two feet from the bottom. The cross member is optional because it does not provide any stability to the trellis. It is used only as a method of driving the upright into the ground with a maul, and a gauge for how deeply the upright should be installed. If you choose to use a fence post driver, the cross member can be eliminated.

We use 1/8" thick 1¼" angle iron available in 1994 at steel suppliers for about 42¢ per foot. A fifty foot

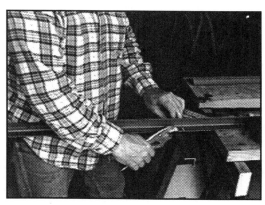

bed requires six uprights, and five ten-foot horizontal supports for a total of $41 if cross members are used. The mesh costs about 10¢ per running foot and we replace that each year. Construct the trellises as follows:

The uprights. Cut one 7' piece and one 1' piece of angle iron. Weld the 1' piece centered and perpendicular 5' down on the 7' piece. (See figure 13-2) Drill a 5/16" hole ½" down from the top of the post on the opposite side of the angle from the crosspiece.

The horizontal supports. Cut a 10' piece of angle iron. Drill holes in each end of the 10' piece about ½" from the end and centered on the angle iron. Since we will be using ¼" bolts, it is best to use at least a 5/16" drill bit. The reason for this will become obvious when you install the horizontal support to the uprights.

This completes the construction of trellis components. We order the mesh from Mellingers in 120' lengths.

Cloches

Cucumbers do not transplant easily, and cloches assure a higher percentage of transplant survival. Our success with cukes over the past few years has been a direct result of these cloches. Cool spring weather delayed non-protected plants, and we had two to three weeks of uncontested markets.

The cloches are made from a 2½' section of concrete reinforcing wire. Construct the cloches as follows:

Cut the cloche from the roll or reinforcing wire. It is possible to cut the reinforcing wire from a *full* roll without rolling out the wire. As the roll gets smaller, it may become necessary to tie one end to a stationary object, and roll out the wire so it can be cut. Measure out 2½'. The

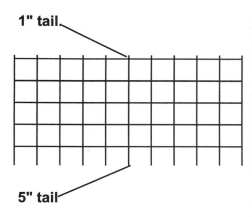

1" tail

5" tail

13-3. The Cloche. *This drawing illustrates the size of the cloche as it is cut from the roll of reinforcing wire. The roll is five feet wide. Each square is six inches square.*

13-4. Installing the plastic. *Notice that the roll of plastic is at the far end of the set-up. The boards between the two saw horses help support the wire during installation of the plastic.*

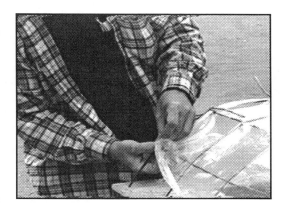

13-5. Tying the plastic. *This corner of the cloche is the most difficult because of the extra plastic from both directions. However, with a little practice, it can be tied securely quite quickly. Notice that on the end of each cloche we have ties on every wire. We tie every other wire along the length of the wire. We have had no problem with wind ripping the plastic using this tying arrangement.*

wires are spaced every six inches so count out five wires. Cut the wires 1" from the cross-wires so five inches is available to stick into the bed, and the other inch stabilizes the cloche along the trellis wire. It is sometimes necessary to adjust the diameter of the cloche. Cloches cut from the outside of a full roll do not have as much curvature as necessary. Those cut from the middle have too much.

Attach the plastic. Lay the wire on a table or a pair of saw horses. Position the roll of clear 3' plastic at one end of the cloche. The plastic is cut long enough to roll up along all ends, providing sufficient strength to withstand our windy days. Use short sections of twine to attache the plastic to the wire. Tie every six inches on the ends and every foot along the sides.

The cloches are sturdy enough to last for three to four years before they must be recovered with plastic.

Bonus Tip - Cutting Twine

We use a tremendous quantity of twine so we have experimented with the best way to cut it to the lengths we need.

Cut a board a little longer than the length you need. Wrap the twine around the board about twenty times. Then use a long, sharp kitchen knife and cut through one end with a sawing motion while holding the twine in place on the board. Carefully remove the other end and form a loop with the twine. Then cut through that loop with the same sawing motion .

COMMERCIAL PLANNING

Varieties

Open-pollinated varieties are mononecious. That is, they have both female and male flowers, usually in a ratio of about 15 to 1. Their primary advantage is that they will bear consistently all season. Hybrids on the other hand, bear heavily and early,

131

CUCUMBER DATA

Planning

Propagation	Direct Seed or Transplants
Frost Tolerance	Very Tender
Earliest transplant date	FFD+10
Maturity date	50-70 days
Seeds per ounce	1250-1750
Seed viability	5 years
Intensive Spacing	18-36"

Starting Transplants

Planting depth	1/4-1"
Germination Temp	60°-105° (95°)
Germination time	3-10 days
Wks to transplant size	14-28 days
Growing Temp (Day/Night)	70°-75°/65°-70°

Growing

pH	5.5-6.8
Nutrient requirements	Heavy feeder
Pests	Cucumber beetles, aphids, cutworms, squash bugs
Diseases	Bacterial wilt, mosaic, anthracnose, downy mildew
Watering	flowering & fruit development

Harvest

Harvest when	Slicers - different sizes; Pickles - To fit in jar
Average price	Slicers -33-50¢/each; Pickles 50-75¢/pound
Average income per square foot	$2.50 - $3.50

but tire out towards the end of the season.

Hybrids are usually *gyonecious* which means they have mostly female flowers and will produce more fruits. This is especially important for pickle production where fruit set is critical to profitability. However, to set fruit, they must still be pollinated by the male flowers. Consequently, seed companies include a few seeds of a pollinator. These seeds are usually dyed a different color so growers can ensure that sufficient pollinators are present. We do not leave the pollinators to chance. We take the pollinators out and plant an open-pollinated slicer like Marketmore. This way we can ensure that we have sufficient mononecious plants in the patch for optimum pollination.

Parthenocarpic varieties have mostly female flowers, and will set fruit without pollination. This makes them ideal for greenhouse growing, because they prefer not to be pollinated. The most common parthenocarpic pickle is County Fair 83. The most famous slicer is Sweet Success.

The following characteristics apply to the selection of both slicing and pickle varieties:

Disease resistance. Resistant cultivars have been developed for cucumber mosaic virus (CMV), Powdery mildew (PM), downy mildew (DM), anthracnose (ANTH), angular leaf spot (ALS), and scab. If you have had problems with any these diseases, choosing a resistant cultivar could solve the problem.

Yield. Commercial catalogs will usually identify those varieties with the best yields. This is a very important factor because it determines profitability in a long season.

Maturity dates for cukes are a real jungle of information. Published maturity dates are sometimes for direct seeding, and sometimes for transplants. The better seed catalogs list which date they are using. If the dates are for direct seeding, we can deduct 10-14 days from this date since we are using transplants. However, maturity dates are not a major factor in variety selection because there is not a wide diversity. Pickling varieties mature in a small range of 52-58 days, hardly significant. Slicers mature a bit later, and vary from 55 to 68 days, slightly more significant but hardly an overpowering selection factor. Our best advice is to develop your own data by keeping meticulous records and experimenting with different options and varieties.

Stress tolerance. Unfortunately, you won't find this characteristic in the catalogs. In 1992 we had an extremely cold season in North Dakota. We had about an equal number of Calypso pickles and Saladins. The cool weather caused stress on both varieties. However, the Calypsos did not get bitter, and the Saladins did. Consequently, we lost half of our crop because we could not sell the bitter cukes. Only experience and talking to other growers will provide this information, but it is critical to success during stressful weather.

Slicing. Plant breeders have isolated the cucumber gene that causes the fruits to become bitter when the plant is stressed. By removing this gene, they have developed "burpless" cucumbers. After having many requests from customers for burpless cucumbers, we added Sweet Slice to our inventory. We soon discovered that many customers refused to purchase a nonbitter cucumber because they considered them too bland for good eating. On the other hand, there are customers who can only eat burpless cukes.

Quantities

There is tremendous demand for cucumbers because fresh ones are more attractive and tastier than the waxed, pale-green, shriveled specimens at the supermarket. We recommend error on the side of growing too many, up to 1/3 of your garden space. For a few weeks, cucumbers can be very profitable, and by growing pickle varieties as slicers, we can convert to pickles and profit from that secondary market as well.

Planting Dates

There are two important cucumber dates, the date for sowing and the date for transplanting. Cucumbers will not grow well in cool weather and are very sensitive to frost. Consequently, there is always the possibility of losing the crop to a late-season frost. Home gardeners can wait until the last frost is past. Commercial gardeners cannot do that because a significant part of profit is determined by our ability to bring cucumbers to the market early. Let's lay out the facts and the options.

Cucumbers will not survive 32°. Cloches will provide a few degrees of protection depending upon the wind. Blankets could be used for an additional few degrees of protection. That's a lot of work, but is it worth it? Consider the potential return on investment. Early cucumber demand is almost unlimited. Therefore, we can sell every cucumber we bring to market. With good weather, the nine rows of cucumbers in the model plan could produce 3000-3500 slicers per week. At 3 for $1 that is over $1000 per week. With plant protection we should be able to get a two-week head start on other growers. That is a return of $2000, and we would recoup our total investment in a single year. And the season has just begun. By being early, we will have developed customers that like our produce, and will return throughout the remainder of the season, In addition, the pickle market will provide a steady market for our cucumbers after the slicer market has weakened.

Calypsos are a 53 day variety when two-week transplants are used. If we are to sell by the middle of July, we must transplant them the last week in May, or about one week after our last frost. With protection, this plant

THE CUCUMBER PLAN

The seed plan

Number of beds 9
Total number of feet 450
Spacing .... 1½"
Number of hills required 300
Number of seeds per hill 5
Number of seeds required 1500
Safety factor for damping off, etc 300
Total seeds required 1800
Seeds per ounce 1000
Seed order .... 2 oz
Variety .... Calypso
Source .... Stokes
Price .... $3.65 per ounce

The planting plan

Planting date .... May 1st
Transplanting date .... May 15th
Bed location 16-24

The marketing plan

Estimated yield .... 12,000 slicers, 40 bushels of pickles
Selling price .... Slicers - 3 for $; pickles 75¢ per pound
Gross income $3,725
Income per square foot $2.75

date reduces the possibility of loosing the crop to frost.

GROWING TRANSPLANTS

Cucumbers do not tolerate damage to the roots, so special care must taken when handling young plants. Obviously they cannot be repotted. Therefore, they will remain where we plant them until we set out the plants in the garden. Consequently, we must make several changes in our greenhouse procedures. We recommend the following:

Use the large plastic trays and paper dividers. Divide the large trays into 35 sections, each about 3" square. If you plan to keep them beyond three weeks, use larger divisions in the trays, otherwise the plants will get leggy because of crowding. Cucumbers present two problems at this time of the season. The first is a shortage of these large trays as peppers and tomatoes may still be using some of them. A second problem is greenhouse space. Cucumbers must be planted in the large trays immediately. Tomatoes and peppers are at their peak space demands. The size of the greenhouse must accommodate this peak period. Purchase additional trays if necessary. It is well worth the investment.

Layer the soil. With other crops, we are able to repot, and can use different soils to meet the changing needs of the plants. We cannot do that with cucumbers. Therefore, we start filling the trays with a mixture that is mostly soil and compost. This will provide necessary nutrients and hold the cell together during transplanting to reduce root shock. The second layer has more peat moss and vermiculite to increase oxygen and improve water holding capabilities. The top layer is sterile germination mix to provide the proper environment for germination.

If you are planting a gyonecious hybrid, remove the pollinators. Some suppliers mark them with a different color seed. If your supplier doesn't, find one that does. We leave nothing to chance in our growing system. Select a good mononecious variety and plant in a well-marked, separate tray.

Plant at least four times as many as you need. First plant four seeds per cell so you can thin to two. Then, plant twice as many cells as you need. Seed is cheap.

Cukes grow quickly. If all four seeds in a cell germinate, they will quickly become crowded. Thin to two plants. Do not pull the plants, pinch them off. This will reduce root damage to the remaining plants.

There is no need to harden the plants off as they will be protected by the cloches immediately after transplanting.

TRANSPLANTING

Spring is a busy time for the commercial gardener. Fortunately, preparing the cucumber beds can be done whenever time is available. In fact, it is advisable to do it early so the plastic mulch can help warm the soil. Cucumbers should not be transplanted until the soil temperature reaches 70°. The plastic mulch will raise the soil temperature so planting can start earlier in the season. We have found the following sequence to work best.

Installing the trellis

This is not difficult or time consuming job but it does require two people.

Position the plastic. Place a 4' black or clear plastic roll at one end of the bed. Install the first upright through the plastic to hold it in place.

Install the uprights. To install the first upright, one person holds the upright plumb while the second pounds it into the ground, until the crosspiece is level with the bed. Roll out the plastic about 10-12 feet. Lay the 10' horizontal support on the ground, even with the first upright to determine the location for the second upright. Install the next upright. Continue this process until all uprights are in place. (Figure 13-6)

Install the horizontal supports. (Figure 13-7) This task requires two people because sometimes the holes do not line up and adjustments are necessary. Install 1/4x20x1" bolts to keep the support in place. Then tighten the bolts.

The installation of the plastic is easiest when done just ahead of the uprights, expecially if wind is a problem. The cross member on the upright holds the plastic in place.

Install rebar on the plastic. (Figure 13-8) This task also requires two people. Position the rebar on the side of the plastic. Roll the plastic on the rebar an inch or so. Tie in four places with short pieces of twine. Four 10' sections of 3/8" reinforcing rod along the 50' bed is sufficient to keep the plastic in place all season.

Install the irrigation hose. We have tried laying the hose on top of the plastic but it seems that some of the water runs off regardless of how carefully we cut the holes. The only disadvantages is that it is almost impossible to check for plugged emitters. Cut the plastic around one side of the cross member on the upright. (Figure 13-11) Slide a single

13-6. Installing the uprights. *One person attempts to keep the upright plumb while the other pounds it in with a post maul. Notice that the horizontal support has been used to estimate the correct distance between the first upright and the second.*

13-7. Installing the horizontal supports. *This is a job for two people because of the length and weight of the support and the difficulty of installing the bolts.*

(I apologize for this fuzzy picture. Most of the pictures in the book are actually taken from the video used in our video tape. We captured the scenes on the computer, did a little image editing, and then used them in the book. This one was enlarged a bit, so resolution became a problem.)

13-8. Installing the plastic. Roll the plastic up an inch or two and tie securely with four short pieces of twine. Cannot be done effectively alone. Works much better with two people.

13-9. Installing the irrigation hose. This picture is a bit difficult to understand so I'll draw a few lines. My left hand is holding up the rebar with the plastic attached. My right hand is sliding the irrigation hose under the plastic.

13-10. Installing the mesh. We install ties on every other square and that held the mature vines without breaking.

13-11. Cutting out for the cross-members. (Above) For those that use cross members, it is necessary to cut the plastic on both sides, and slide the irrigation hose to the middle of the bed.

irrigation hose under the plastic and next to the mesh. (Figure 13-9) Water if necessary to ensure that the ground is well watered prior to transplanting and to give the water time to warm up.

Install the mesh. (Figure 13-10) Make sure you install the mesh on the flat side of the angle iron. If you put it on the narrow side, the wind will eventually rub through strings and break them. Tie the mesh very securely to the angle iron frame. Cucumbers in full production get heavy, and we do not want to lose support in the middle of the season.

We have severe winds in North Dakota so we take one more precaution. We install 3/8 inch rebar at the bottom of the mesh to ensure that the wind cannot whip the young plants out of the ground. (Figure 13-12) We secure the rebar with wood stakes. (Figure 13-13) If you do not have a wind problem, this precaution is not necessary.

Setting out the plants.

We do not harden off the cucumber transplants. Since they move from a protected greenhouse to the protection of the cloches, we have not found hardening off necessary.

Try to pick an afternoon when the wind is reasonable as the cucum-

13-12. Install the rebar at the bottom of the mesh. (Left) We weave a 3/8 inch rebar in the bottom of the mesh to secure the mesh from possible wind damage. This may not be necessary in areas that do not have a problem with wind.

ber plants are still very tender. Dig holes where you cut the plastic next to the emitters. (Figure 13-14) Add a tablespoon of starter fertilizer to the hole. Place at least two plants at every other emitter on the drip line along one side of the trellis, and carefully tamp the plants in place. Then work the other side of the trellis, placing plants at the vacant emitters.

Install the cloches

Place the cloche with the five-inch tails at the edge of the bed. (Figure 13-15) Push the tails firmly into the soil with your foot. Lean the cloche against the mesh.

Tie one side to the other with twine. (Figure 13-16) This ensures that the wind won't send the cloches into the next county. Our success with transplanting cukes is enhanced by the immediate protection we provide them with cloches. We tried leaving a few plants unprotected once, and they lasted only a few days before the wind destroyed them.

GROWING

Once the cloches are installed, there is little to do until it is time to take them off. Watering is necessary because very little rainfall can get through the cloches. Weeding is difficult except along the edges.

Removing the cloches

Timing the removal of the cloches is sometimes difficult. Removal usually occurs incrementally because of the following factors:

Heat. Spring weather can be erratic, sometimes producing a few days of extreme heat long before we are ready to remove the cloches. Then it becomes necessary to remove every other cloche from one side of the trellis to provide cooling circulation.

13-13. Securing the mesh. We use these stakes to keep the mesh from moving in the omnipresent North Dakota wind. This completes the installation of the trellises. This can be done anytime during the spring whenever time is available.

13-14. Cut holes for the plants. Cut holes in the plastic at each emitter on the irrigation hose. The spacing here is for a single crop. Please review the 'Hits and Misses' section for alternate spacing.

13-15. Installing the Cloches. Make sure the tails are pushed into the ground as far as possible to keep the wind from getting under the cloches.

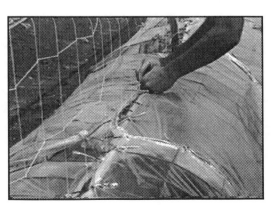

13-16. Tying the cloches together. This keeps the cloches in place until we are ready to remove them.

137

13-17. Starting up the trellis. *At this point it is necessary to train the vines up the trellis and clip the ends of some of the vines to thin them out a bit.*

If wind or cool weather returns, they can be quickly replaced.

Wind. Clocies provide a protective environment similar to a greenhouse. Consequently, the plants are very tender, and need to be hardened off to survive the wind. If strong winds are forecast within two or three days, we do not remove the cloches unless absolutely necessary.

Size of the plants. We let the plants grow to the top of the cloches before removing them. Growth is never uniform, so we remove them from the plants that have outgrown the protection.

Pollination. A few bees will venture under the cloches but full pollination is probably not possible until the cloches are removed. This sometimes is an advantage because we do not want the bees to pollinate until the plants are large enough to sustain production. Hybrids start to blossom long before the plant is ready for both growth and production. We can delay production by leaving the cloches in place.

Training the vines to the trellis

To fully understand this section, it is necessary to discuss how cucumbers grow. Each plant starts with a main runner, but the plant soon develops subordinate stems. These stems create more subordinates and before long we have a tangled mess along the bottom of the trellis that cannot be managed. Therefore, we must thin, trim, and train the stems onto the trellis.

Calypso cucumbers do not climb the trellis naturally. They need to be coaxed a bit, and during the early part of the season, this job is quite time consuming. The secret is to do it right from the beginning. After considerable practice, we have settled on the following system.

As soon as the main stem is long enough, we start it up the trellis. Our trellis has vertical strings every seven inches. Our plants are on 18" centers so we have a few extras strings during this initial trellis training. That will quickly change as subordinate stems become available.

It appears that two plants per hill is optimum. Three plants produces too many vines, which limits production and makes picking difficult. However, do not thin until the plants are well established, about the time you start training the vines. This is very painful for most growers as the plants are healthy and well on their way to a productive lives. Do not pull the extra plants as this may damage the root systems of the remaining plants. Instead, cut them or pinch them off. If a hill did not produce any plants, (cutworm damage, for example) use a third plant in adjacent hills to make up the difference. Let the stem run along the trellis and then up the vertical string.

There are many ways to 'attach' the cucumber to the trellis. You can hook an individual leaf. (They have a small 'V shape next to the stem for this purpose.) However, we have found the best method to wind the stem around the string as many times as possible, and then attach a leaf.

A few cautions are necessary. There will be times when you get behind. A long vine is available along the bed and you are tempted just to stretch it up on the trellis as far as it will go. Don't! It is probably better to leave it there and use it in place. If you attach it to the trellis, it jams all of the vines between it and the trellis into a jumbled mess where cucumbers can hide from the harvest. In addition, stems that grow along the ground are not accustomed to the sun, and will scald much like a tomato. Although they continue to grow and produce, it is impossible to believe that they are at full production. Stems that are trained up the trellis from the beginning adapt to the sun, and are not damaged.

Once the stems are climbing up the trellis, it is a very simple matter to get subordinate stems to follow, Just tuck them through and the vines will hold them in position.

The payoff for this demanding task is during harvest. If the vines are on the trellis, they can be harvested in a fraction of the time it takes if they are on the ground. They are cleaner, and because the bees can get at the blossoms easier, they are also more numerous.

Watering

It is important not to over water cukes early in the season. This will cause shallow root systems because the plant is not required to search for water. Shallow roots may become a problem later during hot weather when plants need tremendous amounts of water. The root system will not be sufficiently developed to provide the water required.

With intensive spacing and vines up on trellises, cucumbers need tremendous amounts of water. Experienced gardeners claim that it is difficult to over water a cuke. We soak them down every day when the vines are in full production. On hot, windy days, we sometimes water them twice a day. Plastic mulch helps conserve moisture and provides a more consistent water supply.

It is not difficult to determine when cucumbers are not receiving enough water. Inadequate or inconsistent water supply creates misshapen fruits, either pointed at the ends or with reduced diameters in the middle. As you harvest, identify areas where fruits are substandard. Perhaps there is a plugged emitter.

Fertilizing

Stokes recommends that hybrids receive 50% more fertilizer than open pollinated varieties. We fertilize lightly once a week.

Use a foliar feed like Spray-N-Grow once a week. Cost is negligible and if just a few more cukes grow, the fertilizer is paid for.

Pest control

Weeds grow under the clear plastic, but usually one weeding solves the problem. Black plastic would provide better weed control but not as much warming. Since cukes thrive in heat, the trade-off is worth it.

We haven't had any serious problems with disease or insects. I believe the secret to our success is cleanliness. Our garden is completely clean of weeds and debris in the fall. Cucumber beetles survive the winter in plant residue. If they have no place to live, they do not reappear in the spring.

Americans eat the worst-tasting cucumbers in the world. The standard long green slicers do not have goot eating quality. They have tough skin, a pithy flesh; they're either bitter or bland.
Rob Johnston [2]

13-18. The bee hive. *A single bee hive is all that is necessary to get optimum pollination, provided sufficient male flowers are present.*

Pollination

Cucumbers have male and female flowers, but only the female flowers produce fruit. Bees must carry pollen from the male flower to the female flower for fruit to set. This complicates the life of the grower in two ways. First, we do not want too many male flowers as this will limit production. Second, bees must be present for optimum pollination.

It is impossible to grow large quantities of cucumbers without bees. A hive of honey bees is recommended for maximum production. Bees can provide a special fascination and with the proper equipment, they are quite harmless. Several recommendations:

Check local ordinances. If there are restrictions on growing bees, you have a few other options. Some commercial growers are now using bumblebees because they claim they get better pollination. There are also non-stinging pollinators such as mason bees that can be attracted to the garden with the proper habitat and flowers.

If there are no ordinance problems you still might have problems with neighbors. You may be able to mitigate neighbor problems by following the suggestions that follow.

Do not overwinter the hive. Overwintered colonies can become very strong by late spring, often reaching populations of over 80,000 bees. This will create problems with neighbors simply because of the numbers involved. Buy package bees instead, late in the spring, just before pollination. Your initial bee population will be just a few thousand, but it doesn't take but a few bees to pollinate the cucumbers. Package bees will increase throughout the summer, but will rarely reach numbers that would concern neighbors.

Use a *single brood chamber,* a queen excluder, and supers. This will limit the space the hive uses for raising young bees. The smaller hive will also be easier to camouflage if necessary.

Kill the bees as soon as the cucumber season is over. Remember, the purpose of the bees is not for honey, but for pollination. To raise honey, larger and more obvious populations would be required.

Place the hive as *close to the cucumbers* as possible. Then the young bees will pollinate the cucumbers as they first venture out of the hive.

PREPARING FOR MARKET

Harvest

Planning the harvest. Start with slicer production and stay with it as long as possible. We have twelve 50' rows capable of producing 750-900 slicers four times a week. At three slicers for a dollar we gross $1000 - $1200 per week. Pickles production won't get close to that. When the slicer market softens, convert only a few rows at a time to pickles. Conversion destroys future slicer production on those rows since it takes a week or two for the small cukes to reach slicer size. It is much better to throw a few slicers than to miss sales caused by dips in slicer supply.

Following the other suggestions in this chapter will guarantee the earliest slicers on the market. Keep picking slicers until the market is obviously overloaded, until you have thrown substantial numbers of cukes away for at least two consecutive markets. Cucumbers need sunshine and temperatures above 80° and warm nights for maximum production. A few sunny warm days will spike slicer production, giving a false signal of production potential. When cool or cloudy weather returns, production falls and the slicer market returns. A second reason for caution in converting to pickles is that individual growers can also spike the supply, especially the first time they pick their cukes. There is always a significant 'first flush' of fruit. This may signal oversupply. However, the next market the supply may return to normal, and if demand is steady, you might run short.

Marking the rows is critical to avoid missing an entire row. Begin picking by placing pails at the end of each row. Use those pails to pick the rows. When production is heavy we have extra pails available, but the 'marking' pails remain in place to identify those rows yet to be harvested. This is particularly important when more than one person is picking.

Controlling slicer production. Weather causes tremendous fluctuations in production. As the rows are picked, rough estimates are made for the next picking based on the number of 'almost large enough' slicers on the vines. This estimate is matched with the weather forecast and the market to determine how small to pick. For example, as we pick Thurs-day morning we know we have only a day and a half before we pick again for our strongest market on Saturday. If the weather is expected to be cloudy, we may pick very light to protect future production. On the other hand, when we pick Tuesday morning we know we have two full days until the next picking for the weaker Thursday market. If production and the weather are favorable, we may pick quite small, knowing that we can sell them easier at the Tuesday market, giving us fewer cucumbers to sell on Thursday.

Slicers

The secret to cucumber harvest is multiple angles. In my more paranoid moments, I am convinced there is a conspiracy among cucumbers plants to hide as many cukes as possible. Look forward while moving down the row, straight ahead as you search closely, and then backwards before you move again. This will assure that most cucumbers of proper size are picked. As you move down one side of the trellis, pick those pickles on the other side of the trellis that might be hidden as you go down the other side.

In the early markets we can pick slicers rather small and still sell them. By small we mean 4-5 inches in length. As the season matures, better slicers must be brought to market. The deformed or curved ones can be sold as bread and butter pickles or held in reserve for an unusually strong slicer market.

Pickles

Pickles present special harvesting problems. If picked too small, future production is reduced. If picked too large, customers are unhappy since most picklers want the

Once the plants are up, don't let them dry out. Inconsistent moisture causes the fruits to be bitter and misshapen. Mulching will help keep moisture in and weeds out.

Emily Stetson [3]

141

small "stuffers" for maximum jar utilization. Pick them every two days or some of them may get too large.

Do not pick pickles much before going to market as they begin to loose moisture as soon as they are picked. We pick them in the mornings before the 11 a.m. and noon markets and they are still fresh when we arrive at the market. When we pick on Friday evening for the Saturday morning market, we sell the pickles before the market and ask customers to come to the garden to get them. Since this is the beginning a weekend, we rarely have problems getting customers to agree to this arrangement.

Pickles need to be sorted after picking. Normal pickles need to be slender and no more than 4" in length. Smaller pickles are needed for jar stuffers to fill in between the big pickles. Bread and butter pickles can be a bit larger but smaller than slicers. We set up a sorting arrangement for four categories, pickles, slicers, large pickles, and rejects. The marketing stand works well for this task. We put boxes on the top of the stand for pickles, slicers, and large pickles. The rejects go in a pail on the floor. We set up the scale to weigh the pickles, and put them in 5-pound bags as we sort them.

MARKETING

There are three phases to marketing cucumbers. The early phase is characterized by the shortage of slicers. At this point it is ridiculous to pick pickles since all production can be used more profitably as slicers.

The middle phase is more difficult as it involves fluctuating supplies caused by changes in the weather. A short period of warm sunny weather may quickly produce an oversupply in slicers. A cold cloudy period will almost shut off the supply. During this phase, pickle demand is still high so it is advisable to convert at least part of production to pickles.

The final phase involves over-supply of both pickles and slicers. The entire crop is now devoted to pickle production and those that are missed adequately supply the slicer demand. Drop prices only as a last resort to move the pickles. However, don't hesitate to cut prices for high volume customers as these people are necessary to move supplies at this point.

Slicers

Cucumbers are one of those crops that benefit from flaunting quantity. We pile them high in the boxes to let customers know we have sufficient quantities for a good selection. This is true because most customers know what size of cucumber they want, and if there is plenty to choose from, they are attracted to our stand.

A critical point in marketing cucumbers is the constant review of the produce. After the cukes get picked over, there are always a few that missed the reject pail. Take them out. Keep the boxes filled by reducing the number of boxes on display. If cucumbers are not selling, display them more prominently in the total display. Push them by suggesting them to customers. Give a few away.

We start the season at 50¢ each for large slicers, and 3 for $1 for the large pickles. We stay there until the market starts to saturate with slicers and then go to 4 for $1 for the remainder of the season. Sometimes we drop our price towards the end of the market to customers that are willing to buy in bulk. I suppose this breaks the pricing rules, but it gives our customers a good deal and permits us to go home and kill some weeds.

Pickles

There are two options used to market pickles, take names and deliver, or sell them by the pound at the market. The choice depends on the supply. If supplies are short, profits are higher selling by the pound at the market. If supplies are plentiful, a list of customers is invaluable.

Pickle pricing is more difficult. Often customers need dill and garlic as well, so it becomes a matter of pricing the pickles high enough to give the dill away, or add the dill to a lower price. We start at $1 per pound for five pounds or less and throw in ten heads of dill. This has been a going rate at the market for some time and it would be counterproductive for us to change that. It takes about a pound of pickles to make one quart, and most recipes call for two dill heads per quart.

Historically, pickles have been sold by the bushel, about 40 pounds. We display the pickles in bushel, half-bushel, and fourth-bushel baskets. These display baskets can be purchased from wholesale seed or packaging suppliers. Several are listed in the sources section of this chapter. We sell the pickles by the pound because it is the most equitable way to sell. Customers can then compare our price with other vendors by asking how many pounds are in a bushel. In 1993 pickles were in very short supply and we got about 70¢ per pound. I have heard of prices as low as 40¢ but we sell most of ours at 60¢ and provide garlic and dill.

We maintain a customer list, and send them advance notice when our pickles are ready. We encourage them to reserve their pickles for a specific day so we can guarantee them pickles on the day they have chose for canning. This customer list is extremely valuable from year to year as we increase our repeat sales.

PAST AND FUTURE HITS AND MISSES

Our cucumber experience is a good example of learning from experience and adjusting to the market. For that reason, we will spend some time to illustrate this key concept.

In 1991 we grew 150' of Calypso pickles and 150' of Marketmore slicers all on trellises. The season was hot and dry and because of a design problem with the water system, we under watered the pickles and had very little production from them. Home gardens were very strong and the slicer market died in mid-August. Since we didn't have any pickle varieties, we could not sell cucumbers.

In 1992 we decided to plant only pickles, since we had been burned so badly the year before with too many slicers. We let the pickles grow up early in the season and sold them as slicers. The slicer market never died, and we sold large pickles throughout the season at 3 for $1, even in late September. This experience validated the idea of growing pickles for slicers and demonstrated the exceptional demand for slicers.

In 1993 one of the larger pickle producers dropped out of our farmers market so we expanded production. The cool weather created superb sales opportunities for early cucumbers. We sold $3,738, 24% of our gross, from 13% of our garden space. Slicer sales remained strong all season. On one Tuesday we brought 900 slicers to market. We brought some back so decided to convert several of the rows to pickles. We shouldn't have done that. The weather turned cooler and slicer production dropped. Hindsight indicates that we could have sold most of our slicers from the entire cucumber crop without ever converting to pickles. However, we had loyal customers who needed the pickles. . .there are always compromises.

At the end of the 1993 season we developed the concept that 1/3 of the garden should be in cucumber production. This decision was based upon the exceptional demand of the past two unusually cool years. So in 1994 we again increased production to 1/3 of our garden space. The season was close to normal and home gardens started producing cucumbers by the bushel. By mid-August we could only sell about $50 in slicers at five cukes for one dollar. The pickle market was extremely weak as well, and we had filled most of our orders. Unfortunately, a hailstorm destroyed our crop and we were not able to determine actual income in a normal year. Prior to the storm we had grossed $1.89 per square foot, which is a respectable income but below our target of $2 per square foot and far below the $3.56 we received in 1993. Our best projections are a potential of $2.50-$2.75 per square foot, but only if production remained level even though the vines were showing signs of fatigue.

In 1994 we changed from steel wire to fabric trellis netting. The change was dramatic and profitable. For the first time, we had vines at the top of the five foot trellis and with only minimum time spent training vines.

We also used plastic mulch extensively for the first time. The most noticeable benefit was in watering. The plastic kept ground evaporation to a minimum so we had fewer misshapen cukes. The second benefit was early production. We direct seeded a bed without plastic mulch and without plastic cloches. Even though the spring was warm, this bed was a full ten days behind those that were direct seeded with the benefit of plastic mulch and cloches. The moral of the story, cucumbers need heat! Use plastic!

I'm not convinced that we had enough male blossoms for optimum pollination. We purchased our seed from a company that did not identify the pollinators with color. Consequently, it was impossible to determine if we had sufficient pollinator plants. Next year we will grow the pollinators in a marked tray to make sure that we have at least three hills along each row.

1994 also demonstrated that cucumber production can be too early in areas with seasonal farmers markets. We could have had our cucumbers in two weeks earlier because of the warm spring. Had we done that, we would have had cukes long before the market was strong enough to sell them. On the other hand, if we could get tomatoes to arrive at this same time, it would be well worth our investment to do some advertising. Cucumbers alone will not bring out the early shoppers, but a combination of cukes and tomatoes would make it almost irresistible.

The affect of home gardens on the farmers market was particularly pronounced with cucumbers during 1994. The weather was almost perfect for cucumbers and the slicer market weakened during the first week in August. There was also plenty of pickles in home gardens and even that market remained weak.

An August hailstorm destroyed our remaining cucumber harvest. (Figure 13-19) The slicer market had already been reduced to about $50 per market so we had converted the entire crop to pickles. We probably could have saved some of the crop because the hail damage wasn't complete, and after about two weeks, the youngest vines probably would have been mildly productive. We probably lost close to $1,500 through the lost cucumber production.

We will make a major change next year in starting cucumbers in the greenhouse. There are two problems with cuke transplants. The first is potential significant losses from poor germination and damping off. The second is spindly plants caused by crowding. Both of these problems can be solved by using individual pots. We have purchased 4" square pots with vacuum-formed trays. We can then space them out when they get larger, and replace those that do not survive. We have chosen a system that holds twenty four-inch pots per tray. This provides the easiest way to spread them out. We will grow our transplants outside as often as weather permits.

We will also make one additional change. Cucumber vines tire after five to six weeks of full production. The fruits become fat in the middle or curved, and they are harder to sell. Pickle production is sometimes difficult because of the misshapen pickles. If you look at Figure 13-13, you will notice that we alternate planting from side to side by each emitter. There is no compelling reason to do that since the vines crawl to both sides anyway. Consequently, our first planting next year will be on one side and about a foot away from the trellis. We will train all of the vines up the trellis, leaving the remaining side free for a later planting. If we plant that side about the first of June, it will be ready for

13-19. Hail damage. *Cucumbers do not survive hail very well. The broad leaves and exposed vines are easily damaged even with the smallest stone. If they recover at all, production will be limited.*

production in early August when the other vines start to tire. We will leave the older vines on the mesh, but sever them at the root. Please remember this is an untested idea. If you are interested in the results, please subscribe to our newsletter.

Except for these two significant changes, we have cucumber production almost where we want it. We may try to find a hybrid pickle that climbs the trellis better then the Calypso variety. We will also do more direct seeding and use the transplants as a back up for a late frost. This planting plan will depend on the spring weather, but we believe it will work in most seasons. The key is to be ready, and have the trellises, plastic, and cloches in place for a break in the weather.

In retrospect, I suspect we underestimated the demand for cucumbers when we entered the market six years ago. This miscalculation was a costly mistake during those early years. On the other hand, cucumber production on 1/3 of the garden might be a bit heavy during normal years unless full production is

145

achieved early in the season, and advertising is purchased to attract customers in sufficient numbers of sell this early produce.

FOR THE HOME GARDENER

There are several ideas here that can be very useful to you. The most significant is the use of trellises. Gardeners with limited space might pass up cucumbers because they need space to spread out. Growing on trellises solves this problem and makes cucumbers a viable crop even for the very small garden. The trellis

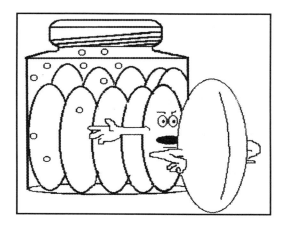

"But, Mom! The guy said only the best would be chosen. So I tried out. And I won!"

is not difficult to build. A ten-foot trellis can be built with just three pieces of angle iron. Most suppliers will cut it to length for you for a nominal charge. Then you need to drill just three holes and you are in business. As stated earlier, the cross member is optional, so no welding would be required.

The mesh is also widely available from garden catalogs. For example, Burpee has a five by fifteen foot piece for less then five dollars. Johnny's Select Seeds also has six-foot high netting.

This mesh would also work for peas and beans, so in one ten foot section you could grow several vegetables vertically without using much precious garden space.

If you like to can pickles, don't overlook the possibility of using your pickle variety as a slicer as well. Try them, you'll probably never grow another slicer!

The protective cloches we describe in this chapter have much wider application than just cucumbers. They can be used for almost anything you want to grow early, even cabbages, carrots, peas and other early crops. They do not need a trellis for support. However, you will still need to tie the two pieces together if you have any wind problems.

Chapter Fourteen

Onions

Most hobby gardeners grow onions from sets, those dime sized onions that invade every store that sells vegetable seeds each spring. They are easy to grow, and produce good quality onions every year. As with most things easy, there are some problems. Onions are a biennial, that is, they go to seed their second year. Onion sets are actually the remains of the first year, so some of the sets go to seed when you would rather they grew into large onions instead of seed tops.

The second problem involves storage capabilities. It is the sulfur content in onions that determines both the sweetness and the storage capabilities of the onion. High sulfur onions store the longest but are also the most pungent. In order to grow onions from sets, the variety must be a good storage onion, otherwise the sets will wither away before spring. To store that long the variety must have high sulfur content, which also means it is a pungent onion. There is a market for strong onions, but not nearly as large a market as there is for the sweet ones.

If we want sweet onions, we must grow them from seed. Onions are a long season crop so they are the first seeds planted each spring. They are very hardy so they are also the first plants set out into the garden in late spring. Onions require considerable care early in the season, but then can almost be ignored. This helps balance the work load. If all of our crops demanded time at the same point in the season, it would complicate our lives and make commercial gardening more difficult than it is.

Onions form bulbs in response to the length of day. 'Short-day' onions begin to bulb with 12-14 hours of daylight. 'Long-day' onions require 14-16 hours of daylight before they begin to bulb. If you plant a long-day onion in the south the day will never get long enough to trigger bulbing. If you plant a short-day onion in the north it will try to bulb long before the top is strong enough to support bulbing. Since we live in the north, we must grow a long-day onion.

COMMERCIAL PLANNING

Varieties

In selecting the varieties we grow, two factors must be considered, day-length and taste. In the extreme north and south, the day-length

North of a line running from Atlanta to San Francisco, you should choose a "long day" onion; south of that latitude, "short day" onions are best.

Shepherd Ogden [1]

147

ONION DATA

Planning

Propagation	Transplants
Frost tolerance	Very hardy
Earliest transplant date	FFD - 28 days
Maturity date	90-120 days (direct seeded)
Seeds per ounce	8,000-10,000
Seed viability	1 yr, use fresh seed
Intensive spacing	4-6"
Planting depth	1/4-1/2"
Germination temperature	32°-95° (80°)
Germination time	7-12 days
Days to transplant size	42-75 days
Growing temperature (Day/Night)	60°-65°/55°-60°

Growing

pH	6-6.5
Nutrient requirements	Light feeder
Pests	Onion maggots and thrips
Diseases	Downy mildew, pink rot, smut
Critical watering	During bulb enlargement

Harvest

Harvest when	¼ lb and up
Yield	Average ½ pounds per plant
Average Selling price	50¢-$1 per pound
Average income per square foot	$2.25 - $3.50

choice is obvious. If you live somewhere in the middle, ask your extension agent or another grower which varieties grow best.

We recommend growing mild onions for market because they do not store well and supermarkets cannot stock them throughout the growing season. This provides an opportunity for premium prices for your produce. We raise the sweetest long-day onion available, the Walla Walla Onion. Vidalia is the most widely grown mild short-day onion.

Storage onions are an excellent option if you have the extra space. If you choose to cater to the salsa canning market, pungent onions will be required. Some of these onions can be sold at normal market prices. The remaining onions can be sold at bulk prices in the fall. We have sold both types of onions at the same market. The mild onions are gone, and we often bring the storage onions home to sell another day. That is the primary benefit to the more pungent varieties. They can be bagged, and brought to market as many times as necessary to sell them. Mild onions need to be sold the day they are picked.

Quantities

The first draft of the model garden, figure 4-2, had 1/6 of the garden in onions. This was based upon our experience with onions as a successful niche crop. However, we reduced the amount because marketing that many onions may not be possible the first few years until your niche market has been established. If someone else is already filling this niche, you may choose not to grow onions at all.

Planning Dates

Onions grow well in cool weather and if planted early enough, are ready for opening market. Even this far north, we can sell onions over a three month period. If all onions are treated equally, they will grow at about the same rate, and in the final month of the market, we will have tons of 2-pound onions. This would, of course, provide maximum production per square foot. However, many customers prefer the smaller onions, and it is the customer that determines what we grow. The final size of the onion is determined by the following:

Size of the transplant. If we set out a plant that is ¼" in diameter it will produce a large and early onion. If the plant is very small it will still survive but will never reach full size. Growing a ¼" plant requires planting about 90 days prior to setting the plants out in the garden. Onion plants grown 1" apart will be much larger than those planted ¼" apart even though they were planted on the same day and given the same growing conditions.

Transplant date. Here's where it starts getting a bit complicated, especially in the north. A long-day onion will start to bulb when the nights get short, regardless of the size of the plant. A small plant cannot support the bulbing effort so neither the bulb nor the plant have a chance to grow because the plant concentrates on bulbing. If we transplant too late, our production could be severely reduced. Consequently, we don't vary this date much. Onions can be transplanted into the garden about a month before the FFD.

To recap: The ultimate size of the onion is determined by the timing and size of the transplant. The size of the transplant is determined by when we plant and how closely we plant the seeds.

Now a few words about economics. We want to make the garden profitable, so we must control our costs, and make decisions based upon which option costs the least. Greenhouses are expensive to operate, especially in late winter. Onions must be started long before any of the other crops. The second crop is peppers, planted about the first week in March. Peppers will not need the greenhouse until mid-March at the earliest. If we start the greenhouse just for onions, we will be growing very expensive transplants. There are two options:

• Purchase a few early plants from the Piedmont Plant Company or another supplier. This delays starting the greenhouse for about a month and is the most economical option. If you choose this option, make sure you air freight the plants to reduce transplanting stress.

• Keep the first few trays under lights for a month. We plant on the 1st of February. We do not start the greenhouse until the peppers need the space in March. The onions grow slowly under lights and in the cool greenhouse.

Growing Transplants

There are four factors that affect the quality of onion plants.

Timing. It takes at least 10 weeks to grow a ¼" onion, regardless of the other conditions involved. Our first few seasons we planted on January 1st but mistakes in spacing negated any advantage of the early start. Then we moved the planting date to February first and corrected some of the mistakes. We had early onions of decent size. Finally, we moved the planting date to March 1st and increased the spacing. The transplants were about the same size. It appears that spacing is more important to size than the planting date. For future years, we will use February 1st as our planting date.

Depth of container. We use 4" deep large trays. This depth gives the onions sufficient room to establish good roots.

Growing mix. Over the past few seasons, we have experimented with various growing mixes. The challenge is that we do not repot onions, so the original mix must provide for the needs of the onion plants for two to three months. We are currently using a mix of 1/3 soil and compost, 1/3 peat moss, and 1/3 perlite and vermiculite.

All onions have about the same sugar content, but pungent onions contain more sulfur compounds, which give them their characteristic bite.

Gardening [2]

149

THE PLAN FOR ONIONS

The seed plan

Number of beds .... 3 beds
Variety .... Walla Walla
Spacing .... 4"
Onions per running foot 3
Rows per bed 9
Onions per running foot of bed 27
Onions per bed 1300
Total number of plants 3900
Germination rate 81%
Safety factor 25%
Seeds required 6420
Seeds per ounce 9000
Seed order .... 1 ounce

The planting plan

Planting date .... February 1st
Tranplant date .... April 15th
Location 11-13

Marketing plan

Average size when sold .... 1/2 pound
Total production .... 1950 pounds
Average selling price .... 60¢ per pound
Gross income $1,170
Income per square foot $2.60

Seed spacing. If the seeds are planted too closely, the plants will never mature. It appears that this factor is the most important. If plants are crowded, it doesn't matter when you plant them, they will never grow very large.

Sprinkle the seeds with spice jar, and cover the seeds with ½" of germination mix. Set the germination room to 80° and adjust as necessary to maintain a soil temperature of 70°. When plants emerge in 7-8 days, set the room temperature to 65° during the day and 55° at night. Move the trays to the light racks and provide 14 hours of light per day. Position the lights as close to the racks as possible to provide maximum light to the small plants.

Transplanting

Most references recommend transplanting onions when plants are a minimum of ½" in diameter. These certainly grow the largest and earliest onions. However, many customers do not want one-pound onions. Consequently, plant all onions, regardless of size. This provides a range of sizes for market, even at the end of the season.

Till the bed one last time leaving it soft and fluffy. A level bed is critical for optimum irrigation as the beds can become saturated and runoff can be a problem. We level the bed with a rake and sometimes make a second pass with the tiller.

Cut the tops off the plants before planting them. We like a plant about 5" tall.

14-1. The planting guide. This jig ensures uniform spacing. The holes are created by a sharpened one-inch dowel with an old bearing pounded on the end at about the right depth. The secret is to have the soil moist so the holes don't fill in again.

Punch holes in the soil with a dowel or rebar. The exact depth of the hole is not critical as the onion will push itself out of the soil as it develops. The hole must be deep enough, however, for the entire root. Drop the plants into the holes burying the root. Press the plant firmly into the soil. Soak the bed with a sprinkler hose. At this point, a sprinkler works better than the irrigation hose because it waters the plants evenly.

GROWING

Once the onions are transplanted, growing them is quite simple. We weed the beds several times, since they do not tolerate weeds well.

Watering

After transplanting, we install three irrigation tubes and immediately start the irrigation. When the onions start bulbing, we water them once a day. Even Walla Walla onions will get strong if they are short of water. The triple hose ensures an ample water supply. A double hose on the storage onions is sufficient since they are pungent regardless of water supply.

Fertilizing and mulching

We mulch with compost to help retain moisture and protect the onions from the sun. We do not add any other fertilizer during the season.

It is important to restrict the application of gypsum and elemental sulfur to lower soil pH. We have very high sulfur content and high pH in our soil, which is common throughout the region. Before we realized this relationship between sulfur and mild onions we tried to lower our pH with sulfur and gypsum. We now use peat moss which is slightly acidic. It is much more expensive but improves soil quality in addition to lowering pH.

Pests

We have had some problem with onion maggots. We pull the damaged plants immediately and destroy them. Otherwise the maggots will go from one plant to another, destroying large parts of the early crop. To control the population, remove all onions from the garden at the end of the season. This removes a primary habitat for surviving the winter.

HARVESTING AND MARKETING

Harvest

The primary concern in marketing onions is cleanliness. A good wash rack, such as the one pictured in figure 8-3 on page 95, is essential for many crops, but particularly onions. Cleaning varies with the stage of onion development. Early in the season we spray them down with water, peel off any damaged layers, cut the roots off, and cut the tops off the smaller onions to a uniform length, usually 8-10 inches. We cut the tops completely off the larger onions. After the skins have started to set in late summer, the easiest way to clean onions is with an air compressor. Blow off the outer layer, cut off

14-2. Planting the onions. With the holes already in place, planting the onions is an easy task.

14-3. Early onions.
Notice the triple irrigation hoses and the intensive spacing.

the roots and tops, and spray them down with water.

Marketing

There is a temptation to market onions too early because they are usable at any stage. However, this reduces production and profits considerably. The counter argument is that we need to sell early onions to establish the market, and to get customers into the habit of purchasing onions from us. A review of our onions sales for the past few years clearly indicates that early sales are insignificant. If we started selling later and stayed longer in the fall, our total sales would increase substantially.

Onions illustrate this late market/early market dilemma. Please understand that North Dakota has a very seasonal market which is dependent entirely upon weather for an opening day. If the spring is warm, we may open the last week of June. If the weather is cool, it may be after July 4th. In either case, the selection and quantity is limited and the customers are somewhat scarce. Onions can be brought to this market at about ¼ to 1/3 pounds. At 75¢ per pound we average less than 25¢ per

onion. If we let them grow up and bring them to a late market in September, we would get 50¢ per onion because they would average over one pound. That's twice as much money for the same garden space.

We want to sell as much produce as possible from a garden with limited space. If income per square foot was the only factor, the decision would be easy, we would hold the onions until the late market. However, weather and competition can complicate the issue. If there is a strong onion market, it might be wise to go early to establish yourself as a quality onion grower. Habits are sometimes hard to change, and if customers becomes accustomed to purchasing onions from a competitor, you might not be able to lure them away. In addition, if the weather is conducive to home garden production, the late season market might be weak and you may be left with many pounds of onions left over. However, wholesale market sales to fast food restaurants are easily done with mild onions, and they will pay the going rate, usually about 30¢ per pound. At that price, you still make more money wholesale than pulling the onions early and going to the early market.

There is no one solution to the early/late market problem. Each grower must analyze the market, and determine which factors are most important, and decide if the early market can be justified.

Early sweet onions sell for $.75 per pound without complaint and we hold that price all season for individual onions. We leave about 8-10" of the tops on a few of the onions, because some customers use the tops for salad and garnish. However, we have discovered that most customers will purchase more often if the tops are removed. I suspect they do not want to pay for something they will just throw away.

When most of the onions have reached marketable size, we start bagging them in three and five pound bags and sell them at 50¢ per pound. Customers are accustomed to seeing onions in the traditional fabric onion bag, so they sell very well. We also offer them loose for those customers that prefer to pick out the ones they want, or those that want only one onion.

We replace any onion that is hotter than expected, and include the following statement in a weekly newsletter or in our brochure:

"We guarantee the sweetness of our Walla Walla onions. If any onion is too hot for your taste, let us know the next time you come to the market and we will replace it free, with no questions asked.

The sweetness of an onion is determined by the variety, the soil, and sufficient water. We use drip irrigation, and sometimes the emitters get plugged up. If we do not catch the problem right away, the surrounding onions sometimes run short of water and get stronger then normal. If you get one of these onions, it is an inadvertent mistake on our part and we will gladly replace it for you."

PAST AND FUTURE HITS AND MISSES

Storage Onions. In 1993 we planted one bed of storage onions, 1/3 white, 1/3 yellow, and 1/3 Bermuda. We didn't get maximum production because it was a newly constructed bed and we had severe weed problems. We cured the onions and bagged them in five pound fabric bags. We sold them all, but had to bring some of them to market several times. However, this is the one advantage to storage onions. If they don't sell, they will be just as marketable at the next market. They do not sell as easily as mild onions, nor with the same volume. Sweet Sandwich is a storage onion that starts getting sweeter after three months of storage. It might provide a nice niche market to complement the Walla Wallas or Vidalias.

Soil mix for raising plants. The onions must spend two to three months in the same growing medium since we do not transplant them. Consequently, we used mostly soil the first year. However, the onions were very small because water and oxygen could not get to the roots. The next year we used a mix of 1/3 compost, 1/3 peat moss, 1/3 soil. This still didn't provide enough oxygen, and water didn't reach the bottom of the tray very easily. Finally, we settled on a mix of 1/3 soil and compost, 1/3 peat moss, and 1/3 perlite or vermiculite. This continues to work very well.

Seed spacing. We have tried many experiments in seed spacing. We purchased a small scale used for loading shotgun shells that measured in grains. We tried various amounts from 50-85 grains. All of these amounts were too crowded for optimum growth. So the next year we tried to estimate the correct amount by scattering seeds until the spacing appeared to be between ½ and 1". This worked just as well as weighing the seed. In future seasons we will give the seeds more room to grow by planting more trays with fewer seeds in them. It appears to be the only way to get large onions for the opening markets.

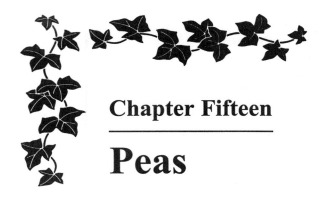

Chapter Fifteen

Peas

"Look Zork! Quadruplets! Doesn't it make you miss the kids?"

Weather, as well as variety, can dramatically influence pea yields.

Diane Bilderbach[1]

We grow peas because they are one of the most popular crops at the market. They can be profitable if grown on trellises and interplanted with other crops to include carrots, lettuce, cabbage, and other cole crops.

We do not grow many peas because they can be adversely affected by warm weather. They like it cool, so the chance of good production is always in question. In addition, even the arrival of the crop is fully dependent upon the weather.

COMMERCIAL PLANNING

Since peas are an early crop it is possible to have them ready for market long before other produce is ready. And other than summer heat, timing is quite irrelevant. Regardless of when you bring peas to market, you will have no trouble selling them if they have been picked properly.

Varieties

Peas fall into three general categories, English, snap, and snow. English are the traditional varieties that must be shelled. Snow pea pods are used in stir-fry, and snap peas fall somewhere in between.

Maturity dates are only important to ensure you do not get your peas to market too early. Maturity dates range from 52 days to over 70.

Yield is perhaps the most important factor in variety selection. Yield is determined by the average number of peas in each pod, and the number of pods per plant.

Heat tolerance varies and should be considered if warm weather is a problem.

You may be tempted to market immature pea pods for stir-fry. They sell for $3 per pound, but it takes many pods to make that pound. Make sure there is a good market for the edible pods. Demand at our market is not capable of supporting many edible pod growers.

GROWING

Planting

We use the same trellis frame to grow peas that we use for cucumbers. Then we use the 2x3 inch welded wire that didn't work for cukes. It works just fine for peas. We install the trellis before we plant the seeds.

We plant about four weeks prior

to FFD. We space the peas very closely, about two inches apart on either side of the trellis wire. Since we have had some problems with germination, we may decrease that spacing even more in the future. We keep the seedbed moist to encourage maximum germination. After the seedlings are two inches high, we thin to our final spacing of 3-4". If you do not thin the peas, it can be difficult to pick the peas closest to the trellis.

You will find references that recommend tighter spacing. However, it important to remember that we are commercial growers and picking time must be an important consideration. A home gardener doesn't mind spending a little extra time picking peas. We can't afford that. Therefore, final spacing is a function of variety and ease of harvest. Adjust your spacing to provide maximum production given the time you are willing to spend picking them.

Fertilizing

Peas are a legume so additional nitrogen is not required. However, they do require adequate potassium and phosphorous. Soil with plenty of organic material will supply these nutrients. Fresh manure should be avoided as too much nitrogen will produce lush foliage, but few peas.

Watering

Make sure the peas have adequate water during germination, then reduce watering to about ½" per week until the plants start to bloom. Then provide about 1" until the pods fill out.

Providing support

Once the peas have climbed two feet up the trellis, support the vines with twine interwoven in the mesh. If

---

PEA DATA

Planning

Propagation	Direct Seed
Frost tolerance	Very hardy
Earliest plant date	3-4 weeks prior to FFD
Maturity date	55-90 days
Seeds per pound	2000
Seed viability	3 years
Intensive spacing	2-6"
Planting depth	1-2"
Germination temp	40-85° (75°)
Germination time	6-15 days

Growing

pH	6-7.5
Nutrient requirements	Soil builder
Pests	Aphids, cabbage looper, cucumber beetles
Diseases	Damping off, powdery mildew, blights, root rot
Critical watering	Pollination and pod development

Harvest

Harvest before	Seeds get too large
Yield	1/8 lbs per plant
Average selling price	$1.50-$2.00/lb
Average income per square foot	90¢-$1.25

---

this is not done, the vines may fall, covering the interplanted crop, and making harvest difficult.

HARVEST AND MARKETING

Harvest

Peas should be harvested while they are small because they are best for eating raw at this stage. If allowed to ripen and get hard, peas loose much of their flavor. A high percentage of your customers purchase peas to eat raw, only a very few will be cooked. Therefore, it is critical that we focus on this customer preference, and pick peas that taste good raw. If

THE PLAN FOR PEAS

The seed plan

Quantity	2 beds
Spacing	2-3", thinned later to 4-6"
Seeds per running foot of row	4-6
Plants per row	200-300
Rows per bed	2
Plants per bed	400-600
Total seeds required	1200
Seeds per pound	2000
Seed Order	1 pound
Variety	Multistar
Source	Johnny's Select Seeds
Cost	$4.75 per pound

The planting plan

Planting date (Approx)	April 18
Location	Beds 29 & 30

The marketing plan

Estimated yield	50 pounds per bed
Selling price	$2.00 per pound
Groos income	$200
Income per square foot	$1.33

Peas are hardy down to the teens until they flower, but the blossoms (and later, the developing pods) are not.

Shepherd Odgen[2]

we follow this practice religiously, we will never have any trouble selling all of our peas, regardless of the supply at the market.

Harvesting peas is time consuming. Beans can be picked by the handfuls because they can be used at almost any stage of development. Peas, on the other hand, must have full pods which requires constant attention from the picker. If you have your fingers on beans you can pick them. Peas need to be checked individually. That takes time and is extremely hard on the back if peas are not grown on trellises.

Marketing

We get $2 per pound and haven't brought any home for several years. We pre-bag them like we do beans.

PAST AND FUTURE HITS AND MISSES

In 1990 we planted 300 square feet of peas without trellises. We sold $115 before the 15th of July because it was a very warm spring and we planted the peas early. However, picking peas without a trellis is hard on the back so we gave up on peas for the next two seasons.

In 1993 we planted Green Arrow peas on trellises and sold $224. If we had interplanted with cabbage we would have averaged almost $1.50 per square foot. That's very respectable pea production.

In 1994 we grew Multistar from Johnny's, a 70-day variety that climbs to the top of the five foot trellis. We were delighted with the growing characteristics of Multistar, but were not happy with the yield. However, we planted the peas too late and had horrible germination. Consequently, it would be unfair to blame production problems on the variety.

FOR THE HOME GARDENER

A few suggestions to make your pea patch more productive.

Use trellises if you are not doing that already. There are many designs less complicated than the one we use. For many varieties you do not need supports that are five feet tall.

Plant very early in the spring, long before the rest of the garden is planted. Peas will not produce well in warm weather.

Do not presoak your seeds. The outside of the seed will expand faster than the inside, and break the seed apart.

Try reducing your spacing for increased production.

Chapter Sixteen

Peppers

According to the National Gardening Association, peppers are the second most popular vegetable grown by home gardeners. Unfortunately, we have not experienced that popularity in our Farmers Market. There is a steady market early in the season but when peppers are in full production, we often bring some home. Consequently, we have found it necessary to limit pepper production.

The primary market is for sweet bell peppers. There is always demand for well-formed fruits for stuffing and we see an increasing demand for fresh peppers for salads. In this section of the country there is a very limited demand for hot peppers. However, there is a growing number of salsa canners that use fairly large quantities of hot peppers. We consider hot peppers a niche market that should be entered only if demand warrants it.

Peppers are easy to harvest but not always easy to grow or sell. They are very sensitive to weather extremes and take great care to get them growing. However, once they are established they can be very prolific producers.

COMMERCIAL PLANNING

Varieties

Peppers have more variety differences than any other crop that we grow. However, if you go beyond the standard 3 or 4 lobed, dark green, thick-walled sweet bell pepper, you are flirting with a niche market.

Color. Discriminating buyers understand the value of a sweet red pepper. However, most customers do not realize that a red pepper is simply a green pepper left to fully ripen. Beyond red and green lie a rainbow of yellows, purples, and browns that could be developed as a niche market.

It is widely accepted that yellow peppers are the sweetest. It would take time to develop a clientele as most customers demand the standard green variety. However, once they taste the sweeter pepper, they might become loyal customers.

Size. Size varies significantly between varieties from 3½" to 6½".

Thick walled. A thicker wall produces more edible pepper. Consequently, it is a very desirable characteristic and should be a primary consideration for variety selection.

Three or four-lobed. The traditional pepper has four lobes and there

I've had excellent results with much earlier seeding in late January or early February, which for me is a good 12-14 weeks before the frost-free date.

Nancy Bubel[1]

157

PEPPER DATA

Planning

Propagation	Transplants
Frost tolerance	Very tender
Earliest transplant date	FFD + 10 days
Maturity date	50-100 days
Seeds per ounce	3400-4900
Seed viability	2-4 years
Intensive spacing	12-15"

Starting Transplants

Planting depth	1/4-1/2"
Germination temperature	60°-95° (85°)
Germination time	8-20 days
Days to transplant size	42-56 days
Growing temperature (D/N)	65°-75°/60°-65°

Growing

pH	6-7
Nutrient requirements	Light feeder
Pests	Cutworms, aphids, flea beetles, Colorado potato beetles
Diseases	Mosaic, bacterial spot, anthracnose.
Critical watering	Flowering through harvest

Harvest

Harvest when	Firm and green
Yield	6-8 peppers per plant
Average selling price	33-50¢/ea
Average income per square foot	$2.00

16-1. Providing heat in the greenhouse. *This system has dramatically improved the profitability of our pepper crop by providing larger transplants. The heating system is available at most building centers.*

are customers who look for these 'perfect' peppers for stuffing.

Fruit set and blossom drop. Pepper blossoms are fussy. Heat, drought, and early fruiting can cause blossoms to fall off, reducing production. Cool weather may deter fruit set. Varieties differ in their abilities to handle these growing extremes so we want a variety that will set fruit early.

Quantities

The model garden plan, figure 4-2, contains one bed of peppers. Based upon our experience this might be a little light, depending upon the season and your market for peppers.

We use 12" spacing with four plants across the bed, or about 200 plants per bed. There are about 4500 pepper seeds per ounce so we order $\frac{1}{16}$ ounce.

Planning Dates

Peppers take 50-75 days after setting out before they are ready for market. We do not try to have peppers for opening market because peppers are too sensitive to cool soil to justify taking the chance. We are satisfied if we can get production by the middle of July which is two weeks into the season.

If we use a 50 day pepper, and assume that we can gain one week with larger plants and plant protection, we must set them out the end of May, or about two weeks after our FFD. The actual date will vary with soil temperature, but in a normal year, this will be about right.

Most references recommend starting peppers 6-8 weeks prior to setting them out which can occur two

1/2 inch plywood

Flexwatt system

1x4 boards

1-1/2 to 2 inch styrofoam

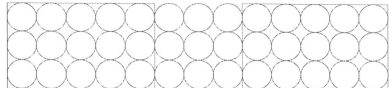

16-2. Pepper spacing. We use rectantular cages to allow maximum spacing. The cages are 3' by 5'. We leave room between the cages for three plants on 1' spacing. This space between cages also provides for the installation of lath to tighten the plastic for wind protection.

This drawing shows three plants across the bed. We have experimented with four across and initial production looks encouraging. This would require, of course, that the cages be made a bit wider. However, if it could be done, the additional plants would increase production by almost a third.

to three weeks after the frost free date. Since we want larger than normal plants, and since we plan to set them out on May 30th, we start ours during the first of March.

GROWING

The key to early peppers is to set out a large plant that has had room to grow. Then we must protect it from the elements, particularly the wind.

Protection

We protect peppers like we do tomatoes, but with larger rectangular cages rather then the 18" round cages we use for tomatoes. The pepper cages are constructed from concrete reinforcing wire, 3' x 5'. The wire must be straightened a bit, and squared off on the corners. This squaring off is very important for maximum production. The first few years we did not square off the corners so our spacing between the cages was sometimes erratic, thereby wasting precious space.

Installation is similar to tomatoes with 3' plastic and lath ties. We use the larger cages because peppers seem to produce better when they are touching the plants around them. You can also plant more peppers with the larger cages.

It is critical to stake down the cages securely. In 1993, we didn't stake the cages very well. We assumed that the few laths used to tighten up the plastic would be sufficient. A 40+ MPH wind ripped through the garden in June, and tore off half the cages, damaging many of the plants. We corrected the mistake with stakes on each corner of the cage, as detailed in figure 16-3.

Growing Transplants

We plant peppers much like tomatoes, initially in flats. When the first true leaves appear, we transplant them into 1204s. Peppers like it a bit warmer so are kept in the germination rack at 85° and they germinate in about six days. As soon as the first plants germinate, we move the trays to the greenhouse.

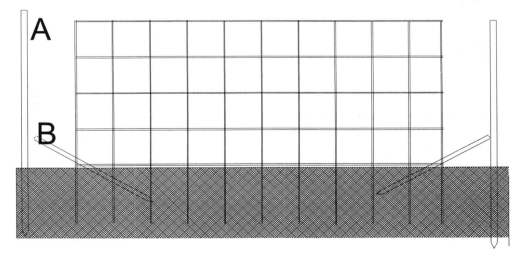

A

B

16-3. Staking the cages. The stakes installed at (B) are critical in areas that have high winds. The lath (A) keeps the plastic tight. We haven't had any problems with loose plastic since we developed this system.

THE PLAN FOR PEPPERS

The seed plan

Quantity .... 1 bed
Spacing .... 12" on center
Plants per running foot of row 1
Rows per bed 4
Plants per bed 200
Seeds required 300
Seeds per ounce 3400-4900
Seeds ordered .... 1/16 ounce
Variety .... Ace Hybrid
Source .... Stokes
Cost $7.80

The planting plan

Planting date .... (FFD-78) March 1st
Transplanting date .... (FFD+7) May 25th
Bed location 10

The marketing plan

Estimated yield .... 1000 peppers
Selling price .... Average 40¢ each
Gross income $400
Income per square foot $2.67

Supplemental heat is needed, particularly at night as peppers are extremely sensitive to cool growing conditions. We discovered this in 1992, when the plants seemed to stagnate, remaining the same size for weeks. When we checked the soil temperature, it was much too cool for optimum pepper growth. We installed a system normally used to heat bathroom floors, figure 16-1.

We transplant them into the paper pots, snipping off the weakest of the two plants. If they get too large for these trays, we transplant them to 5" pots.

Transplanting

It is counterproductive to try to rush setting out pepper plants. They do not tolerate cool weather as tomatoes will. We wait until the ground temperature is 55 degrees at 2" and average daytime temperatures are about 65 degrees and nights above 50. (Bubel uses 65° at 8AM at 4".) Then we look at the long range weather forecast. If it seems to favor taking chances, we transplant the peppers.

Should we remove the blossoms? When we grow a plant that is 10-12 weeks old, there will be plenty of blossoms when we are ready to set the plant out in the garden. Research has indicated that if we remove some or all of these blossoms, total production for the season will increase. But total production is not as important to us as early production. The Ace hybrid seems to produce well even though the blossoms were left on at transplanting time.

The transplant sequence for peppers is similar to tomatoes with a few exceptions. We take off the cages while we are transplanting because there are so few of them, and because it dramatically speeds the transplant process. The plastic mulch might have to be secured if it is a windy day.

We mark the holes every foot with a 50' tape down the length of the bed. We cut slits in the plastic, and dig the holes by hand. Fertilizing, watering, and transplanting occurs in a fluid motion as we work our way to the end of the bed.

Watering

Careful water management is necessary for the pepper crop. Too much water will dilute the sugar content thereby reducing sweetness. Too little water can cause blossom end rot later in the season.

Peppers prefer a minimum soil moisture above 50%.

Fertilizing

Peppers need nitrogen throughout the season. However, care must be taken early in the season, so excess foliage is avoided. Commercial growers use 150-300 pounds per acre, or 4-8 ounces per 100 square feet. We apply nitrogen through the water system once a week during the fruiting stage.

Pest Management

We have had a heavy infestation of aphids the past few years, but a ½ pound of labybugs cleans them out every time. On one occasion we used some insecticidal soap which seemed to help some. However, that is sticky, smelly stuff and required additional work to prepare the fruits for market.

HARVEST AND MARKETING

Harvest

When harvesting peppers, do NOT twist peppers off as this may damage the delicate plants, and reduce future production. We use a small pruning scissors, and cut the stems. Many of the fruits get wedged among the branches and this method removes them without damage to the plant.

Spray them with water, and sell them. We do not let them turn red as this diminishes production substantially and there is not enough premium in red ones to make up the difference.

Marketing

Peppers won't sell like tomatoes in July, but they are a steady product. It is important to find out how many you can sell, because peppers can certainly be overplanted.

Peppers are a 'nice-to-have' item in many families so they are much more sensitive to price and quality than many other vegetables. Early peppers still bring a premium but not like tomatoes.

There is some price resistance at 50¢ each, but that price is attainable for large peppers early in the season when peppers are in short supply. Our standard price is 3 for $1 and depending upon supply, we sometimes have to go to 4 for $1 for part of the market.

Peppers are a very tender crop, so they must be picked before the first frost. Thousands of peppers in various sizes will come from this single picking. This requires marketing bushels of peppers at a single market. This can be a problem if not advertised properly. We take orders through our newsletter.

Peppers provide opportunities for the development of niche markets. In many sections of the country, hot peppers are in great demand. The smaller, colored, sweet peppers also might be developed into a profitable niche market.

16-4. The pepper cage. This picture was taken in 1992. We have made a few changes since then. We have improved the cage design by squaring off the corners providing more space for the peppers. We have also added anchor stakes to keep the cages in place in a high wind. You can see the double irrigation hoses through the plastic mulch. On the top of the picture you can see the laths and twine that keeps the plastic tight in the wind.

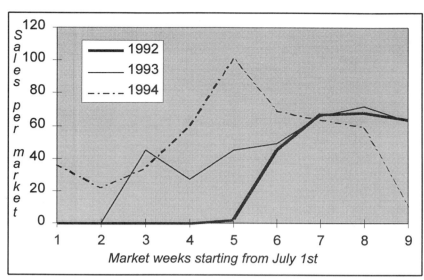

Sales per market

1992
1993
1994

Market weeks starting from July 1st

16-5. Pepper sales.
This chart compares pepper sales from 1992 through the 1994 season. We do not have the figures on how many peppers we brought home, if any. That is, did we have a production problem or a sales problem.

HITS AND MISSES

In 1992 we sold $370 from two 50' beds, each with about 150 plants. Since we made some greenhouse mistakes, we did not bring any peppers to market until after the 1st of August. We did not have sufficient nitrogen because the peppers were a little small and we averaged only 4-5 peppers per plant.

In 1993 we sold $721 from three 50' beds. However, we did suffer wind damage on half the plants. One half-bed was Jalepeno M peppers, and we didn't sell more than $25 of this variety. The other half of the bed was Lipstick, a single-lobbed variety that didn't produce well in our cool season. It is safe to assume that we sold about $600 from the two Ace hybrid beds or about $2 per square foot, or 6-10 peppers per plant.

In 1994 we again adjusted production and made some new mistakes. We tried Habenaro peppers to compliment our canning tomatoes for our salsa customers. They need more warmth than the season provided, and we didn't harvest any for sale. We underplanted the Ace hybrids and purchased some Better Bells locally. They did not produce well. We planted the Ace peppers four wide instead of three and that was just a bit too close for good picking. We sold our first peppers the first week of July and production remained steady throughout the summer until we quit watering in September. Then many of them rotted on the vine. We sold $433 from one bed with only an occasional pepper from the Better Bells. That $2.89 per square foot return proves peppers can be a very profitable crop if we plant the right variety in the right quantity.

Peppers provide a good opportunity to conduct a comprehensive market analysis using the chart at figure 16-5.

There are a number of facts that do not show up on the chart. In 1993 we sold over $700 in peppers, but $298 was in late season sales. In 1994 hail in mid-August severely reduced production.

We can safely draw the following conclusions:

• Even the early market will sustain sales of close to $40 per week.

• Late market sales can average almost $70 per week.

• We lost many sales because of production problems. That is, the market was there, and we had sufficient space allocated to peppers. We just didn't do things right.

In retrospect, I must admit we have made more mistakes on peppers than any other crop. Some of them were understandable given our inexperience, particularly the greenhouse problem in 1992.

FOR THE HOME GARDENER

Try protecting your peppers with plastic. It has improved our production and made peppers available all summer.

162

Chapter Seventeen

Tomatoes

Tomatoes are the most popular plants grown in home gardens across America. If only a few square feet are available for vegetable gardening, tomatoes will usually be grown there. Those that do not garden look for fresh tomatoes at farmers markets, making them the most popular item there as well.

Tomatoes provide a unique opportunity for the small commercial grower because supermarkets cannot compete with locally grown tomatoes. A bright red succulent fruit from a healthy tomato plant grown in real earth will outsell the pale, 'cardboard-tasting' supermarket tomato every time.

Tomatoes are our highest profit product but *ONLY* because we are early. Every penny spent on being the first grower to the market with tomatoes, pays off many times. But it does take considerable capital and time to get there first. Tomatoes are not difficult to grow but do need warm weather to ripen properly. With a little pampering, they can be coaxed into early production.

Start with the production of stocky transplants with dark green foliage and thick stems. Grow them beyond those normally sold by local nurseries into plants that are just beginning to blossom. Transplant them to the garden into well protected cages.

COMMERCIAL PLANNING

Quantities

One-third of the model garden is tomatoes. We explained the reasons for that decision in earlier chapters. The success of such a plan depends upon our ability to bring the first tomatoes to market, and the strength of the canning market. However, because of the extreme popularity of this crop, I doubt an intelligent garden plan should go much below the one-third rule for tomatoes.

Varieties

There are hundreds of tomato varieties on the market. Selecting the right variety is critical to hit the early market. Choose varieties with the following characteristics:

Determinate. Indeterminate plants continue to grow all season. Determinate plants grow to a certain point and then quit growing new foliage. The first few years we wanted as many tomatoes as possible so chose indeterminate varieties. We

Two new exciting varieties proven in the Pacific North west are Santiam and Oregon Spring. They consistently set fruit from their first flowers even in cold weather.
    Warren Schultz [1]

TOMATO DATA

Planning

Propagation .... Transplants
Frost tolerance .... Tender
Earliest transplant date .... FFD
Maturity date .... 50-90 days
Seeds per ounce 11,500
Seed viability .... Hyb 1-2 yrs, OP 3-4 yrs
Intensive spacing .... 18-24"

Starting Transplants

Planting depth .... 1/4-1/2"
Germination temp .... 50°-95° (80°)
Germination time ....6-8 days
Days to transplant size .... 42-70 days
Growing temp (Day/Night) .... 65°-75°/60°-65°

Growing

pH 6-7
Nutrient requirements .... Heavy feeder
Pests .... Tomato hornworm, spider mites, aphids, nematodes
Diseases .... Verticillium and fusarium, blights, tobacco mosaic
Critical watering .... Flowering through harvest

Harvest

Harvest when .... starting to ripen
Yield.. 4-5 lbs per plant
Average selling price .... $1-$2/lb
Average income per square foot .... $2.50-$3

spent many hours pruning the plants to keep them from crawling out of the cages. Our plan now is to maximize early production and to limit late production after prices have dropped. A determinate variety provides this early production and does not require time for pruning.

We experimented with indeterminate varieties for late summer production. We used a five-foot high cage and pruned back some of the growth twice during the season. Production was at least double that of the determinate plants.

Easy fruit set. We cannot sell tomato foliage, we must have fruit. To produce for the early market our plants must set fruit during cool weather.

Early. We use a relatively new variety, Oregon Spring, developed by Dr. Bagget from Oregon State University. It produces six to eight ounce fruits that are often seedless. We have received many compliments on the fine taste of this variety, available from Nichols and Garden City Seeds. The only problem with Oregon Spring is that it is not a fancy tomato and suffers from green shoulders in cool weather.

Medium to large fruits. Customers will purchase small tomatoes if they are the only ones available, but they prefer medium to large ones.

Disease tolerance. Tomatoes are susceptible to many diseases. Choose varieties that have resistance or tolerance for the diseases in your garden.

Planning Dates

The published maturity dates on tomatoes assume our transplants are of the average size, and weather is fairly normal. Oregon Spring tomatoes have a published maturity date of 52 days. If we want a few tomatoes to open the market the first of July we must transplant our tomatoes about the 10th of May, or about one week prior to our frost free date.

Most reference recommend planting tomatoes six to 10 weeks before setting them out. We use 10 to 12 weeks to give us a transplant that is well on its way to full production.

If we select a hardy variety, and have adequate protection, we can transplant tomatoes prior to our frost free date. We take that risk with only a portion of our crop, on the supported beds. We have cloth covers and supplemental heat available for these beds in case of threatening weather.

The remainder of our tomatoes are well protected so are set out about the frost free date. We keep close watch on the weather and if there is no cold weather in the forecast, we set them out. For safety, we plant a second crop in late March. Then if something goes wrong, we still have these reserve plants.

GROWING

Transplants

We use 1020 trays filled with good germination mix to start the tomatoes. We sprinkle the seeds from the package until the seeds are about ½" apart. Trays are placed in the germination room at 75°. The seeds germinated in six to eight days. As soon as the first seeds germinate the trays are placed under lights in the germination room for a few days before being moved to the greenhouse.

As soon as the first true leaves develop, in about 12-14 days, we transplant the seedlings into 1204 trays filled with germination mix. We plant 150% of our final requirement. That is, if we need 600 plants to set out in the garden, we transplant 900 into 1204s at this stage. We wet the germination mix, and use a short ½" pointed dowel to poke a hole in the mix. We prick out the plant with a short pointed stick, place the plant in the hole, and pack it firmly it into place. We keep the newly transplanted tomatoes under lights for a day or two before putting them into the greenhouse.

The second transplanting takes place when the tomatoes are about three inches high, about 15 days after the first transplanting. We fill the bottom of a 35 cell large plastic tray with an inch of compost. This time the plants are buried until only their top leaves show through. We cull out the weakest plants and leave about 150 extras for the final transplanting.

The final transplanting is into 5½" pots. These larger pots provide the space and nutrients to grow the strong healthy plants we need to achieve the earliest tomatoes. We do this one month prior to our projected set-out date to give them a chance to grow as large as possible. Since we have culled weak plants the first two times, we leave only about an extra 10% to provide replacements for cutworms, and plants damaged during setting out.

We do not harden off our tomatoes because they move directly from the greenhouse into a smaller 'cage greenhouse' as described below.

There appears to be an optimum time to set plants out into the garden. This occurs shortly before they have blossomed. If the plants have blossoms when they are set out, and the weather is warm, they will set fruit. This causes a diversion of energy to the fruit; sapping energy that should be spent on a better root system. The plants remain small throughout the season, reducing overall production.

Protection

Tomatoes are very tender plants and like it warm so protection from the elements is critical. We accomplish that with wire cages wrapped with plastic and covered with spun fabric.

The wire cages are made from a 150' roll of standard 5' reinforcing wire. For the purposes of this construction explanation, we refer to the

The biggest payoff of such root-richness, however, it that the plant adjusts easily at transplant time; unlike commercial transplants that typically have had their roots stunted by six-packs, your plants will suffer little or no setback, even if blossoming already has started.
Andrea Chandler [2]

165

THE TOMATO PLAN

The seed plan

Number of beds	9
Spacing	18 inches
Plants per row	30
Rows per bed	2
Plants per bed	60
Total number of plants	540
Seeds required	1080
Seeds per ounce	11,500
Seeds required	1/8 ounce
Variety	Oregon Spring
Source	Johnny's Selected Seeds
Cost	$5.25

The planting plan

Plant date	(FFD-64) March 15th
Transplant date	(FFD-17) May 1st
Tomato location	Beds 1 through 9

The marketing plan

Estimated yield	8-10 pounds per plant
Selling price	Average $1.25 for slicers, 45¢ for canners
Gross income	$4725
Income per square foot	$3.50

17-1, 17-2. Safety! (Above, right) I am securing the end of the roll to the garage door handle. (Above, left) Then we roll a loaded wheel barrow on the other end to hold the roll in place while we work.

eleven wires that run the length of the roll as vertical wires. After making almost 900 cages, we have found the following sequence to work best.

Tie the end of the roll securely to a stationary object. (Figure 17-1) This is a very important safety issue. If the roll comes loose, it could cause serious injury.

Roll out the wire 40-50 feet. Since this is steel, the wire has a strong tendency to roll back together. Use a wheelbarrow or other heavy object to keep the roll in place. (Figure 17-2)

Using a small bolt cutter, cut the wire into 5½' sections. Cut only the interior vertical wires. (Figure 17-3) This will cause the section to curl, taking the pressure off the wire. Finally, cut the two end wires from each section. (Figure 17-4) Since the pressure to roll back has been weakened by cutting the interior wires, the sections will lay right where they are.

Set the full sections on end. Cut off the tails so you have a five foot section with vertical wires on both ends. (Figure 17-5) This will make a cage about 18" in diameter.

Cut on both sides of the center wire, six wires down from the top. (Figure 17-6) This leaves tails on both sections. When we install the cage, the exposed wires are driven into the ground, stabilizing the cage. This leaves a 2' high cage, adequate for the determinate plants we use.

17-3. Cutting the vertical wires. Cut ONLY the nine interior wires. The two outside wires will hold the roll of wire in place until the interior wires of all of the sections have been cut.

Tie the ends of the cage together with wire. (Figure 17-7) We use the wire used for tying concrete reinforcing rods together. It is available at most lumber yards. This is a bit stronger than stove pipe wire, but still pliable. (Reverse the following sequence if you are left handed.) Grab the two ends with your left hand, maintaining pressure downward on the ends with your forearm parallel with the wires. Wrap the wire around the two vertical wires a few turns, and then loop over the horizontal wire. This keeps the tie wire in place.

Make the cage round by pushing on the splice. This is particularly a problem on a new roll of wire. As you move towards the center of the 150' roll, the wire naturally takes on a tighter diameter and less straightening is required.

We are also using some indeterminate tomatoes that require a taller cage. The 5' cages are a bit different in that one end is cut off rather than cutting down the middle. It is necessary to install the center wire tie first when hooking the ends together.

Transplanting

The sequence for setting out tomatoes is as follows:

Fertilize and cultivate the bed. If it is extremely dry, you may want to water for a few days to build up some reserve. Eight hundred cages present problems in the spring. Rather than moving them many times, we prepare the tomato beds as soon as the ground can be worked and put the cages in place.

Lay down the irrigation hose and check that all emitters are working properly. You will not see these emitters for the remainder of the season so it is critical that they work properly from the start.

17-4. Final cuts off the roll. As soon as you cut the outside vertical wires at the roll end, the wire becomes very manageable. Cut the remaining vertical wires.

17-5. Cutting off the tails.

17-6. Cutting the section in half. Cut on both sides of the center wire.

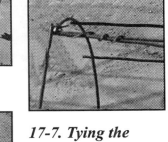

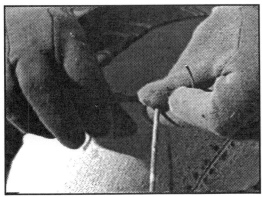

17-7. Tying the cages. The wire must be wrapped on the ends of cage and then around the top wire. Otherwise it can slip down the cage.

167

17-8. Digging the holes. *The post hole digger goes through the plastic easily saving the time of cutting with a knife.*

17-9. Fertilizing. *We believe this step is important to get the plants off to a healthy start. (This is my sister, Ethel. Made the mistake of visiting in the spring.)*

17-10. Placing the plants. *My sister, Mary, slaps the bottom of the pot and the tomato slips out easily.*

17-11. Tamping in the plants. *This can be done through the cages or from the top depending on which is easier on your back.*

Start laying the plastic, placing the cages as you go to keep the plastic in place. This can be done early in the spring. Cut slits in the plastic where the tomatoes will be planted. (It is advisable to do this step when you install the cages. Otherwise any rain will drain off the bed and will be lost. However, if you have a severe weed problem, you may wish to opt for better weed control, and provide additional irrigation water prior to planting.)

Use a post hole digger to dig the holes. (Figure 17-8) Square the holes off and make them deeper as necessary. If you have some leggy plants, it is helpful if you place them in the cage prior to final hole preparation. That way you can estimate the proper depth required for each plant.

Fertilize and water. (Figure 17-9) We use one teaspoon of Epsom salts to provide magnesium and one tablespoon of bone meal. Mix in with the soil in the bottom of the hole. Fill the holes with 400 ppm fertilizer water. Cut off all developing fruit from the plant, leaving blossoms and buds. Set the plants in the hole, pulling them firmly into one corner. (Figure 17-10) Pack the soil into the remaining two sides. (Figure 17-11) If the plants are dry, water immediately.

Wrap the cages with plastic. We use four people. Two hold the roll. (Figure 17-12) (This could be done with a well-designed stand.) The third pulls the plastic, and the fourth guides the plastic around the far end of the bed. Tie off the end of the plastic to an end cage in three spots, top, bottom, and middle. (It is easiest to punch a hole in the plastic right next to the wire.) We have found it best to use two people to initially stretch the plastic around the cages. One keeps the plastic taut, the other ties the plastic to the top of every 6th to 8th cages. (Figure 17-13) Secure the end of the plastic to the cage you started with. Tie the plastic to the tops of the remaining cages using a single knot.

Install 3' laths in between each cage, pushing in the bottom towards the center of the bed to make the plastic taught, leaving about 2-3 inches sticking out above the cage. (Figure 17-14)

Cover the cages with spun fabric. (Figure 17-15) This material is tied using the tails of the ties used to secure the plastic. Use a double knot so the wind cannot break it loose. Install ties between laths on opposite sides, pulling the plastic tight so the wind cannot work the plastic free. (Figure 17-16)

Watering

Careful watering is critical for healthy tomatoes that taste good. If they get too much water, they may crack, or taste may degrade. If they get too little, production will suffer. Tomatoes have a very extensive and deep root system. Consequently, twice a week watering seems to work well except in extreme heat, when more frequent watering is necessary.

Fertilizer

Proper soil for tomatoes should have adequate phosphorus and potassium, but should be free from excess nitrogen which will cause large plants but few fruits. The soil should be well-drained and have plenty of organic material.

Too much nitrogen may degrade the taste as the fruits grow too large. We begin the season with the application of ½ pound of granular fertilizer per 50' bed during bed preparation. We apply additional fertilizer each week after most of the foliage has developed.

17-12. Installing the pastic. Two of us hold the roll. One person is at the far end guiding the plastic around the bed, and my wife, Caroline, is pulling the plastic into place.

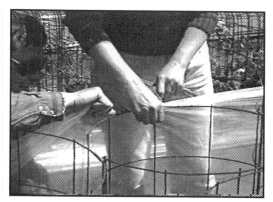

17-13. Making the first ties. One end is secured, then we tie a few cages to get the plastic in place to protect the tender plants from any wind that might be present. Then ties are placed on every cage, but with only a single knot.

17-14. Installing the lath. We have found it necessary to install these lath to tighten the plastic. Otherwise the wind will win the war.

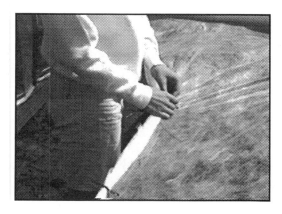

17-15. Installing the spun fabric. This is accomplished using the ends of the ties used to secure the plastic. It is important to stretch this fabric tight so the wind can not whip it against the cages.

169

17-16. The final step. We tie the lath to keep the plastic tight. (The distinguished gentleman on the right is my brother-in-law, Larry Thompson.)

Disease and Pest Control

The most serious problem with tomatoes is disease. They seem to be susceptible to most of the diseases in the garden. Fortunately, plant breeders have developed tomatoes resistant to many of the most common diseases. In addition, prevention measures are effective against many of the remaining diseases. Fungus diseases include blights, leaf spot, and bacterial spot. These can be successfully treated with periodic application of fungicide. Viral diseases include tobacco mosaic virus, and cucumber mosaic virus. These can be contained by controlling aphid populations. Physiological disorders such as blossom end rot, catfacing, and sunscald can be reduced by good growing practices.

We have had some problems with blight and leaf spot since our intensive spacing and plastic wrapping encourages disease during wet weather. As soon as the tomatoes start to crowd, we pull the plastic up about six inches from the bottom to provide some circulation. When the plants are almost full grown, we remove the protective plastic. This has usually reduced our blight problem and the plants usually recover well.

Insects are a constant problem, requiring close monitoring, and quick remedial action. Birds and rodents also sneak a few meals.

Hail Protection

We use 32" sections of 1/4" chipboard to protect our tomato crop from heavier hail. (See Figure 7-9) We hold them down with half-sections of 1" concrete tiles. We watch the weather radar and if a storm approaches, we can put the boards on in about 20 minutes. Early in the season the spun fabric will protect the plants from small quantities of hail up to marble size.

Pruning

We have mostly determinate plants so we do not do a lot of pruning. However, some is necessary to gain access to the bottom of the cage where the early fruit is. We are careful to leave as many leaves as possible to protect the fruit from sun scald.

PREPARING FOR MARKET

Harvesting

Let the tomatoes start to ripen on the vine, and then pull them to protect them from local varmints. Damage from gophers, mice, and insects increases as tomatoes ripen. A fully ripe tomato is easily damaged during harvest while a slightly green tomato survives harvest in much better condition. If tomatoes require more than a day or two to ripen, you are picking them too green. Look for the following when picking tomatoes:

Any tomato that is ripening uniformly is ready to pick. Customers will purchase a 'not quite ripe' tomato if it looks good. In fact, many customers prefer a mixture of ripeness as they do not intend to eat them all at one time anyway.

If a tomato has dark green blotches on top, turn the tomato over to see if the bottom is ripe. If so, pick it as it will not ripen completely anyway. Sell these as seconds. If the bottom is not ripe, leave it for the next picking as some of the green may ripen.

Most growers roll the stem off as they pick to limit the damage from punctures. Our variety has a tough stem so this is not always practical. We put them in 5-gallon pails, being careful not to stack them too deep.

We sort the tomatoes into beverage flats we get from a local wholesale beverage dealer. (There are thousands of these flats that are thrown out every week. If we run short, we contact local gasoline stations and they willingly save them for us in return for a few ripe tomatoes. Beverage stores will do the same.) This takes considerable space in the garage but does allow close management of the ripening fruit. We built two special racks to relieve the space problems.

At the end of the season we always wonder if we should pull all of the tomatoes before that killing frost. Tomatoes ripen only if temperatures are above 55°. If daytime temperature are consistently below that, it doesn't do any good to leave the tomatoes on the vine. Our experience indicates that the fruit will stand about 28° before it will be damaged. The plants will die at this temperature but the fruit can be left on the vine. With minimum protection some of the vines can be salvaged.

Over 80% of the fruit that is picked light green will ripen. However, this can be justified only during a strong canning market. At this point in the season we are attending only the Saturday markets, so we advertise canning tomatoes in the local newspaper. We drop the price to 25-30¢ per pound **and bring them to the market by the trailer-load.**

Marketing

We were able to get $2.00 a pound for all of our early tomatoes. Prices quickly slipped to $1.00 when the home gardens came in. I think a base price of $1 per pound for good quality table tomatoes is possible even towards the end of the season. Canners ran from $.30 - $.50 per pound. People don't seem to be willing to can tomatoes at prices much higher than that.

We market tomatoes at various stages of ripeness. Most customers know they will ripen just fine at home, and they don't want to eat them all at once anyway.

To sell small tomatoes use plastic quart containers and fill them with 8-10 small tomatoes, and sell them by the quart. A second option is to place them all in a single tray. Some customers are looking for the small ones.

PAST AND FUTURE HITS AND MISSES

The Seasons

In 1992 we planted almost 500 plants and sold $3287. We didn't sell any tomatoes until late July because of the extremely cool weather. The slicer market held firm until late in August. The canning market was fairly active, though we didn't pursue it actively. We didn't pull the fruit before frost, probably tilling in over a ton of tomatoes.

In 1993 the cool wet season kept most tomatoes off the market as most growers did not protect their tomatoes from the weather. Home garden tomato production was never a factor. We had an adequate supply but did not sell our first tomato until late in July, almost four weeks after the market opened. We sold $6054 from 750 plants.

To get the most flavorful tomtoes, you should pick them just as they begin to change from orange to red and then keep them at 59° to 70°F in normal room light for four or five days until they finish ripening to rull red.

Marita Cantwell[3]

171

In 1994 we planted 804 plants, including 120 Stokes indeterminate tomatoes in 5' cages. The warm spring weather pushed the plants until they were under considerable stress. Then a neighbor sprayed some weeds with 2-4-D, and the overspray damaged over half of our tomato crop. Unfortunately we were not able to get an accurate assessment of the production potential of the indeterminate varieties.

We tried Johnny's 361 and early fruit set was noticeably better than the Oregon Springs. These also got nicked by 2-4-D so we will not have a complete comparison until next season. However, it appeared that total production was considerably greater than the Oregon Springs.

We designed a method to protect the plants in the cool spring. We went to rummage sales and purchased old blankets and curtains at bargain prices. Then we stripped them up into pieces 26-30" wide. We clipped these blankets to the top of the wire cages with standard 3/8" binder clips available from any office supply store, then put the hail boards over the top. This provides several degrees of protection. If supplemental electric heat is available, we believe we could survive temperatures close to 20° if the wind was not too strong.

Our next project is tunnels for even earlier tomato production. Next year we plan to construct small greenhouses over three of our beds. This will allow us to set out the tomato plants in April and have full production when the market starts in July. It has a few challenges, such as heat and ventilation, but we believe we can solve these problems. The profit potential is almost staggering. If you are interested in the results of our experiments, please subscribe to our newsletter. (See page 207)

THE HOME GARDENER

This chapter contains the best reason for a hobby gardener to purchase this book. Tomatoes are the most popular vegetable grown in gardens across the country. Unfortunately, they can be frustrating because they never ripen soon enough. Some recommendations for the earliest tomatoes on the block:

Grow the earliest variety available. There is a tremendous variance in tomato maturities, perhaps more than any other crop. Unfortunately, most greenhouses have a limited number of varieties. Early Girl will probably be available, and it isn't a bad choice. However, it is not the earliest. If you choose the wrong variety, and follow every suggestion in the next few paragraphs, you still won't get the earliest tomatoes.

Consider growing your own transplants. Tomatoes are the easiest transplants we grow. They seem to thrive on repotting, and are fairly tolerant of less-than-ideal growing conditions. However, give the roots room to grow by repotting several times. You want a short, stocky, healthy plant with blossoms. You can't get that without a larger pot.

Use plastic. Tomatoes need warmth throughout the season. Plastic on the ground will make the soil warm quicker. Plastic around the cages will protect the plant from the wind and capture some of the sun's heat for earlier maturing tomatoes.

NOTES ON THE VIDEO

The video covers the most difficult parts of raising early tomatoes, the construction and installation of the cages.

Chapter Eighteen

Zucchini

This chapter should probably be named summer squash since the concepts discussed here apply to most popular types of summer squash. However, at present we are raising only zucchini. Zucchini is the Rodney Dangerfield of vegetables, it doesn't get much respect. However, it is becoming more popular and entire cookbooks are now devoted to this versatile vegetable. If grown in moderation, and sold small, it is a consistent seller and can be very profitable.

COMMERCIAL PLANNING

Planning for zucchini is very simple because transplants are not required, and it matures very quickly and bears heavily all season.

Quantities

Caution is advised because zucchini can easily be overplanted. Demand is steady but does decrease late in the season. Therefore, it is important to adjust production to the right level. Based on our experience, 1.5%-2% of garden space would be a good starting point.

However, check your markets very closely to determine how many small zucchini are available. Adjust your production accordingly. The garden model provides one partial bed for zucchini. Use only what you think you can sell. The remainder should be used for experimenting with other potential crops. For simplicity, we will use the full bed for planning purposes.

Varieties

There are only minor differences between varieties. Yield isn't much of an issue because they all produce so well. Taste isn't even mentioned. Some of the varieties have some disease tolerance. We use Zucchini Select, a 47 day variety from the Stokes seed company. They produce very early, compact plants which work well on our raised beds.

Timing

In only takes about 1½ months for zucchini to begin production. Consequently, it is easy to have this crop ready for the opening of the season. In fact, we encourage early

18-1. Zucchini spacing. Notice the alternating 18" spacing across the 38" bed. This places one hill by each emitter on the single irrigation hose.

173

ZUCCHINI DATA

Planning

Propagation	Direct seed
Frost tolerance	Tender
Earliest plant date	FFD
Maturity date	50-60 days
Seeds per ounce	300
Seed viability	4-5 years
Intensive spacing	18-36"
Planting depth	1"
Germination temperature	60°-105° (95°)
Germination time	3-12 days

Growing

pH	6-7
Nutrient requirements	Heavy feeder
Pests	Cabbage loopers, corn earworms, cucumber beetles
Diseases	Downy & powdery mildew, mosaic, anthracnose, wilt
Critical watering	Bud development and flowering

Harvest

Harvest when	1-1½" in diameter
Yield	15-20 fruits per plant
Average selling price	33-50¢/each
Average income per square foot	$2.50-$3.00

over production because it takes a week or so to reach full production. And these plants will continue to bear heavily all season. Therefore, if you must throw a few away early in the season, this is much better than missing early sales.

GROWING

Planting

Direct seed zucchini around your FFD by placing six zucchini seeds in hills perpendicular to the emitters along the irrigation hose. Alternate sides and place the hills towards the edge of the beds (Figure 18-1). This gives the plants room to grow and makes harvesting easier. We dig a small trench from the emitter to the hill to ensure sufficient moisture for germination.

Install plastic gallon milk containers with the bottoms cut off over the seeded hills. This protection encourages germination and early growth.

Caring for the plants

Thinning. When the plants become crowded in the container, remove the protection and thin to three plants per hill. Later in the season, when full production is achieved, it may be possible to thin to two plants per hill. This gives the remaining plants more room to spread out.

Fertilizing. Zucchini is a heavy feeder so we start with our standard granular application in the spring. Then we provide two applications of liquid fertilizer during the season.

Pests and diseases. Zucchini is usually not bothered by many insects or diseases.

Mulching. We have found it very beneficial to mulch the bed heavily to conserve moisture and provide a clean growing environment. Without a thick mulch, rains splash soil on the fruits requiring more time for market preparation.

HARVESTING AND MARKETING

One of the primary attractions of raising zucchini is the easiness of harvest and marketing.

Harvesting

Harvest zucchini when they are small, about six to eight inches long. We harvest them with a long-bladed knife rather than twisting them off. We want the vines to remain healthy all season, and by using care in harvest, we have never had problems with vine damage. We usually miss a few so we are able to satisfy those customers who want the larger ones.

Zucchini must be handled carefully as they nick very easily. They rarely need to be washed, just wiped off and brought to market.

Marketing

The most important concept in this entire chapter is the issue of size. Customers want small fruits, not baseball bats. Yet in a market of over 30 growers we are the only ones that bring a consistent supply of small zucchini to market.

I had the opportunity to visit a farmers market in another town in the state. I was comparing prices and noticed they had a well established zucchini price of 50¢ each. That is a bit higher than our market, so I started to look closer. I could not find a small zucchini, they were all the size of a large baseball bat.

I will beat on this a bit more because I suspect it is not peculiar to North Dakota. Our job as growers is to provide our customers with the produce they want. We see an occasional customer that wants to make zucchini bread and might use a large one. But the majority of customers want them small for stir-fry and salads. If we meet this need, zucchini can become very profitable.

We maintain a consistent price of 3 for $1 all season. For the past three years, we have averaged over $2.75 per square foot. Only tomatoes can consistently beat that gross sales figure.

PAST AND FUTURE HITS AND MISSES

Several years ago we grew a few yellow crooked neck squash. They sold quite well at times, but were often erratic because this squash is not very popular in this area of the

---

THE ZUCCHINI PLAN

The seed plan

Number of beds 1
Spacing .... 18"
Hills per bed 33
Plants per hill.. 6
Total seeds required 198
Seeds per ounce 300
Seed ordered .... 1 ounce
Variety .... Zucchini Select
Source .... Stokes
Cost $4.30

The planting plan

Planting date .... (FFD-8) May 10th
Location .... Bed 25

Marketing plan

Price... 3 for $1
Estimated yearly sales $450
Gross income per square foot $3.00

---

country. However, I believe we would be able to develop a small niche market for it. This would take some of the mid-season sales pressure off zucchini by reducing zucchini production and providing an alternative specialty crop to the market. Next year we will try not only yellow squash but a few scallops as well.

Our zucchini was affected by a neighbor's 2-4-D overspray this spring. In fact, it looked so sick we considered pulling it up and reseeding. But we left it and it started to produce almost on schedule, and remained in full production all season. It's a tough plant.

Later in the season we also had hail damage. The broad leaves were almost completely destroyed. However, within about ten days we were almost back to full production. By the end of the season the hail damage was hardly noticeable.

Chapter Nineteen

Other Crops

As you become comfortable with the vegetables described in the past few chapters, you may wish to add other crops that you enjoy growing. Diversification can be useful as a 'hook' to get customers to your stand. Every market needs variety, some of the 'exotic' species that may not be available at the supermarkets.

What follows is a discussion on the merits and disadvantages of various fruits and vegetables that we have tried, some extensively, and others halfheartedly. The crops are listed in the order in which they merit inclusion in your garden.

GARLIC

We have been pleasantly surprised by the steady market for garlic. We raised about 100 square feet this past year, and will triple that for next season. One of the primary advantages to garlic is that it stores well. If it is not sold at the market, we take it home and sell it at the next one.

We have had considerable difficulty growing regular garlic. We cannot plant garlic in the fall without providing some mulch protection for our potentially frigid winters. We will experiment with that option to determine the depth of mulch that would be required.

In 1991 we planted garlic in the middle of a very warm May. Very few plants came up. In 1992 we planted Elephant garlic around the first of April. Again, very few plants came up. About midsummer the local seed supplier told us he had some problems with mold which caused poor germination. The Elephant garlic that germinated grew well, and we sold all the garlic we had in a single market.

In 1993 we planted regular garlic on April 3rd. The weather was cold, cloudy, and fairly wet. The garlic thrived and we got almost 100% germination. The bulbs were not as large as they should be for optimum production, but the garlic sold easily.

In 1994 we finally got it right, and planted the garlic in March as soon as the raised beds could be worked. Garlic seems to need the warming and cooling spring weather to break dormancy in the spring. We had a superb crop, and sold $375 over three weeks for a return of $2.60 per square foot. We sold $72 of garlic in a single market.

To plant garlic, separate the cloves, select the largest ones, and plant them 3-4" apart and 2" deep. We use the same planting system we use for onions. (See figures 14-1 and 14-2) Make sure the blunt ends are facing down and the pointed end is up.

Once the garlic is growing, keep the beds free of weeds and cultivate lightly in between the plants to ensure that the soil remains loose to allow the bulb to expand. When the tops are 6-8 inches high, nitrogen fertilizer should be discontinued. Watering should be limited when the bulbs are in the final maturing stage.

Garlic is a biennial so will develop flower stalks. These should be removed as they will become seed pods and result in smaller bulbs.

The bulbs are ready for harvest when the leaves become yellow or brown, and they start to fall over. When this happens, the entire crop should be harvested. If you wait much longer than this, the outer wrapper will begin to deteriorate if there is still moisture in the bed. The segments will become exposed which detracts from the normal appearance of the bulbs making them more difficult to sell.

DILL

Dill is essential for all pickle producers. In our area it is given away with the pickles to those that need it. Since we are a large pickle producer, we must plant dill. If you do not produce pickles, you could still raise dill profitably, but only if you could get a fair price. Check your local market before you consider dill as a separate crop.

We interplant dill with onions. The seed must be planted soon after the onion plants are set out. Dill takes up to 21 days to germinate in cool soil.

19-1. Garlic ready for harvest. *Once the garlic starts to fall over, it is time to harvest the bed.*

If the onions get a good head start, they will shade out the tender dill plants. We plant two to three seeds next to the emitters on the drip hose. Since we use a triple hose on onions, this provides a spacing of about 10-12 inches. We also plant dill in any open areas of the garden created by poor germination. This gives us some late season dill for the late pickle market.

Timing with dill is a bit difficult because it is impossible to know when the first pickles will be sold. If the slicer market stays strong, we might not sell large quantities of pickles until very late in the season. On the other hand, if warm weather comes early creating a surplus of slicers, pickles may be ready long before the dill. Our problem is that with interplanting, we do not have much choice on when we plant the seeds. Succession planting is not a viable option.

Another problem with dill is that it self-sows easily, creating volunteer patches all around the garden if the plants are allowed to go to seed. Consequently, the dill should be harvested when ready, and brought to market.

Dill creates an opportunity for superb customer service. We include dill data in our pickle customer database. Many experienced picklers have a preference for when the dill is harvested. Some like the seeds

177

harvested. Some like the seeds brown, some green, and some in the flower stage. Some like only a few heads, others put several in each jar. We make an attempt to determine these preferences, so we know what to deliver the next year.

BROCCOLI

Broccoli provides an alternative to cabbage in our gardening system. However, it is a bit more difficult to make a profit from this crop without the help of some cool weather.

Spacing for broccoli should not be reduced below 15", or 1.56 square feet per plant. This limits the 50' bed to three rows or 120 plants. It also limits interplanting with peas or beans to a single row on either side of the trellis.

A good broccoli head will sell for $1 - $1.50 early in the season, depending upon size. That provides an income range between 65¢ per square foot for a single crop at $1 head, and $1.92 per square foot for a double crop at $1.50 per head.

The secret to profitability is the side shoots, which sell for $1 per pound. The advantage to side shoots is that the crop develops very quickly because the plant is mature. If we can squeeze another pound from each plant, broccoli quickly becomes a very profitable crop per square foot. The disadvantage to side shoots is that it takes awhile to pick a pound. But it does happen early in the season before other crops have reached full production.

Side shoots will continue as long as the weather remains cool. That means the plants might remain in place after initial harvest, creating a problem for succession planting. If the weather is warm, the plants can be removed after harvesting the main head, and the bed can be replanted.

WINTER SQUASH

We have grown Buttercup squash over several seasons with great success. It sells extremely well in the early fall, and produces sufficient quantities to make a nice profit.

The problem with winter squash is that it requires considerable real estate. We plant it along the edge of the garden and let it sprawl into the pasture. Occasionally, we need to clip some vines that are invading the other raised beds.

Winter squash is that rare vegetable where freshness isn't an issue. It keeps extremely well for months without any degradation in taste. This is a tremendous advantage because we can bring the produce that does not sell to our next market. That allows us to maintain a price that is fair throughout the season. However, supermarkets sometimes run loss leader sales with squash that can destroy the market.

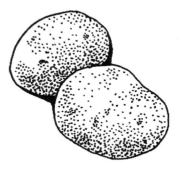

POTATOES

Potatoes sell well all season. However, they are not a profitable crop when returns are calculated by the square foot. In other words, potatoes are not a high value crop compared to tomatoes and cucumbers. Since our entire system is based upon maximum return from minimum space, planting potatoes has not been an option for us.

Some of us look at plants as a source of livelihood, while others find them intriguing subjects for scientific study. But most enjoy plants for the sheer delight of having them in their every-day surroundings, to savor the varied colors, textures, tastes, and aromas that they alone can offer.

Brian Capon [2]

178

We have experimented with potatoes and found them very easy to grow. They can be planted early in the spring. If they freeze, they will come back. A large commercial grower in our area plants his potatoes about six weeks prior to our FFD and has had marvelous success.

We use a double row on our three-foot wide raised beds, spacing the hills every 18 inches. Potato pieces should be between 1.5 to 2.0 ounces, and planted two per hill. With a little experimentation, this planting formula could be tweaked for optimum production.

Timing the harvest is an important decision. Farmers that have 40 acres of potatoes can start harvesting as soon as the market opens. Our prices start at 50¢ per pound so early potatoes are bringing a premium. For those of us with limited space, reduced early production may not pay off, even with a slightly higher price. We might be better off waiting until the potatoes are a bit larger, limit harvest, and try to get a fair price from customers that want a few to compliment the other produce they buy from us.

Production can be erratic. We have harvested a hill that has large quantities of nice medium sized potatoes. The hill next to it might be filled with two very large potatoes and scores of little ones. This may have been our inexperience or may have been peculiar to the variety or the season.

Another problem with potatoes is the physical act of harvesting. It is backbreaking work when done by hand. Large producers have mechanical harvesting equipment pulled behind air-conditioned tractors. The potatoes are washed, graded, and bagged mechanically.

If we had the space, we would grow potatoes simply because many of our customers want them. But it would not be done without a mechanical digger and a larger wash setup than we currently have installed. We would grow an early red variety, probably Norland. These seem to be the earliest and have the broadest customer acceptance. Russets are probably a niche crop that could be developed over time.

LETTUCE

Lettuce comes in four models; crisphead, butterhead, romaine and loose leaf. Traditional head lettuce is a crisphead variety often referred to as iceberg lettuce. We tried head lettuce a few years ago and quickly discovered that customers want leaf lettuce instead.

We believe that lettuce is a possible niche crop. It is easy to grow and sells well. However, it is difficult to keep fresh at the market because it wilts so quickly. Some refrigeration would be necessary to make it a viable quantity crop.

We start the season with lettuce because it grows well in the cool, spring weather. However, lettuce is difficult to grow all summer as it tends to bolt (go to seed) when the weather gets warm. With the right varieties it is possible to grow lettuce even if the weather turns warm for a few days. We haven't found the right combination and we are still experimenting with different varieties.

All across the U.S., farmer's markets are alive and thriving—in big cities and rural communities alike. From huge permanent structures, to pickup tailgates in a shopping mall parking lot, to card tables set up around a town square, today's farmer's markets are as varied as America's countryside. [3]

179

Leaf lettuce sales are limited by the number of people at the early markets. If we receive unusually warm, early summer weather the lettuce may bolt and we may loose this production. Consequently, during our experimental stage, we limit our exposure to about 50 plants.

STRAWBERRIES

Strawberries share the same problem as lettuce, normal June-bearing varieties are in production before our market starts. We recommend that you try some late bearing varieties or day-neutrals to hit the later market when other produce is also available. The strawberries will sell very well, and might attract additional business to your stand if you have sufficient quantity.

There are many ways to grow strawberries, but probably the easiest is to keep the runners cut and every three years grow a new bed. This might not provide the optimum production, but it would yield the most income for the least amount of work. We plan to take a good look at strawberries in a year or two.

RASPBERRIES

We started with raspberries our first year of gardening with canes we got from a friend. At one time we planned to have 800 feet, but trimmed down to about half that, and then eliminated them altogether.

When we quit growing raspberries, we were still experimenting with how to get the biggest yields with the least work. We started with rows eighteen inches wide, and trimmed them back to about one foot. The wider rows were too hard to harvest, and the fruiting canes shaded the new canes, making them smaller than they should be.

Raspberries need to be supported which requires constant attention as the new canes grow taller. We used a simple two-wire system.

We recommend that you prune several times each year. The first pruning should be done as the new canes start developing. Cut out all but the most promising canes, thinning to two to three per running foot. Take out the canes that winterkilled at this time as well. The second pruning occurs about in mid-July when the new canes must be thinned one more time. The final pruning occurs after the fruiting is over, to remove the old canes. This allows a month or so of unrestricted growth for the new canes to reach full height.

Recommendations: Don't take canes from a friend unless you know it is a variety that grows well in your area. We got Lathams when we should have been planting a new variety, Boyne.

We sold raspberries at $3 per pint even though there is considerable price resistance at that level. There just were not enough on the market so we never took any home. I have trouble asking $3 because I believe it borders on price gouging. But . . people paid it.

FLOWERS

When we started gardening commercially we planned to grow dried flowers for a sideline craft business. We quickly discovered there was much more to drying that we had anticipated. We also discovered that vegetables could be very profitable, so we reduced our dependence on flowers.

But after talking to growers in other farmers markets across the state, we learned that flowers are well worth the trouble if you grow the right ones. We grow flowers because they add important color to our marketing stand and they are challenging to grow. However, to make money at flowers, observe the following general rules:

Design your cut flower garden around color and blooming dates. You cannot sell many all-white bouquets. A variety of colors is required at all times of the seasons. That requires the right selection of plants.

Use a mix of annuals, perennials and bulbs. We grow perennials because they do not require as much work since they come back each year. We have some problems with winter kill when we have limited snow cover and harsh temperatures. However, we simply replant as necessary as there are always additional perennials we wish to try.

Use a well executed insect control system. Since most of our flowers are not eaten, we are willing to use chemical insecticides when necessary. Insects seem to be attracted to the flower garden first. If we can control them here, they are less of a problem on the vegetables.

Use mechanical supports for taller flowers. This assures that all blooms will be brought to market rather than trampled because they fell over.

Flower selection

The proper selection of flowers has been the most frustrating part of

our operation. Part of the problem was self inflicted because we attempted to hit a moving target. We started growing flowers to support a dried-flower craft business. Our selection criteria was not whether they would make good cut flowers, but if they would dry well. The cut flower market and good drying flowers are not always satisfied by the same flower. When we abandoned the dried objective, we found ourselves with flowers that did not belong in a cut flower operation. So, step one in the selection of flowers, is to define a clearly stated objective.

Flowers usually have several names that may apply to a family of the same species. Most have a common name and a scientific name. In addition there are varieties within a species that differ considerably in their worth as a cut flower. We recommend that you learn the scientific names for those you grow, and research the varieties within that species. Be very sensitive to varieties as they many times hold the key to success in cut flowers.

Planning

If you thought planning for vegetables was a bit complicated, you 'ain't seen nothing yet'. Proper planning for flowers must consider the following:

Blooming time. We want to sell flowers over a two month period from

There are few businesses that can be initiated from a small garden—but growing and selling herbs is one. With a modest investment of time, energy, and perhaps some money, you are an entrepreneur, free to dream on to success, the pursuit of happiness, and perchance, a major enterprise.
Bertha Reppert [5]

181

mid-July to mid-September. There are many flowers that bloom earlier that must be eliminated from our plan regardless of how compelling growing them might be.

Color. A variety of colors is needed throughout the season.

Vase life. This factor is important to repeat customer business. If a cut flower arrangement does not last about a week, customers will be reluctant to purchase another boquet.

Stem length. A dwarf variety won't cut it (pardon the pun) in the cut flower market. Longer stems provide more options to the flower arranger.

Planting time. Most of our annuals are started as soon as we start the greenhouse in March. Unfortunately, there are exceptions.

Growing flowers is the fascinating part of our cut flower operation. Flowers provide challenges often absent from vegetable gardening simply because of the wide diversity among flowers. These fascinations start with germination.

Germination

Germination of flower seeds is complicated by these factors:

Light. Some seeds require light to germinate, some complete darkness, and the remaining seeds will germinate under either condition. This requires a germination environment that can provide light.

Duration. Some seeds require months to germinate, many take several weeks. During this time growing conditions must remain conducive for germination or the seeds will dry out and die.

Size of the seed. Some flower seeds are so small they are almost like powder. These are extremely difficult to work with and to keep alive when the plants are very small.

Germination rates. Many seeds have slow or irregular germination. This means they will not all germinate at the same time. Since those that do germinate need light, light must be provided or they will die. The addition of light may change the ideal germination conditions for those seeds that have not yet germinated.

Temperatures. Fluctuating temperatures may damage a seedling in its early stages of growth.

Harvesting Flowers

To bring repeat bouquet business we must ensure that our flowers have a reasonable vase life. If we bring them to market, sell them, and they wilt by that evening, we will have lost a flower customer. To extend vase life, we must cut them at the right time, and we must harvest them properly.

To understand proper harvesting, we must first understand what happens to the flowers when we cut them. When a flower is growing, it is full of water, (referred to as turgidity) and food. This varies with the time of day. By late afternoon the flowers are full of food, but have lost some water to evaporation. In early morning, the flowers are full of water but have used some of the stored food during the night. We can cut successfully at either of these times, but never during the heat of the day. If you cut in the morning, wait until after the dew has evaporated.

Much of what occurs in a flower is specific to a particular species. Daylillies, for example, will last one day regardless of what we do to them. Gladiolas, if handled properly, will last for more than a week. There is also considerable differences in varieties within a species. So the first thing we must do is select only flowers that make good cut flowers.

Cut flower sales in this country are definitely on the upswing with big increases predicted for the future. What should interest a small or backyard grower of cut flowers in these predictions is that the big interest is coming in old fashioned garden flowers—like those your mother or grandmother grew.
        Lee Sturdivant[6]

When we cut a flower, we must continue to provide it water and food. Otherwise it will wilt and die quickly. Have warm water (about bath temperature) with you in the garden when you are cutting flowers. We use five-gallon pails and fill them to a depth of half the stem length of the flowers we are cutting. Cut the stems slightly longer than needed for the bouquets. Remove damaged leaves and those that will be under water. Immediately place the stem in the water pail.

The right time to cut a flower varies from flower to flower but is usually determined by the stage of flower development. If the flower is too tight, it may not open. If it is too loose, it may not last long in the vase. For those flowers for which you cannot find solid information, try cutting a few at various stages of flower development. Put them in water and preservative, and leave them at room temperature for a few days.

Flowers we have grown

Now let me save you some money. Over the years I have purchased more books on flowers than on any other aspect of gardening. In retrospect, I needed only one. "Specialty Cut Flowers" by Allan M. Armitage, ISBN 0-88192-225-0, published by Varsity Press/Timber

Press. It provides all of the details you need to grow and harvest hundreds of flowers. For that reason I will not discuss the specifics on how to grow or prepare flowers for market. Instead I will strongly recommend you purchase a copy of this wonderful book. The following is a list of those plants we have tried successfully.

German Statice sells well because it is used as a base for many dried flower crafts. We dry it if not sold fresh at the market and sell it later in the season.

Annual Statice. We grow annual statice because it sells just as well dried as fresh. Therefore, if we grow too much and cannot sell it all at the market, we dry it and sell it later. Start these seeds as soon as you start the greenhouse in the spring. They will require repotting into larger containers, but will bloom earlier when you desperately need the colors. Order specific colors rather than a variety .

Strawflowers are excellent cuts and will also dry well. We recommend you experiment with some of the new varieties as they will sell better.

Gladiolas sell very well and are profitable if thrips can be controlled .

Hybrid lilies are spectacular in our display, and are not difficult to grow. However, they are a bit pricey to purchase, and we have some winter kill.

You will also need filler material such as *Baby's Breath* or *Sea Lavender.* These perennials are easy to get started and to grow.

In this chapter we have introduced optional crops that provide diversification for your market, and add considerable fascination to the planning and growing process. We hope you have time and space to try a few of them.

Marketing is often forgotten when a new market garden venture is set up. Yet it can make or break the developing business. A well-devised marketing strategy can give the business a much greater chance of success right from the start; it is far better than forming a marketing strategy out of necessity over a number of years.

Ric Staines [7]

183

This Business of Gardening

Chapter Twenty

This Business of Gardening

Commercial gardening is a business and realizing that is an important step in the transition from hobby to commercial gardening. A hobby gardener is concerned about production and diversity. A commercial gardener is concerned about profit. How do we become profitable? How should we run our business? What management tools are available to us? What essential skills must we develop? Here are a few suggestions to get you started.

Market aggressively. Here's that word "marketing" again. To be profitable we must sell our produce for the highest price we can get. We do that through effective marketing.

Reduce costs. This is particularly true of labor since gardening is so labor intensive. If you must hire help, do so very carefully.

Look at the long run. It takes time to develop niche markets and in the early phases, we may be spending considerable time for very little return. But in the long run, the time will pay off handsomely. We are doing that with cut flowers. We know cut flowers are sold successfully in many places across the country. We believe we can develop our market. And it is so much fun trying!

Don't loose track of the details. Carry a 3x5 card with you at all times. (My T-shirts all have pockets in them.) I've got a great memory, it's just short. As we work in the garden, ideas surface that will improve our operation. Some of them are blinding flashes of the obvious, and will not be forgotten. However, many of them are small things that get lost if we do not write them down. It is the collective affect of these small details that make us different from other marketers. Don't lose those precious details!

Start small and grow larger. Regardless of how experienced you are at gardening, and regardless of how detailed this book may be, you will still make mistakes. If you start small, you will be able to recover from those mistakes, and make adjustments that will prove profitable.

Cut your losses short. There are some things that do not work in a given market. Give up on the idea. Perhaps it will work at another time. At this point you might raise a good question, "How can you advise me to go for the long run, and then a little later you advise me to cut my losses short? How can you expect me to develop a niche market if I give up right away?" The answer lies in another piece of advice, start small and grow larger. Suppose you want to develop a market for dried and fresh herbs. Start small with a few of the most popular herbs. Test the market. After a season or so, you must honestly answer the question, "Is there a need for this product?" You must answer that question honestly regardless of how you personally feel about herbs. Losses occur because we try to force our preferences upon a market with a mind of its own. I guarantee one thing, if there is a genuine need, you'll know it. If there isn't, cut your losses short.

Finally, have fun! How can that possibly help make money? Because it affects everything you do. It is contagious. Your employees have fun, your customers have fun.

ESSENTIAL SKILLS

In chapter one we discussed the need for a business plan. In chapter four we outlined the principles of planning the garden. In this section we will articulate basic business skills that are necessary for commercial gardening success.

Planning

Decisions. Inherent in this planning process, is the ability to make decisions at the right time. In many cases, the decision is not as important as when it is made. A few years ago we decided to expand our perennial flower operation. We reviewed the catalog and selected those varieties we thought were right for us. We called the company and almost all of them were sold out. The problem? It was May. That decision should have been made in January.

Anticipation. The ability to anticipate requirements comes from research and experience. It is for this reason that we recommend that you start small and grow. Last year we didn't anticipate some key greenhouse supplies and had to pay several times normal wholesale prices. In the process, we lost about $50. That is not enough to break the operation, but if enough of these mistakes are made, it can be devastating.

Details. Management in large corporations starts with lofty concepts like vision. And those are important, even to a small business. But much of successful management revolves around how well we handle details, how well we care for the little things. And it is for this one reason, more than any other, that I strongly recommend the use of a computer. That is what computers are for, to remember the details.

Focus

Many businesses fail because the entrepreneurs loose site of their objectives, because they loose track of their customers. That can easily happen in gardening because you can be pulled in so many directions so easily. You may enjoy raising herbs and enjoy using them. But if you focus on herbs and the customers are focusing on tomatoes, you will fail, not because herbs aren't a great idea, but because the customers aren't there.

OPERATIONS

So far we have developed a brilliant business plan, honed our superb marketing skills, and developed a great list of products. What operational skills do we need to execute that plan and sell our produce?

Making intelligent investments

Throughout the book we have emphasized the need to go after the early market. Our system requires capital expenditures far above most other production systems. So let me explain why that can be justified with a discussion of the concept of return on investment.

We will use tomato cages as an example. Most growers do not take the time to wrap the tomato cages in plastic and spun fabric. Lets look at the costs.

Each cage requires 2½ feet of reinforcing wire. At $45 per 150' roll, each cage costs 75¢. There are 60 cages per 50'-bed, for a total of $45. We need 60 3' laths which cost about $10. This $55 per tomato bed is a capital cost since these cages will last for many years. We need to factor in some replacement costs for broken lath.

Plastic costs $75 for 4000'. We use about 110' for a cost of just over $2.

Spun fabric costs about 11¢ per foot for a cost of $5.50 per bed.

Recurring costs, then, are about $8 per year per row of tomatoes if we add a few cents for broken lath and the twine required to tie the system together.

Eight dollars! Can I recover that cost each year? At $1 per pound I would need to sell eight pounds of tomatoes that I would not have had to sell without the system. If I can have tomatoes just a few days before the other growers, this will be easy.

But suppose . . .suppose I can also get a better price for my early tomatoes, let's say $1.50 per pound. Now I don't have to raise more tomatoes, I just need to bring them to market earlier. To recover my cost I need 16 pounds of early, $1.50 per pound tomatoes from those 60 plants, and I will get $8 more than I would at $1 per pound. Guaranteed!!

But what about the $55 in capital costs? In 1993 we averaged between 7 and 8 pounds per tomato plant. That isn't real good but the weather was horrible. Many growers didn't harvest any tomatoes at all. That means that the $6000 we sold was a direct result of our willingness to make an intelligent capital investment in the cages and covers.

Growers who have seen our tomato production system claim they can't afford to spend the money or time. My reply is, "You can't afford not to." By the time their tomatoes come to market I have sold thousands of pounds and have established a clientele of customers who have developed confidence in the taste of my tomatoes.

Cages are just one example out of many. Marketing, drip irrigation, trellises, cloches, and raised beds all cost time and money. Will they pay off? Certainly! If there is one common mistake among the growers I talk to, it is this. They are unwilling to spend the time and money required to save them time and make more

money. This shortsightedness limits production and market share, and locks them into a marginally profitable operation.

Controlling costs

Now that I have convinced you to spend money on investments, I will try to convince you to be frugal with expenses. Profits are directly related to our success in this area of management.

Materials. The easiest way to save money is to purchase in sufficient quantities to get price breaks. Purchases should be consolidated whenever possible to save shipping costs. On the other hand, there are items we do not skimp on, most notably seeds and water. Buy the seeds you want and use what-ever water you deem necessary. With drip irrigation very little water is wasted.

Labor. The biggest opportunity for savings is here because labor is expen-sive and so easily wasted. This is such an expensive and important category that we have included it in a separate section.

Administrative expenses. These costs are not usually a large part of the budget so there are not many opportuni-ties to save money.

Advertising. The temptation with advertising is to "save" money by not spending enough. This is particularly true if we consider advertising to be an expense rather than an investment. On the other hand, a tremendous amount of money can be wasted here on the wrong kinds of advertising. We must determine what pays off for us and then use our advertising dollars wisely.

Labor

Use part-time help. Use labor only when you need it. This might seem obvious but it is often abused. We do not have set hours for our help. They are on-call. There are many days when we do not need help, so we don't call. Many high school students and retirees welcome whatever work they can get, and are willing to work under such circumstances. But the secret is to deal with expectations early. Explain the erratic working conditions up front, before they agree to work for you. We encourage our employees to find a different job if they want steady employment, not because we are unhappy with their performance, but because we understand they may want more stable working conditions.

Use a job description. There are times when we need to go beyond part-time help. I have a full-time job and at times it dominates my summer schedule. I must then rely on my employees to keep the garden running without much supervision. I do that with a job description that includes the following elements.

• Weed the garden completely once a week.

• Foliar feed once a week.

• Pick for and attend the Tuesday and Thursday markets.

• Water and irrigate according to the printed schedules.

• Remove the residue from harvesting the Tuesday and Thursday markets.

Keep them informed. Employees want to be involved, they want to make a difference and they want to contribute to the success of the business. If you need data on a new variety, let them know that so they can help collect the information on their own. We share financial data with our employees, because it is an easy measure of success, and they deserve to be a part of that celebration.

Keep them motivated. I read a brilliant one-page article a few years ago on how we do that. The author said we can easily motivate employees if we meet these four needs: The need to achieve, the need for recognition, the need to belong, and the need to be treated fairly. In other words, give them challenging work when possible, reward them for work well done, make them an "owner", and treat them well. It's not that hard to do and the results are amazing!

Marketing

Sarah Vogel, North Dakota's Commissioner of Agriculture sponsors an innovative Marketplace conference to bring successful and potential entrepreneurs together to share information. Workshops are conducted on a wide range of topics from management to production to marketing and everything in between.

In a recent conference, over 100 people attended the workshop on how to grow garlic, yet less than 10 attended a marketing workshop. Therein lies the problem. Entrepreneurs are interested in production, but they are not interested in the most critical aspect of success, marketing. But production is a cake-walk compared to effective marketing. Production will give us more produce, marketing will get us a better price. If we focus on production we may well produce more than what we can sell. If we focus on marketing we will sell all that we produce at the best price.

Marketing must become an obsession. It is the one factor that will push us from the mediocre into the very profitable. So how do we improve marketing skills?

Purchase marketing books. In chapter three we have listed two that are on the market, packed with ideas on innovative marketing. Eric Gibson's *Sell What You Sow* is the better of the two, and should be your first purchase.

Visit other markets. Business trips and vacations are opportunities to visit other direct marketers to gather ideas, to see what is working for them. Talk to them, ask them specific questions. I have not encountered a market gardener that is not willing to share marketing ideas.

Subscribe to marketing newsletters. We have provided reviews for several excellent publications in chapter three. These provide a constant source of fresh marketing ideas.

Experiment. Hours of reading cannot achieve results. You must try those new ideas and see if they work for you. If you have doubts, reread the section in this chapter on intelligent investments. Marketing is an investment worthy of the same commitment of funds that we apply to production.

GARDEN RECORDS

If we do things right, and make a profit, the law requires that we keep records. We keep records for that reason, but we also keep records that directly affect our ability to remain profitable, or become more profitable. Therefore, we will approach our record keeping from both angles. We begin with operational records.

Operational records

Careful record keeping is necessary for maximum production and profit from commercial gardening. It is difficult to make adjustments each year to improve yields if no record exists of what worked and didn't work the year before. Success also demands execution of a well designed plan. The master plan for the year should be entered on a calendar and then adhered to religiously. That is, if you plan to plant your tomato seeds on March 12th, then do that. If you vary by a few days, write that information down so you can make your adjustments for the following year based upon actual data. We consider the following records to be the minimum required for a well managed commercial garden.

The plot plan, figure 4-2 on page 43. This plan should be developed for the next season during your current season. It is a great way to record what you have learned. The underlying plan is driven by the requirement to rotate crops for effective disease control.

The planting plan, figure 5-2 on page 57, is the culmination of the planning process. It incorporates the lessons learned from previous years. For example, if our peppers were not quite large enough on the transplant date the previous year, we adjust our planting by a week of two to correct the problem for the coming season.

The seed plan, figure 5-3 on page 58, provides a means of verifying that all seeds have been identified, ordered, and received. This is critical because we need the right seeds on hand at the right time.

Sales records, figures 5-6 and 5-7 are required to make intelligent quantity adjustments for the next year. Total sales figures do not help much, we need figures by market and product.

Optional records

The following records are highly recommended but are technically optional:

Crop rotation plan, figure 5-4 on page 59. This plan is a convenience because the plot plans for each year can serve as a historical record for crop rotation planning.

Experimentation plan, figure 5-5 on page 61. The most important thing here is that the comparisons need to be documented carefully to determine which experiments work and which should be discarded. This plan is not optional if you intend to conduct extensive variety trials.

The master calendar and diary falls somewhere in between required and optional. I suppose many successful gardeners get by without these management tools. However, I believe they are important and should be included in your management system. These bring the entire planning process together in one place. Projected planning dates are entered on the calendar, and daily notes are recorded on all aspects of the garden. Such records are extremely helpful when planning the garden for the next year.

Paying taxes

Earlier in the book I talked about the potentially traumatic transition required to transcend hobby gardening and enter the world of commercial enterprise. For many people, paying taxes is a large part of that trauma. You are now self-employed. You are now required by law to document your income and expenses. Scary, isn't it? Let me attempt to make this as painless as possible.

• If you don't have a computer, get one. For awhile this purchase may add to your trauma, but in the long run, it will substantially reduce your frustration with accounting and the tax process. Later in this chapter I make specific recommendations on the computer you should purchase.

• Purchase Quickbooks by Intuit. If you plan to have employees, add QuickPay to your purchase. (The Quicken software is so good that the software giant, Microsoft, recently purchased Intuit.) The street price for both of these programs will add only $150 to your investment. [1]

• Get in the habit of saving all of your receipts. You will need these in the case of an audit by the IRS. For example, we purchase some of our marketing bags from our local supermarket. Without a receipt, the IRS has a legitimate suspicion that the check we wrote was for milk and eggs.

• Document your business related travel. Keep a log in your vehicle to record starting and ending odometer readings, and the date and purpose of the trip. This is a nuisance, but automobile deductions are a leading trigger for IRS audits. And audits are not on our short list of neat things to do.

• Be careful about taking a deduction for a home office. Make sure you research the complex rules carefully before you make this decision. It might

create more problems than it will solve. The recent Republican victory promises to ease the restrictions, but only time will tell.

• Show a profit. Take your losses the first two years while you are making your capital investments. But then, show a profit, or the IRS will claim that you are not a serious commercial gardener, that you are just claiming your hobby expenses to reduce your taxes.

THE COMPUTER

We have discussed the records that are necessary for a well documented operation. All of these can be kept manually, but it is so much easier to use a computer. It takes time to learn how to make the computer do what we want done, but in the long run it saves many hours of precious time during those "crazy seasons" that afflict the gardener throughout the year.

If you do not have a computer already, I will attempt to convince you to buy one. If you have one, I will try to teach you new ways to make the machine productive. The power of the computer is the ability:

To handle recurring tasks. Gardening repeats its processes every season. The plans, the documents, the calculations are still there from last year. We do not need to repeat them. This saves time, but it also saves mistakes caused because we forgot something.

To make changes easily. The most obvious use of this power is word processing. I can no longer imagine life without a word processor, without the ability to edit endlessly. But this power also pertains to gardening, as we adjust our plot plan, as we adjust our water and fertilizer, and add names to our list of pickle customers.

To compute things. This is actually an extension of the first element because mathematical computations are just the execution of recurring requirements. However, it warrants special inclusion because of the long list of potential applications, accounting being the most obvious.

Software

Software makers have given us some powerful tools. Trainers have taught us the keystrokes. But in the process, both parties made a tragic mistake. They assumed that the connection between keystrokes and production would be automatic, that the implementation would be obvious to the user. That hasn't been true, and some of the billions of dollars corporate America spent on personal computers has been wasted.

It is this approach I will take in my quest to convince you of the merits of automation in commercial gardening. I will show you what can be done, and in the process hope that the wisdom of a PC purchase will become obvious.

Microsoft Windows and improved computing speeds have made computing available to anyone willing to spend a little time learning. Early software relied on specific keystrokes using the function, shift, control, and alternate keys in a dizzying array of combinations. To make good things happen quickly you needed to memorize these combinations. If you didn't remember, you could use help screens or look it up in the manual.

The next generation of software used drop-down menus, which were much easier to use if you forgot the required keystrokes. However, even with a pointing device these menus were still clumsy.

Windows is a graphical interface between the software and the user. With Windows you simply point at what you want to do with a pointing device, and click the item you want. Many menus are similar so learning times are reduced considerably. Personal computing has matured and is now capable of increasing productivity.

So Windows based software is the key to productive computing. But graphics require considerable computing power.

Fortunately, computers capable of handling Windows graphics are available at very reasonable prices. It is the combination of these two conditions, powerful software, and affordable computers, that makes increased productivity through automation available to the small business.

Software some in hundreds of packages, but like most things, you get what you pay for. It is for that reason that I strongly recommend Microsoft Office. If you are currently a computer user, you can trade up for less then $300. If you are purchasing your first machine, buy one that comes with Office. I recommend the Microsoft Office suite of programs for four reason:

Economy. The competition in the software market is brutal. And the "big" war is being fought over these "suites" of programs. The individual programs retail for about $500 with a street price of $300. When you buy them together, you get them for the price of one program sold separately. Even if you do not plan on using them right now, buy them anyway. They are almost free.

Power. The suites have recently been upgraded to where they are at the cutting edge of current software technology. They have more capability than we might need initially, but the power may come in handy later on as we develop more uses for the computer.

Ease of Use. One of the main thrusts of the Microsoft upgrade process was to develop software that would be easier to use. They have simplified many of the more difficult tasks.

Upgrade. Part of the attraction of this suite is that it is very doubtful if subsequent upgrades will be necessary. These programs have developed over many years, and have finally reached maturity. Improvements will be minor and inconsequential, saving the upgrade costs.

Hardware

To run Windows you need at least a 486 computer with 4MB of RAM and 200 megabytes on the hard drive. However, this minimum configuration does not give you much room for expansion, and it will be a little sluggish. Current prices run around $1000. If you wish to go beyond the minimum, add more RAM because current software has an almost insatiable thirst for it. This will do more to speed up your computer than any other factor.

Any dot matrix printer is fine for what we will be doing unless you want to publish a professional looking newsletter. Then a laser or ink jet printer would be required. Prices of personal laser printers have fallen dramatically over the past few years, and are currently around $600. Ink jets are around $250.

USING THE COMPUTER

We will discuss four tasks that a commercial gardening computer can accomplish for us:
- Track the details to include a calendar, project management, and a to-do list.
- Word processing to include newsletters, correspondence, personalized direct mail.
- Accounting to include tax preparation.
- Database management if you track customers for direct mail or product preferences.

An information manager

I will begin with the most compelling reason to use a computer for management of your garden, tracking the details. Once our business plan is in place, and our direction is clear, success is often determined by how well we handle the details. What details do we need to track?

Events are those items on our calender that require us to be at a specific place at a specific time. There can only be one place where this information is tracked. Deconflicting the calendar requires that we have only one for all aspects of our life. We cannot schedule a business dinner on our anniversary. I suppose we could . . . . but . . .

Projects are those things on our calendar that require tasks to be completed before we arrive at a certain date. Events may be projects. Projects may be events, particularly if our work is not completed on time. Successful completion of projects requires that we fully identify those tasks that must be completed, and then assign milestones to assure they get done.

Details are those mundane but necessary things that must be done everyday to keep the business going, the correspondence, the bills, the phone, and ad nauseam.

The to-do list is composed of pieces of all three of the above categories.

We wrap all of these tasks into a program called a Personal Information Manager, or PIM. There are a number of them on the market to include, Lotus Organizer, OKNA DeskTop Set, Day-Timer, ECCO, and others. Most any of them will work just fine. We use the personal information manager to track the following:

Ordering materials. This supports the concept of anticipation. We start this list very early in the season and add to it as other materials become necessary. This way we can lump our purchases together to save shipping costs. It also ensures that we order the materials so they arrive on time.

The seed plan. After we have completed our planning process, we enter our planting dates in the master calendar.

Experiments. As we go through a season, we often identify ideas that should be tried in future years.

This seems like a lot of work. However, it provides an invaluable historical

191

record for future seasons. It also reduces the work for next year because all we must do is adjust this schedule. Making a personal information manager work requires considerable self discipline, first, to write it all down, and second, to review the data religiously. If we don't do that, we are wasting our time. However, there is tremendous peace of mind in knowing that we haven't lost something, or forgotten to do something.

If you are like most of us, the garden isn't the only thing happening in our lives. We have other roles and responsibilities, and all of these have requirements, and schedules, and details that need to be tracked. Religious use of a PIM makes this tap-dance manageable.

Word Processing

In Annex A we introduce some of the possibilities for newsletters and direct mail advertising. You can hire someone to do that for you, but with a word processing program like Microsoft Word, you can do it yourself at a fraction of the cost.

Word processors have become more powerful but at the same time easier to use. We use Word 6, the latest version from Microsoft. It allows us to do our own newsletter layout, without the hassle of learning a difficult desktop publishing program.

Most word processors have a mail-merge capability. This is what generates the "personalized" mail that you receive from AT&T and Ed McMahon. The letters are generated off a list of names, a database of customers. In the latest generation of computer software, this is much easier than it sounds.

Accounting software

I discussed the use of the computer for accounting earlier in the chapter. In 1992 I purchased Personal Tax Edge for tax preparation. It is capable of reading totals from Quicken and other home accounting software packages. It saves a

tremendous amount of time, and also a few dollars if you are in the habit of having someone else do your taxes.

Database programs

If you decide to do a direct mailing, you will need a database program. Probably the easiest option is to use your word processor or your spreadsheet. Both of these are capable of simple sorting, and searching. The spreadsheet option would provide more capabilities.

Beyond that, database programs run the gamut from relatively simple to extremely complex. Even simplest program will require a few hours to program it to do what you want. I have used Approach from Lotus, and Access from Microsoft. Either of these programs will do an excellent job of database management.

THE EPILOGUE

We have come to the end of the book. I hope it has been an interesting and informative experience. I also hope it has given you a realistic idea of what commercial gardening is, and what it is not. It is a lot of hard work, but work that can be rewarding and profitable. It is not a quick way to get rich.

If you decide to remain a hobby gardener, we hope the ideas presented here make your garden more productive and more enjoyable. If you decide to take the plunge into commercial gardening, we welcome you to this marvelous brotherhood of hard work, and we wish you the best of luck.

If you are serious about implementing some of the ideas presented in this book, we recommend you consider our video and our annual newsletter. A description of both products is on page 207.

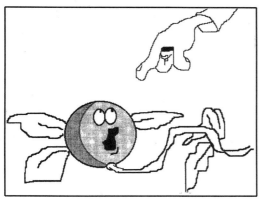

*"Please—don't have cold fingers,
don't have cold fingers, don't have . . ."*

Newsletters and Brochures

Newsletters and brochures can be very effective marketing tools. Fortunately, recent improvements in computers and printers have made these tools available to all of us at a reasonable cost.

A SAMPLE BROCHURE

A brochure is different from a newsletter in that the information should pertain to the entire season. Our real desire is for our customers to keep the brochure for reference throughout the season. In the following paragraphs we include ideas that you can use for your brochure.

What is 'fresh from the garden'?

The following article starts the differentiation process for us. We believe we have the freshest produce at our market. We want customers to know that.

When a home gardener wants fresh beans, he walks into the garden, picks the beans, washes them, cuts them up, cooks them, and serves beans for dinner. That's fresh! Our objective is to get as close to that as possible.

We pick Friday evening for the Saturday morning market. We are not satisfied with this situation but here is no other way to make this market work. The exception is pickles, which we either pre-sell Friday night, or pick early Saturday morning for delivery to the market about 10 AM.

We pick Sunday, Tuesday, and Thursday mornings for those 11 AM and 12 PM markets. If you buy a cuke on those days, it has been picked only hours before. Peppers, zucchini, cabbage, lettuce, peas, onions, and broccoli are always picked in the morning. Beans are sometimes picked the night before and refrigerated. Other exceptions are:

Carrots. Normally carrots are picked the same day they are sold. However, if we know we have too much produce to prepare for market, we sometimes pick carrots the evening before and keep them in water overnight. We have not seen any degradation in quality.

Tomatoes. We pick them after they are mostly ripe on the vine. Why don't we wait until they are complete ripe? Because at that point in the ripening cycle the fruits are very easily damaged. We pick hundreds of pounds each day so we must put the tomatoes in pails, bring them to the preparation area, sort them, and place them in boxes for market. A completely ripe tomato will not stand that much handling without getting soft. And soft or damaged tomatoes don't sell very well.

Flowers. Flowers need to be conditioned in a cool place for several hours. Consequently, we pick our flowers the day before and keep them refrigerated until the next day.

We will never achieve true 'garden fresh'. However, our promise to you is that we will get as close as possible given the quantities we must prepare for market.

The Organic Issue

If you are organic, then make that point clearly. Many people are concerned about chemical use. This is an important distinction to make in a competitive market.

Occasionally we get questions concerning whether we are organic. We are not certified, but we do not spray our vegetables with any insecticides or herbicide. We do use a small amount of synthetic fertilizer to obtain optimum production from our small space.

Meet the gourmet gardeners

We believe it important to introduce yourself to your customers in the brochure with just a few paragraphs. Then elaborate on that with pictures and additional details in the newsletters throughout the season.

Special events

If you have events that will continue throughout the summer, explain them in your brochure. Here are a few examples.

Recipe contest. We are interested in your favorite recipes and are willing to reward you with free vegetables. We will be providing our customers with recipes throughout the season, and if we use yours, we will send you a $5 gift certificate for any purchase at the Gourmet Garden. Please write the recipe on a 3x5 card, and be sure to include your name and address.

Gift Baskets. Last year a friend of ours needed a birthday gift for her boss who had one of almost everything. She asked that we put together a gift basket of flowers and vegetables. It worked great, so this year we have expanded the idea to include a number of different baskets and options.

Have your order ready! If you know what you want to purchase during the next market, just fill out an order form, and we will have it ready for you to pick up when the market opens. This saves time for us at the market, and ensures that you get what you want. Orders will be filled in the order they are received.

What's new this year

You may wish to draw attention to changes you have made in services or products. You will most likely only have space for a few lines concerning each topic. Than additional information can be provided in the newsletters.

The newsletters. For the first time, we will attempt to keep you informed about what is happening at the Gourmet Garden. We will let you know when vegetables will be available, and in what quantities. We will explain what varieties we are

growing and why. And we will provide recipes for using our fresh homegrown garden vegetables. We hope you enjoy the newsletter.

Tomatoes. For the past several years, we have limited our tomato variety to Oregon Spring because they were the earliest we could find. However, they are not a fancy tomato, and by the end of the season, we cannot compete with the fancier varieties.

Therefore, we have added two varieties to our production. Stokes seeds has an Ultrasweet tomato which provides a unique balance of sugar and acids for a tasty sweet flavor. It is an indeterminate variety so we should be able to get good late harvests. Johnny's 361 is a 'beefsteak' variety from Johnny's Selected Seeds. It has 8oz meaty fruits that should arrive short after the Oregon Springs.

Edible flowers. Caroline is experimenting with edible flowers. Our research indicates that both coasts have a big market for edibles. They look marvelous in fresh salads and taste good as well.

Beans. We have returned to pole beans for our green bean customers. They are a better tasting bean, and will produce all season. However, they mature a bit later than bush beans, so we may not always have the first beans at the market.

You will notice that we pick our beans much smaller than many at the market. Optimum taste is achieved when the beans are picked before the seeds start bulging through the pod. Give ours a try and we are sure you will return for another pound of these delicious green beans.

NEWSLETTERS

Newsletters differ from the brochure in that the information is perishable. We recommend that you include the following information:

How is the weather affecting production? Customers know what the weather has been but they may not know what that means to your garden. Many of them have been gardeners in the past, and take a vicarious interest in what is happening in the garden from which they purchase their vegetables.

How are your experiments going? We must always work at improving our service to our customers. One of the ways we do that is by improving production and by adding products to our operation. For example, we are trying to grow lettuce all season because so many customers prefer fresh leaf lettuce over supermarket head lettuce. It is a simple spring crop, but summer presents challenges that could be explained in the newsletter without getting too technical.

How are different varieties producing? I believe that one of our marketing opportunities is to educate our customers. Many of them know little about gardening, even though the subject may fascinate them. To many customers, the hundreds of available varieties are a complete mystery. By explaining the difference, we establish credibility as a professional gardener.

What promotions are coming up? We know that cucumbers will soon be in oversupply. Perhaps a simple promotion might move a few for us.

Recipes. Include at least one recipe for the vegetable currently in oversupply.

Promote canning and start early. Our first issue starts customers thinking about canning. We include a simple pickle or salsa recipe starting with the second issue.

The following paragraphs provide some useful ideas for your newsletter.

Pickles and Slicers

If you do something unique, draw attention to it! This article could be in the brochure if room is available.

We grow pickles and sell them for slicers. You might think that a bid odd, but listen to the experts. The first quote is from Lenard Pike, professor of horticulture and cucumber breeder at Texas A&M University.

"I never eat slicers. In fact, of all the people I know in cuke research, I don't know anyone who will take a fresh market slicing cucumber home and eat it. I wish we could get that across to the home gardener. The pickling types have such a thin skin — you can just pick them up and eat them, adding a little salt and lemon juice if you like. Plus they're crisp. And they're dual purpose — you can pickle them or eat `em fresh."

The second quotation is from Joanna Poncavage, a senior editor for Organic Gardening magazine. In the May/June 1992 issue she published an entire article on the advantages of growing pickles for fresh eating.

"I confess. I like a pickling cucumber better than slicing cucumber for fresh eating. A pickler's flesh seems smoother and more fine-grained; and its skin is usually thinner so you don't have to peel it. I eat them straight off the vine."

Case closed!!

The best way to pick a melon

Customers are always interested in useful information, particularly if it pertains to produce and the market.

There is no comparison between the taste of a fresh melon and the taste of one shipped from 400 miles south. The sweetness of a melon is determined by variety, growing conditions, and when it is picked. Melons that must be shipped are picked a bit green so they can survive the trip without damage. Although they will ripen and sweeten, they will never achieve the sweetness of a melon picked at the right time. It is for these reasons that melons are very popular at the Farmers Market.

The trick is to pick out the right melon, the ripe one that is ready to eat as soon as you get home. Sometimes you see customers knocking on cantaloupes to see if they are ripe. If you are experienced, this might work since the seeds of ripe melons are less firmly attached than unripe ones. You might be able to hear them rattle if your hearing is superb. However, there are easier, more reliable ways to check for ripeness.

1. Smell. A ripe cantaloupe gives off a sweet aroma when they are ready to eat.

2. Press on the blossom end where the melon was attached to the plant. If it feels soft when pressed on, the melon is most likely too ripe.

3. Check the netting. It should be cream colored and the background should be golden yellow. If either is green, the melon isn't ripe.

We do not grow melons because we do not have the space. However, if the season is warm enough and long enough, melons should show up in mid to late August.

Order your pickles

The pickle season is approaching rapidly. Last year pickles were in extremely short supply. This year it appears that quantities will be adequate to satisfy the demand. An early frost might change that, but that is impossible to forecast.

The best pickles are made from fresh cucumbers. Consequently, we want to provide you with the produce when you are ready to make your pickles. We can do that in several ways.

1. Order you pickles for delivery at the market on a given day. This is available on Sundays, Tuesdays, and Thursdays.

2. Pickup your pickles at the garden on Friday night.

3. Volunteer for short notice delivery of excess pickles. We never know exactly what the garden will produce on a given day. Experience allows us to get quite close, but sometimes we have a few that are not spoken for. Once they are picked, we must sell them quickly or they will start to wilt. Early in the season we simply bring them to market. However, as the number of pickle customers diminishes, this becomes harder to do. Therefore, we like to have a list of customers who would be willing to take pickles on short notice. We start calling the customers on this list until we sell the pickles. In return for this convenience, we discount the price by one third. This is the best option for quantity pickle producers.

Please fill out the form at the bottom of this page, and we will contact you if we need any more information. Normally, we will call to verify delivery. If you opt for delivery at a market, we will only hold the pickles until 30 minutes after the market has opened unless other arrangements are made.

What do you want?

For the past few years we have concentrated on producing the standard crops and a limited number of varieties. Our production and marketing system is now capable of adding specialty crops and varieties.

What do you want us to grow? Perhaps you know of a unique variety of eggplant, or an heirloom tomato. Perhaps you have a craving for okra, or Chinese cabbage.

Let us know and we might be able to deliver next year. There is no obligation on your part, and no guarantee that we will be successful in growing your special request. However, it's worth a try.

Garden tours

We will provide customer tours of the Gourmet Garden during the first two weeks of August because some of you may be interested in seeing how your produce is grown. We use raised beds, drip irrigation, trellises, protective cloches, and many other intensive gardening techniques that have fascinated many of the visitors to the garden. Highlights of the tour are:

• The 63 raised beds that grow your vegetables.

• A discussion on the techniques we use to bring produce to the market early.

• Drip irrigation principles including fertilization through the system and our control system.

• Our market preparation area that allows us bring you the freshest vegetables possible.

Tours will be conducted at 7 PM on Tuesday, Thursday, and Sunday evenings. Because of parking limitations, we will only take twenty people for each tour. Drop off the registration card the next time you visit the stand, and we'll get you scheduled for the tour.

Extend your pepper season!

In a few weeks, the first frost will destroy our pepper plants. Peppers are very sensitive to frost so it may be impossible to protect them.

We will pick all of the peppers on the plants and offer them to you at a very good price. These peppers can be used for freezing, canning, or drying, and will provide 'fresh' peppers throughout the winter.

We will sell these peppers for $10 for a full bushel basket, $5 for a half, or $2 for a large sack and $1 for a small sack. If you want some of these peppers, please let us know so we can reserve some for you. Obviously we do not know exactly when this will happen. We will call you when we pick them and arrange for delivery.

Peppers are easy to freeze. Wash well, remove stems, cut in half and remove seeds and membranes. Slice into strips. You can pack them directly into the freezer bags, or flash freeze them in the open and then bag them. They can also be blanched for 2 minutes, and cooled rapidly in ice water. They can be stored for about a year.

When you use your frozen peppers, they cut much easier while they are still they are still frozen. This tip comes from *Horticulture* magazine, September 1988. "The only vegetable that we freeze a winter supply of is green peppers. The price of peppers shoots sky-high every winter, making it worthwhile to lay by a homegrown supply. Furthermore, they require no blanching before freezing. Consequently we simply slice up the end-of-season surplus into strips and pack them in small plastic bags (The kind with the built-in zipper), one pepper per bag. These bags take so little space in the freezer and the contents are so welcome in stir-fried dishes, that they have become a family staple."

This suggestion comes from Herb Johnson, Raleigh, NC, *National Gardening,* December 1988. "When frost finally threatens, I gather the last of my pepper crop, set aside those of table quality, then core and puree the rest in my blender. I pour the course puree in ice-cube trays, freeze them, and store the cubes in plastic bags. They're wonderful added to spaghetti sauce, Creoles, chilies, and jambalayas."

The final tomato packs.

As the end of the season approaches, and frost become eminent, our attention turns to the tomatoes remaining on the vines. It seems such a waste to just put them on the compost pile. So we will offer them to you in special packs that will extend the tomato season for a month or so.

Immature tomatoes are very hard and solid green. These will not ripen and we will not bring them to market. *Mature green tomatoes* are still quite firm and the bottom may be slightly yellow-green. Most of these will ripen. The more yellow there is, the more likely the tomato will ripen. *Breakers* are starting to turn pink. These will ripen in about ten days at room temperature.

To hasten ripening. A mature tomato produces ethylene gas which triggers the ripening process. If you place a very ripe tomato in a bag with a greener tomato, the green tomato will ripen faster because of the ethylene gas from the riper fruit.

To retard ripening. Tomatoes need oxygen to ripen. You can slow down the ripening process by placing two pounds of tomatoes in a freezer bag. That will reduce the oxygen level and slow down the ripening process. Temperature is the other factor that can be controlled. At 80° tomatoes ripen too quickly, at 55° they will turn into a mealy mess. (That is why tomatoes should never be refrigerated.) You can store mature tomatoes in a plastic bag at 59° (basement temperature) for about three weeks. Open the bag, let the oxygen in, and you will have deep-red fruit in 4-7 days.

If you mix breakers with mature tomatoes in the bag, the mature fruits will have a much higher chance of ripening because of the ethylene gas given off by the breakers.

So what's the point of all this? We will provide a flat of tomatoes at various stages of maturity. Some will be almost ready to eat, others will be breakers, and then we will add a few mature green tomatoes. If you follow the suggestions above, you should have ripe, homegrown tomatoes 3-5 weeks after frost has destroyed the crop.

So how many tomatoes do you need? If you eat an average of four pounds of tomatoes a week, you will need 16-20 pounds of tomatoes. A flat is 7-8 pounds, so you will need 2 or 3 flats.

We ask that you order these because they will all come at once, after that first frost. We will call you to set up a delivery time.

Canning

Beans. Planning to can some green beans? Within a few weeks, bean harvest will be in full production. We will offer our beans at $1.15 per pound for purchases of 5 pounds or more. Please let us know in advance when you want them so we can have the beans ready for you.

Dill Pickles

   13 cups water
   6 cups vinegar
   1 cup canning salt
   1 pinch powdered alum
   1 clove garlic
   dill
   Combine water, vinegar and canning salt. Boil for 15 minutes. Pack cukes in jar leaving 1 inch space at the top. Add 1 or 2 heads of dill per quart jar. Put 1 pinch powdered alum, 1 garlic clove in each jar. Pour hot brine over and seal tight.

Make sure you use fresh picklers. They must be picked only a few hours before using for best results. If they are a day old or more, they will be soft, mushy, and possibly hollow.

A few canning tips

To prepare your jars for canning, run your finger around the rim to check for nicks. A jar will not seal if the lip is not smooth. Use the jar for something else, because it is no good for canning.

To sterilize the jars, run the jars through a cycle on the dishwasher or boil them in a kettle of water. You should also sterilize your lids by placing them in boiling water. Let them boil for at least 15 minutes.

Now you are ready to start canning. A plastic wide mouth funnel will come in handy (metal funnels sometimes gets too hot to handle). Place the funnel in the mouth of the jar. Using a soup ladle, fill the jars to an inch from the top. Wipe the mouth of the jars off with a clean damp cloth to remove any particles that may keep your jar form sealing. Remove the lid from the boiling water with tongs, place on the jar and screw on band.

Make sure you have space between the jars while cooling. Once they've sealed, they can be put in storage.

RECIPES

Here are a few useful recipes. Always include one or two in your newsletters that use produce that is in oversupply. It will help sell a few.

Zucchini Relish

10 cups zucchini, grated
4 large onions
4 red peppers
5 tbls salt
2 tsp celery seed
1/2 tsp pepper
2 1/2 cups vinegar
6 cups sugar
1 tbls nutmeg
1 tbls turmeric
1 tbls cornstarch

Chop vegetables and sprinkle with salt. Let set 4 hours. Drain. Add vinegar, sugar and spices to

vegetables and cook 30 minutes. Seal in jars. Makes about 7 pints.

Good for hot dogs, hamburgers or in tartar sauce.

Combo Salsa

24 cups or 6 qts. Skinned tomatoes
3 cups chopped onions
3 chopped green peppers
6 Tbls crushed chili peppers
3 cloves garlic or 2 1/2 /tbls garlic powder
1/2 cup chopped jalepeno peppers
1 Tbls canning salt
1 Tbls chili powder
2 Tbls cumin
1 Tbls sugar
1-2 Tbls vinegar (to taste)

Mix and boils 15 minutes. Add 2 cans of tomato paste. (May need more depending on how thick you like it) Make sure salsa is boiling put in jars and seal..

Tip: To peel tomatoes, dip tomato into boiling water for 30 seconds. Skins should slip off.

Tomato relish

9 lbs. Tomatoes (cut, peeled, don't scald these to peel on this recipe)
2 lbs. Celery cut fine
7 large onions cut fine

Mix in 1 cup canning salt, let set 30 minutes. Drain overnight. In the morning, mix 2 cups vinegar, 4 1/2 cups sugar, 1 1/2 oz. Mustard seed

2 red and 2 green peppers cut fine. Mix together with tomato mixture and stir well. Put in jars. Don't seat tight. Keeps in refrigerator indefinitely.   Yields 8 pints

We hope these ideas will help you publish an interesting and effective newsletter.

This annex provides additional information on sources that you might find helpful in your continued research. Numbered paragraphs refer to the footnotes found in each chapter.

Most of the magazine articles mentioned here should be available at your local library.

The books referenced here are available from your local book store. We include the ISBN number because they all use this system to order books when they are not available.

Chapter 1 - Introduction

1. From the promotional literature for "Growing for Market", a monthly newsletter edited by Lynn Byczynski. Ordering information is on page 14.

2. Jon P. Goodman is the director of the University of Southern California Entrepreneur Program. His article, *What Makes an Entrepreneur* was in the October 1994 issue of INC, Magazine. This magazine is highly recommended because as commercial gardeners we are also entrepreneurs.

3. From the book, "Gardening; The Complete Guide to Growing America's Favorite Fruits and Vegetables", National Gardening Association, page 11. Charles Scott was president of the association when this book was published in 1986. ISBN 0-201-10855-0

4. From the book, "High Yield Gardening", by Marjorie Hunt and Brenda Bortz, published by Rodale Press in 1986. ISBN 0-87857-599-5

Chapter 2 - Commercial Gardening

1. Jim Hightower is a former Commissioner of Agriculture in Texas. This quote is from the foreword to Andy Lee's book, "Backyard Market Gardening", published in 1993 by Good Earth Publications.

2. From the foreword of "Sell What You Sow" by Eric Gibson, published by New World Publishing in 1994. ISBN 0-9632814-0-2 Bud Kerr, Jr is the director of the USDA Office for Small-Scale Agriculture. Ordering information for his newsletter is on page 14.

3. See 1-2.

4. From an editorial in the American Vegetable Grower, September 1994. This monthly magazine is well worth the $14 subscription price. It provides many articles of interest to the small grower. Write

Footnotes

to AVG, 37733 Euclid Avenue, Willoughby, OH, 44094-5992. Gary Acuff lists three conditions that all small operations to thrive: Direct marketing, unique products, and intensive production. Amen!

Chapter 3 - Marketing

2. Andy Lee is the author of "Backyard Market Gardening". Notice that he says "maximum profitability". He's absolutely right. However, there are other problems with a farm stand that might remove it from your list of possibilities.

The following quotes are from the book, "Sell What You Sow" by Eric Gibson.

1. Kelso Wessel is an agricultural economist.

3. Bob Reynolds is a marketing consultant from Moraga, CA

4 and 8. Matty Matarazzo operates Matarazzo Farms in New Jersey.

5. Wayne Weber is from North Fairfield, OH.

6. Steve Hall is from Wayne, NE

7. Dan Block is an agricultural marketing consultant from California.

Chapter 4 - Commercial Design and construction

The Nuts and Bolts of Drip Irrigation from National Gardening magazine, June 1988, pages 40-43. This is an excellent introduction to drip irrigation. There are also several other articles in this issue related to water use.

Chapter 5 - Planning

If you plan to conduct variety trials, I recommend an article by Deborah Wechsler in the February 1987 issue of Organic Gardening entitled, *Do Your Own Variety Trials*. It contains solid advice on how to make the trials accurate and productive.

Chapter 6 - Growing Transplants

1. Piedmont is a very reputable firm that specializes in transplants. They can be reached at (912) 883-7029 or at PO Box 424, Albany, GA 31703. We have ordered from them several times, and have had excellent success. We do recommend that you air freight the plants.

2. If you plan to grow any transplants, get a copy of Nancy Bubel's book, "The New Seed Starters Handbook" from Rodale Press. It is absolutely essential, ISBN 0-87857-752-1.

3. Large plastic trays are available from Gardeners Supply, 128 Intervale Rd, Burlington, VT 05401. 802-863-1700

4. See 6-2.

5, 6, 7. From an article in the February 1989 issue of Horticulture magazine, *The Art of Transplanting* by Shepherd Odgen. Pages 24-26.

Chapter 10 - Beans

1. As quoted in an article by Shepherd Ogden, National Gardening, May 1993, *The dean of beans*. A superb article from an interview with an expert.

2. From *The Care and Feeding of Beans* by Betty Besal in the June 1987 issue of National Gardening. A superb six-page article that covers the gamut of growing beans. A side-bar provides the most complete explanation of inoculants I have seen.

3. If you live in an area of temperature extremes, or want to grow early beans, read Diane Bilderbacks article in the August 1987 issue of Organic Gardening, *Better Beans*.

Bush bean varieties are discussed in Kent Martin's article in the April 1991 issue of Organic Gardening, *Forgiving filets, full-flavored wax, big-yielding blues, and technicolor romanos.*

Chapter 11 - Cabbage

1. *Sweeter Cabbages* by Jack Cook, Organic Gardening, April 1988. Excellent general article on raising cabbages. If you are interested in filet beans, the same issue has an article by Shepherd Ogden.

2 and 4. *Quality Cabbage* by Diane Bilderback, National Gardening, September 1987. Best article I have seen on explaining the differences between varieties.

3. *Plant Yourself a Cabbage Patch* by Vicki Mattern, Organic Gardening, December 1994. Complete article on variety selection through growing and harvest.

Mastering Chinese Cabbage by Shepherd Ogden, Horticulture, June 1990, pages 32-36. Excellent article on varieties and specific growing requirements.

Chapter 12 - Carrots

1. *Garden-Grown Gold* by Kent Martin, February 1988 issue to Organic Gardening. Excellent article on the best tasting carrots. Since taste is the most important factor in variety selection, the article is worth finding in the library.

2. *Carrots* by Warren Schultz, horticultural editor for National Gardening Magazine, in their December 1986 issue. Another superb article on all varieties. Contains advice for southern gardeners.

3. We include this quote to bring attention to the many fine references available from the universities across the country. The University of Illinois has a number of publications tailored to growing conditions in that state. However, these circulars provide plenty of useful information to us all. We recommend that you look to the extension service or university in your state for publications that might address growing problems in your area.

4. Our final quote is from Shepherd Odgen in the Jul/Aug 1993 issue of National Gardening, *Carrot Tricks*. He discusses the finer points of growing carrots.

Chapter 13 - Cucumbers

1. As quoted by Joanna Poncavage in her May/June 1992 Organic Gardening article, *Cukes: Plant Now, Pickle Later!* Dr. Wehner is the cucumber breeder at North Carolina State University. I believe this article puts to rest the issue of eating picklers fresh. If you have doubts, look up this reference.

2. As quoted in *Put up yer cukes!* National Gardening. June 1988 by Warren Schultz. This article explains the differences between cucumber varieties and outlines the advantages of each. Rob Johnston is president of Johnny's Selected Seeds.

3. *Cucumber Complex,* National Gardening, July 1990 by Emily Stetson, the magazine's managing editor. Another good article on the differences between varieties.

Chapter 14 - Onions

1. *Mild-mannered onions*, National Gardening, August 1988, by Shepherd Ogden. This article provides growing guidelines for mild onions as well as selection recommendations.

2. From the book, "Gardening", page 182. We include this quote to draw attention to this marvelous reference by the National Gardening Association. It has been one of our primary sources of information since we started.

Dave Skilton has an article in the January 1987 issue of Organic Gardening on *Onions from Seed*. This provides the basics for starting your own onions, regardless of variety.

Chapter 15 - Peas

1. From the April 1987 issue of National Gardening, Diane Bilderback's article entitled, *More peas, please*. This is an excellent article on all phases of pea production.

2. From the February 1989 issue of National Gardening. Shepherd Odgen's article, *Easy pickin's* covers various varieties with a side bar on growing fall peas. It also contains drawings on building a trellis for peas, and a complete explanation on succession planting.

Chapter 17 - Tomatoes

1. From a February 1987 National Gardening article by Warren Schultz, *Earliest tomatoes ever*. The article is worth looking up because it describes additional techniques that can be used for growing early tomatoes.

2. From a February 1991 article in Organic Gardening by Andrea Ray Chandler, *Ruby Red by Memorial Day*.

3. As quoted in an article by Scott Meyer in the September 1994 issue of Organic Gardening, *Pick No Produce Before its Prime!*. This is one of the finest articles I have seen on the right time to pick vegetables. Since we are concerned with optimum taste at the market, I strongly recommend you look at this entire article.

4. This is the introduction to an article by Vicki Mattern in the November 1994 issue of Organic Gardening, *Get Your Earliest Tomatoes Ever!*. I believe that many of these season extending

techniques have commercial potential. We will try protective tunnels next spring to attempt full tomato production by the opening of market. The investment required will be substantial but we believe we can recoup that cost in the first few weeks.

Chapter 19 - Other Crops

In this chapter we include quotes from several books on market gardening. They all have their strengths and should be considered by anyone serious about commercial gardening. I don't believe you can do too much research. Every reference contains ideas that will more than pay for purchase price of the book.

1. First written in 1974, John Jeavon's "How to Grow More Vegetables than you ever thought possible on less land than you can imagine", has become a classic. Many of our intensive gardening techniques originated from this book. ISBN 0-89815-073-6

2. It is fascinating, if not helpful, to learn more about botany. The best book I have found on the subject is Brian Capon's "Botany for Gardeners". It was published in 1990 by Timber Press. ISBN 0-88192-258-7

3. From the "Farmer's Market Cook Book" published by Better Homes and Gardens. This book contains recipes listed by crop which makes it useful for peak season surpluses. ISBN 0-696-01985-X

4. Michael Olson's "Metrofarm, The Guide to Growing for Big Profit on a Small Parcel of Land" is a recent addition to my library. It was written as a textbook but has good information for growers as well. ISBN 0-963787-60-8

5. There are several books on starting a herb business. This quote is from "Growing your Herb Business" by Bertha Reppert. ISBN 0-88266-612-6

6. From "Flowers For Sale, Growing and Marketing Cut Flowers" by Lee Sturdivant. ISBN 0-9621635-1-1

7. From "Market Gardening, Growing and Selling Produce" by Ric Staines. Though based upon produce markets in England, it has much useful information for growers in this country. ISBN 1-55591-100-5

Chapter 20 - The Business of Gardening

I purchase my software from Micro Warehouse in Lakewood, NJ, 1-800-367-7080. I have had superb service from this company and their prices are very competitive.

Computers are generally cheaper from mail-order companies. We have had excellent success in using these suppliers. However, we do recommend that you purchase from a company that has been in business for a few years. And a few extra dollars spent for a Dell, an IBM, or a Compaq is probably well invested.

SUPPLIERS

In this final section we provide phone numbers and addresses of vendors that supply products required for a successful commercial garden.

Commercial seed companies

Most of the seed company catalogs are advertised in gardening magazines, and the business reply cards are the easiest way to get them. Many of these companies also have commercial divisions that cater to those of us with larger gardens. However, you must request their commercial catalogs. These companies include:

W. Atlee Burpee, 300 Park Ave., Warminister, PA 18991-0002

Harris Seeds, PO Box 22960, Rochester, NY 14692-2960

Johnny's Selected Seeds, Foss Hill Road, Albon, ME 04910

Stokes Seeds Inc., Box 548, Buffalo, NY 14240

Park Seed, Cokesbury Rd., Greenwood, SC 29647

We use a regional commercial supplier for many of our standard seeds. They also have a good supply of other growing and marketing items.

Jordan Seeds, Inc, 6400 Upper Afton Road, Woodbury, MN 55125, 612/738-3422

Then there are some companies that are not quite so obvious, but are important commercial and specialty seed sources:

The Cook's Garden, PO Box 535, Londonderry, VT 05148

Garden City Seeds, 1324 Red Crow Rd., Victor, MT 59875

Fred C. Gloeckner Co., 15E. 26th St., New York, NY 10010

G.S. Grimes Seeds, 201 W. Main St., Smethport, PA 16749

Harris Seeds, PO Box 22960, Rochester, NY 14692-2960

Mellinger's, 2310 W. South Range Rd., North Lima, OH 44452

Nichols Garden Nursery, 1190 N. Pacific Hwy., Albany, Or 97321

Shepherd's Garden Seeds, 6116 Hwy 9, Felton, CA 95018

Thompson & Morgan, PO Box 1308, Jackson, NJ 08527 (THE catalog for flowers.)

Basket and packaging suppliers

Once we have our seeds planted, we must turn our attention to marketing. These companies provide a complete line of packaging supplies.

Monte Package Company, 1-800-653-2807

Putnam Plastics, 1-800-457-3099

ITC Orchard and Turf Supply, 1-800-468-0649

A final piece of advice

We could continue listing suppliers for many pages. The best advice we can give you is to subscribe to some of the industry publications. They will supply articles and advertising to introduce you to the other suppliers you need to fulfill your commercial gardening requirements. Here are a few suggestions.

The address from the American Vegetable Grower is on page 199.

The address for the newsletter, Growing for Market, is on page 14. They have an annual Buyer's guide that lists hundreds of suppliers.

New World Publishing has many books on related topics. Eric Gibson's book, "Sell What You Sow", has the finest resource list available anywhere. New World's new address is 3085 Sheridan St., Placerville, CA 95667. The phone number is 916-642-1212

Finally, contact your state agricultural department or direct marketing association. These organizations are sources of invaluable information for your area. Most states also have annual conferences where you can get great information and talk to other growers who may be struggling with the same problems you have.

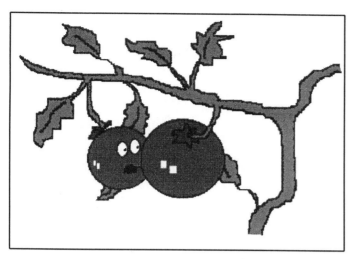

"You mean we get eaten alive, and he makes $10,000 bucks?"

Index

A

Accounting 191
Accounting software 192
Acre 15
Adjusting production 61
Advertising 37, 186
Andrew W. Lee 38
Annual Statice 183
Annuals 181
Armitage, Allan M. 183
Aster Yellows 125

B

Baby's Breath 183
Bacillus thuringiensis 115
Backyard, defined 11
Backyard Market Gardening 38
Base price 30
Beans 57, 62, 194
  diseases 105, 108
  growing 105, 107
  harvesting 105, 109, 96
  marketing 107, 109
  pests 105, 108
  planning 104, 105, 106, 107
  varieties 105, 107, 109, 110
  varietites 104
Bees 138, 140
Bismarck farmers market 31
Blossom end rot 170
Bolt resistance 113
Books, recommended 14
Broccoli
  growing 178
  marketing 178
Brochures 36, 193

Bulbs 181
Burpee 146

C

Cabbage 57, 61
  diseases 112
  growing 112, 114
  harvesting 112, 115
  havesting 96
  interplanting 115
  marketing 114, 116
  pests 112, 113, 115
  planning 111, 112, 114
  varieties 112, 114
Cabbage worms 88
Cages 50
  construction 165
Calcium 81
Canning tips 197
Carrot 61
Carrots 57
  diseases 120
  growing 120, 123
  harvesting 96, 120
  harvets 126
  marketing 122, 126
  pests 120
  planning 119, 120, 122
  varieties 120, 122
Cauliflower 118
Certified organic growers 65
Chlorine 41
Cistern 40
Cloches 50, 110, 146
  construction 130
  installation 137
  removal 137

Color
  effective use of 28
Commercial garden, defined 9
Community supported agriculture 23, 24
Composting 13, 71, 83, 151
  equipment 83
  materials 83
  procedure 84
  water content 84
Computers 189
  hardware 191
  software 190
Construction planning 51
Controlling costs 186
Crop placement 60
Crop rotation 60
Crop selection 53
Cucumbers
  growing 132, 137
  harvesting 132, 140, 96
  marketing 134, 142
  planning 131, 132
  varieties 131, 134
Cultivator 49
Customer education 35
Customer service 18
Cutworms 88

D

Database management 191
Database programs 192
Determinate tomatoes 163
Developing loyalty 27
Developing strategies 22
Dill
  for pickles 177
  interplanting 177
Direct mail 36
Direct marketing 24

Disease control 90
Disease resistance 132
Disease tolerance
  beans 106
Diseases 79
Double-cropping 115, 117, 120
Drainage 18, 42
Dried flowers 183
Drip irrigation 13, 19, 49
  construction 45
Dual-chambered hose 46

E

Early market 22
  defined 21
Edible flowers 194
Entertainment agriculture 23, 25
Entrepreneur 10
Equipment for harvesting 94
Eric Gibson 38, 187
Esthetics 18
Experimentation plan 60

F

Farmers markets
  fees 27
  joining 27
  pricing policies 27
  principles 31
  starting 27
Fence 44
Fertilizer, liquid 82
Fertilizing 80
Financing expansion 10
Florists 23
Flowers 21
  garden design 181
  germination 182
  harvesting 182
  planning 181
  selection 181
Food preservation 35
  dill pickle recipe 197
  freezing 106
Food processing 32
Frost free date 56, 99
Frost tolerance 99, 118

G

Garden cleanup 98
Garden design 44
Garden timing
  for the home gardener 63
Garden tours 34, 196
Gardening methods 22

Garlic
  growing 176
  harvest 177
  timing planting 176
German Statice 183
Germination
  mix 72
  problems 107, 110, 119, 124
  racks 73
  temperature 100
  time 100
Gift baskets 194
Gladiolas 183
Grass clippings 83
Grasshoppers 88
Greenhouse 13, 50
  construction 67
  equipment 67
  fertilizing 75
  kits 67
  operations 73
  soils 71
  space estimates 69
  temperature 77
  ventilation 77
  watering 75
Greenhouse problems
  light 77
  temperature 77
  water 77
Grocery stores 23
Growing mix 72
Growing temperature 100
Growing transplants
  advantages 65
  disadvantages 65
Gyonecious 132
Gypsum 151

H

Hail 91, 144
  protection 170
Hail damage 175
Hardening off 76, 138
Harvest
  management 97, 140
  records 97
  residue 83
Heat tolerance 154
Home delivery 23
Home gardens
  competition from 12
Home office deduction 189
Hoop houses 67
Hybrid lilies 183

I

In-line emitters 46
Indeterminate tomatoes 163
Inoculant 108
Insect life cycles 89
Insecticide
  damage from 175
Insects 79, 115
Integrated pest management 87
Intensive gardening 18
Intensive spacing 121, 99
Interplanting 19,
    107, 110, 115, 120, 127, 154
Investment
  estimated 49
Investments 185
Irrigation 85
  calculating water needs 85
Irrigation hose
  installation 135
Irrigation manifold
  construction 48
Irrigation system
  construction 48

J

Job description 187
Johnny's Select Seeds 156
Johnny's Select Seeds 146
Johnny's Selected Seeds 156, 194
Jordan Seeds 107

L

Labor 186
Lady Bugs 88
Leaf spot 170
Lettuce
  growing 179
  varieties 179
Light racks 73
Lime 41
Location 11

M

Magazines 14
Magnesium 81
Manure 45, 84
Market 11
Market analysis 26
Market manager 27
Market phases 28, 142
Marketing 9, 11, 17, 187
  budget 35
  cooperative 27
  equipment 50

method 22
stand 32, 95
strategies 104
Master planting plan 58
Maturity dates 56, 99
Mechanical planter 123, 128
Media 33
Melon, how to pick 195
Microsoft Windows 190
Money-back guarantee 18
Mononecious 131
Mulch 13, 19, 84,
    108, 144, 151, 174

N

Name recognition 33
Newsletters 13, 36, 193
Newspapers 38
Niche Market 21
Nitrogen 41, 80, 81, 109, 125, 155,
    177
    developing estimates for 81
Nutrient deficiencies 79

O

On-farm sales 23, 25
Onion sets 147
Onions 58, 61
    as a niche crop 54
    diseases 148
    growing 148
    harvest 148, 151
    harvesting 97
    long-day 147
    marketing 150, 152
    pests 148, 151
    planning 147, 148, 150
    short-day 147
    storage 148, 153
    sulfur content 147
    sweet 147, 152
    varieties 147, 150
Organic fertilizers 82
Organic gardening 42, 193
Organic matter 41

P

Packaging 32
Parthenocarpic 132
Peas 58
    diseases 155
    growing 154, 155
    harvest 155
    harvesting 96
    marketing 156

pests 155
    planning 154, 155, 156
    varieties 154, 156
Peat 71
Pelletized seed 128
Pelletized seeds 123
Pepper 62
    harvest 161
Peppers 58, 196, 197
    growing 159
    harvesting 97
    marketing 161
    planning 157
    protection 159
    varieties 157
Perennials 181, 183
Perlite 71
Personal Information Manager 191
Pest control 14
Pests
    chemical controls 88
    organic controls 88
pH 40, 41, 100
Phases
    garden development 20
Phosphorous 155
Phosphorus 41, 80, 109
Photosynthesis 80
Pick-your-own 23, 25
Pickles 141, 143, 145, 195
Piedmont Plant Company 65, 149
Planning 185
Plant hardiness 56
Plant protection 21, 165
Planting depth 100
Plastic bags 32
Plastic mulch 85
Pollination 138, 140, 144
Potassium 41, 80, 109, 155
Potatoes
    growing 178
    harvest 179
Press releases 34
Price cutting 12
Price resistance 30
Pricing
    problems 143
Pricing produce 29
Propagation 99
Public presentations 34

Q

Quickbooks 189

R

Radio 37
Raised bed 16
Raised beds 13, 18
    construction 44
    supported, construction 52
Raspberries
    growing 180
    marketing 180
    pruning 180
    varieties 180
Recipe contest 194
Recipes 35
Refrigeration 109
Restaurant 24
Restaurants 23
Retail marketing 25
Retail sales 26
Roadside stand 23, 25

S

Salsa
    recipe 198
Sawdust 124, 128
Sea Lavender 183
Seed plan 58
Seed starting equipment 50
Seed viability 99
Sell What You Sow 38, 187
Shredder 49
Signs 17, 28
Site selection 39
Soaker hoses 46
Soil
    analysis 41
    compaction 18
    condition 41
    mix 134, 153
    preparation 119
    test 81
    texture 119

Soil temperature 105
    guide for planting 106, 107
Spaghetti tubes 46
Specialty Cut Flowers 183
Spray-N-Grow 81, 139
Spun fabric 124, 125, 169, 186
Squash
    crooked neck 175
    marketing 178
    winter 178
Stokes 134, 114, 122, 194
Storage 95
Storage building 50

Strategies for success 16
Strawberries
    growing 180
    varieties 180
Strawflowers 183
Stress tolerance
    cucumbers 133
Submatic 47
Subscription marketing 24
Subscription sales 26
Subscription services 23, 24
Succession planting 111, 120
Sulfur 41, 81
Summer squash 173
Supermarkets 26

T

Taxes 189
Television 34, 37
Thinning 108, 125
Tomato relish recipe 198
Tomatoes 194
    diseases 170
    growing 165
    harvest 170
    harvesting 97
    how to ripen 197
    marketing 171
    pests 170
    planning 163
    pruning 170
    varieties 163
    watering 169
Transplants 21
    cucumber 134
    onions 148
    optimum age 57
    peppers 159
    tomatoes 165
Trellis 13, 50, 110, 146, 154, 156
    construction 129
    installation 135
    netting 144
    training vines on 138
Twine, cutting 131

V

Vermiculite 71
Vertical growing 19

W

Walla Walla onions 20, 21, 153
Wash rack 95, 151

Water 39
    hauling 40
    quality problems 40
    requirements 39
    problems 80
    shortage problems 40
Weather 102
    effects on market phases 29
Weeds 19, 84, 91
Weeks to transplant size 100
Wholesale marketing 23
Wide rows 19
Winds, problems caused by 136
Word processing 37, 191, 192

Z

Zucchini 58, 62
    diseases 174
    growing 174
    harvesting 97, 174
    marketing 174, 175
    planning 173
    relish 198
    varieties 173

If the order form on page 207 has been used, please photo copy this one.

Product	Quantity	Price	Total
Small Commercial Garden Book		17.95	
Small Commercial Garden Video		19.95	
Annual Newsletter		5.95	
		Sub-total	
		Sales Tax	
		Shipping	2.95
		Total	

North Dakota residents, please add 6% sales tax. ->

I understand that if I am not fully satisfied, I may return the merchandize and my money will be refunded.

Name _____

Address _____

City _____ State ___ Zip Code _____

Method of payment: Check ☐   Credit Card ☐

Card # _____ Exp Date ___ / ___

Signature _____

Phone orders: **1-800-871-4296**

Mail orders to: **PC-Services
PO Box 7294
Bismarck, ND 58507-7294**

Ordering Information

THE VIDEO

We have tried to explain as precisely as possible how we garden. We have included many pictures taken from this video.

However, words and pictures can only do so much. If you are serious about trying some of the techniques in this book, we recommend this 30 minute video. It covers the following topics:

- Raised bed construction
- Construction of trellises
- Installation of trellises
- Tomato cage construction
- Tomato cage installation
- Transplanting tomatoes
- Construction of cloches
- Installation of cloches

We used state-of-the-art digital video on a personal computer to edit the video. This technology is still emerging so the quality of the video is about what you would get if you taped a TV program on your VCR. By doing it this way we were able to keep the cost at a very reasonable $19.95. The video will be available March 1, 1995.

THE ANNUAL NEWSLETTER

Throughout the book we have shared the many experiments and mistakes that have made our commercial garden a success. We aren't finished yet, and we will continue to update our readers on what worked and what didn't work so you can use that information to increase your profitability.

The 32-page newsletter will be available by December of each year, at a reasonable price of $5.95 per year, postage paid.

OTHER POSSIBLE PRODUCTS

At this point we are not sure what the demand would be for other products that might be useful. Please let us know if you would be interested in any of the following:

- A set of plans for building the marketing stand.
- Plans for the light and germination racks.
- Irrigation system plans.

Product	Quantity	Price	Total
Small Commercial Garden Book		17.95	
Small Commercial Garden Video		19.95	
Annual Newsletter		5.95	
		Sub-total	
North Dakota residents, please add 6% sales tax. ->		Sales Tax	
		Shipping	2.95
		Total	

I understand that if I am not fully satisfied, I may return the merchandize and my money will be refunded.

Name _____

Address _____

City _____ State ___ Zip Code _____

Method of payment: Check ☐ Credit Card ☐

Card # _____ Exp Date ___/___

Signature _____

Phone orders: **1-800-871-4296**

Mail orders to: **PC-Services
PO Box 7294
Bismarck, ND 58507-7294**

SECOND CANADIAN ED

Educational Psychology

A Learning-Centred Approach to Classroom Practice

R.R. McCOWAN
DUQUESNE UNIVERSITY

MARCY DRISCOLL
FLORIDA STATE UNIVERSITY

PETER ROOP
APPLETON AREA SCHOOL DISTRICT

DONALD H. SAKLOFSKE
UNIVERSITY OF SASKATCHEWAN

VICKI L. SCHWEAN
UNIVERSITY OF SASKATCHEWAN

IVAN W. KELLY
UNIVERSITY OF SASKATCHEWAN

LEONARD P. HAINES
UNIVERSITY OF SASKATCHEWAN

ALLYN & BACON CANADA
SCARBOROUGH, ONTARIO

Canadian Cataloguing in Publication Data

Educational psychology : a learning-centred approach to classroom practice

2nd Canadian ed.
ISBN 0-205-29070-1

1. Educational psychology. 2. Teaching. I. McCown, R. R., 1952- .

LB1051.E37 1999   370.15   C98930902-9

Allyn and Bacon, Inc., Needham Heights, MA
Prentice-Hall, Inc., Upper Saddle River, New Jersey
Prentice-Hall International (UK) Limited, London
Prentice-Hall of Australia, Pty. Limited, Sydney
Prentice-Hall Hispanoamericana, S.A., Mexico City
Prentice-Hall of India Private Limited, New Delhi
Prentice-Hall of Japan, Inc., Tokyo
Simon & Schuster Southeast Asia Private Limited, Singapore
Editora Prentice-Hall do Brasil, Ltda., Rio de Janeiro

ISBN 0-205-29070-1

Vice President, Editorial Director: Laura Pearson
Acquisitions Editor: Dawn Lee
Marketing Manager: Christine Cozens
Production Editor: Andrew Winton
Copy Editor: Imogen Brian
Production Coordinator: Sharon Houston
Permissions/Photo Research: Susan Wallace-Cox
Cover Design: Liz Harasymczuk
Cover Image: Sandra Dionisi
Page Layout: Joan M. Wilson

Original English Language edition published by Allyn and Bacon, Inc., Needham Heights, MA. Copyright © 1996, 1992.

1 2 3 4 5   03 02 01 00 99

Printed and bound in the United States of America

Visit the Prentice Hall Canada web site! Send us your comments, browse our catalogues, and more at **www.phcana-da.com**. Or reach us through e-mail at **phabinfo_pubcanada@prenhall.com**.

Contents

Preface xxiii

1 Views of Teaching and Learning   1

Teacher Chronicle: Teacher Talk   2
Focus Questions   2
What Are Teaching and Learning?   3
How Can You Develop a Theory of Teaching?   4
Discovering Metaphors for Teaching and Learning   6
Analyzing Metaphors in Teacher Problem Solving   7
How Can You Learn to Think Like an Expert Teacher?   11
Differences between Expert and Novice Teachers   11
Teachers' Thought Processes   13
The Processes of Reflective Construction   15
On What Theory of Teaching Is This Book Based?   17
Working Assumptions about Teaching and Learning   17
The Teaching Approach of This Textbook   18
    Teacher Chronicle   18
    Insights on Successful Practice   18
    Here's How   19
    Key Concepts and Margin Notes   19
Internet Resources   **20**
Here's How To Use This Book   20
Teacher Chronicle Conclusion: Teacher Talk   21
Application Questions   21
    Chapter Summary   21
    Key Concepts   22

Part I Development

2 Cognitive Development   23

Teacher Chronicle: Does It Work?   24
Focus Questions   24
What Are the Dimensions of Human Development?   25
Development Capabilities   25
Influences on Development   26
    Maturation   26
    Active Experience   26
    Social Interaction   26
    Cultural and Situational Contexts   27

How Do Individuals' Cognitive Abilities Develop?   **28**

Organizing and Adapting Mental Constructs   28

   Schemes   28

   Assimilation   28

   Accommodation   29

   Equilibration   29

Constructing Knowledge through Active Experience   30

   Physical Knowledge   30

   Logico-Mathematical Knowledge   30

   Social-Arbitrary Knowledge   31

Piaget's Stages of Cognitive Development   31

   Sensorimotor Stage   32

   Preoperations Stage   33

   Concrete Operations Stage   35

   Formal Operations Stage   36

What Is the Social Basis for Cognitive Development?   **38**

Acquiring Tools to Understand the Environment   38

   Human Activity Systems   40

   Internalization   40

Vygotsky's Zone of Proximal Development   41

   Scaffolding   42

   Intersubjectivity   42

Using Learning to Facilitate Development   43

How Does the Ability to Process Information Develop?   **44**

Increasing Attention   44

Acquiring Knowledge   45

Here's How To Address a Student's Difficulties with Problem Solving   47

Monitoring Cognitive Processes   47

How Do Individuals Develop Language Skills?   **47**

Syntax   48

Semantics   49

Pragmatics   50

How Can You Accommodate the Developmental Differences and Needs of Your Students?   **50**

Assessing Student Thinking   50

Here's How To Discover Student's Zones of Proximal Development   52

Providing Concrete Experiences   52

Using Authentic Activities   53

Here's How to Scaffold an Authentic Activity   53

Encouraging Student Interaction   54

Here's How To Organize Cooperative Learning Activities   54

Using Many Sign Systems   55

Cognitive Instructional Programs Developed in Canada   55

Teacher Chronicle Conclusion: Does It Work?   56

Application Questions 57
   Chapter Summary 57
   Key Concepts 58

3 Personal and Interpersonal Growth 59

Teacher Chronicle: Adolescent Identity Issues 60
Focus Questions 60
How Do Individuals Develop Self-Concepts and Self-Esteem? 61
Development of Self-Concept 61
Cultural Diversity and Sense of Self 64
The Development of Self-Esteem 65
How Does Social Interaction Influence Personal Growth? 68
Erikson's Theory of Psychosocial Development 68
   Stage 1: Trust versus Mistrust 69
   Stage 2: Autonomy versus Shame and Doubt 70
   Stage 3: Initiative versus Guilt 70
   Stage 4: Industry versus Inferiority 70
   Stage 5: Identity versus Role Diffusion 70
   Stage 6: Intimacy versus Isolation 71
   Stage 7: Generativity versus Stagnation 71
   Stage 8: Integrity versus Despair 72
Marcia's Work on Identity Statuses 72
   Identity Diffusion 72
   Moratorium 72
   Identity Achievement 73
   Foreclosure 73
The Significance of Developmental Crises for Teachers 73
Here's How To Help Students Develop Positive Self-Concepts 74
The Importance of Parental Involvement 74
Key Socioemotional Issues at Different Grade Levels 76
   Gender Roles in the Elementary Grades 76
Here's How To Encourage Gender Equity 77
   Puberty and Peer Relationships in the Secondary Grades 78
What Social Problems Affect Students' School Lives? 78
   Risks to Security and Comfort 79
Here's How To Help Students When They Are at Risk 80
   Risks to Health and Safety 81
   Bullying in Canadian Schools 83
How Do Individuals Develop Moral Reasoning? 84
Piaget's Framework of Moral Reasoning 84
   Morality of Constraint 85
   Morality of Cooperation 85
Kohlberg's Stages of Moral Development 85
   Preconventional Morality 86

Conventional Morality   86
Postconventional Morality   87
Criticisms of Kohlberg's Theory   87
The Question of Stages   87
The Question of Applicability   87
The Question of Generalizability   88
Gilligan's Theory of Gender-Based Morality   88
Lickona's Integrative Model of Personal and Interpersonal Development   90
Building Self-Esteem and Social Community   91
Cooperative Learning and Helping Relations   92
Moral Reflection   92
Participatory Decision Making   93
Teacher Chronicle Conclusion: Adolescent Identity Issues   **94**
Application Questions   94
Chapter Summary   94
Key Concepts   95

Part II Diversity

4   Cultural Diversity and Values in the Classroom   **96**
Teacher Chronicles: Grandma Tales   97
Focus Questions   97
What Are Some Sources of Diversity?   **98**
Cultural Diversity   98
Racial and Ethnic Identity   99
Language and Culture   102
Bilingualism and Biculturalism   102
Dominant Bilingualism   102
Dialects and Regional Culture   104
Socioeconomic Status   104
Here's How To Build on the Language Skills of Your Students   **105**
Gender and Sexual Identity   107
Here's How To Create a Gender-Fair Classroom   **109**
Exceptional Ability and Disability   110
How Can Cultural Conflicts Arise in Your Classroom?   **111**
Cultures of the School and Home   111
Learning Styles and Classroom Organization   111
Communication Styles   113
Here's How To Create a Culture-Fair Classroom   **114**
What Are the Dimensions of Multicultural Education?   **115**
Education for Integration and Assimilation   115
Education for Cultural Pluralism   116

Multiculturalism in Canada   117
Bilingual-Bicultural Education   118
Multicultural Curricula and School Reform   121
    Education for Cultural Awareness   123
    Education for Equity   124
    Education for Social Harmony   125

**Here's How To Use Cooperative Groups in Support of
Social Harmony**   125
    Education for Accountability   126
Multicultural Education in Canada   127

**How Can Your Knowledge of Diversity Enhance Teaching
and Learning in Your Classroom?**   **128**
Accepting Student Diversity   129
Here's How To Help Students Accept Diversity in Others   129
Using Multicultural Teaching Strategies   129
Teacher Chronicle Conclusion: Grandma Tales   132
Application Questions   132
    Chapter Summary   133
    Key Concepts   133

5   **Individual Variability in the Classroom**   **134**
Teacher Chronicle: My Name Is Robo   135
Focus Questions   135
How Do Students Vary in Intelligence?   **136**
The Definition and Measurement of Intelligence   136
Cultural Views of Intelligence and Student Performance   137
Three Traditional Theories of Intelligence   137
    Piaget's Dynamic View   138
    Wechsler's Global View   138
    Guilford's Multifactor View   139
Gardner's Theory of Multiple Intelligences   139
    The Seven Intelligences   140
    Gardner's Theory in Practice   141

**Here's How To Engage Multiple Intelligences in
Teaching Math and Science Concepts**   143
Sternberg's Triarchic Theory of Intelligence   144
    Componential Intelligence   145
    Experiential Intelligence   146
    Contextual Intelligence   146
A Canadian Contribution: The PASS Model and PREP Program,
by J.P. Das   147
How Do Students Vary in the Ways They Think and Learn?   **149**
Thinking and Learning Dispositions   149
Here's How To Gauge the Thinking Dispositions of Students   151

Learning Styles and Cultural Differences 152
    Learning Styles of Canadian Aboriginal Children 152
How Do Students Vary in Abilities and Disabilities? **154**
Exceptional Learners 154
Exceptionality and Diversity 156
Students with High-Incidence Disabilities 157
    Emotional and Behavioural Disorders 157
    Specific Learning Disabilities 158
    Communication Disorders 159
Students with Low-Incidence Disabilities 159
    Mental Retardation 159
    Sensory Disorders 160
    Physical Disabilities 162
    Other Health Impairments 162
Students Who Are Gifted and Talented 162
What Provisions Are Made for the Education of Students at Risk and Exceptional Learners? **163**
Compensatory Education 164
Intervention and Prevention Programs 165
Special Education and Inclusion 166
How Will You Use Your Knowledge of Individual Variability to Enhance Teaching and Learning? **166**
Accepting Individual Differences 167
Creating an Inclusive Classroom 168
Adapting Instruction 168
Here's How To Adapt Instruction To Meet Individual Needs **168**
Using Alternative Assessments 169
Teacher Chronicle Conclusion: My Name Is Robo 170
Application Questions 170
    Chapter Summary 171
    Key Concepts 171

Part III Learning

6 **Environment and Behaviour** **172**
Teacher Chronicle: Out of Control 173
Focus Questions 173
What is Behavioural Science? **174**
Principles of Classical Conditioning 175
Principles of Operant Conditioning 175
How Does Reinforcement Influence Behaviour? **176**
Antecedents of Behavior 177

Kinds of Reinforcers   178
   Primary Reinforcers   178
   Conditioned and Generalized Reinforcers   179
   Self-Reinforcement   179
Principles of Reinforcement   180

How Can You Develop Strategies for Changing Student Behaviour?   **181**
Strengthening Desirable Behaviours   181
   Positive Reinforcement   181

Here's How To Use Positive Reinforcement   **181**
   Premack Principle   182
   Negative Reinforcement   182
Weakening Undesirable Behaviours   183
   Punishment   183
   Reinforcement Removal: Extinction   183
   Reinforcement Removal: Time-out   183

Here's How To Use Time-Out Effectively in Your Classroom   **184**
   Reinforcement Removal: Response Cost   184
Teaching New Behaviours   184
   Shaping   185
   Fading   185
   Chaining   186

How Can You Maintain Newly Established Behaviours?   **186**
Continuous Reinforcement   186
Intermittent Reinforcement   188
   Fixed Interval Schedules   188
   Variable Interval Schedules   189
   Fixed Ratio Schedules   189
   Variable Ratio Schedules   190

**How Can Behavioural Principles Enhance the
Teaching-Learning Process in YourClassroom?**   **190**
Working with Individuals to Change Behaviour   191

Here's How To Work with Students To Change Their Behaviour   **191**
   Set Behavioural Goals   191
   Determine Appropriate Reinforcers   191
   Select Procedures for Changing Behaviour   192
   Implement Procedures and Monitor Results   192
   Evaluate Progress and Revise as Necessary   192
Managing by Rules   193

**Here's How To Encourage Rule-Following Behaviour in
Your Classroom**   **193**
Managing a Token Economy   195
Using Praise Effectively   195
Here's How to Use Praise Effectively in Your Classroom   **196**
Making Behavioural Principles Work for You   196

Teacher Chronicle Conclusion: Out of Control   **197**
Application Questions   198
    Chapter Summary   198
    Key Concepts   199

7 Thinking, Remembering, and Problem Solving   **200**
Teacher Chronicle: Chinese Proverbs   **201**
Focus Questions   201
What Is Involved in Thinking, Remembering, and Problem Solving?   **202**
Differing Views of Cognition   202
Learning How to Learn   202
How Can You Teach in Ways That Facilitate the Processing of Information?   **203**
Transferring Information in the Sensory Register   206
    Gaining Attention   206
    Perceiving Information   207
Here's How To Gain Attention and Facilitate Selective Perception   **209**
Encoding Information in the Short Term Store (STS)   209
    Maintenance Rehearsal   210
    Elaborative Rehearsal   211
Retrieving Information from the Long Term Store (LTS)   212
    Retrieval   212
    Reconstructive Retrieval   213
Why Is It Important to Activate Students' Prior Knowledge?   **213**
Episodic Memory   215
Semantic Memory   216
Procedural Memory   217
Conditional Memory   218
Here's How To Facilitate Metacognitive Awareness in Your Students and Help Them Use Conditional Knowledge Effectively   **218**
How Can You Help Students to Remember What They Learn?   **219**
Enhancing Imagery   219
Using Mnemonic Devices   220
    Rhymes   220
    Letter and Sentence Mnemonics   221
    Peg Mnemonics   221
    Story Mnemonic   222
    Keyword Mnemonic   222
Generating Metaphors and Analogies   223
Encouraging Automaticity through Practice   223
How Can You Help Students Learn to Solve Problems?   **225**
Strategic versus Tactical Problem Solving   225

Expert versus Novice Problem Solving 226
Teaching Problem Solving 227
 Identifying, Defining, and Representing the Problem 227
 Predicting Candidate Solutions 228
 Trying Out and Evaluating Solutions 228
 Reflecting on the Problem-Solving Process 229
Here's How To Create a Context for Solving Ill-Defined Problems 229
**How Can a Constructivist Approach Enhance the
Teaching-Learning Process in Your Classroom?** **230**
Active Learning 232
Authentic Activity and Situated Learning 232
Communities of Learning 234
A Constructivist Classroom 235
Here's How To Plan a Constructivist Classroom 235
Teacher Chronicle Conclusion: Chinese Proverbs 236
Application Questions 236
 Chapter Summary 236
 Key Concepts 237

8 Social Learning 238

Teacher Chronicle: A Social Learning Solution 239
Focus Questions 240
What Are the Dimensions of Social Learning? **240**
Models and Observers 240
Learning versus Performance 241
Vicarious Learning and Enactive Listening 243
Other Cognitive Capabilities 245
 Ability to Symbolize 245
 Capacity for Forethought 246
 Self-Regulation and Self-Reflection 246
Reciprocal Determinism 248
 Links between Personal Factors and Behaviour 249
 Links between Personal Factors and Environment 249
 Links between Behaviour and Environment 249
What Is Modelling and How Does Modelling Influence Learners? **250**
Inhibitory and Disinhibitory Effects 250
Facilitative and Environmental Effects 251
Arousal Effects 252
Observational Learning Effects 252
What Are the Processes of Observational Learning? **254**
Attention 254
 Influence of Models on Attention 254

Here's How To Facilitate Attention to Modelled Events   **255**

     Influence of Observers on Attention   255

Retention   256

Production   257

Here's How To Foster Good Production Decisions   **257**

Motivation   258

How Can Your Knowledge of Social Learning Make You a More Effective Teacher?   **258**

Selecting Effective Models   260

     Perceived Similarity   260

     Perceived Competence   260

Using Cognitive Modelling as an Instructional Approach   261

Helping Learners Build a Sense of Self-Efficacy   263

Teaching Goal-Setting and Self-Regulation Skills   265

Here's How To Encourage Goal Setting and Self-Regulation   **267**

Selecting Diverse Models   267

Using Peer Models   268

Being a Model   268

Social Learning Interventions for Exceptional Children   269

Teacher Chronicle Conclusion: A Social Learning Approach   **270**

Application Questions   270

     Chapter Summary   270

     Key Concepts   271

Part IV Motivation and Classroom Dynamics

9 Facilitating Student Motivation   **272**

Teacher Chronicle: An Outer Space Opportunity   **273**

Focus Questions   273

What Is Motivation to Learn?   **274**

Intrinsic and Extrinsic Motivation   274

Internal and External Sources of Motivation   275

Different Perspectives on Motivation   275

How Do Students' Needs and Wants Affect Their Motivation to Learn?   **276**

Maslow's Hierarchy of Needs   276

The Need to Achieve   279

The Need for Autonomy   281

Students' Goals   281

How Do Students' Beliefs Affect Their Motivation to Learn?   **282**

Beliefs about Knowledge and Ability   282

Beliefs in Self-Efficacy   283

Attribution of Causes for Success and Failure 284

Learned Helplessness 284

Impacts of Cultural Beliefs and Values on Students' Motivation 286

How Do Teachers' Beliefs Affect Student Motivation? **286**

Beliefs about Students 286

The Impact of Teacher Expectations 287

Here's How To Avoid the Negative Effects of Teacher Expectations **288**

Beliefs about Teaching Efficacy 289

How Can You Enhance Your Students' Motivation to Learn? **290**

Arousing Curiosity 291

Here's How To Arouse and Maintain Students' Curiosity in Learning **292**

Using Reinforcement Effectively 293

Varying Classroom Goal Structures 293

Here's How To TARGET Learning Goals in Your Classroom and Enhance Intrinsic Motivation **295**

Motivational Training 296

Setting Goals and Changing Attributions 296

Developing Self-Regulation 297

Here's How You Can Help Students Become Self-Regulated Learners **297**

Applying the ARCS Model 298

Attention 299

Relevance 299

Confidence 300

Satisfaction 301

Here's How To Identify and Solve Motivational Problems in the Classroom **301**

Teacher Chronicle Conclusion: An Outer Opportunity **303**

Application Questions 303

Chapter Summary 303

Key Concepts 304

10 **Leading Learning-Oriented Classrooms** **305**

Teaching Chronicle: And Then There's Sam **306**

Focus Questions 307

What is Classroom Management and Leadership? **307**

Metaphors for Managing Classrooms 308

Processes and Products of Classroom Management 310

Managing for Discipline 311

Instructing for Learning 312

Classroom Leadership and Authority 314

How Can You Create a Learning-Oriented Environment? **315**

How Can You Create a Learning-Oriented Environment? 315

Arranging the Classroom 316

Here's How To Use Walls and Bulletin Boards 318

Establishing Rules and Procedures 319

Building a Positive Atmosphere 320

Here's How To Begin the School Year in an Elementary Classroom 321

Here's How To Begin the School Year in a Secondary Classroom 322

Constructing a Democratic Classroom 322

**Here's How To Create a Learning–Oriented Classroom Based on
Collaboration, Community, and Democracy** 323

**How Can Instruction Be Managed to Support a
Learning-Oriented Environment?** 323

Giving Clear Instructions 323

    Precise Directions 325

    Student Involvement 325

Gaining Attention 325

Maintaining Attention 326

    Recognizing Students 326

    Encouraging Student Interaction 327

Pacing 328

Summarizing 328

Making Smooth Transitions 330

**How Can Misbehaviour Be Addressed and the
Learning Orientation Restored?** 331

A Self-Correctional Approach to Student Misbehaviour 331

Here's How To Resolve Conflicts without Creating Losers 333

The Control Theory Approach to Misbehaviour 333

The Applied Behaviour Analysis Approach to Misbehaviour 334

    The Role of Rules 334

    Token Economies 335

    Contingency Contracting 336

The Assertive Discipline Approach to Misbehaviour 337

**How Can Your Knowledge of Classroom Management
Help You Become an Effective Teacher?** 339

Teaching Self-Responsibility 340

**Here's How To Develop a Sense of Self-Responsibility and
Self-Direction in Your Students** 341

Accommodating Cultural Diversity and Special Needs 341

Teaching Ourselves to Share the Power 342

Teacher Chronicle Conclusion: And Then There's Sam 344

Application Questions 344

    Chapter Summary 345

    Key Concepts 345

Part V Effective Instruction

11 **Planning and Teaching to Learning Outcomes**   346
Teacher Chronicle: Giving Something Back   347
Focus Questions   348
What Are Possible Outcomes of Learning?   **348**
Gagné's Taxonomy of Learning Outcomes   348
    Verbal Information   349
    Intellectual Skills   349
    Cognitive Strategies   352
    Attitudes   353
    Motor Skills   353
Bloom's Taxonomy for the Cognitive Domain   354
Krathwohl's Taxonomy for the Affective Domain   355
Harrow's Taxonomy for the Psychomotor Domain   355
Thinking in the Content Areas   356
How Do Teachers Determine and Specify Instructional Outcomes?   **357**
Deciding on Instructional Goals   359
Specifying Performance Objectives   360
How Do Instructional Events Facilitate Learning Outcomes?   **361**
Gagné's Events of Instruction   362
    Preparation Phase   362
    Acquisition and Performance Phase   362
    Transfer Phase   365
    Integrating Multiple Instructional Goals   365
Bruner's Discovery Learning   366
Ausubel's Reception Learning   368
Here's How To Construct and Use Advance Organizers   **369**
Transfer of Learning   369
    Vertical and Lateral Transfer   369
    Low-Road and High-Road Transfer   370
A Cultural Approach to Teaching Thinking   370
Here's How To Create a Culture of Thinking in the Classroom   **371**
How Can You Make Instructional Decisions That Will
Help All Students Learn?   **371**
A Systematic Approach to Planning Effective Instruction   372
    Set Goals   372
    Select or Write Objectives   373
    Analyze Student Characteristics   373
    Select or Develop Assessments of Student Performance   373
    Select Textbooks and Other Materials   373
    Develop Instructional Activities and Choose Instructional Media 373
    Implement Instruction and Revise as Necessary   375
    Adapt Instruction for Students with Special Needs   377

A Flexible Approach to Delivering Instruction: Accommodating
Student Diversity   377
Teacher Chronicle Conclusion: Giving Something Back   **379**
Application Questions   380
    Chapter Summary   380
    Key Concepts   380

12   **Teaching for Active Learning**   **381**
Teacher Chronicle: Plugging In   382
Focus Questions   383
What Is Active Learning?   **383**
Student Thinking   384
Here's How To Cultivate Good Thinking Dispositions   **385**
Critical Thinking   385
Teaching that Yields Active Learning   386
How Can Teacher-Centred Instruction Support Active Learning? **386**
Lecturing   388
**Here's How To Deliver a Lecture that Encourages
Active Learning**   **390**
Explaining   391
Questioning   393
    Structure   393
    Solicitation   394
    Reaction   395
    Reciprocal Questioning   396
Independent Practice   396
How Can Student-Centred Instruction Support Active Learning? **398**
Small Group Discussions   399
Here's How To Intervene in Small Group Discussions   **400**
Peer Teaching and Learning   400
Cooperative Learning   402
    Student Teams-Achievement Divisions   403
    Teams-Games-Tournaments   404
    Team-Assisted Individualization   405
    Cooperative Integrated Reading and Composition 405
    Cooperative Learning: Cultural Considerations 405
Interactive Instructional Technology   407
    Computers and Instruction   407
    Computers and Thinking   408
    Computers, Cultures, and Communication   409
    Computers and Students with Special Needs   410
**How Will Your Knowledge of Active Learning
Techniques Help You Become a More Effective Teacher?**   **412**

Teacher Chronicle Conclusion: Plugging In — 413

Application Questions — 413

    Chapter Summary — 414

    Key Concepts — 414

Part VI Evaluation

13 Assessing Student Performance — **416**

Teacher Chronicle: Testing Trials — 417

Focus Questions — 417

What Is Assessment and How Are Assessment Practices Changing? — **418**

Defining Assessment — 418

Views of Assessment in Canada — 419

Authentic Assessment — 421

Types of Assessment Goals — 422

How Do You Plan and Construct Classroom Tests? — **424**

Planning Objective Tests — 425

Here's How To Produce a Table of Specifications for Test Writing — 426

Constructing Selection-Type Items — 427

    Binary-Choice Items — 427

Here's How To Construct Binary-Choice Test Items — 428

    Matching Items — 429

Here's How To Construct Matching and Double Matching Items — 429

    Multiple-Choice Items — 429

Here's How To Construct Multiple-Choice Items — 431

Constructing Supply-Type Items — 432

    Short Answer Items — 432

Here's How To Construct and Score Short Answer Items — 433

    Essay Items — 433

Here's How To Construct Essay Items — 434

Here's How To Score Answers to Essay Items — 435

How Can You Construct Alternative Assessments? — **435**

Observation-Based Assessment — 437

Portfolio Assessments — 438

Here's How To Design and Use Portfolio Assessments — 440

Performance Assessments — 441

Here's How To Design and Use Performance Assessments — 443

How Can You Ensure Sound Assessment Practices? — **445**

Validity — 446

Reliability — 446

Conducting Item Analysis — 447

Here's How to Perform an Item Analysis — 448

Avoiding Pitfalls in Assessment   449
    Principles for Fair Student Assessment Practices for
    Education in Canada   450
    Part A: Classroom Assessments   451
    Part B: Assessments Produced External to the Classroom   453
How Can You Use Assessment to Improve Teaching and Learning?   **454**
    Providing Effective Feedback   454
    Involving Students in Assessment   456
    Modifying and Improving Instruction   456
    Creating a Positive Assessment Environment in the Classroom   458
Teacher Chronicle Conclusion: Testing Trials   **459**
Application Questions   459
    Chapter Summary   460
    Key Concepts   460

14   Communicating Student Progress   461

Teacher Chronicle: Benefit of the Doubt   **462**
Focus Questions   463
What Are the Benchmarks of Student Progress?   **463**
Criterion-Referenced Benchmarks   464
Norm-Referenced Benchmarks   465
How Do You Interpret Assessment Results?   **467**
Qualitative and Quantitative Information   468
Summarizing Quantitative Information   469
How Do You Interpret Standardized Test Results?   **472**
Types of Standardized Tests   472
The Normal Distribution   474
Standardized Test Scores   476
    Z Scores and Percentile Ranks   476
    IQ Scores   476
    T Scores   477
    Stanine Scores   477
    Grade Equivalent Scores   478
Confidence and Test Scores   479
Here's How to Read a Standardized Test Report   **482**
Issues in Standardized Testing   483
    Test Bias   483
    Bias and Anxiety   485
Here's How to Help Students Overcome Test Anxiety   **486**
Minimum Competency Testing   487
Computerized Adaptive Testing   488
**How Can Criterion-Referenced Judgments Help You
Assign Grades?**   **489**

Grading Systems   489

Achievement or Effort?   490

Pass/Fail Grading   491

Contract Grading   492

Here's How To Ensure a Sound Grading System   **492**

Research on Grading   493

**How Will Your Knowledge of Student Progress Help
You Become a More Effective Teacher?**   **496**

Reporting Student Progress   496

Involving Students and Parents   497

Here's How To Conduct Parent-Teacher Conferences   **499**

Involving Parents from Culturally and Socially Diverse
Backgrounds   499

**Here's How To Involve Parents from Culturally and Socially
Different Backgrounds**   **500**

Standards of Assessment Quality that Support the
Teaching-Learning Process   501

Teacher Chronicle Conclusion: Benefit of the Doubt   **503**

Application Questions   503

Chapter Summary   503

Key Concepts   504

References   **505**

Glossary   **533**

Name Index   **541**

Subject Index   **548**

Photo Credits   **556**

Preface to

Educational Psychology

A Learning-Centred Approach to Classroom Practice, Second Canadian Edition

We are most pleased to have been asked to write a second edition of the Canadian adaptation of *Educational Psychology: A Learning-Centred Approach to Classroom Practice*. The original text written by Rick McCown, Marcy Driscoll, and Peter Roop has all of the essential ingredients of a successful educational psychology textbook. However, our experience suggested that this book would be even more meaningful and relevant to Canadian education students if the theories, research, and practice so comprehensively covered in the original text could be further placed within the Canadian context. Thus we set out to rewrite or add material to the first edition that would clearly provide this Canadian focus. While some chapters required only a few changes, others, such as Chapter 4 on cultural diversity, were substantially rewritten to reflect Canadian culture and values.

This second edition provided us with the opportunity to add new information about teaching and learning and to ensure an even greater coverage of important Canadian contributions. The retirement of Joel Gajadharsingh from the University of Saskatchewan created the opportunity to add Len Haines to the authoring team. We were further guided by the helpful feedback from students, colleagues, reviewers, and the editorial staff at Allyn & Bacon Canada. For example, it was suggested that we add learning objectives at the beginning of each chapter to further complement the questions raised by the Teacher Chronicles. We were also requested to ensure that students across the grade and age range were represented, where appropriate, while recognizing that this text is intended to provide a broad survey of theory, research, and practice. Given the increase in access to information via the internet, we were asked to provide a list of the more important and accessible web pages. We have incorporated these and other suggestions into this second edition.

At the same time, we have remained committed to the basic premises that initially guided the text by McCown, Driscoll, and Roop:

1. Teaching and learning are aspects of the same process
2. Your view of the teaching-learning process affects your classroom practice
3. Reflective construction is necessary for the development of teaching expertise.

Their description of the teaching-learning process is cast within a social constructivist framework. The learning and skills acquired during your undergraduate education program must have meaning, significance, and utility, and transfer to the very real world of diverse Canadian classrooms. It is essential that your courses, textbooks, and pre-teaching experiences provide you with the information and opportunities to begin to construct your own theory of teaching, one that is dynamic and will invariably change with opportunity and experience. Such theory building is also essential to the development of your identity as a teacher.

Authentic classroom experience is reflected throughout the text —more than in any competing text. Case studies, essays by teachers, and examples derived from actual classroom experience help connect theory to real practice.

Teaching experience is necessary but not sufficient for the development of expertise. Expert teachers are also expert learners. The metaphors, knowledge, information, facts, and principles that comprise expert teachers' cognitive schemata and contribute to their teaching theory will, in turn, provide the basis for continuous reflection and reconstruction of all that is critically important to successful teaching and student learning.

It is at this point in your training that textbooks such as this one are so very important in providing you with the kinds of knowledge you will need in the process of becoming the best teacher you can be. Educational psychology is that branch of psychology that addresses such basic questions as: what is learning? who is the learner? how do we assess learning? and what can I do as a teacher to ensure that my students learn the content of classroom instruction but also become effective and life-long learners?

Certainly many of the theoretical principles and research findings drawn from the numerous experts cited in the original version of this text are quite robust. Thus views on child development, research on the effects of reinforcement, models of memory, and so forth will be of either direct or heuristic value to all teachers. Yet, to ensure that this information is meaningful and relevant so that you may "begin practising the hallmarks of expert teaching" (i.e., reflection, testing ideas, construction of a theory of teaching), we have continued to provide a Canadian context whenever appropriate. We have especially highlighted the important theoretical and practical contributions made by Canadian psychologists and educators.

We are most grateful to Imogen Brian, our copy editor, and to Carol Steven, Laura Forbes, Andrew Winton, Dawn Lee, and Cliff Newman of Allyn and Bacon Canada for both inviting and supporting the development of this second edition. Nancy Stevens and Carolynn Archibald provided invaluable assistance in revising the supplemental materials. We thank our students and colleagues, both those from the University of Saskatchewan and from across Canada, for their most helpful advice and encouragement in the preparation of this book.

Don Saklofske
Vicki Schwean
Ivan Kelly
Len Haines

Instructional Aids

We have provided a rich array of materials that we trust will support and enhance the use of this text in your course. Within the textbook, the addition of websites will allow students to access contemporary and relevant information related to the course content. The Instructor's Resource Manual highlights cooperative and collaborative strategies and student assignments, and incorporates a case-based approach. For each chapter, interactive cases are provided in the form of handout MASTERS, and questions are provided to support case analysis as a class activity or in assessment. Our IRM also includes a chapter-at-a-glance feature, learning outcomes, a summary, a list of key concepts, teaching suggestions for introducing chapter content and using the pedagogical text features, and cross-references to the Assessment Package. A Transparency Package is also available.

The Assessment Package is far more than the usual test item file. In addition to multiple-choice and essay items with answer feedback, our assessment package provides alternative, authentic assessments for every chapter along with criteria for scoring them or creating your own scoring rubrics. These features provide opportunities for you to use performance or portfolio assessments in teaching the course—a great way to model these concepts for your students.

A Study Guide supports the learning of students using our text package.

The following pages explain how the book is organized and present the pedagogical features.

Organization of the Book

We have tried to be very clear about our view of the teaching–learning process, including how it works, what it affects, and what factors affect it. By making our view explicit—in the form of assumptions—students will have a basis of comparison for the development of their own views. In the opening chapter students are asked to think about their view of teaching and learning and you will encounter the three basic assumptions that underlie our view. The first of these assumptions will come as no surprise to those who have read the preface to this point.

1. Teaching and learning are aspects of the same process.
2. Your view of the teaching–learning process affects your classroom practice.
3. Reflective construction (explained in Chapter 1) is necessary for the development of teaching expertise.

The remainder of the book is organized into six parts. The working assumptions associated with each part are listed below. These assumptions further explicate our view of the teaching-learning process and are the main themes of this book. Each assumption is explained fully in chapter content.

Part I Development (Chapters 1, 2 & 3)
• Development is complex and multifaceted.
• Development affects learning.
• Life conditions affect development.

Part II Diversity (Chapters 4 & 5)
• Learners are diverse.
• Students' diversity and individuality affect their learning.
• Inclusive classrooms provide learning opportunities.

Part III Learning (Chapters 6, 7, & 8)
• Learning is shaped by the learner's environment.
• Learning is a function of complex mental activities.
• Learning is active construction in social contexts.

Part IV Motivation and Classroom Leadership
(Chapters 9 & 10)
• People are naturally motivated to learn.
• Needs and values affect motivation.
• Classroom management is a shared concern.

> To encourage reflection on the teaching-learning process, each chapter concludes with the question: "How can your knowledge of _____ make you a more effective teacher?"

Part V Effective Instruction (Chapters 11 & 12)
• Teachers and students are both learners.
• Teachers coordinate the context for learning.
• Instructional technologies support teaching and learning.

Part VI Evaluation (Chapters 13 & 14)
• Assessment serves multiple purposes.
• Assessment improves teaching and learning.
• Authentic activity provides a basis
  for assessment.

The assumptions are derived from the theoretical principles of educational psychology that inform classroom practice. In order to help students learn those principles and how they can be used to enhance the teaching-learning process, we have incorporated several instructional features in the design of each chapter.

Features of the Book

The instructional features of this text have been designed to help learners integrate the theory of educational psychology with classroom practice and, consequently, to enhance their understanding of the teaching–learning process. These instructional features are described briefly below. The features and a strategy for their use are discussed in greater detail in Chapter 1.

Weblinks. The Web sites included with this text were carefully selected to ensure that students would have easy access to some of the best sources of current information relevant to the content of this book. While the listings are not exhaustive, these World Wide Web sites should provide a good source of additional information. The Canadian listings reflect the intent of providing a Canadian context for many of the topics found in this book.

Teacher Chronicle. Each chapter begins with a *Teacher Chronicle*, a brief, unresolved case based on actual classroom events. The case provides a practical context and a rich source of examples for the key theoretical concepts and principles presented in each chapter. Each *Teacher Chronicle* introduces an issue or problem that a teacher has faced in a real classroom.

Focus Questions follow each *Teacher Chronicle* and are designed to help students anticipate how the content of the chapter relates to the teaching– learning process that is represented in the *Teacher Chronicle* case.

The *Teacher Chronicle Conclusion* at the end of each chapter shows how the teacher addressed the problems or issues described in the *Teacher Chronicle*. Because the teacher's course of action is not given until the end of each chapter, students have the opportunity to reflect on the theoretical concepts of the chapter in an attempt to anticipate how the teacher solves the problem.

The *Teacher Chronicle Conclusion* is followed by *Application Questions*, the final component of the Teacher Chronicle feature. *Application Questions* refer specifically to the events in the *Teacher Chronicle* and allow students to reinterpret those events through the application of key concepts from the chapter. We have changed or rewritten more than half of the original Teacher Chronicles based on feedback from our students and reviewers, and from our new experiences.

A Teacher Chronicle opens and closes each chapter, presenting a single case drawn from real-life classroom experience. The case is referenced throughout the chapter to help relate topics in the text to actual practice.

Learning Outcomes. The learning outcomes that open each chapter are further intended to guide student learning as they study each chapter. The objectives will provide a focus as students explore each chapter and provide them with a means for evaluating their learning when they reach the end of the chapter.

Insights on Successful Practice. The text not only encourages reflection, but models it as well. *Insights on Successful Practice* are the reflections of expert teachers on how theories of educational psychology are used to teach effectively. There are multiple *Insights on Successful Practice* in each chapter. Each insight gives students the opportunity to study how an expert teacher uses chapter concepts and principles to enhance the teaching-learning process in his or her classroom. We have added a number of new insights that we feel are even more revealing of successful teaching practices.

Each chapter includes Insights on Successful Practice presenting the responses of teachers to questions linking theory and research. Special Insights annotations in the margins encourage critical thinking about the teachers' responses.

Here's How. As an aspiring teacher, one of the questions that students should ask constantly as they read is, "How can I use this theoretical concept to enhance my classroom practice?" In each chapter, they will find a number of *Here's How* lists that can help them answer that question. Each *Here's How* list presents specific suggestions for classroom practice that are based on the research and theory of educational psychology. After a discussion of Gardner's Theory of Multiple Intelligences, for example, students encounter "Here's How To Engage Multiple Intelligences in Teaching Science and Math Concepts." *Here's How* lists are action plans for enhancing the teaching-learning process in a variety of classroom situations.

Key Concepts and Margin Notes. Key concepts throughout the book are printed in boldface. The key concepts are defined in the text itself and in a running glossary that appears in the margins of the text. The concepts are also listed at the end of the chapter as a study aid and in a Glossary at the back of the book.

Margin notes appear throughout the entire text. These notes annotate the text and are designed to provide students with additional opportunities to reflect on the knowledge base, develop their views of the teaching-learning process, and discover conceptual connections to other portions of the text. The categories of margin notes include the following:

- Point—reminders of the basic assumptions of this text, statements of main ideas, and statements of key principles in educational psychology.

- Reflection—questions that help students to reflect on their assumptions and values and to relate chapter content to their prior experiences.

- Example—additional illustrations of chapter concepts and their applications in practice.

- Critical Thinking—questions that help students link and apply chapter concepts and develop practical problem-solving strategies.

- Connection—cross-references to related concepts and information in other sections or chapters.

- Try This—active learning opportunities that students can undertake to expand their knowledge and apply that knowledge in authentic situations.

- Insights—questions that invite students to respond to the commentaries of the expert teachers featured in *Insights on Successful Practice*.

Weblinks for Educational Psychology

Site Name & Location	Site Description	1	Development 2	3	4	Diversity 5	6	Learning 7	8	Motivation 9	10	Instruction 11	12	Evaluation 13	14
American Educational Research Association (AERA) http://aera.net/	A comprehensive overview of the organization. Resources include a searchable ERIC database of AERA publications, directories of members and researchers, online articles and commentaries, and special interest group sections.	•	•	•	•	•	•	•	•	•	•	•	•	•	•
American Psychological Association http://www.apa.org	Describes the organization and includes online versions of journals, press releases, briefs, and media references. Includes a student link and member service information.	•	•	•	•	•	•	•	•	•	•	•	•	•	•
* Association canadienne d'éducation de langue française (ACELF) http://www.acelf.ca	Encourages and supports the education of students in French language and culture. Devoted to facilitating and supporting the effective uses of media and technology in education.	•			•	•			•						•
* Association for Media and Technology in Education in Canada (AMTEC) http://www.camosun.bc.ca/~amtec	A variety of useful articles, links, features, and professional development resources and services.	•					•	•	•	•	•	•	•	•	•
Association for Supervision and Curriculum Development (ASCD) http://www.ascd.org/ index.html	Promotes girls' and women's rights to safe, useful, empowering education and training.	•			•	•	•		•						
* Canadian Congress for Learning Opportunities for Women (CCLOW) http://www.nald.ca/cclow.htm	Promotes girls' and women's rights to safe, useful, empowering education and training.	•													
* Canadian Departments of Education: Alberta http://www.ednet.edc.gov.ab.ca	Each province or territory has a variety of information, services, programs, links, professional development information and opportunities, publications, articles, and lists of or links to related organizations.	•	•	•	•	•	•	•		•	•	•	•	•	•

Weblinks for Educational Psychology

Site Name & Location	Site Description	1	Development 2	3	4	Diversity 5	6	Learning 7	8	Motivation 9	10	Instruction 11	12	Evaluation 13	14
British Columbia http://www.educ.bc.ca **Manitoba** http://www.gov.mb.ca/education **New Brunswick** http://www.gov.nb.ca/education **Newfoundland** http://www.gov.nf.ca/edu **North West Territories** http://www.gov.nt.ca/ECE **Nova Scotia** http://www.ednet.ns.ca **Ontario** http://www.edu.gov.on.ca **Prince Edward Island** http://www.gov.pe.ca/educ **Quebec** http://www.eduq.risq.net/DRD **Saskatchewan** http://www.sasked.gov.sk.ca **Yukon** http://www.yukonweb.wis.net/education															
* **Canadian Psychological Association** http://www.cpa.ca	Describes the association and includes event information, news, discussion groups, online and print publications information, a listing of online psychological resources and the Canadian Journal of Behavioural Science.	•	•	•	•	•	•	•	•	•	•	•	•	•	•
* **Canada's Schoolnet** http://schoolnet2.carleton.ca/ english	Dedicated to bringing educators and students together to enhance learning. Offers a wide array of programs and services, resources, and technology skills development for students and teachers. Includes a comprehensive list of web-based library resources.		•	•	•	•				•	•	•	•		

Weblinks for Educational Psychology

Site Name & Location	Site Description	1	Development		4	Diversity		Learning		Motivation		Instruction		Evaluation	
			2	3		5	6	7	8	9	10	11	12	13	14
Council for Exceptional Children http://www.cec.sped.org	Dedicated to affecting the education of exceptional, disabled and/or gifted students. ontains information on events, professional standards, jobs, publications, ERIC resources, policy, and legislation. Includes student, Canadian and International areas.		•	•		•	•	•							
FreudNet http://plaza.interport.net/ nypsan	Information and library-services server to the Brill Library of the New York Psychoanalytic Institute, one of the largest libraries of that type in the world.		•	•		•		•							
Global School Network (GSN) http://www.gsn.org	Devoted to facilitating and encouraging internet use in teaching. Includes projects, professional development opportunities, resources, and tools.	•			•	•	•			•		•	•		
Mental Health Net http://www.cmhc.com	Large and comprehensive guide to mental health online. Information on various disorders, professional resources in psychology, psychiatry, and social work, journals, and self-help magazines. Also, recent news in the field, glossaries, and discussion forums.		•	•		•	•			•					
Mid-continent Regional Educational Lab (McREL) http://www.mcrel.org	Accesses a wide variety of educational journals; links to internet resources such as lesson and curriculum plans; recent news about education and developments in the field.	•	•	•		•	•	•	•	•	•	•	•	•	•
National Centre for Research Evaluation, Standards and Student Testing (CRESST) http://www.cresst96.cse.ucla. edu/index.htm	A focused, searchable site. Features libraries of reports and newsletters, discussions, and samples of assessments. Includes a page of related assessment links.													•	•

Weblinks for Educational Psychology

Site Name & Location	Site Description	1	Development		4	Diversity		Learning	8	Motivation		Instruction		Evaluation	
			2	3	4	5	6	7	8	9	10	11	12	13	14
Psych Central: Dr. John Grohol's Mental Health Page http://www.grohol.com	A collection of mental-health related articles, mailing lists and newsgroups. Features an online interactive chat, book reviews, and a comprehensive page of mental health, psychology, and support resources on the internet.		•	•	•	•									
Special Education Resources on the Internet (SERI) http://www.hood.edu/seri/seri-home.htm	A collection of internet-accessible information related to special education resources for teaching.		•	•	•	•						•	•		
Stanford University's Department of Psychology: *Cognitive and Psychological Sciences on the Internet* http://www-psych.stanford.edu/cogsci.htm	An index of internet resources relevant to research in these fields.		•	•	•	•		•							
Teaching Ideas http://www.usask.ca/education/ideas/ideas.htm	A variety of articles on teaching and sample lesson plans and curriculum plans in many teaching areas.	•							•	•	•	•	•	•	
* The Integrated Network of Disability Information and Education http://www.indie.ca	A directory of disability information on the internet. Includes addresses and phone numbers for the Directory of Disability Organizations in Canada.		•	•	•	•									

* *Denotes a Canadian Website*

1 Views of Teaching and Learning

LEARNING OUTCOMES

When you have completed this chapter, you will be able to

1. discuss the teaching-learning process
2. recognize the value of developing a theory of teaching
3. outline your own personal theory of teaching
4. create metaphors for teaching and learning
5. list key differences between expert and novice teachers
6. describe the process of reflective construction
7. use this book as an effective learning resource

Teacher Chronicle

Teacher Talk

Kris and Sylvie greet each other in the teachers' lounge one day after school. They are members of an interdisciplinary team at a middle school. Both teach grade seven. Kris, in his first year, teaches social studies and Sylvie, in her twelfth year, teaches math and science. They get together every day in their team to discuss student performance and student behaviour. The third team member, who teaches language arts, hasn't yet arrived.

"What a day!" begins Kris. "I knew I was in trouble when Jamie challenged me during third period. I was trying to get across the idea of finding locations on a map using the grid system. First, she put her head down on her desk, and I thought she was just going to snooze for awhile. But then she threw down the gauntlet. She deliberately ignored my directions to work out the problem in their groups, and it was a real battle to keep her on task."

"I know what you mean," agrees Sylvie. "Jamie can be a real handful. She needs a tight rein."

"Well, by fifth period, I thought I had been thrown to the lions. Sabrina kept punching Beckie in the arm. Mary wouldn't talk to the other members of her group. She insisted on doing all the work herself. And Jayson … he was just being himself, I guess. He kept waving his hand and if I didn't call on him right away, he left his group and started disrupting the groups working around him. I never thought my first year of teaching would be so hard! Why can't these kids cooperate with each other?"

"They will," reassures Sylvie. "But it takes time. Have you done any team-building activities with the students?"

"No." Kris looks blankly at her.

"How did you decide who to put in what group?"

"It was more or less random, I guess. I did think about personalities a little. I figured that putting Matt and Dana together would be like lighting the fuse to dynamite."

Sylvie laughs. "Yes, that would be an explosive combination all right. They're both pretty strong-minded individuals. How often do you change the groups?"

"I haven't thought of that," Kris replies.

"Well," Sylvie suggests, "you have some more planning to do. For one thing, when you put students into groups, you have to remember that it takes time for them to learn how to be a group. And just as some students take longer than others to work out a problem or understand a concept, so do some groups take time to mesh. I remember one group in my class last year that just couldn't seem to get it together. I can't even recall now what got them moving smoothly, but the results were dazzling. They worked out a system for generating hypotheses, systematically testing them, and keeping track of the results. Each member of the group took a specific role that determined what tasks he or she would perform. I've read research since that says assigning roles within a group is a good strategy for achieving cooperation. And my four students, whom I'd about given up on, connected it all up for themselves."

Kris sits silently contemplating Sylvie's story.

"So teaching is kind of like flying a kite," he says finally. "You have to let out the string enough to let each group find its own wind. Say, do you have some material on cooperative learning that I could take a look at?"

Focus Questions

1. How can teaching and learning be conceptualized as an integrated process?

2. What is your theory of teaching? How will your theory affect your professional development as a teacher?

3. What are your metaphors for teachers and learners? What are your assumptions about teaching and learning?

4. What knowledge base and thought processes will allow you to become an expert teacher?

What Are Teaching and Learning?

Kris and Sylvie are talking about teaching and learning, which are the subjects of this book. **Teaching** is action taken with the intent to facilitate learning. **Learning** is change in thought or behaviour that modifies a person's capabilities. Although these statements are simple, their implications could fill several books.

Note that the definition of teaching subsumes the definition of learning— that is, teaching results in change in thought or behaviour that modifies a person's capabilities. Because you intend to teach, it is crucial that you conceive of teaching in terms of learning. Entering the teaching profession means intending to change the thought and behaviour of students to enhance their capabilities. Imagine a person who considers his or her teaching to be independent of learning. After delivering an unsuccessful lesson, this person might explain the outcome by saying, "I taught that, but they didn't learn it." The error in this explanation is the assumption that teaching and learning are separate, distinct processes. No one would accept a salesperson's statement, "I sold the item, but the customer didn't buy it" (cf. Postman & Weingartner, 1969). If an item has to be bought in order to be considered sold, we should consider that knowledge and skills are taught only if they have been learned. Just as effective selling results in buying, so does effective teaching result in learning. When a teacher's efforts fail to produce learning, he or she does not accept the situation, but tries again.

Teaching and learning are integrated. When we discuss either teaching or learning in this book, we are simply choosing to focus on one of two aspects of the same process: the **teaching-learning process.** Consider, for example, the shared reflections of Sylvie and Kris in the Teacher Chronicle. Although they are discussing teaching, they have a lot to say about student learning. Recall that one of the primary reasons they meet daily in the teachers' lounge is to discuss student performance and behaviour. Kris seeks advice from Sylvie that might help him improve the cooperative efforts of his students. In essence, he seeks to teach differently in an effort to enhance the performance of his students. Sylvie reflects on a class in which her students were having difficulty working in cooperative-learning groups. She describes how her students discovered that by taking specific roles, their learning improved. Sylvie also mentions having read research that supports the assignment of roles to individuals working in cooperative-learning groups. In the Teacher Chronicle, both teachers view their teaching in light of student learning. Also, both teachers are themselves learners. They learn from their own teaching experiences. That teaching is a source of learning for both students and teachers is an important insight for those who aspire to teach (McLaughlin & Talbert, 1993).

The teaching-learning process operates under all kinds of conditions and in all kinds of settings. Teaching occurs not only in schools, but also in homes and hospitals, churches and child care centres, museums and meeting rooms, camps and clubs, garages and garbage trucks. Teaching also occurs across time and distance in the form of print, art, technology, and mass media. In some cases, the learner is also the teacher. For example, a person who studies independently takes actions that he or she believes will result in a modification of his or her capabilities. Independent learning, therefore, can be viewed as self-teaching. In other cases—when students engage in cooperative learning, for instance—learners teach each other. Teaching is a universal human activity. It occurs among and between humans of all cultures, in and across all times and places.

teaching Action taken with the intent to facilitate learning.

learning Change in thought or behaviour that modifies a person's capabilities.

teaching-learning process The process of taking action to produce change in thought or behaviour and subsequent modification of capabilities.

All of this is not to say that teaching always produces learning. The definition of teaching includes "the intent to facilitate learning," and even the best intentions do not always produce positive results. Have you ever observed or experienced teaching that failed to facilitate learning? Why does some teaching succeed while other teaching fails to enhance—or even diminishes—a learner's capabilities? Why are some people more capable of facilitating learning than others? How can one become a better facilitator of learning? How can you become, in the true sense of the word, a teacher? That is, not just someone who holds a position on a school's payroll, but someone who facilitates learning and who continually learns and improves as a facilitator of learning.

Classroom practice that reflects an understanding that teaching and learning are aspects of the same process is a hallmark of expert teaching. A conceptual integration of teaching and learning is necessary for teaching expertise. This book is based on the following basic working assumptions:

- Teaching and learning are aspects of the same process.
- Your view of the teaching-learning process affects your classroom practice.
- Reflective construction is necessary for the development of teaching expertise.

This chapter explores these basic assumptions, which are foundational to our view of teaching. Additional assumptions that we point out in this book build on these basic working assumptions and are based on our knowledge of the theory and research of educational psychology; our knowledge of classroom practice; and our reflections on theory, research, and professional practice. The assumptions underlie our descriptions, explanations, and predictions of the phenomenon called teaching. They are part of our theory of teaching. What is your theory of teaching and how will your theory affect your growth as a teacher?

How Can You Develop a Theory of Teaching?

What is the first thing that comes into your mind when you hear the word *teaching*? What images are evoked by the word *learning*? Do the images of teaching imply that someone is learning?

Your vision of teaching and learning will guide your actions as a teacher. Your vision will influence how you plan your lessons, what instructional and assessment strategies you implement in the classroom, and how you reflect on your teaching experiences. Your reflections will be based partly on your expectations according to your prior experiences. Aspiring teachers often think a great deal, for example, about what their ideal classroom will look like. Some choose to become teachers because they are convinced that teaching and learning can be vastly different from what they experienced as students in elementary and high school. However, many beginning teachers have not reflected enough on their views of teaching and learning. When asked "What is *your* theory of teaching?" they are stumped. Only by actively reflecting on your implicit views and making them explicit can you consider adopting alternative views (cf. Unger, Draper, & Pendergrass, 1987; Cunningham, 1987). Unfortunately, there is ample evidence to suggest that many teachers have not devoted time and thought to developing—to any serious degree—their views of teaching. They simply teach as they were taught, without reflecting on the effectiveness of those methods (Huling-Austin, 1994). Dennis Sumara and Rebecca Luce-Kapler (1996) published a most enlightening paper in the *Canadian Journal of Education* arguing for the necessity

Insights on Successful Practice

What suggestions do you have for novice teachers on applying principles of educational psychology to better understand students and classrooms events?

We often hear beginning teacher-education students say "I know how to teach; I just have a way with kids" or "teaching can't be that hard, after all, I spent twelve years in school as a student." On their own, these statements are at worst a bit naive. But when they are followed by "I don't see how a knowledge of psychology will help me be a better teacher" or "psychology is just common sense," they can get in the way of successful teaching practice.

If you close your eyes and think back to your public school teachers, you can probably quite easily describe what made each of them good teachers or not-so-good teachers. There is also no question that we can visit a classroom and fairly quickly get an impression of a positive learning environment, an effective teacher, or a well-presented lesson.

But how does one become a good teacher? How do effective teachers introduce a new concept so that it is meaningful and can be remembered? How do they get and hold student attention, ensure transfer of learning, and recognize individual differences in student learning rate and style? When the lesson content is not all that exciting, but important, how do good teachers motivate students? How do they decide when guided-discovery approaches are likely to be more effective than structured lessons in achieving learning outcomes? How do they accurately measure and evaluate student learning, while taking into account students' development, ability, and exceptional characteristics such as learning disabilities, and cultural and family factors?

Educational psychology has several ways of helping you become the best teacher you can be. This specialty area relates the findings from psychology to classroom teaching practices, to learning environments, and to our understanding of the learner. Educational psychology also examines issues of relevance to teaching and learning with the aid of scientific psychology. Thus educational psychology strives to address the following questions: what is learning, who is the learner, under what conditions does learning occur, and how do we know that learning has in fact occurred?

Teaching is both a science and an art. All of the current tools and contemporary knowledge will not make you a good teacher if you don't also have a commitment to children, and to the importance of education in the life of every child and to society. But to ignore the tremendous and useful knowledge that has accumulated from literally millions of studies of teaching and learning will leave this most important role of teaching to chance outcomes. Your own theory of teaching, essential to your success as a teacher, should be built from insights gleaned from practice and observing or interacting with master teachers, but also from the rich information base of educational psychology.

DON SAKLOFSKE
Educational Psychology
Professor

Your Insights

According to this teacher, in what ways is educational psychology a foundation for teaching practice? Why are both self-knowledge and the knowledge gleaned from educational psychology essential to forming the foundation for successful teaching?

---

of incorporating the identity "teacher" into your personal identity. Even at this point in time, "beginning teachers must negotiate at least three teaching identities: those they bring with them into teacher education, those they develop while doing university course work, and those they develop during student teaching practicums" (p. 65). By way of further developing your identity as a teacher, we would encourage you to peruse the article published in the *McGill Journal of Education* (1989) by Rodney Clifton of the University of Manitoba entitled "Knowledge and mythology in teacher education." This challenging and "hard-hitting analysis of current teacher education" programs in Canada offers a number of proposals to offset the tendency for university faculty and student teachers to believe that "myth has precedence over knowledge ... opinion is knowledge ... knowledge must be practical and ... tradition has precedence over scholarship" (p. 277).

Whether they have reflected carefully on their views of teaching or not, all prospective teachers have implicit assumptions about the nature of learning and what it means to teach. These assumptions are formed through experiencing more than 10 000 hours of teaching and learning during their school years. The wealth of images and impressions from this long observational experience contributes to the tendency to teach the way one was taught (Feiman-Nemser, 1983). In order to develop a **theory of teaching**, in other words, it is important to make explicit your assumptions and examine them for the implications they hold for classroom instruction. A useful way of discovering your assumptions is to consider possible metaphors for teaching and learning and to decide which of the metaphors reflects your ideal classroom.

Discovering Metaphors for Teaching and Learning

Lakoff and Johnson (1980) argue that **metaphors** reflect the very essence of thought, that "the human conceptual system is metaphorically structured and defined" (p. 6). In other words, we represent and talk about our experiences in terms of other more familiar or more commonly shared events that seem comparable. If you listen carefully to conversations among people, you will hear metaphors implicit in almost every sentence. Reread the Teacher Chronicle at the beginning of this chapter, for example. What metaphors does Kris use in describing problems with student behaviours in his classroom? What is Sylvie's metaphor for cooperative learning? What metaphor expresses Kris' theory of teaching?

Examining the metaphors that teachers use when they talk about their experiences in the classroom is an approach to understanding their professional knowledge (Munby, 1987). The notion is that teachers have particular conceptualizations of teaching and learning that become evident in the language they use to describe events in the classroom. In a recent study, for example, interview transcripts of two teachers (Alice, a grade eight English teacher with five years of experience, and Bryn, a grade eight history teacher with eight years of experience) revealed that both teachers used a travel metaphor in describing their classes. Alice, who used the metaphor extensively, employed the following phrases in describing her students and lessons: "I just went ahead," "these kids need a push in every direction," "if he's lost ... he's just going to get further behind," and "they like to get off the subject on to different topics" (Munby, 1987, p. 384). Statements such as "they're going to pick up on that" also suggested that Alice viewed learning as students gathering up information as the lesson travelled by them.

Because metaphors can structure our thinking, they can also affect our behaviour (cf. Munby, 1987; Munby & Russell, 1990; Tobin, 1990; Marshall, 1990). Teachers' metaphors can guide the roles they choose to take, the ways they interact with students, and the approaches they take to solving problems in the classroom. In one case, for example, a high school science teacher conceived of his classroom management role in terms of a ship's captain. He emphasized whole-class activities, where he was in charge of the class, he called on nonvolunteers, to make sure that all students were paying attention, and he acted assertively and goal-directed in class (Tobin, 1990).

theory of teaching
Description, explanations, and prediction of actions taken with the intent to facilitate learning.

metaphor A way to represent and talk about experiences in terms of other, more familiar, or more commonly shared events that seem comparable.

What might be this teacher's metaphors for teachers, learners, and the teaching-learning process? How might understanding these metaphors help this individual become a better teacher?

By contrast, another teacher in Tobin's study saw herself as a comedian. She believed that "students will be captivated by charm, humour, and well-organized presentations, which they will find enjoyable and easy to learn" (Tobin, 1990, p. 124). Unfortunately, students responded to this teacher with aggressive and uncooperative behaviour. Despite her belief in the teacher as a facilitator of learning, her classroom was not an environment conducive to learning. There seemed to be a mismatch between the teacher's expressed view of the teaching-learning process and her behaviours in the classroom. The results of Tobin's study suggest two conclusions. First, when teachers act in accord with various metaphors, different classroom cultures can emerge. Second, the cultures that emerge may not always reflect what teachers expect. Consider, for example, the teacher who thought her comedic approach to teaching would create an enjoyable and captivating atmosphere. Her behaviours, however, did not yield an effective learning environment. As a result, students in her classroom did not act as she expected.

Analyzing Metaphors in Teacher Problem Solving

Discovering and reflecting upon their metaphors for teaching and learning can help teachers understand problems occurring in their classrooms. Examining a metaphor in light of classroom reality can also suggest possible solutions to problems. Recall how in the Teacher Chronicle Kris realized that his teaching behaviour, based on a battleground metaphor, did not match his hopes and beliefs about the teaching-learning process. Making metaphors explicit and then reflecting on the metaphors to discover classroom implications is one way in which teachers can learn from their classroom experience and the classroom experiences of others. These discoveries can lead to beneficial changes in how teachers relate to students and organize and implement lessons. Consider, for example, this reflection of a student teacher:

> When my cooperating teacher referred to my view of teaching as "constant companion," I realized I was taking on more than I could be to my kids. I had been having lots of problems with management because I found it so hard to call anyone down—because I wanted everyone to know that I liked them the

Insights on Successful Practice

How did your experience working with a mentor help you to become a more effective teacher?

Finally, I had my own classroom, and after only a few weeks I was afraid I was becoming the teacher I swore I'd never become: arbitrary, gruff, and cynical. Enter the mentor. She taught down the hall from me. The same children who were making me crazy seemed to be transformed under her influence.

One evening, drained and in doubt, I walked down to her room and started drawing from her the first of many real-life lessons. She gave me some suggestions for working with Jackie, who had some serious learning problems. They were good ideas. As the year went on, she shared tips on organization, demonstrated a positive approach to discipline, and could even help me find a teacher's manual when I needed one. It meant a lot that year to have someone to listen, suggest, role model, and support.

I've been teaching for nearly twenty years now, and I just do not remember all the little things she shared with me. But it occurs to me now that those on-the-job lessons I got from her were not the most important things that she gave me. What were the important things? First, the knowledge that I wasn't alone in my work. She helped me see how I could work with other staff members, parents, and children for our common ends. Second, she managed to transmit her belief in children and their possibilities: she *knew* they were going to succeed in her class. Finally, she modelled respect for our children, the kind of respect that gets children in touch with the good things in themselves. Respect that demands the best work from students. Respect that is not afraid to challenge failings, but never attacks the person.

I think that the early positive, practical support I got has helped give me attitudes that allow me to love my work now. Connectedness, confidence, and respect are powerful shapers of success for teachers as well as students. New teachers all have to find personal paths to these things, and a mentor can help show the way.

EDWARD VALENT
Elementary School Teacher

Your Insights

What are the benefits of mentors for beginning teachers? What steps might you take to develop a mentorship relationship as you begin to teach?

same, and I very much wanted them to like me. I wanted them to know I would be there for them. Part of me still wants that very much, but that conversation certainly clarified for me that I would lose any hope of winning anyone over if the classroom turned to chaos (Carter, 1990, p. 114).

Analyzing metaphors is a problem-solving strategy; that is, **reframing** an event or problem in terms of metaphors provides teachers with novel ways of "seeing" professional puzzles (Munby & Russell, 1990). Insights gained in this way help teachers to resolve issues or problems in their teaching.

Exposing implicit beliefs about teaching and learning also helps teachers to detect inconsistencies in their metaphors. Beginning teachers, especially, often have stated beliefs about learning that are not reflected in their actions in the classroom. Recall Kris's comments in the Teacher Chronicle. Although he stated a belief in cooperative learning and shared knowledge construction, he initially described events of the day in terms of metaphors that conflict with these beliefs. Statements such as "Jamie challenged me" and "she threw down the gauntlet" suggest a conflict or war metaphor, in which the teacher and student are on opposite sides. The words "I was trying to get across ..." suggest the notion that knowledge is a commodity to be handed from teacher to student.

reframing Rethinking an event or problem in terms of metaphors in order to gain a new perspective.

Sylvie, in contrast, uses the metaphor of the well-oiled machine, which is consistent with a view of group dynamics in which students learn to work well together and each student plays an important part.

Teaching and learning can be viewed from many different metaphorical vantage points. Researchers and theorists often employ metaphors in an attempt to describe and explain teaching and learning. One example is the agricultural metaphor: a view of teaching and learning that focuses on student growth. As you can see from Table 1.1, every metaphor has certain consequences for what happens in the classroom—who defines the problem or task, the resources to be studied, how and with whom the work is accomplished, and with what anticipated outcomes. As you read each metaphor in Table 1.1, try to visualize what is happening in the classroom that is consistent with the metaphor. Consider the following aspects of classroom operation:

- how a teacher might deliver a lesson
- what classroom rules might be in place
- how much student-teacher and student-student interaction might take place
- what kinds of assessment techniques might be used
- what sorts of learning outcomes would be valued

Some teachers, for example, see themselves as captains whose role is to lead the troops into battle. They see themselves as being in charge, issuing directions, and providing relevant information. The role of the student, then, is to follow orders and to use the information as directed. Learning is a matter of conquering problems and overcoming barriers that may stand in the way of performance and achievement. Regardless of which metaphor of the teaching-learning process you adopt, there are consequences for the role of the learner, the role of the teacher, and the types of instructional strategies deemed most appropriate for helping students learn.

So, how can you, an aspiring teacher, develop your view of the teaching-learning process? The first step is to make explicit your own metaphors of teaching and learning and to reflect on them. Your general metaphor is the foundation of your theory of teaching. It influences your description, explanation, and predictions about teaching. As a consequence of studying the theory, research, and practice presented in this text, your theory of teaching—and the metaphor on which it is based—will probably change. Your next step is to examine other metaphors to consider their contributions to your understanding of teaching and their implications for classroom practice. Your job will be to consider those implications as they apply to learners, learning tasks, learning environments, and learning contexts—such as students' cultural backgrounds—in which the teaching-learning process occurs.

The research on metaphorical reasoning, particularly on the metaphors used by teachers, suggests strongly that aspiring and practising teachers can improve by explicating and examining their metaphors of teaching. In the Teacher Chronicle, Sylvie, the veteran teacher, commented on how her view of teaching changed when she reflected on both her experience in her classroom and research she had read. Even though she has considerable teaching experience, her theory of teaching continues to change. This is true of all expert teachers. Even so, the thinking of expert teachers differs in some significant ways from the thinking of novice teachers. What are these differences and how can such differences help aspiring teachers prepare to enter the profession?

CRITICAL THINKING: Write your own metaphor of teaching and learning. In small groups, ask each member to share their metaphor and what it expresses.

CRITICAL THINKING: Write your own metaphor(s) on the inside back cover of this text. At the end of the course, revisit this metaphor to determine if it still expresses your views on teaching and learning. Write new metaphors as required.

TABLE 1.1 *A Sample of Metaphors Used by Teachers to Express Their Views of Teaching and Learning*

TEACHER METAPHOR	EXPRESSION OF METAPHOR
Teacher as forest ranger	"I see myself as a protector of the learning environment. A protector takes care of everyone's common property, for the benefit of all."
Teacher as air traffic controller	"There are so many decisions to make in teaching. It's hard to get one thing settled before another plane full of passengers is ready to land."
Teacher as flood control director	"Things don't always work in teaching. Or maybe they don't work the way you expect. Sometimes, you do something that just opens the floodgates, and you have to wait for the flow to subside before you can redirect it."
Teacher as bird-watcher	"I try to be vigilant for the rare birds who can create such chaos in a classroom. But I have to be careful that spotting only that special species will make me miss lots of other birds in flight."
Teacher as gourmet chef	"I was coming in every day trying to serve up the most delicious instructional activities, and I was growing increasingly angry that the students weren't appreciating my delicious academic treats."
Teacher as scientist	"I'm experimenting all the time, trying different things to see how they work. I try to figure out what happened."
Teacher as traffic cop	"I'm trying to change my view of discipline, because I realized seeing myself as a traffic cop put all the responsibility on me and assumes that students will be trying to break the law."
Teacher as preacher	"I lecture in class, because I think an important part of my role is taking the opportunity to share what I know."

STUDENT METAPHOR	EXPRESSION OF METAPHOR
Student as pathfinder	"At the beginning of the term, Ashley seemed so lost all the time. Now, she's beginning to find her way."
Student as scientist	"You pose a problem and the students have to try to hypothesize how to solve the problem. They look at all the variables and then go about doing their experimenting."
Student as plant	"With some kids, you really don't have to provide much structure. I just water them and they grow."
Student as detective	"Learning is like solving puzzles. Students have to find all the clues and then put them together in the right way to find the answer."
Student as sponge	"Some subjects—math is an example—just require more soak time."

Source: Some of the metaphors in this table were suggested by aspiring teachers at Florida State University; others were discussed in articles appearing in the special issue of *Theory Into Practice*, "Metaphors We Learn By," 29 (2), Spring 1990.

How Can You Learn to Think Like an Expert Teacher?

Teaching the way you were taught might be satisfactory if the nature of schools and the society they serve did not change and if the teaching practices of days gone by were uniformly effective. But society has changed. The responsibilities given to schools and to teachers have changed. Fenstermacher (1990) likens the changes in the demands of teaching to changes in aviation:

> Thirty or forty years ago, much of what is known as ... aviation was a matter of skill with stick and rudder, dead-reckoning navigation, and carefully nurtured seat-of-the pants instincts. These relatively simple skills and instincts still form the core of flying, but no one can fly in heavily trafficked airways with just these skills. The crowding of modern airports, the amount of airplane traffic, and the horrible consequences of aviation accidents have resulted in the development of complex requirements and skills for flying (pp. 139–140).

The conditions of teaching and learning in schools have grown so complex that educators are experimenting with major changes in the way schools are organized, the way they are administered, and the way the teaching-learning process is implemented. You will enter the teaching profession at a time when the old paradigms of teaching and learning are being cast off in favour of efforts to reform and restructure education. As schools continue to respond to the complex problems of our society, it will be necessary for teachers to continue learning throughout their careers (Huling-Austin, 1994). The complexity of teaching requires that those who pursue it as a profession accept the challenge of continuous learning.

Not only has teaching practice changed, but so has our understanding of teaching. The recognition of teaching as a complex activity has spawned research designed to investigate how novice teachers differ from expert teachers. The rationale for such research is that if we can determine how teaching expertise develops, it may be possible to facilitate that development. How do expert teachers think? What do they think about? What do they see in classroom behaviour that novice teachers can't see?

Differences between Expert and Novice Teachers

Expert teachers see classrooms differently than do novices. The reason they see different things is that they know different things. The knowledge that expert teachers bring with them into their classrooms allows them to infer accurately and efficiently, to determine relevant from irrelevant information, and to comprehend the meaning behind classroom activity. Experts can read classrooms better than novices (Swanson, O'Connor, & Cooney, 1990).

An experienced teacher was asked what novice teachers need to know in order to become successful teachers. The teacher responded, "I think what you have to learn is how to deal with mental jumbling. You have to learn how to manage the ... excuse the term ... 'mental mess' provided by all the action you see in the classroom and how to stay in control of yourself and the situation in such a way that it continues to be a productive learning environment" (Carter, 1987, p. 5). This teacher's advice is consistent with much of the research on the differences between expert and novice teachers.

Much of the research on expert–novice differences in teaching indicates that expert teachers are more able to comprehend complex classroom phenomena. This research has often compared the perceptual abilities of experts, novices, and postulants—people who are planning to become teachers after a midcareer shift (Berliner, 1986; Carter, Sabers, Cushing, Pinnegar, & Berliner, 1987). In one study, experts, novices, and postulants viewed a series of approximately fifty slides taken in science and math classes and were asked to discuss their reactions (Carter, Cushing, Sabers, Stein, & Berliner, 1988). The sequence in which the slides were shown portrayed a classroom session from beginning to end. Subjects were free to stop the sequence at any point to comment on any slide.

The results of the study indicated that experts were better able than novices or postulants to determine what was important and unimportant information. Experts were better able to form connections between and among pieces of information. Experts were also better at identifying both instructional problems and classroom management problems. An additional finding from this study was that experts, to a much greater degree than either novices or postulants, agreed among themselves. Whenever one expert commented on one part of the classroom sequence, other experts tended to comment on the same part. This was true for slides taken at the beginning, the middle, and the end of the classroom session. Furthermore, the nature of the comments among experts was similar. For example, the following comments were made by three different expert teachers in response to the fifth slide in a sequence:

> "It's a good shot of both people being involved and something happening."
> "Everybody seems to be interested in what they're doing at their lab stations."
> "Everybody working. A positive environment" (Carter et al., 1988, p. 30).

Other findings supported the similarity among expert responses. Recall that the procedure used in the study allowed the subjects to interrupt a sequence of fifty slides at any time in order to comment on what they had seen and that the slides were in a reasonable but imperfect chronological sequence. Novices and postulants made no comments about the chronology of the sequence. Experts, however, noticed several instances of slides out of sequence. For example, one expert commented, "See here's everybody; this is everybody sitting back down again. Obviously, this is not in sequence with the other pictures" (Carter et al., 1988, p. 30).

The investigators, while photographing a math class for slides to show to subjects, noticed a student who seemed very unhappy. At one point during the class, tears appeared in the student's eyes. The student was inattentive and did not interact with any other students or with the teacher. This student was more noticeable in the slides near the end of the sequence than in earlier slides. Only one subject, an expert, was able to discern from the slide sequence what the investigators had seen in person. The expert made the following comments: "I feel kind of sorry for the one girl in the front. It doesn't appear that she is part of the group.... There is definitely a problem there ... she's having problems other than what's going on with the classroom" (Carter et al., 1988, p. 30).

The differences Kathy Carter and her associates found between expert teachers on the one hand and novice and postulant teachers on the other were not

TRY THIS: Observe or interview both novice and experienced teachers in order to further appreciate the differences between them.

attributable to attitudes alone. All novices eligible to participate in the study had been judged competent, and of those, only the novices who were judged by their superiors to have the greatest potential to develop into excellent teachers were selected. Assuming that novices who are "good" beginning teachers have good work habits and positive attitudes toward teaching, then the differences between them and the experts must be attributed to other causes.

Chances are, you have a high level of confidence in your ability to teach. People entering teacher education programs generally do have high levels of confidence in their abilities to teach (Brookhart & Freeman, 1992). If you are a male, you might be more confident than your female classmates (Book & Freeman, 1986; Kalaian & Freeman, 1990; Knight, Duke, & Palcic, 1988). And if you entered your teacher education program directly from high school, you might be less confident than those who entered education after a previous degree (Brookhart, Miller, Loadman, & Whordley, 1990). All those entering teacher education report high levels of confidence and high levels of commitment to the teaching profession. However, research shows that the way you feel about teaching and your abilities to teach, your affective responses, are not the major difference between you and expert teachers. The major difference is cognitive; that is, expert teachers think differently than do novices.

> **schemata** Theoretical knowledge structures that contain information, facts, principles, and the relationships among them.

Teachers' Thought Processes

Carol Livingston and Hilda Borko (1989) conducted an analysis of differences in the way expert teachers and novice teachers think. They compared the planning, the actual interaction with students while presenting a lesson, and post-lesson reflections of both experts and novices. The authors explained the expert–novice differences they found in terms of cognitive schemata (Anderson, 1984). **Schemata** are theoretical knowledge structures that contain information, facts, principles, and the relationships among them. For example, you probably have a restaurant schemata that contains information about menus, waiters, cheques, and how those aspects of eating at a restaurant are related.

According to research on expert and novice teachers, what might be some differences in awareness and attitudes between this experienced teacher and a novice? Are there also differences in the ways beginners and experts think?

Furthermore, you can use this restaurant schemata to interpret new experiences. The next time you eat at an unfamiliar restaurant, notice how much of the experience you are able to predict or anticipate based on your prior knowledge. Teaching schemata include mental representations of teaching experiences. The teaching schemata of expert teachers are, predictably, richer collections of facts, principles, and conceptions of teaching than the teaching schemata of novices. Livingston and Borko describe the difference as follows:

> [The] cognitive schemata of experts typically are more elaborate, more complex, more interconnected, and more easily accessible than those of novices.... Therefore, expert teachers have larger, better-integrated stores of facts, principles, and experiences to draw upon as they engage in planning, interactive teaching, and reflection (1989, p. 37).

The authors reported that experts described extensive mental plans for the lessons they delivered. The mental plans included a general outline of the content to be covered and the processes by which learning was to occur. The experts' plans did not include specific details such as how much time would be spent in any particular learning activity or the specific problems or examples to be covered. Rather, the specifics were determined in class as reactions to student questions or responses. However, the mental plans of two of the three experts studied included specific actions that would be taken, depending on the reactions of students.

Basing their interpretation on the notion of schemata, Livingston and Borko described experts' planning as matching existing information from their knowledge structures—information about instructional activities, the content to be learned, typical student behaviours—with the needs of a particular lesson. Experts were able to make these matches, and thus construct their plans, very efficiently. Novices do not have the extensive information that experts have, nor can they access what information they do have as readily. In constructing their teaching plans, novices often have to interrupt the process in order to build or modify their teaching schemata. One way to think about these findings is that for experts, schemata facilitate the construction of plans, whereas for novices, planning facilitates the construction of schemata.

Another advantage enjoyed by experts in the Livingston and Borko study is their ability to discriminate what is relevant to their planning and interaction decisions from what is irrelevant. For example, experts are better able than novices to compare student questions, concerns, or behaviour with appropriate schemata to determine what should be taken into account in deciding the next step and what can be safely ignored. Because experts deal only with information that is relevant to decisions that must be made while teaching, they consider only information that is relevant to teaching decisions in their post-lesson reflections. Novices, however, cannot automatically discriminate relevant from irrelevant information. Just as the process of planning is disrupted because schemata need to be modified, so can a novice teacher become confused or thrown off by a student's question. Imagine a novice teacher who is attempting, without prior experience, to respond to a student who says, "I don't understand anything we've been talking about the whole period." The novice teacher, who wants very much to address the student's frustration, might feel lost and think, "Should I start over? Are they confused because I'm not sure of the content? Have I made a mistake in explaining a concept? Did I mix up that crucial distinction? Did I go too fast? Is this student just trying to frustrate me?" The novice, not sure of the appropriate way to respond, must evaluate all of the possibilities in order to make a decision.

The expert, in contrast, has probably responded to that student question innumerable times. Through experience, the expert may have developed a routine of questioning that helps the student (and the teacher) get closer to the source of the student's confusion. Instead of considering many possible courses of action, as was the case with the novice teacher, the expert begins probing the student's confusion without hesitation.

Novices' schemata do not contain routines developed as a consequence of responding to numerous similar teaching situations. Because they lack experience, their schemata do not include routine approaches to many of the situations they encounter early in their teaching careers. Novices must consider more information than experts both while planning and while making interactive decisions (Livingston & Borko, 1989). The comparative complexity and richness of expert schemata account well for the differences between experts and novices reviewed here. The richness of expert schemata also explains how experts are better able to use their interpretations of classroom activity to make instructional and classroom management decisions (Berliner, 1987, 1988; Borko & Shavelson, 1990; Carter et al., 1987; Leinhardt & Greeno, 1986; Peterson & Comeaux, 1987).

The Processes of Reflective Construction

The schemata of expert teachers allow them to describe, explain, and predict teaching and learning phenomena better than novices. Thus, one way to conceptualize the difference between expert and novice or aspiring teachers is to think of expert teachers as possessing more sophisticated theories of teaching. Is teaching experience necessary for the development of expertise? Yes. Is teaching experience sufficient for the development of expertise? No. Experience alone will not make you an expert teacher. You must be able to make sense of your experience. You must know how to learn from your experience. To become an expert teacher, you must become an expert learner, and the key to learning about teaching is **reflective construction** (cf. Carter et al., 1988; Cochrane-Smith, 1991; Cochrane-Smith & Lytle, 1990; Livingston & Borko, 1989). But upon what should an aspiring teacher reflect? And what should an aspiring teacher construct? Take a look at Figure 1.1.

Figure 1.1 is an attempt to portray the dynamic processes that connect the knowledge base of teaching and one's theory of teaching. The **knowledge base of teaching** includes **educational psychology**, the scientific study of the teaching-learning process, and classroom practice. This book presents both the research and the theoretical principles derived from research that constitute educational psychology and accounts of classroom practice. Further, we have included relevant Canadian research and experiences wherever appropriate to assist you in building a knowledge base that is contextually meaningful.

Both components of the knowledge base are necessary. Beyond acquiring the knowledge base, you must begin practising the hallmarks of expert teaching: reflection, the testing of ideas, and the active construction of a theory of teaching.

We also encourage you to consult and examine the many excellent Canadian publications that focus on educational and instructional psychology and related topics. The following journals, while not an exhaustive listing, include up-to-the moment articles on theory, research, and practices relevant to novice and experienced teachers: *Alberta Journal of Educational Research, Canadian Journal of Education, Canadian Journal of Special Education, Canadian Journal of School Psychology, Canadian Journal of Native Education,* and *The McGill Journal of Education.*

reflective construction
Thinking critically about the principles and concepts of educational psychology and classroom practice in order to develop a theory of teaching.

knowledge base of teaching
The source from which a theory of teaching can be reflectively constructed; that which is known from educational psychology and classroom practice.

educational psychology
The scientific study of the teaching-learning process.

FIGURE 1.1
The Continuous Process of
Reflective Construction

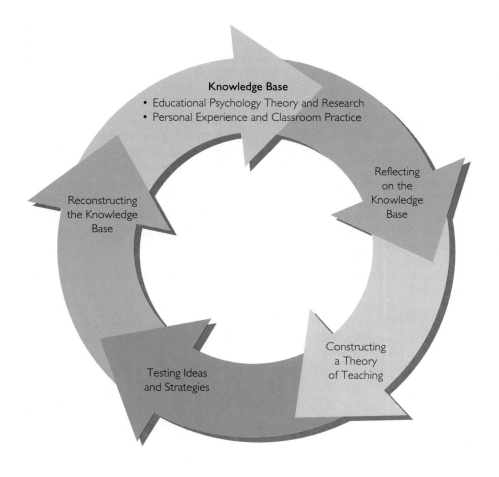

Knowledge Base
- Educational Psychology Theory and Research
- Personal Experience and Classroom Practice

Reflecting on the Knowledge Base

Reconstructing the Knowledge Base

Constructing a Theory of Teaching

Testing Ideas and Strategies

In the Teacher Chronicle at the beginning of the chapter, Kris was engaged in reflection. He thoughtfully considered his own practice in light of his purposes and goals. Sylvie contributed to his reflection by sharing her knowledge of pertinent research and some of her own classroom experiences. The product of Kris' reflection was a set of ideas of how the teaching-learning process would work in the context of his classroom. What his reflection produced was a change in his theory of teaching with regard to the use of cooperative-learning tasks. Kris' description of cooperative learning was different, his explanation of cooperative learning changed, and his predictions of the outcomes of cooperative tasks were altered because he reflected—with the help of an expert.

The ideas that are tested by teachers come from their theories. If a teacher tries an idea in his or her classroom, the resulting experience augments the knowledge base. As long as a teacher tests his or her ideas, the knowledge base available for reflection will continue to expand. As long as a teacher continues to consult the research and principles that are generated by educational psychologists, the knowledge base will grow. And as long as the knowledge base continues to expand, a teacher will always have an opportunity to reflect on new knowledge and thus to construct and reconstruct an ever-evolving theory of teaching.

A career in teaching is a career in learning. You may not be an expert teacher by the time you leave this course, and you may not enter the teaching profession as an expert, but you can begin the process of reflecting on the knowledge base that you will encounter in this book. You can begin constructing a theory of teaching. The importance of reflective construction is our third basic assumption about teaching: Reflective construction is necessary for the development of teaching expertise.

On What Theory of Teaching Is This Book Based?

To answer this question directly, the theory of teaching you will encounter in this book is the theory that we, the authors, have constructed through reflecting on the research and principles of educational psychology, on the classroom experiences of dozens of other teachers, and on our own teaching experiences.

In this chapter we have stated our three basic assumptions about teaching.

1. Teaching and learning are aspects of the same process.
2. Your view of the teaching-learning process affects your classroom practice.
3. Reflective construction is necessary for the development of teaching expertise.

These are the foundations from which our theory of teaching derives. That theory, which has evolved from our understanding of educational psychology and classroom practice, yields other working assumptions. These are all assumptions we continue to work from and continue to test in our own teaching and research and continue to reflect on in the teaching and research of others.

Working Assumptions about Teaching and Learning

The book is organized into six parts. The working assumptions that underlie our theory of teaching and, therefore, our understanding of the knowledge base of teaching and learning are listed below. These statements represent the main themes of this book.

Part 1   Development (Chapters 2 and 3)
- Development is complex and multifaceted.
- Development affects learning.
- Life conditions affect development.

Part 2   Diversity (Chapters 4 and 5)
- Learners are diverse.
- Students' diversity and individuality affect their learning.
- Inclusive classrooms provide learning opportunities.

Part 3   Learning (Chapters 6, 7, and 8)
- Learning is shaped by the learner's environment.
- Learning is a function of complex mental activities.
- Learning is active construction in social contexts.

Part 4   Motivation and Classroom Dynamics (Chapters 9 and 10)
- People are naturally motivated to learn.
- Needs and values affect motivation.
- Classroom management is a shared concern.

Part 5   Effective Instruction (Chapters 11 and 12)
- Teachers and students are both learners.
- Teachers coordinate the context for learning.
- Instructional technologies support teaching and learning.

Part 6 Evaluation (Chapters 13 and 14)

- Assessment serves multiple purposes.
- Assessment improves teaching and learning.
- Authentic activity provides a basis for assessment.

Understanding the teaching-learning process means understanding the factors that can influence it. The factors that influence the teaching-learning process are implied by the assumptions stated above. In this book, we have attempted to integrate the principles of educational psychology and the experiences of classroom practitioners for the purpose of helping you develop a theory of teaching that can be tested in your own classroom.

That integration of theory and practice will come from your own "systematic inquiry of teaching, learning, and schooling" (the primary context in which your theory of teaching will be tested) (Cochrane-Smith, 1991, p. 283). The features in this text have been designed to help you conduct that systematic inquiry.

The Teaching Approach of This Textbook

This book may not be the only learning resource at your disposal, but we have assumed that it is an important one. In writing it, we have incorporated a number of instructional features that are designed to help you acquire and use the knowledge base of teaching. This preview will serve as a basis for a learning strategy that you can employ to achieve the **Learning Outcomes** as you study this book.

Teacher Chronicle. There are several components of the Teacher Chronicle feature. The Teacher Chronicle at the beginning of this and every chapter serves as a focal point for the ideas presented. Teacher Chronicles are events in teaching practice. These events are discussed in the body of a chapter and are concluded or resolved at the end. After reading this chapter, for example, you can find out how Kris modifies and retests his theory of teaching.

Focus Questions following the Teacher Chronicle are designed to help you anticipate how the content of the chapter relates to the teaching-learning process that is represented in the Teacher Chronicle event.

The Teacher Chronicle Conclusion at the end of each chapter is followed by "Application Questions," the final component of the Teacher Chronicle feature. Application Questions refer specifically to the events in the Teacher Chronicle and allow you to reinterpret those events through the application of key concepts from the chapter.

Insights on Successful Practice. Earlier in this chapter we identified classroom practice as part of the knowledge base of teaching. In addition to the Teacher Chronicles, descriptions of classroom practice are provided in three or four features called Insights on Successful Practice that are found in each chapter. The sources of the Insights are practising master teachers. These expert teachers wrote essays in response to specific questions we asked that relate to the chapters in which the essays appear.

The essays are opportunities for you to share the experiences of expert teachers and to broaden the classroom practice portion of your knowledge base. These accounts of how experts use the principles and concepts of educational psychology to handle practical situations are potential solutions to the problems you will encounter in your teaching. Further, the master teachers who share their insights on classroom practice are models for developing your theory of teaching. What better way to begin the journey toward expertise than by studying the practice of experts? Opportunities to reflect on the insights of expert teachers are provided through Insights margin notes, which also invite you to think critically about the views presented.

Here's How. Learning about the knowledge base of teaching is the beginning of your journey toward teaching expertise. Your goal should be to use the knowledge base to reflectively construct a theory of teaching and, ultimately, to add to your knowledge base by testing teaching ideas and strategies. To help you construct your theory of teaching and test ideas, we present features in every chapter called Here's How. These features list specific actions teachers can take in situations that all teachers face.

Here's How features also list steps you can take to turn a theoretical principle or concept into classroom practice. These lists are action plans for teaching and learning. The Here's How that concludes this chapter, for example, is an action plan for using this book as a resource for your professional development.

Key Concepts and Margin Notes. Key concepts throughout the book are printed in boldface. The key concepts are defined in the text and in a running glossary that appears in the margins of the book. The terms are also listed alphabetically at the end of the chapter as a study aid.

We hope you have been reading and responding to the margin notes in this chapter. You will encounter margin notes throughout the entire book. These notes annotate the text and are designed to provide additional opportunities to reflect on the knowledge base, construct your theory of teaching, and discover conceptual connections to other portions of the text. The categories of margin notes include the following:

- Point—reminders of the basic working assumptions of this book, statements of main ideas, and statements of key principles in educational psychology.

- Reflection—questions that help you to reflect on your assumptions and values and to relate chapter content to your own prior experiences.

- Example—additional illustrations of chapter concepts and their applications in practice.

- Critical Thinking—questions that help you link and apply chapter concepts and develop practical problem-solving strategies.

- Connection—cross-references to related concepts and information in other sections or chapters.

- Try This—activities and field experiences you can undertake to expand your knowledge base and apply your learning in authentic situations.

What might be this teacher's assumptions about students and the teaching-learning process? How might these assumptions influence teaching practice?

- Insights—questions that invite you to respond to the commentaries of the expert teachers featured in Insights on Successful Practice.

We conclude this chapter with suggestions for using this book and its features. You may have already begun thinking about how you might use the text features in your learning. As with all the Here's How features in this book, we encourage you to test the ideas in the following list and to modify and improve those ideas.

Internet Resources. The computer age has made readily available a plethora of information about topics and issues of interest to teachers. However, like any published or printed material, the quality is variable and this is especially evident when "surfing the 'net." We have included a brief list of www. sites that provide high-quality information about the topics covered in this book. We have selected sites developed by the major education and psychology associations, as well as a number of www. listings of relevance to Canadian teachers. While there are many more listings which we would encourage you to seek out and explore, we are confident that you will find a wealth of contemporary and relevant information in the sites we have listed.

Here's How

Here's How To Use This Book

- **Preview/Question.** Use the Learning Outcomes at the beginning of each chapter to speculate on the issues of teaching and learning that will be addressed in the chapter. As you read the Learning Outcomes, think about your experiences as a student, your teachers, and your assumptions about teaching and learning. The Teacher Chronicle and Focus Questions at the beginning of each chapter and the Chapter Summary at the end of each chapter can also be used to preview additional questions that you hope to answer as you study the chapter. Check the Insights on Successful Practice, for example, to see what questions the expert teachers who are featured in the chapter have addressed. Check also the Application Questions at the end of the chapter and questions in the margin notes.
- **Read/Relate/Reflect.** Make your reading of each chapter active. Relate the events in the Teacher Chronicle to the principles and concepts you encounter. Seek to answer your own questions as you read, using the features and margin notes to prompt reflective construction. Read each chapter with the goal of discovering relationships between theory and practice.
- **Share.** Share with classmates or colleagues your questions, insights, and developing theory of teaching. Share your interpretations of Teacher Chronicles, reactions to Insights on Successful Practice, and answers to Application Questions. Discussing with others how the material in a chapter informs your views is part of the social construction of knowledge.
- **Test Ideas.** Knowing is not the end of learning. Test the knowledge you acquire through reading, reflecting, and sharing by applying Here's How features and Try This margin notes. Try This is a source of ideas for additional learning activities such as teacher interviews, field observations, and journal writing.

Teacher Chronicle Conclusion

Teacher Talk

A few days after their conversation in the teachers' lounge, Sylvie and Kris arrive early for a staff meeting after school.

"How are your groups faring?" asks Sylvie.

Kris smiles. "Much better. I realized that I was asking students to work cooperatively when they really didn't know how. And without adequate guidance on my part, I was pushing them out of the plane without a parachute. No wonder they were acting out. The more I thought about your story and my experience and looked at the material you gave me, the more I realized that my actions in the classroom weren't very consistent with sound professional practice and my own beliefs about teaching. I really believe that kids can take responsibility for their own learning and that they learn by exploring their environment. But I acted as though teaching is telling. I told them what to do and expected them to learn it."

Sylvie nods. "As you gain more experience, I think you'll find that your theory of teaching shifts over time. I know mine did, and my beliefs are still evolving."

Application Questions

1. How does Teacher Talk reflect the idea that teaching and learning are two aspects of the same process?

2. How do the events in Teacher Talk support the three basic assumptions that serve as the foundation for the theory of teaching espoused in this book?

3. How do Kris' metaphors for teaching and learning change?

4. How do Kris' and Sylvie's thinking reflect known differences between expert and novice teachers?

5. How do Kris' schemata for teaching change?

6. On what parts of the knowledge base does Kris draw to reconstruct his theory of teaching?

7. In what ways do you expect this textbook to provide a knowledge base for you to develop a theory of teaching through reflective construction?

CHAPTER SUMMARY

What Are Teaching and Learning? (L.O. 1, p. 3)

The definition of teaching (action taken with the intent to facilitate learning) subsumes the definition of learning (change in thought or behaviour that modifies a person's capabilities). One of the assumptions on which this book is based is that teaching and learning are aspects of the same process: the teaching-learning process.

How Can you Develop a Theory of Teaching? (L.O. 3, p. 4)

Developing one's theory of teaching starts by becoming aware of one's metaphors for the teaching-learning process. Exposing and examining one's metaphors helps to focus one's views of teaching and to identify inconsistencies between beliefs and practice. Various metaphors of the teaching-learning process are examined for their instructional implications. Research on metaphorical reasoning and on teachers' metaphors is presented.

How Can You Learn to Think Like an Expert Teacher? (L.O. 5, p. 11)

Research on the differences between expert and novice teachers is discussed. The differences between expert and novice teachers are explained by the comparable richness and complexity of the schemata of expert teachers. Expert teachers interpret classroom situations differently than novices and, for that reason, can operate more efficiently and effectively than novices.

To become an expert teacher, aspiring teachers must become expert learners. Aspiring teachers must approach the knowledge base of teaching—including both educational psychology and classroom practice—through a process of reflective construction.

On What Theory of Teaching Is This Book Based? (L.O. 7, p. 17)

The authors' theory of teaching is described by presenting the basic working assumptions of the text. In addition to viewing teaching and learning as integrated, two other basic assumptions are made. First, it is assumed that your view of the teaching-learning process will affect your classroom practice. Second, it is assumed that reflective construction is necessary for the development of teaching expertise.

The instructional features of the text and a strategy for using those features to enhance your study of the text are presented.

KEY CONCEPTS

educational psychology p. 15

knowledge base of teaching p. 15

learning p. 3

metaphor p. 6

reflective construction p. 15

reframing p. 8

schemata p. 13

teaching p. 3

teaching-learning process p. 3

theory of teaching p. 6

2 Cognitive Development

LEARNING OUTCOMES

When you have completed this chapter, you will be able to

1. recognize that development is influenced by both internal (nature) and external (nurture) factors

2. describe the four main factors that influence development: maturation, active experience, social interaction, and cultural and situational contexts

3. define the central Piagetian concepts: assimilation, accomodation, and equilibration

4. describe and give examples of the three types of knowledge: physical, logico-mathematical, and social-arbitrary

5. summarize the central characteristics of Piaget's four stages of development : sensorimotor, preoperations, concrete operations, and formal operations

6. describe and give examples of the two basic types of tools (material and psychological) that people use to interact with and understand their environment

7. define Vygotsky's notion of *zone of proximal development* (ZPD) and give two implications for classroom teaching

8. contrast information-processing theory from the approach of Piaget and Vygotsky

9. define the three central components of information processing theory (code information, store, and retrieve)

10. define and give examples of metacognition

11. define the linguistic terms *phonology*, *syntax*, *semantics*, and *pragmatics*

12. describe the steps that discover a child's ZPD

13. describe how to provide concrete experiences along with authentic activities and cooperative learning to advance children's cognitive development

Teacher Chronicle

Does It Work?

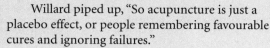

Hillary Olson was in the middle of her high school biology lesson when Willard put his hand up. "Yes, Willard." "Ms. Olson, does acupuncture work? My uncle says it helps him, but my aunt says it's all in his mind." Ms. Olson considered the opportunity that had been presented to her. This might be a good time to introduce the topic of designing a study to test various claims.

"How do we know whether a treatment works or not?" she shot at the class.

"Ask the patients," said Jeremy, leaning forward in his desk.

Louise wasn't convinced, "No, that's not good enough, Mr. May in history class said that blood-letting was used for several centuries as a cure-all. And that it didn't cure the plague or boils or sick people."

Willard grew animated, "How can people use a treatment that doesn't work—it doesn't make sense."

"Well," Ms. Olson interjected, "We know that some people with fatal diseases get better without treatment. So we might selectively remember the successful cases and forget or ignore the failures."

Susan raised her hand, "I've also heard about something called the Placebo effect".

"What's that?" Arlene burst out.

Ms. Olson watched the student interchanges with interest. The class was bringing up the important basics by themselves. "Who knows about the Placebo effect?" she asked the class.

"Isn't it something psychological?" said Brian, who had just been listening so far.

"You're on the right track, Brian. Sometimes people are helped if they are given a sugar-coated pill but believe it is a real medicine. The effect of a placebo is entirely due to a person's belief."

Willard piped up, "So acupuncture is just a placebo effect, or people remembering favourable cures and ignoring failures."

"No, if we say that we are claiming to know the answer before we check it out," said Arlene.

"Yes," Ms. Olson added, "So what have we learned so far?"

"Well," Brian said carefully, "Just because people believe a treatment works doesn't mean it really works."

"So how could we study whether acupuncture works or not?" asked Ms. Olson. "Any suggestions?"

Focus Questions

1. What factors influence intellectual development?

2. How do students mentally organize their experiences in an adaptive way?

3. At what age can students conduct experiments to test "cause and effect"? What differentiates the high school student's approach to experimentation from that of a young child in grade one or two?

4. Why might the age of students be a factor in what they are capable of learning? What are the stages of cognitive development?

5. Can cognitive development be accelerated?

6. How might experience influence learning and development?

7. How are the acquisition of language and cognitive development related?

8. What is developmentally appropriate teaching practice?

What Are the Dimensions of Human Development?

How will you know when your students are capable of doing what you will ask them to do? How will you help each student realize his or her potential? *Developmental psychology* is the study of how humans grow toward their potential and of the capabilities that accompany that growth. Physical, cognitive, and social development are three dimensions of human development. **Cognitive development,** the subject of this chapter, is the growth in our capabilities as learners. *Cognitive development theory* attempts to explain how humans acquire and construct knowledge of themselves and their world.

CONNECTION: Social, personal, and moral development are the subjects of Chapter 3.

As humans develop, *what* they are capable of knowing changes, but so does *how* they are capable of knowing. What infants can know, for example, is probably limited to the world immediately surrounding them, and they come to know this world through physical interaction and manipulation of it. What do infants do with any object presented to them? They put it in their mouths, of course. This is an infant's primary means of learning about his or her world. Adults, in contrast, are capable of learning a great many things and have available to them many ways of doing so.

Theoretical descriptions of development are based on observations of change from inability to ability. For example, suppose that Cassie is unable to swim in June. But in August, she is observed swimming competently. Why did this change occur? Is this a matter of development or of learning?

Development theories differ from learning theories in that development focuses on human capabilities, whereas learning focuses on the realization of these capabilities. So in the example above, maturation enables Cassie to become capable of swimming, but learning provides the means by which she can transform the capability into proficient performance. The difference between development and learning has important implications for teaching. If teachers understand the capabilities—the potential abilities—their students bring to the classroom, they can do a better job of helping them realize those capabilities.

cognitive development
Changes in our capabilities as learners by which mental processes grow more complex and sophisticated.

Development Capabilities

Although humans all develop cognitive abilities in generally the same way, the specific capabilities they acquire will be unique to them as individuals. No two people have precisely the same knowledge of the world, for instance. Nor do any two people think and learn in exactly the same way. Genetic inheritance combined with life experience produces tremendous variability in individuals. Therefore, as you study the models of development presented in this chapter, you should be aware that, because of individual variability in developmental capabilities, the models will not always apply to every student in your classroom.

POINT: *Development is complex and multifaceted.* The instructional decisions you make in planning developmentally appropriate instruction will depend upon your knowledge of a great many things about your students.

Not only will students naturally vary in their developmental capabilities, some will show signs of disability or exceptionality. They may have difficulties or special talents (Hallahan & Kauffman, 1994). Students are considered exceptional learners when they "require special education and related services if they are to realize their full human potential" (Hallahan & Kauffman, 1994, p. 7). The special needs of these students are discussed in Chapter 5.

Influences on Development

REFLECTION: Describe something that you learned easily and something that was difficult to learn. Were the breakthrough and the difficulty due to development or learning?

Development is influenced by factors both internal and external to the individual. In the swimming example, physical maturation influenced the development of Cassie's ability to swim. This is an internal, or innate, factor. Physical growth occurs at a different rate for everyone, and everyone reaches a different endpoint of physical development. These differences will affect a person's individual capabilities. One of the authors, for example, will never be capable of world-class basketball because she is only five feet tall. On the other hand, she is not limited by her physical development in a sport such as sailing. Factors outside the individual also influence development. For instance, the active experience of manipulating objects influences the cognitive development of infants; they develop knowledge and capabilities through this interaction.

Developmental psychologists differ in the emphases they place on the roles of *nature* (internal factors) versus *nurture* (external factors) in human development. As you will see, emphasizing one over the other also has implications for the design of instruction and teachers' interactions with students in the classroom. Development is believed to be influenced by four factors: (1) maturation, (2) active experience, (3) social interaction, and (4) cultural and situational contexts. The latter is very important. As Judith Bernhard (1995) of Ryerson Polytechnic University has pointed out, Canada is a land of increasingly diverse populations. Developmental norms (typical performances) are often derived from studies of white, Western, middle-class children and may be inappropriate when dealing with children with other linguistic, ethnic, and cultural backgrounds.

TRY THIS: Observe children in a playground, noting the ages at which they play different games. How do maturation rates help account for your observations?

Maturation. Two children of identical age may differ in size, athletic skill, reasoning ability, intelligence, and emotional reactions. Differences in the rate of maturation lead to the differences—physical and psychological—that you will see among the students in your classroom. Because students usually reach puberty during their middle school years, middle school teachers often witness the greatest variability in development. In a single grade seven class, for example, there may be girls who have reached their full adult height and boys whose voices have not yet begun to deepen. *Maturation*, or "the unfolding of inherited potential" (Wadsworth, 1984, p. 29), establishes the limits of human development throughout the stages of growth.

Active Experience. *Active experience* refers both to manipulating objects in one's environment and to reorganizing one's thought patterns. An adolescent can figure out the parts of a carburetor by handling one—turning it over and peering into it. By thinking about the carburetor, the adolescent can also think about its function in a new way. As development proceeds, students become increasingly able to reorganize their thoughts without the prior necessity of physically manipulating objects in their environments.

Social Interaction. *Social interaction* comprises the experiences people have with others in their environment, including the exchange of ideas. At a very basic level, people negotiate the meanings of things in their world through their interactions with each other. For example, a boy grasps at an object that is just outside his reach. His mother interprets his behaviour as pointing and responds by giving him the object for which he was reaching. Gradually, as the boy apprehends the same meaning for the gesture as his mother does, he will deliberately use it to mean pointing (Vygotsky, 1978).

People also exchange and negotiate ideas through conversation. Consider the example of a girl who is given a dog for her birthday. She plays with, pets, and feeds her dog. She also talks with her parents about the concept of "loyalty," which reminds her of her experiences with the dog. The social interaction with her parents actually gives meaning to the girl's experience with the dog. It is through this social interaction that she gains her knowledge of loyalty.

Cultural and Situational Contexts. "What does it mean [for development] to grow up in one cultural milieu and not another?" (Bruner, 1973, p. 20). The cultures in which people live make specific and unique demands on individuals that influence the capabilities they develop. For example, if culture and language affect cognitive growth, then the cognitive styles of many Canadian Aboriginal children may vary from the dominant culture. Littlejohn (cited in Greenough-Olsen, 1993) has summarized the research on the child-rearing practices characteristic of Canadian Aboriginal peoples:

> The early child rearing promotes a value of independence and non-directive social interaction. Native children have been found to be generally more spatially than verbally oriented. They learn best from visual stimulation and are less efficient processing auditory information. They avidly absorb the world by sight and touch. Early learning occurs through a process of observation, imitation, private practice, and then successful display. The teaching-learning process within the Native home is primarily non-verbal, non-directive. It has been found to persist long after the family has been urbanized … question-asking was generally not found to be a verbal strategy employed by Native people in their day-to-day speech habits. This is in strict conflict with research on white middle-class families which has shown that questioning is the dominant interactive strategy.

Situational context influences development in a similar fashion. Saxe (1990) studied how different children in Brazil developed mathematical competence. Children who sold candy on the streets developed different mathematical understandings than their non-candy-selling peers. They developed a variety of procedures for making currency exchanges, whereas the non-candy-sellers acquired a mathematical symbol system for doing calculations on paper. The different situations in which the students were operating led to the development of different capabilities.

CONNECTION: Cultural diversity and the role of cultural beliefs and values in learning are discussed in Chapter 4.

As individuals develop cognitively, their attention spans increase, they become able to reason about complex ideas, they acquire language, and they construct knowledge about the world around them. The Swiss biologist Jean Piaget (1896–1980) developed a theory of cognitive development that provides a comprehensive description of the cognitive changes people experience during development and the cognitive structures that come with development. The Russian scientist Lev S. Vygotsky (1896–1934), who was influenced by Piaget's work, offered a theory for understanding cognitive development as a process of learning affected by the sociocultural environment of the child. This chapter explores these and other theories of cognitive development and their implications for teaching.

How Do Individuals' Cognitive Abilities Develop?

Piaget is best known for his extensive accounts of how children think at different times in their lives. Watching his own children at play, he wondered how children adapt to their environment, how they acquire knowledge of the world, and how that knowledge changes as they grow. A person's intellectual progress is a matter of constructing increasingly adaptive knowledge of his or her environment. The important question that Piaget posed is, "By what means does the human mind go from a state of less sufficient knowledge to a state of higher knowledge?" (Piaget, 1970, pp. 12–13).

Organizing and Adapting Mental Constructs

Organization is the human tendency to arrange experiences, thoughts, emotions, and behaviours into a coherent system for constructing meaning. Piaget believed that people use their intellect to make sense of their environment and to form useful mental representations of it. For example, suppose you are handed a small, roundish, red object, the likes of which you have never seen before. It is hinged in the middle, and when closed into a half-moon shape, it has a small handle on one end and what appears to be a spout on the other. What is it? In order to make sense of this object, you must use your logical powers and prior knowledge.

Schemes.   A small child is likely to approach this mystery object actively by feeling it, putting it in the mouth, shaking it, hitting another object with it, or throwing it. You might do some of the same things, such as feeling it and opening and closing the hinge. Piaget proposed that **schemes** are generalized ways of acting on the world, and they provide the basis for mental operations (cf. Gruber & Voneche, 1977; Wadsworth, 1984; Siegler, 1986). In other words, from your actions you would derive some knowledge about this object, such as it's made of hard plastic, the hinge allows it to be opened flat, but the two sides of the hinge cannot be put back-to-back.

Schemes have also been described as modes of organization (cf. Brainerd, 1978), such that acting on the world results in like objects or events being organized together into larger mental structures, such as concepts. With respect to the mystery object, then, your physical actions, which are very rudimentary schemes, probably would not produce enough information to allow identification of the object. Other, more abstract schemes must therefore be used, perhaps relating to the possible uses for such an object.

Assimilation.   Suppose you have seen or experienced things similar to the mystery object. Perhaps you observed a relative using something like it in preparing to serve tea. If so, you would immediately recognize our mystery object as an example of a previously known concept. One way in which mental constructs, such as schemes, change is to simply incorporate new experiences into existing structures. Piaget (1952) called this process **assimilation**.

Fitting the new experience into an existing scheme builds the overall cognitive structure, but it does not change the scheme's essential nature. For example, people who eat frog legs for the first time often comment that frog legs taste like chicken. They have organized their perceptions of taste according to their previ-

---

EXAMPLE: Schemes change continually as a person gains experience with his or her environment. When a child uses the "dog" scheme to understand the experience of seeing a cow, he or she is actively constructing meaning. Once interpreted, the new item becomes part of the scheme that was used to interpret it.

EXAMPLE: Infants are born with the reflex to grasp objects placed in their hands. If you have ever placed your finger in the palm of an infant's hand, for example, you have observed that the infant will automatically grasp your finger. Infants are also born with the reflex to suck. They have schemes for grasping and sucking. After some experience grasping some objects, infants begin to grasp an object and then move the object to their mouths. The grasping scheme and the sucking scheme become coordinated in a new scheme.

schemes In Piaget's theory, generalized ways of acting on the world that provide the basis for mental operations.

ous experiences. Therefore, having eaten chicken a great deal, they have a cognitive representation, their "taste of chicken" scheme, that allows them to understand the new experience of eating frog legs. Thus, they perceive the experience of eating frog legs as similar to that of eating chicken.

The ability to assimilate new experiences increases our sense of understanding our environment. Mistakes can occur, however, when we change the nature of an experience in order to preserve our current understanding. When a high school chemistry student refers to a colloid as a solution, he or she is assimilating the new experience incorrectly into an existing scheme. If we can fit our experiences into ways of understanding that already exist, the job of understanding the environment is less complex or difficult. Much of what happens in schools, however, is designed to change students' cognitive structures.

Accommodation.   Not all new experiences can fit easily into existing schemes. The mystery object is probably still a mystery to most of you, because no prior knowledge comes readily to mind that will help you understand what the object could be. **Accommodation** is the process Piaget identified by which we modify existing cognitive structures or create new ones as a result of experiences that cannot be easily assimilated. In such situations, the person's way of understanding is forced to change to fit the new experience. Together, assimilation and accommodation account for intellectual adaptation (cf. Piaget & Inhelder, 1969).

What about experiences that cannot be assimilated or accommodated very well? If a student experiences an event that is so unfamiliar that it cannot be filtered through existing schemes, then neither assimilation nor any subsequent accommodation will occur. For example, if a teacher were to begin writing Greek on a chalkboard, students may respond by trying to make sense of the symbols. If they are unsuccessful in doing so, they will probably stop trying to organize the information. Likewise, after trying unsuccessfully to make sense of the mystery object, you might simply give up. Under these circumstances, guidance may be required to assist learners in constructing appropriate schemes. In the previous example, the teacher would have to provide guidance to help the students make sense of the unknown symbols. In the example of the mystery object, someone may have to demonstrate that it is a device for squeezing lemon wedges, shown in Figure 2.1.

Equilibration.   What causes a child to seek experience and interaction that lead to significant reorganization in the child's thinking? For Piaget, the answer is **equilibration**, a process that regulates other influences on cognitive development and governs how people organize knowledge to adapt to their environment. Assimilation and accommodation are both necessary for development, but a balance between them is as necessary as the processes themselves. Equilibration is the self-regulating process through which people balance new experiences with what they already know.

If new experiences do not fit into an existing scheme, then *disequilibrium* results. Any event—through active experience, social interaction, and cultural context—can cause disequilibrium in a child's thinking. Changing the existing scheme to accommodate the new experience is a way of achieving equilibrium. Our continual attempt to achieve equilibrium is what leads to adaptive changes in our cognitive organization.

POINT: *Learning is shaped by the learner's environment.* Instruction is often an attempt to develop new ways to understand and interact with the environment. Assimilation contributes to cognitive development by providing greater experience and thereby strengthens an existing scheme. Changing the ways in which we understand our environment requires accommodation and equilibration.

assimilation In Piaget's theory, a process through which new experiences are incorporated into existing cognitive structures such as schemes.

accommodation In Piaget's theory, a process of modifying existing cognitive structures or creating additional ones as a result of new experiences.

equilibration The self-regulating process in Piaget's theory through which people balance new experiences with present understanding.

FIGURE 2.1
A Mystery Device: Kitchen Device Used for Squeezing Lemon Wedges

EXAMPLE: When students move magnetized letters around on a board, they discover that the letters stick to the board; they abstract the magnetic property of the objects they are handling. Other physical qualities can probably be abstracted as well. Perhaps a student will put a letter in his or her mouth to form an idea of how magnet letters taste.

EXAMPLE: Another example of a logico-mathematical experience would be discovering, while reading Shakespeare, that *anon* means "now," "immediately," or "even as we speak."

physical knowledge In Piaget's theory, any knowledge about objects in the world that can be gained through experiencing their perceptual properties.

logico-mathematical knowledge In Piaget's theory, knowledge that goes beyond physical experience and depends upon inventing or reorganizing patterns of ideas.

Constructing Knowledge through Active Experience

The experiences that people assimilate and/or accommodate influence the kinds of knowledge they construct. Piaget distinguished among three types of knowledge that people construct about their environments: physical, logico-mathematical, and social-arbitrary (Piaget, 1969; Driscoll, 1994).

Physical Knowledge. Children construct **physical knowledge** about their environment through the use of their senses to perceive object properties. When children see, hear, smell, taste, or touch objects, they experience physical, perceptual qualities that enable them to form mental representations of the objects. Listening first to a clarinet and then to a trumpet, a student might say, "I like the clearer, stronger sound the trumpet makes. The clarinet sounds too gushy to me." The physical experience of the sounds gave the student ideas—mental abstractions—of the sounds, which are reflected in the words used to describe them.

The process of constructing knowledge based on physical experience is called *empirical abstraction. Empirical* means "of or relating to observation and experience." Children observe various physical properties of objects encountered in the environment and abstract the qualities of these properties. For example, playing with wooden blocks yields knowledge of their "hardness," picking apples provides knowledge of their "shininess," and smelling roses yields knowledge of their "sweet" scent.

Logico-Mathematical Knowledge. When people construct knowledge that goes beyond physical experience and depends on inventing and reorganizing patterns of ideas, they are developing **logico-mathematical knowledge**. For example, Newton is said to have formulated the notion of gravity while pondering apples falling from a tree. His construct was not built on an empirical abstraction of the properties of apples—it didn't matter if they were red or rotten or shiny. Rather, it was his thinking about apples in another sense that led to a new idea. The same is true when students first learn the concepts of addition and subtraction. Whether they learn using pennies, or cookies, or oranges, the result is the same. Physical properties of these objects do not contribute to knowledge of addition and subtraction. But manipulations of them and mental operations—forming and re-forming patterns of ideas—do. Logico-mathematical knowledge is generated through the process of *reflexive abstraction. Reflexive*, using Piaget's definition, means "turned back on itself."

Empirical and reflexive abstraction differ with regard to their sources of knowledge. They also differ in that empirical abstraction requires some object in the environment. Reflexive abstraction can be triggered by something in the environment, such as a falling apple, but it is also possible for reflexive abstraction to occur in the absence of concrete objects. Children can acquire the ability, for example, to add and subtract numbers mentally, without using concrete objects to carry out the operations.

Social-Arbitrary Knowledge. The knowledge that people acquire through their interactions with other people in their own social and cultural groups is what Piaget termed **social-arbitrary knowledge.** People are the source of this knowledge, which includes values, moral rules, language, and cultural symbol systems. For example, children learn different systems of counting depending on their cultures. Anglo-European children learn to count using numbers, whereas many children in Asian cultures may learn to count using an abacus. Similarly, children from certain southern African cultures learn to count using parts of their body (each finger, palm, backside of hand, inside of wrist, etc.). Knowledge of these symbol systems can be acquired only through interaction with people who already know them; they are culturally transmitted.

How do physical, logico-mathematical, and social-arbitrary knowledge develop?

Piaget's Stages of Cognitive Development

Piaget's account of the processes, experiences, and structures involved in cognition describes how people come to know about their world. The experiences we have and the schemes we use for understanding those experiences change as we mature. A grade seven student not only knows more things than a grade two student but also knows things in a different way. The child in grade seven has developed cognitive capabilities that are not yet in the repertoire of the grade two child.

What are the capabilities of students who have reached different levels of cognitive development? All teachers need to know what the cognitive capabilities of their own students are. Teachers of younger children also need to know the capabilities of older children in order to understand the direction that their students' development should be taking. Likewise, teachers of older students need to understand the capabilities that their students developed earlier. The development of new capabilities builds on earlier ones. Moreover, not all behaviours reflect a student's highest level of functioning. Any experienced teacher can tell you that just because a student is capable of complex reasoning doesn't mean that the student will always reason that way.

From his observations of children, Piaget formulated four stages of cognitive development that reflect the dominant schemes which thinking children use and the ages at which they use them to organize and interact with their environment. Piaget's stages are summarized in Table 2.1. Others, such as Pat Arlin (1975,1990) of the University of British Columbia, consider the possibility of a fifth stage. According to Arlin, Piaget's formal operational stage can be considered a *problem-solving* stage. However, many of the problems we face are not clear-cut or do not have unambiguous solutions. She contends that some people reach a fifth stage she terms *problem-finding*. This is characterized by looking at problems in new ways or even perceiving problems where none were seen before.

CRITICAL THINKING: A junior high math teacher switched to teaching at the grade one level. She learned that junior high and primary grade students have very different understandings of the concept of time. The grade one children, while knowing the words *hour* and *half-hour*, had no concrete understanding of what those lengths of time meant. They constantly asked when recess would begin. The frequent interruptions decreased when the teacher compared a half-hour with the amount of time it took the students to watch a popular TV program. Explain this teacher's experience.

POINT: *Development affects learning.* Piaget believed that the dominant schemes of thinking associated with a given stage made students ready to learn some things but precluded them from learning other things.

social-arbitrary knowledge In Piaget's theory, knowledge gained solely by one's interactions with other people within one's cultural group.

TABLE 2.1 *Summary of Piaget's Stages of Cognitive Development*

Stages	Approximate Ages	Nature of Schemata*
Sensorimotor	0–2	Sensations and Motor Actions
Preoperations	2–7	Illogical operations; symbolic representations; egocentric; self-centred
Concrete operations	7–11	Logical, reversible operations; decentred; object-bound
Formal operations	11–Adult	Abstract—not bound to concrete objects

*It is important to remember that the stages are cumulative. The adaptive characteristics of earlier stages are present in later ones.
Source: Piaget's Theory of Cognitive Development (2nd ed., p. 29), B. J. Wadsworth, 1979, New York: Longman. Copyright 1979 by Longman Publishing Group. Adapted by permission of the Longman Publishing Groups.

EXAMPLE: The names of the stages describe the nature of the schemes at each stage. For example, the schemes of typical grade four students allow them to perform concrete operations.

TRY THIS: Repeat the test for object permanence with young children of different ages. Can you pinpoint the approximate age at which it occurs? Why do you think young children love the game of "peekaboo"?

TRY THIS: Observe young toddlers, perhaps in a day care center. Try to distinguish *imitation* from *deferred imitation* in the children's behaviour. What are the implications of deferred imitation for teachers of young children?

sensorimotor stage The earliest stage in Piaget's theory of cognitive development, during which infants learn about their environment through their senses and motor actions.

Piaget (1952) saw development as a process of successive, qualitative changes in children's thinking. The changes that children undergo at each stage derive from the cognitive structures of preceding stages. New structures do not replace prior structures. Instead, they incorporate prior structures, which results in the qualitative change. Let's take a look at the benchmarks associated with each stage of development.

Sensorimotor Stage (birth to approximately 2 years). Infants obtain knowledge at the **sensorimotor stage** through physical experience with the environment. Infants use their senses to experience the environment and their physical or motor actions to interact with it. The reflexes that newborns use to build schemes are the starting point for cognitive development, and the intellectual changes that occur during the sensorimotor period are quite dramatic. For teachers, the two most significant benchmarks of the sensorimotor stage are object permanence and imitation.

Think back to a time when you may have played with an infant. Can you recall playing a version of hide-and-seek in which you hid an object from the child's view and she, rather surprisingly, failed to search for it? What occurred in this case was, quite literally, out of sight, out of mind. A child who exhibits *object permanence* understands that an object can continue to exist whether or not he or she perceives it.

Object permanence is an important foundation for later development. The concept that objects have an existence that is separate from the child and permanent enables children to conceive of objects and actions that are not in their immediate environment.

Imitation, the other benchmark of the sensorimotor stage, is the ability to copy behaviours, and it begins with behaviours that are already part of the child's repertoire. For example, very young children open and close their hands, a behaviour which is related to the grasping reflex. If a parent, playing with the child, begins opening and closing a hand, the child will likely imitate the behaviour. The adult's action prompts the child to perform the same action. Many of the games that parents and infants play together are forms of imitation.

Imitation continues to become more complicated as the child's repertoire of behaviours increases. Toward the end of the sensorimotor stage, toddlers begin to display novel behaviours that are often not especially recognizable to the adult. Ask them what they are doing, and the likely response will be, "I'm being an airplane," or "I'm being a monkey." In deferred imitation, pretending to be something or somebody does not require prompting. A child does not need to see the mother combing her hair before combing a teddy bear's head, for example. The pretending and dramatic play-acting that preschool, kindergarten, and primary grade teachers see in students have their roots in deferred imitation.

Acquiring the capabilities of object permanence and imitation prepares the child for symbolic thinking, a benchmark of the next developmental stage. However, because students develop the capacity for symbolic thinking does not mean they no longer need to handle objects and observe models. The need for tangible objects, models, analogies, and concrete examples never disappears. Students always need concrete examples of the increasingly complex and abstract ideas that they are asked to learn.

Preoperations Stage (approximately 2–7 years). Piaget used the term *operations* to refer to actions based on logical thinking. The actions of a child at the preoperations stage are based on thought, but the actions do not always seem logical from an adult perspective. Thus, the child's thinking is considered prelogical or **preoperational**, because illogical thinking does not prevent youngsters from mentally representing or symbolizing. Preschoolers can easily pretend that a wooden building block is a car or a baby in a carriage or a piece of cheese. Symbolizing of this kind is based on imitation. This capability to replace one object with another or to use words to talk about actions and experiences is called symbolic representation.

Symbolic representation is the process whereby children learn to create their own symbols and to use existing symbol systems to represent and operate on the environment. The most important symbol system is language, which grows tremendously during the preoperations stage. Children's vocabularies increase several thousand percent. The complexity of their grammatical constructions also increases dramatically. From a developmental point of view, using language enhances the capability to think about objects that are not present. Remember, however, that using language to symbolize objects does not mean that children can think logically about them.

The other benchmarks of the preoperations stage are cognitive characteristics that actually prevent logical thinking: perceptual centration, irreversibility, and egocentrism.

If you have ever witnessed a child responding to one of Piaget's classic conservation tasks (e.g., conservation of number, of volume, of mass), then you have probably seen dramatic evidence of perceptual centration. In conservation tasks, children are presented with two identical objects. One is then transformed in some way and the child is asked whether the objects are now the same or different. *Perceptual centration* occurs when the child tends to focus on or perceive

CRITICAL THINKING: A kindergarten teacher built a tepee in her classroom as a place for silent reading. After reading a story about Native Canadians and buffalo, children began an elaborate game, which they played intensely for weeks. They became Native Canadian parents and children, hunters and horses, buffalo and bears. Is this an example of imitation or deferred imitation?

CONNECTION: The process by which children acquire language is discussed later in this chapter.

TRY THIS: Perform a conservation task with kindergarten and grade one students. Look for evidence of perceptual centration and irreversibility. How does preoperational thinking limit learning?

preoperational According to Piaget, the stage at which children learn to mentally represent things.

Children at the preoperational stage of cognitive development have not yet acquired the principle of conservation of number. This child will not understand, for example, that, given ten pegs, the number of pegs remains the same whether collected in a container or placed in the holes. Even when told or shown that the number is the same, the child will insist that there are more pegs when they are in the holes than when they are in the container.

only one aspect of an object or problem to the exclusion of other salient features. In the conservation task for liquid, for example, children are shown two identical beakers of water. The water from one beaker is then emptied into a tall, slender cylinder. When asked to judge whether the cylinder and the remaining beaker contain the same or different amounts of water, preoperational children will consistently say that the "taller one" contains more water. Their perceptions focus on the height of the liquid in the containers to the exclusion of width, circumference, and volume.

Irreversibility, a characteristic of the preoperations stage, refers to a person's inability to mentally reverse actions. A grade two child who is preoperational may know that 4 plus 2 equals 6 but may not be able to solve the subtraction problem of 6 minus 2. Likewise, a preoperational child who recognizes her doll as an old plaything believes she has a new toy when the doll is dressed in new clothes.

Finally, children who are preoperational assume that everyone's experience of the world is the same as their own and that they are, quite literally, the centre of everything. Piaget called this tendency *egocentrism*. Consider, for example, the case of the young girl seated at the dinner table who feels called on to "translate" her parents' conversation:

EXAMPLE: Picture a family on a long drive. The preoperational child in the back seat is listening through earphones to a song. (One lyric is "Jeremiah was a bullfrog. ...") Egocentrically, the child asks a parent in the front seat, "What did that singer say Jeremiah was?"

Father: Would you please pass the potatoes?
Child: Mommy, Daddy wants you to pass the potatoes.
Mother: Here, do you need the salt and pepper?
Child: Daddy, Mommy wants to know if you need the salt and pepper.
Father: Yes, please.
Child: Mommy, Daddy wants the salt and pepper.

Another form of egocentrism can be seen in parallel play and the collective monologue. In parallel play, children play near one another using similar materials, but they do not interact or attempt to influence each other. The collective monologue refers to the phenomenon of children talking in groups without having a conversation. One child may be talking about the colours in his painting, another child may be asking whether or not there is applesauce for today's snack, and a third child may be arguing for a game of tag when playground time comes. Each child addresses the others, but no one responds. Very little linguistic interaction occurs, owing to the egocentric nature of each child's communication.

Because preoperational children develop the capabilities to create and use symbols—language and other symbolic representations—adults begin to consider them thinkers. Teachers should remember, however, that preoperational thinking is not logical. A child who insists that one, and only one, perspective is correct, who talks but doesn't listen, who monopolizes social situations, who refuses to consider all aspects of a problem, is not so much a troublemaker as a child functioning at the preoperations stage.

Concrete Operations Stage (approximately 7–11 years). Concrete operations is the first stage of operational or logical thought in which schemes become organized into operations that can be used to reason about the world. Because logical operations are still new at this stage, students can best use them when considering problems that are concrete in nature. Many educators refer to the concrete operations stage as the "hands-on" period of cognitive development. Although the child can reason, the ability to reason is based on tangible objects and direct experiences.

Benchmarks of concrete operational thought include reversibility and decentration, which contribute to understanding the principles of conservation and the ability to perform multiple classification.

When children enter the concrete operations stage of development, usually around grade two, they become able to mentally reverse events, such as the steps of the amount-of-water problem. Students at this stage can imagine the results of pouring the water back and forth between containers of different shapes and sizes. *Reversibility* is also evident in students learning the related processes of multiplication and division. Given the numbers 12 and 6, for example, they can supply the answer "2" as the number that when multiplied by 6 equals 12 *and* that when divided into 12 equals 6.

Children in this stage have also acquired the capability of *decentration*,

Students in this class are learning the concept of estimation through the use of math manipulatives. Research shows that children at the concrete operational stage of cognitive development learn abstract concepts best when those concepts are represented by objects or direct experiences.

CRITICAL THINKING: A grade one teacher could not understand why Myra, a bright student, was having difficulty learning to read and was also so demanding of attention. Myra had appropriate language skills, but couldn't sit still or concentrate for longer than five minutes. In her teacher's words, "She's driving me crazy." Myra was falling behind her classmates. When the teacher checked Myra's birth date, she understood the problem. Myra had turned six only three days before school started; she was nearly a year younger than the majority of her classmates. Why would Myra's age make such a difference in her ability to learn how to read?

TRY THIS: Interview elementary teachers to collect ideas for hands-on activities. How are those activities developmentally appropriate for students at the concrete operational stage?

concrete operations
Piaget's first stage of operational thought during which children develop skills of logical reasoning, but only about problems that are concrete.

which means that they can consider more than one aspect of an object or problem at a time. Doing multiplication and division, for example, requires that students can think about a number in two different ways: as a multiplier and as a divisor. Students capable of concrete operations can solve problems that have more elements and that are significantly more complex than those that preoperational children can solve.

Together, reversibility and decentration allow concrete operational students to perform conservation tasks that stymie preoperational children. *Conservation* is the ability to recognize that properties do not change because form changes. By applying logic, operational students understand that the amount of water does not change when the shape of the container holding it changes.

It is important to note, however, that when cognitive development is assessed, the culture and first language of the child must be considered. Nyiti (1982) found that 10- to 11-year-old Native Canadian children who lagged behind white, English-speaking children of the same age on selected Piagetian conservation tasks presented in English performed the same tasks better when the problems were presented in their own language.

EXAMPLE: The concrete operational child may be able to classify animals into separate groups of carnivores and herbivores and also to classify both carnivores and herbivores as belonging to another group called mammals.

Reversibility and decentration are also the basis for *multiple classification*, an important reasoning skill that allows children to organize objects according to more than one characteristic. Suppose a student is presented with several cardboard cutouts in shapes of circles, squares, and triangles. The cutouts also vary in colour and size: red, yellow, and blue; small, medium, and large. Asked to classify these objects, a preoperational child would depend upon only one dimension, perhaps putting all the red ones together, all the blue ones together, and all the yellow ones together. The concrete operational child would use more than one dimension to classify the objects.

Concrete operations is only the beginning of logical reasoning. Students still have difficulty thinking about hypothetical problems, such as "If people could know the future, would they be happier than they are now?" (Siegler, 1986). Instead, they need to see things, touch things, experiment with things. They can reason when given concrete objects and experiences to reason with, but abstract reasoning doesn't develop until the final stage of cognitive development—formal operations.

CONNECTION: Problem-solving processes and strategies for teaching problem-solving skills are presented in Chapters 7 and 12.

Formal Operations Stage (approximately 11 years through adult). **Formal operations**—the final stage in Piaget's theory—begins roughly around eleven or twelve years of age and continues into and throughout adulthood. Abstract reasoning is the primary benchmark of formal operations.

Abstract reasoning is the ability to think logically about intangibles. Students who reach the stage of formal operations can begin to deal with possibilities. They can think in terms of a hypothesis: If X, then Y. They can see beyond the here and now. They can verbalize the mental rules they use in solving problems. The logical operations of the concrete operations stage can now be performed outside of the presence of concrete objects.

formal operations
According to Piaget, the stage of development in which the abilities to reason abstractly and to coordinate a number of variables are acquired.

For example, imagine you are standing directly in front of a chair. As you look at the chair, imagine a lamp to the right of it, a table to the left of it, and a rug behind it. Now imagine yourself standing in a new position so that the chair is behind the table. In this position, where is the lamp? A concrete operational student would have trouble with this problem, unless he or she could stand in proximity to the objects or symbolize them on paper. Being able to reason through this problem in the abstract is a characteristic of formal operations. (If you have difficulty working out this problem, do not fear for your stage of cognitive development. As Piaget noted, the ability to operate formally in one situation does not guarantee that the person operates formally in all situations.)

Consistent with Piaget's theory, Bennett and colleagues (1992) found developmental trends with fears in Canadian children. More realistic and abstract fears were expressed over time. Young children were mainly concerned with physical harm from others. Middle school children expressed fear of violence and fears regarding peer rejection, whereas older adolescents were more likely to report concerns with more abstract issues such as the environment, world peace, and political instability. Bonnie Janzen (1995) found a similar trend in fears and concerns with her survey of more than one thousand school youth in Swift Current, Saskatchewan. Older adolescents were also more likely to be concerned about the future and finding a job.

Inhelder and Piaget (1958) created a reasoning problem that illustrated the difference between concrete operational students and those in the formal operational stage. To solve the problem, students were supplied with objects to use in testing a principle of physics—that the length of a pendulum influences its speed.

The length of the pendulum could be shortened or lengthened; the weight at the end of the pendulum could be changed so that it was lighter or heavier. The height from which the pendulum was released could be changed, and the force with which the pendulum was pushed could be changed. Given these four variables, students were asked which of the factors influences the speed at which the pendulum would swing.

Their findings indicated that a student who is formally operational approaches the problem in a very systematic fashion, generating and testing various hypotheses. To illustrate, a formal operational student might choose one weight and one length, and push the pendulum at constant force, while varying the height from which the pendulum is released. Discovering that the height does not influence speed, the student would then proceed to manipulate other factors one at a time in an effort to eliminate possible solutions to the problem. A concrete operational student, by contrast, is likely to approach this task in a haphazard or much less systematic way, sometimes re-testing a hypothesis that has already been discarded. Figure 2.2 shows an analogous experiment. In this case, how might you determine if students are using formal operational reasoning to solve the problem?

Piaget's stages paint human cognitive development in broad strokes. Teachers must remember that an individual student's thinking does not progress in neat, unambiguous steps according to a precise timetable. This is especially true for students who come from diverse cultural backgrounds. Cross-cultural research on development has generally revealed that children from different cultures progress through more or less the same stages but not at the same rates (cf. Siegler, 1986). There are gaps in the experiences of every individual that affect development within and between stages. Students do not advance from one stage to the next overnight, and even those students who seem firmly established in a stage may regress to the previous one.

It is also important to keep in mind that children's answers to Piagetian problems have to be interpreted. Ivan Kelly (1980) of the University of Saskatchewan has pointed out that some of Piaget's dialogues with young children are not as clearly supportive of his theory as he makes them out to be.

CRITICAL THINKING: In terms of what teachers need to know about their students, what are some strengths and weaknesses of Piaget's stage theory of cognitive development?

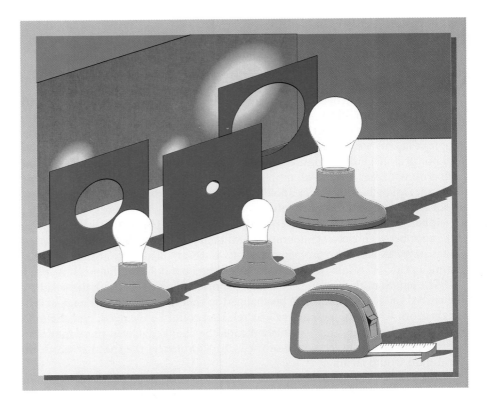

What Is the Social Basis for Cognitive Development?

CONNECTION: Teaching
approaches based on the
social mediation of learning
are presented in this chapter
and in Chapters 8 and 12.

Think for a moment about your own experiences in learning to read. Did your parents or an older sibling read aloud to you? Did you read to them, with their guidance as you stumbled over words that were unfamiliar? Do you recall reading in groups or with a teacher at school? Although current theories of reading acquisition tend to focus on the individual processes of the reader, some researchers argue that "acquiring the ability to read is most decidedly *not* an individual process" (Cole & Engestrom, 1993, p. 23). Rather, it is thought to be a joint meaning-making activity between teachers and students, between students and their parents or siblings, and among groups of students.

Reading is not the only capability whose development is thought to be influenced by the social environment of the child. Vygotsky believed that the social environment is critical to cognitive development (1978, 1987). In fact, he claimed that all capabilities acquired by children actually appear twice, first among people in the child's cultural environment and then within the child; that is, social processes enable the development of personal psychological processes. Let's examine how this occurs.

Acquiring Tools to Understand the Environment

According to Vygotsky, people use tools to engage and understand their environment. Think of what an infant learns about the environment by wielding a small wooden block with which a satisfying noise can be made by hitting it against the high chair or with which peas can be reduced to a pile of mush. Alternatively, imagine what students learn who use computers to access large databases of

Insights on Successful Practice

How do the developmental characteristics of your students influence your interactions with them as their teacher?

Three messages have been on the walls of every classroom in which I have taught for the past twenty years. One is in the form of a poster showing ten runners ready to burst from their blocks at the sound of a starting gun. The caption reads: "You have failed only if you have failed to try." The other two messages are handmade signs. The words have faded over the years, but their meanings are clear: "SUCCESS Lies Not in *BEING* the Best, But in *DOING* Your Best," and "THINK POSITIVE!" I teach these messages to my students.

Each child is the product of countless and immeasurable influences, whether they be biological, social, economic, or political. To teach each child, therefore, means I must first learn from the child before he or she can learn from me. I have to learn who the child is. I cannot come with preconceived notions about the student and what he or she is capable of. Rather, I have to listen and reflect on the many confusing and contradictory messages the child gives and gear my efforts to these often subtle signals. I realize that the understanding I have of the student today will be invalid tomorrow, next week, next month, or next year. If life changes for all of us, it never changes so rapidly as it does for a child.

It is often said that students must trust us if we are to be successful teachers. I rather think it is the other way around. As a teacher, I have to trust that my students want to participate in the learning process, that they want to grow and master their environment, and that they will give me clues as to how I might help them reach their individual potential. I believe that if I listen to my students and respect them, I might become the teacher who makes a difference in their lives.

PAM MANIET-BELLERMAN
Teacher

Your Insights

What are some examples of influences upon development? How might principles of cognitive development help you interpret children's messages? How will you find out about your students' individual capabilities?

---

information or to simulate complex scientific processes. But tools do not always have to be material things. They can also be psychological, such as language and mathematics. Words are tools used to converse and to exchange ideas with one another, and mathematical symbols are tools used in logical operations.

Material tools, then, are those that mediate between people and the natural world (cf. Strauss, 1993). *Mediate* means to "come between and meet halfway, or help to reconcile." So material tools are things that people produce to help them accomplish some task or purpose, such as driving a nail into two boards to bind them together. A variety of tools, some more efficient than others, might enable one to succeed in doing this task.

Psychological tools, by contrast, mediate between individuals in their social interactions. These are signs, symbols, and conventions that have been socially negotiated. For example, putting up a hand is a sign to the teacher that a student wishes to speak. Likewise, turning the lights on and off when students are engaged in cooperative group activities is a sign to them that the teacher wants their collective attention. The happy faces that some teachers use on student papers are symbols of approval and sometimes humour.

Psychological tools can also form coherent systems of signs, such as language. Children must acquire not only individual tools but also the rules by which the individual tools relate to each other and are used. How do children acquire psychological tools and rules for understanding their use in the environment? How do they learn to use material tools in an appropriate fashion? For Vygotsky, the answers are found in human cultural activity and in the process of internalization. What is important is not the tools themselves but how they are used.

Human Activity Systems. People play an important role in the development of others by the activities in which they engage as part of a cultural community (Vygotsky, 1987; Newman, Griffin, & Cole, 1989; Cole & Engestrom, 1993). Human activities, or activity systems (Leont'ev, 1978, 1981), are historically conditioned systems of relations between individuals and their environments. In their homes, for example, people might engage in activities such as cooking, cleaning, gardening, and entertaining. Each of these activities requires that they assume certain roles and use certain tools in particular ways. One would not use a gardening hoe in the kitchen, for instance, any more than a teaspoon would be used to dig holes for installing a fence in the backyard. Similarly, the manner of greeting a guest is likely to differ from the casual interactions of family members around a board game.

POINT: *Life conditions affect development.* Socioeconomic status, for example, affects activity systems as well as access to material and psychological tools for thinking.

In their interactions, parents guide their children in the appropriate use of material tools, as well as their development of appropriate psychological tools and rules. The same is true of teachers in school. By the activities in which you engage children, you help them develop the capacity to use material tools (such as word processors or calculators) and psychological tools (such as mathematical symbols and language) in appropriate ways. "Appropriate ways" are defined by the surrounding culture, which, it is important to note, is constantly changing and evolving as people interact with each other. Math teachers often have students use calculators in some activities (e.g., where computation is subordinate to the intended goal, such as problem solving) but not others (e.g., estimating). But using calculators in schools at all is a relatively recent development in Western cultures.

CRITICAL THINKING: How would Vygotsky (whose theory is discussed in the section, What Is the Social Basis for Cognitive Development?) regard Piaget's social-arbitrary knowledge?

Activity systems provide the basic structures for social contact in which children acquire the tools of their culture. Internalization is the process by which these social and cultural understandings become personal understandings.

Internalization. "Any higher mental function necessarily goes through an external stage in its development because it is initially a social function" (Vygotsky, 1981, p. 162). Remember the example of pointing given earlier in the chapter. The gesture takes on its meaning only through the social interaction between the child and his or her mother. Pointing at an object in the absence of the mother (or another person) would have had no effect. Likewise, if the mother had ignored the gesture, the child would be unlikely to reproduce it when he or she wanted some other object. *Internalization* occurs, then, when the child appropriates the gesture for pointing and uses it in other situations and contexts.

Vygotsky believed that the process of internalization provided a reasonable explanation for the egocentric speech Piaget observed in preoperational children. Remember that preoperational children hold conversations that are really collective monologues. Each child speaks, as though to himself or herself, but no one responds. Is this evidence of egocentric patterns of thinking where children cannot understand the perspectives of their peers? Piaget thought so, but Vygotsky believed that collective monologues could be evidence of internalization of complex cognitive skills, such as self-monitoring. Children speak to themselves as a means of self-guidance and internalize this external speech as thought processes.

To test this hypothesis, Vygotsky conducted a series of experiments in which children worked alone, in cooperative groups with deaf children or children speaking a different language, and in situations where it was difficult to hear vocalizations. In each case, children talked less to themselves than when they worked with other children who could hear and understand them. Vygotsky concluded that egocentric speech showed "a developing abstraction from sound, the child's new faculty to 'think words' instead of pronouncing them" (1962, p. 135). With ensuing development, then, egocentric speech is internalized as private speech and becomes entirely inner-directed and subvocal.

In recent years, other studies have been conducted that support Vygotsky's findings (Berk, 1994). Children tend to use private speech when working on difficult tasks or when confused about what to do next (Berk, 1992). For learners of any age, using private speech can lead to improved performance on tasks (e.g., Bivens & Berk, 1990).

Vygotsky's Zone of Proximal Development

On the one hand, Piaget posited specific stages of cognitive development through which children progress, and he described what children are capable of doing at each stage. Vygotsky, on the other hand, sought to understand how children develop by studying "those functions that have not yet matured but are in the process of maturation" (1978, p. 86). Vygotsky distinguished between the actual development of the child and the *potential* development of the child. Actual development is determined by what a child can do unaided by an adult or teacher. Potential development, in contrast, is what a child can do "through problem solving under adult guidance or in collaboration with more capable peers" (Vygotsky, 1978, p. 86). This area of potential development Vygotsky termed the **zone of proximal development (ZPD)** (Figure 2.3).

To better understand the ZPD, consider the experiences of grade one students in learning to read. Most students in grade one are beginning to read, but some have difficulty making the connections between sounds and written letters. These students exhibit the potential for acquiring prereading capabilities, but reading is still beyond their zone of proximal development.

What is important about the ZPD? For one thing, it helps teachers realize that two children who are capable of the same performance now may not achieve the same level of performance six months from now. By observing how students perform on problems when they are assisted, teachers have a better indicator of potential performance than they do by considering just what students can do on unaided tests. Armed with this knowledge, teachers are better able to determine just what experiences will best support the development of their students.

Another important implication of the ZPD is the emphasis it places on social interaction for facilitating development. When students do much of their work in school by themselves, their development may be slowed (Gage & Berliner, 1992). To develop fully, students must work with more skilled partners who can systematically lead them into more complex problem solving. Through successive turns of talk and action, students negotiate new meanings with their partners that they appropriate and internalize for their own subsequent use. A consequence of this process is that students learn to self-regulate.

What are the conditions for effective social interaction between learning partners? Two characteristics that seem to be important are scaffolding and intersubjectivity.

zone of proximal development (ZPD) In Vygotsky's theory, the gap between actual and potential development—that is, between what a child can do unaided by an adult and what he or she can do under the guidance of an adult or in collaboration with more capable peers.

FIGURE 2.3
Vygotsky's Zone of Proximal
Development: Areas of
Opportunity Between One's
Actual and Potential Cognitive
Development

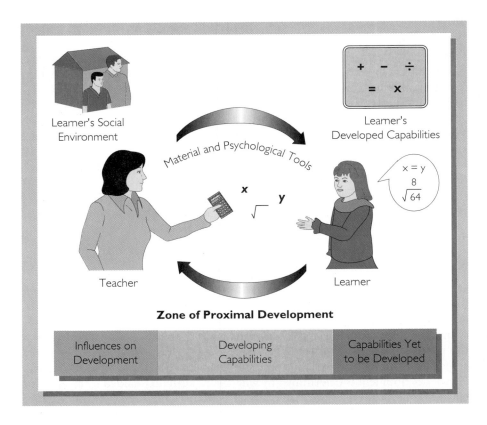

Scaffolding. Scaffolding, a term coined by Jerome Bruner, is a process in which the more advanced partner changes the amount or kind of support provided to the less skilled partner as he or she becomes more proficient in the skill (Wood, Bruner, & Ross, 1976). The use of scaffolds in building construction is the metaphor for this process. To scaffold appropriately, the more knowledgeable partner must know the needs of the less advanced partner, because "information presented at a level too far in advance of the child would not be helpful" (Tudge & Rogoff, 1989, p. 24). Quite often, the teacher serves as the more knowledgeable partner in instruction. For example, Malicky, Juliebo, Norman, and Pool (1997) from the University of Alberta found that teachers coaching young childrens' reading was associated with more self-correction on the part of the children and also served as a platform for the reinforcement of correct reading responses. But sometimes you will find that other students are best at scaffolding instruction for individual students.

Intersubjectivity. The intersubjectivity that exists between learning partners is also an important characteristic of social interaction that advances cognitive development. **Intersubjectivity** occurs when learning partners negotiate a mutual understanding of the task and how to proceed with its solution. They depend on each other in solving problems and accomplishing tasks. Thus, the teacher or more skilled peer does not dominate the interaction or simply demonstrate a solution to the problem. This would be like Ms. Olson in the Teacher Chronicle telling her students how to design the study rather than requiring them to work together to create their own test. The more advanced partner adjusts his or her perspective to that of the student and then attempts to draw the student into a more advanced approach to the problem (Rogoff, 1990).

scaffolding The process in Vygotsky's theory whereby a more advanced partner changes the degree and quality of support provided to the less skilled partner as he or she becomes more proficient.

intersubjectivity In Vygotsky's theory, the process in which learning partners negotiate a mutual understanding of the task and how to proceed with its solution.

Insights on Successful Practice

How can teacher mentorship, according to Vygotsky, promote higher-level thinking in students?

I have taught high school English for fifteen years in Ontario. During this time I have become more and more appreciative of the writings of Lev Vygotsky. According to Vygotsky, the sociocultural context is the background for learning both inside and outside the school. The specific culture we are immersed in may offer us advantages in some areas and disadvantages in other areas. For example, one village in Papua, New Guinea, until recently, counted using body parts starting with the right thumb. The maximum total that can be counted here is 29, limiting the culture to relatively simple arithmetic operations. You might ask yourself whether other cultural groups such as North American Native cultures or Asian cultures might offer levels of functioning that are poorly developed in our Western cultures.

Vygotsky also emphasizes the importance of social interaction and mentorship in the development of higher level thinking. In my English classes I make use of small-group work as often as possible, utilizing interns or teacher aides in cooperative roles with the students. The adults work along with the students, collaboratively, to analyze and explore the themes of novels and the meanings of poems. The more difficult aspects of the process are completed by the adult. She prompts the students to attempt similar thinking with later sections of the novels/poems and with new ones.

We have successfully worked with students on novels such as W. O. Mitchell's *Who Has Seen the Wind*, Harper Lee's *To Kill a Mockingbird*, and *All Quiet on the Western Front,* by Erich Maria Remarque. The latter novel brings up issues to explore collaboratively, such as: does what is real and important to people vary according to circumstances?, the importance of humour and friendship in difficult times, the issues of power differences among people, nature versus nurture, the lasting effect of war on people, the distance traumatic experiences can create between those who have such experiences and those who do not, and differing stances people take against impossible odds.

Chapters and issues are raised and considered, and these are related to the students' own experiences and world events. The goal is to eventually have students thinking independently at more complex cognitive levels. As the term progresses, the adult guidance, where appropriate, is lessened as the students show ability to complete the tasks by themselves. The adult role slowly becomes less that of a collaborator than one of a supportive observer.

It seems to me that this is what education is all about.

IRIS BOLTON
High School English Teacher

Using Learning to Facilitate Development

For Vygotsky, learning occurs in the zone of proximal development and actually *pulls* development along; that is, a capability that has already developed does not need to be learned and therefore does not benefit from instruction. For example, once students comprehend the abstractness of numbers, using manipulatives to work regrouping problems is no longer so valuable. Beyond the upper bounds of one's ZPD, however, learning will be fraught with difficulty. Students who do not understand how numbers work will be frustrated in learning if teachers use only abstract examples.

Learning is most effective when it occurs within the zone of proximal development with those capabilities that are in the process of developing. This view stands in contrast to Piaget's that learning cannot occur until certain capabilities have been developed. For Vygotsky, learning pulls development, but for Piaget, development pushes learning. This difference in views leads to different

TRY THIS: Determine how you might scaffold instruction to support a student's acquisition of a skill you plan to teach.

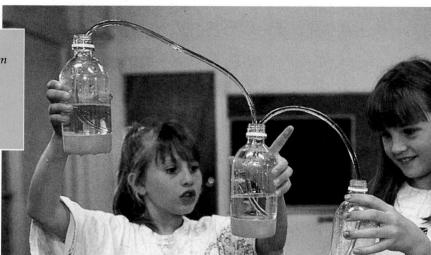

Cognitive development and learning are enhanced through social interaction between learning partners. In scaffolding and intersubjectivity, for example, students are stimulated to grow intellectually through interaction with teachers and more skilled peers.

CRITICAL THINKING: Why can students who have recently mastered a concept best teach that concept to others?

POINT: *Learning affects development.* According to Vygotsky, the more children learn, the more they become capable of learning.

CONNECTION: The information-processing view of learning is examined in more detail in Chapter 7.

implications for teaching. According to Vygotsky, teachers should tailor their instruction to each child's ZPD, because that's where it will be of greatest benefit in furthering the child's development. Vygotsky's view suggests a more "aggressive" approach than Piaget's in helping students reach beyond their current capabilities: Cognitive development can be accelerated.

How Does the Ability to Process Information Develop?

Piaget and Vygotsky were similar in their beliefs that development depends on children's active interaction with their environment. Piaget attempted to describe universal changes in cognition that occur with development, whereas Vygotsky emphasized social and cultural origins of cognitive development. Neither theorist, however, had much to say about how thought and learning occur in the brain. One theoretical model of what happens in the brain is *information-processing theory*, which describes how children and adults operate on different kinds of information. How do people *code, store,* and *retrieve* information for later use?

Information-processing theory derives not from the work of a single individual but from a school of thought that applies a computer metaphor to human thinking. As computers have evolved in complexity, so has information-processing theory. Initially thought of as a linear process, information processing is now conceived in terms of multiple and simultaneous linkages, or neural networks, that develop during learning and account for memory. Primarily a theory of learning, information-processing concepts can be applied to classroom practice.

Increasing Attention

attention The process used to focus on one or more aspects of the environment to the exclusion of other aspects.

Attention is the process used to focus on one or more aspects of the environment to the exclusion of others. When a teacher notices a student looking out the window and says, "Will you *please* pay attention to what's going on here?" the teacher is asking the student to focus on what the teacher is doing to the exclusion of the activity outside. There are four ways that attention can change as children mature (Flavell, 1985).

First, the ability to *control* attention increases with age. Control refers to the length of time a child can attend to a stimulus—sometimes referred to as the attention span—and the ability to concentrate. The attention span increases because the child also becomes less easily distracted. If every new sound, sight, or smell pulls the child's mind away from the task at hand, his or her attentional control is poor.

Second, the ability to *match task demands* increases with age. This refers to the child's ability to focus on several task variables at once and is similar to Piaget's concept of multiple classification. Suppose, for example, that a map-reading problem requires a student to focus on both the location and elevation of a place as it relates to a river. An older child is better able than a younger child to attend to the location and elevation variables.

Third, the ability to *plan* attention increases with age. Older students are better able to determine what is important to focus their attention on. They can interpret cues that tell what is important and, therefore, where they should direct their attention. High school students, for example, often become expert at reading teacher cues for determining what is important, such as writing on the board or repeating information.

Fourth, the ability to *monitor* attention increases with age. With increases in attentional control, task matching, and planning comes a greater ability for students to monitor themselves and to notice when they need to pay more or less attention. For example, older students are more likely than younger students to notice that they are daydreaming instead of focusing on the learning task.

Acquiring Knowledge

Theories of cognitive development, such as Piaget's and Vygotsky's, focus on mental and social processes. In theories of cognition, such as information-processing theory, memory structures and processes are the focus. Information processing and memory are taken up in more detail in Chapter 7.

As they develop, children's ability to store, remember, and use information changes. They can solve increasingly complex problems involving more operations to be kept in mind. A neo-Piagetian approach has been proposed by Robbie Case (1984, 1985, 1993) at the University of Toronto that emphasizes the importance of increasing working short-term memory capacity (amount of information kept in mind) in cognitive development. As children get older, many of their skills become more automatic because they practice, they improve their ability to shift attention between tasks, and they develop better ways of organizing information in order to remember it. These developments, together with neurological maturity, allow children to make better use of short-term working memory. Greater short-term memory capabilities allow one to engage in more advanced sophisticated tasks and thinking.

Short-term memory holds the information a person is working on at any point in time—the information residing in a person's consciousness. An important characteristic of short-term memory is its limited capacity. A person can only deal with a limited amount of information at any given moment, but this capacity increases during cognitive development.

The space available in short-term memory can function as either *operating space*, where the necessary operations to solve a problem are executed, or *storage space*, where additional problem information is stored (Figure 2.4). Young children who are just learning to solve particular kinds of problems must use all their

short-term memory The phase of processing at which a limited amount of information is stored for a limited time.

FIGURE 2.4
Memory Capacity in Two
Stages of Development

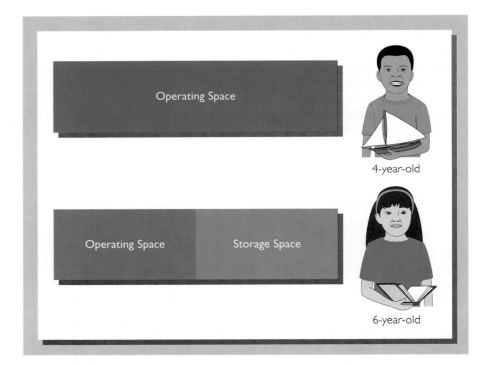

EXAMPLE: To relate automaticity to operating space, think about the difference between a child who knows multiplication tables and a child who has not yet mastered multiplication facts. When each child encounters the problem, "9 times 3," the former responds "27" automatically, without effort. The child who is unable to respond automatically must use memory capacity to carry out mental calculations to get the answer.

REFLECTION: Reflect on the shortcuts you discovered and the shortcuts you were given by teachers. Which shortcuts were more effective in your learning?

automaticity The point at which a mental operation can be executed without conscious effort.

capacity to execute the required operations. As they gain experience with the problems, the operations used require less and less memory capacity. This means that more space is available to store problem information, so that problems with more steps or operations can now be tackled. **Automaticity** is achieved when an operation can be executed without conscious effort. Automaticity reduces the amount of operating space necessary to solve problems. When operating space is reduced, storage space increases. Children attain automaticity through repeated practice on problems requiring the same operations.

By practising operations to the point of automaticity, students can increase their efficiency. A second way to do this is to discover shortcuts. Most students look for ways to simplify the steps they must take in order to solve a problem. Older students are better at finding shortcuts than are younger students. They discover more efficient ways of processing information, but they keep the necessary steps in mind. The older student is also better able to keep track of the elements of a problem. This monitoring capability, which we discussed in relation to attention, also plays a role in memory. Younger students often overlook crucial steps. They oversimplify problems (Case, 1985).

Oversimplifying a problem can be due to failure by young children to encode certain aspects of the problem. *Encoding* is a process of relating new information to prior knowledge so that it can be later retrieved and used. Siegler (1983, 1984, 1986) has found that younger students tend to overlook features of a problem that are critical for solving it, similar to the perceptual centration that Piaget described in preoperational children. Siegler attributed this tendency to the limited content knowledge of children and to their strong preferences for simple rules. With tutoring and practice, he discovered, children can learn to consider all relevant aspects of a problem.

In addition to automaticity, encoding, and the discovery of shortcuts, biological maturation of the brain contributes to "operational efficiency" (Case, 1984). The biology of the brain is a factor over which teachers have no control, but teachers can use automaticity, shortcuts, and encoding of relevant problem features to help students process problem-solving tasks more efficiently.

Here's How

Here's How to Address a Student's Difficulties with Problem Solving

1. Observe the student carefully. Is the problem a lack of automaticity in some critical operation, oversimplification of the task, or both?
2. If a lack of automaticity seems to be the student's problem, provide appropriate practice.
3. If the problem seems to be oversimplification of the task,
   a. determine what the student is leaving out;
   b. emphasize the missing step or steps by demonstrating how the oversimplification does not work;
   c. demonstrate a set of operations that accomplishes the task; and
   d. break the task down into discrete steps and have the student practise each one. In this way, the student learns to encode and use relevant aspects of the problem as well as to make these actions automatic.

EXAMPLE: Younger students oversimplify problems. They tend to focus on one aspect, such as calculating the amount of water by observing only its height in a container.

Monitoring Cognitive Processes

Metacognition is the capability to monitor one's own cognitive processes. It is, simply, one's thinking about thinking. As students develop, they become more aware of their own thought processes and how they work. Donald Meichenbaum (1985) at the University of Waterloo has shown that teaching students to talk to themselves about what to do in certain school-related situations improves their behaviour. Younger students can be taught to apply knowledge of their own thinking in a particular situation, but they seldom transfer metacognitive knowledge to new situations (Forrest-Pressley, MacKinnon, & Waller, 1985). The ability to think about one's own thinking aids the planning of attention, the attainment of automaticity, and the discovery of shortcuts in solving problems. Strategies for teaching metacognitive skills to students are presented in Chapters 7 and 8.

CONNECTION: Metacognition is examined in relation to information-processing views of learning in Chapter 7.

How Do Individuals Develop Language Skills?

Language accounts for much of the communication that occurs in classrooms. Teachers and students talk. Words, phrases, and sentences are written on the board. Textbooks are read. But not all communication is done in a spoken or written language. Students raise their hands, furrow their brows, slump in their chairs. Teachers raise their fingers to their lips, lift their eyebrows, and shake their heads at slumping students. A language comprises symbols, sounds, meanings,

metacognition Knowledge about thinking and the capability to monitor one's own cognitive processes, such as thinking, learning, and remembering.

CONNECTION: Limited English proficiency and bilingual education are discussed in Chapter 4.

CRITICAL THINKING: How would Vygotsky explain these examples of communication in the classroom?

phonology The study of the sound system of a language and the structure of those sounds.

syntax The grammatical arrangement of words in sentences.

semantics The study of the meanings of words and sentences.

pragmatics An area of language that refers to the effects of contexts on meaning and the ways to use language to create different contexts.

and rules that govern the possible relations among these elements. Language is also arbitrary. Why do we call a cow a cow? Why do we associate the letter *R* with the sound "errrr" instead of "sssss"? Why do you recognize those sounds even though they are ink marks on a page? How do children become capable of using language to communicate?

Linguists, those who study the structure and function of language, identify the *grammar* of a language as a system of implicit rules that relate sounds to meaning (Clark & Clark, 1977). Grammatical rules operate on three major elements of language. The first is **phonology**, the sounds of a language and the structure of those sounds. When writing a poem, for example, you may look for words that rhyme. When you do, you are concerned about phonology, how the words will sound in the poem. The second is **syntax**, the way the words of language form sentences. When you convert a passive sentence to its active form, you are changing the syntax. The third is **semantics**, the meaning underlying words and sentences. Although "the man was a bore" is the same syntactically and phonologically as "the man was a boar," they have quite different meanings. The second sentence must also be understood metaphorically, in the sense that the man is similar to a boar (a wild pig) in some way.

There is one other element of language, pragmatics. **Pragmatics** refers to the contexts in which language is used and the way language can be used to create contexts. For example, "the man saw a cow in his undershirt" is an ambiguous sentence without the appropriate context for interpreting it. Either the man was in an undershirt when he saw the cow, or he saw a cow that was wearing his (the man's) undershirt. The latter interpretation could be appropriate if the cow got loose from its pasture, ran under a clothesline, and managed to hook the man's undershirt. Similarly, a single sentence can take on different meanings depending on the context in which it is said, the tone of the speaker's voice, and the intention of the speaker. A linguist who focuses on pragmatics studies intonation, gestures, the conventions by which conversations occur, the meanings of pauses, the intention of a writer or speaker, and the like.

The most dramatic language developmental changes occur before a child reaches school age. The early stages of language development are presented in Table 2.2 (LeFrancois, 1994, 8th ed.)

The stages of grammatical development reflect changes in phonology, syntax, semantics, and pragmatics. Grammatical development occurs rapidly. This is especially true of phonology, the sounds of a language. The majority of English-speaking children can pronounce properly most of the sounds of their language by the time they reach school. The speech sounds that take the longest to develop are *s, z, v, th,* and *zh* (Rathus, 1988). The "lisping" quality in the speech of children in the primary grades can be traced to the lack of development of these sounds. Let's look briefly at some benchmarks of development in the other areas of language, especially those pertinent to school-age children.

Syntax

Children use adultlike sentences by approximately age four (Wood, 1981). However, these are very basic forms: simple declarations and questions. Although early elementary school-age children tend to use simple syntax when they speak, they are capable of understanding more complicated forms, such as the passive voice. For example, they are more likely to say "Mary threw the ball," but they can understand "The ball was thrown by Mary." The complexity of the forms they produce increases as they form compounds, learn to use conjunctions, add

TABLE 2.2   *The Stages of Grammatical Development*

Stage*	Characteristics	
	Middle of Range (years)	Grammatical Capabilities
Sounds	less than 1	Phonological experimentation; crying, cooing, babbling
Holophrases	1	Single words carrying sentential meaning; inflections
Telegraphic utterances	1½	Two word "sentences"; key word modified; declarations, questions, imperatives, and negatives used
Short sentences	2-2½	Real sentences, subjects and predicates; tense changes
Complex sentences	3-4	New elements and clauses embedded; use of parts of speech in various ways
Adultlike structures	4	Structural distinctions made

*The descriptions are relative. Remember the developmental changes outlined in this table occur before most children enter school.

Source: Psychology for Teaching (7th ed., p. 169), G.R. LeFrancois, 1991, Belmont, CA: Wadsworth. Copyright 1991 by Wadsworth. Adapted with permission.

relative clauses, and master tenses. It is important that elementary school teachers recognize that students can understand forms that they do not use yet. When thinking about syntactic development, the rule is that comprehension precedes production (cf. Clark & Clark, 1977).

Semantics

One aspect of semantics is vocabulary. A child begins to use his or her first words around the time of the first birthday. Once the child learns to use words, a single word is often used to communicate a variety of messages. For example, *milk* can mean "I want milk," "The milk is all gone," "That is milk," or "The milk fell" (Bates, O'Connell, & Shore, 1987; Snyder, Bates, & Bretherton, 1981). It takes approximately three to four months for the first ten words to appear. Once the child has acquired approximately ten words, he or she adds another word to the vocabulary every few days. A typical eighteen-month-old child has a vocabulary of approximately forty to fifty words. The average twenty-four-month-old child knows approximately 300 words and by age six, a child may know upwards of 14 000 words (Carey, 1977; Templine, 1957). Reading and other language-based activities that occur in the early grades may contribute to the roughly 5000 additional words the child gains by age eleven (cf. Berger, 1986).

TRY THIS: Document the sentence constructions of children of various ages. Read a complex sentence aloud to the children and ask them to repeat it back to you to observe the changes they make in syntax. How do your observations reflect stages of grammatical development? What are the implications of this effect for teaching?

Aside from the development of a vocabulary, a benchmark of semantic development is the ability to understand complex language functions. For example, many children and some adolescents have difficulty with metaphors, similes, sarcasm, and facetious remarks. Teachers who like to joke and kid with students must be careful when speaking with those whose semantics do not embrace these complex structures.

Pragmatics

Pragmatic development occurs as a child becomes capable of using his or her grammatical competence to communicate in a variety of contexts. A collective monologue may contain grammatically correct language, but it is not communication. By adolescence, students have learned the conventions of conversation and can use them to gain information.

Using language to gain information is just one aspect of pragmatic development. Language can also be used poetically, persuasively, humorously, artistically, tactfully. The language experiences provided by teachers influence pragmatic development throughout a student's career.

How Can You Accommodate the Developmental Differences and Needs of Your Students?

In this chapter, we have looked at patterns of cognitive development and the development of language. At the least, you have probably reached these three conclusions:

1. Your students are likely to think very differently from the way that you think.
2. Your students are likely to use different forms to communicate than you use.
3. There will be great variability in the thinking and communication of your students.

What can you do, then, to accommodate your instruction to the developmental differences and needs of your students? Let's explore some possibilities.

Assessing Student Thinking

Knowing that students think differently from you and that their thinking changes as they mature suggests the importance of assessing student thinking during instruction. To begin with, you will need to know something about your students' stages of cognitive development and ZPDs relative to your goals in order to appropriately tailor instruction. Following are some suggestions for finding out about their ZPDs.

Questions that help you assess the level of your students' thinking can serve another purpose. In order for learning to pull development along, instruction should push students' current competencies to their limits. Questions can do this by guiding students to make new discoveries and to become aware of conflicts or inadequacies in their ways of thinking. Bruner (1960) called these **medium-level questions** after an experienced teacher of mathematics expressed the following point:

> Given particular subject matter or a particular concept, it is always easy to ask trivial questions or to lead the child to ask trivial questions. It is also easy to ask

Insights on Successful Practice

How have you used whole language in your classroom successfully?

I have considered myself to be a whole language teacher for the past nine years. Adopting the whole language philosophy has forced me to continually reexamine my understandings of how children learn and perhaps more importantly what motivates them to learn. As I reflect on my teaching and my interactions with students I ask myself, "Is this activity meaningful to students? Do they see a real purpose for the activity? Are the children immersed in whole texts and invited to participate as readers, writers, speakers, and listeners?" In answering these questions I am evaluating activities to determine whether or not they will motivate students to learn.

As a kindergarten teacher for five years and a grade one teacher for four years I have discovered that inviting children to participate as readers and writers motivates them to become readers and writers. By providing support and accepting their approximations, children are intrinsically driven to actively participate in the reading and writing processes and seek to make sense of the rules governing written language.

Rather than telling children what and how to read and write, I encourage them to choose their own personally meaningful topics for writing and their own books for reading. In addition, I support my students as they use available strategies to make sense of text and to record their messages. I help children become consciously aware of what it is they know and can do.

It was as I watched Becky become a reader that I realized how powerful invitations can be. Each year I invite the children in my grade one class to choose their own books to learn to read. One year Becky chose *Green Wilma* as her goal. This was November and Becky was just beginning to acquire a sight vocabulary and was also just beginning to learn about sounding out words. Most grade one teachers (including myself) would never have thought that Becky would be able to successfully learn to read this book. The vocabulary was difficult, there were few picture clues, and only a subtle rhyming pattern to support her predictions of the text. So why would Becky choose this book for independent reading? Ted Arnold, the author and illustrator of *Green Wilma* had just visited our school and spent an hour talking with the children about his stories and pictures. The children were captivated as he read his favourite stories to them. Becky spent thirty minutes a day for the next four weeks actively studying the words in her book. During this time I questioned whether or not spending four weeks on one book would make a significant impact on Becky's growth as a reader. As a whole language teacher I knew I needed to follow her lead. I provided support when she "got stuck" on a word and encouraged her to continue working toward her goal. At the end of four weeks she not only learned to read *Green Wilma*, but she was also on her way to becoming an independent, fluent reader.

We can learn so much from watching children, extending invitations, supporting their efforts, and following their leads. Children want to become readers and writers, and if we allow them, they will show us what they want to read and write. Many times what they show us unexpectedly exceeds our expectations!

LYNDA F. HAYES
Elementary School Teacher

---

impossibly difficult questions. The trick is to find the medium questions that can be answered and that take you somewhere. This is the big job of teachers and textbooks (p. 40).

Understanding and making students aware of the need for conceptual change is a hallmark of **developmentally appropriate instruction.** Students need a basis for deciding to give up naive beliefs or simple rules in favour of more

developmentally appropriate instruction Instruction that is child-centred and provides activities appropriate to the developmental level of the student.

accurate and useful ones. For example, young children's experience of the earth is that it is flat and stationary. When a teacher attempts to teach them that the earth is "round like a ball," they are likely to assimilate this contradictory information by constructing a representation of the earth as "round like a pizza" (Vosniadou, 1988). When you ask questions that lead students to conflicts or inconsistencies in their thinking, you prepare them to adopt new conceptions. Piaget and Vygotsky would agree that asking questions that throw the students out of equilibrium within their ZPDs can cause them to equilibrate (assimilate and accommodate) until an answer is reached.

Providing Concrete Experiences

Throughout the chapter, there have been examples of how experiences with concrete objects and real problems facilitate development, especially for children in stages from sensorimotor to concrete operations. Children who miss working with manipulatives at an early age may later experience difficulty in learning abstract concepts and operations. This is true in subject areas from mathematics to science to language arts. But even high school students, who are presumed to be formal operational thinkers, can benefit from instructional activities that provide them with concrete experiences and material representations of concepts.

Whenever you anticipate that students will know very little about a subject matter or skill that you intend to introduce, begin by making instruction concrete. In a beginning course on computers, for example, adult students had such difficulty understanding how the computer worked that the instructor built a board with slots that represented addresses in computer memory. Students moved index cards into and out of slots to represent, and therefore understand, the functions of input and output (Driscoll, 1994).

One of the benefits of providing concrete experiences to students is that they don't need you to provide feedback. They can obtain feedback from their own actions. The young child who mashes peas with a wooden block, for example, does not need to be told that the block is a tool capable of this task. The child sees the evidence in the pile of mush. Similarly, students investigating the pendulum problem described earlier do not need the teacher to tell them that the length of the pendulum influences its speed. They have evidence from the trials they conducted in which they varied different elements of the problem.

Using Authentic Activities

Experimenting with tools and investigating phenomena are examples of authentic activities. **Authentic activities** are instructional tasks that provide culturally and situationally relevant contexts for learning and development. Based on Vygotsky's notions of human activity systems, an authentic activity for acquiring arithmetic competence, for example, might entail shopping for the best buys at a supermarket in order to stay within a particular budget. This is typical of an ordinary dilemma that arises in the context of everyday situations. Presenting students with real-life dilemmas to solve helps them to internalize the competencies and tools of their culture.

How do you devise and appropriately scaffold an authentic activity? Here are some guidelines derived from recent research (e.g., Cognition & Technology Group at Vanderbilt, 1991, 1993; Driscoll & Rowley, 1993).

> **POINT:** *Authentic activity provides a basis for assessment.* As you plan authentic activities for your students, consider how these activities might also be used for assessment purposes.

Here's How

Here's How To Scaffold an Authentic Activity

1. Select an activity that provides a motivating reason to learn the knowledge and skills involved in it. For example, middle school students can learn a great deal about friction by designing objects to run down a ramp.
2. Help students determine and define subgoals necessary to be solved before the larger goal can be attained.
3. Teach subordinate skills as they become needed in the solution of subgoals.
4. Help students begin to regulate their own problem solving by gradually withdrawing task assistance and providing feedback on students' task management skills.

> **authentic activities**
> Instructional tasks that provide culturally and situationally relevant contexts for learning and development.

The Kamehameha Elementary Education Program (KEEP) is a good example of the use of authentic activities and scaffolding (Gallimore & Tharp, 1990). In KEEP classes, students work on meaningful goals for which the teachers provide a variety of scaffolds:

- *Modelling*, to introduce children to unfamiliar skills.
- *Instructing*, to direct children toward the next specific act they need to learn in order to move through the ZPD.
- *Verbal feedback* (or reinforcement), to let children know how well they are progressing in relation to reasonable standards of performance.

- *Questioning*, to encourage children to think about the task.
- *Explaining*, to provide strategies and knowledge necessary for thinking in new ways (Berk, 1994, p. 259).

Encouraging Student Interaction

POINT: *Learning is actively constructed in social contexts.* Cooperative learning can help to provide a classroom structure in which students can explore the views of others at the same time they develop their own views.

CONNECTION: Cooperative learning is examined in relation to motivation in Chapter 9 and as a support for active learning in Chapter 12.

Both Piaget and Vygotsky believed that children's interactions with their peers is an important source of cognitive development, but Vygotsky took a step further in describing the kinds of interactions that are most likely to advance development. When you encourage interaction among your students, you enable them to accomplish two goals. First, students are forced to confront the views of others. This helps them to become able to approach an issue from various perspectives and to understand a view that contradicts their own. Second, students learn to express and defend their own understandings and beliefs. Argumentation that was once social becomes personal and available for regulating their future thoughts and actions.

A useful strategy you can use to encourage interaction among your students is cooperative learning (e.g., Slavin, 1991). Cooperative learning, which is discussed in more detail in Chapter 12, means more than simply putting students to work in groups. For **cooperative learning** to be most effective, students must be dependent on each other to achieve a learning goal, they must be responsible for both their own work and for the group product, and they must know how to cooperate. You can effectively implement cooperative learning in your classes by following these guidelines.

Here's How

Here's How To Organize Cooperative Learning Activities

1. Choose complex tasks that require several students working together in order to be achieved. In middle school science, for example, groups can be assigned to develop, build, and test a rocket that will reach certain heights or trajectories.

2. Assign roles to students within a group (e.g., primary investigator, hypothesis generator, time manager). Having different roles means that students will become the more advanced learning partner with respect to the tasks and competencies involved in their role. When you rotate the roles on subsequent assignments, students can serve as models to those newly assigned to their roles.

3. Provide a set of norms or rules that govern the behaviour of students in groups—for example, group members must help any member who requests it, all group members must have the same question before the teacher can be consulted, only one member of the group interacts with the teacher.

4. Prepare students for the new norms that come with cooperative learning by role-playing these norms through games and exercises (cf. Cohen, 1986).

Using Many Sign Systems

As children acquire symbolic thinking around the age of two, they create their own symbols, and they begin to use the symbol systems of their culture, such as language. Vygotsky believed that language is most important in developing higher cognitive functioning, and it is certainly true that language dominates as a mode of communication in school. However, different subject areas have different language structures that must be mastered for content understanding to occur. When you and your students mean different things by the words you use, you are likely to talk at cross-purposes, as occurred in a study of a high school class in earth science (Lemke, 1988). The teacher meant one thing by "light" and "heat," but the students understood another.

Another aspect of language predominance in schools is that students from minority group cultures may be disadvantaged by language habits that differ from their teacher's. Although this will be discussed in greater detail in Chapter 4, it suggests that you should consider language difficulties as a possible source when your students exhibit misconception or misunderstanding. This is also true with respect to classroom pragmatics. You may take for granted that students know they should line up to leave the classroom or raise their hands to be recognized. But these typical (and often unstated) rules may be unfamiliar to students from diverse cultural backgrounds. You should not automatically assume, therefore, that their failure to follow the rules is a sign of either willful disobedience or lower levels of cognitive functioning. The most effective teachers use a variety of alternative sign systems in their instruction.

Cognitive Instructional Programs Developed in Canada

Several cognitive instructional programs have been developed in Canada. In Chapter 5, a program created by Dr. J.P. Das of Edmonton will be described. Summarized here are two other programs that hold considerable promise for classroom use.

Dr. F. French of Mount Saint Vincent University has developed a program entitled Learner Strategies Enabling Thinking (LSET). This program can be used by classroom teachers to develop students' problem-solving, cognitive processing, and reasoning strategies within the context of curriculum instruction. In the LSET program, thinking is viewed as an active process which incorporates both language and language development. The capacities to monitor one's performance, critically reason, and select alternative strategies when current strategies are not successful constitute the thinking process. According to French, both individual-specific and generic or linking strategies are used when problem-solving. In order for individuals to be effective learners, they must feel responsible for their learning outcomes and must be confident that they are capable of achieving success. The LSET program focuses on a collaborative and dialogical approach to learning. A problem-solving paradigm is outlined, as well as prerequisite skills, program objectives, and instructional strategies. In order to facilitate the effective implementation of LSET, sample lesson plans and a teacher training program are provided. Although this program was originally designed for high school teachers, it has been shown to be effective in experimental settings with younger students (grades four to nine) of varying ability levels. To date, a number of schools in Alberta and Nova Scotia have begun to use this program (French, 1987, 1991).

cooperative learning An instructional strategy whereby students work in cooperative groups to achieve a common goal. Conditions that promote effective cooperative learning include positive interdependence among group members, face-to-face interaction, clearly perceived individual accountability to achieve the group's goals, frequent use of interpersonal skills, and regular group processing to improve the group's functioning.

The Strategies Program for Effective Learning and Thinking (SPELT) was developed at the University of Alberta by Dr. R. Mulcahy and his associates. The program incorporates both instructional strategies and active learner involvement. Three phases of instruction are outlined. First, teacher-directed strategies are taught and modelled for the students within specific subject areas. Many of the strategies used in this phase are based on the work of Deshler and his associates (e.g., comprehension and organizational strategies). During the second phase, the notion of teaching for transfer is emphasized. Students are encouraged to apply the strategies taught during phase one; an interactive approach is advocated which allows students to discover whether the strategies work in new situations and determine how they might be altered. In the third phase, students are encouraged to develop their own strategies. They are required to analyze the task, generate strategies, and evaluate the potential effectiveness of the strategies generated. This program is designed for students from grades four to twelve, is applicable in all curriculum areas, and has been successfully pilot-tested in several Canadian school districts (Mulcahy, 1991; Mulcahy, Marfo, Peat, Andrews, and Clifford, 1986).

Teacher Chronicle Conclusion

Does It Work?

Ms. Olson was aware that this section of her biology class consisted of a number of students who would be classified by Piaget at the formal operation stage in reasoning about scientific issues.

"We can't start with a study that is too wide," Lucy piped up, "let's narrow our investigation down to treating headaches." "Very good," said Ms. Olson; "If we make the study too complex, that will make the interpretation of our results more complicated." Jeremy put his hand up, "Let's get a large group of people who suffer headaches weekly and give one group real acupuncture and another group fake acupuncture." "What's fake-acupuncture, using fake needles?" said Willard. "Fake acupuncture might be placing needles in random places around the body instead of the special places that acupuncturists use" suggested Louise. "Great idea," said Ms. Olson. Arlene suggested that "We could give the groups each a treatment twice a week for three months and record the number of headaches each group experienced." "Yes," said Dan, "if the real acupuncture group experienced less headaches, on average, this would be some support for the view that acupuncture really works, at least for headaches!" Ms. Olson was noticing how the students were thinking about testing hypotheses, isolating variables, and utilizing baseline (control) groups—all indications that her students were thinking at the formal operations level.

Ms. Olson decided to capitalize on her opportunity. "Notice, class, that we can use a similar approach to the testing and investigation of claims in other areas such as diet plans, psychological treatments, comparing different fuel-saving measures, and so on. Let's all bring clippings from the newspaper or magazines and talk about how we could test the claims made. Perhaps some of you could do such a study for a science fair."

Application Questions

1. How would concrete operational students respond to the request to design a study to examine the merits of acupuncture or a new diet plan?

2. How would concrete operational individuals respond to the question "Does acupuncture (blood pressure pills, penicillin, etc) work?"

3. Do students need prior knowledge in an area to think effectively in that area? What about medical treatments? Psychological treatments? Does our everyday experience give us a sufficient background to address basic questions in these two areas?

4. Were all students in Ms. Olson's class thinking at the formal operational level?

5. Can you think of alternative ways to those given in Ms. Olson's class for testing claims about new drugs or medical treatments?

CHAPTER SUMMARY

What Are the Dimensions of Human Development? (L.O. 1, 2, p. 25)

The study of human development involves assessing the capabilities we possess as we grow into and develop our potential. There are several areas of human development that have been identified for the purpose of study: cognitive development, personal development, and social development. This chapter has focused on cognitive development and the development of information-processing and language capabilities.

How Do Individuals' Cognitive Abilities Develop? (L.O. 3, p. 28)

Piaget's theory of cognitive development is comprehensive in its description of universal capabilities that children acquire through four stages of development, from birth to adulthood. Although everyone passes through these stages in the same way, there is considerable diversity in the rates at which individual development proceeds. Piaget emphasized the role of active experience in the child's construction of knowledge about the world, and he demonstrated how children's thinking is qualitatively different at different points in their lives.

What Is the Social Basis for Cognitive Development? (L.O. 6, 7, p. 38)

Vygotsky's theory of cognitive development highlights the central role of the social and cultural environment of the child. Higher cognitive functions develop from the child's social interactions with more knowledgeable others in everyday situations. Learning, and consequently instruction, is most effective in the child's zone of proximal development, where it supports capabilities in the process of development.

How Does the Ability to Process Information Develop? (L.O. 8, p. 44)

As children mature, their attention spans grow longer, they are able to make better use of limited memory space, and they encode additional elements of complex problems that they once ignored. With maturation, students are also better able to monitor their own thought processes.

How Do Individuals Develop Language Skills? (L.O. 11, p. 47)

A language is a set of grammatical rules covering phonology (sounds), syntax (structure), semantics (meaning), and pragmatics (context). Grammatical abilities develop rapidly. Children can use relatively complex structures by the time they reach school. Pragmatic development continues indefinitely.

How Can You Accommodate the Developmental Differences and Needs of Your Students? (L.O. 12, 13, p. 50)

Five strategies were presented and discussed that can help you accommodate your instruction to the developmental differences and needs of your students: (1) assessing student thinking, (2) providing concrete experiences, (3) using authentic activities, (4) encouraging student interactions, and (5) using many sign systems in instruction.

KEY CONCEPTS

accommodation, p. 29

assimilation, p. 29

attention, p. 44

authentic activities, p. 53

automaticity, p. 46

cognitive development, p. 25

concrete operations, p. 35

cooperative learning, p. 55

developmentally appropriate
  instruction, p. 51

equilibration, p. 29

formal operations, p. 36

intersubjectivity, p. 42

logico-mathematical knowledge,
  p. 30

medium-level questions, p. 50

metacognition, p. 47

phonology, p. 48

physical knowledge, p. 30

pragmatics, p. 48

preoperational stage, p. 33

scaffolding, p. 42

schemes, p. 28

semantics, p. 48

sensorimotor stage, p. 32

short-term memory, p. 45

social-arbitrary knowledge, p. 31

syntax, p. 48

zone of proximal development
  (ZPD), p. 41

3 Personal and Interpersonal Growth

LEARNING OUTCOMES

When you have completed this chapter, you will be able to

1. define and distinguish self-concept and self-esteem
2. describe how children's self-concept changes from preschool to high school.
3. identify the emphasis of Erikson's theory of psycho-social development and provide a basic description of his eight stages.
4. describe Marcia's four types of identity statuses

5. describe existing social problems that increase the risk of failing in school
6. outline the stages of moral reasoning according to Piaget, Kohlberg, and Gilligan
7. provide a description of Lickona's integrative model of the moral agent, and outline the four basic processes in his model of moral education

Teacher Chronicle

Adolescent Identity Issues

Mr. Bolen is teaching high school for the second year and has noticed distinct differences in the way his students view themselves and their (possible) future careers. These differences seem related to how they approach school and how well they do in their studies. These differences among students are a puzzle to him.

Marilyn seems quite self-confident and a high average student. She is interested in pursuing a career in graphic arts in Toronto after graduation. Susan has a job after school working at an autoparts store. She seems quite confident and is popular with peers. Her parents would like her to go to university or technical school, but Susan isn't really sure what she wants to do.

Mark, on the other hand, obtains high average grades but lacks the self-esteem of Marilyn and Susan. He has always worked on the farm with his family and has not considered doing anything else. He mentions that this father has always looked forward to the day when Mark can "take over the reins" of the family farm and perhaps expand the property.

Theresa and Roger are different again. Although they come from diverse backgrounds—Roger's parents are very well off—both don't have any plans at all for after graduation. Roger spends most of his time after school playing computer games with friends, while Theresa spends most of her time at various coffee shops around town. Both contend that they are not sure what they want to do or what they might be best able to do.

Mr. Bolen finds these students fairly representative of other students in the school. At a staff meeting, Ms. Weber, the principal, asks teachers how they find the students this year and whether they have any concerns they would like to discuss. After relating his experiences with Marilyn, Susan, Mark, Theresa, and Roger, Mr. Bolen finds other teachers have noticed the same themes in many of their students. The principal leans forward with interest, "Last year a number of principals were concerned with just these issues. You may be interested to know that adolescents have, for generations, varied greatly in the way they react to the complexities of trying to integrate choices regarding vocation and philosophy of life. Do you remember learning about Erikson and Marcia at your college of education?"

Focus Questions

1. How does a teacher judge a student's self-esteem?
2. Is positive self-esteem a prerequisite to learning?
3. How does Mr. Bolen recognize differences in self-esteem among his students? Would an elementary school teacher view the self-concepts and self-esteem of students in the same way that Mr. Bolen does?
4. In what ways do one's peers affect one's actions?
5. Is a teacher's perception of a student important to the student's learning? Success or failure in school?
6. In what ways are teachers role models?

How Do Individuals Develop Self-Concepts and Self-Esteem?

Students' personal and social development are as important as their cognitive development. Teachers understand intuitively that it is important for students to think well of themselves, to have a positive rather than a negative self-concept. Experienced teachers have seen students who can't wait to try new things, who welcome opportunities to interact with adults and peers, who radiate confidence in themselves. (Marilyn in the Teacher Chronicle is such a student.) Teachers have also seen students who are hesitant to embrace both academic and social challenges. More important, teachers can influence the feelings students have about themselves. Hess and Zingle (1995) from the University of Alberta have argued that there is not only a strong link between self-concept and learning, but that teachers play an important role in the development of a student's self-concept. They contend that the enhancement of students' self-concepts should be a primary goal of teachers. Hess and Zingle state that "children who have a healthy self-concept will be intrinsically motivated to learn ... they will have the tools to be truly educated" (p. 177). In a similar vein, research conducted by Ian Brown (1992) from the Scarborough Board of Education indicates that teachers can be trained to use behaviours that both elicit and maintain self-control behaviours in their students. This in turn has positive consequences for student achievement and self-esteem and further encourages the development of functional attitudes about themselves as learners. To prove the point, ask a few classmates, a room-mate, or friends to join you in reflecting on the teachers you had in elementary through high school. Did a teacher ever say or do something that influenced, positively or negatively, your feelings about yourself? Chances are one did. Ask the group if a teacher ever gave them confidence. Ask if a teacher ever made them feel inadequate or "invisible." Analyze your own experiences and those of your friends. Do you think that, in all cases, those instances of influencing a student's feelings were intentional on the part of the teacher? Probably not.

> **CONNECTION:** The nature of values and how they are acquired will be examined in Chapter 4.

As a teacher, however, you need to be aware of your influence on students' beliefs about themselves; their self-perceptions. Much of what students learn about themselves comes from their interactions with others, including teachers. Conversely, the interactions students have with other people are influenced heavily by their self-perceptions (Marsh, 1984). Given the influence that teachers can have on a child's or adolescent's self-perception, therefore, it is important for aspiring teachers to understand how self-perceptions are formed.

Development of Self-Concept

Teachers, parents, and administrators recognize the importance of students' self-perceptions. It is not surprising, therefore, that the way students view themselves is the subject of much discussion in educational circles. However, self-concept is a very complex variable and one that is frequently not all that well understood. This complexity is illustrated in several recent articles published in the *Canadian Journal of School Psychology*. For example, Schicke and Fagan (1994) suggest that the relationship of self-concept and intelligence to the prediction of school achievement is not a simple one. Furthermore, self-concept must be viewed from a developmental perspective and can be complicated when children with special needs are present (Obiakor & Algozzine, 1994). Another problem relates to terms that are thrown around and used indiscriminately. A prime example is the confusion between the terms *self-concept* and *self-esteem*. The terms are often used interchangeably, but there is an important difference between them (Beane & Lipka, 1980; Marshall, 1989). **Self-concept** is a person's description of himself or herself in terms of roles, attributes, or characteristics (Beane & Lipka, 1986; Berk, 1994). **Self-esteem**, which will be examined shortly, refers to a person's evaluation of his or her self-concept and the feelings associated with that evaluation. Two people may describe themselves as possessing the same attribute—stubbornness, for example—but one person may judge stubbornness as being positive while the other judges stubbornness as being negative, depending on their values.

The way in which people describe themselves changes with age. For instance, when preschoolers think about themselves and are asked to describe themselves, they tend to focus on concrete characteristics (Berk, 1994). Although such descriptions include characteristics of physical appearance and favourite possessions, research has shown that the most frequent type of description among preschoolers is typical behaviours (e.g., Keller, Ford, & Meacham, 1978). Examples of typical behaviours described might include the following statements: "I can dress myself," "I go to church," and "I play with Shana." Note that these statements, as well as descriptions of physical appearance and possessions, are observable attributes.

One question to raise about such early research is whether the concrete descriptions are the only types of descriptions of which preschoolers are capable. More recent research on the self-concepts of preschoolers has attempted to use other techniques to probe self-concept. One example is the presentation of pictures that depict children either succeeding or experiencing difficulty with tasks (Harter & Pike, 1984). Another technique is to present descriptions and then to ask preschoolers if they recognize the statements as being true of themselves. Recognizing descriptions of self is easier than generating those same descriptions. Using this technique, researchers have shown that children as young as three-and-a-half years old are capable of consistent self-descriptions. These descriptions go beyond observable characteristics to descriptions of typical emotions and attitudes (Eder, 1989; 1990). Examples of statements of emotion or attitude might include, "I don't like going to the library," "I am happy when I'm with my teacher," or "I feel like being quiet when I get mad."

Evidence that self-concept is a developmental phenomenon can be seen in the shift that occurs in self-descriptions between the ages of eight and eleven. You might recall that in Piaget's theory of cognitive development this is roughly the period of concrete operations when children begin to think logically and to classify hierarchically (Marshall, 1989). Data suggest that children are able to apply these capabilities to their conceptions of self. The descriptions of characteristic attributes, behaviours, and internal states typical of preschoolers are, as children reach intermediate grades, categorized into dispositions or personality traits (Berk, 1994). When given the opportunity simply to describe themselves, school-age children are less likely to describe typical behaviours than preschoolers and more likely to emphasize competencies. The self-description of a grade four student, for example, might include statements such as "I am good at arithmetic" or "I can play the piano" (Damon & Hart, 1988). Self-descriptions at this age also contain comparisons of self with peers, for instance, "I can ride a bike better than Joey" (Damon & Hart, 1982; Ruble, Boggiano, Feldman, & Loebl, 1980). Finally, self-descriptions during this period of development include generalizations of personal qualities or traits such as "I am smart," " I have a temper," or "I am kind to others."

TRY THIS: To gather information about your students, develop statements that indicate students' feelings about various aspects of classroom activity and then ask students to identify those statements that describe themselves.

CONNECTION: Self-descriptions or attributions can be used to understand motivation, which is the subject of Chapter 9.

self-concept One's description of self in terms of roles and characteristics.

self-esteem One's judgments about self and the feelings associated with those judgments.

The transition from childhood to adolescence is a time of dramatic changes in a person's life. The changes include self-concept and are discernible in the self-descriptions of adolescents. The categories that elementary-age children use in their self-descriptions are qualified as they enter adolescence and the middle or junior high grades. The self-categorization of "I am kind to others" by a grade four student becomes "I am kind to most people, most of the time" in grade seven. The self-descriptions of adolescents indicate that their self-concept takes into account the situations they have experienced (Barenboim, 1977). One's response to others depends on many factors that change from situation to situation. Consequently, what an adolescent learns about him- or herself is that he or she is generally kind to others, but there are situations in which kindnesses are not easily given. The general sense of self that develops during adolescence is evidenced in self-descriptions that emphasize social virtues—such as kindness or cooperativeness—as well as concern for how one is viewed by others (Rosenberg, 1979).

From the preschool years through high school, what students learn about themselves culminates in a sense of identity. One's sense of identity is the extent to which one enjoys a sense of well-being, a feeling of knowing where one is going, and an inner assuredness that one will receive social recognition from those who count. Whether one develops a sense of identity depends on the overall nature of social interactions. As we will see in our examination of Erikson's theory of psychosocial development, identity is the positive resolution of the developmental crisis of adolescence. Negative resolution at this stage results in confusion about where one fits into the social fabric, a lack of a sense of identity.

POINT: Changes in self-descriptions suggest that students are learning to view themselves in different ways, which is one way in which *development affects learning.*

The changes in self-descriptions described above can be viewed as representing three levels of self-concept: situational, categorical, and general (cf. Beane & Lipka, 1986). Preschoolers describe themselves in terms of concrete characteristics, activities, or emotions that are situationally specific. Elementary-age children create categories from the specific descriptions, thus their self-descriptions include statements of competencies. The change in self-concept from preschoolers to elementary students is a move from the specific toward the general. This pattern continues into adolescence. The self-descriptions at this stage include statements of a general sense of self. The statements, although very general, are likely to be qualified.

An important aspect of the development of self-concept is that as self-descriptions or perceptions change from specific to general, they also become more stable. Another way to think about the development of self-concept is that the self-perceptions of a grade nine

Children's self-concepts and sense of self-esteem develop in social contexts. These social contexts are influenced profoundly by cultural norms, beliefs, and values as expressed in the family and community that together define an individual's social environment

student are more resistant to change than those of a grade two student. Keeping in mind that self-concept refers to the way in which a person describes him- or herself, this means that a high school student's sense of self is not easily changed. Whether a student's sense of self is in need of change depends, of course, on whether the student views him- or herself in a positive or negative way. This evaluative aspect of a student's sense of self is what is referred to as self-esteem.

Cultural Diversity and Sense of Self

Self-esteem is one's evaluation of one's concept of his or her characteristics and competencies. A person whose self-concept includes the characteristic "solitary" may judge that characteristic to be positive or negative. Whether a person judges a characteristic to be positive (thus enhancing one's self-esteem) or negative (thus lowering one's self-esteem) depends on the personal value placed on that characteristic. Some people might value solitariness highly. Others might place no value whatsoever on that characteristic. The point is that one's self-esteem is based on his or her values; judgments about self are value judgments.

REFLECTION: What personal characteristics do you value? Did you ever have a teacher who valued personal characteristics that you did not? How did that influence your relationship with that teacher?

Values, as you will discover in the next chapter, are acquired from the culture in which you are raised. You will likely encounter cultural diversity—differences among people of varying cultural backgrounds—in the classrooms in which you teach. Stalikas and Gavaki (1995) reported that more than 10 000 children of various ethnic backgrounds attended thirty-four private, ethnic, and religious schools in Quebec in 1992. Many more culturally diverse children are enrolled in French or English public schools but also participate in heritage language schools. They conducted a study to demonstrate the importance of ethnic identity among second generation Greek-Canadian secondary school students in Quebec. They found a strong relationship between ethnic identity, self-esteem, and academic achievement. Similarly, Bhatt and Tonks (1992) reported that about a third of Canadians feel that ethnic, ancestral, or cultural roots are important in their definition of self.

Consider the experience of Jason Lopez as he taught in his high school classroom in Toronto, a classroom in which the cultural backgrounds of his students were highly diverse. Most of Jason's students valued assertiveness as a personal characteristic. One manifestation of that characteristic was direct eye contact. Jason himself had learned that teachers should make direct eye contact with students and did so with most of his students. There was one group of students in his class, however, with whom he was unable to make direct eye contact: female students of Asian heritage whose families were recent immigrants. After much effort and no success, he discussed the situation with both female and male students of Asian heritage. What he learned was that assertiveness in general, and direct eye contact in particular, were not culturally valued for females. If his female students of Asian heritage were to make eye contact, they would have felt as though they were defying his authority. Out of respect for his authority, they did not meet his eyes.

REFLECTION: What cultural values shape your self-concepts and measures of self-esteem?

CONNECTION: Learning about oneself often happens through experiences with others. Acquiring self-knowledge is examined again in Chapter 7 in relation to Bandura's concept of self-efficacy.

Researchers have found that some children judge their own competencies in relation to other children. They establish their self-esteem through social comparison (Stipek & McIver, 1989). Children who use social comparison to judge their own worth place value on their standing compared to others. To illustrate, many children from the U.S. mainland use social comparisons in their self-descriptions, such as "I'm the best skater in my class," but children from Puerto Rico almost never describe themselves in relation to others (cf. Damon & Hart, 1988). As a group, Taiwanese students exhibit higher academic achievement than American children. However, American children possess higher self-esteem than the Taiwanese. In Taiwan, competition in classrooms is extremely intense; there is great pressure to achieve. Although students in Taiwan do achieve highly as a group, they also compare themselves to their classmates. Given the high level of competition, very few Taiwanese students will compare favourably with their classmates and consequently do not hold themselves in high esteem (Chiu, 1992–1993).

The values of a child vary not only from country to country but also from cultural group to cultural group within the same country, and even within cultural groups. Because your students will not all value the same personal characteristics, and because self-esteem is based on value judgments, it will be important for you to understand the values each student brings to your classroom. Understanding cultural diversity is necessary for effective teaching as the diversity of students in our schools will continue to increase into the twenty-first century.

The Development of Self-Esteem

A person's self-concept can be clear or vague, accurate or inaccurate, realistic or unrealistic, comprehensive or incomplete (cf. Beane & Lipka, 1986). These dimensions focus on how well a person's self-concept is formed. They do not indicate whether a person feels good or bad about him- or herself. Self-esteem is a person's evaluation of his or her self-concept and, more particularly, the feelings associated with that evaluative judgment. Self-esteem is usually discussed using terms such as *high self-esteem* and *low self-esteem*. What do these phrases mean in terms of a student's feelings about him- or herself? Students with high self-esteem are basically satisfied with themselves, even though they may recognize faults or weaknesses that they hope to overcome (Rosenberg, 1979). Students with low self-esteem are not satisfied with themselves as persons; they judge their worth as a person as low.

Children begin at a young age to show their feelings about themselves; they smile when they succeed at a task and frown and might avoid eye contact with adults when they fail (Stipek, Recchia, & McClintic, 1992). Also, children often act bored if they cannot perform a task. Given the obvious relationship between self-concept and self-esteem, it is not surprising that the pattern of specific to general development of self-concept seems to hold for the development of self-esteem as well. Preschoolers make judgments about various characteristics and competencies. In essence, they form separate self-esteems that are integrated only later into a general evaluation of self (Harter, 1990). Although children develop an overall sense of self-worth, the development of self-esteem is characterized by increasing numbers of dimensions of self.

One way of investigating the self-esteem of young children is to make statements and then ask if the children agree with those statements. The difference between using this technique to investigate self-concept and self-esteem is that the latter uses statements that focus on self-evaluation. Examples of such statements include, "Most kids like me," and "I am good at homework" (Harter 1982, 1986). The results of this research suggest that children under seven years of age judge their social acceptance by how well they are liked by others and their competence by how well they can do things. If young children are questioned using pictures to supplement the verbal statements, evidence suggests that children's self-esteem is subdivided even further (Marsh, Craven, & Debus, 1991).

CRITICAL THINKING: What are the characteristics of concrete operational thought that allow students to develop continually more refined dimensions of self-esteem?

EXAMPLE: Given what you know of Mark in the Teacher Chronicle, how would you describe his self-esteem, taking into account the dimensions of academic, social, and physical self-esteem?

REFLECTION: How did you view yourself in elementary school with regard to academic, social, and physical dimensions? How did you view yourself in high school?

Around seven or eight years of age, about the time that children develop the classification capabilities associated with Piaget's concrete operations, at least three dimensions of self-esteem have developed. These dimensions include academic, physical, and social self-esteem. As children continue to gain developmental experience, these dimensions of self-esteem are refined even further. For example, a child's sense of academic self-worth may be differentiated by content areas. A child's sense of social self-worth may be judged separately in relation to peers and adults. During this period when the dimensions of self-esteem are expanding, children are also forming an overall self-evaluation (Harter, 1990). Two dynamics seem to be operating at once: a child's self-esteem is being differentiated into multiple dimensions and, at the same time, an overall estimate of self-worth is being formed. The results of the operation of both dynamics during this period and the hierarchical structure of self-esteem are presented in Figure 3.1.

Other dimensions are added to self-esteem as children become adolescents. Adolescents become concerned with the complexities of close friendships, same-sex, and opposite-sex relationships. Academic self-esteem becomes complicated by issues of career decisions. Physical self-esteem is influenced by physical maturation and an increased emphasis on one's appearance and attractiveness to

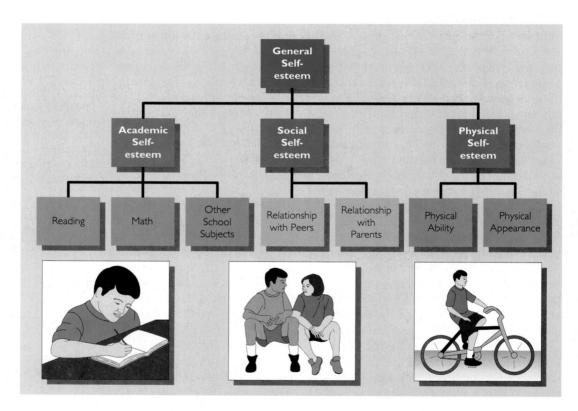

FIGURE 3.1
Hierarchical Structure of Self-Esteem for Children in Intermediate Grades

Source: "Self-Concept: Validation of Construct Interpretations," R. Shavelson, J.J. Hubner, & J.C. Stanton, 1976, *Review of Educational Research*, 46, 407–441. Adapted by permission.

Insights on Successful Practice

What approaches have you used successfully to help students improve academic achievement through positive self-image and higher self-esteem?

To promote the building of self-esteem among my grade two students, I have used a "Student of the Week" program. At the beginning of the year, I assign each child a special week. A letter goes home to the family explaining what the special week means. Children look forward to it, and meanwhile the child and his or her family can be making plans for each day of that week.

During his or her special week, the student leads the class in morning exercises, posts the calendar date, conducts "Show and Tell" and "Daily News," and serves as "Line Leader," "Messenger," and classroom assistant for distributing materials. The Student of the Week has a special bulletin board to decorate with baby pictures and family photographs and has the opportunity to tell the class about the photos. The student also has a special table set aside on which to display and demonstrate favourite toys, souvenirs, collections, hobbies, or crafts. During the week, the student is encouraged to read one of his or her favourite books to the class, play a favourite record-book, and tell favourite jokes or riddles

Students of the Week can make arrangements to bring pets to school to show the class and tell all about them. The children can also invite visitors to the classroom—family members, friends, or neighbours—to tell about their jobs or show slides or demonstrate a craft or hobby.

Students of the Week can bring a treat to pass out to the class and are encouraged to bring treats that they and their family have made together. This year, I added a new component to the program. I take the Student of the Week out to lunch.

In my twenty years of teaching, I have found that this program has always done a lot to increase each child's self-esteem, not only during the special week, but in the anticipation and planning stages and in the involvement of the family.

NANCI MAES
Elementary School Teacher

Your Insights

What other benefits might "Student of the Week" have for students in inclusive, culturally diverse schools? How might this activity be integrated into the curriculum and used in assessment?

---

others (Berk, 1994). White, Mendelson, & Schlieker (1995) from Concordia University studied both global self-esteem and appearance-esteem to determine if esteem was related to being overweight or obese. Their sample of adolescent boys and girls in grades nine to eleven did not report poor self-esteem. However, appearance-esteem decreased with weight increases and was most apparent for students who were obese. As well, girls rated themselves lower in appearance-esteem than boys. Gender differences become more apparent in these and other areas during adolescence. Later in this chapter, we will encounter Gilligan's theory of moral judgment, which suggests that females and males use different criteria to evaluate right and wrong.

A student's academic self-esteem is a powerful predictor of achievement and motivation (Marsh, Smith, & Barnes, 1985). Students with high social self-esteem are liked better by their peers than students with low social self-esteem (Harter, 1982). A student's self-esteem can have a significant impact on the quality of a student's experience in and out of school. In the next section, we examine how interactions with others shape one's view of self.

CONNECTION: One's social environment—other people—provides potential models. The perceived competence of the models can influence one's self-esteem. This relationship is described in detail in Chapter 7.

REFLECTION: Identify messages other people communicate to you that make you feel good about yourself. How might you use similar messages to support the self-esteem of your students?

psychosocial development According to Erikson, the process whereby relationships with others influence one's search for his or her own identity.

critical periods Erikson's eight stages of psychosocial development are defined by these periods; each stage identifies the emergence of a part of an individual's personality.

developmental crisis According to Erikson, there is a conflict faced at each stage of psychological development. The way the crisis is resolved has a lasting effect on the person's self-concept and view of society in general.

How Does Social Interaction Influence Personal Growth?

The hierarchical structure of self-esteem grows more complex as students grow older. One reason for this increase in complexity is that development is accompanied by an expanding social environment. Very young children have a fairly small social environment. When a child starts preschool, day care, and eventually, school, the social environment expands. Ellen Jacobs and Donna White from Concordia University, together with Madeleine Baillargeon of Université Laval and Raquel Betsalel-Presser of Université of Montréal (1995) describe the relationship between social behaviour and school-age child-care experiences based on several studies conducted in Quebec. While there is a relationship between social behaviour and attendance in preschool daycare, these behaviours (e.g., compliance) continued to be manifest for those children who received after-school care.

As children get older and become adolescents, peers become more and more important. The interactions with the other people that constitute one's social environment provide challenges and experiences that influence one's self-esteem. Indeed, the development and/or the enhancement of one's self-esteem cannot be accomplished in isolation. As Damon (1991) puts it: "One cannot 'find' self-esteem in isolation from one's relations to others because it does not exist apart from those relations" (p. 17). Other people have a powerful influence on our sense of self. One way to think about this is to say that one's psychological development is affected by one's social environment.

Erikson's Theory of Psychosocial Development

Erik Erikson developed an important theory about the impact of one's social environment on one's psychological development. His theory of **psychosocial development** emphasizes how relationships with others influence one's search for his or her identity. By virtue of our cultural traditions, teachers occupy a potentially important position in the lives of young people. Teachers not only establish relationships with students but also influence the environment in which relationships between students are established. Erikson's theory gives us a way of understanding how the relationships young people build influence their sense of identity.

Erikson's theory of psychosocial development focuses on the tasks our culture sets before an individual at various points along the continuum of development. The eight stages postulated in Erikson's theory are summarized in Table 3.1.

Erikson's stage theory describes and explains the development of the human personality. Erikson viewed psychosocial growth as consisting of **critical periods** when the "parts" of the individual's personality developed. It is these critical periods that define Erikson's eight stages of psychosocial development. Each stage identifies the emergence of a part of an individual's personality.

Each stage in Erikson's framework is structured as a dichotomy (e.g., trust versus mistrust, intimacy versus isolation), indicating the positive and negative consequences for each stage. Each dichotomy defines a **developmental crisis**, a psychosocial issue that will be resolved in either a positive or negative way. The resolution of each developmental crisis will have a lasting effect on the person's view of him- or herself and of society in general. What follows are brief descriptions of the developmental crises associated with the different stages in Erikson's theory.

TABLE 3.1 *Erikson's Eight Stages of Psychosocial Development*

Stages	Approximate Age	Important Event	Description
1. Basic trust vs. basic mistrust	Birth to 12-18 months	Feeding	The infant must form a first loving, trusting relationship with the caregiver, or develop a sense of mistrust.
2. Autonomy vs. shame/doubt	18 months to 3 years	Toilet training	The child's energies are directed toward the development of physical skills, including walking, grasping, and sphincter control. The child learns control but may develop shame and doubt if not handled well.
3. Initiative vs. guilt	3 to 6 years	Independence	The child continues to become more assertive and to take more initiative, but may be too forceful, leading to guilt feelings.
4. Industry vs. inferiority	6 to 12 years	School	The child must deal with demands to learn new skills or risk a sense of inferiority, failure, and incompetence.
5. Identity vs. role confusion	Adolescence	Peer relationships	The teenager must achieve a sense of identity in occupation, sex roles, politics, and religion.
6. Intimacy vs. isolation	Young adulthood	Love relationships	The young adult must develop intimate relationships or suffer feelings of isolation.
7. Generativity vs. stagnation	Middle adulthood	Parenting	Each adult must find some way to satisfy and support the next generation.
8. Ego integrity vs. despair	Late adulthood	Reflection on and acceptance of one's life	The culmination is a sense of acceptance of oneself as one is and feeling fulfilled.

Source: Psychology (6th ed.), L. A. Lefton, 1996, 6th ed. Needham Heights, MA: Allyn & Bacon. Copyright 1996 by Allyn & Bacon. Reprinted by permission.

Stage 1: Trust versus Mistrust (birth–18 months). If the interactions infants have with the other people in their environment are positive, then the infant will learn that people in their environment can be trusted. According to Erikson (1963), an outcome of trust is the result of consistent experiences over time. If the constancy of interaction between the infant and others meets the basic needs of the infant, then trust is developed. If, however, the interactions lack warmth and caring and the basic needs of the infant go unsatisfied, the developmental crisis is resolved in a negative way. The infant will learn to mistrust those around him or her.

Stage 2: Autonomy versus Shame and Doubt (18 months–3 years). The developmental crisis at this stage occurs as the child enters toddlerhood. It is important for the toddler to explore his or her environment in an effort to establish some independence from parents. The toddler, who is now less dependent on others, seeks to develop a sense of independence and freedom through such exploration. If the child is encouraged to discover what is inside the book on the shelf, if his or her attempts to dress are uninterrupted, if the mess made while pouring cereal is tolerated, the crisis will more likely be resolved in the direction of **autonomy**, a sense of independence. If the toddler's exploration and attempts to be independent are discouraged, he or she will likely feel ashamed of these efforts, and develop doubts about his or her ability to deal with the environment. A parent or caregiver who is unable to allow the toddler to make mistakes, to persist, and to make further mistakes, manifests the kinds of interactions that lead to a negative resolution of the developmental crisis of learning autonomy at this stage.

Stage 3: Initiative versus Guilt (3–6 years). During this stage, children are attempting to develop a sense of initiative, that they are operators on the environment. According to Erikson, **initiative** "adds to autonomy the quality of undertaking, planning, and attacking a task for the sake of being active and on the move" (1963, p. 225). The child's imaginative play often allows the child to imitate adults in performing various tasks. If you have ever seen a child pretend to read or "fix" a clock or "nurse" the family dog, you have seen evidence of the child's attempt to undertake grown-up tasks. It is during this period that children typically learn to identify and imitate same-sex models. Exploration in play during this period is as important as it was during the previous stage. Given the increased linguistic abilities of preschool children, their explorations often take the form of questions to adults. If their interactions and explorations during play are encouraged, if their questions are recognized and answered sincerely, positive resolution of the developmental crisis is more likely. If the child's efforts to explore or his or her questions are treated as a nuisance, the child may feel guilty about "getting in the way."

Stage 4: Industry versus Inferiority (6–12 years). As the child enters school and advances through the elementary grades, the developmental crisis focuses on the child's ability to win recognition through performance. The notion that elementary students need generous encouragement and praise for their accomplishments is consistent with Erikson's view of psychosocial development at this stage. People in education know the importance of early success in school. The child who is encouraged to complete tasks and who receives praise for his or her performance is likely to develop a sense of **industry**, an eagerness to produce. If the child does not experience success—if his or her efforts are treated as unworthy and intrusive—the child will develop a sense of inferiority.

Stage 5: Identity versus Role Diffusion (adolescence). The developmental crisis of adolescence centres on the youth's attempt to discover his or her identity—to identify those things about himself or herself that are unique. For Erikson, **identity** "is experienced merely as a sense of psychosocial well-being ... a feeling of being at home in one's body, a sense of 'knowing where one is going,' and an inner assuredness of anticipated recognition from those who count" (1968, p. 165). An important aspect of an adolescent's sense of identity is his or her choice of occupation (Marcia, 1980). Reflect on the groups, or cliques, from your own

During the industry-versus-inferiority stage of psychosocial development, children need to gain self-confidence through successful performance. Self-confidence grows through others' recognition of successes based on personal effort, productivity, and persistence.

high school. Did not most members of any particular clique share similar aspirations about careers, if not about identical occupations? Another important contributor to the adolescent's sense of identity is his or her emerging sexuality (Marcia, 1980). Adolescence is the period of puberty, dramatic physical maturation, and an increase in relationships with those of the opposite sex. If the nature of the adolescent's interactions support the sense of who he or she is, the resolution of the developmental crisis is positive. A positive resolution instills a sense of self-confidence and stability; whether fulfilling the roles of friend, child, student, leader, boyfriend, or girlfriend, the adolescent feels at ease. Negative experiences that do not allow a student to integrate his or her various social roles into a unitary, stable view of self lead to a sense of diffusion. The adolescent who feels torn apart by what he or she perceives as inconsistent expectations exhibits **role diffusion.**

Stage 6: Intimacy versus Isolation (young adulthood). The young adult's personality—stemming from his or her sense of self—is influenced by efforts to establish an **intimacy**, a close psychosocial relationship, with another person. Typically, this is the period when a young adult who has just finished his or her education or training strikes out on his or her own to begin work and establish a life away from the childhood family. Among young adults, the need for intimate relationships can be seen at any number of places: work, health clubs, singles bars, church functions, athletic teams, recreation groups. Many young adults who are interviewing for jobs in a new town take into account the town's supply of eligible partners. Failure to establish a close relationship with another leads to a sense of **isolation**, a feeling of being alone.

Stage 7: Generativity versus Stagnation (young adulthood–middle age). Erikson identifies **generativity** as a concern for future generations. Childbearing and nurturing occupy the thoughts and feelings of people at this stage in the life span. Many people who decide against having a family and raising children are concerned with questions about their role regarding future generations. The classic career-versus-family decision reflects the developmental crisis that epitomizes

TRY THIS: Observe the behaviour of primary grade students. See if you can infer from their behaviour those who have a sense of industry and those who have a sense of inferiority. Share your observations with the teacher in order to check the accuracy of your impressions.

role diffusion The negative outcome of Stage 5 of Erikson's theory of psychosocial development, whereby an adolescent is unable to develop a clear sense of self.

intimacy The state of having a close psychological relationship with another person. Intimacy versus isolation is Stage 6 of Erikson's theory of psychosocial development.

isolation Failure to establish a close psychological relationship with another person leads to this feeling of being alone. The negative outcome of Stage 6 of Erikson's theory of psychosocial development.

generativity A sense of concern for future generations, expressed through childbearing or concern about creating a better world. Generativity versus stagnation marks Stage 7 of Erikson's theory of psychosocial development.

POINT: Erikson's view of psychosocial development supports the point that *development is complex and multifaceted.*

this stage. Unsuccessful resolution leads to a sense of stagnation, the feeling that one's life is at a dead end.

Stage 8: Integrity versus Despair (later adulthood–old age). According to Erikson, **integrity** is a sense of understanding how one fits into one's culture and accepting that one's place is unique and unalterable. An inability to accept one's sense of self at this stage leads to despair—the feeling that time is too short and that alternate roads to integrity are no longer open.

This summary of Erikson's stages has highlighted the dichotomies that make up each developmental crisis. Although each dichotomy describes well the nature of the crisis to be resolved, it is a mistake to assume that each crisis will be resolved in favour of either the positive or negative qualities of the dichotomy. A student's personality contains positive and negative qualities. Positive resolution of any developmental crisis simply means that the positive quality of that stage is present to a greater degree than the negative quality.

Marcia's Work on Identity Statuses

James Marcia's work on the different types of identity—called **identity statuses**—is among the best known work derived from Erikson's own. Marcia was interested in conducting empirical research based on Erikson's theory. During interviews with male adolescents, Marcia explored concerns and opinions regarding occupational choice, sexuality, religion, and personal value systems (1967). As a result of his analysis of these interviews, Marcia proposed four identity statuses:

1. Identity diffusion types
2. Moratorium types
3. Identity achievement types
4. Foreclosure types

integrity A sense of understanding how one fits into one's culture and the acceptance that one's place is unique and unalterable. Integrity versus despair marks Stage 8 of Erikson's theory of psychosocial development.

identity statuses Different types of identity, as identified by Marcia.

identity diffusion To Marcia, adolescents who avoid thinking about lifestyle decisions and are unable to develop a clear sense of self.

moratorium According to Marcia, adolescents who have given thought to identity issues but have not reached any decisions.

Identity diffusion. A young person who is unable to commit to decisions and who is unable to postpone decisions by declaring a psychosocial moratorium may seek another solution to the developmental crisis—a solution that Erikson (1968) called a negative identity, an aspect of **identity diffusion**.

> The loss of a sense of identity is often expressed in a scornful and snobbish hostility toward the roles offered as proper and desirable in one's family or immediate community. Any aspect of the required role, or all of it—be it masculinity or femininity, nationality or class membership—can become the main focus of the young person's acid disdain (pp. 172–173).

Young people who adopt a negative identity are often those who rebel against authority—parents and teachers. According to Marcia, identity diffusion also describes adolescents who avoid thinking about life-style decisions. Typically, they are disorganized; they act impulsively; they are not goal-oriented. They often avoid commitment to schoolwork or to interpersonal relationships.

Moratorium. The urgency of identity decisions can overwhelm some young adolescents. Rather than deal with life-style decisions they are not prepared to make, they enter a state Erikson called psychosocial **moratorium**. A psychosocial moratorium is a suspension of any decisions that commit the adolescent to a certain occupational or social role. The adolescent buys time. A moratorium period that is used to gain new experiences, to taste adventure, can often contribute to sound decisions when the moratorium ends.

According to Marcia, moratorium types have given thought to identity issues but have not reached any decisions. Their relationships are often intense but usually short-lived. They seem distracted a good deal of the time. It is not unusual for moratorium types to try on a negative identity for a short time before adopting the status of identity achievement.

Identity achievement. **Identity achievement** is ascribed to those who have made life-style decisions, although not in all areas. For example, a young woman might decide, against the advice of her parents, to pursue a medical career. The same young woman may still be confused about sexuality, but she is determined about her occupational choice. The decisions made by identity-achievement types are their own; they have not simply followed the advice of parents, teachers, or counsellors. Identity-achievement types may not have all the answers, but they have made some decisions that give their development direction.

Foreclosure. Adolescents who adopt a **foreclosure** form of identity avoid crises by simply accepting the decisions made for them by others. Often, the decisions they accept were made by their parents. It is typical of foreclosure types to make—or perhaps more appropriately, adopt—their decisions early. With no decisions to make, the crises of identity are averted.

The Significance of Developmental Crises for Teachers

A teacher who is knowledgeable about developmental crises will be alert to the kinds of emotional baggage students might carry into the classroom. Imagine that a grade five teacher learns through a parent conference that one of her students never receives encouragement at home, that the child is viewed as a bother. The teacher might then observe the child carefully for a sense of inferiority, hypothesizing that the child needs to experience success and to receive praise to offset that effect.

Some research suggests the use of caution when interpreting a student's psychosocial well-being in terms of Erikson's stages. One reason is the suggestion that Erikson's stages are better descriptions of personality development in males than in females. During the industry-versus-inferiority period, for example, females appear to be concerned not only with achievement but also with interpersonal relationships (cf. Marcia, 1980). Carol Gilligan (1982) suggests that during adolescence, young women deal with the crisis of intimacy as well as with the crisis of identity.

Another point to keep in mind when making judgments based on Erikson's stages is that the crises that begin in toddlerhood and continue through the preschool, elementary, and middle school years are quite similar. The crises of autonomy, initiative, and industry all stress the need for independence and encouragement. Classroom tasks that allow students to succeed and that result in recognition for accomplishment are as critical for grade six students who are working through the crisis of industry as for preschoolers who are working through the crisis of initiative.

In summary, Erikson's theory suggests several ways in which teachers can facilitate healthy psychosocial development in their students. The suggestions listed in Here's How are possible actions that teachers might take.

TRY THIS: Interview college students to discover if they experienced a period during which they adopted a negative identity. What were the social ramifications? academic ramifications? What can you infer about respondents' identity statuses?

POINT: Emotional baggage influences a child's behaviour, self-esteem, and motivation in the classroom, which supports the point that *development affects learning.*

CRITICAL THINKING: Some students may be perceived as experiencing negative resolutions, which raises the question, "Is a teacher's perception of a student important to the student's learning?"

identity achievement According to Marcia, adolescents who have made life-style decisions, although not in all areas.

foreclosure According to Marcia, adolescents who simply accept the decisions made for them by others. These decisions are often made by their parents.

Here's How To Help Students Develop Positive Self-Concepts

1. Use the dichotomies as a basis for interpreting your observations of students. For instance, does a child's behaviour indicate a lack of industry? a sense of inferiority? confusion about his or her future?

2. Look for or design opportunities that encourage independent action on the part of students. For example, you might have students interview other students, parents, other teachers, and/or friends outside of school on some appropriate topic.

3. Reward independent efforts. Using the interview example, even if the interview is not particularly fruitful, you can praise the effort it took to conduct the interview. While discussing reasons why an interview was not successful, you can point out that the student's efforts have provided a learning opportunity that would not have existed otherwise.

4. Recognize that gender differences may exist. Specifically, keep in mind that research suggests that females may be as concerned with interpersonal relationships as they are with achievement. This difference should be taken into account when interpreting observations of student behaviour.

5. Use parent conferences to determine whether and in what ways students are encouraged at home.

The Importance of Parental Involvement

Current efforts to reform or restructure schools include ways to work with families in the education of their children (Elam, Rose, & Gallup, 1992). Schools in the twenty-first century will not be places for only students and teachers. Parents and community members will be involved as well. Other adults can be a tremendous asset to teachers, especially in their efforts to enhance the self-esteem of their students.

Although school is an important part of a student's social environment, home and community must be considered just as important. Some recent research has shown that parental involvement contributes significantly to children's social and academic progress. This finding also holds for special-needs children such as those identified with Attention-Deficit Hyperactivity Disorder (ADHD). Charles Cunningham of McMaster University and his colleagues have described how a school-based systems-oriented parenting course can increase the availability, accessibility, and cost effectiveness of services for families of ADHD children (Cunningham, Bremner, & Secord-Gilbert, 1993). Similarly, Charlotte Johnson and Kim Behrenz (1993) from the University of British Columbia have offered some constructive recommendations to enhance parents' collaborative child-rearing efforts for children with ADHD who varied in aggressive behaviour. In Calgary, Barb Blakemore and colleagues have developed an effective problem-solving therapy program for parents of children with ADHD (Blakemore, Schindler, & Conte, 1993). What these and many other studies demonstrate is that parents may not only influence their children's behaviour in positive and negative ways, but that they can also be important allies in working

Insights on Successful Practice

What do you do to create a social environment in which students can develop positive self-concepts and positive peer relations?

As the former director and teacher of a program for gifted high school students, I learned that many very bright, sensitive, talented students struggle academically, socially, and emotionally. School was not necessarily an enjoyable place to be for these students, some of whom developed serious personal problems, failed their courses, or dropped out.

I developed a program to motivate the underachievers and to help the achievers deal with the stress that comes from their own and others' high expectations of them. I set up noon-hour discussion groups to bring them together—achievers and nonachievers, affluent and low-income, the ever-popular and those who struggle socially. They met in groups of ten to discuss the "burdens of capability."

The program was a success. Discovering their commonalities, the students could drop their adolescent facades, break down stereotypes, and share personal and school issues as mere human beings. They could relate to and learn from each other. They gained skills in articulating personal concerns, learned to support each other, achieved greater self-awareness, and at the same time affirmed their gifts. I believe we all left each meeting feeling more motivated, and more at peace with ourselves.

JEAN SUNDE PETERSON
Retired Teacher

Your Insights

Why should teachers be concerned about students' affective and social needs? What other student groups might benefit from discussion groups of this kind? What else might you do to help students develop positive social relations?

---

with teachers to enhance children's personal and social well being and school learning. If family members can be recruited as coworkers in an effort to enhance a student's self-esteem, the probability of success increases significantly. As Robin Alter (1992) from York University writes, "if education is ever going to achieve its stated goal of maximizing potential for all students, then a true partnership between parents and schools must be created" (p. 109). How, then, can you recruit parents to join the effort?

One way to approach parent recruitment is to be proactive. Garlett (1993) argues that proactive teachers will make certain that parents know (1) the curriculum being taught and the methods being used to teach; (2) the class rules and regulations, including the consequences of breaking class rules; and (3) the value that the uniqueness of each child adds to the classroom. The last of the three pieces of information will be the most difficult to provide. It may be difficult for some teachers to provide because it requires reflection and careful writing, or because some teachers have difficulty finding the special delights of each student. In some cases, teachers must find opportunities to learn more about certain students. Persistence in such instances will help you find the special qualities of each student. Once found, those qualities can become the building blocks for enhancement of self-esteem. Opportunities to learn about students come to teachers in a variety of ways, many of them unexpected.

If values are the basis of self-esteem and if families are the primary shapers of values, then teachers who want to know the values of their students should get to know their students' families. Visiting the homes of your students is an excellent way to learn about their values. In many instances, however, such visits may

TRY THIS: Brainstorm specific ways of learning about students at the grade level you plan to teach.

prove impractical. If you can't go to the parents or caregivers, then invite them to school. Many parents do not visit schools, even though teachers issue an invitation. However, persistence and explicitness can improve parent participation. Use letters, phone calls, and face-to-face conferences or meetings to say something like the following to parents:

- "Visit our classroom on your way to work."
- "Have lunch with us in the cafeteria."
- "Come join us for our music rehearsal."
- "Check out library books with us when we visit the library." (Garlett, 1993)

Parents or caregivers can be invited to class presentations, either as observers or assessors. Parents can be invited to serve as academic coaches, career consultants, volunteer aides, tutors, field trip or other class activity chaperones, or class videographers, for example.

If parents or caregivers gain knowledge about your classroom, they can better help their children function there. If you meet parents or caregivers, you can better understand the values that your students use as the basis for their self-evaluations. Understanding how students judge themselves will help you structure activities that will contribute to increased self-esteem.

Key Socioemotional Issues at Different Grade Levels

REFLECTION: Reflect on the ways in which you have used stereotypic knowledge in dealing with people.

Groups are different from individuals. Mr. Bolen, in the Teacher Chronicle, may have been influenced in his views of students by such factors as their parents' occupations or the area of the city in which they live. Opinions formed about students based on these factors only would be stereotypic. A *stereotype* is the impression one has of a person based on that person's group. If we look closely enough, all students turn out to be different from our stereotypes of them. Knowing what is typical of a group of students does not inform a teacher about the unique qualities that each individual brings into the classroom. Nevertheless, knowledge of what is considered typical is helpful. By understanding the types of social and emotional issues that your students are likely to encounter, you will be more effective in facilitating their personal and interpersonal growth. As you read, keep in mind that students encounter issues as individuals. Helping students deal with developmental issues requires more than knowledge of their developmental stage. To help, teachers must know their students as individuals.

Gender Roles in the Elementary Grades. The primary grades offer the child a number of challenges: achieving in school, establishing new peer relationships, and developing a new independence from family. With their new roles, primary students are broadening their self-concepts.

An important social issue for young students is meeting the expectations of society. One area in which society communicates its expectations, for better or for worse, is how one's gender should influence one's behaviour. Students acquire these expectations through a process called *gender role socialization*. The socialization process yields knowledge of society's expectations regarding gender-appropriate behaviour. The knowledge students acquire is called **gender role stereotypes**. Research indicates that primary-grade children typically have acquired knowledge about society's expectations for the roles of each sex (Wynn & Fletcher, 1987).

gender role stereotypes
Commonly held expectations about the roles of each sex.

Parents have taught their children behaviours that are appropriate for boys and for girls before these children reach the primary grades (Grossman & Grossman, 1994). One way parents teach is through the toys they give their children. Parents tend to provide their children with gender-appropriate toys (Sidorowicz & Lunney, 1980). Parents also interact with their children in ways that communicate their aspirations for their children. Parents encourage achievement, independence, competition, and control of emotions in boys. Daughters are encouraged to be warm, dependent, and nurturing (Bempechat, 1990; Block, 1983; O'Brien & Huston, 1985).

Other children reinforce gender role stereotypes. Gender role stereotypes are often reflected in cooperative play. Preschoolers are likely to praise and to join in their peers' sex-appropriate behaviour and to criticize what they perceive as sex-inappropriate behaviour (Eagly, 1987; Fagot, 1977, 1985; Langlois & Downs, 1980; Shepherd-Look, 1982).

Elementary students are well versed in the language of gender role stereotypes. Whether these stereotypes will continue to be reinforced or not depends, in part, on teachers' responses to student behaviour. For example, gender role stereotypes suggest that girls are more likely to request assistance than boys (Brutsaert, 1990; Stewart & Corbin, 1988). A teacher who wishes to combat stereotypes will take care to provide assistance to girls only when it is truly needed. Responding to requests from a female student who is quite capable of completing a task on her own reinforces dependence. Here's How provides some additional ideas for correcting stereotypical beliefs held by students (Grossman & Grossman, 1994).

TRY THIS: Visit a day care centre or preschool to observe young children at play. What evidence of gender role stereotypes can you infer from behavioural and verbal interaction?

Here's How

Here's How To Encourage Gender Equity

1. Reward young students for playing with toys and engaging in activities that are nontraditional. (Example: Praise boys for playing with dolls and girls for building models.)

2. Expose students to nonsexist roles and instructional materials. (Example: Avoid materials in which women are portrayed only in stereotypic roles or in which they are "invisible.")

3. Use nonstereotypic role models as guest speakers. (Example: Invite female engineers and male nurses to speak with your students about their careers.)

4. Design units that allow students to participate in nonstereotypic ways; at the secondary level, recruit students into courses in nontraditional patterns. (Example: Encourage males in a food and nutrition unit and females in a mechanics unit.)

5. Reduce the documented dominance of males over females in mixed-gender groups (see Scott, Dwyer, & Lieb-Brilhart, 1985; Women's Educational Equity Program, 1983). (Example: Use cooperative learning groups in which the rights and obligations of each member are clear and in which roles are not stereotypically assigned. For instance, the group recorder role should be shared by males and females.)

REFLECTION: How does your body image affect you? How did you view yourself as an adolescent? a child? In what ways might you be sensitive to your students as they develop physically and mature?

CRITICAL THINKING: Sarah towered above her middle school classmates. Although she was well liked, she felt awkward and uncomfortable. Her work and attitude began to slip. Then a long-term substitute teacher—a very tall woman—took over Sarah's math class. As Sarah spent time talking with the new teacher, her grades picked up and the smile returned to her face. Why did Sarah's contact with this teacher help?

Puberty and Peer Relationships in the Secondary Grades. Toward the end of the elementary grades, the **growth spurt**, a dramatic increase in height and weight that signals the onset of **puberty**, begins to occur (cf. Dusek, 1987). The social implications of this growth spurt, which may occur in some students as early as grade five, reverberate through the junior high grades and into high school.

Because girls mature more quickly than boys, and because, in both sexes, there is considerable variability in physical maturation, some junior high students appear quite mature while others do not. Because appearance is an important aspect of social and emotional experience, the wide-ranging differences can cause problems for students in these grades.

As suggested in Chapter 2, an issue that some junior high school students face is the social consequences of early or late physical maturation. Most girls complete their growth spurt around grade seven. The growth spurt for boys is usually not completed before grade eight or nine (Tanner, 1978a, 1978b). Within each sex, there is a wide variation in maturation rates. Early-maturing girls, therefore, can be as much as four or five years ahead of late-maturing boys.

Because early and late maturation have significant effects on the social life of students, teachers should be prepared to help students deal with some of the problems they will face. This is especially true for early-maturing females and late-maturing males. How might teachers be helpful?

- Avoid using physical characteristics (such as height) to group students for activities.
- Expose students to role models who demonstrate that physical size, maturity, or lack of physical disabilities is not a prerequisite for accomplishment.
- Use cooperative learning techniques that stress contributions to the group instead of individual performance. (This item is addressed later in the chapter in relation to the integrative model of moral education.)
- Encourage students to participate in the establishment of classroom rules and procedures that address people's sensitivities to being treated as different.

What Social Problems Affect Students' School Lives?

Many of the social problems that exist in our society place students at risk of failing in school. Some of those problems deny students the measure of security and comfort that most of us need to pursue our goals. Other problems threaten our health and safety. For teachers to understand the needs of their students, they must first understand the problems their students face. As an example, what do you think are the most predominant fears of Canadian adolescents? A study by Gupta and colleagues (1995) compared the fears of adolescents from Montreal and Vancouver. They summarized their findings as follows:

Issues of acceptance by peers, the formulation of one's identity, discovering intimate relationships, and the uncertainty of their future are all typical adolescent concerns. Substantial interindividual variability was found to exist in the manifestation, acquisition, and persistence of fears. Findings revealed that as a whole the three most commonly reported fears concern their future, issues relating to the environment, and AIDS. With respect to location, adolescents in Vancouver report significantly more fears, especially fears of violence and pain and death, than do those from Montreal. Montrealers most frequently expressed fears of the future, AIDS, and political instability. Developmental

growth spurt A dramatic increase in height and weight that signals the onset of puberty.

puberty The time of physical change during which individuals become sexually mature.

trends revealed an increase in fears of the future, the environment, and political instability, and a decrease in fears of violence and peer pressures as they get older. Females in general were found to express more fears than their male counterparts in most categories (Gupta, Derevensky, Tsanos, Klein, Bennett, & Kanevsky, 1995, p.10).

Consider how the problems discussed below might affect the behaviour of students who face those problems.

Risks to Security and Comfort The number of adolescents who experience family stress has increased. Family stress is introduced by many conditions, such as separation, divorce, and remarriage; single parenthood; birth of a sibling; illness, disability, or death of a family member; loss of income; and poverty. At a time when the adolescent is struggling to develop a sense of identity, turmoil within the family can make the task more difficult. Linda Kurtz (1995) from McGill University has reported on the behavioural outcomes and coping process in children of divorced families. While the number of divorces in Canada was almost 30 000 in 1971, this number had tripled by 1991. Kurtz's study of elementary school children and their parents living in Montreal supported previous findings that children from divorced families had an increased incidence of problem behaviours. In another article from the same issue of the *Canadian Journal of School Psychology*, Motta (1995) contends that an increase in family violence as well as school violence and other stressors (sexual assault, natural disasters) can be implicated in childhood Posttraumatic Stress Disorder.

Linda Kurtz & Jeffrey Derevensky (1993) have further examined the relationship between family factors and suicide in adolescents. They write that:

> In the last decade, the adolescent suicide rate in Quebec has doubled, and continues to be well above the national average. Parental conflict and divorce are acknowledged as important factors that may increase psychological vulnerability during the developmental phase of adolescence, consequently augmenting the risk of suicidality. Suicidal behaviour during adolescence is a concomitant of prolonged and progressive family disruption, inadequate family relationships, and ineffective parent-child interaction (p. 204).

Consider the circumstances of a student who is temporarily living in a shelter for homeless persons. Now, compare the homeless student to another student who lives in an affluent suburb. Which of the two students is most likely to succeed in school? Which is most likely to experience difficulties in school? Because there are more factors that augur against success for the homeless student, we could say that the homeless student is at risk. **Students at risk** is a phrase much used by educators and the general public, but it is not clearly defined. Generally, the phrase "refers to students who perform or behave poorly in school and appear likely to fail or fall short of their potential" (Hallahan & Kauffman, 1994, p. 21). Just as a person who smokes too much, avoids exercise, and eats too much saturated fat is at risk of a heart attack, so too is a student who has no home, receives inadequate nourishment, and suffers from bouts of depression at risk of failing in school.

Poverty is an increasingly serious problem in Canada and has a negative influence on educational attainment. As Benjamin Levin (1995) at the University of Manitoba has pointed out, while schools cannot eliminate poverty, they can contribute to alleviating the effects of poverty. They can do so by improving instruction, providing more preschool education, and forging stronger links between families and communities.

CONNECTION: Students at risk are discussed in Chapter 5.

students at risk Students whose life circumstances make them more likely to fail in school

CRITICAL THINKING: How might Erikson have defined students who are at risk?

CONNECTION: Students with special needs and exceptional learners are discussed in Chapter 5.

Therefore, some of the factors that place students at risk of failure are the circumstances of their lives, such as homelessness, poverty, or a dysfunctional family. Poor life circumstances often deny children and adolescents opportunities to develop and grow normally. In some cases, however, life circumstances can cause more than just developmental delays. Imagine a dysfunctional family, rich or poor, in which the parents are alcoholics or addicted to crack cocaine. A child born to an addict of crack cocaine (a "crack baby") or an alcoholic (fetal alcohol syndrome) faces problems ranging from neurological damage to organ dysfunction to behavioural, social, and learning problems. Severely detrimental life circumstances can lead to physical or psychological disability.

The accommodation of disabilities in the learning environment is an important aspect of teaching and one to which we will return shortly. Physical disabilities, described in greater detail in Chapter 5, include hearing or visual impairments, traumatic head injury, spina bifida, and acquired immunodeficiency syndrome (AIDS), among others. Psychological disabilities include emotional or behavioural disorders, communication disorders, mental retardation, and learning disabilities.

There are also temporary situations that might place a student at risk of performing or behaving poorly, at least for the short term. Think about a student whose family moves to a new city, a new neighbourhood, a new school. Starting at a new school can be traumatic for a student. Although the student will likely adjust to the new setting, eventually make new friends, and begin to feel comfortable in his or her new surroundings, it may take some time. Until the student has adjusted, however, the student is at risk.

It is important to remember that students who live in the best of circumstances and who have no disability can also be at risk of performing or behaving poorly in school, even if they are at risk for only a relatively short period. Every experienced teacher knows that events in their students' lives can influence their actions and accomplishments in the classroom.

Consider the case of Charlie, a nine-year-old who had to change schools in the middle of the academic year (Brodkin & Coleman, 1994). Charlie's father lost his job, and his family had to sell their home and move in with relatives. His new teacher expected Charlie to have some difficulties just after his arrival, but as time went by, he isolated himself from the other students more and more. At the same time, he made very little effort to complete his schoolwork. Charlie was clearly at risk. If his father remains unemployed and the family is unable to get back on its feet, then Charlie's circumstances might persist. If, however, circumstances change and Charlie's family becomes independent once again, this episode will be transitory. Either way, Charlie is at risk now and his teacher is looking for ways to help him in this period of transition.

Adele Brodkin and Melba Coleman (1994) suggest several ways in which Charlie's teacher might be able to help him. Some of the suggestions for helping Charlie include:

Here's How

Here's How To Help Students When They Are at Risk

1. Enlist a buddy—the teacher can assign a classmate, who can be relied upon, to be Charlie's buddy, to include Charlie in games on the playground, and generally "show Charlie the ropes."

continued

2. Empathize out loud—the teacher can let Charlie know, in a casual way, that he or she understands how hard it is to leave friends from his old school. The teacher might also reassure Charlie that he will soon make new friends and that the teacher is already one of those new friends.

3. Assign responsibilities—the teacher can give Charlie jobs, such as playground helper, safety guard, or ball monitor.

4. Cooperative learning—the teacher can take this opportunity to form new cooperative learning groups so that Charlie will not work alone and will share with classmates the experience of assimilating into a new group and learning the group's norms.

5. Parent involvement—the teacher should take care not to infringe on the family's privacy or to offend their pride, but the parents can be informed of opportunities for them to become involved at school. The parents can be invited to share their hobbies with the class, tutor individuals or a small group, or accompany the class on field trips. Charlie's parents can be invited to help other parents coach sports teams, assist in the computer lab or library, call the parents of absent students, or help with school beautification projects.

6. Selected book lists—the teacher can consult with the school librarian to generate a list of books and resources for Charlie's parents that would help them understand how their son's problems have placed him at risk. One such book is *My Daddy Don't Go to Work* by Madeena Spray Nolan (published by Carol Rhoda, 1978).

TRY THIS: Find and read several of the "Kids in Crisis" columns in *Instructor* magazine. What are the causes of the crises faced by the students profiled? What conditions placed the students at risk? How did teachers and others help the students overcome their difficulties?

Another possibility is an alternative school. These schools have been shown to be effective for many marginalized or at-risk youth. Contact School in Toronto is one example of a successful alternative school you may be interested in learning more about (see Gagné, 1996). The schools-within-a-school model is another approach. This approach has been used in the Vancouver Technical Secondary School in British Columbia (Kelly, 1996). Here, larger schools are broken up into schools-within-a-school. Such mini-schools may focus on elite students, dropout prevention, or a vocational or cultural emphasis. Students in each "school" engage in learning together for at least half of each school day in their own location.

Other research has centred on "resilient at-risk students"—those who overcome their social and personal disadvantages. Some of the factors that protect or compensate for social disadvantages include family factors, school factors, community factors, and other human relationships (Johnson, 1997).

Risks to Health and Safety

There are other risks to school success that derive from physical conditions or injury. Some of these conditions are caused at the hands of others (e.g., an abusive adult), and some are self-imposed.

One physical condition that has reached high proportions is traumatic head injury (Bigge, 1991). The most frequent causes of traumatic head injury are automobile accidents, in many of which young children were not properly restrained or in which older passengers did not wear seat belts, and motorcycle and bicycle accidents, in many of which the cyclists were not wearing protective headgear. Tragically, violence—including child abuse—is another major cause of traumatic head injury (Hallahan & Kauffman, 1994).

The disabilities that result from traumatic head injury vary from temporary to permanent and from mild to severe. The symptoms most associated with traumatic head injury include cognitive difficulties such as inability to focus or maintain attention, inability to remember information or learn new information, and inability to organize and think abstractly. These cognitive difficulties often make it hard for injured students to re-establish social relationships. The effects of traumatic head or brain injury are not always immediately seen. In some cases the effects may not become apparent for months or even years after the initial injury (Allison, 1992). Of those who receive serious traumatic brain injury, about half will require special education programs. The half that returns to the general classroom will likely require special accommodation if they are to succeed (Mira & Tyler, 1991).

Another major cause of health and safety risks to children is child abuse. Child abuse includes both physical and sexual abuse as well as neglect. While it is almost impossible to precisely determine the incidence of child sexual abuse, it has been estimated that during childhood one in three girls and one in ten boys have been recipients of sexual advances, and this situation worsens during adolescence (Canadian Committee on Sexual Offenses Against Children and Youths, 1984). In Canada, we have heard of sexual abuse charges brought against teachers that may go back many years. But we also hear of instances of physical abuse and neglect that can lead to the death of the child. The causes of child abuse by adults are many and range from substance abuse and parent stress to mental health problems. A lack of parenting skills, a history of abuse when the parent was a child, and raising a 'difficult' child are other factors implicated in child abuse and neglect. Child abuse is not limited by such factors as socioeconomic status, education, religion, race, or ethnicity.

The results of abuse and neglect can range from mild to severe, both physically and psychologically, or even result in death.

Teachers are in a unique position to detect and report child abuse. Indeed, teachers have a legal, professional, and moral responsibility to report suspected cases of child abuse or neglect. Because failure to report child abuse or neglect is professionally irresponsible, and because it may result in your being held liable in a court of law, one of the first things to do after securing a teaching position is to determine the procedures you are to use in reporting suspected cases of abuse and neglect.

At the same time, various kinds of abuse and neglect are not always easy to spot and may be clouded by our own misconceptions. Rosemary Moskal (1994) conducted a study with Edmonton university education students to determine their knowledge and any myths they held about sexual abuse. The finding that there were various misconceptions about sexual abuse prompted Moskal to conclude that "student and practising teachers, administrators, and their school boards are in need of inservice training both in how to recognize the subtle signs of sexual abuse in children and adolescents and to receive the encouragement they need to report it to the proper authorities" (p. 43). It is incumbent upon all educators to become proficient in recognizing the signs of sexual and physical abuse as well as neglect and to be clear on the actions that can and must be taken as described by Canadian law and the policies of the provincial department of

POINT: The risks to security, comfort, health, and safety that affect students' lives illustrate the point that *life conditions affect development.*

TRY THIS: Call social service agencies that deal with cases of child abuse. Identify yourself as a future teacher and ask for information on the identification and reporting of child abuse.

education and local school boards. You can recognize abuse and neglect by the following signs (Berdine & Blackhurst, 1981):

- evidence of repeated injuries or new injuries
- frequent complaints of abdominal pain
- evidence of bruises, especially newer and older bruises
- evidence of welts, wounds, burns—especially those with well-defined shapes
- clothing that is inappropriate to the weather
- poor skin hygiene or body odour
- unprovided health services, eye glasses, dental work
- consistent sleepiness in class, frequent absence, chronic tardiness

Tragically, the problems faced by students are sometimes perceived to be so devastating and so intractable that suicide is considered as an alternative. Suicidal students, those who threaten or attempt suicide, are likely to give many clues. It is critical that teachers recognize these clues. Suicidal symptoms include the following:

- mention of suicide (80 percent of suicidal people discuss their intentions)
- significant changes in eating or sleeping habits
- loss of interest in prized possessions
- significant changes in school grades
- constant restlessness or hyperactivity
- loss of interest in friends

Every teacher should know what referral process for suicidal students is available in his or her school district. Teachers should also mentally rehearse what actions can be taken from various locations in the school in an emergency situation. In the event that you discover that one of your students is suicidal, it is critical that you remain with the student. Suicidal individuals remain suicidal for limited periods of time. *Do not leave the student alone!* (cf. Bell, 1980; Meyer & Salmon, 1988).

Bullying in Canadian Schools

Bullying at school has existed as long as children have been going to school. Most adults can remember incidents in which they, or friends, were bullies or the victims of bullies. Bullying can have short- and long-term negative consequences for both bullies and victims (Olweus, 1995). Several studies have been conducted that examine the prevalence of bullying in Canadian schools.

Ziegler and Rosenstein-Manner (1991) reported that 15 percent of the Toronto students they surveyed admitted that they bullied other students more than once during the school term. Noelle Bidwell (1997) surveyed an entire school division in Saskatoon, Saskatchewan and found that 10 percent of students reported being bullied on an ongoing, weekly basis. About one-third of the teachers surveyed by Bidwell considered bullying a serious problem in their classrooms. The type of bullying most often experienced by students was to be teased in an unpleasant way, followed by being called hurtful names, being left out of things on purpose, being hit or kicked, and being threatened with harm. Boys were more likely than girls to be threatened with harm, and much more likely to be hit or kicked. Bidwell also found, consistent with the Ziegler and Rosenstein-Manner study (1991), that about 15 percent of students admitted to bullying other students on a weekly basis. Both Canadian studies found that playgrounds, followed by hallways, were the most common locations for bullying.

What can teachers do to stop bullying in their schools? Many schools in Ontario have adopted a zero-tolerance policy toward disobedient behaviour. If such a policy is adopted by a school district, it needs to be clearly communicated to all students and teachers within the school.

Teachers might also discuss bullying with students at the beginning of the school year, and devise activities (stories, films, etc.) to enhance students' empathy and understanding of what it feels like to be bullied. School meetings with students, parents, and teachers may be productive when multiple perspectives can be shared (see Olweus, 1993 for other suggestions).

How Do Individuals Develop Moral Reasoning?

The social problems faced by students influence the way they see the world. Their experiences can influence their judgments about what is right and what is wrong. But maturation also influences the way in which students make moral judgments. These judgments change with age. A student may behave in one way at age six and in a very different way at age sixteen. In both instances, the student may consider him- or herself as behaving in the right way. Let us begin our study of moral development by examining how judgments of right and wrong change as people grow.

Piaget's Framework of Moral Reasoning

Piaget loved to observe children as they reacted to their environment. As a way of eliciting certain reactions, he made up the following pair of stories and asked children of different ages to discuss them.

> There was a little boy called Julian. His father had gone out and Julian thought it would be fun to play with father's ink-pot. First he played with the pen, and then he made a little blot on the table cloth.

> A little boy who was called Augustus once noticed his father's ink-pot was empty. One day when his father was away he thought of filling the ink-pot so as to help his father, and so that he should find it full when he came home. But while he was opening the ink-bottle he made a big blot on the table cloth (Piaget, 1948, p. 118).

Piaget questioned children about these stories. "Who was the naughtiest?" "Were Julian and Augustus equally guilty?" Piaget began to formulate a description of how **moral judgments**—judgments about right and wrong—develop, based on the variety of responses children of different ages gave and the consistency of the responses among children of similar ages.

Piaget concluded that there are general types of moral thinking. The first type—**morality of constraint**—describes judgments made by children up to approximately age ten. The second type of moral thinking—**morality of cooperation**—refers to the moral judgments of older children.

moral judgments Judgments about right or wrong.

morality of constraint According to Piaget, a type of moral thinking made by children under ten years of age; rules come from some external authority and strictly define what is right and wrong.

morality of cooperation According to Piaget, a type of moral thinking made by older children; rules provide general guidelines but should not be made blindly without considering the context.

Morality of Constraint. Morality of constraint is sometimes referred to as *moral realism*. Rules define what is right and what is wrong and come from some external authority. Because these rules are established by authoritative people—those who know—the rules should be obeyed. For students in early elementary grades, rules are sacred. There is no allowance made by the young realist for the context in which events occur. The intention of a person, for example, is not taken into account when judgments of right and wrong are made. Furthermore, the seriousness of a crime is determined by its consequences (cf. Lickona, 1976; Piaget, 1965).

Augustus made a bigger blot on the tablecloth than did Julian. Therefore, Augustus was more guilty than Julian.

Morality of Cooperation. Older children practice the morality of cooperation, alternatively called *moral relativism* or *moral flexibility*. The older child is a relativist; rules are not "carved in stone." A hallmark of cognitive development is decentration. As applied to moral judgments, it is evident in older children's awareness that others may not share their perceptions of rules. Rules, as older children understand them, provide general guidelines. It is inappropriate to follow rules blindly without considering the context in which they are applied. Rules should be obeyed not just because some "authority" has established them, but because they guard against violation of the rights of others. A person with good intentions who causes an injury or damage is not as culpable as a person with premeditation who commits a wrongful act (cf. Lickona, 1976; Piaget, 1965).

Older children who apply the morality of cooperation judge Julian to be more guilty than Augustus, who was attempting to do something nice for his father when he stained the tablecloth.

Kohlberg's Stages of Moral Development

Lawrence Kohlberg, during his graduate studies, became fascinated with Piaget's views on moral development. He followed Piaget's lead in using stories as a vehicle for investigating moral reasoning. Kohlberg wanted to apply his Piagetian-informed ideas on moral thinking to all ages, through adulthood. As a consequence, Kohlberg's stories were more elaborate and afforded a deeper analysis of an interpreter's reasoning. The stories Kohlberg created have become well known as *moral dilemmas*. The following is a classic example that has been used by Kohlberg and others in research on stages of moral reasoning.

> In Europe a woman was near death from cancer. One drug might save her, a form of radium a druggist in the same town had recently discovered. The druggist was charging $2000, ten times what the drug cost him to make. The sick woman's husband, Heinz, went to everyone he knew to borrow the money, but he could only get together about half of what it cost. He told the druggist that his wife was dying and asked him to sell it cheaper or let him pay later, but the druggist said "No." The husband got desperate and broke into the man's store to steal the drug for his wife. Should the husband have done that? Why? (Kohlberg, 1969, p. 376).

By classifying the reasoning his subjects used to respond to this and other moral dilemmas, Kohlberg formulated six stages of moral reasoning. Kohlberg's stages are divided into three levels: preconventional morality, conventional morality, and postconventional morality. Each level subsumes two stages. The levels and stages are presented in Table 3.2.

TRY THIS: Adapt the story about Julian and Augustus to reflect a contemporary situation. Then ask the same questions of a variety of students. How might the responses be classified in terms of Piaget's model?

REFLECTION: How would you respond to Kohlberg's dilemma of Heinz and the drug?

TABLE 3.2 *Kohlberg's Stages of Moral Development*

Level I   Preconventional Morality
Stage 1: Punishment and Obedience Orientation
Stage 2: Instrumental Exchange Orientation

Level II   Conventional Morality
Stage 3: Interpersonal Conformity Orientation
Stage 4: Law-and-Order Orientation

Level III   Postconventional Morality
Stage 5: Prior Rights and Social Contract Orientation
Stage 6: Universal Ethical Principles Orientation

Source: Psychology (3th ed., p. 326), L.A. Lefton, 1991, Needham Heights, MA: Allyn & Bacon. Copyright 1991 by Allyn & Bacon. Adapted by permission.

Preconventional Morality (birth–9 years). **Preconventional morality** refers to judgments made before children understand the conventions of society. Children at this level base their reasoning on two ideas. First, one should avoid punishment, and second, good behaviour yields some kind of benefit.

- *Stage 1: The Punishment–Obedience Level.* The child behaves in order to avoid punishment. Bad behaviour is behaviour that is punished; good behaviour, therefore, is behaviour that is rewarded. For example, children who do not talk without seeking permission do so because authority, the teacher, deems the act of talking without raising one's hand as punishable. Consider the moral dilemma Heinz faced and the question, "Should Heinz have stolen the drug?" A typical Stage 1 answer is, "No, he could get arrested for stealing."

- *Stage 2: The Instrumental Exchange Orientation.* This stage represents the beginnings of social reciprocity; the thinking here is, "You scratch my back and I'll scratch yours." The moral judgments that children make at this stage are very pragmatic. They will do good to another person if they expect the other person to reciprocate or return the favour. In response to the Heinz question, a typical Stage 2 response is, "He shouldn't steal the drug and the druggist should be nicer to Heinz."

Conventional Morality (9 years–young adulthood). **Conventional morality** refers to judgments based on the rules or conventions of society; behaviours that maintain the social order are considered good behaviours. The reasoning at this level is based on a desire to impress others. Peer relationships become very important during this period.

- *Stage 3: The Interpersonal Conformity Orientation.* Reasoning about morality focuses on the expectations of other people, particularly the expectations of people in authority and peers. In order to create and maintain good relations with other people, it is important to conform to their expectations of good behaviour. By being nice or good, approval from others is likely. A typical Stage 3 response to the Heinz question is, "If Heinz is honest, other people will be proud of him."

- *Stage 4: The Law-and-Order Orientation.* The conventions of society have been established so that society can function. Laws are necessary and, therefore, good. The moral person is one who follows the laws of a society without questioning them. A typical Stage 4 response to the Heinz question is, "Stealing is against the law. If everybody ignored the laws, our whole society might fall apart."

TRY THIS: Observe children in a school or neighbourhood playground. How do the children decide about taking turns in the games they play? What stages of Kohlberg's model do their decisions reflect?

preconventional morality
Rules of conduct of children (birth–9 years) who do not yet understand the conventions of society. This is Level 1 of Kohlberg's theory of moral reasoning.

conventional morality
Rules of conduct of older children (9 years–young adulthood) based on the conventions of society. This is Level 2 of Kohlberg's theory of moral reasoning.

postconventional morality
Rules of conduct of adults who recognize the societal need for mutual agreement and the application of consistent principles in making judgments. This is Level 3 of Kohlberg's theory of moral reasoning.

Postconventional Morality (adulthood). **Postconventional morality** is typified by judgments that recognize the societal need for mutual agreement and the application of consistent principles in making judgments. Through careful thought and reflection, the postconventional thinker arrives at a self-determined set of principles or morality.

- *Stage 5: The Prior Rights and Social Contract Orientation.* At this stage, laws are open to evaluation. A law is good if it protects the rights of individuals. Laws should not be obeyed simply because they are laws but because there is mutual agreement between the individual and society that these laws guarantee a person's rights. A typical answer to the Heinz question is, "Sometimes laws have to be disregarded, for example, when a person's life depends on breaking the law."

- *Stage 6: The Universal Ethical Principles Orientation.* The principles that determine moral behaviour are self-chosen; they unify a person's beliefs about equality, justice, ethics. If a person arrives at a set of principles, the principles serve as guidelines for appropriate behaviour. A typical Stage 6 response to the Heinz question is, "An appropriate decision must take into account all of the factors in the situation. Sometimes, it is morally right to steal."

REFLECTION: What does your own response to Kohlberg's dilemma tell you about your moral judgment?

Criticisms of Kohlberg's Theory

Kohlberg's theory is a landmark in the scientific literature on moral development. A good scientific theory is one that generates new research. In this regard, Kohlberg's theory has proven very successful. Much of the research done in response to Kohlberg's theory has raised questions about the theory's utility. A discussion of some of those questions follows.

The Question of Stages. Kohlberg (1971) shared Piaget's view about the ordinality of stages; that is, Kohlberg held that all people progress through the stages of moral development in sequence. There is evidence, however, that calls into question Kohlberg's assumption of ordinality. For example, Holstein (1976) found that responses to moral situations did not consistently and unambiguously place subjects at a particular stage. Holstein also found that females and males differed systematically in their judgments. Other researchers have found that the level or stage of a person's moral reasoning is dependent on the particular moral dilemma that the person responds to (e.g., Fishkin, Keniston, & MacKinnon, 1973).

CRITICAL THINKING: The way a student reasons in response to a hypothetical dilemma may or may not be the way in which that student will behave in real-life situations. Why is this the case?

Although Kohlberg assumed ordinality, he did not assume that all people arrived at Stage 6—the universal ethical principles orientation. After others began to question the validity of his stages, Kohlberg went back and reexamined some of his original data (Colby & Kohlberg, 1984) and subsequently discounted the sixth stage in his theory (cf. Kohlberg, 1978).

The Question of Applicability. Very often, teachers need to reason with a student about the student's classroom conduct. If a teacher knows how a student reasons when confronted with a decision about what's right and what's wrong, the teacher can encourage the child to make a change in behaviour in terms he or she will best understand. If classroom rules are central to students' decisions of what is right and wrong, for example, then a simple reference to classroom rules by the teacher is likely to be effective. With older students, a teacher might use the approval of parents or peers to encourage appropriate behaviour.

Direct attempts by teachers to facilitate moral development in students have resulted primarily in group discussions of moral dilemmas. Moral dilemmas can be of the type used by Kohlberg in his research, hypothetical situations that require a judgment about what is the correct or incorrect action to take in that hypothetical situation. There can also be real-life situations in the classroom or school (e.g., Reimer, Paolitto, & Hersh, 1983). Real-life dilemmas can deal with episodes of aggressive behaviour, cheating on tests, copying homework, or abusing rules.

One technique used to enhance moral reasoning is called *plus-one matching* (Lockwood, 1978). In using this technique, the teacher determines a student's stage of moral development and then presents conflicting views that are consistent with the next higher stage. The goal of plus-one matching is to create some disequilibrium in the student so that he or she is encouraged to entertain other points of view on the issue under discussion.

The Question of Generalizability. For Kohlberg, moral development culminates in the recognition of individual rights and individually generated ethical principles. It is not surprising that Kohlberg, having grown up in a Western culture, would emphasize the Western value of individualism. The question is whether Kohlberg's stages would apply to cultures that prize the good of the group or of the family more highly than the good of the individual. Attempts to apply Kohlberg's scheme to other cultures have met with mixed results (e.g., Hwang, 1986; Vasudev & Hummel, 1987).

Gilligan's Theory of Gender-Based Morality

Another question of generalizability refers to gender differences (Gilligan, 1982; Holstein, 1976). Kohlberg developed his stages based on a longitudinal study of males. In other studies classifying males and females according to Kohlberg's stages, a disproportionate number of women have been placed in Stage 3 as compared with Stage 4. One explanation is that women are generally more empathetic and compassionate toward others and more sensitive to social relationships than men (Gilligan, 1977; Holstein, 1976). Based on these and other studies, Gilligan has developed a stage model of moral development.

Gilligan's theory, presented in Table 3.3, comprises three levels and two transitions. The first level of Gilligan's theory, **individual survival**, identifies selfishness as its primary concern. The transition from individual survival to self-sacrifice and social conformity leads to the realization that caring for others rather than just caring for oneself is good. Gilligan's second level, **self-sacrifice and social conformity**, is similar to Kohlberg's Stage 3. Brabeck (1986) identifies the second level as "the conventional view of women as caretakers and protectors" (p. 70). The transition from the second to the third level involves a growing realization that in order to care for others, one must also take care of oneself. Note the different motives for self-care in this second transition as opposed to the motives in the first transition. The third level of Gilligan's theory is the **morality of nonviolence**. The ethic of this third level is the equality of self and others: It is wrong to serve oneself at the expense of others.

Brabeck (1986) has compared Kohlberg's view on moral development with Gilligan's. Brabeck labels Kohlberg's theory a "morality of justice" that stresses rights, fairness, rules, and legalities. Gilligan's theory, by way of comparison, is called a "morality of care and responsibility." This theory stresses relationships, care, harmony, compassion, and self-sacrifice. Some researchers regard Gilligan's model as a theory of female moral development. Perhaps a better way to think about Gilligan's theory is that it stresses different values than Kohlberg's. Support

individual survival The first level of Gilligan's theory of moral reasoning, in which selfishness is identified as the primary concern.

self-sacrifice and social conformity The second level of Gilligan's theory of moral reasoning, in which there is a realization that caring for others rather than just caring for oneself is good.

morality of nonviolence The third level of Gilligan's theory of moral reasoning, in which there is a realization that it is wrong to serve oneself at the expense of others.

TABLE 3.3 *Gilligan's Stages of Moral Development*

Stages
1   Individual Survival
1A*   From Selfishness to Responsibility
2   Self-Sacrifice and Social Conformity
2A*   From Goodness to Truth
3   Morality of Nonviolence

* Marks a transition stage.

Source: "Moral Orientation: Alternative Perspectives of Men and Women," M. Brabeck, 1986, in *Psychological Foundations of Moral Education and Character Development: An Integrated Theory of Moral Development* (p. 71) by R.T. Knowles and G.F. McLean (eds.), Lanham, MD: University Press of America. Copyright 1986 by University Press of America. Adapted with permission.

for this view comes from a study by Walker, deVries, and Trevethan (1987). These researchers asked children and adults to describe personal experiences that involved some kind of moral conflict. The descriptions indicated that some subjects valued justice while others valued caring, but the values were not tied to the gender of the subject.

Gilligan's theory presents us with a new perspective to consider. It is not confined to moral reasoning (i.e., cognitive judgments of right and wrong) but stresses affect (i.e., feelings, attitudes, emotions). Gilligan's approach is also consistent with our everyday concern with character. Some people possess characteristics that enable them to do more good and resist hurting others. Jean Pettifor (1997) at the University of Calgary suggests that psychology itself could benefit by incorporating moral principles in finding acceptable strategies to achieve acceptable goals.

While Kohlberg's framework informs us about how children think, we must remember that there is more to moral development than cognition. Peters (1977) characterizes Kohlberg's theory as cognitive, with little or no attention paid to affective feelings and attitudes. Peters argues that any attempt to facilitate moral development should address not only how to think but also how to feel. Among the attitudes that accompany sound moral decisions, Peters places caring for

CRITICAL THINKING: In what ways does Gilligan's theory integrate affect and cognition?

Identity formation and moral development during adolescence are influenced by the emergence and validation of self-image, sexuality, expectations for adulthood, and lifestyle choices. Research has raised questions about differences between males and females in habits of thought and the origins of those differences in biology or culture.

CRITICAL THINKING: An honour student cheated to get a
passing grade in English. After
he was caught, he explained,
"I knew that one way or the
other—either failing or getting
caught cheating—I would be
off the honour role." How do
you think the other members of
the council responded to the
student's explanation?

others at the top. Gilligan's framework introduces affect into the mix and certainly emphasizes caring as an important element of morality. Even so, the question is whether a student's reasoning and his or her attitudes are applied consistently in all situations that require a moral judgment.

Lickona's Integrative Model of Personal and Interpersonal Development

In a classic study, Hartshorne and May (1930) found that for many children moral behaviour is situation specific. Children who are generally honest and trustworthy will, under certain circumstances, cheat, especially if the stakes are high enough. Lickona (1976) concluded that "variations in the situation produce variations in moral behaviour" (p. 15). Lickona added, however, that there is evidence to suggest that some children are more morally integrated or consistent than others. What appears to be needed is educational practice that does not rely solely on reasoning exercises but that integrates cognition, affect, and behaviour. We will return later in this chapter to the notion of integrative classroom practice. Before doing so, we examine some of the issues that students encounter in the social environment of schools.

The Council for Research in Values and Philosophy, a group of scholars concerned with the moral dimension of education, share a view of moral development, an **integrative model** that combines cognition, affect, and behaviour. The integrative view postulates moral development as occurring along two dimensions, vertical and horizontal. The *vertical dimension* refers to growth as an increased ability to coordinate the perspectives and needs of others, to discriminate values that advance the human condition from values that do not, to make principled decisions, and to be aware of one's moral weaknesses (Knowles & McLean, 1992; Ryan & Lickona, 1987). Vertical growth is the kind described by Kohlberg and Gilligan as advancement to higher levels of cognition and affect.

The *horizontal dimension* of moral growth refers to the application of a person's moral reasoning and affective capacities to an increasingly wider range of real-life situations. Horizontal growth requires that a person not only think and feel but also act in accordance with his or her cognitive and affective capacities. Suppose that a business executive reasons that laws must be determined through agreement and, at the same time, protect the rights of individuals (Stage 5 in Kohlberg). Suppose further that our executive decides to eliminate a company policy of job sharing without consulting employees. The lack of consistency between the executive's moral capacity to reason and the actions taken reveals weak horizontal development. (Note that the notion of horizontal development could be used to explain the classic Hartshorne and May findings: Good intentions do not always mean moral actions.)

An integrative model of character education requires that attention be paid to vertical growth issues: reasoning, clarifying values, pursuing moral principles. It means also that students should use their thinking and feelings in a wide variety of ways; that is, that they pay attention to horizontal development.

Thomas Lickona presented an integrative model of character education in *Character Development in Schools and Beyond* (Ryan & McLean, 1987). Lickona's model specifies four processes that need to operate in classrooms if teachers are to influence the developing character of their students: (1) building self-esteem and social community, (2) encouraging cooperative learning and helping relations, (3) eliciting moral reflection, and (4) effecting participatory decision making. Keep in mind that Lickona's model is aimed at both vertical and horizontal development.

EXAMPLE: Lickona's model
has also been called an "integrative model of the moral
agent," in which each person
is a moral agent.

integrative model A view
of moral development that
combines cognition, affect,
and behaviour; method of
lesson presentation that
combines inductive skills,
deductive skills, and content
in one model.

Insights on Successful Practice

What advice do you have for novice teachers about dealing with ethical or moral issues in daily classroom life?

In today's increasingly unstructured world, one thing most teachers agree on is that children need to be responsible for the consequences of their actions. Thus, guiding children toward taking this responsibility has become a purpose all teachers share. To help accomplish this purpose in my classroom I have compiled a core of teaching principles that help me lead children toward more responsible behaviour.

My core of principles derives from what seems to me to be a universal wisdom that recognizes affection, courage, honesty, generosity, justice, tolerance, kindness, compassion, and self-reliance as essential attributes in a decent society. I use these attributes as my personal behaviour templates. They have become the mental bumper stickers that flash through my mind while I am engaged in the process of building significant relationships with the children in my charge.

My core of principles based upon these attributes provides me with an economy of ethics, enabling me to respond quickly and consistently without starting from scratch to construct a moral position for every dilemma that arises in my classroom. Just a sampling from my code of principles would include the following three:

1. It is my responsibility to meet the learning needs of my students, not the students' responsibility to meet my ego-centred needs.

2. It takes a courageous, determined adult to see through irresponsible behaviour without rejecting the student. Teacher and student must find a better way.

3. There is no third state or condition in the teacher-learner reciprocal relationship. Either both parties are in it or they are not.

Applying my core of personal principles to use in the classroom requires the design and implementation of a strategy. My design is based on the concept that reciprocity is essential to all constructive relationships. A successful learner-teacher relationship depends on a quid pro quo agreement that recognizes that learning is a transaction.

On the first day of a class, I claim the authority to establish the first rule: "Listen to me when I speak." I justify this first rule by agreeing to listen to any student who wishes to speak. Then I present the concept of reciprocity and discuss the nature of the teacher-learner agreement.

My core principles act as my compass as I guide the group to collectively compose a short list of principles that we all agree to live by while we are in class. The agreement is posted for everyone in class to see and may be amended as the need arises. When dilemmas arise, I refer students to the agreement and ask if we can find a solution.

Thus, I use my set of personal principles to establish my relationship with the students and lead them to establish a set of principles of their own in the form of an agreement by which we can all live in mutual respect. Such an agreement allows those "instants" of teacher-student reciprocity to occur. Those instants are the essence of learning.

STEVE KORPA
High School Teacher

Building Self-Esteem and Social Community. This process involves building a child's self-esteem, a sense of competence and mastery, in the social community of the classroom. This process also requires that students come to know each other as individuals, respect and care about each other, and feel that they are members of and accountable to the group.

As suggested in Chapter 2, self-esteem can be fostered in the classroom in a number of ways. Lickona reports a grade three teacher's practice of learning something special about each student at the beginning of the school year. The teacher asks each student to tell her of an award, a skill, or something else he or

CRITICAL THINKING: Starratt (1987) reports a small group exercise in which each student writes his or her name at the top of a sheet of paper. The paper is passed to the next student who writes something likable about the student named on the page. The page continues around the circle until each student has named something likable about every other student in the group. Why has this technique proved effective?

she is proud of. In the teacher's words, "I then make this something important to me. I stress to the child how important it is to me and it's something just the two of us share" (p. 185). The teacher values each student, and each student tends to value himself or herself more highly.

One grade six teacher who felt that too many of her students viewed themselves negatively decided to write a note to each child. In each note, the teacher mentioned a characteristic in the student that she admired. The notes also invited the students to write back to the teacher, telling her about characteristics they admired in themselves. The teacher reported that following the note exchange, the students more frequently displayed in class the characteristics identified as positive. This kind of affirmation exercise has also been reported as effective in a high school classroom (Starratt, 1987).

Any sort of public effort to share personal feelings and perceptions can contribute to a sense of community. In developing this sense of community, it is important that each student feel that he or she is being listened to with respect.

Cooperative Learning and Helping Relations. The spirit of cooperation and the skills to realize that spirit are essential to adult living (Wynne, 1987). Cooperative learning—students learning from and with each other—can be fostered in classrooms at any grade level. Furthermore, research on classroom learning indicates that cooperative efforts result in higher self-esteem than competitive or individualistic efforts (Johnson & Johnson, 1989, 1992, 1994; Slavin, 1991).

For example, a grade three teacher, teaching a unit on measurement, assigned pairs of children to collect physical measurements. The children were given the tasks of measuring the length of their jumps on a sidewalk, how far they could spread their feet, how high they could reach on the building, and so on. The teacher suggested that when one partner jumped or reached, the other partner should mark the effort. The teacher reported that children enjoyed the active nature of the exercise and the interaction with their partners.

TRY THIS: Observe a cooperative learning activity and identify student behaviours that promote and those that subvert cooperative efforts.

Establishing cooperation and helping as an integral part of one's classroom is not always "sweetness and light." In many cases, children who have not been in highly cooperative classrooms before will unintentionally subvert cooperative efforts by reverting to the skills required in classrooms emphasizing individual effort and achievement. One way of making cooperation easier for students is to help children learn to support each other socially. One grade five teacher, attempting to establish cooperative learning, instituted a daily "appreciation time." At the end of the day each student could speak about something that another student did that day that the speaker appreciated. Appreciation time became the favourite classroom activity. Such acknowledgments allowed students to value helpfulness and thoughtfulness; it also gave students practice in delivering and receiving compliments.

Moral Reflection. The third process in Lickona's model is moral reflection, which focuses on the cognitive aspects of moral development. It might involve reading, thinking, debate, and/or discussion.

CRITICAL THINKING: What might be some advantages and disadvantages of using a thematic curricular approach rather than Kohlberg-type dilemmas in fostering moral development?

A grade five teacher organizes her whole social studies curriculum around the theme of the Middle Ages. The classroom is turned into a "Scriptorium," enabling students to approximate the experience of monks. They work on artistic ornamentation and calligraphy in the manuscripts they produce, which requires slow, painstaking effort. These efforts give the students "a great sense of achievement and appreciation of the artist monk" (Frey, 1983, p. 33). The medieval theme is carried through in the historical fiction that the students read.

Reading and discussing good literature, which engages the mind and the heart, can go far beyond a contrived moral dilemma in eliciting moral reflection.

A teacher who attempts to pursue goals of moral education must be alert to the real-life moral situations that arise in every classroom. Lickona tells the story of a grade two teacher whose class was incubating chicken eggs. One day, the teacher suggested that it might be instructive to open one egg each week as a way of studying embryonic development. Later that day, one of her students objected to the suggestion because it seemed cruel to him. The teacher saw the opportunity to engage the class in meaningful moral reflection. The class discussed the merit of the objection; alternative, though less satisfying, ways of finding out about chick embryos; and even questions about whether the embryos were really live chickens. Here was a moral dilemma that required reasoning, a clarification of feelings, and ultimately, action.

Participatory Decision Making. The fourth process in Lickona's model of moral education is participatory decision making, which holds students accountable for decisions that influence the quality of classroom life. This process is not simply a matter of having students participate in defining classroom rules; it is also a matter of establishing a sense of responsibility and genuine participation in the welfare of the classroom community. The process, when practised well, yields a set of norms that guides students' behaviour.

If students have participated in establishing class rules, the sense of collective responsibility will facilitate the development of norms. Suppose that a class meets to discuss some problems: for example, too much noise during seat work or too little help during cleanup. These problems are not treated as isolated issues, and the students involved in them are not singled out for special attention. The issues are considered by the class as a whole. The theft of one student's lunch money needs to be solved by the whole class. Helping a transfer student make friends and figure out the school's routine is a problem the class has to solve. In effect, the teacher can ask students to identify problems that they would like others in the class help them solve.

To make his point, Lickona relates the experiences of a young substitute teacher. She was asked to take over the class of a teacher who found the children incorrigible and had taken a six-week mental health leave. The substitute was greeted with an announcement from the class that they were the worst class in the school. The substitute immediately brought the class together to decide what rules were needed and why they were necessary. The discussion went on for some time and ended with consensus on one last student-generated rule: "Care about each other" (Lickona, 1987, p. 200).

The meetings continued on a daily basis. Caring for each other became the class ethic. When the substitute left at the end of six weeks, the students asked her to teach the returning regular how these class meetings worked. The substitute advised the regular teacher that the class meetings had had a wonderful effect on the class. The regular chose not to continue the meetings, and by all accounts, the class reclaimed its dubious reputation.

The four processes of Lickona's model are not effective in isolation. If the classroom sense of community is weak, it will be difficult to generate the kind of discussion and debate that makes useful reflection possible. If students do not participate in establishing the rules and norms of their community, it is less likely that a truly cooperative environment will develop. The Lickona model has been applied successfully in a variety of classrooms. But its application requires a teacher who believes deeply in the value of moral education, a teacher who will persist through rocky beginnings and find a way to develop the sensitivity necessary to help students find character.

TRY THIS: Interview a practising teacher regarding his or her efforts to involve students in participatory decision making or to establish a more democratic classroom.

REFLECTION: Reflect on the teachers in your own experience as a student who practised participatory decision making and those who did not. What were your experiences in those classrooms? Did those teachers influence your personal and interpersonal growth differently?

Teacher Chronicle Conclusion

Adolescent Identity Issues

Mr. Bolen expressed concern about a number of his students' attitudes toward themselves and their future at a staff meeting. The principal inquired about whether the staff was familiar with Erikson and Marcia.

"Yes, Erikson viewed the developing of an identity as a central issue for adolescents. Those who have difficulty experience role confusion," said Mr. Bolen. "I see where you are going; these students are experiencing problems associated with the forming of self-identity."

Mr. Marby, the English teacher, pointed out, "Marcia expanded Erikson's theory by detailing four alternatives that adolescents can take when coping with the options and difficulties confronting them."

"That's right," the principal, Ms. Weber, added. "Marcia has provided us with a framework with which we can think about these students. While many students won't fit exactly into Marcia's categories, the ones mentioned seem to be pretty representative of the four identity statuses. Marilyn seems to be identity achieved, Susan at a situation of moratorium, Mark in identity foreclosure, and both Theresa and Roger seem to be identity diffused."

The frameworks established by Erikson and Marcia gave the teachers a starting point to consider options that will foster self-esteem and self-understanding, and that will allow them to think about various occupation alternatives for their students..

Application Questions

1. When you were beginning high school, how would you have classified yourself and your friends according to Marcia's identity statuses?

2. What factors (parenting, socio-economic background, etc.) might contribute to the identity status of a high school student ?

3. What might teachers and schools do to help students who are in identity confusion and moratorium?

4. Do you think identity-foreclosed individuals will have problems later on in life?

CHAPTER SUMMARY

How Do Individuals Develop Self-Concepts and Self-Esteem? (L.O. 1, p. 61)

Self-concept is the way in which a person describes him- or herself. Self-esteem is related to self-concept in that self-esteem is one's evaluation of his or her sense of self. The feelings that one has about self come from self-evaluation. Because one's self-esteem requires a value judgment, the values one learns from one's culture can influence self-esteem.

How Does Social Interaction Influence Personal Growth? (L.O. 2, 3, 4, p. 68)

Erikson proposes eight stages of psychosocial development. Each stage's developmental crisis is identified as a dichotomy of qualities, positive and negative. If the social experiences during that period are generally positive, positive qualities result. If experiences are generally negative, the crisis is resolved negatively.

James Marcia extended Erikson's work as it applied to adolescents' search for identity. He identified four identity statuses. Identity diffusion types are confused, disorganized, and avoid commitment. Moratorium types (not to be confused with Erikson's psychosocial moratorium) have given a great deal of thought to identity issues but have not yet arrived at any conclusions. Identity achievement types are those adolescents who have made life-style decisions on their own. Foreclosure types do not experience a crisis of identity; they simply adopt decisions made for them by others.

If a teacher uses Erikson's theory to make decisions about a student's psychosocial needs, he or she should keep in mind the evidence that suggests that Erikson's framework is a better description of males than of females. There is also a good bit of overlap in the stages: Crises that begin in toddlerhood and continue through the middle school years are quite similar.

What Social Problems Affect Students' School Lives? (L.O. 5, p. 78)

Minor social problems—such as the developmental crises in Erikson's theory—are faced by all students. Some students, however, are at risk of failing in school because the social problems they face go beyond those faced by students who are raised in safe environments. Social situations that result in risk to students' security, safety, and health place a special responsibility on those students' teachers.

How Do Individuals Develop Moral Reasoning? (L.O. 6, 7, p. 84)

Piaget distinguishes between the moral reasoning of younger and older children. Younger children follow the morality of constraint; they follow rules without question. Older children, who follow the morality of cooperation, take into account the context of behaviours in order to judge whether an action is right or wrong.

Kohlberg based his framework on Piaget's views. Kohlberg identified stages of moral reasoning that exist at three levels. At the first level, preconventional morality, reasoning about right and wrong is based on the idea that correct behaviour is that which avoids punishment and yields some kind of reward. The second level, conventional morality, is based on respect for authority and a desire to impress others. The third level is postconventional morality. The reasoning at this level recognizes the need for societal agreement and the consistent application of moral principles. Gilligan's theory extends Kohlberg's work to suggest that moral judgment is gender based.

Lickona identified four overlapping processes that should occur in classrooms where moral education is addressed. The first process focuses on building healthy self-esteem through social support and a sense of belonging to the community of the classroom. The second process operates to establish cooperative learning; the emphasis is on students learning to help each other. The third process, moral reflection, is similar to Kohlberg's—and more similar to Gilligan's—moral reasoning. The final process encourages participatory decision making on questions of behaviour in the community of the classroom.

KEY CONCEPTS

autonomy, p. 70

conventional morality, p. 86

critical periods, p. 68

developmental crisis, p. 68

foreclosure, p. 73

gender role stereotypes, p. 76

generativity, p. 71

growth spurt, p. 78

identity, p. 70

identity achievement, p. 73

identity diffusion, p. 72

identity statuses, p. 72

individual survival, p. 88

industry, p. 70

initiative, p. 70

integrative model, p. 90

integrity, p. 72

intimacy, p. 71

isolation, p. 71

moral judgments, p. 84

morality of constraint, p. 84

morality of cooperation, p. 84

morality of nonviolence, p. 88

moratorium, p. 72

postconventional morality, p. 86

preconventional morality, p. 86

psychosocial development, p. 68

puberty, p. 78

role diffusion, p. 71

self-concept, p. 62

self-esteem, p. 62

self-sacrifice and social conformity, p. 88

students at risk, p. 79

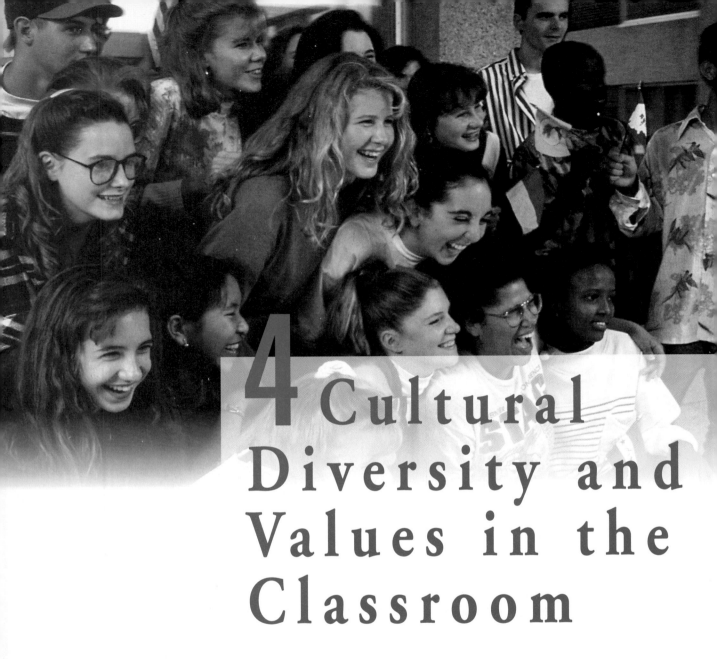

4 Cultural Diversity and Values in the Classroom

LEARNING OUTCOMES

When you have completed this chapter, you will be able to

1. describe sources of cultural diversity
2. explain how ethnic and linguistic differences contribute to diversity
3. give examples of the importance of socioeconomic factors in contributing to diversity
4. discuss how gender and disability can serve as the basis for discrimination
5. compare and contrast the reasons for cultural conflicts in the classroom

6. outline the dimensions of multicultural education
7. describe the position on cultural diversity taken by Canadian schools
8. give reasons for the curriculum to reflect Canada's cultural mosaic
9. create a metaphor to reflect your views on multicultural teaching strategies
10. evaluate Canada's record on multicultural education

Teacher Chronicle

Grandma Tales

Kevin is the star storyteller of Ms. Walker's grade eight English class. He tells stories that captivate his listeners, stories with strong beginnings, intriguing middles, and powerful endings. He tells stories about his older brother the artist, his Aboriginal ancestors, his aunt, his peers, and his recent trips. Kevin is proud of his heritage and frequently refers to it.

However, Kevin's reading skills are weak, and he constantly struggles with written work. He seems unable to organize his thoughts on paper. He cannot write the stories he tells so well. There seems to be no way to head off an F at report card time.

One day his class is discussing tall tales in preparation for a writing assignment. Students share the tales they had been given as a preparatory reading assignment: Johnny Chinook, Glooskap, Sam McGee, and Dalbec. Kevin, having read only one of the tales, does not participate in the discussion.

Near the end of the period, Amy notes, "You know, there aren't any tall tales about women."

Kevin pipes up, "You mean you haven't heard about my Grandma digging the Great Lakes?"

Ms. Walker looks at Kevin, trying to determine if spinning a story now is a stalling tactic on Kevin's part. Sensing student interest in Kevin's question, she tells him to go ahead.

"Many years ago," he begins, "where the Great Lakes are now, there was an open prairie. Grandma came along, saw the prairie, and decided to make her garden there. She reached inside her leather pouch and took out five seeds: the long green bean seed, the fat pumpkin seed, the flat squash seed, the hard maize seed, and the round eye of the potato. Then she took her hoe and began to dig the right hole for each seed: a long skinny hole for the green bean, a fat hole for the pumpkin, a flat hole for the squash, a hole in granite for the hard corn seed, and a potato-shaped hole for the potato. It took her only one day to dig the five holes. She took all the dirt she dug and threw it to the west where she made the Rocky Mountains. Then, just as she got ready to drop in the seeds, along came this huge thunderstorm. It rained and rained for more days than Grandma could count (she hadn't gotten around to creating numbers yet). She stayed under her hoe to keep dry. Well, finally it stopped raining and Grandma looked out. The five holes she had dug were filled to the brim with water. And that's how Grandma dug the five Great Lakes and why they are shaped the way they are."

An appreciative silence follows Kevin's story until Luthien asks, "Is that a story the Mohawks tell?"

Kevin shakes his head. "I just made it up," he beams.

"Do you know any other Grandma tales?" Brent calls out.

"I could tell you about the time Grandma made the Earth from an old basketball."

Ms. Walker glances at the clock and says, "We'll have to save that for tomorrow."

As the students hop up to leave, someone asks Kevin, "Did Grandma make the Atlantic Ocean?"

"Oh, sure, but it took her a little longer than making the Pacific because the ground is harder."

Focus Questions

1. In what ways might Kevin's cultural background influence his learning?

2. How might Kevin's storytelling skills relate to his cultural background?

3. How might Ms. Walker's cultural background be different from Kevin's? How might cultural background differences affect her teaching?

4. What strategies might Ms. Walker use to build on Kevin's storytelling skills? For example, how might Ms. Walker use Kevin's storytelling ability to help him improve his writing skills?

5. How might Kevin's cultural identity increase his classmates' awareness of diversity?

What Are Some Sources of Diversity?

POINT: *Learners are diverse.* In this chapter, many sources of diversity are examined that affect teaching and learning in the classroom.

In recent years, enormous demographic changes in Canada have diversified the makeup of Canadian classrooms. Dramatic increases in the number of immigrants arriving in Canada have occurred over the past decade as a result of changing governmental policies that were largely in response to concerns about an aging population (Sorensen & Krahn, 1996). Sorensen and Krahn present statistics to show that while in 1985 only 84 000 immigrants were admitted to Canada, by 1992 the number of immigrants arriving annually had risen to close to 250 000. They further underscore that over the past few decades the source countries have also changed to include a substantial increase in the number of immigrants from third-world countries. Prior to 1961, 90 percent of immigrants arriving in Canada were European-born: between 1981 and 1991, only 25 percent had been born in Europe. In addition, an increase from 373 265 persons in 1986 to 470 615 persons in 1991 occurred for individuals reporting Aboriginal single origins (Herberg, 1989). By the turn of the century, demographic projections indicate that racial and ethnocultural minorities will rise to almost half the population in some urban areas (Samuel, 1992). Solomon and Levine-Rasky (1996) point out that, in response to these demographic changes, political pressure has succeeded in persuading provincial and local school jurisdictions to develop and implement educational policies that explicitly address the realities of cultural diversity in schools. As a Canadian teacher, you will face girls and boys, students from a variety of ethnic backgrounds, students with exceptional abilities, and students with disabilities. These differences among students influence the skills, knowledge, experiences, values, and strengths that they bring with them into the classroom. Understanding such differences can tell you how some students are likely to learn, make friends, interpret social messages, and approach school work.

EXAMPLE: In one school in the city of North York, it is estimated that at least eighty countries of origin and fifty languages are represented. Sixty percent of all students do not have English as their first language (Campbell, 1996). In Toronto, 50 percent of secondary students are from racial minorities (Carr & Klassen, 1997), while in Edmonton, more than one school child in eight is classified as an ESL student (Carson, 1996).

Cultural Diversity

Culture, broadly speaking, is a way of life in which people share a common language and similar values, religion, ideals, habits of thinking, artistic expressions, and patterns of social and interpersonal relations (Lum, 1986). Some have suggested that people live in five intermingling cultures:

Universal-humans are biologically alike

Ecological-peoples' location on earth determines how they relate to the natural environment

National-people are influenced by the nation in which they live

Local and Regional-local, regional differences create cultures specific to an area

Ethnic-people reflect their ethnic heritages (Baruth & Manning, 1992).

CRITICAL THINKING: Why do students approach learning tasks differently? How do cultural differences contribute to diversity in learning styles among students?

A shared national culture is considered a **macroculture**, representing the core values of a society. Because public schools are embedded within the macroculture, schools tend to emphasize particular values. Cultures exist at other levels as well, however. These smaller groups are called **microcultures** (Banks, 1994a), and they share many, but not all, of the dominant values. Religious practices can define a microculture. People from similar economic backgrounds can form a microculture. Even a single school or classroom can represent a microculture in which people learn a set of values, beliefs, and behaviours valued by the teacher.

Cultural diversity is a complex matter, more so when the focus narrows from the cultural values, beliefs, and behaviours of a group to those of an individual stu-

culture A way of life in which people share a common language and similar values, religion, ideals, habits of thinking, artistic expressions, and patterns of social and interpersonal relations.

macroculture A larger shared culture representing core or dominant values of a society.

microcultures Groups within cultures that share particular values, knowledge, skills, symbols, and perspectives.

dent. To begin with, the extent to which individuals identify with a particular micro-culture varies greatly from person to person. Moreover, individuals identify themselves in relation to a number of different microcultures; they are not just Aboriginal peoples or Asian Canadians, male or female, poor or wealthy, hearing or deaf, Catholic or Jewish. Because all of the microcultures with which people identify will have some influence on their belief systems, understanding and responding appropriately to the needs of a particular student in your class can be challenging indeed.

Although race is frequently used to differentiate among groups of people, contemporary social theorists have rejected the theory that race exists as an objective fact and have argued that race is a complex, dynamic, and changing construct that is related to economic and political factors (Solomon & Levine-Rasky, 1996). Alladin (1996) states that race must be examined as a consequence of unequal relationships, produced and maintained by differential power between dominant and subordinate groups. He contends that racial groups

> ... are constructed on the basis of social relationships and are not based on genetic differences or primordial features ... Physical and cultural traits are the basis of defining social groups only insofar as they are socially recognized as important. The dominant group has the power, and therefore capacity, to use physical and social features to define socially a subordinate group (p. 6).

Thus, while Black/African-Canadian students may represent a heterogeneous group with respect to ancestral heritage, they are linked in their common experience of social oppression (Dei, 1996). Carr and Klassen (1997) argue that it is imperative that teachers understand the importance of race and racism in education and how institutional, structural barriers reinforce inequitable power relations; addressing the issues of racism and the interlocking systems of oppression is dependent on an understanding of the impact and consequences of racism on individuals.

CRITICAL THINKING: Does defining race as a social construct facilitate our understanding of social differences based on class, sex, gender, language, and religion?

What are characteristics or categories of diversity commonly identified as important for education? In the sections that follow, we discuss racial and ethnic identity, language and culture, social class, and cultural identification based on gender, sexual orientation, and exceptionality.

Racial and Ethnic Identity

As indicated, racial identity is not, in and of itself, a good predictor of cultural difference, but as you will see, it is sometimes a component of **ethnicity**. People from the same **ethnic group** derive a sense of identity from their common national origin, religion, and sometimes, physical characteristics (Baruth & Manning, 1992). They share common values, beliefs, language, customs, and traditions. Major ethnic groups in Canada are as follows (Statistics Canada, 1991):

ethnicity A term used to describe the cultural characteristics of people who identify **themselves** with a particular ethnic group.

ethnic group The people who derive a sense of identity from their common national origin, religion, and sometimes physical characteristics.

race A socially constructed, complex, dynamic, and changing construction that is related to economic and political factors.

Approximate percentage of the majority Canadian population

French origins	22.8%
British origins	20.8%
European origins	15.4%
Asian, African, and Pacific Islands origins	6.1%
Aboriginal origins	1.7%
Black origins	0.8%
Other origins	2.9%

REFLECTION: What cultural groups do you identify with? How does your identification with these groups affect your behaviour? your learning?

POINT: Students' backgrounds and individual characteristics affect learning. The values and habits of thinking shared by members of a culture influence how students interpret and react to experiences at school.

TRY THIS: Interview a teacher regarding the teacher's knowledge of his or her students' cultural identities as they affect teaching and learning.

It is important to remember, however, that these groups are themselves characterized by diversity. Even though the term Aboriginal is used as an all-inclusive term referring to status Indians, nonstatus Indians, Inuit, and Métis, major cultural and structural differences exist among these categories. Frideres (1993) states, for example, that even within the more narrow category "Indian," major cultural and linguistic differences exist. He elucidates on the diversity and heterogeneity by pointing out that within Canada there are eleven major linguistic Indian groups who live within six recognized cultural regions (p. 545). American, Australian, New Zealander, and Canadian ethnic backgrounds are several groups comprising the "Other" origins category. Peoples of Black ethnic origins include Caribbean, Ghanaian, and African Black groups. Asian, African, and Pacific Islands groups include people who are Iranian, Lebanese, Ethiopian, East Indian, Chinese, Japanese, and Polynesian, to name a few. Europeans trace their ancestry to Austria, Germany, Scandinavia, Czechoslovakia, Poland, Russia, Italy, Greece, Spain, and surrounding areas in Western, Northern, Eastern, and Southern European countries. French Canadians include French, Acadian, and Quebecois peoples of Canada. Finally, British Canadians have ethnic backgrounds that are English, Irish, Welsh, and Scottish.

What is important for teachers to know about these ethnic groups? How are they different or similar to one another? Much research has been done on racial and ethnic differences, with some interesting results. For example, despite having different values, beliefs, and norms, the experiences of several visible minority groups in Canada were founded on a history of racism that has taken on an institutional form and is reflected in current educational achievement patterns, income, and stereotypes, among others.

Historically, Aboriginal peoples in Canada have faced colonization, assimilation, segregation, and deculturation (Berry, 1981). Harsh measures undertaken by the Canadian government marginalized Aboriginal people by reducing their ability to participate in the educational, political, and economic institutions of the society (Woodward, 1989). Today, the effect of these policies is apparent in statistics showing that Aboriginal peoples' incomes are less than two-thirds of the non-Native income. Current educational data show that "only about one-quarter of Native people fifteen years and older have completed high school compared with nearly three-quarters of the remainder of the Canadian population" (Frideres, 1993, p. 555).

Piper (1993) points out parallels between Black and Chinese Canadians. Black Canadians entering Canada during the American Revolution were subjected to marginalization through educational and residential segregation and reduced employment opportunities. Chinese immigrants, too, faced educational segregation, employment oppression, and discriminatory immigration policies as recently as 1967. Friesen (1993) reminds us that the history of the Japanese in Canada during the Second World War was characterized by the confiscation of their property and the eradication of their rights.

While Canada has a reputation of being a tolerant and compassionate country, contemporary evidence points to continued institutional discrimination against minority immigrants. Satzewich (1993) presents data showing that families born in nontraditional source countries were more likely than Canadian-born and immigrant families from the United States, Britain, and Europe to have a low level of income. "Thus, 24.2 percent of families from the Caribbean, 21.2 percent of families from Western Asia, 14.5 percent of families from East Asia,

15.1 percent of families from Southeast Asia, and 19.9 percent of families from South and Central America possessed a low-income status" (p. 172). Educational statistics provide further evidence of institutionalized racism. Statistics Canada (1991) reported that while 15 percent of the English-speaking population had attained less than a grade nine education, 30 percent of French-speaking adults and 37 percent of other adults had less than a grade nine standing. Most discouraging are statistics revealing that racism in Canada is increasing. Reporting on a study conducted by the Canadian Council of Christians, Alladin (1996) presents statistics to show that a significant number of Canadians feel that a "great deal of racism exists in Canada" with Canadians of African origin, Native Canadians, Canadians of South-Asian/East-Indian descent, Asians, and Jews most likely to be discriminated against (p. 10). Canadian teachers should be aware that as a primary agent of socialization, schools have played an instrumental role in reinforcing structural inequalities.

Racism is "often defined as the domination of one social or ethnic group by another" (Baruth & Manning, 1992, p. 159) and it remains all too evident in Canada (Satzewich, 1993). As pointed out earlier, these acts of domination lead to inequalities in access to education, wealth, and political power. Racism is built upon a belief system that regards one's own group as inherently superior to others, whether the differentiating factors are ethnicity or some physical distinction (such as skin colour). Carl's story illustrates this well:

> Carl recently accepted a teaching position in an inner city school in Regina where students are of predominantly Cree ancestry. Upon first arriving at the school, Carl attempted to implement the same Euro-Canadian classroom pedagogical practices that he had successfully used when teaching in a suburban school. Over time, he was becoming increasingly disillusioned with the inability of these practices to have students display their individual ability and to respond in predictable ways to his disciplinary techniques.
>
> One day, Carl's daughter in grade eight brought home a book written by two local Cree university students. The book provided information about Cree family structure, values, customs, traditions, and world view. Carl's initial reaction was ambivalent when his daughter asked him to read it.
>
> Yet when he did read the book, he realized just how little he had actually known about his Cree students and their rich traditional culture. Of particular interest to him was that Cree students have been raised to believe that the good of the collectivity is more important than the good of the individual. A student who publicly demonstrates superior ability is likely to be seen as showing off and not worthy of respect (Pauls, 1996). He was also intrigued to learn about the belief structure that underlies the Cree approach to child socialization and how it contrasted with European beliefs. Through his reading, he began to appreciate how European ethnocentric interpretations of Cree childrearing practices led to assimilation policies that served to undermine and damage Cree socialization and family life and contribute to academic achievement problems amongst Cree children today. The more Carl read, the more he realized just how discriminatory he had been, consciously and subconsciously. And he was a social studies teacher! Armed with the information in his book, Carl began looking at his Cree students in a different light. As he changed his response to them, he found his Cree students opening up to him and sharing aspects of their culture with his classes. Reflecting on this, Carl realized his own ignorance fed his discrimination. He became determined to learn more about his newest neighbours.

EXAMPLE: Factors such as limited English proficiency, low family income, homelessness, drug abuse, HIV infection, child abuse, or racial discrimination increase the likelihood that students may experience difficulties in school, be referred for and placed in special education programs, and drop out of school.

Language and Culture

Many students come to school speaking either a language other than English or a dialect that is considered nonstandard English. Their language or dialect links them to particular ethnic microcultures; language, as an important form of communication, is the primary medium through which ethnicity is shared. When microcultures do not share many of the values prized by the cultural group that is dominant in the local public schools, the stage is already set for potential conflicts. When teachers and students are also linguistically different, there is the additional potential for communication difficulties to occur. These may cause a student to experience academic problems or to withdraw from the school's society (Banks, 1994a). Let's examine two sources of language differences: bilingualism and dialect.

Bilingualism and Biculturalism. The term for the ability to speak fluently in two different languages is **bilingualism**. In rare cases, bilingual persons can read, write, speak, and think as well in one language as the other. This occurs when they have grown up using both languages in natural social settings for practical, communicative functions (Williams & Snipper, 1990). More often, however, bilingual people favour one language over the other, having acquired their first language in the social setting of home and the second language in the formal setting of school.

Competence in two languages appears to influence academic achievement in three ways (Banks, 1994a). **Additive bilingualism** enhances academic achievement due to the complete literacy of the speaker in the two languages. Because of conceptual interdependence between languages, a concept learned in one language means that it is also learned in the other language. Additive bilinguals appear to enjoy an advantage over monolingual children in a number of specific cognitive tasks. For example, they appear better able than monolingual students to step back and reflect on the structure and function of language (Bialystok & Ryan, 1985). Being fluent in more than one language gives them a broader perspective. The ability to think about one's own knowledge of language is called **metalinguistic awareness**.

Dominant bilingualism. **Dominant bilingualism**, by contrast, has neither a positive nor a negative effect on achievement (Banks, 1994a). In this case, bilingual people are fully competent in their first language and nearly so in their second. **Subtractive bilingualism** exerts a negative influence on achievement. These students, although conversationally competent in both languages, have not developed the thinking skills necessary for full literacy in their first language. Without those skills available for transfer to the second language, achievement in the second language suffers (Banks, 1994a).

Some students have **limited English proficiency**, which means that their first language is not English, and they depend primarily on their first language for communication and understanding. Their English language skills are limited, and they find it difficult to communicate in the dominant language of the classroom.

In Canada, **bilingual education** is generally "thought of as enriched learning whereby students gain a second language at no cost to their regular academic program or first language. Integral to such programs is the potential for an increased awareness of the culture of the second language and presumably an increased cultural appreciation and tolerance …" (Carey, 1991, p. 335).

With the initiation of the British North America Act in 1867 a two-nation culture was conceived, based on the concept of the *charter nations*, England and France.

---

bilingualism A term used to describe the ability to speak fluently in two different languages.

additive bilingualism A form of bilingualism in which students have achieved complete literacy in two languages. Because of conceptual interdependence between languages, learning in one aids achievement in the other.

metalinguistic awareness The ability to reflect on one's own knowledge of language.

dominant bilingualism A form of bilingualism in which students are fully competent in their first language and nearly so in their second.

subtractive bilingualism A form of bilingualism in which students, although conversationally competent in both languages, are not fully literate in either one; this has an adverse effect on achievement.

limited English proficiency A phrase used to describe students whose first language is not English and who depend on their first language for communication and understanding.

bilingual education Enriched learning whereby students gain a second language at no cost to their regular academic program or first language.

Students with limited proficiency in both English and the language of the home are at the greatest disadvantage in school. However, research suggests that fully bilingual children have greater meta-linguisitic awareness that can enhance academic achievement.

This Act recognized the official character of both languages in the various territories of Canada. It is interesting to note that no acknowledgment was made of the Aboriginal peoples who already occupied Canada (Friesen, 1993). Following the recommendations of the Royal Commission on Bilingualism and Biculturalism, launched in 1965, the Official Languages Act of 1969 reaffirmed that Canada had two founding peoples—the French and the British—and that the nation would have two official languages—French and English (Bibby, 1990). In 1971, a further recommendation of the Royal Commission—multiculturalism—was set in place. The policy of multiculturalism encouraged the preservation of other cultures and languages, but stopped short of advocating additional official languages (Bibby, 1990). The Charter of Rights and Freedoms of 1982 guaranteed the freedom of individuals and declared that all Canadians are equal, unequivocally giving legal protection to the rights of every individual. It further endorsed laws, programs, and activities aimed at "the amelioration of conditions of disadvantaged individuals or groups" (Bibby, 1990, pp. 56-57).

CONNECTION: Cultural pluralism and multiculturalism are discussed later in this chapter.

CONNECTION: Metalinguistic awareness relates to the concept of metacognition, which is discussed in detail in Chapter 7.

While discrimination continues to exist in Canada, statistics show that the effect of these policies has been a slow but increasing inclination for the country as a whole to accept the federal policies of bilingualism and multiculturalism. Bibby (1990) writes:

> As of late 1989, 58 percent of Canadians endorsed the two-official-languages-policy, compared with 55 percent in 1980 and 49 percent in 1975. ... In 1987, a comprehensive national survey of fifteen-to-twenty-four-year-olds found that 69 percent of the emerging generation support bilingualism ....
>
> Research also shows that there has been an increase in the acceptance of multiculturalism since the mid-1970s. As of late 1989, 68 percent of Canadians endorsed multiculturalism. The 1987 national youth survey found the support level for multiculturalism among the country's fifteen-to-twenty-four-year-olds to be 74 percent (pp. 51-52).

While Canada has given official-language status to the languages of the colonizers, it has not elected to give official-language status to the languages of its Aboriginal peoples. Corson (1996) states that although "Canada's action is a desirable and necessary recognition of the importance of French and English to this country, our policy makers' failure to give some matching legitimacy to the country's Aboriginal languages seems unjust" (p. 85). Evidence for this assertion is found in statistics showing that few schools in Canada use an Aboriginal language as the medium of instruction. Those schools offering Aboriginal first-language education are relative neophytes and are for the most part located in the Northwest Territories.

> Many Inuit ... recalled the late 1960s and early 1970s when English was often the only language used for instruction in schools and their Aboriginal language was suppressed (Maguire & McAlpine, 1996).

> Language is inextricably interwoven with cultural identity: Canada's failure to recognize the importance of preserving Aboriginal languages has resulted in both linguistic and cultural assimilation of our Aboriginal peoples. There is immediate "need for more coordinated language planning at the national level to revitalize Aboriginal languages under threat, to maintain and develop those capable of survival, and to foster and promote mother-tongue education ..." (p. 98).

Dialects and Regional Culture. A **dialect** is a distinctive version of a language or a variation within a language. The differences among dialects may be in pronunciation, "wash" in Western Canada is "worsh" in parts of the Maritimes; grammar, "I have saw" or "them theirs cars" in some parts of the midwest; or vocabulary, "nuisance ground" in rural Saskatchewan is "garbage dump" or "landfill site" in most other geographical locales. Dialects differ in other ways as well, and factors other than location define dialect groups. People who share dialects often share an ethnic heritage, geographic regional culture, or a particular social and economic background.

Like language itself, all dialects enable their speakers to create meanings and express understandings. Teachers should respect the cognitive abilities of students who speak in nonstandard dialects, because these students will span the same range in other abilities as students who speak standard English. This does not mean that a teacher should accept nonstandard dialect in all settings. The physician who addresses a professional meeting of the Canadian Medical Association speaks in one way. When she addresses her children, she speaks in a different way. The language she uses on the basketball court is different still. She can shift her codes to suit the situation. What of the students who know only a nonstandard dialect? Unless these students learn the standard form of English, the situations that call for it are likely to remain out of bounds.

Today, Banks (1994a) recommends that teachers view students' languages or dialects as a source of strength and a resource for learning standard English. Rather than placing linguistically different students in separate language programs, he suggests that they be accommodated in regular classrooms. In cases where a large number of students speak the same language, a bilingual teacher may be a feasible option. Otherwise, monolingual English-speaking students or more proficient bilingual students can help classmates with limited English proficiency or with nonstandard dialects to learn standard school English, a practice that benefits tutors as much as tutees.

Socioeconomic Status

Just as students reflect racial, ethnic, and language diversity, they also come from families differing widely in socioeconomic status. **Socioeconomic status**, a family's relative standing in society, is measured by a number of variables including income, occupation, education, access to health coverage and community

CRITICAL THINKING: A disproportionate number of students from culturally and linguistically diverse backgrounds are in special education classes. Is this an example of discrimination in schools?

TRY THIS: Interview a teacher regarding his or her approach to language skill development. How does the presence of bilingual students, students with limited English proficiency, and students with regional dialects affect his or her teaching?

dialect A distinctive version or variation of a language in pronunciation, grammar, vocabulary, and usage.

socioeconomic status Relative standing in society as measured by variables such as income, occupation, education, access to health coverage and community resources, and political power and prestige.

Here's How

Here's How To Build on the Language Skills of Your Students

- Become familiar with the dialects and language skills of your students. You will be better able to detect when miscommunication or misunderstanding occurs.

- Use reading materials with predictable and familiar text structures. Knowing the text schema will help students better comprehend the text and figure out the meanings of unfamiliar words.

- Use visual aids to supplement printed and audio materials. Using multiple modalities to express a concept will facilitate student comprehension.

- Have students make up stories and conversations using different dialects and speech styles. Discuss with them the situations and contexts where each style would be appropriate.

resources, and political power and prestige (Macionis, 1994). The unfortunate truth is that large proportions of the Canadian population face problems associated with poverty and inadequate incomes. Human Resources Development Canada (1997) reported that in 1994, 17 percent of children in two-parent families and 68 percent in single-parent families lived in poverty. Infants were over 20 percent more likely than 11-year-olds to be living in poverty, primarily because younger families have higher poverty rates. One in ten Canadian children were living in households supported primarily by social assistance.

Although poor students come from every ethnic origin, in Canada the percentages are greater for students from ethnic groups born in the Caribbean, Western Asia, South and Central America, Southeast Asia, and East Asia (Satzewich, 1993). Aboriginal peoples are among the most economically impoverished groups in Canada. Frideres (1993) reported that in 1980, nearly 80 percent of Aboriginals lived in families where the average income per person was less than $5000; this compared to five percent for other Canadians. Over one-quarter of the Aboriginal population had no earned income during that year.

There is also considerable regional inequality in per capita income across Canada. In 1986, the income per capita for the Atlantic provinces was only 74 percent of the Canadian average. Quebec's per capita income was reported at 95 percent of the national average, Manitoba's at 91 percent, and Saskatchewan's at 94 percent. Ontario, Alberta, British Columbia, and the Yukon reported per capita incomes above the national average, 111 percent, 109 percent, 107 percent, and 106 percent, respectively (Felt, 1993). Of importance to educators is that regions that perform less well on such economic measures as income per capita typically have certain social structural characteristics which are claimed to reinforce their laggard status. Felt illustrates this point by presenting statistics showing that while the less-advantaged provinces have increased their share of university graduates compared to the Canadian average, they have also increased dramatically their residents with less than grade nine education—a level frequently used as a yardstick for literacy. For example, the percent of Newfoundlanders over the age of fifteen with less than a grade nine education has increased from 132.4 to 152.0 percent of the Canadian average in the last thirty-five years (p. 247).

Insights on Successful Practice

What strategies do you use with students in your classroom to promote acceptance of cultural differences?

Several weeks ago, a linguistics professor from the university came to my class to talk about her country, China. The children seemed to enjoy the visit as much as our guest. When I brought the thank-you notes written to her by my students, she told me, "Your students were very attentive. They showed a great interest. You must be doing something right—they seemed to have a great respect for other people's cultures."

Walking back to my car, I began to think, what is it that I've supposedly done right? All of a sudden, many memories began to cross my mind. I remembered the two-year project we did about Aboriginals. Before we began our project I realized that I could not talk to my students about Aboriginals. I didn't know what important information needed to be transmitted. I also realized that the students needed a role model. They needed to see me learn from other people, from other cultures, and to respect other points of view. During those two years our students heard several guest speakers talk about legends, computers, weather, tepees, laws, buffaloes, medicine, family, beliefs, and languages. All the speakers were from different Native cultures. Some were parents from our school; others were members of our community.

Why is it so important to show our students we value other people's customs and traditions? Because our students are part of their own customs and traditions. They need to feel they are being respected for what they are so they can begin to respect others. Being a bilingual teacher, I want to model respect toward one another at every moment. If a child laughs about the sounds other languages make, the students and I discuss the issue. We talk about language, cultures, and differences right then and there. Languages are made out of many different sounds. There are many different groups of sounds, and they come from many different groups of people from all over the world. Our role as teachers is to bring knowledge to our students about the world and its people, not to say who is better than whom but to appreciate their strengths and struggles. With this knowledge, the students will become aware of differences and similarities among all of us. They won't be afraid of differences—on the contrary, they will be sensitive toward others. This is what it means to me to prepare students for the future.

Mmmm, maybe I am doing something right.

DELIA TERESA DE GARCIA
Elementary School Teacher

Children in poverty face hardships on a daily basis that can be difficult to understand for a teacher who comes from a different background. For example, families living in poverty experience low wages, un- or underemployment, little property ownership and no personal savings, and lack of food resources (Baruth & Manning, 1992). Canadian statistics reveal that in 1989, 1.4 million persons, or about five percent of the Canadian population, annually received food aid from food banks, with children under the age of eighteen comprising about 45 percent of such recipients. The operation of school meal programs and other forms of community support further illustrates that large numbers of Canadian individuals and families lack adequate incomes (Wotherspoon, 1993).

The effects of poverty can include students "at a high risk for dropping out of school, experiencing academic failure, and engaging in antisocial behaviour" (Banks, 1994a, p. 36). Statistics compiled by Human Resources Development

Canada (1997) reveal that school readiness is linked to household income; while 9 percent of children from upper-income families and 16 percent of children from middle-income households present with developmental delays, 25 percent of children from lower-income households exhibit developmental disabilities. Household income also emerges as an important factor determining how well families in Canada function. An estimated 15 percent of lower-income children live in households considered dysfunctional, compared to eight percent of middle-income children and five percent of those whose families have higher incomes (pp. 4-5). Moreover, data indicate that the "more socioeconomically disadvantaged the family, the higher the risk that the children will make use of indirect aggression, as well as physical aggression" (Human Resources Development Canada, 1997, p. 18).

However, it would be a mistake to assume that feelings or experiences associated with low social class alone necessarily lead students to lowered ambition or a lack of desire to improve themselves. In a review of nearly 140 U.S. studies conducted between 1960 and 1990, no evidence was found to support several commonly held assumptions about the achievement motivation of African-American students (Graham, 1994). Contrary to the beliefs that initiated this line of research, "African Americans appear to maintain a belief in personal control, have high expectancies, and enjoy positive self-regard," regardless of social class (p. 55). Although comparable studies taking into consideration the multicultural texture of Canadian society and its effect on the psychological development of the individual are scarce, a study by Stalikas and Gavaki (1995) found that amongst Greek-Canadian secondary schoolchildren, a strong and positive relationship existed between ethnic identity, self-esteem, and academic achievement.

Gender and Sexual Identity

Many individuals in our society mistakenly associate *sex* and *gender*. Sex is a biological difference that is relatively fixed at birth. Gender, however, is a social construct that refers to the thoughts, feelings, and behaviours that have been labelled as predominantly "masculine" or "feminine." Actions that are sometimes identified as gender-specific might, in fact, be generated by ethnicity, socioeconomic status, or the expectations of one's context. Moreover, males and females behave differently in same-sex versus mixed-sex groups. Once again, it must be noted that not all males and females will behave in gender-stereotypic ways.

Research has raised questions about the sources of differences in the way boys and girls learn. Sources might include cultural values and expectations, sex-role socialization, gender bias in the classrooms, and the biopsychology of males and females. Are these girls more likely than boys to avoid disobedience, conflict, and competition?

EXAMPLE: Figures show that in Canada women constitute about 95 percent of child care providers, 72 percent of elementary teachers, but only about 35 percent of secondary teachers and 17 percent of university teachers.

CRITICAL THINKING: A disproportionate number of male students are in special education classes. Is this an example of gender discrimination in schools?

TRY THIS: Observe a class for how boys and girls communicate verbally and nonverbally. Are there differences in styles of communication or discussion? How do these differences affect the teaching and learning in the class?

CONNECTION: At the end of the Stone Fox story, Stone Fox picks up Willie's dead dog and carries it across the finish line of the sled race, thus making himself and Willie both winners.

"Even in situations in which people tend to behave in a gender-stereotypical manner, their actual behaviour cannot be predicted on the basis of their sex alone" (Grossman & Grossman, 1994, p. 3). Therefore, you should consider the generalizations discussed here as broad characteristics that do not necessarily hold for all of your students. Nevertheless, they can alert you to anticipate how your students might react when their actions are based upon gender stereotypes.

"In general, females have a lower dropout rate than males. They also are less likely to get into trouble for behavioural problems, less likely to be disciplined by their teachers or suspended from school, and less likely to be placed in special education programs for the learning disabled, behaviour disordered, or emotionally disturbed" (Grossman & Grossman, 1994, p. xi). Many gender differences seem to surface at different ages. Infants and toddlers, for example, show few gender-related differences in behaviour, but by the time they have reached preschool age, they typically demonstrate marked differences in how they prefer to play. Girls tend to prefer structured activities where they assign specific roles, such as teacher, student, and bus driver in playing school. Boys, by contrast, tend to prefer more unstructured play activities with few rules.

In school, boys and girls exhibit differences in their emotions, their relations with others, and their communicative styles. Girls are more likely to be cooperative and to share their thoughts and feelings, whereas boys are more likely to be competitive and to express anger (Grossman & Grossman, 1994). In a recent American study on how students in grades four and five reason about important issues that arise in their reading, Waggoner, Chinn, Yi, and Anderson (1993) discovered interesting differences between girls and boys. They first had students read *Stone Fox*, a story about a boy named Willie whose grandfather is ill and can't pay taxes on their farm. To raise money for the taxes, Willie enters a dog-sled competition and leads most of the race. Ten feet from the finish line, Willie's dog dies from exhaustion. Stone Fox, a Native American who usually wins the race and needs the money to buy back land originally belonging to his people, is running in second place. The researchers then posed this question to the students: Should Stone Fox win the race himself or let Willie win?

The boys who participated in the discussion tended to argue from a rule-based position—that is, Willie's dog died so there is no way for him to win the race. In that case, Stone Fox should go ahead and collect the prize. The girls, in contrast, showed empathy for Willie and argued that Stone Fox should help him. They searched for ways to get around the indisputable fact that Willie's dog had died, and they related personal experiences of similar events to engender sympathy for Willie. These differences in argumentation between boys and girls reflect general differences in communicative styles, where girls are more apt to avoid conflict, preserve harmony, and promote egalitarian roles than boys (Grossman & Grossman, 1994).

Do these differences between girls and boys stem from biology or culture? It is certainly true that boys and girls are treated differently from birth. Parents tend to play more roughly with their sons than their daughters, reacting positively to assertive behaviour in boys and to emotional sensitivity in girls (Lytton & Romney, 1991). Despite parents' best efforts to raise their children in the absence of gender-role stereotypes, it is virtually impossible to completely avoid them. Department stores offer tools and trucks for boys, but dolls and cookware for girls. The differentiation also extends to gendered names for the same toy; girls play with *dolls* while boys play with *action figures*.

As for learning and preference for certain types of instructional activities or learning environments in school, gender differences are complex and not clearly understood. For instance, it is well documented that boys begin to outpace girls in science achievement during middle school (e.g., Haertel, Walberg, Junker, & Pascarella, 1981; Zerega, Haertel, Tsai, & Walberg, 1986), but the reasons for this are speculative at best. The achievement difference could be a function of gender difference, or it could as easily be a consequence of cultural upbringing in which boys are expected to achieve in science and girls are not. Canadian studies also show that there are sex differences in access to and use of computers (Chiareli, 1989). In a review of the research on course enrollment by gender in computer studies programs, Chiareli shows that boys routinely outnumber girls enrolled in computer courses by ratios of more than two or three to one and emphasizes the gender bias in favour of males in educational activities that are supposed to encourage computer use.

Canadian data also indicate there is evidence of a gender gap in mathematics achievement (Randhawa, 1988; Randhawa & Hunt, 1987; Randhawa, 1991), but the gap appears to be closing (Randhawa, 1991). Differences in mathematics achievement appeared to be most pronounced amongst high school students; however, the differences were limited to specific microcomponents (Randhawa & Randhawa, 1993). While Canada has made efforts to redress the inequity of women in nontraditional occupations, statistics suggest that little has been accomplished since 1970: there is still an absence of women in technological and scientific careers (Ontario Royal Commission on Learning, 1994).

In class, males and females differ in their preferences for instructional activities, with males preferring to work independently and with active learning tasks. Females, by contrast, tend to prefer working in cooperative groups or under the direct supervision of the teacher. Boys tend to demand more attention from the teacher than girls, often by calling out answers that prompt a teacher's response (Bailey, 1993). Whether or not this is always the cause, teachers generally pay more attention to boys, asking them more questions and giving them more feedback. Even when teachers are aware of the difference and try to call equally upon girls and boys in class, they still tend to pay more attention to boys, especially in science classes (Kahle & Meece, 1994). The unfortunate effect of these differences in attention is that by the time girls reach college age, they have received an average of 1800 hours less instruction (Sadker et al., 1991).

The findings about gender differences suggest that teachers should try to be aware of how they interact with boys and girls. On the one hand, teachers should consider gender differences in structuring their class to meet the needs of both boys and girls. On the other, they should not discriminate against either girls or boys, and they should avoid perpetuating gender stereotypes that get in the way of effective learning.

TRY THIS: Observe a class and focus on how the teacher pays attention to the boys and the girls. Does the teacher call on one group more than the other? What does the teacher do to assure equal participation by boys and girls?

EXAMPLE: Teachers should also consider differences in sexual orientation. As many as 10 percent of students are homosexual and are often the targets of ridicule, discrimination, and hate crimes. They may be placed in special education programs intended for students with emotional and behavioural disorders. More than one-third of deaths by suicide involve homosexual youths.

Here's How

Here's How To Create a Gender-Fair Classroom
- Examine your own attitudes and behaviour for possible gender bias. Teachers can inadvertently communicate gender-role expectations and stereotypes.

continued

- Model the behaviour you want students to adopt, and reinforce students for behaving in nonstereotypical ways.
- Expose students to a variety of gender roles, illustrating both women and men in nonstereotypical roles. Choose curricular materials with a balance of gender roles, and select a variety of role models for guest speakers, tutors, and mentors.
- Encourage students to use nonsexist language, and help them to identify linguistic bias in the materials they read or the programs they view.
- Use a variety of instructional strategies to meet students' individual needs and to help them develop strengths in areas where their skills are weak. For example, although girls are generally able to work cooperatively better than boys, both can benefit from instruction on how to function effectively in a cooperative setting. Similarly, help girls to function effectively in a competitive role when the situation calls for it.
- Encourage students to consider nontraditional careers and occupations (Grossman & Grossman, 1994).

TRY THIS: Interview a teacher regarding his or her strategies for creating a gender-fair classroom.

Exceptional Ability and Disability

Exceptional students are those who require special education or special services to reach their full potential. They may have mental retardation, learning disabilities, emotional/behavioural disorders, communication disorders, impaired hearing, visual impairment, physical disabilities, or special talents. In Chapter 5, we describe the nature of these exceptionalities and the types of accommodations that teachers can make to help these students reach their full potentials. When exceptional students identify with others who share their ability or disability, they form a kind of microculture. For example, students with hearing impairments, who often communicate in ways that make it difficult for hearing students to join their conversations, form a "deaf culture."

Much literature has criticized the use of standardized norm-referenced tests for categorization and educational placement of minority students. Research shows that misinterpretation and misapplication of such tests results in the channelling of a disproportionate number of minority children into inappropriate remedial, occupational, and special education programs (Pauls, 1996). Other studies have shown that some minority children may be less likely than other students to be provided with appropriate programs to meet their special needs. In a report on the delivery of special education services to First Nations students in band-operated schools in Manitoba, Hull, Phillips, and Polyzoi (1995) argue that the need of First Nations students for special education services may be greater and more complex than the needs of the general student population in Canada. Despite this, statistics show that unreasonably low numbers of First Nations students in Manitoba have been identified as special education students. The authors attribute the relatively low proportion of identified special needs students to the lack of special education resources, both human and financial, that are available for First Nations students attending schools on the reserve (p. 47). Teachers must be aware that an absence of curricular options and special programs for minority students is just as likely to promote structure inequities as is the inappropriate classification and placement of these students.

How Can Cultural Conflicts Arise in Your Classroom?

Cultural differences become most obvious in school when problems arise from mismatches between the students' beliefs and values and those of the teacher or larger school culture. Teachers must be alert for such mismatches and be prepared to provide experiences that may be more compatible with students' backgrounds.

REFLECTION: What value orientations of the home influenced your attitudes toward school?

Cultures of the School and Home

Students learn cultural values and behaviours at home that may or may not prepare them for the expectations of the school. To understand how the discrepant values and behaviours of the culture of the school and home may foster racism, consideration must be given to the *hidden curriculum*. The hidden curriculum "involves the norms and values and mores relating to what is seen by teachers, principals, and the schools in general as proper behaviour" (Nock & Nelson, 1993, p. 338). Many Canadian ethnic groups share in common a traditional culture in which extended families play an important role in the socialization of children. Their educational systems, embedded in a philosophy of being one with nature and communalism, respect children's freedom to develop naturally by searching, exploring, and discovering their world; in close proximity to parents and elders well known to them, children are taught through the instructional techniques of observation and imitation (Johnson & Cremo, 1995; Nock & Nelson, 1993). Such systems can come into conflict with the hidden curriculum of many schools which emphasizes individualism, competition, and conformity. Ungerleider (1991) elucidates further:

> For children whose backgrounds deviate from the school's definition of a normal identity, participation in school is potentially problematic. Through social interaction these children may be called upon to abandon the bases of previous self-identification in order to earn full membership in and benefit from the program of instruction. For some children, there is a disjuncture between the way they are expected to behave at home or in their home communities and the way they are expected to behave at school. The majority of Canadian teachers expect that children will display what they have learned by speaking publicly before their peers at the teacher's initiation. This arrangement inhibits the participation of children from some ethno-cultural backgrounds. At home, these children are expected to observe others, participate with others in a given activity, and, when they are ready, initiate a self-designed test of their abilities. For such children, the public display of what they have learned at the initiation of the teacher is an arrangement quite different from the cultural practice to which they have become accustomed (pp. 201-202).

CONNECTION: Identity formation is discussed in detail in Chapter 3.

Learning Styles and Classroom Organization

Another source of potential cultural conflicts occurs when the organization of classrooms or the instructional strategies used by teachers does not match the learning styles of students. This can be a problem for any student, not just members of ethnic groups, but cultural differences are often so subtle that they are difficult to recognize. For example, Koenig (1981) argued that a major reason for lack of success is teaching processes which have failed to recognize students' preferred cognitive and learning styles. While More (1987) cautions that over-emphasis on

CRITICAL THINKING: In what kinds of instructional situations might a teacher need to accommodate students' cultural backgrounds?

learning style differences between Aboriginal and non-Aboriginal students may lead to new forms of inaccurate labelling and stereotyping, much can be learned about appropriate educational process by considering this area.

CONNECTION: Learning styles of Canadian Aboriginals are discussed in Chapter 5.

Many Canadian classrooms, despite the increasing adoption of cooperative learning structures, are organized so that students work individually and learn alone (Nock & Nelson, 1993). Grading on the curve still promotes competition in some classrooms, and many are teacher-centred, with activities that call for students to provide one right answer (Eggen & Kauchak, 1994). Contrast this classroom organization with the predominantly cooperative learning styles of many ethnic groups. Conflict might occur not only because members might be uncomfortable with individualistic or competitive learning situations but also because other students are unaccustomed to working in cooperative groups when these are used in the classroom. Ungerleider (1991) explains how this may create dissonance in Canadian classrooms.

> In Canadian classrooms it is customary that the teacher initiate activity. Some take this arrangement for granted because, from their cultural perspective, the teacher is the most important person and, thus, may legitimately initiate activity designed to elicit behaviour from the children that can be observed and judged. In this arrangement, the low-status individuals, the students, perform for the high-status individual, the teacher. For students from some backgrounds this practice is peculiar because, from their cultural perspective, high-status people perform activities so that low-status people can learn them. In fact, in some ethno-cultural groups the public display of one's achievements is considered ill-mannered. People from such groups do not draw attention to themselves. Group membership and group cohesion are especially important; self-promotion is seen as a threat to group maintenance. Thus, arrangements such as show-and-tell or practices such as public praise for individual achievement—practices that are conventional in the context of Canadian schools—run counter to the practices of some ethno-cultural groups (p. 202).

Concern with the disengagement from school that many Black students express has led to calls for the establishment of African-centred schools in Ontario. According to Dei (1995), such schools would be guided by Afrocentric principles and classroom pedagogical styles would stress holistic learning and teaching about African cultures as historically, ideologically, politically, and spiritually collective and communitarian. Dei (1996) contends that by empowering Black students with knowledge about African cultural values and traditions that emphasize community belongingness, group unity, and social responsibility, Black students can be provided with the requisite coping and surviving skills to deal with the competitiveness and rugged individualism that are the hallmarks of the Eurocentred school system (p. 58).

When teachers become aware of cultural conflicts between the learning styles of their students and the instructional styles of the classroom, they can incorporate a variety of alternative instructional strategies. Teachers can examine the classroom's cultural norms and modify them to better match the cultural diversity of the students.

Insights on Successful Practice

What strategies have you found work best for increasing parental involvement?

For several years one of our building-wide goals has been an effort to improve parental involvement and communication in the school community. In order to facilitate this discussion, the staff met with a group of interested parents. While we had a solid core of very involved parents, we knew we needed to expand our base to include more parents.

With this in mind, we first brainstormed the things we currently did to involve parents in their children's education: regular and invitational conferences, monthly newsletters, notes about class activities, parents as field trip volunteers, workers in the library, parents as listeners for our reading incentive program. The list went on. We were pleased to see just how much involvement was already happening.

Next we listed (with the parent committee's input), what areas we could expand: more parents on school committees (budget, technology, school improvement), informal lunches or breakfasts with teachers and students, parental help in the classroom on projects, a phone message system to update parents on classroom activities, parental sharing of individual expertise, help with drama productions, creating a school calendar of events, help in the computer lab. This list grew longer and longer as we talked.

Our school is composed of teams, with three to four teachers per team. After the all-staff discussion the teams met individually and put into place their strategies.

For example, our team now begins the school year with a special open house for just our parents, during which we introduce ourselves and explain our program. We emphasize our open door policy in which parents are invited any time to drop in and see what's happening. We now send home a weekly note for each student highlighting successes and, if necessary, indicating behaviour difficulties. Almost weekly we have parents in to share cultural heritage, occupations, or hobbies. This month, for instance, one parent shared his hobby of raising iguanas, another her expertise at quilting, another her life in Laos, another the traditions of Hanukkah. We call home when a student does something exceptionally well. We have a team calendar focusing on what we are teaching during the month and what events are happening. We post messages on the informational phone computer.

As we worked toward our goal, we realized that we needed to open more lines of communication. It is one thing to ask parents to become more involved, and quite another to actually involve them. We are experimenting and learning. We have more ideas now: businesses providing release time so that working parents can come to school, a goal of requesting two hours of school time per month for parents to help, broadening our outreach to include parents of former students and others in the school community. This list grows and grows.

One of our cornerstones now is that it takes the whole village to educate each child. Our village partnership of parents and teachers is becoming a reality.

PETER ROOP
Elementary School Teacher

Your Insights

Why is parental involvement important for students' success in school? What forces make it difficult for families to be involved? What other strategies can you think of for increasing parental involvement?

Communication Styles

Students and teachers can experience communication difficulties when they are culturally dissimilar, because either may misread the verbal and nonverbal cues of the other. Consider, for example, the findings of a study that compared the interactions of school counsellors with students who were culturally similar or dis-

CRITICAL THINKING: How might a teacher find out about communication values to enhance students' participation in classroom interactions?

Here's How

Here's How To Create a Culture-Fair Classroom

- Look for ways to present diverse perspectives, experiences, and contributions. Present concepts in ways that represent diverse cultural groups.
- Include materials and visual displays that represent members of all cultural groups in a positive manner.
- Provide as much emphasis on contemporary culture as on historical culture, and represent cultural groups as active and dynamic.
- View your instruction holistically, so that multicultural aspects will permeate all subject areas and all phases of the school day.
- Draw on your students' experiential backgrounds, their daily lives, and their experiences.
- Make sure all students have equal access to instructional resources, including computers and special programs as well as yourself (Adapted from Baruth & Manning, 1992, pp. 175-176).

TRY THIS: Interview a teacher regarding his or her strategies for creating a culture-fair classroom.

TRY THIS: Observe students' verbal and nonverbal communication in and out of classrooms. What differences in communication styles might relate to cultural differences? What effect might these differences have in the classroom?

similar (Erickson & Schultz, 1982). In conversation, the culturally dissimilar students did not acknowledge the individual counsellor's comments; the culturally similar students did. The acknowledgment difference was due to the fact that the culturally dissimilar students did not want to interrupt the counsellor when he or she was speaking. The counsellors interpreted this lack of acknowledgment as a lack of understanding. Counsellors repeated their messages several times, simplifying them each time. After the conversations, the counsellors judged the culturally dissimilar students as less bright than students who were culturally similar to themselves. The culturally dissimilar students reported that the counsellors made them feel stupid. Neither the students nor the counsellors seemed to understand the subtle cultural differences that affected their judgments of each other.

Problems can also occur in instruction when teachers expect students to actively participate in discussions and students are not accustomed to these interactions. In Canadian schools, teachers typically engage children in conversation when they first come to school as a means of getting to know them. Among the members of some ethno-cultural groups, this is the opposite of conventional practice; such people speak to one another only after they have become familiar with one another through careful and prolonged observation (Ungerleider, 1991, p. 202). When students are accustomed to a particular type of interaction at home, they may find it difficult to adjust to alternate demands in the classroom. Likewise, teachers can feel frustrated by what they perceive to be a lack of response to their teaching efforts. Recognizing that cultural differences in communication styles exist can enable teachers to better understand their students and to help them feel comfortable with the interactive styles used in class.

In an article focusing on Qitiqliq Secondary School in the hamlet of Arviat in the Keewatin region of the Northwest Territories, Macquire and McAlpine (1996) detail the difficulties that mainstream teachers have in communicating with Aboriginal children and their families:

... problems of communication between Aboriginal and mainstream English-speakers stem from basic differences in the social organization of discourse and communication patterns between the two groups, as well as from different expectations of teaching and learning. These differences lead to miscommunication and misunderstanding and frustrate the efforts of teachers and students to work effectively. Through the organization of home visits, members of the Inuit and Qallunaat cultures in Arviat and this community school are attempting to transform the negative images that are frequently attributed to each of them in the literature on home-school discontinuities (p. 230).

What Are the Dimensions of Multicultural Education?

Multicultural education currently means many things to many people (Bibby, 1990; Friesen, 1992, 1993). Views of diversity and the impact it should have on teaching and school curricula reflect different ideologies about the nature of ethnicity and its place in modern societies such as ours (Friesen, 1993). Some believe that too much emphasis on diversity denies the importance of the larger, national culture and might cause divisiveness in society. Others have argued that ethnic diversity provides strength to democracy and should be an integral part of education. These two positions reflect the assumptions of ideologies at two ends of a continuum: assimilation at one end and pluralism at the other. Multiculturalism, as a basis of school reform efforts, is most closely aligned with the pluralist end of the continuum. Let's examine each of these approaches to diversity.

Education for Integration and Assimilation

The ideologies of integration and assimilation might best be understood through the melting pot analogy, which has been used to describe U.S. society and culture. In the melting pot, individual ethnic groups merge into a single, shared culture; this is **integration**. Although some characteristics of the original cultures remain, they blend in support of the new whole. They are coequal in contributing to the national culture, but they do not coexist with it. Just as the ethnic cultures change in response to the national culture, so does the national culture subtly change each time a new ethnic group is added to the mix.

Conversely, with **assimilation**, different ethnic groups learn the ways of the dominant culture and become one with it. A hierarchy of values is assumed where those of an incoming ethnic group are subordinate to those of the national culture. It is expected, then, that people from different cultural groups will adopt and live by the dominant values. They are neither coequal with the national culture nor allowed to coexist with it. "Difference" in this case becomes "deficit."

In education, an integrationist or assimilationist view is characterized by the assumption that living in a common culture requires certain universal skills that must be attained by everyone. To support this goal, curricula should be geared to such skills in order to prepare all students for participation in and commitment to the national culture. The effect on ethnic groups of this educational plan depends on whether they are viewed as coequal with the national culture (as in integration) or unequal (as in assimilation). When educators expect socialization practices of some ethnic groups to put members of those groups at an early

integration A view of diversity in which individual ethnic groups merge together to form a single, shared culture.

assimilation A view of diversity in which a hierarchy of values is assumed so that members of ethnic groups are expected to adopt and live by the values of the dominant culture.

REFLECTION: Examine your own beliefs about diversity. Are they most similar to assimilation, integration, or pluralism? What is the basis for your beliefs?

CRITICAL THINKING: Consider the problem in the Teacher Chronicle in terms of assimilationist and pluralist views of diversity. If Ms. Walker believes in the deficit model, how would she be likely to interpret Kevin's problems with writing? What strategies might she use to help Kevin? If Ms. Walker identifies with cultural pluralism, how might she respond to Kevin's writing problem?

disadvantage, and they recommend compensatory programs to help these students catch up, they adhere to a **deficit**, or unequal, **model** (Banks, 1994a); that is, some groups are deficient in skills that they must make up in order to contribute to the national culture. Students without these skills are considered to be **at risk**, likely to drop out of school if they are not quickly brought to the same level of skill as other students.

Another form of compensatory education has been offered in the recommendation that disadvantaged ethnic minority groups should study ethnic content. The reasoning is that "members of ethnic groups who have experienced discrimination and structural exclusion have negative self-concepts and negative attitudes toward their own racial and ethnic groups" (Banks, 1994a, p. 108). Negative self-concepts and low achievement strivings must be some of the reasons for the characteristically lower academic achievement of minority group children (Graham, 1994). Therefore, studying ethnic content should enhance the self-concepts, thereby raising the achievement levels of these groups (Assante, 1991). Evidence now suggests, however, that these assumptions are not entirely true.

For one thing, comparisons among members of ethnic groups have revealed no systematic differences in their self-concepts or aspirations (Graham, 1994). For another, all students, not just ethnic minorities, can benefit from an approach to education that helps both teachers and students understand cultural differences. As Banks (1994a) put it, "the school should be a cultural environment in which acculturation takes place: both teachers and students should assimilate some of the views, perceptions, and ethos of each other as they interact" (p. 116).

Education for Cultural Pluralism

As the term suggests, **cultural pluralism** is a view of diversity that embraces cultural differences. Cultural pluralism relies on the process of compromise characterized by mutual appreciation and respect between two or more ethnic groups (Friesen, 1985). It implies a commitment to the development of all cultural groups. As an expression of a social goal, it suggests respect for and support of the heritages and cultures of the various ethnocultural groups within a given society, with the end-in-view of providing equity for all citizens (Friesen, 1993, p. 93). As a policy, pluralism contributes to collective and personal freedom by legitimizing diversity. It resolves the question of how different individuals who want to be free can live in a community. Pluralism diplomatically and optimistically declares that the whole is best served by the contribution of varied parts (Bibby, 1990, p. 1). A salad bowl analogy has been used to describe pluralism. All the ingredients that go into the salad are equally important to the final product, so they are coequal. But they also coexist in the final product; each contributes something to the salad, but each maintains its integrity and uniqueness.

Unlike the United States, where there is pressure to discard one's cultural past and conform to the dominant culture, Canada has been at the forefront in endorsing pluralism: in Canada, we have rejected the melting pot for the pluralist mosaic (Bibby, 1990). The central goal of Canadian life has become harmonious coexistence, the central means equality and justice. As Canadians, we aspire to accept and respect the ideas and lifestyles of one another, to be equitable and fair. Beyond mere platitudes, Canada has enshrined good intentions in bilingual and multicultural policies (1971), along with a Charter of Rights and Freedoms (1982; Bibby, 1990, p. 7). With the exception of Newfoundland, Yukon, and the Northwest Territories, all provinces in Canada have responded to the federal government's initiative by formulating multicultural programs of their own (Friesen, 1993).

deficit model The assumption that students who are members of ethnic minority groups are deficient in knowledge and skills required to contribute to the national culture.

at risk Students whose characteristics or life experiences make them likely to fail in school or drop out.

cultural pluralism A view of diversity that embraces cultural differences.

The Canadian government's multicultural policy initially had four aims: (1) to assist all cultural groups to grow, develop, and contribute to Canada; (2) to assist members of cultural groups to overcome the cultural barriers to a full participation in Canadian society; (3) to promote creative encounters and interchange between all Canadian cultures; and (4) to assist immigrants to acquire at least one of the two official languages of Canada (Breton, 1986, p. 51). An evaluation of the impact pluralism has had on life in Canada yields both positive and negative effects. Clearly, statistics presented earlier demonstrate that "prejudice and racism have not yet been subdued despite the best efforts of multicultural proponents" (Friesen, 1995). However, it is encouraging to note an increasing acceptance of multiculturalism by Canadians. Bibby (1990) reports that as of late 1989, 68 percent of Canadians endorsed multiculturalism. A 1987 comprehensive national survey of fifteen-to-twenty-four-year-olds found that 74 percent of the emerging generation supported multiculturalism (p. 52).

In education, two consequences of cultural pluralism arise. First, it is assumed that students from different cultural groups will have unique learning styles and therefore different learning needs. This is the **difference model**, which suggests that curricula should be revised to be more consistent with the experiences of different cultural groups. They should reflect students' different learning styles, cultural histories, and present experiences. In addition, the goal of such curricula is to help students develop strong attachments to their ethnic groups, so that they will be able to function effectively within those groups. This is quite different from the goals of assimilationist curricula.

Both assimilation and cultural pluralism have their problems when taken as a basis for responding to cultural diversity in schools (Banks, 1994a). With assimilation, ethnic groups have had to make all the accommodations. Moreover, the assimilationist assumption of universal learning styles does not seem to be completely true, and to the extent that research is conducted with members of the dominant culture only, we will fail to determine just what cultural differences are important for education. Yet, in Canada, critics of pluralism argue that concentrating on the differences among cultural groups to the exclusion of what groups face in the common culture ignores the fact that people participate in a variety of subcultures at different levels. According to Bibby (1990), pluralism as presently pursued in Canada has resulted in an imbalance between the individual and the group. In Bibby's view, Canada has done a good job of laying a pluralistic foundation. "Now we need to consolidate our gains and move on. Maximum well-being requires that we find a balance between the individual and the group, and that together we pursue the best kind of life possible. Such a Canadian dream is not beyond our grasp" (p. 180).

Multiculturalism in Canada

Within Canada, the essence of **multiculturalism** is a positive, supportive commitment to our diversity, one that builds on cultural diversity as a strength of our society. Friesen (1993) argues that multicultural education in Canada must incorporate a constantly changing and flexible policy, and be supportive of its underlying pluralist values. To achieve this end, he proposes that multicultural education must advance past merely being tolerant of others towards developing a deeper level of interaction through cultural understanding and acceptance. "Understanding," according to Friesen, implies taking time to

> walk in someone else's shoes for a while, to study other lifestyles and value systems, to take relativity seriously.

difference model The assumption that students from different cultural groups will have unique learning styles and therefore different learning needs.

multiculturalism A recognition that ethnic groups make up and contribute to a national culture while they maintain an individual identity.

To understand implies that new knowledge has been attained, but the *use* of knowledge can also be directional. In other words, varying applications can be made of knowledge. Knowledge, when it is attained, is usually categorized by the learner in terms of being useful or not useful, positive or negative. Knowledge is rarely left in a non-evaluated state. Here, multiculturalism reveals its subjectivity because it is commonly held among multiculturalists that knowledge about cultures should be *appreciated*, and not treated in a neutral sense nor disregarded. This belief imparts a specific value mandate upon classroom teachers who thus have the responsibility of helping their students *accept* new data as valid and useful with the encouragement to students that they add it to their repertoire of *valued* knowledge (pp. 85-86).

As a final step toward completing a multiculturally inspired education, Friesen proposes an *encouragement* of diversity. The challenge of seeking to *enhance* differences requires teachers to understand the theoretical conceptions of ethnic pluralism and multiculturalism, study philosophical assumptions concerning multicultural education, study the different characteristics and sociopolitical experiences of ethnocultural communities, and learn skills and techniques for teaching ethnically different students (pp. 86-87). Moreover, Friesen stresses that teachers must be cognizant of interpreting multicultural concerns in the language of the dominant social science disciplines and learn how to develop a pluralist atmosphere in the classroom. This involves helping students to accept themselves with all of their characteristics, and learning to see others as having equal worth and dignity.

As noted earlier, Canada's response to cultural diversity has been to set in place a policy of multiculturalism within a bilingualism framework. When policies of diversity become institutionalized, they typically take the form of special programs, curriculum reform, and school restructuring. For example, bilingual programs are offered to English-speaking students learning French, and summer math and science institutes are designed to enhance the achievement of girls in these subjects. In school reform, efforts are generally undertaken to change parts of the curriculum to reflect multicultural concerns or to change the very norms and values of the school itself.

Bilingual-Bicultural Education

The Canadian policies of bilingualism and multiculturalism drive three broad groupings of language-learning programs: those designed to teach English-speaking students French, those developed to increase competence in English for students with limited English proficiency, and those designed to teach heritage languages other than English or French. A variety of language-learning contexts are employed to achieve these ends including French immersion programs, English as a second language (ESL) classes, and heritage language schools. Within each of these contexts, several different programming options can be identified (e.g., self-contained programs, withdrawal programs, transitional programs, mainstreaming) (Piper, 1993).

French immersion programs in school systems have been a Canadian phenomenon for over twenty years (Carlson & Cole, 1993). Since the first program began in 1965 in St. Lambert, Quebec, French immersion has spread in popularity all across Canada. The broad intent of **language immersion** programs is to promote functional bilingualism through a policy of home and school language switch. The basic premise underlying immersion education is that students

TRY THIS: As a teaching resource, develop a contact list of selected local, provincial, and national professional organizations for multicultural education, bilingual education, and the education of students at risk.

language immersion A form of bilingual education in which students study the second language intensively for extended periods of time.

receive more instruction in the target language than core programs allow, and that the students are learning through the medium of the target language (Bell, 1991).

In Canada, immersion programs may be categorized into early, middle, late, and partial immersion (Bell, 1991). Early immersion programs are the most common and effective for developing second language proficiency (Swain, 1984). Tucker (1981) elucidates the commonalities of early French immersion programs across Canada:

1. Typically, the kindergarten curriculum stresses vocabulary development and passive comprehension skills in French along with other traditional kindergarten activities.

2. At grade one, reading, writing, and arithmetic are introduced exclusively via French. No attempt is made to teach the children to read in English, and parents are specifically urged not to do so in the home.

3. In grade two or three, two daily half-hour periods of English-language arts are introduced. The rest of the curriculum remains essentially the same, with reading, writing, arithmetic, and elementary science being taught via French.

4. The amount of instruction via English is increased gradually and by grade six approximately 50 percent of the curriculum is taught in English and approximately 50 percent in French.

5. Programs for secondary school have been less well articulated, with most graduates of early immersion programs following an accelerated or native speaker French language arts program.

Cummins and Swain (1986) have summarized the literature focusing on the comparison of linguistic competence and academic achievement of French immersion students and their peers in the English program. They conclude that the goals of the program have been met in four significant areas: (a) French immersion students have achieved high levels of proficiency in French; (b) normal levels of English have been maintained and developed; (c) bilingualism has been obtained without any long-term deficits in academic achievement; and (d) French immersion students express positive attitudes toward the program and the target language group while maintaining a healthy self-identity. Bell (1991) indicates that the success of immersion programs in Canada may rest on three factors. First, there has been substantive parental involvement in establishing and ensuring the continuation of the immersion programs. Second, the program is optional and therefore nonthreatening, and third, the language program is additive in nature, in that the target language is learned as an enhancement to the lives of learners rather than as a prerequisite for survival in a new community.

ESL programs are an important part of Canadian school curricula given that in many larger communities half of the children entering school do not speak English as their native language (Bell, 1991). A 1994 *Maclean's* article points out, for example, that 60 percent of all immigrants settle in Canada's three largest cities—Montreal, Toronto, and Vancouver. In Vancouver, ESL instruction is required for nearly half of its 55,000 public school students.

The main objective of ESL programming is to teach English-language skills to students with limited English proficiency. Piper (1993) identifies several key types of programs for ESL students in Canada. *Self-contained programs* are generally reserved for new Canadians having little or no English. They may take the form of a full "reception class" in which the students spend all day in the same

TRY THIS: Visit several schools in your area. What types of bilingual programs are being used in these schools? What was the reason for implementing an immersion or ESL approach?

ESL programs Programs that teach English language skills to students with limited English proficiency.

group with a qualified ESL specialist teacher, or a half-day reception class where students may be bused to a central ESL class for half of the day, while returning to their regular schools for the other half. In *withdrawal programs,* a special resource room for ESL students is set up. ESL students can be withdrawn from the mainstream to work on a one-to-one basis either with their teachers or with English-speaking students in a "buddy system." *Transitional programs* are generally used for upper elementary or secondary students, and are designed to bridge the gap between language and curriculum content. Finally, *mainstreaming* provides a fourth option. As Piper points out, however, the danger of mainstreaming without prior placement in other types of programs or adequate support is that it will result in *submersion,* a programming option known to have a particularly deleterious effect on students' psychological and academic well-being.

In contrast to the immersion methodology, **submersion** refers to the 'sink or swim' approach where no adjustments are made in the school program to take account of the minority child's cultural and linguistic differences. Rather than being additive in nature, submersion programs are subtractive. Subtractive bilingualism is defined as a form of second-language education that attempts to deny or minimize the importance of students' first cultures (Piper, 1993).

> Children in submersion programs may often become frustrated because of difficulties in communicating with the teacher. These difficulties can arise both because the teacher is unlikely to understand the child's [first language] and also because of different culturally determined expectations of appropriate behaviour. Since the child's home language is often viewed as the cause of his difficulties in learning the school language, no attempt is made to encourage [first language] competence and a decrease in the child's desire and ability to speak [the first language] is sometimes viewed as desirable. As one might expect from a program which attempts to widen the cultural gap between home and school and obliterate deeply rooted aspects of children's identity, submersion programs have resulted in widespread academic failure among minority language groups (Cummins, 1984, p. 154).

In Northern Canada, submersion programs are often the only option available to English-as-a-second-language Aboriginal students and likely play a causal role in the academic underachievement and misdiagnosis of exceptionality in many students. One of the authors recalls an incident in Northern Canada in which a significant number of grade one Cree-speaking children were referred for assessment of "dyslexia." Investigation revealed that the referred children had limited proficiency in English yet were being required to conform to a reading curriculum designed for middle-class monolingual English-speaking students! Alternative programs in which the minority students' first language skills and cultural identity are strongly reinforced before English is introduced appear to be a more culturally sensitive option (Cummins, 1989).

In recent years, there has been a proliferation of **heritage language schools** throughout Canada. By the late 1980s, there were nearly 130 000 minority children enrolled in established heritage language schools, which offered classes in nearly sixty different languages other than French and English (Pelech, 1988). Viewed as a means of preserving and promoting cultural identity, most heritage language schools function individually as separate units (Lan, 1993). This autonomy, together with a lack of recognition on the part of Canadian educators of the importance of a strong first-language competence, has weakened the impact of heritage language schools and rendered them "measures of accommodation rather than effective multicultural policy" (Friesen, 1993).

submersion The 'sink or swim' approach to teaching students from different cultures in which school programs do not take into account cultural and linguistic differences.

heritage language schools Programs designed to promote and preserve cultural identity by providing instruction in a heritage language other than English or French.

Insights on Successful Practice

How have Canadian schools innovatively responded to the needs of diverse students?

A number of Canadian schools have responded to the needs of ethnically and linguistically diverse students in innovative ways. Campbell (1996) introduces the reader to George Vanier Secondary School, a large, composite secondary school in North York, Ontario. It is estimated that at least eighty countries of origin and fifty languages are represented in this school. Approximately 60 percent of all students do not have English as their first language. To accommodate the widely varying needs of their diverse student population, George Vanier Secondary School has developed an expanded range of curricular options and special programs. While continuing to offer a strong traditional academic program, the school also provides a wide range of technological and vocational programs as well as a proliferation of special programs, including community-school partnerships, adapted credit course options, cross-curricular integration, learning centre, peer tutoring program, transition and mentoring program, Change-Your-Future Program, and Successful Beginnings Program. According to Campbell, a belief pervades the school that Vanier can find a place or develop a program for any and every student (p. 281).

Kelly (1996) provides us with a snapshot of Vancouver Technical School, an inner-city comprehensive school serving an ethnically diverse clientele. Vancouver Technical School has responded to students' varying needs by implementing a schools-within-a-school (SWS) model. The SWS model is based on the premise that smaller high schools are associated with student gains in achievement and engagement; thus, larger schools are broken up into smaller ones. Participants in each SWS engage in teaching and learning together for at least half of the school day in a distinct location.

The main school gives SWS teachers the autonomy to alter the timetable, select students, create or refashion curriculum, and establish codes of student behaviour. SWSs typically have distinct names and purposes: they aim to serve particular groups or emphasize different themes. SWS programs include flexible studies, various career programs, and dropout-prevention programs. Teachers report that since the implementation of the SWS model, student behaviour and attitudes have improved, dropout rates have fallen, and students show an increase in self-esteem and cultural pride.

Alladin and Ramsankar (1996) allow us to review the myriad of equity programs that have been implemented by Alex Taylor Community School in Edmonton, an inner-city elementary school serving students from diverse ethnic and racial backgrounds. One of the oldest schools in Edmonton, it was once considered one of the most violent and difficult schools in the province. It has responded to concerns of parents and students and developed a co-creative effort to address the concerns of the whole community. The idea that the school consists of a family, regardless of race, creed, or ethnicity, is continuously emphasized. In addition to the regular, prescribed curriculum, the school staff has developed programs and services that relate to the needs of the community. Innovative programs include a baby-sitting service that enables parents to attend adult education classes at the school, a nutrition program, a self-esteem program, cultural exchange and travel programs, food and clothing banks for needy families, ESL classes, voluntary summer program for inner-city children, social, physical, and mental health programs, and citizenship programs, among others.

VICKI SCHWEAN
Special Education Professor

Your Insights

Seek out the articles describing George Vanier Secondary School, Vancouver Technical Secondary School, and Alex Taylor Community School. See if you can identify the strategies used for combating systematic discrimination and student disengagement. How might you use these ideas in your teaching career?

Multicultural Curricula and School Reform

Multicultural education is still undergoing change as a concept. There is a growing consensus among scholars, however, "that an important goal of multicultural education is to increase educational equality for both gender groups, for students of diverse ethnic and cultural groups, and for exceptional students" (Banks, 1994b, p. 16; cf. Banks & Banks, 1993; Sleeter & Grant, 1988). Going further, most scholars agree that multicultural education should prepare all students—including students of the dominant cultures, English and French—to live in a society that is growing ever more culturally diverse. A third aim of multicultural education is **global education**, or helping students to understand that all peoples living on Earth have interconnected fates (Banks, 1994b; Becker, 1979).

What do multicultural curricula look like that are designed to meet these goals? Several different approaches have been used, always with the aim of reforming curricula, and each with different results. In the *contributions approach* (Figure 4.1), teachers conduct activities to celebrate holidays or other cultural observances of ethnic groups. For example, in addition to Christmas or Hanukkah celebrations, a school might plan activities to coincide with Aboriginal ceremonial dances. In the *additive approach*, multicultural concepts and themes are added to an existing curriculum without changing its basic structure, goals, or functions. This occurs when a unit or course on multicultural studies or on a particular cultural group is added. What is important to note about both the contributions and additive approaches is that neither challenges the status quo of the existing curriculum. In fact, as Banks (1994b) has noted,

> [W]hen these approaches are used to integrate cultural content into the curriculum, people, events, and interpretations related to ethnic groups and women often reflect the norms and values of the dominant culture rather than those of cultural communities ... (p. 26).

FIGURE 4.1
Approaches to Multicultural Curriculum Reform

Source: Adapted from "Approaches to Multicultural Curriculum Reform" (1–3), *Multicultural Leader,* Vol. 1, No. 2 Spring 1988.

global education An aim of multicultural programs that helps students to understand that all peoples living on Earth have interconnected fates.

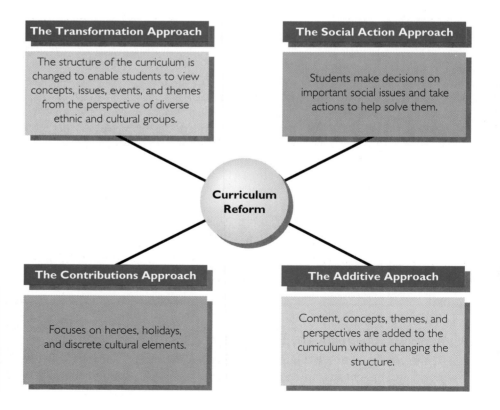

The Transformation Approach

The structure of the curriculum is changed to enable students to view concepts, issues, events, and themes from the perspective of diverse ethnic and cultural groups.

The Social Action Approach

Students make decisions on important social issues and take actions to help solve them.

Curriculum Reform

The Contributions Approach

Focuses on heroes, holidays, and discrete cultural elements.

The Additive Approach

Content, concepts, themes, and perspectives are added to the curriculum without changing the structure.

By contrast, a *transformation approach* results in major changes to curricula, enabling students to experience the perspectives of different cultural groups. Through this approach, for example, the discovery of North America by Christopher Columbus takes on new meaning. After all, it wasn't uncharted territory for everyone, because Aboriginals were already living there. Finally, a *social action approach* extends the transformative curriculum. Students may decide to pursue projects that build on the issues and problems they have studied previously, projects likely to result in personal, social, or civic action (Banks, 1994b).

These approaches to reforming curricula are consistent with five dimensions that Banks (1994a) has defined for multicultural education. The dimensions themselves can serve as the primary foci of curricula and school reform efforts that benefit all students. They also provide a means of interpreting and evaluating existing educational programs that purport to be multicultural. Banks' five dimensions of multicultural education are presented in Figure 4.2:

1. content integration
2. the knowledge construction process
3. prejudice reduction
4. an equity pedagogy
5. an empowering school culture and social structure

Education for Cultural Awareness. To help students learn about and appreciate cultural perspectives other than their own, teachers use content and examples in all subject areas that reflect both genders, diverse cultures, and different social classes. The extent to which they do this determines the degree of **content integration** achieved. Often, the first step toward implementing this guideline is in the selection of bias-free textbooks and other teaching-learning materials (Baruth & Manning, 1992).

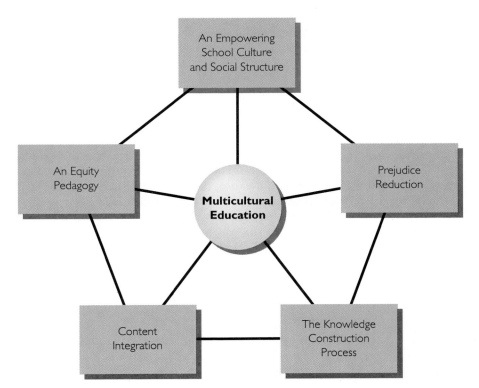

FIGURE 4.2
The Dimensions of Multicultural Education

Source: Multiethnic Education, James A. Banks, 1994, Needham Heights, MA: Allyn & Bacon.

content integration The degree to which teachers use content and examples in all subject areas that reflect both genders, diverse cultures, and different social classes.

TRY THIS: Examine a textbook you might consider using in your classroom. Are there examples of culturally diverse people portrayed in a meaningful, nonstereotypical way? Are various social classes portrayed? Are women, people with disabilities, or elderly people included? What would you conclude about the extent to which this book is bias-free?

CONNECTION: Knowledge construction from a constructivist viewpoint is discussed in Chapter 7.

Materials can have a tremendous impact on student attitudes both by what they include and by what they omit. For example, some textbooks have depicted Asians as excellent students, but show Aboriginals as savage and uncivilized. These images can perpetuate inaccurate stereotypes just as surely as when images of women or elderly people are omitted from textbooks. With omissions, some groups are virtually invisible in textbooks, which has the effect of devaluing these groups in Canadian society.

The content of textbooks can also lead to distortions or unbalanced impressions of various cultural groups. For example, a single point of view presented on a controversial topic may be technically correct but misleading, failing to present the other side. Bias-free materials, then, include culturally diverse images, provide multiple perspectives on complex social issues, and use nonsexist language.

Multicultural perspectives can be integrated with all content areas, not just social studies or literature, with which they are most frequently associated. Multicultural views are also valid and important to examine in the sciences, mathematics, health, and physical education (Baruth & Manning, 1992).

Once the content of multicultural perspectives is in place, teachers can investigate the **knowledge construction process** with their students (Banks, 1994a). In the Western tradition, knowledge is often taught to students as a body of truths that are not to be questioned or critically analyzed. However, even the most apparently objective experiment is influenced by the scientist's prior conceptions and personal biases. Teachers can help students understand how implicit cultural assumptions and perspectives influence the construction of knowledge by juxtaposing conflicting interpretations of the same event. In exploring these interpretations, students should consider which point of view the interpretations represent and why one interpretation may have become the dominant account in history.

When students weigh evidence and think critically about how knowledge is constructed within a cultural context, they participate in a transformative curriculum. Whether reading or listening, they become able to "consider the author's purposes for writing or speaking, his or her basic assumptions, and how the author's perspective or point of view compares with that of other authors" (Banks, 1994a, p. 10).

Education for Equity. "An equity pedagogy exists when teachers modify their teaching in ways that will facilitate the academic achievement of students from diverse racial, cultural, ethnic, and gender groups" (Banks, 1994a, p. 13). To do this, teachers must know the cultural characteristics of students that significantly influence their performance and achievement in school. Instructional strategies can then be developed that will be effective in accommodating those characteristics. We have already discussed how students are diverse in race, ethnicity, social class, and gender, and how general characteristics associated with these microcultures may influence student learning. What can teachers do to implement an equity pedagogy?

To begin with, teachers can get to know their students as individuals, rather than classifying them into stereotypical categories (Tyler, 1989). Just because a student is female and Islamic does not mean she will automatically identify with these microcultures or exhibit characteristics commonly associated with them. However, one must be alert to the possibility that she could. Coming to know students as individuals helps a teacher identify their unique needs and makes instructional accommodation possible.

An instructional strategy that has proven useful with different cultural groups is cooperative learning. When cooperation and sharing are cultural traits of a group, members of the group tend to benefit from cooperative learning activities.

knowledge construction process A process by which knowledge is socially and culturally constructed.

The aims of multicultural education include teaching cultural awareness and acceptance of diversity, promoting educational equality for all students, reducing prejudice and social disharmony, and transforming the culture of schools.

For example, evidence has mounted in favour of using cooperative learning with Aboriginal students (Miller, 1973; Miller & Thomas, 1972). Girls also seem to perform better in all-female groups than in groups where boys are mixed with girls. Not only has cooperative learning been shown to improve the achievement of students who work cooperatively (Sharan, 1985; Slavin, 1995), but in one Canadian study was also shown to improve relations among multicultural-multiethnic students (Ziegler, 1981).

Teachers must communicate clearly and fully the rules of the classroom and expectations regarding school activities and performance, taking into consideration students with limited English proficiency. Teachers may use communication signals that are different from those used by culturally different groups; it is essential, therefore, for teachers to develop communication styles that avoid confusion and respect students' linguistic or cultural differences (Bowman, 1989).

Education for Social Harmony. This dimension of multicultural education concerns helping students overcome racial prejudices and develop more democratic attitudes and behaviours. Prejudice is "an emotional, rigid attitude . . . toward a group of people . . . in the mind of the prejudiced person" (Simpson & Yinger, 1985, p. 21). A prejudiced person categorizes a group of people based on some perceived attribute. Racial and cultural prejudices have very complex causes that are not yet well understood. However, they are likely to include personality variables (aggression, insecurity) and sociocultural variables (norms, traditions, power structure). These and other variables also influence the extent to which individuals act on their prejudices and discriminate against others.

From the research conducted thus far, Banks (1994a) concludes that "systematic experiences must be structured to reinforce and perpetuate the desired attitudes" (p. 245). Once again, cooperative learning can be a means to help combat racist attitudes.

EXAMPLE: Consider the student whose parents would not allow him to exchange valentine cards at school. His teacher, not wanting him to feel left out, devised a unit that included Valentine's Day letters, but revolved around the workings of a post office. Activities such as making stamps and mailing and delivering letters kept him involved but did not require that he exchange valentines. Note how the teacher respected the parents' wishes without disrupting a traditional activity.

REFLECTION: Have you ever experienced discrimination on the basis of your race, sex, ethnicity, or religion?

Here's How

Here's How To Use Cooperative Groups in Support of Social Harmony

- Arrange for heterogeneous groups where students can work with others who come from different cultural backgrounds and where no one group predominates.

continued

TRY THIS: Visit a model school in your area. What do you notice about the bulletin boards, school decorations, and cultural composition of the teaching and administrative staff? Is there evidence of a commitment to multiculturalism?

Education for Accountability. In order for students from diverse cultural groups to experience equality, Banks (1994a) and others contend that schools themselves must be conceptualized as cultural systems with values and norms that support multiculturalism. Each of the previous four dimensions deals with an aspect of the school and school culture. But viewing the school holistically provides a unifying framework for examining not just teaching practices but counselling programs, sports activities, attitudes and behaviour of school staff and administrators, and even what goes on in the school cafeteria (Banks, 1994a).

Table 4.1 shows eight characteristics proposed for multicultural schools (Banks, 1994b). Many of these have already been discussed in this chapter but several deserve particular mention.

The explicit curriculum of a school comes primarily from curriculum guides and other official documents that provide the framework and direction for what teachers are supposed to teach. It is therefore expressed in the goals and objectives that teachers adopt and in the instructional strategies and assessment procedures they use to teach and test for goal attainment. The **hidden curriculum**, however, comprises lessons and messages that, although not explicitly taught by teachers, are nonetheless learned by students. For example, the well-meaning teacher who puts Bible verses above her classroom door each week sends a message to students about religion and which religion is valued.

Attitudes of the school as a social system are conveyed in myriad ways, from the pictures posted on bulletin boards to the way students are grouped for assemblies, to the representation of diverse cultures and both sexes in the teaching staff. In a multicultural school, these attitudes are regularly examined to be sure that messages of diversity are conveyed to students rather than messages of racism or sexism.

Similarly, assessment and testing procedures are scrutinized for potential bias against ethnic, racial, or gender groups. In Canada, procedures designed to minimize bias in testing are described in the *Principles for Fair Student Assessment Practice for Education in Canada* (discussed more fully in Chapter 13). Even when such precautions are taken, however, using standardized tests for placement purposes can result in low-income and minority students being overrepresented in some programs (e.g., those for people with learning disabilities) and underrepresented in others (e.g., those for the gifted) (Schwean & Greenough-Olsen, 1992;

hidden curriculum The tacit lessons and messages taught to students by the way teachers and schools operate.

TABLE 4.1 *The Eight Characteristics of the Multicultural School*

1. The teachers and school administrators have expectations for all students and positive caring attitudes toward them. They also respond to them in positive and caring ways.
2. The formalized curriculum reflects the experiences, cultures, and perspectives of a range of cultural and ethnic groups as well as both genders.
3. The teaching styles used by the teachers match the learning, cultural, and motivational styles of the students.
4. The teachers and administrators show respect for the students' first languages and dialects.
5. The instructional materials used in the school show events, situations, and concepts from the perspectives of a range of cultural, ethnic, and racial groups.
6. The assessment and testing procedures used in the school are culturally sensitive and result in students of color being represented proportionately in classes for the gifted and talented.
7. The school culture and the hidden curriculum reflect cultural and ethnic diversity.
8. The school counsellors have high expectations for students from different racial, ethnic, and language groups and help these students to set and realize positive career goals.

Source: *An Introduction to Multicultural Education*, James A. Banks, 1994, Needham Heights, MA: Allyn & Bacon.

Schwean & Saklofske, 1994). Employing a variety of testing formats to assess students' talents and achievements is likely to be more equitable and more accurate, because students do not perform equally well on all formats (Shavelson, Baxter, & Pine, 1992). Assessment methods such as performance tests, long-range projects, and portfolios developed over a semester can provide greater sensitivity to both student diversity and the wide range of curriculum activities that students experience during the school year (Berliner, 1992).

Achieving the eight criteria for a multicultural school that are listed in Table 4.1 requires taking a *systems approach* to school reform because the school is a complex system of many interconnected variables. Unless these variables are all considered in the context of school reform, it is unlikely that the norms of the school will change. For example, teachers may begin to use culturally sensitive materials in their classes, but if practices continue to exist in the school that discriminate, however subtly, against certain groups, then no real change will be effected. Becoming a truly multicultural school takes the collaborative efforts of the teachers, administrators, students, and parents (Comer, 1988).

Multicultural Education in Canada

At this juncture, it is important to query the status of multicultural education in Canada.

The additive approach to multicultural education is most commonly used in Canada; however, its efficacy for modifying racist attitudes and behaviours has been questioned by several researchers. For example, Rymer and Alladin (1996) argue that additive approaches do not go far enough to question the social organization of knowledge. They state that such approaches operate from the premise that exposure to sensitivity training in human relations and ethnic studies programs will alter racist attitudes towards minorities. Unfortunately, studies have shown that exposing white teachers and students to sensitivity training does not reduce or eliminate prejudice (p. 169).

The failure of conservative multicultural education to transform individual behaviours, attitudes, institutional policies, and racist practices has led to calls for the implementation of transformation and social action approaches. Often referred to as *antiracist education*, transformative and social action approaches seek to eradicate racist ideas and beliefs as well as individual and institutional practices that support and perpetuate racism in society by making a connection between institutional discrimination and inequality of race, class, and gender (Solomon & Levine-Rasky, 1996). According to Harper (1997),

> Antiracist education examines how racial difference is produced in all school subjects, policies, and practices. It assumes that because racism exists in society, it must exist in schools. It highlights the relationship between personal prejudices and systemic discrimination, exposing the ways in which social structures limit some students and advantage others on the basis of race . . . Antiracist education . . . moves us beyond the comfortable aspects of each other's culture, the food and the festivals, to examining the more controversial dimensions of culture which have led to change and can lead to change (p. 9).

How willing are Canadian teachers to implement antiracist education? Solomon and Levine-Rasky (1996) surveyed teachers, schools administrators, and antiracist education policy advisors in five urban Canadian schools to determine their attitudes towards the implementation of antiracist education. Their results showed that many teachers are reluctant to use antiracist curriculum because of their commitment to traditional pedagogy, conservative political views, and conservative views on race and antiracism. Furthermore, they found that while some educators articulate a commitment to antiracist education, they fail to use it in their pedagogical practice. When it is implemented, the integration is often piecemeal. Other researchers contend that a stronger commitment to antiracist education will come from recruiting greater numbers of racial minority and immigrant educators (Bascia, 1996). Studies have found that racial minority teachers are much more supportive of antiracist education than are white teachers and thus, they can contribute positively to equity in education by enhancing cultural compatibility, demystifying the hidden curriculum, developing positive attitudes toward persons from a variety of backgrounds, expressing lived experiences, connecting with the students, and connecting with the communities (Carr & Klassen, 1997). It is discouraging to note that the racial composition of Canada's teaching corps remains largely white (Carr, 1995).

How Can Your Knowledge of Diversity Enhance Teaching and Learning in Your Classroom?

Teachers who are effective in a multicultural environment first learn to know themselves. You, like your students, will come to the classroom with your own cultural experiences and perspectives, as well as possible stereotypes and misperceptions. As a teacher, you are the mediator of messages and symbols that are communicated by the curriculum to your students. You are also a role model for your students. Therefore, it is important for you to be aware of your own personal and cultural values and identity and how these affect your actions in the classroom. This is at the heart of being an effective multicultural teacher.

In addition, effective multicultural teachers both understand the complex nature of diversity and feel a commitment to a multicultural ideology (Banks, 1994a). This means that you accept cultural diversity in your students and help them to accept diversity in each other. Effective multicultural teachers have the ability to view events in their classrooms from various cultural perspectives and the skills to accommodate their instruction to the differences they perceive.

Accepting Student Diversity

Often without thinking about it, people assume that their own cultural ways are the right ways and universally appropriate to others. When the cultural lens through which they view the world extends to evaluating other cultures by their own cultural standards, then **ethnocentrism** is the result. People who have strong ethnocentric beliefs can find it difficult to accept diversity or to understand cultural perspectives that are different from their own. They tend to perceive the traits of other cultural groups as odd or inferior in some way (Baruth & Manning, 1992). You can help students to reduce their ethnocentrism first by recognizing and accepting their diversity. This entails recognizing cultural stereotypes as well.

POINT: *Teachers and students are both learners.* In a multicultural classroom and school, students and teachers together learn to accept diversity by examining their own beliefs and values and becoming aware of others' beliefs and values.

Here's How

Here's How To Help Students Accept Diversity in Others

- Instill in children and adolescents the idea that cultural differences should not be considered right or wrong, superior or inferior.
- Arrange teaching-learning situations (cooperative learning and cross-age tutoring) whereby learners of varying cultures can have firsthand experiences with each other.
- Model acceptance and respect for all people.
- Respond appropriately to statements indicating a lack of understanding or acceptance of cultural differences.
- Encourage respect for all differences—cultural and ethnic, socioeconomic, disabling conditions, gender, and other characteristics which contribute to diversity among individuals (Baruth & Manning, 1992, p. 157).

In facilitating students' acceptance of diversity, remember that change comes slowly. You are challenging long-held beliefs that may have been taught or encouraged at home.

Using Multicultural Teaching Strategies

Regardless of the grade level or subject matter you expect to teach, there are many teaching strategies you can use to support the goals of multicultural education. In your school, start a resource file of ideas and materials that you and other teachers have used and found effective. Some ideas to try are presented in the following lists.

ethnocentrism The assumption that one's own cultural ways are the right ways and universally appropriate to others.

Strategies for School-Wide Cultural Awareness

1. Take a cultural census of the class or school to find out what cultures are represented; let students be the ethnographers.
2. Form a multicultural club.
3. Select a theme to tie various multicultural activities together; hold school programs with art, music, and dramatic presentations; hold a multicultural fair or festival featuring music, art, dance, dress; adopt a multicultural theme for existing activities.
4. Hold a school cross-cultural food festival.
5. Have multicultural celebrations and teach-ins with school-wide activities in all classes.
6. Decorate classrooms, hallways, and the library media centre with murals, bulletin boards, posters, artifacts, and other materials representative of the students in the class or school or other cultures being studied. Posters and other information are available from foreign government travel bureaus and education agencies, private travel agencies, consulates, the United Nations, or ethnic and cultural organizations, for example.
7. Designate a permanent bulletin board for multicultural news and displays.
8. Hold a video film festival dealing with various cultures and multicultural issues.
9. Feature stories in the school newspaper on multicultural topics; publish a multicultural newspaper or newsletter.
10. Hold mock campaigns and elections based on multicultural issues.

Strategies for Cultural Awareness in the Classroom

1. Have students write to foreign consulates, tourist bureaus, or minority organizations for information and decorative materials.
2. Supplement textbooks with authentic material from different cultures taken from newspapers, magazines, and other media of the culture.
3. Use community resources: representatives of various cultures talking to classes; actors portraying characters or events; musicians and dance groups, such as salsa bands or bagpipe units.
4. Work with the library media centre for special bibliographies, collections, displays, and audio-visuals.
5. Hold a mock legislature to debate current or historical issues affecting minorities and cultural groups.
6. Hold oratorical, debate, essay, poster, art, brain brawl, or other competitions with a multicultural focus.
7. Develop a radio or television program on multicultural themes for the educational or local community access channel.
8. Study works in science, literature, and fine arts of various cultures, focusing on the contributions of minority individuals.
9. Have students write short stories or essays on multicultural topics.
10. Have student debates, speeches, and skits on multicultural topics, and present them to classes, parent-teacher organizations, nursing homes, and other community groups.
11. Study the provisions and freedoms of the Canadian Charter of Rights and Freedoms as they relate to minorities.
12. Compare and contrast other cultures with those of mainstream Canada.

13. Discuss the issues and personalities involved in various cultures from a historical, political, and literary standpoint.

14. Have students of other cultures, or their parents, share their native songs with classmates; have students share instruments or recordings of their native cultures.

15. Take field trips to local multicultural sites, such as a neighbourhood, ethnic recreation/social centre, workplace, historical site, museum, restaurant, grocery.

16. Establish pen pals or video exchange programs with students from other cultures.

17. Focus on the everyday artifacts that differentiate the way people behave in various cultures, such as greetings, friendly exchanges, farewells, expressing respect, verbal taboos, ways of using numbers, body language and gestures, gender roles, folklore, childhood literature, discipline, festivals, holidays, religious practices, games, music, pets, personal possessions, keeping warm and cool, cosmetics, fashions, health and hygiene practices, competitions, dating and courtship, transportation and traffic, sports, radio and television programs, hobbies, foods, family mealtimes, snacking, cafes and restaurants, yards and sidewalks, parks and playgrounds, flowers and gardens, movies and theaters, circuses, museums, vacations and resort areas, careers.

18. Discuss what it means to be a member of a minority or different cultural group.

Strategies for Cultural Equity

1. Be sure that assignments are not offensive or frustrating to students of cultural minorities. For example, asking students to discuss or write about their Christmas experiences is inappropriate for non-Christian students. Instead, let students discuss their similar holidays.

2. Help students develop the skills needed to locate and organize information about cultures from the library media center, the mass media, people, and personal observations.

3. Use skills and information from various disciplines (math, social studies, geography, language arts) to compare population, economy, politics, lifestyle, culture, and other data about different cultural groups in Canada during different historical periods and as they are today. Discuss the meaning of the differences.

4. Discuss the relevance of the Charter of Rights and Freedoms and government in dealing with today's problems that relate to minorities and cultural diversity.

5. Focus on geography skills and knowledge in geography courses as part of related courses.

6. Discuss the importance of international trade and the skills needed to be employed in that area.

7. Discuss what it means to be a Canadian citizen.

Strategies for Accountability

1. Make newcomers feel welcome through a formal program.

2. Form a school-wide planning committee to address the implementation of multicultural education.

3. Contact your school division's multicultural coordinator for ideas and assistance.

4. Let teachers knowledgeable about multicultural topics present inservice workshops for others or teach their classes occasionally.

5. Make reminders during daily announcements about multicultural activities (Adapted from Baruth & Manning, 1992, pp. 211-214).

Teacher Chronicle Conclusion

Grandma Tales

As Ms. Walker made her lesson plans for the next day, she reflected on Kevin and his storytelling ability. How could he use his skills to become a better writer? Could his telling stories orally replace written assignments? The next day Ms. Walker met Kevin at the classroom door.

"Kevin," she asked, "Do you tell many stories at home?"

"Oh, sure. We tell stories all the time. My aunt says that telling stories to the whole family is much better than reading."

"Why?" Ms. Walker asked.

"She says that when you tell a story, everyone gets to be part of it. But when you read a story, only one person hears it."

"How would you like to tape-record your stories so that you could share them at school and home, too?" Ms. Walker asked.

"Can I really?" Kevin said.

"Yes, and then with a partner's help you can write them down for your written work. I think that your writing will improve, don't you?"

Kevin smiled. "Then maybe I might pass English?"

"Yes."

Application Questions

1. Rewrite the conversations between Kevin and Ms. Walker for a different ending.

2. What other strategies might Ms. Walker have used to capitalize on Kevin's strengths?

3. Is tape-recording an appropriate strategy? Why or why not?

4. Will writing the stories after telling them help Kevin's writing abilities?

5. What other cultural insights might Ms. Walker have gained in understanding Kevin better?

6 How might Ms. Walker become a more effective teacher in dealing with other students whose cultural backgrounds differ from hers?

7. How does culture influence learning?

8. How does culture influence teaching?

9. If Ms. Walker shares Kevin's stories with a math teacher, how might that teacher use this knowledge to aid in Kevin's math instruction? geography? science?

CHAPTER SUMMARY

What Are Some Sources of Diversity? (L.O. 1, p. 98)

As Canadian society continues to diversify, so do Canadian schools. Students come from many different racial, ethnic, and socioeconomic backgrounds. They speak many languages and dialects in addition to standard English and French. They come with a variety of abilities and disabilities that can become cultural traits to the extent that students identify with others having the same exceptionality. All of these characteristics influence how students learn and interact in the school environment.

How Can Cultural Conflicts Arise in Your Classroom? (L.O. 4, 5, p. 111)

When your students come from different backgrounds and experiences, there is a potential for conflict. You may organize your classroom, use instructional strategies, or communicate in ways that are either unfamiliar to your students or conflict with the values with which they were raised. It is important for you to examine your own values and beliefs in relation to those of your students and consider ways in which you can best meet their needs.

What Are the Dimensions of Multicultural Education? (L.O. 6, p. 115)

Recent Canadian approaches to multicultural education are based on the concept of pluralism and endorse the notion that all ethnic groups contribute equally to Canadian society. The current purposes of many multicultural programs include enhancing cultural awareness, increasing educational equity, and overcoming racist attitudes. To do this, a systems (or school-wide) approach to multicultural education is recommended.

How Can Your Knowledge of Diversity Enhance Teaching and Learning in Your Classroom? (L.O. 9, p. 128)

By becoming familiar with the diversity of your students, you can help them to be more accepting of cultural differences in one another. You can also use a variety of multicultural teaching strategies to facilitate cultural awareness, educational equity, and social harmony.

KEY CONCEPTS

additive bilingualism, p. 102

assimilation, p. 115

at risk, p. 116

bilingual education, p. 102

bilingualism, p. 102

content integration, p. 123

cultural pluralism, p. 116

culture, p. 98

deficit model, p. 116

dialect, p. 104

difference model, p. 117

dominant bilingualism, p. 102

English as a second language (ESL) programs, p. 119

ethnic group, p. 99

ethnicity, p. 99

ethnocentrism, p. 129

global education, p. 122

heritage language schools, p. 120

hidden curriculum, p. 126

integration, p. 115

knowledge construction process, p. 124

language immersion, p. 118

limited English proficiency, p. 102

macroculture, p. 98

metalinguistic awareness, p. 102

microculture, p. 98

multiculturalism, p. 117

race, p. 99

socioeconomic status, p. 104

submersion, p. 120

subtractive bilingualism, p. 102

5 Individual Variability in the Classroom

LEARNING OUTCOMES

When you have completed this chapter, you will be able to

1. outline several traditional views of intelligence

2. compare and contrast the contemporary intelligence theories of Gardner and Sternberg

3. provide examples of how these theories describe individual differences

4. describe how thinking and learning dispositions are related to student learning

5. assess the relationship between culture and learning

6. describe some of the high-incidence disabilities you will likely encounter as a teacher

7. list several low-incidence disabilities that will require special education services

8. discuss the relative advantages and limitations of current special education provisions

9. explain the interaction between student needs and classroom instruction

Teacher Chronicle

My Name Is Robo

Mrs. Chiu is preparing her grade one room in anticipation of the beginning of the school year. It is new student visiting day, and parents and students are dropping in to meet her.

"Good morning, Mrs. Chiu. My name is Dr. Kotre and this is my son, Heath. We just stopped by to say a quick hello."

Heath buzzes past Mrs. Chiu and heads straight to the play corner. Picking up a toy robot, he begins manipulating its arms, saying in a mechanical voice, "My name is Robo. I am model 2005." Dropping the robot, Heath grabs a shell from the science table and howls into it. "WHOOOOOOOO!" Seconds later, he is building a tower with wooden blocks.

Mrs. Chiu quickly tries to recall what she had learned about Heath from his cumulative record folder. He has an IQ of 145, is already selected for the gifted and talented program, is not yet a reader, and is thought by his kindergarten teacher to be highly creative.

Dr. Kotre smiles. "He's going to love your room, Mrs. Chiu."

"I hope so," she says. "If he's happy here, I can teach and he can learn."

Heath had stacked the blocks and was running a toy fire truck into them.

"Okay, Heath, it's time to go," says Dr. Kotre as the blocks tumble down.

"No," he answers defiantly.

"Yes, Heath, I have an appointment."

"NO!" he shouts.

Dr. Kotre looks at Mrs. Chiu.

"Heath, you will have plenty of time to play with those toys when school starts next week."

Heath bangs the blocks together and starts crying. "I'm not through yet."

"Yes you are," Dr. Kotre says, frustration creeping into her voice. She takes him by the arm, but he pushes away.

"No!" he screams.

Mrs. Chiu remembers another comment from Heath's kindergarten teacher. Heath was recommended for observation by the resource teacher.

After several embarrassing minutes, Heath is finally coaxed with a bribe into leaving.

"Yes, Heath, I will buy you that new transformer toy," Dr. Kotre says. On the way out, her eyes meet Mrs. Chiu's with a look that says "Good luck."

Focus Questions

1. In what ways did Heath exhibit the intelligence suggested by his high IQ score? Other than the robot, what are Heath's manipulation skills? Are these skills a sign of intelligence? Are there gaps in his intelligence? If so, what are they?

2. Consider the ways in which you think Heath would learn best. How would you characterize his preferred style of learning? What factors might place Heath at risk of failing in school? What evidence supports your choice of factors?

3. In preparing to consult with other professionals concerning Heath's needs, what behaviours should Mrs. Chiu document from her classroom observations? Will interactions with other students provide important information? How can information about Heath's relationships with other children be communicated without invading his or other students' privacy?

4. Would you predict that Heath can be helped through behavioural training? Will medication be necessary? What role would Mrs. Chiu play in such decisions? If medication is prescribed, what responsibilities would fall on Mrs. Chiu?

5. What kind of special program might be established to help Heath? Are there legal requirements for such a program? Who should participate in its development? Why?

6. Do you think Heath's behaviour might prove disruptive for other students? How? What strategies should Mrs. Chiu use to make Heath feel included in the class? What strategies should she use to help him learn? How should she assess Heath's learning?

How Do Students Vary in Intelligence?

Heath, in the Teacher Chronicle, presents a unique challenge for his teacher. But so will each student in Mrs. Chiu's class. Ultimately, the question for Mrs. Chiu, and every other teacher, is "How can I adapt the teaching-learning process to meet the unique needs of each individual student?" The first step in solving this problem is to recognize the role that individual student characteristics play in learning. The next step is to acquire an understanding of the ways in which students differ from one another.

An analysis of research data on relationships among variables thought to influence school learning shows that student characteristics are among the most important variables (Table 5.1) (Levin, 1993; Wang, Haertel, & Walberg, 1993). Student characteristics include demographics and academic placement histories as well as social, motivational, cognitive, and affective characteristics.

It is important for future teachers to recognize that the characteristics of their students will vary and how those characteristics influence students' learning.

In this chapter we focus on the key factors that determine the individual characteristics of your students and, therefore, their learning. We begin by examining a student characteristic that has long been linked to success in school, intelligence.

The Definition and Measurement of Intelligence

REFLECTION: How do you define intelligence? How does that definition help you explain differences among people?

Although we examine several variations, the term **intelligence** is generally defined as one's capacity to learn. Intelligence is included on most permanent records of students. Indeed, in many school districts, the measured intelligence of a child is used in concert with other information to make instructional decisions concerning that student's future.

The measurement of intelligence yields an index called an *intelligence quotient* (IQ). A person's IQ is typically represented by a single number. For example, someone with an IQ of 102 is considered to have average intelligence; an IQ of 120 is considered above average. In and out of educational circles, when we talk about a person's intelligence, we usually think of it as a unitary thing that can be reflected in a single number. Incidentally, while we usually talk about IQ as a single value, it is more accurate to speak of the probable range of a person's IQ. The measurement of intelligence will be further discussed in Chapter 13. In this section, we examine the meaning of the term *intelligence* rather than its measurement.

There has been a long and animated debate among psychologists as to the meaning of *intelligence*. Intelligence is a **construct**, an idea devised by a theorist to explain something else. Intelligence, for example, has been used to explain why some students graduate from law school and others can't finish high school; why

intelligence: A personal capacity to learn, often measured by one's ability to deal with abstractions and to solve problems.

construct: An idea devised by a theorist to explain observations and relationships between variables.

TABLE 5.1 *Ranking of Variables Found to Influence School Learning*

1. Student characteristics
2. Classroom practices
3. Home and community educational contexts
4. School demographics, culture, climate, policies, and practices
5. Provincial and district governance and organization

Source: Adapted from "Toward a knowledge base of school learning" (Table 3, p. 270), M. C. Wang, G. D. Haertel, & H. J. Walberg, 1993, in *Review of Educational Research*, 63 (3), 249–294.

some complete tasks with ease and others struggle; why some succeed and others fail. It is a measure of differences among students. Some psychologists suggest that there is a general overriding mental ability that can be referred to as a person's intelligence. Others take the view that there are multiple intelligences.

Cultural Views of Intelligence and Student Performance

Beliefs about intelligence vary with culture. When researchers (Okagaki, Sternberg, & Divecha, 1990) asked parents to characterize an intelligent grade one student, Cambodian, Filipino, and Vietnamese families rated noncognitive attributes, such as motivation for school tasks, self-management, and social skills, as more important than cognitive skills, such as problem solving and verbal skills. This conception of intelligence as a strong motivational element was particularly strong for the Filipino and Vietnamese parents. This finding is similar to a study of Japanese and Chinese mothers (Stevenson & Lee, 1990). For these parents, an intelligent child is one who exerts effort in pursuit of goals. This conception of intelligence differs considerably from that of Anglo-American parents, who view intelligence as a function of innate cognitive abilities. Hispanic parents rated cognitive and noncognitive as equally important aspects of intelligence. Of the noncognitive factors, however, social skills were particularly important to their concept of intelligence. Okagaki and Sternberg (1991) found that "the more important parents believe that social skills are to a child being an intelligent individual, the lower children's scores."

Cultural norms influence not only parents' concepts of intelligence but also the types of intellectual abilities that are likely to develop. Anglo-European North American culture tends to emphasize logic-mathematical and linguistic intelligences. The Anang people of Nigeria, in contrast, emphasize musical intelligence. Children raised in the Anang culture are expected to be able to sing hundreds of songs by the age of five. They are also expected to play several instruments and to perform complicated dances (Hetherington & Parke, 1993).

Children's beliefs about their own intelligence can also influence their performance in the classroom. Children who believe that intelligence is incremental—that is, something that can be developed—view their performance in terms of improving their skills and abilities. In contrast, children who believe intelligence is a fixed entity view their performance as a test of ability. When faced with failure, children with an incremental belief tend to adopt a mastery orientation; those who hold entity beliefs tend to feel helpless (Cain & Dweck, 1989; Dweck, 1989). Such beliefs may also be related to observations that some children tend to cope well with criticism of their work, while for other children criticism damages their self-images (Heyman, Dweck, & Cain, 1992).

CONNECTION: Beliefs about intelligence can contribute to one's self concept and self-esteem, as discussed in Chapter 3.

CRITICAL THINKING: Why would a belief that intelligence is incremental rather than fixed yield a different orientation toward mastery?

Three Traditional Theories of Intelligence

The nature of intelligence has been debated since the earliest days of scientific psychology. Francis Galton (a cousin of Charles Darwin) was an early participant in the debate and one of the first to measure intellect directly (Gardner & Hatch, 1989). The result of the debate has been a multitude of definitions of the construct and, by implication, a considerable degree of disagreement among the experts in the field (Hetherington & Parke, 1993).

The debate on the causes, distribution, and measurement of intelligence reached a high point with the publication of the controversial book by Herrnstein and Murray entitled *The Bell Curve* (1994). Since the issues raised in this book continue to be argued, we would encourage you to consult a series of informed papers published in a special issue *of The Alberta Journal of Educational Research* (volume XLI, 3, September, 1995).

Three views of intelligence are presented that illustrate the variety of perspectives that psychologists have traditionally taken. Piaget's view of intelligence is based on his concern with explaining cognitive development. In the course of explaining the way in which cognitive capabilities grow and change, Piaget addressed the construct of intelligence. David Wechsler's view illustrates the general position that intelligence is most usefully considered as a single mental capacity. A third view, J.P. Guilford's multifactor view, represents the school of thought that intelligence is best seen not as a single entity but as a range of separately identifiable factors.

Piaget's Dynamic View. In Piaget's view, a person's intelligence is dynamic—that is, it changes as a person's interaction with the environment changes. Recall Piaget's stages of cognitive development, as discussed in Chapter 2. Each stage defines a person's intelligence. According to Piaget, an infant organizes his or her environment into sensorimotor schemata; he or she is using sensorimotor intelligence to understand the environment. As the infant accommodates and assimilates new experiences, he or she constructs new types of cognitive structures, called preoperational schemata. Development proceeds through concrete operational schemata and formal operational schemata. The type of schemata a person uses defines the type of intelligence a person has. Because schemata change throughout the course of a person's cognitive development, a person's intelligence is dynamic. In Piaget's view, cognitive development is the development of new forms of intelligence.

Piaget's dynamic view suggests that there are dangers in thinking about intelligence as some intellectual "substance"—such as the ability to reason abstractly—that students should acquire in greater quantities as they proceed through school. To use only one yardstick to measure intelligent behaviour is to deny the differences in cognitive capabilities that exist among students at different stages of intellectual development.

Wechsler's Global View. David Wechsler became well known as a developer of intelligence tests for preschool children, school-age children, and adults. Although he died in 1981, one of the most respected and often-used IQ tests for children of ages six to sixteen years is the Wechsler Intelligence Scale for Children, now in its third edition (WISC-III; Wechsler, 1991). The test has also been normed for Canadian children. A number of articles have been published by Canadian psychologists describing the use of the WISC-III for children with learning disabilities (Beal et al. 1996), attention deficit hyperactivity disorder (Schwean & Saklofske, 1998), and intellectually gifted children (Beal, 1995). Currently, the most recently published adult scale, the WAIS-III (Wechsler, 1997) is also being standardized on a sample of Canadian adults (Hildebrand & Saklofske, 1996). From his work, Wechsler developed a global view of intelligence: "Intelligence is the aggregate or global capacity of the individual to act purposefully, to think rationally, and to deal effectively with the environment" (1958, p. 7). Wechsler viewed people's intelligence as an overall ability to deal with the world around them. Wechsler's view, derived as it was from concerns about testing the construct, suggests that a test of spatial ability, a test of mathematical computation, or a test of verbal reasoning may tell us very little about a student's overall ability to deal with the world. Intelligence, from the global view, is more than the sum of its parts.

CONNECTION: Piaget's stages, described in Chapter 2, identify essentially different ways of thinking.

Guilford's Multifactor View. While Wechsler focused his efforts on defining intelligence as a single entity, Guilford worked to establish a definition of intelligence that recognized a range of factors that constituted it. Guilford sought some way of organizing appropriate factors into a framework. The result of his efforts was the "three faces of intellect" model, which organized intellectual capabilities along three dimensions, or faces (Guilford, 1967; see also 1980, 1985).

The first face in Guilford's model describes the types of operations a person performs. An operation is a kind of intellectual activity or process, such as knowing, remembering, making judgments. The second face in Guilford's model is the content of the operation. Content refers to the nature of the information being operated on, such as images, and abstract systems of codes, such as numbers or words. When a person operates on some kind of content, a product results. The information that defines the content is transformed through processing into independent items of information, sets of items that share properties, and ways of organizing information. Guilford's model gives us a way of thinking about what mental operations students perform, what content they operate on, and what mental products they generate.

TRY THIS: Using one kind of operation and one type of content, try to predict what type of product would be generated.

Gardner's Theory of Multiple Intelligences

Piaget, Wechsler, and Guilford represent perspectives that have been part of the debate on intelligence for several decades. In the 1980s, two new intelligence theorists arrived on the scene. The work of Howard Gardner and Robert Sternberg has captured the imagination of many educators. Although there are critical differences between the two formulations, both theorists have caused educators to reexamine the relationship between learning and intelligence.

Gardner's **theory of multiple intelligences** sprang, as many theories do, from discontent. In Gardner's case, the discontent was twofold. First, Gardner's own research in the area of cognitive development (1975, 1979, 1982) ran counter to Piaget's notion that the use and interpretation of various symbol systems were all aspects of one intellectual function. Gardner (and his colleagues) supported the notion that discrete psychological processes are used for linguistic, numerical, pictorial, and other types of symbol systems (Gardner, Howard, & Perkins, 1974; Gardner & Wolf, 1983). The second part of Gardner's discontent came from his observation of the types of symbolization processes that were—and in many cases still are—typical in schools: linguistic symbolization and logic-mathematical symbolization. Although these two forms of symbolization are important for most of the tasks required of students in school and are the symbol systems that underlie most items on intelligence, aptitude, and achievement tests, there are other symbol systems that are important to learning and performance both in and outside of school (Gardner & Hatch, 1989).

EXAMPLE: Think back to Erikson's theory in Chapter 3. How did discontent contribute to his theory of psychosocial development?

As Gardner contemplated the importance of additional symbol systems in human cognition, he realized that he was extending traditional notions of human intelligence. For this reason, Gardner theorized that there are autonomous human intelligences. Thus, Gardner's definition of intelligence is applied to seven different forms of thinking: "the capacity to solve problems or to fashion products that are valued in one or more cultural settings" (Gardner & Hatch, 1989, p. 5). In the Anang culture in Nigeria, for example, the capacity to perform songs is highly valued and is considered a sign of intelligence. Gardner

theory of multiple intelligences Howard Gardner's theory of seven distinct intelligences or talents.

The capacity to use symbol systems, such as language, math, and logic, is a common indicator of intelligence. Defined more broadly, intelligence is the ability to solve culturally valued problems or to create culturally valued products.

REFLECTION: Why should culture be an important aspect of one's view of intelligence? How does your cultural background influence your view of intelligence?

TRY THIS: Using Table 5.2, try to determine how all of the intelligences might manifest themselves in the life of a surgeon. What about the life of a musician? A politician? A teacher?

POINT: This research supports one of the basic assumptions of this book: *Learners are diverse.*

CRITICAL THINKING: According to Gardner, what type(s) of intelligence(s) represents Heath's strengths in the Teacher Chronicle? His weaknesses?

has also established criteria that determine what is and what is not a human intelligence. Of particular significance in Gardner's definition is the recognition of cultural values as an important element in human intelligence(s). We return to the educationally impor-tant connection between culture and intelligence before concluding our examination of intelligence. First, however, we examine the product of Gardner's discontent and subsequent contemplation, his seven intelligences.

The Seven Intelligences. Gardner's seven intelligences are presented in Table 5.2. The core components of each intelligence provide an essential description of the abilities, capacities, and sensibilities of each type of intelligence. The *endstates* are typical occupations associated with each intelligence. Although the endstates can serve as instructive examples, it is important to recognize that real people represent a blend of intelligences. A skilled surgeon, for instance, must possess both the spatial intelligence necessary to recognize the correct point and length of incision as well as the bodily-kinesthetic intelligence needed to wield the scalpel. A religious leader, whose intra- and interpersonal intelligences afford insight into the spiritual nature of humans, also needs the linguistic intelligence to communicate that insight (Gardner & Hatch, 1989).

The theory of multiple intelligences predicts that individuals will differ in their particular profiles of intelligence. Clifford Morris and Raymond LeBlanc (1996) have suggested that both teachers and students are able to recognize different kinds of intelligence. They found a strong agreement between the self-perceived intelligence of students and teacher nominations based on Gardner's seven intelligences. A preschool study illustrates the kinds of data that have been collected in support of the theory of multiple intelligences. The performances of children in ten different activities were assessed. The activities included storytelling, drawing, singing, music perception, creative movement, social analysis, hypothesis testing, assembly, calculation and counting, and number and notational logic. Using statistical comparisons, the twenty children in this study were classified as below average, average,

TABLE 5.2 *Gardner's Seven Intelligences*

Intelligence	Core Components	End States
Logic-mathematical	Logical or numeric patterns; long chains of reasoning	Scientist, Mathematician
Linguistic	Sounds, rhythms, meanings of words; different functions of language	Poet, Journalist
Musical	Rhythms, pitch, timbre; forms of musical expression	Composer, Violinist
Spatial	Visual-spatial relationships; transform perceptions	Navigator, Sculptor
Bodily-kinesthetic	Control of body movements; object manipulation	Dancer, Athlete
Interpersonal	Moods, temperament, motivations, desires of others	Therapist, Salesperson
Intrapersonal	Own feelings, strengths, weaknesses, desires, intelligences	Person with detailed accurate self-knowledge

Source: "Multiple Intelligences Go to School: Educational Implications of the Theory of Multiple Intelligences," H. Gardner & T. Hatch, 1989, *Educational Research, 18* (8), 4–10.

or above average on each activity. Above-average performance was taken as an indication of strength; below-average performance was taken as an indication of weakness. An analysis of the performances indicated that fifteen of the children had a strength in at least one area. Twelve of the children's performances indicated one or more weaknesses. Only one child performed in the average range on all activities—and her performances varied considerably within the average range. The particular strengths and weaknesses revealed in this study were not similar across children, indicating distinct profiles (Gardner & Hatch, 1989).

Gardner's Theory in Practice. Recent efforts by Gardner and his colleagues have focused on the development of appropriate assessments and on instructional materials and activities that support the forms of thinking represented by the seven intelligences. One such effort, called "Project Spectrum," has developed curriculum materials, activities, and assessments that have a student-centred learning focus (cf. Malkus, Feldman, & Gardner, 1988; Krechevsky, 1991; Ramos-Ford & Gardner, 1990). The study of preschool children described in the previous section was part of Project Spectrum.

In Project Spectrum, each activity is designed to tap one or more of the seven intelligences. Project Spectrum classrooms are supplied with materials that invite manipulation and experimentation. As students work and play with the materials, teachers are afforded the opportunity to observe unobtrusively the strengths and interests of students.

The Key School, an elementary school, used the theory of multiple intelligences to design special classes and activities that encouraged students to discover their intellectual strengths and develop the full range of their intelligences (Olson, 1988). Over the course of the school year, each student engaged in a number of projects, which were videotaped. Researchers developed criteria for assessing the videotaped presentations.

TRY THIS: Interview teachers to discover if any are familiar with the theory of multiple intelligences. If they are, ask how the theory has influenced their teaching.

At the junior and senior high school levels, Gardner and his colleagues have collaborated on a project called Arts PROPEL (Armstrong, 1994; Magee & Price, 1992; Wolf, 1989; Zessoules, Wolf, & Gardner, 1988). The project yielded a series of modules called domain projects, which focus students' efforts on exercises and activities in music, creative writing, and the visual arts. The products generated by students, including early drafts or preliminary sketches, are collected in portfolios that are assessed by both teacher and student. This type of assessment allows students to reflect on their own work and on the feedback they receive; the portfolios also provide an opportunity for feedback from external evaluators, which can provide extra incentive for students to do their best work.

Gardner's theory of multiple intelligences is significant for aspiring teachers because it provides an understanding of the variety of talents that students might bring to the classroom, talents that may or may not be seen easily in the context of traditional school learning. Consider the cases presented in Table 5.3. Gardner studied the highly accomplished people portrayed in the table—some would call them geniuses—in an attempt to discover the connection between their intelligences and creativity. These cases of exceptional creativity are taken by Gardner and other proponents to be evidence in support of the theory of multiple intelligences.

TABLE 5.3 *Creativity and Success in School*

Name	Childhood Characteristics	Degree of School Success
Sigmund Freud	Avid reader, articulate, self-learner, well-behaved	Very high
Albert Einstein	Spoke late, loner, loved to build and manipulate objects, usually quiet but capable of tantrums and disruptive behaviour	Low in early grades, High in middle and later grades
Pablo Picasso	Loved to observe people and patterns, learned to read and write with difficulty, suffered in arithmetic, school-phobic, socially dependent on father, cheating	Very low
Igor Stravinsky	Privileged life-style, surrounded by adult intellectuals, early interests in painting and theatre, preferred improvisation on the piano, disinterested in formal schooling, self-learner	Low
T.S. Eliot	Affluent family of considerable accomplishment in religion and education, sensitive, observant, when very young generated sounds —not words—in the rhythm of sentences, fascinated by sensory impressions	Very High
Martha Graham	Mother was strict, daily prayers, church; father entertained Martha by singing; close to her father who caught her in lies by reading her body language; quiet but respected by classmates	High
Mohandas Gandhi	Born into a family with high ethical and moral standards, advised and mediated adult conflicts, pondered social and ethical issues of everyday life, not physically robust	Average

Source: Creating minds: An anatomy of creativity seen through the lives of Freud, Einstein, Picasso, Stravinsky, Eliot, Graham, and Gandhi, H. Gardner, 1995, New York: Basic Books.

For teachers, an important aspect of the theory of multiple intelligences is the connection between intelligence and thinking. The various types of intelligence define forms of thinking. The way a person thinks and the types of questions, problems, and issues about which a person thinks are, perhaps, the most defining feature of that person. Whether a child grows up to be a composer, physician, mechanic, engineer, or teacher; whether a child becomes an environmental advocate, patron of the arts, volunteer firefighter, community fundraiser, or president of the local PTA depends greatly on what occupies his or her thinking and how he or she thinks.

Teachers need to find ways of encouraging the use of all kinds of intelligences, not just the linguistic and logic-mathematical intelligences that are tapped by typical academic tasks. How can teachers tap the talents that are less obviously related to academic learning? How can they facilitate learning with students in whom such talents are predominant? How can bodily-kinesthetic, inter-, or intrapersonal intelligences, for example, be used to teach abstract concepts in math or science? The following ideas are based on lessons developed by Thomas Armstrong (1994).

REFLECTION: Think about your own aspirations when you were a child. How do you think they may have influenced your thinking and learning in school?

Here's How

Here's How To Engage Multiple Intelligences in Teaching Math and Science Concepts

- When teaching multiplication tables (for the fours, let's say), have students count to forty. Have students stand or clap on every fourth number. [bodily-kinesthetic intelligence]
- When teaching the function of an unknown x in algebraic equations, have students act out an equation. For example, using the equation $4x - 3 = 9$, arrange a group of four students next to a student wearing a mask to represent the unknown x. Then place a student representing subtraction, a group of three students, one student representing equals, and a group of nine students on the right side of the equation. As the class takes steps to solve the equation, students in the equation leave or join groups in an effort to isolate x and thus determine x's value. [interpersonal, bodily-kinesthetic]
- The concept of an algebraic unknown could also be addressed by asking students to reflect on the mysteries—the unknown x's—in their own lives and to discuss how they solve for x when handling personal issues. [intrapersonal]
- When teaching Boyle's law (when mass and temperature of a gas are fixed, pressure is inversely related to volume) in a high school physics class, have some students act as individual molecules of air. The molecule students move at a constant rate (temperature). Other students confine the molecules in a corner of the room by stretching a string that becomes one boundary of the container. The students holding the string begin to move toward the corner (reducing volume). As the volume decreases, the molecules will begin bumping into each other (pressure) more frequently. [interpersonal, bodily-kinesthetic]
- Boyle's law could also be addressed by having students discuss how they feel when they are under lots of pressure in their personal lives. Have them discuss the sense of personal space they feel when under pressure and when they feel very little pressure. [intrapersonal]

How do you accommodate students' individual differences in the ways they learn best?

I teach a mixed-ability grade five class. I have to be on my toes to keep the interest of such a diverse group. I have begun some of my lessons by running into class wearing my jogging suit and a bronze medal. My entrance caught their attention. The students' reading lessons at the time were about sports figures; they were eager to bring in their own trophies and medals to share with the rest of the class. It seemed that from then on, I had created an environment in which they were much more willing to learn.

Another activity I have used is having students read how-to books and then bring in homemade projects based on their readings. Their projects have included ecology boxes, stationery, and doll houses. The students are proud of their accomplishments, and we display them in the main hall of the school so other students can enjoy them as well.

I have also asked students to complete a unique kind of book report: a hanging mobile! I am usually amazed at the creativity they display in these assignments. One child read the mystery, *Ten Little Indians*. His report consisted of a bow from which he suspended each of the characters from the story.

English grammar can be taught in a multisensory way. For example, my students were having difficulty with complex sentences. I made signs that read "main clause" and "conjunction" and "subordinating clause." Then I chose three students and made up an elaborate story about the "main clause" being so independent. Each student became a part of the sentence through a comical identity. Through the hilarity, the students were able to learn and enjoy English grammar.

All ages benefit from experience rather than lecturing. In the elementary years, the subjects taught are more readily learned and accepted when creative activity accompanies the lesson. Hands-on teaching also creates a classroom with fewer behaviour problems.

DIANNE BAUMAN
Elementary School Teacher

Your Insights

What is meant by teaching in a multisensory way? How did this teacher use humour and hands-on activities to help all her students reach their full potential in her class regardless of their abilities?

Sternberg's Triarchic Theory of Intelligence

Gardner's theory of multiple intelligences is important for teachers because the theory helps us recognize that the talents students bring to our classrooms come in a variety of forms. Although this is a valid reason for examining Gardner's theory, it has also been raised as a criticism. Robert Sternberg, who joins Gardner as a major contemporary figure in the study of intelligence, argues that Gardner's theory of intelligences is, in reality, a theory of talents (Sternberg, 1989). To distinguish talent from intelligence, Sternberg provides an illustrative comparison between a person who is tone-deaf, and thus lacks some aspects of musical talent, and a person who lacks the cognitive ability to plan ahead. The former is capable of functioning quite well in the world—many of us have done it for years; the latter might very well require substantial assistance or resident care to carry out everyday functions. "Intelligence is general: without it we cannot function independently. Talents, however, are specialized" (Sternberg, 1989, p. 42).

Sternberg's approach to the study of intelligence focuses on how it functions in everyday life. He views intelligence as a kind of mental self-management. Mental self-management has three elements that form the basis of his formal definition of intelligence. Sternberg's definition is that intelligence is "purposive adaptation to, selection of, and shaping of real-world environments relevant to one's life and abilities" (Sternberg, 1989, p. 65).

CRITICAL THINKING: What would be the difference between a theory of intelligence and a theory of talent? How could you test Gardner's theory to determine if Sternberg is correct?

Sternberg identified three kinds of intelligence: componential, experiential, and contextual, hence the name, triarchic ("ruled by three") theory. The triarchic theory is presented in Figure 5.1.

Componential Intelligence. **Componential intelligence** identifies the mental components of what we call intelligent behaviour. Components are mental processes that underlie behaviour and are classified by the function they serve. *Metacomponents* are processes that identify problems, determine goals, plan strategies, and monitor and evaluate performance. *Performance components* are processes that are used to execute the plans or to carry out the tasks that have been selected. *Knowledge acquisition components* are the processes by which new learning occurs (Sternberg, 1996).

To illustrate componential intelligence, consider a student—perhaps this happened to you as well—who is working on a word problem in science or math. The student reads the problem to determine its nature, how to solve it, what information is required, and what information is irrelevant. This aspect of problem identification and planning is a metacomponent function. The student then begins carrying out the appropriate calculations, a function of performance components, to solve the problem. Along the way, the student discovers that there is a calculation needed that he or she does not know how to perform. This

CONNECTION: How do the metacomponents described here relate to the notion of metacognition described in Chapter 2?

componential intelligence Part of Sternberg's theory of intelligence, referring to a person's ability to reason abstractly, process information, and determine the kind and sequence of operations required for a task or problem.

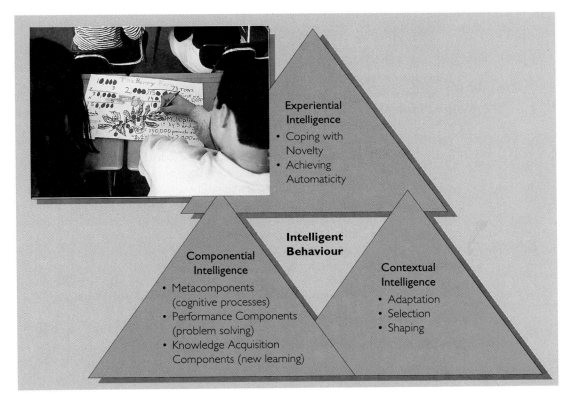

FIGURE 5.1
Sternberg's Triarchic Theory of Intelligence

Source: Based on *The Triarchic Mind: A New Theory of Human Intelligence*, R.J. Sternberg, 1989, New York: Penguin Books.

discovery halts work on the problem and serves as feedback to the metacomponents. This feedback allows the metacomponents to determine that what is required is to learn the procedure needed to continue work on the problem. The new procedure is learned (through knowledge acquisition components) and is performed (through performance components) as the student continues toward the goal of solving the problem.

Experiential Intelligence.   The second part in the triarchic arrangement is experiential intelligence. **Experiential intelligence** explains how intelligence is related to novel tasks or new ideas in one's environment. Learners who exhibit a high degree of experiential intelligence are those who deal effectively with novel situations. This type of intelligence allows a student to analyze new tasks and to access knowledge and skills that will allow completion of the task. After several encounters with a new task or problem, those high in experiential intelligence will have automated the procedures required to complete the task. If a set of procedures becomes automatic, those procedures can be carried out with little or no effort which, in turn, frees cognitive resources for other activities. An individual with little experiential intelligence is less capable of "automating" procedures and must, therefore, reason through a particular kind of problem each time it is encountered.

Contextual Intelligence.   **Contextual intelligence** is reflected in one's ability to adapt, select, or shape one's environment to optimize one's opportunities. An implication of this type of intelligence is that measuring it requires judgments of the quality of one's existence within his or her environment. Sternberg (1986) provides a cross-cultural example to illustrate what he means by contextual intelligence and why he feels that the measurement of intelligence must be sensitive to the context in which it occurs.

Suppose that a traditional intelligence test developed in North America were used to assess the intelligence of an African Pygmy. The type of intelligence tapped by North American tests is not likely to be the type of intelligence that allows a Pygmy to survive and flourish in his or her everyday environment. While the North American tests used in this hypothetical situation might measure something, it would not be contextual intelligence. The test would serve little purpose unless, of course, the Pygmy had as a goal adapting to North American culture.

If adaptation to an environment is a form of intelligent behaviour, consider the intelligence displayed by the mentally retarded student who was incapable of telling time. The student spent part of each day in a work program away from the school. Because the student had to catch a bus back to school, it was important that he keep track of the time. Every day, the teacher wondered if the student would miss the bus back to school, but he never did. The teacher discovered that at work the student wore a watch, something he never did at school. More important, the watch was broken. Whenever the student needed to know the time he would look at his watch and then say to someone, "Excuse me, but my watch is broken. Could you tell me the time, please?" His practice of putting on a nonfunctional watch on arriving at the work program was an adaptation to his new environment, and a rather ingenious one at that.

Ingenious adaptations are contextually intelligent behaviours. Students—and adults in the work force—who can't read but find ways to get by demonstrate contextual intelligence. Students who find shortcuts or exploit loopholes to avoid classroom work also demonstrate this type of intelligence.

TRY THIS: Observe children or adolescents solving problems. After observing, interview the students to see if you can document their use of componential intelligence.

TRY THIS: Find difficult historical situations for your students to study. Have your students brainstorm ways of adapting, selecting, and shaping the environments to improve the situations.

experiential intelligence
Part of Sternberg's theory of intelligence, describing a person's capacity to deal with novel tasks or new ideas and to combine unrelated facts.

contextual intelligence
Part of Sternberg's theory of intelligence, relating to one's ability to adapt, select, or shape one's environment to optimize one's opportunities.

People who exhibit contextual intelligence may not always adapt to an environment; sometimes the most intelligent move is to select an environment. Selection is a second form of contextual intelligence that is related to an individual's ability to find an appropriate environment. Consider, for example, those who chose to leave or deselect the environment of Nazi Germany rather than to remain and adapt to it. Another example of selection comes from a book entitled *Whatever Happened to the Quiz Kids* (Feldman, 1982). The Quiz Kids, who all had very high IQ scores, appeared on radio and television in the 1940s and 1950s. A follow-up study of the Quiz Kids found that only those who found work that interested them and who persevered in that field had successful careers. The less successful Quiz Kids were unable to find a niche for themselves and, despite their high IQs, exhibited little contextual intelligence.

A third form of contextual intelligence is shaping. There are times when adapting to an environment or selecting a new environment is not possible. In such instances, contextual intelligence can still be used to shape or change the environment rather than the person. Oskar Schindler, whose story was portrayed in the movie *Schindler's List*, shaped his environment in Nazi Germany rather than adapt to or deselect it. Schindler was an industrialist who employed Jewish workers and bribed Nazi officials, thus saving many Jewish people from the death camps during the Holocaust. Shaping environments occurs in many less dramatic or historically significant contexts as well. A person whose talents are unrecognized or undervalued by a company might propose a new position or division that would match more closely his or her strengths.

Recent research and theory on the nature of human intelligence, particularly the work of Howard Gardner and Robert Sternberg, have broadened the concept of intelligence from the traditional views. The new views have emphasized that intelligence needs to be understood in context, including the context provided by cultural norms. The notions of multiple intelligences and multiple components of intelligence suggest that there are different ways in which students can exhibit intelligent behaviour (Bransford, Goldman, & Vye, 1991). If this is so, teachers and parents should look for and acknowledge students' strengths—not just in the traditional academic areas, but in other areas as well. Teachers can also help students broaden their views of what intelligent behaviour is. If students who have not experienced success on traditional academic tasks can learn to see themselves as intelligent, their self-esteem should be improved. As we learned from Chapter 3, enhancement of a student's self-esteem is critical to facilitating psychological growth. Intelligence is one characteristic that contributes to variability in classrooms. Another source of variability is the way students prefer to think.

REFLECTION: What ingenious adaptations have you displayed in order to disguise a disability?

CRITICAL THINKING: What other historical figures have demonstrated contextual intelligence by shaping their own environments?

TRY THIS: Interview a teacher to discover the methods by which he or she determines the strengths and weaknesses of students.

A Canadian Contribution: The PASS Model and PREP Program by J.P. Das

Dr. J.P. Das, University of Alberta, and his colleagues including John Kirby (Queen's University), the late Ron Jarman (University of British Columbia), and Jack Naglieri (Ohio State University), have developed a cognitive functioning model comprising Planning, Attention, Simultaneous, Successive (PASS) processing. The PASS model is based on cognitive psychology research and the model of brain functioning proposed by A.R. Luria, a Soviet neuropsychologist. Attentional processes depend on an appropriate level of arousal. Two broad classes of attention can then be obtained: selective attention (focusing on relevant stimuli and disregarding extraneous stimuli) and divided attention (performing several tasks without losing efficiency). Simultaneous and successive processing are responsible for taking in, processing, and retaining information from the external world. Simultaneous processing is an integrative process which categorizes stimuli into groups. Successive processing is also integrative; however, stimuli are organized temporally and serially. Planning processes provide the means for analyzing cognitive activity and developing, assessing, and modifying problem-solving strategies. These planning processes "provide the individual with the means to employ simultaneous and successive processes for tasks that are the focus of attention" (Das, Naglieri, & Kirby, 1994, p. 27). In order to assess individual PASS processes, tasks that require specific processes regardless of content or modality are used (Das et al., 1994).

Dr. J.P. Das, together with Jack Naglieri, recently developed a comprehensive test to measure the PASS processes. The Das-Naglieri Cognitive Assessment System (Naglieri & Das, 1997), as well as the various earlier versions of the individual subtests that are included in this new instrument, have been used in research projects with many different groups of children, including those who are developmentally delayed and learning disabled. An example of one such study was published by Saklofske and Schwean (1993) from the University of Saskatchewan. In order to examine the short-term effects of methylphenidate (Ritalin) in the treatment of children with Attention Deficit Hyperactivity Disorder (ADHD), an experimental version of the CAS was administered to twenty-nine children with ADHD in a double-blind study. There was evidence to suggest that Ritalin did enhance performance on selected simultaneous and planning tasks, but had little or no effect on tests measuring attention and sequential processes. The PASS model and CAS hold considerable promise for furthering our understanding of cognitive processes.

A major criticism of other models and tests of intelligence is that they lack prescriptive validity. In other words, knowing that a child scores average on a traditional IQ test, but is having difficulties in mathematics and spelling, does not help the teacher develop an intervention or remediation program. Das argues that the PASS model is useful not only for describing cognitive processes but also for developing appropriate programs.

PREP is a remediation program based on the PASS model. The purpose of PREP is to "induce successive or simultaneous processing while involving the training of planning and promoting selective attention" (Das, Naglieri, & Kirby, 1994, p. 172). The program focuses on remedial training in reading, spelling, and comprehension. Remediation tasks consist of global processing (internalization of strategies) and content bridging (strategies relevant to reading and spelling) forms (Das, 1993). Student progress is monitored through the use of pre- and post-tests and instructors' qualitative observations. PREP is designed for administration to one or two students at one time and takes approximately fifteen to twenty hours to complete.

Several studies have examined the usefulness of PREP with students who are learning disabled. L.W. Krywaniuk at the University of Alberta conducted a study with low-achieving Aboriginal students. Students completed remedial instruction tasks which emphasized successive processing. Research results indicated that students improved in successive processing and were able to transfer these skills to nontaught successive processing tasks as well as reading tasks. D. Kaufman, also from the University of Alberta, implemented a training program which emphasized successive processing tasks. Both above-average and below-average students participated in the program. The results were similar to Krywaniuk's in that student improvement in successive processing tasks and skill transference to other subjects occurred. A study was conducted by Parmenter in which students who were educable mentally handicapped (EMH) were trained on four successive processing tasks selected from the Krywaniuk and Kaufman studies. After the training sessions were completed, the students were unable to demonstrate transfer to either new successive or simultaneous processing tasks or reading tasks. According to Parmenter, these students continued to use their inefficient strategies rather than adopting the more effective strategies. These and other studies together with a full description of both the PASS model and PREP are included in the book *Assessment of Cognitive Processes* by Das et al. (1994). As well, an overview of the DNCAS by Denise Hildebrand has been published in the *Canadian Journal of School Psychology* (1998).

How Do Students Vary in the Ways They Think and Learn?

Watch your classmates as they discuss a question, read their textbooks, listen to a presentation, or prepare a lesson plan. How do they engage in these activities? What are the differences in preparation? Do their study outlines look different? Do some incorporate drawings? Are some of the textbooks read by your colleagues highlighted heavily? Do some of your fellow learners ask a lot of questions in discussion? offer lots of suggestions? speak only infrequently? Do they persist in the face of difficult problems? Do some have difficulty getting organized on projects? Any group of students, including the groups you will teach, represents a variety of dispositions and preferences for thinking and learning.

Thinking and Learning Dispositions

Thinking is central to the teaching-learning process and is, therefore, a consistently recurring theme in this book. In this section, we examine thinking as a source of individual variability. There are at least two ways that thinking varies among students. The first is thinking skills. Some students think better than others because they have better thinking skills. The development of thinking skills was addressed in our examination of cognitive development in Chapter 2 and will be addressed further in Chapters 7, 11, 12, and 13. The second way in which thinking varies among students—and the one on which we focus in this section—is in the ways students are disposed to think. **Thinking dispositions** are mental habits, inclinations, or "abiding tendencies in thinking behaviour exhibited over time and across diverse thinking situations" (Tishman, Perkins, & Jay, 1995, p. 37).

People have all kinds of behavioural inclinations or dispositions. Some people are inclined to eat too much, to be kind, to rise early, or to sleep late. People also are disposed to think in various ways. Some people think by asking lots of questions, some are persistent when they think about a problem, some routinely take multiple perspectives. As we saw in the last chapter, one's cultural background and home environment influence what behaviours are considered appropriate and, therefore, valued. For instance, a student raised in a home where family members routinely consider points of view other than their own is likely to develop that disposition in his or her own thinking. Likewise, a student who is raised in a family that dismisses as wrong all viewpoints that differ from those of the family will likely be close-minded in his or her thinking.

REFLECTION: Did you see any evidence in the Teacher Chronicle that Heath might have been influenced by his mother's thinking? If so, how?

thinking dispositions
Mental habits, inclinations, or tendencies in thinking behaviour exhibited over time and across diverse thinking situations.

It would be possible, of course, to speculate endlessly on different ways in which people are disposed to think. Some dispositions, however, are obstacles to learning. A student who is inclined to ignore instructions, for example, is not likely to become a competent problem solver.

Rather than speculating on all of the thinking dispositions that might exist, Shari Tishman and her colleagues (1995) have focused on identifying dispositions that foster learning. Tishman and her colleagues suggest that good learners tend to exhibit curiosity, flexibility, precision, organization, and patience in their thinking. To understand the dispositions in context, assume that a grade seven class has been challenged by their teacher as follows: "Water is a precious natural resource. As good citizens, we have a responsibility to conserve it. What is our class going to do to conserve water? This is not a paper assignment. We are going to take some actions that conserve water. Now, what are we going to do?"

For each disposition, general descriptions are followed by examples (in italics) of thinking dispositions that would contribute to solving the water conservation problem.

TRY THIS: Give this idea to a teacher. See if the teacher is willing to try it in his or her classroom and if you can observe.

- Curiosity: Curious thinkers ask questions, look for additional information, probe, and reflect. *We should find out if there are other groups who have taken steps to conserve water and find out what they did. Maybe we could get some stuff from the Water Department or even interview some of their experts.*

- Flexibility: Flexible thinkers take alternative points of views, venture new ideas, are open-minded and playful. *Maybe we should divide into teams and let each team brainstorm a bunch of ideas. One of the things we might want to think about is whether water is the best resource to conserve.*

- Precision: Precise thinkers seek clarity, are thorough, and take care to avoid errors. *Do we have to think of things that only we can do, or can we teach other people to help conserve? If we are going to teach others, we had better try out our ideas on ourselves first.*

- Organization: Organized thinkers are orderly and logical, they plan ahead, and work methodically. *I think we should figure out how much water we need to conserve and then think about how we are going to measure water that won't be used. That will take some thought.*

- Patience: Patient thinkers are willing to give themselves time to reason and are persistent in their efforts. *This should be a big project. I think we should do it, but if we are really going to do this, let's make sure we will have enough time each week to work on it* (cf. Tishman et al., 1995).

Tishman and her colleagues do not claim that this is an exhaustive list; other positive dispositions surely exist and there are other descriptions of learning styles. For example, Dr. Robert Sternberg, who developed the Triarchic Theory of Intelligence described earlier in this chapter, has also developed an interesting description of thinking styles which he defines as the personal way in which someone uses his or her intelligence. Grigorenko and Sternberg (1995) contend that this theory of thinking styles and "mental self government" has important applications in education, ranging from addressing the potential for bias in the evaluation of student learning to helping teachers to understand the ways in which students use their intelligence and helping students to develop and manage their own intelligence. A succinct overview of Sternberg's (1998) theory may be found in the *Canadian Journal of School Psychology.*

However, the description provided by Tishman may be considered to be the "bottom-line" dispositions that support classroom learning. If curiosity, flexibility, precision, organization, and patience are benchmarks, then they can be used to gauge the degree to which a student is disposed to good thinking. How can the benchmark dispositions be used by a teacher to determine variability among the individuals in his or her classroom?

Here's How

Here's How To Gauge the Thinking Dispositions of Students

- Give students opportunities to display their thinking dispositions. This means setting up tasks, such as the water conservation challenge, that require students to initiate investigations, make decisions, and solve problems. We have a colleague, for example, who challenges his students to find the best chili recipe in the world (Shank, 1995).

- Have students document their own thinking. As students work on the thinking challenges you give them, have them stop from time to time to talk about, write about, or otherwise record how they are thinking. Our colleague has students keep a journal of their investigations of the best chili recipe in the world. The younger students' thinking might be documented through checklists or interviews that determine, for example, what questions students have asked, their attempts to clarify a problem, or their persistence (Woditsch & Schmittroth, 1991).

- Ask students to critique demonstrations of your thinking. Set up a thinking challenge for yourself and then perform a thinking scene for your students. Your thinking scene could take place in the library, at a computer, or with other thinkers. First, display poor thinking dispositions: Make guesses instead of asking questions, take only one point of view, give up on difficult parts. Then, using the same challenge, act the scene again, but this time display the benchmark dispositions. Ask students to identify the differences between the first and second scenes. Use students' responses—which could be either written or oral—to gauge thinking dispositions (see Woditsch & Schmittroth, 1991).

- After small group or class discussions, ask students to identify ways in which the group's thinking might be improved in future discussions. Have students focus on the group's thinking processes rather than on any specific product of the discussion. Monitor the discussion to ensure that all students have a chance to evaluate thinking processes and that, as a consequence, you have a chance to note those students who do and do not display the dispositional benchmarks suggested by Tishman et al.

- Allow for a variety of observations over a reasonable period of time. Keep in mind that thinking dispositions are "abiding tendencies in thinking behaviour exhibited over time and across diverse thinking situations" (Tishman et al., 1995, p. 37). Judgments made on the basis of one observation may or may not represent a student's tendencies.

Learning Styles and Cultural Differences

The work on thinking dispositions reported here builds on several decades of what is referred to as "learning styles" research. However, the bottom-line thinking dispositions account well for the findings of this earlier research. For example, Guilford's (1967) three faces of intellect model suggests a distinction between convergent and divergent styles. Convergent thinkers tend to react to instructional materials in conventional ways. Divergent thinkers tend to respond in unconventional or idiosyncratic ways. This distinction can be understood in terms of the flexibility disposition presented earlier. Thinking flexibly (including divergently) contributes to learning.

CRITICAL THINKING: Before reading ahead, speculate as to why the authors are accounting for the findings of learning styles research using thinking dispositions.

Another example of earlier research on learning styles distinguishes impulsive or reflective styles of learning (Kagan, 1964a, 1964b). Impulsive students tend to answer questions quickly; reflective students take their time, preferring to evaluate alternative answers. Reflective students are more concerned with being accurate than with being fast. From the perspective of thinking dispositions, these learning styles can be interpreted in terms of the bottom-line dispositions of patience and curiosity. These dispositions indicate that reflectivity supports learning to a greater extent than impulsivity.

TRY THIS: Ask practising teachers why it is dangerous to categorize students.

Dispositional differences among students vary. The thinking dispositions postulated by Tishman and her colleagues (1995) have an advantage over earlier research on learning styles, which attempted to categorize and test for specific learning styles (Dunn, Beaudry, & Klavas, 1989). Although the reliability and validity of many of these tests have been questioned, the tests have been used to categorize students. Once learners were categorized, specialized instructional programs were developed for learners in the various categories. Programs were developed that focused on visual styles, auditory styles, and left-brain and right-brain styles. There is a danger in this approach to the teaching-learning process:

> People are different, and it is good practice to recognize and accommodate individual differences. It is also good practice to present information in a variety of ways through more than one modality, but it is not wise to categorize learners and prescribe methods solely on the basis of tests … The idea of learning styles is appealing, but a critical examination of this approach should cause educators to be skeptical (Snider, 1990, p. 53).

The danger of categorizing students is further complicated by some research findings suggesting that there are learning-style differences among various groups of people. Some researchers have investigated whether a person's cultural or ethnic heritage might predict one's learning style. For example, some researchers have identified learning-style differences between Aboriginal Canadians and non-Aboriginals.

Learning Styles of Canadian Aboriginal Children. The Canadian First Nations (or Aboriginal) population is composed of 596 bands located on 2284 reserves and Crown land (Norris, 1990). Eleven languages and some fifty to seventy dialects are spoken. In addition, statistics vary regarding the percentage of Native people residing on reserves, ranging from 25 percent to 59 percent of the Native population (Census Canada, 1986). Consequently, Murdoch (1988) reminds us of the dangers of viewing any group of people as being similar in all/most ways. He suggests that while Canadian Cree children, for example, may have a visual-spatial orientation, they are not a homogeneous people, with five dialects of Cree spoken in Canada.

An analysis of the interrelationship among culture, language, and cognition in Aboriginal Canadian children is discussed by Sally Greenough-Olson of Saskatoon in her Master's thesis entitled "The influence of language on non-verbal intelligence test performance of Saskatchewan Aboriginal children" (1993). A paper presented by J. More at the World Conference of Indigenous Peoples Education (1987) held in Vancouver reinforces this argument. He cautions that an overemphasis on learning style differences between Aboriginal and non-Aboriginal students may lead to new forms of inaccurate labelling and stereotyping of students. At the same time, he suggests that we can increase our understanding of what educational processes and opportunities are appropriate by considering this research. While noting important cultural and linguistic differences between Aboriginal students, More summarizes the research literature as follows:

a) higher frequency and relative strength in global processing on both verbal and non-verbal tasks;

b) relative strength in simultaneous processing, but a possibility that sequential processing skills develop more slowly than simultaneous skills because they are not used in primary grades;

c) the possibility of using strengths in simultaneous processing to develop sequential processing;

d) higher frequency and relative strength among Aboriginal students in using imagery and relative weakness in verbal coding and understanding;

e) higher frequency and relative strength in processing visual/spatial information;

f) lower frequency and relative weakness in verbal coding and understanding; and

g) reflective more than impulsive (watch-then-do rather than trial-and-error) (More, 1987, p. 8).

John Berry of Queen's University is one of the most prolific and informed scholars on cross-cultural psychology. Canadian teachers are urged to consult his many articles and books. With respect to fully understanding the relationship between cognition, learning, and culture, Berry states:

> The cross-cultural study of cognitive development then, must attend to three issues. One is the nature of the ecological and cultural context in which cognitive development takes place. A second is the kind of cognitive abilities which are developed in that context. And a third is the nature of the relationships which may exist between the cultural context and cognitive development (Berry, 1979, p. 395).

Studies of learning-style differences among groups have been criticized for at least two reasons. First, as mentioned earlier, the tests used to determine a person's learning style have questionable value. Second, research that stereotypes people fosters instructional practice that reinforces stereotypes rather than addressing the learning needs of each individual (Gordon, 1991; Yee, 1992).

Categorizing learners by ethnic group ignores differences that exist among individuals within that group. Likewise, categorizing individuals according to tests of learning style ignores the different ways an individual can think. The bottom-line thinking dispositions are not categories into which students are sorted. They are standards of thinking that support learning. Individuals may differ in regard to which dispositions they use, but knowledge of such differences fosters teaching that addresses each learner's needs.

CONNECTION: Do you think that Heath, in the Teacher Chronicle, will be categorized? How might that influence his progress in school?

How Do Students Vary in Abilities and Disabilities?

CONNECTION: Recall the discussion of students at risk in Chapter 3.

The needs of individual students are a function of their life circumstances and their abilities. Some students need special attention because they are raised in difficult circumstances; other students need special attention because they have exceptional abilities. In the Teacher Chronicle at the beginning of this chapter, Heath has a very high IQ, and he comes from a family that has at least one parent who is a professional and also interested enough to come to school for a meeting. If we stop there, Heath's profile would suggest that he should do well in school. However, the events in the Teacher Chronicle also allow inferences about Heath's behaviour and emotions that suggest he may be at risk of performing or behaving poorly in school.

Exceptional Learners

The needs of some students require special accommodations in the classroom. Special needs students—called **exceptional learners**—are either impaired by mental retardation, learning disabilities, emotional/behavioural disorders, communication disorders, hearing loss, visual impairment, physical disabilities, or they are gifted. In both cases, such students require special instruction and services to reach their full potential (Hallahan & Kauffman, 1994). Estimating the prevalence or total number of children presenting with exceptionalities in the Canadian population is difficult because of varying definitions and descriptions of disabilities, disparate data collection methods, and the high co-occurrence of disorders amongst children. Recent statistics suggest that approximately 15.5 percent of Canadian children present with some kind of disability (Winzer, 1996). Many children with disabilities also have some kind of learning disability (25 percent). Approximately 12 percent of the group have behavioural/emotional difficulties; 10 percent are cognitively challenged. Approximately 26 percent of students with disabilities participate in some kind of special education program: special school, special class within a regular school, or individualized program (Oderkirk, 1993).

exceptional learners
Learners who have special learning needs and who require special instruction.

Flynn, Kelly, and Janzen (1994) found, however, that students in the College of Education at the University of Saskatchewan estimated the prevalence of learning disabilities to be four times higher than upper limits established by experts. Other studies have found similar results.

Programs designed to help students at risk of school failure because of their life circumstances include early intervention, prevention, and compensatory education. In addition, many schools offer an increasingly comprehensive array of social services for students and their families.

Insights on Successful Practice

In your experience, what strategies work best for reinforcing self-esteem in students with disabilities?

My interactions with exceptional children have informed me that many of these youngsters exhibit low self-esteem. Their words capture their despair, lack of confidence, and loss of hope, with messages such as "I'm stupid," "I always do things wrong," "I'm so ugly, I was born with half a brain" being common. Others do not express their low self-esteem as directly. Instead, it can be inferred from the coping strategies they use to manage stress, frustration, and failure; they rely on coping behaviours that are counterproductive and that actually exacerbate their difficulties. Behaviours such as quitting, avoiding, cheating, clowning, bullying, denying, or making excuses often signal that the child is feeling vulnerable and is desperately trying to escape from a situation that he or she feels will lead to failure.

In working with these children, we must not lose sight of the courage and many strengths they possess. We must actively identify and reinforce each child's "islands of competence" for if we do not, we will continue to have children burdened by intense feelings of inadequacy. We must make every effort to establish realistic expectations and goals and to make appropriate accommodations based on the unique qualities of each child. To instill a sense of ownership and pride, we must provide all children with ample opportunities for assuming responsibilities, especially those that help them to feel they are making a contribution to their home, school, and/or community environments. To enhance self-efficacy, we must create opportunities to learn the skills necessary for making choices and solving problems, as well as opportunities to apply and refine these skills.

Self-esteem is nurtured when we communicate realistic appreciation and encouragement to exceptional children. Words and actions that help children to feel genuinely special are energizing and demonstrate to children that there are those who accept and believe in them. Most of all, self-esteem and self-efficacy are promoted through supportive relationships. It is essential that each student develop a close and nurturing relationship with at least one caring adult. Students need to feel that there is someone within the school whom they know, to whom they can turn, and who will act as an advocate for them.

ADAPTED FROM ROBERT B. BROOKS (IN PRESS)

Your Insights

Who are students at risk? What special educational needs might these students have? What are some other strategies you might use in your classroom to increase the academic success of students at risk?

The special needs of exceptional students have received formal recognition in Canada. Although there is no federal legislation, aside from the Declaration of Human Rights, outlining or guaranteeing the rights of children with exceptionalities, each of the provinces is responsible for passing legislation and developing policies pertaining to the education of children within its respective jurisdiction (Winzer, 1995). In Ontario, for example, provincial legislation adopted in 1980 requires that school divisions provide services to students with disabilities. Within this legislation, principles such as universal access, financial responsibility of the province for the education of exceptional students, the appeal process, and ongoing assessment, diagnosis, and programming are outlined (Winzer, 1995).

Most types of exceptionality stem from a disability. The terms *disability* and *handicap* are often used interchangeably in everyday language. Even so, the terms are distinctive, and the distinction is important for teachers to understand. "A **disability** is an inability to do something, a diminished capacity to perform in a specific way. A **handicap,** on the other hand, is a disadvantage imposed on an

disability A diminished capacity to perform in a specific way.

handicap A disadvantage imposed on an individual.

TRY THIS: Contact your local school district, and inquire about their services for students with disabilities.

REFLECTION: Did you ever experience a time when a disability became a handicap? What were the circumstances? How did you handle it? How did you feel about it?

CONNECTION: Think back to Lickona's model for moral education in Chapter 3. In the context of that model, how is diversity in a classroom an opportunity for learning?

TRY THIS: Consider creating an Ethnic Feelings Book for your students during practice teaching. Seek the advice of your cooperating teacher and your supervisor.

individual. A disability may or may not be a handicap, depending on the circumstances" (Hallahan & Kauffman, 1994, p. 6, emphasis added). In your classroom, you will encounter students who are disabled in some way. Their disabilities may or may not be handicaps, depending on the accommodations you make in your classroom.

Exceptionality and Diversity

Understanding the impact of cultural diversity is especially important for teachers of exceptional students because of sociological concerns. Although culturally diverse groups are represented in all areas of exceptionality, a disproportionate number of some minorities may be represented in special education and remedial settings. This may be due to a variety of factors such as assessment and placement procedures in the school, biased testing, biased expectations or attitudes of teachers and school personnel, and misunderstanding of a student's culture and language (Winzer, 1996).

Cultural diversity can be viewed as a strength in a classroom, as an expanded opportunity for learning (cf. Banks, 1994). Research on cooperative learning, for example, shows that heterogeneous groups achieve better than homogeneous groups (Johnson & Johnson, 1994). Heterogeneity provides a richer source of experience to a learning group than homogeneity, in which every member of the group brings a similar background and experiences to the work of the group.

Because some students with disabilities suffer from low self-esteem, and because cultural differences sometimes lead to conflicts of values, it is particularly important for teachers to attend to students' self-concepts. Charles Jones taught in a self-contained classroom of twelve disabled students. All of the students were Black. The students had negative self-images and denigrated their own heritage. Ethnic name-calling was common among members of the class. In an effort to improve the situation, Jones had his students create an "Ethnic Feelings Book." Students worked together and individually to learn about their heritage, discussed negative terminology and stereotypes, listened to Black people from the community who visited the class, participated in role playing, and focused on the positive attributes of relatives and community leaders. They documented what they learned in the book. The result of the project was a substantial decrease in name-calling—including peer reprimands—increased enthusiasm, and cooperative behaviour (Ford & Jones, 1990). Cultural, ethnic, linguistic, religious, and even regional factors seem to be important in the self-descriptions of Canadians. We can sense the pride expressed in identifiers such as Maritimer, Aboriginal, Westerner, Torontonian, French-Canadian, and Sikh.

At the heart of the matter of cultural diversity, exceptionality, or any other source of variability of students is the importance of recognizing the individual needs of students. Heward & Orlansky (1992) ask the following question: "If a student cannot speak, read, or write English well enough to progress in the school curriculum, does it make any difference whether the limited English proficiency is caused by cultural differences or by a disability?" (p. 491). Yes and no. No, in the sense that, in either case, the student and teacher face a problem: The student is at risk of performing poorly. Yes, in the sense that the instructional solution depends greatly on the origin of the problem.

Students with High-Incidence Disabilities

Categories of exceptionality are general descriptions. Students who enter your classroom with a particular disability or who are gifted will differ from one another in the same way that nonexceptional students differ from one another. As you prepare yourself for the variety that exceptional learners will introduce to your teaching situation, there is an important point to keep in mind. The point, which we will examine more closely later in the book, is that good teaching practice serves the individual needs of learners, regardless of the label they have been given.

One aspect of exceptionality to recognize is that some types of exceptionality are much more common than others. You can expect to teach many more students from the high-incidence exceptionalities described in the following discussion than students from the low-incidence exceptionalities described in the next section.

Emotional and Behavioural Disorders. **Emotional/behavioural disorder (E/BD)** is a disability that has proven difficult to define in a widely accepted way. Definitions may also vary between and across geographical, social, political, and judicial regions. No single definition of behaviour disorder exists in Canada. Of the twelve Canadian provinces/territories, eight allow local school systems to modify their definitions of behaviour disorder (Saskatchewan, Ontario, Prince Edward Island, and Newfoundland do not allow changes). Of the ten provincial jurisdictions that have official definitions, there are eight different definitions (Robert, 1995). Despite the lack of a generally accepted formal definition, E/BD students are easily noticed in a classroom (Hallahan & Kauffman, 1994). Through advanced statistical analysis, researchers have identified patterns or dimensions of disordered behaviour (e.g., Achenbach, 1985; Quay, 1986; Quay & Peterson, 1987). In spite of the advances in identification and treatment, Dworet and Rathberger (1990) suggest that Canadian children suffering from serious emotional or behavioural problems were receiving less attention in 1988 than was provided in 1981.

Various studies have attempted to determine the incidence of behaviour disorder in Canadian schools (Csapo, 1981; Dworet & Rathberger, 1990). The more recent Ontario Child Health Study (Offord, Boyle, & Racine, 1989) reported that approximately 5 percent of school-age children present serious behavioural concerns. In his paper on depression in Canadian Natives, Armstrong (1993) noted that Native children were excluded from this research. A study by Robert (1995) suggests a higher rate of behaviour disorders in the children of one Saskatchewan tribal council.

One broad category of disordered behaviour is externalizing—that is, acting out against others. Acting out in the form of classroom disruption—showing off, fights, temper tantrums—is a particular kind of externalizing called *conduct disorder*. Experienced teachers recognize that these behaviours occur in normal students as well as in E/BD students, the difference being that E/BD students cry, scream, and fight much more impulsively and with much greater frequency. Acting out that occurs in the company of others is called *socialized aggression*. The aggressive, illegal, and disrespectful behaviour of gangs is an example. Statistics reveal increasing levels of aggression in Canadian schools coupled with student dissatisfaction with how victims and perpetrators of aggression are dealt with by school staff (Gabor, 1995; MacDonald, 1997). These factors, together with the serious long-term personal and emotional implications of such externalizing behaviours and their

REFLECTION: Think back to your days as a student. Did you ever know an E/BD student? What kinds of behaviors did he or she display?

emotional/behavioural disorder A disability in which people have difficulty controlling their feelings and behaviour.

tremendous cost to society, have resulted in considerable attention being directed towards identifying intervention strategies. For example, Phillips, Schwean, and Saklofske (1997) from the University of Saskatchewan have outlined a cognitive-behavioural intervention that was found to be effective in reducing the frequency of externalizing behaviours. Ellis (1997) described a volunteer mentorship program that will be implemented in Alberta schools to reduce the incidence of serious disruptive behaviour.

Another category of behaviour that has received considerable attention is Attention Deficit Hyperactivity Disorder or ADHD (Hohn, 1995). Students with ADHD often have difficulty concentrating and remaining seated and are sometimes aggressive. A special issue of the *Canadian Journal of School Psychology*, volume 9, number 1, 1993, is an excellent source of information on ADHD. Of particular interest to teachers is the article by Schwean et al. entitled "Educating the ADHD child: Debunking the myths." An understanding of the nature of a student's problem allows both teacher and other classmates to accommodate the problem and thus enhance the disabled student's participation in school activities.

Another broad category of disordered behaviour is internalizing—that is, behaviour that reflects emotional problems, such as depression or debilitating anxiety. More specific types of internalizing are immature or withdrawn behaviours. Students who exhibit immaturity tend to have shorter attention spans, are easily distracted, and answer questions impulsively. Behaviours symptomatic of withdrawal include embarrassment, self-consciousness, sadness, and anxiety (Hallahan & Kauffman, 1994).

Specific Learning Disabilities. **Learning disabilities** is a generic term referring to a disorder in cognitive processing. It emerged as a field of study for educational researchers in the early 1960s. Since that time, a number of different definitions of learning disabilities have been posited. Winzer (1995) has outlined a number of commonalities among the different definitions:

1. Neurological impairment—students with learning disabilities may have some dysfunction in their neurological processing which interferes with learning.

2. Uneven growth patterns—students with learning disabilities may have marked strengths and weaknesses in their functioning.

3. Difficulty with learning tasks—compared to their peers, students with learning disabilities perform poorly on academic tasks.

4. Discrepancy between aptitude and achievement—"students with learning disabilities are perhaps best described as those who manifest educationally significant discrepancies between their tested potential for academic tasks and their performance in academic and social domains" (p. 292).

learning disability A generic term for disorders in cognitive processing that interfere with learning.

5. Intelligence scores that are average or above average.

6. No other causes—students with learning disabilities do not have other known causes of learning deficits such as mental retardation or hearing difficulties.

Many provincial special education policies include a definition of learning disabilities in order to facilitate the identification and designation of students. In Saskatchewan, for example, a student may be identified as severely learning disabled if assessment results indicate that a student is of average or above-average intelligence, exhibits a significant discrepancy between aptitude and achievement, and the student's average progress rate on academic tasks is less than half that of average pupils (Saskatchewan Special Education Policy Manual, 1989). Despite provincial policies regarding the identification of children with learning disabilities, recent Canadian studies show that few teachers are alert to the possibility of students' learning disabilities and underscore the need for increased awareness (Nielsen, 1997).

Communication Disorders. **Communication disorders** fall into two major categories: speech disorders and language disorders (American Speech-Language-Hearing Association, 1982).

Speech disorders include articulation, voice, and fluency problems. Sounds are sometimes omitted, substituted, added, or distorted. Voice quality problems, such as abnormal pitch, loudness, or quality, also fall into the category of speech disorder. A lack of fluency in the flow of verbal expression—stuttering—is another form of speech disorder. Stuttering can begin in childhood and persist into adulthood. However, stuttering is chiefly a childhood disorder. With the help of a speech therapist, most children stop stuttering by the end of adolescence.

Language disorders are problems in using symbol systems to communicate, resulting in difficulty in understanding or generating messages. Language disorders may involve phonological impairment (see Chapter 2); they may also be experienced by students who use a nonvocal system of symbols such as sign language. Children who experience communication disorders may or may not experience other types of disorders, including cerebral palsy, mental retardation, and learning disabilities.

Communication is basic to social interaction and to our intuitive judgments of a student's general intellectual ability. It is important to remember that although a student's ability to send and receive messages may be impaired, that impairment does not necessarily mean that the student's intellect is also impaired.

Students with Low-Incidence Disabilities

You can expect to have students with high-incidence disabilities in your classes frequently throughout your career. Depending on the type of district or school in which you will teach, you will probably encounter students with the types of disabilities described here less frequently.

Mental Retardation. A widely accepted definition of mental retardation is as follows:

Mental retardation refers to substantial limitations in present functioning. It is characterized by significantly subaverage intellectual functioning, existing concurrently with related limitations in two or more of the following applicable adaptive skills areas: communication, self-care, home living, social skills, community use, self-direction, health and safety, functional academics,

TRY THIS: Interview a student with a learning disability—perhaps there is one in your class. Find out what kind of disability he or she has and how the disability has affected him or her.

POINT: That communication disorders require special instruction supports a basic assumption of this book: *Students' background and individual characteristics affect learning.*

TRY THIS: Volunteer some time with your local chapter of the Association For Community Living, Learning Disabilities Association, or Children with Attention Deficit Disorder. Use your time to observe and reflect on the challenges faced by people with disabilities, and do some research on the programs designed to help them reach their goals.

communication disorder Speech (voice) and language (symbols) disorders.

mental retardation Significantly subaverage intellectual functioning, usually present at birth, resulting in or associated with impairments in adaptive behavior and manifested during the developmental period.

TRY THIS: Volunteer some time with a local agency that serves people with mental retardation. Use your time to observe and reflect on the challenges faced by people with mental disabilities, and do some research on the programs designed to help them reach their goals.

leisure, and work. Mental retardation manifests before age 18 (American Association of Mental Retardation [AAMR] Ad Hoc Committee on Terminology and Classification, 1992, p. 5).

Mental retardation is not an all-or-none phenomenon. The AAMR system of classification lists four levels of mental retardation: mild, moderate, severe, and profound. Mild mental retardation is by far the highest incidence of these four categories.

Although there are four levels of deficiency in the classification system, the AAMR also emphasizes the importance of shifting the emphasis away from estimating an individual's deficiency level to "estimating the intensities of needed supports (intermittent, limited, extensive, pervasive)" (Schalock, Stark, Snell, Coulter, Polloway, Luckasson, Reiss, & Spitalnik, 1994). Assessing the needed supports of the student facilitates the development and implementation of an appropriate individual education plan.

Instruction for mildly retarded students [or students with cognitive disabilities] focuses on developing readiness skills in the early elementary grades. Readiness skills include sitting still, following directions, discriminating sounds and visual stimuli, self-help (e.g., dressing, using the washroom), and working cooperatively with peers. Instruction in later elementary grades addresses functional academics. Mildly and moderately retarded students are taught to read ads in the newspaper, the telephone book, and labels at the supermarket rather than social studies or fiction. The purpose of such a reading program is to allow them to function independently. Junior high and high school instruction encourages the development of community living and vocational skills (Epstein, Polloway, Patton, & Foley, 1989). The major instructional goal for severely and profoundly retarded students is independent behaviour. Practical skills, such as eating, dressing, and personal hygiene, are emphasized. The reader may wish to consult a book chapter written by the Saskatchewan team of Bruce Gordon, Don Saklofske, and Denise Hildebrand (1998) that discusses issues related to assessment, classification, and programming needs for children with mental retardation.

Sensory Disorders. **Sensory disorders** refer to disabilities in using sensory information from the environment. Hearing and visual impairment are sensory disorders. Hearing impairment includes students who, on one end of the continuum, are hard of hearing and, on the other end, are deaf. *Otitis media*, or middle ear infection, causes mild hearing loss in children. Although most cases of otitis media occur before children enter school, approximately one third of elementary school-aged children will experience middle ear infection at least once. Otitis media is also more prevalent among lower socioeconomic groups, Aboriginal populations, children with craniofacial abnormalities (e.g., cleft palate), and affects more males than females (Winzer, 1995). Students who have hearing impairments can, with the aid of special amplification devices, use their sense of hearing to good advantage. Deaf children must be instructed through other senses. Because a child with a hearing impairment may have difficulty speaking or understanding speech, he or she is often assumed to have below-average intelligence. Language deficits are not deficits in intellectual ability.

Many hearing-impaired students need only amplification devices and articulation therapy. Others must learn special communication techniques. In addition to auditory training, which can help students make use of whatever hearing they possess, the techniques include speech reading, finger spelling, and true sign languages. Speech reading is a more accurate name for what most people call

sensory disorder
Disorders such as hearing and visual impairments.

lipreading. Speech readers use not only visual cues from the speakers' mouths but also gestures and body language cues. Finger spelling is a way of translating spoken English and differs from a true sign language (Figure 5.2).

A true sign language has its own grammar and, contrary to the opinion of many, can be used to convey abstract ideas (Sacks, 1989). The communication techniques used by those with hearing impairments make it difficult for those who do not have hearing loss to join them in a conversation, and vice versa. Because communication plays a critical role in social interaction, deaf people socialize with those who share their disability to a greater extent than do people in other exceptional categories (Hallahan & Kauffman, 1994).

Visual impairment is legally defined by a person's acuity and field of vision. A legally blind person is one whose acuity is 20/200 or less. (A person with 20/200 vision sees at twenty feet what a person with normal vision sees at 200.) Field of vision refers to the width, measured in angles, of a person's peripheral vision.

Educators define visual impairment in terms of the method of reading instruction a student with visual impairment requires. A child with low vision is able to read print through the use of magnification technology; a child who is blind must use braille or audio tapes. These and other technological advances make it possible to teach students with visual impairments in regular classrooms. In addition to using devices that enlarge viewing material or vocalize printed matter, students with vision loss may need aids, such as guide dogs or sensor devices, to move about.

CRITICAL THINKING: What is the difference between a language and a translating system?

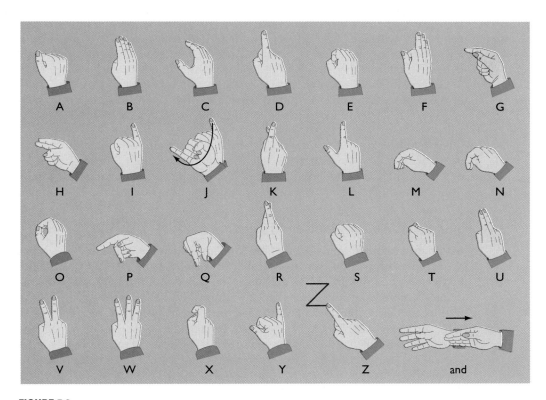

FIGURE 5.2
Finger Spelling Alphabet

Source: Exceptional Children (5th ed., p. 284), D.P. Hallahan and J.M. Kauffman, 1991. Copyright 1991 by Allyn & Bacon. Reprinted by permission.

Physical Disabilities. Physical disabilities include disorders of the skeleton, joints, and muscles or health conditions that interfere with students' educational performances. Some physical disabilities, such as cerebral palsy and epilepsy, are due to neurological impairments. Cerebral palsy is not a disease in the proper sense of the word. It is neither contagious, remittable (with periodic relief from symptoms), nor progressive (although poor treatment can cause complications). It is a syndrome that includes motor and/or psychological dysfunctions, seizures, behaviour disorders, or any combination of symptoms due to brain damage.

Epilepsy is a condition that periodically causes abnormal amounts of electrical activity in the brain, resulting in seizures. Seizures vary in duration, frequency, and intensity. Some seizures last only a few seconds; others may last for several minutes. Some children with epilepsy have seizures every few minutes, others have them only once a year. The most intensive seizures involve major convulsions, which can be frightening to an observer. Minor seizures, a common indicator of which is rapid eye blinks, sometimes go unnoticed.

Skeletal/muscular disabilities, such as muscular dystrophy and arthritis, can limit a student's movement and, as a result, his or her participation in some school activities. Other disabilities caused by health problems can also limit participation in school activities.

Perhaps no health-related disability has been so readily turned into a handicap as acquired immune deficiency syndrome (AIDS). The devastating nature of the disease and its epidemic proportions (Church, Allen, & Stiehm, 1986) have made it difficult for children who have contracted it to interact normally with their peers. The HIV virus that causes AIDS is transmitted through intimate sexual contact with infected partners, through blood transfusions from those who are infected, from an infected mother to a child in utero, or from using contaminated hypodermic needles. It is not transmitted through casual social contact. Sex education to help adolescents prevent infection is helping to curb the spread of the disease. Programs to educate classmates of infected students and to help alleviate social stigma and enhance social interactions are also available.

Other Health Impairments. Other health-related conditions can either limit a student's activity or require special accommodation by teachers and sometimes by other students. Table 5.4 provides brief descriptions of additional health conditions that might be experienced by students in your future classrooms.

Students Who Are Gifted and Talented

Gifted and talented students are able to meet academic challenges better than the majority of their peers in any number of areas. Renzulli (1982) distinguishes between "academic" giftedness and "creative" giftedness. Students who are academically gifted are able to learn quickly and easily. They generally score well on tests of intelligence, aptitude, and achievement. Creatively gifted students tend to solve problems in new and effective ways. Interestingly, academically gifted students tend, as a group, not to be any more or less successful in later life than the general student population, whereas creatively gifted students are more likely to achieve later success.

There are underachieving gifted students. Schoolwork that does not challenge gifted students is considered a major reason for underachievement (Hallahan & Kauffman, 1994). Gifted underachievers often have negative attitudes toward school and toward themselves (Delisle, 1982; Ribich, Barone, & Agostino, 1991). One approach to working with underachieving gifted students

TRY THIS: Contact your local school district and ask to receive materials that explain the division's policies and procedures for accommodating students or staff who are HIV-positive.

physical disability
Disorders of the skeleton, joints, and muscles, or health conditions that interfere with students' educational performances.

gifted and talented
Students who are able to meet academic challenges better than the majority of their peers in any number of areas.

TABLE 5.4 *Additional Physical Conditions*

Condition	Description
Asthma	Chronic respiratory condition characterized by repeated episodes of difficulty in breathing, especially exhalation
Cystic Fibrosis	Inherited disease characterized by chronic respiratory and digestive problems, including thick, sticky mucus and glandular secretions
Diabetes	A hereditary or developmental problem of sugar metabolism caused by failure of the pancreas to produce enough insulin
Nephrosis and nephritis	Disorders or diseases of the kidneys due to infection, poisoning, burns, crushing injuries, or other diseases
Sickle-cell anemia	Severe, chronic hereditary blood disease in which red blood cells are distorted in shape and do not circulate properly
Hemophilia	A rare, sex-linked disorder in which the blood does not have a sufficient clotting component and excessive bleeding occurs
Rheumatic fever	Painful swelling and inflammation of the joints (typically following strep throat or scarlet fever) that can spread to the brain or heart
Tuberculosis	Infection by the tuberculosis bacterium of an organ system, such as lungs, larynx, bones and joints, skin, gastrointestinal tract, genitourinary tract, or heart
Cancer	Abnormal growth of cells that can affect any organ system

Source: Exceptional children: Introduction to special education (6th ed.), D. P. Hallahan & J. M. Kauffman, 1994, Boston: Allyn & Bacon.

involves observing carefully their performances and behaviours in various instructional situations, sharing those observations and hypothesized causes for underachievement with the students, and developing a partnership with the students (and their parents, if possible) aimed at solving the problem (Whitmore, 1986).

Historically, it has been assumed that between 3 and 5 percent of students in schools are gifted and talented. For this reason, gifted and talented is usually considered among other low-incidence exceptionalities. There are, however, experts who believe that a much larger percentage of students—perhaps 15 to 25 percent—could benefit from programs for gifted and talented students (Hoge & Renzulli, 1993; Renzulli and Reis, 1991).

What Provisions Are Made for the Education of Students at Risk and Exceptional Learners?

Exceptional learners and those whose life circumstances place them at risk are served through educational programs that augment the regular instruction in classrooms. These programs fall into three categories: compensatory education, early intervention, and special education. Compensatory education programs are designed to remediate the delayed development that occurs when students are denied opportunities because of difficult life circumstances. Early intervention programs are designed to prevent developmental delays and thus eliminate the need for later remediation. There are other types of intervention programs—such as dropout prevention—that may not start until the elementary or middle grades, but most interventions are designed to be preventative and are, therefore, begun in early childhood. Special education programs serve students who have disabilities, either physical or psychological, that are relatively long term.

REFLECTION: Think back to your classmates in high school who did very well in school. Try to identify characteristics that would allow you to infer whether they would have been considered academically or creatively gifted.

TRY THIS: Interview a principal or a director of special education services. Ask his or her opinion of the claim that 15 percent to 25 percent of students could benefit from programs for the gifted and talented.

Insights on Successful Practice

What do you do to help both your low-ability and your high-ability students succeed academically?

One way that I accommodate learners of varying abilities is by using contemporary literature. The short fiction of writers such as Jamaica Kincaid, Donald Barthelme, Isabel Allende, and Gabriel Garcia Márquez forces all readers to reexamine their preconceptions about text. These authors break with so many narrative traditions that every student, gifted and challenged, must struggle to understand the work. Fortunately, these writers are such extraordinary storytellers that the struggle is hardly painful.

In Kincaid's short story "Girl," for example, an Antiguan mother lectures her daughter on how to behave. In the two-page diatribe, the daughter only gets to pipe up twice to defend her behaviour. Talking about the story, students immediately respond to the conflicting directions parents so often give them: Be independent, think for yourself, do as I say. They are reminded of how their own mothers beat them up with instructions for living. When I ask students to write a similar piece, modelling Kincaid's style but itemizing the warnings they've heard, they jump to the task.

One student wrote, "Serve from the right, clear from the left. Don't look for love. It will find you. This is how to balance a chequebook. Be a designated driver. Keep your head up, shoulders out. Don't slouch." Like Jamaica Kincaid's girl, theirs could only speak out twice. Like her, theirs were dismissed out of hand. "Don't give me those looks." The imitations helped students understand the literature they had read. They didn't need a lesson or quiz on tone, they felt what Kincaid had done with language in their bones.

Often less confident, less well-read readers are put off by the demands of traditional literature. When asked to navigate Herman Melville's waters, they flounder, and their failure becomes the more evident in comparison with well-prepared students. Reading contemporary texts, all students face the same challenges. No one, not even the teacher, has privileged information. The class unlocks the text's meaning and discovers its richness together.

CAROL JAGO
High School Teacher

Before turning to a description of school programs for exceptional children, it may be helpful to provide an example of the kind and extent of such initiatives in Canada. In a cross-Canada survey of educational programs for students with behavioural disorders, Shatz (1994) reported that 85 percent of school districts surveyed provide programming for these students. More than 40 percent of Canadian school districts have written program descriptions for students with behaviour disorders in the areas of student needs identification, and program philosophy, goals, design, and operations.

Compensatory Education

compensatory education
Educational programs designed to combat the presumed effects of poverty on school performance.

Compensatory education programs were started to counteract the presumed effects of poverty on school performance. It was assumed that children raised in poverty were often denied the kind of stimulation that fosters readiness to achieve in school. Research has since confirmed the assumption (Kennedy, Jung, & Orland, 1986). Compensatory education programs, such as Head Start and Follow Through, are designed to combat the effects of poverty and thus prepare students for success in school.

A number of Canadian school districts, particularly those in large urban centers, have implemented compensatory programs. Many of these programs offer preschools, smaller class sizes, additional supports for teachers such as teacher assistants, and close contact between community and school associations ("Inner-City Schools," 1988). These elements are indicative of the movement within compensatory programs to emphasize collaboration between teachers and other educational professionals who serve disadvantaged students. Other types of programs for exceptional learners and for learners at risk, such as intervention and prevention programs, also call for collaboration.

Intervention and Prevention Programs

Compensatory education programs were motivated by an effort to remediate the difficulties that placed students at risk. More recently, there has been an increase in programs designed to prevent the need for remediation through early intervention (cf. Slavin, Karweit, & Wasik, 1994). Programs for infants and preschoolers that provide stimulation, parent training, and other services have shown long-term positive effects on school performance (Berrueta-Clement, Schweinhart, Barnett, Epstein, & Weikart, 1984; Wasik & Karweit, 1994). One such program, called "Success for All," provides reading instruction, individual tutoring, family support, and other services. The goal of the program is that students from disadvantaged homes will not fall behind in the early grades. This goal is pursued tenaciously. When problems arise, changes are made quickly to solve the problem and maintain student achievement. As a result, students who experienced Success for All compare favourably to control students in reading performance throughout the elementary years (Madden, Slavin, Karweit, Dolan, & Wasik, 1993).

Another program designed to prevent learning problems through early intervention is called "Reading Recovery" (Clay, 1993, 1994; DeFord, Lyons, & Pinnell, 1991). The program focuses on grade one students who are most at risk of failure to read. Teachers who work in Reading Recovery programs are specially trained in the program's instructional model and in the nature of teacher-student interactions during instruction. Students receive one-on-one tutoring for thirty minutes each day from the specially trained teacher. Research has shown impressive results for the program. Grade one students at risk from approximately two-hundred school districts participated in Reading Recovery. Of those grade one students, 83 percent attained the average reading level for their grade (cf. Huck & Pinnell, 1991; Pinnell, 1989). Reading Recovery is a national program in New Zealand and has been widely used in Canada, the United States, and Australia.

Reading Recovery and Success for All are examples of intensive intervention programs. The professionals who work in these programs understand that failure to intervene early and decisively increases the risk that a child will fail. These programs demonstrate that intensive intervention can give students at risk a good start and that a good start in school can prevent many students from becoming academically disabled.

Social skills interventions have also been implemented in an effort to ameliorate the social problems often associated with disorders like learning disabilities, attention deficit/hyperactivity disorder, and hearing impairment, among others. For example, Conte, Andrews, Loomer, and Hutton (1995) report on an Alberta study designed to see if a social skills intervention involving coaching, role playing, and information sharing would lead to improved sociometric status for children presenting with learning disabilities. Results demonstrated that relative to controls, children who participated in the program showed superior

TRY THIS: Contact an urban school board to inquire whether they offer a compensatory program. Ask if you can visit a school which has a compensatory program. Record the services offered and share your findings with colleagues.

REFLECTION: Think back to your own teachers in elementary and high school. How much coordination did you perceive among your teachers? Why do you think there was or was not sufficient coordination? What could be done to improve coordination?

CONNECTION: The instructional effects of individualized instruction are examined in Chapter 12: Teaching for Active Learning.

sociometric status and improved social problem-solving skills. Because early social problems may be an important marker of later psychological maladjustment, social-skills interventions that have demonstrated efficacy should be an integral aspect of comprehensive prevention programs.

Special Education and Inclusion

"**Special education** means specially designed instruction that meets the unusual needs of an exceptional student" (Hallahan & Kauffman, 1994, p. 14). Designing instruction to meet the needs of exceptional learners may require special materials, special teaching techniques, or special equipment or facilities. The instructional needs of a student with a hearing impairment, for example, may require that the teacher use sign language or closed caption video. Exceptional students may require related services—that is, services that allow students to participate in specially designed instructional activities. A gifted student may require transportation to a local college to take an advanced course. A student with a physical disability may require physical or occupational therapy to participate in job training. A student with an emotional disability may require counselling to work cooperatively with classmates. These services—both instructional and related—are provided by professionals and staff members in a variety of settings.

The relationship between general and special education has been the focus of much policy making. Many school districts have adopted policies which encourage mainstreaming students with special needs. Recently, an increasing number of parents and educators are advocating the concept of full inclusion. **Full inclusion** refers to the notion that all students with disabilities, no matter how profound or severe, should be educated in the general education classroom. Advocates of full inclusion argue that labelling is harmful and that people with disabilities should not be viewed as a minority group. As a result, the concept of mainstreaming does not promote the complete inclusion of students; rather, sociocultural realities within mainstreaming distinguish between the members of the mainstream and those wishing to join it (Winzer, 1995). Not all educators are proponents of full inclusion. Opponents of full inclusion often argue that the needs of many exceptional students cannot possibly be met in general education classrooms: Some students need the special attention or care that is more readily available in the resource room or other settings. The movement towards inclusion will continue to be an issue of debate and experimentation and will influence the way professional teams deliver instruction.

How Will You Use Your Knowledge of Individual Variability to Enhance Teaching and Learning?

There is an old story that has passed, in one form or another, from teachers' lounge to teachers' lounge for years and years. It is the story of the new history teacher and the old history teacher. Meeting for the first time, the old teacher asks the new teacher, "What are you going to teach this year?"

The new teacher responds enthusiastically, "World history." The new teacher launches into a long and nauseatingly detailed description of the content topics, the key historical events, and the important documents that students will study. The old teacher listens politely and without interruption. Finally, with pride and the satisfaction of having demonstrated impressive knowledge, the new teacher says, "And what are you going to teach?"

TRY THIS: Conduct a survey of faculty in a university department of education. Try to find out what the faculty views are of full inclusion.

special education Specially designed instruction to meet the needs of exceptional learners.

full inclusion The inclusion of all students, regardless of their disabilities, in the regular classroom.

Insights on Successful Practice

What advice can you give novice teachers about successfully including students with disabilities into their classrooms?

Including students with disabilities into the classroom is no different than successfully including all students into the classroom. After twenty-five years of teaching high school English, I think I am finally beginning to learn this lesson. From *Multiple Intelligences* by Howard Gardner, *Gifts Differing* by Isabel Briggs Myers, and *Please Understand Me* by David Keirsey and Marilyn Bates, I learned that there are many different ways humans learn and relate to one another. I learned that the highest dropout rate in our country occurs among students who are active, hands-on learners. The kid who can't sit still for a lecture on *Romeo and Juliet* blossoms when we act out a scene. The student who won't write a fifty-word essay on anything will work and rework almost everything if she can use the computer.

So new teachers need to forget about teaching the way they were taught. Most of us went into teaching because we were successful in the average Canadian classroom. Memorizing, comprehending what we read, and working alone were techniques that worked for many of us. But for the average Canadian student, and most certainly for the student with a disability, these techniques don't work. Many students learn their literacy skills from the TV, not the tradebook. To judge a student's ability on how they learn is to doom many of our students to assignments and assessments in which they will seldom shine.

I learned this lesson from Mark, a special education teacher who worked right alongside me in a grade nine English classroom. I learned that students with behaviour disorders such as attention deficit disorder (ADD) are not intentionally trying to disrupt the classroom. I learned that graphic organizers help learning-disabled students understand a novel better than study questions. And most important, I learned that teaching can be a very isolated profession. We walk into our classrooms alone and retire thirty years later without ever having seen a colleague in action. I can't think of another profession so cut off from itself.

So the most important advice I can give novice teachers about successfully including students with disabilities into their classrooms is to seek out advice from other teachers, to open your classroom door, to volunteer for collaboration. We have so much to learn from one another.

Working in collaboration with special education teachers has opened my eyes to all my students. Appreciating their different gifts and their ways of knowing is the key to reaching all students.

MAUREEN F. LOGAN
High School Teacher

The old teacher smiles and says, "Students."

The point the old teacher in the story was making is that teaching is not simply covering the content. Theoretically, it would be possible for a teacher to cover the content in a classroom without students. Teaching is inextricably tied to the learning that results. How can a teacher say that he or she has taught if no student has learned?

Accepting Individual Differences

Modelling acceptance in your own interactions with students who are at risk or disabled is an important instructional strategy. There are, however, other techniques that you can employ in your classroom. One of these techniques is simulation exercises in which nondisabled students are artificially—and temporarily—disabled. An example would be to blindfold sighted students so they

CONNECTION: The effects of modelling are discussed in Chapter 8: Social Learning.

can experience visual impairment. Such simulations allow disabled students to teach the nondisabled students how to handle the demands of a disability. Another example of how acceptance can be enhanced is to invite successful adults with disabilities to meet and talk with students. Such models illustrate to disabled and nondisabled students alike that a disability does not prevent people from achieving success (Salend, 1994). There are also materials—films and books, for example—that portray protagonists with disabilities. Class discussions of these materials can enhance the acceptance of individual differences related to disabilities. Teaching techniques that allow nondisabled students to benefit from the work of disabled students, such as cooperative learning, can also be employed to advantage. Cooperative learning, which requires students to depend on each other in order to be successful, is described in detail in Chapter 12: Teaching for Active Learning.

Creating an Inclusive Classroom

The movement for inclusion means that students with disabilities will be placed in regular classrooms. Simply placing students with disabilities in regular classrooms, however, does not guarantee that those students will feel a part of that classroom group. An inclusive classroom is one in which students are socially integrated, not just physically present.

The feelings of students toward one another (especially students with disabilities) can be influenced considerably by the interaction patterns and attitudes displayed by the teacher (Simpson, 1980). Thus, if a teacher models a positive attitude toward students with disabilities, regular students are more likely to interact positively with their disabled peers.

An inclusive classroom makes those present feel like part of a community. The teacher plays a critical role in creating a feeling of community in a classroom and making all of the students feel as though they are members of that community. The processes in Lickona's model (see Chapter 3) are an excellent source of ideas for building a sense of community in the classroom.

Adapting Instruction

Knowledge of the characteristics of students is necessary for effective teaching but so is concern that students' needs are met by the instruction that is delivered (Oser, 1994). The descriptions of individual variability in this chapter (and in Chapters 2, 3, and 4) are a good start on acquiring the requisite knowledge. The requisite concern must come from an attitude that student learning is the most important measure of teaching. Knowledge of the ways in which students differ and concern that the needs of students be met are both necessary if a teacher is to adapt his or her instruction to the needs of students.

Adapting instructional practices to the needs of individual students is something that good teachers do. But how can adaptations be made? Here are ten ideas suggested by Maniet-Bellermann (1986).

Here's How

Here's How To Adapt Instruction To Meet Individual Needs

- Present material on tape for students who cannot read successfully.
- Allow students to tape-record answers if writing is difficult or their handwriting is illegible.

continued

- Provide lots of visual reminders (pictures, maps, charts, graphs) for students who have trouble listening or attending.

- Break directions and assignments into small steps. Completion of each step is an accomplishment.

- Give tests orally if the child has trouble with reading, spelling, or writing. Testing that demonstrates what the student knows, rather than language skills, gives you a clearer picture of the student's abilities.

- Emphasize quality rather than quantity of writing.

- Carefully establish routines so that students with disabilities do not become further handicapped by the confusion of unclear expectations.

- Arrange desks, tables, and chairs so every person can be seen easily and every word heard easily. Remember, students with hearing deficits need to see your face as you speak.

- Provide carrels or screens—an "office"—for students who are easily distracted.

Adaptations should emphasize the abilities of students rather than their disabilities. Because instructional adaptation is something that good teachers do, we will revisit the notion in Chapter 12: Teaching for Active Learning.

Using Alternative Assessments

Assessment is part of instructional practice. The methods you select to assess learning performance can themselves be positive learning experiences for your students. If instructional adaptation is part of good teaching practice, it makes sense that adaptations of assessment activities are also good teaching practice.

Traditional paper-and-pencil tests may be difficult for some disabled students to take. Accommodations might include giving the test orally or without a time limit. Such adaptations make sense. If a student who has cerebral palsy is incapable of writing answers, then it makes sense to give the test in a way that will allow for a fair assessment of what he or she has learned. The point is to find ways to assess fairly what students have learned. But this is the point no matter who the student is, no matter what strengths or weaknesses he or she has, no matter what his or her cultural background.

In an effort to enhance the quality of information gained from classroom assessments, new approaches are being proposed and tested. These new approaches are referred to as *alternative assessment, authentic assessment*, and *portfolio assessment*. These new approaches to assessment attempt to make the assessment of learning more relevant and more descriptive of the capabilities of learners. Such assessment is appropriate for all learners and is examined closely in Chapter 13: Assessing Student Performance.

The individual characteristics of your students will influence profoundly the teaching-learning process in your classroom. Knowing your students as individuals will allow you to understand and honour how each is different from you and from each other. Knowing their individual characteristics will allow you to include them in the community of your classroom; to adapt your instruction to their needs; and to assess their abilities, not their disabilities. Each student displays intelligent behaviour. Each student is at risk at some time. Each student is exceptional in some way.

CONNECTION: The use of alternative assessment is expanding in schools. We look closely at assessment techniques in Chapter 13: Assessing Classroom Performance.

Teacher Chronicle Conclusion

My Name Is Robo

At the end of September, Heath's mother requested a special conference with Mrs. Chiu to review Heath's progress. On the positive side: he had already learned to read and now reads at a grade-two level. He had created a comic strip, shared it with the class, and helped another student create her own. Every time an animal was mentioned in storytime he made that animal sound (something Mrs. Chiu enjoyed and encouraged). He displayed a high degree of accuracy in his science drawings, frequently turning to reference books (and using the index) for more knowledge. In large group discussions he shared his knowledge on every topic from robots to the Latin names of jellyfish. His artwork was exceptionally creative and detailed.

On the negative side, he rarely followed the exact directions given by Mrs. Chiu, as he always added his own wrinkle to his work. He never played with other children at recess. Instead, he just swung by himself, back and forth, for fifteen minutes and was frequently late coming in, as he ignored the bell. On impulse, he had hit three students one day with blocks. Each time he was placed in a cooperative group, it ended in his throwing a tantrum or the other children complaining about him. His impulsive behaviours of wandering around or focusing on something else interfered with his math instruction, and he rarely finished an assignment. He had no real friends with whom he played.

Mrs. Chiu told Dr. Kotre that the teacher of emotionally disturbed children had made several observations of Heath and would be providing her with a report. When that report came, she suggested that they meet again with the special needs teacher.

Dr. Kotre shook her head and thanked Mrs. Chiu for her patience and understanding.

"Somehow I had hoped that this year would be better than kindergarten for Heath. Maybe I'm in over my head."

"I think we all are," Mrs. Chiu said, "but we'll find the best way to keep Heath learning and to help him develop his social skills."

Application Questions

1. How would you characterize Heath's intelligence in My Name Is Robo? Which view of intelligence provides the best description of Heath? Why? From what you have learned about student diversity, add to the list of Heath's strengths and weaknesses.

2. What aspects of Heath's situation place him at risk of failing in school? What steps, other than those indicated, should be taken by Mrs. Chiu?

3. What strategies could Mrs. Chiu use to encourage Heath to participate more fully in group activities?

4. How could you model acceptance of Heath in your classroom? What steps would you take to encourage Heath's classmates to accept him?

5. Could Mrs. Chiu make any instructional adaptations that would help Heath be more successful? How would you build on Heath's strengths to encourage growth in his areas of weakness?

6. How might other professionals help Mrs. Chiu and Dr. Kotre meet Heath's needs?

CHAPTER SUMMARY

How Do Students Vary in Intelligence?
(L.O. 1, 2, 3, p. 136)

What is considered intelligent behaviour depends on the view of intelligence being considered. Piaget's view assumes that intelligence changes as students develop cognitively. Wechsler assumes that intelligence is a global capacity. Newer views of intelligence, such as Gardner's theory of multiple intelligences and Sternberg's triarchic theory, expand the notion of intelligence beyond what is measured on traditional IQ tests to a consideration of talents and abilities to behave adaptively in one's environment.

How Do Students Vary in the Ways They Think and Learn? (L.O. 4, 5, p. 149)

Students are disposed to think in different ways. Research on thinking dispositions indicates that there are some bottom-line dispositions that contribute to learning. Variability in thinking has also been documented in research on learning styles. A dispositional approach to thinking establishes standards against which students can be compared. Categorizing students according to learning styles or identifying the predominant learning style of a group is seen as dangerous teaching practice.

How Do Students Vary in Abilities and Disabilities? (L.O. 6, p. 154)

Students are sometimes placed at risk of failing in school. The factors that place students at risk often arise from conditions over which the student and the teacher have no control—for instance, the student's home environment. The factors that place students at risk may be temporary or permanent. Exceptional students require special help to learn effectively. Cultural minorities are disproportionately represented in exceptional populations. Emotional and behavioural disorders and learning disabilities account for the largest number of exceptional students. Other, low-incidence disabilities include students with mental retardation and students with communication disorders, sensory disorders (such as hearing and visual impairments), physical disabilities, and health-related impairments, such as AIDS.

What Provisions Are Made for the Education of Students at Risk and Exceptional Learners? (L.O. 8, p. 163)

Students with special needs—because they are at risk or because they are exceptional—are served by a variety of educational programs. Compensatory education seeks to compensate for the effects of poverty. Intervention and prevention programs are designed to monitor at-risk students closely and provide special instructional interventions to ensure student success. Special education and inclusion programs provide the accommodations that exceptional learners need to succeed.

How Will You Use Your Knowledge of Individual Variability to Enhance Teaching and Learning? (L.O. 9, p. 166)

Knowledge of students as individuals is key to teaching. Recognizing that students are individuals with individual needs is the first step in accepting students and helping them to accept each other into the community of the classroom. Creating a classroom that includes all students regardless of ability or disability requires accommodating needs. Various ways of adapting instruction and assessment are discussed.

KEY CONCEPTS

communication disorder, p. 159

compensatory education, p. 164

componential intelligence, p. 145

construct, p. 136

contextual intelligence, p. 146

disability, p. 155

emotional/behavioural disorder, p. 157

exceptional learners, p. 157

experiential intelligence, p. 146

full inclusion, p. 166

gifted and talented, p. 162

handicap, p. 155

intelligence, p. 136

learning disability, p. 158

mental retardation, p. 159

physical disability, p. 162

sensory disorder, p. 160

special education, p. 166

theory of multiple intelligences, p. 139

thinking dispositions, p. 149

6 Environment and Behaviour

LEARNING OUTCOMES

When you have completed this chapter, you will be able to

1. describe the basic principles of classical and operant learning

2. recognize the role of antecedent and consequent conditions in learning

3. distinguish between the kinds of reinforcers

4. compare and contrast methods for strengthening and weakening behaviours

5. explain strategies for teaching new behaviours

6. describe the differential effects of reinforcement schedules

7. discuss the pros and cons of using behavioural principles in the classroom

8. outline how you might implement behavioural principles in various school grades

9. explain why behavioural principles are more or less likely to work in schools

Teacher Chronicle

Out of Control

Shareen Nasdid sits at her desk at the end of the worst day of her two-year teaching career. Her grade two class is out of control and she knows it.

She is feeling manipulated by several students, most notably Leah. She is discouraged and wondering if teaching is really for her. As she reflects, she thinks about Sarah O'Dell's class next door. There is always a buzz of activity and excitement in Ms. O'Dell's room; the kids are talking quietly with each other, they're interacting with Ms. O'Dell individually and in groups, they're doing independent projects. When the time comes to shift to another activity, some kids put away the materials being used, while others are helping Ms. O'Dell get new materials out, all without apparent direction from the teacher. The kids never seem out of control. She makes it appear so easy, Shareen thinks. But how? she wonders. What is *she* doing that *I* can't do? Why do her students seem so on task when mine are like a bunch of wild chimpanzees? Sarah has been so approachable . . . maybe she should ask her for some advice.

That evening Shareen calls Sarah to discuss her situation. "Just when I have them settled and on task, Leah blurts out something. Then Jeremy joins in and pretty soon they're in charge. When it comes time to start another activity, I wind up doing all the cleanup. No matter what directions I give, I find myself running from one side of the room to the other—taking one thing away from Leah, telling Jeremy to get back in his area, trying to make sure that every table has the materials they need to get started."

"What have you tried to get them organized and on task?" Sarah asks.

"First I offered them extra free time if everyone finished their work. But then some finished early, got their free time, and the others wanted it and. . . ." Shareen hesitates. "Then I tried punishing Leah every time she broke one of the rules. None of the punishments seem to matter to her anyway—losing recess, staying after school, seeing the principal."

"Have you given her time-out?"

"Yes, but she does so many distracting things that the others can't focus. I'm at the end of my rope."

"I tell you what. Tomorrow, I'll go to Mrs. Lucka and arrange for you to come observe me for a morning. You'll see more than I can possibly tell you about. And Shareen, don't worry. I was in the same situation early in my career."

"Not you!" Shareen exclaimed.

Sarah laughed. "Oh yes, and I was having so many problems I was almost fired."

"And last year you were District Teacher of the Year?"

"I had some mentors to help me along, and so now I want to continue the tradition. Then someday, you'll be Teacher of the Year."

Focus Questions

1. How might a behavioural scientist approach Shareen's problem?
2. What role does the classroom environment play in learning?
3. How are behaviours reinforced?
4. How can student behaviours be changed?
5. How is behaviour learned?
6. What is a possible reason for the persistence of Leah's off-task behaviour?
7. What principles should guide decisions about student behaviours?
8. Will your students perceive reinforcement or punishment the same way you do?

What Is Behavioural Science?

When your first group of students walks into your classroom on your first day as a certified teacher, they will respond to you and to the classroom you have prepared for them. When you present a lesson, administer a test, lead a discussion, monitor study hall, ask and answer questions, review a test, organize a lunch line, or referee a scuffle in the hall, students will respond to you. How will they respond? Will they do what you ask of them? Will they ignore you? Will they defy you? Shareen Nasdid's students in the Teacher Chronicle go off task when Leah and Jeremy interrupt a class activity, and they ignore her directions to put away materials when it is time to begin a new activity. What are her students responding to? Let's examine the principles of behavioural analysis as they apply to human learning, and see what answers they provide to these questions.

The **behavioural approach** to learning represents a school of thought in which learning is explained through observable aspects of the environment. Imagine, for example, that a student answers discussion questions at the end of a textbook chapter by taking notes on chapter content. On the chapter test, the end-of-chapter questions appear in a modified form as essay items. The student earns the highest possible score on the essays and, for all remaining reading assignments, takes notes based on the chapter discussion questions. What did this student learn?

CRITICAL THINKING: Give an example of the distinction between observable behaviour and inferences based on observation.

A behavioural scientist would approach this question by first observing the student's behaviour—taking notes from textbook chapters—and analyzing what happened to the behaviour—it increased. The apparent reason for the increase in note-taking behaviour is also an observable event. That is, the consequence of taking notes was a high score on the essay items. By linking the behaviour with its consequence, the behavioural scientist infers that the student learned to take notes from textbook chapters. Although cognitive or mental processes may accompany the student's change in behaviour, they are not thought to be important in understanding learning (cf. Skinner, 1987a, 1989). Thus, it doesn't matter what the student thinks about note-taking from textbook chapters as long as the behaviour continues to result in high test scores. If that contingency holds, the note-taking behaviour is likely to be maintained.

The behavioural approach to learning offers strategies for classroom management and student learning and suggests ways to prevent and resolve discipline problems. (Incidentally, classroom management, as you will see in Chapter 10, is much more than student discipline. It involves managing the classroom environment and learning activities of students as well.) Behaviourism defines, for educators, the concept of reinforcement. **Reinforcement** refers to consequences of responses that establish and maintain desirable behaviour. The high score on the essays served as reinforcement of the note-taking response.

The term *behaviour*, when used in everyday conversation, comprises an immense body of activities. From a behavioural scientist's point of view, however, the term includes only observable behaviours. What students *think* is of relatively little concern to behaviourists; what they *do* is the focus of importance. In linking environmental events to behaviour, the behavioural scientist also seeks to understand the cues prompting learners to act and the consequences determining whether learners will continue to act in the same way. These environmental cues and consequences govern whether a particular behaviour is appropriate or inappropriate in a particular situation.

behavioural approach   A school of thought in which learning is explained through observable aspects of the environment instead of mental or cognitive processes.

reinforcement   The process by which the consequences of behaviour establish and maintain it.

The appropriateness of behaviours is judged within the context of the environment in which they are displayed. In schools, teachers establish the environmental conditions that, in effect, control student behaviour in their classrooms. Students learn to respond appropriately to teachers' cues so that they know, for example, when tossing an eraser at the teacher will earn them a smile and a chuckle or a scowl and detention.

Environmental events can come to control the behaviour of those who find themselves in that environment. Important questions for any teacher to ask, and especially a novice teacher, are: How do I increase and maintain desirable student behaviour and decrease undesirable behaviour? How do I teach students self-management skills so that they control their *own* behaviour? Principles of behavioural psychology help provide answers to these questions.

TRY THIS: Observe a child for 15 minutes and record your observations. Then examine your notes to see how often you have described actual behaviours in contrast to making inferences about internal states or making evaluative and judgmental comments.

Principles of Classical Conditioning

Ivan Pavlov, who won a Nobel prize in 1904, conducted conditioning experiments that became classics in the history of psychology. Pavlov studied how a dog's salivation reflex might be conditioned—that is, brought under control of the environment. Pavlov's procedure began by simply presenting food to the dog. The dog salivated. The food is an unconditioned stimulus, a stimulus that automatically elicits a response. Salivation is an unconditioned response, an automatic reflex. Reflexes do not need to be learned or conditioned; they occur automatically in the presence of particular stimuli. People flinch when they see they are about to be hit. They blink when a puff of air hits an eye during a glaucoma test. They draw back in haste upon touching a hot surface, such as a burner on the stove.

In the case of Pavlov's experiments, the trick was not to get the dog to exhibit a reflex (salivating in the presence of food) but to get the dog to salivate predictably before food was presented. Pavlov conditioned the dog to salivate to a particular sound, a stimulus that does not normally elicit salivation. The sound, or tone, is the conditioned stimulus, a stimulus that is paired with an unconditioned stimulus. The tone preceded slightly the presentation of food. After several pairings of the conditioned stimulus (tone) with the unconditioned stimulus (food), the tone elicited salivation. Salivation elicited by the previously neutral tone is a conditioned response, a response to a conditioned stimulus. Figure 6.1 illustrates how Pavlov's **classical conditioning** works.

Principles of Operant Conditioning

B. F. Skinner, after carefully analyzing Pavlov's work, became interested in behaviours that were not simply elicited reflexes but that operated on the environment to produce consequences (Skinner, 1938). Skinner called behaviour that operates on the environment **operant behaviour**. He believed that organisms are inherently active in their environments, so that most behaviour is of this type. Birds, for example, peck at things, perhaps looking for food or gathering twigs with which to build a nest. When Skinner put pigeons into an enclosed compartment with a recessed light (known as a key) and food hopper, they pecked randomly at the walls, the key, and the edge of the food hopper. When he systematically presented food after certain pecks—at the key, for example—these pecks became conditioned. Thus, the operant behaviour of pecking the key resulted in the consequence of getting food. Because getting food was a desirable consequence for the pigeon, it pecked at the key more often. Through **operant conditioning**—learning through responses and consequences—the pigeon learned how to obtain food in the Skinner box.

classical conditioning The process of bringing reflexes under control of the environment. Also known as Pavlovian and respondent conditioning.

operant behaviour According to Skinner, behaviour that is not a simple reflex to a stimulus but an action that operates on the environment.

operant conditioning According to Skinner, learning through responses and their consequences.

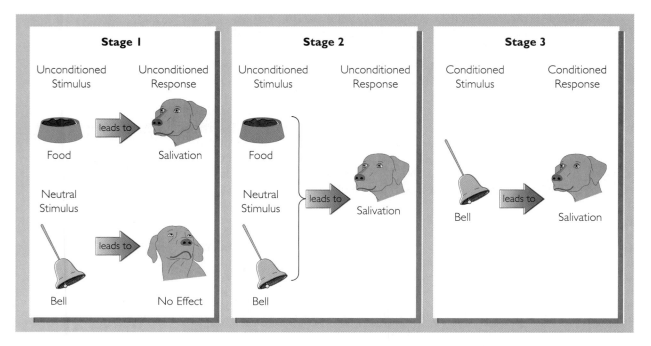

FIGURE 6.1
The Three Stages of Classical Conditioning

Through responses and consequences, students can learn how and when to raise their hands during a classroom discussion, how to write in a cursive style, how to operate the class computer, and other behaviours that support learning. Because operant behaviour is the type most often encountered in classrooms, our examination of behaviour and environment concentrates on operant conditioning.

How Does Reinforcement Influence Behaviour?

To understand why some operant behaviours are learned and others are not, Skinner (1953) argued that behaviour should be studied in terms of its antecedents and its consequences. Antecedents refer to environmental events that come before a behaviour and provide the context for it to occur. They are the cues that signal the availability of reinforcement for a given behaviour. Consequences are what result from a behaviour and, according to Skinner, determine whether the behaviour ever occurs again. If a pigeon did not receive food for pecking at the key in the Skinner box, for example, it would peck at the key no more often than it pecked anywhere else in the box. When pecking at the key does result in food, then the pigeon pecks at the key much more often than it pecks anywhere else.

The concept of reinforcement is critical to Skinner's operant conditioning, and it was first expressed by E. L. Thorndike (1913) as the **law of effect**. According to Thorndike, when a response is made that results in a "satisfying state of affairs," the response becomes more likely to occur again. Conversely, when a response is made that results in an "annoying state of affairs," the response becomes less likely to recur. Two important relations between a behaviour and its consequence are expressed in Thorndike's law. First, the consequence

law of effect Thorndike's law of learning, which states that any action producing a satisfying consequence will be repeated in a similar situation. An action followed by an unfavourable consequence is unlikely to be repeated.

is *contingent upon* the response, which means that it occurs only when the response occurs. Second, the nature of the consequence, whether satisfying or aversive to the learner, determines its effect on the behaviour. Satisfying consequences lead to a strengthening of behaviour, whereas aversive consequences lead to a weakening of behaviour.

The **contingencies of reinforcement**, or what Skinner (1969) called the learning principles based on the law of effect, can be identified in any learning episode by analyzing the episode for the three components of antecedent, response, and consequence. In Shareen's class in the Teacher Chronicle, for example, the shift to a new activity appears to signal students to go off task; the consequence of this behaviour is individual attention from the teacher, which acts as a reinforcer. This kind of analysis can be useful in helping teachers to identify problem behaviours and opportunities for new behaviours in their classes and to develop strategies for increasing desirable behaviours and decreasing undesirable behaviours.

TRY THIS: Observe a student in a class. Record, in strictly behavioural terms, his or her behaviour and the antecedent and consequent events. What can you infer about learning?

Antecedents of Behaviour

Once the pigeon has learned that pecking a key results in food, the behaviour of pecking can be brought under further control of the environment by making food available only when the pigeon pecks at a *lighted* key. The lighted key becomes a signal for when pecking will result in food. In a sense, the lighted key has acquired the ability to control the pigeon's behaviour. It serves as a **discriminative stimulus**, which cues the learner that a particular behaviour will be reinforced when it is present.

Suppose a teacher begins a discussion in a science class by walking around her desk and sitting on the edge nearest the students. She smiles and says, "Okay, let's see if we can figure out the concept of aerodynamics together." She then asks a question about the material. A student raises his hand, is called on, and answers the question. The teacher praises the student's response. The teacher's pattern of positive reactions is consistent for all students who respond, even when an answer is not what it should be. For instance, a teacher might ask the class how an airplane is able to fly. If a student responds, "By going real fast," the teacher may reinforce the attempt by saying, "Speed is a very important part of the answer. Your answer shows me that you are thinking. Keep it up, Aisha. Now, Aisha has identified speed as an important reason airplanes can fly. What are some of the other reasons?"

The teacher's question, her smile, and her position on the desk are all aspects of the stimulus situation present during reinforcement of student responses. Asking the question, smiling, and being seated on the desk are potential signals, or discriminative stimuli, to participate in the discussion. Students may participate in future discussions even when the teacher is not seated on the desk, but the probability of "participation behaviour" is enhanced by the presence of the additional discriminative stimuli.

Now, further suppose that the same teacher is in the habit of pacing quickly up and down the rows while asking drill-and-practice questions in a rapid-fire manner. The questions during drill and practice are factual questions. Quick recall is sought, but student responses are not praised or elaborated in the way they are during discussions. The teacher's smile is gone.

If reinforcement is delivered when the teacher is seated and smiling but not while she is pacing and stone-faced, the nature of the class participation will be different. Students will learn to discriminate between questions asked while she is seated and smiling and questions asked while she paces. The students may vol-

contingencies of reinforcement According to Skinner, learning principles based on the law of effect, the relationship between antecedent, response, and consequence.

discriminative stimulus A stimulus that is present consistently when a response is reinforced and comes to act as a cue or signal for the response.

By raising their hands, these students are exhibiting operant behaviour. What discriminative stimulus are they responding to? What consequence will reinforce their behaviour? How will their responses act as a contingent stimulus for the teacher's behaviour?

unteer less frequently during drill and practice, causing the teacher to call on students who have not raised their hands. (This may be precisely what the teacher wants to have happen.)

Teachers are largely responsible for the environment in which students respond; they are a source of discriminative stimuli. If discriminative stimuli are *signals*, remember that students of all ages are enthusiastic readers of the signals that teachers give. You may even be sending signals of which you are unaware. An entire junior high health class once decided that quizzes always came the day after the teacher wore a particular blue dress. (Lest you doubt the ability of students to identify discriminative stimuli, think back to your days in junior and high school and the time you spent analyzing, critiquing, and in many cases, making fun of the dress, mannerisms, and behaviour of some of your teachers.)

Let's now turn to Shareen Nasdid's predicament in the Teacher Chronicle. What signals, or discriminative stimuli, might she be emitting inadvertently that trigger disruptive behaviour in her class? Despite her desire to have students put away their own materials at the conclusion of a class activity, perhaps her running around the room, taking materials away from some students and giving new materials to other students, tells them that she will do everything if they wait long enough.

Kinds of Reinforcers

Discriminative stimuli can exist as antecedents to behaviour only when a consequence of the learner's response also exists. In the Skinnerian model of learning, the consequence of a response alters its probability of recurrence. The most common consequence is one that is satisfying, or *reinforcing*, to the learner and results in increasing the likelihood that the learner will repeat the response. However, consequences of behaviour can also be aversive to the learner, with the result that the response becomes less likely to recur. For example, the student whose answers in class discussion are always met with a frown from the teacher is likely to participate less over time.

The use of reinforcement as a consequence of behaviour is perhaps the most important management skill a teacher can possess. Understanding the effects of reinforcement entails recognition of the different types of responses that can serve as reinforcers.

Primary Reinforcers. A **primary reinforcer** is basic to biological functioning. Food, water, shelter, physical comfort, and affection are reinforcers that contribute to human functioning. Primary reinforcers can be used effectively in

REFLECTION: Recall *signals* used by your teachers. What effect did they have on your behaviour and that of classmates?

EXAMPLE: A teacher might use a secret code as a discriminative stimulus, such as pulling the left ear as a signal for a student to stop an undesired behaviour.

primary reinforcer
Something that satisfies a basic biological need, such as food, water, or shelter.

instructional settings (cf. Rachlin, 1991). Teachers find that some autistic children, for example, learn to make eye contact or to speak when rewarded for their behaviour with small bits of food. Middle school students also cite gum and pop as favourite rewards for which they will behave appropriately in class. However, the reinforcers used in classrooms are usually conditioned reinforcers.

Conditioned and Generalized Reinforcers. A **conditioned reinforcer** is a neutral object, gesture, or event that acquires the power to reinforce behaviour as a result of being paired with one or more primary reinforcers. Perhaps the most common conditioned reinforcer for humans is money. Pieces of paper, authorized as legal tender, have become associated with many of the necessities of existence. The potency of money as a reinforcer is extraordinary. Consider all of the behaviours people engage in to receive it in sufficient quantities. Money is sometimes used to reward students' academic progress, a practice that has met with criticism because progress tends to halt when the money stops (Kohn, 1993). However, Chance (1993) points out that, in many cases, no progress was made prior to the use of money as a reinforcer. He says, "If students show little or no interest in an activity, it is silly to refuse to provide rewards for fear of undermining their interest in the activity" (p. 789).

Some kinds of conditioned reinforcers are social in nature. A gesture of affection, a word of praise, a hand placed on a shoulder, a handshake, a physical threat, or a verbal reprimand are examples. Can you recall from your own childhood a teacher or other adult who could comfort you with a smile, or one whose look ignited terror? What is a reinforcing stimulus? This question is crucial for teachers; it is one that each teacher must answer for her- or himself. Furthermore, it is a question that each teacher must answer for each student; not every student is motivated by a good grade or a kind word. Shareen, in the Teacher Chronicle, has not yet discovered effective reinforcers to motivate Leah. Perhaps this is because Shareen has concentrated on punishing Leah's inappropriate behaviour rather than looking for ways to reinforce her on-task and appropriate behaviours. We see later in the chapter that behavioural procedures are preferable that involve motivating students toward the achievement of positive goals, rather than away from aversive circumstances.

Self-Reinforcement. Skinner (1987b) proposed the simple idea that many reinforcers offer learners the opportunity to manipulate the environment successfully. What is the attraction of video games? Why do people bowl or play billiards? Why do people enjoy hobbies such as painting or gardening? Why do people engage in behaviours "just for the fun of it?" (Nye, 1979, p. 38). Perhaps because these activities allow them to manipulate and control a portion of their environments without having to rely on other people or other aspects of the external environment, people are using self-reinforcement.

Self-reinforcement is an important concept for teachers. When students learn to reinforce their own behaviour, they begin to exert control over themselves and their immediate environments. Shareen observed that Ms. O'Dell's students appeared to pick up and put away instructional materials without the teacher's apparent direction (or reinforcement) of this behaviour. Students learn to self-reinforce when they understand the contingency between their behaviour and its consequences and when they value or desire the consequences. Ms. O'Dell's students, for instance, may have learned the contingency between putting materials away and having an uncluttered work space. Alternatively, they may have learned that putting materials away leads to easy access of these materials in the future. If students value either an uncluttered work space or easy

REFLECTION: What kinds of reinforcing stimuli do you prefer to use in the classroom? What means of communicating these stimuli are most comfortable for you as a teacher?

CRITICAL THINKING: Why should a teacher attend to discriminative stimuli when testing possible reinforcers?

conditioned reinforcer   A neutral object or event that acquires the power to reinforce behaviour as a result of being paired with one or more primary reinforcers, for example, money.

access, then putting materials away is a behaviour they can use by themselves to add something desirable to their environment.

Principles of Reinforcement

When the consequences of behaviour are examined for the potential effect they have on the behaviour itself, specific principles of reinforcement result. These principles are shown in Figure 6.2.

The nature of the reinforcer refers to whether the consequence of behaviour is satisfying or aversive. What makes a reinforcer satisfying or aversive is a crucial point for teachers who seek to influence students' behaviour. A satisfying consequence is something the learner wants and will work to obtain. An **aversive** consequence is something the learner does not want and will try to avoid. In Figure 6.2, behavioural contingency refers to the relationship between a response and its consequence. A student behaviour might lead the teacher to present a reinforcer or to terminate or remove a reinforcer.

Depending on the behavioural contingency and the nature of the reinforcer, then, there are four general principles that increase or decrease behaviour. Positive reinforcement and negative reinforcement both serve to increase behaviours, and reinforcement removal and punishment both serve to decrease behaviours. Positive reinforcement occurs when a satisfying consequence is presented and results in strengthening the response. For example, a teacher rewards a student's participation in class discussions, which increases the student's participation. Negative reinforcement also strengthens behaviour, but it does so through the removal of an aversive consequence. This means that something undesirable to the learner is removed to increase the desired behaviour. Teachers who give weekly quizzes, for example, might exempt students

TRY THIS: Observe behaviour during a lesson and identify all the contingencies of reinforcement.

FIGURE 6.2
Basic Principles of Reinforcement

Source: Adapted from *Psychology of Learning for Instruction,* M. P. Driscoll, 1994, Needham Heights, MA: Allyn & Bacon.

aversive Undesirable.

| | Nature of Reinforcer | |
	Satisfying	Aversive
Stimulus Presented Contingent on Response	**Positive Reinforcement** *Example:* Student turns in neater assignments when teacher praises neatness	**Punishment** *Example:* Student is sent to suspension for fighting (Behaviour Weakened)
Stimulus Removed Contingent on Response	**Negative Reinforcement** *Example:* Student exempts weekly quiz for exemplary homework (Behaviour Strengthened)	**Reinforcement Removal** *Example:* Students lose earned free time for playing with lab equipment

Behavioural Contingency

who achieve a certain score on graded homework. The impetus to complete the homework is strengthened because it enables students to avoid the aversive consequence of weekly quizzes.

To weaken a response, punishment can be used to present an aversive consequence to the learner, such as assigning students to detention for fighting in school. Reinforcement removal also weakens undesirable behaviours, because it involves taking away reinforcers from students who behave inappropriately. For example, a student who has earned free time on the class computer may lose some of that time for interfering with other students' learning.

How Can You Develop Strategies for Changing Student Behaviour?

In any classroom, students behave in ways that either support their own and others' learning or that get in the way of learning. Through behavioural analysis and the principles of reinforcement, you can strengthen desirable behaviours and weaken or eliminate undesirable behaviours.

Strengthening Desirable Behaviours

There are many behaviours that teachers wish their students would display more often in class. These might include, for example, turning in assigned homework, participating in class discussions, paying attention, putting away materials at the end of an activity, writing neatly, and behaving courteously toward other students. Students might already know how to do these things, but they just don't do them often enough or at the appropriate times. To strengthen desirable behaviours, teachers use positive reinforcement, the Premack principle (a special case of positive reinforcement that we will discuss shortly), and negative reinforcement. However, a study conducted by McGill University researchers, Jeff Derevensky and Randie Leckerman (1997) reminds us that reinforcement is not used similarly, or even systematically, by all teachers. They observed that teachers in special education classrooms used all types of reinforcements more often than teachers in other classroom settings. However, they noted an opposite trend in integrated classrooms "with regular students receiving more praise and reinforcement than special population students" (p.15). This finding reminds us that we must be aware of not only *what* we are reinforcing but *who* is being reinforced.

Positive reinforcement. **Positive reinforcement** occurs when a satisfying consequence is presented contingent upon some behaviour, which results in strengthening that behaviour. How can you use positive reinforcement?

EXAMPLE: Correctly identifying the value of a consequence can be tricky. One teacher kept putting a disruptive student out in the hall, assuming that he would prefer to participate in class and would be persuaded to control his behaviour. However, the student loved going into the hall, seeing the activity near the office, and talking with everyone who passed by. What might the teacher do to correct the situation?

Here's How

Here's How To Use Positive Reinforcement
- Identify a possible reinforcer for the student whose behaviour you wish to reinforce.
- Present it to the student each time the student exhibits the desired behaviour.

positive reinforcement
The presentation of a satisfying stimulus, contingent on a response that results in strengthening the response.

A teacher who wants students to participate more in class may smile and nod each time a student offers a comment. Shareen, in the Teacher Chronicle, was attempting to use positive reinforcement when she offered extra free time as a reinforcer for getting work done.

Premack Principle. David Premack (1959, 1965) reviewed the conditions under which positive reinforcement influences behaviour. His analysis yielded what is known as the **Premack principle**: A high-probability behaviour can be used to reinforce a low-probability behaviour.

What is a high-probability behaviour? If as a student you were given the choice between working on the computer or doing seat work, which activity would you choose? The activity you choose is your high-probability behaviour. The Premack principle is like "Grandma's rule," the contingency millions of grandmothers have used to get kids to eat vegetables: "Eat your green beans and then you can have some ice cream." Given a choice, most kids would choose to eat ice cream rather than green beans. The high-probability behaviour—eating ice cream—is promised to increase the incidence of the low-probability behaviour— eating green beans.

Perhaps you have observed a classroom in which the teacher says something like, "Okay, we are going to have ten minutes of free time now so that we will be ready to concentrate on those verb conjugations during language arts." Assuming that using free time is a high-probability behaviour, such an attempt misses the point of the Premack principle, because the free time is not used to reinforce verb conjugation. A better way for the teacher to proceed would be to say, "If we all work together on our verb conjugations in language arts, we can take ten minutes at the end of the period for free time."

Using the Premack principle increases a teacher's chance of selecting effective reinforcers. How do you select a reinforcer that will be effective for a particular student? Why not ask? Just as restaurants give their customers menus from which to choose, teachers can use a reinforcement menu to determine what students would like to receive as a consequence of their behaviours. What might happen, for example, if Shareen asked Leah what should be the consequences of her (mis)behaviour? Once you have identified high-probability behaviours, you can use those behaviours to reinforce other behaviours you desire for your students.

Negative reinforcement. **Negative reinforcement** occurs when an aversive consequence is removed or terminated following a desirable response to strengthen that response. Think about how car manufacturers prompt people to buckle their seat belts, and you will have a good example of negative reinforcement. A person who instantly buckles up (the desirable behaviour) can avoid the sound of the buzzer (the aversive consequence) that begins when the car is started.

Negative reinforcement is sometimes called "escape conditioning" (see Sulzer-Azaroff & Mayer, 1986). Skinner (1987b) argued that our culture, in general, relies too heavily on negative reinforcement, when positive reinforcement is a better solution. Too many times we may do something just to keep a boss, a parent, or a teacher off our backs. In these cases, we're not motivated toward the behaviour; we're motivated against the aversive consequence.

Weakening Undesirable Behaviours

Just as teachers want students to behave in some ways more often, they also want students to behave in other ways less often. Behaviours deemed undesirable are those that disrupt the class and interfere with students' learning. These could include, for example, talking out of turn or without being recognized, fighting in class, passing notes to a friend, and throwing food in the cafeteria. Teachers can deal with these behaviours by either presenting an aversive consequence or removing a desired consequence. The learner sees both responses as undesirable. In the Teacher Chronicle, the teacher views sending students to the principal as an undesirable consequence of inappropriate behaviour, but the student clearly does not share this view, because being sent to the office did not change her behaviour as the teacher expected.

Punishment. Weakening undesirable behaviours through **punishment** entails presenting an aversive consequence. This occurs, for example, when the gym teacher assigns extra laps to a student who misbehaves. Similarly, teachers might punish fighting or cursing by assigning students to detention after school or for some part of the school day. Punishment is most effective when a warning against misbehaviour precedes it and when the punishment is used to communicate to students what behaviour is not appropriate in particular situations (Azrin & Holz, 1966; Walters & Grusec, 1977). Punishment should be used sparingly, however, because it can have negative side effects, such as engendering fear or aggression in the transgressor. Although some school districts may permit physical punishment, it is not recommended because of a host of potential harmful effects. The side effects of punishment are a serious concern when they result in running away or truancy. A student who is punished for doing poorly in school, for instance, may come to view school or home with anger and fear. If running away or staying out of school enables the student to avoid those feelings, then undesirable behaviour is being inadvertently reinforced.

Reinforcement Removal: Extinction. People sometimes ignore the wails of a child who has just been put to bed or denied something. By ignoring the behaviour, thereby removing the reinforcement that was sustaining it (your attention), you succeed in eliminating the offending behaviour. This is known as **extinction**. Teachers practice extinction on a daily basis when they ignore annoying, but not exceedingly disruptive, behaviours of students. The boy who wanders around the room, the girl who taps your elbow to get your attention while you work with another student, the child who fusses when it's time to come in from recess are all examples of situations in which teachers may withhold their attention from the student and ignore the annoying behaviour.

Extinction works best when coupled with positive reinforcement for establishing more desirable alternative behaviours. Students can be distracted from misbehaving and then rewarded for behaving appropriately.

Reinforcement Removal: Time-out. **Time-out** removes reinforcement by separating a disruptive student from the rest of his or her classmates in order to decrease the disruptive behaviour. The rationale for this practice is that if a child misbehaves to receive the attention of the teacher or other students, separating the child from his or her audience removes a desirable aspect of the environment.

REFLECTION: What is your view on the use of physical punishment in schools? On what knowledge and values is your view based?

TRY THIS: Interview a teacher to find out the types of behaviours that can and cannot safely be ignored.

punishment The presentation of an aversive stimulus immediately following a response in order to weaken the incidence of the response.

extinction Removing reinforcement that is maintaining a behaviour in order to weaken that behaviour.

time-out The practice of separating a disruptive student from the rest of his or her classmates in order to decrease the probability of the response that precedes it.

TRY THIS: Interview a teacher who uses time-out as a consequence. Does the procedure work with all students? How does the teacher decide when and with whom to use time-out?

CRITICAL THINKING: Why might an emphasis on aversive consequences in the classroom have a negative effect on the learning environment?

EXAMPLE: Using small steps to successively approximate behaviour increases the likelihood of success and, therefore, reinforcement. Successively raising expectations and standards of performance has the same effect.

response cost A fine is exacted from an individual as punishment for misbehaviour.

Reinforcement Removal: Response Cost. Like extinction and time-out, response cost results in the removal of reinforcement contingent on a behaviour in order to decrease or eliminate that behaviour. In **response cost**, however, the removal consists of taking away specified amounts of some previously earned reinforcer (Weiner, 1969)—that is, the individual must pay a fine for misbehaviour. In society, response cost commonly occurs in the form of fines for overdue library books, exceeding the speed limit, and parking in restricted areas. It is important that the fine be high enough to deter the person from behaving in the same way again.

Response cost can work well in the classroom when students decide for themselves what the fines should be for behavioural transgressions. In a middle school, for example, students earn scrip (currency in the form of tokens or play money) that they can exchange for privileges such as free time or extra time on the school's computers. At the same time, they are fined in scrip for such misbehaviours as arriving late to class and being impolite to another student.

Teaching New Behaviours

To this point, we have discussed how teachers change behaviours that are already in their students' repertoires. Sometimes you want to increase some of these behaviours and reduce or eliminate other behaviours. What do teachers do when they want students to behave in new ways?

To teach students new behaviours, teachers use shaping, fading, and chaining, among other methods. Some goals teachers have for students are rather like holes on a golf course. A golfer rarely makes a hole in one. Instead, the golfer starts by taking his or her best shot with a driver. The object of the initial shot is to get as close to the green as possible so that the next shot will carry to the general vicinity of the hole. As the golfer gets closer and closer to the hole, he or she needs to be more precise in selecting clubs to use and shots to make. So it is in a classroom. The behaviours that teachers set as their goals cannot be reached with one shot. Teachers must choose their environmental tools and make their shots with increasing finesse until they reach their goals, the change in students' behaviour that they wish to effect.

This child's placement in to time-out is designed to weaken an undesirable behaviour by removing access to positive consequences (being with peers). What conditions will help to ensure the effectiveness of the time-out?

Shaping. The process of reinforcing successive approximations of a target behaviour is called **shaping** (Reynolds, 1968: Skinner, 1954, 1963). Successive approximations are behaviours that, over time, come closer and closer to some complex action. The first approximation of a forehand stroke in tennis is to grip the racquet correctly. Shaping behaviour can be accomplished in a number of ways with a wide variety of behaviours. By simply paying attention to a child on the school playground, a teacher shapes the child's play on the jungle gym, encouraging various stages of proximity to the jungle gym, touching, climbing, and finally, extensive climbing—the target behaviour (Harris, Wolf, & Baer, 1967). Skinner (1958) discussed shaping academic behaviours by using teaching machines, before the days of instructional computing. The presentation of material—either on audiotape, on a video monitor, or in a book—is called *programmed instruction*. Skinner described programs that provide reinforcement of correct responses and that gradually increase in difficulty. Small steps, or frames, that proceed from simple to complex, help to ensure that students respond correctly and are reinforced as often as possible.

Shaping is necessary because many of the behaviours we desire of students are complex. If we waited for students to learn multiplication on their own or to speak French spontaneously before we reinforced their learning behaviours, we might wait a very long time. So teachers have to take an active role in modifying behaviour. In Chapter 8, we discuss how teachers (and other students) model behaviour as a first step in the shaping process.

Fading. Recall that discriminative stimuli can exert a measure of control over behaviour. Suppose Leah has learned to stay on task whenever Shareen is walking around the room monitoring students. The monitoring aspect of the environment has come to control Leah's seat-work behaviour. Shareen is happy with Leah's effort but also wants her to work effectively on her own.

CRITICAL THINKING: A teacher used bear-shaped note paper to send home her grade one students' weekly reports. Good notes were written on the front and notes about negative behaviour on the back. The teacher decided mid-year to stop writing the notes but did not tell the students. Much to her surprise, only two students asked why they weren't getting their bears anymore. Why didn't more students ask about the notes?

shaping The process of reinforcing responses that are successively closer to the ultimate desired behaviour.

CONNECTION: How is fading similar to the notion of scaffolding that was discussed in Chapter 2?

TRY THIS: Interview a teacher to find out how complex behaviours are broken down so that they can be successfully approximated or chained.

CONNECTION: In Chapter 7, you will encounter a cognitive view of how information is committed to memory and motor performances are learned.

fading The gradual withdrawal of a discriminative stimulus while the behaviour continues to be reinforced.

chaining Successively linking together discrete, simpler behaviours already known to the learner in order to establish complex behaviours.

continuous reinforcement A schedule of reinforcement in which reinforcement is delivered after every correct response.

Using an approach called fading could accomplish Shareen's goal. **Fading** is the gradual withdrawal of a discriminative stimulus while the behaviour continues to be reinforced (Terrace, 1963a, 1963b). Shareen could use fading to make Leah's seatwork behaviour less dependent on her own behaviour. Here's how she might do it.

Shareen knows that Leah stays on task whenever Shareen walks around the room monitoring students' work. Because Leah is working well, she is getting good marks on her papers. Shareen could begin the fading procedure by spending less time next to Leah's desk as she strolls around the room. Each day, she could decrease her proximity to Leah, checking Leah's work carefully to ensure that she is still earning good marks. Shareen must be careful to reinforce Leah's good work with laudatory comments on her papers or with verbal praise. She must also be careful to fade the discriminative stimulus slowly, because too great a change would have the reverse effect. If Shareen finds that the quality of Leah's work suffers or that off-task behaviour increases, then she must again increase the discriminative stimulus—her presence—until Leah's work improves. Fading a discriminative stimulus requires a delicate balance between supporting a student's efforts and requiring a little more self-direction at each turn.

Chaining. Sometimes complex behaviours must be learned that are made up of simpler, discrete tasks. **Chaining** occurs when these simpler behaviours are successively linked prior to the presentation of reinforcement. Driving a car is an example of a behavioural chain that consists of the following sequence of behaviours (once the person is behind the driver's seat of a car with automatic transmission): adjust seat, adjust rearview and side mirrors, insert key, turn key to start, put in gear, press accelerator. Reinforcement occurs at the end of the chain in successfully backing out of the driveway. Often, the simpler tasks are acquired through shaping, as when a driver learns how much pressure is required on the gas pedal to accelerate at a reasonable speed.

Other typical examples of behaviours learned through chaining include memorizing long passages of prose (sentences are added in succession until the entire passage can be recited without mistakes) and performing a dance (each discrete step is added until the entire dance can be performed).

How Can You Maintain Newly Established Behaviours?

Consequences of behaviour are contingent on changes in behaviour. As we saw in the last section, the nature of the consequences that follow a response influences whether it is strengthened or weakened. The frequency of consequences also plays an important role. In practice, consequences of behaviour do not always occur uniformly. Not every student who raises his or her hand to participate is called on. Not every smile from the teacher serves to reinforce. Not every misbehaviour is reprimanded. A student doesn't have to make the correct response to every item on every test to be rewarded with an A. How, then, can you effectively maintain behaviours that have been newly established in your students?

Continuous Reinforcement

When you provide reinforcement after every correct response, then you are using a schedule of **continuous reinforcement**. Continuous reinforcement is important when first establishing a pattern of correct responding. For example, in try-

Insights on Successful Practice

How have you applied behavioural learning principles successfully in classroom management?

I taught a public school class for intermediate students with moderate cognitive disabilities. There were ten students in the classroom—nine boys and one girl. One student in particular, who had been referred by at least two teachers for emotional problems, was often in control of the classroom. His behaviours included making threats on the life of the teacher by imaginary uncles, kicking the wall, saying that absent students had been misbehaving, attributing behaviours to students who were incapable of performing those behaviours, and chanting.

I decided to use a form of response cost that emphasized good behaviour from the children in the classroom. In other words, I wanted to catch my students being good and then reward that behaviour. The system was colour coded, using green, yellow, and red tokens. At the beginning of the day, everyone started out in the "green." This meant that everyone had two smiley faces in the green, two in the yellow, and two frowning faces in the red. A child who exhibited a negative behaviour was given a warning. If the behaviour occurred again, the child lost a smiley face from the green and was sent to time-out for three minutes. At the end of the three minutes, if the child was calm, he or she was allowed to rejoin the class. If the child was not yet calm, the timer was reset for another three minutes. If, at the end of that time, the child was still not calm, he or she was given a choice of being calm or losing another smiley face. I explained to the child that although he or she had lost one smiley face, he or she was still in the green, but if he or she chose to continue the negative behaviour, he or she would then be out of the green. Once out of the green, the child was reminded that he or she was still in the yellow.

At the end of the day, if a child was still in the green, the child was allowed to have popcorn while watching a movie. If the child was in the yellow, the child was allowed to watch the movie and still had tomorrow's recesses. If a child lost all of the smiley faces, then the child was in the "red," which meant no movie and no popcorn, but he or she could have recesses the following day. A child who had lost all of his or her frowning faces was no longer in the red and would lose recesses for the following day.

The colour coding and rewards were combined with verbal feedback. For me, this feedback was the most important part. For example, if a child had an extremely bad day and was in the red at the end of the day, I would say to that child as he or she was leaving, "Tomorrow, you *will* have a good day." This technique resulted in a transference of external control to internal control. For example, eventually, as the students were leaving for the day, they would say, "Ms. V., tomorrow I *will* have a good day!" I would then praise them.

A problem with this technique occurred between the time the movie and popcorn were given and the time the school bus arrived. The problem student would display disruptive behaviours, knowing that he had received his reward for the day. When this occurred, I began passing out candy to those who were exhibiting desired behaviours. Those who acted disruptively were ignored. This technique was successful in reducing the negative behaviours prior to bus arrival.

The technique I used has proven to be successful in reducing negative behaviour. It does need to be used with other strategies to maintain or increase positive behaviours. Also, it has not been found to be effective in increasing production or quality of work. However, it was successful in reducing the amount of time the child spent out of the classroom (e.g., in the principal's office). The best part of this approach is that I regained control of my class in a positive way.

J. BROCK VINSON
Elementary School Teacher

Your Insights

Which principles of behavioural psychology did this teacher use? How do response cost systems work? What role did locus of control play in this teacher's strategy? Why might behavioural methods be appropriate for some students with disabilities?

---

ing to encourage a reticent student to participate in class discussion, you might reinforce the student with praise or acknowledgment every time he or she joins in. The result of continuous reinforcement is a pattern of behaviour that occurs at a steady, though not necessarily frequent, rate. A behaviour that is continuously reinforced is also relatively easy to extinguish when reinforcement is stopped. To increase the overall rate of behaviour, or to maintain it over time, then intermittent reinforcement should be used.

Intermittent Reinforcement

Intermittent reinforcement is contingent not on each response but on some schedule or combination of schedules (cf. Ferster & Skinner, 1957). For example, you might acknowledge or praise a student every other time the student entered a class discussion. In another situation, you might praise students for every ten minutes of remaining on task.

There are two types of schedules of intermittent reinforcements: interval schedules and ratio schedules. Interval schedules are based on time, so that reinforcement is available only after a certain interval of time has elapsed. Ratio schedules are based on the number of responses exhibited by the learner (Skinner, 1953).

In addition to conditions of time and number of responses, schedules of reinforcement are defined by the consistency with which reinforcement is delivered. Fixed schedules, whether they are interval or ratio, deliver reinforcement at a constant rate. Variable schedules deliver reinforcement at an unpredictable rate. Figure 6.3 identifies four schedules of intermittent reinforcement: fixed interval, variable interval, fixed ratio, and variable ratio.

Fixed Interval Schedules. A fixed interval schedule provides reinforcement for a correct response only after a certain period of time has passed. Classrooms are full of fixed interval schedules: the weekly spelling test on Friday, the unit test every six weeks, Friday afternoon films. All are schedules in which reinforcement is available only after a fixed period of time has passed.

EXAMPLE: Piecework, such as being paid for each garment you sew, is an example of a ratio schedule.

FIGURE 6.3
Types of Reinforcement Schedules

Source: Adapted from *Psychology of Learning for Instruction,* M. P. Driscoll, 1994, Needham Heights, MA: Allyn & Bacon.

intermittent reinforcement A schedule of reinforcement in which reinforcement is delivered on some, but not all, occasions.

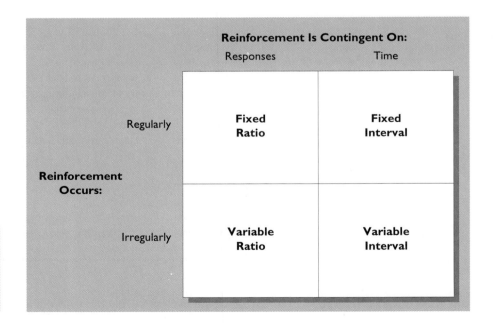

What happens to student behaviour when it is reinforced on a fixed interval schedule? Imagine your own study behaviour in a course where you have a weekly quiz on Friday. Over the weekend and at the beginning of the week, you probably think little about studying for the quiz, but as the time for it approaches, you spend more and more time studying, perhaps even cramming on Thursday night. A scallop shape, where behaviour occurs most frequently at the end of the time interval, is characteristic of fixed interval schedules (Figure 6.4).

Variable Interval Schedules. A variable interval schedule produces a more uniform rate of response than a fixed interval schedule. If you expect a quiz but are not told on what day it will be administered, you are more likely to study a little each day than to cram the night before. Overall, you might study no more than under a fixed schedule, but your studying is distributed throughout the week rather than crammed into one evening. Because distributed practice is more effective at facilitating learning than massed practice, many teachers prefer to administer pop quizzes than to schedule quizzes at regular intervals.

Fixed Ratio Schedules. A fixed ratio schedule provides reinforcement for a consistent number of responses regardless of how long it takes to produce these responses. A student working through a computer tutorial, for example, may have to answer five questions correctly before being permitted to advance to a new topic. Likewise, a student in reading may earn free time at the library for every three books read.

TRY THIS: Keep a journal reflecting on your own study behaviour in classes where pop quizzes are given and in classes where tests are given on a predictable schedule.

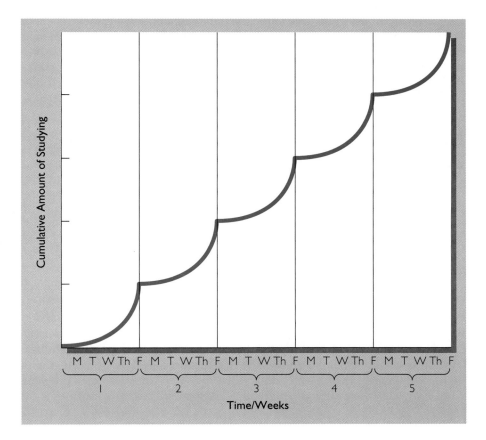

FIGURE 6.4
Cumulative Responses Under a Fixed Interval Schedule

Source: From *Theories of Learning* (5th ed., p. 180), G. H. Bower and E. R. Hilgard, 1981, Englewood Cliffs, NJ: Prentice-Hall. Copyright 1981 by Prentice-Hall. Adapted by permission.

The fixed ratio schedule, like the fixed interval schedule, produces an uneven pattern of responses. Immediately after a reinforcement is delivered, the rate of response slows. It's as if the learner has taken a break to savour the reinforcement just received. So, for example, the student who has just finished reading her third book and received free time in the library may not begin a new book for several more days.

Variable Ratio Schedules. A variable ratio schedule provides reinforcement after a varying number of desired responses. This type of schedule produces a frequent and consistent pattern of responding.

One high school teacher wanted to use extensive practice to teach math concepts in her remedial classes. She faced a major problem in encouraging her students to complete their homework. She used a variable ratio schedule to solve her problem. For each homework assignment a student completed with at least 90 percent accuracy, he or she got some number of chances to spin the "wheel of fortune." (Some assignments were worth more spins than others.) The wheel contained each student's name. If the student's name came up on one of his or her spins, the student won points that could be used to exchange for certain privileges. The teacher found that homework performance improved dramatically and, consequently, so did test scores. The teacher's scheme is an example of a variable ratio schedule because the number of spins that led to winning varied.

Intermittent reinforcement, if there are sufficiently long intervals or ratios, can be a powerful controller of behaviour. Behaviour maintained using these schedules is more resistant to extinction than behaviour that is continuously reinforced, with variable ratio schedules producing a behaviour pattern most resistant to extinction. Setting up an environment and providing appropriate consequences is part of the teacher's job. The other part of the job is determining what responses should be reinforced and helping students to learn strategies for self-reinforcement.

How Can Behavioural Principles Enhance the Teaching-Learning Process in Your Classroom?

Envision, if you will, a well-functioning classroom. Everyone's vision is probably a little bit different. For most people, however, a well-functioning classroom is one in which students know what they are supposed to do, work busily on task, and have facial expressions ranging from alert attentiveness to smiling satisfaction. The teacher may be working with one student, a small group, or the entire class. What does it take to achieve this vision?

From the examples so far provided in this chapter, you may have realized that problems in a class can come from a single individual who misbehaves or fails to behave in the desired fashion. Alternatively, problems can stem from a misunderstanding of what the rules are by the entire class. Either situation can wreak mayhem for the teacher as he or she attempts to solve the problem and get students back on task. The remaining sections of this chapter show how you can employ behavioural management techniques to solve individual or whole-class problems and design a learning environment that will facilitate all students' learning.

POINT: *Teachers coordinate the context for learning.* By using behavioural principles, teachers can work with individual students, as well as the entire class, to manage their behaviour and maintain an environment conducive to learning.

Working with Individuals to Change Behaviour

Most teachers can tell you who, in their classes, are the "quiet ones," the "social ones," the "active ones," the "passive ones," the "immature ones," and so forth. These are the students about whom teachers are heard to remark, "I wish Nicole would participate in class more often. She has so much to offer the other students." Or "I wish Kieran would take just a little more time to organize his work. He can be so impulsive." There are also students whom teachers identify as behaviour problems, students whose disruptive behaviours interfere with class activities and students' learning. Whether you identify a problem behaviour to eliminate in one student or a behaviour you'd like to encourage in another student, you can help students change their behaviour.

Here's How

Here's How To Work with Students to Change Their Behaviour

- Decide on behavioural goals.
- Determine appropriate reinforcers.
- Select procedures for changing behaviours.
- Implement the procedures and monitor results.
- Evaluate progress and revise as necessary (Driscoll, 1994; Sulzer & Mayer, 1972).

Set Behavioural Goals. To change a student's behaviour, you must know how you want the student to behave. What is the student doing now that you want to reduce or eliminate? What should the student do to behave appropriately in your classroom that he or she is not doing now? By observing the student carefully in class, you can determine just how frequently the student engages in both wanted and unwanted behaviours. From this baseline, and by enlisting the student's participation, you can establish specific goals for decreasing an undesired behaviour and increasing a desired behaviour. For example, with one student, you may set a goal for reducing temper tantrums from two or three times per day to no more than once a week. With another, you might set a goal for increasing the neatness with which assignments are prepared from less than one a week to at least 90 percent turned in neatly. Knowing the baseline of behaviour before you implement procedures to change behaviour provides a basis for evaluating progress toward the goals you and your students have decided on.

Determine Appropriate Reinforcers. As we have indicated throughout this chapter, what is reinforcing to one person may not be for another. What you choose as reinforcers for a particular student should depend on careful observation of the student to determine likes and dislikes. A conference with the parents or student can also reveal wants or desires that can serve as potent reinforcers in a behaviour change program. Alternatively, you can arrange for students to choose their own reinforcers. Often, the most effective reinforcers are those that individual students choose for themselves.

POINT: *Learners are diverse.* The reinforcers and contingencies of reinforcement that are effective with one student may not work for another.

REFLECTION: Recall a situation in which you had a choice of reinforcers. How did your choice influence your behaviour?

Select Procedures for Changing Behaviour. Whether your goal is to increase or decrease a behaviour determines the type of procedure likely to be most effective in reaching the goal. When increasing a behaviour, using positive reinforcement and the Premack principle is the best choice because negative reinforcement is a form of aversive control. For teaching entirely new behaviours, you may decide to use shaping, fading, or chaining, depending on the behaviour or task to be learned. When reducing or eliminating a behaviour, some form of aversive control is probably necessary for at least a short time. However, by using a combination of procedures, you can emphasize the acquisition of desired behaviours as alternatives to those being eliminated.

Implement Procedures and Monitor Results. Once goals, appropriate reinforcers, and behaviour change procedures are all determined, you and the student are ready to implement the plan. The most important aspect of implementing a program of behaviour change is consistency. If you are not consistent, you are likely to inadvertently maintain behaviours you are trying to change. During the period of implementation, you should also observe the student's behaviour carefully to determine whether the procedures you selected are having the desired effect.

Evaluate Progress and Revise as Necessary. The final step in working to change behaviour is to evaluate whether the procedures implemented are indeed working as intended. Is the undesired behaviour that was targeted for change actually occurring less often? Is the desired behaviour you or the student wish to establish occurring more often, or is at least some progress being made toward its achievement? If the answer to these questions is no, then you should reexamine every aspect of the program. Perhaps the reinforcer being used with the Premack principle is not a high enough probability behaviour to reinforce the desired low-probability behaviour. Perhaps you have emphasized aversive control procedures without planning for positive reinforcement of alternative behaviours. Whatever the cause, you should make adjustments to the program and continue to monitor their effects.

Suppose, in contrast, that the program is effective. In this case, you should consider gradually changing the schedule of reinforcement, so that the student's behaviour becomes more under his or her control and less affected by the external reinforcement. In the following episode, which took place in Peter Roop's classroom, can you detect the five steps to changing behaviour? What were Peter's goals for changing Rodney's behaviour? How did he enlist Rodney's participation in achieving these goals? Based on Peter's experience, what advice would you give to Shareen in the Teacher Chronicle?

Rodney was a handful in the classroom. If he could disrupt a lesson, he did. If he could hit someone, he did. If he could avoid work, he did. If he could cause trouble in the playground, he did.

Nothing in my bag of tricks seemed to work in my attempts to manage his behaviour. Not only did I want to control his outbursts and problems with others, I wanted him to eventually internalize some control over his own behaviour.

One day I discovered Rodney's desire to play football at recess. Not only did he want to play, he wanted to be the one to take the football out to the playground. At times, his need to take the ball superseded his wish to play. Once I finally saw his desire to have the ball, I used it in the classroom to effect a change in his behaviour preceding recess. Together we decided that he could take the ball on those days when he was nice to others. For several weeks he took the ball on good days and couldn't play with it on bad days. Each morning he checked with me to see how he'd done, although he already knew ahead of time whether the ball would be his. Then a day came when he was good and forgot all about the ball as a reward. For the next two days, he behaved himself without needing the ball. After that, his behaviour backslid and the football became necessary again—but only for the rest of the week. Unfortunately, we had a spell of rotten weather; with recess inside his behaviour deteriorated. But as the weather got better, the football once again became an important tool for eliciting appropriate behaviour.

Managing by Rules

The contingencies, or the rules, that students learn and that come to govern their behaviour can be learned by responding in an environment. Behaviour that is controlled by rules is called rule-governed behaviour. When students enter school, they must learn what the rules are. After spending several years in school, however, many of the rules are givens. Much of the behaviour you will expect of students in your classes is rule-governed behaviour (cf. Rachlin, 1991).

For students to behave as you expect them to, they must know the rules. You can tell students what the contingencies are in the classroom environment or learning situation. You can also elicit students' input in determining what the rules of the classroom should be. When students have a hand in deciding rules (and possibly consequences), they exercise some degree of control over their environment. This is likely to bring them one step closer to self-reinforcement and the management of their behaviour.

Knowing rules and following rules, however, are two separate things. Following rules is something a person does, a kind of behaviour. Rule-following behaviour, like any behaviour, is influenced by the consequences of the behaviour. Whether or not your students follow the rules in your classroom, then, is determined by the consequences they experience and the consistency with which they experience these consequences.

REFLECTION: Recall teachers you had whose actions did not match their words. How effective were these teachers?

Here's How

Here's How To Encourage Rule-Following Behaviour in Your Classroom

- Respond immediately. Although it is unlikely you can reinforce every student who is following a rule, you should respond immediately when any student breaks a rule.
- Be consistent. One teacher developed a system where he drops a yellow card on the desk of any student caught breaking a rule. The first yellow card is a warning. If the student earns a second yellow card, the

continued

Insights on Successful Practice

How have you used behavioural methods to increase student motivation?

It's vital for a young child entering school or preschool to build a positive self-concept and develop an enjoyment of learning as well as to become responsible. In order for young students to feel good about themselves, they need to become self-reliant. A clip system that I started about ten years ago and still use works beautifully with most young children. A successful positive approach to discipline makes both teaching and learning a joy in the classroom.

The classroom rules should be discussed thoroughly and should be posted so that the student is aware of rules, rewards, and consequences before the process begins. After the child is aware of what is expected, the classroom management begins. The child is responsible for picking up two clips (I use colourful plastic clothespins) upon entering the classroom each day. Anytime during the day, if a school or class rule is broken, the teacher will ask the child for a clip and either remind the child of the rule, or better still, ask the child to state the rule or the reason for losing a clip. It takes only a few seconds to direct a student back on task with minimal interruption to the teaching procedure.

At the end of the day, the student with one or two clips will be rewarded. One clip is exchanged for a sticker card, and an additional treat is given for the second clip. If the child loses both clips, he or she will be given a "You Can Do Better" sad clown stamp card. When ten stickers are collected, the student may trade them in for something out of the class treasure chest.

A cooperative communication between home and school makes the system work much more successfully. The parents have already been notified of how the clip system works, have a copy of school and class rules, and have been asked to follow up by providing reinforcement at home. I have received positive feedback from parents through the years, adding a little more responsibility each time. This also keeps the system from becoming old hat to the students and helps them become more self-reliant. By the end of the year, each child is finding his or her own clips with his or her name on them and at the end of the school day is responsible for putting the more sophisticated magnetic clip on a magnet board ready for the next day.

Discipline was my greatest dread when I first started teaching, and I experimented with many different methods. This system has helped me tremendously by relieving a lot of pressure from me and has also improved my students' self-discipline. I have shared this system with other teachers in my school and my school district. Other teachers in day care centres, kindergarten classes, and grade one classes are also using it. They have relayed to me that it makes classroom management a much more pleasant task.

EDNA LOVEDAY
Elementary School Teacher

Your Insights

What were the goals of this teacher's response cost system? What role did parental involvement play? Why might behavioural models be appropriate for younger students?

---

student is to see the teacher after class or after school. For the third infraction, the teacher drops a red card on the student's desk, which means "Gather your materials quietly and report to the principal's office."

- Be fair. Breaking a particular rule should merit the same consequences whether the student is the class clown or the class leader.

When managing by rules in your classroom, remember the old teaching maxim: Practise what you preach and model appropriate or desired behaviour. If you follow that rule, your consequences will be desirable.

Managing a Token Economy

Sometimes teachers develop token economy systems for managing rule-governed behaviour. In a **token economy**, students earn objects (e.g., poker chips, marbles, stickers, play money) that they can redeem for reinforcers. Each reinforcer has a price. After students earn the requisite number of tokens through correct responses, they obtain the reinforcer. In many respects, token economies are fixed ratio schedules. The fixed ratio is different for each reinforcer: A dinosaur pencil may cost seven tokens, whereas thirty minutes of free time on the computer may cost twenty-four. For a particular reinforcement, however, the ratio of responses to reinforcer is fixed.

Token economies have been shown to work in a variety of settings, including with patients in mental hospitals (cf. Ayllon & Azrin, 1968). In a remedial classroom, a token economy was used effectively to help students stay on task and to ask questions (Wolf, Giles, & Hall, 1968). Bushell, Wrobel, & Michaelis (1968) demonstrated the effective use of a token economy with children in a regular classroom, who, as a result of their participation, increased their attention to task instructions and became quieter.

Token economies differ from simple token collection systems, such as those set up by libraries to encourage children to participate in summer reading programs. Typically, children are rewarded a star or a point or a sticker—which is displayed on a chart—for reading a certain type or number of books. After the children have completed the requirements of the program, they receive a certificate and have their names posted at the library. Similar systems are used in many classrooms: behaviour charts, reading charts, multiplication charts, for example. In such systems, unlike the true token economy, collecting stars or checks does not allow the learner to choose a reinforcer. True token economies allow the learner some choice in determining reinforcement. In a token economy, the tokens acquire the status of conditioned reinforcer. Conditioned reinforcers can, of themselves, be powerful motivators of behaviour.

Token economies also permit the use of response cost that, together with positive reinforcement, helps to manage all sorts of rule-governed behaviour. In a sense, the management system becomes something of a minisociety. Remember the middle school mentioned earlier. Class or school rules are posted, with tokens earned for exemplary conduct or owed for rule transgressions. Students may not be happy about losing tokens when they break a rule, but they understand what they did wrong when you question them about their behaviour and exact the fine.

Using Praise Effectively

Behavioural principles are so widely used to support rule-governed behaviour of students in classrooms that we sometimes forget their usefulness in supporting other kinds of learning outcomes. Praise is a powerful reinforcer for learning more than rules or how to behave appropriately in various environments. It is also a powerful reinforcer for learning subject-related and self-management skills. Haven't you felt that glow of satisfaction when a teacher praised you for doing a good job or

TRY THIS: Observe a token economy and interview teachers who use it. What are the strengths and weaknesses of this approach? Ask if the teachers have plans for stretching the ratio or fading.

token economy   A behavioural program that allows students to earn objects for good behaviour. The objects can be redeemed for desirable goods or privileges.

TRY THIS: Observe a classroom in which the teacher enjoys a good rapport with his or her students. How does the teacher reinforce desirable behaviour?

accomplishing a difficult task? Haven't you worked that much harder after a teacher praised your progress toward an instructional goal? Praise can affect a student's persistence at a task, strategies for learning, and confidence in achieving a goal.

Here's How

Here's How To Use Praise Effectively in Your Classroom

- Praise students' accomplishments and progress during an instructional activity, not just their participation in it. For example, "I can see from your answers that your measurements are becoming more and more accurate. Accuracy is so important in conducting experiments."
- Praise students when they demonstrate self-management skills, such as monitoring their time in order to complete a task during an allotted period. A grade seven teacher is careful to praise students working in groups when they carry out their assigned roles in an efficient and cooperative fashion.
- Make praise truly meaningful. Don't give undeserved praise, either because the student hasn't earned it or because task accomplishment is too easy to be especially praiseworthy. In either case, students may begin to question whether they have the ability to earn genuine recognition (Woolfolk, 1995).

Making Behavioural Principles Work for You

No matter what behavioural principles you decide are useful for enhancing teaching and learning in your classroom, there are three important points you should keep in mind. First, behavioural strategies designed to change student behaviour must be used responsibly. There are important ethical issues for you to consider when you use behavioural strategies. There is evidence to suggest, for example, that rewarding students for learning what they are already interested in will undermine their interest in learning (see further discussion of the undermining effect in Chapter 9). Some researchers are also concerned about the message of teacher control that is conveyed by behavioural strategies at a time when student autonomy in learning should be facilitated (Lebow, 1993). Finally, it is important to consider the effects of these strategies on individual students. A behavioural program involving reinforcement at home may backfire and lead to increased abuse if the student has experienced a history of being punished by parents for poor progress reports (Woolfolk, 1998).

Second, the actions you take to reinforce a student do not constitute positive reinforcement unless behaviour increases. For reinforcement to occur, the consequence must be desirable to the learner. You cannot assume that verbal praise—or candy, free time, or high grades—is always desirable. Likewise, the punishment you mete out is only punishment if behaviour decreases, which means that the consequence is undesirable to the student. One of the basic assumptions of operant conditioning is that the individual is the appropriate source of information about learning. Individuals differ in what they find desirable and undesirable.

CONNECTION: What suggestions for effective reinforcement are offered by the developmental theories that were presented in Chapters 2 and 3?

Finally, you must be comfortable with the consequences you use in your classroom. There are any number of potential positive reinforcers. Many are tangible and obvious. An equal number are subtler: a smile, a nod, a casual comment (Nye, 1979). Moreover, there is the matter of the particular classroom environment and the group of students with whom you are working. In some schools, a teacher may be able to use a trip to the computer lab as a reward or to implement a token economy. In other schools, the school's structure and rules may not permit this. Knowing your strengths and weaknesses, and what can and cannot be used as reinforcement in your particular environment allows you to offer students realistic choices among reinforcers. Finally, although students learn through the operation of behavioural principles, as you have seen in this chapter, they also learn through cognitive processes and social interactions, which are the subjects of Chapters 7 and 8.

Teacher Chronicle Conclusion

Out of Control

The following Monday, Shareen spends the morning in Sarah O'Dell's classroom. Again she marvels at the control Sarah has without being overbearing. The students understand the room rules, they frequently monitor themselves without Ms. O'Dell's intervention, and when there is an occasional disruption, Sarah handles it quietly. While the children are working independently after a reading lesson, Sarah walks around the room, praising and questioning students.

Every so often Sarah drops a penny into a large bear-shaped jar on her desk. The students who see her do it smile at each other and get back to work. Twice before recess she drops in three pennies, once after all students had finished their work and once when three students cleaned their desks. At recess, Shareen asks Sarah about the penny jar.

"That's the secret for this semester. When we discussed room rules at the beginning of the year, they all had their input." Pointing to the rules posted on the wall, she says, "See, none of them start with DON'T. They all are positive, like 'We will work quietly.' After we established the room rules, then we decided on how to enforce them. The solution is the penny jar. When I

catch them being good as a class or individually, I quietly drop in a penny. Not every time, but frequently."

"What happens when the jar is full?" Shareen asks.

"Two things. They get to choose extra gym time, extra free time, watch a video, or even have a party. Then we split the pennies, and I start all over again."

"I tried something similar with my kids," Shareen says. "I put a piece of candy in a jar at the end of the day if they were good. That fell apart real soon."

Sarah laughs. "I tried that, too. But the more frequently I can reinforce the positive behaviours, the more involved they become in acquiring them."

"I can't tell you how much just watching you has helped," Shareen says. "Now I think I can make it to the end of term!"

"You'll make it far beyond that," Sarah says, just as the kids rush back in.

Application Questions

1. What did Shareen do to reinforce good behaviours?

2. What kind of reinforcement schedule did Sarah employ with the penny jar? Shareen with the candy jar? Why did Shareen's use of the candy jar fail?

3. Would the penny jar work with high school students? Why or why not? What would work?

4. Imagine if Shareen tried the penny jar approach now. Why might it fail or succeed for her?

5. How important is it for students to have input into class rules?

6. How should Shareen make Leah an ally, instead of an enemy?

7. Are rewards more effective if a person can choose the rewards for certain behaviours?

8. Imagine you are teaching a middle school English class. How would you involve the students in controlling their own adolescent behaviours?

9. Write a set of classroom rules for grade one, grade six, grade nine, grade twelve. What similarities and differences did you find?

10. Will what works for one teacher work for every teacher? Work every year?

CHAPTER SUMMARY

What Is Behavioural Science? (L.O. 1, p. 174)

Behavioural science is an approach to learning that relies on the observable environment and observable behaviours. Skinner's model of operant conditioning came from his study of Pavlov's work with behaviours that were reflexes to environmental stimuli. Skinner's theories address behaviours that lead to environmental consequences and thus operate on the environment.

How Does Reinforcement Influence Behaviour? (L.O. 2, 3, p. 176)

Skinner's basic model of learning involves three components: antecedent, response, and consequence. Antecedents are aspects of the environment that, in the presence of reinforcement, come to signal and control behaviour. Consequences of behaviour influence the probability that a given response will reoccur. Teachers systematically design reinforcement contingencies to increase or decrease the behaviours of their students.

How Can You Develop Strategies for Changing Student Behaviour? (L.O. 4, 5, p. 181)

Teachers strengthen desirable behaviours through positive reinforcement, negative reinforcement, and the Premack principle. Although it is possible to use primary reinforcers (such as food) to reinforce behaviour, teachers generally use conditioned reinforcers, such as grades, praise, or other forms of recognition. To weaken undesirable behaviours, teachers can use aversive measures such as extinction, punishment, time-out, and

response cost. For the most effective use of these procedures, teachers should pair them with more positive measures to reinforce alternative behaviours.

To teach entirely new, often complex, behaviours, teachers use shaping to reinforce successive approximations of a goal or chaining to link previously learned discrete skills into a more complex target behaviour. Fading, the gradual withdrawal of discriminative stimuli while the response continues to be reinforced, is used to make student behaviour less dependent on the teacher or other aspects of the student's environment.

How Can You Maintain Newly Established Behaviours? (L.O. 6, p. 186)

Once a behaviour is established using continuous reinforcement, you can maintain it by gradually changing the reinforcement schedule so that the response is less dependent on external reinforcement. Eventually, behaviour may come to be entirely self-reinforced. With interval schedules, the time is lengthened and varied until reinforcement is delivered. With ratio schedules, the number of responses required for reinforcement, regardless of the time it takes to produce them, is increased and varied.

How Can Behavioural Principles Enhance the Teaching-Learning Process in Your Classroom? (L.O. 7, 8, p. 190)

To change the behaviour of an individual student, you can work with the student to set a behavioural goal, determine appropriate reinforcers, select procedures to change behaviour, implement procedures and monitor results, and evaluate progress and revise as necessary. To ensure that students follow class or school rules, consequences of following or violating the rules must be established and consistently applied. One means of doing this is through a token economy, where students earn objects as a result of appropriate behaviour that they can use to buy reinforcers. Transgressions of the rules require paying fines by giving back previously earned tokens.

As a teacher, you must decide how and when behavioural principles will work best for you. Some teachers are opposed to the use of external reinforcers, whereas others do not feel comfortable using particular social reinforcers, such as jokes, with students. By understanding your own personal strengths and biases, as well as the effects of behavioural techniques, you will be in a position to make realistic decisions about the management of behaviour and learning.

KEY CONCEPTS

aversive, p. 180

behavioural approach, p. 174

chaining, p. 186

classical conditioning, p. 175

conditioned reinforcer, p. 179

contingencies of reinforcement, p. 177

continuous reinforcement, p. 186

discriminative stimulus, p. 177

extinction, p. 183

fading, p. 186

intermittent reinforcement, p. 188

law of effect, p. 176

negative reinforcement, p. 182

operant behaviour, p. 175

operant conditioning, p. 175

positive reinforcement , p. 181

Premack principle, p. 182

primary reinforcer, p. 178

punishment, p. 183

reinforcement, p. 174

response cost, p. 184

shaping, p. 185

time-out, p. 183

token economy, p. 195

7 Thinking, Remembering, and Problem Solving

LEARNING OUTCOMES

When you have completed this chapter, you will be able to

1. explain how to know that students are learning

2. describe techniques that enhance student learning

3. identify the processes children use to remember information

4. summarize the three stages of memory (sensory register, short-term store, long-term store)

5. distinguish between maintenance rehearsal and elaborative rehearsal in encoding information

6. describe the four types of memory (episodic, semantic, procedural, conditional) and their relevance to learning

7. explain the roles that metaphors, analogies, and images play in remembering information

8. describe how student attention affects the learning of new information

9. explain how the relevance of a lesson affects mastery of the material

10. identify ways in which teachers can simplify lessons to enhance student understanding

Teacher Chronicle

Chinese Proverbs

Michael Harvey was hired in September to teach two classes of grade four social studies. It is his first teaching job and he is eager to demonstrate to his students, the parents in the community, and his colleagues that he will be an asset to the school.

Over the last two months he has presented new information on the early history of Canada. Much of this has focused on the Native peoples of Canada and their lifestyles before the arrival of Europeans. He has provided them with detailed facts about the cedar houses and advanced tribal and social organizations of the Natives along the Pacific coast in British Columbia; the dome-shaped half-buried houses of the Natives of the B.C. interior; the tepees and hunting skills of the Plains Natives; the toboggans, canoes, and wigwams of the northern subarctic forest Natives; the lives of the nomadic woodland Natives of northern Ontario and Quebec, and the Lowland (Southern Ontario and Quebec) Natives who excelled at growing beans, corn, pumpkin, and tobacco and who invented lacrosse. The students in his social studies class were very interested in learning about Canada's First Nations peoples. However, after the unit, Michael gave his first exam and was very disappointed with the results. While they did well on basic facts, they did less well on describing the social organization and lifestyles of the tribes. Most of the students had seemed to be paying attention during the lessons. Why, then, hadn't they learned the material?

The next day as he is walking down the hall Michael notices a sign on another teacher's door:

Tell me, I forget

Show me, I remember

Involve me, I understand

—*Chinese Proverb*

The words rattle in his head all day long. He had told his class about the different Native groups and their unique languages and cultures. He had shown them pictures and videos of their different lifestyles. But he realizes now that he hadn't involved them. He makes new plans that night.

Focus Questions

1. How does a teacher know if his or her students are learning?
2. What techniques can a teacher use to enhance student learning?
3. What difference does a student's previous knowledge about a subject make in learning?
4. Why is student application important in mastering new knowledge?
5. How can teachers use what students already know to enhance their learning?
6. How can knowing how you learn as an individual be an important factor in your learning?
7. Why might sharing an experience or teaching another student improve learning?
8. What processes do students use to remember information?
9. What roles do metaphors, analogies, and images play in remembering information?
10. How does one process new information?
11. Why might Mr. Harvey's students have done poorly on questions relating to the social organization and lifestyles of Canadian Aboriginal groups?
12. How does the amount of student attention affect learning new information?
13. How important is the relevance of a lesson to student mastery?
14. How much should teachers help students integrate new knowledge with what they already know?
15. In what ways should teachers simplify lessons to enhance student understanding?

What Is Involved in Thinking, Remembering, and Problem Solving?

You learned in Chapter 6 that behavioural scientists focus exclusively on the stimulus, response, and associated environmental changes that occur with learning. Although these may be accompanied by changes internal to an individual learner, behavioural scientists argue that such changes need not be investigated in order to understand learning. Learning is conceived in terms of changes in observable behaviour. Cognitive learning theorists, in contrast, believe that events occurring within the learner are just as important for understanding learning as the environmental events external to the learner. The term *cognition* has to do with the act of knowing. Therefore, cognitive theorists conceive of learning in terms of the acquisition of knowledge.

Differing Views of Cognition

CRITICAL THINKING: Sherlock Holmes once used the analogy of storing items in an attic to describe human cognition. Why might the computer analogy be more accurate?

What does it mean to acquire knowledge? And how is knowledge a part of thinking, remembering, and solving problems? Cognitive theorists offer different answers to these questions. In this chapter, we examine several views of cognition. Information-processing theory is based on a computer metaphor that assumes humans may process information in much the same way as computers do. In this view, learning is a matter of inputting information from the environment, transforming it for storage in memory, and then retrieving it from memory to produce a response.

Extensive research on the properties of memory has extended the information-processing view and demonstrated how important prior knowledge is to the comprehension and encoding of new knowledge. Students come to school already knowing a great many things. What they know and how they have organized this knowledge in memory will greatly influence what they are able to learn from the lessons you teach.

Finally, an opposing view of cognition is represented in constructivism. Based on a construction, or "mind as laboratory," metaphor, the constructivist view proposes that learning is a matter of constructing knowledge in a learning community. In this view, learning is a process not only of individual knowledge construction but also of enculturation into the practices of intellectual disciplines (Cobb, 1994). As you will see, all of these views have important implications for teaching.

Learning How to Learn

CONNECTION: Learning how to learn is a process of developing metacognitive skills. This is discussed in Chapter 2 and later in this chapter.

For students to develop the critical reasoning skills that are an essential part of thinking and problem solving, they must, in effect, learn how to learn. They must become aware of their own cognitive processes. They must become capable of regulating these processes in appropriate ways so that specific learning goals may be attained. And they must monitor their own learning, recognizing when particular strategies are ineffective and should be revised.

It can be argued that learning how to learn is the most important outcome of schooling. A student who leaves school knowing how to learn has options that are not available to a student who does not learn well. Both the effective learner and the poor learner may possess basic reading and math skills, but the effective learner can use those skills to augment his or her opportunities. An effective learner is equipped not only to find and secure employment but also to improve and advance as an employee. One who knows how to learn is capable of continuously discovering opportunities and of critically analyzing those opportunities. The challenges that await our students when they have left our classrooms require that we help them develop their ability to learn. Being able to augment their knowledge and skill in any area they choose empowers them to identify and solve problems. For instance, an effective learner may not know upon graduation what opportunities exist in the field of outdoor recreation but will be able to reason, to apply strategic knowledge, and ultimately to discover what opportunities do exist or what opportunities might be created. Helping our students become able learners will allow them to pursue better jobs, better interpersonal relations, better educations, and better ways of living. Becoming an able learner involves possessing skills that allow one not only to learn effectively, but also to evaluate information accurately. Even good students often lack the latter critical thinking skills. Students are confronted with a rapidly changing world along with a continual media bombardment ranging from dubious claims about health treatment and popular psychology to pseudo-documentaries on the occult. As Ivan Kelly and Don Saklofske (1994) at the University of Saskatchewan point out, it is imperative that students develop an awareness of both the psychological biases, which foster and maintain fallacious beliefs, along with the critical thinking skills that will allow them to assess the believability of claims. Keith Stanovich, at the Ontario Institute for Studies in Education, has written an excellent book entitled *How to Think Straight about Psychology* (1996) that contributes to this end.

But learning how to learn is by no means easy. University professors regularly encounter students who study in ways that are ineffective or who tackle problems using strategies that are not appropriate for the particular problem at hand. In many cases, these students are not aware that their actions will not produce the desired result, and they are puzzled when this happens. "But I studied for so many hours!" they protest. As you will see in this chapter, learning comes about not only from being cognitively engaged but also from being engaged in particular ways. As you examine the ways in which cognition can be engaged effectively, compare your own cognitive activity to that discussed in the chapter. If you intend to use this chapter to improve your own learning, you must first reflect on your own cognitive efforts. How do you think about new material that you are supposed to learn? How do you go about trying to remember information that you need to know? How do you first define and then work on problems you are required to solve? After you have carefully considered the way you go about the work of learning, you will be in a position to experiment with some of the principles and techniques of learning that you will encounter in this chapter.

How Can You Teach in Ways That Facilitate the Processing of Information?

Psychologists were among the first to use computers to help them in their work (particularly in conducting statistical analyses). These psychologists became knowledgeable about the ways in which computers processed information; they began to theorize that humans processed information in an analogous way (Hunt, 1971). Human **information-processing models** borrow heavily from the vocabulary of the computer with terms such as input, output, storage systems, capacity, encoding, retrieval, and executive control.

information-processing models Models of learning that rely on an analogy between the human mind and the computer to explain processing, storage, and retrieval of knowledge.

Much of the information students encounter in classrooms is coded information. Making sense out of written or spoken information is a matter of using a linguistic code. Using numerals and symbols to define and solve mathematical problems requires another code. How do students learn these codes? And, once learned, how do they use the codes to comprehend new information, understand concepts, and put to good effect what they have learned? The information-processing view assumes that certain types of mental structures form a mechanism by which information is acquired, comprehended, stored, and retrieved for later use.

Figure 7.1 shows a flowchart illustrating the human information-processing model. Most information-processing models can be traced to Atkinson and Shiffrin (1968). Let's follow the flow of information through the various stages. Then we look more closely at the major stages of processing and the specific means by which information is transformed at each stage. These stages also provide ideas for strategies you can use to facilitate students' information processing. Refer to Figure 7.1 as you read.

The *environment* is the source of input into the information-processing system of the learner. Through sense *receptors*, humans take in stimulus information from the environment, which they see, hear, smell, taste, or feel. Receptors are the

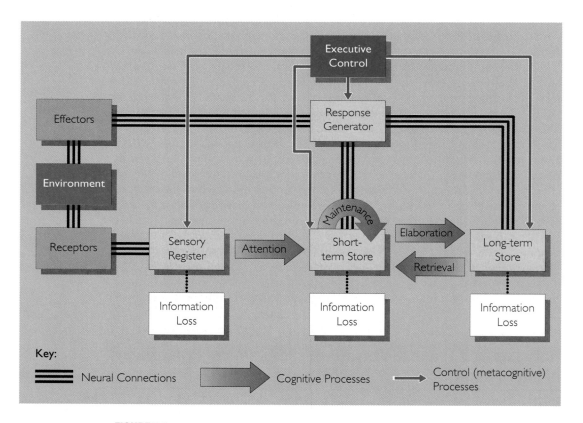

FIGURE 7.1
The Human Information-Processing Model

Source: Essentials of Learning for Instruction (2nd ed., p. 13), R. M. Gagné and M. P. Driscoll, 1988. Copyright © 1988 by Allyn and Bacon. Reprinted by permission.

physical connection between the organism and the environment. Each receptor has a corresponding *sensory register*, where information is stored very briefly.

From the sensory register, information that receives the learner's attention moves into *short-term store* (STS), where it meets one of four fates. Information may be lost, maintained in STS, used to make a response, or transferred by means of elaboration to long-term store.

Information reaching *long-term store* (LTS) can remain there, reenter STS through the process of retrieval, or be used to make a response. To generate a response, the learner converts cognitive information into neural messages that activate effectors. *Effectors* are the muscle systems that produce a response, such as speaking, writing, or moving in a specified way. The effectors are the physical means by which the learner operates on the environment.

Finally, *executive control* monitors the flow of information throughout the system. It governs the use of various processes to transform, store, and retrieve information. The monitoring and governing functions are executed by means of control processes.

Following the trail of information takes us from the environment (stimulus input), through the cognitive mechanism of the learner, and finally back to the environment (response output). Information-processing theory is a stage theory, postulating that information goes through a series of transformations as it passes through the cognitive system (Table 7.1). Although information-processing theory has undergone many modifications since it was first introduced, its essential stages—sensory register, STS, and LTS—have remained intact. It is tempting to think of these stages as having analogous physical structures in the brain. Indeed, we tend to refer to them as structures. Keep in mind, however, that the stages represent constructs made up by theorists to account for what seems to happen to information as people learn. Indeed, as more and more brain research is conducted, evidence is mounting that information is processed in parallel by multiple structures at once, rather than serially as originally illustrated by information-processing models (Iran-Nejad, Marsh, & Clements, 1992; Kesner, 1991; McClelland, 1988). Nonetheless, important implications for teaching accrue from an examination of the stages involved in information processing.

TRY THIS: Have a look at Michael Shermer's *Why People Believe Weird Things* for an entertaining exploration of the need for critical thinking, along with evaluations of a number of controversial popular claims.

TABLE 7.1 *Summary of Memory Stages*

	Stages		
Properties	**Sensory Register**	**Short-Term Store**	**Long-Term Store**
Capacity	Large	Small	Large
Code	Literal copy of physical stimula	Dual code —verbal —visual	Episodic
Permanence	0.5 seconds	20–30 seconds	Permanent
Source	Environment	Environment and prior knowledge	Effective encodings from STS
Loss	Decay	Displacement or Decay	Irretrievability

Transferring Information in the Sensory Register

The sensory register is the memory stage most closely connected to the information in the learner's environment. The sensory register stores information in a form that is very close to the physical stimulus, a literal copy of the input. For example, when you are listening to a friend speak, the information in your sensory register takes the form of sounds, not words. You turn those sounds into words at a later stage of processing.

The information in the sensory register is not very durable. Information can reside in the sensory register for about one-half of a second (Houston, 1986), and it decays quickly unless further processing takes place.

Although the sensory register holds information in an undeveloped state for only the briefest period, its capacity is quite large. A lot of information from the environment enters the sensory register. At any time, an incredible amount of information is available for a learner to process. A student sitting in a classroom receives sensory information from the teacher, a neighbour's whisper, the chalkboard, the bulletin board, the ticking of the clock, the aroma from the cafeteria, the buzz in the lights, the breeze from the window, the clouds rolling by, the graffiti on the desk. All of that information enters the student's sensory register, but not all of it is being noticed by the student. It is only the information that is noticed that moves on to STS.

Gaining Attention.   For students to process information further, they must pay attention to important aspects of the information. In the information-processing model, attention is a process that acts on information to transform it in some way. Attention determines which information is transferred from the sensory register to STS and which information is not. What causes a learner to attend to information?

Attention can be engaged selectively or automatically. **Selective attention** is under the control of the learner. Learners have the ability to orient their cognitive effort toward a particular source of information in the environment. A student in a classroom can make a conscious effort to attend to the speech and actions of the teacher. A student can also direct his or her attention to other information available in the classroom environment.

Imagine, for example, that you are a member of a discussion group for the class in which you are reading this book (you may actually remember a similar episode to the one we describe). There are twelve discussion groups in the room, each consisting of between three and six people. The task is to develop recommendations for teaching based on the developmental theories discussed in Chapter 2. Each group is to examine recommendations for elementary or high school. You have unwittingly joined a group that is discussing elementary school, while you plan to teach high school. As a consequence, you pay less attention to the discussion than perhaps you should. You do at least look at the other members in the group as they speak, and from time to time, you nod in reaction to particular comments. You are allocating just enough attention to the discussion so that you can nod, but you are not really following what is being said. Rather, you are listening to a conversation that is occurring in the group adjacent to yours. A woman in the adjacent group is describing her recent experience trying out a lesson plan she developed for a high school history class.

You selectively attend to the high school teaching story at the expense of recommendations for elementary school teaching. Should a group member ask you for your opinion on a particular strategy, you would be at a loss for an answer. The reason is that selective attention, the gatekeeper of STS, uses up some of the limited capacity available in STS. Attending to some aspects of the environment precludes the processing of other information.

You continue your nodding at the elementary school discussion while attending to the high school story when, three groups over, you hear someone mention your name. Suddenly, you hear neither the elementary school discussion nor the high school story as you strain to hear what is being said in that faraway group. The switch of attention, a cognitive phenomenon, is almost a physical sensation. You can almost feel your ear growing in the direction of your name.

Why did you hear your name spoken? You have no idea what was said just prior to the mention of your name, but suddenly, you hear the conversation quite clearly. The explanation is **automatic attention**—processing information without effort.

The conversation occurring three groups away has been entering your sensory register. (Remember, sensory register has a large capacity.) Prior to the mention of your name, you were not attending to that conversation. Therefore, the conversation did not enter your STS. The mention of your name automatically drew your attention. The conversation thus became part of the information in your STS, a part of your consciousness. Information is transferred from the sensory register to the STS by means of the process of attention, which can occur in either a selective or an automatic fashion.

Controlling, or at least guiding, the attention of students is something teachers attempt every hour of every school day. Reflect on the teachers whom you have had who were adept at keeping your attention focused on the content of the class. Reflect on those teachers who could direct your attention to themselves but not to the material you were supposed to learn. Reflect on those teachers who did not control your attention at all. Finally, consider the ways in which you control and direct your own attention. Effective learners employ a variety of strategies for attending to important aspects of instruction.

TRY THIS: Interview teachers for the strategies they use to direct student attention. What are similarities and differences in their strategies? What effect do the strategies appear to have on students' learning?

Perceiving Information. Gaining attention is a necessary condition of information processing but not a sufficient one. Students must also appropriately perceive information, recognizing familiar patterns that can serve as a basis for further processing. Children learning to read, for example, must be able to perceive the input b as the letter b and not the letter d in order to correctly interpret certain words. **Selective perception** is the process of selectively attending to specific features of the stimulus information in order to process it further. Perception is influenced by the nature of the stimulus itself, by the tendency of the cognitive system to organize and find meaning in stimulus inputs, and by the context in which a given stimulus appears.

To illustrate, examine these symbols: -   )   :

Chances are that you recognized, from their physical shapes, that these symbols represent a dash, a parenthesis, and a colon, respectively. Now look at the same symbols in the following rearranged format. What do you perceive? :-)

Arranged together in this way, the symbols appear to form a smiling face oriented sideways. Even though the physical stimulus inputs have remained the same, you perceived them differently. This demonstrates the tendency of the human cognitive system to form a *gestalt*, or a meaningful interpretation of physical patterns. Finally, the influence of context on perception can be seen in the following sentence.

I love the month of March, because that's when
the cold snows of winter give way to flowers in the
the spring.

automatic attention The process of attention that occurs without effort.

selective perception The process of selectively attending to important aspects or details in stimulus information in order to process them further.

Insights on Successful Practice

What strategies have you used successfully to help students process information and retain learning?

Every teacher encounters the problem of students not being able to remember what they learned last week, last month, or last semester. It is a typical problem. Students remember what they need to recall for the next test and then promptly forget the material. Then when cumulative tests come, students fall apart. They do not seem to remember material they should readily have at their fingertips. Whether the test is a teacher-made exam or a national standard of measurement, students and teachers look bad.

There is a solution, however. It is a game called "Around the World" that teachers and students can enjoy. Played daily or whenever time permits, the game can be adapted to all subjects and age levels. There are virtually no limits to how the game can be employed.

Simply stated, the teacher calls out questions and students answer. Two randomly selected students seated next to each other begin. They stand and the teacher asks a question such as "What is the continent on which we live called?" The first of the two students to say "North America" wins and advances to the next student. That student stands to face the challenger. The teacher asks another question. If the student who previously won wins again, he or she advances to the third student. If not, that student sits down in the seat of the second student, and the second student advances. The game continues for several rounds or as long as time permits. Each student tries to go "Around the World" or around the classroom by defeating all the other students. A prize may be offered for doing so.

Competition requiring calculations takes students to the chalkboard. With chalk in hand, the two competitors listen to the problem and work it as quickly as possible. When they are finished, they step back and point to the correct answer. If neither is correct, the teacher might allow students to work the problem again. Normally, whoever finishes first with the correct answer challenges the next student. Variations could include letting one-half of the room challenge the other half. Points for right answers are tallied. Sometimes points are awarded to both teams if students come up with correct answers within a certain time limit.

"Around the World" works beautifully with English grammar questions. A teacher might ask students to find the verb in the sentence. "John walked to school" or the proper noun in the sentence, "I asked Mary to come to the game." In science, questions could focus on scientific terms, body systems, parts of the universe, or animals and their habitats. Social studies is perhaps the easiest subject in which to formulate questions because there is seemingly no end to the number of geography questions a teacher can generate.

The game can be lots of fun and very effective even on a field trip. While on the bus, teachers and students can review material applicable to that particular extended classroom experience. The teacher asks questions as usual but calls on one student from each side of the bus beginning with the first student. Two new students may be called each time or the winner may continue and face a new challenger each time. Regardless, students do not stand up. They keep their seats, and everyone must be very quiet in order to hear the questions and answers.

There really are no limits to this game. Teachers and students will see its advantages immediately and think up a number of variations. If played regularly, students will remember material from earlier classes and surprise themselves and test administrators with the knowledge they have accumulated.

WILLIAM D. SMYTH
Teacher

Your Insights

How does this teacher's "Around the World" game work to facilitate the retention of learning? Would this approach be appropriate for all kinds of learning? What might be some advantages and disadvantages of classroom competitions?

Did you detect the error in this sentence? Chances are you read right over the second *the* in the part of the sentence that reads "flowers in the *the* spring." Prior knowledge sets up expectations for perception, so that students perceive what they expect the stimulus information to be. This is why, for example, proofreading is such a difficult task. It requires paying attention to the stimulus input of letters, while at the same time ignoring the meaning their arrangement provides.

To facilitate selective perception, teachers draw students' attention to particular features in the instruction that are important to process further. In reading, students learn to distinguish similar letters. They also learn to use contextual information to interpret the meanings of unfamiliar words in sentences or paragraphs. In science, students learn to perceive the units of measurement on graduated cylinders. In music, students learn to distinguish the sounds of different instruments, different scales, and different rhythms.

Here's How

Here's How To Gain Attention and Facilitate Selective Perception

- Use gestures, voice inflections, and other signals to alert students and indicate important points in the lesson.
- Ask questions to stimulate curiosity and interest in the lesson.
- Tell students what they will learn in the lesson to establish an expectancy for learning. Help them to find relevance in the lesson to their own interests and goals.
- Compare and contrast similar features to help students focus on essential details.

Encoding Information in STS

In some versions of the information-processing model, STS is called **working memory** (cf. Bell-Gredler, 1986); STS is where the learner *works on* the information from the environment. In STS the learner encodes information: Sounds become spoken words; visual patterns on a page become written words.

To *encode* means to convert a message into a code. In information-processing theory, **encoding** is the process of converting a message from the environment to a cognitive code so that the information can be stored and later remembered (Kulhavy, Schwartz, & Peterson, 1986). Encoding is one kind of work done in STS, and from an instructional perspective, it is the most important. Making codes—constructing cognitive representations—is the primary business of the human cognitive mechanism. This is the work we want our students to do in our classrooms. The codes that learners create in STS allow them to say they understand or do not understand the material that has been presented to them. The codes also allow students to perform tasks of varying complexity.

As we have already discovered, information from the environment arrives in STS through the sensory register. The knowledge that allows us to encode sensory input is stored in LTS. Creating meaningful codes requires integration of information from the environment with the knowledge stored in LTS. STS is a busy place because it is where what students know comes together with the information they are to learn.

Another reason why STS is such a busy place is that it has a limited capacity. If you have ever had thirty students all asking you questions at the same time, you know what limited capacity means. In his classic article, Miller (1956)

CRITICAL THINKING: A kindergarten teacher begins each math session with a game. She asks certain students to stand up, choosing the students by a particular attribute: patterns in seating, initials, colours of clothing, eyes, hair, types of shoes. The other students guess why the students are standing. Why would this game help young students with mathematics?

EXAMPLE: The making of meaning occurs in STS. It is in STS that information from the environment is brought together with prior knowledge—that is, information from LTS.

working memory In some models, another term for STS because this is the stage at which a learner works on information from the environment.

encoding The process of converting a message from the environment to a cognitive code so that the information can be stored and later remembered.

identified the capacity of STS at about seven pieces of information. Pieces of information are known technically as "chunks." Chunks may not sound much like a scientific term, but it is a good descriptor. What follows is a row of numbers, fifteen pieces of information—DON'T LOOK YET. Study the digits for about ten seconds and then cover the list with your hand. Here are the fifteen digits you will be asked to remember in order:

1 4 9 1 6 2 5 3 6 4 9 6 4 8 1

Now, with the list covered, see how many of the digits you can remember in order. (By the way, if you cheated and looked ahead at the digits, try this little experiment with a friend by reading the numbers to him or her.)

If you tried to process each digit separately, you were taxing the limit of your STS. As a result, you probably did not recall all of the digits. If you grouped the digits into two- or three-digit numbers (e.g., 149, 162), you probably recalled more of the information. Grouping the digits into numbers is an example of chunking (Miller, 1956; Simon, 1974). When the digits are chunked, the number of pieces of information to remember is reduced. The amount of information per se has not changed, but the limited capacity of STS has been used more efficiently. This is especially true if the chunks form a meaningful pattern. Can you detect a pattern in these numbers?

An item of information in STS can last for approximately twenty to thirty seconds (Miller, 1956; Peterson & Peterson, 1959). Items may not last that long if they are displaced by new information arriving from the sensory register. Have you ever tried to take verbatim notes during a lecture? As you will see, there are a number of reasons why this isn't a good way to learn. In the context of STS, the problem with transcribing is that it taxes capacity. Unless you are a very fast writer, you are working on the new information that the lecturer is presenting while attempting to remember old information long enough to write it down on paper. We have all tried this kind of note-taking at one time or another; most of us gave it up about the time we realized that we had very little idea of what the lecturer was trying to convey.

Items in STS can be maintained for longer than thirty seconds if they are rehearsed (Anderson & Craik, 1974). Rehearsing information in order to maintain it in STS has a positive side effect. Rehearsal can lead to the transfer of information from STS to LTS. Transfer is not guaranteed, but the longer information is rehearsed, the more likely it will be transformed to LTS (cf. Atkinson & Shiffrin, 1971; Jacoby & Bartz, 1972).

Maintenance Rehearsal. Maintenance and elaboration are the two process arrows that originate in STS (see Figure 7.1). **Maintenance rehearsal** maintains the availability of information in STS by keeping it activated. Repeating a telephone number over and over to maintain the information long enough to dial it is maintenance rehearsal. With enough rehearsal, it is possible to transfer the information to LTS. You've probably stored a lot of information in LTS simply because of repetition. Do you remember a poem you once learned in high school? Through sheer repetition—maintenance rehearsal—the information may have been stored in LTS.

Maintenance rehearsal is a type of encoding that could be called brute force learning. Repeating information doesn't guarantee that information will be stored permanently, but it can lead to permanent storage. Information stored in this way, however, may not be all that meaningful.

REFLECTION: In what ways do you chunk information to make it easier to learn? Are these strategies useful for teaching as well as learning?

TRY THIS: Observe students in high school as they take notes in class. Are they attempting to take verbatim notes? What can you infer about their learning?

maintenance rehearsal
Rote memorization, which does not guarantee understanding.

These students will remember their lines through maintenance rehearsal. At the same time they will encode key elements of the play, such as plot sequence and characterization. Based on this knowledge, their capacity for elaborative rehearsal will enable them to improvise if they forget their lines during a performance.

Memory does not equate understanding. How many times have you memorized a formula or a definition of some concept that you did not truly understand? Maintenance rehearsal, or rote memorization, is helpful or necessary in many situations, both in and out of the classroom. For example, students can solve many types of arithmetic problems quickly and easily when they have committed the multiplication tables to memory. For most people, this requires maintenance rehearsal. Likewise, maintenance rehearsal is useful for learning spelling rules, the genders of French and Cree nouns, and the dates of historic events. However, because many of the learning outcomes we seek for students are outcomes of understanding, another type of encoding is required, elaborative rehearsal.

Elaborative Rehearsal. Elaborative rehearsal is a type of encoding that relates new information to information already stored. The stimulus information becomes transformed because the learner elaborates on it in some way (cf. Driscoll, 1994). A student, after reading a description of a concept, might generate an example of that concept. Another student might create a mental picture of stimulus information, such as the solar system in order to visualize the relative distances planets are from the sun. Stimulus information might be supplemented with additional information that aids recall—for example, learning to spell "arithmetic" by memorizing the sentence, "a rat in the house may eat the ice cream."

Do you recall learning the names of the Great Lakes? Perhaps your teacher wrote the names of the lakes on the chalkboard:

Huron, Ontario, Michigan, Erie, Superior.

Your teacher, after writing the names on the board, may have asked the class to look closely at the names. "Does anyone in the class notice anything about the names of the Great Lakes? Don't answer aloud, but does anyone notice something about the first letters of each lake? Look at the first letters and see if they form a word. What is the word?" Using the word HOMES to store the names of the Great Lakes is a form of elaborative rehearsal known as a mnemonic device, specifically an acronym.

Whether you, as a teacher, decide to use maintenance rehearsal or elaborative rehearsal in the classroom has important implications for the way students will encode information effectively. The teacher who asks students to continually repeat information takes on an additional burden: Drill and practice can be boring. Using maintenance rehearsal as an instructional technique makes it hard to maintain a high level of attention in the classroom. It is easier to keep students interested and on task if they are transforming information rather than merely repeating it.

EXAMPLE: To learn, it is necessary to remember information. However, memorization is not always the learning goal.

EXAMPLE: Elaborative rehearsal may take more effort than maintenance at the point of encoding, but in the long run it is a more efficient learning tactic.

CONNECTION: Mnemonic devices are discussed in greater detail later in this chapter.

REFLECTION: Think about times you have used maintenance and elaborative rehearsal in learning. What was the result in each case? Which was more effective in helping you to achieve a learning goal?

elaborative rehearsal A type of encoding that relates new information to information already in LTS.

Another implication of your choice relates to students' cognitive efforts. Both maintenance and elaboration require STS capacity, but the student who elaborates is doing more with information than the student who merely maintains. Maintenance rehearsal occurs in STS. Maintenance rehearsal may cause information to be transferred to LTS, but the encoding itself is an STS activity. Elaboration requires the use of knowledge in LTS. In order to integrate stimulus information with prior knowledge, prior knowledge must be transferred from LTS to STS.

Retrieving Information from LTS

LTS is considered to be the permanent store of the human information-processing system (Driscoll, 1994). LTS houses many different kinds of information: episodes that you have experienced in childhood, facts, abstract rules that allow you to understand language, strategies for solving problems, smells, sounds, tastes, feelings, and visual images. There is information in LTS that you may not know is there.

"How many windows were in the house or apartment in which you were raised?" Our guess is that no one has ever asked you for that information. Therefore you have never retrieved it from your LTS. The number of windows is not the kind of information you use every day, but let us see if we can find the information somewhere in the recesses of your LTS.

First, picture in your mind the house or apartment that you grew up in. Do you have the place in mind? If it had multiple stories, concentrate on the main floor. Now, imagine that you are inside your childhood home. Picture yourself just inside the front door. As you stand there, turn to your right. Now begin walking around the main floor. If there is a wall, follow it to an opening. If there are doors, open them and proceed slowly. Walk through all of the rooms on that floor and look out each window, keeping track of the number of windows you encounter. How many windows are there?

LTS contains much of what we learned intentionally and much that we never made a conscious effort to learn. As learners, we bring the contents of our LTS to school with us. Our experiences are represented there. Our knowledge is represented there. We call that knowledge and experience *prior knowledge*.

Retrieval. **Retrieval** is the process that transfers information from LTS to STS. It is the utilization of stored information. For information stored in LTS to be used by the learner, it must be brought into working memory. How is information stored in LTS brought to bear on stimulus information being encoded in STS? What can a teacher do to facilitate retrieval? Recall the teacher who used the word HOMES to help students elaboratively encode the names of the Great Lakes. At some later time, the teacher will be able to use HOMES as an effective retrieval cue. The cue—HOMES—is specific to the encoding of the names of the Great Lakes.

Another connection between encoding and retrieval is evidenced by the nature of the codes created during elaborative encoding. The prior knowledge a learner retrieves in order to make sense of incoming information influences the comprehension of the stimulus. For example, students use their general knowledge about war to interpret an account in the local newspaper about an armed conflict in a particular region of the world. Although the report may include no information about atrocities perpetrated by the aggressors, students are likely to believe that these acts took place nonetheless. They infer from previously learned information meanings that are not explicitly presented.

retrieval The process that transfers information from LTS to STS in order to be used.

Reconstructive Retrieval. Although cues, such as the HOMES acronym, can make retrieval very efficient, some information in LTS is not so readily available. Earlier you were asked to retrieve the number of windows in your childhood home. The cues we provided to help you retrieve that information were not memory tricks (like HOMES) or something you inferred (e.g., that "aggressors perpetrated atrocities on their victims"). Instead, we suggested that you create a visual image of your home, which helped you to reconstruct the information you were asked to retrieve.

Retrieval of this sort can be viewed as a type of problem solving. The learner uses logic, retrieval cues, and prior knowledge to reconstruct information (Lindsay & Norman, 1977). Reconstructive retrieval is highly sensitive to the particular knowledge and experiences stored in a learner's LTS. In reading and remembering the details of a story set in Calgary, for example, students who live in Halifax or St. John's are likely to construct and retrieve understandings that differ from those of students who live in Vancouver.

Instructionally, when you help students solve the problem of accessing information you help them make sense of the material they are to learn, facilitating the process of retrieval. The knowledge students retrieve from LTS influences their understanding.

EXAMPLE: Inferential comprehension, which involves reconstructive retrieval, is an important milestone in the development of fluent reading.

TRY THIS: Identify a topic you anticipate teaching in your own classroom. Think about how you will conceptualize the topic. Describe from a student's point of view how he or she might process the information you give, allowing him or her to conceptualize the topic.

Why Is It Important to Activate Students' Prior Knowledge?

Prior knowledge—knowledge that has already been acquired— influences the quality and quantity of what students learn. Human beings intuitively understand that prior knowledge is useful in understanding new information. Recall a time in high school when you were listening to a teacher's explanation of some concept. If its meaning somehow eluded you, what did you do? You probably knitted your brow, raised your hand, and said something to the effect, "I don't understand what you are talking about. Could you give me another example?"

The prior knowledge learners bring to a learning situation influences their understanding of new information. Indeed, part of the understanding constructed by a student is due to his or her prior knowledge (Rumelhart, 1980; Leinhardt, 1992). Tobias (1982) argued that students' prior knowledge is the most important factor in determining the outcome of any instructional situation. Tobias suggested further that we should worry less about ability or other individual differences. Instead, we should concentrate on discovering methods of instruction that will best tap the learner's prior knowledge and capitalize on what a student brings to the lessons we are teaching.

It is important to remember that prior knowledge can inhibit learning as well as facilitate it. Have you ever tried to learn racquetball after years of playing tennis? Although both are racquet sports, the way in which the racquet is swung requires entirely different movements of the arm and wrist. As a consequence, it can be very difficult for a tennis player to learn the wrist movements required in racquetball. Leinhardt (1992) offers another example involving the use of base ten blocks (Dienes blocks) in teaching arithmetic.

Dienes blocks are very helpful in providing students with a concrete representation of regrouping in addition. When the concept of regrouping is later encountered in subtraction, those students with prior knowledge of Dienes blocks are better prepared than students without this prior knowledge. However, when students are asked to use Dienes blocks to represent decimals, their learn-

POINT: *Learners are diverse.* The students who come into your classroom will vary tremendously in the prior knowledge they bring with them.

prior knowledge
Knowledge that has already been acquired and stored in long-term memory.

Insights on Successful Practice

What memory games or mnemonic devices have you used successfully to help students remember information?

One of several junior high school teaching positions that I have held was in a large inner-city school. While the students were classified as mildly learning impaired, they were all from economically disadvantaged homes where learning was not valued. The students lacked motivation for learning and seemed to be merely marking time until they were able to drop out. They offered a challenge to teachers to make learning opportunities not only meaningful but also exciting and memorable.

I relied significantly on the use of mnemonics to make learning "stick" and found that they were successful because the students enjoyed using them. Mnemonics are those wonderful devices that place memory tracers on essential but seemingly unrelated bits of information. Just as metaphors are devices to make the unfamiliar seem familiar, mnemonics are devices to make the illogical seem logical. In whatever manner teachers make use of mnemonics, research has shown them to be very effective as teaching devices—not just for classrooms, but I use them personally. My favourite, which I use every time I have to replace a lightbulb or put a screw in a fixture is "Righty, tighty. Lefty, loosey." Another mnemonic I use regularly is one I discovered to help remember the spelling of "absence," my own personal memory hurdle. I finally realized that "There is no *sense* in your ab*sence*."

In one of my junior high classrooms, the students were relatively proficient in mathematics computation and enjoyed the challenges of multiplication. I soon noticed, however, that, without exception, when they had obtained the sum they would liberally sprinkle spaces into the answer without order or meaning, as if they knew that all long figures required a few spaces to be complete. I tried explaining the system for placement of spaces, but without success.

One day I wrote a figure "1" on the far left side of the chalkboard, and then proceeded to follow that with zeros across three contiguous boards. I then gave each student a piece of chalk, had them line up behind me, and going from right to left we sang "One, two, three, a space! One, two, three, a space!," and marked spaces as we conga-lined around the room. Never again did a single student misplace a space in a computation answer. I would often notice students with heads bowed, softly saying "One, two, three, a space!" as they counted off places in their answers.

VIRGINIA L. PEARSON
College of Education Professor

---

ing is often hindered. It is difficult to make the switch in meaning from a block representing, for example, one hundred to a new representation of the block meaning one-hundredth (Leinhardt, 1992).

When you begin planning lessons for your students, keep in mind this quote at the beginning of a book by Ausubel, Novak, & Hanesian (1978).

> If I had to reduce all of educational psychology to but one principle, I would say this: The most important single factor influencing learning is what the learner already knows. Ascertain this and teach him [or her] accordingly.

As a teacher you want your instructional messages to make sense to your students. If they are to do so, you must find ways to tap your students' prior knowledge, connecting the information you want them to learn with what they already know. Let's see how students mentally represent their prior experiences and examine ways teachers can build on them.

What prior knowledge does each of these children bring to school? According to educational psychology theory and research, why is it important for teachers to ascertain students' prior knowledge?

Episodic Memory

Episodic memories are those associated with a particular time and place or those connected with events (Tulving, 1972). The memory you have of a phone call you made this morning, the breakfast you ate, and the birthday gift you received when you were twelve years old would all be episodic memories.

Episodic information tends to be stored in the form of **mental images**. We usually think of these as visual representations (i.e., pictures in your mind), but they can be representations that involve any of your other senses as well. Can't you imagine the spicy smell of your mother's special recipe or the fumes of the school bus you used to ride?

Memories that are represented in images can also be represented verbally. For example, the memory of Shakespeare's *Macbeth* can be represented verbally, as in recalling that Lady Macbeth's "Out, out damn spot!" speech refers to blood she imagines she has on her hands and that she rubs over and over to get off. But if one sees the play performed, the speech is likely to be remembered as well in a vivid image of the experience.

The existence in memory of multiple codes is the essence of **dual-code theory** put forward by Allan Paivio of the University of Western Ontario (Paivio, 1971, 1975, 1978). Two systems are assumed to represent information in memory, one for verbal information and the other for nonverbal, or imaginal, information. When both systems are used to represent a particular piece of information, as in Lady Macbeth's speech, memory for the event will be particularly strong.

The organization of images in memory is based on the temporal and spatial relations of events. As evidence of these time and space relations around which episodic information is organized, imagine yourself in the following situation:

You are taking a multiple-choice test. You have gone through the exam, completing all of the items that you are sure of. Now you are contemplating an item that has two plausible alternatives: A and C. You ponder the alternatives, knowing that you read the pertinent information somewhere in the text. You try to recall exactly what you read. You can't seem to remember what you read, but you do know that it was located on the upper left-hand part of the page.

Why is it that you remember the location of the information, but not the information itself? You search memory in an attempt to find the specific information you need. What you recall is the location of the information you seek but not its content. Because the information is stored episodically, it is natural for the spatial nature of the information to be retrieved.

Many episodic experiences follow a pattern (e.g., one family dinner is very much like any other family dinner). Because many events fit into the same pattern, the distinctiveness of each specific instance is lost. A departure from the

CRITICAL THINKING: A teacher begins a review session with the question, "Who can remember what we were doing when we talked about ellipses?" Why might this be an effective retrieval method for some students?

REFLECTION: Recall times when you reminisced with friends or family. Identify some of the images that were elicited by those remembrances. How important were those images in remembering?

episodic memories Memories associated with specific personal experiences, including the time and place they occurred.

mental images Cognitive representations of, for example, pictures, sounds, and smells.

dual-code theory The assumption of two systems of memory representation, one for verbal information and one for nonverbal, or imaginal, information.

pattern can make one episode very distinctive and therefore easily remembered. For example, people tend to remember where they were and what they were doing when they heard about history-making or catastrophic events.

To take advantage of episodic memory, teachers can include distinctive and interesting events in their lessons as a context for learning information and skills. In learning about geography, for example, students on an excursion who walked through the mud of a mangrove shore, waded in the sea, and tasted foliage for salinity remembered more than students whose guides merely pointed out geographic areas of interest (MacKenzie & White, 1982). Likewise, acting out scenes from *Macbeth* can enhance literature students' memory for aspects of the play, and designing a space station can provide a distinctive context for learning history, science, mathematics, and nutrition.

Semantic Memory

Semantic memories differ in nature from memories of specific episodes. Semantic memories make up one's general knowledge, for example, that "*i* comes before *e*, except after *c*" and that "what goes up must come down." When and where did you learn those rules? Most of us know many rules but have forgotten the exact circumstances in which we acquired them.

For the most part, we structure the memory of our experiences around certain patterns. These stored patterns tend to subsume the details of those experiences. We can remember the general pattern, but we lose the autobiographical tags of these events. Each general pattern of experience is stored in memory as a knowledge structure. Just how knowledge structures are organized in memory, and how they are modified or used, has been a matter of some debate among memory theorists. Proposals for the structure of knowledge in memory have ranged from vast conceptual networks (cf. Anderson, 1983, 1990) to connections among subsymbolic units (called *parallel distributed processing models*; cf. McClelland, Rumelhart, & the PDP Research Group, 1986).

Two related structures in which knowledge is hypothesized to be organized are the schema and the mental model. The term *schema* is used in much the same way that Piaget used the idea of scheme. (For a review of Piaget's theory, see Chapter 2.) Concepts that we acquire as the result of various experiences are thought to be stored as schemas. Richard C. Anderson (1977) provides a clear description.

> A **schema** represents generic knowledge; that is, it represents what is believed to be generally true of a class of things, events, or situations. A schema is conceived to contain a slot or a place holder for each component. For instance, a Face schema includes slots for a mouth, nose, eyes, and ears (p. 2, emphasis added).

Take as an example an event schema. By the time they graduate from high school, students have had considerable experience taking standardized tests. They know that no materials except pencils are permitted at the test site, that no talking is allowed, that a certain type of answer sheet is used, and that they will work on each subtest for a specified amount of time. If they were to appear for a test and find the desks arranged in groups of four, they would be surprised. Their expectations for standardized test-taking would be violated.

Students understand new experiences and new information in terms of the schemata they already possess. What students understand as they read their text-

CRITICAL THINKING: How might a teacher use unusual experiences to teach material effectively?

CRITICAL THINKING: Give another example of an event schema and describe its contents.

TRY THIS: Interview students to construct a representation of their mental models of using a calculator (or word processor, or some other concept/principle of interest to you). How might you use their representations to inform your teaching of that concept?

semantic memories Memories of facts and general knowledge, but not including the time and place they were learned.

schema A mental structure for organizing information and representing knowledge. Any set of objects, experiences, or actions that is consistently classified forms a schema.

books, for example, depends on their text structure schemata, such as compare/contrast, cause/effect, and problem/solution (Armbruster, 1986). When information is presented in ways that fit students' expectations, their comprehension of the information is enhanced. To help students comprehend unfamiliar information, teachers can provide practice in recognizing and interpreting different types of text structures. Similarly, students solve arithmetic word problems more effectively when they access relevant schemata for particular problem types (DeCorte, Verschaffel, & De Win, 1985; Cooper & Sweller, 1987). Helping students to recognize and represent problem types in arithmetic leads to their greater ability to solve a variety of problems (Lewis, 1989; Fuson & Willis, 1989).

A **mental model** is a schema-based representation of experience, but it also includes a learner's perceptions of task demands and task performances. A mental model governs how a person approaches a learning task.

Students approach learning tasks with mental models that are usually incomplete, idiosyncratic, and utilitarian. Remember the preference for simple rules that has been observed in young children (see Chapter 2). The same is true with mental models. Students will cling to understandings that have served them well in the past, even though these may contain contradictory, erroneous, or unnecessary concepts (Driscoll, 1994).

In order to build effectively on students' prior knowledge, teachers must ascertain the mental models they possess, which means getting in touch with the naive or informal knowledge students have about things (Prawatt, 1989). Armed with this information, teachers can help students to see inherent contradictions or errors in their naive theories by explicitly modelling and providing guided practice in more accurate conceptions (cf. Gagné & Glaser, 1987).

Procedural Memory

Prior knowledge that includes knowledge of how to do things is called **procedural knowledge**. Procedural knowledge is thought to be stored as a series of stimulus-response pairings. Assume that you have procedural knowledge of how to ride a bike. It is difficult to explain the procedure verbally, but it is easy to demonstrate it. It is also difficult to engage in the correct bike-riding responses unless a bike is part of the stimulus situation. If you doubt this, put down your book and try to display bike-riding behaviour without a bike.

The stimulus-response pairings stored as part of procedural knowledge allow learners to respond to certain stimuli automatically. You jump into water and start to swim (if swimming procedures are stored). Procedural knowledge is acquired through practice. With enough practice, the appropriate responses are stored permanently and can be retrieved automatically, without conscious effort.

Although procedural knowledge is a large part of motor skills, it is also involved in many cognitive tasks. For example, knowing how to multiply and divide are examples of procedural knowledge. Knowing how to construct grammatical sentences while speaking is another example of procedural knowledge. It is important for this type of procedural knowledge to become automatic. In speaking, for example, we want to concentrate on the meaning of what to say, not on how to say it. Similarly, when procedural knowledge in mathematics or other subject areas becomes automatic, it facilitates problem solving. Many experts cannot tell you how they solved a complex problem in their fields, but they know their solution is accurate.

mental model A schema-based representation of experience, including perceptions of task demands and task performances.

procedural knowledge Prior knowledge that involves knowing *how* to do something.

Conditional Memory

Prior knowledge also includes knowledge of when and how to use certain schemas and/or procedural knowledge. A student may have the procedural knowledge that allows him or her to read fluently. But some reading tasks may require that a text be skimmed rather than read closely. Conditional knowledge allows a student to match procedures and semantic knowledge to the task at hand (Schunk, 1996).

This kind of regulation of knowledge and processes is referred to as **metacognition**, which means, literally, cognition about cognition (Flavell, 1985). One metacognitive function is the application of conditional knowledge. For example, a student who has learned to skim a textbook to locate desired information could skim the newspaper at home for information about his or her favourite sports team. Another function of metacognition is to monitor and evaluate thinking processes. Students who are metacognitively aware question their comprehension of ideas and make decisions about how to study based not only on the material to be learned but also on their own cognitive strengths and weaknesses.

Instructionally, metacognition is referred to as learning how to learn. Students learn specific strategies for controlling their own processes of attention, encoding, and retrieval in order to attain particular goals. A teacher interested in encouraging metacognition might have students read a humorous story or a set of instructions or listen to a lecture at the planetarium or a political debate. A discussion of purposes for listening or reading would precede the event (e.g., enjoyment, specific directions, concepts, decision making). When students can distinguish between reading for enjoyment and reading for making a decision, then these different concepts can be applied to other learning situations from which students will derive further benefit (Schunk, 1996).

EXAMPLE: Students who are metacognitively aware can think critically and reflectively about what they know and the ways in which they learn.

TRY THIS: Consult *The Skeptical Inquirer,* which critically evaluates fringe and other popular claims in society. Ask students to choose articles from the magazine and debate the issues. Write to Box 703, Amherst, N.Y. 14226-0703.

metacognition Knowledge about thinking, and the capability to monitor one's own cognitive processing, such as thinking, learning, and remembering.

Here's How

Here's How To Facilitate Metacognitive Awareness in Your Students and Help Them Use Conditional Knowledge Effectively

- Demonstrate a variety of strategies to help students attend to, encode, remember, and retrieve information.
- Point out when, where, and why a given strategy is effective.
- Provide opportunities for students to practise using strategies. Complex or involved strategies may require extensive practice to be used effectively.
- Remind students to use strategies. Younger or less experienced students are less likely than older or more experienced students to use the strategies they know.
- Provide positive feedback when students use strategies appropriately. This serves to reinforce students and to enhance their awareness of when strategies will help them learn.

How Can You Help Students to Remember What They Learn?

Learning outcomes are the joint product of what students know when they enter a classroom and the instruction they encounter while they are there. What should this instruction be to make the most of what students already know? The answer depends on the desired outcomes. Are students supposed to simply remember information? Are they supposed to create concepts, solve problems, apply a procedure, or make judgments? We want students to acquire high-level outcomes that characterize skilled performance within a knowledge domain. In many cases, however, students must be able to remember information before they can pursue other goals.

Enhancing Imagery

Imagery is a form of elaborative encoding. Mental images are mental pictures, sounds, smells, and so on. We can retrieve mental images that are already in LTS, as in the exercise to count your windows that prompted you to conjure a mental image. We can also construct images during encoding to help us remember information better (see Corbett, 1977).

When students generate their own images to help them remember things, they are actively processing information. The more active students are in processing information, the more likely it is that they will retain and elaborate on that information. When using images for instructional purposes, it is important to keep in mind the distinction between interactive and noninteractive images.

Let's suppose, for example, that a teacher begins a history lesson on the Wars of the Roses. Some children may create an image to represent these wars on their own. They may start with two visual symbols, a white rose for the Yorks and a red rose for the Lancasters. Picturing the roses separately would be a noninteractive image of the two symbols. An interactive image could have the Yorks' white rose to the north and the Lancasters' red rose to the south scratching England with their tangled thorns.

Although the generation of images by students is a more active form of processing, evidence suggests that images provided by a teacher can also be beneficial (Wollen & Lowry, 1974). Either their own or a teacher's images can help students make connections between the material to be learned and their prior knowledge. Most of the research on the use of imagery as a memory aid has dealt with fairly simple stimuli. Even so, there exists compelling evidence that interactive imagery is more beneficial as a retention aid than separation imagery and that both of these types of imagery seem to work better than no imagery at all (Houston, 1986).

The ability to generate images develops along with other cognitive abilities. Young children can benefit from images provided by a teacher for use during learning, but they cannot readily generate images of their own (Reese, 1977). As children develop, they become more effective in generating their own images than in using those provided by a teacher. The more cognitively advanced students become, the more likely it will be that images introduced by an instructor will interfere with the tendency to generate images on their own.

Using Mnemonic Devices

mnemonic devices Techniques that help us to organize or elaborate information we wish to retain.

rhymes Words that are identical to others in their terminal sound.

Mnemonic devices are techniques that help us to organize or elaborate information we wish to retain. Mnemonics work by relating the information to be remembered to well-known or familiar information (Houston, 1986; Norman, 1968). Although we think of mnemonics as procedures that help improve one's memory, the word *mnemonics* also refers to the art of memory, which served an important function for the ancient Greeks. The art was taught to Greek scholars as a technique to help them remember long speeches. The mnemonic method used familiar locations as a way of organizing material.

Unlike imagery, mnemonic devices have been demonstrated to be useful for students of all ages, including preschool students (Levin, 1985; McCormick & Levin, 1987). There are at least five different types of mnemonic devices: rhymes, letter and sentence mnemonics, peg mnemonics, stories, and keyword mnemonics. Used alone, these devices have been shown to enhance memory, but imagine the effects of combining these techniques with imagery (Figure 7.2).

Rhymes. Many mnemonic devices make use of sound patterns or **rhymes**. Consider many of the memory aids you learned as a child: "Thirty days hath September, April, June, and November...." "*I* before *e*, except after *c*." The rhyming pattern makes it easier to remember. Most people learn the alphabet by reciting it in a singsong manner. If you silently sing the alphabet song to yourself, you will

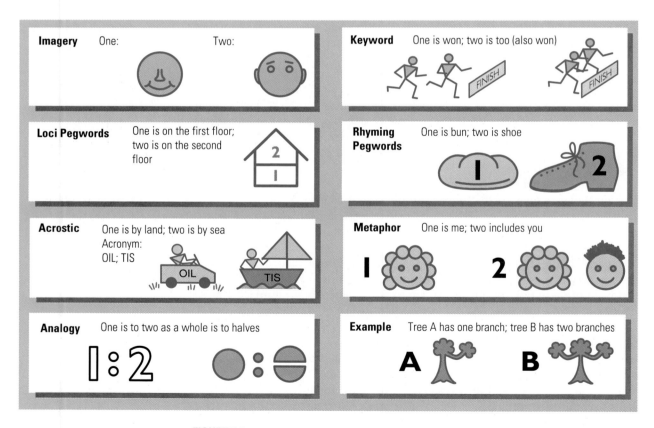

FIGURE 7.2
Thinking, Remembering, and Problem Solving

discover that the song makes use of rhyme. The alphabet song also aids memory by virtue of its being a song (with a familiar rhythm and notes to sing). A grade five teacher of our acquaintance uses the familiar theme to *The Flintstones* to teach her students the names of the countries in Central America. If you sing along, we guarantee you won't forget them either:

Bel-ize. Guat-e-ma-la.

Hon-duras. El Sal-va-dor.

Nica-nica-ra-gua.

Costa Rica and Pan-a-ma.

Letter and Sentence Mnemonics. A second type of mnemonics makes use of letters or sentences. The memory device we used to encode the names of the Great Lakes (HOMES) is an example of an **acronym**, or first-letter mnemonic. Another example is ROYGBIV (pronounced as a name, Roy G. Biv). This name stands for the colours of the spectrum of visible light: red, orange, yellow, green, blue, indigo, and violet. A technique very similar to the acronym is the acrostic.

An **acrostic** is a mnemonic that uses a sentence as a memory cue for information. For example, remembering the nine planets in order can be achieved with: Men Very Easily Make Jugs Serve Useful New Purposes. Learning the notes represented by lines on a musical scale is easy when you remember the sentence, Every Good Boy Does Fine.

Peg Mnemonics. Peg mnemonics are mnemonic devices that make use of visual imagery. Peg mnemonics are organizational in nature. The learner uses known information as organizational pegs from which to hang new information. Some peg mnemonics require that the learner first learn the pegs and then use the pegs to remember additional information. One peg mnemonic is the method of loci, mentioned earlier in reference to Greek scholars learning their speeches. (*Loci* is from the Latin word *locus*, which means "place.") The pegs used in the method of loci are familiar locations. For example, a student can be asked to remember the route he or she takes when walking home from school and to identify several distinctive landmarks along the route. With the well-known locations serving as pegs, new information can then be imagined and mentally stored. Suppose you wanted your students to learn the names of the ten provinces and the order in which they were established. The method of loci could be used to remember the names of the provinces. By placing the provinces along a familiar route, they could be recalled by mentally walking the route.

A more direct application of the method of loci, as it was used by the Greeks, would be to store images that represent topics for an informational speech. The images would be stored in various locations around the student's home or even in the classroom in which the speech will be delivered.

Another peg mnemonic is called the *peg-word method*. The peg words are learned by the student for use in a variety of situations requiring sequential recall. Note that the peg words make use of rhyme.

One is a bun.	Two is a shoe.
Three is a tree.	Four is a door.
Five is a hive.	Six is sticks.
Seven is heaven.	Eight is a gate.
Nine is a line.	Ten is a hen.

EXAMPLE: The peg-word method is used to teach children their telephone numbers. Students also use number peg words as an aid in remembering the order of species along a phylogenetic scale. For double-digit numbers, the images are combined. For example, twelve is a "bun-shoe"; twenty-one is "shoe-bun." The visual image for twelve is a foot wearing a dinner roll. The visual image for twenty-one is a shoe inside a sliced roll, described as a shoe sandwich

acronym A word formed from the initial letters of a group of words (e.g., NASA).

acrostic A sentence used as a memory cue for information to be remembered.

peg mnemonics A strategy for memorization in which items of a list to be learned are associated with cue words and images.

Imagery is a powerful tool in learning. How does imagery strengthen metaphors and analogies? Which mnemonic devices include the use of imagery? How is imagery used to represent a problem in problem solving?

With the exception of *heaven*, the peg words are concrete. All of the peg words, however, can be easily imaged. By integrating new material with the familiar peg words, the new information can be more easily recalled. The value of this peg-word mnemonic is in remembering information in a particular sequence. The key to using this mnemonic is to learn the peg words themselves so that they can be recalled automatically.

Story Mnemonic. Another mnemonic technique that helps in recalling ordered information is the **story technique**, which combines the elements to be remembered in their correct order in a brief story. Suppose you wanted students to remember the order of the elements in a simple declarative sentence: subject, verb, object.

A short "story" is as follows: "The subject verbed the object." Using the word *verb* as a verb is a bit whimsical, but the elements serve their defined function. The passive voice might be illustrated this way as well: "The object was verbed by the subject."

Memory experts who present mnemonic techniques in business seminars or to the general public tout the story technique as a good way of remembering a list of chores or errands.

Keyword Mnemonic. Most mnemonics have been in use for quite a long time. The final mnemonic discussed here is of recent vintage. The keyword method was developed specifically for learning foreign language vocabulary (Atkinson, 1975; Atkinson & Raugh, 1975). The keyword method requires first that a known word be chosen from the learner's first language. The chosen word must sound similar to part of the foreign language word to be learned. The Spanish word for *letter* is *carta*. The English word *cart* becomes the keyword. The German word for *newspaper* is *zeitung*. The last syllable is similar to the English word *tongue*.

The second step is to generate a visual image combining the keyword and the meaning of the foreign word. To remember the word *zeitung*, the student might use an interactive image of a person reading a newspaper with his or her tongue sticking out. Or a more bizarre image—giving the newspaper a tongue of its own—might be generated. What image would you create to remember the Spanish word *carta*?

The keyword method has been used in other content areas—for example, as an aid in absorbing data about important people in history: chronological, biographical, and statistical information (Levin, Dretzke, McCormick, Scruggs, McGivern, & Mastropieri, 1983; McCormick & Levin, 1987). The keyword method has also been demonstrated to be an effective learning technique for students with reading difficulties and for students with learning disabilities (see Goin, Peters, & Levin, 1986; Peters & Levin, 1986).

TRY THIS: Create a lesson in which you would use a mnemonic device (rhyme, acrostic, peg words, or story technique) to help students learn and remember information.

TRY THIS: Identify several key elements of a concept you expect to teach. Then generate a story that students could use in a classroom situation to aid them in remembering the information.

TRY THIS: Consider using the keyword mnemonic as a way of remembering new vocabulary in this chapter.

story technique A memorization technique that helps in recalling ordered information by combining the elements to be remembered in the correct order in a brief story.

Generating Metaphors and Analogies

In addition to using imagery techniques and mnemonic devices, you can help students make connections between new information and prior knowledge by using metaphors, analogies, and examples. Houser (1987) identified the role of analogy and metaphor by using an example. "When the teacher . . . says that the sun is the mother of the earth, the metaphor is intended to present an immediate object that the student would otherwise not associate with the sun and the earth, but which informs the student of something important about their relationship" (p. 272).

When learners are presented with concrete analogies, their retention of abstract information improves significantly. In a study conducted by Royer and Cable (1976), subjects read an abstract passage about the flow of heat or the conduction of electricity. Some readers were provided with a relevant physical analogy: The molecular structure of the conductor was presented as a Tinkertoy structure. In this way a connection was made between the students' knowledge of Tinkertoys and the new information about the way that heat or electricity is conducted through a solid object.

The connections between prior knowledge and new information can be made by the students (through the use of imagery or mnemonic devices) or by the teacher (through the use of examples, metaphors, or analogies). In either case, the integration yields lasting and organized representations that can then be retrieved and used for other learning tasks. The instructional goal of integration is not simply the retention of the new information; the goal is to make the new information available so that it enhances additional learning in the future.

TRY THIS: Observe language arts classes to discover how metaphors and analogies in reading material are interpreted in class discussions.

Systematic use of imagery, mnemonics, metaphors, and analogies can help students remember a great deal of information, some of it apparently arbitrary and unconnected to larger bodies of knowledge. Spelling rules are an example. Although spelling is an essential part of language arts, the spelling of some words can only be memorized or the rule for spelling them memorized. Moreover, such knowledge is a necessary, but not sufficient, prerequisite to skilled performance in writing. But skilled performance in writing is an example of a desired high-level learning outcome. How can teachers make the most of their students' prior knowledge to help them reach these higher-level learning outcomes? One way is to make automatic the basic skills that comprise higher-level outcomes.

Encouraging Automaticity through Practice

As you saw earlier in the chapter, attention is a limited resource. Because of this, the teacher's task is to help students focus on critical features of the instructional environment while fostering the development of automatic processing (Grabe, 1986). Fostering **automaticity** helps the learner in several ways. The development of automaticity allows a learner to perform cognitive tasks without any cost in capacity. This is a crucial point for a teacher. Bloom (1986) called automaticity "the hands and feet of genius." He argued that automatization of basic skills, not simply mastery, would be a desirable objective in the primary grades.

CRITICAL THINKING: Beginning readers tend to sound out words. Why might sounding out words diminish readers' capacity to focus on their meaning?

Picture two students reading aloud. One is a skilled reader; one is a poor reader. How do their performances differ? The poor reader stumbles over words and uses little inflection to signify a deep understanding of the material. He or she expends a great deal of effort sounding out difficult or unfamiliar words. The poor reader has to devote much of his or her cognitive capacity to the task of word recognition and pronunciation, leaving little capacity for the business of constructing meaning. The good reader, on the other hand, recognizes words automatically and is able to devote the majority of attention to understanding what is read.

automaticity Automatic processing of information from the environment that results in the automatic execution of certain skills.

Insights on Successful Practice

What techniques work best for you in gaining student attention and activating their prior knowledge at the start of a lesson?

Getting the students' attention is essential if any learning is to take place. The teacher who makes any attempt at instructional delivery without first gaining student attention is doomed to fail and to promote student failure. Activating prior knowledge empowers the student to construct new learning around that which is already familiar. Thus, the student realizes that there is a relatedness to all learning and that no knowledge, skill, interest, attitude, or appreciation exists in isolation.

During the course of my teaching career I have found that using models, using illustrations, and raising questions that require reflective thinking have been successful in both getting the students' attention and activating prior knowledge. These techniques have been useful when used alone or in any combination. When teaching a lesson about the nature and cause of water pollution, for example, a container of polluted water can be placed before the students to get their attention. Their prior knowledge can be called upon in an introductory discussion of how the water may have become polluted. To introduce a lesson on mammalian characteristics, small mammal pets can be displayed to serve as an attention-getter. These are only two examples of bringing the real thing into the classroom to begin a lesson. The possibilities are limited only by teacher creativity.

Models serve as excellent attention-getters when the real thing is unavailable or when it simply is not feasible to bring in the real thing. When teaching the distribution of the Earth's water, for instance, a globe can be used to show the amount of water compared to the amount of land on the surface. Model airplanes can be used to get the students' attention when the teacher begins a lesson on the principles of flight. Illustrations can be used to paint a picture in words, drawings, paintings, pictures, charts, graphs, or some other form. Illustrations enable students to get a picture in their minds that, when coupled with any prior knowledge or previous experiences on the topic, will make the new learning much more meaningful for them.

Certain questioning strategies set the scene for and orient the student to what is to follow. Rhetorical questions, such as "What is matter?," can be used to introduce a lesson and get students ready to explore matter and its behaviour. Analysis, synthesis, and evaluation questions encourage a different kind of thinking and require reflection on the students' part. Reflection is quite an effective way of activating prior knowledge. When students are allowed time to reflect, whether they are faced with models, illustrations, or questions, they are better able to link previous experiences to the current situation. This helps them to better attend to what they are learning and even to make predictions or develop hypotheses about some future action or occurrence.

LOEVENIA MAGEE GAFNEY
Elementary School Teacher

Your Insights

What are the steps in direct instruction? According to this teacher, what are good ways of engaging students' attention? In classes you teach, how might you introduce a lesson to arouse curiosity and activate prior knowledge?

TRY THIS: Interview teachers in the elementary grades for ways they employ to help students develop automaticity in basic skills. Do they use similar or different techniques for different skills (such as reading vs. math facts)?

In reading, as well as other content areas, component skills must be learned to the point of automaticity if learners are to be considered truly skilled or fluent (LaBerge & Samuels, 1974). Students learning a second language must acquire the ability to use rules of grammar automatically. Aspiring tennis players must be able to act automatically when they set up and serve a ball. Driver education students must learn to operate the car automatically while they attend to possible hazards in the road.

Developing automaticity of basic skills such as reading is mostly a matter of practice (cf. Shiffrin & Schneider, 1977). Although component part skills can sometimes be practised independently of the larger complex skill of which they are a part (as in memorizing the multiplication tables), others (such as driving) must be practised in their entirety.

How Can You Help Students Learn to Solve Problems?

When students acquire a foundation of information, automatic basic skills, and an arsenal of metacognitive strategies, they have the essential tools for solving problems. **Problem solving** is defined as the activity of applying rules, knowledge, and cognitive strategies to move from the current situation, or initial state, to a desired outcome, or goal (Anderson, 1993; Eggen & Kauchak, 1996). For example, suppose you are invited to visit a friend or relative who lives in a different city. The goal is to reach that location at a specific time. Suppose the initial state is that you do not own a car (or any other means of transportation). The problem, then, is how to get from your home to the home of your friend or relative.

To solve this problem, you would bring to bear other knowledge of your initial state, such as how much money you have for public transportation and whether you know of anyone else driving in the same direction at the time you wish to go. You would also employ specific skills and knowledge to acquire train, plane, and/or bus schedules and fares. You might use rules of arithmetic to compare costs in money and time of alternate modes of transportation. And you might employ various cognitive strategies to generate other candidate solutions to the problem.

This problem is relatively well defined, in that the rules to solve it are known and can fit into a simple algorithm specifying what steps to follow (Figure 7.3). Other problems, such as diagnosing a patient's symptoms when they match those of more than one disease, are complex and ill defined. Solving ill-defined problems may require a lengthy process of defining and redefining the problem, trying out and monitoring the success of candidate solutions. This is why solving problems is often a matter of creating or generating solutions, applying known rules in unique and insightful ways (Gagné, 1985; Woolfolk, 1995).

Unfortunately, many, if not most of the problems we encounter in everyday life are ill-structured and open-ended. As Rowell, Gustafson, and Gilbert (1997) point out, real world problem solving involves social, economic, political, and technical features that cannot easily be simulated in classroom settings. Students need to consider problems structured by themselves rather than the teacher, along with the balancing of real-life social and technical realities.

REFLECTION: Recall some of the problems you have solved in school. Were they well defined or ill defined? In what ways did your teachers help you identify the nature of a problem?

Strategic versus Tactical Problem Solving

Researchers who study problem solving have discovered that problems are typically approached on two levels. On a broad or *strategic* level, learners employ an overall approach to solving problems, such as breaking the problem into parts and determining subgoals that must be solved. Usually, subgoals are identified that, when solved, reduce the difference between the initial state and the desired end state. Most people are very reluctant to identify and solve subgoals that temporarily increase this difference or seem to take them in a direction away from their goal (Anderson, 1990).

Once a problem has been defined and subgoals identified, then *tactical* problem solving takes over; that is, learners apply domain-specific methods that depend on subject-matter knowledge. In geometry, for example, proving that two triangles are congruent requires recognizing vertical angle configurations. In planning your trip in the preceding example, you know to check schedules and fares before making a decision about what mode of transportation to select. The specific steps taken to solve a problem, then, depend upon the subject-matter domain to which the problem belongs. The more students know about a subject, the better able they are to think of divergent ways to solve a problem. Divergent thinking leads to greater success in problem solving.

problem solving The activity of applying rules, knowledge, and cognitive strategies to move from the current situation, or initial state, to a desired outcome, or goal.

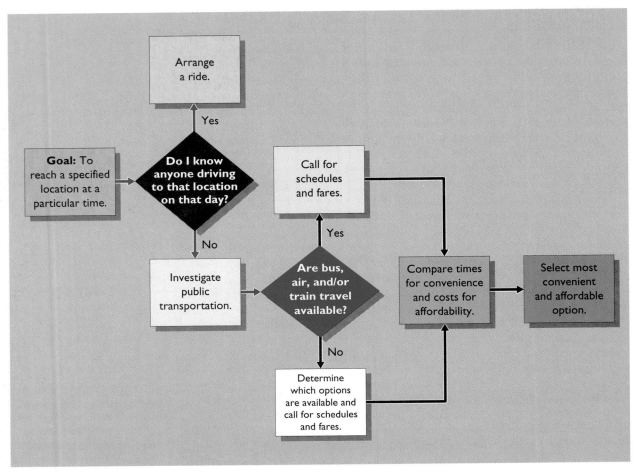

FIGURE 7.3
A Simple Algorithm for Solving a Transportation Problem

Expert versus Novice Problem Solving

Experts in a subject area differ from novices in more than the actions they take to solve problems in the domain. They also differ in how they define and represent problems in the domain. Experts appear to understand a problem in terms of deeper features, whereas novices tend to focus on superficial aspects of the problem (Chi, Feltovich, & Glaser, 1981; Anderson, 1993). For example, experienced teachers and prospective teachers were asked to identify instructional problems from student comments such as, "Why do we have to learn this stuff?" and "I never figure out what we're supposed to do before the teacher moves on to the next chapter." Prospective teachers tended to interpret the problems in terms of surface features of a lesson, such as pacing. Experienced teachers, however, did not see pacing as the problem. Rather, they recognized that decisions about pacing are based on a teacher's awareness of student prior knowledge. Too fast a pace is a sign that the teacher misjudged the prior knowledge of students, assuming that they knew more than they actually did (Driscoll, Klein, & Sherman, 1994).

Experts in a subject matter are also more likely to ask questions and seek additional information to clarify the nature of a problem than they are to accept a problem as stated. This means that their efficiency in solving problems is greatly enhanced compared to the novice, because in better defining the problem, they take fewer wrong turns to reach a solution.

Experts also have background knowledge of the basic methodologies that are used in various disciplines. Competence in evaluating claims involves learning ways of applying systematic reasoning approaches to problems. Many novice teachers lack these skills and do not model appropriate problem-solving strategies. This is especially the case in the sciences where students (and unfortunately a number of teachers) view science as a catalogue of facts rather than an approach to asking and testing answers put to the natural and social world.

Bikkar Randhawa (1994), at the University of Saskatchewan, points out that high competence in an area is characterized by a rich knowledge base of that area along with utilization of metacognitive strategies. Furthermore, he indicates that expertise is acquired gradually along with a lot of specific learning involving extensive exposure to worked-out examples of problem solving in the domain. A useful resource for high school science teachers interested in this issue is *Scientific Thinking* (1997), by Robert Martin from Dalhousie University. Martin provides real-life cases of research from the physical, biological, and social sciences along with stimulating questions and exercises that would benefit high school students.

Teaching Problem Solving

So how can novices become more expert at problem solving besides learning more about a subject matter? Listed in Table 7.2 are seven steps that constitute a general approach to solving problems that teachers can model with their students in any domain.

Identifying, Defining, and Representing the Problem. To begin with, students must determine what the problem is that they are to solve. This involves identifying the problem in context, determining why it is a problem, and finally, setting out all

TABLE 7.2 *Teaching Problem Solving*

1. Identification: What is the problem in context?

2. Definition: Why is it a problem? What does it mean?

3. Representation: What does it look like? How can we visualize the problem?

4. Hypothesis formation or prediction: How might we solve it? What do you think is the solution?

5. Experimentation: What happens if we . . . ?

6. Evaluation of solution: Does this solution really work?

7. Reflection on problem-solving process: What did we do to solve the problem?

Source: Based on *The Ideal Problem Solver,* J. D. Bransford and B. S. Stein, 1984, New York: Freeman.

the parameters of the problem (including subgoals). For example, a grade seven teacher and his students arranged an experiment to investigate the effects of air pressure, amount of water in a two-litre plastic bottle, and rocket design on the height of the bottle's trajectory when it was launched as a bottle rocket. After comparing the data collected on a particularly windy launch day to data collected when the winds were calm, the students decided they had a problem: The wind affected both the bottle's trajectory and their measurements (*identification*). This was a problem because the wind introduced an additional, confounding variable (*definition*). And not only was the wind an additional and confounding variable, it was also unpredictable and uncontrollable (*representation*). Hence, the effect of the wind was likely to mask whatever true effects were caused by aerodynamic shape, pressure, and water.

These students represented their problem conceptually by describing the unanticipated variable (wind) and its projected effects on their experiment. However, problems and their elements can also be represented visually (or graphically). Producing a visual representation often helps students to better understand the nature of a problem. An important aspect of identifying, defining, and representing a problem is ensuring the accuracy of the determination. In this case, students had to ask themselves whether the wind was the *only* difference between the two launch days that could account for the difference in the results.

Predicting Candidate Solutions. Once a problem has been defined as completely as possible, then predictions can be entertained as to what might be done to solve it. It is often useful to have students generate as many hypotheses as possible, no matter how farfetched they may seem. Then each prediction can be subjected to critique and analysis on its likelihood of success. In addition, advantages and disadvantages, or costs and benefits, of each candidate solution can be weighed. In the rocket example, the students discussed possible orientations for the rocket launcher to minimize the effect of wind. They considered their schedule and the possibility of launching only on calm days. They noted the fact that seven teams were taking the same measurements from different vantage points during each launch and wondered whether calculating an average would conquer the problem—that is, a steeper angle of launch recorded by the team who viewed the rocket coming toward them would be offset by a shallower angle recorded by the team who viewed the rocket going away from them.

Trying Out and Evaluating Solutions. After the possible solutions that have been judged least likely to succeed have been winnowed out, students can try out those that remain and evaluate their success. In the rocket example, the teacher and students decided that launching only on calm days was not feasible. They reasoned that wind direction on any given day would be a constant for all launches, provided that the launcher remained in the same position, so they chose a single position facing away from the school. They also chose to average

TRY THIS: An entertaining psychological approach to critical thinking can be found in David A. Levy's *Tools of Critical Thinking: Metathoughts for Psychology*. Each chapter includes many exercises that apply the skills to everyday issues.

their measurements as a means of pooling errors caused by the wind. Since the same patterns were revealed in the data over different launch days, the students judged their solution to be reasonably effective.

A solution that does not work should be examined in terms of whether it was implemented as planned before it is judged unworkable. If no solution works, then you can encourage students to reexamine their definition and representation of the problem. Perhaps they overlooked an important variable or factor that had to be accounted for.

Reflecting on the Problem-Solving Process. When students have concluded an activity that involved solving problems, encourage them to reflect upon what they learned from the problem-solving process. What solution worked, and why did it work? Was their process of solving the problem efficient, and if not, why not? What else might they have done to improve the process? In the case of the rocket-launching experiment, the teacher held discussions with students on a regular basis to reflect on the process. As a consequence, some students built additional rockets at home that might be more impervious to wind effects, whereas others made suggestions to improve the design of the rocket launcher. Reflection of this nature helps students to become more metacognitively aware and makes it more likely that they will be successful in future problem-solving endeavours. This is especially true of ill-defined problems, which are typical of the problems students will face in the world outside school. Roth, from the University of Victoria, and McGinn (1997), from Simon Fraser University, emphasize that solving ill-defined, complex problems that occur in everyday life often involves exploiting the expertise of individuals with conflicting views, the use of tools such as computers, statistics, and graphing programs, and a lot of just "mucking about."

Here's How

Here's How To Create a Context for Solving Ill-Defined Problems

- Look for broad, interdisciplinary problems with more than one right answer.
- Emphasize the importance of identifying, defining, and representing the problem. Ill-defined problems can often be defined and represented in several ways. How they are represented will affect the subgoals that are solved.
- Have students reflect upon their tactics and strategies throughout the problem-solving process. Sometimes they need to examine problems from a new perspective to make progress in finding a solution.

Insights on Successful Practice

What strategies have you found work best for your students in remembering information, transferring knowledge, and solving problems?

If you provide children with trust, meaningful content, adequate time, choice, and an enriched environment, they will have the tools to be successful. Special needs children need to know that we will give them adequate time to finish work, take tests, and finish projects.

Academic content must be meaningful to children. One important approach to this is the integrated thematic instruction model. This teaching model enables teachers to write their own curriculum so that it branches out to embrace the several learning modalities of children. The thematic model at our school relies on creating a theme that will integrate several subject areas. The theme and curriculum are broken down into learning components. Students and teachers identify key points that embrace the ideas of the components. Children show their knowledge of key points through inquiries—projects that show a student's knowledge and provide the students with several options to apply their learning. For special-needs children, thematic inquiry-based instruction is a welcome relief from reading books, memorizing information, and taking tests.

As a special educator, I have learned much from my general education colleagues. They are not bound by labels. They see each child as a potential learner, and the results usually indicate that their professional and personal intuition and initiative were right on target. Our students who came from self-contained special education classes achieved more learning goals more quickly in a general education setting than in self-contained classrooms. Special educators are the facilitators that break down the needs of each child, determine how those needs can be met in a general education setting, and provide the best service possible to those children. Our results have been phenomenal. We attend to reading discrepancies on an individual basis, but we also read to our students during class time to close the gap between students with and without disabilities. We give students tools to learn to study. We help them map out a timeline for an inquiry and the steps for completion. We adapt spelling tests by introducing the whole list phonetically, visually, and through stories about words. We teach them guided reading to help them read for content. We teach them to study what they have read and to store the information away until they need to connect it to other parts of the curriculum.

Inclusion has been the bridge that has allowed our children who learn differently to come home to the classroom and be at peace with themselves and others. The academic expectations are very high for them. We are building a great program based on an understanding of disabilities, a willingness to shift the teaching paradigm, and a strong conviction that children learn best when they are included.

CINDY FARREN
Elementary School Teacher

How Can a Constructivist Approach Enhance the Teaching-Learning Process in Your Classroom?

What does it mean to "understand?" To "know?" There is a distinction between *understanding* as it is used in an everyday setting and *understanding* as it is used by cognitive psychologists (Royer & Feldman, 1984). The everyday sense of the word conveys a subjective experience of empathy or comprehension. If a friend tells you about his or her disappointment and anger at not being accepted into a graduate program, you might say, "I understand how you feel." When you use *understand* in this sense, you mean that you can empathize with your friend's emotional state.

Consider the use of the word *understanding* to denote comprehension. For example, "For best results, squeeze tube from bottom." After reading the sentence, you probably have a sense of what it means. However, consider this sentence: "The trip was delayed because the bottle broke" (Bransford & McCarrell, 1974). This sentence most likely leaves you with a sense of uncertainty. The words are familiar but you are not sure what they mean. As a message, the sentence is difficult to decipher. Many times, students have a sense that they follow a teacher's message and so they respond, if queried, that they understand the lesson. If Mr. Harvey in the Teacher Chronicle had asked his students prior to the test if they understood the early lifestyles of different Canadian Aboriginal peoples, they probably would have said they did.

From a cognitive perspective, understanding is the most important outcome of learning. However, understanding means more than comprehending or following the gist of an instructional message. When students have acquired information in a way that enables them to solve problems, serves as a foundation for mastering additional material, or motivates them to seek applications of what they know, only then has understanding been achieved (cf. Royer & Feldman, 1984).

To take an example, understanding the concept of *remainder* means more than being able to say "a remainder is the amount left over from the division of one number into another." The student who truly understands remainders should be able to use this knowledge to solve problems and interact successfully in the world. Unfortunately, only 23 percent of thirteen-year-olds in a study could give the right answer to the following problem, despite the fact that 70 percent successfully performed the long division (Schoenfeld, 1988).

An army bus holds 36 soldiers. If 1128 soldiers are being bused to their training site, how many buses are needed?

What happened? Students failed to connect the computation of a remainder with its practical consequences in this problem. Almost a third gave the answer as "thirty-one remainder twelve." However, if soldiers are left over after the number of full buses is determined, then one more bus is needed to carry the remainder.

This example illustrates the problem of what constitutes necessary conditions for developing and displaying understanding. How do teachers know when their students have understood? Does the student who is able to work the problems at the end of a textbook chapter understand the chapter's material? Do students actually have to assign soldiers to buses in order for us to conclude that they understand remainders?

Finally, understanding involves reflection on alternative perspectives and commitment to one's own beliefs. The students who truly understand the concept of remainder will not be dissuaded from their belief that thirty-two buses are needed to carry 1128 soldiers if each bus seats 36 people. An important part of learning is the consideration of alternative views and explanations and a rejection of those that are inconsistent with available data. Conversely, situations in which not all the facts are known call for a willingness to adopt a tentative explanation and remain open to the possibility that it will be wrong. This, too, is a part of understanding. Alice Yuet Lin Lee (1997) at the University of British Columbia advocates a constructivist approach to the popular media-education movement in schools. In her "cultural reflective model," the emphasis is on how different contemporary issues are interpreted by the media. The media usually offer an incomplete and one-sided perspective. Students are encouraged to consider alternative interpretations of news events, including those from other social and cultural perspectives.

CRITICAL THINKING: A teacher who was convinced that the key to understanding a subject was the ability to understand and use a subject-appropriate vocabulary hit on a fun way for students to learn new vocabulary. The teacher had them write jokes. Extra credit was given for jokes, and jokes regularly appeared on tests. Why might joke writing help in remembering and using subject-linked vocabulary?

POINT: *Learning is a function of mental activity.* In the constructivist view, this mental activity consists of constructing knowledge through experience.

CONNECTION: How does the constructivist view of learning relate to Piaget's view of cognitive development? To Vygotsky's view?

In the remainder of this chapter, we present a view of learning that represents a paradigmatic shift from the information-processing and memory models discussed earlier. Although still cognitive in orientation, the **constructivist view of learning** stems from the assumption that knowledge is constructed by learners as they attempt to make sense of their environments (e.g., von Glasersfeld, 1988; Lave, 1988; Leinhardt, 1992; O'Loughlin, 1992). It implies the development of principled knowledge that is a function of the activity, context, and culture in which it is used (McLellan, 1993; Cognition and Technology Group at Vanderbilt, 1993); knowing cannot be separated from doing (Brown, Collins, & Duguid, 1989).

Active Learning

A natural consequence of the idea that knowing and doing are inseparable is the belief that students must be actively engaged in the instructional task for learning to occur. The notion of **active learning** is not particularly new; we stressed earlier in the chapter that the more active students are in processing information, the more successful they will be in encoding and retrieving it. However, active learning from a constructivist perspective requires qualitatively different interactions between students and content than is achieved through more practice or more feedback (Semb & Ellis, 1994). Rather, active learning calls for students to engage in meaningful tasks in which they have *ownership* of content (Honebein, Duffy, & Fishman, 1994).

For example, elementary school students were asked to use LOGO (a computer language designed for children) to write a program that would teach fractions to students one year behind them in school. Although fractions are usually heartily disliked, these students tackled the project with great enthusiasm, learning not only fractions but also computer programming and instructional design in the process (Harel & Papert, 1992; cited in Honebein, Duffy, & Fishman, 1994). Similarly, students who learned research methods by designing their own studies and collecting and analyzing data remembered these procedures for a very long time, more than ten years (Conway, Cohen, & Stanhope, 1991, 1992). Conway et al. (1992) attributed the findings to active learning, which "may have led to the creation of more stable long-term memory structures than did the *passive* learning characteristics of other parts of the course and, hence, the high level of memory performance for research methods" (1992, p. 475).

In a recent review of what students remember from knowledge taught in schools, Semb and Ellis (1994) concluded that instructional strategies that promote higher levels of original learning enhance retention over the short term, but only instructional strategies that involve active learning prevent forgetting over the long term. In summary, cognitive research clearly points to the conclusion that teachers who foster active learning enhance the outcomes of learning for their students. The question for teachers who seek to apply these research findings in their classrooms becomes, how do we establish instructional situations that foster active learning on the part of our students? From the constructivist perspective, the answer comes in two parts: the nature of the task and the nature of the interaction among learners. The issues of task and interaction are examined, in turn, in the last two sections of the chapter.

Authentic Activity and Situated Learning

An important issue in active learning is the type of activity in which learners engage. Many constructivist researchers argue that for students to learn the skills and knowl-

constructivist view of learning A cognitive view of learning whereby learners are assumed to construct knowledge in the context of the activity of the culture and knowing cannot be separated from doing.

active learning Students engaging in meaningful tasks in which they have *ownership* of content.

edge of a given discipline, they should engage in activities that are authentic to the discipline. What makes a context for learning or a particular instructional activity authentic? Leinhardt (1992) summarized it well:

> A task can be **authentic** because it is part of the world outside of school (for example, a grocery store) or because it is part of the culture of a particular discipline (such as mathematics or chemistry) (p. 24, emphasis added).

CONNECTION: Authentic tasks are also discussed in relation to cognitive development in Chapter 2, and again in Chapter 13.

The first sense of authenticity emphasizes the need for many skills and knowledge learned in school to be transferred to contexts outside of school. For example, arithmetic skills are needed to comparison shop in a grocery store or to balance the family budget. Likewise, learning to communicate well both orally and in writing is essential for participating in a debate on whether to ban the use of nets in commercial fishing. During the debate, one might be required to speak at a public forum or write letters to the local newspaper. When these kinds of activities can be incorporated into instruction, students see the relevance of certain knowledge and skills, and they practise these skills in appropriate ways.

Authentic tasks can also imply the activities performed by people who are proficient in their respective disciplines. Not only do we want students to be able to learn mathematics skills that can be applied in real-world contexts, but we also want them, in some degree, to think like mathematicians (or scientists or historians). To do this requires working on problems common to the discipline, where answers are not always known in advance and the teacher can take part in the problem-solving process. All too often, working on problems that can be solved relatively quickly leads to a belief that *all* problems can be solved quickly, if only one understands the material (Schoenfeld, 1988; Doyle, 1988).

CRITICAL THINKING: Why do "experiments" attract students' attention so readily and facilitate learning so well?

When students work on complex and authentic problems, the teacher serves as a guide, modelling strategies and processes during class activities. For example, a teacher of Canadian history decides to adopt the theme of *conflict* in units on the settling of Canada, the War of 1812, and westward expansion. In each case, students face the problem of how to represent and understand the conflict—who were the adversaries, why were they fighting, what conditions of the time influenced their actions, and so forth. The students examine the conflicts from retrospective and modern perspectives, including their own. The teacher provides resources to the students in the form of textbooks, historical novels, critical analyses of the events, and videotaped documentaries, but the students must make their own selections of information to access as their investigations proceed (L. Scott, personal communication, December 1994). The activities in which these students engage are authentic to the discipline of history; they represent what historians do in trying to understand an historical event.

An approach very similar to authentic activity can be seen in the concept of **situated learning**. In situated learning, students are engaged in solving realistic or simulated problems that require the use of disciplinary knowledge and skills. For example, the Cognition and Technology Group at Vanderbilt (CTGV) has developed a series of interactive video lessons for mathematics called the *Jasper Woodbury Problem Solving Series* (CTGV, 1991). In paired lessons, Jasper experiences various adventure-related problems, and students are challenged to find an optimal way for Jasper to resolve them. In one lesson, they must figure out how Jasper can get home from a boat trip before sunset without running out of gas. The problem involves mathematical concepts of distance, rate, and time, and it requires students to determine a series of subproblems to be solved (CTGV, 1990, 1991, 1993). The goal of the series is to provide realistic and interesting ways for

authentic task An instructional task that is part of the world outside of school (e.g., comparison shopping) or part of the culture of a particular discipline (e.g., "exploiting extreme cases" in mathematics reasoning).

situated learning Students engaging in problem solving of realistic or simulated problems that require the use of disciplinary knowledge and skills.

students to do and learn mathematics. Moreover, the lessons are paired in order to provide transfer of skills learned during one Jasper adventure to another, analogous one.

Evidence from the implementation of the Jasper series in several schools suggests that it is effective in helping students see connections between the problems they solved with Jasper and everyday problems they encounter at home where mathematics could be applied (CTGV, 1993). In class, students also appear motivated to engage in problem solving and to persist in their efforts to solve Jasper's adventures (CTGV, 1991).

Besides computer simulations or microworlds (Rieber, 1991), hands-on projects, theme-based units, and complex scenarios and cases provide other means for implementing authentic or situated activity. We hope, for example, that the Teacher Chronicles used in this book, which come from the experiences of real teachers, will help you to learn and solve problems related to teaching in a more authentic way. Moreover, the cases involve more than one principle or idea, illustrating the complexity of the teaching-learning environment and enabling you to examine them from multiple perspectives (cf. Spiro, Feltovich, Jacobson, & Coulson, 1991).

Communities of Learning

Ms. McKay's students are working on a lesson in thermodynamics. They work in four-person teams, making predictions about what kinds of materials will keep baked potatoes hot and cold drinks cold. Myra, the Principal Investigator, is in charge of directing the team's experiments and keeping things going. Karl records predictions in his role of Hypothesizer. Cheyenne, as Researcher, selects options on the computer simulation and reads out results as they appear on the screen. The students discuss the results of each trial, but Lena's job is to summarize the group's conclusion prior to their generating the next hypothesis.

"Okay," says Myra. "Let's start with potatoes at 150 degrees internal temperature. What do we use to keep them hot?"

"Aluminum foil. That's what my mom always uses," offers Cheyenne.

"Good idea," agrees Karl. He writes as he says aloud, "Beginning temperature equals 150 degrees. Material is aluminum foil. What is it called—what we're doing?"

"Insulating, dumbo!" shouts Lena.

"Oh, yeah. Insulator is aluminum foil. Time for fifteen minutes. Predict no temperature change."

Cheyenne types in the group's selections and groans as she reads out the result. "Temperature loss: 25 degrees."

"That can't be right," exclaims Karl. "You must have typed something wrong. Do it again."

"No, wait a minute," says Lena. "Remember we talked in class about metals being good *conductors* of heat. Aluminum foil is a metal. It can't be a good insulator as well as a good conductor."

"But if that's true," insists Karl, "why do restaurants use aluminum foil to keep baked potatoes hot?"

In this example, you see students confronting a misunderstanding that might have lain hidden and unquestioned without both the experiment and the exchange of ideas among students. In the constructivist view, learning is inherently a social process, because knowledge is distributed across individuals. For understanding to occur, students must accept or refute ideas proposed by their peers and teacher, offer interpretations and explanations of their own, and eventually build on or reconstruct the network of concepts and principles that make up their knowledge—that is, learning occurs in a community. "When students talk to each other, they rehearse terminology, notational systems, and manner of reasoning in a particular domain, thus reducing the individual burden of complete mastery of material while keeping the visions of the entire task in view" (Leinhardt, 1992, p. 24).

CONNECTION: How does this episode exemplify cooperative learning as discussed in Chapters 2 and 12?

When students assume particular roles within a group, as they do in this example, they are often able to collaborate more fully, with each member contributing something essential to the success of the entire group. Another way of achieving such a learning community is offered by Brown and Campione (1990), who described a middle school science curriculum in which students also worked in research groups. However, these groups, like the elementary school students who designed computer programs to teach fractions, were responsible for becoming experts on a topic they would teach to the others in the class. Each group researched its topic and wrote a booklet they would use to teach the topic. Then the students were regrouped into teams made up of one expert from each of the original research groups, so that they could learn the other topics. Expertise was thus distributed throughout the classroom, and dialogue among students was an essential part of the learning process, as "students force each other to sort out their own misunderstandings" (Brown & Campione, 1990, p. 118).

A Constructivist Classroom

A primary goal of constructivist educators is to foster critical thinking skills, and they argue that this is best done through learning communities engaged in authentic, situated learning tasks. As Brown and Campione (1990) put it:

POINT: *Teachers and students are both learners.* In constructivist classrooms, teachers do not know all the answers, and students can act as facilitators of learning as much as do teachers.

> The goal is reading, writing, and thinking, in the service of learning about something. Teaching is on a need-to-know basis, with experts (be they children or adults) acting as facilitators. Student expertise is fostered and valued by the community. A community of discussion is created with distributed expertise. This change from traditional teaching and learning practices results in significant improvements both in the students' thinking skills and in the domain-specific knowledge about which they are reasoning (p. 124).

Here's How

Here's How To Plan a Constructivist Classroom

- Choose themes or learning contexts that provide authentic activities for students to engage in. These are likely to span several weeks or months, involve complex problems with many possible solutions, and cross disciplinary boundaries to integrate aspects of different subject matters.
- Model the processes (such as defining a subproblem or managing the activities of a learning team) that you want students to learn.
- Support students' activity with helpful hints and instruction on an as-needed basis, but endow them with responsibility for task completion and learning.
- Provide ample opportunity for students to engage in meaningful dialogue, among themselves, with you, and with experts in the topics they are studying.

Teacher Chronicle Conclusion

Chinese Proverbs

As the morning social studies lesson gets underway, Michael Harvey tells the class to close their books.

"Today, we are going to do something different. We will be dividing into seven groups of four. Each group will represent one of Canada's early Native groups: Pacific Coast, British Columbia Interior, Plains, Northern Forest, Eastern Canada Woodlands, Eastern Canada Lowlands, and the Arctic peoples."

The students all look at him. He continues, "John, Mabel, Abel, and Max will be the Lowland Natives of Southern Ontario and Quebec. I want you to learn about your own Native group's everyday living. One of you will be a chief, others will take on other roles in the tribe. You will make a presentation to the class in two weeks. You can make clothes, demonstrate games or other activities of your own Native group. Be creative."

"Wow," John exclaims. "We can make a model of a village. I can make some longhouses out of boxes."

"Great idea," Mabel says, "I like gardening and can find out how they set up their crops, and Max can make plasticine models." As the other students learn what Native groups they will be representing, similar enthusiasm occurs as students suggest activities they can engage in and present to the other students.

Michael knows he has connected with the class.

Application Questions

1. Why did Mr. Harvey's group work suggestion generate such enthusiasm? How might the projects on early Canadian Native people support active learning?

2. How might students' prior knowledge help them work on their projects?

3. How might Mr. Harvey evaluate the projects?

4. Why is metacognition a valuable tool for a student to possess?

5. Describe a lesson you remember from elementary school, middle school, and high school. Why do you remember these lessons over others? Did they make use of imagery, mnemonic devices, or stories? Did they promote active learning? Did they involve authentic tasks?

CHAPTER SUMMARY

What Is Involved in Thinking, Remembering, and Problem Solving? (L.O. 1, p. 202)

Cognitive theories of learning are built around the premise that events occurring within the learner are important for understanding the process of learning. Information-processing models of cognition rely on a computer metaphor to explain processing, storage, and retrieval of knowledge, whereas constructivist views propose that learning is a matter of constructing knowledge in a social environment. In both perspectives, learning how to learn— becoming aware of and regulating one's own cognitive processes—is essential for developing critical reasoning and problem-solving skills.

How Can You Teach in Ways That Facilitate the Processing of Information? (L.O. 2, 3, p. 203)

To help students process information during instruction, teachers gain and direct their attention to important aspects or details that are to be further processed. Attention can operate selectively, as when a student consciously directs his or her concentration to some stimulus information. Attention can also operate automatically, as when a learner is able to focus on information without conscious effort. Further processing occurs through encoding, which is the process of integrating new knowledge with prior knowledge. Effective teachers prompt students to elaborate on new information, thereby forming many connections to prior knowledge and ensuring understanding.

Why Is It Important to Activate Students' Prior Knowledge? (L.O. 4, 5, 6, p. 213)

The prior knowledge they bring with them to the classroom has an enormous influence on what and how students learn. Facts and concepts that make up a learner's prior knowledge can be organized as episodes (episodic knowledge) or as general knowledge of the world (semantic knowledge). Procedural knowledge is prior knowledge of how to do things, such as how to apply facts and concepts. Conditional prior knowledge is knowledge of when and under what conditions facts, concepts, and procedures should be used.

How Can You Help Students To Remember What They Learn? (L.O. 7, 8, p. 219)

You can help students use their prior knowledge in many ways to remember information. Imagery is the basis for many types of elaborative encoding, including the use of mnemonic devices. Mnemonics are processing techniques that make information more memorable. Metaphors and analogies are useful in helping learners to integrate their prior knowledge with the information they are asked to learn. Practice on component basic skills helps to make them automatic, so that learners can direct their attentional resources to more complex tasks.

How Can You Help Students Learn to Solve Problems? (L.O. 9, p. 225)

Learners develop specific tactics for solving problems of particular kinds as they acquire knowledge of a subject matter. You can help students become effective problem solvers by teaching them to identify, define, and represent a problem; predict candidate solutions; try out and evaluate solutions; and reflect on the problem-solving process.

How Can a Constructivist Approach Enhance the Teaching-Learning Process in Your Classroom? (L.O. 10, p. 230)

According to the constructivist view, learning occurs by actively constructing knowledge in a learning community. Active learning is best facilitated with tasks that are authentic to the world outside school or to a subject matter discipline and with interactions among learners that prompt them to sort out their own understandings and misunderstandings.

KEY CONCEPTS

acronym, p. 221

acrostic, p. 221

active learning, p. 232

authentic task, p. 233

automatic attention, p. 207

automaticity, p. 223

constructivist view of learning, p. 232

dual-code theory, p. 215

elaborative rehearsal, p. 211

encoding, p. 209

episodic memories, p. 215

information-processing models, p. 203

maintenance rehearsal, p. 210

mental images, p. 215

mental model, p. 217

metacognition, p. 218

mnemonic devices, p. 220

peg mnemonics, p. 221

prior knowledge, p. 213

problem solving, p. 225

procedural knowledge, p. 217

retrieval, p. 212

rhymes, p. 220

schema, p. 216

selective attention, p. 206

selective perception, p. 207

semantic memories, p. 216

situated learning, p. 233

story technique, p. 222

working memory, p. 209

8 Social Learning

LEARNING OUTCOMES

When you have completed this chapter, you will be able to

1. outline Bandura's social-cognitive theory
2. distinguish between learning and performance
3. give examples of vicarious and enactive learning
4. outline the basic cognitive abilities
5. explain the idea of reciprocal determinism
6. discuss how modelling influences learning

7. explain Bandura's five categories of learning outcomes
8. describe the processes of observational learning
9. provide illustrations of the effective classroom use of social learning theory

Teacher Chronicle

A Social Learning Solution

Fourteen-year-old David recently transferred to Ms. Werther's grade eight classroom. Prior to David's arrival, Ms. Werther reviewed his cumulative folder and noted that David had a history of aggressive behaviour. Shortly after David's placement in her classroom, Ms. Werther observed that whenever David was frustrated, he reacted by threatening to hurt his peers, breaking their possessions, or verbally abusing them. Within a very short time, David was socially rejected by his classmates. David was not the only child in her class who exhibited unacceptable aggression; the aggressive behaviour of several other boys also presented a constant challenge to her management skills. Moreover, she noted that the behaviour of some of these youngsters seemed to be admired by their peers.

Ms. Werther had recently attended a workshop on aggressive children where she had learned that children who effectively manage their anger demonstrate good problem-solving abilities; that is, they accurately perceive and interpret social cues, generate a number of alternative solutions to the cues, evaluate the consequences of these solutions, act out the optimal solution, and then modify the solution if it is not effective. She also learned that aggressive children are deficient in many aspects of this problem-solving sequence. For example, she was told that aggressive children tend to interpret ambiguous social situations as aggressive, search for fewer clues before reaching a conclusion about another child's intentions, generate fewer competent solutions, offer solutions that are more aggressive than do other children, and believe that aggression produces positive outcomes.

At the workshop, Ms. Werther was introduced to an anger-control program for children that was based on social learning theory. She thought this program would be beneficial not only to David but also to the other aggressive children in her class. Although the anger-control program was designed to be implemented in a small group setting, Ms. Werther felt that it could be adapted for the classroom. She wanted to include all of the children in her class because she believed that those youngsters who demonstrated assertive and altruistic behaviours were good examples to the aggressive children and that all adolescents could benefit from learning to problem solve more effectively. After careful consideration, Ms. Werther decided to administer the program twice weekly for 40-minute sessions. Prior to implementing the program, Ms. Werther conducted behavioural observations of the target aggressive children to determine the frequency of their aggressive behaviours and whether certain environmental events precipitated their inappropriate behaviour.

For the sessions, Ms. Werther grouped the students in a semi-circle, with the front being reserved for the leader(s). Authors of the anger control program had conducted a very careful task analysis of the anger cycle and had developed sessions around each of the components. Each session began with a detailed description of the skill that was being taught followed by models role-playing an anger-producing situation that was relevant to the children's lives. Models were asked to augment their role-play with verbalizations that revealed their cognitive efforts at problem solving. Sometimes the models were successful in controlling their anger and were given reinforcement for their actions; at other times, their efforts did not lead to a positive outcome and it was necessary for them to role-play how they might cope with this type of situation. Children who could benefit most from the program (i.e., David and other adolescents who were prone to aggression) were then asked to role play anger-producing situations drawn from their own lives. Following each role play, actors were given performance feedback from group members. To ensure that the skills learned in the group would generalize to other settings, Ms. Werther kept other teachers and parents informed as to the skills that were being taught so that they could further reinforce their use in contexts outside of the classroom.

In addition, Ms. Werther made efforts to model effective problem-solving strategies and to consistently reinforce students for their use of these strategies in ongoing interactions within the school environment.

Focus Questions

1. Do you think all of the aggressive students will benefit equally from the anger control program? Should Ms. Werther have more carefully evaluated the role of the peers for its impact on sustaining the boys' aggression? What should she have looked for? What components of the program might she have modified to ensure a successful outcome for all target children?

2. What components of the anger-control program attempted to enlist the attention of the participants? Do you think the outcome of the role plays will have an impact on whether or not the target children learn the skill being taught? Will each of the aggressive boys attend similarly to the same models?

3. What strategies did Ms. Werther use to ensure that the target boys not only retained the skill being taught but used it at later times? How successful do you think these strategies will be? Do you think exposing the boys to coping models as well as mastery ones will help cement anger-control skills?

4. How might faulty reasoning and poor problem solving have sustained aggression in the target boys? What techniques did Ms. Werther employ to alter these cognitions? What strategy is likely to be effective in helping the boys learn how to more effectively gauge the social impact of their behaviour? Do you think this program is going to be successful in instilling confidence in the target boys that their needs can be met without the use of aggression?

What Are The Dimensions of Social Learning?

CONNECTION: The influence of the environment and the effects of reinforcement on learning are discussed in Chapter 6.

Rather than relying only on disciplinary measures to curb aggression in her students, Ms. Werther adopted a social learning approach that emphasized teaching alternative behaviours. In adopting this approach, Ms. Werther endorsed the notion that through observation or vicarious experience, her aggressive students could become more proficient at evaluating and regulating their behaviour. Models are the vehicle through which observational or vicarious learning occurs; they are a significant source of learning and motivation in and out of classrooms. In this chapter, we examine how people can learn by observing others. As we begin our examination of learning through modelling, reflect on your reaction to the program Ms. Werther implemented. Do you think aspects of your behaviour might be changed through participation in such a program?

social cognitive theory A learning theory, originated by Bandura, that draws on both cognitive and behavioural perspectives.

According to the theory, people learn by observing the behaviour of others in their social environment.

Models and Observers

The Teacher Chronicle clearly illustrates several principles of social learning. The theoretical perspective in which those principles are embedded is called *social cognitive theory*. Its major proponent, Albert Bandura, takes a broad view of learning. Bandura's (1986) **social cognitive theory** stresses concepts of operant conditioning (the environment and reinforcement) as well as the concept of mental activity or cognitive processes to explain learning.

Social cognitive theory has its origins in Bandura's early research on the phenomenon of observational learning (imitation). His investigations were partially motivated by a dissatisfaction with the operant-conditioning explanation of learning. Operant conditioning holds that a student learns by doing. Bandura felt that much of what humans learn they learn by watching what other people do.

In his early work (1962, 1965, 1971a, 1971b), Bandura investigated a number of variables that influence the outcomes of observational learning. In all of these studies, the learner is an **observer**. The stimulus is the behaviour of another person, acting as a **model**. Bandura studied the effects of age, sex, and the perceived status and perceived similarity of the model. (An observer's perceptions of a model have important instructional implications; we examine those implications later in the chapter.) In addition to investigating the perceived characteristics of the model, Bandura also investigated the type of behaviour that the model exhibited, including displays of skills unknown to the observer, hostile and aggressive behaviours, and standards of reward that the model accepted.

In a series of classic investigations known as the "bobo doll" studies, children who observed models kick and punch a large inflatable doll (the bobo doll) demonstrated this aggressive behaviour more often than children who did not observe such behaviour (e.g., Bandura, Ross, & Ross, 1963; Bandura & Walters, 1963). Another early finding suggested that observers tend to imitate the types of moral standards exhibited by a model. If an observer sees a model behave in questionable ways, the observer is more likely to lower his or her standards of appropriate behaviour.

To illustrate, picture yourself at a banquet or wedding reception, some kind of gathering where each table has a floral centrepiece. As the festivities wind down, a few people wonder aloud if it would be appropriate to take a centerpiece home. Conversations about the flowers take place at a number of tables. These discussions end with someone saying, "Well, if we don't take them home with us, they'll just be thrown out." Finally, one of the guests picks up a centrepiece and leaves. No one stops or even questions the flower-toting guest. A model is born. The observers, even some who initially questioned the correctness of taking the centrepieces, imitate the model.

> **EXAMPLE:** During a review of an exam, student A convinces the teacher that her answer should be considered correct. Student B reports that he used the same reasoning as student A. Most of the students join in the chorus, "Yeah, that's what I thought, too."

Another example of a model influencing an observer's standards of appropriate behaviour might be found in the old notion, "People don't usually give their correct weight on their driver's license." How many of us have observed people in our immediate social environment model questionable behaviour when it comes to the issue of reporting our weights?

Observational learning is not limited to aggression or questionable moral behaviour; not all models beat up bobo dolls or cheat on their income tax. Many positive outcomes can be gained by observing models. If teachers are to find and use models to their advantage, they must first understand the cognitive capabilities that allow students to learn not only by performing activities but also by observing others perform.

Learning versus Performance

Bandura raised a key point with his research in the early 1960s: Learners need not experience punishment or reinforcement to learn what is and is not appropriate behaviour in a given situation. Much human learning can be done vicariously, by observing another person responding in a situation. From Bandura's point of view, learners need not be behavers; they can be observers.

> **observer** The learner is an observer, according to Bandura.
>
> **model** A person whose behaviour acts as a stimulus to learning, according to Bandura.

REFLECTION: Think of a behaviour demonstrated by one of your friends at a party that you later tried. What were the characteristics of the demonstration that prompted you to try it?

Bandura's early studies examined how the consequences of a model's behaviour affected imitation by the observer. Behaviours that are rewarded instead of punished or ignored lead to a higher degree of imitation by the observer. You have already considered whether the outcome of a role play is likely to affect whether aggressive boys in the Teacher Chronicle will adopt the behaviour being modelled. If they perceive the consequence as negative, do you think they will use that solution during their next altercation? Bandura (1971b) also examined the effects that various levels of motivation had on an observer's imitation of modelled behaviour. In an interesting manipulation, Bandura (1982) demonstrated that regardless of whether the model's behaviour is rewarded or punished, the observer's imitative performance increases in the presence of a reward. Bandura rewarded observers for imitating behaviour for which the model was punished in order to see if the observer *could* imitate unrewarded behaviour. In interpreting Bandura's findings, Bower & Hilgard (1981) stated, "Thus it was found that the observer had learned the 'bad guy's' responses, even though he did not perform them until the incentive to do so was offered" (p. 463).

Bandura's research provides a basis for distinguishing **learning**—becoming capable—from **performance**—exhibiting a capability. In this respect, the social cognitive perspective differs from the operant-conditioning perspective. Operant-conditioning theory says that learning is behaviour; social cognitive theory separates what observers learn from the behaviours they perform.

Bandura (1986) enlisted the concept of cognitive processes to explain how observers can learn without performing. As we will begin to see, the social cognitive theory of learning is a hybrid of behaviourist and cognitivist notions. The processes that Bandura postulated to explain observational learning are cognitive processes of the type found in information-processing theory that was examined in Chapter 7.

POINT: The information-processing theory and the constructivist notions discussed in Chapter 7, as well as Bandura's theory, support one of the themes of this book: *Learning is a function of mental activity*.

Bandura's research has been truly programmatic. His research moved from issues of model effectiveness, reward of model, and reward of observer to consideration of the ways in which an observer's personal factors influence learning and performance (Bandura, 1986). Understanding the role that an observer's perceptions of a

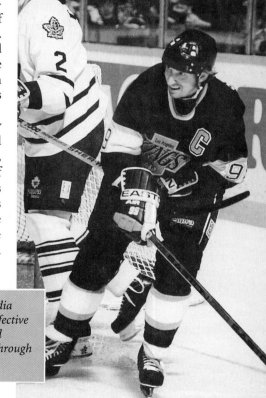

According to social cognitive theory, media characters and sports heroes are often effective models. Children learn the thoughts and behaviours of these models vicariously through observation.

learning Becoming capable.

performance Exhibiting a capability.

model, or of him- or herself, play in the learning process will make us more aware of issues of student motivation. Social cognitive theory is not only a hybrid of behaviourist and cognitivist learning theories, it also bridges the gap between issues of learning and issues of motivation.

As Bandura (1986) has pointed out, the technological age has provided observers with a multitude of models in a variety of communicative contexts. We observe models in our homes, religious institutions, classrooms, and malls. Much has been written on the role of television and other media in promoting aggression in children, and one might suspect that the aggressive behaviour of the boys introduced in the Teacher Chronicle is sustained, in part, by the violence they are exposed to on a daily basis through such media. The behaviours that we observe in others and the consequences of their actions are part of our social environment. Observing others can teach us a great many things about ourselves.

Operant-conditioning theorists explained learning by focusing on the interaction between the environment and behaviour. Cognition was considered an interesting phenomenon—something that might accompany behavioural change—but unnecessary for the explanation of learning. Social-cognitive theory, however, treats human cognition as an essential concept in understanding learning. The importance of cognition in social cognitive theory can be seen in two ways: first, in the distinction that is drawn between enactive and vicarious learning and, second, in the way that cognition is thought to influence and be influenced by both environment and behaviour.

Vicarious Learning and Enactive Learning

From the perspective of social cognitive theory, "Learning is largely a [cognitive] processing activity in which information about the structure of behaviour and about environmental events is transformed into symbolic representations that serve as guides for action" (Bandura, 1986, p. 51). Clearly, this definition implies that cognitive activity mediates learning and therefore is absolutely distinct from the operant-conditioning view described in the previous chapter. Enactive and vicarious learning are different modes of learning in social cognitive theory. It is important to keep in mind that both modes of learning are thought to involve cognition, because enactive learning may appear, at first, to be identical to operant conditioning. As we will see, it is not.

A student learns enactively by performing and learns vicariously by observing others perform. **Enactive learning** occurs when one learns from the consequences of one's behaviour. Behaviours that lead to favorable consequences are retained by the learner and used again in similar situations. Behaviours that lead to unfavorable consequences are discarded. To this point, enactive learning sounds like operant conditioning. Indeed, the behavioural consequences are the same.

The difference between enactive learning and operant conditioning is how the consequences of behaviour function. "Social cognitive theory [of which enactive learning is a part] contends that behavioural consequences, rather than strengthening behaviours as postulated in operant theory, serve as sources of information and motivation" (Schunk, 1996, p. 103). Learners use the consequences of their actions to determine whether their actions are appropriate or inappropriate, correct or incorrect. Learners also evaluate the desirability of consequences and seek to learn behaviours that lead to desirable outcomes. Enactive learning is learning by performing and then processing the information provided as a consequence of those performances.

CRITICAL THINKING: Although theories of motivation are addressed in Chapter 9, consider the following question: What is the relationship between learning and motivation? Does motivation always precede learning? How might learning enhance motivation?

TRY THIS: List the ways in which a student's environment and behaviour might influence his or her cognitive activity.

CONNECTION: Look back at the consequences of behaviour in Chapter 6.

REFLECTION: From your student experience, identify the most significant learning that occurred through the observation of another. Did you learn a concept? A skill? Both? What kinds of outcomes do you think are most likely to occur through vicarious learning?

enactive learning Changes in thought or behaviour that are a function of environmental consequences experienced by the learner.

Vicarious learning occurs when one learns by observing the performance of others without overtly performing oneself. Vicarious learning is a common mode of human learning, perhaps because it has significant advantages for the learner.

Vicarious learning saves time. Imagine students trying to learn how to use a microscope or a new software program without a teacher demonstration or an instruction manual. Vicarious learning is adaptive because it prevents learners from learning about dangerous situations "the hard way." Having read, heard, or watched accounts of the devastating effects of tornadoes causes most of us to take precautions when a funnel cloud is reported. Fortunately, people do not always have to experience consequences to learn that some behaviours are not adaptive.

While it is important to understand that enactive and vicarious learning are distinct modes of learning, it is critical to recognize that much of the learning in classrooms requires both. Observing models (usually, but not necessarily, teachers) who explain and demonstrate a skill enhances learners' (usually, but not necessarily, students') first attempts at performing that skill. The initial role plays of more assertive and altruistic peers in the Teacher Chronicle provide such models. Think of all the skills that require some orientation and explanation for the learner to attempt performance: writing; reading; performing long division or algebraic manipulation; playing a musical instrument; operating tools; searching databases; using sewing machines, stoves, TV cameras; checking out library books. Now, consider the degree to which any of those skills would be learned if the learner was prevented from enacting what he or she had learned vicariously. How well can one learn to write by listening to someone explain writing or by reading about the mechanics of writing, the function of plot, and the purpose of character development? Teachers provide the modelling—via demonstrations, explanations, and presentations—that supports vicarious learning, and they provide the consequences, in the form of informative feedback and motivation, of student performance.

In the course of distinguishing enactive and vicarious learning, mention was made of multiple sources or media by which learners can observe the performance of models. Humans are capable of learning vicariously via live performances, written accounts, photographic or videographic presentations, and oral stories or reports. A discussion of the capability to learn through vicarious experience—as well as other human capabilities—follows shortly, after an examination of the relationships among behaviour, environment, and personal factors, factors such as a learner's cognitive activity.

As mentioned earlier, the social cognitive point of view assumes that learning can be vicarious as well as enactive. By observing other people's behaviours and the consequences of those behaviours, we can learn what courses of action are and are not effective. Such observations allow us to build up our own store of knowledge and then to use our symbolizing capability to plan courses of action. The vicarious capability affords us a major advantage. Because we can learn by watching others make mistakes or succeed, we do not have to learn everything by trial and error. We do not have to spend as much time acquiring experience.

Many skills and much knowledge in our culture could not be transmitted very efficiently without vicarious learning. What would happen if everyone had to learn to drive a car by means of trial and error—that is, through selective reinforcement of the correct responses? What would happen if medical students had to learn the techniques of surgery in a trial-and-error fashion? Indeed, what would happen if aspiring teachers had no models from whom to learn? Many complex skills could not be mastered at all were it not for the use of modelling.

Children who had no models of linguistic behaviour in their environments would be hard-pressed to develop the linguistic skills necessary to communicate with fellow members of their society.

The technology of communication has increased the symbolic environments from which both children and adults learn vicariously. We learn not only ways of behaving but also patterns of thought, life-styles, values, and attitudes from television, film, and print media. We are able to learn from symbolic environments because we possess this vicarious capability.

Other Cognitive Capabilities

A basic assumption of this theory is that people have the following basic cognitive capabilities: symbolizing capability, forethought capability, self-regulatory capability, self-reflective capability, and vicarious capability, which we just discussed. Let's look at each of the other capabilities in turn.

Ability to Symbolize. People use symbols in virtually every aspect of their lives, as a way to adapt to and alter their environment. This capability results from a cognitive process that transforms the environment into some kind of cognitive representation. This perspective is shared by Bandura's social cognitive theory as well. Humans **symbolize,** or process symbols, that help us transform our experiences into internal or cognitive codes. These codes serve as guides to future action. Humans can cognitively play out scenarios of action by using prior knowledge and their power to symbolize. Playing out scenarios releases us from the need to perform all possible courses of action in order to decide which action to take. Testing ideas symbolically saves people from many mistakes. Think, for example, of the many role play solutions that children participating in the anger-control group presented in the Teacher Chronicle will be exposed to. In real-life situations, proficient problem solvers will cognitively appraise the relevance and likely outcome of several alternatives prior to choosing any one solution. It would be socially disastrous to try out every one.

Using symbols also helps people communicate with one another across great distances and even across time. Technological advances have taken advantage of this use of symbols. Essentially, the use of symbols assumes that people's behaviour is based on thought. Behaviour based on thought, however, does not mean that thoughts and the consequent behaviour will always be rational. Rationality depends on the skills of the learner. An individual, for example, may not have fully developed the ability to reason, which is at the foundation of rationality. (We will see later in this chapter that social cognitive theory accounts for many of the cognitive developmental characteristics that we discussed in Chapter 2.)

Even if an individual is capable of sound reasoning—of logical reasoning—that individual will make mistakes because of faulty information. We may reason possible outcomes based on inadequate knowledge of a situation, faulty interpretation of events, or failure to consider all of the possible consequences of a particular choice of action. Suppose, for example, that a teacher assigns a student extra homework because the student was not paying attention in math class. The teacher takes the action because the student was unable to answer questions about the addition problems on the board. Two days later, the school nurse, in the course of a visual screening, informs the teacher that the child has poor eyesight. Symbolizing capability accounts not only for accomplishment, but also for poor judgment, and even irrational behaviour.

TRY THIS: Ask some students to identify characters from television or movies that influence the way they act. Ask them to give specific examples of behaviours and situations.

CRITICAL THINKING: How did Piaget, discussed in Chapter 2, describe the development of reasoning? Why should the development of reasoning be an important factor in the ability to symbolize?

symbolize To form mental representations of modelled events.

CONNECTION: The importance of metaphors in the development of teaching expertise is discussed in Chapter 1.

TRY THIS: Interview a junior high or high school student in an attempt to discover how he or she handles peer pressure.

POINT: A basic assumption of this book is: Reflective construction is necessary for the development of teaching expertise. The point here is that the substance of the reflection is also important.

forethought Anticipation of the future.

self-regulation The act of applying an internal set of standards and criteria to regulate one's own behaviour.

self-reflection The act of thinking about one's own experiences and reflecting on one's own thought processes.

self-efficacy A human being's judgment about his or her ability to deal effectively with tasks that need to be faced.

Capacity for Forethought. Human beings do not simply react to their immediate environment but are guided by their past experiences as well. Using knowledge of the past, humans are capable of **forethought,** of anticipating the future. They can consider possible courses of action and anticipate the outcomes of those actions. People set goals for themselves and plan for what Bandura (1986) calls "cognized" futures, planned courses of action. Anticipating that one's goals will be met by following these plans provides the motivation to do so. The capability of forethought—the ability to plan, to carry out intentions, to achieve a purpose—is based firmly in symbolic activity.

We often use a metaphor or an analogy to represent our past experiences and imagine future events. Using these symbolic representations, we plan possible courses of action. For example, viewing one's job as *war* leads one to think about colleagues and/or competitors as either friends or foes. Our course of action would likely be a *militant* one. Viewing the job as a *public educational campaign* would lead to a different course of action. Our cognized futures can have a strong causal effect on our present action. A student might focus great effort on academic study because he or she envisions a university scholarship. Our capability to think ahead, to imagine the future, serves as an impetus for present action.

Self-Regulation and Self-Reflection. Bandura (1986) assumes that humans do not behave solely to please others in their environment, that they also behave in ways that please themselves; that is, people are self-reinforcing. To this end, they develop a technique of **self-regulation,** by applying a set of internal standards and evaluative reactions to their own behaviour. Through evaluative self-reactions, they are able to detect discrepancies between their performance and their internal standards of behaviour. By taking particular actions and evaluating those actions against personal standards of performance, they are able to adjust their behaviour. Although behaviour is undoubtedly influenced by others in one's environment, Bandura assumes that self-produced influences also play a role. For example, junior high and high school students are under immense social pressure to follow the crowd, but not every adolescent bows to peer pressure.

People are capable of thinking about their own experiences and reflecting on their own thought processes. For Bandura, **self-reflection** leads to self-knowledge—that is, knowledge about our effectiveness under certain circumstances and, more generally, knowledge about our ability to adapt to our environment. People gain an understanding of themselves, evaluate, and, on the basis of that evaluation, alter their thought processes and enhance their future actions.

The self-reflective capability, however, does not guarantee that future actions will always produce positive consequences. If we operate on faulty or mistaken beliefs, such beliefs can lead to erroneous thought, and therefore, erroneous action.

Suppose, for example, that a teacher believed that fear was the only effective way to motivate students. Such a teacher might reflect on the methods he or she used to make students fearful: Were my threats taken seriously? Was the exam sufficiently difficult to scare them into studying harder? Could I have gotten Elizabeth suspended for her inadequate reading of the assignment? Our fear-monger is capable of self-reflection, but reflecting on ways to motivate solely through aversive consequences will not lead to sound instructional decisions.

Self-reflection leads to evaluative judgments about our own thought and action capabilities. Central among these judgments of self is a sense of **self-efficacy,** a person's judgment about his or her ability to deal effectively with tasks he or she faces (Bandura, 1986). Self-efficacy is an important concept in social cognitive theory and

Insights on Successful Practice

What advice can you give novice teachers about helping students become reflective, self-regulating, self-advocating learners?

Soon after I began teaching, I became frustrated with students' lack of responsibility, so I developed a responsibility education program to solve the problem. The program's goal is to have children become responsible, independent learners. They learn to set goals, evaluate their progress, and use organizational skills to succeed.

To help students become independent learners, I designed a child-centred grading system. I feel that grades should make sense to children. How else can students evaluate progress toward their own goals? Unfortunately, we often use grading systems that were designed for adults' convenience instead of children's understanding. For example, to a child limited to Piaget's "concrete operational thought," abstractions such as weighted grades seem more like magic than useful, relevant information. Furthermore, issuing report cards weeks after the work is done compounds students' confusion. I solved the problem with a weekly grading system based on concrete operations that students can understand and use as independent learners.

The skills students learn in the responsibility education program allow them to grow beyond being merely responsible. They learn to be independent and to strive for excellence. The "payoff" comes when the students take over the class.

For example, one year my grade five class designed, organized, and carried out a very successful read-a-thon for world hunger. The students used their skills to set goals and organize committees. They gathered information, arranged publicity, designed ways and means to implement the project, and handled the money they raised. Along the way they taught themselves lessons in geography, earth science, political science, nutrition, and English. To further educate themselves and others, they obtained a speaker and arranged a school assembly. The students examined charitable agencies to compare how well each would use their contributions to help the hungry. And of course, each student read 500 pages. In five weeks, the "500 For Food" read-a-thon raised about $800 for world hunger.

As is demonstrated by the "500 For Food" read-a-thon, students can learn to be responsible, self-directed learners. It was designed, organized, and carried out by grade five students who had learned not only to feel responsible for themselves and for others, but also how to be responsible.

CHUCK BOWEN
Elementary School Teacher

Your Insights

According to this teacher, what is the key to helping students become independent learners? How do student-centred instruction and student-centred assessment contribute to this process?

---

it is important to teachers. The sense that students develop about their abilities to perform tasks influences their motivation and, ultimately, their learning performances. Several sources of information contribute to our self-judgments of efficacy. We look at those variables later in this chapter.

The human ability to use and generate symbols along with the ability of forethought, to cognize futures, allows us to set goals and plan courses of action. Because we can symbolize and anticipate, we are able to learn by observing others. We gather information about ourselves through direct and vicarious experiences. Our self-knowledge includes the set of internal standards by which we judge the effectiveness of our own thought and action and thereby regulate our own behaviour. Self-regulation of behaviour is one source of information that influences our all-important sense of self-efficacy. The capabilities reviewed here are clearly cognitive in nature and interrelated. For Bandura, these capabilities are a major part of what the observer contributes to learning outcomes. The capabilities of the learner are but one reason why humans learn and behave as they do.

CONNECTION: The importance of prior knowledge—which is related to these capabilities—that learners bring to a learning task is discussed in Chapter 6.

Reciprocal Determinism

The capability for vicarious learning that Bandura (1986) ascribes to humans reveals his assumption that cognition plays a major role in determining behaviour. Cognition that produces thoughts, beliefs, values, and expectations is subsumed into a category that Bandura called "personal factors." Noncognitive characteristics—the learner's size, sex, physical attractiveness, race, and social skills—are included in the category as well. Personal factors interact with the environment and with behaviour to influence learning and performance. Both behaviour and environment are modifiable. Each controls the other, to some extent. The relationship that exists among personal factors, environment, and behaviour is called **reciprocal determinism.** The relationship has also been referred to as triadic reciprocality (Bandura, 1986; Schunk, 1991) to emphasize that each element is related to the other two elements. Bandura (1986) described reciprocal determinism (depicted in Figure 8.1) as follows:

> In the social cognitive view people are neither driven by inner forces nor automatically shaped and controlled by external stimuli. Rather, human functioning is explained in terms of a model of triadic reciprocality in which behaviour, cognitive and other personal factors, and environmental events all operate as interacting determinants of each other (p. 18).

We examine the reciprocal interactions by focusing, in turn, on the three sides of the triangle in Figure 8.1.

FIGURE 8.1
The Relationships of Reciprocal Determinism

Source: Reprinted with the permission of Simon & Schuster, Inc. from the Macmillan College text *Learning and Instruction,* M.E. Gredler. Copyright 1992 by Macmillan Publishing Company, Inc.

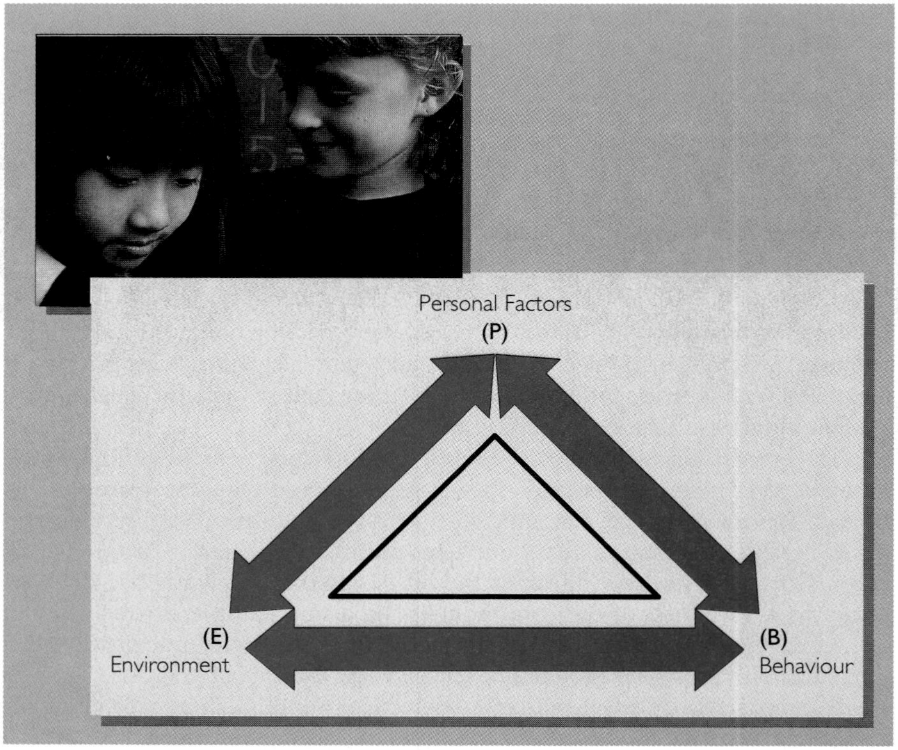

reciprocal determinism In cognitive social theory, the three-way relationship that exists among personal factors, environment, and behaviour.

Links between Personal Factors and Behaviour. To describe the interrelations, let's start from the top of the triangle with the personal factors at the apex. The personal-factors category influences and is influenced by behaviour and environment. Personal factors (P) such as cognition, a sense of self, attitudes, appearance, and demeanour influence behaviour (B) by means of basic human capabilities we've just discussed (P→B). David, the new student in Ms. Werther's class, believes that aggression is likely to lead to positive outcomes. Thus, when another student gets an object he wants, he reacts by pushing and verbally degrading him. David's personal factors influence his behaviour.

Behaviour also influences personal factors (B→P). David's aggressive behaviour towards his peer results in the peer relinquishing the object to him. David cognitively appraises this as a positive outcome thereby reinforcing the notion that aggression serves to get his immediate needs met. Personal factors influence a learner's behaviour. The behaviour, once evaluated, influences personal factors.

Links between Personal Factors and Environment. In addition to cognition, other personal factors, such as physical characteristics, size, sex, and social attributes, influence (or activate) the reactions from the environment (E) (P→E). A friend of ours who uses a wheelchair tells us that many of the people she encounters in her daily travels ignore her presence. It is unusual for people she sees every day to make eye contact or nod a casual acknowledgment as they pass in the halls where she works. She tells the story of how she was heading to the parking lot one day with her ambulatory office partner. Another employee said hello to the office partner and chatted about office matters for a couple of minutes. Not once during the chat did the employee acknowledge our friend's presence with a word or look. The environment responds to the personal factors one displays to the environment.

The social environment provides us with feedback that influences personal factors, such as thoughts and attitudes (E→P). Once activated by personal factors, differential social treatments from the environment influence personal factors. The environment informs an individual's perception of self, including a sense of self-efficacy that grows out of various social situations.

Links between Behaviour and Environment. Behaviour operates on the environment to produce certain consequences (B→E). For example, David's aggressive behaviour towards his peers leads to them forming a perception of him as hostile which, in turn, increases the likelihood that they will socially reject him.

Environmental consequences also influence the likelihood that a behaviour will occur in similar environmental situations (E→B). The rejection David experiences at the hands of his classmates further reinforces his perception that the world is a hostile place (a personal factor) and increases the chances that in subsequent interactions, he will behave aggressively (a behaviour factor).

Reciprocal determinism reflects the social cognitive view that humans are neither driven wholly by inner forces nor controlled entirely by their environment (Bandura, 1986). Understanding learning from the social cognitive view means understanding not only the interrelationship between environment and behaviour but also how cognitive and other personal factors influence and are influenced by environment and behaviour.

REFLECTION: Think about the decisions you have made regarding your appearance and your demeanour. How have those decisions influenced your behaviour? Give specific examples.

TRY THIS: Interview a friend or colleague who is disabled. Ask for comments on the ways other people typically respond to his or her disability in professional situations and in social situations. Are there any differences? If so, how does your friend or colleague account for the differences?

CRITICAL THINKING: How does this characteristic of Bandura's theory qualify as a hybrid learning theory? Have you studied any other theories thus far in this book that could be characterized as hybrid theories?

EXAMPLE: As an example of this point, consider the difference between learning how to whistle and learning the conditions under which whistling is or is not appropriate.

What Is Modelling and How Does Modelling Influence Learners?

Modelling is a generic term in social cognitive theory (Bandura, 1986) that refers to psychological changes (e.g., changes in thought, action, attitude, emotion) that can occur when a learner observes one or more models (cf. Rosenthal & Bandura, 1978; Schunk, 1996). Modelling produces a variety of effects or outcomes. Teachers can, by means of their own attention to the task at hand, make students more or less task oriented.

Because teachers and students acting as teachers are potential models for all learners, it is important that they understand the outcomes of modelling. Too often theorists and clinicians use the term *modelling* as a synonym for *imitation*. Modelling involves more than just mimicking behaviour; the acquisition of new behaviours is just one type of change brought about through modelling.

Bandura (1986) has identified five categories of modelling outcomes: inhibitory and disinhibitory effects, response facilitation effects, environmental enhancement effects, arousal effects, and observational learning effects (Figure 8.2). A teacher who understands the distinctions between these outcomes can use modelling as an effective classroom tool.

Inhibitory and Disinhibitory Effects

Inhibitory effects strengthen previously learned inhibitions. By observing a model, an observer acquires information about the feasibility and probable consequences of modelled actions and in this way learns restraint. For example, suppose that student O, the observer, has recently acquired the ability to whistle loudly. Suppose also that another student, M, the model, in the class also possesses this ability and demonstrates this ability in response to a group presentation on branches of government. Student M receives glares from the presenters as well as an under-the-breath comment, "What a jerk," from a popular student in the class. By observing the consequences of whistling by student M, student O learns not to engage in that behaviour. Student O's whistling behaviour is inhibited, but only in situations that are the same or similar to the model's situation. Student O may refrain from whistling in the classroom, but not on the way home from school.

Disinhibitory effects occur when a behaviour already known by the observer, but infrequently performed, increases

modelling Learning by observing the behaviour of others.

inhibitory effects Consequences of modelling that reinforce previously learned inhibitions.

disinhibitory effects Consequences of modelling that increase a behaviour already known but infrequently performed by the observer, by removing the inhibitions associated with that behaviour.

According to social cognitive theory, individuals do not respond to environmental reinforcement alone but are self-reinforcing. People reflect on their own thoughts and experiences and exercise self-regulation.

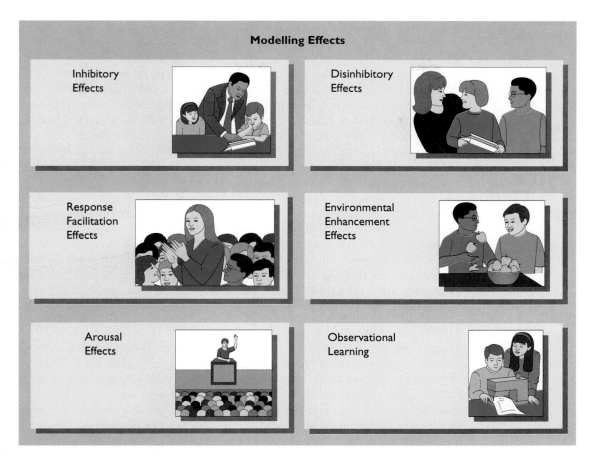

FIGURE 8.2
Modelling Effects
How do each of these scenes depict the modelling effect represented?

as a result of observing a model. If, in our whistling example, the model had received reinforcement, or at least had not experienced discouraging consequences as a result of whistling in the classroom, our observer's whistling behaviour would be disinhibited. The observer would be more likely to whistle as a result of observing the model.

Facilitative and Environmental Effects

Response facilitation effects serve as social prompts for previously learned behaviour. Bandura refers to response facilitation as "exemplification" (1986). Response facilitation effects are similar to disinhibitory effects. Both result in previously learned behaviour being performed as a result of observing a model. The difference is that response facilitation increases behaviours not by lifting inhibitions, but by introducing behaviour inducements. The simple observation of a model's behaviour is often sufficient inducement for the observer to engage in the same type of behaviour. Take, as an example, applauding in the middle of a speech given at a school assembly. If one student begins applauding, other students will likely join in. The modelled behaviour cues a known response by the learner. Bandura

response facilitation effects
Consequences of modelling that promote previously learned behaviour by introducing inducements to perform that behaviour.

TRY THIS: Interview a practicing teacher in an attempt to discover how he or she uses the response facilitation effect to generate student interest.

TRY THIS: Observe a class for a period of time sufficient to allow you to identify class leaders. Observe the leaders in an attempt to determine if they facilitate the types of effects discussed here more than other students.

environmental enhancement effects Consequences of modelling that direct an observer's attention to certain aspects or objects in the model's environment.

arousal effects Consequences of modelling that change an observer's physical and psychological reactions caused by the model's expressed emotions and actions.

observational learning effects Consequences of modelling that lead to the acquisition of cognitive and behavioural patterns that had no chance of occurring prior to modelling.

(1986) uses the example of one person looking up at the sky. Once one person looks up, others will imitate the behaviour and look up, too.

Meaningful classroom behaviour can also be facilitated or exemplified by models. Research has shown that models can activate altruistic behaviour, conversation, discussion, questioning, and brainstorming (cf. Bandura, 1986). Schunk (1996) presents as an example of response facilitation a new display in a classroom. If the display causes one student entering the room to examine it closely, a group is likely to form around it. If the group begins discussing the display, other students will join the group even though they do not know why their schoolmates have gathered.

Environmental enhancement effects direct an observer's attention to certain aspects or objects in the model's environment. If a model's behaviour includes the use of certain objects, an observer will focus more on those objects than on other objects in the environment. As a result of having their attention thus directed, observers are more likely to select those objects used by the model than other objects. This result holds true even if the observer uses the object in a different way or for a different purpose than does the model. Picture a student demonstrating her recently acquired ability to juggle. It is easy to imagine other students picking up one of the balls and tossing it, squeezing it, or bouncing it off the floor.

Arousal Effects

Arousal effects are changes in an observer's emotional level caused by a model's expressed emotion. Although an emotional model may cause an observer's emotions to be aroused, the observer may not display the same emotion that the model does. Recall or imagine a situation in which you observed two angry people arguing in public, perhaps in a store or a restaurant. As you observed the argument, you probably felt a surge of emotion, but the emotion you felt might not have been anger. It is more likely that you felt embarrassed by this public display. If the argument appeared to be on the brink of becoming an altercation, you might have felt anxiety or fear.

Positive emotions can also be aroused by models. Ms. Werther anticipates that the target aggressive boys will feel a sense of satisfaction and empowerment following a role play experience that culminates in a proactive resolution to a conflict situation.

Observational Learning Effects

Observational learning effects involve the acquisition of cognitive and behavioural patterns that, prior to modelling, had a zero probability of occurring. A model may teach an observer new behavioural skills, such as juggling, or cognitive competencies, such as long division. An observer may learn new standards of socially acceptable behaviour or rules for generating such behaviour. The observational learning effect includes new ways of organizing existing component skills. For example, when a student learns to pronounce a new word, he or she is learning to combine previously known sounds in a new way.

To summarize, modelling can result in cognitive, affect, and/or motor outcomes, depending on the context and consequences of modelled actions. Inhibitory or disinhibitory effects occur when a model plays a role analogous to that of either a subject in a research study or a test pilot. Response facilitation effects occur when a model serves as a prompter who cues certain behaviours. Environmental enhancement effects occur when the model serves as a prop handler or tour guide who highlights certain objects or aspects of the

Insights on Successful Practice

In your experience, how have strategies based on social learning theory benefitted you and your students?

Education can be seen as a simple transaction between the knower and the learner. The goods labelled knowledge are packaged and passed unmodified from one person to another. Tidy as this model may seem, in my experience it just doesn't work. For learning to be meaningful, it must be interactive. Teacher and students together must wrestle with text, discover what it means in their worlds, and construct or create meaning for themselves. In this process, the teacher is primarily a catalyst, but she or he must also serve as model, resource, and manager of time and space. The goal is to create a total environment in which students learn how to learn.

Pleasure is a key ingredient in an interactive classroom: the pleasure of figuring out something for yourself, the pleasure of working with friends on a project, the pleasure of watching students encased in aluminum foil perform "The Idylls of the King." I could fill a hope chest with the bed sheets that have been left behind from a decade of Caesar skits.

Emotional responses to literature stay with us long after we've forgotten the characters' names. Learning that is attached to feeling lasts.

In my opinion, an outstanding teacher is one who is also a lifelong learner and who has developed strategies for helping students become the same. When I watch my students struggle together with a poem—matching wits, defending their views, finding meaning, if not consensus—I feel that my classroom is a laboratory for the human experiment. I see growth.

CAROL JAGO
High School Teacher

Your Insights

What principles from social learning theory can be inferred from this teacher's essay? What role does social interaction play in meaningful learning? What does it mean to say "learning that is attached to feeling lasts?"

---

environment. Arousal effects occur when the model serves as a cheerleader, a cheerleader charged with whipping up not enthusiasm, but emotions. Observational learning effects occur when a model serves as an instructor or training demonstrator.

The outcomes examined here occur in classrooms because students observe and learn from models. Some of the models that affect classroom learning and performance are internal to the classroom. These internal models include the teacher, classmates, and fictional characters and historical figures encountered in assigned readings. Other models—such as television, movies, sports, and rock stars; cartoon characters; parents; and religious leaders—are external to the classroom. Any model, no matter who or what it is, is capable of generating one or more of the modelling effects described in these sections.

If a teacher is to use modelling as an effective tool, he or she must understand modelling outcomes. Teachers who understand the various kinds of information that models can convey understand the roles a model can play. Armed with such knowledge, teachers can select models to play the role or roles students need to observe. However, just because a teacher selects good models does not ensure that students will accept those models as their own. Knowledge of modelling outcomes is necessary, but not sufficient. Teachers need to know about the effects models can have, but they must also understand that it is the observers who must acquire the information, attitudes, and behaviours conveyed by these models. The cognitive processes of observational learning explain how an observer learns from a model.

TRY THIS: Interview a teacher about the ways in which he or she uses models in the classroom. Who are the models? How are they selected? For what specific purposes are models used?

What Are The Processes Of Observational Learning?

REFLECTION: Who were your models in school? Why did those people become your models? Why did they attract and hold your attention?

Bandura (1986) characterizes observational learning as a cognitive processing activity. Information from modelled events is transformed into symbolic representations that guide future action. There are four processes that operate as observers learn from models: attention, retention, production, and motivation (Figure 8.3).

Attention governs the aspects of the modelled event that learners observe or fail to observe. **Retention** converts modelled events into cognitive representations. **Production** allows the observer to organize his or her observations so that he or she may perform the modelled behaviour. **Motivation** determines the likelihood that observational learning is turned into performance. Let us examine each process in turn.

Attention

Unless people pay attention to modelled events, they cannot learn much from them. This conclusion is consistent with the attention process as it is understood in the information-processing model. Attentional processes in observational learning allow the observer to determine which aspects of the modelled events are relevant and which are irrelevant. Selectively attending to aspects of the modelled event is an important subfunction in observational learning. There are a number of factors that influence the observer's selectivity. Some are properties of the model and the modelled behaviours; others are properties of the observer.

attention The ability to observe modelled behaviour.

retention The capacity to remember modelled behaviour.

production The act of producing modelled behaviour.

motivation The desire to produce the modelled behaviour.

Influence of Models on Attention. The quality and quantity of observational learning can be affected by the *salience* of modelled actions, the extent to which these actions stand out from other aspects of the environment. In a classroom filled with potential models, one classmate may behave in a highly conspicuous manner. The conspicuous model may jump up and sing "O Canada." Such an event would likely be considered salient.

Relevance—the extent to which relevant and irrelevant behaviours can be discriminated—is another property of modelled events that influences the attention process. Suppose an observer is watching a professional tennis player on television. The observer may attend not only to the position of the racquet prior to the swing

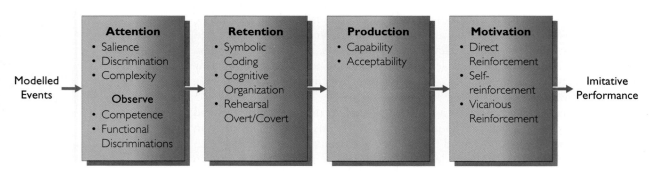

FIGURE 8.3

The Four Processes of Observational Learning

Source: Social Foundations of Thought and Action: A Social Cognitive Theory (p. 52), A. Bandura, 1986, Englewood Cliffs, NJ: Prentice-Hall. Copyright 1986 by Prentice-Hall. Reprinted by permission.

and to the footwork of the professional player, but also to the particular tennis clothing worn by that player. Attending to the position of the racquet and the footwork of the player are relevant aspects of the model's behaviour; such attention will allow the observer to better imitate the model's tennis stroke. Imitating the model's style of dress may occur as a function of observation, but the style of dress is irrelevant for imitating the model's tennis stroke.

An observer's attention can be influenced also by the *complexity* of the modelled events. Complex modelling requires that the observer acquire the rules for generating behaviour rather than simply imitating the behaviour itself. If an observer is to learn chess by observing a model, he or she must watch how the various pieces are moved and, from those moves, abstract the rules that govern each piece. If the observer is to acquire some level of competence, he or she must also abstract the strategies and tactics that govern a series of moves.

The salience, relevance, and complexity of modelled events affect an observer's attention. But remember that a basic assumption of social learning theory is reciprocal determinism: Aspects of the environment and personal factors determine each other. In terms of attention, this means that what is salient, relevant, and complex about a modelled event is influenced by the personal factors an observer brings to the modelled event. How can a teacher make modelled events salient, relevant, and appropriately complex?

EXAMPLE: Examples of what is meant by relevant aspects of behaviours can be found in various instruction manuals such as a book on how to improve your tennis game.

Here's How

Here's How To Facilitate Attention to Modelled Events

- Ask or survey your students' interests. Find out what recreational activities they pursue, who are their favourite performers, what are their favourite books and movies.

- Use the interest surveys to select models. For example, if you are going to teach a science unit, select several scientists of both genders and various cultural backgrounds whose work is related to the unit. In addition to readings, select a film or a movie excerpt that is related to the topic. Give students options as to the resources they can choose to consult. Let them choose what is most salient to them.

- Ask students to help you determine what the outcomes of the unit should be. Should we take a test? Create a project? Teach other students through demonstration? Allow students to help make the work relevant.

- Create follow-up activities for students who desire to pursue a topic in depth. Don't stifle a student's interest in pursuing a topic at a more complex level.

Influence of Observers on Attention. The attentional process can be influenced by properties of the observer, in addition to properties of the model's behaviour. An experienced chess player will attend to different aspects of a televised chess match than will a chess novice. As we saw in Chapter 1, expert teachers interpret classroom situations differently from novice teachers. The complexity of the modelled event is better appreciated by the expert observer because the expert observer has a knowledge base that allows him or her to make more critical discriminations of the actions taking place. Similarly, a chess master's cognitive competencies and prior knowledge influence what he or she sees as salient and relevant in the modelled activity. The cognitive competencies of the observer, therefore, influence the perception of the modelled events.

Observers make a determination of the functional value of modelled events. An observer who expects to function in an environment similar to that of the model will pay closer attention to the behaviour of the model than will an observer who does not expect to function in such an environment. A junior high student who studies ballet may watch both ballet and gymnastics on television. The student will perceive the salience, understand the complexity, and make better discriminations of relevant and irrelevant behaviours of the ballet dancers than those of the gymnasts.

There is a developmental effect in observational learning that is associated with attentional processes. Bandura (1986) reports that young children cannot attend well to modelled events for long periods of time. Furthermore, they do not easily distinguish relevant aspects of modelled behaviour from irrelevant aspects. Rather, it seems that salience is the most important factor, even though the most salient aspect of a modelled event may not be the most relevant. As children mature, they develop a more extensive knowledge base and are better able to make use of various memory strategies. Maturation influences the capacity for observational learning. As children develop cognitively, they get better at symbolically representing vicarious experiences.

Retention

Retention processes include symbolic coding, organization of what has received attention, and rehearsal. For the observer to form and retain a cognitive representation of the modelled behaviour, it is necessary that he or she code and store observations. The cognitive representation that results is the basis for further action by the observer. Think of what students in the anger-control program will store in their memory following exposure to a role play.

In order to perform a modelled behaviour, a student must form an accurate cognitive version of the model's behaviour—what Bandura refers to as symbolic coding and organization. Retaining the information requires more than simply coding and organizing a model's behaviour, however. Some sort of rehearsal is necessary if the observer is to perform. Bandura (1986) refers to two types of rehearsal: cognitive rehearsal and enactive rehearsal, also known as *covert* and *overt* rehearsal. Overt rehearsal is of the type that most of us think of as practising. It usually involves a physical action. Imagine, for example, the prospective dancers who arrive at an audition for a Broadway show. Typically, the choreographer of the show brings the hopefuls to the stage and demonstrates a series of dance steps. Those auditioning are given the opportunity to briefly rehearse the dance steps in an overt fashion—that is, to actually do them. After being shown the steps, the auditioners go into the wings to await their turn to perform the steps for the director of the show. As the dancers wait in the wings for their opportunity to perform, they practise the dance steps. Because there is insufficient room in the wings for them to perform the series of steps fully, they tend to abbreviate their actions.

In some cases, you can see auditioners sitting quietly, perhaps with their eyes closed, dancing to themselves. This is covert rehearsal. Perhaps you have heard or read that Olympic athletes, especially gymnasts or figure skaters, who

CONNECTION: The effects of perceived relevance on motivation are discussed in the ARCS model presented in Chapter 9.

CRITICAL THINKING: Speculate as to which kind of rehearsal might be most effective in learning a skill. Are there learning activities that would facilitate one more than the other? Other activities that would enhance both?

must perform a prescribed program of action, engage in a kind of covert rehearsal called *imaginary practice* (Bower & Hilgard, 1981). Reports by Olympic athletes indicate the effectiveness of such covert rehearsal. Greg Louganis, a gold-medal-winning diver, choreographed his dives to music. The music was not played aloud, but covertly, in his head. After much covert and overt practice, the music became part of his symbolic code. The dive could be covertly rehearsed by mentally playing the musical accompaniment. More formal evidence also exists to suggest that covert rehearsal is an effective way to improve actual performance (see Corbin, 1972; Feltz & Landers, 1983).

TRY THIS: Talk with gymnasts, figure skaters, or ballet dancers. Ask them if they use covert rehearsal. If so, ask them how they use it.

Production

After the observer attends to and retains modelled behaviours, he or she is ready to produce the behaviours. Production processes are influenced most immediately by the observer's physical capabilities. Later, production is influenced by the self-observation and self-feedback associated with the performance.

The cognitive component of production processes can be thought of as decisions that the observer must make. The first of these is whether or not he or she is physically capable of producing the modelled behaviour. The second decision is whether or not producing the modelled behaviour is socially acceptable.

Suppose you read about a teacher with an unusual way of energizing her students at the beginning of class. From time to time she dons a cape and runs into the classroom to the taped strains of a trumpet fanfare. As she reaches the front of the classroom, the taped music switches to a rock tune. She invites the class to stand and dance with her. After a minute or so of dancing, the music fades, and she removes her cape and begins the day's lesson.

What would you do with this modelled event? Would you imitate the behaviours? You have two decisions to make. Am I capable of producing the modelled behaviours? If so, do I judge the behaviours to be acceptable? To make those decisions, you need to consult your knowledge of self. Having observed and judged your own past behaviour, you can anticipate the consequences of modelling the caped dancer. The decision of capability is more than simply determining whether or not you are physically capable of the modelled behaviours. The question, Is this behaviour acceptable? means deciding if you can bring yourself to display such behaviours. What if you tried the cape-and-music gambit and it led not to energy, but to embarrassment? The point is that decisions of capability spill over into decisions of acceptability. But what if students never tried new activities? What if their production decisions prevented them from taking small risks? How can you help your students make sound capability and acceptance decisions?

REFLECTION: Would you use these particular tactics with your own students? Why or why not?

Here's How

Here's How To Foster Good Production Decisions

- Establish an atmosphere where risk taking is encouraged. Students who feel they are unable to risk certain behaviours may never try new activities.
- Take risks yourself. Try to learn new skills and demonstrate your progress—mistakes and all—to your students. Show students that learning new concepts and skills can be all the more rewarding for the mistakes that are made along the way.

continued

- Support effort. When students attempt to play a new song, sculpt for the first time, apply a new math concept, write their first haiku, you can reward the effort even if the product of that effort is flawed.
- Talk about decisions. Ask students to share their decisions of capability and acceptance. Help students reflect on their reasoning and encourage them to test their decisions. A student who chooses not to participate in a folk dance because he or she fears embarrassment can be encouraged to test his or her prediction.

Motivation

CONNECTION: The facilitation of self-regulation skills is examined in the next section of this chapter.

Motivation is the last component of Bandura's (1986) observational learning model. Motivational processes include three kinds of reinforcement: direct reinforcement, self-reinforcement, and vicarious reinforcement.

Direct reinforcement is provided by the external environment. If the production decisions are positive, the observer performs the modelled behaviour. The observer's behaviour yields an environmental consequence: direct reinforcement.

Self-reinforcement is derived from the observer's evaluation of his or her own performance independent of environmental consequences. The caped teacher may perform her musical lesson staging simply because she enjoys it or because she feels competent doing it. Jugglers do not always need an audience—a source of direct reinforcement—to perform. Juggling is often performed in solitude because the juggler finds reinforcement in the act itself.

Vicarious reinforcement is derived from viewing a model engaged in the behaviour. Vicarious reinforcement explains why you might stay up late to watch, for example, Harrison Ford movies. You may be neither capable nor particularly desirous of producing the behaviours you observe, but you do derive vicarious pleasure from watching Ford perform them repeatedly.

If students learn behaviours by observing others in their social environment, and if through the processes of observational learning they come to decisions about their capabilities and their efficacy in performing behaviours that they have learned, an important instructional question arises. What makes an effective model? Furthermore, how can we, as teachers, provide and serve as effective models for our students?

If we consider the questions developmentally, the most obvious candidates for potential models change as children change—as they grow older. For very young children, prominent adults in their social environment have an advantage as potential models. As children grow older, the influence of significant adults in their environment decreases. As children enter the intermediate elementary grades and proceed through junior high and high school, the importance of peers increases. Think of how important it was for you to feel accepted and supported by adults when you were very young and then by your classmates in junior and senior high.

direct reinforcement Using direct consequences from the external environment to strengthen a desired behaviour.

self-reinforcement Using consequences that come from within to strengthen a desired behaviour.

vicarious reinforcement Using consequences derived from viewing a model engaged in a desired behaviour to strengthen that behaviour.

How Can Your Knowledge of Social Learning Make You a More Effective Teacher?

Teachers who know the processes and outcomes of observational learning are better able to decide when and under what conditions models might prove useful. If,

Insights on Successful Practice

How do you use peer modelling in your
classroom, and with what results?

Another important aspect of morning business periods is our daily sharing. Daily sharing is a particular kind of sharing designed for each day of the week. Mondays are teacher's sharing days. This practice gives me an excellent opportunity to model and set standards indirectly. I share poems, books, current events, and teach songs.

The students share from Tuesday to Friday. Each student is scheduled so that he or she knows what and when to share during the month and can plan accordingly. The class is divided into five groups. Each group is scheduled to present in one of three categories—current events, poetry, or books—during the week.

When sharing current events, the students search for articles related to the science, social studies, or literature units of study. For example, last month the students had to apply their newspaper reading skills in selecting articles related to our science units on plants, animals, and ecology. The following articles were shared: "Be Wary of Breakfast Foods," "How to Keep Costs Down, Nutrition Up," "Spoilage Signs in Cans," and "Guilty Dog Still Sought on Big Isle." The students prepare for the sharing by locating an appropriate article, reading it, and then writing a short summary. During their oral presentations, they point out the location of the incident discussed in the article on a map. These sharings bring additional real-life dimensions to our units.

When sharing poetry, the students choose poems related to the social studies and science topics and literature themes. They also attempt to identify specific literary elements previously taught within the poem of their choice. For example, Malie chose a poem by X. J. Kennedy, "The Whale Off Wales," and demonstrated her recognition of personification and simile in this poem. In addition, the students' own understanding of personification and simile enhances their appreciation and comprehension of her piece. The students enjoy and appreciate the range of poems shared: these poems also serve as models for their own writing. Through exposure to poems on subjects about which they have done reading, they realize there are many ways to express ideas about a topic.

When sharing books, the students select books related to our study of literature and other social studies topics for the month. They read, prepare, and creatively present their books. For example, upon selecting and reading a myth or tall tale, each student pretended to be a director or a member of a cast of characters for a play based on the story. In the context of enjoyable book-sharing activities, the students analyzed the qualities of the characters and identified similar qualities among their classmates.

I have found that students extend their range of reading, expand the ways they "sell" books to others beyond the traditional book report, and stimulate their own perceptions when interpreting stories through these book-sharing activities. The daily integration and application of content and communication areas has far-reaching benefits for my students by providing the necessary involvement and practice to help them internalize content and refine their communication abilities.

BETSY F. YOUNG
Elementary School Teacher

for example, a teacher wants to motivate students—to arouse some interest in an upcoming project—employing a model to demonstrate the project would be a reasonable plan. Indeed, this is the strategy Ms. Werther adopted when she included assertive and altruistic students in the anger-control program. Making use of models in the classroom is not, however, simply a matter of deciding when to use a model. Decisions about the instructional use of models is complicated by the fact that not all models are equally effective.

CRITICAL THINKING: Why should modelled events more effectively arouse interest than a simple verbal preview?

Selecting Effective Models

In order to select the right model, a teacher must know what makes a model more or less effective. Effectiveness depends on the perceptions of the observer; model effectiveness is in the eye of the beholder. We now examine two types of observer perceptions, similarity and competence, and ways in which those perceptions relate to peer modelling.

Perceived Similarity. **Perceived similarity** is an observer's perception of similarity between him- or herself and the model. As is the case with other characteristics of a model, the observer's perception influences the model's effectiveness.

Rosenkrans (1967) showed children a film of a model playing a war game. The children were then led to believe that they were similar or dissimilar in background to the model. The high-similarity condition produced more modelled behaviours than the low-similarity condition. Rosenkrans' study supports the notion that models who are perceived by observers to be similar to themselves are more effective models.

Schunk (1987), in reviewing the literature on model effectiveness, recognizes that when it comes to the question of how many models are needed, more are better. Studies have shown that multiple models increase the likelihood that observers will perform the model behaviour. (This is a form of response facilitation, which we examined earlier.) But why should an increased number of models increase response facilitation effects? Schunk reasons that increasing the number of models increases the likelihood that observers will see themselves as being similar to at least one of the models.

Spence (1984) reviewed research to determine what influence the sex of the models had on observational learning. Spence concluded that the sex of the model seems to affect performance more than it does learning. Children learn behaviours from models of both sexes; they also judge the sex-appropriateness of those behaviours. Because some behaviours are judged more appropriate for members of one sex or the other, students who observe an opposite-sex model may decide that the behaviour is not, to use the term from the production process of observational learning, acceptable. The tendency to imitate behaviours performed by same-sex models can therefore be attributed to perceived similarity.

Perceived similarity is an important element of model effectiveness. If an observer sees him- or herself as being similar to the model and then observes the model succeeding in a particular situation, the observer is more likely to infer self-efficacy. Thus, perceived similarity means that the observer is likely to say to him- or herself, "If he (she) can do it, I can do it."

Perceived Competence. **Perceived competence** is an observer's evaluation of how expert a model is. Simon, Ditrichs, & Speckhart (1975) found that children are more likely to follow the behaviour of models they perceived as being competent than they are to follow models they perceive as being less than competent in the displayed skill. This is especially true when they are learning a novel response.

A model who masters a situation is perceived as being competent. However, this competence can itself be perceived in at least two different ways. Suppose that a teacher brings in two published novelists to talk about creative writing. The first novelist reads a scene from her latest book and discusses her characters' motivations and their symbolic meanings. The second novelist brings in marked-up copies of his first five drafts of a scene and describes the frustrations

TRY THIS: Identify a particular outcome you intend for your students. List as many models as you can that might be used to help your students attain the outcome.

REFLECTION: Make a list of the five most influential models you had in high school. How many were of the same gender? Were there any of the opposite sex? If so, identify the characteristics that most influenced you.

perceived similarity An observer's perception of similarity between himself or herself and the model.

perceived competence An observer's evaluation of how expert a model is.

involved in getting from the rough draft to the published version. Both models have mastered the skill of creative writing. The first novelist presents her mastery as an accomplished fact; she can be called a *mastery model*. The second novelist demonstrates how he overcomes problems on his way to mastery; he can be called a *coping model* (cf. Schunk, 1996).

When learners are fearful about a particular situation, they are more likely to improve their performances and gain self-confidence when they observe coping models rather than mastery models. Coping models initially demonstrate the typical fears and deficiencies of the observers. A model who copes with a situation, rather than mastering it instantly, may be a model who helps observers enhance their sense of self-efficacy (Schunk, Hanson, & Cox, 1987).

There is one other aspect of perceived competence that merits mention here. Perceived competence can be influenced by an observer's perception of a model's social status. One attains high social status by distinguishing her- or himself from others in a field of endeavour. A well-known political figure has been elected ahead of others. A well-known movie actor has been cast in more leading roles than other actors. A professional athlete has been selected over other athletes. If a model has high social status, he or she is often given credit for competence outside his or her area of expertise. We buy breakfast cereals because they are endorsed by athletes, not nutritionists.

A teacher who is judged by students to be a really great teacher has attained high status within the school community. The teacher may have attained that status because he or she is a recognized authority in a particular academic field or is recognized as a teacher who fosters student success.

Using Cognitive Modelling as an Instructional Approach

One of the implications of the social cognitive view is that modelling expands instructional opportunities beyond the process of shaping (Ormrod, 1990; Schunk, 1991). Shaping, an instructional process based in operant-conditioning theory, begins by reinforcing existing behaviours and then selectively reinforces changes in those behaviours to bring about complex behaviour. Modelling, however, is an instructional process by which new behaviours, concepts, and skills can be introduced, demonstrated, practised, and reinforced. Consider, for a moment, how difficult it would have been for Ms. Werther in the Teacher Chronicle to have used shaping as a way of decreasing aggressive behaviour in her students.

Teachers typically model cognitive skills that they want their students to acquire. The usual instructional sequence is for the teacher to explain and demonstrate the skill to be learned. After the skill is presented, students are given the opportunity to practise with guidance from the teacher. As the teacher monitors the students' practice, he or she checks for understanding and provides feedback to improve performance. If students experience severe problems, the skill is retaught, perhaps using a different explanation and demonstration. If students perform adequately during guided practice, they move to independent practice with only periodic checks by the teacher.

Cognitive modelling is an instructional approach that builds on modelled explanation and demonstration by augmenting the demonstration of the skill with model verbalization (Meichenbaum, 1977). As the model—usually the teacher—demonstrates the skill, he or she speaks aloud his or her thoughts, reasons, and decisions. To illustrate, imagine you are a student in a class in which the skill being taught is long division. The teacher writes the following problem on the board: $4\overline{)116}$

TRY THIS: Observe various classroom teachers. Identify those teachers who exemplify mastery models and those who can be classified as coping models. Which of the two types of teachers would you consider to be more effective? Explain your choice.

CONNECTION: This aspect of cognitive modelling is related to the notion of fading, discussed in Chapter 6.

cognitive modelling An approach to instruction that combines demonstration of skill with verbalization of cognitive activity that accompanies the skill.

As the teacher begins working on the problem, you hear the following verbalization: "Okay, let's see. First I have to decide what number I divide four into. I start with the first digit of the dividend, which in this problem is one. Four won't go into one, so I move to the right to see if it will go into that number. By moving one number to the right, I now have eleven. Four will go into eleven three? No, four times three is twelve and that's bigger than eleven. Four will go into eleven two times. So, my quotient begins with two, which I write above the eleven. Okay, the next step is to multiply two times four, which is eight. I write the eight under the eleven, subtract and end up with three. Now, I bring down the six that is left in the dividend...." And so the verbalization goes. By modelling not only the skill but also the thoughts, reasoning, and decisions that accompany the performance of the skill, the teacher is modelling his or her cognition. You will recall that cognitive modelling was an integral component of the anger-control program Ms. Werther adopted; she encouraged her models to augment their role play with verbalizations that revealed their cognitive efforts at problem solving. This approach is consistent with the concept of thinking dispositions presented in Chapter 5.

Verbalization during cognitive modelling can also include statements that indicate the model's motivation. Statements that imply self-reinforcement, such as, "This is going well, " "I think I'm getting this," or "That looks like it was a good decision," show students that making progress on a problem or task has positive consequences. Sharing the positive feelings of success seems a worthwhile reason to use cognitive modelling, but what would happen if, while verbalizing, a teacher makes a mistake? After all, teachers who use cognitive modelling run the risk of revealing their own weaknesses, especially if they are working on novel problems or if they are truly attempting to discover a new understanding in partnership with students. The research on model effectiveness suggests that making mistakes is okay and that verbalizing one's difficulties may, in the long run, prove helpful to students who are struggling. If a teacher's verbalization acknowledges a problem, determines what steps he or she might take to solve the problem—including the possibility of rereading an assignment or consulting an additional source of information—and ultimately solves the problem, that teacher will probably establish him- or herself as a coping model. Recall that both coping and mastery models are perceived as competent, but the coping model is more effective (Schunk, 1996). So, what if you use cognitive modelling in your own class and you make a mistake? Acknowledge it. Determine how to correct it. Persevere until the correct solution is found. Modelling the process by which you learn from mistakes might be one of the most valuable lessons you will ever teach.

TRY THIS: Observe one-on-one tutoring. Make a note of the number of times the tutor uses these kinds of statements in working with the learner. After the tutoring session, share your notes with the tutor as you discuss the session.

An instructional approach that is conceptually similar to cognitive modelling is called cognitive apprenticeship (Brown, Collins, & Duguid, 1989). In secondary and higher education, apprenticeships have usually taken the form of internships. Internships are opportunities for students to apply the knowledge and skills they have acquired in school to real work situations (Driscoll, 1994). Although most classroom teachers may not be able to establish internships, they can model skills and then structure learning activities that require students to apply those skills in meaningful and realistic ways (cf. Honebein, Duffy, & Fishman, 1994). Suppose, for example, that a science teacher assigned a project, the outcome of which was transforming the classroom into a science museum, complete with hands-on exhibits and guided tours for other students in the school, parents, and administrators. The exhibits could be developed on the basis of the units in the school's curriculum. The teacher could function as the director of the museum, while students functioned as other personnel—for example, members of exhibit teams, evaluators of other exhibits, guides, resource persons, brochure writers, exhibit caption writers, and publicists. This type of project allows the teacher to model skills, coach students, and evaluate student learning in ways similar to those used by the master in whose charge the apprentice was placed.

REFLECTION: Think back to a situation in which you worked with an expert. How did the experience influence your learning? What was the nature of the relationship between you, as the apprentice, and the master?

Helping Learners Build a Sense of Self-Efficacy

One of the most important outcomes that a student can acquire is the ability to learn. Bandura postulates the existence of a self-regulating system within the learner, which permits the learner to observe and evaluate his or her own performance. The judgments that the learner makes by means of self-evaluation influence his or her belief that he or she is capable of learning. Learning to learn is an outcome of instruction. To the extent that observational learning occurs in classrooms—and it occurs a great deal—self-efficacy is also an outcome of classroom instruction. Bandura (e.g., 1977, 1982, 1986) suggests four possible sources by which students can gain information relevant to their sense of self-efficacy: outcome of performance, vicarious experience, verbal persuasion, and physiological states.

The first source of information about self-efficacy is the outcome of performance. Successful performance on a given task enhances one's sense of self-efficacy.

A second source of efficacy information is vicarious experience. Students who observe models who attain success can use those observations to determine their own efficacy. If the role model attains success, the student will make judgments about the similarity between him- or herself and the model. The observer, seeing that the model has successfully completed the task, will also infer competence. If the competent model is perceived as being similar to the observer, the observer's sense of efficacy will be enhanced. If, however, the competent model is seen as being dissimilar, the observer may attribute the model's success to those qualities that he or she does not possess.

A third source of information that can influence self-efficacy is what Bandura refers to as "verbal persuasion." Other people in the learner's social environment—peers, teachers, parents—can persuade the learner verbally that he or she is capable of success at a particular task. Verbal persuasion by others is a substitute for the self-evaluation that occurs normally in observational learning. Verbal persuasion can occur internally as well, taking the form of what might be called positive self-talk.

TRY THIS: Ask practising teachers if the success of one student has a ripple effect on the motivation of other students. Ask whether the "If he or she can do it, so can I" attitude is noticeable in the classroom. If it is, ask for examples. If it is not, ask why.

REFLECTION: Think back to an episode in which a teacher responded to your class in a way similar to that indicated here. How did the teacher's comments make you feel? Were they motivating? If so, how? If not, why not?

POINT: Although the concept of self-efficacy is related to self-esteem—discussed in Chapter 3—there is an important difference. Self-efficacy is situation-specific.

Physiological states provide a last source of information about self-efficacy. Bandura refers to the gut feelings that convince a learner that he or she can or cannot achieve a goal. By taking into account factors such as perceived ability of the model and of self, the difficulty of the task, the amount of effort that needs to be expended, and aids to performance, students may experience physical sensations of increased alertness or excitement.

Teachers must try to provide the type of information that will enhance students' sense of self-efficacy. For example, suppose you were to respond to a sense of difficulty in your class by saying, "I don't understand why you people can't do this; the class last year had no problems." Such a response would require students either to perceive themselves as dissimilar to last year's class or to perceive themselves as less capable.

The degree to which a sense of self-efficacy has been developed is an outcome of observational learning (Driscoll, 1994). As there is with all learning and motivation issues, the relationship between self-efficacy and motivation is a strong one. Bandura (1977, 1982) argues that students with a sense of high self-efficacy will produce greater effort and persist longer in a task than students with a sense of low self-efficacy.

The relationship between academic self-efficacy and motivation is illustrated in several Canadian studies. McLean (1997), in a study of attitudinal factors related to students' success in high school, found that high-achieving students were significantly more likely to see themselves as academically competent, able to control their own academic destiny, and favourably viewed by peers, parents, and teachers than were low achieving students. In a series of studies examining the relationship of self-efficacy in mathematics to mathematics achievement, Randhawa and colleagues demonstrated that mathematics self-efficacy is a powerful mediating variable between mathematics attitudes and mathematical achievement (Randhawa, 1994; Randhawa, Beamer & Lundberg, 1993). Gender-related differences were also reported, with boys exhibiting stronger mathematical performance and placing a higher value on the relevance of mathematics to society and a higher perception of their ability in mathematics than did girls.

Motivational overtones are also present in the relationship between self-efficacy and choice of activity. Bandura argues that self-efficacy influences a student's choice of activity. Students with low self-efficacy in a particular area take measures to avoid tasks in that area. In contrast, students with high-efficacy expectations toward a particular task tend to approach that task eagerly.

Self-efficacy involves a belief that one can produce some behaviour regardless of whether one actually can or cannot produce that behaviour. Bandura (1977) proposes that the concept of self-efficacy is an indicator of both performance and achievement. He states that "individuals can believe that a particular course of action will produce certain outcomes, but if they entertain serious doubts about whether they can perform the necessary activities, such information does not influence their behaviour" (p. 193).

Therefore, outcome expectations and efficacy expectations must be met before a person will enact a behaviour that leads to an anticipated outcome (Figure 8.4). Efficacy expectations, which are predictions of how effective or competent one will be in his or her performance, differ from outcome expectations. Outcome expectations refer to a person's predictions about the likelihood that a given behaviour will lead to particular consequences. In this sense, outcome expectations are the judgments that observers make about the functional value of modelled behaviours.

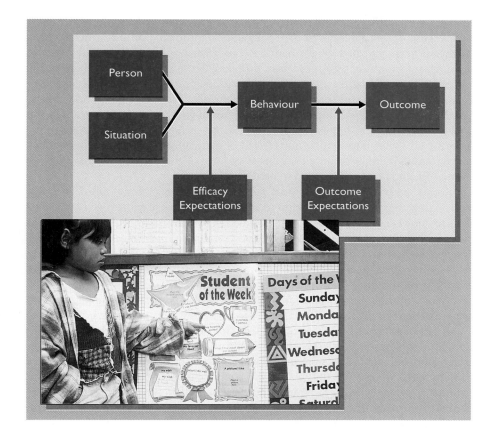

FIGURE 8.4
The Relationship among
Efficacy Expectations, Outcome
Expectations, and Behaviour

Source: Social Learning Theory
(p. 79), A. Bandura, 1977,
Englewood Cliffs, NJ: Prentice-
Hall. Copyright © 1977 by
Prentice-Hall. Reprinted by
permission.

As we will discover in Chapter 9, the learner's expectations and the teacher's expectations of learners are important determiners of motivation, especially in classroom achievement situations. Goal setting is an important component of the self-regulation system and, therefore, an important determiner of a student's sense of self-efficacy.

This point is illustrated in a Canadian study that examined resiliency factors in at-risk students. Resiliency factors are personal and situational characteristics that compensate for or protect individuals from risk. Johnson (1997) reported that resilient at-risk adolescents were more likely to be described as exhibiting a strong sense of self-worth, and as being motivated, academically successful, and prone to establish and work toward specific goals to overcome their adverse situations.

Bandura (1977, 1986) suggests that when individuals set goals, they determine a desired standard against which they compare internally their present levels of performance. Bandura suggests further that delaying self-reward until goals are met increases the likelihood that individuals will sustain their efforts until the goals are attained. Bandura's observations have led to additional research on the practice of goal setting and its influence on the individual student's sense of self-efficacy.

Teaching Goal-Setting and Self-Regulation Skills

Learners who are good at regulating their own learning activities are likely to set more realistic goals for themselves. Positive efficacy expectations motivate students to achieve (Schunk & Zimmerman, 1994). It is important to remember, however, that a sense of self-efficacy results from gathering information from the environment and from one's own performance. Because learners must gather and interpret so much information, they may make mistakes. Setting unrealistically high goals, for example, would be the result of erroneous beliefs or inaccurate observation of models. The same could be said for setting unrealistically low goals. Locke, Shaw, Saari, and Latham (1981) identify the properties of goals as being important to the goal-setting process. They note that setting goals using specific standards of performance is better than setting nonexplicit or general goals for improving performance. In addition, assuming that one is capable of performing the goal, setting more difficult goals tends to lead to better performance.

Goals can be long range or short range. Short-range goals are called *proximal* goals. Long-range goals are referred to in social cognitive literature as *distal* goals. Schunk and Gaa (1981) argue that it is better to set proximal goals than distal goals for improving self-motivation and performance. They suggest that the result is especially important for young children who may not be capable of cognitively representing distal goals. They also maintain that learners who set proximal goals may be promoting self-efficacy; as they observe their progress toward these goals, the quality of their performance increases. Successful performance helps children maintain their motivation and enhance their sense of self-efficacy.

The evaluation of one's own performance is part of the self-regulation system. Students can evaluate themselves in terms of the internal standards that are part of the self-regulation system. In a social environment, however, it is difficult for students to escape the reality of social comparison. Ruble, Boggiano, Feldman, & Loebl (1980) provided a developmental analysis of the role of social comparison in self-evaluation. They found that very young children make little use of comparative information when performing evaluations of their own performance. However, by grade four, students utilize social information in evaluating their own competence. For example, a preschool child may not compare his or her drawing with those of other students before judging the drawing's quality, but a grade five student would judge his or her drawing by comparing it with the drawings of others. This use of social information, according to Bandura (1986), can have a vicarious influence on self-efficacy.

Think back to Ms. Werther's anger-control program; including performance feedback following a student's role play provided a means by which the target boys could begin to integrate self-evaluation into their behavioural repertoire.

Additional research on the relationship between goal setting, social comparison, and self-efficacy was undertaken by Schunk (1983). Schunk compared the effects of social comparative information against proximal goal setting. Four groups of children were studied. The first group was given comparative information about problems solved by other children in a division-skills program. A second group pursued the goal of a set number of problems in each session. A third group received both of the treatments. A fourth group served as the control, receiving neither treatment.

The third group, which operated with both information about the performance of others and a clear goal, demonstrated the highest perceived self-efficacy and achieved the highest skill level. These results indicate that the combined use of social comparison information and an internal standard leads to higher levels of self-efficacy. If the information from others and having goals can help performance, how can we teach our students to set goals?

TRY THIS: Interview students in an attempt to discover their long-range goals and their short-range goals. Ask them if they consciously set goals for themselves. If so, how? If not, have they ever considered doing so?

CRITICAL THINKING: How might the results of this study be explained using the concept of scaffolding discussed in Chapter 2?

Here's How

Here's How To Encourage Goal Setting and Self-Regulation

- Encourage students to compare their work and their products with each other and to discuss the standards they use in judging their work and the work of others.

- Encourage students to set both distal and proximal goals. After setting a long-term goal, have students work together to determine the steps that can be taken to reach that goal.

- Give feedback regarding not only the quality of student products but also the quality of the work process. Encourage students to think of ways they can improve their work habits and, thereby, improve the final outcome.

- Help students learn to judge their internal standards. A student who establishes unrealistic goals may do harm to his or her sense of self-efficacy.

Selecting Diverse Models

The research, discussed earlier in the chapter, on the effects of perceived similarity on model effectiveness indicates that students are more likely to model someone whom they view to be like themselves. Given the cultural diversity and the inevitable gender differences that will exist in any classroom, not all of your students will perceive you to be similar to themselves. One answer to this problem is to provide multiple models for your students. Multiple models have been shown to be more effective with learners than a single model because, by providing a number of models, learners are more likely to perceive similarity between themselves and at least one of the models. The use of multiple models not only enhances the probability of perceived similarity but also provides an opportunity to celebrate diversity.

Women are underrepresented among science and math teachers. Men are underrepresented among English and art teachers and also among all elementary teachers (Grossman & Grossman, 1994). These patterns reinforce sex-role stereotypes. If the teacher is the only adult that students observe, and the teacher does not attempt to expose the students to other adults, the stereotypes will be perpetuated. One way to combat this problem is to seek out female scientists and male artists, those people who function successfully in non-stereotypic roles. In addition to gender, cultural groups are also underrepresented among school teachers. Invite Aboriginals, both male and female, who can model success in nontraditional occupations to share their experiences. Although little research has been done on the effectiveness of this approach, the research that has been done indicates that providing female students with female models improves girls' participation in math. Research has shown that same-sex models for boys enhance their achievement in a variety of academic areas (Brody & Fox, 1980; Mitchell, 1990).

TRY THIS: Contact organizations such as the National Action Committee on the Status of Women or Assembly of First Nations and ask if they have a speakers' bureau. Many organizations have speakers' bureaus and are happy to help teachers.

Using Peer Models

Peer models are people who are from the same social environment as the observer. In a classroom, students who model behaviour for other students are peer models. The literature on peer modelling suggests that classroom peers can help in training social skills, enhancing self-efficacy, and remedying deficiencies in a variety of skill areas (Schunk, 1987). In another study of the effects of peer models, Gresham (1981) examined the acquisition of social skills in children with physical disabilities. Those children who observed peer models engaging in a variety of social interactions showed enhanced social skills.

The effectiveness of coping models is reinforced when coping models are the observer's peers. Peer models who must cope with difficult or stressful situations can enhance the self-efficacy of observers. It is not surprising that peer models who can enhance the self-efficacy of observers under stressful or difficult conditions are effective in situations that require remedial instruction.

What is called *peer modelling* when seen from a social cognitive point of view becomes *peer tutoring* when put into practice in a classroom. The teacher who uses peer tutoring in his or her classroom should do so with an eye toward model effectiveness. A student chosen to tutor another student is a potential model; the student to be helped, the observer. Social cognitive theory holds that the observer's perceptions of the model determine the model's effectiveness.

CONNECTION: Peer tutoring is examined in some detail in the context of cooperative learning techniques in Chapter 12.

Generally, research evidence suggests that peer tutoring works. Such evidence can be explained in terms of perceived similarity—a model who is a peer is likely to be perceived as being similar by the observer. Although peer tutoring has the built-in advantage of perceived similarity, the evidence on peer modelling suggests that coping models benefit observers as well. Finding a good match between students in terms of competence provides a reasonable basis for forming peer-tutoring pairs in the classroom.

Being a Model

Social cognitive theory provides us with an explanation of how observers learn from models. As instructional leaders, teachers are in a unique position to choose models for their students and to serve as models. As we learned earlier in this chapter, the perceived competence of a person influences his or her effectiveness as a potential model. When students walk into a classroom, the teacher is in a position of defined competence. What the teacher does with that status influences his or her ability to model behaviours for the students. Although social cognitive theory tells us that perceived competence makes for an effective model, it is important that we realize that our defined status of authority will not maintain our effectiveness. Students may attend to us initially because we are teachers. But unless we can maintain our status as competent models, students will soon stop attending to our behaviours. If the attention process is not supported by the model in the environment, then the retention, production, and motivation processes of observational learning will not occur.

CONNECTION: Think back to the information- processing theory described in Chapter 7. Attention—either selective or automatic—is necessary for additional processing of information.

peer models Models who are from the same social environment.

We are often told as teachers that we should model enthusiasm for the content we are going to teach. If teachers are not enthusiastic, then the students won't be either. But think back to your own elementary and high school experiences. Weren't there teachers in your classrooms who seemed to be enthusiastic yet who attracted little of your attention? One explanation is that their competence was mitigated by a lack of perceived similarity. One of the authors of this book can recall a high school teacher who displayed competence but was perceived by his students as being so dissimilar to them that he was not an effective model. It was not unusual for this teacher, who taught chemistry, to walk into the classroom and exclaim that he did not understand why we did so poorly on our tests. Our reaction as observers in this situation was that this particular teacher was absolutely correct in his reaction to us. He simply could not understand that we did not understand the material. Because he was so dissimilar from us as students, his enthusiasm for the content was not enough to make him an effective teacher. Did you ever have a teacher like that?

If we assume that as teachers we must serve as models, we must find ways of connecting with students. In Chapter 6, when we considered connections, we examined ways of connecting the content we teach to students' prior knowledge. Social cognitive theory requires that we look for ways to connect ourselves with our students. How can we be an effective model for Monica? For Jamal? Whether the outcome we seek for our students is discipline, understanding, or self-efficacy, making connections remains an important part of the job.

Reflecting on our characteristics as models is one way of pursuing avenues of connection. If our students experience difficulties, we can set ourselves up as coping models. If we show that we have or have had difficulties with material, and then provide examples of how we mastered the material in the face of those difficulties, we are more likely to be perceived as similar—and competent—by our students and therefore more likely to serve as effective models.

> **POINT:** Reflecting on our characteristics as models supports one of the basic assumptions of this book: *Reflective construction is necessary for the development of teaching expertise.*

Social Learning Interventions for Exceptional Children

Research has shown that exceptional children are vulnerable to the development of psychosocial problems (Anderson, Williams, McGee, & Silva, 1989; Offord, Boyle, & Racine, 1989). Interventions based on social learning principles have, however, demonstrated efficacy for mitigating the long-term impact of these psychosocial problems. For example, the PATHS curriculum, a program designed for hearing impaired school-aged children, uses role playing, modelling by teachers and peers, social and self-reinforcement, and verbal mediation to improve students' self-control, emotional understanding, interpersonal cognitive problem solving, and social competence (Greenberg & Kusche, 1993).

Social learning programs to alter the maladaptive attributions about success and failure exhibited by students with learning disabilities, as well as interventions designed to improve their self-regulation and coping skills, can be found in the research literature (Shelton, Anastopoulos, & Linden, 1985; Kamann & Wong, 1993). Powers, Swoers, Turner, Nesbitt, Knowles, & Ellison (1996) have recently introduced a program designed to promote self-determination in adolescents with physical disabilities. The program is aimed at developing self-efficacy appraisals through enactive attainment (repeated performance accomplishments), vicarious experience (role model interactions), social persuasion (feedback, reinforcement, and challenge), and physiological feedback (relaxation training and positive self-talk). Problem solving and coping strategies are integrated throughout. Our Teacher Chronicle has already introduced us to an anger-management program consistent with one proposed by Lockman, Lampron, Gemmer, and Harris (1987).

Teacher Chronicle Conclusion

A Social Learning Approach

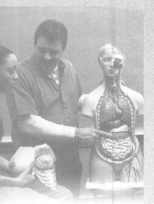

After offering eighteen sessions of the anger-control program, Ms. Werther thought it important to carefully evaluate the impact of the program on decreasing aggressive behaviour in her target students. Once more, she gathered frequency data on their aggressive behaviour. She was pleased to note that David had made significant progress; not only was he less aggressively reactive but he also seemed to make efforts towards understanding other students' perspectives. Ms. Werther was particularly excited to note that David's classmates also seemed to have altered their perception of him and were more tolerant towards his behavioural lapses.

Unfortunately, little change was observed in two other boys. Ms. Werther noted that these youngsters appeared to use their aggression in a planned way and were held in high esteem by other members of the class. Having made this observation, Ms. Werther determined that the roots of aggression in children may be quite diverse and that multiple interventions are likely necessary.

Application Questions

1. What might have happened had Ms. Werther used models who were greatly admired by all the students because of their success in careers requiring considerable self-control (for example, a noted boxer or football player). Do you think that the higher status aggressive boys might have responded differently? What other modifications might Ms. Werther consider to enhance the likelihood that these boys will benefit from a social learning intervention?

2. Suppose the target children use their newly learned anger-management skills in another environment and the result is negative. What effect is this going to have on their subsequent use of these skills? How might Ms. Werther use these experiences advantageously?

3. List the people after whom you model yourself. Defend your selections. How many of your models are peers? If some are peers, explain why. If not, why not?

4. Imagine that a grade two teacher decided to implement a program similar to the one used by Ms. Werther. Do you think it would be successful? Are there developmental considerations that the teacher would need to keep in mind? How might the program be modified?

5. While a decrease in David's aggressive behaviour likely led to altered peer relationships, what other components of the anger-control program might account for the increased tolerance of his peers? What social learning activities might Ms. Werther incorporate on a day-to-day basis to enhance tolerance and acceptance in all children?

6. To what extent do you think that role-playing anger-management skills influenced learning and retention? Would the students have acquired as much learning had they been exposed to anger-control strategies through text? Why or why not?

CHAPTER SUMMARY

What Are The Dimensions Of Social Learning?
(L.O. 1–5, p. 240)

Social learning occurs when a learner observes a model. What the observer learns may or may not be performed. Social cognitive theory suggests that we need not engage in a behaviour to learn that it is or is not appropriate in a particular situation. We can learn the consequences of behaviours by observing others. Vicarious learning is possible because humans have cognitive capabilities that allow them to symbolize, anticipate, and reflect. Social learning theory recognizes the relationship among behaviour, personal factors, and the environment.

What Is Modelling and How Does Modelling Influence Learners? (L.O. 6, p. 250)

The effects of observing models can cause an observer to engage in behaviours that are not normally performed or to refrain from exhibiting known behaviours. Observing a model can also highlight aspects of the environment that would not have been otherwise perceived. Observation of a model can also arouse emotions—either positive or negative—in the observer.

What Are the Processes of Observational Learning? (L.O. 8, p. 254)

Learning by observing others occurs when the learner attends to the model's behaviour and undertakes overt or covert rehearsal to retain the observed behaviour. Once cognitively represented or retained, the learner must decide whether the behaviour can and should be exhibited. Reinforcement can be delivered by others in a learner's environment or by oneself, or it can be experienced vicariously through observation.

How Can Your Knowledge of Social Learning Make You a More Effective Teacher? (L.O. 9, p. 258)

Social learning principles govern the properties that make models more or less effective. Perceived similarity and competence contribute to a model's effectiveness. Cognitive modelling—modelling not only overt behaviour but also the cognitive processes that underlie that behaviour—can be used as an effective instructional tool. Social learning principles also help teachers build self-efficacy, select models, and encourage relationships between model and observer.

KEY CONCEPTS

arousal effects, p. 252

attention, p. 254

cognitive modelling, p. 261

direct reinforcement, p. 258

disinhibitory effects, p. 250

enactive learning, p. 243

environmental enhancement effects, p. 252

forethought, p. 246

inhibitory effects, p. 250

learning, p. 242

model, p. 241

modelling, p. 250

motivation, p. 254

observational learning effects, p. 252

observer, p. 241

peer models, p. 268

perceived competence, p. 260

perceived similarity, p. 260

performance, p. 242

production, p. 254

reciprocal determinism, p. 248

response facilitation effects, p. 251

retention, p. 254

self-efficacy, p. 246

self-reflection, p. 246

self-regulation, p. 246

self-reinforcement, p. 258

social cognitive theory, p. 240

symbolize, p. 245

vicarious learning, p. 244

vicarious reinforcement, p. 258

9 Facilitating Student Motivation

LEARNING OUTCOMES

When you have completed this chapter, you will be able to

1. describe the internal and external factors that motivate students to learn, participate in class, and complete learning tasks

2. distinguish between deficiency and growth needs in Maslow's hierarchy of needs and describe their relevance to the classroom

3. tell how students' self-concept and explanations of success and failure influence their motivation to strive for academic achievement

4. explain how expectations and uses of reinforcement influence students' motivation

5. suggest several teaching strategies that increase students' motivation to learn

6. define *self-efficacy* and describe three ways that students develop expectations of self-efficacy

Teacher Chronicle

An Outer Space Opportunity

Opportunities for teachers to reach a student often appear at the most unexpected times. These moments often provide the best teaching of the day.

Jerry Bird walks around his room observing his grade nine writing class. The board is covered with the results of a brainstorming lesson the class has just completed. Lists of words fill the board, connected by a web of lines linking one idea to another. The class is prewriting for an assignment on space exploration.

All are intently punching their keyboards except Bronson. Bronson has his hand up for help. He followed the brainstorming session, but rarely joins in classroom activities. He has a good sense of humour and is reading at his grade level. He doesn't seem to find English interesting, however, and spends much of his time day-dreaming in class. Most of his assignments are incomplete and not well done.

"Does the assignment have to be on what we are now doing? Could I write on the future?" Bronson whispers as his teacher approaches.

"What are you thinking?" Jerry asks, noticing that he has nothing on his screen.

"I have been playing a computer game called Wing Commander Prophecy and it's really cool. You travel around the galaxy in a space craft encountering an alien race which thinks differently from us. Some of the space missions are really intense."

Jerry hasn't seen Bronson so animated before. He thinks for a moment, considering the options. His goal in the lesson is to have the class write a short term paper on space exploration so that they learn to use the library and Internet as resources, and at the same time learn about the contribution to space exploration by Canada and the United States. If Bronson writes about his video game and ties it in to possible future technology he would be accomplishing most of the objectives of the assignment, although from a different perspective.

"Sure," Jerry tells him, "Why don't you write on how video games portray the possible technologies and exploration of space in the future?"

Bronson smiles and begins hitting the keys furiously. Jerry thinks about Bronson's interest while he continues walking around. This is the first time Bronson has expressed a real interest in a writing assignment. Perhaps he can use Bronson's interest as a base to extend his enthusiasm into other topics. In the meantime, Jerry can't wait to read Bronson's assignment.

Focus Questions

1. What internal and external factors might affect Bronson's motivation to learn? to participate in class?

2. How does Jerry's modification of the assignment reflect his understanding of the importance of student motivation in learning? Did he make the right decision?

3. What would you do in Jerry's situation with Bronson?

4. What teaching strategies might Jerry use to increase students' motivation to learn?

What is Motivation to Learn?

Reading this chapter is a learning activity focused on the topic of student motivation. As you embark on this activity, consider your reasons for doing so. Are you reading this chapter now because your instructor assigned it? Are you reading the chapter because you have a quiz at the end of the week? Are you reading the chapter because you want to understand why students differ in their pursuits of academic achievement? Are you reading the chapter because you will be a student teacher soon and you are concerned about motivating your students? What motivates you to do what you're doing right now? What motivates you to continue reading a textbook when you find its subject matter uninteresting? What motivates you to learn new things even when you have no particular use for them at the moment?

When students develop a **motivation to learn**, they initiate learning activities, they stay involved in a learning task, and they exhibit a commitment to learning (Ames, 1990). These are all outcomes that we desire of students in school, and effective schools are those that help students acquire the goals, beliefs, and attributes that will sustain a long-term engagement in learning. In the Teacher Chronicle, for example, Jerry wants to involve Bronson in the writing activity, and there are many ways she could go about doing this. As you will see in this chapter, however, some ways are more effective than others, especially when it comes to promoting an ongoing commitment to learning.

Intrinsic and Extrinsic Motivation

Why do students initiate or engage in some learning tasks and not others? One aspect of motivation to learn concerns the reasons students behave as they do. **Intrinsic motivation** occurs when learners work on tasks for internal reasons, such as pleasure or enjoyment in the activity, satisfaction in learning something new, or curiosity about and interest in the topic. The child who reads during recess, on the bus to and from school, and in the family car on vacation, for example, is said to be intrinsically motivated toward reading. Likewise, the student who is fascinated by trains and seeks out information about them is intrinsically motivated to learn about the subject of trains.

Extrinsic motivation occurs when learners work on tasks for external reasons. They may want to please a teacher or parent or avoid getting in trouble that would be certain to follow if they failed to complete the task. Students who engage in tasks for the sake of achieving some reward or anticipated outcome also are extrinsically motivated. For example, an aspiring teacher may take a particular course, not because he or she is especially interested in the subject matter, but because it is required in order to obtain certification. Similarly, some students memorize the multiplication tables in order to achieve a good grade rather than for the satisfaction of learning math and becoming prepared for more complex problem solving.

What is important about the reasons students possess for learning is that two students may well engage in the same behaviour but do so for quite different reasons. Whereas one is interested in the topic, the other may be working to achieve a certain grade. Their reasons have consequences for the quality of cognitive engagement in the learning task and, hence, the quality of learning that results. Different reasons also have different consequences for continuing motivation. The intrinsically motivated person is more likely to stay involved in and demonstrate a com-

---

POINT: *People are naturally motivated to learn.* Sometimes, however, the activities in which students have intrinsic interest to learn are not the same as those teachers want them to learn.

---

motivation to learn A disposition of learners that is characterized by their willingness to initiate learning activities, their continued involvement in a learning task, and their long-term commitment to learning.

intrinsic motivation When learners work on tasks for internal reasons, such as pleasure or enjoyment in the activity.

extrinsic motivation When learners work on tasks for external reasons, such as to please a parent or to avoid getting into trouble with the teacher.

mitment to learning than is the extrinsically motivated person. For the latter, task engagement is likely to cease when the extrinsic reasons for learning no longer exist.

REFLECTION: Think about your motivation to learn in this class. Are you primarily extrinsically or intrinsically motivated? Why?

Internal and External Sources of Motivation

Student motivation is an extremely complex matter. Many sources of motivation arise from within the learner, but just as many come from the learning environment. Listed in Figure 9.1 are various sources of student motivation to learn. A study by Canadian researchers Vallerand and Bissonnette (1992) from the University of Quebec in Montreal shows the relationship of intrinsic motivation to task commitment. Vallerand and Bissonnette reported that college students who persisted to the end of a compulsory course were more likely to be intrinsically motivated than were students who dropped out. Identifying internal sources—such as a student's goals, beliefs about his or her ability, or willingness to take risks—can help you understand why students appear motivated or unmotivated to engage in certain learning tasks. Understanding these factors can also aid you in helping students to develop adaptive motivational patterns. For example, you could work with students to increase their self-confidence when they have the capability of achieving a goal but don't believe they can do it. Knowing how aspects of the learning environment can influence motivation enables you to arrange learning conditions to best support the intrinsic motivation of your students.

CRITICAL THINKING: What are the sources of motivation according to behavioural learning theory (Chapter 6)? According to cognitive learning models (Chapter 7)? According to social learning theory (Chapter 8)?

Different Perspectives on Motivation

The sources of motivation that are shown in Figure 9.1 are associated with different views of motivation that emphasize some factors over others. Recall the behavioural perspective on learning (Chapter 6), for example. Reinforcement was described as a process that increases the incidence of existing behaviour and facilitates the establishment of new behaviours. If you consider motivation from a behavioural perspective, you can see that reinforcers serve as extrinsic motivators

FIGURE 9.1
Sources of Student Motivation

Within the Learner	From the Learning Environment
• Personal goals and intentions • Biological and psychological drives and needs • Self-concept, self-esteem, and self-confidence • Personal beliefs, values, expectations, and explanations for success or failure • Self-knowledge, prior experiences, and sense of self-efficacy • Personality factors, e.g., willingness to undertake risk, ability to manage anxieties, curiosity, and persistence in effort • Emotional states and levels of arousal	• Goals of teachers, parents, and peers • Classroom goal structures • Outcomes of social interactions • Social and cultural beliefs and values • Classroom reinforcements; incentive and disincentive systems • Instructional stimuli involving complexity, novelty, and ambiguity • Teachers' and others' expectations of the learner • Performance models • Instructional practices that attract attention, provide relevance, foster confidence, and lead to satisfaction

of behaviour. To the extent that learners find a reinforcer satisfying or desirable, they will be motivated to engage in the behaviour that leads to the reinforcer.

From a cognitive perspective, by contrast, the focus is on intrinsic motivation as it is influenced primarily by thoughts and beliefs. Learners hold beliefs about their abilities to accomplish tasks and achieve certain goals, which influence their motivation to undertake a task in the first place. Similarly, their thoughts about their own success or failure in achieving a goal will affect their motivation to continue a learning activity. Cognitive theorists are also concerned about the influence of the teacher's beliefs and expectations on student motivation.

A third perspective on motivation stems from humanistic theories, which focus on biological and psychological needs and drives. Examples of needs that influence motivation include the need to achieve, the need for self-fulfillment, and the need for autonomy. Humanists believe these needs propel learners to seek certain goals and to act in certain ways in much the same way that hunger causes you to seek food. In some of these theories, needs are arranged hierarchically; that is, basic needs such as safety and self-esteem must be satisfied first before learners can go about the business of satisfying growth needs such as knowing and understanding.

Finally, social learning theories integrate intrinsic and extrinsic sources of motivation as they focus on both the goals and expectations of learners and the consequences of reaching those goals. Expectancy x value theories, for example, regard motivation as a function of the learner's expectation of achieving a goal and of the learner's perceived value of that goal—that is, learners must expect to achieve a goal *and* they must value such achievement to be motivated and willing to take actions toward goal attainment.

This chapter provides a multidimensional picture of student motivation that draws from all four perspectives, so that you will be well prepared to understand and solve problems related to motivation in your classroom.

How Do Students' Needs and Wants Affect Their Motivation to Learn?

To help your students improve their motivation to learn in your classroom, you must understand the needs and wants of your students and how these influence motivation. What needs will your students bring to school? What do they want that they might work hard to attain? What are sources of motivation for academic achievement?

Maslow's Hierarchy of Needs

Human beings need water to drink; they need food to eat; they need shelter and love. They need to feel safe, both physically and psychologically. Part of being human is the need to feel good about oneself. Part of being human is the need to understand the world around oneself. Different people have different needs, and their needs vary in degree. For some, the need for shelter is most important; for others, the need for food is the primary motivation. Individuals' needs change as well—during a day, a year, a lifetime.

The concept of human needs is basic to the theory formulated by Abraham Maslow (1943, 1954), known as Maslow's **hierarchy of needs** (Figure 9.2). At the

EXAMPLE: A grade four student really wants to be in the top reading group but is not willing to work on his reading enough to make the top group. His parents offer him extra TV time in exchange for extra reading. This arrangement works for awhile. The boy makes progress, but not enough to merit moving him into the top group. Then his parents hire him to read: They offer to pay him by the hour. Soon, he is reading far more than his parents expect him to, and the teacher moves him into the top reading group. What elements of motivation are in action here?

POINT: *Needs and values affect motivation.* Understanding the needs and wants of your students can help you plan lessons that will meet their needs and stimulate their interest in learning.

hierarchy of needs A theory proposed by Abraham Maslow in which human needs are arranged in a hierarchy from basic needs to self-actualization, or self-fulfillment.

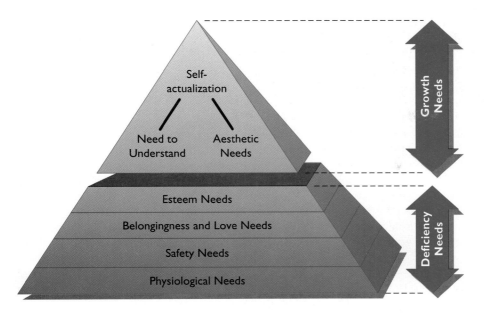

FIGURE 9.2
Maslow's Hierarchy of Needs

Source: Psychology (4th ed., p. 406), L.A. Lefton, 1991, Needham Heights, MA: Allyn & Bacon. Copyright 1996 by Allyn & Bacon. Reprinted by permission.

lower levels of the hierarchy are basic needs that humans require for physical and psychological well-being: **deficiency needs**.

Deficiency needs must be at least partially satisfied before a person can be motivated to pursue satisfaction of higher-level needs. The higher-level needs, which, when satisfied, enable the human being to grow psychologically, are called **growth needs**. As growth needs become satisfied, a person is able to fulfill his or her personal potential and achieve **self-actualization**.

As an example of how the hierarchy of needs helps explain motivation, consider a child who comes from an unhealthy, abusive home environment. Any student who comes to class from such a neglected environment has unfulfilled basic needs. Given his or her life circumstances, that student may not feel very safe. If a student has an unfulfilled need as basic as safety, it will be very difficult for that student to focus on higher-order needs, such as the need to understand. Parents play an important role in satisfying the deficiency and growth needs of their children. Parents who wish their children to become capable of pursuing growth needs must help their children satisfy the more basic needs of health, safety, belonging, love, and self-esteem (Nystul, 1984).

The same argument can be made for adult learners (Sappington, 1984). Teachers of adult learners must also help those learners satisfy basic needs before expecting them to be motivated to understand and to grow in other ways. For both children and adults, one basic need is an emotionally safe learning environment. Establishing a safe environment enables students to address constructively any fears they may bring to the learning situation. It also allows learners to take risks in the classroom, to participate more fully, and, thereby, to grow psychologically.

How can Maslow's theory provide a means for teachers to identify problems in students who appear to be unmotivated—that is, who appear to be motivated by goals other than academic achievement and who take nonacademic routes to their goals? Observe such a student and, starting at the bottom of the hierarchy, ask yourself some questions. Are the student's physiological needs being met? Is

CONNECTION: Principles of human development discussed in Chapters 2 and 3 relate to Maslow's theory.

deficiency needs According to Maslow's hierarchy of needs, the basic needs that humans require for physical and psychological well-being.

growth needs According to Maslow, the higher-level needs, the satisfaction of which enables human beings to grow psychologically.

self-actualization Fulfilling one's personal potential.

Insights on Successful Practice

What can you do to increase your students' motivation to learn?

I have been teaching high school science in Northern Manitoba for the last three years. Motivating students and creating interest in our subject helps solve several potential classroom problems simultaneously. First of all, interested students are far less likely to provide discipline problems. The two are incompatible. Interested students don't throw spit balls or spend their time jabbing other students. They are also more likely to bring other students in line when they act out of order.

Second, when our students are motivated—so are we! There is nothing so gratifying as having students who are interested in what we are teaching. Otherwise teaching can become just another nine-to-five job, and who wants that?

And, third, students learn more effectively when they are attentive.

If I had to summarize the secret to motivating students in one word it would be *variety*. Bring in guest speakers and the occasional film and audio-visual materials. But keep in mind that these can be overused—a film every week defeats the purpose.

Collect anecdotes about the lives of famous scientists mentioned in class. Did you know that Archimedes' alleged feat of setting attacking Roman ships on fire at Syracuse in 214 b.c.e. was duplicated on a small scale in 1923 by an engineer? Using seventy flat mirrors (each 1 m x 1.5m), he focused the sun's image onto a rowboat fifty metres from shore. It began to burn within a few seconds and soon sank.

The skilful use of questions is a time-honoured approach to successful teaching. In my science classes I put up a question of the week. Some of these have been: Why do the wheels on cars move backwards in films? How do boomerangs come back? Why are some substances trans-parent? There are many resource books that provide questions such as these (and, yes, answers too). One recent favourite source of mine is Robert Wolke's *What Einstein Didn't Know* (Carol Publishing Group, 1997).

Ask students to explain phenomena that can be understood (with some thinking) using high school science. Ask them to explain how someone can lie on a bed of nails (if they need help, mention snowshoes as a hint). Ask them to explain walking on a bed of hot coals (If they need help, remind them that the air in an oven and a cake pan are both at the same temperature. The distinction between temperature and heat conductivity of wood/coal and metals is important here).

By far the best source of fascinating material to enrich our classes can be found in books by good science-writers. I've really mined DeSalle's and Lindley's *The Science of Jurassic Park and the Lost World, or How to Build a Dinosaur* (Basic Books, 1997) for my high school biology class and Lawrence Kraus' *The Physics of Star Trek* (Basic Books/Harper Collins, 1996) for my physics classes. You can do the same and really have some fun. To promote critical thinking, my students find enlightening the late Carl Sagan's *The Demon-Haunted World* (Ballantine Books, 1997) and Peter Huston's *Scams From the Great Beyond: How to Make Easy Money off ESP, Astrology, UFOs, Crop Circles, Cattle Mutilations, Alien Abductions, and other New Age Nonsense* (Paladin Press, 1997). Remember—always be enthusiastic about your subject. Enthusiasm is catching!

CHRISTOPHER PIKE
High School Science Teacher

Your Insights

For this teacher, what was the key to increasing student motivation to learn?

---

the student receiving adequate food and shelter? If physiological needs have been met, what about the safety of that student? Does the student feel physically safe at home and in school? An interview with the student might give you some clues about the student's feelings of safety. Next, what about this student's needs to belong to a group and to feel loved? In this regard, you can think about Lickona's model of moral education (examined in Chapter 3). Observing this student's social interactions can give you some clues about the extent to which his or her needs to belong and to be loved are being gratified. Richard McLean (1997), at the University of Alberta, found that academically good students were more likely than academically poor students to feel that their parents, peers, and teachers were positive about their school performance and believed they had the ability and potential to be successful.

If the student appears to have positive relations with peers, if he or she is not a social isolate, if the student exhibits a sense of community in the family and at school, and if the student seems to feel loved, then the next set of questions to ask should address the student's self-esteem and his or her sense of self-efficacy. You may want to assign tasks that you feel sure the student can perform successfully in order to gauge the student's views of his or her abilities. Finding out the student's expectations of efficacy could give you some clues about academic self-esteem.

The failure to gratify a need results in a related form of dysfunction or disturbance. If your observations reveal a dysfunction related to deficiency needs, some kind of action is needed. For example, safety, belongingness, and esteem needs might be gratified in a classroom that operates on the basis of Lickona's model (1987). For the most part, teachers can exert influence only at school. If problems related to deficiency needs cannot be met at school, a teacher must seek outside help. One of the first things a new teacher should do is learn the school district's referral system. Find out what student services and other professional help are available for students.

A student whose deficiency needs have been met is said to be growth motivated. Growth-motivated students have a need to understand and to know. They also have aesthetic needs. A student in physics might appreciate the beauty inherent in the phenomena of astronomy, for example. Another student might appreciate the rhythm of a sonnet or the elegance of a mathematical formula. Growth-motivated students tend to seek a tension that they find pleasurable, usually in the form of a challenge. Learners who attempt independent studies, for example, seek to solve problems of their own devising.

It is important to note here that students who are growth-motivated tend to be self-directed. These students take the responsibility to satisfy their need to know and understand and their aesthetic needs. Recalling the earlier distinction between intrinsic and extrinsic motivation, we can see that growth-motivated students tend to rely more on intrinsic rewards than extrinsic rewards. Teachers who work with such students should provide them with opportunities to pursue self-directed learning and take care not to undermine their intrinsic motivation with unnecessary extrinsic rewards.

A growth-motivated person has had his or her deficiency needs met and therefore seeks the challenge of meeting growth needs. This suggests that you should arrange learning situations that students will view as challenging, but not threatening. If students perceive your classroom as threatening, they are likely to play it safe. They will not take risks academically; they will not seek out the challenge. From Maslow's perspective, therefore, the best classrooms are those that maximize the opportunities for growth by reducing the possibilities for failure and embarrassment. Risk-taking behaviour, in an academic sense, is to be encouraged.

The Need to Achieve

Achievement motivation is a desire or tendency to overcome obstacles and to accomplish some difficult task through the exercise of power. Achievement motivation can manifest itself as an attitude of competitiveness and willingness to take certain risks (e.g., McClelland, 1965).

TRY THIS: On the basis of classroom observations, brainstorm with your classmates to define an emotionally safe environment. What elements contribute to such an environment?

REFLECTION: As a student in elementary and secondary school, how did your unmet needs influence your experiences in school?

CONNECTION: Lickona's model of moral education in Chapter 3 relates to the satisfaction of deficiency needs in Maslow's theory.

TRY THIS: Gather information from a school district or interview a school administrator regarding the referral system used in the district.

EXAMPLE: Many of the problems encountered by growth-motivated students are problems they have devised themselves. The tension created by such problems is imposed by the student and hence becomes a source of pleasure.

achievement motivation A person's desire or tendency to overcome obstacles and to accomplish some difficult task through the exercise of power.

According to Maslow's theory, what are every learner's basic human needs? How might the satisfaction or frustration of those needs affect a student's motivation to learn?

The level of the need to achieve that students project gives us an index of the amount of risk-taking behaviour they are capable of and, to some extent, the types of goals that motivate them. In a classic study, McClelland (1958) asked children to play a ring-toss game. The children were allowed to choose the distance from which they would toss a ring over a peg. McClelland found that high-need achievers preferred to toss the ring from a medium distance. Low-need achievers tended to choose a distance either very near or very far from the ring. The interpretation that McClelland offered was that high-need achievers stand in the middle distances because the probability of success is estimated to be around 50 percent. This probability of success, balanced with the value of winning, maximizes the challenge of the game. A child who stands very near to the peg increases the probability of success, but such a success is easily won and does not present much of a challenge. When a child chooses to stand very far from the peg, he or she decreases the probability of success to such a point that the goal of tossing the ring onto the peg is not likely to be achieved very often. Success from a great distance is more a matter of luck than a matter of achievement.

How do people develop a need for achievement? McClelland believes that achievement motivation is a stable trait resulting from the home environment and how parents raise their children. Children who are permitted to solve their own problems and make their own mistakes are more likely to develop a high need for achievement than children whose parents intervene when they experience failure (McClelland & Pilon, 1983). Other, more contemporary theorists emphasize the effects of conscious beliefs and values and recent experiences in achievement situations on the development of achievement motivation (Stipek, 1993), suggesting that experiences in school as well as those at home can influence the need to achieve.

If we interpret McClelland's study in terms of academic goals, the children high in need to achieve appear to pursue goals that are at once challenging and realistic. This does not tell the whole story, however. Atkinson (1964) concluded that people have a need to avoid failure as well as a need to achieve. Depending on which need is stronger in a given situation, students can perceive a challenging situation as threatening instead. In that case, they may withdraw from the situation or play it safe by pursuing goals they know they can achieve. For example, consider two gymnasts preparing for an important competition. One, whose need to avoid failure is stronger than the need to achieve, practises an old routine that has served her in the past and that she is confident of performing well. The other, whose need for achievement outweighs any fear of failure, works on a new routine with difficult movements. Done well, this new routine is likely to win the meet for the team, but doing it is a risk, a risk the second gymnast is willing to take. Although they are in the same situation, the two gymnasts, with their differing needs, respond differently to the challenge (Woolfolk, 1995).

EXAMPLE: A grade nine math student always proclaims "I can't do that" whenever his teacher introduces new material. He often does have a difficult time mastering new material, especially when compared with his more math-oriented peers. This negative comment is always his first reaction. What purpose do repeated negative comments serve? How do they affect success as a learner?

CRITICAL THINKING: What is the relation between Maslow's growth and deficiency needs and the emotions of hope of success and fear of failure?

The Need for Autonomy

Can you recall a situation in which you offered help, perhaps to a younger friend or sibling, only to be told, "I want to do it *myself*" or "Let me do it *my way*"? Not only do people have a need to achieve and demonstrate competence, we also have a need to initiate and regulate our own actions. This is referred to as the **need for autonomy**, or self-determination (Deci, Vallerand, Pelletier, & Ryan, 1985; Deci, et al., 1991). According to Deci's self-determination theory, actions can be motivated by forces that fall on a continuum from external regulation to self-regulation. External regulation is itself a continuum. At one end is doing something because of an external contingency, such as behaving in class to avoid punishment by the teacher. At the other end is doing something because its outcome is valued, such as learning to use a computer in order to gain access to resources on electronic networks. **Self-regulation**, in contrast, occurs when a person is motivated to engage in an activity purely by choice and by virtue of his or her interest in the activity. So, for example, another gymnast on the team may learn a new routine, not to help the team win but simply because she wants to learn it for herself.

Motivation that is more autonomous in nature has been linked to positive educational outcomes, such as greater conceptual learning, better academic performance, and more enjoyment of school and academic tasks (Deci et al., 1991). According to Deci and his colleagues, teachers can support autonomy in the classroom by using a noncontrolling style of presentation in class, providing choices to students with information about the personal utility of various activities, and creating a climate of acceptance. A variety of means by which teachers can help students develop self-regulatory skills is presented later in this chapter.

Students' Goals

Whether students engage in learning tasks for intrinsic or extrinsic reasons affects the kinds of academic goals they willingly pursue. An aspect of goals related to student motivation is the distinction between performance goals and learning goals (Dweck, 1986; Elliott & Dweck, 1988; Dweck & Leggett, 1988; Ames, 1992). A **learning goal** is a goal through which a student seeks to increase his or her competence; it reflects a challenge-seeking, mastery-oriented approach (hence, a learning goal is sometimes referred to as a mastery goal). For example, you might have as a learning goal to "find and use effective strategies for gaining students' attention." A **performance goal** is a goal through which a student seeks to gain favourable judgment of his or her competence or to avoid negative judgment. A performance goal would be reflected in your statement that you "want to get an A in educational psychology."

Different types of goals promote different motivational patterns in students. Performance goals lead students who lack confidence in their abilities to avoid challenge and to display helplessness. For example, an undergraduate student who, when asked if he wishes to retake a quiz in hopes of raising his grade to an A declines and says, "Oh no, Ma'am. I'm not an A kind of guy." Offered the chance, students will give up rather than persist in a learning task. Conversely, students confident of their own abilities react to performance goals by rising to the challenge, but only if they can avoid taking risks. For example, a student might choose to retake a quiz only if the score can result in a higher grade and not a lower one.

need for autonomy The need to initiate and regulate our own actions; self-determination.

self-regulation Motivation to engage in an activity purely by choice and by virtue of one's interest in the activity.

learning goal An aim of students who place primary emphasis on increasing competence.

performance goal An aim of students who place primary emphasis on gaining positive recognition from others and avoiding negative judgments.

REFLECTION: Recall courses you took in university in which your goals and the professor's goals did not match. How did these mismatches influence your behaviour? Your motivation to learn?

With learning goals, however, students display a mastery-oriented pattern of motivation (Dweck & Leggett, 1988). They tend to seek challenging tasks and to demonstrate persistence in those tasks. In one study, Clark and Tollefson (1991) found that students with learning or mastery-oriented goals were more motivated to write, had greater confidence in their writing, and more positive attitudes toward writing than students with performance goals. Instead of thinking about their ability in relation to learning goals, students consider what strategies must be applied to achieve the goal. For example, consider the case of Kelly, who wants to learn how to sail a windsurfer. Although she has never done this before and does not see herself as especially athletic, she is determined to master boardsailing. Rather than question her ability to perform the correct movements, she concentrates on the instructor's directions, and when she falls numerous times, it is because "I didn't put my feet in the right place."

How Do Students' Beliefs Affect Their Motivation to Learn?

How long students will persist in their efforts to attain an academic goal depends to a large degree on beliefs they hold about their own abilities and about learning in general. This section examines those beliefs and the effects they have on student motivation.

Beliefs about Knowledge and Ability

REFLECTION: Reflect on your own beliefs regarding learning. How do your beliefs relate to the strategies you use to learn? How do your beliefs influence your actions when you are faced with a difficult or challenging task?

Recent studies investigating the epistemological beliefs of students reveal that academic performance and motivation are both related to what students believe about the nature of knowledge. Four possible beliefs are hypothesized (Schommer, 1990, 1993). The first is that knowledge consists of isolated facts, as opposed to integrated, complex systems of information. A student with this belief is likely to seek simple answers to questions and ignore connections across topics. The second belief is that knowledge is absolute. Students who believe in the certainty of knowledge are likely to accept the word of the teacher or the textbook as the authority and not question it. Students who believe that the ability to learn is innate—the third belief—view learning as unaffected by effort or strategic behaviour. Finally, students who adhere to the fourth belief, that learning occurs quickly or not at all, tend to think that success is unrelated to hard work, so that concentrated effort is a waste of time.

Not all of these beliefs have yet been investigated with respect to motivation. However, there is evidence that children with a strong belief in innate ability tend to feel helpless when faced with a difficult task (Dweck and Leggett, 1988). Children who believe that ability is more malleable perceive the same task as a challenge. Moreover, performance goals, discussed earlier in the chapter, seem to promote a greater belief in fixed ability, whereas learning goals promote a greater belief in the possibility that ability can be changed. Mathematics educators have also pointed out that experience with problems that are easy and quick to solve promotes a belief in quick learning, so that students tend to give up when faced with lengthier, more complex problems (Doyle, 1988; Schoenfeld, 1988).

The relation between students' epistemological beliefs and their motivation to learn merits thoughtful examination. Schommer (1993) suggests that teachers may want to assess students' beliefs and consider how they may be influencing those beliefs during instruction:

Do [teachers] test to teach facts or to understand concepts? Do they assign tasks that are quick to complete or do they give students challenging tasks that take time? Do all test items have only a single right answer or do some test questions allow for several possible answers? (p. 411)

The answers to these questions can determine the teacher's role in motivating students to engage and persist in learning tasks and the subsequent effect on their academic achievement.

Beliefs in Self-Efficacy

When students observe their own successful completion of academic tasks, they develop a belief in their ability to continue such accomplishments—a belief called **self-efficacy** (Bandura, 1977, 1982). Students' beliefs about their own ability to perform successfully influence their motivation. From experiences with multiple-choice tests, for example, students may classify themselves as good or poor test takers. On future tests of this nature, students who believe they can't do well will not put forth the effort required to perform well. Subsequent poor performance then serves to reinforce the initial belief.

Students develop expectations of self-efficacy from a number of sources.

The first source of self-efficacy is simple self-observation. Past success leads you to expect you will succeed in the future on similar tasks; such success enhances your sense of self-efficacy.

A second source of self-efficacy is the observation of others. When you observe others whom you perceive to be similar to yourself, you attend to their behaviour. You view yourself as being capable of achieving the same outcome they do. You say to yourself, "If that person can do it, I can do it."

A third source of self-efficacy is encouragement, usually in the form of verbal praise. Verbal encouragement may come from a teacher who says, "I know that you have the ability to accomplish this particular task and I'm confident that you will be able to perform well." Verbal encouragement can also come from within, an internal pep talk called positive "self-talk."

A fourth source of expectation for self-efficacy is emotional arousal. Some kind of emotional event can spur your determination to attain a particular outcome. Perhaps you have experienced, in your own academic career, a teacher who expressed doubt in your abilities to do well in school. As a result of your indignance at the doubt expressed by the teacher, you set out to prove to him or her, to others, and to yourself that you are indeed capable of attaining what they thought was, for you, unattainable. If a student has expectations of efficacy, if a student believes he or she is capable of accomplishing a particular goal, the belief will serve as motivation. This is true even in cases where there are many obstacles to success.

Some of your students will be physically, emotionally, or cognitively challenged in some way. When such students overcome obstacles and succeed in attaining the goals they've set, they can be assumed to harbour expectations of efficacy. Learners who persist, learners who believe in their abilities under certain conditions, and learners who exert an extraordinary amount of effort in pursuit of a particular academic goal are motivated by their sense of self-efficacy. They use their capabilities in a focused way. The mental effort that a student exerts in pursuit of an academic goal can be an index of that student's motivation.

When students attain or fail to attain a particular goal, they explain their success or failure in ways that influence their sense of efficacy and their subsequent engagement in similar academic tasks. Looking at motivation from this perspective requires an understanding of attribution theory.

TRY THIS: Interview teachers about their goals for helping students to develop sophisticated epistemological beliefs. What means do they employ to help students develop more sophisticated beliefs?

REFLECTION: In what areas do you feel you have a sense of strong self-efficacy?

CRITICAL THINKING: How does social cognitive theory (Chapter 8) support this discussion on the development of self-efficacy?

TRY THIS: Observe teachers to discover how they use verbal encouragement and model positive self-talk.

REFLECTION: Recall teachers who made you want to prove yourself to them. What role did emotional arousal play in your decision to increase your efforts?

self-efficacy A learner's beliefs about his or her ability to successfully perform a task or attain a goal.

Attribution of Causes for Success and Failure

The explanations, reasons, or excuses that students give for succeeding or failing at tasks are called *attributions*. For example, a student who says, "I got a good grade on the test because it was easy," is attributing his success to the test, whereas the student who says, "I did well on the project because I worked really hard," is attributing her success to her own efforts.

Weiner's **attribution theory** of motivation is based on three dimensions of attribution: locus, stability, and responsibility (1980, 1986, 1992). The first dimension, locus, refers to the location of the cause of success or failure. A student may cite, as the cause for his or her success or failure, something that is internal or something that is external. For example, attributing success on a test to one's effort is an internal attribution, whereas attributing the same success to luck is an external attribution.

The second dimension, stability, refers to whether an attributed cause is consistent or inconsistent from one situation to the next. Effort is an unstable attribution because a student might exert a great deal of effort in studying for a history exam and little or no effort in preparing for a math exam. Ability, in contrast, tends to be stable in that, for instance, previous musical facility is likely to predict future musical facility.

The third dimension in Weiner's formulation is responsibility, that is, whether a perceived cause of success or failure is under the student's control. From the point of view of a student, effort is a controllable attribution; the difficulty level of a test is not. Therefore, depending on the reasons given for success or failure, the situation may or may not have been under the student's control. Weiner's dimension of responsibility is related to Rotter's (1954) locus of control, which was proposed as a generally stable trait concerning one's sense of control over life. People with an internal locus of control believe they are mostly in control of their own fates, whereas people with an external locus of control believe that what happens to them is mostly a matter of luck.

When Weiner's three dimensions are combined, the result is a set of attributions that is commonly used by students to explain their failure on a particular learning task (Table 9.1). Recall your own experiences as a student. Which attributions in Table 9.1 best reflect your own thinking? How did your thinking influence your motivation?

REFLECTION: Think about your attributions for success and failure. Do you emphasize an internal or external locus of control?

attribution theory The explanations, reasons, or excuses students give for their own successes or failures in learning.

TABLE 9.1 *Weiner's Attribution Theory*

Dimension Classification	Reason for Failure
Internal-stable-uncontrollable	Low aptitude
Internal-stable-controllable	Never studies
Internal-unstable-uncontrollable	Sick the day of the exam
Internal-unstable-controllable	Did not study for this particular test
External-stable-uncontrollable	School has hard requirements
External-stable-controllable	Instructor is biased
External-unstable-uncontrollable	Bad luck
External-unstable-controllable	Friends failed to help

Source: Human Motivation: Metaphors, Theories and Research (p. 253), B. Weiner, 1992, Newbury Park, CA: Sage Publications, Inc. Copyright © 1992 by Sage Publications. Reprinted by permission of Sage Publications, Inc.

Whatever reason is given for success or failure, a central assumption of attribution theory is that students will seek in their reasoning to maintain a positive self-image (Frieze & Weiner, 1971; Kukla, 1972; see also Aronson, 1972). Students who perform well on a standardized achievement test, for instance, are most likely to attribute success on the test to their own ability. The locus is internal. Students who perform poorly on such a test, however, are likely to attribute their failure on the test to some external factor, such as the difficulty of the test or poor instruction by a teacher, or to something that is uncontrollable, such as illness during the test.

Particularly important for teachers to realize is that low achievers tend to attribute their failure to lack of ability (internal and relatively stable). They also, incidentally, tend to attribute their successes to luck (external). A recent study in several high schools in northwestern Alberta found that students who were good academically were much more willing to report that they were responsible for their own academic successes than were academically less successful students. The latter were more likely to attribute their academic outcomes to external influences (McLean, 1997). Failure-prone learners also tend to be sensitive to indirect cues from the teacher that reinforce their low ability attributions. "Seemingly positive teachers' behaviours such as praise for success at easy tasks, the absence of blame for failure at such tasks, and affective displays of sympathy or compassion can communicate to the recipients of this feedback that they are low in ability" (Graham & Barker, 1990, p. 7). High achievers attribute failure to lack of effort (internal and unstable) and so are not especially attuned to the teacher's behaviour. This attribution leads them to try harder on subsequent occasions.

Learned Helplessness

An ability attribution for failure provides learners with a negative self-perception. They have failed and the reason they have failed is that they lack ability, an internal, stable source. Students who fail consistently and attribute these failures to causes that are not under their control can develop a serious motivation problem called **learned helplessness** (Dweck, 1975; Seligman & Meier, 1967). Students who have a learned-helplessness orientation feel that nothing they do matters. They tend to attribute failures to reasons that are internal and stable. For example, "I do not succeed because I am dumb. Therefore, nothing I do will improve my situation. I will always fail."

Learned helplessness as a condition can also arise from teacher-mandated consequences that are inconsistent and therefore unpredictable. In such situations, the students cannot predict what sorts of behaviour will bring about a particular consequence, such as a good grade or punishment for misbehaviour. The environment operates on the students rather than the students being instrumental in bringing about changes in the environment. Perceiving themselves as being unable to alter events by their behaviour, students develop low expectations, which cause deficits in future learning as well as motivational and emotional disturbances (Seligman, 1975).

Learning to be helpless can influence not only students' perceptions of themselves, their self-efficacy and sense of self-esteem, but also the instructional treatment they receive in school. In a study of 164 children who had been referred to a school problems clinic, the primary cause of difficulty for 80 of them was identified as a lack of motivation (Landman, 1987). When the 80 "unmotivated" children were compared with the 84 who were perceived as "motivated," it was found that the unmotivated children were further behind academically and received less remedial help in school.

REFLECTION: Think of times when you rationalized outcomes in a way that helped you maintain a positive self-image.

CRITICAL THINKING: For teachers, what is the value of attributional style as a tool for understanding individual students?

POINT: *Life conditions affect motivation.* Students who come from homes where they are constantly denigrated by parents or siblings may develop a learned-helplessness orientation.

TRY THIS: Interview teachers about learned helplessness in students. How might teachers inadvertently contribute to this condition? What are some interventions teachers might try to overcome learned helplessness in students?

learned helplessness A depressed state when a person feels that no matter what he or she does, it will have no influence on important life events.

CONNECTION: The topic of learned helplessness relates to the education of children at risk, discussed in Chapters 3 and 5.

Attribution theory gives us a way to identify motivation problems that could have serious consequences. How can teachers respond to motivational problems in children? Possible answers to this question appear later in this chapter, which presents a variety of strategies teachers can use to enhance the motivation of their students toward academic goals.

Impacts of Cultural Beliefs and Values on Students' Motivation

Do attributions as defined by Weiner and others exist across cultures? In a study of 140 school children from Sri Lanka and 149 children from England, the attributional dimensions of locus of cause, stability, and controllability were present, but there were differences in the frequency with which certain attributions were used (Little, 1987). Weiner's attribution theory identifies *luck* as a major attribution. For children from Sri Lanka, however, *luck* was not a frequent attribution, but *karma* was. This suggests that attribution theory should be used along classification dimensions that are consistent with the culture of the child rather than with the culture of the researcher (or teacher).

CONNECTION: Review the discussion of cultural differences in Chapter 4.

Three dimensions of attribution theory—locus, stability, and responsibility—appeared to be useful in identifying differences between male and female children in the Philippines (Watkins & Astilla, 1984). For females in this study, on the one hand, attributions that are external and uncontrollable led to a preference for rote learning approaches. Males, on the other hand, tended more to internal and controllable attributions, which led to an emphasis on internalizing and approaches to study that resulted in higher achievement.

These studies suggest that cultural background influences attributions. When you use a child's attributions to gauge motivation, you should take cultural differences into account. These studies indicate macrocultural differences (see Chapter 4), but it is possible that the microcultural differences in a classroom might also affect your judgment of student motivation.

CRITICAL THINKING: How can cultural differences influence motivation? Why is it important to know a student's background when attempting to understand a student's motivation?

How Do Teachers' Beliefs Affect Student Motivation?

Imagine yourself in the classroom conducting a group activity. Some students are participating actively, others are sitting quietly but apparently paying attention to the comments of their peers, still others are staring out the window, doodling in a notebook, or wandering around the room. Based on their behaviour and your knowledge of the students, you can make some reasonable predictions about who is motivated in this situation and who is not. You also know that many different factors can influence the motivation of students to participate in this particular task, or in learning activities in general. Now consider your expectations about whom you expect to succeed in the task and how much influence you believe you can have toward motivating those students who seem unmotivated. What effect might your beliefs have on your actions in the classroom? What effect might these beliefs have on student motivation?

Beliefs about Students

Teachers acquire a variety of beliefs about students from a number of sources. Have you had an older brother or sister precede you through school? The experiences your teachers had with your sibling created certain expectations that they probably applied, albeit unintentionally, to you. Many students go through school trying to live up to or live down an older sibling's reputation. Teachers also acquire beliefs about students from other teachers, from medical or psychological reports in school records, and from standardized test scores. To the extent that these sources enable a teacher to construct an accurate understanding of a particular student's characteristics and needs, there is no need for concern. A problem arises, however, when teachers maintain beliefs about their students that are inaccurate. This could happen because of stereotypes held by the teacher or because the teacher fails to adjust his or her perception of a student over time even though the student's behaviour or performance has changed.

For example, teachers commonly believe that boys have more behaviour problems than girls and that physically attractive students will achieve at higher levels than less attractive students (Woolfolk, 1995). Knowledge of ethnic background, language differences, and disability can also affect a teacher's beliefs about students. A number of Canadian studies (Herbert, Hemingway, & Hutchinson, 1984; Hutchinson & Hemingway, 1984; Myles & Ratslaff, 1988) have found evidence for teacher bias in referral and placement of students as a function of ethnicity and gender. Even the students' behaviour in class can be the source of inaccurate beliefs by the teacher about the students' motivation. For example, a middle school teacher realized that the fidgety behaviour of her students wasn't always a sign of inattentiveness or lack of motivation. Sometimes, the students just needed to get up and move about after sitting still for a period of time. In an interesting twist, a Canadian study reported by University of Alberta researchers Wild, Enzle, and Hawkins (1992; in Baron, Earhard, & Ozier, 1995) found that students' perceptions regarding teacher motivation had a significant impact on learning. Students who viewed their teacher as intrinsically motivated showed higher task engagement and enjoyment than did students who perceived the teacher as extrinsically motivated.

The Impact of Teacher Expectations

The **Pygmalion effect** refers to one way teachers' expectations may influence the behaviour of students. The term comes from the myth of a Greek sculptor, Pygmalion, whose expectations of a statue he created caused the statue to come to life. (George Bernard Shaw's *Pygmalion,* the story of the transformation of a cockney flower girl, Eliza Doolittle, into a refined lady of aristocratic demeanour, was the basis for the musical, *My Fair Lady.*) Forgett-Giroux, Richard, and Michaud (1995) at the University of Ottawa found that student self-confidence and self-concept, as well as school performance in mathematics and French, were affected by teacher expectations, pupils' probability of success on school tasks, and pupils' personal values.

The term *Pygmalion effect* was applied to teachers' expectations by Rosenthal and Jacobson (1968). Rosenthal and Jacobson measured the intelligence of children in grades one through six in a school. After the test was administered, the teachers of certain students were told that the test predicted substantial intellectual gains for those students in the coming year. In reality, the students identified as potential achievers performed no better or worse than other so-called average children who took the test. At the end of the school year, the group of children took the intelligence test a second time.

The results of the second test showed that the potential achievers did in fact show significant gains in intelligence. The gains were attributed to the heightened expectations of the students' teachers. This result was labelled the

> **Pygmalion effect** The influence that a teacher's expectations may have on the behaviour of students. Also called the teacher expectancy effect and the self-fulfilling prophecy.

REFLECTION: How did self-ful-filling prophecies and teacher expectancy effects influence your motivation and performance as a student?

EXAMPLE: A teacher has one of her best friend's daughters in class. Because the teacher already knows the student well, the teacher has high expectations for the child. In addition, the teacher does not want to disappoint her friend in terms of her daughter's accomplishments that year. Therefore, the teacher gives the student extra responsibilities and extra attention, in some cases bending the rules. One day the teacher overhears the student say, "I wish she would treat me the same as everyone else." How should the teacher resolve this situation?

REFLECTION: What do you want to know about your students before they enter the classroom? What do you *not* want to know? Why?

Pygmalion effect. These and similar results have also been referred to as *self-ful-filling prophecy* and the *teacher expectancy effect,* terms that are still used to identify any situation in which the communication of expectations by a teacher is thought to influence student behaviour.

Rosenthal and Jacobson's study was intensely scrutinized. Additional research studies directed toward the effects of teacher expectations were also undertaken. Close inspection of Rosenthal and Jacobson's results showed that the self-fulfilling prophecy operated in grades one and two but not in grades three through six. Some questioned the test used to measure IQ, arguing that better measures of IQ should have been used. Others pointed out that even the positive results in grades one and two could not be construed as convincing evidence that negative expectations necessarily lead to low performance (cf. Wineburg, 1987).

The interest of researchers in teacher expectancy effects has remained high, and recent research has yielded important qualifications regarding the influence a teacher's expectations may have on student behaviour. For one thing, self-fulfilling prophecies appear to operate in a three-stage process (Jussim, 1986). During the first stage, teachers develop expectations of individual students. In the second, teachers begin differential treatment based on those expectations. In the third, students behave in expectancy-confirming ways. However, it appears that, in the second stage, both the frequency and nature of teachers' interactions with low-achieving versus high-achieving students must be considered. In one study, teachers tended to interact more *frequently* with high-achieving and high-expectancy students, but they spent more *total time* waiting for and interacting with low-achieving and low-expectancy students (Leder, 1987). This suggests that if we balance our interactions with students, we interrupt the process by which self-fulfilling prophecies come to fruition.

Finally, the results of a recent study emphasize the importance of teachers' actions over teachers' expectations. In the cases of two students, year-end achievement was opposite to that predicted and expected by the teacher. What happened? In one case, "the teacher had failed to take corrective action when she should have *because she had expected* [the student] to do well on her own" (Goldenberg, 1992, p. 539). In the other case, "*in spite of the teacher's low expectations* for [the student's] success, the teacher took actions that appear to have influenced [her] eventual grade one reading achievement.... Low expectations were clearly evident, but they were irrelevant in determining the teacher's actions" (p. 539).

To the extent that we allow our expectations about students to influence our actions with them, we risk creating a classroom of haves and have-nots. If we are aware that expectancies can influence interactions in our classrooms, we can guard against differential treatment.

Here's How

Here's How To Avoid the Negative Effects of Teacher Expectations

- Examine your own beliefs and teaching practices for possible stereotypes and prejudices. Do you tend to give boys different tasks than girls? Do you call on or involve all students equally in a learning activity? Do the instructional materials you use show both genders and a wide range of ethnic groups? Try to ensure that your instruc-

continued

tional materials and strategies, including evaluation and disciplinary procedures, treat all students fairly.

- Be careful how you use information about students that comes from their personal records, standardized tests, and other teachers. Although these sources of information can be helpful in determining individual students' needs, they can also create expectations that do not hold true in the context of your classroom.
- Be prepared to change your expectations of students as they acquire and demonstrate new competencies.
- Monitor your verbal and nonverbal responses to students in your class. Try to ensure that all students have equal access to you—your critical feedback, your encouragement, your smiles as well as your frowns.

TRY THIS: Interview teachers about the ways they guard against teacher expectancy effects.

REFLECTION: What are your beliefs about the ability of teachers to influence the motivation and performance of their students? How might your beliefs affect decisions you make in the classroom?

Beliefs about Teaching Efficacy

Just as students have beliefs about their own abilities that affect their motivation, so teachers have similar beliefs that can affect whether they employ effective motivational strategies with students in their classes. Vern Stenlund (1995), from the University of Windsor, emphasizes that motivation is a two-way street. Students who exhibit low motivation while in the classroom produce professional job discouragement for teachers. In recent years, the concept of self-efficacy has been applied to teachers' general beliefs about the influence of teaching on learning, as well as to their specific beliefs about their abilities to motivate students. **Teaching efficacy** refers to a teacher's belief that teaching, in general, will have an influence on students' learning. Personal teaching efficacy is the teacher's belief in his or her ability to motivate students (Ashton & Webb, 1986). For example, a teacher who largely agrees with the statement, "When it comes right down to it, a teacher can't really do much because most of a student's motivation and performance depends on his/her home environment" (Woolfolk & Hoy, 1990), is said to be low in teaching efficacy. However, a teacher who says, "I am confident I can get my students interested in learning," is likely to be high in personal teaching efficacy.

teaching efficacy A teacher's belief that teaching, in general, will have an influence on students' learning.

Teachers who are high in teaching efficacy and personal efficacy tend to provide students with tasks that are challenging and opportunities to take responsibility for

In what ways will your expectations of the students you teach affect their motivation to achieve? What beliefs and values as a teacher will contribute to your ability to enhance students' motivation to learn?

Insights on Successful Practice

What advice can you give novice teachers about the effects of teacher expectations on student motivation?

Motivation is undoubtedly the crux of the learning process. Encouraging love of learning remains our challenge, and if teachers examine their own motivations for teaching they might become more successful in enhancing students' motivation to learn. For instance, do you love both your subject and your students? Are you interested and excited by words, ideas, and concepts? Do you have faith in your students' innate yearning for knowledge and ability to recognize what is important? Do you have high expectations for them?

Are you willing to look for the particular key that will unlock this unique personality, that individual mind? Not every teacher will succeed every day with every student, because we are limited in our understanding of all that goes on in each of their lives. Nevertheless, we are given the charge not only to show the way, but also to encourage the journey.

Once your students have embarked on the journey—shown an interest in the subject (however great or small the journey might be)—it is the teacher's responsibility to act as a guide. You become their mentor, encouraging them to continue their quest and strive for excellence. Because your students leave your classroom does not mean they leave your life—or that you have left theirs. Your influence continues. Your expectations for them become part of their expectations for themselves.

PATRICIA WOODWARD
Junior High School Teacher

---

their own learning (Ashton & Webb, 1986). These teachers also tend to be more committed to teaching (Coladarci, 1992) and more likely to use effective motivational strategies with exceptional students (cf. McDaniel & McCarthy, 1989). Results of one recent study indicated that general and special education teachers with high personal and teaching efficacy were most likely to agree with general class placement of an exceptional student (Soodak & Podell, 1993).

By contrast, teachers who are low in teaching or personal efficacy are more likely to be authoritarian in style and less likely to try teaching strategies that might challenge their own capabilities. As a consequence, these teachers are also less likely to find ways of helping students who experience difficulty in their classes (Ashton & Webb, 1986).

How can teachers develop high teaching and personal efficacy? Probably in much the same way that students develop high self-efficacy toward specific learning tasks. You can imagine how successful experiences in teaching may build confidence in your ability to make a difference in students' learning. These experiences could occur in your teacher preparation program, in your student teaching, and in your teaching as a professional employed at a school. It has also been found that a healthy school climate directly relates to a positive sense of teacher efficacy (Hoy & Woolfolk, 1993).

CRITICAL THINKING: How are expert and novice teachers likely to differ on teaching efficacy? Why?

CONNECTION: How does this discussion of teaching efficacy relate to implications for inclusion that are discussed in Chapter 5?

How Can You Enhance Your Students' Motivation to Learn?

Motivating students and creating interest is important for maximizing learning in the classroom. Willoughby (Brock University), Motz (York University), and

Wood (Wilfrid Laurier University) (1997) contend that creating high levels of interest may be especially important when teaching adolescents. High interest may serve as an energizing factor for attending to the material for older students. This may not be as necessary for young children.

How can you enhance motivation in a systematic and effective way? This final section of the chapter presents an integrated model of motivational design that you can use to identify potential sources of motivational problems in your classes and to select motivational strategies to help solve those problems. Also discussed are ways you can arouse and maintain students' curiosity during learning, use reinforcement effectively, and help students attribute their successes and failures to motivational and learning strategy variables, viewing ability as something they can change.

Arousing Curiosity

Curiosity is a knowledge state caused by stimuli that are novel, complex, or in some way incongruous (Berlyne, 1965). Intuitively, you will recognize that curiosity is a strong source of motivation. Consider the following example of arousing curiosity in a classroom context:

"Before we begin the next science chapter," the teacher said, "I'd like to tell you a story. Then," she added, with a slight smile, "I'll ask you a question."

The grade six students looked at their teacher expectantly.

"A man was out driving his car," the teacher began, "when he noticed something quite unusual. A truck stopped in the middle of a block and the truck driver got out with a baseball bat in his hands. He walked back to the centre of the truck and suddenly hit the side several times with the bat. Then he got back in and drove on."

Several children who had been somewhat indifferent when the teacher started now looked at her raptly.

"As the man in the car followed the truck," she continued, "he saw the truck again stop after about three blocks and again the driver got out, beat his truck a few times with the bat, returned to his seat, and drove off."

Every eye in the room was now riveted on the teacher.

"Once more," the teacher went on, "the man in the car followed the truck and, sure enough, in another three blocks it stopped, the driver got out and banged away with his bat."

The teacher paused and glanced around the room. Satisfied that she had the class's attention, she continued. "The man in the car," she said, "was fascinated. He followed the truck for almost three kilometres trying to figure out what the truck driver was doing. Finally he gave up."

The teacher again paused, scanning the intent faces in front of her.

"The next time the truck stopped," she went on, "the man jumped out of his car, ran over to the truck driver, and said, 'Sir, forgive me for bothering you. But I've been following you for almost three kilometres. Why on earth do you drive exactly three blocks, get out with a baseball bat, and hit your truck a few times?' The truck driver said, 'It's really very simple. I've got a two-tonne truck and inside I've got three tonnes of canaries. So I've got to keep one tonne of them in the air at all times.'"

A few of the students looked puzzled, some seemed skeptical, and several laughed. As the teacher waited, the laughter gradually spread until the entire class was smiling.

"Now," she said, "let me give you a question."

Looking pointedly at the class, she said, "Was the truck driver stupid?"

curiosity An eager desire to know caused by stimuli that are novel, complex, or strange or that involve fantasy and ambiguity.

There was a sudden silence as the children pondered the query.

"Yes," a sandy-haired boy said suddenly. "He still had three tons in his truck."

The teacher remained silent watching her students. Then a bright-eyed girl in the corner of the room raised her hand shyly.

"Beth."

"He really wasn't being stupid," the girl said, "because if one ton was flying around inside the truck, they wouldn't add any weight."

With this the teacher smiled and walked to the board. She then began a lesson on the principle of air support (Rubin, 1985, pp. 129-130).

Using novelty, as the teacher in the example did, is one way of creating the perceptual arousal that is one aspect of curiosity. Novel or incongruous situations alert students' attention. Consider what would happen, however, if the teacher telling the story of the canaries were to use such a story to begin every lesson. Would the novelty of such incongruous stories wear off? If so, would she be less likely to engage her students' curiosity? Curiosity, as a source of motivation, has a somewhat limited use in the classroom unless it can be sustained. How do teachers sustain curiosity?

Here's How

Here's How To Arouse and Maintain Students' Curiosity in Learning

- Use fantasy to provide a meaningful context for learning. Students find it easy to augment a situation involving fantasy with their own imaginations (Rieber, 1991). For example, a unit on the solar system could be set in the context of space travel and preparing to explore "strange new worlds where no one has gone before" (cf. Star Trek).

- Use problem-based scenarios that require students to seek additional information in order to solve them. Computer-based simulations (e.g., Sim City, Sim Earth) and technology-based instruction (e.g., the Jasper Woodbury Problem-Solving Series on videodisc) are good examples of this strategy. They provide complex problems to students along with numerous clues and information regarding their solution. Moreover, there are typically several ways in which the problems can be solved, which adds to the challenge and curiosity engendered in students.

continued

TRY THIS: Observe classrooms to discover how teachers use curiosity to introduce lessons and maintain attention.

- Give assignments to students that are somewhat ambiguous in nature to generate curiosity and prolonged task engagement (Woolfolk & McCune-Nicolich, 1984). For example, groups of students can be given the same set of oddly assorted materials in a science class and be told to "invent something" or "create a vehicle" or in a language arts class to "create a story involving these materials."

Using Reinforcement Effectively

The **undermining effect** is the result that external rewards can have on behaviour that is intrinsically motivated (Deci, 1971, 1975; Morgan, 1984). For example, a student who begins reading biographies of World War II figures and who brings the subject to the attention of a parent or teacher may find the parent or teacher delighted with the student's new-found interest. As a function of this delight, the parent or teacher tells the student that for every new World War II biography read, the student will receive some sort of reward—either free time in the classroom to pursue a hobby, or release from a household chore or some more tangible reward. According to Deci and other researchers, establishing external rewards in a situation like this might undermine the student's intrinsic motivation. The student might continue her reading not out of curiosity about the figures in World War II, or a need to understand the events of that war, but because of the rewards delivered from external sources—the parent or the teacher.

It is tempting for a teacher to encourage academic pursuits, especially in a student who has not demonstrated a keen interest in reading or writing or other cognitive activities. However, teachers should take care in identifying those areas in which students require motivation from external sources and to allow intrinsically motivated behaviour to flourish on its own terms. The undermining effect appears to operate at all ages. The intrinsic motivation of young children is especially susceptible to being undermined by extrinsic rewards (see Lepper, Greene, & Nisbett, 1973; Sarafino, 1984).

You have learned from other chapters that reinforcement is a powerful teaching tool. Teachers should not, however, reinforce student behaviour indiscriminately. To reinforce effectively, a teacher needs to know students' goals and their intrinsic motivations. Part of the reason is that such knowledge helps a teacher decide when to provide external sources of motivation and when to allow the intrinsic motivation of a learner to determine classroom activity.

Varying Classroom Goal Structures

Teachers can have a strong impact on student motivation to pursue particular types of goals by the classroom structures they create (e.g., Ames & Ames, 1984; Dweck, 1986). A classroom **goal structure** is the way in which teachers manage learning and evaluate and reward student performance. Johnson and Johnson (1987) described three types of goal structures: cooperative, competitive, and individualistic.

A **cooperative goal structure** is present when rewards are bestowed on a group based on their performance as a group, rather than to members of the group based on individual performance. As a consequence, students perceive

CRITICAL THINKING: How might teachers inadvertently undermine students' motivation?

EXAMPLE: A teacher uses a system of plus and minus marks to monitor student behaviour. At the end of the week, students with two pluses get a treat. This system works well with grade one students. With grade six students, however, it does not. Why?

REFLECTION: Recall an activity in which your motivation was undermined by external rewards.

undermining effect Consequence that an extrinsic reward can have on behaviour that is intrinsically motivated.

goal structure A means by which teachers manage learning and evaluate and reward student performance.

cooperative goal structure A class management structure in which rewards for performance are given to a group, not to individuals within the group. As a consequence, students view attainment of goals as possible only through cooperation with members of their group.

CONNECTION: Cooperative goal structures also relate to models for active learning discussed in Chapter 12.

cooperation as the best means for successfully attaining goals. If the group is given the task of publishing a volume of poetry, for example, then the anticipated group product—the volume of poetry—provides the basis for evaluation and subsequent rewards. One student cannot receive a higher grade than another student for his or her contribution to the book of poetry. In such instances, students are motivated to put forth their best efforts in cooperation with their group, not just to help themselves but out of a sense of obligation to the other members of their group.

Think back to your own high school experience. Perhaps you were in a group—the band, the cast or crew of a play, the French club, an athletic team, or the school yearbook staff. The success of the product or performance depended on cooperation. If you contributed to such an effort, part of your motivation was likely a sense of obligation; you may have worked harder because you didn't want to let the other people down. To be sure, you invested time and effort in the group because the group was doing something you liked. But there were probably times when you went above and beyond the call of duty.

Cooperative goal structures are effective for several reasons (Johnson & Johnson, 1987, 1990):

1. Group work requires discussion, promotes the discovery process, and leads to a higher level of learning.

2. Discussion promotes diversity of ideas, opinions, and positions. In arguing for a position, explanations are sought, repeated, and—through repetition—clarified. Comprehension and retention are enhanced.

3. Members in the group provide feedback and, because it is a group project, encouragement for each other.

CRITICAL THINKING: How might a competitive goal structure be focused on effort rather than ability?

In a cooperative goal structure, students attain the goal only if other students also attain the same goal. In a **competitive goal structure**, students view attainment as possible only if other students do not attain the goal. By definition, competitive goal structures ensure that some students will be unsuccessful. In general, students who experience a classroom managed by means of a competitive goal structure tend to have low expectations, show little persistence on achievement-oriented tasks and, as just indicated, avoid tasks in which they have experienced little success (cf. Johnson & Johnson, 1987).

Although students may show improvement in performance under a competitive goal structure, this improvement should not be interpreted as success. Students appear to reward their own behaviour only if they win a competition (Ames & Ames, 1984). When they win, they tend to think of their success as due to ability, whereas when other students win, they attribute that success to luck. Competition also fosters social comparisons.

competitive goal structure A class management structure in which students must compete for rewards so that they view attainment of goals as possible only if other students do not attain them.

Are there any classroom situations in which a competitive goal structure is appropriate? Consider a spelling bee. In a spelling bee, there is only one winner. In order to attain the goal of winning the spelling bee, others must lose. Does this mean that spelling bees should be avoided? Not necessarily. If a class spelling bee were conducted at the beginning of a spelling unit, the competition would highlight the differences among learners in terms of prior skill or ability. If the spelling bee were conducted at the end of the unit, when all students have had a chance to master the list, the results would be more easily attributed to effort. At the end of the unit, more students have a chance of winning. Failure for any one student is less likely because all students have mastered the material or are approaching mastery. The outcome of the game or competition is more in doubt and, therefore, more fun. In sum, competitive goal structures can be used effectively if the competition is based on effort toward mastery rather than on the ability levels the students bring to the learning situation.

An **individualistic goal structure** is one in which rewards are provided on the basis of an individual's performance, unaffected by the performance of other students. An individual is not a contributor to a group performance nor are rewards available to only one or a few winners. An individualistic goal structure allows each student to compete against a criterion. If all students achieve the criterion, all students are rewarded.

Individualistic goal structures probably constitute the most common form of evaluating and rewarding student performance. Although students are judged and rewarded on the basis of their own work, they also learn, however, that there is no payoff for cooperation. In addition, some students may perceive an individualistic goal structure as competitive and exhibit competitive behaviour even though such behaviour is neither required nor desired.

The goal structures used in classroom learning situations can also orient students toward learning (or mastery) goals rather than to performance goals. At least six organizational variables in schools and classrooms affect student motivation: task, autonomy, recognition, grouping, evaluation, and time (Ames, 1990; Maehr & Anderman, 1993). These six variables are expressed in the acronym TARGET, which refers to an approach being tried in schools to establish a greater task or learning focus while at the same time minimizing an ability or performance focus. Here's How outlines this approach.

CRITICAL THINKING: What kinds of attributions would mastery-oriented students exhibit?

Here's How

Here's How To TARGET Learning Goals in Your Classroom and Enhance Intrinsic Motivation

- Choose *Tasks* that are challenging, interesting, worthy of consideration, and meaningful to your students.

- Support *Autonomy* and responsibility in learning by providing choices to students along with the opportunity to set their own learning agenda.

- *Recognize* progress toward goal attainment, as well as student achievement of learning goals. Make sure the efforts of all students are recognized.

- In *Grouping* students (organizing them for instruction), provide opportunities for students to participate equally in decision making and other classroom roles. Create a climate of acceptance and encourage participation of all students.

- Use *Evaluation* practices that reduce emphasis on social comparisons among students and provide opportunities for students to demonstrate progress, as well as their best work. Encourage students to evaluate their own work and help them to develop skills to do so.

- Schedule *Time* for interdisciplinary units and complex problems to facilitate lengthy student engagement in learning (adapted from Maehr & Anderman, 1993).

TRY THIS: Observe a number of classrooms to identify the types of goal structures being used. How do differences in goal structures affect student motivation and learning?

individualistic goal structure A class management structure in which rewards are given on the basis of an individual's performance, unaffected by the performance of other students.

Insights on Successful Practice

What do you regard as the most important aspect of your role as a teacher who influences students' motivation to learn?

If someone were to write a "teacher's epitaph" for me, I would want it to say, "She listened." As a teacher, the single most important activity for me is to listen to my students rather than listen for prescribed answers. By listening, and by providing a student-centred learning environment, I contribute to my students' motivation to succeed academically.

A classroom that is student centred will always be more conducive to the educational process than one in which student-teacher interaction is dependent on materials or instructional approaches alone. Student-centredness is at the heart of trends toward literature-based curricula or whole-language classrooms. What else are these approaches but attempts to get teachers to pay attention to the needs and interests of their students? We know from research in response to reading programs that conditions intrinsic to the learner, which are part of the subjective nature of reading, are integral to reader engage-ment and understanding. This appears to be true in both narrative and expository text. When a student finds personal meaning in a lesson, this meaning becomes the key to sustained and continuing learning, the springboard for knowledge development. No number of workbook pages or computer programs or creative bulletin boards can substitute for the subjective response. For this reason, the human communication aspects of education are crucial, including my role as one who listens.

SUE MISHEFF
University Professor

Your Insights

According to this teacher, why is student-centredness the key to effective teaching? What are the hallmarks of student-centred instruction, and what part does intrinsic motivation play in student-centred learning?

Motivational Training

Besides organizing your classroom and your instruction to facilitate motivation, you can employ a variety of means with students to help them self-regulate. According to McCombs (1984, 1988; McCombs & Marzano, 1990) teaching students to become self-regulated learners is motivational training. This training should include attention to cognitive, metacognitive, and affective strategies. Thus, students must acquire motivation-related skills, such as setting realistic learning goals that interest them and using appropriate self-talk when they experience difficulty or failure in a learning task. Students must also acquire motivation-related will, which involves recognizing "the power of their choices—the power of the self as agent" (McCombs & Marzano, 1990, p. 64).

Setting Goals and Changing Attributions. Programs have been developed that help teachers address achievement motivation and attributions of their students. For example, several programs have been designed to help students at risk of dropping out of school (Alschuler, 1973). These programs focus specifically on the use of self-paced materials, games and activities intended to enhance the student's sense of personal responsibility for success and failure. In effect, the programs provide **attribution training**, attempting to change the attributional style of the student.

DeCharms' work (1976, 1980) provides the best known examples of attribution training. In his attributional training program, DeCharms uses the analogy of origins and pawns: Origins are people who are masters of their own fate, those

attribution training
Attempting to change the student's style of explaining his or her own learning successes or failures.

who exhibit an internal locus of control; pawns are people who do not exert a control over the events in their environment but, rather, are controlled by them. Pawns have an external locus of control. Children in the DeCharms classic study were trained to become origins. They were taught to plan their actions, starting with the establishment of realistic goals—goals that are neither so difficult that they precluded successful completion nor so easy that success in completing them is perceived as meaningless.

DeCharms demonstrated that one way to combat the problem of the pawn syndrome or the characteristics of learned helplessness is to teach children how to set realistic goals. When these goals are learning goals, as opposed to performance goals, self-concept and an internal locus of control are also likely to be enhanced (e.g., Smith, 1986). Parents, teachers, and students should together seek opportunities for success, change attributions from external to internal reasons, and learn to use feedback in a positive manner (Greer & Withered, 1987). The keys to the success of this kind of program seem to be the establishment of adaptive goal-setting behaviour; learning the difference between realistic and unrealistic goals; and, having established these goals, planning actions that will lead to their attainment. Attributional training programs that implement these suggestions have been found to be successful. For example, students trained in DeCharms' program attended school more regularly than those who did not participate in origins and pawns training. Participants in the DeCharms' program were also more likely than untrained students to graduate from high school. Attribution training has been shown to affect the motivation and performance of educationally at-risk children and of adults with mental retardation. Participation of students, their parents, their peers, and teaching and counselling professionals in such programs may also help to reduce informal (and possibly inaccurate) labelling of students by teachers and other professionals.

Developing Self-Regulation. Attribution training, with its emphasis on students learning to control their own environment and their own learning, also supports self-regulation and the development of autonomy. But there are other ways as well to help your students become autonomous self-regulated learners.

TRY THIS: Develop a plan for attribution training that you could use with students you plan to teach. What goal-setting activities will you include?

Here's How

Here's How You Can Help Students Become Self-Regulated Learners

- Model strategies for setting goals, planning actions, monitoring progress, and making appropriate attributions. Show students what they can expect as a result of applying these strategies to help them understand the personal utility of self-regulated strategies (Deci et al., 1991).
- Provide opportunities for students to make meaningful choices and decisions about their own learning with a minimum of pressure to respond in a particular way. For example, a grade seven history teacher collects a variety of resources to make available to students—including textbooks, reference books, historical novels, videotapes, and newspapers. From this extensive database, the stu-

continued

TRY THIS: Develop a plan from the Here's How strategies for helping students become self-regulated learners. How will you monitor your behaviour in supporting autonomy and minimizing teacher control?

dents choose what they wish to investigate when the class studies an event or period in history.

- Convey expectations and confidence in students' ability to regulate their behaviour. There is evidence that teachers who believe students will regulate themselves are more autonomy-supportive and less controlling toward those students. In contrast, when teachers think students have to be extrinsically motivated, they become more controlling and less autonomy-supportive (Pelletier & Vallerand, 1989).

- Acknowledge individual students' feelings and perspectives as valued. Let students know that it's okay to feel confused during a difficult learning activity or resentful about limits placed on their behaviour. Providing a context of socioemotional support for students is an important aspect of developing self-regulation (McCombs & Marzano, 1990).

CRITICAL THINKING: What conditions have to exist for students to be motivated to achieve academically?

ARCS model A model teachers can use to identify and solve motivational problems in their classrooms. The ARCS model defines four categories of motivation that must exist for students to be motivated to learn: attention, relevance, confidence, and satisfaction.

Applying the ARCS Model

Let's take a look at some of the conditions that should exist if achievement motivation is to develop within a student. The conditions can be referred to by the acronym ARCS. The **ARCS model** is a general model of motivation that was developed by Keller (1983, 1984, 1987a,b) and described by Driscoll (1994). There are four elements in this model of motivation, representing conditions that must exist in order for a learner to be motivated: *Attention, Relevance, Confidence,* and *Satisfaction* (ARCS). These conditions are illustrated in Figure 9.3.

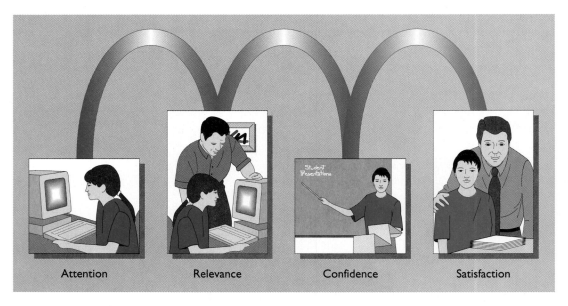

| Attention | Relevance | Confidence | Satisfaction |

FIGURE 9.3
The ARCS Model: Conditions Needed for Motivation to Learn

Attention. The term *attention* has been examined as part of the discussion of information-processing and social cognitive theories. In those discussions, *attention* referred to a process. In the ARCS model, *attention* is a state or condition of the learner. A student in the classroom is either attending or not attending to the achievement-related stimuli. In the ARCS model attention is a necessary condition for motivation.

One of the things that new teachers worry most about is their ability to gain students' attention so they can learn. It's possible to study many different attention-getting devices by observing teachers in the field. Some teachers will clap their hands or make some sudden noise that will automatically get the attention of students. Other teachers will engage in a particular routine that signals to students that it's time for them to pay attention.

CONNECTION: How do information-processing theory (Chapter 7) and social cognitive theory (Chapter 8) relate to this discussion of attention?

If we want students to learn the pronunciation of a single word, we need to attract their attention only for a moment. However, in the context of student motivation, attention must be sustained over long periods of time. Maintaining attention is even more important than attracting it.

Consider the children's program, *Sesame Street,* which is designed not only to capture but also to sustain attention. The program's attention-sustaining ability appears to stem from the use of humour, incongruity, and encouragement of viewer anticipation (Lesser, 1974). This anticipation comes in the form of known characters, such as Big Bird, Oscar the Grouch, Grover, Bert and Ernie, and the Count. Viewers come to know these characters' personalities and anticipate their actions. When they see Oscar the Grouch emerge from his residence, a garbage can, viewers anticipate the kinds of comments Oscar will make. To satisfy their curiosity and to determine whether their anticipations are correct, viewers listen to Oscar the Grouch to see what he has to say.

REFLECTION: How do educational programs on television maintain viewers' attention?

Perhaps you are a fan of a particular soap opera on television. If so, you know the personality characteristics of the soap opera characters quite well. You can, therefore, predict the types of behaviours they are likely to display. Your attention to their activities is sustained because you are curious to see how their personalities will influence events.

The attention condition in the ARCS model appeals to a particular kind of learner interest. It is the interest that people have in events that makes them curious.

Relevance. Relevance, the second condition in the ARCS model, requires the engagement of learner interest; that is, learners must perceive that the content of the material presented is important to them.

CRITICAL THINKING: What makes lessons relevant to students?

Beginning teachers are often advised to make their lessons relevant to students' lives by relating the lesson to the experiences of students. One way to demonstrate the relevance of material is to convince students that the material will enable them to achieve an instructional goal. For example, in the Teacher Chronicle at the beginning of this chapter, Jerry might have demonstrated how brainstorming makes story writing easier. Demonstrating relevance is an effective approach for students who view instructional goals or learning outcomes as important, for either intrinsic or extrinsic reasons.

For some students, lessons can be made relevant by the use of humour or by the use of the unexpected. Recall the teacher who told the story about a truckload of canaries. The story itself is relevant for some students, not because it illustrates the principle of air support, but because it is funny. They can take the story home and entertain their parents with it. The entertainment value of the story makes it relevant for students who fancy themselves storytellers. For a student with story-telling goals, the story establishes a condition of motivation. Other students may find the information relevant because it provides a unique example of a scientific principle.

Suppose that you were going to teach a lesson about the solar system. Part of your job is to teach the students about the dimension and properties of the Sun. The size of the Sun, for example, could be communicated in any number of ways.

It could simply be communicated by numbers. The Sun's diameter is approximately 1.4 million kilometres; it weighs 330 000 times as much as Earth, and its mean distance from Earth is approximately 149 million kilometres. Each square centimetre of the Sun's surface radiates 1500 calories of energy per second. Unless your students are studying for an imminent appearance on a television game show, these numbers may hold little relevance for them. Suppose, however, that after providing the appropriate numbers you then describe the size of the Sun in the following terms:

> The Sun could be hollowed out so that half of it were hollow. We could place Earth with the Moon still orbiting around it in the hollow half. At the turn of the century, Sir James Genes calculated that if he could remove matter the size of a pinhead from the core of the Sun, and place that bit of matter on Earth, the heat from that pinhead of matter would kill a human being 151 kilometres away.

Describing the dimensions of the Sun in these terms rather than only in terms of statistics might, for some students, prove relevant to their interests and, therefore, motivate them to attend to the rest of the lesson.

The notion of relevance takes us back to the importance of goals in considering the motivation of students. If you understand what goals students bring with them to your classroom, then you are better able to present information in a way that will be relevant to them.

Confidence. Confidence refers to students' beliefs that they can perform competently in a particular learning situation. Learners are motivated when they believe that they can be successful in learning new material and performing new tasks. Confidence relates to self-efficacy and contributes to achievement. Studies have shown that confident learners are better able to attain goals than learners who do not have confidence in their own abilities (Bandura, 1977; Jones, 1977). When students have successful learning experiences, they infer that they can perform effectively. Such success builds confidence and enhances expectations of efficacy.

How can you build confidence in your students? Besides providing learning opportunities during which students can experience success, you can help them to expect success by making your own expectations clear. This means clearly communicating both the behaviours necessary for goal achievement and your beliefs that students are capable of performing these behaviours. You can also build confidence in students with challenging but not overwhelming tasks, during which you provide decreasing amounts of assistance as learners become capable of independently achieving the task.

Finally, consistent with attribution theory, you can help students to become more confident in their abilities by encouraging them to see learning as a consequence of their own efforts and effective study strategies. When you give detailed feedback explicitly showing students what they did wrong and why, they are able to attribute poor performance to specific problems that can be corrected.

EXAMPLE: Making a connection with prior knowledge by means of concrete imagery makes that information relevant and enhances retention of the information in memory.

CONNECTION: How does confidence relate to self-efficacy, described earlier in this chapter?

Satisfaction. Satisfaction occurs when expectations about learning are met. For example, a student who has successfully completed all required tasks in a course may expect to receive some sort of extrinsic reward, such as a good grade, teacher praise, or parental encouragement. However, the satisfaction of learning expectancies may lead also to self-reinforcement, as in the case of a student who achieves competence in a skill that he or she wanted to learn. Finally, the condition of satisfaction is met when a student fulfills his or her need to achieve.

How can you assure that students' expectations about learning will be satisfied? For students who are intrinsically motivated, it is important that they be able to use their newly acquired knowledge or skills in a meaningful way. In math, for example, students could solve problems from situations in their lives, such as how many squares on their block, how many worms in their yard, or how many goals their favourite hockey player scored this season. Jerry, in the Teacher Chronicle, helps to assure Bronson's satisfaction in learning to write by allowing him to write about something of personal interest.

When students are extrinsically motivated, they will be satisfied when their learning results in the anticipated reward. When you have done well on all course assignments and exams, you expect to receive an A in the course and are satisfied when you do. Imagine your feelings, however, in a situation where you believe you have done well on a course project, successfully meeting all of the instructor's preset criteria, but you receive a grade of B without so much as an explanation for why the grade wasn't an A. It is likely that you would feel very unsatisfied with the learning experience and probably unmotivated to work hard on the next assignment. This aspect of satisfaction concerns equity, or how consistently standards and consequences for achievement are applied. Students must perceive that they are being fairly and equitably treated to derive satisfaction from a learning experience.

The ARCS model identifies four conditions that must be met if students are to be motivated to learn. Although these conditions should exist within the learning situation in your classroom, it is important to keep in mind that many of these conditions may arise from earlier events in your students' experiences. How do you determine, then, if there are motivational problems in your class and what motivational strategies you should incorporate into your instruction?

Here's How

Here's How To Identify and Solve Motivational Problems in the Classroom

- Develop a profile of your students' motivation in terms of the categories of ARCS—attention, relevance, confidence, and satisfaction.
- Based on the student profile, define motivational objectives.
- For each motivational objective, select corresponding motivational strategies to incorporate into your lessons.
- Try out the strategies you selected and observe the results. If student motivation does not improve, revise your analysis of the problem(s) and your selection of motivational strategies.

TRY THIS: For a class you teach or plan to teach, try out the ARCS model to identify motivational problems you may face and to plan ways you could avoid or overcome those problems.

In the first step, you should think about your students in terms of the ARCS model and develop a profile of their motivation. Who are your learners? Are they likely to experience problems paying attention or finding relevance in the subject matter of the lesson? Do they have little confidence in their abilities? If the answer to any of these questions is yes, then satisfaction in learning could also be a problem. From your knowledge of the students in your class, you can identify the variables that are likely to be potential sources of motivational problems.

From the student profile, you can determine the likely motivational needs that exist in your class, providing the basis for defining specific motivational objectives (the second step). For example, suppose you are teaching a class of students who have tested below average in reading. The self-efficacy of these students as readers is likely to be low, which means that their confidence in their ability to read will be low. With this knowledge in mind, you may define a motivational objective: Students will gain confidence in reading. In defining a motivational objective, you should also give some thought to how you will know when it has been achieved. What is an indicator of increased confidence in reading, for example? In the Teacher Chronicles, Bronson demonstrates reading confidence by his willingness to read aloud in class.

The third step is to select corresponding motivational strategies to integrate into your instruction that will help meet the identified motivational objectives. For instance, Jerry's setting up Bronson to write a story about his favourite computer game is a strategy designed to enhance his motivation.

The final step is to try out the strategies you selected, observe the results, and revise if necessary. For example, Jerry learned that allowing a student to complete a writing assignment by using a topic of personal interest is an effective means of establishing relevance and sustaining attention for this task. He recognized Bronson's need, tried the strategy, and found that it worked. He is now likely to add this strategy to his repertoire and use it again with students who exhibit similar needs.

The ARCS model provides a systematic means of improving the motivational appeal of instruction. It is one of the tools teachers can use to help their students become and stay motivated.

Teacher Chronicle Conclusion

An Outer Space Opportunity

Jerry Bird stands in front of his class, ready to hand back the writing assignments. "I want to tell you how pleased I was with how you completed the assignment. Most of you put a lot of thought into your writing. I suggested some changes on your papers, and we will get to those in a minute. But first I want to ask you a question." He pauses, looking at Bronson, "What do you think space exploration will be like in the future? What kind of technology might we have? For example, what about the technologies of spacecraft we find in computer games?" Everyone shifts to look at Bronson, who is grinning like a jack-o-lantern.

Normally Bronson doesn't like to be the centre of attention, but Jerry has made a connection with him by allowing him the freedom to do the assignment differently from the others. "Bronson, would you be willing to read your assignment to the class?" Jerry asks. Bronson hesitates momentarily then starts talking about his interest in space computer games and how they sparked his interest in outer space. Bronson astonishes the class by saying he thinks real travel between the stars would be a problem because of Einstein's theory of relativity. He tells the class that as a spacecraft nears the speed of light its mass increases so much that light speed is a barrier that cannot be broken. So much of Star Trek and other science fiction shows go beyond what is possible. He also suggests that advanced civilizations might not exist because once they develop beyond a nuclear technology they are most likely to blow themselves up. This started a lively debate among the students which continued even after the recess bell had rung.

Jerry says, "Bronson, thank you for a very stimulating talk," as Bronson beams back. Bronson is off to a new start in his grade nine writing class.

Application Questions

1. In terms of the concepts and theories presented in this chapter, what motivational factors influenced the behaviour of Bronson? What are the sources of those factors?

2. What might Jerry have done if Bronson did not want to read his story?

3. How is Bronson's self-efficacy for writing likely to be enhanced by this experience?

4. How might learned helplessness come into play with Bronson? What other techniques could Jerry or Bronson's other teachers use to help him overcome learned helplessness?

5. Is Jerry high or low in teaching efficacy? Why? What can you do to develop your own teaching efficacy?

6. Analyze the events in this Teacher Chronicle in terms of the ARCS model. How did Jerry design instruction to enhance students' motivation for accomplishing his instructional goals? Using the ARCS model, analyze a lesson you plan to teach and develop motivational strategies that you could incorporate into your instruction.

CHAPTER SUMMARY

What is Motivation to Learn? (L.O. 1, p. 274)

All students are motivated, but not all students may be motivated to do the things that teachers ask of them or for the reasons that teachers expect. When students develop a motivation to learn, they initiate learning activities, they stay involved in a learning task, and they exhibit a long-term commitment to learning. Understanding the internal and external sources of student motivation enables you to provide a learning environment that is motivating and to assist students in developing adaptive motivational patterns.

How Do Students' Needs and Wants Affect Their Motivation To Learn? (L.O. 2, p. 276)

Some students work toward a goal because they wish to satisfy some personal need or interest. Others pursue a goal in order to obtain rewards from the environment or people in that environment. The needs and wants of students affect their choice of goals and their willingness to engage in certain types of activities.

How Do Students' Beliefs Affect Their Motivation To Learn? (L.O. 3, p. 282)

Students are likely to persist in learning goals that are challenging but still within their perceived competence to attain. They are also likely to remain motivated when they attribute their successes and failures to their own effort and study strategies, rather than to ability or luck. These attributions are associated with beliefs that ability is malleable, that knowledge is complex and multifaceted, and that learning takes time and effort.

How Do Teachers' Beliefs Affect Student Motivation? (L.O. 4, p. 286)

When teachers communicate differential expectations to their students, they can adversely affect student behaviour and motivation. You can avoid negative effects of teacher expectations by becoming aware of your own beliefs and monitoring your behaviour in the classroom to ensure that you treat all students fairly. Moreover, the more you believe that you can influence learning and motivation, the more likely you are to use effective strategies for motivating your students.

How Can You Enhance Your Students' Motivation to Learn? (L.O. 5, p. 290)

By arousing your students' curiosity, using reinforcement strategies prudently, and organizing your classroom to support cooperation, you can enhance students' motivation to learn. Motivational training—that is, teaching students how to set realistic goals, plan for goal attainment, and make appropriate attributions about their successes and failures—is a means for helping them develop self-regulation and intrinsic motivation. Finally, using the ARCS model, you can identify potential motivational problems in your classes, select appropriate motivational strategies, and implement these strategies in your instruction.

KEY CONCEPTS

achievement motivation, p. 279

ARCS model, p. 298

attribution theory, p. 284

attribution training, p. 296

competitive goal structure, p. 294

cooperative goal structure, p. 293

curiosity, p. 291

deficiency needs, p. 277

extrinsic motivation, p. 274

goal structure, p. 293

growth needs, p. 277

hierarchy of needs, p. 276

individualistic goal structure, p. 295

intrinsic motivation, p. 274

learned helplessness, p. 285

learning goal, p. 281

motivation to learn, p. 274

need for autonomy, p. 281

performance goal, p. 281

Pygmalion effect, p. 287

self-actualization, p. 277

self-efficacy, p. 283

self-regulation, p. 281

teaching efficacy, p. 289

undermining effect, p. 293

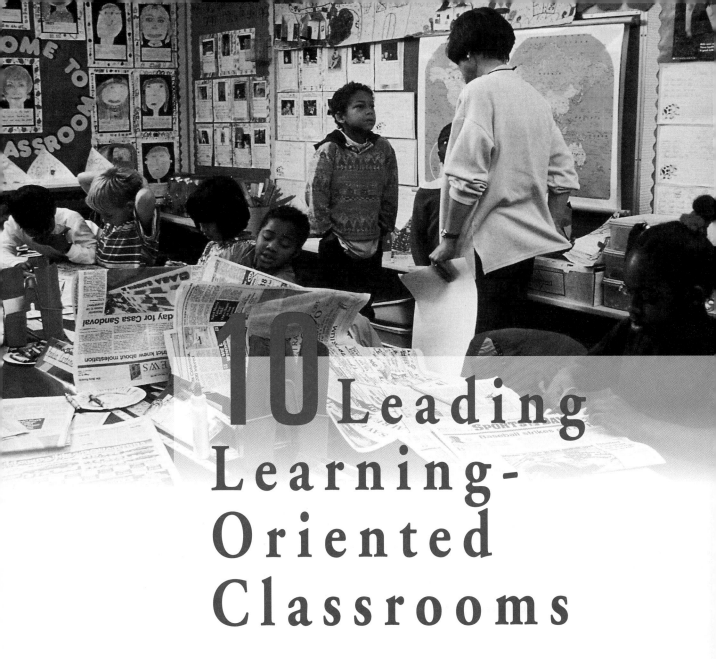

10 Leading Learning-Oriented Classrooms

LEARNING OUTCOMES

When you have completed this chapter, you will be able to

1. identify and describe characteristics of, and distinctions between, work-oriented and learning-oriented classrooms

2. define the terms *classroom management, discipline,* and *instruction,* and describe their interrelationships

3. describe and explain the classroom management continuum, from collaborative to authoritarian

4. describe the classroom arrangement, rules, and routines that lead to learning-oriented environments

5. explain how a teacher's instructional planning, presentation, and responding skills lead to learning-oriented classrooms

6. describe a range of teacher responses to inappropriate student behaviour

7. explain the importance of student self-responsibility and commitment in pursuing learning goals

8. explain why it is important to take into account different cultural norms while planning for classroom management

Teacher Chronicle

And Then There's Sam

Tracy Briand sits at her desk after her grade three students have been dismissed for the day. It's quiet now, but this has been another busy day. She thinks back over the events of the day, then of the week. "I'm generally pleased with how things are going. The class layout and routines have been effective. This desk arrangement in pods of four has worked out well for whole group instruction and for the cooperative groups that I've set up. Even though it's only October, the children have settled in and are learning the small group routines. The class rules that we worked out together and posted on the bulletin board have helped to establish positive classroom behaviour and a good climate for learning."

Tracy moves around the pods of empty desks, tidying up gym shoes and work materials that are out of place, noticing the names of the students taped to the desks. Yes, everyone is settling into a good work pattern ... but then there's Sam.

The day's events involving Sam come rushing vividly back to Tracy, "Sam, please don't shout. Sam, remember our rule about pushing and fighting. Sam, get to work. Sam, go to the principal's office, right now."

Despite all her efforts to guide him gently and consistently, Sam's behaviour leads to regular confrontations, both with Tracy and with his classmates. He pushes, shoves, speaks out of turn, refuses to take part in group activities, and wanders around the room bothering others. These behaviours have not endeared him to his classmates, and he has developed no real friendships. The other children have, for the most part, responded well to the class rules and gentle reminders. Why not Sam?

She thinks, I know how important it is to help Sam find success and become the person he can be. He has many endearing qualities, and at times his behaviour is very acceptable. How can I help him turn his negatives into positives? Ms. Briand sits at her desk and begins to organize her memories of Sam's classroom behaviour over the past week.

There are so many negatives and so few positives! Is it simply because she has not often noticed Sam engaged in appropriate behaviour? She realizes that in her busy role of teacher, it has been difficult to assemble a clear picture of Sam's behaviour, aside from the negatives. She decides, "I think I'll ask Warren, the resource teacher, to spend some time in the class. While he is here, we can make a plan for the two of us to observe Sam's behaviour carefully."

The next week, the resource teacher spends several hours working and observing in Ms. Briand's classroom. On Friday after dismissal, they meet to pool their observations and construct a profile of Sam as a learner. Together they assemble a list of interests, strengths, and needs:

Positive	Negative
enjoys math manipulatives	physically aggressive (pushes others)
arrives on time	leaves seat during work time
responds well to praise	often disrupts cooperative group work
likes computer	often does not finish assigned work
likes art work	interrupts during verbal interactions
	fights with others on the playground

Looking over the list, the two teachers notice that there are some patterns of positives that can be built upon, and that some of the negatives are related to each other.

Next, Warren and Tracy share their observations of the ways that Tracy and the other students respond to Sam's positive and negative behaviours. They are looking for patterns that might help to explain why Sam chooses to engage in negative behaviours rather than more appropriate alternatives. They notice some important trends in how Ms. Briand responds to Sam. When Sam engages in positive behaviour, he rarely receives feedback or recognition. When he engages in negative behaviour, Ms. Briand first gives him a verbal reprimand, then applies punishment. Punishments have been loss of privileges, "time out" of class activities, and removal from the classroom, usually in that order. The other students in the classroom respond in different ways to Sam. Most have learned to ignore his negative behaviour. However, Rob and Darren have sometimes deliberately tried to provoke Sam's negative behaviour, laughing when he gets into trouble.

"Thanks, Warren," says Tracy. "I think that, with your help, I now have a clearer picture of Sam. Now we can all begin to work together to create a more positive learning environment, and help Sam build on his positive behaviours."

Focus Questions

1. Does Ms. Briand approach classroom management more as a leader or a manager?

2. What do Ms. Briand's reflections reveal about her beliefs about management, discipline, and learning?

3. Using the behaviour list compiled by Ms. Briand and the resource teacher, list four rules that you think are posted on the class bulletin board? How do classroom rules contribute to student learning?

4. Why is it important that students be actively involved in deciding on classroom rules? What steps would you take to involve students in establishing rules and routines in the classroom?

5. Would you consider Ms. Briand to be an effective classroom manager? Why or why not?

6. Why is the beginning of the school year so important in establishing classroom routines? What preparations do you think Ms. Briand made before the school year began?

7. What steps do you think Ms. Briand will take to help Sam improve his behaviour? Should these steps fail, what additional options might she pursue?

What is Classroom Management and Leadership?

The way a teacher manages his or her classroom says a great deal about what that teacher values. Consider the case of Ms. Briand in the Teacher Chronicle, for example. Although you do not see her interacting with her students, you can infer that she takes her responsibility for managing her class quite seriously. But why does she go to the trouble to ponder the problems of one child? Is it because she values a quiet classroom and Sam is noisy, or does she value learning and is seeking ways to help Sam learn? The way one teaches reveals what one considers to be important, and classroom management is central to teaching.

Classroom management has long been recognized as one of the primary responsibilities of teaching (e.g., Bagley, 1907). It is important because it influences students' behaviours, feelings, and learning. Your knowledge of and skill in classroom management will, to a great extent, determine the success with which you facilitate student learning. Therefore, your management skills will also influence how others perceive you as a teacher. Students who find themselves in a poorly-managed classroom must fight an uphill battle to learn and will judge the teacher in that classroom as ineffective. Students may not submit a formal evaluation, but their views of teachers are shared and teachers' reputations are quickly established.

TRY THIS: Interview a retired teacher who had a long career in the classroom. Ask the teacher to describe ideas and practices concerning how classroom management changed over the course of his or her career.

A parent whose child is in a poorly managed classroom will—at the very least—fail to become the teacher's ally. An administrator who observes a poorly managed classroom will submit negative evaluations of the teacher. The converse is also true. Well-managed classrooms provide an environment for student learning, make good impressions on parents, and are positively evaluated by administrators.

Teachers who work in well-managed classrooms enjoy their work, enjoy their students, and feel a sense of accomplishment (cf. Cangelosi, 1993). Teachers who enjoy their work are likely to be more enthusiastic about their teaching and the students whom they teach. The knowledge and skills discussed in this chapter can make a difference in your self-esteem as a teacher, your sense of self-efficacy as a teacher, and ultimately, the degree to which you are satisfied with a career in teaching. Classroom management is one of the keys to effective teaching because it affects all who have a stake in education, but especially learners.

Given the importance of classroom management to educational stakeholders, it is not surprising that serious efforts to reform education are beginning to focus on the way classrooms and, by extension, schools are managed (McCaslin & Good, 1992). Classroom management will continue to be the focus of efforts to improve education because it is central to the work of schools, the work accomplished through the teaching-learning process. Understanding classroom management requires understanding how management is related conceptually to discipline, instruction, and ultimately learning. Becoming an effective classroom manager also requires that you identify the outcomes you value for your students.

Whether a teacher values obedience or learning, solitary effort or social interaction is revealed not only in classroom practice but also in the metaphors he or she uses to conceptualize how classrooms should operate. Our management metaphors are frameworks that define what we view as possible in our classrooms (Randolph & Evertson, 1994). In turn, our views of what is possible influence how well our students learn. Ms. Briand, in the Teacher Chronicle, tried for a month to improve Sam's behaviour so that he could learn. Her efforts failed, but as we leave Ms. Briand in her reflections, it is clear that she thinks it is possible to find ways of helping Sam learn.

Metaphors for Managing Classrooms

Research has shown clearly that one of the most perplexing challenges faced by novice teachers is managing student behaviour (Lashley, 1994; Veenman, 1984). Furthermore, some of these difficulties can be traced to the metaphors beginning teachers use to think about classroom management (Weinstein, Woolfolk, Dittmeier, & Shanker, 1994).

Researchers have identified metaphors ranging, for example, from *prison guard* to *boss* to *negotiator* to *facilitator* (Lashley, 1994; Randolph & Evertson, 1994; Weinstein et al., 1994). The first two metaphors conjure images of the teacher as overseeing students, initiating student activity through orders, and holding those in his or her charge accountable for getting their work done. The last two metaphors suggest something different about the nature of the interaction between teacher and students and the outcomes of that interaction. Negotiation and facilitation suggest that teachers work with students to help them learn. Teachers, especially beginning teachers, who see themselves as overseers of students' work rather than as facilitators of students' learning are more likely to experience difficulties in managing student behaviour (cf. Good & Brophy, 1994; Marshall, 1990).

CRITICAL THINKING: How will classroom activities and teacher responsibilities change if curricula become integrated across subject areas? If bell schedules in junior high and high schools are eliminated?

REFLECTION: Review the metaphors of teaching discussed in Chapter 1. How do the metaphors relate to those mentioned in this section? How does your own metaphor of teaching compare to those mentioned in the book?

POINT: The differences between work-oriented and learning-oriented classrooms illustrate one of the assumptions of this book: *Teachers coordinate the context for learning.*

The research on metaphors used by teachers to conceptualize classroom management and the effects associated with those metaphors have led to a useful distinction between classrooms that are work oriented and those that are learning oriented (Evertson & Randolph, 1995). **Work-oriented classrooms** are those in which students tend to be directed by a teacher who values production. Students are expected to follow directions closely because, by doing so, they will complete the work efficiently. **Learning-oriented classrooms** are those in which students are encouraged, rather than directed, by a teacher who values learning. Following directions in learning-oriented classrooms is important as well, but students are encouraged to question directions and explore possibilities. An effectively managed work-oriented classroom is likely to be orderly and quiet, a well-oiled machine. An effectively managed learning-oriented classroom is likely to be noisy, a beehive of activity. Students in work-oriented classrooms are more likely to reconstruct information, whereas students in learning-oriented classrooms are more likely to construct knowledge (Evertson & Randolph, 1995). Obedience is valued in work-oriented classrooms; taking responsibility for one's learning is valued in learning-oriented classrooms (cf. Curwin & Mendler, 1988; McLaughlin, 1994).

Thomas Good and Jere Brophy (1994) describe a system of critical attitudes that exists in well-managed, learning-oriented classrooms. They call it a system because each of the three attitudes supports the others and because all attitudes are supported by a value of learning. A depiction of the system is given in Figure 10.1.

The most important aspect of this system is the value context. Effective classroom managers value learning and communicate that value through their actions. Imagine a teacher who promises that, "If you all behave yourselves until the end of the period, I will not assign homework tonight." What sort of message does this send to students? By establishing this contingency, the teacher ignores the learning that homework might foster and treats what could be a legitimate learning activity as something to be avoided or used as a bargaining chip. Teachers who devalue learning often use a *factory* metaphor to

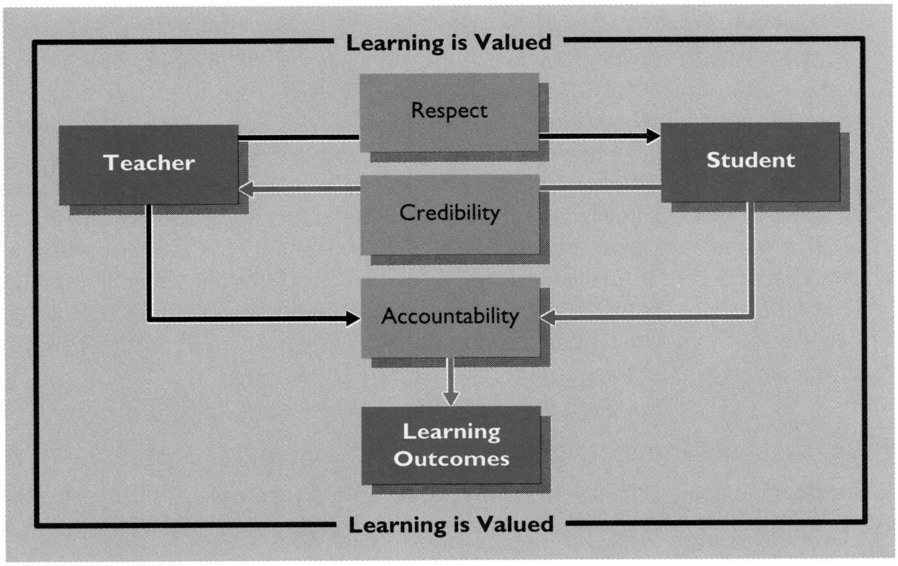

TRY THIS: Ask friends and colleagues to identify the best classroom they were ever in and the worst. How was each of those classrooms managed? What sorts of learning activities were used? What were the rules and procedures in those classrooms? How was misbehaviour managed? Characterize your data in terms of contrasting metaphors.

work-oriented classrooms Classrooms in which the teacher values production and is directive of student activity.

learning-oriented classrooms Classrooms in which the teacher values learning and facilitates, rather than directs, student activity.

FIGURE 10.1
A System of Attitudes that Supports Learning-Oriented Classroom Management

Source: Based on the discussion of essential teacher attitudes in *Looking in Classrooms* (6th ed., pp. 133–134), T. Good and J. Brophy, 1994, New York: Harper Collins.

think about classroom management (Randolph & Evertson, 1994). In a factory metaphor, students are labourers who complete work in exchange for grades, privileges, or other incentives. Teachers are bosses or paymasters who focus on the work and not on what might be learned by doing the work. Good and Brophy (1994) describe teachers who devalue learning as those who "think of school-related tasks as unrewarding drudgery and do not expect students to enjoy them. Their students soon learn to wince, sigh, or protest at the mention of assignments" (p. 134). However, a teacher who values learning views the classroom in terms of the learning, not just the work, that takes place there. The essential ingredient of learning-oriented classrooms and the foundation of Good and Brophy's system of critical attitudes is a teacher who values learning (Marshall, 1990, 1992).

Building on a foundation of the value of learning, the first critical attitude is respect for students. Good and Brophy's observations of classrooms suggest that teachers who successfully manage classrooms like and respect their students. It seems unlikely that a person who does not enjoy working with children or adolescents would be likely to earn their respect in return. In their discussion about teachers' attitudes toward students, Good and Brophy emphasize the importance of a teacher's concern for students as individuals. Consider Ms. Briand in the Teacher Chronicle at the beginning of the chapter. Although the class as a whole demonstrated a level of discipline that was resulting in positive growth, she was spending time carefully reflecting on the behaviour and accomplishments of one student. Her efforts indicate her concern not just for the class as a whole but for each individual in the class and, therefore, an attitude of respect.

The second critical attitude is credibility. Students perceive teachers who manage effectively as credible, as people who do what they say they will do. Credibility requires that teachers practise what they preach and that they practise and preach consistently. According to Good and Brophy (1994), unless a teacher is willing to say to students, "I intend to treat each of you fairly and if I do not, I want to know about it immediately," credibility will be difficult to establish. Unless a teacher is willing to follow through on such claims, credibility will be difficult to maintain.

The teachers and students of well-managed classrooms jointly maintain the third critical attitude: Teachers who manage effectively hold themselves and their students accountable for learning. Furthermore, in a learning-oriented classroom, teachers encourage students to develop an attitude of self-accountability. Teachers who take an interest in their students and who deal with them credibly must adopt the attitude that the important outcome is what students learn. This may require some tough-mindedness from time to time. It may be easy to overlook a lack of achievement in a student who has shown considerable improvement in his or her effort. While a teacher, in this case, would certainly want to encourage the student to continue his or her effort, the teacher must help the student keep in mind that effort without learning is not good enough.

Processes and Products of Classroom Management

A summary of research on effective schools and classrooms, published by the Association for Supervision and Curriculum Development (ASCD), found a

REFLECTION: Which of your teachers did you find most credible? How did they establish that credibility with you? What are some of the ways in which your credible teachers were similar? How will you establish yourself as credible in the eyes of your students?

CONNECTION: You have already encountered the concept of active learning in Chapter 7 and will encounter it again in Chapter 12. Active learning relates to the idea that effort and activity are necessary for, but do not guarantee, learning.

relationship between high achievement in students and the skills possessed by teachers. Students who achieve consistently had teachers who demonstrated skill in managing, in preparing and organizing classroom activities, as well as establishing and maintaining learning environments. Teachers whose students achieved well were also found to be skilled at guiding student learning (Squires, Huitt, & Segars, 1983).

If these are the teaching skills that are associated with student learning, how are they related to each other and how do they affect learning? One way to conceptualize these important relationships is to view managing and instructing as processes. This chapter first examines the relationship between the process of management and its product, discipline. Then instruction and learning are added to the conceptual mix.

Managing for Discipline. The terms *classroom management* and *discipline* are often used interchangeably (Bellon, Bellon, & Blank, 1992). This is true of people both outside and inside the world of education. Even those who are preparing to teach often use the terms synonymously. We asked aspiring teachers and veteran teachers identified as effective classroom managers to reflect on what classroom management meant to them. The vast majority of aspiring teachers seemed to assume that classroom management means dealing with discipline problems. They wrote of the disciplinarian role of a teacher, handling disruptive students, making students listen, keeping students under control, and making sure students know who's the boss. Two themes emerged from the written comments of aspiring teachers. One was that classroom management required control. The other was that classroom management is strictly reactive. Although reacting to problem behaviours is a part of classroom management, prevention is at least as important. This proactive aspect of classroom management, involving cooperation and collaboration, was reflected in the comments of veteran teachers.

Veteran teachers, in reflecting on the meaning of classroom management, rarely used the word discipline in their descriptions. For the veteran teachers, classroom management meant establishing rules, involving students in decision making, organizing for instruction, finding and preparing materials for lessons, and creating active learning experiences that maintain interest and keep students focused on the material being taught. Essentially, veterans' answers revolved around planning and organization. The best way to establish discipline in the classroom, say the veterans, is to be organized. This advice from expert practitioners is supported by a considerable body of research findings (Brophy, 1988; Doyle, 1986; Emmer & Ausiker, 1990; Evertson & Harris, 1992; Gettinger, 1988; Jones & Jones, 1995; McCaslin & Good, 1992). One review of this research, for example, concluded that teachers who view "classroom management as a process of establishing and maintaining effective learning environments tend to be more successful than teachers who place more emphasis on their roles as authority figures or disciplinarians" (Good & Brophy, 1994, p. 129).

Classroom management and discipline are related but are not synonymous. According to Emmer (1987), **classroom management** refers to the actions taken by teachers to encourage student learning, while **discipline** is the extent to which students act appropriately and are involved in learning activities. Discipline, therefore, is a function of sound classroom management. Poor classroom management yields a lack of discipline. Thus, classroom management is viewed as a process and discipline as a product of that process. The next section examines another process and

CRITICAL THINKING: Some educators use the term *discipline* to refer to actions taken by teachers to deal with problem behaviour. In this chapter, the term is used to refer to student behaviour because it helps in thinking about how management and discipline are related to learning. Why should this product view of discipline make it easier to think about the relationship of discipline to learning?

classroom management Actions taken by a teacher to facilitate student learning.

discipline The extent to which students are engaged in learning or other classroom-appropriate activities.

product that are based on the management-discipline relationship. As you move to the discussion of instruction and learning, keep in mind that both management and discipline are defined with reference to learning.

Instructing for Learning. Classroom management is central to teaching, but the instructional process is at least as important as management. While management is critical to success as a teacher, it is important that instruction does not become subordinate to management (e.g., Allington, 1983; Brophy, 1982; Duffy & McIntyre, 1982). Instruction is of such importance that we will revisit it in a later section in this chapter and in the chapters that follow. Planning for instruction is the focus of Chapter 11. Instructional techniques are discussed in Chapter 12. Chapter 13, on classroom assessment, also has an instructional focus; indeed, it argues that assessing student learning is a form of instruction. The focus of this section, however, is on defining the process of instruction, identifying the product of that process, and determining how it is related to management and discipline. How is classroom management related to the teaching-learning process?

Driscoll (1994) defines **instruction** as "the deliberate arrangement of learning conditions to promote the attainment of some intended goal" (p. 332). One obvious commonality between the definition of teaching and instruction is that of intent. Teaching is undertaken with the intent to facilitate learning. Instruction, however, is defined more specifically. The intent that underlies the process of instruction focuses on a particular learning goal. Intent is further implied in the definition of instruction through the phrase "deliberate arrangement of learning conditions." What are the conditions of learning for a particular goal? Consider the following example, taken from Driscoll (1994).

> Suppose we are interested in students learning how to calculate averages of groups of numbers. From our knowledge of motivation, we know that for students to acquire this skill, they must have some confidence in their ability to learn it, and they must see some value in learning it. Information processing theory suggests additional conditions required for learning. Students must already know how to add, multiply, and divide, because these skills are components of the rule for calculating averages. Furthermore, the new information (i.e., the rule itself) should be presented to learners in a way that facilitates encoding (p. 332).

Thus far, the example identifies the conditions of learning that need to be met in order for the particular learning goal to be attained. How might a teacher establish those conditions and motivate students to assume responsibility for their own learning? He or she might choose to demonstrate the rule and to follow the demonstration with meaningful problems for students to solve. These problems might be presented in a worksheet constructed by the teacher, assigned from a textbook, or embedded in a long-term project—such as tracking the performance of stocks in an investment portfolio—that requires students to identify and solve problems involving the calculation of averages. Thus, by determining ways of establishing the learning conditions necessary for students to attain the intended goal, the teacher has devised a certain plan for instruction tied to a particular learning goal.

If the conditions of learning are established properly, and if instruction is effectively implemented, then the outcome of instruction is student learning. In a sense, the process of instruction builds on discipline. If the management

Insights on Successful Practice

In your experience, what role does teacher planning play in successful classroom management?

Planning for instruction is an essential teacher activity because it directly influences the effectiveness and efficiency with which we teach. This in turn influences our approaches to classroom management. A well-planned lesson and its related activities not only engage students in productive work, but also contribute to the students' realization that they are learning and achieving. Students develop a feeling of success and consequently the teacher gains their attention and cooperation.

After teaching my first lesson on expository writing, I realized that the entire lesson was teacher-centred, that the content was presented in a vacuum, and that it lacked the conceptual specificity that would have resulted in more effective learning. I decided that the entire unit of work should be replanned. I developed a unit of work in which expository prose as a concept in writing was divided according to the principles governing the development of expository paragraphs: enumeration, analysis (subdivisions=partition, classification, process analysis), definition, comparison, and contrast. I collected examples of each kind of paragraph from novels, magazines, and student textbooks in science and social studies. I carefully planned each subdivision of exposition as a separate lesson. Transparencies were constructed and for each lesson, paragraphs illustrating the particular principle were selected from the students' literature, science, and social studies texts and used as examples. A learning centre appropriate for each of the sub-concepts was also organized and in it were placed examples of the sub-concept clearly illustrating the principle of paragraph development used, reference materials containing additional examples, question sheets for discussion, and group activities. Each major lesson was organized to include: a direct-teaching segment of ten minutes; a fifteen-minute search for individual examples of paragraph development from materials in the learning centre; and group discussions on the specific principle used in the paragraph. Follow-up lessons included the application of the principle learned in responding to actual questions students were given in literature, science, and social studies.

This planning resulted in several positive teacher and student behaviours. I taught lessons that were specific and more focused; my instruction was brief, effective, and efficient because the concepts were placed in concrete contexts, and because abstractions were now connected to concrete examples which students could see, read, and discuss. Students began to respond with added interest because they realized that "exposition" was to be found in the daily reading or writing activities in which they were engaged in different subject areas. Their discussions were more animated because they learned that their personal lives and experiences were filled with examples of this subject matter. Their expository writing skills improved because they used actual questions from other subject areas in oral discussions as well as in the follow-up writing activities. Although the lessons presented resulted in much student talk, movement, and other related activities, all of it was purposeful. Students were motivated; they knew what they had to do; they were on task; they knew that they were learning. Because each lesson was well planned and the related materials and activities were carefully organized, I had little or no need to "discipline" students. Carefully-planned lessons can contribute to effective teaching, can motivate students to learn, and can eliminate undesirable and unproductive behaviour.

SANDRA E.
High School Teacher

Your Insights

What aspects of instructional planning does this teacher make it a point to consider? How might planning or the lack of it affect classroom management?

process is successful, then students are prepared to learn—the conditions of learning identified by Driscoll are in place. The teacher can then instruct with greater probability of success (Evertson, Emmer, Clements, & Worsham, 1994). The relationship between management and discipline, can now be expanded to include the process of instruction and the outcome of that process, learning.

Classroom Leadership and Authority

Teachers are leaders of learning and learners. In order to establish discipline, teachers must essentially gain the cooperation of their students (cf. Good & Brophy, 1994). In order to bring about learning, teachers must guide students to engage in the instructional tasks that lead to the attainment of learning goals. Leading students means engaging students' minds, finding ways of eliciting their active participation in the teaching-learning process, and assisting students to stay focused on the goal of learning. As Goodlad (1983) stated: "Being a spectator not only deprives one of participation, but also leaves one's mind free for unrelated activity. If academic learning does not engage students, something else will" (p. 554). If discipline is not established through effective management techniques and if instruction fails to engage students, problem behaviours will develop.

Leadership is a difficult concept to define, as evidenced by the number of definitions that have been supplied by scholars who study it (Hoy & Miskel, 1991). Even so, there are some elements in definitions of *leadership* that occur with considerable frequency. One of those elements is the concept of *goals*. Fiedler and Garcia (1987) suggest that a leader is someone who directs or coordinates a group's efforts to attain a particular goal. A leader is also someone who can shape or articulate the goals. In classrooms, one of the responsibilities of a teacher is to lead students toward the attainment of learning goals. How should a teacher direct students toward learning goals? In what manner should a teacher lead?

The answer is that it depends on the kind of classroom atmosphere you wish to create. Do you expect your students to *comply* with your requests or demands? Do you want them to *identify* with you and to emulate you? Do you want them to *internalize* attitudes and behaviours and thus demonstrate autonomy and independence (see Kelman 1958; 1961; McCaslin & Good, 1992; Kohn, 1996)? At one level, complete compliance with classroom rules and procedures is desirable. Suppose that, for instance, in the case of a fire drill, students are to line up in alphabetical order (in order to account for everyone in the class). A lack of compliance in this case could be a threat to safety. At another level, however, students need to act of their own accord, use their own judgment, or take the initiative in formulating and pursuing their own goals. In such instances, there may be little or no guidance available from outside sources; that is, there may be no external guidelines with which to comply.

Management styles can be likened to a classic model of parenting styles (McCaslin & Good, 1992). The model formulates a continuum from little or no control (permissive) to a great deal of control (authoritarian) (Baumrind, 1971, 1991). Authoritarian parents control decision making and issue orders to their children with little effort to discuss or explain their orders. Their purpose is to gain obedience.

In the middle of this continuum is the authoritative style, in which parents provide firm guidelines for the behaviour of their children but are flexible in the interpretation of those guidelines. Authoritative parents communicate their standards through discussion and explanation and value self-realization in their children's behaviour. A position further along this continuum, perhaps best described as **collaborative**, has been advocated by Kohn (1996). Kohn draws a contrast between "doing to" and "working with" classroom environments. The "doing to" classroom is characterized by teacher control. In this kind of classroom, the teacher makes the decisions about curriculum and classroom rules. A variety of rewards and punishments are deployed to ensure that students comply with the teacher's wishes. In the "working with" classroom, students play an

---

EXAMPLE: Consider persons you regard as great leaders in history. What were the goals they pursued? Consider how their ability to articulate goals and vision contributed to their ability to lead others.

CRITICAL THINKING: Why are guidelines for a child's behaviour important? Would it be better to allow children to discover their own guidelines of behaviour? Why or why not?

TRY THIS: Ask a teacher to characterize his or her leadership style. Then, with the teacher's permission, ask students to characterize the teacher's leadership style. The teacher may be very interested in discussing your findings with you.

authoritative leadership Authority established through the flexible implementation of standards and characterized by discussion with and explanation to followers.

collaborative leadership Guidance through shared planning, decision making, and problem solving.

active role in constructing a **learning community**. To accomplish this, the teacher works toward creating an environment in which the students' interests and questions drive the curriculum. The goal is to focus upon the students' underlying motives, thereby encouraging the development of positive values and self-regulation of learning and behaviour. Kohn argues that the "working with" environment can only emerge when the teacher shares decision making, rule formulation, and problem solving with the students. The challenge for the teacher is to provide the structure that will permit the "working with" climate to thrive.

Reflect for a moment on the metaphors that were suggested at the beginning of the chapter. Most of the approaches to classroom management would be considered either authoritarian or collaborative. For instance, work-oriented classrooms are more authoritarian while learning-oriented classrooms are more collaborative (see Evertson & Randolph, 1995). The outcomes of collaborative leadership in the classroom are more consistent with learning goals such as critical thinking, self-understanding, self-evaluation, and other higher level thinking skills. "We cannot expect that students will profit from the incongruous messages we send when we manage for obedience and teach for exploration and risk taking" (McCaslin & Good, 1992, p. 12).

How can teachers lead collaboratively? How can you display the values and attitudes that are characteristic of classrooms that are learning communities? Generating a classroom management plan that respects students and values learning is an important first step in establishing the classroom discipline on which instruction and learning can be built.

How Can You Create a Learning-Oriented Environment?

Even before we examine the elements of a sound classroom management plan, it is important to note that planning is associated with the development of positive learning environments (Evertson & Emmer, 1982). Planning enables a teacher to avoid inappropriate student behaviour by organizing the classroom and materials so that the physical environment is conducive to learning. Advanced planning also allows teachers and students to decide upon classroom rules and procedures that will help prevent problem behaviour (Brophy & Evertson, 1976; cf. Jones & Jones, 1995; Kounin, 1970). In this section, we will examine the research and the recommendations for organizing a classroom, establishing rules, and developing classroom procedures. These research-based recommendations can be used as the foundation of a plan for effective classroom management.

POINT: Your metaphors of teaching are frameworks for what is possible in your classrooms. The importance of this type of reflection is signified in one of the basic assumptions of this book: *One's view of the teaching-learning process affects one's classroom practice.*

TRY THIS: Ask teachers to share with you their classroom management plans. Also call school districts to see if there are classroom management requirements or recommendations that teachers in the district follow. How do the plans compare to the recommendations in this book?

learning community A classroom environment built on ideals and values of kindness, fairness, and responsibility.

Arranging the Classroom

A good place to begin developing a plan for classroom management is with the physical environment. Teacher Peter Roop begins preparing for each school year by spending time in his classroom a few days before students return from summer break. He describes his thoughts and feelings in the following brief passage, called "Room for Improvement."

> My room seems so empty when I walk in at the beginning of the school year—nothing on the walls, the bookcases covered with paper to keep off the summer dust, the desks in a jumble in one corner, my desk in another. I am reminded of Ichabod Crane's one-room schoolhouse after Brom Bones plays his Halloween prank and changes everything around.
>
> My first inclination is to begin arranging the desks. This is a ritual for me. I know, however, that over the next three days I will move everything at least three more times before the kids come to class. Nonetheless, I move the desks, thinking how much easier it would be to sketch a floor plan on paper or on the board. I could sketch where my desk will be, which board I will be using most often and where I want their attention directed, where my activity table will be placed, where my big armchair for reading aloud will be. But there is something about physically moving furniture that helps me reenter the world of the classroom, so I keep shoving things around.
>
> I am satisfied with my first arrangement. For now. I sit down and think about the room. It really is a world. There is the immediate physicalness—the space, the desks, the shelves—that part of the environment that must be accepted but can also be improved. There are other, less tangible aspects of our world that become apparent only when the students arrive: their needs, my goals and expectations, interactions between the students and myself, and how I will lead.
>
> Picking up a class roster I read down through the names: Ernesto, Paula, Raeanne, Surrinder, James, Meghan, Karl, Matt, Daniel. How well will this world meet their social needs? Will my management style match their learning needs? Patrick, Jonathan, April, Melissa, Takeda, Lida, Adam, Pam, Scott, Nick, Brad. Who will find this environment stimulating, engaging, demanding, and intriguing? Who will prefer another environment, less open, more controlled, less demanding?
>
> It takes sunlight about eight minutes to reach Earth, I thought. How long will it take me to reach some students? I wonder. And I only have three days to get ready for this world of human emotions, ideas, thoughts, problems, interests, feelings, and growth.
>
> Enough daydreaming. Hopping off my desk, I wonder, wouldn't a circular arrangement encourage more peer interaction?

REFLECTION: What are your favourite types of physical spaces for learning? Which of your classrooms was most physically appealing to you? Most comfortable? Draw a floor plan of your favourite classroom from memory. What other memories of your experiences in that classroom are brought to life as you draw the physical layout?

The physical arrangement of your classroom will not, by itself, guarantee effective management. However, a thoughtful arrangement can contribute to the learning outcomes you seek. Emmer, Everston, Clements, and Worsham (1994) specify several aspects of good classroom arrangement.

The most important aspect is to select a room arrangement that is consistent with your learning goals and instructional activities. If your instruction will consist primarily of presentations, demonstrations, and teacher-led discussions with the whole class, you will want to be sure that all students have a clear view of the main instructional area, including the chalkboard and overhead or computer-generated projections (Figure 10.2). If your instructional approach calls primarily for small group work, however, an arrangement like that depicted in Figure 10.3 might be more appropriate.

Although the classroom arrangements in Figures 10.2 and 10.3 are quite different, they are similar in one important aspect. They both afford the teacher

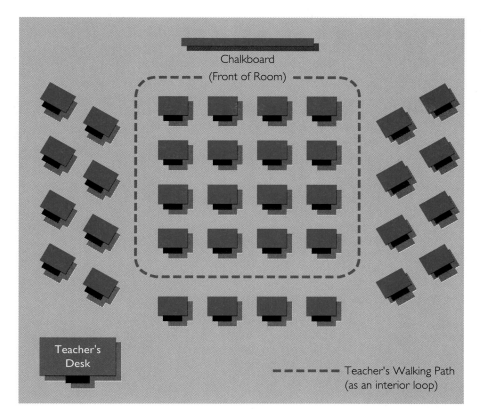

FIGURE 10.2
A Possible Classroom
Arrangement

*Source: Solving Discipline
Problems* (3rd ed., p. 216), C.
H. Wolfgang, 1995, Needham
Heights, MA: Allyn & Bacon.
Reprinted by permission.

Chalkboard
(Front of Room)

Teacher's
Desk

Teacher's Walking Path
(as an interior loop)

proximity to students (Wolfgang, 1995). In either of these arrangements, a teacher can move easily around the room and bring himself or herself into fairly close proximity to any student. By using such arrangements teachers are less likely to attend to one group of students at the expense of others.

In a classroom that is arranged in traditional rows, there is a tendency for teachers to spend most of their time in the front of the classroom and to direct most of their attention to students seated there. The front of the room becomes what is called an action zone. **Action zones** are those areas in a seating arrangement where teachers direct most of their attention. Students who are not in the front of the classroom tend to contribute less to class discussions, are judged to be less attentive, and achieve at lower levels than students who are in the front (Adams & Biddle, 1970; Daum, 1972; Delefes & Jackson, 1972; Schwebel & Cherlin, 1972). Daum (1972) demonstrated that low-ability students who are moved to an action zone improve their level of achievement. Coincidentally, high-achieving students who were placed farther from the teacher in the classroom did not suffer a decrease in achievement. As a way of maintaining the attention of all students, the seating arrangement is not simply a matter of arranging the desks but of also arranging the students who sit at those desks.

Another key to good room arrangement is keeping high-traffic areas—such as frequently used bookcases, supply areas, the pencil sharpener, and the waste basket—clear of furniture. It is also a good idea to arrange the room so that high traffic areas are dispersed throughout the space. Other keys to good room arrangement include maintaining clear sightlines—between the teacher and students and, for classrooms in which peer interaction is valued, sightlines among students—and keeping frequently used materials easily accessible (Emmer et al., 1994).

CRITICAL THINKING: What are the advantages and disadvantages of the classroom layouts in Figures 10.2 and 10.3?

CONNECTION: Student groupings are discussed in greater detail in Chapter 12.

action zones The areas in a classroom where a teacher directs most of his or her attention.

Here's How To Use Walls and Bulletin Boards

- At the beginning of the school year, you should have, at the very least, a display area that can be used to list daily assignments and a decorative display that welcomes students to the room.

- You should have a wall or bulletin board display of classroom rules. If you plan to establish classroom rules in collaboration with your students, the display can be labelled Classroom Rules—To Be Decided Jointly.

- You should setup instructionally relevant displays. For younger students you might display a number line and alphabet letters. For older students you could post an example of the format that written assignments will need to follow, and a display depicting a topic that will be covered in class.

- If you run out of ideas, visit other classrooms to see what other teachers do to make their rooms feel welcoming and alive. There are also commercial bulletin board materials and books on bulletin board design at school supply stores.

- If you are stuck for time as you prepare for the beginning of the school year—a likely possibility for any new teacher—simply cover the bulletin boards with coloured paper and invite students to construct their own displays.

FIGURE 10.3

A More Interactive Classroom Arrangement

Source: Classroom Management for Secondary Teachers (3rd ed., p. 13), Emmer, Evertson, Clements, and Worsham, 1994, Needham Heights, MA: Allyn & Bacon. Reprinted by permission.

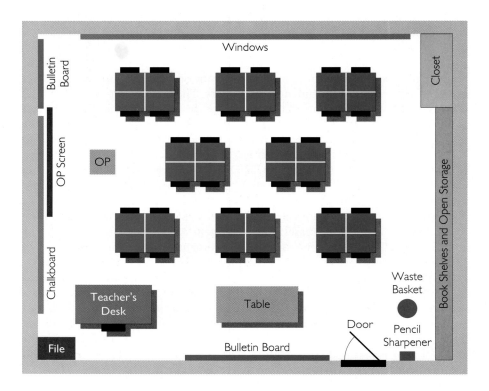

Imagine that because you value peer interaction and wish to establish a learning-oriented classroom, you have selected the arrangement shown in Figure 10.3. Now imagine that when your students enter the room on the first day of class, the walls, bulletin boards, and chalkboard are empty. If you want your room to become a "beehive of activity," that should be part of your students' first impression. But how can you establish that expectation? Here's How lists some ideas (cf. Emmer et al., 1994).

Establishing Rules and Procedures

Rules and procedures both refer to expectations of student behaviour. **Rules** are general statements of standards of behaviour that are meant to apply across all classroom situations. An example of a rule is: Be helpful and polite to others. **Procedures** also identify standards of behaviour but apply to specific activities. For instance, you will probably establish procedures for collecting homework, making up missed work, contributing to class discussions, and leaving the room (Emmer et al., 1994; Evertson et al., 1994).

Rules should be simply stated and relatively few in number (Charles & Senter, 1995). The following are examples of classroom rules that might be used in an elementary classroom (Evertson et al., 1994).

1. Be helpful and polite.
2. Respect the property of others.
3. Listen while others speak.
4. Respect all people.
5. Obey school rules.

In order to make only a few statements that apply to most situations in the classroom, rules are necessarily general statements. In order to help students understand such general statements, you should provide explanations of the rules along with numerous examples. To help primary grade students understand the preceding rules, for instance, you will probably need to explain terms such as *polite* and *respect*. One example of being polite might be, "saying 'please' when you want to borrow something and 'thank you' when you get it." Examples can also include what not to do, such as, "Respecting people means that you don't hit them." Another way to help students learn rules is to point out events in the classroom when rules have been and have not been followed.

Classroom rules for older students should address points similar to rules for elementary students and may include additional, task-oriented statements, such as: Be ready to begin work when the bell rings (cf. Emmer et al., 1994). Even though students in junior high and high school can be expected to comprehend rule statements more easily than their younger peers, it is still advisable to provide secondary students with illustrations.

Although examples or illustrations of these rules might include inappropriate behaviour, note that the rules are stated positively. In general, stating rules positively is preferable to negative statements. Positively stated rules make it easier for teachers to encourage positive student behaviour (Burke, 1992). Consider the rule: Respect all people. A negatively stated version of that rule might be something like: Do not call people names. If students have worked very well together to complete a group brainstorming task, the message to them is much clearer if a teacher comments on their respect for each others' opinions rather than congratulating them for getting through the session without calling anyone

TRY THIS: Go to a local teachers' store and browse through the materials available for bulletin boards, or borrow materials catalogues from a teacher. How might you use such material? How might your students construct their own bulletin boards?

EXAMPLE: One of the classroom rules is: Respect other people's property. When a student picks up a pencil from another student's desk, the teacher asks, "Lisa, I am wondering if you remembered our rule about respecting other people's property and asked Sam's permission to use his pencil."

CRITICAL THINKING: From an operant-conditioning point of view, why would positively stated rules work better than negatively stated ones?

rules General standards of behaviour that are meant to apply across all classroom situations.

procedures Standards of behaviour that are specific to a particular classroom task or set of related tasks.

a name. If positively stated rules are more easily reinforced, students who follow the rules are more likely to serve as models for classmates. In terms of Bandura's social learning theory, discussed in Chapter 8, reinforcing a student for appropriate behaviour provides other students with an opportunity to learn those behaviours vicariously.

Procedures are methods for completing all sorts of routine activities in a classroom (Emmer, 1987). Another way of thinking about procedures is that they provide a how-to plan for routine activities in a classroom. In formulating the procedures that will be part of your classroom management plan, you will need to account for academic work routines. These routines should answer the how-to questions that students might ask about academic work in your classroom. The procedures you establish for academic work should answer the following questions for students (Emmer, 1987).

1. How do I find out what my assignments are?
2. How do I complete work missed when I am absent?
3. How do I get help if I need it?
4. How do I find out how well I am progressing in this class?
5. How do I earn grades in this class?

REFLECTION: Think about your own questions when you entered this class on the first day. Compared to your concerns, how complete is Emmer's list? What else might students want to know?

TRY THIS: Interview a practising teacher about making preparations for the school year. What specific goals does the teacher have for the first week of school? The first month? Ask for recommendations for how you should prepare for your very first teaching assignment.

In addition to academic activities, there are other routine tasks that require procedural planning (Evertson, 1987; Weinstein & Mignano, 1993). These nonacademic procedures include use of equipment and learning centres, using the washroom and drinking fountain, leaving and returning to the room (as, during a fire drill), housekeeping chores (such as watering plants or changing bulletin board notices), beginning and ending the school day. Procedures for both academic and nonacademic classroom routines need to be explained to students just as rules are explained. Having a management plan that meticulously addresses every possible classroom procedure is of little use if students are unaware of or do not understand procedures (Good & Brophy, 1994.)

Building a Positive Atmosphere

Some of the most influential classroom management research of the past 15 years are the beginning-of-the-school-year studies conducted by educational psychologists Emmer, Evertson, Anderson, and their colleagues (e.g., Emmer, Evertson, & Anderson, 1980; Emmer et al., 1994; Evertson, 1987; Evertson et al., 1994). In these studies, the researchers made frequent observations of a large number of classrooms during the first few weeks of the school year. They continued making observations as the year progressed, although the frequency of the observations decreased. During some of the later visits, the researchers discovered that some classrooms were operating very well and some were not. Furthermore, the well-managed classrooms, where discipline had been attained, were producing considerably higher levels of student achievement than the poorly managed classrooms.

After determining which teachers were the effective classroom managers and which were less effective, the researchers went back to their observations made at the beginning of the school year. They discovered differences in how the good managers and poor managers started the year. Thus, their observations suggested that establishing a positive classroom atmosphere—one in which students display disciplined behaviour and achieve well—is influenced by early student-teacher interactions. To test the validity of their conclusions further, the researchers developed principles of classroom management from their observations of effective teachers. These principles were then taught to other teachers who used them in their own classrooms. The results attained by the new teachers supported the conclusion that there are techniques that can be used at the beginning of the school year to establish a positive learning environment. What are those techniques? How can you start the year in a way that will increase discipline and learning? Here's How presents two lists, one for elementary students and one for secondary students.

REFLECTION: From your experience as a student, identify examples of classes in which discipline and learning did not occur. Try to recall how those classes began. Do you think the first class meetings made a difference?

Here's How

Here's How To Begin the School Year in an Elementary Classroom

- Greet the students. A warm greeting of each student as he or she enters the room helps students feel welcome in their new learning environment. Have name tags prepared ahead of time, with some extras for unexpected students, so that you can give students a name tag when they enter the room. Have an independent activity for students to work on at their desks as you greet other arriving students.

- Conduct introductions. Once students have arrived, introduce yourself and tell them something about yourself. A long autobiographical presentation would be inappropriate, but take a moment to share some of your interests. Have students introduce themselves to the class as well.

- Describe the room. Begin acquainting your students with the various areas of the room. Make sure to point out any areas or materials that they will be using on the first day.

- Present and discuss rules and procedures. First present any major school rules—for example, "No running in the halls." Together with the students, brainstorm and discuss ideas about why that rule is necessary. Next, present and discuss the classroom rules and the consequences of rule violation, or indicate where the rules to be developed by the class will be posted.

- Communicate with parents. If not the first day, then certainly during the first week of school, send a letter home to parents. Include information about materials their child will need for school, how parents may contact you, and special events such as parent-teacher conferences and open-house. Take time to craft a letter that presents yourself well. Use the letter to establish your professionalism. Have a colleague read a draft to ensure clarity, correct grammar, and correct spelling. You may include a list of the school rules and class routines with the letter. Have parents sign and return part of the letter. This allows you to check that all parents have received the letter and informs parents that you invite their involvement (see Evertson et al., 1994).

Here's How

Here's How To Begin the School Year in a Secondary Classroom

- On the first day of class, stand near the door to help students find the correct room. Greet students as they enter your class, but avoid long conversations. Tell students that they may choose their seats for this first class meeting. When most students have arrived, enter the room, stay in prominent view, and monitor student behaviour. You can do this while engaging students in pleasantries.

- When the bell rings, state your name, the name of the subject, and the grade level—which should already be written on the chalkboard—so that students can check their schedules to ensure they are in the correct room.

- Check attendance. Get to this administrative task quickly. As you call the names on the roster, have students raise their hand, rather than call out, to indicate their presence. Calling the roster gives you a chance to start associating names and faces. Using the hand-raising technique communicates the idea that being recognized is more desirable than calling out. If you intend to establish hand raising as a procedure for speaking in class, this technique helps to establish that norm early.

- Conduct introductions. Tell students something about yourself: your interests, hobbies, and why you enjoy teaching the course they have just started. If students do not know each other, a brief, get-acquainted activity would be in order. You might administer a brief interest survey. After introductions, give students an overview of the course, and describe some of the more interesting activities that they can anticipate in the course.

- Present and discuss rules and procedures. Some secondary school teachers prefer to call these "guidelines." In any case, design your presentation of rules and procedures to eliminate student uncertainty. As you present each rule, provide examples and a rationale. Invite students to contribute examples and reasons for a particular rule. If you anticipate that one of the class rules or procedures will be difficult to follow, you should acknowledge that possibility and assure students that you will help them develop appropriate behaviours (see Emmer et al., 1994).

Constructing a Democratic Classroom

British Columbia teacher Donald Fleming has described how he began the school year by developing a class constitution that included rules of conduct for both teacher and students (Fleming, 1996). His goal was to lead his seventh grade students through design of a classroom community and culture built upon such values as civic spirit, compassion, and trust. "Here's How" traces a series of lessons designed by Fleming in the collaborative construction of a democratic classroom.

Here's How

Here's How To Create a Learning-Oriented Classroom Based on Collaboration, Community, and Democracy

- Students think and write about their personal talents and learning styles in a series of guided interviews with adults (teachers, parents) and one another.

- In groups of four, students design an "ideal society" that would best accommodate each person. Each group presents their vision orally in parliamentary fashion.

- Student groups then discuss the role of schooling in the realization of their vision. Parents are interviewed for input. Groups produce a concise written statement.

- Student teams use the "role of schooling" statement to generate five classroom rules applicable to both students and teachers. The rules are compared across groups, sorted, revised, and voted on to arrive at a set of collective rules.

- Based on the set of collective rules, the teacher drafts a constitution, which is discussed, revised, and voted on.

- Four non-punitive steps are devised to deal with rule infraction by student or teacher (e.g., verbal reminder, written reminder, class meeting, parent or principal meeting)

How Can Instruction Be Managed to Support A Learning-Oriented Environment?

A good start to the school year is critical to the atmosphere that will develop in your classroom. A good start is just that, however—a start. Building and maintaining a positive, learning-oriented environment requires attention to the procedures for managing the instructional activities you employ to facilitate student learning (Good & Brophy, 1994).

One of the best ways to maintain discipline is to engage students in interesting activities that, when completed, yield a feeling of accomplishment. But finding an interesting activity does not ensure that the activity will prove a success. The activity must be managed well if it is to produce learning. Students must become involved with the activity; the activity must engage their cognitive efforts. Vernon Jones and Louise Jones (1995) describe instructional management skills that facilitate the active engagement of learners in the instructional task (cf. Rosenshine, 1983). Some of the instructional management skills examined in this section were first addressed by Kounin (1970). These skills, to be discussed in turn, are (1) giving clear instructions, (2) gaining attention, (3) maintaining attention, (4) pacing, (5) summarizing, and (6) making smooth transitions.

CONNECTION: This chapter focuses on managing learning activities. In Chapter 12, the focus will be on the activities themselves. Both here and in Chapter 12, it is important to realize that management and instruction occur interdependently.

CONNECTION: This discussion relates to instructional goals and their influence on motivation, as discussed in Chapter 9.

Giving Clear Instructions

Disruptive behaviour in classrooms often occurs when students are unsure of what to do when assigned a particular task (Brophy, 1988). Students who are

Insights on Successful Practice

In your experience, what role does teacher communication play in successful classroom management?

Presenting a clear and consistent message to everyone in the school and parent community is vital for the success of my classroom management. I firmly believe that both parents and teachers want to see children develop as happy, well-adjusted students who are successful and confident. Because we have the same goal in mind, it is imperative to work side by side and continue a consistent and clear line of communication between home and school. Parents need to feel that they are a vital link in the success of their child's educational experience, which encompasses academic, emotional, and social success in the classroom, school, and larger community. As the teacher, it is my responsibility to foster and reinforce the concept of a three-way partnership. It is a chain that connects parents to teachers, with the most important link in the middle—the student. When the students understand that the significant adults are working together with the goal of helping them succeed, they are motivated to do their best and strive to reach the high expectations we have of them for becoming all that they can be.

The first week of school, I make personal contact with each family by phone and invite them to attend Back-to-School Night, at which time I go over the program for their child and how they can help at home. I am always amazed at the reaction I get, for there are always those who express surprise and appreciation for this small professional courtesy. Many have the perception that a phone call from the teacher is an indication of a problem! It's nice to break that pattern and show them that I am fostering the three-way partnership.

Students call home if a recurring problem arises that prevents others from getting the most out of the day and focusing on their responsibilities. Often a few minutes on the phone with the parent helps the student get refocused through reinforcement from that critical link in the chain. But parents also receive calls that validate their child's efforts and successes in school, and success in itself is a powerful motivator. Parents sign newsletters attached to their child's homework. When students return their homework completed on time I give them a ticket that enters them into a monthly draw for breakfast with the teacher. I am communicating that their efforts and responsibility lead to satisfaction and it is my way of supporting and reinforcing that behaviour.

I ask that parents communicate with me as well so that I gain a better understanding and appreciation of the unique dynamics of each family. I have seen so many changes happen in a child's life at home, and for some the classroom structure provides consistency in an otherwise chaotic home environment. Communication must travel two ways to be most effective. I expect students to be active participants at their parent-teacher conferences. It is an opportunity for students to share openly with their parents and teacher their concerns, surprises, and future goals, and then we brainstorm together as a team on strategies toward successfully meeting those goals and how each person in this three-way partnership has a role. Through this spirit of mutual support and cooperation I see children thrive and become empowered as they are validated as being capable individuals.

JENLANE GEE MATT
Elementary School Teacher

Your Insights

What three-way communication link does this teacher nurture? Why is this link important to student success, and what pragmatics of classroom life are served by it? What guidelines for effective communication can you infer from this essay?

---

on-task behaviour Any time a student is engaged with an academic task.

unsure of how to ask for assistance or move to a new activity when a task is completed are more likely to display disruptive behaviour than students who know what procedures to follow and what actions to take after the task is completed (cf. Brophy & Evertson, 1976; Jones & Jones, 1990; Kounin, 1970). Giving clear instructions is one of the skills Jones and Jones identify as increasing the time students spend engaged with academic tasks, referred to as **on-task behaviour.** By increasing on-task behaviour, teachers reduce the amount of disruptive behaviour in their classrooms.

Precise Directions. Teachers can take several steps to make sure their instructions are clear. First, you should make sure that directions to students are precise. These directions should include information about what students will be doing, the reason for doing it, how students can find help if it is needed, and what they should do when their work is completed. Students express their uncertainty about tasks in a number of disruptive ways. As an example, they might ask questions repeatedly about the task they have been assigned. Other forms of disruption might occur as expressions of boredom or acting out.

Providing precise directions tells students *what* they are to do. Expectations can be made clearer by also describing *how well* students should perform. Jones and Jones report that one teacher uses three labels to inform students of the desired quality of their work. The first label, *throwaway,* is for practice material, material that will not be handed in. The second label, *everyday learning*, is applied to work that will be turned in and graded. This work, therefore, should be neatly done. The presentation does not have to be perfect, however; the main purpose of everyday learning work is to check the student's understanding of the material. The final label, *keepers,* refers to work that the students may want to retain permanently or work that may be displayed.

Student Involvement. One way to check if students understand your instructions is to ask them to paraphrase the directions they have received. Checking students' understanding of instructional content is an important part of active instruction. It is helpful to check students' understanding of the instructions to make sure they are engaged correctly in a task.

Write instructions on a chalkboard or bulletin board so that students may refer to them, or ask students to write out the instructions before beginning the activity to ensure that they have understood them correctly. If students are experiencing some difficulty in following a complex set of instructions, you can break down the instructions into smaller units. Directions should always be given immediately prior to presenting the activity that the students are being asked to do.

No matter how clearly teachers present instructions to their students, and no matter how well students listen to those instructions, there will be times when students must ask questions about what they are to do. Applying Maslow's hierarchy of needs (Chapter 9) suggests that student questions should be accepted in a positive manner. If you accept students' questions in a positive way, that acceptance contributes to the classroom atmosphere in which students work. If they find the teacher to be a willing helper, who will support their efforts, the atmosphere in the classroom will seem safe. A safe atmosphere encourages risk taking by students who will now attempt to meet higher-level needs because the lower-level need of safety has been satisfied.

Gaining Attention

The best time to engage students in a learning activity is when it begins. A lesson that fails to capture attention at the beginning is not likely to turn into an exciting learning experience (see Kounin, 1970). Experienced teachers have developed a number of strategies for gaining attention at the start of a lesson (Jones & Jones, 1995).

One strategy is to select or teach a cue that signals to the students that a lesson is about to begin. Using phrases such as "OK, we're just about ready to get started here, so everyone pay attention" or "OK, let's get ready to start" are so common that they tend to be ineffective in capturing students' attention.

TRY THIS: Observe a primary grade classroom and a secondary classroom. In particular, observe the way in which directions are presented. What are the similarities? Do the guidelines in this book apply to both classrooms?

EXAMPLE: Another example of a theoretical justification for responding to students' questions is Lickona's model of character education, discussed in Chapter 3.

Effective cues used by teachers include flashing the classroom lights, ringing a tiny bell, and placing an attention-grabbing transparency on the overhead projector. We observed a grade eight teacher in Saskatoon use a visual cue to effectively and efficiently gain his students' attention. Without speaking, he raises his arm. Students immediately follow suit, raising one arm while they stop talking and focus upon the teacher. This action serves as a signal to other students and soon the class is silent and ready for this teacher's instructions.

Some signals can serve additional purposes, such as communicating the teacher's interest or enthusiasm to the students. For example, one teacher always wears a sport coat to class but never wears it while teaching. The sport coat is merely a prop. When the administrative details at the beginning of a period are complete, the instructor always removes his coat. On those occasions when he is wearing long sleeves, he rolls them up to indicate that he is ready to get to work.

The use of a verbal or visual cue must be followed by a waiting period. If the catch phrase or signal succeeds in directing students' attention to the teacher, then the delay will be short. It is important for the teacher not to begin until everyone in the classroom is paying attention, however long the delay. The effectiveness of the signal is diminished if the teacher begins the lesson before all students are paying attention.

Many students are easily distracted. Before beginning a lesson, you should look around your classroom and remove any potential distractions. For instance, if there is noise coming from the hallway, close the door. Such preparations can serve as additional signals that the lesson is about to begin.

Maintaining Attention

The time that students spend directly engaged in learning activities relates positively to their level of achievement (Fisher, Berliner, Filby, Marliave, Cahen, & Dishaw, 1980; Fisher, Filby, Marliave, Cahen, Dishaw, Moore, & Berliner, 1978). If students are to be engaged in instructional tasks, the teacher must develop strategies to help them maintain their attention during a lesson. Fisher et al. (1978) report that the amount of time students spend working directly on instructional tasks varies from less than 50 percent for some teachers to more than 90 percent for others. Earlier in this chapter, you learned about seating arrangements and how an effective arrangement can enhance student attention. Other attention management skills include recognizing students and encouraging student interaction.

Recognizing Students. One way to keep students alert during a lesson is to avoid establishing a predictable pattern when calling on students to respond in class. Achieving unpredictability is not as complicated as it may sound. *Random* calling means that each student has an equal probability of being selected to answer a particular question. You can, with a bit of practice, approximate random selection. One helpful tip is to monitor the extent to which you call on low-achieving students. The tendency, for many teachers, is to call on high-achieving students disproportionately more often (Brophy & Good, 1974; Cooper & Good, 1983). Another tip is to return occasionally to a student who has recently responded to a question. Such practices keep students alert because they are unable to predict accurately who the teacher will call on next.

A more systematic approach, suggested by Jones and Jones (1995), is to keep a tally sheet and mark it each time a student is called on. You can also inform students—as you present classroom procedures on the first day of class—that you intend to call on each of them. If students understand your intentions, it is less likely that students who volunteer frequently will experience frustration if you do not call on them as often as they would like.

You will enhance attention if you ask the question before calling on a particular student. When you ask the question prior to calling on a student and use an unpredictable pattern of selection, all students tend to listen more carefully to the question. When a teacher selects a student before asking a question, the other students in the classroom are relieved from responsibility. Consider the reaction of students in a class where the teacher says, "Ronald, what do we call a word that modifies a verb?" In this case, Ronald is on the spot, and the other students in the classroom are more likely to respond to the fact that they were not called on than to the question being asked. Questioning can have powerful effects on students' attention. We will examine this skill in more detail in our discussion of active learning in Chapter 12.

Encouraging Student Interaction. Another way to maintain attention is to encourage students to interact with their classmates. One way to do this is to ask students to elaborate upon the answers that other students have provided. Keep in mind that it is helpful to avoid repeating the answers that students give to questions. Jones and Jones (1995) have observed that many teachers parrot nearly every answer that students give, which teaches the students that they do not have to speak clearly or loudly when answering. Students learn that the teacher is the only one who is required to hear the answer. They pay less attention to peers because they have learned that the teacher will provide the answer. Finally, students learn that the teacher is the source of all information in the classroom. These effects, taken together, decrease the attention that students pay.

Students will listen carefully to their classmates' answers when they are encouraged to do so by the example of their teacher. If teachers pays close attention to what students say, they are modelling good listening behaviour for students. A teacher can demonstrate careful listening by asking students to repeat, clarify, or elaborate what they have said. This practice indicates that you not only are interested in what the student has to say but also want to understand clearly the student's point of view.

Maintaining attention can be facilitated by a teacher who is animated. The animation in the teacher's voice and facial expression is indicative of a high level of energy for the topic being discussed. This demonstrated enthusiasm can be further enhanced by using more positive than negative verbal statements. Verbal reinforcement should be sincere. If the teacher follows every student response by saying, "Oh, what an insightful answer!" students will learn that any response will receive verbal reinforcement, and that will diminish the reinforcing effect of verbal praise.

It is important to keep in mind that the silences between utterances also communicate information to the students. The research on wait-time (discussed in Chapter 12) indicates that silence can give students an opportunity to think more clearly about the question at hand. Silence can also gain attention. Silences serve to separate verbally related thoughts from each other. When writing, we can separate thoughts by using periods, paragraphs, and sections. Silences in the classroom are the auditory equivalent to that separation and can signal to students when an idea is important.

TRY THIS: Observe several lessons, focusing on the questioning techniques of the teacher. Note the nature and length of students' responses as well as the class' overall level of attention. What are your observations about the effectiveness of the questioning techniques?

EXAMPLE: Teacher modelling of active listening is an excellent way to encourage that behaviour in other tudents. Another way to encourage active listening is to ask a student to paraphrase another student's answer.

CONNECTION: Chapter 12 presents a discussion of *wait-time,* which refers to the interval between asking a question and calling on a student to respond as well as to the interval between the student's response and the teacher's reaction.

Pacing

Pacing refers to the tempo a teacher establishes while teaching. The tempo with which you present your lessons is partially dictated by your teaching style. Some people speak faster than others. Some are more likely to digress, telling a story or providing other examples. Some prefer rapid-fire drill and practice to a more leisurely seat-work assignment. But pacing is determined by more than just our own personal styles. It is determined by the way you organize your material and by your ability to observe students' responses. As you reflect on your performances in the classroom, you will become more skilled at judging the appropriateness of your pacing. As you gain field experience or as you videotape lessons in your teacher education program, ask others and yourself questions such as, Did I speak too quickly? Did I exhibit enthusiasm? Did I pace the lesson by modulating my voice? Did I use silences effectively? Did I repeat myself too often?

Asking these questions of your students can yield useful information about pacing. You may also ask students whether you are accurately picking up their cues when they do not understand or if you provide sufficient time for them to complete seatwork. You can obtain this feedback after a lesson, in either an informal question-and-answer period, or through written evaluations. One high school teacher reported that he wanted to improve his pacing without interrupting the class and without spending time after the lesson reviewing the form of the lesson rather than its substance. The teacher taught his students several hand signals that they could use during a lesson to inform him of the appropriateness of his pacing—whether he was talking too much or repeating himself, talking too fast, or presenting material that they did not understand (Jones & Jones, 1995).

Kounin (1970) found that teachers who were able to scan their rooms and to respond to problems effectively before they became serious had fewer discipline problems. For example, if a student appears restless—shifting in his or her seat, playing with materials on the desk—the teacher can avoid disruptive behaviour by simply recognizing the student's restlessness and asking the student for an explanation. There are two reasons for asking a student why he or she is having difficulty paying attention. First, the student's answer provides you with direct feedback on your pacing. Second, this approach encourages students to share their feelings because the teacher is taking their observations and opinions seriously.

Summarizing

Providing students with summaries of what has been taught during a particular lesson or, in the case of primary grades, over the course of a day is a way of helping them organize information. By stepping back at the end of an instructional unit and putting the material into perspective, you facilitate the development of organized knowledge structures, or schemata.

There are several ways in which students can become actively involved in summarizing activities. One way is to have them write, perhaps in a daily journal, something that they have learned in the lesson or during the instructional day. Such an activity also provides the teacher with an opportunity to diagnose problems (e.g., if a student has difficulty writing down something he or she has learned).

Role playing can also be used as a summary-generating technique. Students might play the role of a reporter and provide a news summary of the learning events that occurred during the lesson. A teacher might say something like, "We go now to our classroom correspondent, Christopher Yee, who will report on the

POINT: Informal surveys of students are helpful not only in improving a teacher's instructional delivery but also in showing the students that the teacher is serious about teaching well, thus enhancing credibility.

CONNECTION: This chapter also examines approaches for handling disruptive behaviour. One of those approaches assumes that misbehaviour always represents a problem that the student is experiencing and is, therefore, an opportunity to help the student identify and solve the problem.

Insights on Successful Practice

What advice can you give novice teachers about preventing discipline problems?

Effective teaching and learning can be achieved in classroom environments in which there are few or no disruptions. Some kinds of disruptions such as the ringing of bells and telephones or the knocking on doors for routine inquiries are uncontrollable. Disruptive student behaviours, however, can be minimized if not completely eliminated. The key to this, naturally, is the teacher's planning for teaching and the careful organization of the day's activities. If the teacher has thoughtfully completed those tasks and students understand what their responsibilities are, they will generally make a genuine effort to meet the standards or expectations. But there are occasions in which students will resort to disruptive behaviours. As teachers, we can anticipate these occasions and make plans for eliminating them. These plans should encompass the cooperative formulation of guidelines or rules.

After several years of teaching in Northern Manitoba and Ontario, I learned that standards of behaviour must be established early and with the students' cooperation. Timing is crucial. For example, talking while another student is responding to a question is unacceptable behaviour. The teacher must deal with the problem immediately, explaining why such behaviour is unacceptable. That would be the opportune moment to spend some class time in developing the required guidelines or rules. This activity must be a cooperative effort. It can be achieved in small group discussions, or in a large class discussion, or both.

Having had some minor disruptive behaviour problems, I divided the class into five small groups. Each group was asked to list what it expected of me, the teacher; what it expected of other students in my class; and what it expected of each member of the group. I also listed what I expected of myself and what I expected of my students. Each group summarized its list of expectations and presented it to the entire class. I also presented mine. A committee consisting of one member from each group evaluated the suggestions, categorized them, and prepared the final list. The entire class had the opportunity to revise the list. This cooperative effort revealed that almost all the students had similar expectations of the teacher, other students, and themselves. Because the rules were developed cooperatively, the students felt some ownership of them. The result was a healthy growth of peer pressure in enforcing the rules. A noticeable decline in disruptive behaviours soon occurred. Instead, there was a quick development of positive responding behaviours among and between students and between the students and me.

Even though rules for behaviour are established, there are times when a student might continue to exhibit unacceptable behaviour. Be discreet in dealing with such situations. Some minor problems, such as interrupting a speaker, can be addressed directly and immediately. Some problems, such as truancy, may be more serious and will require time for discussion and resolution. In such situations, avoid the tendency to be confrontational and, above all, avoid embarrassing the student. Acknowledge the existence of the problem immediately, and let the student know that you will deal with the problem privately. Give the student the opportunity to say why the problem arose. Elicit alternate ways of resolving the problem. I will suggest ways of resolving the problem if the student is unable to do so.

When students are provided with these kinds of experiences, they view the teacher as a source of support, respect, understanding, and assistance. When you are viewed in this way by your students, they will no doubt genuinely attempt to assist you in developing a well-disciplined classroom environment.

GRAHAM B.
Junior High School Teacher

Your Insights

According to this teacher, what are the most important aspects of establishing standards of behaviour? How does this contribute to effective classroom management?

covert activities of Canadian spy Laura Secord. Come in, Christopher." Summaries can also be facilitated by asking students to create learning displays or to develop newspaper articles or schematic drawings indicating the key points in the lesson.

If student-centred summarizing is not possible, the teacher can provide the summary. In that case, frequent reviews should be provided in order to increase the chances that the information will be retained and to reinforce the concept that learning builds on previous learning. Frequent reviews also encourage students to synthesize the concepts from one lesson with information from another lesson.

Finally, tests can be used as summarizing tools. Going over a test after it has been completed provides students with feedback about the correctness or incorrectness of their responses. Such a review provides students who have made errors with an opportunity to correct those errors. It also acts as an additional presentation of important information from the unit.

Too often, our students perceive the academic tasks we present as a set of unrelated hoops to jump through. By summarizing material we can show them how what they are doing relates to what they have been doing in past lessons and what we hope to accomplish in upcoming class sessions.

Making Smooth Transitions

A great deal of classroom time is spent in transitions—that is, moving from one activity to the next. Consider a junior high or high school, where students change classes approximately every forty to fifty minutes. Packing up from one class, moving into the hall, meeting friends, talking, stopping at the locker, and moving into the next class where materials are retrieved, notebooks are opened, and pencils are readied are major transitions in themselves. Add to this any change of focus or topic that may occur during a period. In elementary schools, nearly 15 percent of classroom time is taken up with approximately thirty major transitions each day (Gump, 1967; Rosenshine, 1980). An important difference between master teachers and less-skilled classroom managers is the way in which they handle transitions (Arlin 1979; Doyle, 1984). Because students are not engaged in an academic task during transitions, the time is ripe for disruptive behaviour.

The physical arrangement of the classroom should enable students who need to retrieve or turn in materials at different times to do so without disturbing other students. In addition, a daily schedule can be posted for easy reference by the students, and any changes in the schedule can be discussed each morning (Evertson et al., 1994; Charles & Senter, 1995; Weinstein & Mignano, 1993). Scheduling is especially important in elementary classrooms. Having materials prepared in advance—including possibly an outline of the lesson for the next period—or a videotape or software package loaded and ready to switch on decreases the time that students spend in transition. A teacher who must spend time preparing materials during class is inviting the students in the classroom to move off task.

When you end one lesson, do not relinquish the students' attention until you have introduced or provided instructions for the following activity. The "packing-up syndrome" is common at all instructional levels. It is important to keep students focused through the end of one lesson and to give them on-task directions before packing up is permitted.

Another way of shortening transitions is to ask students to do certain management tasks. For example, if you can have a student take attendance, hand out papers, or collect materials, you will have more time to engage in other tasks in preparation for a lesson, thus reducing the transition time. If students perform administrative and logistical tasks, you will also have more time to monitor the classroom and attend to individual needs.

TRY THIS: Ask teachers who are recognized for their classroom management expertise to describe their techniques for moving the whole class from one activity to the next. How do they handle small group transitions? Transitions in individualized instruction? Transitions to labs or library sessions?

CONNECTION: Look at Figures 10.2 and 10.3. Do those classroom arrangements facilitate the efficient retrieval and distribution of materials? In which of those two arrangements would you expect that the teacher would have to play a more prominent role in distribution and collection of materials?

How Can Misbehaviour Be Addressed and the Learning Orientation Restored?

The instructional management skills discussed in this chapter are meant to keep students engaged in learning. If students are actively involved in learning activities, they are unlikely to disrupt learning by misbehaving. **Misbehaviour** is any behaviour, by one or more students, that violates classroom rules or interferes with learning activity in the classroom (Doyle, 1986, 1990). If a sound management plan is implemented and if instructional management is done well, then misbehaviour will be minimized. Even in the best managed classrooms, however, not all misbehaviour is prevented. How will you manage misbehaviour? The management techniques examined in this section are ways to respond to misbehaviour.

Jacob Kounin identified two skills that are key to the effective management of misbehaviour: *withitness* and *overlapping* (Kounin, 1970). Kounin coined the term *withitness* when the phrase "being with-it," meaning being alert or aware, was popular. "**Withitness** is knowing what is going on in every part of the classroom at every moment, in a way that is evident to students" (Charles & Senter, 1995, p. 135). Teachers who possess withitness skills have the ability to identify misbehaviour quickly and accurately. **Overlapping** is the ability to attend to two issues simultaneously. For example, suppose that two students in the back of the room are working together while the teacher is consulting with a group in the front of the room. Student A grabs a pencil from Student B's desk. Student B shouts out, "Hey, give me that back." A teacher who possesses overlapping skills might address the disruption with a quick glance at both students, making eye contact that sends the message, "That is inappropriate behaviour; get back on task." At the same time, the teacher continues addressing the question from the group with whom she is consulting.

Withitness and overlapping skills develop with experience and are more likely to exist in the classroom of a teacher who projects an image of being in charge (Charles & Senter, 1995). Reflect for a moment on the earlier discussion of classroom management as collaborative leadership. A teacher who has not established a learning-oriented environment, has not communicated respect for students, and is not perceived as credible by students will have a more difficult time resolving disruptions. As you consider the approaches to managing misbehaviour presented in the following sections, consider how a learning-oriented environment and being perceived as a collaborative leader contribute to the efficacy of these approaches.

A Self-Correctional Approach to Student Misbehaviour

Minimum uses of teacher power leave the student in control of rectifying behaviour. As the use of teacher power in handling misbehaviour escalates, the student has fewer options and, as we shall see, so does the teacher. The self-correctional approach described here maximizes student involvement in resolving conflict. The idea is to help students view their misbehaviour as a problem and to help students solve that problem for themselves.

This approach to handling misbehaviour was first developed by Thomas Gordon and is sometimes called the Teacher Effectiveness Training (TET) Model, after the title of the book Gordon wrote in which he presented his ideas (Gordon,

TRY THIS: Discuss with your classmates the distinction between prevention and reaction with regard to classroom management. How did you think about classroom management before you read this chapter and how do you think about it now?

POINT: The idea that teachers' use of power determines the amount of control that students can exercise supports the basic assumption that: *Classroom management is a shared concern.*

misbehaviour According to Doyle, any behaviour, by one or more students, that competes with or threatens learning activities.

withitness According to Kounin, the teacher's ability to observe all situations in the classroom and to deal effectively with misbehaviour.

overlapping A teacher's ability to deal with more than one issue at the same time.

What management and leadership models are available to the teacher for responding to this student misbehaviour? What might be the most effective way to restore this classroom to a learning-oriented environment?

1974, see also Gordon, 1988). There are two essential assumptions of the approach. First, student misbehaviour can be self-corrected, and second, misbehaviour is remedied best through authentic communication between teacher and student (Wolfgang, 1995). *Authentic communication* means that the teacher does not simply hear an utterance but also understands the message behind the utterance. Authentic communication can take several forms.

Imagine that a student has just screamed an obscenity in the middle of an exam. One way to deal with the misbehaviour is simply to look at the student. With the right kind of look, a teacher can communicate the message, "I am aware of what you said, but I trust that you can correct yourself. If you need some help, I'm here for you." That is a lot of meaning to put into a look, but if an authentic relationship has been established between the teacher and the student, looks can be very effective. If a look does not lead to a remedy, the student can be encouraged to verbalize his or her discomfort through gestures or a nondirective statement such as, "You must be having difficulty with this exam." The statement acknowledges that some emotion underlies the misbehaviour and invites the student to talk about those feelings. The next step is to issue a direct invitation to discuss the misbehaviour. According to Gordon, if the student accepts an invitation to discuss the misbehaviour, you must take care to avoid offering advice or a solution for the student. Actively listening to the student in order to paraphrase and help the student pinpoint his or her feelings and to understand the reasons underlying the misbehaviour is key. The urge to take control of the problem and solve it for the student may be great, but if students are to learn how to correct their own behaviour problems, they must be given opportunities to do so.

Communicating with students goes beyond active listening. Teachers must be clear about why they perceive a student's action as misbehaviour. One way of achieving this clarity is to use I-messages. An **I-message** addresses the problem behaviour and its effects, expresses the teacher's feelings, but does not attack the self-concept of the misbehaving student (Ginott, 1972; Gordon, 1988). Consider as an example from Wolfgang (1995), "When students run down the stairs (behaviour), I am fearful (feelings) that people will fall and get injured (effect), and my job is to keep people safe" (p. 27). I-messages can be used to express feelings about situations that provoke strong emotions such as anger or frustration in a teacher. For example, a teacher may become angry with a student who talks during sustained silent reading, particularly at the end of a long, hard teaching day. Rather than directing this anger at the student personally, the teacher might say, "The class has established the rule that talking is forbidden during sustained silent reading (behaviour). We have another rule in this class that if you have something to say, at any time, you should raise your hand. Because talking during sustained silent reading interrupts important work (effect), and because it breaks the rules that we all worked on (effect), I get angry (feelings)."

TRY THIS: Observe classroom activities that require the teacher to move about the room to monitor small groups or individual work. Take particular note of the nonverbal communication that occurs. What happens when the teacher is in close proximity? How does the teacher make eye contact? Does the teacher use a special look?

I-message A clear statement by a teacher that tells how he or she feels about misbehaviour but that does not lay blame on a student.

The self-correcting approach recognizes that there are times in all classrooms when serious conflicts between student and teacher arise. One way to resolve conflicts is for the teacher to impose a resolution. This may be necessary in extreme instances where a student may be in danger of hurting someone or being hurt. In most situations, this is not the best way to approach conflict resolution. If the teacher uses his or her power to take control over the student's behaviour, the teacher is not demonstrating respect for the student's ability to self-correct and the student is seen as the loser in the conflict. A second way to resolve conflicts is for the teacher to give in to the student and abandon his or her view of the conflict. There may be times when a student argues so compellingly that the teacher should concede the argument and withdraw from further discussion. This should not become a pattern, however. If a teacher continually loses conflicts, students will have difficulty perceiving the teacher as credible. So, how can a teacher resolve a conflict with a student and at the same time maintain the attitudes of respect and credibility that support learning-oriented classrooms? This question is addressed by the "no-lose method" (Gordon, 1974, 1988).

CRITICAL THINKING: Think back to some of the characteristics of effective models discussed in Chapter 8. How might losing a conflict undermine a teacher's effectiveness?

Here's How

Here's How To Resolve Conflicts without Creating Losers

- Define the problem together. Identify the misbehaviour clearly, and then have each person explain what he or she wants out of the situation. Listening carefully to the other person is critical here.

- Brainstorm resolutions. Together, the participants generate as many resolutions to the conflict as possible. It is critical that ideas not be evaluated at this point. The purpose of this step is to collaborate on generating ideas—both good and bad.

- Evaluate each possible resolution. At this stage in the process, evaluate ideas for resolving the conflict. An important rule here is that any participant may veto any idea. If participants veto all ideas, the process reverts to brainstorming.

- Reach a decision. The participants choose one possible resolution by means of consensus. No votes are allowed. Everyone must be able to live with the decision reached.

- Plan and implement the decision. Reaching a decision is not the end of the process. In order to carry out the decision, ask questions such as: What will we need to resolve the conflict as we have decided? Who will be responsible for what? What is our time frame for implementing our decision?

- Evaluate the implementation. After following the plan for a period of time, reconvene the participants to find out if everyone is satisfied. Ask whether changes should be made in order to improve matters for everyone.

The Control Theory Approach to Misbehaviour

The basic assumption of the **control theory** approach is that students behave or misbehave in an attempt to control for themselves the satisfaction of their own

control theory The view that students need to be empowered to control to meet their own needs and thus experience success in school.

basic needs: survival, belonging, power, fun, and freedom (Glasser, 1986). There are three additional assumptions underlying control theory.

- Students feel pleasure when their needs are met and frustration when they are not.
- Because schools rarely empower students to meet their needs, students rarely work to their potential.
- Schools must create conditions that meet student needs. Teachers should provide encouragement, support, and help. This assumption implies that teachers do not blame, punish, or use coercive management strategies.

Glasser has described these assumptions and their implications in greater detail using the labels *quality schools* and *quality teachers* (1990, 1993). Glasser advocates control theory as a way of creating quality learning environments that allow students to meet their needs and thus experience the pleasure of success. If students can satisfy their needs in a classroom, they experience no frustration and do not misbehave. Even so, he recognizes that his approach will not eliminate all misbehaviour. From Glasser's point of view, misbehaviour occurs when one of two essential rules is broken. Those rules are: Be kind to others and Do your best work (Glasser, 1990; see also Charles & Senter, 1995). If one of these rules is broken, then a problem exists and the teacher's responsibility is to collaborate with students to solve that problem.

Suppose that two students are caught pushing each other in the hall. Following Glasser's approach, the teacher intervenes in a calm, unemotional manner. It is important to avoid fuelling what is already an emotionally charged situation with comments that would put students on the defensive. The teacher might say, "I see there is a problem here. How can I help?" The students will likely start blaming one another, at which point the teacher might say, "I want both of you to calm down. I'm not interested in punishing either of you, I want to help work out whatever the problem is. When you have had a chance to calm down, we will try to solve the problem." Later, after the students are less emotional, the teacher calls them together and says, "What you two were doing is against our rules. Now, what can we do to ensure that this doesn't happen again?" The teacher keeps the focus on a problem that caused the misbehaviour, not on determining who is at fault. Once students are engaged with the teacher in a discussion of the problem that caused the misbehaviour, the no-lose method of conflict resolution discussed in the previous section might be profitably employed.

CRITICAL THINKING: How would implementing the no-lose method in the context of control theory differ from its use as part of the self-correcting approach? Why is control theory viewed as utilizing more teacher power than the self-correcting approach?

The Applied Behaviour Analysis Approach to Misbehaviour

Applied behaviour analysis is the analysis of behaviour problems and the prescription of remedies based on behavioural learning principles, sometimes called behaviour modification (Alberto & Troutman, 1990; Madsen & Madsen, 1981). The approach is based on operant-conditioning principles examined in Chapter 6. From an applied behaviour analysis perspective, misbehaviour is behaviour that the teacher finds undesirable. The natural tendency is to respond to misbehaviour by simply telling the student to stop, which is not always effective. In the Teacher Chronicle at the beginning of the chapter, Ms. Briand learns that reprimands and other punishments do nothing to correct Sam's misbehaviour. What else can she do?

applied behaviour analysis
The analysis of behaviour problems and the prescription of remedies.

The Role of Rules. Rules play an important role in applied behaviour analysis approaches to misbehaviour. One technique, called *rules-ignore-praise* (RIP), works as follows: rules are established, misbehaviour is ignored, students who follow the rules are praised. No consequence for misbehaviour occurs, following Skinner's principle that positive reinforcement is the best way to bring about change in behaviour. The RIP technique has been found to work fairly well at the elementary school level, but not at the secondary school level (Charles, 1992).

A variation on the theme is called *rules-reward-punishment* (RRP). This technique introduces limits and aversive consequences absent from RIP. As in the case of the RIP, RRP starts with the establishment of rules and emphasizes positive reinforcement for students who follow the rules. However, RRP does not ignore misbehaviour. The rules that are established under the RRP approach include not only a statement of the rules but also a statement of the consequences for breaking those rules. Students are informed that they have a choice to make. They can choose to abide by the established rules or they can choose to receive the prescribed punishment. Presenting the contingency in this way means that the teacher does not punish misbehaviour, rather the students choose to punish themselves. Charles (1992) argues that the RRP approach is very effective with older students, especially if they have had a hand in establishing both the rules and the consequences of breaking the rules.

Token Economies. Because Skinner argued that positive reinforcement is a more powerful behaviour change technique than using aversive consequences, one way to deal with misbehaviour is to encourage desirable behaviour. Recall the discussion of token economy technique in Chapter 6, which proposes rewarding students with tokens for exhibiting desirable behaviours. The value of various desirable behaviours is determined in advance so that students know what the positive consequences of their appropriate behaviour will be. In addition to earning tokens, students are given access to tangible goods that they may buy with their tokens. Prizes might include stickers, pencils, some forms of food, a book, magazine, drawing paper, crayons, or other objects that students in the class find desirable. It is important for teachers who use token economies to take care in keeping records so that tokens are distributed fairly and consistently. Using this approach also means that class time must be set aside for shopping (Martin & Pear, 1992).

Tokens can also be used to purchase activities. A student who earns a sufficient number of tokens may purchase, for example, free time on the computer to play games. During shopping time, the teacher can issue a voucher for such activities. In essence, a token economy that sells activities is an application of the Premack principle described in Chapter 6. Students engage in task behaviours (presumably of low probability) that will eventually be rewarded with an opportunity to engage in purchased behaviours (presumably of higher probability).

Charles (1992) suggests that any teacher who chooses to implement a token economy explain clearly and completely to the principal, to parents, and to students how the token economy will work before implementing it. It is necessary to use this approach to minimize misbehaviour. Nothing is quite so disruptive as a token economy gone awry. Token economies have been used successfully in a variety of classroom situations at all grade levels, including classrooms that have students with disabilities.

Token economies delay the delivery of primary reinforcement following a desirable student behaviour by using secondary reinforcement (tokens) as an immediate consequence of behaviour. The effect is to lengthen, sometimes considerably, the time between the appropriate behavioural response and primary reinforcement. If we can instill in our students an ability to delay gratification for

CRITICAL THINKING: Why has the RIP technique been found to be more effective at the elementary level than at the secondary level?

TRY THIS: Visit a classroom in which a token economy is operating. Based on your observations, address the following questions: Does the token economy work well? What criteria would you develop to judge the effectiveness of token economies? Do these criteria focus on learning outcomes?

Insights on Successful Practice

What approaches to dealing with discipline problems have worked best for you and your students?

Because we deal with diverse personalities on a daily basis, we will be confronted with behaviour problems from time to time. There are infinite reasons why behaviour problems occur in a classroom. Generally, however, students need attention and want to be recognized. If this is the case, I capitalize on the students' individual interests which may or may not be directly related to their academic work. I have often used such information to provide the individual students a forum for "strutting their stuff."

For example, I learned that one of my "problem students" (Calvin) was an avid archer. Gradually, I introduced him to a number of books on archery. He read them voraciously and started bringing to class a variety of magazines and history books dealing with archery. During a social studies lesson, I used a segment from the film "Robin Hood" to illustrate the leadership qualities of the major character. One of these qualities was his skill as an archer. Calvin was asked to comment on the kind and quality of the bows and arrows used by the characters as well as on the techniques used by them. Because he had time to view the segments ahead of time and prepare himself for the task, Calvin performed marvelously. Students asked many questions and he sensed that he was teaching them something. Needless to say Calvin's behaviour became more positive. He was then encouraged to present a brief history of the development of the primitive bow and arrow to the modern cross-bow. Again, he excelled in this activity, because he was able to draw on personal experiences based on the stories told to him about hunting and trapping by his grandfather and other elders of the First Nations community in which he lived and attended school.

To continue the behaviour modification process, I discussed with the mathematics teacher the possibility of dealing with math concepts relating to velocity, trajectory, and angles. In that class, Calvin became the leader of one of the small groups, and assisted the teacher in preparing diagrams for use in the class. His self-esteem improved dramatically because of his successful achievements and my "problem student" became a model student. He was instrumental in organizing an archery club which is still attracting keen interest and his grandfather continues to be a valuable resource person in this endeavour. Calvin's new-found enthusiasm and interests were transferred to other school subjects and other classes.

If we want to influence our students positively, we must recognize the worth of every one of them and, above all, we must recognize the need of all students to succeed at what they do. Furthermore, we must provide the opportunities for all students to experience success as often as they can.

DELBERT W.
Junior High School Teacher

> ### Your Insights
> What strategies does this teacher use to change the behaviour of "problem students?" What is the value of encouraging students to "strut their stuff?"

their efforts, we are providing them with an opportunity to learn that sustained effort can bring rewards.

Contingency Contracting. Contingency contracting, which involves drawing up a contract between the teacher and the student, is an applied behaviour analysis technique that can be used to encourage desirable behaviour and discourage misbehaviour. A contract should include terms or conditions under which appropriate behaviours will be displayed or will define the limits on misbehaviour. For example, a teacher might use a contract to increase the amount of seat-work the student completes and, simultaneously, decrease the student's out-of-seat behaviour. In this case, the contract should specify how much out-of-seat behaviour the teacher will tolerate and under what conditions he or she will allow it, as well as the amount of seat-work students must complete. Contracts have been quite successful across grade levels; they can also be helpful with younger children. Many teachers who employ this technique use the contract itself to introduce variety into the learning situation. Figures 10.4 and 10.5 provide examples of contingency contracts.

Considerable research has been amassed to demonstrate the effectiveness of behaviour change programs. However, this approach has not gone without criticism. Before deciding to implement a behavioural program in your classroom, you may wish to consider the argument by Kohn (1996) that the use of rewards and punishments by the teacher to manipulate student behaviour carries damaging side-effects. Kohn's objections to punishment-reward systems are well expressed in this quote:

> "Like punishments, rewards warp the relationship between adult and child. With punishments, we come to be seen as enforcers to be avoided; with rewards, as goody dispensers on legs. In neither case have we established a caring alliance, a connection based on warmth and respect. Like punishments, rewards try to make bad behaviours disappear through manipulation. They are ways of doing things *to* students instead of working *with* them" (p.36).

The Assertive Discipline Approach to Misbehaviour

The approach to discipline called **assertive discipline**, developed by Lee Canter and Marlene Canter, makes use of several of the principles of applied behaviour analysis, including the establishment of rules and consequences prior to the implementation of disciplinary actions (Canter & Canter, 1976, 1992, 1993). In addition to the establishment of rules, assertive discipline emphasizes that teachers follow through with consequences and that the consequences be delivered fairly and consistently.

REFLECTION: Imagine a class in which you sign a contract. How might signing the contract make you feel? How might it influence your motivation? How might you feel about not fulfilling your contract?

assertive discipline An approach to misbehaviour based on principles of applied behaviour analysis.

I'm Leaping in to Say

If: I can play four square
without getting in a
fight at recess

Then: I can play with
the gerbil for
ten minutes

| Date | My Name | Teacher's Name | My Friend's Name Who Will Help Me |

FIGURE 10.4
A Behaviour Contract for an Elementary Student

Source: Comprehensive Classroom Management: Motivating and Managing Students (3rd ed., p. 369), V. F. Jones and L. S. Jones, 1990, Needham Heights, MA: Allyn & Bacon. Copyright 1990 by Allyn & Bacon. Adapted by permission.

Name of Student: Suzy Jones   Grade: 9th   Date: _____

School: _____   Contract Monitor*: Mrs Smith

Reason for Contract: Demonstrates difficulty controlling anger with regard to peer
                     interaction

Student Expectations for Responsible Behaviour

1. Follow all classroom and school rules.
2. Expectations requiring additional instructions and clarification:
   A. When angry, Suzy is expected to remain in control by making responsible choices to handle
      her anger. This applies in the classroom so students can continue working and applies to
      unstructured time outside the classroom.

Student Choices

Responsible choices
(ways to meet expectations)

A. Ignore situation
B. Remove self from situation
C. Ask for five minutes time out at desk
D. Do deep breathing or relaxation
   exercises at desk
E. Write down feelings until I can talk the
   situation over with teacher or counsellor

Irresponsible choices
(choosing negative consequences)

A. Not doing work
B. Refusing to continue working
C. Distracting classmates from work
D. Yelling at peers or teachers
E. Running away
F. Fighting

Student Consequences

Consequences for Responsible Behaviour at School

A. Stay in class
B. Be with friends
C. Learn new things
D. Have a boyfriend
E. Feel good about my ability to control
   my anger

At Home:

If Suzy chooses to control her anger all
week at school, she will earn an extra half-
hour on the weekend to have private time
with mother.

Consequences for Irresponsible Behaviour

A. If the behaviour occurs, Suzy will go to
   the office and fill out a Problem-Solving
   Worksheet; she must be able to control
   herself prior to returning to class.
B. If the behaviour occurs during unstructured
   time, she will be expected to sit on the
   curb until end of free time and then will
   be expected to go to the office to fill out
   Problem-Solving Sheet.

Contract Monitor Agrees to:

1. Consistently apply stated consequences for both responsible and irresponsible behaviour.
2. Regularly review contract with student every three weeks.
3. Review contract at staffings as appropriate.

Contract Termination Criteria:

Contract will be terminated when student consistently makes responsible choices to deal
with her anger for a three-week period.

Student Signature: _____   Date: _____

Contract Monitor Signature: _____   Date: _____

Parent Signature: _____   Date: _____

*Staff member responsible for contract development, application, and review.

FIGURE 10.5
A Behaviour Contract that Emphasizes Student Responsibility

Source: Comprehensive Classroom Management: Motivating and Managing Students (3rd ed., pp.
381–382) V. F. Jones and L. S. Jones, 1990, Needham Heights, MA: Allyn & Bacon. Copyright 1990
by Allyn & Bacon. Reprinted by permission.

A communication that is characteristic of assertive discipline is a clear and succinct statement that identifies the problem and suggests a way of remedying it. Charles (1981) provides three examples of responses to fighting in the classroom. Of the three, the last is characteristic of the assertive approach.

- Nonassertive: "Please try your very best to stop fighting."
- Hostile: "You are acting like a disgusting savage again!"
- Assertive: "We do not fight. Sit down until you cool off so we can talk about it."

Examining the three responses, you can see that the first expresses some dissatisfaction on the part of the teacher, but the response does not help assert the authority of the teacher or suggest a remedy to the situation. Nor is it delivered in terms that are likely to influence the behaviour of students who are engaged in fighting. The hostile response is aggressive, but not assertive; it crosses the boundary of the situation and attacks personality. The third response, an example of assertive discipline, provides a clear message about what the problem is and a clear message about how the problem will be solved.

Imagine that a student talks out during sustained silent reading. Let's see how an assertive discipline approach might be used to respond verbally to the disruption.

The teacher, on hearing the talking out, says, "Marsha, our rules do not tolerate talking out during sustained silent reading. You must not talk out again."

Marsha says, "But I need something."

The teacher responds, "That may be the case, but talking out during sustained silent reading is against the rules. If you have something to say, raise your hand and I will come to you."

"But, but, George is bothering me."

"If it happens again, raise your hand and I will come over. I'll keep an eye on things, but you may not talk out during sustained silent reading."

In this exchange, the teacher asserts the rule that is being broken and follows through by continuing to assert the rule. By reminding the student that she may speak to the teacher after raising her hand, the teacher also provides a remedy to the problem. To summarize, using the assertive discipline approach means that teachers make promises, not threats.

How Can Your Knowledge of Classroom Management Help You Become an Effective Teacher?

Perhaps the most important lesson to learn from the theories and research on classroom management is that it is a process inextricably connected to student learning. The problems that arise from poor classroom management and the benefits that accrue from sound management cannot be isolated from learning. If a teacher manages a classroom poorly, student learning will suffer. Conversely, teachers who do not value learning will experience management problems. Learning is not only an effect of sound management but also a cause. If learning is truly occurring for every student in a classroom, that classroom will be easy to manage.

A second lesson teachers can take from what educational psychologists have learned about classroom management is that communication is a key element in learning-oriented classrooms. Our actions as teachers, and not just

EXAMPLE: The assertive discipline approach enjoys considerable popularity in certain schools. It does, however, have its critics. This approach is an example of a package solution to problems. There are useful ideas in this package, but one should always be wary of assuming that any one technique will work with all students or in all situations.

POINT: Recall the point discussed in Chapter 1: *Teaching and learning are aspects of the same process.*

our words, send messages to our students. Our actions tell our students that we do or do not value learning and value their input or are not concerned about their problems. Without saying a word about it, we tell our students whether we see them as subordinates or partners. Our students send messages to us as well. Their behaviours and misbehaviours are signals that they are learning successfully or that they are not. If we can understand them as individuals, their behaviour can reveal their needs to us and we can then respond to those needs.

A final lesson to learn is that classroom management teaches our students a great deal about themselves. The way we interact with our students allows them to infer how capable they are of making decisions, of taking responsibility, and of contributing to the community of the classroom. Although sound management serves as a foundation for instruction in math, reading, science, and other academic areas, it also instructs directly. And what it teaches directly is important.

In this last section of the chapter, we focus on what our classroom management practices teach our students and on what we, as teachers, can learn through our practices.

Teaching Self-Responsibility

REFLECTION: How many opportunities were you afforded in your classrooms to take responsibility for your own learning and behaviour? How might such opportunities have been structured in those classrooms? How do you think you would have responded to those opportunities?

One of the clear findings from the research examined in this chapter is that management practices contribute significantly to the nature of the learning environment. Depending on a teacher's approach—and the underlying values reflected by that approach—a classroom can afford students a variety of opportunities. Recent work in the general area of motivation and, more specifically, volition, suggests that a critical ingredient in realizing personal goals is environmental affordance. **Affordances** are the opportunities offered a person by his or her environment (Corno, 1995; Snow, Corno, & Jackson, 1995). In some classroom environments, students are afforded opportunities to take responsibility for their own behaviour and learning.

A sense of self-responsibility means establishing goals for oneself and then finding ways to achieve those goals. A sense of self-responsibility is arguably one of the most important learning outcomes that we can help our students attain. And motivation and volition play a significant role in its development. Motivation is connected to volition by means of a "commitment pathway" (Heckhausen & Kuhl, 1985). Corno (1995) explains that pathway as follows:

> Motivation establishes goals, while volition implements them. Motivation promotes goals, while volition protects them. Motivation involves individual thinking about goals; while volition involves the initiation of processes for accomplishing goals. Motivation embraces foresight, while volition embraces follow-through. ... Both motivation and volition are important psychological components involved in getting... "what you want" (p. 3).

This theoretical account of motivation and volition suggests that if we want our students to develop self-responsibility, we need to afford them opportunities to establish their goals and then follow through on them. But how do we afford them appropriate opportunities? Part of the answer is to establish learning-oriented as opposed to work-oriented classroom environments. Here's How outlines the steps suggested by British Columbia educator Maurice Gibbons (1991) to assist students in self-directed learning.

affordances Opportunities offered a person by his or her environment.

Here's How To Develop a Sense of Self-Responsibility and Self-Direction in Your Students

- Each student begins by deciding on a goal they would like to accomplish and writing that goal down clearly.
- The following responsibilities are then set up as a learning contract in worksheet format:
  - decide on a challenge project and products
  - outline the activities needed to achieve the learning goal and products
  - arrange the activities into a time line that shows what will be done when
  - identify the support person(s) needed to help with the project
  - identify the audience to whom the product(s) will be presented
  - decide how to evaluate the success of the project
  - decide how to celebrate the successful completion of the project
  - negotiate the plan with a parent, teacher, and support person. Have them sign to show that all parties agree to the plan.

Accommodating Cultural Diversity and Special Needs

The values that teachers have are reflected in the ways they manage instruction and the ways they respond to misbehaviour. As you learned in Chapter 4, the values students bring to the classroom are at least partially determined by their cultural backgrounds. You also learned that conflicts between value systems can cause problems for both students and teachers. This is especially true when the expectations for classroom behaviour are based on cultural norms that are not shared by teacher and students. Consider, for example, two differences between Anglo-Canadian culture and Native culture. First, Anglo-Canadian youth often tend to demonstrate that they are listening by making direct eye contact. Native youth avoid making direct eye contact (Baruth & Manning, 1992). Second, Anglo-Canadians are accustomed to having rules for almost every possible situation; most Native youth expect few rules (Baruth & Manning, 1992). Now suppose that a teacher has established a classroom rule that says, "Listen while others are speaking." Suppose also that the teacher, because he or she has internalized Anglo-Canadian cultural norms, expects students to follow the rule and to demonstrate their compliance by making eye contact. If a Native student follows his or her own cultural norms, the teacher is likely to interpret the student's behaviour as breaking a rule.

Consider another rule that is commonly used in classrooms, "Respect other people." One's interpretation of what it means is likely to be influenced by one's cultural background. Many Canadian youth of Native, African, and Asian ancestry and other racial, ethnic, and religious groupings have encountered either overt or implied racism. White Anglo-Canadian youth are much less likely to have faced such attitudes. If these minority students have been sensitized by their experience to comments that, by tone or inference, are insulting, then they may feel disrespected by comments thought by others to be perfectly innocent. Given the importance of clear communication in effective classroom management,

CONNECTION: Mismatches of expectations because of differences in cultural norms are discussed in Chapter 4 and throughout this book.

teachers and students must take care to learn about one another's cultural norms and the behavioural expectations they carry.

Many children with special learning needs are also vulnerable to the development of behavioural problems. Imagine having to sit through a series of lectures delivered in an unknown foreign language, day after day, and then being examined on your comprehension of the material. You likely would respond either with total passivity (withdrawal or quitting) or by engaging in antisocial or disruptive behaviours such as cheating, clowning, and/or bullying. Managing such resulting behaviours is not likely to be successful because the "lecture is still being delivered in a foreign language." Modification of the factors that underlie such compensatory behaviours is more likely to lead to positive outcomes. For example, the behaviour of children with Attention Deficit/Hyperactivity Disorder (AD/HD) can significantly disrupt the instructional activities of a classroom. However, with judicious environmental and curricular changes, this disruptive behaviour may be effectively managed. Suggestions include compensating for the lack of internal structure by providing a good deal of external structure (make lists, give reminders, provide repetition, direction, and limits); ensuring that the child is attending (or hearing) by repeating directions and making frequent eye contact; seating the AD/HD child near the teacher's desk or wherever the teacher is most likely to be; and preparing the child for transitions. Attending to reinforcement schedules is particularly important for AD/HD children, as studies have shown they exhibit unique responses to reinforcers. They require more salient reinforcers that are delivered more frequently. Moreover, positive reinforcement, alone, is rarely effective in maintaining appropriate levels of academic and social behaviour among children with AD/HD. Levying mild penalties following inappropriate behaviour has been shown to be effective in promoting consistent behavioural change (DuPaul & Stoner, 1994).

The nature and extent of modifications required for children with other exceptionalities will need to be determined on an individual basis. For teachers, imparting knowledge and skills to exceptional children will require sensitivity to a range of environmental and personal factors.

Teaching Ourselves to Share the Power

The approaches to managing misbehaviour, discussed earlier in the chapter, were presented in a sequence that represents movement along a continuum. The continuum ranges from minimum use of teacher power, such as self-correctional approaches, to maximum use of teacher power, such as assertive discipline. **Teacher power** can be thought of as the extent to which students are given autonomy and control to change their behaviour. There is an inverse relationship between teacher power and student control. If a teacher exerts very little power, students are enabled to exert a great deal of control. If, however, a teacher decides that he or she will exercise maximum power to bring about a change in student behaviour, the student has very little control. The continuum also represents a framework for organizing approaches to managing misbehaviour called *three faces of discipline* (Wolfgang, 1995; Wolfgang & Wolfgang, 1995). The three faces are

- Relationship-Listening
- Confronting-Contracting
- Rules and Consequences

TRY THIS: Interview teachers to investigate the extent to which they exercise their power to control student behaviour. Ask them to describe the techniques they use to address misbehaviour. How does the information you gather relate to information in this chapter?

teacher power The authority that teachers have available to them to manage student behaviour; inversely, the extent to which students control their own behaviour.

The relationship-listening face represents those approaches to managing misbehaviour that employ minimum teacher power (e.g., Kohn, 1996). The focus of such approaches is on establishing a positive relationship with students and listening actively in an attempt to understand the problem that caused the behaviour. The techniques employed by teachers using a relationship-listening approach are typically eye contact and nondirective statements. The self-correcting approach to misbehaviour examined earlier is an exemplar of the relationship-listening face.

The confronting-contracting face represents those approaches to misbehaviour that require a teacher to exert a moderate amount of power. Moving from a relationship-listening approach to a confronting-contracting approach can be viewed as escalating teacher intervention. According to Wolfgang, the teacher who uses a confronting-contracting approach is saying, in effect, "I am the adult. I know misbehaviour when I see it and will confront the student to stop the behaviour. I will grant the student the power to decide how he or she will change, and encourage and contract with the student to live up to a mutual agreement for behavioural change" (Wolfgang, 1995, p. 6). Questioning is a typical form of intervention in confronting-contracting approaches. Glasser's control theory is an exemplar of this face.

The applied behaviour analysis and the assertive discipline approaches examined earlier represent another escalation of teacher power into the category of rules and consequences. A teacher who uses these types of approach to misbehaviour leaves the student very little control over changing his or her behaviour. The teacher's position here is that, "There are rules and behaviours that I desire to see exhibited by students. I will assert my authority and control contingencies in order to bring those behaviours about." Typical interventions in this category include directive statements, altering the environment (as in the case of delivering reinforcements), and demonstrating desired behaviours.

If we use this continuum of teacher power to place (1) the metaphors of management, (2) learning styles, and (3) value orientation in that order, we arrive at a consistent and powerful conclusion. Figure 10.6 shows this continuum.

Recalling the research examined in this chapter, teachers who personify the facilitator metaphor have been found to be more effective classroom managers than teachers who view themselves as boss. Collaborative leaders are better classroom managers than authoritarian leaders. Learning-oriented classrooms are better managed than work-oriented classrooms. And the bottom line is that better managed classrooms produce more student learning.

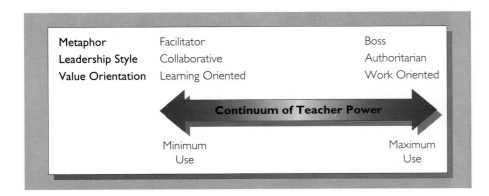

FIGURE 10.6
Metaphors of Management, Leadership Styles, and Value Orientations Placed on a Continuum of Use of Teacher Power

Teacher Chronicle Conclusion

And Then There's Sam

Meeting with Warren, the resource teacher, has led Ms. Briand to some new insights in working with Sam. On the weekend, she looks over the list of positives and negatives that they constructed together. She wants to make a plan that encourages Sam to take control of his own behaviour and, at the same time, makes limited demands on the individual time it will take for the plan to be effective. She also wants the plan to be encouraging and supportive of Sam's learning.

Ms. Briand thinks, I know Sam loves to use the class computer. I could use time on the computer as a reward that he earns for positive classroom behaviour. The behaviour we need to work on first is the hitting and shoving. We don't want anyone to get hurt, and eliminating this behaviour should result in changes in other areas, such as completing work on time. I could make up a self-monitoring check sheet for Sam. I could divide each period into ten-minute time blocks, and have Sam put a check on the sheet for each time period that he does not push others. Then if he gets, say, ten check marks in a row to start with, he could trade that in for ten minutes of computer time. I could have him using instructional software games during his earned computer time. He should find that rewarding, and it would help to reinforce his academic skills, too.

On Monday, Ms. Briand is ready to put the plan into action. She spends some time explaining to Sam that they will be working together to help him stop pushing others, and that his job will be to keep track of this and to put check marks on the sheet. Sam seems enthused at the possibility of earning computer time and willing to follow the plan.

The first day on the plan did not produce a magical transformation of Sam's behaviour. By the end of the day there had been some shoving, and he only earned ten minutes on the computer. But by Friday, Sam had earned the maximum of 30 computer minutes. Incidents of shoving had gone down dramatically, and Sam even seemed to be happier at school.

Ms. Briand thinks, Great! This is working. Time to review the behaviour list and revise the check sheet. I'm so glad for Sam.

Application Questions

1. Why was Ms. Briand's plan for Sam successful? Would a plan like this work for a middle years or high school student? Why or why not?

2. What are the advantages and disadvantages of having Sam keep track of his own behaviour? What could go wrong with this approach? What would you do to find out if this approach is working properly? What would you do if the self-management approach does not work?

3. How could Ms. Briand have involved the other students in the class as part of the behaviour management plan she made for Sam? What advantages and disadvantages could result from involving the other students?

4. Where would you place Ms. Briand on the continuum of use of teacher power? What are her values? What is her metaphor of classroom management? What is her leadership style?

5. Considering the approaches to behaviour management outlined in this chapter, what are some other ways Ms. Briand could have dealt with Sam's behaviour?

CHAPTER SUMMARY

What Is Classroom Management and Leadership? (L.O. 1, 2, 3, p. 307)

Research has shown that the way teachers think about classroom management influences their management practices. Various metaphors of management are discussed along with their implications. Management is viewed as a process whose product is discipline. Management and discipline are related to another product-process pair, instruction and learning. Effective classroom managers are collaborative leaders.

How Can You Create a Learning-Oriented Environment? (L.O. 4, p. 315)

A learning-oriented classroom is one in which assignments and other instructional activities are viewed as a means to learning outcomes, not outcomes in their own right. The contributions of the physical arrangement of the classroom and classroom rules and procedures to a positive, learning-oriented learning environment are described.

How Can Instruction Be Managed to Support a Learning-Oriented Environment? (L.O. 5, p. 323)

Instructional management skills enable a teacher to keep students focused and actively involved in learning tasks. These skills include giving clear instructions, gaining attention, maintaining attention, pacing, summarizing, and making smooth transitions.

How Can Misbehaviour Be Addressed and the Learning Orientation Restored? (L.O. 6, 7, p. 331)

Misbehaviour is behaviour by one or more students that disrupts or competes with the primary activity of learning. Several approaches for addressing misbehaviour are presented. The approaches differ in terms of the amount of teacher intervention or the use of teacher power required by each approach. Self-correctional and control approaches use less teacher power than applied behaviour analysis approaches.

How Can Your Knowledge of Classroom Management Help You Become an Effective Teacher? (L.O. 8, p. 339)

The theories and research on classroom management are interpreted in light of teaching students self-responsibility. The cultural norms of various groups influence the nature of communication and interaction. These potential differences need to be accounted for so that rules and consequences will be understood clearly and applied fairly. Ideas for managing an urban classroom are discussed. The chapter ends by analyzing the continuum of teacher power in relation to management metaphors, value orientations, and leadership style.

KEY CONCEPTS

action zones, p. 317

affordances, p. 340

applied behaviour analysis, p. 334

assertive discipline, p. 337

authoritative leadership, p. 314

classroom management, p. 311

collaborative leadership, p. 314

control theory, p. 333

discipline, p. 311

I-message, p. 332

instruction, p. 312

learning community, p. 315

learning-oriented classrooms, p. 309

misbehaviour, p. 331

on-task behaviour, p. 324

overlapping, p. 331

procedures, p. 319

rules, p. 319

teacher power, p. 342

withitness, p. 331

work-oriented classrooms, p. 309

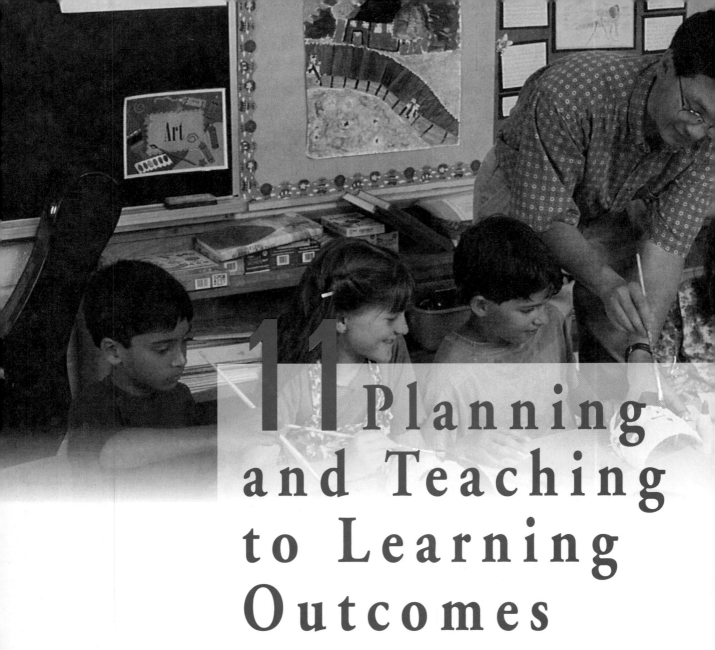

11 Planning and Teaching to Learning Outcomes

LEARNING OUTCOMES

When you have completed this chapter, you will be able to

1. describe learning outcome frameworks according to Gagné, Bloom, Krathwohl, and Harrow

2. write instructional goals for a unit or lesson

3. write performance objectives for a unit or lesson

4. explain how the events of instruction relate to the learning process

5. describe and compare discovery and reception learning

6. explain the concept of transfer of learning

7. list the stages of a model for developing effective instruction

8. write the format for an instructional or lesson plan

Teacher Chronicle

Giving Something Back

Angela Broski has been a middle years teacher for nine years. Her present assignment is a grade eight class of twenty-six students at an urban Regina school. This year is the first that she has volunteered to supervise a student intern from the local college of education. Her principal, Bob Karle, has urged her to take on the mentoring of a student teacher for the twelve-week internship this year. He told her that she is a master teacher with a strong reputation among colleagues and parents, and is well liked by her students. Angela had some misgivings at first—"Surely there are other teachers better prepared than I am to give these students the kind of experience they need." But Mr. Karle's words had reassured her, and she decided "Why not? It's time to give something back to my profession."

During the third week of September, Angela attended the internship workshops conducted at the college to orient both supervising teacher and intern to the practicum experience. Here she met her intern, Jason Michaels, and they both learned what was expected of them as a newly formed team. Angela's task was to serve as a mentor to Jason's progressive growth as a beginning teacher. This would mean modelling many aspects of planning and teaching, assisting Jason to reflect on these practices, providing Jason with strategic opportunities to take on lesson planning and instruction, and continuously expanding these experiences over the internship period. In particular, his in-depth project was to develop and teach an integrated, thematic unit planned jointly with Angela.

It is Monday afternoon at 4:30. Angela sits at her desk reflecting on the two weeks that Jason has spent in her classroom. "He certainly lacked confidence the first week," she thought. "But that is beginning to change. I notice that he has picked up on my classroom management routines. Particularly, he is making sure he has all the students' attention before he gives instructions, and that has made his mini-lessons much more effective. He still needs to work on his questioning skills and the detail of his explanations when modelling skills and strategies for the students. But, even more importantly, I need to provide him with more responsibility in designing sequences of lessons. The basic framework provided by the college is fine, but it is crucial that he starts to get a feeling for the variety of skill levels in this class. He needs to begin to see how one lesson relates to another, and how to sequence skills across the lessons."

"Yikes, I'm beginning to remember my feelings as a beginning teacher . . . 'this is so complicated, there are so many things to think of at once. It's really hard to figure out what level all these students are at, and what they need next.' How did my wonderful supervising teacher, Sandy Black, see me through this crisis? Hmmm, oh, yes! She asked me to think of something that I was good at, would enjoy teaching, and the students would enjoy learning. We did a unit on knitting and sewing. But so many lessons in so many curriculum areas came out of it. All the students had fun and learned a lot. And so did I. This experience really cemented my decision to be a teacher. Thanks, Sandy. Now I know what to say to Jason at our planning meeting tomorrow afternoon."

Next day Angela said to Jason, "I've been thinking. I believe it's time for you to start work on the thematic unit you need to complete this term."

"I know you're right, I've been worrying about that," said Jason. "But I feel so overwhelmed at managing the lessons I'm teaching now, I don't think I can do it. Where do I begin?"

"Jason, just think of something you are interested in and good at; something you think you would enjoy teaching, and that the students would enjoy learning," said Angela. "Put some thought into it and let's begin serious planning on Thursday at our regular meeting".

Jason came to the Thursday meeting sporting a big grin. "I've thought about it, and I know just what kind of unit to work on. When I was younger, I had a big interest in insects. I still do. In fact, I dug out all the materials left over from my old ant colony. I've been thinking of how I could develop lessons in science, language arts, math, and social studies. What do you think?"

"Sounds exciting to me," said Angela with a smile.

Focus Questions

1. What are some of Angela's motives as a mentor to Jason?
2. What are the first steps that Jason will need to take in planning this thematic unit?
3. How can Jason ensure that a range of curriculum goals are included in his unit?
4. What kinds of lessons and activities could be developed in the unit?
5. How can Jason accommodate a range of student interests and abilities?
6. How can Angela best provide Jason with just the right amount of support and guidance in implementing his thematic unit?

What Are Possible Outcomes of Learning?

What are students supposed to learn in school? What *can* they learn? How do teachers determine and specify what their students ought to learn in their classes? These questions concern learning outcomes that teachers use as a basis for planning their instruction. In making decisions about what students should learn, teachers consider the knowledge, skills, and attitudes that can be acquired in a given subject area.

Instructional theorists have found it useful to distinguish among the variety of things people can learn (Driscoll, 1994). In doing this, they make a fundamental assumption that learning proceeds differently depending on what outcome or capability students are acquiring. For example, learning how to throw a softball underhand requires very different instruction from learning how to spell. Likewise, learning to appreciate jazz requires different learning conditions from learning to recite one's part in a school play.

There are different ways to characterize what students can learn, but the result is usually a *taxonomy*, or classification system, of learning outcomes.

Gagné's Taxonomy of Learning Outcomes

TRY THIS: Examine textbooks and accompanying teachers' materials in the content areas you plan to teach, and identify prescribed learning outcomes. Which categories of Gagné's taxonomy do they exemplify?

Robert M. Gagné viewed learning as accounting for all of the attitudes, values, skills, and knowledge acquired by human beings. When people learn, they become capable of a variety of performances (Gagné, 1977, 1985; Gagné & Driscoll, 1988; Driscoll, 1994). According to Gagné, there are five types of learned capabilities or **learning outcomes**:

1. Verbal information
2. Intellectual skills
3. Cognitive strategies
4. Attitudes
5. Motor skills

learning outcomes
According to Gagné, capabilities acquired by students resulting from the interaction of internal and external conditions of learning.

Although we examine each type of learning outcome separately, it is important to keep in mind that most instructional goals include several types of outcomes. It is also important to note that these types of learning outcomes not be thought of as discrete, or separate, from one another. Certainly, they overlap and interact.

Verbal Information. **Verbal information** is one capability that makes communication possible. When a student states that W.O. Mitchell wrote *Who Has Seen the Wind*, he or she is declaring some knowledge. The declaration provides evidence that the student has acquired some verbal information. Being able to make declarations about the environment enables us to communicate. For example, a young child begins asking questions about his or her environment in order to communicate about the environment. The endless chain of questions that parents often hear is the child's search for verbal information.

"What's that, Daddy?"
"A tree."
"Mommy, what's that?"
"A car."
"What's that?"
"An airplane."
"What's that?"
"A giraffe."

Acquiring verbal information enables the child to communicate. Gagné and Driscoll (1988) identified names, facts, principles, and generalizations as units of verbal information. Just because a student is able to make a particular statement of fact, however, does not mean that he or she fully understands the implications of the statement. For example, because students can state the Pythagorean theorem does not mean they can use it to solve problems involving right-angle triangles.

By its nature, the learning outcome that we call verbal information allows us to make statements. The acquisition of verbal information serves other functions for the learner as well. One function of verbal information is that it provides labels that allow us to operate in everyday situations. Preschool students are often quizzed on their home addresses and on emergency phone numbers. Children might be taught that they should wait by an elevator if they become lost while shopping with their parents. In Great Britain, a child would be advised to wait next to the lift. The terms are different, but they both serve the function of labels.

Verbal information also serves as a basis for thinking or as a vehicle for thought (Gagné & Driscoll, 1988). For example, because a mechanic possesses verbal information about car engines, he or she is able to hypothesize about the causes of various engine problems. The ability to hypothesize is evidence of another kind of learning outcome, intellectual skill.

Intellectual Skills. Whereas verbal information refers to knowing "what," intellectual skill refers to knowing "how." **Intellectual skills** include making discriminations, identifying and classifying concepts, and applying and generating rules. When we state that "*a* squared plus *b* squared equals *c* squared," we express verbal information. If we can use the formula to derive the length of one side of a right-angle triangle when the lengths of two sides are given, we show intellectual skill.

Intellectual skills are not necessarily more complex than verbal information, just different. Table 11.1 shows how intellectual skills can be ordered in terms of complexity, from simpler to more complex skills.

The simplest kind of intellectual skill is the knowledge of how to make discriminations. **Discrimination** is the ability to distinguish between two or more environmental stimuli. Detecting a difference in shapes, for example, enables a preschool child to put the round block in the round hole and the triangle block in the triangular hole. Similarly, an inability to detect differences in colour would

---

CRITICAL THINKING: What are examples of verbal information outcomes in the content area you expect to teach?

CONNECTION: How does Gagné's distinction between verbal information and intellectual skills relate to declarative versus procedural knowledge as discussed in Chapter 7?

CONNECTION: Relate the concept of discrimination to the discussion of relevance in modeling (Chapter 8) and in using the ARCS model (Chapter 9).

CRITICAL THINKING: Explain the difference between verbal information and intellectual skills in terms of the possibility of discriminating between types of rocks without knowing their geologic labels.

verbal information A learning outcome that enables learners to communicate about objects, events, or relations; declarative knowledge.

intellectual skills According to Gagné, learned capabilities that enable learners to make discriminations, identify and classify concepts, and apply and generate rules; procedural knowledge.

discrimination Distinguishing between and responding differently to two or more stimuli.

TABLE 11.1 *Categories of Intellectual Skills*

Intellectual Skill	Example of Performance Based on the Capability
Discrimination	Distinguishing printed *p*'s from *q*'s
Concrete concept	Identifying the spatial relation *below*
Defined concept	Classifying a city by using a definition
Rule	Applying the rule for finding the area of a triangle to specific examples
Higher-order rules	Generating a rule for predicting rainfall in a particular location

Source: Essentials of Learning for Instruction (p. 61), R. M. Gagné and M. P. Driscoll, 1988, Englewood Cliffs, NJ: Prentice-Hall. Copyright © 1988 by Allyn & Bacon. Reprinted by permission.

According to Gagné's theory, what types of capabilities might these children be learning in this situation? What other learning outcomes do children achieve as they become capable of more complex thinking?

make it difficult for a student to tell whether the litmus paper had changed colour in testing for acids and bases.

The capability to discriminate requires experience. A baby may learn that the red object rolls and the yellow object rattles. The baby may also learn that the white cylindrical object yields milk, but the blue cylindrical object, mother's antique vase, is not to be touched. As children enter school, they are still acquiring the ability to discriminate. In school, a great deal of their discrimination learning revolves around symbols. Children must learn to discriminate between the letter *T* and the letter *F*, and between the numeral 5 and the numeral 3. As children proceed through school, the discriminations they are required to make become finer and finer. Consider the junior high school student who learns the difference between the pronunciation of the French *R* and the English *R*.

After the child has developed the skill to determine that horses, cows, sheep, and dogs are all different from one another, the child is ready then to learn what these animals are. **Concrete concepts** refer to objects, events, and relations that can be observed or experienced.

Dog is a concrete concept. It is an object, something that can be pointed to in the environment. Humans acquire concrete concepts by making appropriate discriminations in a number of instances—in this case, acquiring knowledge of

CONNECTION: How does Gagné's theory resemble Piaget's theory of cognitive development in Chapter 2?

concrete concepts
Abstractions based on objects, events, people, and relations that can be observed.

the critical features that make an animal a dog but not a horse. If you consider the wide range of features included in the concept dog, you can see that although the concept may be concrete, it is not necessarily simple. For example, a Chihuahua and the Newfoundland are both instances of the concept "dog."

Concrete concepts are not only objects or classes of object features, they can also be events. A student may learn, for example, that one sound is produced by a violin and a different quality of sound is produced by a piano. A child will also learn the critical features that distinguish parades from the lines of people entering a ride at Canada's Wonderland.

Concrete concepts include the spatial relations among objects. Take, for example, the concepts of above and below. A child will learn through experience that the red light is above the green light on a traffic signal. Other relational concrete concepts include the concepts of up, down, higher, lower, near, and far. The successful acquisition of concrete concepts allows students to identify entire classes of objects, events, or relations and point them out in the environment. Keep in mind the difference between the outcome of verbal information and that of intellectual skill. Just because a student can point out an example of a concept in his or her environment does not mean he or she is able to name the concept. In order to communicate about the concept, some verbal information is necessary.

Among the many concepts that we expect our students to acquire or construct are **defined concepts**—concepts that cannot be pointed out in the environment the way that concrete concepts can and, thus, must be defined. Take as an example the concept information. There are many instances of information in our environment and many sources of information as well, but information itself is not a concrete object, event, or relation.

Students who understand defined concepts are able to use them in an abstract fashion. The student cannot point to freedom in the environment. However, the student can learn to use the notion of freedom to discuss the Charter of Rights and Freedoms.

Concrete concepts can acquire the properties of defined concepts. A child who first learns the concept dog by seeing concrete instances in the environment may later become capable of defining the concept in abstract terms. The student who can classify a dog as a quadrupedal mammal with a carnivorous diet has provided a kind of definition for the concept dog. Once a student understands a defined concept, it is not necessarily the case that the student no longer uses his or her concrete concept. In many instances, learners store in memory both a concrete and a defined concept.

Next in order of complexity is an intellectual skill called **rules**. Normally, we think of a rule as a verbal statement such as "*i* before *e* except after *c*." As a learned capability, this rule allows us to spell correctly the word *receive*. Rules allow learners to use symbols. Typically, the symbols used in school are linguistic and mathematical. There are other symbols that operate in a classroom, however. For example, consider the signals that a teacher's body language or facial expressions provide. Students learn these symbols because they have acquired or constructed rules.

Students learn the rules of grammar, the rules of decoding words, the rules of algebraic manipulation, and the rules of verb conjugation. A learner who understands rules is able to interact with his or her environment in generalized ways. In a classroom, for example, a student may be told that his or her name should always appear in the upper right-hand corner of the paper. As a type of intellectual skill, the rule-governed behaviour is the student's ability to remember to put his or her name in the upper right-hand corner of all papers.

CRITICAL THINKING: What is the importance of defined concepts in generating plans or theories? How might defined concepts contribute to your theory of teaching?

REFLECTION: Think of examples from your own experience of each type of intellectual skill.

defined concepts
Abstractions that cannot be observed in the environment but must be defined (e.g., freedom).

rules The ways phenomena work. As a learned capability, rules enable learners to use symbols.

CONNECTION: In the information-processing model (Chapter 7), cognitive strategies are represented by the executive control function. As students acquire the various capabilities discussed in this chapter, they become more adept at regulating the cognitive processes by which they attend, encode, and retrieve information, and solve problems.

Students with an understanding of concrete and defined concepts can, as a result, acquire or construct rules, allowing them to respond to a class of events. Thus, knowing Strunk and White's (1979) rule that "a participial phrase at the beginning of a sentence must refer to the grammatical subject" saves us from writing an incorrect sentence such as: "Being in a dilapidated condition, I was able to buy the house very cheap" (p. 14). Knowing the rule also helps us to respond to sentences that we read and that we have never seen before.

The most complex type of intellectual skill is called higher-order rules. **Higher-order rules** are formed by combining two or more rules, which allows a student to solve problems. In the case of mathematics, the application of higher-order rules is easily seen. For example, in order to calculate an average of a set of numbers, students must use rules of addition (add the set of numbers to find their sum), counting (count the numbers to determine how many there are) and simple division (divide the sum by the count). After practising many such problems, students apply the individual rules in an algorithmic fashion as part of a single, higher-order rule (add the numbers to find the sum, count how many numbers there are, and divide the sum by the count). Through this process, they have generated a higher-order rule. Students solve problems in other content areas as well by generating higher-order rules (Gagné & Driscoll, 1988). When a student attempts to apply the economic principle of supply and demand, he or she is generating a higher-order rule.

In summary, intellectual skills vary in complexity and can be ordered according to that complexity. Learning simple intellectual skills, such as discrimination, allows the learner to acquire more complex capabilities, such as concepts.

Cognitive strategies. Another type of learning outcome, other than verbal information and intellectual skills, is cognitive strategies. Gagné uses the term **cognitive strategies** to identify the capability to internally organize skills that regulate and monitor the use of concepts and rules (Gagné, 1985). Gagné (1985, p. 138) stated that

> [I]n other words, they learn *how* to learn, *how* to remember, and *how* to carry out the reflective and analytic thought that leads to more learning. It is apparent as individuals continue to learn that they become increasingly capable of *self-instruction* or even what may be called *independent learning*. This is because learners acquire increasingly effective strategies to regulate their own internal processes. This new function of control over internal cognitive processes is what distinguishes [cognitive strategies] from the intellectual skills.

Cognitive strategies serve a metacognitive function; they enable students to organize and monitor their cognitive processes, such as perception, encoding, and retrieval. For example, a high school student who is facing a unit test on Margaret Laurence's work may develop a cognitive strategy in order to study effectively for the exam. The student determines as precisely as possible what is expected and then adopts the following approach:

1. Review the vocabulary list handed out at the beginning of the unit.
2. Reread the synopsis written as one of the assignments in the unit.
3. Answer the textbook discussion questions at the end of each of Laurence's stories.
4. Reread part or all of a particular Laurence story to find or develop answers as needed.

higher-order rules Rules formed by combining two or more rules, thus allowing students to solve problems.

cognitive strategies A learned capability that enables learners to organize and regulate their own internal processes.

There is a distinction between *problem solving* and *problem finding* (Bruner, 1971). The student who is preparing for the unit exam on Margaret Laurence may be presented with several problems. One problem may be to compare and contrast the symbolism in *The Stone Angel* with the symbolism in *A Jest of God*. While looking for similarities and differences between the use of symbols in the two stories, the student may discover something about Laurence's use of dialogue that opens up a new line of analysis. In this way, the student has found a new problem; that is, the problem was not assigned by the teacher but was generated by the learner using cognitive processes.

Pressley, Borkowski, and O'Sullivan (1984) recommend that more attention be given to metacognition or the learner's awareness of his or her own thinking process. Metacognitive awareness seems to play a critical role in the learner's ability to develop self-instruction skills and skillfully transfer learning strategies. According to Derry and Murphy (1986), educators should take a two-part approach to teaching learning strategies. First, they should devote the beginning of each school year to training learning skills. Second, they should embed cognitive strategies in the curriculum and apply them across the content areas.

Brown (1988) investigated whether preschool children can learn a principle on the basis of one or two examples and, if so, whether or not the ability to abstract a principle was affected by the ability to explain why a concept is an instance of a rule. The results indicated that preschool children are able to form mind-sets that aid them in looking for analogous solutions to problems. The effect was both rapid and quite dramatic. The results indicated that the effect was facilitated by the elaborations and explanations the students were asked to make. The conclusion is that reflection about one's cognitive activity is important. Metacognition plays a role.

Attitudes. An **attitude** is a personal feeling or belief that influences a student's tendency to act in a particular way (Gagné, 1985; Gagné & Driscoll, 1988; Dick & Reiser, 1989; Driscoll, 1994). We acquire attitudes toward any number of things. For example, a student may acquire an attitude toward teachers that influences his or her behaviour toward them.

Students acquire attitudes that influence other social behaviour. Often such attitudes are instilled at an early age, and, in many cases, they are learned at home. For example, a student may have acquired an attitude toward people of a different religion or race. This attitude influences the student's behaviour toward people who are perceived as different.

In general, attitudes affect the choices that a learner makes. The learner who comes to class on time with the materials needed for the day's lesson is exhibiting an attitude. The simple observation of one action, however, does not provide sufficient information to judge whether a student has acquired a particular attitude. Teachers look for consistent actions over time as evidence that a student has a positive attitude toward school, for example. Examples of attitudes teachers often hope to instill in students include courtesy toward other students and a desire to do one's best. Attitudes related to social issues, such as making a decision to recycle waste, are also targeted as desirable goals by teachers.

Motor Skills. The final type of learning outcome that Gagné discusses is motor skills. **Motor skills** are physical capabilities that require muscle control and hand-eye coordination, such as the ability to ride a bike or use a computer keyboard. Motor skills also involve cognitive and affective outcomes. You have a cognitive representation of riding a bicycle and feelings or attitudes about bike riding.

REFLECTION: Identify a unit or lesson you expect to teach. What intellectual skills will students need to acquire in order to master the topic? What cognitive strategies do you think are important for the students to learn? How would you facilitate the development of cognitive strategies while teaching this unit?

CONNECTION: Metacognition is discussed in detail in Chapter 7.

CRITICAL THINKING: Would asking students to describe how they read help them develop cognitive strategies?

CONNECTION: Cultural beliefs and values of students are discussed in Chapter 4. How these affect motivation is discussed in Chapter 9.

TRY THIS: Interview teachers regarding how they determine student attitudes. What attitudes do they hope to facilitate in their instruction?

attitude According to Gagné, a learned capability that influences a person's choice of personal action.

motor skills According to Gagné, learned capabilities relating to movement or to muscles that induce movement, such as the ability to ride a bicycle or to operate a computer.

Similarly, executing a pas de deux in *Swan Lake* involves motor, cognitive, and affective capabilities.

Bloom's Taxonomy for the Cognitive Domain

Benjamin Bloom, a contemporary of Gagné, conceived of learning outcomes in a somewhat different way. Instead of considering cognitive, affective, and psychomotor domains of learning within the same taxonomy, Bloom developed a taxonomy for the **cognitive domain** alone that has been widely applied in curriculum guides (Bloom, Furst, Hill, & Krathwohl, 1956).

Bloom's taxonomy consists of six levels, progressing from simple to complex. The examples given at each level specify a behaviour a student might be asked to perform.

> *Level 1: Knowledge*—the recall of specific facts, methods and processes, patterns and structures. The focus of these outcomes is remembering. For example, being able to list the four basic food groups is a knowledge outcome.

> *Level 2: Comprehension*—the first level of understanding. At this level, the learner can know what is being communicated and make use of the idea appropriately. For example, a student may be able to distinguish between nouns, verbs, and other parts of speech.

> *Level 3: Application*—ability to use information in new situations. The information can be general ideas, rules, methods, principles, or theories that must be remembered and then applied. For example, students demonstrate application when they use the appropriate formula to solve an equation.

> *Level 4: Analysis*—ability to identify elements embedded in a whole and recognize relations among elements. For example, students might analyze elements of a character, setting, and plot in a story.

> *Level 5: Synthesis*—ability to put elements together to form a new whole. For example, when students design a scientific experiment, draft an essay, or choreograph a dance, they are performing synthesis.

> *Level 6: Evaluation*—judgments based on criteria of value or worth. For example, a student might use the four principles of music appreciation to evaluate Beethoven's Fifth Symphony or use criteria for judging the effectiveness of an argument.

The level of the cognitive taxonomy identifies the level of complexity. The higher the taxonomic level, the more complex the learning involved.

Bloom's taxonomy can be used to plan instruction based on learning outcomes. For example, in the cognitive domain, the teacher decides whether students should know, comprehend, apply, synthesize, or evaluate. The teacher states these decisions as performance objectives—what students will know and be able to do. Table 11.2 shows the words teachers use to identify what students might be expected to do for each level of the cognitive domain (Tuckman, 1988). As the following sections illustrate, we can also specify performance objectives for the affective and psychomotor domains of learning. Later sections discuss how to construct performance objectives.

TABLE 11.2 *A Selected List of Verbs for Writing Cognitive Objectives*

Knowledge	define/describe/identify/label/list
Comprehension	convert/defend/distinguish/estimate/explain
Application	change/compute/demonstrate/discover/manipulate
Analysis	diagram/differentiate/discriminate/distinguish/identify
Synthesis	categorize/combine/compile/compose/create
Evaluation	appraise/compare/conclude/criticize/describe

Source: Testing for Teachers (2nd ed., p. 17), B. W. Tuckman, 1988, Orlando, FL: Harcourt Brace Jovanovich. Copyright © 1988 by Harcourt Brace Jovanovich. Reprinted by permission.

Krathwohl's Taxonomy for the Affective Domain

The five levels in Krathwohl's affective taxonomy represent a progression of capabilities leading to learning outcomes in the **affective domain**—changes in attitudes and emotional responses (Krathwohl, Bloom, & Masia, 1964).

> **REFLECTION:** From personal experience, list one example for each level in each of the three domains of learning.

> *Level 1: Receiving or Attending*—Receiving or attending involve the learner as becoming sensitive to or aware of certain stimuli. These outcomes include a willingness to receive or selectively respond to experiences. An example would be a willingness to listen to a guest speaker.

> *Level 2: Responding*—Responding refers to the learner's motivation to learn. The category includes a willingness to respond and the ability to find satisfaction in responding. For example, students in a computer lab willingly adhere to posted rules for using equipment.

> *Level 3: Valuing*—Valuing is evident when the learner expresses a value or shows that a behaviour has worth. The category includes acceptance of a value, preference for a value, and commitment to a value. An example is a student who, because of a committed belief, chooses to participate in an environmental conservation project.

> *Level 4: Organizing*—Through organization individuals develop a value system. As ideas, opinions, and beliefs become internalized, the learner gives some of them priority over others and in the process conceptualizes values and organizes a value system.

> *Level 5: Characterization*—At the level of characterization, an individual's behaviour consistently reflects the values that he or she has organized into some kind of system. Learners at this level practise what they preach and believe deeply in these values.

Harrow's Taxonomy for the Psychomotor Domain

Harrow (1972) proposed a taxonomy of outcomes for the **psychomotor domain**. This taxonomy, which includes six levels of performance, can be used to specify psychomotor outcomes in areas of physical education, dance, art, theatre, and motor development therapies for students with disabilities (Table 11.3).

> **affective domain** Learning outcomes that relate to emotions, values, and attitudes, as classified by Krathwohl's taxonomy.
>
> **psychomotor domain** Learning outcomes that relate to skilled physical movements, as classified by Harrow's taxonomy.

TABLE 11.3 *Harrow's Taxonomy for the Psychomotor Domain*

Level 1:   Reflex movements—involuntary movements present at birth or developed during maturation
            Example: grasping reflex in infants

Level 2:   Basic movements—fundamental movements as components of more complex actions
            Example: movement of the hand to hold a pencil

Level 3:   Perceptual abilities—the brain's ability to receive sensory stimuli and transmit motor messages to appropriate muscle groups
            Example: perception of properties of a writing surface

Level 4:   Physical abilities—characteristics of a person that, depending on development, permit efficient movement
            Example: ability to write persistently

Level 5:   Skilled movements—simple and complex that are learned
            Example: forming cursive letters; learning to use a word processor

Level 6:   Nondiscursive communication—nonverbal communication
            Example: expression through gestures, facial expressions, mime, or dance

How might you plan for this learning outcome and the events leading up to it using the taxonomies for the cognitive, affective, and psychomotor domains?

Psychomotor outcomes are also evident in many other subjects. In science, for example, well-developed hand and eye coordination is required to operate laboratory equipment. Positioning a microcomputer's mouse to insert the cursor at a particular point on the screen is another example of a psychomotor outcome.

Thinking in the Content Areas

Acquiring various learning outcomes as they are defined in taxonomies does not guarantee that students will use these skills and knowledge. In fact, criticism of education often centres on the fact that students do *not* routinely use the knowledge and skills they learn in school (Brown, Collins, & Duguid, 1989). According to some researchers, one reason for the problem of inert knowledge is that most instruction occurs at the content level and rarely focuses on the cultural level (Tishman, Perkins, & Jay, 1995). Thus, students learn facts, principles, and basic problem-solving skills within a discipline but do not learn what it means to participate in the culture of a discipline—that is, to "do what historians do" or to "think like a mathematician." This participation requires thinking skills and dispositions that are situated and acquired within the cultural context of a subject matter discipline.

According to Tishman et al. (1995, pp. 2-3), there are **six dimensions of good thinking:**

1. *A language of thinking*—the language used by teachers and students in the classroom to talk about thinking and to encourage high-level thinking. For example, students in social studies might use such thinking words as *claim, evidence, research,* and *justify* in discussing the issue of park rules in the national park system.

2. *Thinking dispositions*—habits of mind regarding thinking, such as the disposition to look beyond what's given, to explore alternative points of view, and to remain alert to possible error. Students demonstrate a thinking disposition when they ask a lot of questions about a story they have read, questions that lead them to explore new concepts.

3. *Mental management*—thinking about and controlling one's thinking processes. Science students exhibit mental management when they plan a strategy for conducting an experiment that builds on their individual strengths and assures completion of the investigation in the time allotted.

4. *The strategic spirit*—the attitude of responding to learning challenges with appropriate thinking strategies. For example, given the assignment to select a topic for an independent project, a student plans how to search for a good idea by stating a goal, brainstorming ideas, and thinking about the pros and cons of a few of the most interesting ideas.

5. *Higher-order knowledge*—the ways of solving problems, using evidence, and making inquiries that are specific to a subject area. For example, students in English class explore possible interpretations of a poem by considering the evidence supporting each interpretation.

6. *Transfer*—the application of knowledge and strategies from one context to another and the exploration of how different areas of knowledge connect to one another. For example, students learning about important historical developments come to understand the significance of literary characters' decisions in historical contexts.

Regardless of the subject matter or grade level, teachers must make decisions about what learning outcomes they want students to achieve. How do they do this in a way that will help them plan the daily, weekly, and yearly activities that make up their instruction?

How Do Teachers Determine and Specify Instructional Outcomes?

The business of determining and specifying the learning outcomes that will guide instruction is an important part of the classroom teacher's job. While blue-ribbon panels, provincial departments of education, or school districts largely determine curricular goals, the classroom teacher must translate these goals into specific objectives for instruction.

Decisions about what to teach in schools are shared by local school boards, educational administrators and teachers, taxpayers, parents, and students. Sometimes curriculum committees adopt plans developed outside the community and marketed for wide use. In most cases, local educators are free to exercise their professional judgment regarding site-specific curriculum decisions.

CONNECTION: How does the notion of the cultural level of instruction relate to Vygotsky's theory (Chapter 2) and situated learning (Chapter 7)?

CONNECTION: How does the concept of mental management relate to metacognition, discussed in Chapter 7? To Gagné's cognitive strategies?

CRITICAL THINKING: Are the six dimensions of good thinking reflected in Gagné's learning outcomes or Bloom's taxonomy? How are they alike or different?

six dimensions of good thinking Six aspects that characterize skill in thinking critically, which include a language of thinking, thinking dispositions, mental management, a strategic spirit, higher-order knowledge, and transfer.

Insights on Successful Practice

In your experience, what are the most important aspects of planning and providing effective instruction?

Thoughtful planning is essential for effective instruction. The critical dimensions of planning include selecting, organizing, and sequencing the content to be taught, isolating the objectives both cognitive and affective to be achieved, selecting the instructional techniques and materials to be used, and stipulating the evaluation procedures which will determine the success of the teaching and learning activities.

To organize the content or the unit of work for my students in the Northwest Territories, I use concept maps. The concepts are organized sequentially or developmentally, so that the acquisition of new knowledge is dependent on previously acquired knowledge. Learning activities are then devised. Such activities may include exercises for individual seat work, a variety of cooperative learning group activities, field trips, and other related activities designed to achieve specific goals.

The goals to be achieved are dependent on the content and on the students. These goals are generally structured around three dimensions of student development—cognitive, affective, and motor. These goals ought to be reasonable, observable, and testable. This dimension of planning must include carefully planned procedures for assessing the teaching and learning activities. These may take the form of objective tests based on specific parts of the content, short answer tests, group projects, essay type tests, and review tests. It is important to determine ahead of time the method of marking and the value or worth of each test. Finally, this stage of planning should include the selection of instructional techniques and procedures suited to the content, the students, and the goals to be achieved.

When this aspect of planning is completed, I introduce the unit of work to my class. I then invite their input into finalizing the preparation of the content, goals, and evaluation procedures. The significant thing about this activity is sharing information with students. Students respond more positively to my expectations when they know what the expectations are. The next step in planning for instruction includes the development of a series of related lessons, each with its own objectives and appropriate exercises, review tests, unit tests, and group projects.

Executing the plan is just as important as the planning activity itself. In delivering a given lesson, I review the prior knowledge and experiences that students must have in order to understand and learn the new knowledge. If students do not have the requisite knowledge, I quickly reteach the required concepts or information. Only then do I move to the new information. The development of my lessons is inductive; they are brief and they are followed by practice. Successive lessons follow the same procedure but emphasis is given to the analysis and review of previous lessons. The lesson presentations end with a synthesis of all information studied to that point. Student activities at the end of the lessons are varied in order to provide the necessary interest and to accommodate objectives related to the affective and motor domains.

Obviously, careful planning is essential to effective instruction. A well-developed plan, however, does not necessarily result in the delivery of an effective lesson. The teacher is the key in these endeavours and he/she must be flexible enough to place a plan aside momentarily and reteach appropriate and relevant concepts before proceeding with the planned lesson. The lesson must be brief, focused, and followed by practice. Evaluation of students' performance must follow each lesson. I am always prepared to reteach a lesson if the evaluation reveals weaknesses in teaching or learning.

RICHARD R.
High School Teacher

Your Insights

Planning is crucial, according to this teacher, but teachers must also be able to set aside their plan. Why? In what ways can flexibility in planning pay off?

Teachers are given the responsibility to lead students through a curricular maze. By the end of the year, a student should be able to use certain skills, know certain facts, apply certain concepts, and evaluate certain materials. A good number of the learning outcomes that students are to attain have been prescribed for the teacher by external sources.

In recent years, provincial departments of education have undertaken curriculum development and reform projects with the aim of producing detailed curriculum guides in the required areas of study for their kindergarten to grade 12 systems. These guides provide teachers with not only detailed lists of desired learning outcomes, but descriptions of instructional methods and related assessment procedures. These documents also typically provide lists and outlines of instructional units considered appropriate for each of the grade levels. In many cases, model lessons have been collected and made available for teachers to use in developing their own units of study.

These curriculum development initiatives have also provided Canadian educators with teaching and learning frameworks that detail broad domains of learning outcomes intended to cut across and integrate the required areas of study. In Saskatchewan, this curriculum and instruction framework has been called the Common Essential Learnings (C.E.L.s) (Saskatchewan Education, 1988). These integrative learning strands consist of developing students' abilities in:

- Communication—listening, speaking, reading, and writing
- Numeracy—mathematical ideas, techniques, and applications
- Critical and Creative Thinking—creating and evaluating ideas, processes, experiences, and objects
- Technological Literacy—awareness, exploration, and use of technology; how technology shapes and is shaped by society
- Personal and Social Values and Skills—personal, moral, social, and cultural aspects of school subjects and the school environment
- Independent Learning — capable, self-reliant, self-motivated, and life-long learning

The intention is that teachers will plan units of study with the C.E.L.s in mind, and develop students' abilities in these areas to the extent possible. Some units may offer many opportunities to develop the C.E.L.s, while the topic and focus of other units may limit such opportunities. It is also intended that the C.E.L.s be developed and evaluated simultaneously, not separately, from the subject matter content areas.

Deciding on Instructional Goals

Once teachers have decided generally what they want students to learn, they can specify these outcomes in ways to better guide instructional planning and assessment. Outcomes are first defined generally as goals and then analyzed into component objectives. **Instructional goals** are broad statements of desired learning outcomes that often encompass an array of specific performances to be attained. For example, the goal, "communicate effectively in writing," involves such subordinate performances as "generate a topic sentence" and "provide supporting

instructional goals General statements of what students should be able to do as a consequence of instruction.

details," as well as such grammatical prerequisites as "use appropriate punctuation" and "spell correctly."

Following are examples of instructional goals.

A. Use a recipe to bake a cake from scratch.
B. Demonstrate courteous behaviour in the halls.
C. Perform numeric operations.
D. Employ an efficient strategy for carrying out a class assignment.

Notice that these examples differ in specificity and the degree to which enabling or subordinate objectives are implied. For students to attain the goal in example A, they would have to demonstrate such skills as adjusting the amount of ingredients (intellectual skill) and breaking the eggs and stirring the batter (motor skill). The goal in example B requires that students know what kinds of behaviours are considered courteous. For the goal in example C to be useful to a teacher, the teacher must make it specific to the context in which it is to be performed. The teacher might expect students to perform numeric operations in counting objects, solving a geometry problem, setting up the budget for a school project, or determining the amount of fertilizer needed for a particular size field. Example D is a thinking goal with enabling objectives that would be specific to a particular content area or grade level.

Specifying Performance Objectives

Performance objectives, then, are statements of specific performances to be demonstrated by students as evidence of their goal attainment. Usually, objectives are stated in behavioural terms, because behaviours can be directly observed and measured.

Robert Mager's model of **behavioural objectives** has influenced the way in which generations of teachers have gone about preparing performance objectives (Mager, 1962). Behavioural objectives are based on the operant-conditioning view of learning. Operant conditioning's emphasis on observable behaviour gave educators a way of specifying what outcomes to expect of their students. Behavioural objectives also provided a way to monitor teacher accountability with regard to the outcomes of their instruction. Skinner (1968) said, "The first step in designing instruction is to define the terminal behaviour. What is the student to do as the result of having been taught?" A behavioural objective states what students should be able to do as a result of instruction.

According to Mager (1962), behavioural objectives should contain three elements: (1) a statement of the observable behaviour students are to perform as a consequence of instruction, (2) the conditions under which the behaviour will be demonstrated or exhibited, and (3) the criteria by which attainment of the objective will be judged. Consider the following examples, and identify in each the three elements of a behavioural objective.

A. Using a ruler, students will correctly label centimetres and millimetres.
B. Given an unlabelled sky chart, students will correctly list at least seven constellations.
C. In an essay, students will contrast the postwar economies that developed in Japan and in Canada.
D. From examples, students will compose a formally correct haiku and limerick.

CRITICAL THINKING: Explain the connection between behavioural objectives and operant conditioning by discussing shaping as a way of approximating instructional outcomes.

TRY THIS: Interview a teacher regarding the use of Mager's model for defining objectives and why he or she uses it.

behavioural objectives Specific statements of goals, which include the behaviour students should be able to perform as a result of instruction, the conditions of their performance, and the criteria used to judge attainment of the goals.

Mager's model for defining objectives set the standard. Clearly there are other ways to specify objectives that appear in textbooks, curriculum guides, and provincial regulations. Many curriculum guides, for example, provide objectives in a format that presents a general goal followed by statements that specify subject matter and behavioural outcomes. This approach is based on the work of N. E. Gronlund. Following Gronlund's (1991) model, a curriculum guide for chemistry might include the following entry:

1. General objective: Demonstrate knowledge of acids and bases.
   The student will
1.01. Define the term *ions*.
1.02. Identify common acidic solutions.
1.03. Distinguish between an acid and a base.
1.04. Demonstrate a litmus test.

As a result of recent reform efforts in education, some curriculum guides produced by departments of education include goals and objectives that call for higher-order thinking skills. For example:

2. General objective: Use numeric operations to describe, analyze, disaggregate, communicate, and synthesize numeric data and to identify and solve problems.
   The student will
2.01. Accurately identify and perform appropriate numeric procedures with problems found in numeric, symbolic, or word form.
2.02. Estimate approximate numeric solutions to problems without using calculating devices.
2.03. Accurately analyze, synthesize, and evaluate numeric ideas, concepts, and information through appropriate formulae, symbols, theorems, equations, graphs, diagrams, and charts.

These objectives drive the development of appropriate assessments. Classroom tests and performance assessments should reflect the instructional goals, the conditions under which the performance is to be demonstrated, and the criteria for determining if the goals have been attained.

Behavioural objectives have been criticized for limiting the teacher's focus of instruction and choice of instructional methods. Research results have also been equivocal concerning their effective use by learners (e.g., Klauer, 1984). However, objectives do help teachers remain oriented to desired learning outcomes (Dick & Reiser, 1989).

REFLECTION: In your experience as a student, what are some advantages and disadvantages of teaching to behavioural objectives?

How Do Instructional Events Facilitate Learning Outcomes?

Distinguishing among types of outcomes helps us understand the cognitive processes involved in achieving learning outcomes. Knowledge of outcomes does not ensure, however, that students will achieve them. Teachers must determine the instructional events (the outward conditions of learning) that will support the cognitive processes involved.

Teaching and learning are two sides of the same coin. A teacher who claims to have taught when students do not learn is like a salesperson who claims to have made a sale even though the customer did not buy anything. The teacher's

CRITICAL THINKING: How do instructional events influence a student's cognitive processes?

actions and instructional decisions should engage the learner and support the cognitive processes required for learning.

Gagné's Events of Instruction

Figure 11.1 identifies the learning processes that occur in classroom learning situations in relation to the instructional events that support those processes. The processes represent phases of learning (Bell-Gredler, 1986; Gagné, 1977).

The nine events in **Gagné's events of instruction** follow the typical sequence of a direct instruction lesson, and effective lessons are assumed to include all nine events in one form or another. The order of events and who provides them may change, however, depending on the method of instruction. In cooperative learning, for example, students may search out information relevant to a project on which they are working rather than wait for the teacher to provide them with needed materials. In addition, they may depend on each other, instead of the teacher, for feedback. Likewise, students conducting independent study would provide some of the events of instruction for themselves.

Preparation Phase. The first three events of instruction—gaining attention, informing the student of the objective, and stimulating prior knowledge—comprise the preparation phase of learning (Bell-Gredler, 1986). When the teacher is successful in gaining the student's attention, the student apprehends or becomes aware of relevant stimuli pertaining to the lesson. Teachers use a variety of verbal signals, such as "Listen up!" or "Open your book to page twenty-seven" or "Take a look at this picture" to accomplish this event. Visual and auditory signals (e.g., turning on the overhead projector, shaking a rattle) can also be very effective at gaining and directing students' attention.

The second event of instruction is informing the student of the goals or objectives of the lesson. If students know what they are expected to do, they can make appropriate decisions throughout the lesson. When you orient students toward the goal of the lesson, you activate their motivation. For example, if students know that they will be expected to write a summary at the end of a lecture, they will study differently than if they expect to define terms introduced during the lesson. A student who has a clear sense of what he or she is supposed to do is less likely to procrastinate on a task or fail to meet the goal. Building expectancies for students activates their motivation.

Stimulating recall of prior knowledge is the third event of instruction. By encouraging students to retrieve prior knowledge appropriate to the goals of the lesson, you will enhance their acquisition, construction, and retention of material to be learned. Recall can be stimulated through formal means, such as pretests, or through informal means, such as reviewing with students what they learned previously or inviting reports of relevant personal experiences.

Acquisition and Performance Phase. After students are prepared for learning, the acquisition and performance phase begins (events 4-7 in Figure 11.1). This phase is the essence of classroom instruction (Bell-Gredler, 1986). The fourth instructional event in a typical lesson is the presentation of stimulus material. Teachers or students present material in lectures, discussions, and live demonstrations. Textbooks and overhead transparencies present material in print, diagrams, and pictures. Computers present material in many forms (print, diagrams, video, and audio) that are often sequenced on the basis of the student's responses. In whatever form material is presented, however, it should help students to selectively perceive the

CONNECTION: Gagné's model is based on information-processing theory and combines principles of behavioural and cognitive learning theories (see Chapters 6 and 7).

CONNECTION: How does the instructional event, gaining attention, relate to the ARCS model (Chapter 9)?

CONNECTION: See the sections on prior knowledge and selective attention in Chapter 7.

Gagné's events of instruction According to Gagné, the external conditions required to support and facilitate the cognitive processes that occur during learning.

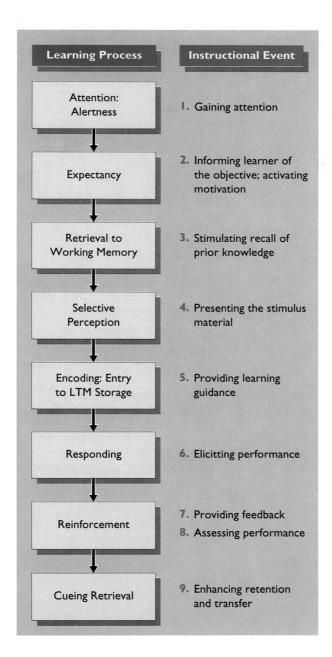

FIGURE 11.1
Gagné's Instructional Events and Learning Processes

Source: Essentials of Learning for Instruction (2nd ed., p. 128), R. M. Gagné and M. P. Driscoll, 1988, Englewood Cliffs, NJ: Prentice-Hall. Copyright 1988 by Allyn & Bacon. Reprinted by permission.

Learning Process

- Attention: Alertness
- Expectancy
- Retrieval to Working Memory
- Selective Perception
- Encoding: Entry to LTM Storage
- Responding
- Reinforcement
- Cueing Retrieval

Instructional Event

1. Gaining attention
2. Informing learner of the objective; activating motivation
3. Stimulating recall of prior knowledge
4. Presenting the stimulus material
5. Providing learning guidance
6. Elicitting performance
7. Providing feedback
8. Assessing performance
9. Enhancing retention and transfer

important stimuli in the situation. By focusing on just the important elements, the student is better able to store the elements in short-term memory.

The form in which material is presented should also be appropriate to the desired learning outcome. To support a learning outcome such as "serve a tennis ball," information is more effectively presented via a live demonstration or a slow motion video than a verbal description in a textbook. Similarly, for an outcome such as "determine the altitude of a rocket launched straight up," information could be presented by the teacher or textbook as a series of steps to follow.

The teacher's actions during the next event of instruction, providing learning guidance, support the student's creation of a mental representation of the

Insights on Successful Practice

As a teacher, how do you model learner characteristics and learning performances for your students?

In adopting performance criteria for our students, our district and community agreed that all students should become self-directed learners and resourceful, innovative problem solvers. In the process of providing training for the staff in the usual instructional strategies associated with cooperative learning, mastery learning, and responsibility training, our district also adapted Dr. Margaret Wang's Adaptive Learning Environment Model to our needs and goals. Our model, Continuous Progress Instruction (CPI), gives us a way to assess student progress, make prescriptives, and guide students toward these two performance criteria.

A CPI unit is designed to allow students to make choices about what material they will cover, how they will use the time allotted to them, and what types of products they will produce. CPI also allows me to prescribe certain types of work for the students based on how I assess their needs at any given point.

In our last unit, the English 9 team looked at the objectives we wanted to cover, the works we had available, and the time we had in which to do all this. We divided the readings into three major groupings and asked students to select their first and second choices from these groupings. For each grouping we developed a series of learning centres, which were designed to allow students a full range of exploratory possibilities.

Some were group oriented while others were individual oriented. We did not limit the products students were to produce for their portfolios to pencil-and-paper products. Drawing on Howard Gardner's work with both multiple intelligences and project-based education, we designed the learning centres so that students also had a choice of products they could produce, including poems and artistic creations. The products had to demonstrate the student's understanding and comprehension of the concepts and works in the unit.

After all these choices were made, each team had to set a work schedule that would allow it to complete all group work while still allowing individuals time to complete their own work. The schedule also had to provide the times when they would take any quizzes and major tests that were included in the unit. In essence, then, students were responsible for their own lessons, for assigning work to be done in and out of school, for scheduling work time and due dates, and for solving problems associated with the learning centres, time management, and group activities.

On a follow-up self-evaluation, one of the questions we asked was: "What do you feel you have gained from this unit?" Representative samplings of student responses include the following statements.

> From the group activities, I have gained the skills of working with people, cooperating in a group, compromising, and making decisions. In the independent unit, I've gained the knowledge of how to map out an independent schedule of goals for myself.

> I learned how to decipher different types of writing. I had to read many poems that were written in different styles. I had to read law books in order to answer my research question.

> I learned to link dissimilar stories together and work independently to find out my learning speed and style.

From the smaller CPI units we run throughout the year in English 9 to the final nine-week unit, I feel that students come to be self-directed learners and creative, innovative problem solvers. They also take a great deal of pride in both their individual portfolios and in the final group presentations.

MICHAEL A. BENEDICT
High School Teacher

Your Insights

What is continuous progress instruction? What role do responsibility training and cooperative learning play? How does CPI affect the assessment of student learning? What clear advantages has CPI had for this teacher and his students?

---

stimulus information that can be stored in long-term memory. In terms of the information-processing model examined in Chapter 7, the student makes meaningful sense of the stimulus information. Meaningful information is more easily stored and is retained longer.

The sixth event of instruction is referred to as eliciting performance. This is practice. Students learning to play tennis must have the opportunity to practice serving. Likewise, students learning to determine altitude using an inclinometer to measure the angle of incidence could practise by determining the height of trees or school buildings in addition to determining the altitude of rockets.

Feedback follows practice and is the basis for both reinforcement and response correction. Feedback functions to confirm the student's expectations about the goal of the lesson. Performance that results in goal attainment is reinforced. Feedback also serves to correct inaccurate performances. Students who compute an entirely different number than the rest of the class for the altitude of a particular rocket launch obtain feedback indicating that they made a mistake.

Transfer Phase. The final two events of instruction, called the transfer phase, support the cognitive processes necessary for the **transfer of learning**. This occurs when knowledge or skills learned in one situation are used in another. Assessing performance requires that the teacher give students opportunities to use or demonstrate what they have learned. If students are truly capable of making a discrimination or applying a rule, they should be able to use the new capability in a variety of situations. Assessment allows students to test their wings and allows teachers to determine that the knowledge is not limited to the specific circumstances in which the initial learning took place. For example, the student who has learned to serve a tennis ball should be able to do so competently in a variety of settings and situations.

Actions that enhance retention and transfer encourage the student to retrieve the learned information in new situations. A student who can generalize beyond the instructional context in which information was learned has developed an elaborate encoding of the information and more retrieval cues for using the information in the future.

Integrating Multiple Instructional Goals. Most lessons are intended to support more than one instructional goal, which means that teachers must ensure that the events of instruction they plan are appropriate for all goals contained in the lesson. One way for teachers to do this is through an enterprise schema. The **enterprise schema** provides an overall learning context that integrates multiple instructional goals and communicates the purpose for learning these goals (Gagné & Merrill, 1990).

Thematic lessons provide an example. A grade five teacher decides to teach a social studies lesson on maps. The overall goals of the lesson are for students to (1) locate specific destinations on a map in relation to their school, (2) determine distances between specified locations using the map's scale, and (3) plan the best route to a particular location, considering factors such as necessary stops along the way and types of roads travelled. To attain these goals, students must acquire intellectual skills (solving distance problems, estimating travel times), motor skills (measuring distances along a route), and cognitive strategies (finding an efficient solution). The enterprise of planning a class field trip provides the context and purpose for acquiring these learning outcomes. It also provides the context for determining and selecting specific events of instruction to be used during the course of the lesson.

Teaching methods also need to be integrated with multiple instructional goals. Consider again the core phases of instruction. How should material be presented? Guidance given? Performance elicited? Feedback provided? The answers to these questions depend on whether a teacher decides to facilitate

TRY THIS: Develop a thematic lesson for a class you expect to teach. What is the enterprise schema in your lesson? What instructional goals does the lesson integrate?

POINT: Teachers coordinate the context for learning. They do this by implementing the events of instruction and by organizing discovery and reception learning.

transfer of learning The application of knowledge acquired in one situation to other situations.

enterprise schema An overall learning context that integrates multiple instructional goals and communicates the purpose for learning these goals.

What multiple instructional goals might this learning enterprise serve? What instructional methods might best serve these goals? In what ways might students transfer this learning to other situations?

learning through discovery or through reception. These methods of instruction are often complementary. Teachers may use both at different times within a lesson in order to support particular goals.

Bruner's Discovery Learning

Discovery learning occurs when students are presented with problem situations that require them to discover the essential concepts of the subject matter (Bruner, 1960). Bruner advocates learning through discovery because it supports active learning. A teacher who uses a discovery learning approach to instruction presents examples or problems and then asks students to examine and think about them inductively with a goal of formulating a general principle. For example, a teacher might give students equal amounts of fresh water and salt water and ask them to experiment with samples to find out the differences between the two—differences in appearance, taste, weight, and other properties. Students could be encouraged to find out how well various objects float in the two containers. By experimenting, the students would discover and articulate the essential properties rather than being told what they are. Discovery learning encourages students to actively use their intuition, imagination, and creativity. Because the approach starts with the specific and then moves to the general, it also facilitates inductive reasoning.

What conditions promote effective discovery learning? To begin with, "discovery, like surprise, favours the well-prepared mind" (Bruner, 1961, p. 22). When students have little or no prior knowledge related to principles they are asked to discover, they can experience frustration and failure. Asking them to make connections to related ideas as they enter a discovery learning environment can help students begin to determine what information is relevant and what steps they should take to solve a problem.

Providing models to guide discovery is another important condition for discovery learning. "The constant provision of a model, the constant response to the individual's response after response, back and forth between two people, constitute 'invention' learning guided by an accessible model" (Bruner, 1973, p. 70). In teaching the concept of alliteration, for instance, a teacher could provide both examples and nonexamples and systematically guide students through an exploration of their similarities and differences. By asking certain kinds of questions and prompting students to generate hypotheses, the teacher also models the inquiry process. What students can learn by discovery, then, includes not just content-specific concepts and information but also critical thinking skills and a disposition toward critical thinking.

A third condition that promotes discovery learning is the use of contrasts to stimulate cognitive conflicts. In science, for example, a teacher could begin a

EXAMPLE: A kindergarten teacher has each of her children pick an object from a box each day and describe it. In the box, she has gathered everything from old records to nuts and bolts. After each child has described the object, the teacher asks him or her how the object might be used. At first, the children's guesses range far afield from the actual use of the object. But as they become more skilled in describing, they also begin to realize the functional attributes of the objects. Why do you think the teacher takes the time to do this exercise, and what value might it have for the children?

discovery learning
Bruner's approach to teaching, in which students are presented with specific examples and use these examples to form general principles. Discovery learning is inductive.

Insights on Successful Practice

As you match teaching methods with learning objectives, how do you incorporate affective outcomes into your lesson plans?

Incorporating affective outcomes into lesson plans begins in the earliest stages of planning any unit of work and its series of related lesson plans. After the content is conceptually mapped and sequentially arranged, the specific learning outcomes or goals must be outlined. At this time, attention must be given not only to the cognitive development of students, but also to their affective and motor development. I teach at the upper elementary school level in Ontario and instruct my students in almost all the disciplines they study. I have found that in almost all of these disciplines I can create opportunities and experiences which will influence their development in each of the three domains.

Because I engage in direct inductive teaching in large as well as small groups, my students have innumerable opportunities to develop their cognitive as well as their interaction skills. This part of the inductive lesson is always followed by a variety of student activities designed to enhance their affective and motor development. These activities may include individual seat work, cooperative learning groups with specially assigned tasks, group projects, independent study, and other related individual or group projects.

After introducing my unit of work on "Wheat Production in the Prairie Provinces" to my grade six class, the students and I agreed upon the formulation of five cooperative learning groups based on specific interests of the students. We collectively outlined aspects of wheat production which we wanted to investigate and each group chose to pursue its area of interest. I arranged a series of field trips to a nearby farm, a grain terminal, a flour mill, a farm equipment dealership, and a bakery. Each group was responsible for researching and collecting relevant information in its area of interest and then for constructing a series of questions which would elicit additional information for completing the report. Before a given field trip, the specific interest group had the opportunity to share its information and questions with the entire class. Other groups were invited to add relevant questions but were also permitted to formulate at least three questions of their own to be used at the time of the visit. The specific interest group, however, divided the questions equally among its members.

After each field trip, the specific interest group began preparing a group report for presentation to the entire class. These reports, finalized in the written composition classes, included graphs, diagrams, drawings, and photographs designed by the students. I organized my math lessons to assist students in learning to use line and bar graphs and in dealing with fractions, decimals, and percentages. My written composition classes were designed to teach outlining, paragraphing, narration, and exposition. After each group had completed its presentation, the students agreed to synthesize all the information into a single report for the school.

Obviously, the unit of work organized in this manner provided ample opportunities for students to develop their cognitive, affective, and motor skills. My instruction and students' research and writing contributed to an increase in their cognitive development and in their interaction skills. Their involvement in monitored cooperative learning group activities enhanced their affective skills such as cooperation, dependability, courtesy, and study habits. Their participation in writing, art work, and the construction of displays contributed to the development of their motor skills.

SHERI A.L.
Elementary School Teacher

Your Insights

How does this teacher match teaching methods with instructional goals? How does she incorporate affective objectives and use student input? What range of methods will you employ when planning your lessons?

---

lesson on air and air pressure with a demonstration that shows water flowing uphill. This is a surprising event because we are accustomed to the force of gravity causing water to flow downhill. In trying to resolve the discrepancy, students discover how air exerts pressure that can overcome the force of gravity.

Discovery learning is an effective approach for facilitating students' acquisition of information, concepts, and problem-solving skills. It is also highly motivational. Most teachers who use discovery learning in their classrooms report that students want to find out the answers to problems and will engage in purposeful activities to do so (Friedl, 1991). Moreover, if students are not successful in finding all the answers, they benefit more from a teacher's explanations than when such explanations are given without the students having first engaged in inquiry.

There are drawbacks to discovery learning. Teachers can find it time-consuming, costly, and complex to implement. There is also a risk that process will begin to outweigh content. Many science programs implemented in the 1970s that were based on the concepts of discovery failed because content was ignored, and teachers found that "process without content did not produce results" (Friedl, 1991, p. 2). It is important, therefore, to keep desired learning outcomes in full view when designing and implementing discovery learning programs.

Ausubel's Reception Learning

Meaningful learning occurs when students actively process the information they are asked to learn. Whereas Bruner advocated a discovery approach to meaningful learning, Ausubel believed that knowledge is best acquired through reception rather than discovery. **Reception learning** occurs when students receive the essential principles or concepts, think about them deductively, and are then shown how to apply them in specific instances (Ausubel, Novak, & Hanesian, 1978).

For Ausubel, active processing of information occurs when the ideas presented are well organized and clearly focused. In order to present effectively, teachers must carefully organize, sequence, and explain the material so that students can process it efficiently. The kind of instruction that leads to reception learning is called *expository teaching*. (*Exposition* means explanation.) An essential element of expository teaching is the advance organizer.

An **advance organizer** is information presented prior to learning that assists in understanding new information (Ausubel, Novak, & Hanesian, 1978). Suppose that a teacher is lecturing about Buddhism. For an advance organizer, the teacher could ask students to read and discuss a passage about the relationship between Christianity and Buddhism (see Ausubel & Youssef, 1963). Advance organizers are thought to provide a context for unfamiliar information by activating prior knowledge. An advance organizer for a lesson on occupational roles might be to ask children what they want to be when they grow up or what jobs family members hold.

Continuing research on advance organizers led Ausubel et al. (1978) to conclude that organizers can enhance learning if two conditions are met. The first condition is that the target information must be a unitary topic or a set of related ideas. Topics that are too broad would require an organizer too general to be meaningful. The second condition for effective use of advance organizers is that the organizing statement or activity must activate the prior knowledge of the learner. If it is unrelated to a learner's prior knowledge, the advance organizer becomes an additional piece of information to be learned rather than an aid to understanding the lesson.

CONNECTION: What is the process by which advance organizers might activate pre-existing schemata (see Chapters 2 and 7)?

reception learning
Ausubel's approach to teaching, in which students are presented with material in a complete, organized form and are shown how to move from broad ideas to more specific instances. Reception learning is deductive.

advance organizer
Information presented prior to instruction that assists in understanding new information by relating it to existing knowledge.

Here's How

Here's How To Construct and Use Advance Organizers

- Examine the new lesson or unit to discover necessary prerequisite knowledge and skills. List.
- Reteach if necessary.
- Find out if students know this prerequisite material.
- List or summarize the major general principles or ideas in the new lesson or unit (this could be done first).
- Write a paragraph or plan an activity (the advance organizer) emphasizing the major general principles and similarities to previous learning.
- Provide verbal or visual information prior to learning of new material that does not contain specific content from the new material.
- Provide a means of generating the logical relationships between old and new topics and elements in the information to be learned.
- Cover the main subtopics of the unit or lesson in the same sequence as they are presented in the advance organizer (Mayer, 1979, p. 392; West, Farmer, & Wolff, 1991, p. 125).

TRY THIS: Observe several classrooms to discover the variety of advance organizers teachers use. Develop an advance organizer for a lesson or unit you might teach.

REFLECTION: How can one instance of learning help or hinder another instance of learning? Think of examples from your own learning experiences.

In expository teaching, advance organizers enable learners to integrate new information and prior knowledge. Whether material is learned through reception or through discovery, students must be able to use what they learn, not only in the circumstances in which learning occurs but in new situations as well.

Transfer of Learning

As defined previously, transfer of learning refers to the influence of learning something in one situation on learning in other situations. We hope, for example, that the problems students learn to solve on Monday will help them solve new problems on Tuesday, on Friday, and next year. How does transfer occur?

Vertical and Lateral Transfer. Gagné (1985) defined two types of transfers, vertical and lateral (see also Royer, 1979). When complex skills are more easily learned because of simple skills that were acquired earlier, *vertical transfer* has occurred. A good example is the acquisition of intellectual skills—learning discriminations facilitates learning concepts. Therefore, one outcome of acquiring the discrimination capability is to facilitate the acquisition of concepts. Likewise, the acquisition of concepts results in easier acquisition of rules.

Lateral transfer is the generalization of knowledge or skill to a new situation—one that is different from the original situation in which the knowledge or skill was acquired but is not more complex. Lateral transfer is promoted when

CONNECTION: How does lateral transfer relate to Gagné's ninth event of instruction? To the transfer dimension of thinking?

students are given novel tasks that require they use what they learned previously. For example, a student who has finished studying a spelling list might work on a word game activity containing the spelling words.

Vertical and lateral transfer can be near or far. *Near transfer* refers to situations in which acquired skills are applied in new ways that are very similar to the original learning situation. *Far transfer* occurs when the skill is applied in situations that are quite far removed from the original learning situation. For example, learning to type on a manual typewriter facilitates using a computer keyboard. The situations are quite similar and would be referred to as near transfer. Learning to type might also facilitate the use of a stenographic machine. However, the situations are quite different and would be an example of far transfer.

Low-Road and High-Road Transfer. Salomon and Perkins (1989) suggested another way of looking at transfer. *Low-road transfer* is the "spontaneous automatic transfer of highly practised skills with little need for reflective thinking" (p. 118). Low-road transfer involves a great deal of practice to attain the automaticity of skills required. Salomon and Perkins use the example of driving a truck after one has learned to drive a car. Low-road transfer would also occur when students begin to read expository prose after learning to read narrative prose.

High-road transfer involves "the explicit conscious formulation of abstraction in one situation that allows making a connection to another" (p. 118). An example is applying math procedures in designing a poster. High-road transfer can occur in a forward-reaching sense when a general principle is so well learned that it suggests itself spontaneously in a new situation. It can occur in a backward-reaching sense when a need arises in a new situation that causes the learner to look back at past experiences for a potential solution. In either case, high-road transfer depends on mindful abstraction. The learner must deliberately use a principle acquired in one context in a new context.

Generating the abstraction and making a decision to use that abstraction in a new way requires the learner to think about his or her own thinking—metacognition.

A Cultural Approach to Teaching Thinking

As we saw earlier in the chapter, transfer of learning can be considered one of the six dimensions of thinking, which also includes aspects of metacognition in mental management. Because thinking is enculturated within subject matter disciplines, Tishman, Perkins, and Jay (1995) advocate "culture-based teaching" as a means for students to acquire good thinking skills. Specifically, they recommend that teachers provide these four **cultural forces**:

1. *Models* of the culture, which are examples or illustrations of good thinking practices. This means that teachers themselves should use the language of thinking in their disciplines and model thinking strategies in solving problems.

2. *Explanation* of culturally important knowledge, such as explaining how a thinking strategy works and why it is important. In discussing a particular interpretation of a poem, for example, an English teacher might describe why it is valuable to identify metaphors in writings.

3. *Interaction* between students and members of the cultural community. Cooperative problem solving, either as a class or in small groups, provides a structure for thinking along with others.

CONNECTION: How does high-road transfer relate to the transfer dimension of thinking? How does low-road transfer relate to automaticity (Chapter 7)?

CRITICAL THINKING: How can lessons support the transfer of learning? Why should they?

cultural forces Four teaching strategies used to help students acquire thinking skills: (1) providing models of the culture, (2) explaining important cultural knowledge, (3) providing interaction among students and other members of the cultural community, and (4) providing feedback on students' use of thinking skills.

4. *Feedback* on students' thinking processes. Teachers can provide direct feedback on whether students have justified their decisions, for example, or they can provide feedback that redirects student effort instead of criticizing it. Questions such as, "Have you considered all the options?" help students to correct impulsive actions that interfere with good thinking.

CONNECTION: How do these cultural forces relate to Vygotsky's theory (Chapter 2) and situated learning (Chapter 7)?

Although these recommendations can be implemented by individual teachers in their classrooms, Tishman et al. (1995) argue that entire schools should become cultures of thinking. As an example, they offer a vision of what a thinking-centred school might look like. At the entrance, a chalkboard greets visitors with the heading, "Things I Wonder about Today," under which both teachers and students write questions. In one classroom, a teacher has posted "Thinking Goals: Be organized, Be curious, Be neat when you make your weather chart, Be patient, and Don't be afraid to ask questions." In another classroom, students are experimenting with what happens to a graph when changes are made to the mathematical equation that represents it. In the gym, the PE teacher has students making up their own calisthenics.

Here's How

Here's How To Create a Culture of Thinking in the Classroom

- Identify the things you already do in the classroom that touch on any or all of the six dimensions of thinking and build on them, making use of the four cultural forces.

- Learn as you go. Start experimenting with one thinking dimension at a time, and be alert to how it naturally draws in others.

- Start small. Think big. Think about multiunit, interdisciplinary projects that might span weeks or months, and start with a pilot project that lasts several days.

- Be explicit with students about what you are trying to do: Make cultural change a joint effort.

- Whenever possible, work with colleagues.

- Try to use the thinking dimensions as bridges across different content areas.

- Be bold: Don't be afraid to plunge in and experiment with thinking-centred activities, even if you feel unsure about exactly what to do (Tishman et al., 1995, pp. 197-199).

How Can You Make Instructional Decisions That Will Help All Students Learn?

Teachers spend most of their instructional planning time in the following ways: allocating time to various learning activities; studying and reviewing content to be taught; organizing daily, weekly, and term schedules; attending to administrative requirements; and assisting substitute teachers (Clark & Peterson, 1986; McCutcheon, 1980). Much of this planning is done to implement the plans and wishes of educational administrators, school boards, and provincial departments of education. As the agent of implementation, however, you will determine how much time is allotted to the various prescribed outcomes, how the outcomes are interpreted, what supplemental materials to use, and how those materials are used. How can you plan instruction to assure effective learning for all your students?

A Systematic Approach to Planning Effective Instruction

Dick and Reiser (1989) define effective instruction as "instruction that enables students to acquire specified skills, knowledge, and attitudes" and "instruction that students enjoy" (p. 2). They offer a systematic planning process that can provide you with an outline for delivering effective instruction. This process consists of interrelated steps as shown in Figure 11.2. Although the figure presents the steps as a linear process, the planning of expert teachers is dynamic, with many of these steps occurring nearly simultaneously (Moallem & Driscoll, 1994). The important thing is, for instruction to be effective, your planning must in some way accommodate these steps. Let's examine each step in turn.

Set Goals This step involves examining and reflecting upon all the various sources of instructional goals that are available to you: provincial or district curriculum guides, textbooks adopted by your school or district, plans developed by school committees or parent/teacher organizations, and your professional judgment. Consider the types of learning outcomes you want students to acquire and within what time framework—during the school year, within a multilesson unit of instruction, in a single lesson. Think about how the goals relate to one another.

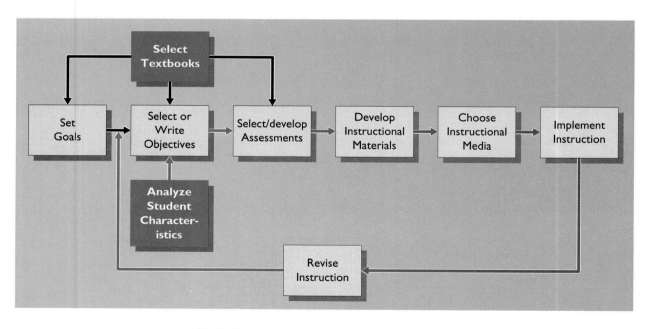

FIGURE 11.2
Dick & Reiser's Model for Developing Effective Instruction

Source: Planning Effective Instruction, W. Dick and R. A. Reiser, 1989, Englewood Cliffs, NJ: Prentice-Hall, Inc. Copyright © 1989 by Allyn & Bacon. Reprinted by permission.

Select or Write Objectives. With this step, you must determine more specifically what you expect students to do as a result of instruction that demonstrates their attainment of instructional goals. It requires you to translate general goals into specific objectives that you can use both to plan instruction and to assess student performance. Thinking about assessment is often a very effective way of generating objectives. This is because writing test items or performance assessments requires you to be very specific about what you mean by goals such as "write effectively" or "employ an efficient strategy." It also requires you to be very specific about the conditions under which you expect students to perform as well as the standards you will use to judge their performance.

Analyze Student Characteristics. While it is important to keep desired outcomes firmly in mind while planning instruction, you also know that learners are diverse in the characteristics they bring to the classroom. This means that you may modify your objectives in order to plan instruction that is appropriate for your particular students. For example, a middle school teacher wants students to manage their own learning to a large extent but knows that they have great difficulty keeping track of time during class assignments. Therefore, while keeping self-regulation of learning as a general goal, the teacher selects time management as a more immediate and achievable objective.

POINT: *Teachers and students are both learners.* An important part of your planning will be learning about the needs of your students, as well as about instructional models and methods and about yourself as a teacher.

Select or Develop Assessments of Student Performance. Assessment of student performance is the means by which you will determine how well students have attained the instructional goals. Although most curriculum series come with tests keyed to objectives listed in the textbook, it is a good idea to examine those tests for what they actually measure. In a recent study, for example, objectives provided in each chapter of a science textbook reflected the higher levels of Bloom's taxonomy (application, analysis, evaluation). The accompanying tests, however, assessed primarily fact and vocabulary learning (Driscoll, Moallem, Dick, & Kirby, 1994). How you assess student performance should depend on what you want students to learn (and what you have actually taught them).

Select Textbooks and Other Materials. Determining the instructional resources you will use to present information or provide learning guidance is a decision ideally made when you plan specific instructional activities related to your objectives. In most schools, however, textbooks remain the mainstay of instruction, and they are generally adopted without much regard for the instructional goals of individual teachers. Whether or not you are involved in the adoption process, you face the choice of using the textbook (or not) in your own instruction.

POINT: Instructional technologies support teaching and learning. Depending on your objectives, you may select various kinds of media as well as textbooks and other print materials.

Dick and Reiser (1989) provide a set of criteria to help teachers in selecting textbooks and other print materials. The criteria pertain to content, presentation, instructional design, and classroom use and are summarized in Figure 11.3.

Develop Instructional Activities and Choose Instructional Media. Instructional activities are what you do in the classroom to help students meet the instructional goals. Both what you do and how you do it should be explicitly oriented to the type of learning outcome you expect students to achieve. Using the recommendations discussed in this chapter, you can devise an instructional plan that identifies your goals of instruction, specific objectives, possible assessment strategies, specific instructional strategies (including events of instruction), and the means or methods you intend to use for implementing those activities. Beginning teachers often find it useful to write detailed plans, so that they have something concrete to

TRY THIS: Interview teachers regarding their instructional plans. How much of each plan is written and how much is mental? Do they follow a particular format in constructing lesson plans? Why?

Content	Instructional Design
Is the content accurate? • Is information factually stated? **Is the content up-to-date?** • Is the copyright date within the last five years? **Is the content comprehensive?** • Is the content congruent with district and/or provincial curriculum guidelines? **Are social issues treated fairly?** • Are ethnic groups, males, and females shown in nonstereotyped roles through words and pictures?	**Are the instructional components congruent?** • Does the content match the objectives and assessments? **Do the instructional characteristics facilitate learning?** • Are summaries included in each unit or chapter? • Are practice activities included in the text or teacher's edition? • Do practice activities match the content and skills? • Do practice activities match the test items? • Are motivational activities included?

Presentation	Classroom Use
Does the text format make learning easy? • Do the chapters address a single, main theme? • Do print size and type ensure legibility for the grade level of students? • Do the illustrations reinforce the text? **Is the content presented at the appropriate grade level for the intended learners?** • Do vocabulary and symbols match grade level of students? **Does the writing style help make learning easy?** • Is the tone appropriate for the intended learners? • Are the directions and explanations clearly stated?	**Are the materials effective with students?** • Are there data indicating that students learn from the materials? • Are there data indicating that students like the materials? **Is use of the instructional materials compatible with the teaching conditions?** • Are preferred settings for conducting instructional activities available in user schools? • Are staff development services available from the publisher? **Do the supplementary print materials help make learning easier?** • Does the teacher's edition match the content of the student text? • Are workbook activities congruent with the content of the text? • Do users state their satisfaction with the materials?

FIGURE 11.3

Criteria for Selecting Textbooks and Supplementary Print Materials

Source: Planning Effective Instruction, W. Dick and R. A. Reiser, 1989, Englewood Cliffs, NJ: Prentice-Hall, Inc. Copyright © 1989 by Allyn & Bacon. Reprinted by permission.

keep them on track during the day. With experience, you will probably find that your written instructional plans will become briefer and more of your planning will take place mentally. A sample format for writing an instructional plan is shown in Figure 11.4.

Implement Instruction and Revise as Necessary.   You have now reached the point of trying out your instructional plan in the classroom. You may have decided to implement a discovery approach or to have students work in cooperative groups. You may be using computers to supplement your teaching or to provide tutorial instruction to students on specific skills or knowledge. You will be using presentation, management, and communication skills as you implement your plan, and you will need to reflect on how well your plan is working.

Sometimes you will get immediate feedback from your students that a particular strategy is ineffective. Perhaps you did not allow enough time for students to complete an assignment, for example. Or perhaps they do not understand the directions for how to complete a task. You can easily remedy problems of this nature during the lesson by allowing additional time or explaining a task in another way. At other times, reflection after action can reveal problems with your instruction. Perhaps a large number of students performed poorly on a unit test, and you realize that additional instruction on prerequisite skills was probably needed. Or perhaps a group of students is having difficulty with a lesson because of a particular thinking disposition or cultural difference. These problems can be overcome by revising the instruction in some way to better meet the needs of the students.

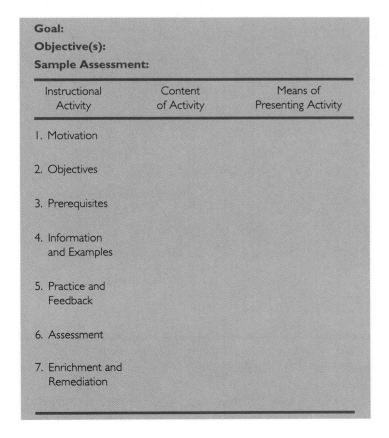

FIGURE 11.4
Format for an Instructional Plan

Source: Adapted from *Planning Effective Instruction,* W. Dick & R. A. Reiser, 1989, Englewood Cliffs, NJ: Prentice-Hall.

Insights on Successful Practice

How have you adapted instructional planning to meet the needs of students with special needs?

I have been the special education resource teacher in this urban elementary school for the past seven years. Five years ago we adopted a philosophy of *Inclusion* in our school. This has meant that some of our students who were previously placed in segregated schools and classrooms for students with disabilities or advanced abilities have been moved back into our regular classrooms. What a challenging and exciting time it has been!

As the school staff, we realized from the beginning that we would need to change the way we do our work. These changes would be a bit different for each one of us, but we would need to move in the same direction so we could provide the best education possible for all the children in our school, including those with special needs. We also knew that to be successful we would need to plan carefully and problem solve as a team when difficulties happened. And happen they did!

We started by asking our district Special Education Consultant to help us through the startup process. It took us a year to do what we called "foundation-building." Creating a vision, working out goals and roles, identifying resources, reviewing "best practices" for assessment and instruction, working on collaboration skills and processes—that year we did it all.

One of the most difficult tasks we faced was to decide on a planning framework that we could all agree would be workable for us as teachers, yet would lead to quality programs for our students with special needs. After some reading, asking, thinking, and talking together, we decided on a planning framework. We used the simple mnemonic **PLAN** to help us remember and stay focused on our process:

Profile the requirements of the classroom environment

Look at student strengths and needs

Adapt the setting, goals, materials, and methods

Nurture the student through continuous assessment and re-planning

As simple as it seems, this framework has had a great deal to do with our success. We developed a computer-based worksheet that sets out the four steps, and the sub-steps of each. We developed on-line assessment tools and action guides to help provide the detailed information we needed. And we began to work together as efficient and effective teams.

We have learned a great deal from our students with special needs. We have learned that not all students need to learn the same thing at the same time; that it is possible to identify students' unique needs and adjust our lessons in small but important ways to help meet those needs. We have learned that teamwork is powerful, and much can be accomplished if we work together. But, most of all, we have learned that our students with special needs are capable of a great deal more than we might have imagined, given the right support. Our students have also learned a lot from us. They have learned about acceptance, togetherness, and caring community. They have learned about competence, persistence, and self-reliance. And, most of all, they are learning how to become full, participating members of society.

SANDRA B.
Special Education Resource
Teacher

> **Your Insights**
>
> *What is Inclusion? How did these teachers prepare for the presence of special needs students in their regular classrooms? What are some of the major obstacles to inclusion? Beyond academic skills, what important outcomes does inclusion address?*

Information that can help you determine what revisions are necessary includes student performance on tests or other assessment measures during and after instruction, student attitudes toward instruction, and observation of student behaviour during instruction. Considering this information in light of your goals, objectives, assessments, and instructional strategies will help you to systematically pinpoint deficiencies in your plan that can be revised for more effective instruction.

Adapt Instruction for Students with Special Needs There is one more factor to consider as you put your instructional plan into action. Does your plan adequately accommodate students with special needs in your classroom? The general planning framework in Figure 11.2 alerts you to the importance of identifying student learning characteristics and modifying objectives to meet individual needs. However, you may find it necessary to plan more intensively on an ongoing basis to meet the needs of some students, especially those with disabilities. You may also find it helpful to enter into a collaborative team effort with a special education resource teacher to assist with this planning and adaptation. Such a team planning environment has been described in the Insights on Successful Practice on page 376.

With a Canadian perspective on planning for inclusion of students with special needs, Hutchinson (Friend, Bursuck, & Hutchinson, 1998) has outlined a systematic series of steps called INCLUDE to assist in adapting instruction for students with special needs:

Identify classroom environmental, curricular, and instructional demands

Note student learning strengths and needs

Check for potential areas of student success

Look for potential problem areas

Use information gathered to brainstorm instructional adaptations

Decide which adaptations to implement

Evaluate student progress

This framework alerts the teacher to consider the demands of the classroom setting and the characteristics of the student while planning lessons. Through such careful analysis, the individual needs of students with disabilities can often be reasonably accommodated with quite minor adjustments. Hutchinson points out that the accommodations and adaptations to your lessons which you decide to make for students with special needs will often assist many other students in the class.

A Flexible Approach to Delivering Instruction: Accommodating Student Diversity

As Figure 11.4 suggests, instructional plans are like blueprints. A blueprint provides a plan for that which will be built. Although the blueprint identifies what elements will be built and how those elements will relate to each other, it does not specify the techniques that will be used to construct the various elements of the building. Instructional plans provide us with the elements of a lesson and suggest the sequence in which those elements should occur. But no plan can be so prescriptive as to eliminate the professional judgments of teachers and remain an effective model for instruction.

Plans may provide the structure for your teaching efforts, but you and your students provide the context. Teaching is a highly personal activity. How you teach depends very much on who you are. Regardless of which techniques you choose, you will adapt them to better suit your own characteristics as a teacher and your students' characteristics as learners. This may be illustrated by examining the research on beliefs that teachers hold about their ability to affect student learning and achievement. A study of elementary school children and teachers carried out in Southern Alberta found that the achievement of grade three students was positively related to teacher personal efficacy beliefs. As well, the beliefs held by students about their own abilities was correlated with school achievement (Anderson, Greene, & Loewen, 1988).

Each student will respond differently to your instructional actions. Assuming your job is to facilitate the achievement of your students, you must make decisions about instructing them while keeping their individual characteristics in mind. There is no one best way to teach, and effective teachers respond to their personal strengths or weaknesses, the characteristics of their students, and the desired instructional outcomes. While there are many opinions about what is a good or ideal teacher, there is no absolute agreement. Each of us can describe our best or favourite teacher, but we soon realize that there are both common and unique qualities when we compare our criteria to those ascribed to someone else's favourite teacher. For example, a group of Ontario adolescent boys and girls agreed that teachers should have a thorough knowledge of the subject they teach and should be effective communicators. However, "while males look to a variety of classroom procedures, among them interesting textbooks, shorter classes, and audio-visual aids to help them in their courses, female adolescents place their trust primarily in the teacher as the centre of a social network within which students seek respect and support" (Cook, 1992, p. 28).

Reflecting in action can help you respond during class to individual students' needs. You might discover, for example, that one group of students requires more time to complete an activity than you had planned or than other groups require. Having to adjust the timing of activities during a lesson is a common occurrence, especially for beginning teachers. Reflecting after action is a way to consider changes in your plan that you might make based on events you observed in class.

At the same time, reflecting before action can help you prepare for unexpected occurrences—either things that go wrong or teachable moments that arise during a lesson. For example, things can sometimes go wrong with even the best laid plans. Equipment to conduct an experiment might fail, or a demonstration might not turn out as expected. If you have considered the variety of possible things that could go wrong with your lessons, then you are in a good position to react appropriately when something does go wrong. Likewise, when you expect the unexpected, you can exploit teachable moments in a positive way to support desirable, if unintended, outcomes.

How do you develop the flexibility with which to respond to the ever-changing needs of your students and yourself? One way is through regular reflection on your teaching and its effects on your students. We have stressed throughout this book that teaching is a continual process of learning—about yourself as a teacher, about instructional models and methods, and about students.

POINT: *Reflective construction is necessary for the development of teaching expertise.* Improving your teaching practices depends on your reflection upon how they work.

Teacher Chronicle Conclusion

Giving Something Back

As Angela prepares for her regular Thursday afternoon mentoring session with Jason, many thoughts run through her head: "It's hard to believe — only two weeks left in Jason's internship experience. But I've seen so much growth in his skills, confidence, knowledge base, and so much more. Jason will be an excellent teacher. I can see that clearly. My goal today will be to get Jason to step back from all the planning and teaching that has been going on, and have him reflect on his unit on ants and what he and the students have learned from it."

Jason has come to value these mentoring sessions with Angela very highly. Her skillful questioning has led him to think very deeply about himself as a teacher —his values, the skills he possesses and those he needs to acquire, and how to get to know the students and their needs.

Angela begins by saying, "Jason, you have just finished the last of your lessons on the ant unit you developed. Let's spend some time looking back and thinking about what we have all learned from it. I'll ask you some questions that I hope will help you in writing up the Reflections part of your assignment for the college. First of all, what have you learned about planning units and lessons?"

Without hesitation, Jason responds, "First of all, I've learned how important it is to be systematic and organized. Remember the lesson I did on ant physiology? It sure did flop, but it was easy to figure out why— the instructions for the cooperative learning activity were not clear enough, and the misbehaviour that followed was really my fault. I'll never let that happen again. I've also found out that learning can be fun, for the students and for me. The main thing is to get them involved in making decisions and in using their learning. I wonder how long some of those kids will keep their ant colonies working?"

"You're right, Jason," says Angela. "Systematic advanced planning with a close eye on the outcomes you want students to achieve is critical to success in teaching. What have you learned about instructional approaches and methods?"

"Well, I've learned that no matter what instructional approach you use, from direct instruction to discovery learning, a teacher's job is to identify a student's conceptions and misconceptions, and provide explanations and modelling that affirm their understanding or help the student rethink those ideas. I have also learned that, with guidance and structure, students can learn a great deal from each other. I was really pleased with the peer tutoring groups we set up in math. It took some work and planning, but the students learned a lot."

"Great, Jason. You have shown me repeatedly over the past month your increasing skill at doing these things effectively with students. What can you tell me about meeting the individual needs of students, particularly those with disabilities?"

"For me, the key to meeting individual student needs is to discover each student's learning interests, skills, and strategies. This was difficult for me. But, with your help, I learned how to listen and watch carefully as they talked, read, and wrote; and to analyze their motives and interests. I was able to use this knowledge to adjust my goals for students as I planned lessons. For example, I puzzled over how to help Tanya overcome her problem completing assignments. I found that using a highlighter to accent the key words in printed instructions worked very well for her."

"You're right, Jason," says Angela. "Students will learn best from us only when we are able to learn from them."

After Jason leaves, Angela is alone again with her thoughts. "I'm glad I responded to Bob's nudge and agreed to take an intern. It has been tremendously gratifying to watch Jason grow as a professional, and to know that I had an important part to play in it. Now I know how you must have felt, Sandy. It really is great to be able to give something back to your profession!"

Application Questions

1. Which aspects of Dick and Reiser's model of effective instruction has Jason used to meet the needs of individual students?

2. How might the six dimensions of good thinking be incorporated into Jason's unit on ants?

3. What could Jason do ensure that students transfer the learning from his ant unit to other situations?

4. How might Jason have built discovery learning into his unit?

5. Considering Bloom's Taxonomy, how could Jason have worked on improving his questioning skills?

6. Think of a thematic unit that you would enjoy teaching. Develop a lesson using Dick and Reiser's format for instructional planning.

CHAPTER SUMMARY

What Are Possible Outcomes of Learning? (L.O. 1, p. 348)

Students learn many different things in school, from specific facts and critical thinking in subject matter disciplines to attitudes and motor skills. By categorizing these different types of learning outcomes, teachers assume that different learning conditions are necessary for students to acquire the various outcomes.

How Do Teachers Determine and Specify Instructional Outcomes? (L.O. 2, 3, p. 397)

Teachers rely on provincial requirements, curriculum guides, district and school guidelines, as well as their own professional knowledge to determine what their students should learn in a school year and within a particular lesson. To help them plan instruction and assessment, teachers can generate specific objectives—which include desired student performance, conditions of performance, and criteria by which to judge performance—from more general goals.

How Do Instructional Events Facilitate Learning Outcomes? (L.O. 4, 5, 6, p. 361)

Gagné's nine events of instruction provide guidelines as to what external conditions should be provided during instruction to facilitate internal processes of learning. These are implemented differently depending on a teacher's decision to use discovery or reception learning in the classroom. To facilitate transfer of learning and other dimensions of thinking, teachers can employ four cultural forces in their instruction—models, explanation, interaction, and feedback.

How Can You Make Instructional Decisions That Will Help All Students Learn? (L.O. 7, 8, p. 371)

By employing Dick and Reiser's (1989) model of effective instruction, you can systematically plan instruction to meet students' individual needs and to facilitate learning of particular outcomes. No matter how thoroughly you plan, however, situations are bound to arise in the classroom that call for a flexible and reasoned response. Cultivating a reflective attitude is one way to be prepared for all eventualities.

KEY CONCEPTS

advance organizer, 368

affective domain, 355

attitude, 353

behavioural objectives, 360

Bloom's taxonomy, 354

cognitive domain, 354

cognitive strategies, 352

concrete concepts, 350

cultural forces, 370

defined concepts, 351

discovery learning, 366

discrimination, 349

enterprise schema, 365

Gagné's events of instruction, 362

higher-order rules, 352

instructional goals, 359

intellectual skills, 349

learning outcomes, 348

motor skills, 353

psychomotor domain, 355

reception learning, 368

rules, 351

six dimensions of good thinking, 357

transfer of learning, 365

verbal information, 349

12 Teaching for Active Learning

LEARNING OUTCOMES

When you have completed this chapter, you will be able to

1. explain the principles underlying the term *active learning*

2. demonstrate how to encourage good thinking dispositions in students

3. describe active learning during teacher-centred, direct instruction lessons

4. explain how lecturing, explaining, and questioning can promote active learning

5. explain the rationale and practices involved in student-centred instruction

6. describe how small group discussions can support active learning

7. describe how peer teaching and learning foster active learning

8. list and describe the main approaches to cooperative learning

9. outline how computer technology can be used to enhance student-directed learning

Teacher Chronicle

Plugging In

Eighth grade teacher Tom Duffy has just finished a science unit on magnetism and is about to begin a unit on electricity. He knows from working with these students for five months that there will be considerable differences among them in the background knowledge they bring into the learning situation. Kam's father is an electronics technician, and he and Kam have built some amazing projects together. Susan, who has a learning disability, lacked interest in the magnetism unit, and probably will bring limited background knowledge to the topic of electricity. Mr. Duffy already has many activities and experiments in mind, but he needs to find out what his students already know so that he can match his lessons and tasks to their present knowledge.

Mr. Duffy asks his students each to draw up a KWL worksheet by ruling a sheet of paper into three vertical columns. Mr. Duffy uses the KWL strategy before each new instructional unit, so the students know well how to use it by now. He watches as they enter the column headings Know, Want to Know, and Learned. Then he says, "Think about the term *electricity* and write down everything you know about it in the Know column. Remember, it's OK to use a concept web to present your knowledge, if you want. I'll be using this information to adjust our science experiments on electricity to fit with what you already know."

After the students have been writing for about fifteen minutes, Mr. Duffy says, "It's time to break into your learning teams for twenty minutes to share what you know. Remember to assign the roles of recorder, encourager, and facilitator. Recorders, please fill out the Know column on a new KWL sheet."

A buzz of productive activity follows. Mr. Duffy circulates among the groups to ensure that students are on task and on time. At the end of twenty minutes he says, "OK teams, I'd like you to break out of your groups. Your job as individuals is to think about the discussion, then complete the second column of KWL—Want to Know. Maybe somebody on your team mentioned a term you don't know, or perhaps a concept or characteristic about electricity caught your attention and caused you to want to learn more. You have ten minutes—go ahead."

The classroom is silent as the students think and write. After ten minutes, Mr. Duffy says, "OK class, I'd like you to break back into teams. This time the job is to share what you have written in the Want to Know column. After we have finished with teams today, I will collect the individual and team KWLs, so recorders, keep good notes."

As the teams work together, Mr. Duffy circulates around the class looking over the individual and group KWL sheets. He notices that Kam has shown an advanced knowledge in the diagrams he has drawn of switches, circuits, and their operation. Susan has made entries reflecting just a basic knowledge, such as "Makes the toaster work." Just as he had anticipated, there is a lot of variation in what he sees on the other KWL sheets. During this hour, Mr. Duffy has gathered some information crucial to the success of his electricity unit.

After the students have gone for the day, Mr. Duffy looks over the group KWL sheets carefully, and takes notes. It becomes clear to him how he will need to set up his lab stations for the next day. He also looks over the individual KWL sheets for patterns of responses and uses this information to create the most productive learning teams possible.

Focus Questions

1. How can you actively engage students in their own learning?
2. Is active learning dependent on the subject matter?
3. When is it advantageous for students to work in small groups? to receive whole-group instruction?
4. When is it important for students to receive direct instruction? To engage in discovery learning?
5. What is cooperative learning and how does it work? What are the benefits of cooperative learning?
6. How can computers and related technology support active learning?
7. How can a teacher make adaptations in the classroom to help exceptional students meet with success? How can technology be used to help these students?

What is Active Learning?

Active learning is a general term for learning that occurs when the learner is mentally involved in a task. The notion of active learning has been around for a long time, but its meaning has evolved considerably over the last four decades. The term was first used by researchers in psychology and education in the late 1950s and early 1960s as they sought to move our understanding of learning away from the behaviouristic explanations that had dominated psychological thought for four decades and toward cognitive explanations. Behaviourism, reflected in the theory of operant conditioning, assumed that learning is reflected in behaviour and that nonobservable mental activity does not have to be considered to understand how human beings learn. As cognitive views of learning developed, the mental activity of learners became the focus of theoreticians and researchers. Thus, active learning was learning in which cognitive activity played a major role.

As cognitive views gained greater currency in the psychological and educational research literature, the meaning of the term *active learning* continued to evolve. By the mid 1970s, for example, Merlin Wittrock had proposed his *generative model of learning* (Wittrock, 1974; Wittrock, Marks, & Doctorow, 1975). The basic premise of the model is that learners comprehend and understand what they are learning in ways that are consistent with their prior knowledge. The implications of this and other models of cognitive activity have fostered research that continues to illuminate the nature of active learning (Kourilsky & Wittrock, 1992; Wittrock, 1990, 1991).

Today, the term *active learning* has a connotation of constructivism that is consistent with one of the working assumptions of this book: Learning is actively constructed in social contexts. The basic idea is that learners construct meaning through their interactions with their environment. As you read this paragraph, you are the one constructing its meaning. And because your prior knowledge and experiences are different from those of other readers, the meanings you construct may differ—slightly or more significantly—from theirs. This view of knowledge construction as building bridges from the

CONNECTION: See the assumptions of operant conditioning in Chapter 6.

POINT: Several chapters in this book have discussed constructivist views. The constructivist view underlies one of the basic assumptions of this book: *Learning is active construction in social contexts.*

active learning Learning that occurs when the learner is mentally engaged in a task.

known to the unknown underlies many of the teaching techniques that are described in this chapter (Haring-Smith, 1994a, 1994b, 1993). The common thread in all uses of *active learning* is that learners are involved in constructing their own knowledge.

New approaches to the teaching-learning process seek to make students active participants in knowledge construction rather than passive recipients of didactic presentations. The teaching approaches examined in this chapter emphasize active learning but include direct instruction. Good teaching—new *and* traditional—has always produced active learning. A lesson or lecture that provokes a student to consider a topic from a new perspective has involved the student in constructing knowledge.

One way to consider the kinds of teaching that yield active learning is to focus on student thinking. What kind of thinking helps students acquire basic skills? Find and solve problems? Think critically? If we can answer these questions we will be prepared to discover the kinds of teaching that yield active learning.

Student Thinking

CRITICAL THINKING: Thinking dispositions were discussed in Chapter 5 as a source of variability among learners. What role do you predict thinking dispositions will play in this chapter on instructional approaches and techniques?

We have addressed the ways students think, directly or indirectly, a number of times in this book. In Chapter 5, we discussed thinking dispositions as a source of variability among individual learners. Thinking dispositions, you will recall, are mental habits, inclinations, or tendencies in a person's thinking that occur over time and across thinking and learning situations (Tishman, Perkins, & Jay, 1995). Shari Tishman and her colleagues suggest that good learners are disposed toward curiosity, flexibility, precision, organization, and patience in their thinking.

In Chapter 7, we examined the way students remember information, how they construct mental representations, how they identify and solve problems. The steps involved in teaching problem-solving skills include identifying, defining, and representing the problem; predicting candidate solutions; trying out and evaluating solutions; and reflecting on the problem-solving process. We also examined the metacognitive skills that allow students to monitor their thinking and problem solving.

In the context of active learning, thinking dispositions and problem-solving skills are equally important. Most efforts to teach higher-level thinking, such as problem solving, however, have focused on skills, and have failed to account for the dispositional differences that exist among students. Yet those who do not have good thinking dispositions are not as likely to use the skills they have been taught. One way to improve the teaching and learning of thinking is to focus on the development of dispositions to use sound thinking. But how do you teach dispositions? How can you facilitate the development of thinking dispositions that contribute to learning? You can incorporate thinking dispositions into the culture of your classroom. Some specific ways of enhancing thinking dispositions (based on suggestions from Tishman et al., 1995; Woditsch & Schmittroth, 1991) are presented in Here's How. As you examine the instructional approaches in this chapter that facilitate active learning, consider how the thinking dispositions might be encouraged.

Here's How

Here's How To Cultivate Good Thinking Dispositions

- Model good thinking dispositions: Show students how you think. Share the questions you ask when learning, demonstrate persistence in the face of difficult problems, and show how you consult additional sources of information. Critically analyze with students the thinking of historical figures. What was Pierre Elliott Trudeau's thinking during the October Crisis, for example? Encourage students to model good thinking dispositions for each other.

- Build an awareness of good thinking dispositions: Encourage and prompt students to take advantage of opportunities to display good thinking dispositions. One teacher kept a poster in plain view and referred to it often during class discussions. The poster addressed the five thinking dispositions with these simple pieces of advice:

  Don't give up.
  Ask lots of questions.
  Generate multiple ideas and explanations.
  Be critical.
  Don't stop too soon (Tishman et al., 1995, p. 47).

- Use "thinking alarms": In addition to encouraging the use of good thinking dispositions, you should also point out instances in which poor thinking dispositions are used by sounding thinking alarms. Here's another poster example that lists both the impetus for the alarm and the good thinking disposition that the alarm should encourage.

Thinking Alarm	*Thinking Disposition*
Lazy thinking	Be curious and questioning.
Narrow thinking	Be broad and adventurous.
Messy thinking	Be clear and careful.
Scattered thinking	Be organized.
Hasty thinking	Give thinking time (Tishman et al., 1995, p. 53).

- Encourage your students to interact: Provide opportunities for student-to-student interaction in your classes. Encourage students to listen for poor thinking and to sound alarms. Likewise encourage students to identify and praise instances of good thinking.

REFLECTION: What were the learning activities that caused you to think at the highest levels? Were they solitary activities or did you interact with others? What role does social interaction play in critical thinking?

Critical Thinking

Cognitive taxonomies such as the one described in Chapter 11 postulate different levels of thinking. Lower levels of thinking such as recall of knowledge and basic comprehension require less complex cognitive activity than higher levels such as synthesis and evaluation, the key ingredients in **critical thinking**. Critical thinking

critical thinking Higher-level thinking used to analyze, synthesize, and evaluate.

can be defined as cognitive activity that allows a learner to analyze or synthesize information in order to make a judgment. The outcomes that we seek for our students involve the ability to think critically. We want students to leave the classroom not only capable of synthesizing and evaluating but also with a desire to apply their critical thinking abilities to problems. We want them to persist when the problem is difficult and to generate creative solutions to those problems. Knowledge is the result of doing, predicting, testing, talking; it is actively constructed in a social context.

Applying critical thinking skills in the classroom can be encouraged whenever students are required to solve problems. For example, as students are attempting to define or clarify a problem, they judge what information is relevant or irrelevant, determine if additional information is necessary, and formulate appropriate questions. Often problems require the student to distinguish fact from opinion, to recognize value judgments and unsupported assumptions, and analyze multiple sources of data to determine if they are adequate for use in formulating a solution (Kneedler, 1985). By encouraging students to analyze, synthesize, and evaluate whenever they have an opportunity to solve problems, we will help them acquire good thinking dispositions as well.

Teaching that Yields Active Learning

There are many ways to facilitate active learning. This chapter examines traditional teaching techniques that have been around for hundreds of years as well as more recent techniques. One of the major distinctions made in this chapter is between teacher-centred instruction and student-centred instruction. This distinction refers to the locus of learning activity. For example, teachers who present the key concepts of a unit through lecture are at the centre of learning activity in their classrooms. If students have a question or are in need of clarification, they go to the source of the information, the teacher. This is **teacher-centred instruction**. In **student-centred instruction**, a teacher may organize students into learning groups, provide them with the necessary resources, materials, and framework for learning, and then expect the students to work together to learn the key concepts. In this case, if clarification is needed, students would consult each other before going to the instructor.

Teacher-centred techniques concentrate the responsibility for guiding the teaching-learning process in the teacher; student-centred techniques spread the responsibility between teacher and students. Both sets of techniques can be used to foster active learning in students.

How Can Teacher-Centred Instruction Support Active-Learning?

Teacher-centred instruction occurs when the teacher exerts a high degree of control over the teaching-learning process. A form of teacher-centred instruction that captures the essence of such approaches is called *direct* or *explicit* instruction, terms coined by Barak Rosenshine (1979, 1986).

Direct instruction refers to academically focused, teacher-directed classrooms using sequenced and structured materials. It refers to teaching activities where goals are clear to students, time allocated for instruction is sufficient and continuous, coverage of content is extensive, performance of students is moni-

TRY THIS: Observe a variety of classroom teachers. Which ones would you classify as characterizing teacher-centred instruction? Why? Which teachers characterize student-centred approaches to instruction? Why?

REFLECTION: Think back to a dynamic teacher you had in elementary school who epitomized direct instruction. What behaviours did the teacher display during instruction? Was the teacher effective? Why or why not?

teacher-centred instruction Instruction in which the teacher is the focus of learning activity.

student-centred instruction Instruction in which the student is the focus of learning activity.

direct instruction A form of teacher-centred instruction in which goals are clear and the teacher controls the material and the pace.

tored, . . . and feedback to students is immediate and academically oriented. In direct instruction, the teacher controls instructional goals, chooses materials appropriate for the student's ability, and paces the instructional episode (p. 38, boldface added).

Direct instruction may be teacher centred, but that does not mean that students are not actively involved. Gagné's events of instruction, discussed in Chapter 7, represent a model of direct instruction that encourages active learning. Another example of a teacher-centred approach to instruction is **mastery teaching**. Madeline Hunter's Mastery Teaching Program, for example (1982, 1984, 1991), is one of the most widely recognized models of teacher-centred instruction among practising teachers. Hunter identifies seven elements that constitute an effective lesson. As you examine the elements, picture where the action is in the classroom. Whom do you envision doing most of the talking? Who controls the pace of the lesson? Who identifies the key questions to be answered or the key issues to be resolved?

1. *Anticipatory set* refers to a mind-set that leaves students curious about the remainder of the lesson. Their curiosity leads them to speculate about or anticipate what is to come. This is the part of a lesson through which the teacher captures the attention of the student.

2. *Objective and purpose,* the second element in Hunter's model, provides students with the explicit objectives or purpose of the lesson. By informing the students of what you expect them to be able to do, you are building on the anticipatory set.

3. *Input* is the presentation of new material. Input, as an element of an effective lesson, requires that information be well organized and presented in a logical sequence. Hunter suggests that presenting information in a verbal and a visual manner can make input effective.

4. *Modelling* means that you should use frequent examples in the lesson to clarify meanings. Hunter refers to the modeling phase of a lesson as "modelling what you mean." When the objective of the lesson is to attain a skill, modelling serves the same purpose as Bandura's observational learning. If the objective of the lesson is to attain a concept or acquire verbal information, modelling calls for the use of examples or analogies or metaphors.

5. *Checking for understanding* is the evaluation of students' comprehension and understanding by asking questions orally or on a written quiz. The teacher may also ask the students to provide an example of the material on their own.

6. *Guided practice* begins the process of transfer by presenting students with a few problems or questions to answer on their own. Immediate feedback guides their practice in answering such questions in the classroom and gives students a way to check their own understanding and receive help on any aspect of the lesson that they may have misunderstood.

7. *Independent practice* encourages students to answer questions or work problems on their own. Providing immediate feedback after independent practice is particularly helpful. However, feedback may occur after students have completed a homework assignment, another form of independent practice.

Studies of the effectiveness of Hunter's method have generally concluded that training teachers in the method does not significantly increase student learning (e.g., Mandeville & Rivers, 1991; Stallings & Krasavage, 1986). In one study, teachers were taught the Hunter method as part of an inservice project that included two years of supervised program implementation and a one-year

CRITICAL THINKING: With reference to Bandura's theory of social learning, in what respects is Hunter's use of the term *modelling* similar and different? What are the outcomes of Hunter's modelling? How do they compare with the outcomes of Bandura's modelling?

mastery teaching Refers to Madeline Hunter's seven-step lesson model.

anticipatory set The first step in Hunter's approach to lesson delivery. This step establishes expectancies or a mind-set in students that anticipates the material to be covered.

guided practice The sixth step in Hunter's approach to lesson delivery. This step begins the process of transfer.

What thinking dispositions on the part of learners should teachers encourage for active learning? How can this teacher provide direct instruction that is effective and that supports active learning?

maintenance follow-up period, during which teachers and administrators were to continue the project on their own. During the two implementation years, teachers increased their use of Hunter's principles; however, they decreased their use during the last year. The amount of time students spent engaged in tasks and achievement of those tasks increased during the two years of implementation. These too decreased during the last year. The research indicates that close monitoring of classroom practice may be required in order for the Hunter method to be as effective as possible (Stallings & Krasavage, 1986).

Although training in the Hunter method and in other forms of direct instruction does not seem to enhance student learning in a consistently significant way, many educators see value in Hunter's method for aspiring teachers. The value is that Hunter's method identifies the minimum skills that all teachers should possess (Gage & Needels, 1989). Perhaps one reason studies have shown little difference between those trained in the Hunter method and those not trained is that the untrained teachers already possessed the skills that the training addressed.

When the teacher is the hub around which learning activities turn, it is likely that the information flow in the classroom is from teacher to student. More important than the direction of the information flow, however, is what happens to the information when it reaches the student. Are students actively processing the information that reaches them? In the next several sections we examine teaching behaviours or techniques that are common in teacher-centred classrooms. For each type of teaching behaviour, we seek to discover how that behaviour can facilitate active learning in students.

Lecturing

Lecturing, that is, presenting information to a group, is the most common teaching behaviour in elementary and secondary schools, colleges and universities, and training programs within business and industry (Johnson & Johnson, 1994). Your own experience probably reflects the prevalence of lecturing. Despite its status as the method of choice among teachers at all levels, lecturing has come under criticism (Good & Brophy, 1994; Henson, 1988). One criticism is that the lecture format assumes that all students need the same information presented in the same way at the same pace. Another criticism is that lectures provide little opportunity for learners to interact either with each other or with the presenter and therefore discourage the social construction of knowledge and skills. A third criticism is that lectures often outlast student attention and are boring, poorly organized, irrele-

lecturing A discourse given in class for the purpose of instruction.

vant, or redundant. You have no doubt experienced lectures that did not meet your needs, did not allow you to talk about your reactions to ideas, or failed to capture and maintain your interest. Such complaints are more properly directed at the lecturer rather than the technique itself, however. Overuse and inappropriate use are to blame for much of the criticism heaped on lectures (Good & Brophy, 1994).

Lecturing is appropriate and effective in some situations and not in others. A number of researchers have identified the conditions under which lecturing is an appropriate instructional technique (e.g., Bligh, 1972; Good & Brophy, 1994; Henson, 1988; McKeachie, 1986; McLeish, 1976; Verner & Dickinson, 1967). The optimal conditions include:

- When information presented in the lecture is not readily available from another source
- When material needs to be organized in a special way for a particular group
- When a new topic of study or a task needs to be introduced
- When the information to be presented is a unique integration of multiple sources
- When it is important to present points of view that differ from assigned materials
- When information needs to be summarized or synthesized.

TRY THIS: Observe teachers using the lecture technique. Which lecturers seem to be most effective? Which lecturers show signs of "reading" the class? What behaviours indicate that they are reading student reactions? Are the more effective lecturers the better readers?

Equally important is lecture preparation and delivery. The following guidelines for effective lectures (Chilcoat, 1989; Duffy et al., 1986) reflect an emphasis on the cognitive processes involved in active learning:

- Start with an advance organizer or an anticipatory set that allows students to create a context for what is to be presented.
- Present the behavioural objectives, instructional goals, or expected learning outcomes of the presentation. This will orient students to expectations and alert them to new material and key concepts.
- Present new material with reference to students' prior knowledge.
- Elicit student responses from time to time to check for comprehension and to ensure learning is active.
- Review the main points of the lecture.
- Follow the lecture with an assignment or questions that require students to paraphrase key concepts and apply them in novel ways.

The guidelines for delivering an effective lecture are designed to help you overcome some of the shortcomings of the technique. In particular, the idea of periodically eliciting student responses during the lecture is designed to combat the problem of maintaining student attention, a fundamental prerequisite for active learning. Even highly motivated learners have difficulty attending actively for extended periods. Research suggests that adults are capable of active attention for only ten to fifteen minutes (e.g., Johnson, Johnson, & Smith, 1991; Penner, 1984; Stuart & Rutherford, 1978).

EXAMPLE: Another example of a learning task that requires relatively long periods of attention is reading. Adults are usually capable of sustaining attention for longer periods. Why should this be the case?

If motivated adults have attention difficulties, how can teachers of children and adolescents maintain the attention necessary for active learning? One solution, which is consistent with the guidelines presented here, is to use lectures with *book ends* and *pair shares* (Johnson & Johnson, 1994). Book ends refer to focused discussions that occur just before and just after a lecture. The prelecture discussion serves

CRITICAL THINKING: From an information- processing point of view, why should book ends and pair shares solve the attention problem that accompanies the use of lecture?

as an advance organizer for the lecture. Instead of the teacher presenting the advance organizer, however, students work on a task that allows them to access pertinent prior knowledge. The postlecture discussion serves to bring closure on the topics presented in the lecture. **Pair shares** refer to short discussions between pairs of students, interspersed with periods of lecture (Figure 12.1). The technique of lecturing with book end and pair share discussions allows students to interact with each other in order to construct their understanding of new concepts actively.

Here's How

Here's How To Deliver a Lecture that Encourages Active Learning

- *Prelecture Focused Discussion.* Have students pair with the person seated next to them. You may wish to have students change seats from time to time so that subsequent pairings will vary. Assign the advance organizing task.
- *First Lecture Segment.* Deliver the first part of your lecture. Make sure that the segment lasts no longer than twelve minutes.
- *First Pair Share.* Give students a task that addresses the material you covered in the first segment of the lecture. Allow three or four minutes for the pair to complete the task. Announce the time allotted and then stick to the deadline. The task may be to answer a question that you pose, to react to a theory or position that you have presented, or to relate the lecture material to past learning. The pairs use the following process to complete the task:
  - Individuals *formulate* their own answers.
  - Students *share* their formulations with their partners.
  - Students *listen* intently to their partners' answers.
  - Together, the pair *creates* a new answer that synthesizes and improves on the answers of both individuals.

  Randomly select two or three students to give thirty-second summaries of each pair's answer. Make sure that students understand that they are not speaking for themselves, but for the pair. It is important to take the time to have students make summary statements. This sends the message that their discussions are to be taken seriously.
- *Second Lecture Segment.* Deliver the second part of your lecture.
- *Second Pair Share.* Assign a task that addresses the second lecture segment.
- *Repeat* the lecture segment-pair share steps until the lecture is complete.
- *Postlecture Discussion.* Assign pairs to complete a discussion task that brings closure to the material presented in the lecture. For example, you could ask students to summarize what they learned from the lecture and how they can integrate the new information into some extant conceptual framework. The closure task could lead students into a homework assignment or preview concepts to be covered at the next class. Students should be given four to five minutes to complete the postlecture discussion.

TRY THIS: How many of your friends are good at explaining? Interview those who are. Ask why they explain well. Ask them a question that requires an explanation. Write down their responses and then analyze the responses to see if you can identify elements that make the explanations effective.

pair shares Short discussions between student dyads. Such discussions are usually interspersed with periods of lecture.

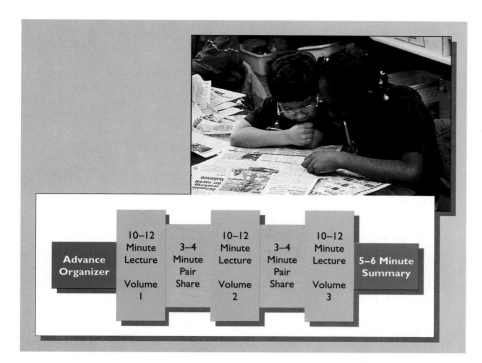

FIGURE 12.1
Lecturing with Book Ends and Pair Shares

Source: Adapted from *Learning Together Alone* (4th ed., p. 130), D. W. Johnson & R. T. Johnson, Needham Heights, MA: Allyn & Bacon.

Explaining

Another form of instructional interaction that, in this case, focuses on teacher-student interaction is explanation. Successful explanations reward teachers with the "lightbulbs" of understanding above their students' heads. Explanations are more focused than lectures. The purpose of **explanation** is to define, clarify, or provide an account of concepts, events, and relationships (cf. Gage & Berliner, 1988). Although lectures often include explanations, explanations are not always presented in the context of a lecture. For instance, an explanation could be triggered by a student's question about a concept from the previous night's reading assignment.

The teacher who presents explanations effectively tends to be more responsive to the specific needs of the student and has a clearer idea of the student's misunderstanding. The explanation that such a teacher offers provides information that goes to the heart of the student's problem. Effective teachers also tend to provide a context or framework for the answers that their explanations provide (Duffy, Roehler, Meloth, & Vavrus, 1986). For example, suppose a student, after reading the assigned chapter, asks the economics teacher for help in understanding the concept of supply. One way of responding to the student's request would be to provide a formal definition of the term such as, "Supply is the amount of goods and services available in the marketplace." A second way of responding would be to provide the definition and then go on to describe how supply and demand operate to influence price. The first response by the teacher, the definition, might help the student memorize the definition by repeating the term and its meaning. But the definition by itself does not help the student put the term into a larger context or framework. The second response in this example does help the student connect the concept of supply to other concepts such as demand, price, and market. Useful

explanation A clarification that provides a context or framework for a concept, event, or relationship.

Insights on Successful Practice

What advice can you give novice teachers about grouping students for instruction?

Grouping students for instructional purposes suggests that the teacher is a flexible practitioner and that he or she believes that students do have multidimensional experiences that can be utilized in collecting, organizing, and presenting information. To be successful, the technique requires a variety of teaching approaches such as large group instruction, conceptual teaching, direct inductive teaching, and individual instruction. Most importantly, it includes opportunities for students to assume control of their learning experiences. The use of this technique also suggests that the teacher is not a dispenser of information, but rather a facilitator, a guide, a motivator, and a positive critic.

Groups may be organized homogeneously or heterogeneously, depending on the nature of the concept or topic being taught and the objectives to be achieved. If the topic is naturally divided into several parts which contain many levels of difficulties, homogeneous groups may serve as an effective option. Generally, however, heterogeneous groups provide more opportunities for student-student interaction, for sharing information, and for cooperation. However students are grouped, the number of groups in a classroom should not exceed five or six. This range will permit the teacher adequate opportunities for monitoring, guiding, and encouraging each group. The number of students in each group may vary but that number should be small enough (four to five) to permit each student maximum opportunities for interaction within the group. Membership within the groups should change so that students do not begin to assume set roles as leaders, thinkers, note-takers, or lapse into the negative role of being followers.

Teaching in Vancouver, I found that grouping students for instruction requires a great deal of planning and organizing, not only of the groups within the class but also of the instructional procedures, group responsibilities, learning materials, and the physical arrangement of the classroom itself. A teacher must be familiar with a variety of teaching techniques and must be willing to use them. Topics or concepts must be carefully chosen so that all students have maximum opportunity for participation in the group effort. Teacher objectives and student objectives must be clearly outlined and shared. These objectives will be helpful in providing appropriate direction and guidance for teachers and students and for evaluating the teaching and learning that have taken place. Teaching materials and learning materials must be selected and organized for efficient use. The organization of a "learning centre" for each topic contributes to the effectiveness and efficiency of gathering information. Questions which may assist students in focusing their efforts must be formulated and shared and should accompany the reading materials placed in the learning centre. Finally, a teacher must recognize that group work has a purpose or an objective that must be evaluated. It is therefore necessary to develop a procedure for any group instruction. If complete closure of the discussion of a topic cannot be achieved in a given period, help students to bring tentative closure to their effort. For example, what facts or tentative details have they proposed? What conclusions or tentative conclusions can they draw? What judgments or tentative judgments can they make at this time?

Specify the responsibility of each group for gathering, organizing, and presenting the information to the large group. Monitor and participate actively in group discussions so as to guide and facilitate the efforts of members of the group. Help students develop skills in analyzing and synthesizing information collected.

SHERYL G.
Elementary School Teacher

Your Insights

According to this teacher, how should small-group instruction be arranged? What are some disadvantages of grouping students with similar knowledge and abilities together?

---

explanations can also include the use of nonexamples as well as examples. For instance, the economics teacher might have pointed out, "An example of supply might be the number of tickets available for a rock concert, but not the number of people who wanted those tickets. The number of people would be demand." Such explanations help students build cognitive structures or schemata in terms of which they make sense of experience. Thus, teachers should attempt to focus clearly on the student's request but should also help the student connect the information being sought with his or her prior knowledge. Explanations are also occasions for instructing students on how to use the information in other learning situations, thus contributing to metacognitive awareness and transfer of learning.

Questioning

Questions are basic to teaching and learning. Teachers and learners both ask and answer questions. This section focuses on the questions that teachers ask of students as a way of facilitating learning. **Questioning** refers to anticipating, soliciting, and reacting to student responses as a means of instruction. But what types of questions should be asked and under what conditions?

Questioning is an instructional technique that reaches back to antiquity and is used in classrooms from preschool to graduate school. Moreover, it is a technique that is used quite frequently. Research has shown that primary grade teachers ask approximately 150 questions per hour. University professors in undergraduate education classes ask approximately 25 questions per class hour (Duell, Lynch, Ellsworth, & Moore, 1992).

Socrates taught by asking questions that challenged students' conceptions and led them to higher and higher levels of thought. A well-known modern teacher, Jaime Escalante, successfully taught calculus to students from disadvantaged backgrounds using questions for drill and practice. He asked questions to help students learn the basic math facts they needed to master in order to understand and use more advanced concepts.

In terms of Bloom's taxonomy of cognitive objectives (see Chapter 11), questions such as those Socrates asked can be used to teach objectives at the higher levels of analysis, synthesis, and evaluation. The drill and practice questions used by Escalante address objectives at the taxonomic levels of knowledge, comprehension, and application. In both cases, the teacher's questions require the student not only to attend to the teacher but also to formulate and deliver responses. The interactive nature of the questioning tactic leads to active rather than passive learning. The nature of the questions, the manner in which teachers elicit responses, and the type of feedback or reaction to the students' answers determine the outcomes questioning will produce in a particular classroom situation.

A useful way for teachers to think about questioning includes three stages: *structure*, setting the stage for the questions that follow; *solicitation*, asking the questions; and *reaction,* responding to the students' answers (Clark, Gage, Marx, Peterson, Staybrook, & Winne, 1979; see also Good, 1988; Tobin, 1987).

Structure. Structure is established through lecture, explanation, assigned reading, or other activities and anticipates students' responses to questions. This stage sets up students, providing them with the appropriate background information and format to use when answering questions. Teachers can establish structure by providing rules that govern the answers students give. For example, a teacher might prepare a class for a review session by saying, "I am going to ask you some practice questions similar to the ones that will be on the test on Friday. As you

> **POINT:** Asking questions seems like a very straightforward idea. Yet there has been considerable study of the questioning techniques of teachers. The questions a teacher asks of his or her students provide a context for learning, which is one of the underlying assumptions in this book: *Teachers coordinate the context for learning.*

> **questioning** The act of asking questions as a tactic of instruction.

CONNECTION: Consider how Mr. Duffy's actions constitute the use of an advance organizer as described in Chapter 11.

TRY THIS: Observe questioning in a classroom. Using Bloom's taxonomy, identify the taxonomic level of each question.

know, Friday's test will require short essay answers. For today's review, I want you to give a brief answer followed by supporting evidence. Let's try the first review question." Providing students with a context allows them to access the prior knowledge they will need to respond appropriately.

From an information-processing perspective, answering questions requires students to retrieve information from long-term store (Duell, 1994; Gagné, Yekovich, & Yekovich, 1993). First, consider a question that requires simple recall of the definition of a key term, a case of drill and practice on basic factual information. An example might be "What is a rheostat?" The student must locate the definition of *rheostat* in long-term store, transfer the definition into short-term or working memory, check to make sure the definition matches the key term, and then generate the answer. Now consider a question that requires a student to apply a concept in a new situation, a higher level of thinking. An example here might be, "How might a rheostat be used to control the temperature of an oven?" In this instance, the student begins as before, retrieving pertinent information from long-term store into working memory. In working memory, the student integrates the retrieved information (not only what a rheostat is but also how it works) with information about the new situation (ovens, temperature) to determine if the prior knowledge is applicable to the new situation. If additional information is necessary—which is often the case when higher-level thinking is required—the student must locate and retrieve the additional information. This process of retrieval from long-term store and evaluation of the resulting integration in working memory is repeated until an answer is generated. The point here is that the level of the question influences the cognitive activity that occurs as students respond to a teacher's questions.

It is important to note that the level of the question can be influenced by the structure provided by the teacher. Suppose, for example, that a teacher sets up the question "What is a rheostat?" as follows. "I am going to ask you to identify some key terms from the unit on electricity. Now, when I ask you about a key concept, your job is to give not only the definition, but to identify a real-life example in which that concept is used and to explain how the concept works." By structuring the question in this way, the teacher is demanding more complex cognitive activity than would be required had the teacher simply solicited definitions. Thus, active learning can be enhanced by asking higher-level questions or by structuring questions so that higher-level responses are required.

Solicitation. If questioning in ways that increase thinking is advantageous, it would be foolish to ask high-level questions without providing students the necessary time to think. We have already seen from the research that wait-time increases the quality of learning. By reacting or calling on students only after some time has elapsed, we give students the time to engage in higher-level thinking. Time to think, however, is also a function of solicitation. To illustrate, think back to a class in which your teacher was asking students in a large group to answer questions. Maybe it was a review of a homework assignment. The teacher structured the questioning session in such a way that you knew the teacher was checking to see who had and had not done the assignment. Suppose that the teacher solicitation routine was to call on a student and then ask the question. What was your reaction each time another student was chosen? Orpha Duell (1994) provides the following analysis of such a situation.

If the teacher names a student before asking a question, although all students could engage in the processing sequence required to respond, it is likely that at least some will not because it is clear they are not expected to answer the question. If the teacher asks questions, pauses, and then names a student to respond, it is more likely that all students will do the processing sequence in an attempt to be ready should they be called upon (p. 398).

Although asking questions is a critical teaching function, it is useful to keep in mind that professionals who elicit information from others—such as psychiatrists, lawyers, pollsters, and teachers—gain more information from their clients when they ask fewer questions and give their clients more time to think and talk (Dillon, 1988, 1990; Kloss, 1993). The research described previously suggests that the keys to facilitating active learning by means of questioning are encouraging students to think at higher levels and providing them with the time to do that thinking.

Reaction. Between solicitation (asking the question) and reaction (responding to the student's answer), there is the period of time, called **wait-time I,** when the student formulates his or her answer and delivers it. The period of time between the student's answer and the teacher's reaction to that answer is called **wait-time II** (Rowe, 1986) (Figure 12.2).

The routine a teacher uses to acknowledge or call on students affects the length of wait-time I. For example, if students in a classroom are allowed to

REFLECTION: Which of your teachers used the technique described here? Was your attention in the class affected? If so, how? If not, why not?

TRY THIS: If you have the opportunity to tutor children or adolescents, take a stop watch to your next session. Each time you ask a question, do not let the student answer for at least three seconds. At the end of the session, review the quality of your students' answers.

FIGURE 12.2
Wait-Times Associated with Questioning

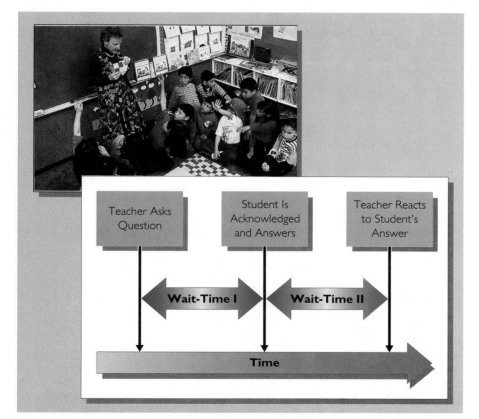

wait-time I The length of time between the teacher's question and the student's response.

wait-time II The length of time between the student's response and the teacher's reaction to that response.

respond spontaneously, without first being acknowledged by the teacher, wait-time I will be decreased. If students are required to raise their hands and be acknowledged before responding, the teacher can control the length of wait-time I, which has its advantages. Research has shown that lengthening wait-time to three seconds is accompanied by increases in the attainment of higher-level outcomes (Rowe, 1986; Tobin, 1987). Other benefits that accrue by extending wait-time include greater student attention, more complex student answers (Fagan, Hassler, & Szabo, 1981; Tobin & Capie, 1982), more relevant student questions, and fewer disciplinary comments from teachers (Rowe, 1986).

Although longer wait-times are generally related to higher-level thinking, the decisions you make about solicitation and reaction must take into account the outcomes you are trying to help your students achieve. "There are many classroom contexts in which shorter pauses between speakers can be justified. For example, when rote memorization or recall of facts is required, drill and practice activities might be conducted at a brisk pace using shorter wait-time" (Tobin, 1987, p. 91).

Reciprocal Questioning. The techniques associated with wait-time are commonly used in teacher-centred instruction. One student-centred approach to questioning is called **reciprocal questioning**. Reciprocal questioning is a technique that encourages students to develop and answer their own high-level questions (King, 1990). Typically, reciprocal questioning occurs at the conclusion of a lecture or other presentation of new material. The teacher organizes students into pairs or triads and gives them the beginnings of questions, called *stems*, that they must complete and then answer. Students complete the stems with reference to the material that the teacher presented in the lecture. Some examples of the question stems are:

- How might you use ... to ...?
- How are ... and ... similar? How are they different?
- What might happen if ...?
- Another example of ... is ...?
- Why is it important to understand ...?
- What are the advantages and disadvantages of ...?

Students who have been trained to use the stems in response to a lecture process the information more deeply than students who merely discuss their reactions to a presentation. The explanation of the technique's effectiveness lies in the reflection, critical thinking, and active learning facilitated by the question stems. Are there some other ways of encouraging the reflective thinking that is characteristic of active learning?

Independent Practice

reciprocal questioning A technique that uses question stems that students complete. The technique encourages critical thinking.

independent practice Tasks that students complete independently either in the classroom or at home.

Independent practice refers to tasks a student completes independently while in the classroom or at home. In many classrooms, seat work constitutes a large proportion of the student's day. This is especially true in elementary school classrooms. Rosenshine (1980) estimates that elementary students spend between 50 percent and 70 percent of their time doing seat work (see also Stigler, Lee, & Stevenson, 1987). One reason seat work is so common in elementary classrooms is that elementary teachers tend to work with their students in groups. While the teacher is working with one group, the other students need to fill the time with a task that does not require the teacher's constant attention. In many instances, the most practical solution to this problem is seat work.

Evertson, Emmer, and Brophy (1980) documented the amount of time grade seven and eight math teachers devoted to lecture versus seat work. The most effective math teachers divided class time between lecture and seat work almost equally. Students of those teachers who were the least effective spent more than three times as long doing seat work as they did learning from lectures or demonstrations. Heavy reliance on seat work can compound the problem of low-achieving students (Anderson, Brubaker, Alleman-Brooks, & Duffy, 1985). Many low-achieving students lack the adequate motivation and confidence necessary for effective independent work. Some of these students lack reading and other basic skills and have not developed the kinds of self-monitoring and organizational skills that would allow them to benefit from seat work. For many of these students, simple completion of the assignments is the goal that guides their efforts on seat work.

CONNECTION: See the discussion of self-efficacy in Chapter 8.

According to principles of direct instruction, examined earlier, independent practice should be preceded by guided practice. If a student enters into independent practice without a clear notion of what the task is, or with a mistaken idea of how a skill is to be applied, the student will practise making errors (Gunter, Estes, & Hasbrouck Schwab, 1990). Thus, in order to use seat work effectively, students must know what to do and how to do it. Likewise, it is important that the teacher circulate around the class, quickly checking to ensure that each student has undertaken the task successfully. It will often be necessary to provide further explanation and guidance to individual students who have misunderstood or are having difficulty with the assignment.

Because seat work does offer practical value, it is likely to stay in the repertoire of many teachers. When you find it necessary or desirable to use seat work in your own classroom, there are several guidelines that can enhance its effectiveness.

If you will use seat work as a regular feature in your classroom, spend time early in the year establishing rules and procedures that will enable students to work independently. Make students aware of rules for talking among themselves during seat work, how to obtain help, under what conditions they can get out of their seats, and what to do when they have completed their seat work (cf. Emmer, Evertson, Clements, & Worsham, 1994). Formulating general rules and procedures will eliminate many nonacademic, procedural questions that might distract you while you are helping other students.

Establishing seat work procedures will allow you to be as available as possible to students during their practice sessions. If students are clear as to how they should work, you are free to walk around the room and spot-check the progress of students so that you can readily intervene when a student is working poorly or incorrectly. Moving about the room while monitoring seat work also sends a message to students that you are aware of their behaviour and that you place some importance on the task at hand (Fisher, Berliner, Filby, Marliave, Cahen, & Dishaw, 1980).

A number of studies have found a strong correlation between the amount of homework assigned and higher grades (e.g., Keith, 1982; Marshall, 1982; Wolf, 1979). A research study of grade three and five students by Gorges and Elliot (1995) published in the *Canadian Journal of School Psychology* found that time spent on homework was a moderate predictor of academic performance. Further, parental involvement in certain homework-helping activities was also related to student achievement. The guidelines that apply to seat work also apply to homework (Good & Brophy, 1994). The obvious difference between homework and seat work is the teacher's ability to monitor the performance of students. Although the teacher can suggest procedures and routines that will help

CRITICAL THINKING: How is preparation for homework related to the structure stage of questioning? How is it different?

students to complete homework more efficiently, the teacher is not available to answer students' questions as they arise. Preparing students in class for their homework assignments is, therefore, a critical element of the tactic. If students are confused or unclear about what they are to accomplish at home or how they are to accomplish it, they are less likely to derive benefits from homework.

Finally, evaluating seat work and homework is likely to increase student engagement in the tasks they are given. If students, especially less-motivated students, perceive seat work and homework as just practice, they will be less likely to put forth their best efforts. Thus, evaluating independent work and incorporating student performance into any grades you assign is a good way of emphasizing the importance of independent work. In the case of homework, you should check the work and give feedback in the form of comments to your students. Using written commentary in evaluating homework enhances achievement (Elawar & Corno, 1985).

How Can Student-Centred Instruction Support Active Learning?

This part of the chapter focuses on teaching behaviours that move the locus of learning activity away from the teacher and toward the students. Student-centred approaches define the teacher as a *facilitator,* not an *orator;* a *coworker,* not a *boss;* a *guide on the side,* rather than a *sage on the stage* (Johnson & Johnson, 1994). Many student-centred teaching approaches are therefore consistent with constructivist views of learning (Prawat, 1992). Before examining student-centred approaches, let's consider some of the key characteristics of the constructivist view of the teaching-learning process. One constructivist benchmark is that learning is best done in real-life environments, complete with the ill-defined problems characteristic of everyday situations. Another benchmark, consistent with Vygotsky's view of intellectual growth, is that social negotiation is essential to learning. A third constructivist benchmark is that ideas and concepts should be learned in diverse ways (Driscoll, 1994; Marshall, 1992). Consider these benchmarks in relation to a learning activity designed by James Ellington, a grade four teacher (Adams Johnson, 1992).

On a bright spring day, Mr. Ellington takes his class outside to a large, carefully outlined rectangle of grass. He is talking with his students about the concept of protective colouration in nature. He sprinkles three hundred coloured toothpicks throughout the rectangle of grass, sixty red ones, sixty blue, sixty yellow, sixty natural, and sixty green. As he does, he asks his students to imagine that the toothpicks are worms and that on such a nice day robins will be hunting for them. He then poses a question, "What colour worm do you want to be?" The students make predictions, such as "I sure don't want to be yellow against the green grass." They get down on their hands and knees and collect as many of the toothpicks as they can find and then analyze the results. The students have found fifty-six of the sixty yellow toothpicks and only seven of the green toothpicks. They discuss fractions and draw a graph to indicate their findings.

Notice how this lesson addresses the constructivist benchmarks presented earlier. Learning about protective colouration in this way is more authentic than hearing a lecture. The social interaction that is facilitated by being outdoors on hands and knees is more natural than that found in the classroom, and the lesson adds variety to the learning activities of the students.

The reason to use constructivist benchmarks in evaluating teaching behaviours is that those benchmarks are the best standards we have for determining the extent to which learning is both active and student centred. For as Pamela Adams Johnson, the chronicler of James Ellington's worm lesson, says, "Schooling should not be viewed as a spectator sport for students, where adults perform while students watch" (Adams Johnson, 1992, p. 67).

Student-centred instruction can be provided in the form of small group discussions, peer teaching, cooperative learning, and interactive instructional technology.

Small Group Discussions

Small group discussions allow students to exchange information and opinions. The groups that worked on the electricity concepts in the Teacher Chronicle would be considered discussion groups. Small group discussion is helpful in fostering a student's ability to think critically because students must express, support, and modify their assumptions, conclusions, and opinions (Gage & Berliner, 1988). A student's reasoning then becomes part of the content of the group's discussion.

If students are to learn effectively in a discussion group, they must develop communication, interaction, and social skills. For example, students need to listen and respond to what they hear. The ability to listen for the purpose of responding to group discussion is different from the ability to listen effectively to a lecturer. Thus, students learn to think through problems as part of a group process.

Students faced with the challenge of marshalling arguments in small group discussions must also learn to reason and think critically about questions, issues, or problems. Evidence suggests that small group discussions can also stimulate changes in attitudes and behaviour. Students who take a position in a group discussion are making a public statement that implies a course of action on their part.

In choosing small group discussion as a means of instruction, teachers are well advised to consider the learning objectives students are to attain. General objectives in low-consensus content areas are most appropriate for discussion formats. *Low consensus* describes the lack of a high degree of agreement as to what is and is not true or important. Topics in social studies or literature, for example, are more suitable for discussion than formulas and equations. Areas of low consensus that are emotionally charged, such as a discussion of legislation and court decisions involving civil liberties, will elicit a variety of opposing views. Many teachers try to avoid controversial topics, but Johnson and Johnson (1994) suggest that they should address controversial topics. A discussion that requires one to take and defend a position against the positions of others forces students to find new information, to organize their thinking, and to negotiate conflicts. In addition, such discussions encourage students to construct logical arguments that can withstand or account for new information and other perspectives. Finally, discussions of controversial topics contribute to the development of self-knowledge.

The teacher's role in small group discussions is to avoid interfering while at the same time facilitating effective group dynamics. Some teachers have a natural tendency to respond to any difficulty students are having and to suggest solutions before the group has had a chance to develop its own ideas. Other teachers

TRY THIS: Ask a number of your friends if they prefer to discuss their reading assignments in their classes or not. For those who voice a preference for discussion, ask them to explain why they think discussion helps.

REFLECTION: In which classes do you find discussion more productive? Is there a connection with the general level of consensus of the material discussed? If you will teach math, how will you structure small group discussions?

small group discussion
Exchange of information and opinion among a small number of students.

might watch helplessly as discussion groups break into quarrels or lapse into silence. The following section, Here's How, presents some strategies for facilitating discussions (Good & Brophy, 1994; Johnson & Johnson, 1994; Gage & Berliner, 1988).

Here's How

Here's How To Intervene in Small Group Discussions

- If several small groups are discussing a topic, briefly monitor all of the groups on a rotating basis.
- If discussion is flagging, ask a leading question.
- If digressions are occurring, remind the group of the task at hand or ask a question that refocuses attention.
- If one student is monopolizing the discussion, ask other members of the group to comment on the group's progress—or lack of it.
- If lengthy pauses occur between contributions to the discussion, intervene. Long pauses may be a sign that students are becoming confused or have forgotten the task at hand.
- If students are having difficulties distinguishing values or opinions from facts, intervene. If you doubt the group's ability to discern the difference, ask a question such as "Is Rodney's statement an opinion or a fact?"
- If logical fallacies stated by one member of the group go undetected by other members, the validity of the discussion is damaged. Logical fallacies may include overgeneralization or reasoning based on unsound premises. Questions such as "Is that true?" or "Does that make sense?" can help focus students' attention on issues of logic as they pertain to the discussion.
- Provide closure to discussions by asking each group to report results or write brief summaries.

Peer Teaching and Learning

CRITICAL THINKING: How might you overcome the so-called social perception problem associated with same-age peer tutoring? What steps could you take in a classroom to prevent the problem?

Peer teaching and learning can take several forms. In some cases, you can assign one student to tutor another student. In such cases, you can easily infer that the student who is being tutored needs help. In other cases, students learn together on a more equal footing by teaching each other. Teachers can also work with students in an effort to transfer gradually the responsibilities for teaching from teacher to students working together.

One form of peer teaching is peer tutoring, which occurs when one student is assigned to help another learn assigned material (see the discussion of peer modelling in Chapter 8). According to research, peer tutoring improves the academic performances and attitudes of both the student who tutors and the student who is tutored (Cohen, Kulik, & Kulik, 1982). The two basic types of peer tutoring are cross-age tutoring and same-age tutoring. There is little research to suggest what specific characteristics of the tutor and the tutored teachers should consider in forming groups. Establishing pairs of students of the same age can be difficult, because when a teacher appoints one classmate to tutor another, it implies a relationship based on ability, and both students are likely to perceive the tutor as superior. One solution is to have study pairs—study buddies—alternate in the roles of tutor and tutee in a way that maximizes each student's strengths. Peer tutoring, in which the responsibility for tutoring alternates between students, is a basic element in cooperative learning techniques (Johnson, Johnson, & Holubec, 1993).

Similarly, teachers can also pair peers so they can learn together without implying teaching responsibilities in the relationship. For example, middle school students who were assigned to learn together outperformed students who worked individually on a cognitive reasoning task (Kutnick & Thomas, 1990). The students who were paired did not necessarily share similar achievement histories. Furthermore, the scores on the reasoning task indicated enhancement in the performance of each partner, not merely an average enhancement for the pair. Not all studies of peer learning have shown such gains, however. In a study of mathematical problem solving, high school students who were paired randomly—with a few students working in triads—performed less well than students working alone (Stacey, 1992). One explanation of the results, however, was that the students working in groups tended to choose simpler, often incorrect, solutions to the math problems. The groups seemed to adopt a norm of minimal brainstorming in considering possible solutions. Perhaps the students were unfamiliar with peer learning or simply perceived this particular task as inconsequential.

Reciprocal teaching is a specialized form of peer teaching designed initially to help poor readers develop and apply metacognitive skills (Palincsar, 1986; Palincsar & Brown, 1984). The instructional arrangement involves the teacher working with small groups of students. The instructional task is to acquire four reading strategies that facilitate reading comprehension and understanding. Those strategies are: summarizing the content of a passage, formulating a question about the key point, clarifying unclear portions of the reading material, and predicting what will be addressed later in the passage.

The teacher begins by explaining and modelling these strategies for students. Gradually, the teacher encourages students to take over the teacher's role by modelling the strategies for peers. Students eventually learn to ask themselves strategic questions about the material they are reading. For example, students may ask themselves the following in response to a passage about the circus:

- What part of the circus did this paragraph address?
- How did the circus start?
- Why was the fire at the P. T. Barnum Museum important? Is that the section I should reread?
- Is the next section about clowns?

TRY THIS: Find a teacher who uses reciprocal teaching as a technique. Ask the teacher to describe cases in which the shift from teacher to student occurred too quickly. Ask the teacher to explain how one should gauge the shift.

reciprocal teaching A technique that begins with the teacher's questions designed to enhance metacognitive skills and that progresses to a gradual transfer of the control of questioning to the students, who work cooperatively.

Research on reciprocal teaching has shown it to be an effective method of improving reading achievement in poor readers (Palincsar, 1987; Palincsar & Brown, 1984; Rosenshine & Meister, 1991). These and other studies have also suggested that the technique is most effective when (1) the shift of responsibility from teacher to student occurs gradually, (2) when the difficulty of the task and the teaching responsibilities are matched to the student's ability, and (3) when teachers observe students carefully as they teach in order to determine how the student is thinking about the reading material.

Cooperative Learning

REFLECTION: Recall learning groups in which you have participated that worked well and not so well. Were there any freeloaders in the group that did not work well? What can a teacher do to ensure that each individual feels responsible to the other members of the group?

Cooperative learning is an instructional technique that calls for students to be teamed together to attain certain goals (Kagan, 1989; Slavin, 1991). Johnson and Johnson (1994) identify five basic ingredients of cooperative learning (Figure 12.3). *Face-to-face promotive interaction* refers to students talking with each other in order to share insights and ideas. *Individual responsibility* refers to the necessity for teachers to hold students accountable for themselves to prevent freeloading in a learning group. *Collaborative skills* include the skills necessary for effective group functioning, such as leadership, team building, and conflict resolution. *Group processing* refers to how well the group is functioning aside from the academic products or performances on which they are working. Addressing the quality of working relationships gives the group opportunities to improve the way it works.

Successful cooperative learning groups also show *positive interdependence* among participants. Positive interdependence exists when students perceive that their individual fates are linked to the fates of others in the group. A belief that "we sink or swim together" fuels the group to interact in positive ways, to hold themselves accountable to others, to collaborate, and to reflect on the quality of group functioning.

Cooperative learning techniques require teachers to place themselves in an entirely different role than do teacher-centred techniques such as lecturing. To some degree, teachers share authority with students over the knowledge students

FIGURE 12.3
Elements of Cooperative Learning

Source: Adapted from *Learning Together and Alone* (4th ed.), D. W. Johnson & R. T. Johnson, 1994, Needham Heights, MA: Allyn & Bacon.

cooperative learning
Students working together to attain common learning goals.

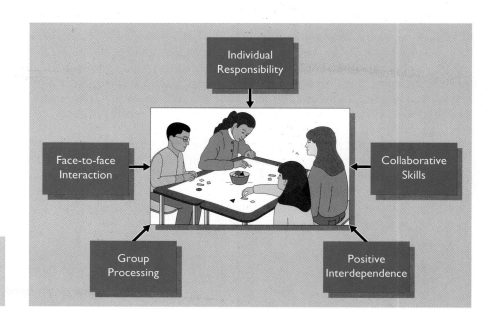

gain. As students become more responsible for their own learning, teachers and students become collaborators, sharing responsibility for determining what is to be learned (Bruffee, 1993). The issue of who determines what is to be learned has been used to distinguish cooperative learning from collaborative learning (Haring-Smith, 1993, 1994a, 1994b).

Canadian authors Clarke, Wideman, and Eadie (1990) have emphasized the importance of providing students with a process to learn about working together effectively. They have described a four-stage cycle teachers can use to assist students in enhancing their cooperative skills and the quality of learning that takes place in groups:

- Reflection—thinking about the experience of working together

- Understanding—developing generalizations about what the group skill is and how to use it

- Practice—using the skill in the next group experience

- Experience—integrating the skill into working in groups

The teacher can guide students toward understanding how the cycle works, and can intervene with individuals, groups, or the whole class to provide information and support.

One approach to collaborative learning is called *teaching for understanding* (Talbert & McLaughlin, 1993). This approach is based on three principles: that knowledge is constructed; that the teacher is a guide, a collaborator in the construction of student knowledge; and that the classroom is a learning community that supports its members. Translated into classroom practice, these principles mean that sometimes topics are generated by students rather than presented by the teacher (Perkins, 1993).

Informal cooperative learning groups are formed on a temporary, ad hoc basis. While the group has a goal to attain, the nature of the work needed to attain that goal is usually short lived, and therefore the group may last for only a few minutes or perhaps a full class period. The purpose of informal learning groups is to focus student attention on the content to be learned and to help students actively process that content. The groups formed in the Teacher Chronicle to review the concepts of electricity are an example.

Formal cooperative learning groups, in contrast, are more structured and may last up to several weeks or months. Members of formal learning groups have two major responsibilities. They are responsible for maximizing not only their own learning but also the learning of all other members of the group. Formal learning groups work to complete a specific task, usually resulting in some performance or product. The outcomes—the performances or products generated by the group— can range from acquiring information to problem solving to cooperative composition. The following sections describe formal cooperative learning programs that were extensively researched and developed during the 1980s and 1990s.

Student Teams-Achievement Divisions. One type of team that can be formed is referred to as **Student Teams-Achievement Divisions (STAD)**, a cooperative learning method that employs a cycle of teaching tactics consisting of lecture, cooperative study in small groups, and quiz (Slavin, 1987). Rewards are given to teams whose members show the greatest improvement over their own past performances, the real-world equivalent of increased productivity. STAD teams work best when each comprises four or five students.

student teams-achievement divisions (STAD) A cooperative learning method that uses heterogeneous groups of four to five students. Rewards are given to teams whose members show the greatest improvement over their own past performance.

A lesson using the STAD procedure begins with a lecture presentation of material, usually conducted over one or two class periods. During the cooperative study phase, which lasts for one or two class periods, the teacher provides each team with worksheets or other materials pertaining to the topic covered in the lecture. Each team is to make sure that all of its members master the material. In order to encourage real teamwork, a teacher can insist that team members work together on just one or two copies of the worksheets.

The team score is the total amount of improvement of each individual over his or her past performances on assessments. Teachers can compute a team score by adding together the number of improvement points earned by the team and dividing that number by the number of team members assessed.

After calculating team scores, the teacher delivers some reward or recognition to any team that averaged two or more improvement points. Rewards are based not on the performance of the team compared with other teams, but with its own past performance.

Consider the following STAD procedure for teaching math. After you have lectured on the objectives of a math lesson and teams have convened for team study, you might distribute worksheets containing math problems based on the lecture just presented. In this case, each student on the team should work each problem. Each student should compare his or her answer with those of the other teammates. If any member of the team has missed a problem, it is the responsibility of the other teammates to provide remediation. The STAD procedure emphasizes that team study is not complete until all members of the team have mastered the material. Students should address questions that arise during team study to teammates before consulting the teacher. After students complete team study, the teacher gives a test to the entire class and calculates team scores. The teacher assigns students to new STAD teams every five or six weeks, and students who were on low-scoring teams have a chance to try again or achieve greater success. This recommendation is similar to the idea of changing the membership of teams on a playground when one team has won a number of games in a row.

Teams-Games-Tournaments. Another form of team learning is **Teams-Games-Tournaments (TGT)** (Slavin, 1987, 1991). As in the STAD procedure, the team is responsible for preparing each team member for competition. In TGT, a team comprises four or five members of varying ability levels. Once the teacher forms the mixed-ability teams, the prepared members leave their teams to compete as individuals in homogeneous three-person competition groups. Each team member competes against members of other teams in weekly tournaments. The competitive groups change each week, but the level of ability within groups remains constant. An individual's performance in the weekly tournament contributes to his or her team's score.

In each competition group, players take turns serving one of three functions: Reader, Challenger I, or Challenger II. The Reader on a particular turn reads the problem or question to the two challengers. The Reader attempts to solve the problem or answer the question. Challenger I can then choose to challenge the reader's answer by giving a different answer, or Challenger I may pass. Challenger II may challenge or pass. Challenger II then checks the correct answer to the problem or question using an answer sheet provided by the teacher. Students exchange roles so that each student plays each role within a tournament. The score received by each player is his or her contribution to the team's total score for a particular tournament.

The three players who compete against each other in a group change each week. The winners in each group are moved to a higher-ability group for the next week's tournament. The low scorer in each group is moved to a lower-level group for the next week's tournament. In this way, each team member has an increased chance of contributing points to the team's overall performance.

Team-Assisted Individualization. The **Team-Assisted Individualization** (TAI) approach prescribes that students work individually at their own pace with programmed materials. However, students also study and practise together in mixed-ability groups as in STAD. Although the assigned content provided to each student is in the form of programmed instruction—usually, but not necessarily presented via computer—the teammates are available to check work and to encourage and remediate. Because the team as a whole is rewarded for the work of individual players, it is to each individual's advantage to assist others on the team. The TAI approach allows teammates to become a source of motivation for individual students. Another advantage of TAI is that teammates can perform some of the clerical work that otherwise the teachers would perform. This variation of cooperative learning has proved very effective in elementary-school mathematics (Slavin & Karweit, 1985). In studies of math classes, classes taught via TAI compared favourably to classes taught in a more traditional way (Good et al., 1983; Slavin, 1985, 1991).

Cooperative Integrated Reading and Composition. In most classrooms where reading groups are used, the groups tend to be homogeneous. This allows the teacher to work with groups using materials that are similar in difficulty and to proceed at a pace that is appropriate for each group rather than at one pace for the entire class. One of the consequences of using homogeneous reading groups is that while the teacher is working with one group, other students must work independently. Typically, the time spent working independently is not used very effectively. Another disadvantage of using homogeneous reading groups is that the achievement benefits of heterogeneous cooperative learning groups are lost (Johnson & Johnson, 1991; 1992; Slavin, 1990).

One solution to both of these difficulties is an approach called **cooperative integrated reading and composition (CIRC).** CIRC combines a pair of students from one reading group and a pair of students from another into a mixed-ability cooperative learning group. While the teacher is busy leading one of the reading groups, CIRC groups—formed from the students in the remaining reading groups—are engaged in a variety of tasks. The four members of a CIRC group take turns reading to each other and answering questions about what they have read. The group practises new vocabulary, spelling, and reading comprehension skills. Group members also write about what they read. Research on the CIRC approach indicates that it has a positive effect on students' reading skills and on standardized scores from reading and language achievement tests (Stevens, Malden, Slavin, & Farnish, 1987; Slavin, 1987).

Cooperative Learning: Cultural Considerations. A thought-provoking paper by Lance Roberts and Rodney Clifton (1988) outlines the unimpressive results achieved in educating Canada's Inuit students. In their study, carried out in the eastern part of the Northwest Territories, it was shown that Inuit students hold traditional, collectively oriented attitudes in contrast to white students from the same schools. While it is conceivable that student attitudes might be modified to

CRITICAL THINKING: How does CIRC avoid the problems that sometimes occur when same-age pairs are brought into a tutoring arrangement? Does having four students in each group contribute to success? Why or why not?

team-assisted individualization (TAI) A teaching tactic in which students work on programmed materials as members of a heterogeneous group. Rewards for completing the work accurately and quickly are given to the team as a whole.

cooperative integrated reading and composition (CIRC) Pairs of students from one homogeneous reading group join another pair from a different reading group to work cooperatively on comprehension and writing skills.

Insights on Successful Practice

How have you and your students benefitted from the use of cooperative learning groups?

The beneficial effects of such cooperative learning groups on my students in Edmonton include the development of the courteous responses we accord one another as human beings, an improvement in academic achievement, a greater sensitivity to and an improvement in race relations and gender relations, and an increase in the social skills of cooperation and collaboration.

If the topic to be investigated is interesting for the students, they will certainly be motivated to express their feelings or test their ideas. In these situations, they quickly learn to listen to one another, to avoid interrupting a speaker, and to respect the views of others. With the teacher's leadership and guidance, they can also learn to compliment others for their contribution, to acknowledge other students' responses, but most importantly, to recognize that they can learn from others.

If the content to be learned is carefully organized and the activities thoroughly planned, the cooperative learning model can be used to improve student performance on crucial academic tasks. If the groups are organized so as to include both high achievers and low achievers, cooperative learning can benefit both, especially when they work on academic tasks together. In such a situation, low achievers will not only learn from listening to their peers but the high achievers generally assume the role of tutors, thereby giving the low achievers special attention. The high achievers, on the other hand, also gain academically because they must verbalize their thoughts for others in the group. This verbalization must help those students to crystallize abstractions and to observe deeper relationships and associations within and among topics and concepts.

If the cooperative learning group is organized to include students from different races and genders and if those students are encouraged to assume leadership roles within the group, it is possible that improvement in race and gender relations will occur. Planning, however, is crucial if this result is to be achieved. The teacher must not only know the students well, he/she must provide opportunities for all students to demonstrate their leadership qualities and their knowledge or their skills. Hence, in planning and organizing the activities for the cooperative learning groups, individual accountability, the development of interpersonal skills, face-to-face interaction, and positive interdependence must be considered.

I believe that whenever students are asked to work in cooperative learning groups, they need guidance and encouragement from the teacher. While some cooperative learning groups may be unstructured and the teacher's role non-directive, there are still goals to be achieved. These goals may be social or affective rather than academic. In either case, the teacher must be sensitive to the need for his/her intervention at critical moments. In this sense, the teacher is the catalyst for success.

I believe that the cooperative learning model is an effective approach for achieving a variety of academic and social goals. If the subject matter for study is carefully selected, if the cooperative learning groups are thoughtfully organized, and if the learning objectives are clear and reasonable, group members can interact positively, then they can learn to cooperate with others for the benefit of the group or the team, they can learn to respect others regardless of race or gender, and in so doing, enhance their own individual knowledge and skills.

SANDRA E.
High School Teacher

Your Insights

According to this teacher, what are some affective benefits of cooperative learning? What are some academic benefits? What will you do to promote effective cooperative learning in your classroom?

---

better fit a classroom grounded in "competitive individualism," a better, more workable, and culturally sensitive approach would be to restructure classrooms using cooperative learning strategies. Roberts and Clifton argue that, while there are no specific studies which examine the effects of cooperative learning strategies on Inuit children, there are some basic reasons to support the use of classroom instruction organized on cooperative principles and learning strategies. Changing student attitudes, especially when they are grounded in the student's very identity, is both difficult and incongruent with Canada's commitment to multiculturalism. Rather, it is easier to change what is within our control as teachers and that includes teaching practices, methods, and the social relationships in our classrooms. In this way we not only respect the attitudes our students bring to school, but also build on and strengthen these attitudes. As the authors conclude:

> Given the serious deficiencies in Inuit schooling, it seems worthwhile to consider reorganizing classrooms along cooperative principles, especially when such suggestions are practical and have empirical as well as theoretical support (Roberts & Clifton, 1988, p. 226).

Interactive Instructional Technology

The majority of schools in Canada use microcomputers and have credit courses at the high school level in computer programming and information processing. Richard Kenny (1992) of the University of Ottawa contends that computer and educational technology can contribute significantly to the improvement of the public school system. This can be most effectively done, he argues, by adopting a "diffusion/adoption" perspective. This approach emphasizes creating instructional materials and designing software with teachers at a local school system level. Clearly, computers are part of the learning environment you will encounter, and they are capable of supporting the teaching-learning process in a number of ways. Computer technology, including data storage systems such as videodiscs, is capable of multimedia presentations of information to learners that include text, graphics, video, sound, and animation. The technology allows learners to enter simulated environments that are remarkably realistic. Computers can help students to be understood in their own classrooms or to communicate with a stranger on another continent.

Computers and Instruction. Educational technology found its foothold in the classroom by means of **computer-assisted instruction (CAI)**. Computer-assisted instruction approaches employ the computer as a tutor to present information, provide drill and practice, simulate problems, assess a learner's level of knowledge, and provide remediation. For example, a student might learn about deforestation through a tutorial program that presents basic facts, maps, and a video clip of a speech made by a legislator in favour of banning the import of lumber from the Brazilian rain forest. After taking a test to determine if the student acquired the background information, the program assesses the student's responses and, if needed, presents a remedial lesson. When the student is ready to move on, the technological environment changes from a tutorial mode into a simulation mode. Simulation programs approximate activities that cannot be done in the classroom because they are too expensive, dangerous, time consuming, or otherwise not feasible. In the simulation mode, the student can learn about the importance of rain forests and the effects of deforestation by using computer models. Students can cut down trees with key strokes and examine the effects of deforestation on the global climate. Programs such as *ScienceVision* and *Science 2000* are simulation programs that allow students to conduct realistic experiments and work on realistic problems at relatively small cost and without dangerous risks (Coburn, 1993; Tobin & Dawson, 1992). Microworlds offer more realistic environments than simulations and are consistent with constructivist

TRY THIS: Interview a teacher who has embraced technology in the classroom. Ask the teacher to explain the advantages of technology in terms of student learning.

REFLECTION: Recall a computer simulation that you found particularly intriguing. If you have not had that experience, try to find someone who has. Why did the simulation hold your attention? Did you feel you had control over the environment created by the computer program? Did your ability to try repeatedly to succeed influence your learning?

computer-assisted instruction (CAI) Instruction delivered by a computer, including tutorial, simulation, drill, and practice.

notions of learning (Rieber, 1991a, 1991b). They are designed to encourage students to explore and discover (Papert, 1993). *TinkerTools,* for example, is software that allows students to explore a series of environments or microworlds while discovering the basic principles of physics (White, 1993).

Schwier and Misanchuk (1993) have described a term with a broader focus than CAI—Interactive Multimedia Instruction (IMI). They describe IMI as instructional, multiple-media sourced, segmented, intentionally designed, and coherent. At the heart of IMI is a computer, with related media such as videodisks, still photos, and audio serving as sources of information input and output. The authors provide a framework with examples of how to use authoring tools such as HyperCard to design and deliver quality IMI.

Robler, Edwards, and Havriluk (1997) have classified instructional software into five categories:

- Drill and practice—programs that allow learners to work on problems or answer questions and get feedback on correctness.

- Tutorial—programs that act like tutors by providing all the information and instructional activities that a learner needs to master a given topic.

- Simulation—programs that model real or imagined systems to show how those systems work.

- Instructional games—programs designed to increase motivation by adding game environments and rules to learning activities.

- Problem-solving—programs that directly teach the steps involved in problem-solving, or provide opportunities to acquire problem-solving skills by solving problems.

Roblyer et al. describe in depth the great range of additional software options (such as word processing, databases, spreadsheets, graphics, multimedia encyclopedias) available to the teacher to support instruction. Your challenge will be to select, from the software available to you, items that you can successfully integrate into your teaching. The most important consideration as you evaluate software for use in your classroom is to ensure that you keep instructional goals and student outcomes clearly in view. You will then be in a good position to decide upon the software that will best support your teaching and learning situation.

Computers and Thinking. Computer technology supports the development of higher level thinking in at least two ways. First, the technology can provide students with opportunities to develop their problem-solving skills. Second, the technology can serve as tool for thinking and problem solving.

The first function is illustrated by an imaginative use of technology that allows students to develop their problem identification as well as their problem-solving skills. The Cognition and Technology Group at Vanderbilt (CTGV) developed a video-based environment for mathematical problem solving called the *Jasper Woodbury Problem Solving Series* (1990, 1991, 1992, 1993). In each pair of lessons, a complex problem is presented via video with both relevant and irrelevant information embedded in the context of an adventure story. Students must decide what problems must be solved in order to reach a resolution to the story. To help them in solving these subproblems,

EXAMPLE: Perhaps you recall the build-your-own-story books in which you, the reader, had to answer questions at various points in the book. Depending on your answer, you were directed to a particular page to finish the story.

they can access any part of the videodisc using a bar-code reader to replay segments that may contain relevant information. In most of the lessons, students can find three or four possible solutions, depending on the approach students take to the problem. The video adventures capture the students' attention and imagination and motivate them to engage in problem solving for extended periods of time.

As a tool for problem solving, computers can extend not only our ability to retrieve information—through networked databases and videodisc encyclopedias—but also our ability to think. We refer to computer programs that are designed to help learners brainstorm, analyze, and organize ideas as cognitive tools.

Well-designed computer programs can facilitate learning by extending a student's ability to think. In other words, they become mind-extension cognitive tools (Derry & Lajoie, 1993).

> Good computer-based cognitive tools can support such social problem-solving processes by providing physical representations of abstract strategies and concepts, making them tangible for inspection, manipulation, and discussion, thereby encouraging generalized metacognitive awareness and self-regulatory ability (p. 6).

One such program called *Inspiration* helps students brainstorm, diagram information, and develop meaningful links among concepts. The program allows students to identify and define concepts, to write and store comments, to establish links between concepts, and to define the nature of those links. The program is especially useful for members of a cooperative learning group. By using both the graphic and text capabilities of *Inspiration*, cooperative groups can develop a concept map of their consensual understandings. The map as a product is not so important as the process group members must go through in negotiating meaning as they construct the map.

Computers, Cultures, and Communication. Perhaps the most exciting instructional prospect to arise from recent enhancements in educational technology is in the areas of telecommunications and telecomputing. *Telecomputing* is a term that has recently gained currency to distinguish computer access at a distance from the more general term *telecommunications*. Telecommunications refers to satellite-based information delivery systems such as telephone links and instructional television (Kearsley, Hunter, & Furlong, 1992; Ryder & Hughes, 1997).

Telecomputing provides access to World Wide Web, Gophers, and the Internet, global networks that can link a student sitting at a computer to vast storehouses of information and to other learners around the world. Access to people who live in different countries or who live differently in our own cities provides enormous learning opportunities. Telecomputing not only allows students to learn about people from other cultures, but to learn with them as well. A geography class in Hull, Quebec, and a class in Bologna, Italy, are comparing the environmental concerns of their respective communities. High school students in Seattle received eyewitness reports of the destruction of the Berlin Wall from their colleagues at the Marie-Curie-Oberschule in Berlin. Students in Juneau, Alaska, and Moscow, Russia, are collaborating on a vision statement about global health in the year 2000 (Kearsley, Hunter, & Furlong, 1992).

CRITICAL THINKING: Given that computer technology can so readily support constructivist approaches to teaching, do you think that the evolution of computer technology has contributed to the emergence of constructivist approaches? Why or why not?

TRY THIS: Interview students who have had the experience of working on a joint project with other students at a distance.

Computers and Students with Special Needs Computer-based technology plays a very important role in the education of students with disabilities. Lewis (1993) and Male (1997) have described the many ways that computers have been used to overcome the limitations students experience as a result of a disability. Lewis has conceptualized the benefits of technology as an ABC model: Technology can

Augment abilities and

Bypass or

Compensate for disabilities.

For example, the computer can be used to augment the remaining vision of a partially sighted student by displaying text in fonts large enough for the student to read. Bypass technologies are frequently used to allow students with physical disabilities to operate computers. On the input side, hardware and software is available to allow students to use alternative keyboards, touch screens, pointers or switches, speech, and even eye movements to control the computer (see Lewis, 1993, for detailed descriptions). On the output side, speech synthesizers for students who cannot speak and Braille printers for blind students allow needed alternatives. Technology solutions can also help to compensate for, or diminish, the effects of a disability. For example, students with learning disabilities who have persistent difficulties with spelling and composing can use such word processing tools as outliners, spell checkers, and grammar checkers to compensate for their disability.

Two recent developments—the world wide web and collaborative models of special education service—have given rise to a new way that computers are being used to enhance the education of students with disabilities. A new class of software called "groupware" has emerged along with development of the world wide web (Schrage, 1993). By using combinations of shared documents, electronic mail, file transfer, and live audio/video conferences, "virtual teams" can be established. Using these technologies, team members can work together on an ongoing basis, sharing the task of designing projects and seeing them through. On the service side, special educators now advocate a collaborative team approach to service delivery for students with special needs (Fishbaugh, 1997). Students, parents, classroom teachers, resource teachers, and other professionals combine their efforts to create a team that works together using the principles and practices of collaboration to deliver quality education for the student with a disability.

Researchers at the University of Saskatchewan have combined concepts of groupware and collaboration to produce computer software called "CoPlanner" (Haines & Robertson, 1996; Robertson, Haines, Sanche, & Biffart, 1997). The software provides a structured set of tools (calendars, worksheets, forms, text, and mail) and a teamwork environment (directories and security) that allow the team members to be systematic in planning and implementing instructional programs for students. The software guides the formation of the team and their ongoing planning through a six-stage process:

- Identification—reaching consensus on concerns, goals, and outcomes
- Information Gathering—assessing the strengths and needs of the student
- Reflection—drawing upon the student's profile to design an instructional plan

Insights on Successful Practice

How do you use computers in your school?

At long last, computers have become a meaningful part of the teaching and learning that go on in each classroom of this school. When I was appointed principal here seven years ago, a large area in the learning resources centre had been converted into a computer laboratory. There were 15 computers set up as workstations. With teams of two at each computer, the lab could handle a class of 30 students. All the computers were networked and had Internet access, and we also had a scanner and laser printer on the network. So, really, we were quite well equipped with technology in this school.

For the first two years as principal, I watched how the lab was being used. First of all, we had ten classes competing for lab time, so we had to use a booking system. The senior students always seemed to get priority. Some teachers used the lab rarely, if at all. I asked these teachers why they did not use the lab more often. I got responses such as "I can't get the booking time I need," "It's time-consuming and disruptive to move a whole class to the lab, or to send a group out," and "The lab separates me from my teaching materials and environment; it breaks up the flow of my teaching and of the students' work."

Clearly, my questions had uncovered some major obstacles to the productive use of technology in our school. I asked the staff if they would rather break up the lab and move the computers to their classrooms. The reception to this idea was lukewarm overall, and hostile from the grades six to eight teachers: "How could I possibly make use of one computer in my classroom?" Seeking some answers, I phoned Sam, the regional technology consultant, and explained the dilemma. He told me that many school staffs struggle with the same problems, but that a new initiative in the division to fund the networking of classrooms had just been announced, and that this might help to overcome the dilemma. We set up a meeting to explore the options.

It took us two years to transform the use of computers in our school. Here's what we did. First, we gathered as a staff so we could plan the changes as a team. The concerns of the senior teachers were reduced when they realized that they could receive the Internet and e-mail in their classrooms. We talked about our vision for technology use and

reached the consensus that the technology should move to the people, rather than the people moving to the technology. We decided to move one computer to each classroom. That would leave five machines in the LRC, so we could still have a small lab for staff development and student use. Then came the creative ideas!

Now when I walk down the hall, work in classrooms, or talk with teachers, here are the kind of things I see. Andrea, the grade five teacher, has the computer set up as a publishing centre. Her class has taken on desktop publishing and produces the school newspaper. They collect write-ups over the network from "roving reporters" in each classroom and do the editing, layout, and distribution. Rick, the grade seven teacher, uses an overhead projector and projection panel to display web sites and CD-ROMs to the whole class. Louis Riel and the Northwest Rebellion will never be the same again! Bob, the grade three teacher, has two students with learning disabilities working on a math tutorial program — they no longer leave the classroom for remedial work. Kathy has her grade four students researching food and culture with their pen pals in Norway through Canada's SchoolNet. There are many more examples, but needless to say, we have transformed teaching and learning here—there is real excitement.

There have been some payoffs for me as an administrator, too. We have moved more in the direction of being a "paperless" school. All communications are sent to the staff via e-mail. I am also able to easily distribute a variety of outside documents to the teachers without going near the photocopy machine!

Our experiences with technology in this school have taught us that computers are most effective when they serve as tools that are integrated into the classroom and into the curriculum.

KEN CROSS
Elementary School Principal

Your Insights

What are the advantages and disadvantages of the computer lab arrangement? Is "one computer in every class" always a better setup? How will you use computer technology in your classroom? What are some ways you can think of to use computers in teaching and learning?

- Teaching—putting the instructional plan developed by the team into action
- Monitoring—checking the student's response to the instructional plan
- Reporting—communicating about student progress to others as needed

The software not only guides the team's planning, but collects the products of their work in a shared environment. Team members can share access to the electronic file, and documents can be sent to team members for input and updates. This allows the team to continue to work together effectively as a "virtual team" when they cannot meet face-to-face. Research conducted by Haines, Sanche, and Robertson (1993) reported positive effects of the use of *CoPlanner* software upon aspects of team functioning.

Advances in computers and related special education technology have hastened the process of inclusion of students with disabilities into regular classrooms and society (Male, 1997). These technologies allow students with disabilities to become more active and successful participants in regular classrooms with their peers. As a teacher, you will probably have the opportunity to work with students who rely on technology to be successful in your classroom. Also, you will find yourself working in collaborative team situations to help your students. With technology and teamwork support, these students can enrich the classroom for all.

How Will Your Knowledge of Active Learning Techniques Help You Become a More Effective Teacher?

As you have seen, teaching for active learning requires a focus on what students do and how they think when they learn. As you use teacher-centred instructional approaches you are thinking about how your behaviours as a teacher influence the cognitive activity of your students. And, as you use student-centred instructional approaches, you are thinking about how your students' behaviours influence their cognitive activity and that of their peers. Therefore, knowing active learning techniques helps you to fulfill your role in the teaching-learning process.

Knowing active learning techniques also helps you advance your own construction of the teaching-learning process as you learn to teach effectively in a variety of ways with a variety of instructional aids. Expert teachers have developed a teaching repertoire—a variety of instructional approaches, strategies, and formats. Using a variety of techniques increases your ability to engage student interest, to respond to situations flexibly, and to match curriculum and instruction to the thinking dispositions and learning characteristics of your students. Research suggests that the effective use of broad-based teaching repertoires fosters higher student achievement (Brown & McIntyre, 1993; Hiebert, 1991).

Teacher Chronicle Conclusion

Plugging In

Before science class the next day, Mr. Duffy has set up eight lab stations, two with computers that run simulations, and others with simple wiring and switch layouts connected to lights, buzzers, and other devices. There is a hum of excitement. The students really look forward to this class.

Mr. Duffy begins the class session by saying, "As you can see, I have been busy setting up electricity workstations. There are eight stations, and your team will need to complete at least five over the next five classes. At each station there is a printed instruction sheet. You will also find a team response sheet which you will need to fill out. You will notice that each station has "essential" and "extension" tasks. Everyone must complete the essential tasks, but you may go on to one or more of the challenging extensions if you finish early. There will be two unit tests on electricity. As usual, you will be graded on the basis of what you accomplish and how well you work as a team. I have set up team lists, so your first task is to check which team colour you have been assigned to, then get together and decide which station you want to start with. Any questions?"

"What if two teams want to work at the same station at the same time?" asks Rick.

Mr. Duffy says, "You will need to problem-solve that one between your two groups. But everyone will have a chance to work at the stations they want over the next few days. No more questions? OK, it's team time."

Amid a buzz of excitement, the students form their groups. After ten minutes, Mr. Duffy informs the class that it is time to move to the first station. The teams begin work, and Mr. Duffy circulates quickly from group to group, making certain that they have understood the instructions and begun the task successfully. As the students experiment, he rotates from group to group asking questions, prompting, and demonstrating. Twice during the lesson, he calls for the attention of the whole class and provides an explanation with diagrams on the board, then returns the teams to their work.

About half way through the period, Mr. Duffy raises his head to check out the operation of the class as a whole. At the various stations, bells ring, lights flash, motors whir, and the conversations of learning rise from the teams. He looks over and sees Kam helping Susan wire a parallel circuit as he carefully explains to her how it works.

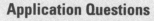

Mr. Duffy thinks, "They sure are getting a charge out of this! I'll have them complete the Learned column of the KWL worksheet at the end of the unit, but I have a feeling there won't be enough space in that column."

Application Questions

1. In what ways is Mr. Duffy's instruction teacher-centred?

2. What specific techniques of effective instruction can you identify in the Teacher Chronicle? In what ways do those techniques support active learning on the part of Mr. Duffy's students?

3. In what ways is his instruction student-centred?

4. What specific instructional choices reflect a constructivist approach to teaching? In what ways do those choices support active learning on the part of Mr. Duffy's students?

5. Create a dialogue among a group of students at one of Mr. Duffy's lab stations that reveals the benchmarks in thinking or cognitive processing that students can attain when they are engaged in active learning in a social context.

6. What opportunities for peer teaching are implicit in Mr. Duffy's lesson plan? What forms of peer teaching might be most appropriate in relation to his instructional goals and the needs of his students?

7. How might the lesson in the Teacher Chronicle be accomplished through formal cooperative learning groups? Which program or technique described in this chapter might you choose for this purpose, and why?

8. What is required to make cooperative learning work? In what ways can cooperative learning approaches benefit students? In what ways can they benefit teachers?

9. What instructional technologies might Mr. Duffy use to support student learning? What specific purposes might those technologies serve in his class?

10. Create a revised lesson plan for Mr. Duffy and his students that integrates multiple uses of instructional technology in the classroom.

CHAPTER SUMMARY

What is Active Learning? (L.O. 1, 2, p. 383)

Active learning refers to student engagement in the process of learning. Thinking is an important aspect of active learning. Good thinking dispositions can support active learning and we examined ways to encourage the development of good thinking dispositions. Critical thinking refers to higher levels of the cognitive taxonomy; critical thinking requires learners to be actively engaged with the learning material. Teaching that facilitates active learning can be either teacher centred or student centred.

How Can Teacher-Centred Instruction Support Active-Learning? (L.O. 3, 4, p. 386)

There are a variety of instructional techniques in which the teacher's behaviour is central to learning. In teacher-centred learning, much of the responsibility for learning rests with the teacher; the teacher must engage the student's attention and thinking. Teacher-centred techniques include lecturing, explaining, questioning, and independent practice.

How Can Student-Centred Instruction Support Active Learning? (L.O. 5–9, p. 398)

Student-centred approaches to instruction take the teacher out of the hub of instructional interaction in the classroom. Students are more responsible for learning outcomes than when teacher-centred approaches are used. Student-centred approaches are theoretically consistent with constructivist views of the teaching-learning process. These approaches to instruction include small group discussion, peer teaching and learning, cooperative learning, and the use of technology.

How Will Your Knowledge of Active Learning Techniques Help You Become a More Effective Teacher? (L.O. 5–9, p. 412)

Whether teacher-centred or student-centred approaches to instruction are employed, the teacher must always focus on the effects of instructional activity on the learner's thinking. It is important to build a repertoire of teaching behaviours by considering new metaphors and ideas for teaching and testing new techniques in the classroom. Reflecting on the results of these efforts will help you build your theory of teaching.

KEY CONCEPTS

active learning, p. 383

anticipatory set, p. 387

computer-assisted instruction (CAI), p. 407

cooperative integrated reading and composition (CIRC), p. 405

cooperative learning, p. 402

critical thinking, p. 385

direct instruction, p. 386

explanation, p. 391

guided practice, p. 387

independent practice, p. 396

lecturing, p. 388

mastery teaching, p. 387

pair shares, p. 390

questioning, p. 393

reciprocal questioning, p. 396

reciprocal teaching, p. 401

small group discussions, p. 399

student-centred instruction, p. 386

student teams-achievement divisions (STAD), p. 403

teacher-centred instruction, p. 386

team-assisted individualization (TAI), p. 405

teams-games-tournaments (TGT), p. 404

wait-time I, p. 395

wait-time II, p. 395

13 Assessing Student Performance

LEARNING OUTCOMES

When you have completed this chapter, you will be able to

1. define *assessment*
2. describe the four related components of assessment
3. build a table of specifications for a unit test
4. write tests items following the construction guidelines
5. compare and contrast the advantages and disadvantages of various test items

6. provide a rationale for the use of alternative assessment methods
7. define *validity* and *reliability*
8. outline the main themes contained in *The Principles for Fair Student Assessment Practices for Education in Canada*
9. explain the role of assessment in teaching and learning

Teacher Chronicle

Testing Trials

Louisa Cardinal, a first-year high school teacher, plops down in a chair in the lounge and lets out a long sigh. Amy Legare, a friend and fellow science teacher, joins her.

"You look bushed," she says. "Good thing it's Friday."

Ms. Cardinal smiles at her concern. "Yes, it has been a long week. But it's not that so much as the disaster my kids made of a unit test I just gave them. I don't know if it's them, my teaching, or the test that's the problem."

She looks at Mrs. Legare, a veteran teacher and asks, "Amy, how do you make up your tests? Your kids always complain about how hard your tests are, but they never complain that they aren't fair."

Amy laughs and answers, "You know I really enjoy creating tests. Creating might seem a funny way to think of what one does in putting a test together, but test making is a creative thinking and writing process for me. For instance, when I create a test for my science classes, I want it to be a fair representation of the material we have covered since the previous test. So I give multiple choice questions related to class lectures and lab experiments. And I include some open-ended questions that can be answered correctly in a number of ways."

Mrs. Legare continues, "I also give them practice tests to familiarize them with my formats. It seems to me that one way to make a test reliable is to eliminate the possibility that someone could miss an item he or she really knows. The test score is only an estimate of a student's knowledge, but it should be the best estimate that I can make it. So I encourage students to read the test questions carefully and consider their responses. I want them to read through every possible answer first before deciding on a solution. My students have difficulty with this at the beginning of the year, but most get to be quite adept at it by the end of the first quarter."

"Are your tests mostly multiple-choice then?" Ms. Cardinal asks.

"No, I ask at least one essay question covering the material presented in the labs. My labs are set up as small group activities. In order to ensure that each student participates to the best of his or her ability, I make the essay question one that links together things they should have learned."

Mrs. Legare pauses before continuing. "In the essays, I give points for details covered in class or discovered in a close reading of the textbook. As a vocabulary extension, I also include jokes and riddles based on the terminology covered in the unit. The students enjoy these jokes, and over the years, I have found that such wordplay actually improves their scientific vocabulary."

Ms. Cardinal shakes her head. "There's a lot more that goes into a good test than I ever thought."

"Yes, Louisa, and you don't always need paper-and-pencil tests either. Sometimes I use performance assessments to test skills. There's a great deal that can be learned from assessments and not just who knows what. I use tests as a check on my teaching and on the instructional materials we're using. It took me a few years to learn to develop good tests. You'll get there sooner, I'm sure."

Focus Questions

1. What purposes do assessments serve?
2. What are the different kinds of assessments, and what are some advantages and disadvantages of each?
3. What is authentic assessment?
4. How should test items be constructed?
5. What is involved in designing alternative assessments?
6. What makes an assessment valid and reliable?
7. How can you best prepare students for assessments?
8. How can assessments be used to improve teaching and learning?

What is Assessment and How Are Assessment Practices Changing?

In the Teacher Chronicle, Louisa Cardinal faces a typical problem of beginning teachers: how to construct and administer an assessment that will accurately measure what the students have learned. When people talk about classroom assessment, they use a variety of terms interchangeably: evaluation, assessment, measurement, test. Although the terms are related, their distinctions are important for the decisions teachers must make about student progress and achievement. In order to understand these distinctions, consider this example: Leland and Darlene correctly answer 90 percent of the questions on a geography test. Now let's examine what this example means in relation to assessment, evaluation, measurement, and test.

Defining Assessment

Assessment is the process of gathering, analyzing, and interpreting information about students and their progress in school. It is a comprehensive and multi-faceted analysis of performance (Wiggins, 1993). As you will see in this chapter, teachers conduct a great deal of assessment, from administering tests to observing student performance on tasks in class. They gather information about student characteristics (thinking dispositions and cultural backgrounds), achievement (skills and knowledge in geography), and attitudes (enjoyment of place names, anxiety about map reading). Teachers assess student characteristics and entry levels of skill and knowledge so that they may better plan more effective instruction. They assess student performance in order to facilitate learning. Successful learning depends upon accurate and informative feedback following assessment of progress toward a goal. And teachers conduct assessments to communicate student progress to a variety of audiences, including students, parents, and the community. Wilson (1996), from Queens University, contends that the assessment of students requires that teachers assume the dynamic roles of mentor, guide, accountant, reporter, and program director.

Assessment is the most general of the four terms and describes all of the activities that yield various sorts of information about students. The geography test, then, is one form of assessment. It provides one kind of information about this student's knowledge of geography. The different kinds of tests given by Ms. Cardinal and Mrs. Legare in the Teacher Chronicle are also forms of assessment.

Assessment provides the context for **measurement**, which is the process of describing a student's particular characteristics. Measurement answers the question, "How much?" (Gronlund, 1993). The geography test is a measurement because it shows how much of the information on the test Leland and Darlene knew. In this case, it is also a *quantitative* description because it answers the question of how much knowledge the student has of geography in numerical terms. How else might teachers judge a student's knowledge of geography? Perhaps the student can locate cities or countries on a map and trace the shortest route between them. Describing students' knowledge in terms of qualities they possess or performances they can demonstrate, rather than in terms of numerical scores on tests, provides a *qualitative* measure of their individual achievement. In the assessment of writing skills, for example, the teacher might say that Leland scored a 5 out of a possible 7 on the essay test (a quantitative description). Or the teacher could say that Leland applied the basic mechanics of writing, used lan-

assessment The process of gathering, analyzing, and interpreting information about students and their progress in school.

measurement The process of describing a student's particular characteristics. Measurement answers the question, "How much?"

guage appropriate to the topic and reader, but failed to fully develop and support ideas introduced in the opening paragraph (a qualitative description). Quantitative and qualitative measurements both provide teachers with valuable information about student progress, but the nature of the information they provide is different and generally complementary.

A **test** is a formal procedure or an instrument used for measuring a sample of student performance. Tests can be constructed in a variety of formats, from objective pencil-and-paper items (e.g., multiple-choice, true/false, fill-in-the-blanks) to performance assessments (e.g., constructed response tests based on realistic tasks). The geography test mentioned earlier is probably made up of objective items, whereas asking students to locate cities on a map and trace routes between them is a form of performance assessment. All tests provide some kind of information about students, but, depending on their format, the information may be quantitative or qualitative in nature. As you will see, there are advantages and disadvantages to using any particular test format.

Finally, **evaluation** is the process by which teachers make specific judgments about their students using information gained from formal and informal assessment. Evaluation enables a teacher to answer the question, "How good?" or "How well?" (Gronlund, 1993). For example, Ms. Stein might judge how good Leland and Darlene are in geography or how well Leland writes by the students' test scores. Likewise, Ms. Stein might judge how good the geography lessons were by how many students in the class achieved scores of 90 percent on the test. Evaluation judgments lead to such decisions as what the students' activities will be for the next several minutes and which students should be placed in a particular reading group or special education program. In the first case, teachers are likely to have conducted an informal evaluation that told them the class needed an extra few minutes to complete a class activity. In the second, it is more likely that the teacher formally evaluated performance to determine how well students were reading.

Assessment is an integral part of teaching and learning, not just a means of monitoring or auditing student performance (although it does serve this purpose as well). Assessment is a way to improve learning, because teachers and students alike can use assessment information to adjust the learning experience. And because learning gives rise to a diversity of understandings, teachers, administrators, and policy makers should all have expertise in a variety of assessment methods. They should be able to construct sound assessments and use them effectively in gathering desired information about students.

Teachers today are experiencing some fundamental changes in the way they view and conduct assessment in schools (Gronlund, 1998; Stiggins, 1991; Wiggins, 1993). At a societal level, assessment reform is calling into question standardized testing practices that have been developed over the last sixty years. At the classroom level, teachers are calling for better ways to determine what their students are learning. It is worthwhile to review some of the changes that are occurring as an introduction to specific assessment methods.

Views of Assessment in Canada

It was only at the beginning of the 20th century that the first intelligence tests, as we know them today, were developed. This was followed by the creation of achievement tests that could be administered to large groups of students. Education systems soon became one of the largest users of standardized tests that

POINT: *Assessment serves multiple purposes.* A score on a test can be used to judge how well students have achieved and how effective was the instruction.

CRITICAL THINKING: Why is the purpose for which evaluation is used so critical to the individual, parents, school, and society?

test A formal procedure or an instrument used for measuring a sample of student performance.

evaluation The process by which teachers make specific judgments by answering the questions "How good?" or "How well?" (e.g., How well have students understood this concept? How good is this instruction?).

CONNECTION: Standardized testing and how teachers can interpret the results of standardized tests are discussed in detail in Chapter 14.

CRITICAL THINKING : Debate continues over what standardized tests should be designed to measure. How are the results of this debate likely to affect teachers' decisions in the classroom?

POINT: *Authentic activity provides a basis for assessment.* Authentic activity is exemplified in tasks such as driving, but it can also be a part of paper-and-pencil tests. Using a protractor to measure an angle is an authentic activity.

CONNECTION: How would the assumptions that constructivists make about learning (discussed in Chapter 7) affect their views of assessment?

could be administered to individuals or groups and that assessed a diversity of variables ranging from intelligence and school achievement, to career interests and behaviour and learning problems. The purpose of testing and assessment has evolved over the past 50 years to include placement (e.g., special education programs), selection (e.g., identifying highly intelligent children for enriched programs), promotion (e.g., departmental high school exams), and evaluating curriculum, teaching practices, and programs. The users and consumers of tests and test information in school systems are, essentially, anyone who is responsible for educational decision making. Thus teachers, administrators, special education consultants, school psychologists, counsellors, and curriculum planners and developers use test information to guide their decision-making tasks, which may range from promoting a student to the next grade to determining if a particular reading program is producing the desired results.

Critics of tests are numerous and vocal. Teacher newsletters published by the various provincial teachers associations as well as local Canadian newspapers still carry articles and viewpoints that question the use of tests in schools. Part of this reaction may be due to observing trends in the United States. Unfortunately, many of the critics who oppose the use of carefully standardized tests seem to misunderstand some critical features of assessment. First, a test is a sample of behaviour and therefore, the more information gathered, the better the decision a teacher is able to make. No teacher would argue that a single spelling test, or performance on one math quiz, or the oral reading of a single paragraph is sufficient to accurately evaluate a student's achievement in these complex domains. Secondly, tests do not make decisions, but are "neutral." An intelligence test does not make the decision to pass–fail, or offer additional remedial instruction, or even recommend a program for gifted children. These decisions are made by school personnel, parents, and students after considering "all" of the information, which may include standardized tests as well as teacher-made tests and observations over a period of a time. This multimethod and multisource assessment gathered in a systematic way over time becomes the information from which decisions are made by educational personnel.

We encourage you to consider some other sources of information on assessment issues and techniques written by Canadian authors. This material should supplement and even extend the information contained in this and the next chapter. In the book *Educational Psychology: Canadian Perspectives* (Short, Stewin, & McCann, 1991) are chapters by Tom Maguire ("Evaluation of classroom instruction"), Verner Nyberg ("Constructing teacher-made tests"), and Henry Janzen and Don Saklofske ("Testing for diagnostic purposes"). Katherine Covell from the University College of Cape Breton has published a book entitled *Readings in Child Development: A Canadian Perspective* (1995). Here, Don Saklofske and Vicki Schwean from the University of Saskatchewan, together with Henry Janzen, University of Alberta, have contributed a chapter outlining the components of assessment, including defining children's needs, decision-making, factors influencing test results, and issues associated with cultural diversity. Don Saklofske and Henry Janzen published a paper in the *McGill Journal of Education* (1990) entitled "School-based assessment research in Canada." They point out the problems associated with "importing" tests from other countries and describe some of the efforts to develop tests that can be more confidently employed in Canadian schools (e.g., Canadian Achievement Test, Canadian Cognitive Abilities Test, Canadian Test of Basic Skills).

The important consideration of cross-cultural assessment practices and culture-fair testing is comprehensively discussed by Don Massey of Edmonton in an article on "Cross-cultural psychology assessment" published in the *Canadian Journal of School Psychology* (1988). More recently, Vicki Schwean and Sally Greenough-Olson (1992) prepared a detailed report addressing assessment strategies for identifying exceptional students of Native ancestry. Assessment issues are also discussed in Canadian textbooks by Bowd, McDougal, and Yewchuk (1998) and Winzer (1995) and in articles published in the *Canadian Journal of School Psychology*. Finally we would refer readers of this book to a special issue of the *Alberta Journal of Educational Research* (March, 1990), in which some of Canada's leading measurement and evaluation experts presented their views, research, and recommendations on the topic "Assessment in the classroom."

CONNECTION: Recall that even major, individually administered, standardized tests, such as the WISC-III, had to be renormed for use in Canada (Chapter 5).

Authentic Assessment

Because "assessment can legitimately be viewed as the manifestation of a system's educational values" (Baron, 1991, p. 307), the move toward new educational values has brought a similar move toward new assessment strategies. Scholars and teachers alike are seeking ways other than **objective tests** of assessing student performance, ways that comprise a reform movement known as authentic assessment. Also called alternative assessment, performance assessment, holistic assessment, and observation-based assessment, **authentic assessment** concerns the measurement of complex performances and higher-order thinking skills in real-life contexts. Often, these higher-order thinking skills are conceived as the standard practices of experts in a subject matter discipline.

As a concept, authentic assessment is not especially new. Examples such as writing assessments, Red Cross swimming tests, and driving tests have existed for years (Hambleton & Murphy, 1992). Imagine how limited a picture of students' winter survival skills in Northern Ontario could be gained by administering a test consisting of 30 multiple-choice, true-false, and matching items questions. The goal of authentic assessment is to make tests more integral to learning tasks so that skills such as problem solving and critical thinking can be measured. Venues for conducting authentic assessment include activities such as projects, exhibitions, demonstrations, observations, science fairs, and peer- and self-assessment (Hart, 1994).

Proponents of authentic assessment have argued that it provides a more direct measure of higher-order learning goals than do more traditional measures such as paper-and-pencil tests (Frederiksen & Collins, 1989; Wiggins, 1989). For example, scores on an objective test may indicate that students know the components of a well-written essay, but can they write one? The only way to know for sure is to ask them to perform the task. Authentic assessment is also thought to reflect a more constructivist orientation to learning because it requires students to demonstrate complex tasks rather than small, discrete skills practised in isolation (Shepard, 1991). Finally, the insertion of authentic tasks into standardized achievement tests is expected to bring an increase in instructional attention to those tasks, just as standardized writing assessments led to an increase in instructional time devoted to composition (Popham, 1993).

So what does this all mean for assessment practices in classrooms? For assessment to improve learning, it should provide a multidimensional picture of what students know and can do. It should respect students' diversity in ways of

objective tests Paper-and-pencil tests made up of items, such as true/false and multiple-choice, that can be objectively scored (i.e., scored in exactly the same way no matter who or what is doing the scoring).

authentic assessment Assessment of higher-order skills such as problem solving and critical thinking in real-life contexts through the use of projects, exhibitions, demonstrations, portfolios, observations, science fairs, peer- and self-assessments.

understanding. It should suggest actions teachers can take to improve the educational development of their students and the quality of their educational programs. To accomplish these goals, teachers have available to them a broader array of assessment techniques than ever before. Taking advantage of them, however, requires understanding of assessment goals, procedures for constructing assessments, and criteria for judging and improving the quality of assessments. It is to these issues that we now turn.

Types of Assessment Goals

CONNECTION: How would Bloom's or Gagné's taxonomies (discussed in Chapter 11) be used to specify knowledge- and skill-goals for assessment?

Look back for a moment to Mrs. Legare's test in the Teacher Chronicle. What might the essay question measure that is different from what is measured by the multiple-choice questions? What kind of learning outcome is implicit in the teacher's statement that she wants to encourage students to "read the test questions carefully and consider their responses"?

Teachers must decide, in any subject area they teach, what to assess. As you have seen from Chapter 11, assessment goals should coincide with instructional goals. It is a useful practice for teachers to consider what and how they wish to assess student progress at the same time they determine instructional goals. Unfortunately, many a teacher has experienced writing a "really good test item" only to discover that he or she hadn't actually taught what the item assessed. Therefore, thinking about assessment first often clarifies instructional goals and keeps one congruent with the other.

CRITICAL THINKING: Does thinking about assessment when setting objectives and planning lessons lead to only 'teaching for the test'?

What types of things do teachers want to assess? The most obvious, perhaps, are the knowledge and skills teachers hope students will acquire. Knowledge and skills are often quite specific and can be defined using any of the taxonomies described in Chapter 11. Examples include tracing the historical development of cultural diversity in Western civilization (knowledge), making observations of birds and communicating these observations through written or verbal descriptions (skills), and comparing and contrasting two systems of government (analysis).

CRITICAL THINKING: What outcomes of active learning, discussed in chapter 12, might become targets of assessment?

Sometimes teachers are interested in assessing more complex goals such as critical thinking and problem solving. These higher-order thinking skills may consist of any number of prerequisite knowledge and skills, but knowing the prerequisites does not guarantee that

How can paper-and-pencil tests be constructed to assess students' higher-order thinking skills? What are all the factors that teachers must take into consideration when planning and constructing assessments?

Insights on Successful Practice

In developing assessments, how do you include measures of students' higher-level thinking?

As a science teacher, I always have realized how important writing and critical thinking skills are to the understanding and learning of science. I have tried several times in the past to encourage students to write about science content in an essay format. However, after years of hearing, "I don't know what to write!" and "How long does this have to be?" I finally found a formula for writing success that has been very useful in teaching writing skills to my science students.

I decided that I wanted my students' writing to demonstrate their knowledge of the subject. The material had to be written in an orderly fashion, emphasizing logic and critical thinking skills as well as the students' opinions, viewpoints, and English skills. To accomplish this goal, I devised a lesson with specific outcomes for each of these objectives. I do not teach English skills to students, but do emphasize the importance of subject-verb agreement, complete sentences, and correct punctuation in their science writing.

Because many students seem unsure of what to write about, I started this writing program by having all students write an essay on the same topic. I gave the writing assignments after we had covered a particular unit of content. This provided each student with a similar background in the subject; the essays would serve as a good review of the material. I have found that sentence statements or topic statements are successful with beginning writers. Instead of telling students to write something about forests, cells, molecules, or the treatment of waste water, I use statements such as "Forests are more than trees," "The pathway of a drop of water through a treatment facility is an important journey," or "A cell is an organism."

I use the sentence topic to accomplish my first science teaching objective—students should be able to demonstrate their knowledge. I write the topic on the board and then ask for student ideas about the topic. Students usually come away from this brainstorming activity and the resultant discussion with lots of ideas about what to write.

I then focus the students' attention on the fact that they can group many of their ideas into categories. Often several different groupings are possible. Students then complete an outline on their topic. The outline helps to accomplish my second objective—student writing should be orderly and stimulate logic and critical-thinking skills. Students use thinking skills—analysis, synthesis, comparison, and contrast—when preparing categories of information.

I focus my comments and criticism on the students' outlines, and after I return the outlines to the students, they write their essay. I emphasize the importance of using correct grammar, punctuation, and spelling in their essays. On the day students turn in their essays, either the students or I read them in class. This allows students to get immediate feedback on their work.

A writing activity of this type helps students to realize that English skills do play an important part in science. This activity helps them strengthen their knowledge of a particular content area and use some critical-thinking skills. It also gives students an opportunity to express their own viewpoints on a topic and deepens my appreciation of the English teacher across the hall.

LINDA VYGODA
High School Teacher

students can successfully synthesize them in the context of a larger problem-solving activity. Therefore, assessments are sought that provide complex problems and require students to integrate previously learned skills and knowledge.

Achievement-related behaviours and achievement-related products can also be goals of assessment that teachers target. *Achievement-related behaviours* are behaviours that students exhibit during activities or assignments that facilitate

CRITICAL THINKING: Think about some of the goals you might want to assess. On what knowledge and skills would you assess student progress? What achievement-related behaviours and achievement-related products would you target for assessment? What attitudes or dispositions do you think are important to assess?

CONNECTION: Issues related to motivation and attribution are discussed in Chapter 9.

their achievement. Cooperating in a group to reach a common goal is an example. Communicating results of an investigation, perhaps in graphical or prose formats, is another. A third example is performing certain motor tasks, such as a floor exercise in gymnastics. Achievement-related products, by contrast, refer to the artifacts students produce that illustrate what they have learned. Project reports, essays, and artwork are all examples of achievement-related products.

Finally, teachers are often interested in assessing the status of student affect. In other words, what achievement-related attitudes do students exhibit toward what they are learning? Are they motivated to learn the material? How confident are they of their ability to succeed? How do they attribute the errors they make in learning? Assessing student affect helps teachers to understand what other conditions affect student performance besides their mastery of the curriculum. The variety of goals that teachers can choose to assess is represented in Figure 13.1.

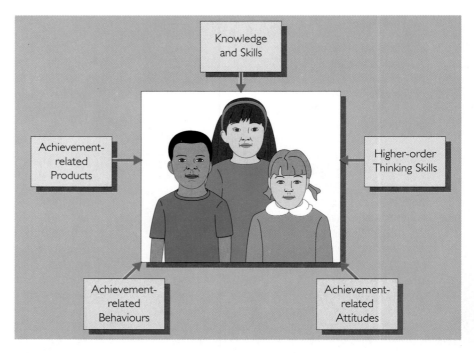

FIGURE 13.1
What Do Teachers Assess?

How Do You Plan and Construct Classroom Tests?

EXAMPLE: One school district uses only the results of an IQ test to place students in its gifted program, while a neighbouring school district places students using peer recommendations, teacher observations, and parental evaluations in addition to IQ test results. Which approach is better suited to the purpose of evaluation and why?

Canadian teachers have many different methods available to them for obtaining the kind and amount of information they need to make the critical decisions expected from them (e.g., Should Mary be promoted to grade five? Does Jason have a learning disability? Is my reading program effective?). Leslie McLean (1988), from the Ontario Institute for Studies in Education, has argued that conventional achievement tests, especially those developed at the national and local levels, are perceived by teachers to have little application to their teaching. Rather, "measurement moves closer to pedagogy as it moves closer to the classroom" (p. 244). A number of Canadian studies conducted in British Columbia (Anderson,

1989) and Ontario (Wahlstrom & Danley, 1976) indicated that classroom teachers prefer to use their own teacher-made tests and other in-class assessment methods (e.g., portfolios, observation). Even then assessment practices may still be somewhat disconnected from instruction and student learning. Reasons for this range from poorly constructed tests to the impact of bias on teacher judgments. A more complete discussion may be found in articles by McLean (1988) and Saklofske and Janzen (1990) published in the *McGill Journal of Education*, and also by Wilson (1989) in the *Alberta Journal of Educational Research*.

Teachers must find or design assessment methods that will succeed in gathering desired information for making sound judgments about their students. In doing this, teachers are wise to consider the effect of different types of test formats and tasks on different students. Students' test scores depend to some degree on the particular methods used to assess their performance, because each method provides a different view of what students know and can do (Shavelson, Baxter, & Pine, 1992).

Some tasks used on tests may even be so inherently interesting as to affect positively students' attitudes toward testing. In a study comparing two approaches to testing student understanding of volume, for example, Wiggins (1993) reported that the performance test so engaged students that some of the worst students were among the best performers on the test. Some also pleaded with their teacher to continue working on the problem after school! It seems advisable, then, for teachers to consider using a variety of different assessment methods within any unit of instruction in order to gain a more complete picture of each student's achievements.

This section discusses paper-and-pencil tests that teachers can administer in class during a single class period. These tests include item formats ranging from multiple-choice to essay. The next section presents alternative assessment methods that are more commonly associated with authentic assessment. For each method, we discuss advantages and disadvantages that should help you in selecting those most appropriate for your assessment purposes.

CRITICAL THINKING: It has been suggested that teacher assessment practices often 'fall short' because of a lack of planning. Give some examples that would illustrate poor planning.

Planning Objective Tests

Teachers use objective tests to help them make a variety of decisions. A test that is given *prior* to the instruction can help teachers determine students' **readiness** for instruction—that is, whether they have the necessary prerequisite skills and knowledge. Testing prior to instruction also helps teachers assign students' placement at particular levels of instruction. Readiness may also include the assessment of attitudes and motivation that can facilitate or interfere with learning. **Placement** tests are commonly used in reading instruction, for example, to determine what level of reading difficulty a student is capable of handling.

Tests that are given *during* the learning process to monitor student progress are called **formative assessments**. Teachers might use these tests to diagnose learning difficulties, to improve instruction, or to provide feedback to students to improve their learning. Daily or weekly quizzes are an example. **Summative assessments** occur at the *end* of an instructional unit for evaluation, for example, to assign a grade (Gronlund, 1993).

When teachers construct a test, they must decide in advance on its purpose, because the purpose will influence the types of items constructed, the length of the test, and the scope and depth of content covered. The purpose of a test can also influence its administration. If its purpose is formative, for

readiness A goal of assessment that shows whether students have the necessary prerequisite skills and knowledge to begin a unit of instruction.

placement A goal of assessment that determines what level of difficulty a student is capable of handling in instruction.

formative assessment An assessment used to diagnose learning difficulties and to provide feedback to students to improve their learning.

summative assessment An assessment administered at the end of an instructional unit for the purpose of assigning a grade.

example, the teacher may consider allowing students to answer the questions using their textbooks or to work in cooperative groups. Tests used for placement purposes, however, must provide information about each individual's capabilities to ensure that appropriate instruction is provided. Therefore, these would be given to individuals to answer without benefit of outside resources.

To plan a test, teachers must be sure that the items they write or choose (e.g., from existing item banks or unit tests accompanying published curricula series) actually measure their goals and objectives. This is most easily done by constructing a **table of specifications**, a framework or matrix that shows the content areas or objectives to be assessed along with the desired level of skill for each outcome (Table 13.1). Here's How lists the steps to produce a table of specifications (Gronlund, 1993; Kubiszyn & Borich, 1987).

TRY THIS: Discuss with a teacher how he or she uses tests for formative and summative purposes. How are these uses different?

Here's How

Here's How To Produce a Table of Specifications for Test Writing

- Identify the learning outcomes and content areas to be measured by the test. Table 13.1, for example, identifies six objectives that relate to the goal of subtracting without regrouping.
- Determine the category of outcome to which each instructional objective belongs. Table 13.1 assigns objectives to the categories of knowledge (K), comprehension (C), and application (A) from Bloom's taxonomy.
- Determine the number of test items that need to be constructed for each objective. This should reflect how much weight to give each outcome on the test. In other words, measure objectives that are most important or that were given the most attention in the instruction by more test items. Table 13.1, for example, assigns objective 1 only one item and objectives 4, 5, and 6 six items each.
- Add the number of items in each column.
- Determine what percent of the test measures each objective and each category of learning. Check to be sure that these percentages match the relative importance of the objectives and desired outcomes.

table of specifications
Used for planning a test, a two-way chart or matrix that shows the content areas or objectives to be assessed along with the desired level of skill for each outcome.

selection-type items A test item format in which students select an answer from possible alternatives.

supply-type items A test item format in which items ask students to generate an answer.

Look at Table 13.1 again. What does it suggest about the importance this teacher placed on application? On solving specific kinds of subtraction problems?

Because the table of specifications shows the types of learning outcomes to be assessed on the test, it also provides guidance to the teacher in selecting or generating types of items that are appropriate for each outcome (Popham, 1981). Items in which students select an answer from possible alternatives are called **selection-type items**, whereas items that ask students to generate an answer are called **supply-type items**. The characteristics of different item types present both advantages and disadvantages in constructing classroom tests that meet teachers' needs (Table 13.2).

TABLE 13.1 *A Table of Specifications for a Test on Subtraction Without Borrowing*

Content Outline	K	C	A	Percentage
1. Distinguishes addition and subtraction signs	1			4
2. Distinguishes addition problems from subtraction problems	2			8
3. Identifies correctly and incorrectly solved subtraction problems		4		16
4. Correctly solves single-digit subtraction problems			6	24
5. Correctly solves double-digit minus single-digit subtraction problems			6	24
6. Correctly solves double-digit problems that do not require borrowing			6	24
Total	3	4	18	25 items
Percentage	12	16	72	100

Key: K = Knowledge; C = Comprehension; and A = Application.

Source: Education Testing and Measurement: Classroom Application and Practice (2nd ed., p. 65), T. Kubiszyn and G. Borrich, 1987, Glenview, Il: Scott, Foresman. Copyright 1987 by Scott, Foresman, and Company. Adapted by permission of HarperCollins Publishers.

REFLECTION: Can you ever recall a test where you thought either "nothing I studied is on this test" or "this test has too many items on things we hardly covered in class."

TRY THIS: Develop a table of specifications to construct a test for a unit in a subject area you plan to teach.

Constructing Selection-Type Items

Selection-type items include multiple-choice; binary-choice items, such as true/false; matching; and interpretive formats (an interpretive item is often a lengthy case followed by several multiple-choice questions). These formats typically require a process of recognition and are especially useful for assessing knowledge of facts, understanding of concepts, and, with interpretive items, problem solving (see Table 13.2). Let's examine how selection-type items are constructed (guidelines are derived from Carey, 1988; Cunningham, 1986; Ebel & Frisbie, 1986; Gronlund, 1998; Hopkins & Antes, 1985; Hopkins & Stanley, 1981; Nitko, 1983; Popham, 1981).

CONNECTION: How might the process of recognition (discussed in Chapter 7) relate to student performance on selection-type items? How might the process of recall relate to performance on supply-type items?

Binary-Choice Items. **Binary choice items** include any selected response item that offers two optional answers from which to select. Examples include true/false items, yes/no items, and items that require the student to classify a statement as fact or opinion, or as cause or effect. Other kinds of classifications may also be assessed with binary items, such as when a teacher directs students to identify words in a list as nouns or verbs.

Binary-choice items offer a number of advantages. They are efficient in covering a great deal of material, and they are useful in covering content topics that can be placed into two categories. Binary-choice items are also easy to score. It takes very little of the teacher's time to correct a binary-choice item test.

One disadvantage of binary-choice items, however, is that the items are subject to guessing. With only two choices, students have a 50 percent chance of answering an item correctly simply by guessing. Constructing longer tests can help to solve this problem, because a longer test will provide a better sample of the item population. In this sense, it is more difficult to guess the correct answers to forty binary-choice items than to guess correctly on twenty items. Another disadvantage of binary-choice items is that poorly written items tend to encourage rote memorization rather than a higher level of cognitive processing.

binary-choice items Any selected response item that offers two optional answers from which to select.

TABLE 13.2 *Summary of the Relative Merits of Selection-Type Items and Supply-Type Items*

Characteristic	Selection-Type Items	Supply-Type Items	
		Short Answer	Essay
Measures factual information	Yes	Yes	Yes
Measures understanding	Yes	No	Yes
Measures synthesis	No	No	Yes
Easy to construct	No	Yes	Yes
Samples broadly	Yes	Yes	No
Eliminates bluffing	Yes	No	No
Eliminates writing skill	Yes	No	No
Eliminates blind guessing	No	Yes	Yes
Easy to score	Yes	No	No
Scoring is objective	Yes	No	No
Pinpoints learning errors	Yes	Yes	No
Encourages originality	No	No	Yes

Source: How to Make Achievement Tests and Assessments, N. E. Gronlund,1993, Needham Heights, MA: Allyn and Bacon. Reprinted by permission.

Here's How

Here's How To Construct Binary-Choice Test Items

- Write items about substantive content (not trivialities), but avoid broad general statements if students must judge them true or false.
- Avoid the use of negative statements, especially double negatives. Do not add the word *not* to make a statement false. Negative statements are more difficult for students to comprehend than positive statements and so become a test of language skills rather than of content knowledge.
- Avoid long, complex sentences that include two ideas in one statement unless the item measures cause and effect or if/then relations.
- If opinion is used, attribute it to some source unless the ability to identify the opinion is what is being measured specifically.
- Make sure that true statements and false statements are approximately equal in length and number.
- Avoid specific determiners that give unintended cues, such as *always*, *never*, *all*, or *none*.
- Paraphrase statements from instructional material, rather than lifting them verbatim, thus requiring students to understand.
- Make false statements plausible to someone who does not know the correct answer.
- Make sure the item is either definitely true or false to avoid ambiguity.
- Avoid constructing a predictable pattern of correct answers. For example, true true, false false, true true, false false.
- Do not create trick statements using petty wording.
- Include directions that specify the type of judgment to be made and how students are to record their answers. This helps to ensure that students who know the material will correctly interpret the questions.

Good binary-choice items should be conceptualized in pairs. Write true and false statements about the same information, but use only one item from the pair on the test.

Matching Items. **Matching items** usually consist of two columns of words or phrases to be matched. Items on the left are called *premises*. Items on the right are called *responses*. Matching items are compact in form and are efficient for measuring associations. They are also easy to score.

The disadvantage of matching items is that they are restricted to material that students can associate based on simple relations. Because classroom learning often requires multiple associations among ideas and concepts, the *double matching* format may prove quite useful (Carlson, 1985; Figure 13.2). Matching items are difficult to write because they require homogeneous material throughout the unit to be tested. Matching items are also susceptible to unintended clues and tend to focus on lower-level outcomes. In short, matching items work well when they are appropriate for the learning outcome and when they are well constructed.

Here's How

Here's How To Construct Matching and Double Matching Items

- Use homogeneous material in a given exercise. A set of matching items must deal with the same material. It is difficult to write matching items across topics.
- Use more responses than premises, providing directions that responses may be used once, more than once, or not at all, to avoid giving away answers.
- Keep the list of premises and responses brief, especially the responses that students have to scan for the correct one.
- List responses in a logical order. This means that if students were to read only the response column, the responses, as a group, make sense.
- Indicate in the test directions the basis to be used for matching premises to responses.
- Place all items for one matching exercise on the same page.
- Label the premises with numbers and the responses with letters.

A variation of the matching items, *tabular* or *matrix* items can be used to distinguish among ideas in a more comprehensive fashion than by matching or double matching (Carlson, 1985). In Figure 13.3, for example, students are asked to make a variety of judgments about sentence structure by indicating on the matrix what structures are present in a set of test sentences. A matrix item can be scored by counting the number of misplaced entries, or by counting only the correct answers and ignoring the errors.

Multiple-Choice Items. **Multiple-choice items** consist of questions or incomplete sentences that are accompanied by three or more alternative responses, one of which is to be selected as the correct or best answer. The question or statement in the multiple choice items is called the *stem*. The responses are called *alternatives*. Incorrect alternatives are called *foils* or *distractors*.

matching items Any test item consisting of two columns of words or phrases to be matched.

multiple-choice items Test items consisting of questions or incomplete sentences that are accompanied by three or more alternative responses, one of which is to be selected as the correct or best answer.

FIGURE 13.2

Example of a Double Matching Test Item

Source: Creative Classroom Testing (p. 133), S. B. Carlson, 1985, Princeton, NJ: Educational Testing Service. Reprinted by permission.

Topic: Biology — The Circulatory System
Objective: Knowledge of Specific Facts

For each of the parts of the circulatory system listed below, determine the direction of blood flow and oxygen content. Place the letter for oxygen content (A or B) and blood flow (A–C) in the appropriate space.

Oxygen Content
A. Blood with oxygen
B. Blood without oxygen

Blood Flow
A. Toward heart
B. Away from heart
C. Not applicable

Oxygen Content	Parts of Circulatory System	Blood Flow
_____	Left Ventricle	_____
_____	Right Ventricle	_____
_____	Right Atrium	_____
_____	Aorta	_____
_____	Pulmonary Artery	_____
_____	Pulmonary Vein	_____
_____	Arteries	_____
_____	Veins	_____
_____	Capillaries	_____

Topic: English Grammar
Objective: Comprehension of Sentence Structure

For each of the following sentences, place an X in the appropriate box(es) of the table:

1. Bill and Joe went to the store and bought candy.
2. The soldiers not only surrounded the enemy base, but they also successfully attacked it.
3. The girls who entered the contest were photographed for the newspaper and a local magazine.
4. If it rains tomorrow, the picnic and the parade will be postponed until next week.
5. Anyone who chooses may go to the movies with us or may stay at home.
6. The teacher assigned math and English homework over the weekend.
7. Ducks and geese are related, but are different species.

	Simple Sentence	Compound Sentence	Complex Sentence	Simple Subject	Compound Subject	Compound Verb	Contains Prepositional Phrase(s)	Contains Direct Object(s)	
1									1
2									2
3									3
4									4
5									5
6									6
7									7

FIGURE 13.3

Example of a Tabular or Matrix Test Item

Source: Creative Classroom Learning (p. 114), S. B. Carlson, 1985, Princeton, NJ: Educational Testing Service. Reprinted by permission.

An important advantage of multiple-choice items is that they can measure a wide variety of learning outcomes, including higher-level outcomes, if they are properly constructed. Two recently published studies in the *Alberta Journal of Educational Research* have described the equivalence of multiple-choice and constructed response questions in relation to the types of solution strategies employed (Barnett-Foster & Nagy, 1995) and to critical-thinking-test performance (Norris, 1995). The flexibility of multiple-choice items also overcomes some of the shortcomings of other objective items. For example, multiple-choice items eliminate some of the guessing that can take place with binary-choice items. They can cover a wider array of material than matching items, and there is no need for the material covered on the test to be homogeneous. If alternatives are well written, multiple-choice items can facilitate diagnosis of learning errors and misconceptions. Multiple-choice items are easy to score and they are relatively unaffected by response patterns.

The primary disadvantage of multiple-choice items is that it is often difficult to write plausible foils that do not provide clues to the correct or best answer. Sometimes foils can also cause unintended interpretations of the item, which could be correct, depending on the frame of reference used by the student in answering the question. One way of overcoming this problem is to ask students to explain or justify their answer choices to multiple-choice items, but the best solution is to make sure that foils are unambiguously wrong.

REFLECTION: What have been your experiences with multiple-choice tests? What strategies have you used in responding to multiple-choice questions? How are these strategies related to the guidelines for writing good multiple-choice items? What test-taking skills might you teach your students?

Here's How

Here's How To Construct Multiple-Choice Items

- Write the stem of the item so that it is meaningful and presents a clear problem without the student's having to look at the alternatives. See the example in Figure 13.4, and refer to it as you read the guidelines.
- Include as much of the item as possible in the stem without providing irrelevant material.
- Use negatively stated items rarely and only if absolutely necessary. If used, emphasize the negative using boldface type or capital letters.

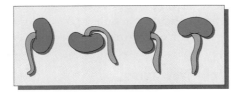

Lupe decided to sprout his bean seeds before planting them in the school garden. The picture above shows several bean seeds that have started to grow. The direction of the growth of the root is a response of the root to
- a. light
- b. heat
- c. oxygen
- d. gravity

continued

FIGURE 13.4
Example of a Multiple-Choice Item in Grade Five Science

Source: "Authentic Assessment: A Systemic Approach in California," by K. B. Comfort, in *Science and Children*, October 1994, 42–43, 65. Reprinted by permission.

- Make the alternatives grammatically consistent with the stem to avoid providing inadvertent clues to the correct answer.
- Make sure there is only one correct or clearly best answer.
- Provide plausible foils to avoid giving away the answer. Use foils that represent likely mistakes of students to help diagnose misconceptions or errors in reasoning.
- Avoid verbal associations between the stem and the answer that give unintended clues.
- Make sure the length of the correct alternative does not provide clues by being either significantly longer or shorter than the foils.
- Make each alternative position (A, B, C, or D) the correct answer approximately an equal number of times. The correct answer position should be arranged randomly. (This can be achieved most of the time by arranging the foils in alphabetical order.)
- Avoid using "all of the above" and "none of the above" unless there are specific reasons for doing so. These add to the difficulty of interpreting the item without necessarily being better measures of students' knowledge.
- Avoid requiring personal opinion, which will lead to the possibility of more than one correct answer.
- Avoid wording that is taken verbatim from the textbook or other instructional materials, as this encourages memorization rather than understanding.
- Avoid linking two or more items together, except when writing interpretive exercises. Items should be independent and not provide clues to other items.

TRY THIS: Locate some old exams in your student union's test file. Examine the multiple-choice items in relationship to the construction criteria listed in this text.

Interpretive items might be a paragraph or two describing a problem or case followed by several multiple-choice or open-ended questions asking students about the case or problem. Teachers can also use graphs, charts, and math problems in interpretive items. Teachers often assess reading comprehension with interpretive exercises in which they give a reading selection followed by comprehension questions asking about the meaning of events in the story. Similarly, interpretive exercises can be useful in science when they provide an experiment and ask students to make predictions or synthesize interpretations about the results.

Constructing Supply-Type Items

When students generate answers to supply-type items, they must recall information from memory rather than recognize an alternative presented. This often makes supply-type items more difficult to answer. In contrast, these items, which include short answer and essay formats, are useful in assessing reasoning and synthesis. Let's examine how supply-type items are constructed.

Short Answer Items. **Short answer items** are supply-type items that include incomplete statements, such as fill-in-the-blanks (completion items) or direct questions requiring a brief response. Short answer items can be answered with a word, a number, a phrase, or a symbol, for example. A form of a short answer

short answer items
Supply-type items that include incomplete statements, such as fill-in-the-blanks or direct questions requiring a brief response.

item called a *statement* and *comment item* can be used to require students to interpret information, predict outcomes, evaluate evidence, and explain their understanding of concepts or their reasoning in solving problems. Consider the following example of a statement and comment item (also called an *open-ended item*):

> Neesha put snails and plants together in a jar of pond water. She sealed the jar and placed it in a spot where it would receive some light. After several days, Neesha checked the jar and found that the snails and plants were alive and healthy. Explain why the snails and plants stayed alive (Comfort, 1994, p. 42).

An advantage of open-ended items like this one is that they ask for students to demonstrate higher-order thinking. Another advantage is that they reduce guessing to a minimum. A disadvantage of short answer items is that they can be difficult to score, arising from the unanticipated answers that must be considered, poor handwriting, and interpretation of phrases used by students.

Here's How

Here's How To Construct and Score Short Answer Items

- Make sure the required answer is brief and specific. Too broad a question makes it difficult for students to figure out what information is being solicited.
- Avoid verbatim statements from the textbook that encourage memorization.
- Word the item as a direct question, if possible.
- For completion items, provide the numerical unit desired where appropriate (e.g., metres, grams, kilometres).
- If fill-in-the-blank items are used, use only one blank per statement and place it toward the end of the statement. The use of more blanks that occur early in the statement can leave out too much information and create ambiguous questions.
- Omit the most important, not trivial, words in completion items in order to assess understanding of relevant concepts.
- Avoid unintended grammatical cues.
- Prepare a scoring key with anticipated acceptable answers or model answers.
- Provide sufficient answer space, making all blanks the same length to avoid providing clues to the correct answer.

Essay Items. **Essay items** require students to construct written responses of varying lengths. *Restricted-response essays* strictly limit the desired response in terms of content and length. *Extended-response essays* allow more latitude in the content of the responses and usually require longer answers. This format is particularly useful when synthesis of content is desired. Following are examples of both types of essay items:

essay items Test items that require students to construct written responses of varying lengths.

Restricted-response essay question	Three theories have been proposed about the nature of light energy. Briefly describe each theory and the evidence that supports it.
Extended-response essay item	For a course that you are teaching or expect to teach, prepare an assessment plan for evaluating student achievement. Be sure to include the procedures you would follow, the assessment strategies you would use, and the reasons for your choice.

REFLECTION: How will your knowledge of cognitive development (Chapter 2) impact on both your teaching and evaluation procedures?

Teachers can use essay items to measure very complex and high-level outcomes, such as analysis or synthesis. These items also assess students' differing abilities to express their thoughts in writing.

The primary disadvantage to the use of essay items, however, lies in the difficulty of scoring them fairly. The use and relative merits of holistic versus analytic scoring is comprehensively described by Hunter, Jones, and Randhawa (1996) in *The Canadian Journal of Program Evaluation*. They note that the authentic-assessment movement in Canada has resulted in a greater interest and use of holistic scoring methods, but that these techniques have both advantages and limitations. Scoring the answers to essays entails some subjectivity on the part of teachers, who can be influenced by their general impressions of the students whose papers they are grading. A halo effect can occur when the teacher, knowing the student by reputation or because other items on the test have been answered well, assumes that the essay answers will be equally as good. Likewise, a teacher may assume that a student who has scored poorly on the rest of the test will also answer poorly on essay items. Scoring essays also consumes a great deal of the teacher's time. Finally, it may take students considerable time to answer each essay question, which means that teachers can ask only a limited number of such questions, and thus can cover only a limited sample of the material from the unit on the test.

Despite these problems, essay tests can be a very useful form of assessment, when conducted following these guidelines.

Here's How

Here's How To Construct Essay Items

- Use essay questions only for high-level outcomes not satisfactorily measured by objective formats.
- Phrase the question to clearly define the task.
- Provide approximate length expectations, point values, and time limits for each question. This alerts students to the relative importance of the item and helps them to gauge their time appropriately during the test.
- Avoid optional questions or extra credit items unless there is a specific reason—for example, individualized instruction.
- Ask a colleague to critique the questions. This helps to keep questions clear and focused and prevents unintended interpretations by students.
- For the most part, ask several short items rather than one or two very long items. Longer items put more emphasis on the writing style and capability of the students rather than on their knowledge of the material.
- Verify the question by writing a trial response.

Here's How

Here's How To Score Answers to Essay Items

1. To obtain an idea of the quality of answers you expect on the essays, review all materials in the text and instructional activities regarding the topic of the essay before scoring. Also read a sample of the answers. Then, prepare an outline of the answer or write a model answer that can be used as a scoring guide.

2. Decide how to handle factors that are irrelevant to the learning outcomes you wish to assess, such as spelling and grammar. You may wish to provide corrective feedback on spelling and grammar even though mistakes do not contribute to the student's overall essay score.

3. Score all answers to one question before going on to the next question in order to avoid a halo effect.

4. Score answers anonymously in order to avoid a halo effect.

5. If the results are very important to the student, as in borderline cases where the score makes a difference between the student passing or failing, obtain a second opinion or reread the papers.

6. Provide feedback to students on their answers. Later sections of the chapter discuss specific ways to provide constructive feedback in detail.

REFLECTION: How do the guidelines for writing and scoring essay items match your current view of the value of essay items?

How Can You Construct Alternative Assessments?

When teachers set instructional goals that involve the use of higher-order thinking skills and the coordination of a broad range of knowledge, they sometimes experience frustration in developing objective tests that will adequately measure these goals. For example, Bateson (1990) states that the four goals for the science curriculum in British Columbia are skills and processes, knowledge, critical thinking, and attitudes. Yet, the measurement and evaluation practices of teachers emphasize the knowledge goal, while almost totally ignoring student attitudes. Conventional test items and procedures function well in assessing unitary skills and discrete aspects of knowledge, but they are less effective in assessing achievement-related behaviours, dispositions, and products (Stiggins, 1991). When these constitute assessment goals, then teachers are likely to find that alternative, authentic assessments provide a more holistic picture of students' learning.

Assessments are authentic when they meet the following criteria (adapted from Wiggins, 1993, p. 229, and Hart, 1994, p. 10):

- Assessments are engaging and worthy problems or questions of importance.
- They represent real-life, interdisciplinary challenges.
- They present students with complex, ambiguous, open-ended problems and tasks that integrate knowledge and skills.
- They require students to produce a *quality* product and/or performance.
- They require students to justify or defend their products or choices.
- They provide criteria and standards that may be modified through discussion.
- They recognize and value students' multiple abilities, varied learning styles, and diverse backgrounds.

CONNECTION: Based on Sternberg's and Gardner's views on intelligence described in Chapter 5, what arguments can be made for alternative assessments?

Insights on Successful Practice

How have you used authentic assessments of students' academic performances and with what results?

One method I have used in the classroom as a way to assess whether my students have learned something—a math problem, science concept, or other lesson—is to have them demonstrate it or teach it to someone else or even to a group. This type of assessment is based on the idea that in order to teach somebody else, the student must have learned and understood the material him- or herself.

The "teaching" can be done through a number of different ways—lecture or demonstration (such as role playing), illustrations (designing posters or charts), or writing (producing books or other publications). Class discussion periods are one way I have used to give the students a chance to teach and help each other and give me the opportunity to assess their progress. The following is an example of how student teaching went far beyond our classroom.

The most valuable lesson my students with learning disabilities can learn is how to become their own advocates—how to help themselves, and how to teach others about their problems and how they best can be helped. This requires the students to learn and understand as much as possible about their own particular problems, their strengths and weaknesses, and what helps them the most. In addition, they must learn to deal with parents, teachers, and classmates who do not understand about learning disabilities.

Numerous class discussions dealing with issues relating to learning disabilities led to the decision by the students to write a book about them. The entire class was involved in the production—writing, typing, illustrating, assembling, mailing, publicizing, and bookkeeping. The lessons and skills learned through the publication of the book were invaluable—but the greatest outcome was the increased self-confidence and self-esteem of the authors as they learned how to deal with their learning disabilities by teaching and helping others. The book, now in its third edition, is being read around the world and has been translated into several languages.

The students also developed and presented workshops on learning disabilities for parents, teachers, and children. By teaching others about their problems, they learned about themselves and it was easy to accurately assess their competence.

PAMELA MANIET-
BELLERMANN
Maniet-Bellermann Foundation
for the Learning Disabled

These criteria stem from the belief that any task worth learning is worth assessing, so that learning and assessment become hard to distinguish as separate activities. Tasks worth learning are also those worth repeating and practising. They may require students to work together in order to complete, and they most certainly require varying amounts of time for different students or groups of students to complete. Finally, authentic assessments often allow for a significant degree of student choice in what product or performance is attempted and how it is completed (Hart, 1994).

Authentic assessments differ from classroom tests not only in format but also in the roles played by teacher and student. Most classroom tests are developed or selected by teachers, so that the student is a passive recipient of assessment. With authentic assessment, however, the student becomes an active partner in the assessment enterprise. Although the teacher serves as the more expert partner in providing appropriate feedback, students involved in authentic assessment activities learn to judge their own work and adopt goals for self-improvement.

The advantages of authentic assessments are numerous. They work well in responding to student diversity, including varying abilities, learning styles, and cultural backgrounds. They tend to be motivational in providing students with tasks that they perceive as worthwhile, interesting, and relevant. Authentic assessments provide teachers with a multidimensional view of student performance, which illustrates not just achievement but also affective characteristics such as motivation to learn. Authentic assessments help students to learn how to monitor their own performance and provide a means of communication among students, parents, and teachers. Finally, authentic assessments have **systemic validity**, which means that they can serve as an impetus for curriculum change (Frederiksen & Collins, 1989). When teachers adopt authentic tasks as a way to assess learning, they tend as well to adjust their instruction to provide more practice with the same kinds of tasks.

Authentic assessments also have their disadvantages, however. Chief among them is the amount of time required to conduct authentic assessment. Whereas objective tests take up a class period or less, authentic assessments are likely to span several class periods and can continue for as long as a grading period or semester. Authentic assessments may also require more resources and considerable effort on the part of the teacher to plan. Careful planning is necessary, though, to ensure that tasks are effective, criteria for completion are clear, and students have access to the resources they will need. Finally, evaluating student performance on authentic assessments is a more complicated matter than counting correct answers on an objective test. In many cases, teachers must rely on their professional judgments without much external guidance for setting performance standards and criteria.

Just as there are different forms of classroom tests and procedures for developing them, so there are different types of authentic assessments and appropriate means of constructing them. Like classroom tests, teachers can also construct authentic assessments to serve different purposes. For finding out about students' needs and characteristics, serving the purpose of diagnosis and placement, observation-based assessment is a useful strategy. For keeping track of and monitoring student development over a period of time, portfolio assessment is appropriate. For checking up on individual student performance and assigning grades, performance assessment is common (cf. Chittendon, 1991). Let's examine each in turn.

Observation-Based Assessments

Teachers observe students in class all the time. Almost without thinking about it, teachers become familiar with various aspects of their students' intellectual, physical, social, and emotional development. They know which students prefer listening to reading as a mode of learning. They know which students work well in groups and which work better alone. To be a useful part of any assessment program, however, observations should be systematic, objective, selective, unobtrusive, and carefully recorded. To make their observations systematic, teachers should follow these guidelines (Hart, 1994):

1. Observe all students.
2. Observe often and regularly.
3. Record observations in writing.
4. Note the typical as well as the atypical. Observations of the routine are just as valuable as observations of the extraordinary.
5. Aggregate multiple observations in order to discern patterns of behaviour.
6. Synthesize evidence from different contexts for a holistic picture of each student.

REFLECTION: How might authentic assessment practices enhance teacher evaluations of culturally different (Chapter 4) or special needs (Chapter 5) children?

POINT: The assessment of student learning is an important and integral part of the teaching-learning process.

TRY THIS: Observe in classrooms where teachers are using various forms of alternative assessment. What goals are being assessed? What are students' reactions to these assessments?

TRY THIS: Interview teachers regarding their use of observation-based assessments. What methods do they use to conduct and record observations? For what purposes do they use observation-based assessment?

systemic validity A property of assessment in which assessment serves as an impetus for curriculum change.

As for what to observe and how to record it, most teachers find checklists of various sorts to be useful. A checklist is composed of a listing of the behaviours or traits that the observer should be assessing. Checklists are best used for making yes/no, present/absent decisions about behaviours. Is a student on task? Does a student participate in small group discussion? Does the group divide labor on a cooperative project? Have students completed all steps in a procedure? Does a student use punctuation correctly when writing an essay? Each of these questions can be answered with a yes or no. The behaviour is either observed or not. When it is desirable to rate the behaviour on a continuum of excellent to poor or some other scale, then a rating scale should be used instead of, or in conjunction with, the checklist. Checklists also serve their function best when they include specific, well-defined behaviours or characteristics to be observed.

Other useful tools for focusing and documenting observations include rating scales and interview sheets. **Rating scales** are measurement instruments used to make judgments about some continuing behaviour or performance. Rating scales allow the teacher to judge the frequency of occurrence of some behaviour or the quality of some performance. Rating scales that use numbers typically consist of a list of attributes that can be rated numerically from "excellent" to "poor" or from "satisfactory" to "unsatisfactory." The following item is an example from a rating scale on student characteristics:

Student turns in homework assignments on time.

1	2	3	4
Always	Usually	Seldom	Never

Interview sheets are useful for recording a teacher's observations during a conference with the student. They generally consist of a list of questions to be asked of each student together with space for recording the student's responses (Hart, 1994). The questions reflect what the teacher wants to observe. In the sample language arts interview sheet shown in Figure 13.5, for instance, the questions can provide insight to the teacher regarding how students reacted to a story they had read.

Recording observations does not have to be burdensome or time consuming to the teacher. The key to minimizing record keeping is developing systems for taking notes, such as checklists and rating scales, that require little writing and recording time. With the increase in computer technologies, electronic performance support tools are available to help teachers record observations in the classroom.

Portfolio Assessments

Several Canadian measurement experts have criticized the over-reliance on tests and traditional assessment methods used in educational decision making. This viewpoint is not limited to student assessment. Bartley (1997) from Lakehead University argues that "portfolio assessment offers significant opportunities to value teacher reflection and promote good assessment practice in a preservice teacher education program" (p. 99). Dan Bachor (1990) states that measurement errors that occur from the use of single or time-bound measurements may be lessened through the use of portfolios cast within the framework of authentic assessment. This viewpoint is supported by Leslie McLean (1990) of the Ontario Institute for Studies in Education. He suggests that test scores are not, by themselves, adequate measures of educational achievement. McLean states:

TRY THIS: Develop a checklist for assessing student performance on a unit in a content area you plan to teach.

rating scale A measurement instrument used in observation-based assessment to make judgments about some continuing behaviour or performance.

interview sheet A means of recording a teacher's observations during a conference with the student, which generally consists of a list of questions to be asked of each student together with space for recording the student's responses.

Literature Review Sheet

Reader's Name _____ Date _____

Interviewer's Name _____

Book Title _____

Author _____

1. Whom did you like most in the story?

2. Whom did you like least?

3. Where does the story take place?

4. When does the story take place?

5. Why did the story keep your interest?

6. Did the author do anything that surprised you?

7. What was the saddest part of the story?

8. What was the happiest part of the story?

9. Did any part of the story make you laugh or cry?

10. What do you wish you could ask the author?

11. What type of person do you think would most enjoy reading this book?

FIGURE 13.5
Example of an Interview Sheet

Source: Assessment and Evaluation in Whole Language Programs, Bill Harp, ed. Copyright 1991 Christopher-Gordon Publishers, Inc. Reprinted by permission.

We have learned a great deal in the past decade about the importance of meaning and context in language teaching, and these ideas are beginning to inform our understanding about the learning of mathematics and science. Achievement takes on new meaning—not as some general or abstract trait to be captured by a single number but instead as performance on meaningful tasks in a recognizable context. The most promising tool for the assessment of authentic achievement in the classroom (and perhaps for accountability as well) is the portfolio, a systematic, cumulative record of performance. Evaluation of portfolios … has shown them to be promising ways to truly integrate student evaluation with the rest of teaching and learning (p. 78).

"A **portfolio** is a container of collected evidence with a purpose" (Collins, 1992, pp. 452-453). Artists and photographers, for example, develop portfolios of their best work for submitting to galleries or potential employers. Financiers develop portfolios containing all of their financial holdings and transactions in stocks, bonds, real property, and other assets. In education, students can develop portfolios for several

portfolio A collection of evidence pertaining to students' developing knowledge and expertise, serving a particular assessment purpose.

These students are having their geography presentation videotaped. What artifacts, reproductions, attestations, and productions might be included in their cooperative learning assessment portfolio?

REFLECTION: Portfolio assessment is becoming more common in classes taken by prospective and returning teachers. What has been your experience in putting together a portfolio? What evidence of your progress did you include? How well do you think the portfolio reflected your achievement during the course?

different purposes that determine what types of evidence are collected and assembled in the portfolio. To show achievement in writing, for example, students might collect samples of their best work—best poem, best short story, best expository piece. To show development or progress in their understanding of how science is integrated with their daily lives, students would collect evidence of improved observational skills and changes in reasoning.

Assessment portfolios have the potential of enabling: teachers to assess student progress; parents, teachers, and students to communicate about a student's work; teachers and administrators to evaluate instructional programs; and students to evaluate and showcase their own achievements (Hart, 1994). For example, in the Middle School Science and Technology project, Powell (1993) used portfolios to document student progress toward particular goals in science. Likewise, portfolios serve several purposes in a project called *Arts PROPEL*, from showing students' best work to documenting their development in writing skill (Wolf, 1989). Teachers must be clear about which purpose they are designing a portfolio assessment to serve, because the purpose will influence what types of evidence they should require in the portfolio.

Collins (1990, 1991, 1992; Collins & Dana, 1993) has distinguished four types of evidence that are routinely collected for inclusion in portfolios. *Artifacts* are documents produced by students during normal instruction, such as a project report, paper-and-pencil test, or drawings to accompany stories they have written. *Reproductions* are documents that display events in which students have participated. These include, for example, photographs of a student's entry in the school science fair or a videotape of a student group presenting two sides of a controversial social issue. *Attestations* are documents prepared by other people that provide external evidence of the student's performance or progress. A letter from the school principal praising a student's plan to recycle waste from the cafeteria is an attestation, as is a music critic's glowing review of a student's flute recital. Finally, *productions* are documents prepared especially for the portfolio, such as reflections on the learning process, captions for other submitted work, and explanations for the inclusion of certain pieces of evidence in the portfolio.

Here's How

Here's How To Design and Use Portfolio Assessments
- Determine the purpose(s) of the portfolio.
- Decide what will count as evidence (artifacts, reproductions, attestations, productions).

continued

- Specify how much evidence should be included, based on the *value-added principle*; that is, for each piece of evidence to be required, ask, "What will be added to the portfolio if this piece of evidence is included?" Including too few items makes it difficult for the teacher to judge achievement or progress in a valid way; including too many items can result in duplication of evidence and confusion.

- Indicate how the evidence should be organized (i.e., chronologically, thematically, or by classes of evidence) (Adapted from Collins, 1992, and Hart, 1994).

When it comes to evaluating portfolios, there are no hard and fast rules for teachers to follow. You can define criteria based on the types of evidence included in the portfolio, the degree to which the evidence shows progress and achievement, and your expectations of what students should have achieved. Once you define specific criteria, you can assemble them in a checklist and scoring rubric. A **rubric** is a "scaled set of criteria that clearly defines for the student and teacher what a range of acceptable and unacceptable performance looks like" (Pate, Homestead, & McGinnis, 1993, p. 25). A general scoring rubric could include the following categories:

Poor: The student did not do the task, did not complete the assignment, or shows no comprehension of the activity.

Inadequate: The product or assessment does not satisfy a significant number of the criteria, does not accomplish what was asked, contains errors, or is of poor quality.

Fair: The product or assessment meets some of the criteria and does not contain gross errors or crucial omissions.

Good: The product or assessment completely or substantially meets the criteria.

Outstanding: All the criteria are met, and the product or assessment exceeds the assigned task and contains additional, unexpected, or outstanding features (Price & Hein, 1994, p. 29).

One purpose of using portfolios is to develop students' abilities in self-assessment. Therefore, teachers may ask students to set their own evaluation criteria (Hart, 1994). Alternatively, expert judgment is a promising means of evaluating portfolios. "Expert judgment implies that the person doing the scoring recognizes the value of the performance as a whole" (Collins, 1992, p. 461), as music or art critics judge an orchestral performance or painting on its entire composition rather than its individual parts. The point to remember is that whatever procedures you use for scoring, they should be consistent with the purpose for which the students developed the portfolios.

Performance Assessments

Performance assessments are a demonstration of learning, or an exhibition of curriculum mastery (Monson & Monson, 1993). They involve tasks that focus on students' use of knowledge and skills in a variety of realistic situations and contexts (Hart, 1994). Tasks that work well in performance assessments are integrative, permit multiple solutions or solution paths, and require sustained effort (Baron, 1991). They can be loosely structured, so that students must not only figure out how to solve the problem, but also decide what the problem is to solve.

TRY THIS: Interview teachers who use portfolio assessment in their classes. For what purpose(s) do they use portfolios? How do they determine what types of evidence should be included? How do they help students learn to assemble a good portfolio? How do they evaluate student portfolios?

CRITICAL THINKING: For what kinds of instructional objectives are performance assessments particularly appropriate?

rubric A scaled set of criteria clearly defining for the student and teacher the range of acceptable and unacceptable performance on a performance assessment.

performance assessment A demonstration of learning, or an exhibition of curriculum mastery, that typically involves tasks focusing on students' use of knowledge and skills in a variety of realistic situations and contexts.

Insights on Successful Practice

In your experience, what is the best way to develop and use a system of portfolio assessment?

At my high school, we have been working on establishing a system of school-wide portfolios. As I reflect on our progress, four key areas seem to surface.

The first is that it is important to develop a small, solid core of individuals who are committed to the use of portfolios. This group becomes the "champions for change." The committee accepts responsibility for developing and synthesizing the theoretical and practical research basis. This group also develops formal and informal methods to explain the proposed program to the entire staff. A further purpose of the committee is to address and alleviate questions and concerns as they arise.

Second, attention must be given to the personal concerns of staff members. During the first year, the majority of our discussions centred on personal considerations rather than educational issues. These concerns centred on procedural, mechanical, and time issues. Until these concerns are addressed, it is difficult, if not impossible, to implement educational reform.

The third area relates to the implementation process. We found that trying to delineate graduation expectations, develop authentic assessments, and implement portfolios as a unified package was too much for some of our staff members. We chose to use what Michael Fullan refers to as the Ready-Fire-Aim approach. We developed the rationale for portfolios (got ready), encouraged teacher participation (fired), and are now attempting to connect graduation expectations, demonstrations, and portfolios (aiming). An alternate method, which may have been more effective, would have been to focus initially on the graduation expectations. Once consensus is reached regarding the expectations, it seems that authentic assessments become a natural consequence. Student portfolios become the obvious method to collect, document, and assess progress toward meeting the expectations.

Finally, it must be recognized that portfolio implementation is a slow and evolutionary process. It has been over four years since we began the process, and there are still several staff members who either do not understand or do not accept portfolios as a viable system. The portfolio-response sheets and other materials have gone through several revisions. In addition, we are continuing to develop methods that provide the time for the effective and efficient use of portfolios by students and staff. Most important, we are just beginning to formally link our graduation expectations, demonstrations, and portfolios.

These key areas are not unique to the implementation of portfolios. They apply to most examples of reform efforts. I would suggest that anyone contemplating the implementation of portfolios first become familiar with the research relating to the change process.

DON DAVIS
High School Teacher

Your Insights

According to this teacher, what are the four key elements of an effective system of portfolio assessment? What are some drawbacks, and why can implementing school-wide portfolios take time? How might you use portfolios in the subject area you plan to teach?

Performance assessment tasks can also be complex enough to require students to work together in small groups.

When deciding whether and how to use performance assessments, teachers should consider, as they do with all forms of assessments, what purpose the performance assessment is to serve. Some kinds of skills can be measured *only* through performance testing. To determine whether a prospective medical lab technician knows how to properly draw a blood sample, for instance, one must observe the person actually doing it. Likewise, the language arts teacher knows whether students can use proper punctuation in a composition only by having students produce a writing sample. However, other targets of performance assessment are not always so clearly identified.

Whether students understand the concept of volume in order to be able to solve problems, for example, can be assessed using the items shown in Figure 13.6(1). If teachers are interested in students' reasoning processes as they answer questions like these, then the test items could be modified to require students to "show all work" or "explain and justify your answer." But when teachers want to know the extent to which students can use their understanding of volume in actual situations where such knowledge is required, then a performance task is preferred, such as that shown in Figure 13.6(2).

Performance assessments are appropriate for measuring metacognitive as well as cognitive development. How well students plan, whether they are proficient at monitoring and evaluating their own work, and how skilled they are at reflection are all possible metacognitive targets of performance assessment. Finally, dispositions are often a target of performance assessment, such as perseverance or flexibility (Quellmalz, 1991). In short, performance assessments are most useful when "essential tasks, achievements, habits of mind, or other valued 'masteries' are falling through the cracks of conventional tests" (Hart, 1994, p. 42).

Once teachers have decided to use performance assessments, how should they go about designing them? Guidelines have been derived from a variety of sources (Baron, 1991; Hambleton & Murphy, 1991; Hart, 1994; Quellmalz, 1991; Wiggins, 1993).

POINT: *Authentic activity provides a basis for assessment.* In performance assessment, the activities are usually complex, problem-oriented tasks that often cross subject matter disciplines.

TRY THIS: Interview teachers on their use of performance assessments. What are some of the advantages and disadvantages they see?

Here's How

Here's How To Design and Use Performance Assessments

- Select or design tasks that are meaningful and interesting to students and require integration of knowledge, skills, and dispositions. The volume problem shown in Figure 13.6(2) is an example of this and the following guidelines.

- Select or design tasks that are complex, well structured, and/or permit multiple solutions.

- Situate tasks in real-world contexts that are developmentally appropriate for students.

- Ensure that students have access to needed resources and have sufficient time to develop assignments and projects.

- Impose authentic constraints on task completion, such as whether students may seek help from others or work in teams.

- Clearly state what performance is expected of students and how this performance will be judged. If self-assessment and/or peer-assessment are used, indicate what procedures will be followed to develop performance criteria.

Like other forms of authentic assessment, performance tasks require careful and systematic planning by the teacher, and they take longer to administer and score. Scoring itself represents a special problem with performance assessment, because there are so many different variables that a teacher may want to measure. When different solutions to a problem are possible, the quality of the solution must be judged, and judging quality depends upon criteria that the teacher has determined are important. When multiple goals are being assessed with a single, multifaceted performance, then criteria must be established for each goal.

FIGURE 13.6

Two Approaches to Testing
Student Understanding of
Volume

*Source: Assessing Student
Performance* (p. 114), G. P.
Wiggins, 1993, San Francisco,
CA: Jossey-Bass Publishers.
Reprinted by permission.

1. Objective Test Questions

1. What is the volume of a cone that has a base area of
   78 square centimetres and a height of 12 centimetres?
   - a. 30 cm³
   - b. 312 cm³
   - c. 936 cm³
   - d. 2808 cm³

2. A round and a square cylinder share the same height.
   Which has the greater volume?

2. A Multiday Performance Assessment on Volume

Background: Manufacturers naturally want to spend as little as possible, not only on the product, but on packing and shipping it to stores. They want to *minimize* the cost of production of their packaging, and they want to *maximize* the amount of what is packaged inside (to keep handling and postage costs down: the more individual packages you ship, the more it costs).

Setting: Imagine that your group of two or three people is one of many in the packing department responsible for M&M's candies. The manager of the shipping department has found that the cheapest material for shipping comes as a flat piece of rectangular paperboard (the piece of posterboard you will be given). She is asking each work group in the packing department to help solve this problem: *What completely closed container, built out of the given piece of posterboard, will hold the* largest volume *of M&M's for safe shipping?*

1. Prove, in a *convincing* written report to company executives, that both the *shape* and the *dimensions* of your group's container maximize the volume. In making your case, supply all important data and formulas. Your group will be asked to make a three-minute oral report at the next staff meeting. Both reports will be judged for *accuracy*, *thoroughness*, and *persuasiveness*.

2. Build a model (or multiple models) out of the posterboard of the container shape and size that you think solves the problem. The models are *not* proof; they will *illustrate* the claims you offer in your report.

Checklists and rubrics, as described earlier, can be useful in scoring performance tasks. Rubrics are especially useful because they can be used to score almost any dimension of performance, including how much assistance the student required to complete a task or the nature of that assistance (Quellmalz, 1991). To develop a rubric for use in scoring performance assessments, teachers should:

- Make a list of important parts of the performance task, such as content, process, mechanics, presentation, source variety, number of cues needed to complete the task.

- Develop a scale for each section showing expected criteria.

- Weight the rubric sections (Pate et al., 1993).

An example of a rubric teachers might use to score student presentations is shown in Figure 13.7. You can see that the teacher has identified six components of the performance to be separately scored. Performance on each component is judged on the basis of criteria defined at three levels. Then an overall score is calculated by multiplying each component score by a weighting factor and adding the results.

	Criterion 1	Criterion 2	Criterion 3	Score × Weight	Total
Section One Eye Contact with Audience	Rarely	Not often	Often	_____ × 6 =	_____ points
Section Two Posture	Often slouches, sways, turns back on audience, fidgets	Sometimes slouches, sways, fidgets, turns back on audience	Stands straight, faces audience, movements appropriate to presentation	_____ × 6 =	_____ points
Section Three Voice Projection	Words not pronounced clearly and volume too low	Words not pronounced clearly or volume too low	Words pronounced and heard clearly	_____ × 6 =	_____ points
Section Four Organization	Information not presented in a logical, interesting sequence; the audience could not follow	Information was interesting, but not presented in a logical order	Information presented in a logical, interesting sequence which the audience could follow	_____ × 7 =	_____ points
Section Five Visual Aids	Two different types of media; information not relevant to outcomes/content; messy; minimal artistic effort	Two different types of media; information relevant to outcomes/content; adequate artistic effort	More than two different types of media; information relevant to outcomes/content; very neat; excellent artistic effort	_____ × 5 =	_____ points
Section Six Time	Less than 10 minutes	10 to 14 minutes	15 minutes or more	_____ × 3 =	_____ points
				Bonus Points	_____ points

FIGURE 13.7
Example of a Rubric for Scoring Performance Assessments

Source: "Designing rubrics for authentic assessment," P. E. Pate, E. Homestead, & K. McGinnis, in *Middle School Journal,* 1993, 25 (2), 25–27. Reprinted by permission.

How Can You Ensure Sound Assessment Practices?

This chapter has examined various types of assessments and guidelines for constructing them. By following these guidelines, you will increase the likelihood that your assessments will be sound. What does this mean? Sound assessment practices yield evaluative information about student performance that is accurate and consistent. With accurate information, teachers can be confident in their diagnoses of student learning problems, their decisions about student placement, and their selection of instructional activities to best meet student needs. For assessment practices to be sound, however, they must have the properties of validity and reliability. Thus, before we evaluate student test performance, we must evaluate our tests to ensure that they offer a fair and accurate estimate of what it is that we want to measure (e.g., learning objectives) (Hopkins, 1998).

Validity

Validity is the most important property of sound assessments and therefore the most important quality for teachers to consider as they construct either classroom tests or authentic assessments. **Validity** concerns the extent to which interpretations of assessment results will be appropriate, meaningful, and useful (Gronlund, 1998; Janda, 1998).

EXAMPLE: Think of content-related evidence of validity in terms of the following question: Does the assessment measure what it purports to measure?

To be sure that the results of a test or authentic assessment are valid, teachers can draw on various sources of evidence. To begin with, assessments typically measure only a sample of the tasks students can perform in the content domain being assessed. For example, a teacher who wants to know how well students use a dictionary cannot construct an assessment that contains all the possible tasks in which a dictionary is appropriately used. Instead, the teacher must depend on a representative sample of tasks that will enable him or her to infer students' competence in dictionary use. *Content-related evidence* of validity, then, refers to how representative the assessment tasks are of those in the overall content domain.

To improve the validity of their assessments, teachers should carefully identify desired learning outcomes. When constructing tests, they should use a test plan (table of specifications) and be sure there are sufficient items to measure each learning outcome. When constructing authentic assessments, they should select tasks that best represent the content domain and types of learning outcomes they want students to acquire.

Criterion-related evidence of validity is important when the purpose of a test or alternative assessment is to accurately measure performance at the present time or to predict it in the future. An assessment may be administered, for example, in order to predict whether a student should be moved into a higher-ability grouping for mathematics class. The test is used to predict the student's achievement in the new class.

An assessment is valid when the students that it predicts will perform well in a new situation actually do so. So, for example, if a student is moved to a higher-ability group in mathematics based on assessment scores and continues to perform well, we can infer that the results of the assessment must be valid.

CONNECTION: Intelligence tests are discussed further in Chapters 5 and 14.

A third type of evidence used to judge the validity of assessments is called *construct-related evidence*. This type of evidence is important if the purpose of an assessment is to measure some psychological trait or construct. Take, for example, the IQ tests discussed in Chapter 5. Intelligence is a construct. It is a concept that theorists literally constructed as an explanation of certain observations. IQ tests are designed to measure the psychological characteristics that make up a kind of intelligence. IQ scores are interpreted to mean that people possess these characteristics in varying amounts. A test of IQ is considered valid on the basis of how well its scores correlate with the characteristics theoretically associated with intelligence, such as school achievement.

validity A property of assessment concerning the extent to which interpretations of assessment results will be appropriate, meaningful, and useful.

reliability A property of assessment that concerns the degree to which assessments are free of measurement errors.

Reliability

Although validity is the most important quality of sound assessment, it is not the only quality necessary. Reliability of assessment is also crucial, and **reliability** concerns the degree to which assessments are free of measurement errors. The results teachers observe of student performance on tests or other forms of assessments are actually estimates of students' true levels of achievement. As such, they always contain a certain amount of error. Errors creep into student performance due to problems in conducting assessments as well as problems internal to the students.

For example, perhaps a fire drill interrupted an essay test and students didn't have adequate time to finish writing. Or perhaps a student was recovering from a severe head cold at the time a music recital was scheduled. Measurement errors can also be caused by student carelessness, variations in motivation, and luck in guessing. Todd Rogers and Ping Yang (1996) from the University of Alberta have also studied "test-wiseness." They state that "if a test taker possesses test-wiseness and relevant partial knowledge, and if a test contains susceptible items ... these factors can result in improved or higher scores" (p. 247). Errors can also be caused by variations in assessment conditions and inconsistent scoring of results.

Assessments are reliable, then, when they give a consistent picture of student performance over time and between one type of measurement and another. What is also important for teachers, however, is whether assessments are reliable in classifying masters from nonmasters. The student who has mastered the material should perform consistently well on measures designed to assess mastery, whereas the student who has not mastered the subject should consistently perform below the established mastery criterion. Remember that Mrs. Legare in the Teacher Chronicle is concerned about writing tests that eliminate the possibility students will miss an item that they really know. She wants her assessments to distinguish consistently between students who have mastered instructional content and met performance criteria from those who have not. When teachers use multiple means of assessment to determine what their students know and can do, they increase the reliability with which they will make sound assessment decisions.

Teachers can also improve the reliability and validity of their assessment decisions by evaluating their assessment practices. Test or assessment **bias** occurs when procedures or items discriminate unfairly among students. For example, when test items draw on the experiences and backgrounds of upper-middle-class or Anglo-Canadian students to the exclusion of poor or minority group students, then the latter are not likely to perform as well even when they are equally competent in the subject matter. Bias can also occur when some students are given more time and resources than other students to complete tasks. Teachers should check for possible bias before administering an assessment, but they can check the quality of test items after administration as well.

Conducting Item Analysis

Teachers who regularly use objective tests for evaluating their students begin to accumulate test items of different types, some of which work better than others for measuring student performance. Evaluating items after tests are administered serves an important instructional function. **Item analysis** allows the teacher to determine whether an item functions in the way the teacher intends it to. By reviewing an item and your students' responses to it, you can determine whether the item is testing the intended objective, whether it measures at the appropriate level of difficulty, and whether it distinguishes those who know the content from those who don't.

For multiple-choice tests, item analysis also allows the teacher to determine how well different foils work within an item. Analyzing items in class—perhaps reviewing the items on the test after grading them—is a way to provide students with feedback at the same time you acquire valuable information that may be used for improving items. Item analysis by means of in-class review also helps the teacher determine common student errors and difficulties. Item analysis can suggest ways to revise curriculum and improve your test-writing skills (Nitko, 1983). Once suitable tests have been developed, their validity and reliability can be improved by using item analysis procedures.

EXAMPLE: Think of reliability in terms of the following question: Would the results obtained on a particular test be the same if the test were given at a different time or if the same questions were asked in a different way?

TRY THIS: Interview teachers to discover ways they try to ensure the validity and reliability of assessment results. In what ways do they deal with potential bias in assessment?

CONNECTION: Referring to Chapters 2 and 4, how can cultural and language factors impact on the reliability and validity of teacher assessments?

bias The result of procedures or items used in assessment that unfairly discriminate among students.

item analysis A procedure used to evaluate test items for the purpose of determining whether the item functions in the way the teacher intends it to.

Here's How

Here's How To Perform an Item Analysis

- **Step 1**. Arrange the test scores in order from the highest score to the lowest. See Figure 13.8 for an illustration of this item analysis procedure.
- **Step 2**. Identify an upper and a lower group. The upper group is the highest scoring 25 percent of the entire class; the lower group is the lowest scoring 25 percent.
- **Step 3**. For each item, count the number of upper-group students who chose each alternative. Repeat the count for the lower group.
- **Step 4**. Record the counts for each item on a copy of the test.
- **Step 5**. Add the two numbers (from the upper and lower groups) for the keyed response (i.e., correct answer). Divide this sum by the number of students in both the upper and lower groups. Multiply this decimal value by 100 to form a percentage. This percentage is an estimate of the *index of item difficulty*.
- **Step 6**. For the keyed response, subtract the count of the lower group from that of the upper group, and divide this number by the number of examinees in one of the groups. You can use the number in either group because both groups are the same size. The result is a decimal that is the *index of discrimination* (Ebel & Frisbie, 1991).

FIGURE 13.8
An Illustration of Item Analysis

Test Item: Students in a religion class draw concept maps as a means of learning differences among the many religions they are studying. This tactic is most likely to influence which process?
a. long-term storage
b. performance
c. search and retrieval
d. semantic encoding

Suppose that 150 students took the test. The upper 25 percent consists of the highest 37 scorers, whereas the lower 25 percent consists of the lowest 37 scorers. Their scoring patterns on this item are shown below.

Item Alternatives	A	B	C	D*
Upper 37	5	0	0	32
Lower 37	8	4	5	20

*correct answer

$$\text{Index of Difficulty} = \frac{\text{Upper Correct + Lower Correct}}{\text{Total Upper and Lower}} = \frac{32 + 20}{74} = .70 \times 100 = 70\%$$

$$\text{Index of Discrimination} = \frac{\text{Upper Correct} - \text{Lower Correct}}{(1/2)\,\text{Total}} = \frac{32 - 20}{37} = .32$$

The *index of item difficulty,* the result of Step 5, estimates the proportion of students who answered the item correctly. This is because the procedure does not include all of the students who took the test, only the upper and lower groups. The difficulty index is a measure of how hard students found each item to be. An index of 50 percent, for example, means that approximately half of the students answered that item correctly. If fewer than half the students correctly answered an item, it is probably too hard and should be modified in some way.

Suppose, on the other hand, that the index of item difficulty for a particular item turns out to be 95 percent, which means that nearly all the students got it right. Does this mean that the item is too easy? Perhaps, but remember that a test should be measuring what students have learned from instruction. If instruction is effective, then most of the students should be correctly answering many of the items. A test that contains too many hard items will simply be discouraging to students and may indicate problems with the instruction or the test.

The *index of discrimination,* the result of Step 6, is a measure of the extent to which an item differentiates students who do well on the entire test from those students who perform poorly overall. The discrimination index can vary between .00 and 1.00. The closer to 1.00, the better the item discriminates between those who did well and those who did poorly on the test, because a discrimination value of 1.00 means that all of the upper group got the item right whereas none of the lower group did. If the same number of students in each group answered an item correctly, then the index of discrimination will be .00.

Unless the index of discrimination is exactly .00, then it will be either positive or negative. It will be positive when a greater number of students in the upper group answered correctly than students in the lower group. When more students in the lower group answered correctly, the index of discrimination will be negative. Good test items should discriminate between well-performing and poorly performing students, so they should have discrimination indices that are positive. A negative index is a signal that the item is bad, either because it is poorly worded or ambiguous, or because it assessed content that was not taught.

By examining the pattern of students' choices of foils in a multiple-choice question, teachers can find clues to what might be wrong with any given item. Suppose, for example, that half of the upper group and most of the lower group chose a particular foil. This could be an indication of more than one correct answer to the question or a strong misconception held by students. A good item is one answered correctly by most of the students in the upper group, with some students in the lower group selecting each of the foils. Reflecting on Ms. Cardinal's problem in the Teacher Chronicle, what might she have learned by conducting an item analysis on the test on which students performed so poorly?

Avoiding Pitfalls in Assessment

With practice at using the guidelines in this chapter and experience in your classroom, you will become accomplished at devising valid and reliable assessments and learn to avoid many of the problems commonly experienced by practising teachers (Ebel & Frisbie, 1991). One problem is that teachers tend to rely too heavily on subjective judgments that stem from informal observations rather than on reliable and valid measurements.

Observations yield necessary and highly useful data, but it is important that they be considered along with other sources of evidence about student achievement, such as formal assessment. Any time two sources of evidence converge toward the same conclusion, you can be more confident that the

TRY THIS: Ask both school teachers and university instructors how they "test their tests."

CRITICAL THINKING: Under what conditions would a low or high index of item difficulty be desirable?

CRITICAL THINKING: How would the results of an item analysis on a multiple-choice test help you determine how students are understanding a particular concept?

TRY THIS: Generate an item analysis that demonstrates a good multiple-choice item.

CRITICAL THINKING: How could you use a table of specifications as a tool for planning instruction?

conclusion is correct. Similarly, if the inferences you draw from observations diverge from assessment results, you have found a problem worthy of additional thought and investigation.

Too many teachers cause themselves problems by putting off assessment planning and preparation until the last minute. One consequence is that paper-and-pencil tests, rather than performance assessments, must be used to save time. Teachers also construct tests sometimes that are heavily weighted toward the material at the end of the unit while ignoring material from the beginning of the unit. Planning ahead will help you make better decisions about what assessment methods you should use in your classes, and using a table of specifications will help you to ensure a more valid and reliable test.

When it comes to objective tests, many teachers construct and administer tests that are simply too short. A test that is too short increases the likelihood that the items on the test will not be representative of the content domain to be measured and thus run the risk of being unreliable. Writing tests that are too short, putting off test preparation until the last minute, and relying on subjective judgments rather than specifying objectives and the cognitive level at which items ought to be written all yield an overemphasis on trivial details to the exclusion of some of the more important principles or applications in the unit.

Failure to use test construction guidelines increases the likelihood that the test results wil not be accurate or meaningful. Many teachers, once they have the test results in hand, forget that all measurement, no matter how carefully designed, is prone to error and imprecision. Frequent assessment and the use of multiple modes of assessment are ways to avoid this problem. The item analysis procedure is another means of overcoming problems with test items. Failure to use item analysis yields tests that, over time, do not improve in quality.

Principles for Fair Student Assessment Practices for Education in Canada

Canadian teachers should be guided in their classroom, school, and province-wide assessment practices by a recently published set of guidelines titled *The Principles for Fair Student Assessment Practices for Education in Canada* (1993). This document contains a set of principles and related guidelines generally accepted by professional organizations as indicative of fair assessment practice within the Canadian educational context. Assessments depend on professional judgment. The principles and related guidelines presented in this document identify the issues to consider in exercising this judgment and in striving for the fair and equitable assessment of all students.

The Principles for Fair Student Assessment Practices for Education in Canada is the product of a comprehensive effort to reach consensus on what constitutes sound principles to guide the fair assessment of students. The principles and their related guidelines should be considered neither exhaustive nor mandatory; however, organizations, institutions, and individual professionals who endorse them are committing themselves to endeavour to follow their intent and spirit so as to achieve fair and equitable assessment of students.

The Principles for Fair Student Assessment Practices for Education in Canada was developed by a working group guided by a Joint Advisory Committee. The Joint Advisory Committee included two representatives appointed by each of the following professional organizations: Canadian Education Association, Canadian School Boards Association, Canadian

Association for School Administrators, Canadian Teachers' Federation, Canadian Guidance and Counselling Association, Canadian Association of School Psychologists, Canadian Council for Exceptional Children, Canadian Psychological Association, and Canadian Society for the Study of Education. In addition, the Joint Advisory Committee included a representative of the provincial and territorial ministries and departments of education.

The principles and their related guidelines are organized in two parts. Part A is also applicable at the post-secondary level with some modifications. Part B is directed at standardized assessments developed external to the classroom by commercial test publishers, provincial and territorial ministries and departments of education, and local school jurisdictions (boards, boroughs, counties, and school districts).

Part A: Classroom Assessments. Part A is directed toward the development and selection of assessment methods and their use in the classroom by teachers. Based on the conceptual framework provided in the *Standards for Teacher Competence in Educational Assessment of Students* (1990), it is organized around five interrelated themes:

1. Developing and Choosing Methods for Assessment
2. Collecting Assessment Information
3. Judging and Scoring Student Performance
4. Summarizing and Interpreting Results
5. Reporting Assessment Findings

Developing and Choosing Methods for Assessment
Assessment methods should be appropriate for and compatible with the purpose and context of the assessment.

- Assessment methods should be developed or chosen so that inferences drawn about the knowledge, skills, attitudes, and behaviours possessed by each student are valid and not open to misinterpretation.
- Assessment methods should be clearly related to the goals and objectives of instruction, and be compatible with the instructional approaches used.
- When developing or choosing assessment methods, consideration should be given to the consequences of the decisions to be made in light of the obtained information.
- More than one assessment method should be used to ensure comprehensive and consistent indications of student performance.
- Assessment methods should be suited to the backgrounds and prior experiences of students.
- Content and language that would generally be viewed as sensitive, sexist, or offensive should be avoided.
- Assessment instruments translated into a second language or transferred from another context or location should be accompanied by evidence that inferences based on these instruments are valid for the intended purpose.

Collecting Assessment Information
Students should be provided with a sufficient opportunity to demonstrate the knowledge, skills, attitudes, or behaviours being assessed.

- Students should be told why assessment information is being collected and how this information will be used.
- An assessment procedure should be used under conditions suitable to its purpose and form.
- In assessments involving observations, checklists, or rating scales, the number of characteristics to be assessed at one time should be small enough and concretely described so that the observations can be made accurately.
- The directions provided to students should be clear, complete, and appropriate for the ability, age, and grade level of the students.
- In assessments involving selection items (e.g., true-false, multiple-choice), the directions should encourage students to answer all items without threat of penalty.
- When collecting assessment information, interactions with students should be appropriate and consistent.
- Unanticipated circumstances that interfere with the collection of assessment information should be noted and recorded.
- A written policy should guide decisions about the use of alternative procedures for collecting assessment information from students with special needs and students whose proficiency in the language of instruction is inadequate for them to respond in the anticipated manner.

Judging and Scoring Student Performance
Procedures for judging or scoring student performance should be appropriate for the assessment method used and be consistently applied and monitored.

- Before an assessment method is used, a procedure for scoring should be prepared to guide the process of judging the quality of a performance or product, the appropriateness of an attitude or behaviour, or the correctness of an answer.
- Before an assessment method is used, students should be told how their responses or the information they provide will be judged or scored.
- Care should be taken to ensure that results are not influenced by factors that are not relevant to the purpose of the assessment.
- Comments formed as part of scoring should be based on the responses made by the students and presented in such a way that students can understand and use them.
- Any changes made during scoring should be based upon a demonstrated problem with the initial scoring procedure. The modified procedure should then be used to rescore all previously scored responses.
- An appeal process should be described to students at the beginning of each school year, or course of instruction that they may use to appeal a result.

Summarizing and Interpreting Results
Procedures for summarizing and interpreting assessment results should yield accurate and informative representations of a student's performance in relation to the goals and objectives of instruction for the reporting period.

- Procedures for summarizing and interpreting results for a reporting period should be guided by a written policy.
- The way in which summary comments and grades are formulated and interpreted should be explained to students and their parents/guardians.

- The individual results used and the process followed in deriving summary comments and grades should be described in sufficient detail so that the meaning of a summary comment or grade is clear.

- Combining disparate kinds of results into a single summary should be done cautiously. To the extent possible, achievement, effort, participation, and other behaviours should be graded separately.

- Summary comments and grades should be based on more than one assessment result so as to ensure adequate sampling of broadly defined learning outcomes.

- The results used to produce summary comments and grades should be combined in a way that ensures that each result receives its intended emphasis or weight.

- The basis for interpretation should be carefully described and justified.

- Interpretations of assessment results should take account of the backgrounds and learning experiences of the students.

- Assessment results that will be combined into summary comments and grades should be stored in a way that ensures their accuracy at the time they are summarized and interpreted.

- Interpretation of assessment results should be made with due regard for limitations in the assessment methods used, problems encountered in collecting the information and judging or scoring it, and limitations in the basis used for interpretation.

Reporting Assessment Findings
Assessment reports should be clear, accurate, and of practical value to the audiences for whom they are intended.

- The reporting system for a school or jurisdiction should be guided by a written policy. Elements to consider include such aspects as audiences, medium, format, content, level of detail, frequency, timing, and confidentiality.

- Written and oral reports should contain a description of the goals and objectives of instruction to which the assessments are referenced.

- Reports should be complete in their descriptions of strengths and weaknesses of students, so that strengths can be built upon and problem areas addressed.

- The reporting system should provide for conferences between teachers and parents/guardians. Whenever it is appropriate, students should participate in these conferences.

- An appeal process should be described to students and their parents/guardians at the beginning of each school year or course of instruction that they may use to appeal a report.

- Access to assessment information should be governed by a written policy that is consistent with applicable laws and with basic principles of fairness and human rights.

- Transfer of assessment information from one school to another should be guided by a written policy with stringent provisions to ensure the maintenance of confidentiality.

Part B: Assessments Produced External to the Classroom. Part B applies to the development and use of standardized assessment methods for student admissions, placement, certification, and educational diagnosis, and for curriculum and program evaluation. These methods are primarily developed by commercial test publishers, ministries and departments of education, and local school systems. The principles and guidelines as presented in Part B are intended to be consistent with the *Guidelines for Educational and Psychological Testing* (1986) developed in Canada.

Developing and Selecting Methods for Assessment

Developers of assessment methods should strive to make them as fair as possible for use with students who have different backgrounds or special needs. *Developers* should provide the information users need to select methods appropriate to their assessment needs. *Users* should select assessment methods that are as fair as possible for students who have different backgrounds or special needs. *Users* should select methods that are appropriate for the intended purposes and suitable for the students to be assessed.

Collecting and Interpreting Assessment Information

Developers should provide information to help users administer an assessment method correctly and interpret assessment results accurately. *Users* should follow directions for proper administration of an assessment method and interpretation of assessment results.

Informing Students Being Assessed

Direct communication with those being assessed may come from either the developer or the user of the assessment method. In either case, the students being assessed and, where applicable, their parents/guardians should be provided with complete information presented in an understandable way. Control of results may rest with either the developer or user of the assessment method.

How Can You Use Assessment To Improve Teaching and Learning?

Although you will use assessment to communicate student progress to parents, other teachers, and the community and to measure the effectiveness of your instruction, you are likely to find its greatest benefit is improving the learning of your students. Besides making sure that assessment results are valid and reliable, you can improve learning by providing effective feedback, involving students in assessment, using assessment results to improve instruction, and creating a positive assessment environment in your classroom.

Providing Effective Feedback

Objective tests have been a predominant form of assessment for so long that many people have come to equate test scores with feedback. After all, test scores provide an indication of how well a student performed in comparison to other students or to some external standard. But consider how much information is conveyed to the learner by a single test score (e.g., 68%, B–, "Good effort"). Not much. There is nothing in a score that tells a learner how to improve his or her performance if it did not come up to standard. Feedback is "information that provides the performer with direct, usable insights into current performance, based on tangible differences between current performance and hoped-for performance" (Wiggins, 1993, p. 182). Feedback enables learners to self-correct, to adjust, and to improve their performances.

What is effective feedback? Many teachers believe they are providing helpful feedback when they assign a grade or write comments on student work that either praise or point out mistakes. Knowing that they have made a mistake, however, is not enough to help students correct their errors. They need to know why the mistake is a mistake and why an alternative answer would be better. For example, a student who has miscalculated in an arithmetic problem can be shown how to solve the problem correctly and encouraged to try again. Effective feedback is descriptive in nature ("you should try to include specific details to support your initial assertion"), not evaluative ("your writing is below average") or judgmental ("you're a poor student").

Depending on how confident students are of their test answers, they will attend to feedback differently (Kulhavy & Stock, 1989). Students who are very sure of an answer they get wrong will likely spend more time trying to understand why they erred than students who are very unsure of their answers. Lack of confidence in their responses can signal that these students lack fundamental understandings that might require additional instruction. Effective feedback helps students to confirm their right answers, debug their mistakes, and reveal their lack of understanding. Effective feedback also provides students with standards and criteria they can use in self-assessment. Table 13.3 displays a comparison of effective and ineffective feedback that can help you in providing constructive feedback to your students to improve their learning.

TRY THIS: Observe teachers to discover ways they provide effective feedback. What feedback do they give students on written work or other achievement-related products?

REFLECTION: Of the many tests and assignments you have completed over the years, what kind of feedback have you found most meaningful?

TABLE 13.3 *A Comparison of Effective versus Ineffective Feedback*

Effective Feedback	Ineffective Feedback
Provides guidance and confirming (or disconfirming) evidence.	Provides praise or blame, and nonsituation-specific advice or exhortations.
Compares current performance and trends against successful result.	Naively assumes that instructions and hard work will bring people to their goal.
Is timely and immediately useful.	Is not timely; suffers from excessive delay in usability or arrives too late to use at all.
Measures in terms of absolute progress; assesses the accomplishment; specifies degree of conformance with the exemplar, goal, or standard.	Measures in terms of relative change or growth; relative to the self or norms, tells students how far they have come (not how far they have left to go).
Is characterized by descriptive language.	Is characterized by evaluative or comparative language.
Is useful to a novice; offers specific, salient diagnoses and prescriptions for each mistake.	Is not useful for a novice; offers a general summary of strengths and weaknesses.
Allows the performer to perceive a specific, tangible effect of his or her efforts.	Obscures any tangible effect so that none (beyond a score) is visible to the performer.
Measures essential traits.	Measures easy-to-score variables.
Derives the result sought from analysis of exit-level or adult accomplishment.	Derives the result sought from an arbitrarily mandated or simplistic goal statement.

Source: Compiled from *Assessing Student Performance*, G.P. Wiggins, 1993, San Francisco: Jossey-Bass.

Involving Students in Assessment

One of the hallmarks of the current assessment reform is that students should be just as involved in the assessment process as their teachers (Hart, 1994). "If we want people to gain control of important habits of standards and habits of mind, then they have to know. . . how to accurately view those things and to apply criteria to their own work" (Wiggins, 1993, p. 54). When students learn to self-assess, they not only begin to internalize performance standards, but also increase their sense of ownership over their learning.

In a kindergarten class, for example, a teacher found that students could accurately judge their writing development on a scale she posted in the classroom (Lamme & Hysmith, 1991). Once they began to view their work in these terms, they also took more risks with their writing.

TRY THIS: Interview teachers regarding whether and how they involve students in the assessment process. What are some advantages and disadvantages in doing this?

Peer assessment occurs when students evaluate each other's work. This happens informally all the time when students look to see what their neighbours are doing in comparison to their own efforts. But when you provide assessment forms or checklists or conduct discussion about individual student products, then you have elevated peer assessment to a more formal process. Peer assessment works especially well in situations where students collaborate on the performance criteria or standards to be used in judging their work. In a sense, setting the criteria also means that students have set goals that they expect their performance to meet. Setting their own goals makes it likely that students will work hard to achieve them and may rely on each other in doing so.

Collaborative or group assessment is a third way in which students can become involved in the assessment process. In some cases, an entire class may set common performance goals, such as "understanding the mathematics that we do," or "being open to new ideas and new approaches" (Hart, 1994). Then, on a regular basis, they examine their common progress toward goal attainment. Asking evaluative and reflective questions helps students to do this, such as "What did you learn doing this assignment?" "Is there another way this problem could be solved?" "What new questions did this activity raise for you?" Having students keep a journal or learning log in which they list goals, keep assignments, draw conclusions, and evaluate their own learning is another means to reflect on individual or class progress and process.

Finally, assessment questionnaires are a useful way of having cooperative groups assess their teamwork and individual contributions to a project or assignment. You can direct questions not only toward the performance criteria to be used in judging the learning product but also toward the process used in completing the project or assignment. Figure 13.9 shows a sample of questions that might be useful for groups in assessing their performance.

Modifying and Improving Instruction

In the Teacher Chronicle, Ms. Cardinal wonders whether the poor performance of the students on her test is a problem with them, her teaching, or the test. By conducting an item analysis, she could discover whether problems existed on the test, and her prior knowledge of the students would give her insight as to whether their performance on this test was consistent with their performance on other measures. Suppose Ms. Cardinal decided that the test was fair but that students' performance on it was simply not representative of what she knew they could achieve. How could the test results help her to pinpoint possible problems in the lesson itself?

FIGURE 13.9
Portion of an Assessment
Questionnaire for Self and
Group Assessment

Directions: Circle the number that best reflects your opinion or assessment.

1. How would you rate your understanding of the material covered in Unit 4?

   Limited   1   2   3   4   5   Full

2. How helpful was your group in discussing the concepts in Unit 4?

   Not very   1   2   3   4   5   Very

3. What was your own level of engagement in your group's discussion?

   Low   1   2   3   4   5   High

4. How would you rate the engagement of each member of your group in the discussion? (*Write in the first name of each person in the space provided.*)

   _____   Low   1   2   3   4   5   High

   _____   Low   1   2   3   4   5   High

   _____   Low   1   2   3   4   5   High

Assessment data of all sorts are useful to teachers in determining what went right and what went wrong with their instruction. By finding out what went wrong, they can modify and improve their instructional strategies. What kind of information might you collect to help you in revising instruction? Dick and Reiser (1989) recommend that essential sources of information include student performance on unit tests and their attitudes after instruction. Additional useful information may include what students knew and how they felt about the subject matter before instruction, their performance on activities and exercises during instruction, and your observations of students during instruction.

Once you have collected assessment data, the task is to organize and analyze it. You could begin by summarizing data according to the objectives dealt with in the lesson. For example, following the table of specifications for the unit test (review Table 13.1), you could list average student performance on each objective and each type of outcome. This would tell you whether students had difficulty with a particular objective (solving double-digit problems that do not require regrouping) or whether they had trouble with a type of outcome (application of concepts they could otherwise define). Depending on the problem you identify, you could provide additional practice, teach the concepts in an alternate way, or find new examples that might be a better fit to your students' backgrounds.

Just as test scores help you to identify possible areas for revising instruction, so does information about student attitudes, both during and after instruction. During instruction, looks of confusion or boredom on the faces of students are potent indicators of a lesson gone awry. Even after instruction, finding out how students reacted to specific aspects of a lesson can help you decide whether to retain an activity you tried out for the first time or to revise it because it didn't keep students' interest. In any event, you can continuously improve your teaching by heeding the things you learn from student assessments.

REFLECTION: Recall an episode from your schooling in which a teacher changed the activities of a class based on the results of a test or quiz. How effective were these changes?

EXAMPLE: One of the purposes of diagnostic evaluation is to determine whether students belong in gifted or special education programs or need modifications of curriculum, instruction, or environment (e.g., inclusive classrooms). Assessment of motor and cognitive skills may be accomplished by using written, oral, and physical tests.

Creating a Positive Assessment Environment in the Classroom

Assessment improves learning and performance when it is respectful of students and in the students' interest (Wiggins, 1993). As Figure 13.10 suggests, teachers should be flexible in their assessments and responsive to individual student needs. More than this, however, teachers can set standards of excellence in their classes and then adopt classroom policies that support student progress toward attaining those standards.

It is important to point out that *standards* of performance are not the same thing as *expectations* of performance. As Wiggins (1993) put it, standards are ideals, always out of reach but eminently desirable nevertheless. He gives the example in industry of "zero defects per million," a standard commonly set by manufacturers. Although this standard is virtually impossible to achieve, and manufacturers don't really *expect* to achieve it, the standard provides a benchmark toward which they can strive. What is *expected* is that everyone will work continuously toward narrowing the gap between present performance and ideal performance.

Ideal performance, it is also important to point out, does not have to be a singular measure of excellence. Standards and criteria depend upon the context and purpose of the assessment (Wiggins, 1993). Writing a letter to the editor, for example, must meet different criteria than writing a report of a scientific investigation. Moreover, while the standards of performance for writing a scientific article might include ability to pass a peer review for publication, you would not expect grade eight students to achieve that standard.

TRY THIS: Teachers have implicit views about assessment that reflect their views of students and learning. Visit several different teachers' classrooms and try to determine the extent to which they adhere to the Principles for Fair Student Assessment Practices for Education in Canada.

FIGURE 13.10
Assessment Bill of Rights for Students

Source: Assessing Student Performance (p. 28), G. P. Wiggins, 1993, San Francisco, CA: Jossey-Bass. Reprinted by permission.

1. Worthwhile (engaging, educative, and authentic) intellectual problems that are validated against worthy real-world intellectual problems, roles, and situations.

2. Clear, apt, published, and consistently applied teacher criteria in grading work and published models of excellent work that exemplify standards.

3. Minimal secrecy in testing and grading.

4. Ample opportunities to produce work that students can be proud of, thus, ample opportunity in the curriculum and instruction to monitor, self-assess, and self-correct their work.

5. Assessment, not just tests: Multiple and varied opportunities to display and document achievement, and options in tests that allow the students to play to their strengths.

6. The freedom, climate, and oversight policies necessary to question grades and test practices without fear of retribution.

7. Forms of testing that allow timely opportunities for students to explain or justify answers marked as wrong but that they believe to be apt or correct.

8. Genuine feedback: Usable information on their strengths and weaknesses and an accurate assessment of their long-term progress toward a set of exit-level standards framed in terms of essential tasks.

9. Scoring/grading policies that provide incentives and opportunities for improving performance and seeing progress against exit-level and real-world standards.

When a positive assessment environment exists in the classroom, assessment serves the functions of determining what you can reasonably expect of students and of helping students continually adjust their performance so that it comes nearer to the standards. The following tips from teachers who have made assessment a positive and integral part of their instruction may help you to get started:

1. *Establish your own personal evaluation plan.* Choose assessment strategies that are most likely to provide you with the information you need to help students learn.

2. *Share your plan with students.* Make your standards and expectations clear. Involve students in determining some of these expectations.

3. *Make assessment part of your daily class routine.* Integrate assessment strategies into your instruction. Have students evaluate their own and each other's work, and discuss the results as a class.

4. *Use volunteer assessment aides.* Solicit the help of parents or other volunteers to collect assessment data or evaluate student work against standards of excellence.

5. *Set up an easy and efficient record-keeping system.* Consider file folders and computer-based systems for compiling and recording student progress. Consider ways of having students keep their own records (adapted from Hart, 1994, pp. 87-88).

A system of continuous progress often depends upon regular and open communication among teachers, students, parents, and the community at large. Sound assessment practices can provide you with a solid foundation for communicating your instructional goals and your students' progress toward goal attainment. How to do this effectively is the focus of Chapter 14.

Teacher Chronicle Conclusion

Testing Trials

During the weekend after her conversation with Mrs. Legare, Louisa Cardinal redesigns the test on which her students did so poorly. Reflecting on her colleague's remarks, she rewrites her multiple-choice questions and includes an essay question. She also adds some authentic problems for students to solve using what they have learned. On Monday she announces the new test.

Application Questions

1. What should Ms. Cardinal do to prepare her students for the new test?

2. Construct a sample of test items for the new test, based on a unit or lesson in a content area you plan to teach.

3. Analyze your sample test. How do the items reflect learning outcomes and instructional goals?

4. How can you be sure the test and its results will be valid? reliable?

5. In what ways could you use the test results and for what reasons?

CHAPTER SUMMARY

What is Assessment and How Are Assessment Practices Changing? (L.O. 1, 2, p. 418)

Assessment is a process of gathering, analyzing, and interpreting data in order to make judgments about student learning. Classroom tests provide one form of assessment commonly used by teachers, but authentic assessment provides an alternative and sometimes more useful means of assessing complex thinking and problem-solving skills. Teachers assess many different knowledge and skill competencies acquired by their students. They also evaluate student dispositions toward learning, as well as achievement-related products and processes. Teachers specify assessment goals based on their professional knowledge, curriculum guides, and input from the community.

How Do You Plan and Construct Classroom Tests? (L.O. 3, 4, 5, p. 424)

To construct classroom tests that best match the content and learning outcomes they want to assess, teachers should use a table of specifications for planning their tests. Depending on their goals, teachers have available a variety of item formats, such as binary-choice, matching, multiple-choice, short answer, and essay items.

How Can You Construct Alternative Assessments? (L.O. 6, p. 435)

Authentic assessments, including observation-based assessment, portfolios, and performance tasks, provide

teachers with the means to assess the development of student knowledge and skill over time and the application of these skills in realistic contexts and situations.

How Can You Ensure Sound Assessment Practices? (L.O. 7, 8, p. 445)

For assessment practices to be sound, they must first be valid, which means that interpretations of assessment results must be appropriate, meaningful, and useful. Assessments must also be reliable, or as free from measurement errors as possible. Teachers can improve the soundness of their assessment practices by evaluating items, planning ahead, using assessment construction guidelines, and using multiple means of judging student learning.

How Can You Use Assessment To Improve Teaching and Learning? (L.O. 9, p. 454)

In addition to following the other suggestions offered in the chapter, you can use assessment to improve learning by providing effective feedback to your students, involving them in the assessment process, revising and improving instruction, and creating a positive assessment environment in your classroom.

KEY CONCEPTS

assessment, p. 418

authentic assessment, p. 421

bias, p. 447

binary-choice items, p. 427

essay items, p. 433

evaluation, p. 419

formative assessment, p. 425

interview sheet, p. 438

item analysis, p. 447

matching items, p. 429

measurement, p. 418

multiple-choice items, p. 429

objective tests, p. 421

performance assessment, p. 441

placement, p. 425

portfolio, p. 439

rating scale, p. 438

readiness, p. 425

reliability, p. 446

rubric, p. 441

selection-type items, p. 426

short answer items, p. 432

summative assessment, p. 425

supply-type items, p. 426

systemic validity, p. 437

table of specifications, p. 426

test, p. 419

validity, p. 446

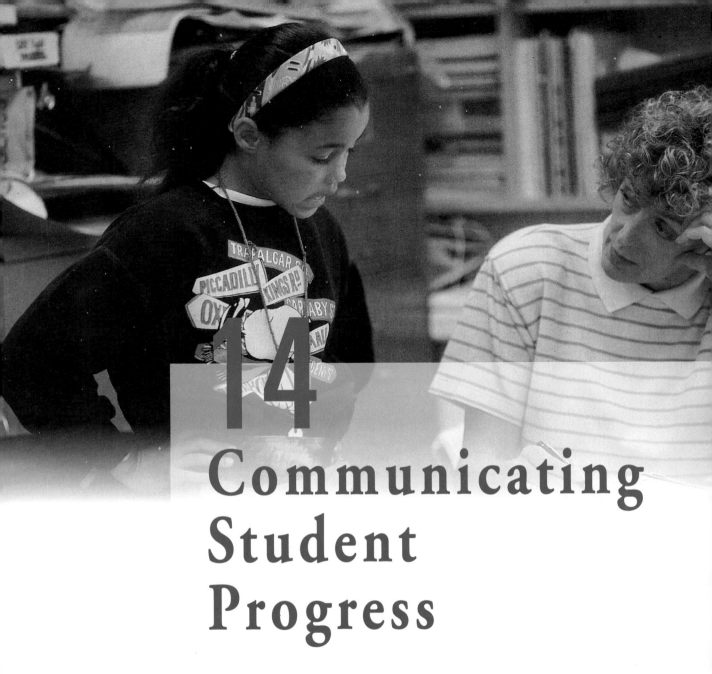

14

Communicating Student Progress

LEARNING OUTCOMES

When you have completed this chapter, you will be able to

1. describe criterion and norm-referenced evaluation
2. distinguish between quantitative and qualitative assessment information
3. understand basic descriptive statistics
4. interpret the scores from standardized tests of intelligence and achievement
5. discuss the factors that can influence test scores

6. compare and contrast the various standards for determining student grades
7. describe the interaction between student assessment and teaching effectiveness
8. demonstrate the relationship between assessment practices and cultural factors
9. examine the relevance of quality assessment in the teaching-learning process

Teacher Chronicle

Benefit of the Doubt

Roy Clark, a middle school math teacher, reaches into his mailbox and takes out a note from Louise Geiger, his principal. The note says, "Could I please see you at your break to discuss math placements for next year?"

Mr. Clark jots a quick response, puts it in Mrs. Geiger's mailbox, and goes to get his math record book. He reviews it during his study hall assignment in the fourth period. He already knows that Mrs. Geiger has decided to make next year's math placements based on the most recent achievement test scores. Anyone with a 7 stanine or higher would automatically be slotted for algebra.

Mr. Clark makes a note beside one name, Heidi Rogers. Heidi is a good, average student who works really hard in math, which does not come easy for her. She had done extremely well on the standardized math test to get a 6 stanine. After the test, Mr. Clark had been pleasantly surprised that Heidi's stanine was 6 because he had expected it to be a 5.

Heidi's study habits, motivation, and support from home indicate to Roy that, even though algebra would be a challenge, Heidi should be placed there. Knowing that the standardized tests are only one measurement tool, he takes a firm grip on his record book and heads for the principal's office, determined to convince Mrs. Geiger.

"Let's sit at the table while we look at the test scores," Mrs. Geiger suggests.

"Fine," Mr. Clark replies, pulling out a chair and opening his grade book.

"Most of your students have done very well," Mrs. Geiger begins. "With 7 as the standard for entering algebra, your class fits the curve." She pauses before asking, "Are there any students about whom you have particular concerns?"

"Yes," Mr. Clark answers. "Heidi Rogers. I realize that she scored in the 6th stanine on this test, but I feel it would be a disservice to her not to place her in algebra next year."

"Why?" his principal asks, scanning the grade book for Heidi's name. Finding it, Mrs. Geiger spends a moment looking at her grades. "She has only a B average in your class."

"For two major reasons," Mr. Clark answers. "Look at her test scores again. Heidi was in the 7th stanine for computation, but only in the 5th for math reasoning. Her daily work reflects this split, too, but to a greater degree. Heidi is an extremely hard worker in class. She is attentive in every lesson, but she has difficulty grasping new concepts without some extra work. For example, Heidi's mother told me at the last conference that she spends an hour every night working on math problems. When the class begins a new unit, she sometimes spends two hours learning the new material. I have seen too many girls drop out of math because we expect them to fail."

Mrs. Geiger nods her head. "What's the second reason?"

"The 5th stanine reflects the difficulty she has in math reasoning. I see it in class and on her homework. She has a hard time figuring out word problems. She often guesses which operation to use. When she does the computation, she is usually correct. However, sometimes, she uses the wrong operation to answer the problem."

"How can she do the work in algebra then?"

"I was planning on coaching her in math reasoning. With her determination, I think she can master it."

"But won't she get discouraged when she finds out how difficult algebra can be?"

Roy laughs. "Not Heidi. Where others see a hurdle too high to jump over, she sees an opportunity. She'll stick with it until she succeeds."

"Well, Roy, You have me convinced. After you've met with Heidi and her mom, let me know what they think."

"Thanks, Louise. I appreciate the opportunity to discuss Heidi's placement with you. This is a good decision for her."

"I appreciate discussing this with you, Roy. It helps me remember that our students are not just numbers on a printout."

Focus Questions

1. How do educators use standardized test scores to make decisions about student placement?
2. What does the Teacher Chronicle suggest about the role of classroom teachers in interpreting standardized test scores?
3. What other assessment tools might Mr. Clark include in evaluating Heidi's progress and predicting her success in algebra?
4. What is the relationship between Heidi's stanine score of 6 and her grade of B in the course?
5. How should Mr. Clark explain the situation to Heidi and her mother?

What Are The Benchmarks of Student Progress?

As you saw in Chapter 13, teachers use assessments of various kinds for various reasons. One important use is to make evaluative judgments about the achievement and the capabilities of students. Some types of assessments are based on the classroom performances of our students. We use such assessments to assign grades. Grades represent evaluative judgments, and the grades we assign to our students stay with them throughout their academic careers.

Another category of assessments, called standardized tests, can also exert considerable influence on a student's future. The results of standardized tests can be at odds with the students' cumulative grades. In other cases, the scores on standardized tests can reinforce the judgments reflected by cumulative grades. In the Teacher Chronicle, the principal was prepared to make a judgment about Heidi based only on standardized test scores; Mr. Clark argued that his classroom assessments should be considered as well. Teachers do not design standardized tests, but they administer them, receive the results, and are asked to make instructional judgments based on those results. As you enter the teaching profession, you too will assess classroom performance and receive the results of standardized tests. Using the information from both types of assessments, you will be expected to interpret them for your students and for their parents, to make professional judgments, and to justify those judgments.

So, what are the bases of professional judgments? How can we justify the inclusion of a student in a program for gifted and talented students, the assignment of a particular letter grade, or the referral of a student for diagnostic testing by the school psychologist? Professionals make judgments on the basis of benchmarks. **Benchmarks** are standards or criteria against which evidence is compared in order to make an evaluative judgment. Lawyers compare a set of events against a particular law—which serves as the benchmark—to see if that law is applicable to the set of events. Physicians compare blood samples against particular criteria—a minimum red blood cell count, for example—in order to render a judgment or diagnosis of the patient's malady. Teachers also use benchmarks as a basis for professional judgments. For example, Saskatchewan educators Daryll Hunter and Trevor Gamble (1996) point to the intense efforts at developing national and provincial educational standards at this time. Those benchmarks are one of two types: criterion-referenced and norm-referenced.

benchmarks Standards against which evaluative judgments are made.

Criterion-Referenced Benchmarks

CRITICAL THINKING: How does a test score communicate meaningful feedback to you in your university course work? Of what use are test scores to you besides simply communicating some level of achievement?

In Chapter 13, we examined various techniques by which teachers assess their students' classroom performances. We also examined how those assessments can be interpreted. Rubrics to score performance assessments and item analysis in multiple-choice tests are examples. The measurements obtained from classroom assessment techniques must then be compared with a standard of performance in order to judge the quality of that performance. Suppose you were informed that a student received a score of 37 on a quiz. How would you judge the student's performance? Does a score of 37 represent mastery of some content? Does it represent failure to collaborate with others? Is it the highest score in the class? The lowest? Evidence must be compared against some benchmark so that a teacher, school psychologist, curriculum supervisor, or principal can determine and then communicate a student's progress. The score of 37 on the quiz might be compared against the number of points possible on the test, say 40. Perhaps the score is compared against the performance of other students who took that same test. A score of 37 might mean that the student has outperformed 80 percent of his or her classmates. If the basis of comparison or benchmark is some external criterion—for example, "the student will score at least 90 percent correct to receive an A"—then the score is being used to make what are called **criterion-referenced judgments**. If the basis of comparison is the performance of other students in the class, then the score is being used to make **norm-referenced judgments** (see Carey, 1994; Hanna, 1993; Popham, 1990). As we will see, the type of benchmark used as the basis for comparison restricts the kinds of judgments that should be made.

CONNECTION: See the discussion of scoring rubrics in Chapter 13.

Criterion-referenced evaluation is undertaken to answer the basic question: What can students do? Criterion-referenced evaluation uses measures of specific domains of competency; it has sometimes been called domain-referenced evaluation. These domains have been conceptualized in a variety of ways since the 1960s, including "mastery criteria," "behavioural objectives," "minimum competencies", and more recently, "performances" and "outcomes." Although there are significant differences between, for example, minimum competencies and outcomes, the underlying concept of criterion-referenced evaluation is that performance is judged against achievement goals (Stiggins, 1994).

CONNECTION: See the discussion of learning outcomes and their specifications in Chapter 11.

The emphasis on student performance and criterion-referenced evaluation grew from the "accountability movement" that began in the 1960s. The fundamental idea of accountability is that educators be held responsible for student learning and performance. In response to this call for greater accountability, Robert Glaser (1963) argued for the use of criterion-referenced evaluation in classrooms in order to assess student attainment of specific learning objectives. Glaser remains committed to the idea that classroom assessment should focus on specific domains of student performance. More recently, he—and many other educational researchers—have advocated for innovations that integrate assessment activity and learning activity (e.g., Herman, Aschbacher, & Winters, 1992; Glaser & Silver, 1994).

criterion-referenced judgments Assessment scores are compared to a set performance standard.

norm-referenced judgments The performance of one student is compared against the performances of others.

The following vignette illustrates the innovative assessment approach. Notice how the teacher, Ms. Inouye, emphasizes active student performance in her assessment and, in turn, how that activity enhances the quality of the learning.

We encounter Ms. Inouye, a teacher at Winston Churchill School, sitting at her kitchen table shortly after returning from a summer trip to Batoche, Saskatchewan. Ms. Inouye has decided to use the idea of a living history as a performance assessment for the unit on Louis Riel and the North-West Rebellion in her Canadian history course. Ms. Inouye was surprised at the lasting controversy over the various interpretations of the perceived long-term personal goals of Louis Riel, the justification of his execution, and the land concerns of the Métis in Manitoba and Saskatchewan. Many plays, films, and books have been written, taking contrasting positions, on these topics. One novel approach to this subject, Ms. Inouye surmises, would be to have students act as "interpreters" of the various protagonists in this Canadian saga. Several students could carefully study the historical circumstances surrounding and leading up to the clash of the two cultures (Métis and Anglo-Protestant immigrants from Ontario) in the later 1880s. Further, each student interpreter might study a particular historical person whom he or she could portray (Louis Riel, Gabriel Dumont, Thomas Scott, Donald Smith, Ambroise Lépine, Sir John A. Macdonald, Colonel Wolseley, Charles Nolin, and so on). These student representatives or interpreters of the past would converse with other students, always speaking in character, so that other students might learn about the history of the North-West Rebellion and its consequences for the present day.

How would Ms. Inouye ensure that her students had acquired basic knowledge of the events leading up to and including the Canadian North-West Rebellion? Traditional criterion-referenced tests and quizzes might be used. An alternative that Ms. Inouye considers, however, is to invite other school students, adults from local Métis organizations, and individuals from historical societies to interact with the interpreters in her classroom. As we leave Ms. Inouye, she is drafting a set of questions that she might encourage people to ask her interpreters of the past, a scoring rubric to document the performances of her students, and forms that the adults from the Métis and local historical societies might use to provide feedback to her students.

Teachers could use the idea of a living history to assess performance for any period of history. They might also adapt the technique for the study of literature, science, or math. Students could perform as interpreters of characters in a novel, authors, scientific or mathematical theorists, or those engineers, architects, and others who have applied scientific theories or mathematical principles. The point of the vignette is that assessment enhances learning because the assessment requires active performance.

TRY THIS: Share the living history idea with a practising teacher. Ask the teacher for ideas on how you might implement this in your classroom.

The criteria by which teachers judge performances (including tests or quizzes) and portfolios (collections of performances) tell us what students can do. Teachers account for and communicate student progress by documenting demonstrations of performance, mastered objectives, and the products of learning. As Richard Stiggins (1994) put it, accountability has pressured schools to become "performance-driven institutions." In terms of classroom assessment, this means that "schools are working effectively only when they articulate clear and specific achievement targets for their students and build instruction around the principle that all students attain those standards" (p. 29).

Norm-Referenced Benchmarks

The benchmark for criterion-referenced evaluation is the achievement goal that a student seeks to attain. The benchmark for norm-referenced evaluation is the performance of other people; that is, norm-referenced judgments about a student are made by comparing that student's performance to the performances of other students. The standardized achievement test that the principal used for

Insights on Successful Practice

What alternatives to conventional criterion-referenced self-made teacher tests have you tried with your students and with what results?

Once a year I had students in all my classes write their own individual exams and respond to their own questions. I used this process with all my students regardless of ability level, and it seemed effective with every group. The process began with keeping organized notebooks during the term, because on exam day all materials used during the term were available for taking one's test. Everything was open notes, open book. It is my experience that the open-book procedure encourages note taking and research skills. As students worked on their questions, I referred them to indexes, glossaries, dictionaries, and encyclopedias to locate details for planning their responses. Some discovered the resource features of their texts for the first time.

Students had ample time to prepare and discuss their test items, which they had to write according to certain specifications. They were to construct twelve task instructions or essay questions at four different learning levels: knowledge, comprehension, application, and analysis. My activity sheet gave them a list of action verbs for each of the four levels to use in constructing test items. With self-made tests in hand, students completed their responses in class during a two-hour open-notes exam block. They also filled out a self-assessment form in which they compared self-testing to teacher tests and noted new knowledge and skills they had gained from the experience. In a class discussion, students reported the processes they used in their work and the triumphs and trials they experienced.

Students always reported that creating their own tests was much more time consuming than reviewing for a teacher-made test. Many also expressed a feeling of pride and accomplishment never experienced in conventional tests. I was always impressed with the depth and detail of the test product and the effort students expended to include creativity and artistry. The detail was such that I usually asked students to mark their four best responses, and those were the ones used for a grade.

DOROTHY SAWYER
Retired High School Teacher

Your Insights

What are some advantages and potential disadvantages of using student-made tests as a basis for evaluation? What forms of alternative assessments might you use with your students?

CRITICAL THINKING: Does the practice of grading on the curve apply to all learning contexts? to the reading performance of a class of grade one students? to a heterogeneous group of grade six students? to an academically talented high school class? to your educational psychology class?

normal curve A mathematically defined function that approximates many educational phenomena.

math placements in the Teacher Chronicle is an example of an assessment that is used to make norm-referenced judgments. The other students who took the achievement test with Heidi are known collectively as the norm group. Norm-referenced evaluation usually uses assessments that are designed to be broader and more general in scope than tests used in criterion-referenced evaluation and are typically more comprehensive.

The famous bell-shaped curve is also called the **normal curve** (Figure 14.1). The practice of grading on the curve is based on the assumption that any group of students represents a range of achievement or ability: There would be very few people in the class who would excel and there would be very few people in the class who would fail. Most of the people in the class would perform somewhere in the middle. Looking at the distribution of grades along the bell-shaped curve in Figure 14.1, we can see how the assumption of variable performance or ability led to the assignment of grades according to the normal curve.

Imagine that you are a high school student who walks into the first class and hears the teacher announce that you will be graded on the curve. As a high school student, you may be unaware of the practice of norm-referenced measurement and what it means technically, but you have an intuitive notion of what it means to be

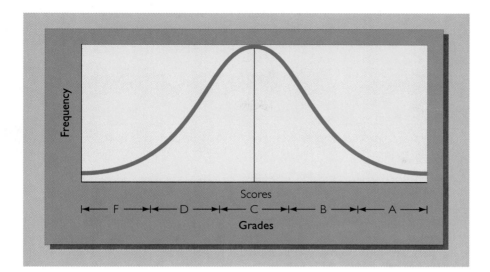

FIGURE 14.1
Grades Based on the Normal
Curve

graded on the curve. Your intuition tells you that only a few people will receive A's. It also means that you will compete for those A's, so you begin looking around to identify the students whom you think will do well in the class. You compare yourself with the top students in order to determine the possibility that you might receive an A in the course. Some of your classmates look around to see which of the other students will likely receive failing grades. They are hoping that a sufficient number of failures occur so that they will be excluded from that category.

The use of norm-referenced evaluation as a way of assigning grades is no longer the predominant practice in schools. As we saw in the last chapter, grades are determined primarily on the basis of criterion-referenced assessments. This is not to say, however, that norm-referenced evaluation is of no value. Norm-referenced evaluation yields legitimately useful information for educators. The scores from standardized tests can be used to make norm-referenced judgments that can improve instructional practices, diagnose individual learning difficulties, and provide benchmarks of student progress.

Regardless of whether the purpose of assessment is to make judgments based on a comparison with achievement criteria or judgments based on a comparison with other people (i.e., a norm group), it is critical that the user of assessment information understand the purpose for which an assessment was designed. An assessment designed to measure inferential reading ability but used to judge decoding skills is being used invalidly. Invalid use of assessment information can also occur if the user of that information inaccurately or inappropriately interprets assessment results.

How Do You Interpret Assessment Results?

Accurate interpretation of assessment results is necessary for valid judgments. In order to accurately interpret results, it is necessary to understand the nature of the information produced by the assessment. Assessment information can be either qualitative or quantitative. **Qualitative information** is communicated through words; **quantitative information** is communicated through numbers (Krathwohl, 1993; Lyman, 1998; Wiersma, 1995). Even when the performance being assessed is not based on a paper-and-pencil test, the assessment of that performance tends to

REFLECTION: Think back to your reactions to the various grading systems your teachers used. Does the grading system influence the atmosphere of the class? The nature of the interactions between teacher and students? Among students?

EXAMPLE: Think about writing a paragraph for a chapter that you might have been assigned as an example of summarizing qualitative information.

qualitative information
Information communicated through words.

quantitative information
Information communicated through numbers.

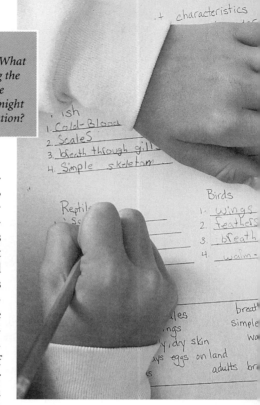

How would you determine if this test is criterion-referenced or norm-referenced? What difference would this make in interpreting the results? What quantitative and qualitative information about student performance might you derive from this instrument of evaluation?

be described in either words or numbers. The assessment of a dance performance, for example, could be either a written critique or a numerical rating. For most people, interpreting assessment results means interpreting numbers, and, for the most part, they are right because educational assessments generally yield numbers. This is one reason why we will focus in this section on the interpretation of quantitative assessment information. The second reason is that qualitative assessment information tends to be verbal descriptions. Of course, verbal descriptions can be either written or oral, but both describe with words. Interpreting verbal descriptions is a task with which most of us are quite familiar. The interpretation of quantitative information—especially from standardized tests—is relatively unfamiliar to most aspiring teachers.

Qualitative and Quantitative Information

CRITICAL THINKING: Are there particular grades or subject areas where qualitative information may be more meaningful than quantitative information, and vice versa?

First, let's consider examples of how qualitative information might be used to make judgments about students. In the Teacher Chronicle, Mr. Clark, the teacher, orally describes the quality of Heidi's work habits and parental support to the principal during the meeting to decide math placements. The description was a succinct summary of the teacher's observations of Heidi in the classroom and of his conference with Heidi's mother, and it was relevant to the placement judgment to be made. Further summarization and interpretation of the description is unneccessary. As another example, assume that a teacher sends home a written report to parents in which the teacher assesses a student's attitude. The teacher does not assign a number to the student's attitude but communicates an appraisal of the student's attitude with words only. The comments represent the teacher's judgment based on observing, among other things, the student's behaviour, general demeanour, and the quality of interaction with classmates. Again, the written description is a summary of student behaviour. In most cases, written assessments are not further summarized because they address directly the criteria used to make evaluative judgments.

Now consider examples of how quantitative information is used in making judgments. Returning to the Teacher Chronicle, the principal bases her initial judgment about Heidi's placement on stanine scores. Stanine scores are numerical categories that result from standardized tests; these and other types of scores from standardized tests will be examined later in the chapter. Teachers collect, and subsequently interpret, a great deal of quantitative information. The scores on a quiz or test are clearly quantitative. Some information that may seem on the surface to be qualitative is quantified. Consider, for example, the use of a simple survey to assess the quality of a student presentation. The teacher may circle "strongly disagree" to "strongly agree" for several statements such as those on the checklist in Table 14.1.

The interpretation of quantitative information usually requires summarization. One way of summarizing the scores from the checklist in Table 14.1 would be to add the ratings of the four statements. Each student would then receive one score for his or her presentation. (The minimum score would be 4, the maximum 20.) If, instead of using the checklist to assess the presentations, the teacher had written comments, the comments would have been the summary. Thus, the quantitative summary would be one number, whereas the qualitative summary would have been written statements of perhaps a paragraph in length. Because quantitative information is more economical, numbers are used frequently to communicate student progress. In most cases, for example, scoring rubrics convert performances into quantitative summaries.

TRY THIS: Contact a local school district or check the curriculum library for performance assessments and their scoring rubrics. Notice how many times the assessments are converted to numbers.

Summarizing Quantitative Information

Suppose, for example, you were to give a test to your class. Suppose, furthermore, that you were asked by your principal to describe your class' performance on that test. You might provide your principal with a statistic: a number that summarizes all of the scores in the distribution.

Every distribution of scores has two properties. One is called the central tendency. The **central tendency** of a distribution is a description of where the middle of the distribution is. For example, in describing the performance of your class to your principal, you might tell him or her what the average score for the

central tendency A score that is typical of a distribution of scores. Mode, median, and mean are three measures of central tendency.

TABLE 14.1 *An Example Checklist that Demonstrates How Judgments of Quality Can Be Quantified*

Student presenter _____

Note to the Teacher: In response to the student's presentation, circle a number from 1 to 5 for each statement below.

The scale is defined as follows:

> 1 = strongly agree
> 2 = agree
> 3 = neutral
> 4 = disagree
> 5 = strongly disagree

1. The student began with a sound premise.	1	2	3	4	5
2. The student cited outside sources.	1	2	3	4	5
3. The student spoke clearly.	1	2	3	4	5
4. The student summarized well.	1	2	3	4	5

class was. If there were 50 possible points on the test and the average performance of your students was 38, you might say to your principal, "The average was 38 out of a possible 50 points." The number 38 is a statistic used to describe the other numbers in the distribution.

A second property of distributions is called **dispersion,** which is an indication of how similar or different the scores in the distribution are from one another. Your principal, having learned the average, or central tendency of the distribution, might inquire further about the performance of the class. If the principal were to ask you what was the lowest score and the highest score on the test, he or she would be inquiring about the dispersion of scores.

Measures of central tendency are numerical descriptions of the average, or typical value in a distribution. There are three different ways to describe the property of central tendency: mode, median, and mean. Each method of describing the central tendency yields a statistic. The **mode** of a distribution is the most frequently occurring score. As illustrated in Figure 14.2, ten students took the test. The distribution of scores is called a frequency distribution because it shows the frequency with which each score occurs in the distribution. (The score of 84, for example, occurs twice in Figure 14.2.) The mode of this distribution of scores is 78 because the score of 78 was attained by more students than any other score.

The **median** of the distribution is that point along the distribution of scores that divides the set of scores into two equal halves. Half of the scores will be above the median; half of the scores below. In Figure 14.2, the median of the distribution is 80.

dispersion An indication of how similar or different the scores in a distribution are from one another.

mode The most frequently occurring score in a set of scores; one of the three measures of central tendency.

median The central score of a set of scores; the score that divides the set of scores into two equal halves; one of the three measures of central tendency.

FIGURE 14.2
A Hypothetical Distribution of Students' Scores

Student Name	Score
Sara M.	79
Andrew B.	84
Kwai J.	78
Brenda W.	78
Lupe E.	85
Sean W.	81
Ruth V.	85
Denora T.	78
Jean-Luc C.	84
Oscar H.	78

The third way to describe the central tendency of a distribution is the mean. The **mean** of a distribution is its arithmetic average. If your notion of taking an average is to add scores and divide the sum by the total number of scores in the distribution, then you have the correct notion of a mean. By adding the ten scores in the distribution in Figure 14.2 and dividing the total sum by 10, we arrive at the index of central tendency called the mean, which in this case is 81.

The mean, median, and mode are three statistics, three numbers that describe the central tendency of a distribution of other numbers. The mean is the preferred index of central tendency because it takes extreme scores into account, which the median and mode do not. To illustrate this point, suppose that the distribution of quiz scores in Figure 14.2 was changed by adding the score of a student who did very poorly on the exam. Perhaps the student felt ill or fell asleep during the quiz. Whatever the reason for the performance, his or her score is now part of the distribution in Figure 14.3.

Adding this extreme score to the distribution does not change the mode at all; the most frequent score is still 78. The median of the new distribution is 79, not much change from the previous median of 80. The mean of the new distribution, however, is changed considerably. The mean of the new distribution is 74.09 compared to the previous mean of 81. Thus, the mean is the index of central tendency that is most sensitive to extreme scores. If it is important to consider all members of the group—as it is for most evaluative puposes—then the mean is the preferred measure of central tendency.

The formula for calculating the mean ($\overline{x}$) of a set of scores is:

$$\overline{x} = \frac{\Sigma\,x}{n}$$

where $\Sigma\,x$ is the sum (Σ) of all scores (x) divided by the number (n) of scores

CONNECTION : See the discussion of reliability and validity in Chapter 13.

mean The arithmetic average of a set of scores; one of the three measures of central tendency.

FIGURE14.3
A Hypothetical Distribution of Students' Scores

Student Name	Score
Sara M.	79
Andrew B.	84
Kwai J.	78
Brenda W.	78
Lupe E.	85
Sean W.	81
Ruth V.	85
Denora T.	78
Jean-Luc C.	84
Oscar H.	78
Jim H.	5

A simple formula for calculating the standard deviation (s.d.) is:

$$s.d. = \sqrt{\frac{\Sigma(x - \bar{x})^2}{n - 1}}$$

where the mean ($\bar{x}$) is subtracted from each score (x) and squared, the squared values are added together (Σ) and this total is divided by one less than the number of test scores (n-1). The square root of this total is the s.d.

Dispersion refers to the extent to which scores in a distribution are similar to one another. One way to describe dispersion is to report the **range** by subtracting the lowest score from the highest score. The range is a relatively crude measure of dispersion, that, although providing a quick estimate of the dispersion of scores, can be influenced considerably by extreme scores. Consider, for instance, how the ranges of the distributions in Figures 14.2 and 14.3 change because of the extreme score. The range, then, tells us only about the difference between the two most extreme scores. If we want an index of dispersion that tells us something about all of the scores in a distribution, we need to use a statistic called the standard deviation.

The **standard deviation** describes the average distance between each score in the distribution and the mean of the distribution. Similar scores in a distribution yield a small standard deviation. A distribution in which scores are highly dissimilar yields a large standard deviation.

As an example, let's consider the following distribution of scores: 20, 22, 24, 26. The mean of this distribution is 23. The first and last scores in the distribution are three units away from the mean. Thus, the score of 20 in this distribution can be said to deviate by a distance of 3 units. The score of 26 also deviates by 3. The middle scores in the distribution (22 and 24) each deviate by 1. By adding the deviations (which equal 8 in this example) and dividing by the number of scores (4 in this example) we get an estimate of standard deviation (in this example, the standard deviation is 2). Conceptually, a standard deviation is the average deviation in a distribution. Although the formulas that are actually used to calculate standard deviations are more complicated than indicated here, what is important is that you understand the essential concept. The concepts of mean and standard deviation underlie the interpretation of standardized tests.

How Do You Interpret Standardized Test Results?

Imagine that you are now seven weeks into your first teaching job. You feel that you are beginning to get a handle on the administrative routine in the school. You are starting to understand and communicate with your colleagues. The students in your classroom have settled into a good working rhythm. As you walk into the office to pick up your mail, you find yourself thinking about the progress you have made during those first seven weeks. You notice in your mailbox that there is an official-looking memo from the superintendent of the school district (Figure 14.4).

You finish reading the memo on the way to the teachers' lounge to grab a cup of coffee and to look over your lesson plans. Although the prospect of parent-teacher conferences is a bit daunting, you feel prepared to discuss and justify the grades you have assigned your students during the first grading period. The idea of discussing the results of standardized tests that you did not design and score, however, is a bit worrisome. You start to wonder, what exactly did those tests measure?

Types of Standardized Tests

Standardized tests are used to make norm-referenced judgments; they are designed to enable the evaluator to make comparisons between one person who

TRY THIS: Ask practising teachers to recount their first parent-teacher conferences. Ask them what they have learned about preparing for them.

range The difference between the highest and lowest scores in a set of scores.

standard deviation A statistic that expresses the variability in a distribution of scores.

standardized tests Tests that are prepared to provide accurate and meaningful data on students' performances compared to others at their age or grade levels.

INTEROFFICE MEMO

Date: October 10, 1998
To: All School Personnel
From: M. Jones, Superintendent
Re: Parent-Teacher Conference

A reminder to all school personnel, especially principals and classroom teachers:

Parent-teacher conferences will be scheduled in your school during the second week of November. In addition to discussing the grade reports that parents of your students will receive next week, parents have also been advised that they may discuss with you the results of the standardized achievement tests that were administered during the first week of school. The achievement tests provide us with important data concerning the academic levels of our students. It is important for parents to understand and appreciate the results of those tests. They have been advised that they may bring any questions they may have about the results of the tests to the conference. Therefore, you should be familiar not only with the classroom work of your students, but with their performances on the achievement tests.

took that test and other members of the norm group. Standardized tests can be used to measure achievement and aptitude or to make diagnoses (see Gronlund, 1990; also Kubiszyn & Borich, 1993).

Achievement tests measure students' knowledge in various content areas. According to Gronlund (1990), standardized achievement tests are useful in five ways:

1. To evaluate general educational development in basic skill areas
2. To evaluate progress during the year or over years
3. To group students for instruction
4. To determine broad areas of strength and weakness
5. To compare achievement with aptitude

A recent trend among companies who design achievement tests is to provide, in addition to the norm-referenced data, criterion-referenced data. Criterion-referenced information is provided through the reporting of results by instructional objective or by specific skill area. Standardized test results may include criterion-referenced information, but they have been designed for other purposes. The number of items used to measure each skill area is usually quite small. Two of the most commonly administered multilevel group achievement tests in Canada are the Canadian Achievement Test and the Canadian Test of Basic Skills.

CRITICAL THINKING: How do the different aspects of validity discussed in Chapter 13 apply to each of the three types of standardized tests described in the text?

Aptitude tests measure learned abilities based on a broader spectrum of in-school and out-of-school experiences. An example of an aptitude test is the Canadian Cognitive Abilities Test that you probably took during your elementary or high school years. A common distinction between achievement and aptitude tests is that achievement tests measure what has been learned and aptitude tests measure learning potential. Gronlund suggests that it is too simplistic to make distinctions in this way. A better way to think about the distinction is that achievement tests measure what is learned from school activities and experiences.

Aptitude tests are usually shorter than achievement tests. They are less likely to be biased with respect to students of differing backgrounds. We will return to this issue later under the label cultural bias. Aptitude tests can be used before training because they are not designed to measure achievement. Aptitude tests are used to identify underachievers in combination with achievement tests.

Diagnostic tests can be used to identify learning difficulties by pinpointing student errors. Such tests do not identify the causes of such difficulties. They do, however, identify specific strengths and weaknesses. Having identified strengths and weaknesses by means of a diagnostic test, a teacher can then engage in careful observation and seek other information in search of the source of a student's learning problem. Diagnostic tests also confirm or disconfirm the judgments made on the basis of other tests. You must always keep the purpose of the test in mind as you interpret results (Worthen & Spandel, 1991). Likewise, you must always remember that norm groups serve as the basis for comparison in norm-referenced tests. In order to compare a grade two student with a grade eight student, both students must have taken the same exam.

The Normal Distribution

Earlier in the chapter, we encountered five statistics that teachers use to describe the score distributions. Three of those statistics serve as indices of central tendency: mean, median, and mode. Two statistics serve as indices of dispersion in a distribution: range and standard deviation. The question that remains is: How do these indices serve as the basis for understanding and then communicating the results of standardized tests? Many such scores conform to the bell-shaped or normal curve mentioned earlier in the chapter. Understanding the properties of the normal curve is critical for communicating where a student stands in relation to other students.

How is this standardized aptitude test different from an achievement test? What are the most appropriate uses of these and other types of standardized tests?

The standard deviation is a ruler applied to the normal distribution. (The normal distribution discussed earlier is given in Figure 14.5.)

Looking at Figure 14.5, we see that the normal distribution is symmetrical and that most of the scores in a normal distribution are located near the centre. Because the highest point in the distribution is in the exact centre of the symmetrical curve, the mean, median, and mode coincide.

The normal distribution is a theoretical distribution. It is derived from mathematical formulas. Even though the normal distribution is theoretical, it describes many naturally occurring distributions. Consider the height of human beings. If we were to measure the height of all human beings over eighteen years of age and construct a frequency polygon of that distribution, the distribution would be normal in shape. Most people would be of average height. As we move to the extremes of the distribution—people who are very tall or people who are very short—we should find fewer and fewer people. The normal distribution matches many actual distributions of psychological characteristics as well.

As mentioned, the mean of a normal distribution resides at the center of the distribution along with the median and the mode. Properties of the normal distribution include the relations of various points on the curve to the standard deviation. Suppose, for example, characteristic X is normally distributed. By adding all of the X scores in the distribution and dividing by the number of X scores in that distribution, we can calculate the average score of the X distribution.

Having calculated the mean of that distribution, we can then determine how far each score in the distribution deviates from the mean by calculating the statistic called standard deviation. The properties of the normal distribution are such that one standard deviation (the average distance of all scores from the mean of the distribution) accounts for certain percentages of the area defined by the normal distribution.

Looking once more at Figure 14.5, we can see that the normal distribution has been divided into areas defined by standard deviation units. If we move in

CRITICAL THINKING: What characteristics of students in a "typical" classroom may or may not be normally distributed?

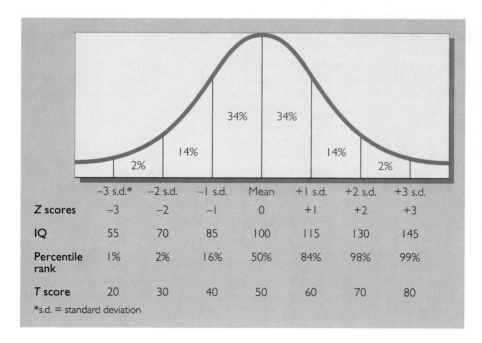

FIGURE 14.5
Standardized Test Scores in Relation to the Normal Curve

Source: Essentials of Educational Measurement (5th ed., p. 69), R. L. Ebel and D. A. Frisbie, 1991, Englewood Cliffs, NJ: Prentice Hall. Copyright 1991 by Allyn and Bacon. Reprinted by permission.

	−3 s.d.*	−2 s.d.	−1 s.d.	Mean	+1 s.d.	+2 s.d.	+3 s.d.
Z scores	−3	−2	−1	0	+1	+2	+3
IQ	55	70	85	100	115	130	145
Percentile rank	1%	2%	16%	50%	84%	98%	99%
T score	20	30	40	50	60	70	80

*s.d. = standard deviation

either direction from the mean of the distribution to a distance that is equal to one standard deviation unit, we find that each unit above and below the mean accounts for roughly 34 percent of the entire distribution. Taken together, the two standard deviation units on either side of the mean account for a total of 68 percent of all of the scores in the X distribution. The area of the normal curve defined by the area between one and two standard deviation units above or below the mean accounts for approximately 14 percent of all of the scores in the distribution. Figure 14.5 also includes the percentages accounted for between two and three standard deviation units. Once we are beyond three standard deviation units above or below the mean, we have accounted for approximately 99 percent of all of the scores in a distribution. This means that by finding a single student in a normal distribution, we can make evaluative statements about that student in comparison to other students in the norm group.

Standardized Test Scores

Standardized scores are assigned by using the standard deviation of a distribution to identify points on a normal curve. Standardized scores tell educators how one person's performance on a test compares with that of other people in the same norm group. Although there are a number of different types of standardized test scores used in educational assessment, all are ways of identifying where a student stands in relation to the others in his or her norm group. As you examine several common standardized scores in the following sections, keep in mind that the type of score reported does not change a student's standing in the norm group. Using different scores merely communicates that standing in different terms. The same idea applies to temperature, which can be measured using either a Celsius or a Fahrenheit scale. Depending on the scale used, the number used to describe the temperature will change, but not the temperature itself.

Z **Scores and Percentile Ranks.** One form of standardized score is called a Z score (shown in Figure 14.5). A Z **score** is a score given in standard deviation units. The mean of any normal distribution is assigned a Z score of zero. Standard deviation units define Z scores above and below the mean. A score on the normal distribution that is one standard deviation unit above the mean is assigned a Z score of +1. A score that resides two standard deviation units above the mean is assigned a Z score of +2. Scores that reside below the mean are given minus or negative Z scores. Note that we can assign Z scores to any normal distribution regardless of the mean and the standard deviation of that distribution. Once Z scores are assigned, we can determine the percentage of people in the distribution who are above or below a particular Z score. **Percentile rank**, another standardized score, defines the percentage of people in the norm group above whom an individual scores. For example, the percentile rank of a person who is at the mean of the distribution is 50. The percentile rank of the individual with a Z score of +1 is 84 (see Figure 14.5).

IQ Scores. A more familiar standardized score is provided by the intelligence quotient (IQ). IQ is based on standard deviation units as well. Once we have assigned the standard deviation ruler to a normal curve, it is possible to compute any of the standardized scores such as Z scores, IQ scores, percentile ranks, or T scores.

Z score A score given in standard deviation units. The mean of any normal distribution is assigned a Z score of 0. Scores above the mean are plus scores; scores below the mean are minus scores.

percentile rank A standardized score that gives the test taker the percentage of people in the norm group above whom he or she has scored.

Before describing some of the other standardized scores, let's look at an example of where IQ scores come from and how they are interpreted in relation to the normal curve. (IQ scores are given in Figure 14.5.) Suppose an intelligence test has a mean of 100 and a standard deviation of 15. Interpreted in terms of these standardized scores, if you had an IQ of 115, you would have an IQ that is higher than 84 percent of the general population. We can calculate that percentage by examining the areas under the normal curve defined by standard deviation units. Note also that an IQ score of 115 is equivalent to a Z score of +1.

CONNECTION: See the discussion of the construct of intelligence in Chapter 5.

T Scores. Another standardized score that has been developed is called the T score. The distribution of a T score has a mean of 50 and a standard deviation of 10. An IQ score of 115 converts to a T score of 60. Any number of standardized scores could be derived in this way. Consider the scores we have examined to this point. They have all been defined in terms of standard deviation units applied to the normal curve. IQ scores, which we use most often and tend to think of as having certain numeric properties, are defined scores. Suppose you invented an IQ test. Your IQ test has sixty-three items on it. You can assign a score to any one person's performance, ranging from 0 to 63. Let's assume that you administer your IQ test to a large number of people, perhaps 5000. After collecting 5000 scores on your IQ test, you could then calculate the mean score. Let's assume that the mean score on your IQ test is 38 items correct. With the distribution of your IQ scores in hand, you can then calculate the standard deviation of the distribution. Let's assume that the average deviation from the mean of all the 5000 scores is 4. This is another way of saying that the standard deviation is equal to 4.

A mean equal to 38 and a standard deviation equal to 4 are based on the obtained scores on your IQ test. Obtained scores are often called raw scores. Because of the size of your sample and the nature of the characteristics being measured, we can assume that the distribution of scores is normal around a mean of 38, with a standard deviation of 4. When the time comes for you to report the results of your IQ test, you could report the raw scores.

For example, a person who scored one standard deviation above the mean would have a raw IQ score of 42. Instead of reporting the raw score, you could also report derived scores. One such score would be the Z score. Instead of reporting the raw score of 42, you could inform the person who received the raw score of 42 that his or her score is a +1 in Z-score terms. Alternatively, you could report a T score of 60, or a percentile rank of 84.

EXAMPLE: Stephen Jay Gould's book, *The Mismeasure of Man*, has an interesting history of intellectual tests.

You could, however, follow the more common pattern of reporting IQ scores by converting the raw score mean into a defined IQ score of 100. You could also define the standard deviation of your IQ distribution to be equal to fifteen IQ-point units. Thus, instead of the person receiving an IQ score of 42 in raw score terms, you could report that person's defined IQ score as 115.

Stanine Scores. Another common standardized score is a stanine. You will recall from the Teacher Chronicle that Mrs. Geiger used stanine scores to make math placements. **Stanine** scores are standardized scores that range from 1 to 9, each of which represents a range or band of percentages under the normal distribution. The stanine bands are depicted in Figure 14.6. A stanine score of 5 represents the middle 20 percent of the distribution and includes those students who scored at the mean of the distribution. Stanine scores greater than 5 indicate performances that are above average. Stanine scores below 5 indicate performances below the average. One advantage of reporting stanine scores is that small differences

T score A standardized score that converts raw scores to a distribution with a mean of 50 and a standard deviation of 10.

stanine A standardized score from 1 to 9, each of which represents a range or band of raw scores.

FIGURE 14.6
Stanine Scores in Relation to
the Normal Curve

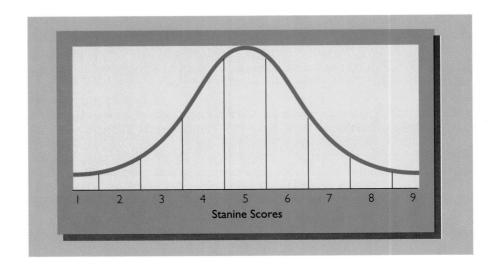

Stanine Scores

between scores are less likely to be interpreted as real differences. It is important that we keep in mind that all standardized tests, as indeed all educational measurement, contain error.

TRY THIS: Ask several teachers to explain grade equivalent scores to you; ask them how they use those and other standardized test scores.

Grade Equivalent Scores. Along with stanines and percentile ranks, perhaps the most popular form of reporting standardized test results is the use of grade equivalents (see Carey, 1994; Kubiszyn & Borich, 1993). Recall the imaginary situation early in this chapter: You learned of parent-teacher conferences and your responsibility to report and interpret the standardized scores of your students. Suppose that one of your grade two students has a reading score that is equivalent to that of a grade four student. On a superficial level, it seems obvious that a student in grade two who scores at a grade four reading level is capable of reading as well as the average grade four student. As obvious as that may seem, it is not the case and is the reason why grade equivalents are so often misinterpreted.

Typically, **grade equivalent scores** are generated by using a test to measure the performance of the target grade, and grades one level below and one level above the target grade. Thus, the norm group and the tables of scores used for that grade two student's norm group come from the performances of students in grades one, two, and three. Grade four students, with whom the grade two student is being compared, are not part of the group who took the grade two student's test. In this example, grade two students and grade four students are not members of the same norm group. Remembering the caveat about norm groups, that only members of the norm group are eligible for comparison, we can see the mistake that a parent or teacher makes who assumes that the grade two student is performing at the same level as the average grade four student.

The reason our grade two student earned a grade equivalent score of grade four is that scores beyond one grade level above and below the target are extrapolated, or estimated, from the obtained scores of the three grades. Grade equivalent scores that are much higher or much lower than the student's actual grade level merely indicate that the student differs considerably from the average performance of his or her own norm group. Extreme grade equivalent scores say nothing about the specific skills that a student may possess.

grade equivalent score A standardized test score that uses grade-level performances to place individuals.

In addition to this common problem of misinterpretation, there are additional problems related to the use of grade equivalent scores. Kubiszyn and Borich (1993) list four problems.

1. Equal differences among grade equivalent scores do not necessarily reflect equal differences in achievement. For example, the difference between Student A who performs at a grade equivalent of 2.6 (sixth month of grade two) and Student B who scores at a grade equivalent level of 3.6 is not the same as the difference between Student C who scores a grade equivalent of 5.6 and Student D who scores at a grade equivalent of 6.6.

2. Grade equivalents are not useful unless a subject is taught across all of the grades that are represented in the grade equivalent scores. For example, to report that a student's achievement in geometry is at the grade equivalent level of 5.4 is meaningless if grade five students do not take geometry. If this is the case, what does it mean to achieve in geometry at the level of the average grade five student in the fourth month of that grade?

3. Grade equivalents are often interpreted as standards rather than norms. Grade equivalents are averages; a grade equivalent of 9.3, for example, represents the median point in a distribution of scores obtained by students in the third month of grade nine. Grade equivalents, then, are based on a comparison with other students; that is, they are norm-referenced, not criterion-referenced, evaluations.

4. It is difficult to compare grade equivalents across various school subjects. A student who is a full grade level behind in math may be further behind in math than the same student who is one full grade level behind in reading. Students progress at different rates in different subjects; therefore, the norms for reading and for math are not comparable.

CRITICAL THINKING: What might account for the variety of standardized test scores? Why do you think grade equivalent scores were invented?

Despite all of these problems, it is very likely that you will receive grade equivalent scores for your students. It is also very likely that at some point you will have to interpret those scores in order to make instructional or placement decisions about your students. You will also be asked to explain the results of standardized tests to curious parents.

Confidence and Test Scores

Use the preceding descriptions of standardized test scores to interpret the report provided in Figure 14.7. This is the type of report that you will use, in combination with criterion-referenced assessments, to discuss student progress at parent-teacher conferences, instructional placement conferences, and other judgments that affect the teaching-learning process.

An important aspect of the report in Figure 14.7 are the bands of scores indicated in the graph of national percentile. ("National" in this report means that the norm group includes students from the entire country.) The bands represent what are called confidence bands or confidence intervals. **Confidence bands** identify a range of scores that are probable limits of a student's true score. Confidence bands are used because assessments are not perfectly reliable. There is always some error that distorts the true score. The more reliable the assessment, however, the less the distortion. (If this does not sound familiar, you may want to review the discussion of reliability in Chapter 13.) How should a teacher interpret the confidence bands and other scores on a report of standardized test results? For purposes of illustration, the following list refers specifically to the reading vocabulary scores in Figure 14.7.

REFLECTION: Try to recall an occasion when you first learned of your score from a standardized test. How did you interpret it? How did you feel when you learned what the score meant?

confidence band An interval around a particular score in which the true score probably lies.

STUDENT INTERPRETIVE REPORT
STUDENT: STEVENS RAINA **GRADE:** 5.7 **BIRTH DATE:** 8/27/88 CODES: ....

[A]	NS	GE	NCE	SS	NP	RANGE
READ VOCABULARY	7	8.5	73	760	87	79-93
READ COMPREHENSION	7	9.5	73	766	86	77-92
• TOTAL READING	7	9.1	73	763	87	81-91
LANGUAGE MECHANICS	4	4.4	59	736	67	56-76
LANGUAGE EXPRESSION	5	5.5	48	728	46	36-57
• TOTAL LANGUAGE	5	4.3	54	732	58	50-64
MATH COMPUTATION	4	5.0	30	706	28	21-37
MATH CONCEPTS & APPL	5	5.6	48	721	46	37-56
• TOTAL MATHEMATICS	4	5.3	43	714	38	31-45
• TOTAL BATTERY	6	6.5	57	736	63	59-68
SPELLING	6	6.6	59	738	66	54-77
STUDY SKILLS	6	6.5	56	735	61	51-71
SCIENCE	6	6.9	57	746	63	52-75
SOCIAL STUDIES	5	5.5	47	728	43	34-54

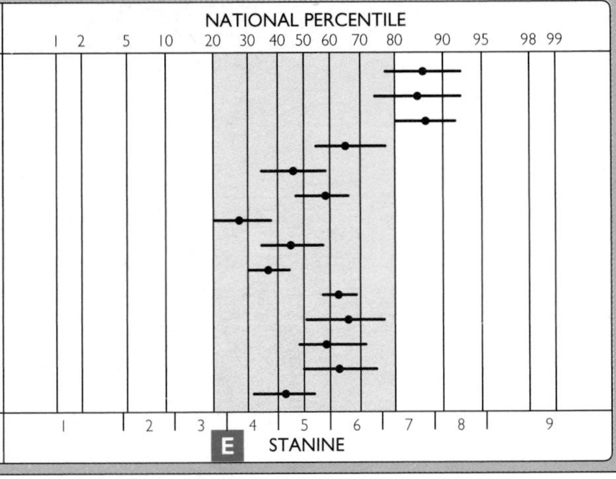

[B]

[C] [D]

NS: NATIONAL STANINE
GE: GRADE EQUIVALENT
NCE: NORMAL CURVE EQUIVALENT
SS: SCALE SCORE
NP: NATIONAL PERCENTILE

[E] STANINE

INTERPRETATION OF SCORES

[F] **NORMS** This student's test performance may be compared with that of the National Norm Group by referring to the National Percentile column (NP) above. Achievement in the basic skills is best summarized by the "Total" scores. The student's Total Battery score is above the national average (the 50th percentile). In Total Reading, the student's achievement was better than approximately 87 percent of the nation's grade 5s; in Total Language, better than approximately 58 percent; in Total Mathematics, better than approximately 38 percent.

OBJECTIVES Content areas included in CTBS/4 are indicated as follows: Reading (R), Language (L), Mathematics (M), Spelling (SP), Study Skills (ST), Science (SC), Social Studies (SS).
The student is strong in skills related to:
[G] APPLYING CONCEPTS OF GEOMETRY (M), RECOGNIZING CORRECT NOUN AND PRONOUN USE (L), APPLYING CONCEPTS OF NUMBER THEORY (M), RECOGNIZING CORRECT ADJECTIVE AND ADVERB USE (L), RECALLING DETAILS STATED IN PASSAGES (R).
The student may need further instruction to develop skills related to:
PERFORMING COMPUTATIONS INVOLVING FRACTIONS (M), APPLYING CONCEPTS RELATED TO ALGEBRA (M), RECOGNIZING ELEMENTS OF PARAGRAPH COHERENCE (L), APPLYING CONCEPTS OF SOCIOLOGY, ANTHROPOLOGY (SS), ASSESSING, APPLYING SOCIAL STUDIES CONCEPTS (SS).

FORM-LEVEL: A-15 **SCORING:** PATTERN (IRT)
NORMS FROM: 1997 **QUARTER MONTH:** 31
TEST DATE: 4/24/98

FIGURE 14.7
A Sample Student Interpretive Report.

Source: Reprinted with permission from a 1992 catalogue of materials for the *Comprehensive Tests of Basic Skills* (4th ed., p. 155), Monterey, CA: Macmillian/McGraw-Hill School Publishing Company.

Insights on Successful Practice

What advice can you give novice teachers about interpreting scores from standardized tests?

Probably the most misunderstood method of student assessment is standardized tests. Such tests can provide the teacher with an invaluable amount of information. Like any approach to assessment, standardized tests are intended to help us make particular decisions about student learning and our teaching. They are not a replacement for carefully constructed teacher-made tests or the many other means that we have for getting useful information about our students' academic growth. Instead, standardized tests are another part of the essential information base needed to make the best decisions we can as teachers.

Our school district employs such group standardized tests as the Canadian Achievement Tests (CAT/2), Canadian Test of Basic Skills (CTBS), and the Canadian Cognitive Ability Test (CCAT). I find the results to be very helpful in getting to know my students and confirm my perceptions of, or even raise questions about, the learning and achievement of particular students. For example, Dan was earning average marks in most of his grade eight classes, but seemed increasingly uninterested in school. Results from the CCAT that was administered to all grade eight students suggested that Dan was a very intelligent lad, although he had never been identified as such. The school psychologist was then requested to administer the Wechsler Intelligence test (WISC–III) and using Canadian norms, Dan scored in the top two percent on nonverbal abilities and the top ten percent on the verbal measures. This was followed up with an individually administered achievement test (Wechsler Individual Achievement Test) and again the results suggested that scores in reading, mathematics, and language were in the superior range, with writing scores falling in the high average range. These findings certainly helped us to better understand and meet Dan's needs for a more challenging program. Standardized tests have been most useful to me in trying to determine if a student's low achievement in the classroom is due to a lack of ability, a learning disability, or some other cause such as low motivation.

However, I am also reminded that in some cases standardized tests may be less useful for various reasons. While standardized tests may allow comparisons to national standards, this may not be the best comparison for the kinds of local decisions we have to make in our school. As well, some tests may less adequately reflect our provincial curriculum and the learning objectives developed for our students. My observations of students have also helped me to place the results from standardized tests in perspective. All of the things that can impact positively or negatively on test performance have to be considered, such as the health of the student, reading skills, test wiseness, and test anxiety. Students may misread a direction and do poorly for reasons unrelated to what the test measures. Or they may work at a particular pace which can be accommodated in the classroom but not on a timed test. Because some students do not demonstrate their best performance on tests, authentic assessments, teacher-made tests, and the use of portfolios are also needed to arrive at a fair and accurate assessment of each student.

My general rule is that the more information I have about a student, the better I can be as a teacher. I never jump to conclusions based on any test score. Rather, I look for corroborating evidence from other sources of information that will then help me decide whether the finding from a test is meaningful or an artifact of other related factors.

JORI HARRISON
Junior high school teacher

Your Insights

According to this teacher, what are the factors you should keep in mind when interpreting, reporting, and using standardized test results? What list of do's and don'ts might you derive from this brief essay?

Here's How To Read a Standardized Test Report

- The Comprehensive Test of Basic Skills is not just one test but a series of subtests. The collection of subtests is called a battery. The first column indicates the various subtests in the entire battery. Focusing on the first row, reading vocabulary, and moving across from left to right, the first score is the national stanine (NS). This student's performance compared with the national norm group placed him or her in the 7th stanine, clearly above average.

- The second score reported is grade equivalent (GE). This student's grade equivalent on reading comprehension is 8.5. This is a grade five student, and although reading vocabulary is probably taught across grades five through eight and nine, the safest interpretation from the grade equivalent is that the student is clearly above average in comparison with his or her norm group. Before making additional interpretations, the test manual should be consulted to determine how the test was normed. One question to ask, for example, is did grade eight students take this form of the reading vocabulary test?

- The next score is the normal curve equivalent (NCE) based on a mean of 50 and standard deviation of 21.06. This student's NCE score is 73. This places the student approximately one standard deviation above the mean. This is no surprise. The other standardized scores, if converted to Z scores, would also be approximately $Z = +1$. Remember that all standardized test scores supply essentially the same information because all are based on the application of the standard deviation ruler to the normal curve.

- The scale score (SS) refers to the score obtained on the reading vocabulary test before being converted into the other standardized scores reported. The illustration of developing your own IQ test and defining a standardized score pertains here. Keep in mind that all of the other reading vocabulary scores in this report are based on the scale score.

- The percentile rank (again, the norm group is grade five students from across the country) is 87. This means that the student performed better than 87 percent of the norm group. Note that the narrative section of the report refers to percentile ranks, but with reference only to total reading, total language, and total math subtests. The reading vocabulary subtest is combined with reading comprehension to form total reading.

- The range is the confidence band around the percentile rank. Although standardized tests are quite reliable, there is some error associated with the student's percentile rank. The interpretation of the range is that it is highly probable that the student's true percentile rank—compared to grade five students nationwide—is between 79 and 93. (The exact probability associated with this range is most likely 95 percent, meaning that you can be 95 percent sure that the student's national percentile rank is between 79 and 93. To determine the exact probability used to construct confidence

continued

bands on this or any standardized test, you could consult the test manual or the guide to interpretation that often comes to teachers with the test results.)

- The graphic results, with national percentile on the top and stanine on the bottom, are redundant. These scores have already been presented in the columns discussed earlier. Nevertheless, the graph can be very helpful in explaining results to students and to parents. (To help you relate the graph to this discussion of standardized scores, imagine that the normal curve in Figure 14.5 or 14.6 is superimposed on the graph. The reading vocabulary score would be slightly to the right of the first standard deviation unit above the mean and within the 7th stanine. Notice the lower limit of the confidence band is in the 6th stanine and the upper limit is in the 8th stanine.)

- The Interpretation of Scores section of the report in Figure 14.7, mentioned in step 5, provides not only a narrative interpretation in the subsection labelled "Norms" but also a qualitative description of the student's strengths and weaknesses in the subsection labelled "Objectives."

TRY THIS: During a school visit or in a university class, ask to see one of the standardized achievement tests used in local schools. How are student raw scores represented as standard test scores?

Issues in Standardized Testing

The use of standardized tests provides a basis for comparing students with each other, for making norm-referenced judgments. In Chapter 13, we looked at classroom assessments that teachers used primarily to make criterion-referenced judgments. In recent years, there has been a greater emphasis on criterion-referenced tests in schools in order to more carefully track the progress of students across objectives. This recent trend—to track carefully the instructional progress of students—has led to another trend—providing criterion-referenced information with norm-referenced test results. The information comes in the form of scores on content or skill clusters. Such information can take the form of an individual profile, the profile of a school, or the profile of an entire district.

Although standardized testing practices continue to evolve in light of changing views of assessment, it is still the target of much criticism, even from within the teaching profession. For example, "Teachers Must Hold Firm Against Standardized Testing" was one of the cover articles of the *1997 Saskatchewan Bulletin* (Vol. 64, No. 3). At the same time, *The Globe and Mail* (page C11, June 26, 1997) reported the comments of Paul Gooch, vice-provost at the University of Toronto, Tom Calvert of Simon Fraser University, Peter Such, associate dean of York University's Atkinson College, and Luke McWatters, Eden program director, regarding the use of internet sites (e.g., www.schoolsucks.com; ren.glaci.com/tpw/) for obtaining tests and the problem of who is actually responding to on-line test sites in distance-education courses. Common complaints about standardized tests themselves are that they are biased against some students, they reduce teaching to only preparing students for tests, and they focus time on lower-order thinking skills (Haney and Madaus, 1989).

Test Bias. In order to communicate student progress based on standardized test results, a teacher must account for or explain why particular results were obtained. One alternative explanation of standardized test results is that they are biased toward certain types of students. Popham (1990) provides a general definition of test bias. **Test bias** occurs whenever an aspect of a test, the way a test is administered, or the way the result is interpreted, unfairly penalizes or benefits individuals who are members of some subgroup. There are a number of ways in which test bias could manifest itself (Flaugher, 1978). For example, a test might be considered biased if the scores of one group of students are lower, on average, than those of other groups. Several recent publications raising the possible relationship between intelligence, social class, gender, and race have once again brought this issue into the limelight (e.g., Herrnstein & Murray, 1994).

Some researchers have argued that a test is biased if the following assumption is made: Tests measure the same characteristics for all examinees. Suppose, for example, that if all examinees taking a math achievement test can read the instructions equally well, then we would attribute any differences in their scores to math ability. However, if students of equal math ability are unequal in their ability to read and follow instructions on the test, differences in reading ability and not math ability would account for differences on the test.

Other critics have argued that the sexist or racist content of a test is a form of bias. When the language and pictures used on a test do not represent the gender and racial balance of the examinees, or when they perpetuate undesirable role stereotypes, the test is culturally biased. A test can also be biased if it predicts performance more accurately for one group than for another group. However, some recent research on this issue indicates that most standardized tests predict school achievement equally well across groups of students (Sattler, 1992).

A test can be biased if it is used in the wrong way. Suppose a company tested its prospective employees using an examination that measured skills and aptitudes that were irrelevant for the job but that systematically excluded one group or another. If the test results did not accurately predict success on the job, the use of that test would result in bias.

Tests can be biased if they are administered under conditions that unfairly affect certain groups. For example, a test might be administered that prevented someone with a physical disability from demonstrating the appropriate knowledge or skills needed to answer a question or questions.

A number of articles published by Canadian writers have provided evidence that many commonly used intelligence tests yield biased results when administered to Aboriginal children. For example, studies by Seyfort, Spreen, and Latimer (1980) with Aboriginal children from three different bands in British Columbia; Mueller, Mulcahy, Wilgosh, Watters, and Mancini (1986) with several age groups of Inuit children from Northern Canada; and Scaldwell, Frame, and Cookson (1985) with two groups of Oneida and Chippewa-Muncey children from Ontario have all raised concerns about the use of individual intelligence tests such as the Wechsler Intelligence Scale for Children (WISC) with Aboriginal children. As an alternative measure, Greenough-Olsen (1993) and Schwean and Greenough-Olsen (1992) recommend the use of non-verbal tests of cognition such as matrices tests when assessing Aboriginal students. Goldstein (1988) from the Vancouver School Board has also called for more careful, sensitive, and fair assessment practices with Aboriginal children.

The issue of test bias has not been limited to Aboriginal students. We are reminded of Canada's cultural diversity when we see articles entitled "A comparison of the K-ABC and WISC-R for Cantonese, English, and Punjabi speaking Canadians" (Gardner, 1986) or read Ester Cole's (1992) article on "Characteristics of students referred to school teams." Dr. Cole states that the Toronto Board of

CRITICAL THINKING: How does the use of a test influence its fairness? Does use of the test influence its reliability or validity? Why or why not?

test bias An unfair disadvantage (less frequently an unfair advantage) that affects members of some subgroups because of some aspects of the test, the way the test is administered, or the way the result is interpreted.

Education "has a long history of receiving immigrant students and fostering multicultural programs," which has resulted in the development of many support systems to meet the needs of ESL (English as a Second Language) students.

Anita Li (1994) from the University of Calgary has addressed the issues of equity assessment in relation to new immigrant students with limited English proficiency. Li proposes a series of questions that should be asked when assessing these new Canadians: Is the assessment nondiscriminatory or fair? Is the assessment interactive and relevant to instruction? Are the assessors self-aware and sensitive to cultural and language diversity? Do we include assessment of native language and English language proficiency in both oral and written contexts? Is the assessment ecologically sound? What is the purpose of this assessment? Don Massey (1988) from the University of Alberta has outlined a practical model which incorporates an experimental problem-solving and clinical approach to cross-cultural assessment.

John Lewis from McGill University and Ronald Samuda of Queen's University have contested the practice of administering single score intelligence tests to culturally different students. They argue that such measures are discriminatory and urge the increased use of comprehensive and dynamic assessment strategies: "Clearly teachers need to become more aware that standardized norm-referenced tests are irrelevant and inappropriate if they are to achieve the ideals of educational equity in the assessment and placement of students who veer from the mainstream by virtue of cultural, linguistic and/or socioeconomic circumstances" (Lewis & Samuda, 1989).

Finally, it is worth mentioning here that there are many other factors that can have an impact on a student's test performance. Some of these reside in the test itself. We frequently find ourselves in Canada 'importing' tests, mainly from the United States. Saklofske and Janzen (1990) have discussed the issues and problems associated with using standardized tests developed in other countries in their article in the *McGill Journal of Education*, and also in their chapter in the book titled *Educational Psychology: Canadian Perspectives* (Short, Stewin, & McCann, 1991). The problem occurs not only with achievement tests, but also with intelligence tests. For example, the Canadian validity study of the American WISC-III indicated that there were score differences between Canadian and American children, necessitating the publication of separate norms for Canada. There are also various non-test factors that influence test scores. Saklofske and Schwean (1992) have outlined some of the causes of poor test performance related to the examiner, the student (e.g., motivation), and the test situation.

One factor that can impact on test performance is termed **test-wiseness**. Todd Rogers and Pin Yang (1996) from the University of Alberta have concluded that higher test scores can result from a combination of test-wiseness and partial relevant knowledge on the part of the student when a test contains susceptible items. Rogers and Bateson (1991) and Rogers and Wilson (1993) have demonstrated that both professionally developed standardized tests and teacher-made tests contain test-wise-susceptible items. Rogers and Yang have suggested that "training programs directed toward the acquisition of test-wiseness be included as a regular part of the school program at the junior high school level" (p. 247).

Bias and Anxiety. Bias can occur because of the anxiety that tests foster. Students come to learn very quickly how much importance is placed on standardized achievement tests. Standardized aptitude tests, especially those given later in a child's academic career, are even more critical to their futures. Hill (1984) sug-

CONNECTION: See the Principles for Fair Assessment Practices for Education in Canada described in Chapter 13.

test-wiseness using test characteristics and formats or the test situation to receive a higher score than expected if only subject matter knowledge was being measured.

gests that test anxiety affects as many as ten million elementary school students in the U.S., the most serious cases occurring in formal testing situations. They know the material, but cannot demonstrate their knowledge in a formal testing situation. For such students, the tests provide low and invalid estimates of their abilities.

Hill's review of the research indicates that there are three characteristics of standardized testing that contribute most heavily to test anxiety. The first is the time limits and pressures of a standardized test. The second is test difficulty. Standardized tests are norm referenced; the goal of the test is to discriminate between students. Such tests are bound to contain difficult items. The final characteristic that contributes to test anxiety is the mechanics of the test, such as the instructions and the question formats. Hill recommends that teachers can help alleviate test anxiety by teaching test-taking skills to students who suffer from this anxiety in standardized test situations.

The picture may be further complicated, as noted in this headline in the *Calgary Herald* newspaper (December 23, 1997): Boys Cope Better with Province's Exams. It has been reported that high school girls score five to six percent lower than boys on the multiple-choice items that comprise part of the Alberta diploma exams. These exams account for fifty percent of the grade twelve final mark in each subject tested. However, it was also suggested that girls may earn better teacher-awarded marks based on their better classroom performance. These findings remind us, as teachers, of the need to be sensitive to the influences of anxiety, test-wiseness, item-type, and a host of other factors when using test scores to reflect a student's kind and extent of learning.

Here's How

Here's How To Help Students Overcome Test Anxiety

- Familiarize your students with various item types, have them read test instructions carefully, and give them feedback on their interpretations of those instructions prior to taking the tests. Such feedback can alleviate some of the student's anxiety, and help the learner gain confidence in his or her ability to take such tests.

- If the test is a criterion-referenced classroom assessment, consider giving anxious students additional time to complete the exam. This is often a necessary accommodation for students with learning disabilities. If the test is a formal, standardized assessment, coordinate with school administrators to provide students with learning disabilities a special administration of the exam that extends the time limit (this is a common practice in most school districts).

- For anxious students who do not qualify for extended-time administrations, pass along guidelines that will help them use the time available to their best advantage. Advise your students to do the following:

  a. Start immediately and work quickly before you get tired.

  b. Keep moving through the items. Answer the easy items; if you get stuck, mark the item so that you can come back later, and then move on!

  c. If you have a doubt about an item, go ahead and answer it, but mark it so that you can return later, and then move on!

continued

> d. If you are working on an essay test, do not leave an item unanswered. If you are running out of time, at least write an outline to communicate to the examiner that you knew something about the question, but were unable to finish.
>
> - Review problem-identifying and problem-solving skills. Remind your students also to monitor their own thinking, and to use the metacognitive strategies you have taught them: considering all the alternatives, questioning the degree to which they are certain or uncertain of an answer, and checking their work to avoid careless mistakes.

Minimum Competency Testing. An important trend in standardized testing in the United States is the use of so-called minimum competency tests. This issue has been raised at various times in Canada as well, but in different ways. For example, a perusal of journals such as the *Canadian Journal of Education* special issue (1995) on *Accountability in Education in Canada* details the provincial efforts in British Columbia, Alberta, Ontario, Quebec, and Newfoundland at setting educational standards and ensuring accountability.

Minimum competency testing came about as a response to the U.S. public's perception that the educational system was not teaching students basic skills (O'Neil, 1991). Most states created laws requiring minimum competency testing, and many are advocating national standards of student competency (O'Neil, 1993). The most common type of minimum competency testing requires students to pass comprehensive exams before being awarded high school diplomas. Minimum competency tests have also been used as a basis for promotion at various grade levels.

The purpose of minimum competency testing, as first designed, was twofold. First, these tests were to ensure that students graduating with a high school diploma had achieved minimum skills. Second, they were to provide schools with an incentive to better educate students in basic skills. As minimum competency testing became more common, legal issues were raised, including the fairness of such tests when administered to special education students and minorities. Again, this is the issue of test bias. A major related problem that remains unsolved is the lack of a precise definition of *minimum competency*. What should be the benchmarks of competency? Many school districts are responding to the trend toward authentic assessment by forming task forces of teachers to investigate and formulate plans that include the assessment of minimum competency (see Cunningham, 1986).

CRITICAL THINKING: Is assessment-driven instruction something to be avoided or embraced? Explain your answer, with reference to reliability and validity.

One result of minimum competency testing has been referred to as assessment-driven instruction, which "occurs when a high-stakes test of educational achievement (because of the important contingencies associated with a student's performance) influences the instructional program that prepares students for the test" (Popham, 1987, p. 680). A high-stakes test is one that qualifies students for promotion or graduation, or one that is used to evaluate instructional quality and acts, therefore, as a curricular magnet.

Popham (1987) argues that measurement-driven instruction can improve the quality of education, if it meets five criteria:

1. Clearly described criterion-referenced tests must be used so that teachers can target their instruction.

2. Tests must measure worthwhile content and skills.

3. Tests should each be limited to a reasonable number of essential skills. (Popham suggests five to ten.)

4. Tests should be constructed so that they lead to effective instructional sequences.

5. Instructional support must be provided.

The general idea is that in those cases where measurement drives instruction, teachers must construct the instruments used for measurement with that effect in mind.

Tests by their very nature have the capability of driving instruction. Take, for example, an American school district whose students were given a state-mandated test, as were students in all of that city's districts. The test was originally designed to measure basic skills and was administered to determine which schools within the districts had an unacceptably high percentage of students who had not achieved basic skills. The department of education would use the test results as the basis for its allocation of monies for remedial instruction. Thus, the purpose of the test was to formulate a plan for the allocation of instructional monies.

After the first administration of this test, a local newspaper printed the results of the test by rank, ordering the performance of the schools within the district. The publicity led some schools in the district to encourage their teachers to focus their instructional efforts on the skills represented on the test. Because of the economic ramifications, the test became a matter of very high stakes for a number of schools and the original purpose of the test was subverted. The assessment began to drive instructional programs. Again, a caveat comes into play: When using tests, we must be aware of the purpose for which they are designed. Bracey (1987) argues that assessment-driven instruction leads to a fragmented and narrow curriculum, to trivialism, and to stagnation of the curriculum and instruction. This threat is one of the reasons for the trend toward the assessment of authentic performances.

CONNECTION: See the discussion of instructional technology in Chapter 12.

Computerized Adaptive Testing. Another trend in standardized testing is computerized adaptive testing (Eller, Kaufman, & McLean, 1986-1987; Geisert & Futrell, 1995). Computerized adaptive testing uses computer programs that gather information about a student's ability and then provide test questions based on that information. The most sophisticated software systems evaluate ability after each question. Computerized adaptive testing is one way in which technology may contribute to alternatives in testing, expanding the range of information obtained from testing. Although the widespread use of computerized adaptive testing has not yet occurred, clearly we will continue to see growth of this technique for obtaining evaluative information.

Some problems with this technology as a basis for assessment have become evident as the use of computer-based testing continues to grow (Sarvela & Noonan, 1988). Given the rapidity with which the technology changes, it is likely that the problems educational researchers will address in the future are not clearly definable in the present (Callister, 1994). The problems of human factors or how humans interact with computers are some of the computer-based testing issues researchers are exploring. Such questions include the degree of feedback provided by computer programs and the timing of that feedback; the nature of the assessment is being addressed as well as the question of motivation. The effect of negative consequences, in particular, is being investigated and also questions about differential motivation effects for high and low achievers.

Using computer-based assessments requires the analysis of many different items that address similar skill areas. This is a problem of nonequivalence of groups. Very often, students will see different numbers of items and items that are different. The order in which the items are presented will change and items will be administered at different times in a course. All of these problems result in nonequivalent comparison groups, and as you have learned, in order to make norm-referenced judgments, norm groups must consist of people who have been tested under identical conditions.

How Can Criterion-Referenced Judgments Help You Assign Grades?

We use assessments and observations of various sorts to collect evidence, which will be the basis of our evaluative judgments. One of the most important judgments we make as teachers are the grades that we assign to students. Although some schools or districts are experimenting with nongraded instruction, aspiring teachers should anticipate the need to develop and use a grading system. A teacher's grading system is the method by which information generated through the assessment techniques discussed in Chapter 13 is interpreted.

TRY THIS: Survey a number of practising teachers to see which side of this issue they take. If possible, sample across grade levels to see if elementary and secondary teachers differ. What would you predict?

Grading is an important part of teaching for several reasons. Grades provide students with a means by which to evaluate themselves. Grades are important for reporting progress to parents, to future teachers, and to potential employers. Grades also provide a basis for future educational decisions. Grades serve to motivate and reward some students as well (Ebel & Frisbie, 1991; Frisbie & Waltman, 1992).

Those who criticize grades argue that they provide extrinsic but not intrinsic motivation. They also argue that grades become more important than what students learn. The counter-argument is that rather than placing less importance on grades, educators should improve the way in which grades are assigned, making sure that they are accurate, valid, meaningful, and correctly interpreted (Ebel & Frisbie, 1991).

The lack of a clear definition of what a grade means is a major problem in grading. As a result, there is a good deal of variability in grading practices and procedures among teachers, courses, and schools. Another major problem is that grades are often awarded on the basis of insufficient evidence or irrelevant criteria. Unsound evidence results in grades that are, from an evaluation standpoint, unreliable. We must establish the criteria that are used to assign grades in conjunction with a plan for evaluating students before the construction of tests occurs. If we follow the guidelines we develop for generating well-constructed tests, we lessen the impact that less-than-reliable grading has.

Grading Systems

One of the decisions educators must make about grading systems is what the standard of comparison will be. Remember, educators make all evaluative statements on a comparative basis. They judge students' performance against some standard. That standard may be absolute or relative. An **absolute standard** is based on the amount of course content the student has learned; its criterion is the content. Students' grades are therefore independent of one another. What they are subject to is called a criterion-referenced evaluation. The basis for the comparison is some external criterion of performance.

absolute standard A grading system in which scores are compared to a set performance standard.

A **relative standard** is based on the student's performance vis-à-vis other students; it is referred to as norm-referenced grading. Teachers decide relative or norm-referenced grading not only on the basis of a student's performance, but also on how well that student performed compared with all other students.

Teachers can report either type of grading, absolute or relative, with traditional letter grades. Table 14.2 provides some descriptors of what the traditional letter grades mean using either an absolute or relative standard (Frisbie & Waltman, 1992).

Achievement or Effort?

Among the questions that teachers must answer for themselves are: Should grading be done on the basis of achievement? On the basis of effort? On the basis of the two in combination? There is a general agreement among measurement specialists that grades should simply reflect achievement. Effort, behaviour, and other factors should be kept separate. But because they are kept separate does not mean that they are precluded from evaluation. Based on attribution research and research on classroom goal structures, many educational psychologists recommend focusing on effort as part of a teacher's general evaluation (e.g., Johnson & Johnson, 1994; Weiner, 1986). In any case, the teacher and anyone who has been assigned a grade by the teacher should understand what the grade reflects.

Some educators respond to the intuitive appeal of grading simply on the basis of achievement as opposed to judging a person's potential or aptitude. Grading on the basis of aptitude takes into account the individual differences that exist among students. Some educators reason that because there are differences in the aptitude of their students, they should take those differences into account. As a result, they try to grade each student on a separate set of criteria

relative standard A grading system in which the performance of one student is compared against the performances of others.

TABLE 14.2 *Descriptors of Grade-Level Performances Using Absolute or Relative Standards*

Absolute Scale Criterion-Referenced	Relative Scale Norm-Referenced
• Firm command of knowledge domain • High level of skill development • Exceptional preparation for later learning	Far above class average
• Command of knowledge beyond the minimum • Advanced development of most skills • Has prerequisites for later learning	Above class average
• Command of only the basic concepts of knowledge • Demonstrated ability to use basic skills • Lacks a few prerequisites for later learning	At the class average
• Lacks knowledge of some fundamental ideas • Some important skills not attained • Deficient in many of the prerequisites for later learning	Below class average
• Most of the basic concepts and principles not learned • Most essential skills cannot be demonstrated • Lacks most prerequisites needed for later learning	Far below class average

Source: "Developing a Personal Grading Plan," *Educational Measurement: Issues and Practice.* D. A. Frisbie and K. K. Waltman. Fall 1992, p. 37. Reprinted by permission.

designed with that student's aptitude in mind. The basic argument, however, is that this is not a good practice, simply because there is not a valid enough case for measuring aptitude.

A similar problem arises when we consider the advisability of grading on the basis of improvement. In order to grade on the basis of aptitude or improvement, it is necessary to have a valid starting point. Grading on the basis of improvement can be done as long as the teacher has available valid pre- and post-measures of achievement. Even if measurements are taken before and after instruction, however, the scores reported for each student are problematic. The scores reported in a pre- and posttest design are called *gain scores*. One problem is that part of the difference between the pretest and posttest might be explained not by what was learned after the pretest, but by the fact that merely taking a pretest improves scores on the posttest. This is referred to as the *practice effect*. If the practice effect were identical for all students, then the problem would not be serious. But if one student's aptitude allows him or her to benefit more from a pretest than another student's, then it becomes more difficult to use gain scores as an index of achievement. Gain scores are unreliable for several reasons, not the least of which is that students can quickly catch on to the idea that they are being graded on improvement and make sure that they score poorly on a pretest.

Pass/Fail Grading

One approach to grading has been to assign grades of passing or failing to student performance rather than traditional letter grades. Hopkins and Antes (1990) have identified the advantages and disadvantages of using a pass/fail grading system.

One advantage of pass/fail grading is that students may experience less anxiety by eliminating some of the competition. The use of pass/fail grading may create an atmosphere that encourages more intellectual risk taking. Suppose, for example, you give your students the following assignment: "Show me that you understand the concepts of time, speed, and distance and how they are related. You are free to demonstrate your knowledge in any way you wish, with one exception: you may not write or speak." Deliberate attempts to encourage creative problem solving require a classroom environment that supports risk taking and that allows students to try again if they fail. A pass/fail grading system seems to fit the bill, especially if students are given more than one opportunity to succeed. An advantage to this type of system is that students may work toward fulfilling requirements with less pressure. And, finally, the teacher and the student may work together to determine the criteria for a pass grade.

REFLECTION: Would (or did) receiving grades based on your effort influence your motivation to learn? Consider this issue in light of the discussion in Chapter 9 on self-efficacy.

TRY THIS: Interview a sample of university students. Try to discover the extent to which these students are aware of working the system in some way to give them an edge in terms of grades.

CRITICAL THINKING: Would Pass/Fail grading be more or less fair if all assessment information were qualitative? Would the nature of the information—qualitative or quantitative—make a difference? If so, why? If not, why not?

What criteria and scoring rubric might you use to evaluate these students' performance? What system might you use for reporting a grade? What are some of the other alternatives for evaluating student progress?

One disadvantage of using pass/fail grading is that the grades themselves provide less information for future teachers, for parents, and for the students. Another disadvantage is that students may do less work without the graduated criteria of letter grades. The students' efforts may fall to the lowest acceptable or pass level. Students who fail in a pass/fail course may experience even greater pressure from such failure than students who fail in traditionally graded courses. Pass/fail grading does not provide information on the specific strengths and weaknesses of a student's work. As with other forms of grading, what constitutes a pass grade varies from instructor to instructor. Although this is true of traditional letter grades, the range of variation within the grade "pass" is, by definition, greater.

In some cases, a pass/fail system has been combined with the traditional letter grade system. In such cases, whether a student passes or fails depends on whether or not he or she is doing enough work to earn a traditional grade of D. The basis for the combined grading system leans heavily on the traditional grading system.

Contract Grading

One of the conclusions that has been drawn from the literature on grading is that students like **contract grading** (see Taylor, 1980). Contract grading is a system in which the performances that are necessary for each letter grade are specified in advance. Further, students decide which grade they intend to pursue and sign a contract that says they understand that in order to earn the grade they have targeted, they will do the work specified. Teachers who used contracts assigned more high grades than those who used conventional methods. In terms of student achievement, however, contract grading was no better than conventional grading. Contract grading appears to be best suited to very small classes or to independent studies. Written agreements should be used in order to avoid misunderstandings of the criteria by which students will be judged. As in all grading systems, but especially those that employ contracts, the achievement targets must be clearly understood by students and teacher. The targets must specify what is to be done by the student as well as what is an acceptable level of performance.

Although the term *contract grading* refers specifically to the practice described here, all grading systems are, in a sense, contracts. Students earn grades by fulfilling the requirements established by the teacher. If the student meets the requirements, then the teacher is expected to hold up his or her end of the bargain. Furthermore, once grades have been assigned, they continue to be a medium of exchange. Parents may reward or punish students for certain grades. Students use grades to gain entrance into programs and universities (Brookhart, 1991). No matter what form of grading they use, teachers should follow certain guidelines to ensure a sound system (Hopkins and Antes, 1990).

contract grading Using an agreement that states what performances are required for a particular grade.

> ### Here's How
> #### Here's How To Ensure a Sound Grading System
> - Collect information from a variety of sources, a number of tests, a number of different types of tests, and a number of evaluative procedures other than tests, including observation.
> - Good grading requires that data be recorded in a systematic fashion. Maintenance of an up-to-date grade book qualifies here.
> *continued*

- Quantify the collected information in some way; that is, give it a numerical value. Although they are important, save value judgments until the final evaluation. Parent-teacher conferences are an ideal place to communicate such judgments.
- Weight the final evaluation more heavily on information collected near the end of a grading period so that the focus of the grade is on terminal performance.
- Base grades only on achievement data. Do reports on other traits separately.

Research on Grading

Researchers have examined the impact that evaluation processes have on students. Natriello (1987) suggests that higher evaluative standards lead to more effort and to higher performance, but only if students view those standards as obtainable. The research also suggests that there is a relationship between evaluative standards and effort in performance such that students should be challenged but not frustrated in their efforts. Figure 14.8 describes the relationship as curvilinear. As evaluative standards increase, so do effort and performance, but only up to a point. As standards continue to increase beyond a certain point, effort and performance decrease.

The effects of absolute versus relative grading on achievement have yielded mixed results, although studies seem to favour absolute standards for assigning grades. Focusing on the individual and using an absolute basis for comparison in deriving grades may be most beneficial to students whose initial performance is poor, who have low self-esteem, and who have an external locus of control. Self-referenced standards (comparison against self rather than

REFLECTION: How might evaluation practices affect self-concept as discussed in Chapter 3 and student motivation as described in Chapter 9?

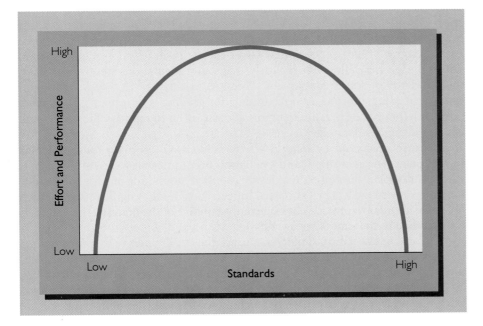

FIGURE 14.8
The Effects of Standards on Effort or Performance

REFLECTION: Did grades have a "social" use for you or your parents or caregivers? Did your grades influence relationships or interactions with family and friends? Does the way grades are used define what a grade means?

against an absolute, and therefore an external, criterion) seem to work best for students with low self-esteem and an internal locus of control. Norm-referenced standards—the type used to generate percentile ranks, stanines, and other standardized test scores—work best for students with high self-esteem. The results of the research suggest that teachers need to consider individual differences in grading (Natriello, 1987).

Research conducted in Canadian schools in British Columbia, Manitoba, and Ontario has indicated that student assessment practices are often of poor quality (e.g., Wilson, 1990). Many university professors we have spoken to across Canada lament the limited training in assessment that teachers receive in their teacher education programs.

In an important study of teachers' grading practices, Brookhart (1993) asked practising teachers questions about the meaning and use of grades. Although measurement experts have for years recommended that grades reflect only achievement and not effort, Brookhart's data suggest that teachers do not follow that recommendation (see also Stiggins, Frisbie, & Griswold, 1989). Teachers think about both the meaning of grades and the consequences of grades as they implement their grading systems. Teachers do not follow the recommendation to consider only achievement as the basis for assigning grades because they are concerned about the use to which grades are put (Brookhart, 1991, 1993). Tom Maguire (1991), an educational psychology professor at the University of Alberta, recommends that teachers' evaluation practices be guided by four considerations: fairness, utility, significance, and responsibility. Thus, our assessment practices should be valid, reliable and free from bias, purposeful for all (students, teachers, administrators, parents), directed at significant rather than trivial outcomes, and should encourage student learning and self-evaluation.

Teachers function in two roles: They are both judges of the students and advocates. As advocates, teachers concern themselves with more than just judging the achievement level of a student. Teachers are concerned with the development of student self-esteem, a sense of self-efficacy, and their motivational consequences (cf. Brookhart & Freeman, 1992). If teachers must function as both judges and advocates, then it will be a difficult matter for them to ignore the effort of students. Maguire (1991) again reminds us that assessment and grading practices must be congruent with both our cognitive and affective educational goals. Stiggins (1994) suggests that effort can be included in a grading system only if the teacher defines effort clearly, treats all students consistently, and meets the standards of sound assessment discussed in Chapter 13. Even so, Stiggins warns that using effort as a source of data for grading is "a mine field." His recommendation (if teachers are to report effort at all) is to report achievement and effort outcomes separately.

Because classroom evaluation affects students in so many ways, teachers should plan their assessment and evaluation procedures very carefully. Teachers who want to plan carefully must devote a sufficient amount of time to generating achievement goals. They also need time to consider the cognitive level of each objective in order to provide coverage representative of the material that students have studied in the unit (Crooks, 1988).

Classroom evaluation should encourage the development of understanding, transfer of learning, and higher-level thinking skills. The active learning techniques described in Chapter 12 and the authentic assessment practices described in Chapter 13 support a basic assumption of this book: Assessment improves teaching and learning. Instructional techniques that support active learning are

Insights on Successful Practice

What system have you developed for assigning grades and why do you use it?

"How can I better motivate my students?" is a perennial question teachers ask themselves. The ways in which students respond to their teachers' efforts vary according to student age and content material. Shaping student commitment and attitudes plays a role in motivating students. Teachers must be particularly concerned with the critical problem of student motivation. Embodied in motivation are factors such as commitment, attitude, and interest.

As a chemistry teacher, I instituted the use of a contract grading system to encourage commitment, elevate level of interest, and enhance positive attitudes among advanced-placement chemistry students. Contracts encouraged students to make a deeper commitment to their responsibility for learning.

Students actively participated in setting standards for grading. They did this in an informal setting through discussions of standards and expectations as one of several preliminaries to beginning the formal course of work. In addition to standards, discussion focused on specific course requirements. The students negotiated with each other and with me for certain stipulations that eventually became a formalized, written grading agreement. The one requirement in the process and its outcome(s) was that the agreement, or any portion thereof, could not violate district or school policies, mandates, or guidelines for student evaluation.

Following the development of the written agreement, each student made a commitment to a set of goals while working within the framework of the established standards for each of four grading periods. Once a contract had been finalized, it usually contained such things as alternatives to certain kinds of work as well as opportunities for make-up work, extra credit, and the like. The contract might stipulate that different kinds of written work be graded in different manners, such as assigned point values, letter grades, and "satisfactory" versus "unsatisfactory." Each student signed the agreement with the understanding that the class and I could mutually renegotiate the agreement, or portions of it, at the beginning of each new grading period if undesirable consequences, impractical items, or unrealistic stipulations surfaced along the way.

The concept of a grading agreement, or contract, lends itself to the achievement of higher levels of competency with an emphasis on quality rather than quantity. It aids students in realizing the importance of long-range planning and established priorities. It encourages student participation in setting standards. It may also be constructed in such a way that it allows alternatives for the student to work at a pace more suited to his or her needs.

GERALD E. WALKER
High School Vice-Principal

Your Insights

What were the outcomes of this teacher's experiment with contractual grading agreements? To what extent do you think grading contracts might benefit all students? Why might you use or not use this approach with your students?

---

useful in enhancing both content goals and thinking skills; assessment procedures can also serve those functions. Think of the logic in terms of Bloom's taxonomy of cognitive learning outcomes. If teachers tie assessments to the learning objectives and if students realize that they must engage in application, synthesis, or evaluation to attain those objectives, then the teacher increases the likelihood of higher-level thinking.

As was discussed in Chapter 13, classroom assessment should assist learning. One way in which assessment supports the teaching-learning process is through feedback. Guidelines for providing useful feedback from assessments were part of that discussion. But what of the feedback that students' grades communicate? Some researchers argue that grades, as a form of feedback, should be deempha-

CONNECTION: See the discussion of feedback in Chapter 13.

sized. By themselves, grades provide the student with little useful information. A letter grade does not identify the specific areas in which the student needs to improve (Jones & Jones, 1995). This information is provided best during teacher-student conferences that outline the effort the student will have to make to improve specific skills. In addition to grades, teachers should provide some detailed comments that honestly identify weaknesses and provide suggestions for improvement in the content area. Teachers who provide students with some possible courses of action are more likely to motivate those students to pursue content goals than those who do not. As Covington & Beery (1976) state, "Grades tend to motivate those students who least need it; that is, those who are already successful; while, perversely, the very students who need motivating the most (poor students) are most put off and threatened by grades" (p. 116).

How Will Your Knowledge of Student Progress Help You Become a More Effective Teacher?

CRITICAL THINKING: Are the standards discussed in this section a cause or effect of the student-centred instructional approaches described in Chapter 12?

As you read in Chapter 13, the landscape of classroom assessment is changing. Not only are the techniques for assessing student performance changing, but so are the methods for communicating student achievement. Collectively, these methods are referred to as *student-centred communication* (Stiggins, 1994).

Reporting Student Progress

Student-centred communication of achievement outcomes goes beyond the traditional practice of providing parents with report cards; student-centred communication supports the teaching-learning process. Table 14.3 summarizes various aspects of assessment communication systems. By contrasting how a traditional system and a student-centred system would address the various aspects, we can see how student-centred communication would change communication practices.

TABLE 14.3 *Traditional and Student-Centered Communication Compared*

Facet of communication	Traditional	Student-centred
Definition of Goals	Simple labels for grades, subject names	Detail regarding components of academic success
Manager of Communication	Teacher with context	Teacher, student, or parent; varies
Keeper of vision	Teacher	All parties share
Assessor/interpreter of results	Teacher	All parties share
Direction of communication	One-way	Bidirectional for all parties
Primary language used	Grades, test scores	Scores, ratings, examples; oral and written reports
Communication methods	Report cards; conferences	Narrative reports; conferences; portfolios

Source: Student-centred Classroom Assessment (p. 400), R. J. Stiggins, 1994, New York: Merrill. Adapted by permission.

As suggested by Table 14.3, student-centred communication means that what is being assessed is described in richer detail than in traditional communication. For example, instead of defining an achievement goal as simply "Reading," as is often the case on traditional report cards, this form provides more precise information. A student-centred communication about reading might address whether a student can use context to infer meaning or whether he or she evidences metacognitive awareness through self-monitoring (Stiggins, 1994). Another important change from the traditional paradigm is that students, parents, and teachers contribute to both the assessments and the communications about the results of those assessments.

If student-centred communication is to provide more information about progress toward achievement targets, then forms of communication other than or in addition to traditional report cards are needed. Some of those forms were described in Chapter 13. Rating forms, anecdotal or narrative reports, and self- and peer evaluations could supplement the summative evaluations provided by report cards.

Consider the *checklist* as an alternative or supplement to grades. The checklist provides statements and the teacher checks the statement that corresponds to the degree to which the student has achieved a target or objective. Checklists are advantageous because they provide detailed information, are easy to understand, and can include information on behaviour, effort, or other nonacademic characteristics. However, teachers need many statements and judgments for each student if the checklist is to provide an accurate profile. If teachers use checklists or narrative reports during the assessment of performance, however, then the only change required is to communicate those data to parents and students rather than just the grade that represents those data.

TRY THIS: Interview teachers about the ways—other than report cards—in which they communicate student progress to students, parents, and administrators.

Involving Students and Parents

Students are the most important users of the information gained through assessments (Stiggins, 1994). If we are to encourage students to continuously progress toward achievement targets, then we must provide them with information that allows them to see their progress and to reflect on the learning activity that has brought them to their current achievement status.

Peer feedback, as discussed in Chapter 12 in the section on cooperative learning, is a source of information for the student that is sometimes ignored in traditional communication systems. Peer assessment in this context would be very useful to teachers, parents, and students in judging the students' progress toward healthy interpersonal relations or team building. For example, a teacher might ask a cooperative learning group to brainstorm periodically on how well the group is learning. The brainstorm session might be initiated with the following question: "What have we done as a group to help each other learn?" Depending on the age of the students and the kind of assessment information sought, the teacher might also ask each member of the group to:

CRITICAL THINKING: What sorts of norms around group processing (as discussed with reference to cooperative learning in Chapter 12) should be in place before encouraging peer assessment? What should peers assess?

- Name one thing the group could do to improve everyone's learning.

- Name at least one thing that each member of the group has done to help others learn.

If a teacher uses such items, he or she might need to take care that some students do not become targets of criticism. One way to avoid this is to stress that the task is to identify what individuals have done to help the group; the task is not to identify ways in which the group has been harmed. Students could also be reminded that listening is an important way to help others learn. By allowing students to talk to each other about their learning, students not only become more aware of the group's purpose and how their peers view their contributions, but the teacher also acquires information about how well students are working with their peers.

An additional source of student feedback, in addition to peer feedback, is self-evaluation. Students can be encouraged to make comments about how well they feel they are learning. For very young students, a checklist with pictures and very simple word categories that indicate how the student feels about his or her own learning might be used as the basis for self-evaluation. In a recent evaluation of instructional practice, for instance, grade one students demonstrated that they are capable of completing such a checklist to indicate how they felt about their effort on a particular assignment, whether they would like more assignments of that nature, and how difficult they found the assignment for each piece of work collected in their portfolios (McCown, Casile, & Brookhart, 1994). Furthermore, after a week or two of training and practice, most grade one students were capable of completing the checklists independently. Older students could be required to keep a journal in which they record their assessments of their own performances. Students can also be encouraged to share their self-appraisals with their peers.

Whether students record their self-assessments on a checklist or in a journal, it is important for the teacher to confer with students about their work and about the students' appraisals of their work. These conferences do not have to be major commitments of time, they can be done informally during seat work or, if students work regularly in cooperative learning groups, the teacher can confer with students a group at a time. Some teachers regularly collect and write brief comments about their students' self-assessments. If teachers give students an active role in monitoring their own progress toward achievement goals and respond to those reports, the students will feel empowered. The opportunity to assess one's own progress and then compare the assessments with those of others includes the student in the communication system. Compare such a system to a situation in which the student generates data for someone else—the teacher—and must await the teacher's judgment.

Report cards are not the only means of communicating with parents or caregivers. Robin Alter (1992) from York University writes that teachers and parents share the same educational goals for children, but that problems may not be resolved because of misunderstandings in parent-school communications. You can bring parents into the assessment communication loop by sending home narrative reports, sharing portfolios, and initiating contact (Hopkins, Stanley, & Hopkins, 1990). A narrative report, in the form of a letter to a student's caregiver, allows the teacher to address the unique strengths and weaknesses of the students. Teachers can suggest specific ways that parents can help their children academically. Letters also open a line of communication between parents and teachers. Although it takes more time, Hopkins, Stanley, and Hopkins consider the use of a letter an advantage to the teacher because it forces the teacher to think about the individual student's achievements. Some schools, especially elementary schools, have replaced report cards with narrative reports (Stiggins, 1994). Letters sent to parents could also invite parent feedback and questions.

Another way to involve parents—one used in most cases in addition to grade reports—is the parent-teacher conference. These conferences offer the parents and the teacher a chance to discuss each student's progress and the instructional plan most suited to that student. Parents can provide pertinent information that

TRY THIS: Observe cooperative learning groups in classrooms and, with the teacher's permission, interview some group members to find out how they tell each other that some improvement is needed in the group.

TRY THIS: Try to locate a district or school that relies solely on narrative reports. Ask the teachers and administrators at the school how parents respond to such reports.

will help the teacher to understand the student in his or her classroom. Experienced teachers view these conferences as important. The first round of conferences for a new teacher usually arouses a considerable amount of anxiety. There are several factors to keep in mind in preparing for and conducting parent-teacher conferences (Carey, 1994; Hopkins, Stanley, & Hopkins, 1990). How should you conduct a parent-teacher conference?

Here's How

Here's How To Conduct Parent-Teacher Conferences

- Review the student's cumulative records and the student's portfolio prior to the conference. If portfolios are not used in your classroom, assemble samples of the student's work.

- Use a structured outline to guide the conference. List questions to ask parents and try to anticipate parents' questions.

- Be professional and maintain a positive attitude. Be willing to listen, be understanding, and encourage two-way communication. Be honest. Begin by describing the pupil's strengths. Accept some of the responsibility for any problems.

- Conclude the conference with an overall summary. Keep a succinct written record of the conference. List problems and suggestions with a copy for the parents.

- Avoid blaming parents or putting them on the defensive. Avoid making derogatory comments about other teachers, other students, or the school. Never argue. A parent who leaves a conference with negative feelings about the school, your classroom, or you will not be an ally.

- Avoid discussing conferences with other parents or caregivers. The only other adults who may need to discuss a parent-teacher conference are other school personnel directly involved with the student.

TRY THIS: During your teaching internship or during school visits, ask if it would be possible to observe a parent-teacher conference.

Involving Parents from Culturally and Socially Diverse Backgrounds

Assessment of a student's progress is, in most cases, the primary focus of the communications between the school and the home. Such communications—in the form of report cards, narrative reports, or parent-teacher conferences—reflect what has been called the school's institutional perspective (Finders & Lewis, 1994). The prevailing institutional perspective is that students who are less successful in school come from homes in which the parents do not become involved in school activities or do not support the goals of the school. This perspective includes a perception that families of less successful students require training in order to support the goals of the school (Mansbach, 1993). The perspective of the school is based on the cultural majority. It is a view that sometimes conflicts with the perspectives of parents from cultural backgrounds that represent minority values. Don Massey (1988) of the University of Alberta has summarized a number of important issues of relevance to cross-cultural assessment in Canada. He discusses the importance of such factors as cultural and ethnic identity, attitudes to education and assessment, language, and "acculturative

CONNECTION: The notion of institutional perspective relates to the values discussion in Chapter 4.

stress" in assessment and interpretation processes. For example, in some cultures, parents and children are not viewed as having equal status. A parent who is not fluent in English might have to rely on his or her child to translate at a parent-teacher conference. This situation places the child and the parent in a social situation that violates a cultural norm and, thus, decreases the likelihood that the parent will participate in the conference at school (Finders & Lewis, 1994). There are, of course, ways to avoid this situation by using another adult to interpret, but the situation illustrates that the school's perspective does not always accommodate a parent's cultural background. Becoming sensitive to the cultural norms of your students' parents and accommodating those norms is one way to enhance parent involvement.

Differences between the school's institutional perspective and the cultural backgrounds of parents are not the only dynamics that prevent parents or caregivers from participating in school activities and supporting school goals. Parents have diverse school histories. The institutional perspective held by most educators does not take into account the parents' experiential histories in school. "For many parents, their own personal school experiences create obstacles to involvement. Parents who have dropped out of school do not feel confident in school settings" (Finders & Lewis, 1994, p. 51). Parents who have had unpleasant experiences with the assessment systems of schools are not likely to anticipate happily a parent-teacher conference.

Parents also have diverse time and other constraints that can prevent participation in the school-home communication loop. Many parents carry workloads or schedules that do not afford them the flexibility to attend meetings or conferences during the school day. Parents who work at night cannot attend an evening open house. Often, financial concerns create an obstacle to participation in or support of school activities. For instance, one mother who was placed in the difficult position of denying her child eight dollars to purchase the school yearbook questioned the school's understanding of her situation. The economic constraints of her home in combination with the economic demands of the school prevented her child from participating fully in the life of the school. This woman's perception of the school is that it cares little for her problems and that perception will likely prevent her from communicating with school officials, including her child's teacher (Finders & Lewis, 1994).

If the institutional perspective of schools prevents some parents from communicating with the school about their children's progress, how can those obstacles be overcome? One way to discover an answer is to ask the parents. What follows are suggestions from parents whose cultural, social, or economic background does not match the institutional perspective (Finders & Lewis, 1994).

Here's How

Here's How To Involve Parents from Culturally and Socially Different Backgrounds

- Clarify how parents can interact with school officials, especially you. Many parents who do not share the institutional perspective do not know what channels of communication with you or other school officials are considered appropriate. Parents want to know: Is it okay

continued

to call? If so, when is the best time? May I call you at home? Should I send a note with my child? How should I, who do not share your language(s), communicate with you? Is there someone besides my child who could translate? Successfully answering these questions for parents may prove difficult because you must first establish a communication link. But if the parents who asked for clarification are an indication, your efforts will be worth it.

- Encourage parents to assert their concerns and frustrations. If parents feel they cannot communicate because of misunderstandings, then part of your professional responsibilities should be first to discover the sources of misunderstanding in order to remedy them.

- Establish trust through a personal relationship. Parents feel that this is a critical element in establishing the home-school communication link. One way to encourage this kind of relationship is to assure parents that they are welcome to drop by anytime they can. When parents do appear, make sure you welcome them warmly.

- Build on, do not denigrate, the home environment. The institutional perspective often carries an assumption that children from economically constrained homes do not have "good living environments." If you communicate this message to your students and their parents, you can destroy the link you are trying to create.

- Use parent experience and expertise. Just because some parents did not experience a great deal of success in school does not mean they have no experience or expertise to share. Find out what the parents of your students do, and then build on their experience. One teacher whose students came from a community in which many of the parents worked in construction built a unit around the field of construction. The parents became enthusiastic guest experts and, subsequently, attended parent-teacher conferences in record numbers.

Standards of Assessment Quality that Support the Teaching-Learning Process

Assessment is an integral part of the teaching-learning process. As such, classroom assessment should support the efforts of the teacher who is attempting to encourage learning and the student who is attempting to learn. One of the problems that teachers face, however, is the expectation that they play the dual roles of judge and advocate (Brookhart, 1993). Some observers have argued that the roles are incompatible and that teachers should serve the role of advocate and leave the role of judge to external assessment (Bishop, 1992). Exclusive use of external assessment procedures would mean a significant change in the way classroom performance is currently assessed and evaluated. One problem would be to find external assessors who were adequately trained in assessment techniques to ensure reliable and valid judgments. Although this is an intriguing idea that should attract serious discussion among those advocating school reform, the idea will probably be impractical for most teachers in the foreseeable future.

TRY THIS: Interview one or two teachers and ask them to respond specifically to their feelings about playing the dual roles discussed in this chapter.

Assessment improves learning and instruction if it is built on a system that clearly defines learning outcomes, accurately assesses those outcomes, and fairly evaluates the results. Clarity, accuracy, and fairness are also the characteristics

CRITICAL THINKING: How does the standard of clear and appropriate goals influence the reliability and validity of performance assessments as presented in Chapter 13?

that must be in place for a teacher to serve as both an advocate for and a judge of student learning. The person who is primarily responsible for building and initiating the assessment system is the teacher. It is imperative, therefore, that teachers understand the standards of assessment quality (Stiggins, 1994) in order to create an assessment environment that supports the teaching-learning process.

The most important standard of assessment quality is *clear and appropriate goals*. If the teacher and student are certain of both the goal and the criteria for its attainment, then the teacher can direct the student's learning efforts and, at the same time, serve as an impartial judge of the student's performance. When students and teachers do not share an understanding of the goal, misunderstandings occur and the teaching-learning process suffers. Suppose, for example, that a goal is to plan and prepare a well-balanced meal, but that no scoring rubric has been established to assess the performance. If the teacher and the student are not clear about what constitutes a well-balanced meal, the student may, in the course of instructional activity, develop criteria for planning and preparing the meal that do not match the teacher's subjective criteria. If this happens, the teacher is likely to judge the performance inadequate. The student, unaware of the teacher's criteria, will feel that the assessment was unfair. This is especially true if the student has made a sincere effort to meet what he or she perceived as the goal.

Misunderstandings between the learner, whose performance is assessed, and the teacher, who is responsible for assessing, are at the heart of any breakdown in the teaching-learning process. The lack of clear and appropriate goals is one source of misunderstanding. The other standards of quality assessment can also be viewed as potential sources of misunderstandings and, therefore, threats to the teaching-learning process. Another standard, for example, is that the *purpose of assessment is clear*. Imagine that a student takes a quiz, believing that the score will not affect his or her grade, only to discover later that the quiz counts. How will this affect the teacher-student relationship? How will that relationship influence the teaching-learning process? There is a standard that the *method of assessment matches the goal*. If a teacher uses an essay to assess an outcome that requires a performance, the student who tries to write the essay is likely to feel that the assessment is unfair.

TRY THIS: Paraphrase this standard using the terms *true score and error score*.

Another standard of assessment quality is that there is a *sufficient and representative sample* of items that measure what students have to learn. Imagine students who worked and studied very hard to learn a mathematical principle. Now imagine that when tested, the exam prevented the students from demonstrating the extent of their learning because only one question addressed that principle. Students who have worked very hard to achieve a goal and then are denied the opportunity to demonstrate their achievements are not likely to feel supported by their teacher.

The final standard of assessment quality is that *sources of extraneous interference are controlled*. This standard is met by following the guidelines for constructing reliable and valid assessments that were the focus of Chapter 13. If the teacher assesses a student by methods that do not reflect what a student has actually learned, or if the teacher misuses the results of the assessment, the student again becomes confused about the connection between what is being learned and what is being assessed.

The standards of quality assessment are standards that you will not attain merely by reading this book, but they are worthy of your pursuit because they support the teaching-learning process. And your major responsibility as a teacher is to facilitate student learning. Attainment of these standards will require experience and reflective construction of your theory of teaching based on that experience and the knowledge base of educational psychology. The challenge is left to you and should you accept it, we hope that what you have learned from this book will help you help your students learn.

CONNECTION: See the discussion on building your theory of teaching in Chapter 1.

Teacher Chronicle Conclusion

Benefit of the Doubt

Mr. Clark welcomes Heidi and her mother to a conference to discuss Heidi's math placement.

"Mrs. Rogers, Heidi, have a seat." Mr. Clark opens a folder with samples of Heidi's math work along with an index card showing her grades and standardized test scores.

"Do you have any questions about Heidi's work so far?"

"Yes," Mrs. Rogers says. "What exactly is a stanine? We were concerned about placement in algebra next year. Heidi really wants to take it, but she says her grades aren't good enough."

"Well," Mr. Clark begins. "In some cases that might be true, but not in Heidi's case. With the extra work she has done this semester in math reasoning and her hard work and determination, I feel certain she should take algebra."

Heidi bursts into a smile. "Really?" she asks.

"Yes. I have no doubts. It might not be easy and you'll have to work over the summer to keep your math skills fine-tuned, but I know you can do it."

Mrs. Rogers looks at her daughter. "With track and soccer and your other classes?"

"Sure, Mom. I know I can pass algebra if I work hard enough. I just have to want to and I do."

Application Questions

1. How did qualitative and quantitative information influence the final decision about Heidi's placement in algebra? How confident are you that Heidi will succeed in algebra?

2. Assume that the principal's guideline that a stanine score of 7 is required for algebra placement is based on evidence and is not just an arbitrary cut-off score. What kind of norm-referenced evidence would be necessary? Criterion-referenced evidence?

3. What does Mr. Clark's grade book look like? What are the entries in the grade book? How many assessments do you think Mr. Clark would have made on Heidi during the six weeks preceding the placement meeting? How did his grade book support his position in the meeting with the principal?

4. Why are confidence bands important in interpreting standardized test scores? Could Mr. Clark have used confidence bands in building his argument for Heidi's placement? Are confidence bands really necessary in interpreting stanines when each stanine represents a range of scores?

5. Heidi's mother sounds a bit apprehensive about Heidi's ability to succeed in algebra. Is this something Mr. Clark should try to address before the end of the conference? If so, how? If not, why not?

6. Assume that Mr. Clark always writes a letter to the math teacher that each of his students will have next year. Write what you think would be his letter about Heidi.

CHAPTER SUMMARY

What Are The Benchmarks of Student Progress? (L.O. 1, p. 463)

Evaluation requires judgments and all judgments require some benchmark or standard that serves as a basis for comparison. There are two kinds of benchmarks used in educational evaluation. The first is criterion-referenced benchmarks. A student's performance is compared against some set of external criteria. The second type is norm-referenced benchmarks, which use the other constituents of the norm group as the basis for comparison.

How Do You Interpret Assessment Results? (L.O. 2, p. 467)

A distinction is made between two types of assessment information: qualitative and quantitative. Qualitative information is communicated with words. Quantitative information is communicated with numbers. Many times information that seems to be qualitative is easily transformed into quantitative because the latter is more easily summarized and more economically described.

How Do You Interpret Standardized Test Results? (L.O. 3, 4, 5, p. 472)

Standardized test scores are based on the application of the standard deviation ruler to the normal curve. The various kinds of standardized test scores (Z scores, T scores, percentile ranks, stanines) are different forms of the same information. Essentially, all standardized test scores provide information about where one student stands in relation to the other students who took the same test, the norm group.

How Can Criterion-Referenced Judgments Help You Assign Grades? (L.O. 6, p. 489)

Grading systems can be based on absolute standards of quality of performance or can be based on student performance relative to that of other students. Many teachers assign grades based on evaluation of both achievement and effort. Guidelines suggest that grades be based on achievement only. This does not mean a teacher cannot evaluate effort separately. Evaluations of classroom work do not have to take the traditional form of grades; they can be presented qualitatively as well as quantitatively. In addition, students can contract for grades, thus participating in the establishment of criteria used to assign grades.

How Will Your Knowledge of Student Progress Help You Become a More Effective Teacher? (L.O. 7, 8, 9, p. 496)

Student-centered communication focuses evaluative information on specific achievement goals. Communicating student progress requires open lines of communication, especially between home and school. Some parents are uncomfortable or anxious about participating in school activities, including parent-teacher conferences. Teachers who understand the barriers that are created when parents' perspectives do not match the institutional perspective can help overcome those barriers. Clear communication of goals is key to quality assessment and communication of assessment information.

KEY CONCEPTS

absolute standard, p. 489

benchmarks, p. 463

central tendency, p. 469

confidence bands, p. 479

contract grading, p. 492

criterion-referenced judgments, p. 464

dispersion, p. 470

grade equivalent score, p. 478

mean, p. 471

median, p. 470

mode, p. 470

norm-referenced judgments, p. 464

normal curve, p. 466

percentile rank, p. 476

qualitative information, p. 467

quantitative information, p. 467

range, p. 472

relative standard, p. 490

standard deviation, p. 472

standardized tests, p. 472

stanine, p. 477

T score, p. 477

test bias, p. 484

test-wiseness, p. 485

Z score, p. 476

AAMR Ad Hoc Committee on Terminology and Classification. (1992.) *Mental retardation: definition, classification, and systems of support* (9th edition). Washington, D.C.: American Association on Mental Retardation.

Achenbach, T. M. (1985). *Assessment and taxonomy of child and adolescent psychopathology.* Beverly Hills, CA: Sage Publications.

Adams Johnson, P. (1992). Hunting for worms. In D. Seymour, T. Seymour, (Eds.), *America's best classrooms: How award-winning teachers are shaping our children's future.* Princeton, NJ: Peterson's Guides.

Adams, R. S., & Biddle, B. J. (1970). *Realities of teaching: Explanations with videotape.* New York: Holt, Rinehart & Winston.

Alberto, P. A., & Troutman, A. C. (1990). *Applied behavior analysis for teachers* (3rd ed.). New York: Merrill-Macmillan.

Alladin, I., & Ramsankur, S. (1996). Dealing with racism in the community: Response from Alex Taylor Community School. In M.I. Alladin (Ed.), *Racism in Canadian Schools* (pp. 147-156). Toronto: Harcourt Brace Canada.

Alladin, M.I. (1996). Racism in schools: Race, ethnicity, and schooling in Canada. In M.I. Alladin (Ed.), *Racism in Canadian Schools* (pp. 4-21). Toronto: Harcourt Brace Canada.

Allington, R. L. (1983). The reading instruction provided readers of differing reading abilities. *Elementary School Journal, 83* (5), 548–559.

Alschuler, A.S. (1973). *Developing achievement motivation in adolescents.* Englewood Cliffs, NJ: Educational Technology Publications.

Alter, R.C. (1992). *Parent-school communication: A selective review.* Canadian Journal of School Psychology, *8,* 103-100.

American Association of University Women. (1992). *How schools shortchange women.* Annapolis Junction, MD: AAUW.

American Speech-Language-Hearing Association. (1982). Definitions: Communicative disorders and variations. *ASHA, 24,* 942–950.

Ames, C. A. (1990). Motivation: What teachers need to know. *Teachers College Record, 91,* 409–421.

__(1992). Classrooms: Goals, structures, and student motivation. *Journal of Educational Psychology, 84,* 261-271.

Ames, C., & Ames, R. (1984). Goal structures and motivation. *The Elementary School Journal, 85,* 39–52.

Anderson, C. M. B., & Craik, F. I. M. (1974). The effect of a concurrent task on recall from primary memory. *Journal of Verbal Learning and Verbal Behavior, 13,* 107-113.

Anderson, J. R. (1983). *The architecture of cognition.* Cambridge, MA: Harvard University Press.

__(1990). *The adaptive character of thought.* Hillsdale, NJ: Erlbaum.

Anderson, J. R. (1993) Problem solving and learning. *American Psychologist, 48,* 35–44.

Anderson, J.D., (1989). Evaluation of student achievement: Teacher practices and educational measurement. *The Alberta Journal of Educational Research, 35,* 123-133.

Anderson, L., Brubaker, N., Alleman-Brooks, J., & Duffy, G (1985). A qualitative study of seatwork in first-grade classrooms. *Elementary School Journal, 86,* 123–140.

Anderson, R. C. (1977). Schema-directed processes in language comprehension. In A. Lesgold, J. Pelligreno, S. Fokkema, & R. Glaser (Eds.), *Cognitive psychology and instruction.* New York: Plenum Press.

__(1984). Some reflections on the acquisition of knowledge. *Educational Researcher, 13* (10), 5–10.

Anderson, R. C., & Ortony, A. (1975). On putting apples into bottles: A problem of polysemy. *Cognitive Psychology, 7,* 167–180.

Anderson, R. C., Pichert, J. W., Goetz, E. T., Schallert, D. L., Stevens, K. V., & Trollip, S. R. (1976). Instantiation of general terms. *Journal of Verbal Learning and Behavior, 15,* 667–679.

Anderson, R.N., Greene, M.L., & Loewon, P.S. (1988) Relationships among teachers' and students' thinking skills, sense of efficacy, and student achievement. *Alberta Journal of Educational Research, 34,* 148-162.

Arlin, M. (1979). Teacher transitions can disrupt time flow in classrooms. *American Educational Research Journal, 16,* 42–56.

Arlin, P. (1975) Cognitive development in adulthood: A fifth stage? *Developmental Psychology, 11,* 602-606.

Arlin, P. (1990). Wisdom. Its nature, origins, and development. New York: Cambridge University Press, pp. 230-243.

Armbruster, B. B. (1986). Schema theory and the design of content-area textbooks. *Educational Psychologist, 21,* 253–267.*

Armstrong, H. (1993). Depression in Canadian Native Indians. In P. Cappeliez & R.J. Flynn (Eds). *Depression and the Social Environment.* Montreal: McGill-Queen's University Press, pp. 218-234.

Armstrong, T. (1994). *Multiple intelligences in the classroom.* Alexandria, VA: Association for Supervision and Curriculum Development.

Aronson, E. (1972). *The social animal.* San Francisco: W. H. Freeman.

Ashton, P.T. & Webb, R.B. (1986). *Making a difference: Teachers' sense of efficacy and student achievement.* New York: Longman.*

Asian and Pacific Islander data: 80 census goldmine (1988). *Census and You, 23,* 3.*

Assante, M.K. (1991). The Afrocentric idea in education. *The Journal of Negro Education, 60,* 170–180.*

Atkinson, J. W. (1964). *An introduction to motivation.* Princeton, NJ: Van Nostrand.

Atkinson, R. C. (1975). Mnemotechnics in second-language learning. *American Psychologist, 30*, 821–828.

Atkinson, R. C., & Raugh, M. R. (1975). An application of the mnemonic keyword method to the acquisition of a Russian vocabulary. *Journal of Experimental Psychology: Human Learning and Memory, 104*, 126–133.

Atkinson, R. C., & Shiffrin, R. M. (1968). Human memory: A proposed system and its control processes. In K. Spence & J. Spence (Eds.), *The psychology of learning and motivation* (Vol. 2). New York: Academic Press.

__(1971, August). The control of short-term memory. *Scientific American*, pp. 82-90.

Ausubel, D. P. & Youssef, M. (1963). Role of discriminability in meaningful parallel learning. *Journal of Educational Psychology, 54*, 331–336.

Ausubel, D. P., Novak, J. D., & Hanesian, H. (1978). *Educational psychology: A cognitive view* (2nd ed.). New York: Holt, Rinehart & Winston.

Ayllon, T., & Azrin, N. H. (1968). *The token economy*. New York: Appleton-Century-Crofts.

Azrin, N. H., & Holz, W. C. (1966). Punishment. (pp. 380–447). In W. K. Konig (Ed.), *Operant behavior: Areas of research and application*. New York: Appleton-Century-Crofts.

Bachor, D.G. (1990). Toward improving assessment of students with special needs: Expanding the data base to include classroom performance. *The Alberta Journal of Educational Research. XXXVI(1)*, 65-77.

Bagley, W. C. (1970). *Classroom management: Its principles and technique*. New York: Macmillan.

Bailey, S. M. (1993). The current status of gender equity research in American schools. *Educational Psychologist, 28* (4), 321–339.

Bandura, A. (1962). Social learning through imitation. In N. R. Jones (Ed.), *Nebraska Symposium in Motivation*. Lincoln: University of Nebraska Press.

__(1965). Influence of models' reinforcement contingencies on the acquisition of imitative response. *Journal of Personality and Social Psychology, 1*, 589–595.

__(1969). *Principles of behavior modification*. New York: Holt, Rinehart & Winston.

__(1971a). *Psychological modeling: Conflicting theories*. Chicago, IL: Aldine-Atherton.

__(1971b). Vicarious and self-reinforcement processes (pp. 228–278). In R. Glaser (Ed.), *The nature of reinforcement*. New York: Academic Press.

__(1977). *Social learning theory*. Englewood Cliffs, NJ: Prentice Hall.

__(1982). Self-efficacy mechanism in human agency. *American Psychologist, 37*, 122–147.

__(1982). Self-efficacy mechanisms in human agency. *American Psychologist, 37*, 122–147.

__(1986). *Social foundations of thought and action*. Englewood Cliffs, NJ: Prentice Hall.

Bandura, A., & Walters, R. (1963). *Social learning and personality development*. New York: Holt, Rinehart & Winston.

Bandura, A., Ross, D., & Ross, S. A. (1963). Vicarious reinforcement and imitative learning. *Journal of Abnormal and Social Psychology, 67*, 601–607.

Banis, H. T., Varni, J. W., Wallander, J. L., Korsch, B. M., Jay, S. M., Adler, R., Garcia-Temple, E., & Negrete, V. (1988). Psychological and social adjustment of obese children and their families. *Child: Care, Health and Development, 14*, 157–173.

Banks, J. A. (1994a). *An introduction to multicultural education*. Needham Heights, MA: Allyn & Bacon.

__(1994b). Multicultural education: Characteristics and goals. In J. A. Banks and C. A. McGee Banks (Eds.), *Multicultural education: Issues and perspectives*. Needham Heights, MA: Allyn & Bacon.

__(1994c). *Multiethnic education*. Needham Heights, MA: Allyn & Bacon.

Banks, J. A., & Banks, C. A. M. (1993). *Multicultural education: Issues and perspectives* (2nd. ed.). Needham Heights, MA: Allyn & Bacon.

Banks, J.A. (1987). *Teaching Strategies for Ethnic Studies* (4th ed.) Boston, MA: Allyn & Bacon.

Barenboim, C. (1977). Developmental changes in the interpersonal cognitive system from middle childhood to adolescence. *Child Development, 48*, 1467–1474.

Barnett-Foster, D. & Nagy, P. (1995). A comparison of undergraduate test response strategies for multiple-choice and constructed-response questions. *The Alberta Journal of Educational Research. XLI(1)*, 18-35.

Baron, J. B. (1991). Strategies for the development of effective performance exercises. *Applied Measurement in Education, 4* (4), 305–318.*

Baron, R.A., Earhard, B., & Ozier, M. (1995). *Psychology: Canadian Edition,* Scarborough, ON: Allyn & Bacon Canada.

Bartley, A.W. (1997). Enhancing the validity of portfolio assessment in preservice teacher education. *The Alberta Journal of Educational Research. XLIII(2/3)*, 99-113.

Baruth, L. G., & Manning, M. L. (1992). *Multicultural education of children and adolescents*. Needham Heights, MA: Allyn & Bacon.*

Bascia, N. (1996). Teacher leadership: Contending with adversity. *Canadian Journal of Education, 21(2)*, 155-169.

Bates, E., O'Connell, B. & Shore, C. (1987). Language and communication in infancy. In J. D. Osofsky (Ed.), *Handbook of infant development*. (2nd. ed.). New York: Wiley.

Bateson, D.J. (1990). Measurement and evaluation practices of British Columbia science teachers. *The Alberta Journal of Educational Research, 36*, 78-84.

Baumrind, D. (1967). Childcare practices anteceding three patterns of preschool behavior. *Genetic Psychology Monographs, 75*, 43–88

Baumrind, D. (1971). Current patterns of parental authority. *Developmental Psychology Monograph, 4* (Number 1, Part 2).

__(1991). The influence of parenting style on adolescent competence and substance abuse. *Journal of Early Adolescence, 11,* 56–95.

Baumrind, D. (1973). The development of instrument competence through socialization. Dr. A. Pick (Ed.) *Minnesota Symposium on Child Psychology* (vol. 7). Minneapolis, MN: University of Minnesota Press.

Beal, A.L. (1995). A comparison of WISC-III and OLSAT-6 for the identification of gifted students. *Canadian Journal of School Psychology, 11(2),* 120-129.

Beal, A.L., Dumont, R., Branche, A., & Cruse, C. (1996) Validation of the WISC-III Short-Form for Canadian students with learning disabilities. *Canadian Journal of School Psychology, 12 (1),* 1-6.

Beane, J. A., and Lipka, R. P. (1980). Self-concept and self-esteem: A construct differentiation. *Child Study Journal, 10,* 1–6.

__(1986). *Self-concept, self-esteem, and the curriculum.* New York: Teachers College Press.

Becker, J. M. (Ed.). (1979). *Schooling for a global age.* New York: McGraw-Hill.

Bell, K.J. (1991). Language learning in Canadian classrooms: Our heritage of multilingualism. In R.H. Short, L.L. Stewin, & S.J.H. McCann (Eds.), *Educational psychology: Canadian perspectives.* Toronto: Copp Clark Pitman.

Bell, R. (1980). *Changing bodies, changing lives: A book for teens on sex and relationships.* New York: Random House.

Bell-Gredler, M. E. (1986). *Learning and instruction: Theory into practice.* New York: Macmillan.

Bellon, J. J., Bellon, E. C., & Blank, M. A. (1992). *Teaching from a research knowledge base: A development and renewal process.* New York: Macmillan.

Bempechat, J. (1990). *The role of parent involvement in children's academic achievement: A review of the literature trends and issues, No. 14.* New York: ERIC Clearinghouse on Urban Education, Institute for Urban and Minority Education.

Bennet, A., Klein, C., & Derevensky, J. (1992). A developmental examination of adolescents' fears. *Canadian Journal of School Psychology, 8,* 69-79.

Berger, K. S. (1986). *The developing person through childhood and adolescence.* (2nd ed.). New York: Worth.

Berk, L. E. (1992). Children's private speech: An overview of theory and the status of research. In R. M. Diaz & L. E. Berk (Eds.), *Private speech: From social interaction to self-regulation.* Hillsdale, NJ: Erlbaum.

__(1994). *Child development* (3rd ed.). Needham Heights, MA: Allyn and Bacon.

Berliner, D. C. (1986). In pursuit of the expert pedagogue. *Educational Researcher, 15* (7), 5–13.

__(1987). Ways of thinking about students and classrooms by more and less experienced teachers. In J. Calderhead (Ed.), *Exploring teacher's thinking.* London: Cassell Educational Limited.

__(1988). The development of expertise in pedagogy. Charles W. Hunt Memorial Lecture presented at the Annual Meeting of the American Association of Colleges for Teacher Education, New Orleans.

__(1992). Redesigning classroom activities for the future. *Educational Technology, 32* (10), 7–13.

Berlyne, D. E. (1965). Curiosity and education. In J. D. Krumbolz (Ed.), *Learning and the educational process.* Chicago: Rand McNally.

Bernhard, J. K. (1995). Child development, cultural diversity, and the professional training of early childhood educators. *Canadian Journal of Education, 24(4),* 414-421.

Bernstein, B.B (1971). *Class, codes and control.* London: Routledge and K. Paul.

Berrueta-Clement, J. R., Schweinhart, L. J., Barnett, W. S., Epstein, A. S., & Weikart, D. P. (1984). *Changed lives.* Ypsilanti, MI: High Scope.

Berry, J.W. (1981). Native peoples and the larger society. In R. C. Gardner & R. Kalin (Eds.), *A Canadian social psychology of ethnic relations.* Toronto: Methuen.

Berry, N. (1979). Cultural and cognitive styles. In L. Friedman, L. Das, & N. O'Conner (Eds.), *Intelligence and learning.* New York: Plenum Press.

Bhatt, G.S. & Tonks, R.G. (1992). Defining self within a multicultural context: An empirical exploration. Paper presented at the Canadian Psychological Association convention, Quebec City.

Bialystok, E. and Ryan, E. (1985). Toward a definition of metalinguistic skill. *McRill Palmer Quarterly, 31,* 235–252

Bibby, R.W. (1990). *Mosaic madness: The poverty and potential of life in Canada.* Toronto: Stoddart.

Bidwell, N. (1997). *The nature and prevalence of bullying in elementary schools.* Research report #97–06, Saskatchewan School Trustees Association (SSTA), 400–2222–13th Ave., Regina, Saskatchewan, S4P 3M7.

Birman, B. F., Oraland, M. E., Jung, R. K., Anson, R. J., Garcia, G. N., Moore, M. T., Funkhouser, J. E., Morrison, D. R., Turnbull, B. J., & Reisner, E. R. (1987). *The current operation of the Chapter 1 program.* Washington, D.C.: Office of Educational Research and Improvement, U.S. Department of Education.

Bishop, J. H. (1992). Why U.S. students need incentives to learn. *Educational Leadership, 49* (6), 15–18.

Bivens, J. A., & Berk, L. E. (1990). A longitudinal study of the development of elementary school children's private speech. *Merrill-Palmer Quarterly, 36,* 443–463.

Blakemore, R., Shindler, S., & Conte, R. (1993). A problem-solving training program for parents of children with Attention Deficit Hyperactivity Disorder. *Canadian Journal of School Psychology, 9,* 66-85.

Bligh, D. A. (1972). *What's the use of lectures?* (2nd ed.) Harmondsworth, England: Penguin.

Block, J. (1983). Differential premises arising from differential socialization of the sexes: Some conjectures. *Child Development, 54,* 1335–1354.

Bloom, B. S. (1986, February). "The hands and feet of genius." Automaticity. *Educational Leadership*, 70–77.

Bloom, B. S., Englehart, M. D., Furst, E. J., Hill, W. H., and Krathwohl, D. R. (1956). *Taxonomy of educational objectives, Handbook I: Cognitive domain.* New York: McKay.

Book, C. L., & Freeman, D. J. (1986). Differences in entry characteristics of elementary and secondary teacher candidates. *Journal of Teacher Education, 37* (2), 47–51.

Borko, H., & Shavelson, R. J. (1990). Teacher's decision making. In B. Jones & L. Idols (Eds.), *Dimensions of thinking and cognitive instruction.* Hillsdale, NJ: Erlbaum.

Bowd, A., McDougall, D., & Yewchuk, C. (1994). *Educational Psychology for Canadian Teachers.* Toronto: Harcourt Brace & Co.

Bower, G. H. (1972). Mental imagery and associative learning. In L. W. Gregg (Ed.), *Cognition in learning and memory.* New York: Wiley.

Bower, G. H., & Hilgard, E. R. (1981). *Theories of learning* (5th ed.). Englewood Cliffs, NJ: Prentice Hall.

Bowman, B. T. (1989). Educating language-minority children: Challenges and opportunities. *Phi Delta Kappan, 71,* 118–120.

Boykin, A.W. (1986). The triple quandary and the schooling of Afro-American children. In U. Neizser (Ed.) *The school achievement of minority children.* Hillsdale, NJ: Erlbaum.

Brabeck, M. (1986). Moral orientation: Alternative perspectives of men and women. In R. T. Knowles & G. F. McLean (Eds.), *Psychological foundations of moral education and character development: An integrated theory of moral development.* Lanham, MD: University Press of America.

Bracey, G. W. (1987). Measurement-driven instruction: Catchy phrase, dangerous practice. *Phi Delta Kappan, 68,* 683–686.

Brainerd, C. S. (1978). *Piaget's theory of intelligence.* Englewood Cliffs, NJ: Prentice Hall.

Bransford, J. D. (1979). *Human cognition: Learning, understanding, and remembering.* Belmont, CA: Wadsworth.

Bransford, J. D., & McCarrell, N. S. (1974). A sketch of a cognitive approach to comprehension: Some thoughts about understanding what it means to comprehend. In W. B. Weiner & D. S. Palermo (Eds.), *Cognition and the symbolic processes.* Hillsdale, NJ: Erlbaum.

Bransford, J.D., Goldman, S.R., & Vye, N.J. (1991). Making a difference in people's abilities to think: Reflections of a decade of work and some hopes for the future. In L. Okagaki and R.J. Sternberg (eds.), *Directors of development: Influences on children.* Hillsdale, NJ: Erlbaum.

Bray, G. (1976). *The obese patient: Major problems in internal medicine* (Vol. 9). Philadelphia: Saunders.

Brenner, D., & Hinsdale, G. (1978). Body build stereotypes and self-identification in three age groups of females. *Adolescence, 13,* 551–561.

Breton, R. (1986). Multiculturalism and Canadian nation building. In A. Cairns & C. Williams (Eds.), *The politics of ethnicity, gender and language in Canada.* Toronto: University of Toronto Press.

Brodkin, A.M. & Coleman, M.F. (1994). Reaching out to a dislocated child. *Instructor, March,* 18-21.

Brody, J., & Fox, L. H. (1980). An accelerative intervention program for mathematically gifted girls. In L. H. Fox, L. Brody, & D. Tobin (Eds.), *Women and the mathematical mystique.* Baltimore, MD: Johns Hopkins University Press.

Brookhart, S. M. (1991). Grading practices and validity. *Educational Measurement: Issues and Practices*, Spring, 35–36.

__(1993). Teachers' grading practices: Meaning and values. *Journal of Educational Measurement, 30,* 123–142.

Brookhart, S. M., & Freeman, D. J. (1992). Characteristics of entering teacher candidates. *Review of Educational Research, 62* (1), 37–60.

Brookhart, S. M., Miller, T. E., Loadman, W. E., & Whordley, D. (1990, October). *Profiles of entering teacher candidates: Gathering baseline data for teacher education program evaluation.* Paper presented at the Annual Meeting of the American Evaluation Association, Washington, D.C.

Brooks, R.B. (In press). Fostering resilience in exceptional children: The search for islands of competence. In V.L. Schwean & D.H. Saklofske (Eds.), *Handbook of Psychosocial Characteristics of Exceptionality.* New York: Plenum.

Brophy, J. E. (1982). How teachers influence what is taught and learned in classrooms. *Elementary School Journal, 83,* 1–13.

__(1988). Educating teachers about managing classrooms and students. *Teaching and Teacher Education, 4,* 1–18.

Brophy, J. E., & Evertson, C. (1976). *Learning from teaching: A developmental perspective.* Needham Heights, MA: Allyn & Bacon.

Brophy, J. E., & Good, T. L. (1974). *Teacher–student relationships: Causes and consequences.* New York: Holt, Rinehart & Winston.

Brown, A. L. (1988). Motivation to learn and understand: On taking charge of one's own learning. *Cognition and Instruction, 5,* 311–321.

Brown, A. L., & Campione, J. C. (1990). Communities of learning and thinking, or a context by any other name. In D. Kuhn (Ed.), *Developmental perspectives on teaching and learning thinking skills: Contributions to human development* (vol. 21), 108–126.

Brown, I.D.R. (1992). The effect of teacher training on special education students' self-control, academic achievement, and self-esteem. *Canadian Journal of School Psychology, 8,* 1-22.

Brown, J. S., Collins, A., & Duguid, P. (1989). Situated cognition and the culture of learning. *Educational Researcher, 18* (1), 32–42.

Brown, S., & McIntyre, D. (1993). *Making sense of teaching.* Philadelphia: Open University Press.

Bruffee, K. A. (1993). *Collaborative learning: Higher education, interdependence, and the authority of knowledge.* Baltimore, MD: Johns Hopkins University Press.

Bruner, J. S. (1960a). *The process of education.* New York: Vintage Books.

___(1960b). Readiness for learning. In Bruner (Ed.), *The process of education.* Cambridge, MA: Harvard University Press.

___(1961). The act of discovery. *Harvard Educational Review, 31* (1), 21–32.

___(1973a). Culture and cognitive growth. In Bruner (Ed.), *The relevance of education.* New York: Norton.

___(1973b). Some elements of discovery. In Bruner (Ed.), *The relevance of education.* New York: Norton.

Brutsaert, H. (1990). Changing sources of self-esteem among girls and boys in secondary school. *Urban Education, 24* (40), 432–439.

Burke, J. C. (1992). *Decreasing classroom behavior problems: Practical guidelines for teachers.* San Diego, CA: Singular.

Bushell, D., Wrobel, P., & Michaelis, M. (1968). Applying "group" contingencies to the classroom study behavior of pre-school children. *Journal of Applied Behavior Analysis, 1*, 55-61.

Butterfield, F. (1982). *China: Alive on the bitter sea.* New York: Bantam Books

Cain, K. M., & Dweck, C. S. (1989). The development of children's conception of intelligence: A theoretical framework. In R. J. Sternberg (Ed.), *Advances in the psychology of human intelligence.* Hillsdale, NJ: Erlbaum.

California Assessment Collaborative. (1993). *Charting the course: Toward instructionally sound assessment.* San Francisco: California Assessment Collaborative.

Callister, T. A. (1994). Educational computing's new direction: Cautiously approaching an unpredictable future. *Educational Theory, 44* (2), 239–256.

Canada. *Ethnic origin. The Nation* (1991). Catalogue No. 93-315.

Canadian Committee on Sexual Offenses Against Children and Youths. (1984). Report (Vol. 1). Ottawa: Canadian Government Publication Centre.

Cangelosi, J. S. (1993). *Classroom management strategies: Gaining and maintaining students' cooperation* (2nd ed.). White Plains, NY: Longman.

Canter, L., & Canter, M. (1976). *Assertive discipline: A take-charge approach for today's educator.* Los Angeles: Lee Canter and Associates.

___(1992). *Assertive discipline: Positive behavior management for today's classroom.* Santa Monica, CA: Lee Canter & Associates.

Carey, L. M. (1994). *Measuring and evaluating school learning* (2nd ed.). Needham Heights, MA: Allyn & Bacon.

Carey, S. (1977). The child as ward learner. In M. Halle, J. Bresnan, & G. A. Miller (Eds.), *Linguistic theory and psychological reality.* Cambridge, MA: MIT Press.

—(1991). Academic achievement and reading comprehension in minority and second languages. In R.H. Short, L.L. Stewin, & S.J.H. McCann (Eds.), *Educational psychology: Canadian perspectives.* Toronto: Copp Clark Pitman.

Carlson, L.D., & Cole, E. (1993). Communication and interaction patterns in French immersion classrooms: Implications for consultation. *Canadian Journal of School Psychology, 9,* 133-149.

Carlson, S. B. (1985). *Creative classroom testing.* Princeton, NJ: Educational Testing Service.

Carr, P.R., & Klassen, T.R. (1997). Different perceptions of race in education: Racial minority and white teachers. *Canadian Journal of Education, 22(1),* 67-81.

Carter, K. (1987). Cooperating teachers' conceptions of teaching. Unpublished paper prepared for the University of Arizona Cooperating Teachers Project, funded by OERI, U.S. Department of Education.

___(1990). Teacher's knowledge and learning to teach. In W. R. Houston (Ed.), *Handbook of research on teacher education.* New York: Macmillan.

Carter, K., Cushing, K., Sabers, D., Stein, P., & Berliner, D. (1988, May–June). Expert-novice differences in perceiving and processing visual classroom information. *Journal of Teacher Education,* 25–32.

Carter, K., Sabers, D., Cushing, K., Pinnegar, S., & Berliner, D. (1987). Processing and using information about students: A study of expert, novice, and postulant teachers. *Teaching and Teacher Education, 3* (2), 147–157.

Case, R. (1984). The process of stage transition: A neo-Piagetian view. In R. J. Sternberg (Ed.), *Mechanisms of cognitive development.* New York: W. H. Freeman.

___(1985). *Intellectual development: Birth to adulthood.* New York: Academic Press.

___(1993). Theories of learning and theories of development. *Educational Psychologist, 28* (3), 219–234.

Census Canada, 1986.

Chadwick, D. (1989). Protecting abused kids. *NEA Today, 8* (5), 23.

Chance, P. (1993). Sticking up for rewards. *Phi Delta Kappan, 74,* 787–790.

Charles, C. M. & Senter, G. W. (1995). *Elementary classroom management* (2nd ed.). White Plains, NY: Longman.

Charles, C. M. (1992). *Building classroom discipline: From models to practice* (2nd ed.). New York: Longman.

Chi, M., Feltovich, P., & Glaser, R. (1981). Categorization and representation of physics problems by experts and novices. *Cognitive Science,* 5, 121–152.

Chiareli, D.L. (1989). Sex and computers: Equity vs. inequity. *Comment on Education, 18,* 12-19.

Chilcoat, G. (1989). Instructional behaviors for clearer presentations in the classroom. *Instructional Science, 18,* 289–314.

Chittendon, E. (1991). Authentic assessment, evaluation, and documentation of student performance (pp. 22–31). In V. Perrone (Ed.), *Expanding student assessment.* Alexandria, VA: Association for Supervision and Curriculum Development.

Chiu, L-H. (1992-1993). Self-esteem in American and Chinese (Taiwanese) children. *Current Psychology: Research and Reviews, 11*, 309–313.

Church, J. A., Allen, J. R., & Stiehm, E. R. (1986). New scarlet letter(s), pediatric AIDS. *Pediatrics, 77*, 423–427.

Clark, C. M., Gage, N. L., Marx, R. W., Peterson, P. L., Staybrook, N. G., & Winne, P. H. (1979). A factorial experiment on teacher structuring, soliciting, and reacting. *Journal of Educational Psychology, 71*, 534–552.

Clark, C., & Peterson, P. L. (1986). Teachers' thought processes. In M. Wittrock (Ed.), *Handbook of research on teaching* (3d ed.). New York: Macmillan.

Clark, H. H., & Clark, E. V. (1977). *Psychology and language.* New York: Harcourt Brace Jovanovich.

Clark, J., & Tollefson, N. (1991). Differences in beliefs and attitudes toward the improvability of writing of gifted students who exhibit mastery-oriented and helpless behavior. *Journal of Education of the Gifted, 14* (2), 119–133.

Clark, R.E. (1983). Reconsidering research on learning from media. *Review at Educational Research, 53*, 445–459.

Clark-Johnson, G. (1988). Black children. *Teaching Exceptional Children, 20*, 46–47.

Clarke, J., Wideman, R., & Eadie, S. (1990). *Together we Learn.* Scarborough: Prentice-Hall.

Clay, M. M. (1993). *Reading recovery: A guidebook for teachers in training.* Auckland, New Zealand: Heinemann.

__(1994). *An observation survey of early literacy achievement.* Auckland, New Zealand: Heinemann.

Clifton, R. (1989). Knowledge and mythology in teacher education. *McGill Journal of Education, 24*, 267-279.

Cobb, P. (1994). Where is the mind: Constructivist and sociocultural perspectives on mathematical development. *Educational Researcher*, 23 (7), 13–20.

Coburn, J. (1993). Opening new technological horizons for middle and high school. *Technology & Learning* (special supplement).

Cochrane-Smith, M. (1991). Reinventing student teaching. *Journal of Teacher Education, 42* (2), 104–118.

Cochrane-Smith, M., & Lytle, S. L. (1990). Research on teaching and teacher research: The issues that divide. *Education Researchers*, 19 (2) 2-10

Cognition & Technology Group at Vanderbilt. (1991). Technology and the design of generative learning environments. *Educational Technology*, 31(5), 34–40.

__(1990). Anchored instruction and its relationship to situated cognition. *Educational Researcher, 19* (4), 2–10.

__(1992). The Jasper experiment: An exploration of issues in learning and instructional design. *Educational Technology Research and Development, 40* (1), 65–80.

__(1993). Anchored instruction and situated cognition revisited. *Educational Technology, 33* (3), 52–70.

Cohen, E. G. (1986). *Designing groupwork.* New York: Teachers College Press.

Cohen, P. A., Kulik, J. A., & Kulik, C. C. (1982). Educational outcomes of tutoring: A meta-analysis of findings. *American Educational Research Journal, 19*, 237–248.

Coladarci, T. (1992). Teachers' sense of efficacy and commitment to teaching. *Journal of Experimental Education, 60* (4), 323–337.

Colburn, D., & Melillo, W. (1987, June 16). Hispanics: A forgotten health population. *Washington Post*, p. 16.

Colby, C., & Kohlberg, L. (1984). Invariant sequence and internal inconsistency in moral judgment stages. In W. Kurtines & J. Gewirtz (Eds.), *Morality, moral behavior, and moral development.* New York: Wiley-Interscience.

Cole, E. (1992). Characteristics of students referred to school teams: Implications for preventive psychological services. *Canadian Journal of School Psychology, 8*, 23-36.

Cole, M., & Engestrom, Y. (1993). A cultural-historical approach to distributed cognition. In G. Salomon (Ed.), *Distributed cognitions: Psychological and educational considerations.* Cambridge, MA: Harvard University Press.

Collins, A. (1990). Portfolios for assessing student learning in science: A new name for a familiar idea. In A. B. Champagne, B. E. Lovitts, & B. J. Calinger (Eds.), *Assessment in the service of instruction.* Washington, D.C.: American Association for the Advancement of Science.

__(1991). Portfolios for assessing student learning in science. In G. Kulm & S. Malcom (Eds.), *Science assessment in the service of reform.* Washington, D.C.: American Association for the Advancement of Science.

__(1992). Portfolios for science education: Issues in purpose, structure, and authenticity. *Science Education, 76* (4), 451–463.

Collins, A., & Dana, T. M. (1993). Using portfolios with middle school students. *Middle School Journal, 25* (2), 14–19.

Comer, J. P. (1988). Educating poor minority children. *Scientific American, 259*, 42–48.

Comfort, K. B. (1994, October). Authentic assessment: A systemic approach in California. *Science and Children*, 42–43, 65.

Conte, R., Andrews, J., Loomer, M.., & Hutton, g. (1995). A classroom-based social skills intervention for children with learning disabilities. *The Alberta Journal of Educational Research, XLI* (1), 84-102.

contradictory responses to antiracist education. *The Alberta Journal of Educational*

Conway, M. A., Cohen, G., & Stanhope, N. (1991). On the very long-term memory of knowledge acquired through formal education: Twelve years of cognitive psychology. *Journal of Experimental Psychology: General, 120*, 395–409.

__(1992). Very long-term memory of knowledge acquired at school and university. *Applied Cognitive Psychology*, 6, 467–482.

Cook, S.A. (1992). Adolescents' perceptions of classroom process. *McGill Journal of Education, 27*, 19-30.

Cooper, G., & Sweller, J. (1987). The effects of schema acquisition and rule automation in mathematical problem-solving transfer. *Journal of Educational Psychology*, 79, 347–362.

Cooper, H. M., & Good, T. L. (1983). *Pygmalion grows up: Studies in the expectation communication process.* White Plains, NY: Longman.

Corbett, A. T. (1977). Retrieval dynamics for rote and visual image mnemonics. *Journal of Verbal Learning and Verbal Behavior, 16,* 233–246.

Corbin, C. (1972). Mental practice (pp. 93–118). In W. Morgan (Ed.), *Ergogenic aids and muscular performance.* New York: Academic Press.

Corno, L. (1995). Working toward foresight and follow-through. *Mid-Western Educational Researcher, 8* (1), 2–10.

Corson, D. (1996). Official-language minority and aboriginal first-language education:

Coulter, R.P. (1996). Gender equity and schooling: Linking research and policy. *Canadian Journal of Education, 21(4),* 433-452.

Covell, K. (1995). *Readings in Child Development: A Canadian Perspective.* Toronto: Nelson Canada.

Covington, M., & Beery, R. (1976). *Self-worth and school learning.* New York: Holt, Rinehart & Winston.

Crooks, T. J. (1988). The impact of classroom evaluation practices on students. *Review of Educational Research, 58,* 438–481.

Csapo, M. (1981). The behaviorally-disordered child in Canada's schools. *Behavioral Disorders, 6,* 139-149.

Cummins, J. (1984). *Bilingualism and special education: Issues in assessment and pedagogy.* Clevedon, UK: Multilingual Matters.

__(1989). A theoretical framework for bilingual special education. *Special Education, 56,* 111-119.

Cunningham, C.E., Bremner, R., & Secord-Gilbert, M. (1993). Increasing the availability, accessibility, and cost-efficiency of services for families of ADHD children: A school-based systems-oriented parenting course. *Canadian Journal of School Psychology, 9,* 1-15.

Cunningham, G. K. (1986). *Educational and psychological measurement.* New York: Macmillan.

Cunningham, J., & Swain, M. (1986). *Bilingualism in education.* London: Longman.

Curwin, R. L., & Mendler, A. N. (1988). *Discipline with dignity.* Alexandria, VA: Association for Supervision and Curriculum Development.

Damon, W. (1991). Putting substance into self-esteem: A focus on academic and moral values. *Educational Horizons, 70,* 12–18.

Damon, W., & Hart, D. (1982). The development of self-understanding from infancy through adolescence. *Child Development, 53,* 841–864.

__(1988). *Self-understanding in childhood and adolescence.* New York: Cambridge University Press.

Das, J.P. (1993). Neurocognitive approach to remediation: The PREP model. *Canadian Journal of Psychology, 9 (2),* 157-173.

Das, J.P., Naglieri, J.A., & Kirby, J.R. (1994). *Assessment of cognitive processes: The PASS theory of intelligence.* Boston: Allyn and Bacon.

Daum, J. (1972). Proxemics in the classroom: Speaker-subject distance and educational performance. Paper presented at the 18th Annual Meeting of the Southeastern Psychological Association, April 6–8, Atlanta, GA.

Davies, A., Hogan, P., & Clandinin, J. (1991). Classroom management: Restoring our relationships. In R.H. Short, L. Stewin, and S. McCann.

DeCharms, R. (1976). *Enhancing motivation.* New York: Irvington.

__(1980). The origins of competence and achievement motivation in personal causation. In L. J. Fyans, Jr. (Ed.), *Achievement motivation.* New York: Plenum.

Deci, E. L. (1971). Effects of externally mediated rewards on intrinsic motivation. *Journal of Personality and Social Psychology, 18,* 105-115.

__(1975). *Intrinsic motivation.* New York: Plenum.

Deci, E. L., & Ryan, R. M. (1985). *Intrinsic motivation and self-determination in human behavior.* New York: Plenum.

Deci, E. L., Vallerand, R. J., Pelletier, L. G., & Ryan, R. M. (1991). Motivation and education: The self-determination perspective. *Educational Psychologist, 26,* 325-346.

DeCorte, E., Verschaffel, L., & DeWin, L. (1985). Influence of rewording verbal problems in children's problem representations and solutions. *Journal of Educational Psychology, 77,* 460-470.

DeFord, D. E., Lyons, C. A., & Pinnell, G. S. (1991). *Bridges to literacy: Learning from reading recovery.* Portsmouth, NH: Heinemann.

Dei, G.J. (1995). Examining the case for "African-Centred" schools in Ontario. *McGill*

Dei, G.J. (1996). The role of afrocentricity in the inclusive curriculum in Canadian schools. *Canadian journal of Education, 21(2),* 170-186.

Delefes, P., & Jackson, B. (1972). Teacher-pupil interaction as a function of location in the classroom. *Psychology in the Schools, 9,* 119–123.

Delisle, J. (1982). Learning to underachieve. *Roeper Review, 4,* 16-18.

Derevensky, J.L. & Leckerman, R. (1997). Teachers' differential use of praise and reinforcement practices. *Canadian Journal of School Psychology. 13(1),* 15-27.

Derry, S. J., & Lajoie, S. P. (1993). A middle camp for (un)-intelligent instructional computing: An introduction. In S. P. Lajoie & S. J. Derry (Eds.), *Computers as cognitive tools.* Hillsdale, NJ: Erlbaum.

Derry, S. J., & Murphy, D. A. (1986). Designing systems that train learning ability: From theory to practice. *Review of Educational Research, 56,* 1-39.

Dick, W., & Reiser, R. A. (1989). *Planning effective instruction.* Englewood Cliffs, NJ: Prentice Hall.

Dillon, J. (Ed.) (1988). *Questioning and teaching: A manual of practice.* London: Croom Helm.

__(1990). *The practice of questioning.* New York: Routledge.

Dorris, M. A. (1981). The grass still grows, the rivers still flow: Contemporary Native-Americans. *Daedalus, 110 (2),* 43–69.

Douvan, E., & Adelson, J. (1966). *The adolescent experience.* New York: Wiley.

Douvan, E., & Gold, H. (1966). Modal patterns in American adolescence. In M. L. Hoffman & L. W. Hoffman (Eds.), *Review of developmental research* (Vol. 2). New York: Russell Sage.

Doyle, W. (1984). How order is achieved in classrooms: An interim report. *Journal of Curriculum Studies, 16,* 259-277.

__(1986). Classroom organization and management. In M. C. Wittrock (Ed.), *Handbook of research on teaching* (3d ed.). New York: Macmillan.

__(1988). Work in mathematics classes: The context of students' thinking during instruction. *Educational Psychologist, 23,* 167-180.

__(1990). Classroom management techniques. In O. C. Moles (Ed.), *Student discipline strategies: Research and practice.* Albany: State University of New York Press.

Driscoll, M. P. (1994). *Psychology of learning for instruction.* Needham Heights, MA: Allyn & Bacon.

Driscoll, M. P., & Rowley, K. (in press). Semiotics: Toward learning-centered instructional design. In C. Dills & A. Romiszowski (Eds.), *Instructional development: The state of the art, Vol. III. The paradigms, models, metaphors, and viewpoints.* Englewood Cliffs, NJ: Educational Technology Publications.

Driscoll, M. P., Moallem, M., Dick, W., & Kirby, E. (1994). How does the textbook contribute to learning in a middle school science class? *Contemporary Educational Psychology, 19,* 79-100.

Driscoll, M.P., Klein, J. D., and Sherman, G. P. (1994, March). Perspectives on instructional planning: How do teachers and instructional designers conceive of ISD planning practices? *Educational Technology, 34-42.*

Duell, O. K. (1994). Extended wait time and university student achievement. *American Educational Research Journal, 31* (2), 397-414.

Duell, O. K., Lynch, D. J., Ellsworth, R., & Moore, C. A. (1992). Wait-time in college classes taken by education majors. *Research in Higher Education, 33,* 483-495.

Duffy, G. G., & McIntyre, L. D. (1982). A naturalistic study of instructional assistance in primary-grade reading. *Elementary School Journal, 83* (1), 15-23.

Duffy, G. G., Roehler, L. R., Meloth, M. S., & Vavrus, L. G. (1986). Conceptualizing instructional explanation. *Teaching and Teacher Education, 2,* 197-214.

Dunn, R., Beaudry, J. S., & Klavas, A. (1989). Survey of research on learning styles. *Educational Leadership, 47* (7), 50-58.

Dunphy, D. C. (1963). The social structure of urban adolescent peer groups. *Sociometry, 26,* 230-246.

DuPaul, G.J., & Stoner, G. (1994). *ADHD in the schools: Assessment and Intervention Strategies.* New York: Guilford Press.

Dusek, J. B. (1987). *Adolescent development and behavior.* Englewood Cliffs, NJ: Prentice Hall.

Dweck, C. S. (1975). The role of expectations and attributions in the alleviation of learned helplessness. *Journal of Personality and Social Psychology, 31,* 674-685.

__(1986). Motivational processes affecting learning. *American Psychologist, 41,* 1040-1048.

__(1989). Motivation. In A. Lesgold & R. Glaser (Eds.), *Foundations for a psychology of education.* Hillsdale, NJ: Erlbaum.

Dweck, C. S., & Leggett, E. L. (1988). A social-cognitive approach to motivation and personality. *Psychological Review, 95,* 256-273.

Dworet, D. & Rathberger, A.J. (1990). Provincial and territorial Government responses to behaviorally disordered students in Canada. *Behavioral Disorders, 15,* 201-209.

Eagly, A. H. (1987). *Sex differences in social behavior: A social-role interpretation.* Hillsdale, NJ: Erlbaum.

Ebel, R. L., & Frisbie, D. A. (1986). *Essentials of educational measurement* (4th ed.). Englewood Cliffs, NJ: Prentice Hall.

__(1991). *Essentials of educational measurement* (5th ed.). Englewood Cliffs, NJ: Prentice Hall.

Eder, R. A. (1989). The emergent personologist: The structure and content of 3 1/2-, 5 1/2-, and 7 1/2-year-olds' concepts of themselves and other persons. *Child Development, 60,* 1218-1228.

__(1990). Uncovering young children's psychological selves: Individual and developmental differences. *Child Development, 61,* 849-863.

Edwards, J. R. (1979). *Language and disadvantage.* London: Wauld.

Eggen, P., & Kauchak, D. (1994). *Educational psychology: Classroom connections.* New York: Merrill Publishing Co.

Elam, S. M., Rose, L. C., & Gallup, A. M. (1992). The 24th annual Gallup/Phi Delta Kappa Poll of the public's attitudes toward the public schools. *Phi Delta Kappan, 74* (1), 41-53.

Elawar, M. C., & Corno, L. (1985). A factorial experiment in teachers' written feedback on student homework: Changing teacher behavior a little rather than a lot. *Journal of Educational Psychology, 77,* 162-173.

Eller, B. F., Kaufman, A. S., & McLean, J. E. (1986–1987). Computer-based assessment of cognitive abilities: Current status/future directions. *Journal of Educational Technology Systems, 15,* 137-147.

Ellerod, F. E., & McLean, G. F. (Eds.). (1986). *Act and agent: Philosophical foundations for moral education and character development.* Washington, D.C.: University Press of America.

Elliott, E. S., & Dweck, C. S. (1988). Goals: An approach to motivation and achievement. *Journal of Personality and Social Psychology, 54* (1), 5-12.

Ellis, J. (1997). Volunteer mentorship programs to prevent and respond to troubled behavior. *The Alberta Journal of Educational Research, XLIII (1),* 53-56.

Emmer, E. T. (1987). Classroom management and discipline. In V. Richardson-Koehler (Ed.), *Educator's handbook: A research perspective.* White Plains, NY: Longman.

Emmer, E. T., & Ausiker, A. (1990). School and classroom discipline programs: How well do they work? In O. C. Moles (Ed.), *Student discipline strategies: Research and practice.* Albany: State University of New York Press.

Emmer, E. T., Evertson, C. M., & Anderson, L. M. (1980). Effective classroom management at the beginning of the school year. *Elementary School Journal, 80,* 219–231.

Emmer, E. T., Evertson, C. M., Clements, B. S., & Worsham, M. E. (1994). *Classroom management for secondary teachers* (3rd ed.). Needham Heights, MA: Allyn & Bacon.

Epstein, C. (1980). Brain growth and cognitive functioning. In *The emerging adolescent: Characteristics and implications.* Columbus, OH: NMSA.

Epstein, M. H., Polloway, E. A., Patton, J. R., & Foley, R. (1989). Mild retardation: Student characteristics and services. *Education and Training in Mental Retardation, 24* (1), 7-16.

Erickson, F., & Schultz, J. (1982). *The counselor as gate keeper: Social interaction in interviews.* New York: Academic Press.

Erikson, E. (1963). *Childhood and society* (2d ed.). New York: Norton.

___(1968). *Identity, youth and crisis.* New York: Norton.

Evertson, C. M., & Harris, A. (1992). What we know about managing classrooms. *Educational Leadership, 49,* 74–79.

Evertson, C. M., & Randolph, C. H. (1995). Classroom management in the learning-centered classroom. In A. Ornstein (Ed.), *Teaching: Theory and practice.* Needham Heights, MA: Allyn & Bacon.

Evertson, C. M., Emmer, E. T., Clements, B. S., & Worsham, M. E. (1994). Classroom management for elementary teachers (3d ed.) Needham Heights, MA: Allyn & Bacon.

Evertson, C. M., Emmer, E., & Brophy, J. (1980). Predictors of effective teaching in junior high mathematics classrooms. *Journal of Research on Mathematics Education, II,* 167–178.

Evertson, C.M. (1987). Managing classrooms: A framework for teachers. In D. Berliner & B. Rosenshine (eds.), *Talks to teachers.* New York: Random House.

Evertson, C.M., & Emmer, E.T. (1982). Effective management at the beginning of the school year in junior high classes. *Journal of Educational Psychology, 74,* 485–498.

Fagan, E. R., Hassler, D. M., & Szabo, M. (1981). Evaluation of questioning strategies in language arts instruction. *Research in the Teaching of English, 15,* 267–273.

Fagot, B. I. (1977). Consequences of moderate cross-gender behavior in preschool children. *Child Development, 48,* 902–907.

___(1985). Changes in thinking about early sex-role development. *Developmental Review, 5,* 83–98.

Feiman-Nemser, S. (1983). *Learning to teach.* East Lansing, MI: Institute for Research on Teaching.

Feldman, R. D. (1982). *Whatever happened to the Quiz Kids?* Chicago: Review Press.

Felt, L. (1993). Regional disparity, resource development, and unequal accumulation. In P.S. Li & B.S. Bolaria (Eds.), *Contemporary sociology: Critical perspectives.* Toronto: Copp Clark Pitman.

Feltz, D. L., & Landers, D. M. (1983). Effects of mental practice on motor skill learning and performance: A meta-analysis. *Journal of Sport Psychology, 5,* 25–57.

Fenstermacher, G. (1990). Moral consideration on teaching as a profession. In J. Goodlad, R. Soder, & K. Sirotnik (Eds.), *The moral dimensions of teaching.* San Francisco: Jossey-Bass.

Ferster, C. B., & Skinner, B. F. (1957). *Schedules of reinforcement.* New York: Appleton-Century-Crofts.

Fiedler, F. F., & Garcia, J. E. (1987). *New approaches to effective leadership: Cognitive resources and organizational performance.* New York: Wiley.

Finders, M., & Lewis, C. (1994). Why some parents don't come to school. *Educational Leadership, 51* (8), 50–54.

Fishbaugh, M. (1997). *Models of collaboration.* Boston: Allyn & Bacon.

Fisher, C. W., Berliner, D. C., Filby, N. N., Marliave, R., Cahen, L. S., & Dishaw, M. M. (1980). Teaching behaviors, academic learning time, and student achievement: An overview. In C. Denham & A. Lieberman (Eds.), *Time to learn.* Washington, D.C.: National Institute of Education.

Fisher, C. W., Filby, N. N., Marliave, R., Cahen, L. S., Dishaw, M. M., Moore, J. E., & Berliner, D. C. (1978). *Teaching behaviors, academic learning time, and student achievement: Final report of phase III-B, Beginning Teacher Evaluation Study* (Tech. Report V-1). San Francisco: Far West Laboratory for Educational Research and Development.

Fisher, C., Berliner, D., Filby, N., Marliave, R., Cahen, L., & Dishaw, M. (1980). Teaching behaviors, academic learning time, and student achievement: An overview. In C. Denham & A. Lieberman (Eds.), *Time to learn.* Washington, DC: National Institute of Education.

Fishkin, J., Keniston, K., & MacKinnon, C. (1973). Moral reasoning and political ideology. *Journal of Personality and Social Psychology, 27,* 109–119.

Flaugher, R. L. (1978). The many definitions of test bias. *American Psychologist, 33,* 671-679.

Flavell, J. H. (1985). *Cognitive development* (2nd ed.). Englewood Cliffs, NJ: Prentice Hall.

Fleming, D. (1996). Preamble to a more perfect classroom. *Educational Leadership, 54*(1), 73-76.

Fleming, M., & Chambers, B. (1983). Teacher-made tests: Windows on the classroom. In W. E. Hathaway (Ed.), *Testing in the schools: New directions for testing and measurement,* No. 19. San Francisco: Jossey-Bass.

Flynn, M., Kelly, I.W. & Janzen, B.L. (1994). Education students' oerestimation of the prevalene of learning disabilities. *Psychological Reports, 74,* 195-198.

Ford, B. A., & Jones, C. (1990). An ethnic feelings book: Created by students with developmental handicaps. *Teaching Exceptional Children, 22* (4), 36–39.

Forgette-Giroux, R., Richard, M., & Michaud, P. (1995). L'influence du climat psychosocial de l'ecole et le concept de soi des eleves. *Revue Canadienne de l'education, 20(3),* 367-374.

Forrest-Pressley, D. L., MacKinnon, E., & Waller, T. G. (Eds.). (1985). *Metacognition, cognition, and human performance.* New York: Academic Press.

Frederiksen, J. R., & Collins, A. (1989). A systems approach to educational testing. *Educational Researcher, 18* (9), 27–32.

Frederiksen, N. (1984). The real test bias. *American Psychologist, 39,* 193–202.

French, F. (1987). Learner strategies enabling thinking (2nd ed.). Halifax: Mount Saint Vincent University.

__(1991). Cognitive instructional practices in today's schools: Promise or fallacy. In R.H. Short, L.L. Stewin & S.J.H. McCann.

Frey, G. (1983, Summer). The Middle Ages: The social studies core of the fifth grade. *Moral Education Forum,* 30–34.

Frideres, J. (1993). Native peoples. In P.S. Li & B.S. Bolaria (Eds.). *Contemporary sociology: Critical perspectives.* Toronto: Copp Clark Pitman.

Friedl, A. E. (1991). *Teaching science to children: An integrated approach.* (2nd ed.). New York: McGraw-Hill, Inc.

Friend, M., & Bursuck, W. D., & Hutchinson, N. (1998, in press*). Including students with special needs: A practical guide for classroom teachers.* Scarborough, ON: Allyn & Bacon Canada.

Friesen, J.W. (1985). *When cultures clash: Case studies in multiculturalism.* Calgary: Detselig Enterprises.

__(1993). *When cultures clash: Case studies in multiculturalism* (2nd ed.). Calgary: Detselig Enterprises.

Frieze, I., & Weiner, B. (1971). Cue utilization and attributional judgments for success and failure. *Journal of Personality, 39,* 91–109.

Frisbie, D. A., & Waltman, K. K. (1992). Developing a personal grading plan. *Educational Measurement: Issues and Practices,* Fall, 35–42.

Fuson, K. C., & Willis, G. B. (1989). Second graders' use of schematic drawings in solving addition and subtraction problems. *Journal of Educational Psychology, 81,* 514–520.

Gabor, T. (1995). School violence and the zero tolerance alternative. Ottawa, ON: Solicitor General Canada.

Gage, N. L., & Berliner, D. C. (1988). *Educational psychology.* Boston: Houghton Mifflin.

__(1992). *Educational psychology.* Boston: Houghton Mifflin.

Gage, N.L., & Needels, M. C. (1989). Process-product research on teaching: A review of criticism. *Elementary School Journal, 89,* 253–300.

Gagné, A. (1996). Success at Contact: The argument for alternative schools for at-risk youth. *The Alberta Journal of Educational Research, XLII(3),* 306-314.

Gagné, E. D., Yekovich, C. W., & Yekovich, F. R. (1993). *The cognitive psychology of school learning* (2nd ed.). New York: HarperCollins.

Gagné, R. M. (1977). *The conditions of learning* (3rd ed.). New York: Holt, Rinehart, & Winston.

__(1985). *The conditions of learning* (4th ed.). New York: Holt, Rinehart & Winston.

Gagné, R. M., & Glaser, R. (1987). Foundations in learning research. In R. M. Gagné (Ed.), *Instructional technology: Foundations.* Hillsdale, NJ: Erlbaum.

Gagné, R. M., & Merrill, M. D. (1990). Integrative goals for instructional design. *Educational Technology Research & Development, 38,* 23–30.

Gagné, R.M., & Driscoll, M.P. (1988). *Essentials of learning for instruction* (2nd ed.). Englewood Cliffs, NJ: Prentice Hall.

Gallimore, R., & Tharp, R. (1990). Teaching mind in society: Teaching, schooling, and literate discourse. In L. C. Moll (Ed.), *Vygotsky and education.* New York: Cambridge University Press.

Garcia, E. E. (1992). Hispanic children: Theoretical, empirical, and related policy issues. *Educational Psychology Review, 4,* 69-94.

Gardner, H. (1975). *The shattered mind.* New York: Knopf.

__(1979). Developmental psychology after Piaget: An approach in terms of symbolization. *Human Development, 15,* 570–580.

__(1982). *Art, mind and brain.* New York: Basic Books.

__(1993). *Creating minds: An anatomy of creativity seen through the lives of Freud, Einstein, Picasso, Stravinsky, Eliot, Graham, and Gandhi.* New York: BasicBooks.

Gardner, H. (1995). Reflection on multiple intelligences: Myths and messages. *Phi Delta Kappan, 77,* 200-210.

Gardner, H., & Hatch T. (1989). Multiple intelligences go to school: Educational implications of the theory of multiple intelligences. *Educational Researcher, 18* (8), 4–10.

Gardner, H., & Wolf, D. (1983). Waves and streams of symbolization. In D. R. Rogers & J. A. Sloboda (Eds.), *The acquisition of symbolic skills.* London: Plenum.

Gardner, H., Howard, V., and Perkins, D. (1974). Symbol systems: A philosophical, psychological and educational investigation. In D. Olson (Ed.), *Media and symbols.* Chicago: University of Chicago Press.

Gardner, J. (1986). Factor structure of the K-ABC for Cantonese, English, and Punjabi-speaking Canadians. *Canadian Journal of School Psychology, 4,* 49-59.

Garlett, M. W. (1993). Making parents into partners. *Teachers in Focus, 2* (3), 7–8.

Geisert, P. G., & Futrell, M. K. (1995). *Teachers, computers, and curriculum: Microcomputers in the classroom* (2nd ed.). Needham Heights, MA: Allyn & Bacon.

Genesee, F. (1985). Second language learning through immersion: A review of U. S. programs. *Review of Educational Research, 55,* 541–561.

Gettinger, M. (1988). Methods of proactive classroom management. *School Psychology Review, 17,* 227–242.

Ghash, R. (1995). New perspectives on multiculturalism in education. *McGill Journal of Education, 30(3),* 231-238.

Gibbons, M. (1991). *How to become an expert: Discover, research, and build a project in your chosen field.* Tucson, AZ: Zephyr Press.

Gilligan, C. (1977). In a different voice: Women's conceptions of self and of morality. *Harvard Educational Review, 47,* 481–517.

__(1982). *In a different voice.* Cambridge: Harvard University Press.

Ginott, H. (1972). *Teacher and child.* New York: Macmillan.

Glaser, R. (1963). Instructional technology and the measurement of learning outcomes: Some questions. *American Psychologist, 18,* 519–521.

Glaser, R., & Silver, E. (1994). Assessment, testing, and instruction: Retrospect and prospect. In Darling-Hammond (ed.), *Review of Research in Education,* Vol. 20. Washington, D.C.: American Educational Research Association.

Glass, G. V., & Smith, M. L. (1977). *Pull out in compensatory education.* Washington, D.C.: Department of Health, Education, and Welfare.

Glasser, W. (1986). *Control theory in the classroom.* New York: HarperCollins.

__(1990). *The quality school.* New York: HarperCollins.

__(1993). *The quality school teacher.* New York: HarperCollins.

Goin, M. T., Peters, E. E., & Levin, J. R. (1986, March-April). *Effects of pictorial mnemonic strategies on the reading performance of students classified as learning disabled.* Paper presented at the Annual Meeting of the Council for Exceptional Children, New Orleans.

Goldenberg, C. N. (1992). The limits of expectations: A case for case knowledge about teacher expectancy effects. *American Educational Research Journal, 29,* 517-544.

__(1988). Cautions concerning assessment of Native Indian students. *Canadian Journal of School Psychology, 4,* 17-20.

Good, T. L. (1988). Teacher expectations. In D. Berliner & B. Rosenshine (Eds.), *Talks to teachers.* New York: Random House.

Good, T. L., & Brophy, J. E. (1994). *Looking in classrooms* (6th ed.). New York: HarperCollins.

Good, T. L., Grouws, D., & Ebmeier, H. (1983). *Active mathematics teaching.* New York: Longman.

Goodlad, J. (1983). A study of schooling: Some implications for school improvement. *Phi Delta Kappan, 64,* 465-470.

Gordon, B., Saklofske, D.H., & Hildebrand, D.K. (1998). Assessing children with mental retardation.. In H.B. Vance (ed.). *Psychological Assessment of Children.* New York: john Wiley & Sons.

Gordon, E. W. (1991). Human diversity and pluralism. *Educational Psychologist, 26,* 99-108.

Gordon, T. (1974). *T.E.T.: Teacher effectiveness training.* New York: Peter H. Wyden.

__(1988). *Teaching children self-discipline: At home and at school.* New York: Times Books.

Gould, S. J. (1981). *The mismeasure of man.* New York: W. W. Norton.

Grabe, M. (1986). Attentional processes in education. In G. D. Phye & T. Andre (Eds.), *Cognitive classroom learning: Understanding, thinking and problem solving.* New York: Academic Press.

Graham, S. (1994). Motivation in African Americans. *Review of Educational Research, 64* (1), 55–117.

Graham, S., & Barker, G. P. (1990). The down side of help: An attributional-developmental analysis of helping behavior as a low-ability cue. *Journal of Educational Psychology, 82,* 7–14.

Greenberg, M.T., & Kusche, C.A. (1993). *Promoting social and emotional development in deaf children: The PATHS project.* Seattle, WA: University of Washington Press.

Greenough-Olsen, S.C. (1993). The influence of language on non-verbal intelligence test performance of northern Saskatchewan Aboriginal children (p. 29-30). M.Ed. thesis, University of Saskatchewan.

Greer, J. G., & Withered, C. E. (1987). Learned helplessness and the elementary student: Implications for counselors. *Elementary School Guidance and Counseling, 22* (2), 157–164.

Gresham, F. (1981). Social skills training with handicapped children: A review. *Review of Educational Research, 51,* 139–176.

Grigorenko, E.L. & Sternberg, R.J. (1995) Thinking styles. In D.H. Saklofske and M. Zeidner (Eds.) *International Handbook of Personality and Intelligence.* New York: Plenum.

Gronlund, N. E. (1990). *Measurement and evaluation in teaching* (6th ed.). New York: Macmillan.

__(1991). *How I write and use instructional objectives* (4th ed.). New York: Macmillan.

__(1993). *How to make achievement tests and assessments* (5th ed.). Needham Heights, MA: Allyn & Bacon.

Grossman, H. (1983). *Classification in mental retardation.* Washington, D.C.: American Association on Mental Deficiency.

Grossman, H., & Grossman, S. H. (1994). *Gender issues in education.* Needham Heights, MA: Allyn & Bacon.

Gruber, H. E., & Voneche, J. J. (1977). *The essential Piaget.* New York: Basic Books.

Guilford, J. P. (1967). *The nature of human intelligence.* New York: McGraw-Hill.

__(1980). Fluid and crystallized intelligences: Two fanciful concepts. *Psychological Bulletin, 88,* 406–412.

__(1985). The structure-of-intellect model. In B. B. Wolman (Ed.), *Handbook of intelligence.* New York: Wiley.

Gump, P. (1967). *The classroom behavior setting: Its nature and relation to student behavior* (Report No. BR-5-0334). Washington, D.C.: Office of Education, Bureau of Research.

Gunter, M. A., Estes, T. H., & Hasbrouck Schwab, J. (1990). *Instruction: A models approach.* Needham Heights, MA: Allyn & Bacon.

Gupta, R., & Derevensky, J., Tsanos, A., Klein, C., Bennett, A and Kanevsky, L. (1995). A comparison of Adolescents' fears from Montreal to Vancouver. *Canadian Journal of School Psychology, 11,* 10-17.

Haertel, G. D., Walberg, H. J., Junker, L., & Pascarella, E. T. (1981). Early adolescent sex differences in science learning: Evidence from the National Assessment of Educational Progress. *American Educational Research Journal, 18* (3), 329-341.

Haines, L., & Robertson, G. (1996). Using computers to support teamwork in inclusive elementary classrooms. In J. Andrews (ed.), *Teaching Students with Diverse Needs: Elementary Classrooms.* (pp. 251-272). Toronto: Nelson Canada.

Haines, L., Sanche, R., & Robertson, G. (1993). Instruction CoPlanner: A software tool to facilitate collaborative resource teaching. *Canadian Journal of Educational Communications, 22,* 177-187

Hale-Benson, J. E. (1986). *Black children: Their roots and their culture* (rev. ed.). Baltimore, MD: Johns Hopkins University Press.

Hallahan, D. P., & Kauffman, J. M. (1991). *Exceptional children: Introduction to special education* (5th ed.). Needham Heights, MA: Allyn & Bacon.

Hallahan, D. P., & Kauffman, J. M. (1994). *Exceptional children: Introduction to special education* (6th ed.). Needham Heights, MA: Allyn & Bacon.

Hambleton, R. K., & Murphy, E. (1992). A psychometric perspective on authentic measurement. *Applied Measurement in Education, 5* (1), 1-16.

Haney, W., & Madaus, G. (1989). Searching for alternatives to standardized tests: Why, whats, and whithers. *Phi Delta Kappan, 70,* 683-687.

Hanna, G. S. (1993). *Better teaching through better measurement.* Orlando, FL: Harcourt Brace Jovanovich.

Harel & Papert, S. (1992). Software design as a learning environment. Dr. I. Harel & S. Papent (Eds.) *Constructionism,* Norwood, NJ: Ablox.

Haring-Smith, T. (1993). *Learning together: An introduction to collaborative learning.* New York: HarperCollins.

__(1994a). *Writing together: Collaborative learning in the writing classroom.* New York: HarperCollins.

__(1994b, June). *Why collaborative learning backfires.* Paper presented at the conference What Works: Building Effective Collaborative Learning Experiences, sponsored by the National Center on Postsecondary Teaching, Learning, and Assessment, Pennsylvania State University, State College, PA.

Harper, H. (1997). Difference and diversity in Ontario schooling. *Canadian Journal of Education, 22(2),* 192-206.

Harris, F. R., Wolf, M. M., & Baer, D. M. (1967). Effects of adult social reinforcement in child behavior. In S. W. Bijou & D. M. Baer (Eds.), *Child development: Readings in experimental analysis.* New York: Appleton-Century-Crofts.

Harrow, A. J. (1972). *A taxonomy of the psychomotor domain: A guide for developing behavioral objectives.* New York: David McKay.

Hart, D. (1994). *Authentic assessment: A handbook for educators.* Menlo Park, CA: Addison-Wesley Publishing Co.

Harter, S. (1982). The perceived competence scale for children. *Child Development, 53,* 87-97.

__(1986). Processes underlying the construction, maintenance, and enhancement of self-concept in children. In S. Suhls & A. Greenwald (Eds.), *Psychological perspectives of the self* (Vol. 3). Hillsdale, NJ: Erlbaum.

__(1990). Issues in the assessment of the self-concept in children and adolescents. In A. LaGreca (Ed.), *Through the eyes of a child.* Needham Heights, MA: Allyn & Bacon.

Harter, S., & Pike, R. (1984). The pictorial scale of perceived competence and social acceptance for young children. *Child Development, 55,* 1969-1982.

Hartshorne, H., & May, M. A. (1930). *Studies in deceit.* New York: Macmillan.

Heckhausen, H., & Kuhl, J. (1985). From wishes to action: The dead ends and short cuts on the long way to action. In M. Frese & J. Sabini (Eds.), *Goal-directed behavior: The concept of action in psychology.* Hillsdale, NJ: Erlbaum.

Henson, K. (1988). *Methods and strategies for teaching in secondary and middle schools.* New York: Longman.

Herberg, E.N. (1989). *Ethnic groups in Canada: Adaptations and transitions.* Toronto: Nelson Canada.

Herbert, W., Hemingway, P., & Hutchinson, N. (1984). Classification and placement decisions of Canadian teachers-in-training as a function of referral information. *Canadian Journal for Exceptional Children, 1,* 56-60.

Herman, J. L., Aschbacher, P. R., & Winters, L. (1992). *A practical guide to alternative assessment.* Alexandria, VA: Association for Supervision and Curriculum Development.

Herrnstein, R. J., & Murray, C. A. (1994). *The bell curve: Intelligence and class structure in American life.* New York: Free Press.

Herrnstein, R.J. & Murray C. (1994). The bell curve: Intelligence and class structure in American life. New York: Free Press.

Hess, G.C., & Zingle, H.W. (1991). Improving self-concept and motivation: The relationship between the affective and cognitive domains. In K. Covell.

Hess, R., Chih-Mei, C., & McDevitt, T. M. (1987), Cultural vaniation in family beliefs about children's performance in mathematics: Comparisons among People's Republic of China, Chinese-American, and Caucasian-American families. *Journal of Educational Psychology, 79,* 179–188

Hetherington, E. M., & Parke, R. D. (1993). *Child psychology: A contemporary viewpoint.* New York: McGraw-Hill.

Heward, W. L., & Orlansky, M. D. (1992). *Exceptional children* (4th ed.). New York: Merrill.

Heyman, G. D., Dweck, C. S., & Cain, K. M. (1992). Young children's vulnerability to self-blame and helplessness: Relationship to beliefs about goodness. *Child Development, 63,* 401–415.

Hiebert, F. (Ed.). (1991). *Literacy for a diverse society.* New York: Teachers College Press.

Hildebrand, D.K. & Saklofske, D.H. (1996). The Wechsler Adult Intelligence Scale- Third Edition: A Canadian Standardization Study. *Canadian Journal of School Psychology, 12(1),* 74-76.

Hildebrand, D.K. (1998) A review of the Das-Naglieri Cognitive Assessment System. *Canadian Journal of School Psychology.* In press.

Hill, K. T. (1984). Debilitating motivation and testing: A major educational problem—Possible solutions and policy applications. In R. E. Ames & C. Ames (Eds.), *Research on motivation in education: Vol. 1, Student motivation.* New York: Academic Press.

Hoge, R. D., and Renzulli, J. S. (1993). Exploring the link between giftedness and self-concept. *Review of Educational Research, 63* (4), 449–465.

Hohn, R. L. (1995). *Classroom learning and teaching*. White Plains, NY: Longman.

Holstein, B. (1976). Irreversible, stepwise sequence in the development of moral judgment: A longitudinal study of males and females. *Child Development, 47*, 51-61.

Honebein, P. C., Duffy, T. M., & Fishman, B. J. (1994). Constructivism and the design of authentic learning environments: Context and authentic activities for learning. In T. M. Duffy, J. Lowyck, & D. Jonassen (Eds.), *Designing environments for constructive learning*. Hillsdale, NJ: Erlbaum.

Hopkins, K. D., & Antes, R. L. (1990). *Classroom measurement and evaluation* (3rd ed.). Itasca, IL: F. E. Peacock.

Hopkins, K. D., Stanley, J. C, & Hopkins, B. R. (1981). *Educational and psychological measurement and evaluation* (3rd ed.). Englewood Cliffs, NJ: Prentice Hall.

Hopkins, K. D., Stanley, J. C, & Hopkins, B. R. (1990). *Educational and psychological measurement and evaluation* (7th ed.). Englewood Cliffs, NJ: Prentice Hall.

Hopkins, K.D. (1998). *Educational and Psychological Measurement* (8th ed.) Boston: Allyn & Bacon.

Houser, N. (1987). Toward a Peircean semiotic theory of learning. *American Journal of Semiotics, 5* (2), 251–274.

Houston, J. P. (1986). *Fundamentals of learning and memory* (3rd ed.). New York: Harcourt Brace Jovanovich.

Hoy, W. K., & Miskel, C. G. (1991). *Educational administration: Theory, research, and practice* (4th ed.). New York: McGraw-Hill.

Hoy, W., & Woolfolk, A. E. (1993). Teachers' sense of efficacy and the organizational health of schools. *Elementary School Journal, 93* (4), 355–372.

Huck, C. S., & Pinnell, G. S. (1991). Literacy in the classroom. In D. E. DeFord, C. A. Lyons, & G. S. Pinnell (Eds.), *Bridges to literacy: Learning from reading recovery*. Portsmouth, NH: Heinemann.

Huling-Austin, L. (1994) *Becoming a teacher: What research tells us*. Booklet. West Lafayette, IN: Kappa Delta Pi.

Hull, J., Phillips, R., & Polyzoi, E. (1995). Indian control and the delivery of special education services to students in band-operated schools in Manitoba. *The Alberta Journal of Educational Research, XLI(1)*, 36-62.

Human Resources Development Canada (1997). Statistical profile of Canada's children. *Applied Research Bulletin, 3(1)*, pp. 1-23.

Hunt, E. B. (1971). What kind of computer is man? *Cognitive Psychology, 2*, 57–98.

Hunter, D. & Gambell, T. (1996). Setting standards for a provincial literacy assessment in Saskatchewan: Premises and procedures. *McGill Journal of Education, 31(2)*, 195.

Hunter, D.M., Jones, R.M. & Randhawa, B.S. (1996). The use of holistic versus analytic scoring for large-scale assessment of writing. *The Canadian Journal of Program Evaluation, 11(2)*, 61-85.

Hunter, M. (1982). *Mastery teaching*. El Segundo, CA: TIP Publications.

__(1984). Knowing, teaching, and supervising. In P. Hosford (Ed.), *Using what we know about teaching*. Alexandria, VA: Association for Supervision and Curriculum Development.

__(1991). Hunter lesson design helps achieve the goals of science instruction. *Educational Leadership, 48* (4), 79-81.

Hutchinson, N., & Hemingway, P. (1984). Educational decision-making of experienced teachers exposed to biasing information. *B.C. Journal of Special Education, 8*, 325-332.

Hwang, K. (1986). A psychological perspective of Chinese interpersonal morality. In M. H. Bond (Ed.), *The psychology of the Chinese people*. New York: Oxford University Press.

Hyde, J. S., Fennema, E., & Lamon, S. J. (1990). Gender differences in mathematics performance. *Psychological Bulletin, 107*, 139–155.

Implications of Norway's Sami Language Act for Canada. *Canadian Journal of Education, 21(1)*, 84-104.

Inhelder, B., & Piaget, J. (1958). *The growth of logical thinking from childhood to adolescence* (A. Parsons and S. Seagrin, Trans.). New York: Basic Books.

Inner-city schools: Vancouver's elementary principals take a position. (1988, June). *The Canadian School Executive*, 10-19.

Iran-Nejad, A., Marsh, G. E., & Clements, A. C. (1992). The figure and ground of constructive brain functioning: Beyond explicit memory processes. *Educational Psychologist, 47*, 473–492.

Iran-Nejad, A., Wittrock, M., & Hidi, S. (Eds.). (1992). Special Issue: Brain and Education. *Educational Psychologist, 27* (4). Washington, D.C.: American Psychological Association.

Jacobs, E.V., White, D.R., Baillargeon, M., & Betsalel-Presser, R. (1995). Peer relations among children attending school-age child-care programs. In K. Covell.

Jacoby, L. L., & Bartz, W. H. (1972). Rehearsal and transfer to LTS. *Journal of Verbal Learning and Verbal Behavior, 11*, 561–565.

Janda, L.H. (1998). *Psychgolgical Testing*. Boston: Allyn & Bacon.

Janzen, B.L. (1995). *The Youth Lifestyle Survey: A survey of youth and parents in Swift Current and area*. Prepared for the Interagency Committee on Child Abuse, Swift Current, Sasktchewan.

Johnson, C., & Behrenz. (1993). Childrearing discussions in families of nonproblem children and ADHD children with higher and lower levels of aggressive-defiant behavior. *Canadian Journal of School Psychology, 9*, 66-85.

Johnson, D. W., & Johnson, R. T. (1987). *Learning together and alone: Cooperative, competitive, and individualistic learning* (2nd ed.). Englewood Cliffs, NJ: Prentice Hall.

__(1989). *Cooperation and competition: Theory and research*. Edina, MN: Interaction Book Company.

__(1990). Cooperative learning and achievement. In S. Sharan (Ed.), *Cooperative learning theory and research*. New York: Praeger Publishers.

__(1991). *Teaching students to be peacemakers*. Edina, MN: Interaction Book Company.

__(1992a). *Creative controversy: Intellectual challenge in the classroom*. Edina, MN: Interaction Book Company.

__(1992b). *Positive interdependence: The heart of cooperative learning*. Edina, MN: Interaction Book Company.

__(1994). *Learning together and alone: Cooperative, competitive and individualistic learning* (4th ed.). Needham Heights, MA: Allyn & Bacon.

Johnson, D. W., Johnson, R. T., & Holubec, E. (1993). *Cooperation in the classroom* (6th ed.). Edina, MN: Interaction Book Company.

Johnson, D. W., Johnson, R. T., & Smith, K. (1991). *Active learning: Cooperation in the college classroom*. Edina, MN: Interaction Book Company.

Johnson, G. M. (1997). Resilient at-risk students in the inner-city. *Revue des Sciences de L'education de McGill, 32*, 35-44.

Johnson, N., & Cremo, E. (1995). Socialization and the native family. In K. Covell.

Johnston, P., Allington, R., & Afflerbach, P. (1985). The congruence of classroom and remedial instruction. *Elementary School Journal, 85*, 465–477.

Jones, R. A. (1977). *Self-fulfilling prophesies: Social psychological and psychological effects of expectancies*. New York: Halsted Press.

Jones, V. F., & Jones, L. S. (1990). *Comprehensive classroom management: Motivating and managing students* (3rd ed.). Needham Heights, MA: Allyn & Bacon.

__(1995). *Comprehensive classroom management: Creating positive learning environments for all students*. Needham Heights, MA: Allyn & Bacon.

Journal of Education, 30(2), 179-198.

Jussim, L. (1986). Self-fulfilling prophecies: A theoretical and integrative review. *Psychological Review, 93*, 429–445.

Kagan, J. (1964a). *Developmental studies of reflection and analysis*. Cambridge, MA: Harvard University Press.

__(1964b). Impulsive and reflective children. In J. D. Krumbolz (Ed.), *Learning and the educational process*. Chicago: Rand McNally.

Kagan, S. (1989). *Cooperative learning: Resources for teaching*. Laguna Beach, CA: Resources for Teachers.

Kagan, S., Zahn, G. L., Widamin, K. F., Schwartz Wald, J., and Tyrrell, G. (1985). Classroom structural bias: Impact of cooperative and competitive structures on cooperative and competitive individuals and groups. In. R. E. Slavin et al. (Eds.) *Learning to cooperate, cooperating to learn*. New York: Plenam Press.

Kahle, J. B., & Meece, J. L. (1994). Research on girls in science: Lessons and applications. In D. Gabel (Ed.), *Handbook of research in science teaching & learning*. Washington, D.C.: National Science Teachers Association.

Kalaian, H. A., & Freeman, D. J. (1990, April). *Is self-confidence in teaching a multidimensional or unidimensional trait?* Paper presented at the Annual Meeting of the American Educational Research Association, Boston.

Kamann, M.P., & Wond, Y.L. (1993). Inducing adaptive coping self-statements in children with learning disabilities through self-instruction training. *Journal of Learning Disabilities, 26*, 630- 638.

Katz, P., & Zalk, S. R. (1978). Modification of children's racial attitudes. *Developmental Psychology, 14*, 447-461.

Kearsley, G., Hunter, B., & Furlong, M. (1992). *We teach with technology: New visions for education*. Wilsonville, OR: Franklin, Beedle, & Associates.

Keith, T. Z. (1982). Time spent on homework and high school grades. A large-sample path analysis. *Journal of Education Psychology, 74*, 248–253.

Keller, A., Ford, L., & Meacham, J. A. (1978). Dimensions of self-concept in preschool children. *Developmental Psychology, 14*, 483–489.

Keller, J. M. (1983). Motivational design of instruction. In C. M. Reigeluth (Ed.), *Instructional-design theories and models: An overview of their current status*. Hillsdale, NJ: Erlbaum.

__(1984). The use of the ARCS model of motivation in teacher training. In K. Shaw (Ed.), *Aspects of educational technology: XVII. Staff development and career updating*. New York: Nichols.

__(1987a, October). Strategies for stimulating motivation to learn. *Performance and Instruction Journal*, 1–7.

__(1987b, November/December). The systematic process of motivational design. *Performance and Instruction Journal*, 1–8.

Kelly, D.M. (1996). Dilemmas of difference: Van Tech's schools-within-a-school model.

Kelly, I.W. (1980). Piaget on the child's understanding of the necessity of logical laws. *Canadian Journal of Behavioral Science, 12*, 104-109.

Kelman, H. C. (1958). Compliance, identification, and internalization: The processes of opinion change. *Journal of Conflict Resolution, 2*, 51–60.

__(1961). Processes of attitude change. *Public Opinion Quarterly, 25*, 57-78.

Kennedy, M., Jung, R., & Orland, M. (1986). *Poverty, achievement, and the distribution of compensatory education services*. Washington, D.C.: U.S. Department of Education.

Kenny, R. (1992). Can educational technologies help change public school education? *Canadian Journal of Educational Communication, 21*, 95-107.

Kesner, R. P. (1991). Neurobiological views of memory. In J.L. Martinez, Jr. & R. P. Kesner (Eds.), *Learning and memory: A biological view* (2nd ed.). San Diego: Academic Press.

King, A. (1990). Enhancing peer interaction and learning in the classroom through reciprocal questioning. *American Educational Research Journal, 27*, 664–687.

Kirshnit, C. E., Richards, M. H., & Ham, M. (1988, August). *Athletic participation and body image during early adolescence*. Paper presented at the 96th Annual Convention of the American Psychological Association, Atlanta, GA.

Klauer, K. J. (1984). Intentional and incidental learning with instructional texts: A meta-analysis for 1970-1980. *American Educational Research Journal, 21,* 323–340.

Kloss, R. J. (1993). Stay in touch, won't you?: Using the one minute paper. *College Teaching, 41* (2), 60–63.

Kneedler, P. (1985). California assesses critical thinking. In A. Costa (Ed.), *Developing minds: A resource book for teaching thinking.* Alexandria, VA: Association for Supervision and Curriculum Development.

Knight, R. S., Duke, C. R., & Palcic, R. (1988). *A statistical profile of secondary education teachers at Utah State University at the completion of their teacher education program.* Logan: Utah State University (ERIC Document Reproduction Service No. ED 292 773).

Knowles, R. T., & McLean, G. F. (Eds.). (1992). *Psychological foundations of moral education and character development: An integrated theory of moral development* (2nd ed.). Washington, D.C.: The Council for Research in Values and Philosophy.

Koenig, D. (1987). Cognitive styles of Indian, Metis, Inuit and non-Native of Northern Canada and Alaska and implications for education. Unpublished doctoral dissertation, University of Saskatchewan.

Koffler, S. L. (1987). Assessing the impact of a state's decision to move from minimum competency testing toward higher level testing for graduation. *Educational Evaluation and Policy Analysis, 9,* 325–336.

Kohlberg, L. (1969). Stage and sequence: The cognitive-developmental approach to socialization. In D. A. Goslin (Ed.), *Handbook of socialization theory and research.* Chicago: Rand McNally.

__(1971). From is to ought: How to commit the naturalistic fallacy and get away with it in the study of moral development (pp. 151–235). In T. Mischel (Ed.), *Cognitive psychology and epistemologies.* New York: Academic Press.

__(1978). Revisions in the theory and practice of moral development. *Moral Development: New Directions for Child Development, 10* (2), 83–88.

Kohn, A. (1993). Rewards vs. learning: A response to Paul Chance. *Phi Delta Kappan, 74,* 783–787.

Kohn, A. (1996). *Beyond discipline: From Compliance to Community.* Alexandria, VA: ASCD.

Kounin, J. (1970). *Discipline and group management in classrooms.* New York: Holt, Rinehart & Winston.

Kourilsky, M., & Wittrock, M. C. (1992). Generative teaching: An enhancement strategy for the learning of economics in cooperative groups. *American Educational Research Journal, 29* (4), 861–876.

Krathwohl, D. R. (1993). *Methods of educational and social science research: An integrated approach.* New York: Longman.

Krathwohl, D. R., Bloom, B. S., and Masia, B. B. (1964). *Taxonomy of educational objectives, Handbook II: Affective domain.* New York: McKay.

Krebs, D.L., & Van Hesteren, F. (1994). The development of altruism: Toward an integrative model. *Developmental Review, 14,* 103-158.

Krechevsky, M. (1991). Project Spectrum: An innovative assessment alternative. *Educational Leadership, 48* (5), 43–48.

Kubiszyn, T., & Borich, G. D. (1987). *Educational testing and measurement.* Glenview, IL: Scott, Foresman.

__(1993). *Educational testing and measurement: Classroom application and practice* (4th ed.). New York: Harper-Collins.

Kukla, A. (1972). Foundations of an attributional theory of performance. *Psychological Review, 79,* 454–470.

Kulhavy, R. W. (1977). Feedback in written instruction. *Review of Educational Research, 47,* 211–232.

Kulhavy, R. W., & Stock, W. A. (1989). Feedback in written instruction: The place of response certitude. *Educational Psychology Review, 1,* 279–308.

Kulhavy, R. W., Schwartz, N. H., & Peterson, S. (1986). Working memory: The encoding process. In G. D. Phye & T. Andre (Eds.), *Cognitive classroom learning.* New York: Academic Press.

Kurtz, L. (1995). Coping processes and behavioral outcomes in children of divorce. *Canadian Journal of School Psychology, 11,* 52-64.

Kurtz, L., & Derenensky, J. (1993). The effects of divorce on perceived self-efficacy and behavioral control in elementary school children. *Journal of Divorce and Remarriage, 20,* 75-94.

Kutnick, P., & Thomas, M. (1990). Dyadic pairings for the enhancement of cognitive development in the school curriculum: Some preliminary results on science tasks. *British Educational Research Journal, 16* (4), 399–406.

LaBerge, D., & Samuels, S. J. (1974). Toward a theory of automatic information processing in reading. *Cognitive Psychology, 6,* 293–323.

Lakoff, G., & Johnson, M. (1980). *Metaphors we live by.* Chicago: University of Chicago Press.

Lamme, L. L., & Hysmith, C. (1991, December). One school's adventure into portfolio assessment. *Language Arts,* p. 632.

Lan, K.S.K. (1993). The Chinese in Calgary: Schooling for cultural identity. In J.W. Friesen.

Landman, G. B. (1987). An evaluation of the effects of being regarded as "unmotivated": Developmental and behavioral disorders; *Clinical Pediatrics* (Special issue), *26* (5), 271–274.

Landry, R. (1987). Reading comprehension in first and second languages of immersion and Francophone students. *Canadian Journal of Exceptional Children, 3,* 103–108.

Langlois, J. H., & Downs, A. C. (1980). Mothers, fathers, and peers as socialization agents of sex-typed play behaviors in young children. *Child Development, 51,* 1237–1247.

Lashley, T. J. (1994). Teacher technicians: A "new" metaphor for new teachers. *Action in Teacher Education, 16* (1), 11–19.

Lave, J. (1988). *Cognition in practice: Mind, mathematics and culture in everyday life.* New York: Cambridge University Press.

Lebow, D. (1993). Constructivist values for instructional systems design: Five principles toward a new mindset. *Educational Technology Research and Development, 41* (3), 4–16.

Leder, G. C. (1987). Student achievement: A factor in classroom dynamics? *Exceptional Child, 34* (2), 133-141.

LeFrancois, G. R. (1991). *Psychology for teaching* (7th ed.). Belmont, CA: Wadsworth.

Lefton, L. A. (1991). *Psychology* (4th ed.). Needham Heights, MA: Allyn & Bacon.

Leinhardt, G. (1992, April). What research on learning tells us about teaching. *Educational Leadership,* 20–25.

Leinhardt, G., & Greeno, J. G. (1986). The cognitive skill of teaching. *Journal of Educational Psychology, 78,* 75–95.

Lemke, J. L. (1988). Genres, semantics, and classroom teaching. *Linguistics and Education, 1* (1), 81–99.

Lenneberg, E. H. (1967). *Biological foundations of language.* New York: John Wiley.

Leont'ev, A.N. (1978). The development of writing in the child. In M. Cole (Ed.), *The selected writings of A. R. Luria.* White Plains, NY: Sharpe. (Originally published 1929).

___(1981). *Language and cognition.* Washington, D.C.: Winston.

Lepper, M. R., Greene, D., & Nisbett, R. E. (1973). Undermining children's intrinsic interest with extrinsic rewards: A test of the overjustification hypothesis. *Journal of Personality and Social Psychology, 28,* 129–137.

Lerner, R. M., & Schroeder, C. (1971). Physique identification, preference, and aversion in kindergarten children. *Developmental Psychology, 5,* 538.

Lesser, G. S. (1974). *Children and television.* New York: Random House.

Levin, B. (1995). Educational responses to poverty. *Canadian Journal of Education, 20(2),* 211-218.

Levin, H. M. (1993). Editor's introduction. *Review of Educational Research, 63* (3), 245–247.

Levin, J. R. (1985). Educational applications of mnemonic pictures: Possibilities beyond your wildest imagination. In A. A. Sheikh (Ed.), *Imagery in the educational process.* Farmingdale, NY: Baywood.

Levin, J. R., Dretzke, B. J., McCormick, C. B., Scruggs, T. E., McGivern, S., & Mastropieri, M. (1983). Learning via mnemonic pictures: Analysis of the presidential process. *Educational Communication and Technology Journal, 31,* 161–173.

Levy, David A.(1997) *Tools of Critical Thinking: Metathoughts for Psychology.* Toronto: Allyn and Bacon.

Lewis, A. B. (1989). Training students to represent arithmetic word problems. *Journal of Educational Psychology, 81,* 521–531.

Lewis, J., & Samuda, R.J. (1989). Non-discriminatory assessment of culturally different students. *The McGill Journal of Education, 24,* 253-266.

Lewis, R. B. (1993). *Special Education Technology: Classroom Applications.* Pacific Grove, CA: Brooks/Cole.

Li, A.K.F. (1994). Equity in assessment: From the perspectives of new immigrant students. *Canadian Journal of School Psychology, 10,* 131-137.

Lickona, T. (1987). Character development in the elementary school classroom. In K. Ryan & G. F. McLean (Eds.), *Character development in schools and beyond.* New York: Praeger.

Lickona, T. (Ed.). (1976). *Moral development and behavior: Theory, research and social issues.* New York: Holt, Rinehart & Winston.

Lindsay, P. H., & Norman, D. A. (1977). *Human information processing: An introduction to psychology* (2nd ed.). New York: Academic Press.

Linn, M. (1991). Gender differences in educational achievement (pp. 11–50). In *Proceedings of the 1991 ETS Invitational Conference: Sex equity in educational opportunity, achievement, and testing .* Princeton, NJ: Educational Testing Service.

Little, A. (1987). Attributions in a cross-cultural context. *Genetic, Social, and General Psychology Monographs, 113* (1), 61–79.

Livingston, C., & Borko, H. (1989, July-August). Expert-novice differences in teaching: A cognitive analysis and implications for teacher education. *Journal of Teacher Education,* 36–42.

Lochman, J.E., Lampron, LB., Gemmer, T.C., & Harris, S.R. (1987). Anger coping intervention with aggressive children: A guide to implementation in school settings. In P.A. Keller & S.R. Heyman (Eds.), *Innovations in Clinical Practice: A Source Book* (Vol. 6, pp. 339-356). Sarasota, F.L.: Professional Resource Exchange.

Locke, E. A., Shaw, K. N., Saari, L. M., & Latham, G. P. (1981). Goal setting and task performance: 1969-1980. *Psychology Bulletin, 90,* 125–152.

Lockwood, A. (1978). The effects of value clarification and moral development curriculum on school age subjects: A critical review of recent research. *Review of Educational Research, 48,* 325-364.

Lopez, J. (1994). Personal communication.

Lyman, H.B. (1998). *Test Scores and What They Mean* (6th ed). Boston: Allyn & Bacon.

Lytton, H., & Romney, D. M. (1991). Parents' sex-related differential socialization of boys and girls: A meta-analysis. *Psychological Bulletin, 109,* 267-296.

MacDonald, I.M. (1997). Violence in schools: Multiple realities. *The Alberta Journal of Educational Research, XLIII(2/3),* 142-156.

Macionis, J. J. (1994). *Sociology* (4th ed.). Englewood Cliffs, NJ: Prentice Hall.

MacKenzie, A. A. & White, R. T. (1982). Fieldwork in geography and long-term memory. *American Educational Research Journal, 19,* 623–632.

Maclean's (1994). Lessons of Vancouver. Toronto: Maclean Hunter.

Madden, N. A., Slavin, R. E., Karweit, N. L., Dolan, L. J., & Wasik, B. A. (1993). Success for all: Longitudinal effects of a restructuring program for inner-city elementary schools. *American Educational Research Journal, 30,* 123–148.

Madsen, C. H., & Madsen, C. K. (1981). *Teaching/discipline: A positive approach for educational development.* Raleigh, NC: Contemporary Publishing.

Maehr, M. L., & Anderman, E. M. (1993). Reinventing schools for early adolescents: Emphasizing task goals. *The Elementary School Journal, 93,* 593–610.

Magee, L. J., & Price, K. R. (1992). Propel: Visual arts in Pittsburgh. *School Arts Magazine, 91,* (8), 42–45.

Mager, R. (1962). *Preparing instructional objectives* (2nd ed.). Palo Alto, CA: Fearon.

Maguire, T.O. (1991). Evaluation of classroom instruction. In R.H. Short, L.L. Stewin, & S.J.H. McCann.

Male, M. (1997). *Technology for inclusion: Meeting the special needs of all students.* Boston: Allyn & Bacon.

Malicky, G. V., Juliebo, M. F., Norman, C. A., & Pool, J. (1997). Scaffolding of metacognition in intervention lessons. *The Alberta Journal of Educational Research, XLIII (2/3),* 114-126.

Malkus, U., Feldman, D. H., & Gardner, H. (1988). Dimensions of mind in early childhood. In A. D. Pellegrini (Ed.), *Psychological bases of early childhood.* New York: Wiley.

Mandeville, G. K., & Rivers, J. L. (1991). The South Carolina PET study: Teachers' perceptions and student achievement. *Elementary School Journal, 91,* 377–407.

Mansbach, S. C. (1993, February/March). We must put family literacy on the national agenda. *Reading Today,* 37.

Maquire, M.H., & McAlpine, L. (1996). Attautsikut/together: Understanding cultural frames of reference. *The Alberta Journal of Educational Research, XLII(3),* 218-237.

Marcia, J. E. (1967). Ego identity status: Relationship to change in self-esteem, "general adjustment," and authoritarianism *Journal of Personality, 35* (1), 119–133.

__(1980). Ego identity development. In J. Adelson (Ed.), *The handbook of adolescent psychology.* New York: Wiley.

Marsh, H. W. (1984). Relations among dimensions of self-attributions, dimensions of self-concept and academic achievement. *Journal of Educational Psychology, 76,* 1291–1308.

Marsh, H. W., Craven, R. G., & Debus, R. (1991). Self-concepts of young children 5 to 8 years of age: Measurement and multidimensional structure. *Journal of Educational Psychology, 83,* 377–392.

Marsh, H. W., Smith, I. D., & Barnes, J. (1985). Multi-dimensional self-concepts: Relations with sex and academic achievement. *Journal of Educational Psychology, 77,* 581–596.

Marshall, H. H. (1989). The development of self-concept. *Young Children, 44* (5), 44–51.

__(1990). Beyond the workplace metaphor: Toward conceptualizing the classroom as a learning setting. *Theory into Practice, 29* (2), 94–101.

__(Ed.). (1992). *Redefining student learning: Roots of educational change.* Norwood, NJ: Ablex.

Marshall, P. M. (1982). *Homework and social facilitation theory in teaching elementary school mathematics.* Unpublished doctoral dissertation, Stanford University, Stanford, CA.

Martin, G., & Pear, J. (1992). *Behavior modification: What it is and how to do it* (4th ed.). Englewood Cliffs, NJ: Prentice Hall.

Marzano, R. J., Pickering, D., & McTighe, J. (1993). *Assessing student outcomes: Performance assessment using the dimensions of learning model.* Alexandria, VA: Association for Supervision and Curriculum Development.

Maslow, A. H. (1943). A theory of human motivation. *Psychological Review, 50,* 370–396.

__(1954). *Motivation and personality.* New York: Harper & Row.

Massey, D. (1988). Cross-cultural psychology assessment. *Canadian Journal of School Psychology, 4,* 21-37.

Mayer, R. E. (1979). Can advance organizers influence meaningful learning? *Review of Educational Research, 49,* 371–383.

McCaslin, M., & Good, T. (1992, April). Compliant cognition: The misalliance of management and instructional goals in current school reform. *Educational Researcher,* 4-17.

McClelland, D. C. (1958). Risk taking in children with high and low need for achievement. In J. W. Atkinson (Ed.), *Motives in fantasy, action, and society.* Princeton, NJ: Van Nostrand.

McClelland, D. C., & Pilon, D. (1983). Sources of adult motives in patterns of parent behavior in early childhood. *Journal of Personality and Social Psychology, 44,* 564–574.

__(1965). Toward a theory of motive acquisition. *American Psychologist, 20,* 321–333.

McClelland, J. L. (1988). Connectionist models and psychological evidence. *Journal of Memory and Language, 27,* 107–123.
McClelland, J. L., Rumelhart, D. E., & the PDP Research Group. (1986). *Parallel distributed processing: Explorations in the microstructure of cognition* (Vol. II). Cambridge, MA: Bradford Books.

McCombs, B. L., & Marzano, R. J. (1990). Putting the self in self-regulated learning: The self as agent in integrating will and skill. *Educational Psychologist, 25,* 51–70.

McCombs, B.L. (1984). Processes and skills underlying continuing intrinsic motivation to learn: Toward a definition of motivational skills training interventions. *Educational Psychologist, 19,* 199–218.

__(1988). Motivational skills training: Combining metacognitive, cognitive, and affective learning strategies. In C. E. Weinstein, E. T. Goetz, & P. A. Alexander (Eds.), *Learning and study strategies: Issues in assessment, instruction, and evaluation.* New York: Academic Press.

McCormick, C. B., & Levin, J. R. (1987). Mnemonic prose-learning strategies. In M. Pressely & M. McDaniel (Eds.), *Imaginary and related mnemonic processes.* New York: Springer-Verlag.

McCown, R. R., Casile, W. J., & Brookhart, S. M. (1994). *Continuous progress instruction: Evaluation report.* Pittsburgh, PA: Fox Chapel Area School District.

McCutcheon, G. (1980). How do elementary school teachers plan? The nature of planning and influences on it. *The Elementary School Journal, 81* (1), 4–23.

McDaniel, E. A., & McCarthy, H. D. (1989). Enhancing teacher efficacy in special education. *Teaching Exceptional Children, 21* (4), 34-38.

McKeachie, W. J. (1986). *Teaching tips: A guide book for the beginning college teacher.* Lexington, MA: D. C. Heath.

McLaughlin, B. (1984). Second language acquisition in childhood: Vol. 1. Preschool children (2d ed.) Hillsdale, NJ. Erlbaum.

McLaughlin, H. J. (1994). From negation to negotiation: Moving away from the management metaphor. *Action in Teacher Education, 16* (1), 75–84.

McLaughlin, M. W., & Talbert, J. E. (1993). Introduction: New visions of teaching. In D. K. Cohen, M. W. McLaughlin, & J. E. Talbert (Eds.), *Teaching for understanding: Challenges for policy and practice.* San Francisco: Jossey-Bass.

McLean, L.D. (1988). Achievement measures made relevant to pedagogy. *McGill Journal of Education, 23,* 243-252.

___(1990). Time to replace the classroom test with authentic measurement. *The Alberta Journal of Educational Research, 36,* 78-84.

McLean, L.D. (1988). Achievement measures made relevant to pedagogy. *McGill Journal of Education, 23,* 243-252.

McLean, R. (1997). Selected attitudinal factors related to students' success in high school. *The Alberta Journal of Educational Research, XLIII (2/3),* 165-168.

McLeish, J. (1976). The lecture method. In N. L. Gage (Ed.), *The psychology of teaching methods: Seventy-fifth yearbook of the National Society for the Study of Education.* Chicago, IL: University of Chicago Press.

McLellan, H. (1993, March). Situated learning in focus: Introduction to special issue. *Educational Technology, 33,* 5–9.

Meichenbaum, D. (1977). *Cognitive behavior modification: An integrative approach.* New York: Plenum.

___(1985). *Stress inoculation training.* New York: Pergamon.

Meyer, R. G., & Salmon, P. (1988). *Abnormal psychology* (2nd ed.). Needham Heights, MA: Allyn & Bacon.

Meyers, J., Gelzheiser, L., Yelich, G., & Gallagher, M. (1990). Classroom, remedial and resource teachers' views of pull-out programs. *Elementary School Journal, 90* (5), 531–545.

Miller, A.G. (1973). Integration and acculturation of cooperative behavior among Blackfoot Indian and non-Indian Canadian children. *Journal of Cross-Cultural Psychology, 4,* 374-380.

Miller, A.G., & Thomas, R. (1972). Cooperation and competition among Blackfoot Indian and White Canadian children. *Child Development 43,* 1104.

Miller, G. A. (1956). The magical number seven, plus or minus two: Some limits on our capacity for processing information. *Psychological Review, 63,* 81–97.

Millsap, M., Turnbull, B. J., Moss, M., Brigham, N., Gamse, B., & Marks, E. M. (1992). *The Chapter 1 implementation study: Interim study.* Washington, D.C.: U.S. Department of Education.

Mira, M. P., & Tyler, J. S. (1991). Students with traumatic brain injury: Making the transition from hospital to school. *Focus on Exceptional Children, 23* (5), 1–12.

Mitchell, T. (1990). Project 2000 gateway to success for some black males. *Black Issues in Higher Education, 7* (18), 49–50.

Moallem, M., & Driscoll, M. P. (1994, April). *An experienced teacher's model of thinking and teaching.* Paper presented at the Annual Meeting of the American Educational Research Association, New Orleans, LA.

Moll, L. C., Tapia, J., & Whitmore, K. F. (1993). Living knowledge: The social distribution of cultural resources for thinking. In G. Salomon (Ed.), *Distributed cognitions: Psychological and educational considerations.* Cambridge: Cambridge University Press.

Monson, M. P., & Monson, R. J. (1993). Exploring alternatives in student assessment: Shifting the focus to student learning in the middle school. *Middle School Journal, 25* (2), 46–50.

More, J. (1987). *Native Indian learning styles: A review for researchers.* Paper presented at the Meeting Their Needs Conference, Winnipeg, Manitoba, and World Conference of Indigenous Peoples' Education, Vancouver, British Columbia.

Morgan, M. (1984). Reward-induced decrements and increments in intrinsic motivation. *Review of Educational Research, 54,* 5–30.

Morris, C. & LeBlanc, R. (1996). Multiple intelligences: Profiling dominant intelligences of grade eight students. *McGill Journal of Education, 31 (2),* 119.

Moskal, R. (1994). Sexual abuse myths held by student teachers. *Canadian Journal of School Psychology, 10,* 43-53.

Motta, R.W. (1995). Childhood posttraumatic stress disorder and the schools. *Canadian Journal of School Psychology, 11,* 65-78.

Mueller, H., Mulcahy, R., Wilgosh, L., Watters, B., & Mancini, G. (1986). An analysis of WISC-R item response with Canadian children. *Alberta Journal of Education Research, 32,* 12-36.

Mulcahy, R. (1991). Developing autonomous learners. *Alberta Journal of Educational Research, 37(4),* 385-97.

Mulcahy, R., Marfo, K., Peat, D., & Andrews, J. (1986). *A strategies program for effective learning and thinking.* Alberta: University of Alberta.

Munby, H. (1987). Metaphor and teachers' knowledge. *Research in the Teaching of English, 21,* 377–397.

Murdoch, J. (1988). Cree cognition in natural and educational contexts. In J. Berry, S. Irvine, & E. Hunt (Eds.), Indigenous cognition: *Functioning in cultural context* (pp. 231-256). Boston: Martinus Nijhoff Publishers.

Murphy, J. M., Jellinek, M., Quinn, D., Smith, G., Poitrast, F. G., and Goshko, M. (1991). Substance abuse and serious child mistreatment: Prevalence, risk, and outcome in a court sample. *Child Abuse and Neglect, 15,* 197–211.

Myles, D.W., & Ratslaff, H.C. (1988). Teachers' bias towards visible ethnic minority groups in special education referrals. *B.C. Journal of Special Education, 12.*

Naglieri, J.A. & Das, J.P .(1997). *Das-Naglieri Cognitive Assessment System.* Itasca, ILL. Houghton Mifflin.

Natriello, G. (1987). The impact of evaluation processes on students. *Educational Psychologist, 22*, 155–175.

Newman, D., Griffin, P., & Cole, M. (1989). *The construction zone: Working for cognitive change in school.* New York: Cambridge University Press.

Newman, P. (1982). The peer group. In B. Wolman (Ed.), *Handbook of developmental psychology.* Englewood Cliffs, NJ: Prentice Hall.

Nielsen, J.Q. (1997). Increasing awareness of learning disabilities. *The Alberta Journal of Educational Research, XLIII(2/3),* 169-172

Nitko, A. J. (1983). *Educational tests and measurement: An introduction.* New York: Harcourt Brace Jovanovich.

Nock, D.A., & Nelson, R.W. (1993). Schooling and inequality. In P.S. Li & B.S. Bolaria (Eds.), *Contemporary sociology: Critical perspectives.* Toronto: Copp Clark Pitman.

Norman, D. A. (1968). Toward a theory of memory and attention. *Psychological Review, 75,* 522–536.

__(1983). Some observations on mental models. In D. Gentner & A.L. Stevens (Eds.), *Mental models.* Hillsdale, NJ: Erlbaum.

Norris, M.J. (1990). The demography of aboriginal people in Canada. In S.S. Halli, F. Trovato, & L. Driedger (Eds.) Ethnic Demography: *Canadian immigrant, racial and cultural variations.* Don Mills, Ont: Oxford University Press, 33-59.

Norris, S.P. (1995). Format effects on critical thinking test performance. *The Alberta Journal of Educational Research. XLI(4),* 378-406.

Nye, R. D. (1979). *What is B. F. Skinner really saying?* Englewood Cliffs, NJ: Prentice Hall.

Nyiti, R.M. (1982). The validity of cultural differences explanations for cross-cultural variation in the rate of Piagetian cognitive development. In D.A. Wagner & H.W. Stevenson, (Eds.), *Cultural perspectives on child development.* San Francisco, CA:Freeman.

Nystul, M. S. (1984). Positive parenting leads to self-actualizing children. *Individual Psychology Journal of Adlerian Theory, Research and Practice, 40,* 177–183.

O'Brien, M., & Huston, A. C. (1985). Development and sex-typed play behavior in toddlers. *Developmental Psychology, 21* (5), 866–871.

O'Loughlin, M. (1992). Rethinking science education: Beyond Piagetian constructivism toward a sociocultural model of teaching and learning. *Journal of Research in Science Teaching, 29,* 791–820.

O'Neil, J. (1991). Drive for national standards picking up steam. *Educational Leadership, 48* (5), 4–8.

__(1993). Can national standards make a difference? *Educational Leadership, 50* (5), 4–8.

Obiakor, F.E., & Algozzine, B. (1994). Self-concept of young children with special needs: Perspectives for school and clinic. *Canadian Journal of School Psychology, 10,* 123-130.

Oderkirk, J. (1993). Disabilities among children. *Canadian Social Trends,* 22-25.

Office of Educational Research and Improvement. (1990). *Grant announcement: National educational research and development center program.* Washington, D.C.: U.S. Department of Education.

Offord, D.R., Boyle, M.H., & Racine, Y. (1989). Ontario Child Health Study: Correlates of the disorder. *Journal of the American and Adolescent Psychiatry, 28,* 856-860.

Okagaki, L., & Sternberg, R. J. (1991). Cultural and parental influences on cognitive development. In L. Okagaki & R. J. Sternberg (Eds.), *Directors of development: Influences on the development of children's thinking.* Hillsdale, NJ: Erlbaum.

Okagaki, L., Sternberg, R. J., & Divecha, D. J. (1990, April). *Parental beliefs and children's early school performance.* Paper presented at the annual meeting of the American Educational Research Association, Boston.

Olweus, D. (1993). *Bullying at school – what we know and what we can do.* Oxford: Blackwell.

Ormrod, J. E. (1990). *Human learning: Theories, principles, and educational applications.* New York: Macmillan.

Oser, F. K. (1994). Moral perspectives on teaching. In L. Darling-Hammond (Ed.), *Review of Research in Education* (volume 20). Washington, D.C.: American Educational Research Association.

Paivio, A. (1971). *Imagery and verbal processes.* New York: Holt, Rinehart & Winston.

__(1975). Coding distinctions and repetition effects in memory. In G. H. Bower (Ed.), *The psychology of learning and motivation* (Vol. 9). New York: Academic Press.

__(1978). Dual coding: Theoretical issues and empirical evidence. In J. M. Scandura & C. J. Brainard (Eds.), *Structural/process models of complex human behavior.* Leyden, The Netherlands: Sijthoff & Nordhoff.

Palincsar, A. S. (1986). The role of dialogue in providing scaffolded instruction. *Educational Psychologist* (Special Issue on learning strategies), *21,* 73–98.

__(1987, April). *Reciprocal teaching: Field observations in remedial and content-area reading.* Paper presented at the annual meeting of the American Educational Research Association, Washington, D.C.

Palincsar, A. S., & Brown, A. L. (1984). Reciprocal teaching of comprehension-fostering and monitoring strategies. *Cognition and Instruction, 1,* 117–175.

Papalia, D. E., & Olds, S. W. (1992). *Human development* (5th ed.). New York: McGraw-Hill.

Papert, S. (1993). *The children's machine: Rethinking school in the age of the computer.* New York: Basic Books.

Parten, M. B. (1932). Social participation among preschool children. *Journal of Abnormal and Social Psychology, 27,* 243–269.

Pate, P. E., Homestead, E., & McGinnis, K. (1993). Designing rubrics for authentic assessment. *Middle School Journal, 25*(2), 25–27.

Pauls, S. (1996). Racism and native schooling: A historical perspective. In M.I. Alladin (Ed.), *Racism in Canadian schools* (pp. 22- 37). Toronto: Harcourt Brace Canada.

Pelech, F. (Ed.). (1988). Proceedings of the tenth conference of the northern Alberta heritage languages association. Edmonton: Alberta Cultural Heritage Foundation.

Pelletier, L. G., & Vallerand, R. J. (1989). Behavioral confirmation in social interaction: Effects of teachers' expectancies on students' intrinsic motivation. *Canadian Psychology, 30* (2a), 404.

Penner, J. (1984). *Why many college teachers cannot lecture.* Springfield, IL: Charles C. Thomas.

Pepitone, E. A. (1985) Children in cooperation and competitions: Antecedents and consequences of self-orientation. In R. E. Slavin et al (Eds.) *Learning to cooperate, cooperating to learn.* New York: Plenum Press.

Perkins, D. N. (1993). Teaching for understanding. *American Educator: The Professional Journal of the American Federation of Teachers, 17* (3) 8, 28–35.

Peters, E. E., & Levin, J. R. (1986). Effects of a mnemonic imagery strategy on good and poor reader's prose recall. *Reading Research Quarterly, 21,* 179–192.

Peters, R. (1977, August 19–26). *The place of Kohlberg's theory in moral education.* Paper presented at the First International Conference on Moral Development and Moral Education, Leicester, England.

Peterson, L. R., & Peterson, M. J. (1959). Short-term retention of individual verbal items. *Journal of Experimental Psychology, 58,* 193–198.

Peterson, P. L., & Comeaux, M. A. (1987). Teachers' schemata for classroom events: The mental scaffolding of teachers' thinking during classroom instruction. *Teaching and Teacher Education, 3,* 319–331.

Pettifor, J. (1997). Ethics: Virtue and politics in the service and practice of psychology. *Canadian Psychology, 37,* 1-9.

Phillips, D., Schwean, V.L., and Saklofske, D.H. (1997). Treatment effect of a school-based cognitive-behavioural program for aggressive children. *Canadian Journal of School Psychology, 13(1),* 60-67.

Phye, G. D., & Andre, T. (Eds.). (1986). *Cognitive classroom learning.* Orlando, FL: Academic Press.

Piaget, J. (1932/1948). *The moral judgment of the child* (M. Cabain, Trans.). Glencoe, IL: Free Press.

__(1952). *The origins of intelligence in children* (M. Cook, Trans.). New York: International Universities Press.

__(1965). *The moral judgment of the child.* New York: Free Press. (Original work published 1932.)

__(1969). *Science of education and the psychology of the child.* New York: Viking.

__(1970). *Genetic epistemology.* New York: Columbia University Press.

Piaget, J., & Inhelder, B. (1969). *The psychology of the child.* New York: Basic Books.

Pinnell, G. S. (1989). Reading recovery: Helping at-risk children to read. *Elementary School Journal, 90,* 161–182.

Piper, D. (1993). Students in the mainstream who face linguistic and cultural challenges. In J. Andrews & J. Lupart (Eds.), *The inclusive classroom: Educating exceptional children.* Scarborough, ON:Nelson Canada.

Popham, W. J. (1981). *Modern educational measurement.* Englewood Cliffs, NJ: Prentice Hall.

__(1987, May). The merits of measurement-driven instruction. *Phi Delta Kappan, 68,* 679–682.

__(1990). *Modern educational measurement* (2nd ed.). Englewood Cliffs, NJ: Prentice Hall.

__(1993). Educational testing in America: What's right, what's wrong? *Educational Measurement: Issues and Practice, 12* (1), 11–14.

Postman, N., & Weingartner, C. (1969). *Teaching as a subversive activity.* New York: Delacorte Press.

Powell, J. C. (1993). What does it mean to have authentic assessment? *Middle School Journal, 25* (2), 36–42.

Powers, L.E., Sowers, J., Turner, A., Nesbitt, M., Knowles, E., Ellison, R. (1996). TAKE CHARGE: A model for promoting self-determination among adolescents with challenges. In L.E. Powers, G.H.S. Singer, & J. Sowers (Eds.), *On the road to autonomy: Promoting self- competence in children and youth with disabilities* (pp. 275-322). Baltimore, MD: Paul H. Brookes.

Prawatt, R. S. (1989). Promoting access to knowledge strategy and disposition in students. *Review of Educational Research, 59,* 1–41.

(1992). Teacher beliefs about teaching and learning: A constructivist perspective. *American Journal of Education, 100,* 354–395.

Premack, D. (1959). Toward empirical behavior laws: I. Positive reinforcement. *Psychological Review, 66,* 219–233.

__(1965). Reinforcement theory (pp. 123–180). In D. Levine (Ed.), *Nebraska Symposium on Motivation* (Vol. 13). Lincoln: University of Nebraska Press.

Pressley, M., Borkowski, J. G., & O'Sullivan, J. T. (1984). Memory strategy instruction is made of this: Metamemory and durable strategy use. *Educational Psychologist, 9* (2), 94–107.

Price, S., & Hein, G. E. (1994, October). Scoring active assessments. *Science and Children,* 26–29.

Principles for Fair Student Practices for Education in Canada (1993). Edmonton, Alberta: Joint Advisory Committee. (Mailing address: Joint Advisory Committee, Centre for Research in Applied Measurements and Education, 3-104 Education Building North, University of Alberta, Edmonton, AB, T6G 2G5).

Quality Education Data. (1993). *Educational technology trends, public schools, 1992–93.* Denver, CO: Quality Education Data.

Quay, H. C. (1986). Classification. In Quay & J. S. Werry (Eds.), *Psychopathological disorders of childhood* (3d ed.). New York: Wiley.

Quay, H. C., & Peterson, D. R. (1987). *Manual for the Revised Behavior Problem Checklist.* Unpublished manuscript.

Quellmalz, E. S. (1991). Developing criteria for performance assessments: The missing link. *Applied Measurement in Education, 4* (4), 319–331.

Rachlin, H. (1991). *Introduction to modern behaviorism* (3rd ed.). New York: W. H. Freeman.

Ramos-Ford, V., & Gardner, H. (1990). Giftedness from a multiple intelligences perspective. In N. Colangelo & G. Davis (Eds.), *The handbook of gifted education*. Needham Heights, MA: Allyn & Bacon.

Randhawa, B. S. (1994) Self-efficacy in mathematics, attitudes, and achievement of boys and girls from restricted samples in two countries. *Perceptual and Motor Skills, 79,* 1011-1018.

Randhawa, B. S., Beamer, J. E. & Lundberg, I. (1993). Role of mathematics self-efficacy in the structural model of mathematics achievement. *Journal of Educational Psychology, 85,* 41-48.

Randhawa, B.S. (1988). Basic skills and macro- and micro-analysis of maathematics achievement of grade ten students as a function of gender and locale. *British Educational Research Journal, 14,* 141-148.

__(1991). Gender differences in academic achievement: A closer look at mathematics. *The Alberta Journal of Educational Research, 37,* 241-257.

Randhawa, B.S., & Hunt, D. (1987). Sex and rural-urban differences in standardized achievement scores and mathematics subskills. *Canadian Journal of Education, 12,* 137-151.

Randhawa, B.S., & Randhawa, J.S. (1993). Understanding sex differences in the components of mathematics achievement. *Psychological Reports, 73,* 435-444.

Randolph, C. H., & Evertson, C. M. (1994). Images of management for learner-centered classrooms. *Action in Teacher Education, 16* (1), 55–63.

Rathus, S. A. (1988). *Understanding child development*. New York: Holt, Rinehart & Winston.

Reese, H. W. (1977). Imagery and associative memory. In R. V. Kail & J. W. Hagen (Eds.), *Perspectives on the development of memory and cognition*. Hillsdale, NJ: Erlbaum.

Reimer, R. H., Paolitto, D. P., & Hersh, R. H. (1983). *Promoting moral growth: From Piaget to Kohlberg* (2nd ed.). New York: Longman.

Renzulli, J. (1982). Dear Mr. and Mrs. Copernicus: We regret to inform you . . . . *Gifted Child Quarterly, 26,* 11–14.

Renzulli, J. S., & Reis, S. M. (1991). The schoolwide enrichment model: A comprehensive plan for the development of creative productivity. In N. Colangelo & G. Davis (Eds.), *Handbook of gifted education*. Needham Heights, MA: Allyn & Bacon.

Research, XLII(1), 19-33.

Resichauer, E. O. (1981). *The Japanese*. Cambridge, MA: Harvard University Press.

Reynolds, G. S. (1968). *A primer of operant conditioning*. Glenview, IL: Scott, Foresman.

Ribich, F., Barone, W., & Agostino, V. R. (1991, February). *A semantic differential: Perspectives on underachieving gifted students*. Paper presented at the Eastern Educational Research Association, Boston.

Richardson, E. H. (1981). Cultural and historical perspectives in counseling American Indians. In D. W. Sue (Ed.), *Counseling the culturally different*. New York: John Wiley.

Rieber, L. (1991a). Animation, incidental learning, and continuing motivation. *Journal of Educational Psychology, 83,* 318–328.

__(1991b, February). *Computer-based microworlds: A bridge between constructivism and direct instruction*. Paper presented at the Annual Meeting of the Association of Educational Communications and Technology, Orlando, FL.

Robert, L.J. (1995). An epidemiological study of behavior disorders in the Saskatoon Tribal Council student population. M.Ed. thesis. University of Saskatchewan.

Roberts, L.W., & Clifton, R.A. (1988). Inuit attitudes and cooperative learning. *McGill Journal of Education, 23,* 213-230.

Robertson, G., Haines, L., Sanche, R., & Biffart, W. (1997). Positive change through computer networking. *Teaching Exceptional Children, 29,* 22-30.

Robler, M. D., Edwards, J., & Havriluk, M. (1997). *Integrating Educational Technology into Teaching*. Columbus, OH: Merrill, Prentice Hall.

Rogers, W.T. & Bateson, D.J. (1991). The influence of test-wiseness on performance of high school seniors on school leaving examinations. *Applied Measurement in Education, 4(2),* 159-183.

Rogers, W.T. & Wilson, C. (1993). *The Influence of Test-Wiseness upon Performance of High School Students on Alberta Education's Diploma Examinations*. Edmonton AB: University of Alberta, Centre for Research in Applied Measurement and Evaluation.

Rogers, W.T. & Yang, P. (1996). Test-wiseness: Its nature and applications. *European Journal of Psychological Assessment, 12,* 247-259.

Rogoff, B. (1990). *Apprenticeship in thinking*. New York: Oxford University Press.

Rosenberg, M. (1979). *Conceiving the self*. New York: Basic Books.

Rosenkrans, M. A. (1967). Imitation in children as a function of perceived similarity to a social model and vicarious reinforcement. *Journal of Personality and Social Psychology, 7,* 301–315.

Rosenshine, B. V. (1979). Content, time, and direct instruction. In P. Peterson & H. Walberg (Eds.), *Research on teaching: Concepts, findings, and implications*. Berkeley, CA: McCutchan.

__(1980). How time is spent in elementary classrooms. In C. Denham & A. Lieberman (Eds.), *Time to learn*. Washington, D.C.: National Institute of Education.

__(1983). Teaching functions in instructional programs. *Elementary School Journal, 83,* 335–351.

__(1986). Synthesis of research on explicit teaching. *Educational Leadership, 43* (7), 60–69.

Rosenshine, B., & Meister, C. (1991, April). *Reciprocal teaching: A review of nineteen experimental studies*. Paper presented at the Annual Meeting of the American Educational Research Association, Chicago.

Rosenthal, R., & Jacobson, L. (1968). *Pygmalion in the classroom: Teacher expectations and pupils' intellectual development*. New York: Holt, Rinehart & Winston.

Rosenthal, T. L., & Bandura, A. (1978). Psychological modeling: Theory and practice. In S. L. Garfield & A. E. Bergin (Eds.), *Handbook of psychotherapy and behavior change: An empirical analysis* (2nd ed.). New York: Wiley.

Rotter, J. (1954). *Social learning and clinical psychology*. Englewood Cliffs, NJ: Prentice Hall.

Rowe, M. B. (1986). Wait time: Slowing down may be a way of speeding up! *Journal of Teacher Education, 37* (1), 43–50.

Rowland, G. (1994). Designing and evaluating: Creating futures and appreciating error. *Educational Technology, 34* (1), 10–22.

Royer, J. M. (1979). Theories of the transfer of learning. *Educational Psychologist, 14*, 53–69.

Royer, J. M., & Cable, G. W. (1976). Illustrations, analogies, and facilitative transfer in prose learning. *Journal of Educational Psychology, 68*, 205–209.

Royer, J. M., & Feldman, R. S. (1984). *Educational psychology: Applications and theory*. New York: Alfred A. Knopf.

Ruben, K., Maioni, T., & Hornung, M. (1976). Free play behaviors in middle and lower class preschools: Parten and Piaget revisited. *Child Development, 47,* 414–419.

Ruben, K., Watson, K., & Jambor, T. (1978). Free play behaviors in preschool and kindergarten children. *Child Development, 49,* 534–536.

Rubin, L. J. (1985). *Artistry in teaching*. New York: Random House.

Ruble, D. N., Boggiano, A. K., Feldman, N. S., & Loebl, J. H. (1980). Developmental analysis of the role of social comparison in self-evaluation. *Developmental Psychology, 16,* 105–115.

Rumelhart, D. E. (1980). Schemata: The building blocks of cognition. In R. Spiro, B. C. Bruce, & W. F. Brewer (Eds.), *Theoretical issues in reading comprehension*. Hillsdale, NJ: Erlbaum.

Rutter, M. (1980). *Changing youth in a changing society: Patterns of adolescent development and disorder*. Cambridge, MA: Harvard University Press.

Ryan, K., & McLean, G. F. (Eds.). (1987). *Character development in schools and beyond*. New York: Praeger.

Ryder, R. & Hughes, T. (1997). *Internet for Educators*. Columbus, Ohio: Merrill.

Rymer, J.E., & Alladin, I.M. (1996). Strategies for an antiracist education. In M.I. Allidin (Ed.), *Racism in Canadian Schools* (pp. 157-170). Toronto: Harcourt Brace Canada.

Sacks, O. W. (1989). *Seeing voices: A journey into the world of the deaf*. Berkeley: University of California Press.

Sadker, M., Sadker, D., & Klein, S. (1991). The issue of gender in elementary and secondary education. In G. Grant (Ed.), *Review of Research in Education*, Vol. 17. Washington, D.C.: American Educational Research Association.

Saklofske, D.H., & Janzen, H. (1990). School-based assessment research in Canada. *McGill Journal of Education, 25,* 5-23.

__(1991). Testing for diagnostic purposes. In R.H. Short, L.L. Stewin & S.J.H. McCann.

Saklofske, D.H. & Schwean, V. (1992). Influences on testing and test results. In M. Zeidner & R. Most (Eds.), *Psychological testing: An inside view* (pp. 89-119). California: Consulting Psychologists Press.

__(1993). Standardized procedures for measuring the correlates of ADHD in children: A research program. *Canadian Journal of School Psychology, 9*, 28-36.

Salend, S. J. (1994). *Effective mainstreaming: Creating inclusive classrooms* (2nd ed.). New York: Macmillan.

Salomon, G., & Perkins, D. N. (1989). Rocky roads to transfer: Rethinking mechanisms of a neglected phenomenon. *Educational Psychologist, 24* (2), 113–142.

Sanders, D. (1987). Cultural conflicts: An important factor in the academic failures of American Indian students. *Journal of Multicultural Counseling and Development, 15*, 81–90.

Sappington, T. E. (1984). Creating learning environments conducive to change: The role of fear/safety in the adult learning process. *Innovative Higher Education, 9* (1), 19–29.

Sarafino, E. (1984). Intrinsic motivation and delay of gratification in preschoolers: The variables of reward salience and length of expected delay. *British Journal of Developmental Psychology, 2* (2), 149–156.

Sarvela, P. D., & Noonan, J. V. (1988). Testing and computer-based instruction: Psychometric considerations. *Educational Technology, 28* (5), 17–20.

Saskatchewan Education Special Education Policy Manual (1989).

Saskatchewan Education, 1988. *Understanding the Common Essential Learnings: a handbook for teachers.* Regina, SK: Saskatchewan Education.

Sattler, J. (1992). *Assessment of children* (3rd ed., rev.). San Diego: Jerome M. Sattler.

Satzewich, V. (1993). Race and ethnic relations. In P.S. Li & B.S. Bolaria (Eds.), *Contemporary sociology: Critical perspectives.* Toronto: Copp Clark Pitman.

Saxe, G. B. (1990). *Culture and cognitive development: Studies in mathematical understanding*. Hillsdale, NJ: Erlbaum.

Scaldwell, W., Frame, J., & Cookson, D. (1985). Individual assessment of Chippewa, Muncey and Oneida Children using the WISC-R. *Canadian Journal of School Psychology, 1*, 15-21.

Schalock, R.L., Stark, J.A., Snell, M.E., Coulter, D.L., Polloway, E.A., Luckasson, R., Reiss, S., & Spitalnik, D.M. (1994). The changing conception of mental retardation: Implications for the field. *Mental Retardation, 32(3),* 181-193.

Schicke, M.C., & Fagan, T.K. (1994). Contributions of self-concept and intelligence to the prediction of academic achievement among grade 4, 6, and 8 students. *Canadian Journal of School Psychology, 10,* 62-69.

Schoenfeld, A. H. (1988). When good teaching leads to bad results: The disasters of "well-taught" mathematics classes. *Educational Psychologist, 23*, 145–166.

Schommer, M. (1990). Effects of beliefs about the nature of knowledge on comprehension. *Journal of Educational Psychology, 82*, 498–504.

___(1993). Epistemological development and academic performance among secondary school students. *Journal of Educational Psychology, 85,* 406–411.

Schrage, M. (1990). *Shared Minds: The New Technology of Collaboration.* New York: Random House.

Schunk, D. H. (1983). Developing children's self-efficacy and skills: The roles of social comparative information and goal setting. *Contemporary Educational Psychology, 8,* 76–86.

___(1987). Peer models and children's behavioral change. *Review of Educational Research, 57,* 149–174.

___(1991). *Learning theories: An educational perspective.* New York: Macmillan.

Schunk, D. H., & Gaa, J. P. (1981). Goal-setting influence on learning and self-evaluation. *Journal of Classroom Interaction, 16* (2), 38–44.

Schunk, D. H., & Zimmerman, B. J. (Eds.) (1994). *Self-regulation of learning and performance: Issues and educational applications.* Hillsdale, NJ: Erlbaum.

Schunk, D. H., Hanson, A. R., & Cox, P. D. (1987). Peer-model attributes and children's achievement behaviors. *Journal of Educational Psychology, 79,* 54–61.

Schwean V.L., & Saklofske, D.H. (1998). WISC-III assessment of children with attention deficit/hyperactivity disorder. In A. Prifitera & D.H. Saklofske (Eds). *WISC-III Clinical Use and Interpretation.* San Diego: Academic Press.

Schwean, V., & Greenough-Olson, S. (1992). Northern Lights School Division: Master plan for the identification and assessment of exceptional students. Unpublished manuscript: University of Saskatoon.

Schwean, V., & Saklofske, D.H. (1994). An epidemiological study of exceptionalities in children of the Saskatoon Tribal Council. Unpublished manuscript, Saskatoon Tribal Council.

Schwean, V., Parkinson, M., Francis, G., & Lee, F. (1993). Educating the ADHD child: Debunking the myths. *Canadian Journal of School Psychology, 9,* 37-52.

Schwebel, A. I., & Cherlin, D. L. (1972). Physical and social distancing in teacher-pupil relationships. *Journal of Educational Psychology, 63,* 543–550.

Schwier, R., & Misanchuk, E. (1993). *Interactive Multimedia Instruction.* Englewood Cliffs, N. J.: Educational Technology Publications.

Scott, K. P., Dwyer, C. A., & Lieb-Brilhart, B. (1985). Sex equity in reading and communication. In S. S. Klein (Ed.), *Handbook for achieving sex equity through education.* Baltimore, MD: Johns Hopkins University Press.

Seifert, K. L., & Hoffnung, R. J. (1987). *Child and adolescent development.* Boston: Houghton Mifflin.

Seligman, M. E. P. (1975). *Helplessness: On depression, development, and death.* San Francisco: W. H. Freeman.

Seligman, M. E. P., & Meier, S. F. (1967). Failure to escape traumatic shock. *Journal of Experimental Psychology, 74,* 1–9.

Semb, G. B., & Ellis, J. A. (1994). Knowledge taught in school: What is remembered? *Review of Educational Research, 64,* 253–286.

Seyfort, B., Spreen, O., & Lahmer, V. (1980). A critical look at the WISC-R with Native Indian children. *Alberta Journal of Educational Research, 26,* 14-24.

Shank, G. (1995). Personal communication.

Sharan, S. (1985). Cooperative learning and the multiethnic classroom (pp. 255–276). In R. Slavin, S. Sharan, S. Kagan, R. Lazarowitz, C. Webb, & R. Schmuck (Eds.), *Learning to cooperate, cooperating to learn.* New York: Plenum.

Shatz, E. (1994). Cross-Canada survey of programs for behaviorally disordered children and youth. M.Ed. thesis,. University of Saskatchewan.

Shavelson, R. J., Baxter, G. P., & Pine, J. (1992). Performance assessments: Political rhetoric and measurement reality. *Educational Researcher, 21* (4), 22–27.

Shelton, T.L., Anastopoulos, A.D., & Linden, J.D. (1985). An attribution training program with learning disabled children. *Journal of Learning Disabilities, 18,* 261-265.

Shepard, L. A. (1991). Psychometricians' beliefs about learning. *Educational Researcher, 29* (7), 2–16.

Shepherd-Look, D. (1982). Sex differentiation and the development of sex roles. In B. Wolman (Ed.), *Handbook of developmental psychology.* Englewood Cliffs, NJ: Prentice Hall.

Shermer, Michael (1997). *Why People Believe Weird Things.* New York: W.H. Freeman & Co.

Shiffrin, R. M., & Schneider, W. (1977). Controlled and automatic human information processing: Perceptual learning, automatic attending, and a general theory. *Psychological Review, 84,* 127–190.

Short, R.H., Stewin, L.L., & McCann, S.J.H. (1991). *Educational psychology: Canadian perspectives.* Toronto: Copp Clark Pitman.

Sidorowicz, L. S., & Lunney, G. S. (1980). Baby X revisited. *Sex Roles, 6,* 67–73.

Siegler, R. S. (1983). Five generalizations about cognitive development. *American Psychologist, 38,* 263–277.

___(1984). Mechanisms of cognitive growth: Variation and selection. In R. J. Sternberg (Ed.), *Mechanisms of cognitive development.* New York: Freeman.

___(1986). *Children's thinking.* Englewood Cliffs, NJ: Prentice Hall.

Simon, H. A. (1974). How big is a chunk? *Science, 183,* 482–488.

Simon, S., Ditricks, R., & Speckhart, L. (1975). Students in observational paired-associate learning: Informational, social, and individual difference variables. *Journal of Experimental Child Psychology, 20,* 81–104.

Simpson, G. E., & Yinger, J. M. (1985). *Racial and cultural minorities.* New York: Harper & Row.

Simpson, R. L. (1980). Modifying the attitudes of regular class students toward the handicapped. *Focus on Exceptional Children, 13* (3), 1–11.

Skinner, B. F. (1938). *The behavior of organisms: An experimental analysis.* New York: Appleton-Century-Crofts.

___(1953). *Science and human behavior.* New York: Macmillan.

__(1954). The science of learning and the art of teaching. *Harvard Educational Review, 24,* 86–97.

__(1958). Teaching machines. *Science, 128,* 969–977.

__(1963). Operant behavior. *American Psychologist, 18,* 503–515.

__(1968). *The technology of teaching.* New York: Appleton-Century-Crofts.

__(1969). *Contingencies of reinforcement.* Englewood Cliffs, NJ: Prentice Hall.

__(1987a). What ever happened to psychology as the science of behavior? *American Psychologist, 42,* 780–786.

__(1987b). *Upon further reflection.* Englewood Cliffs, NJ: Prentice Hall.

__(1989). The origins of cognitive thought. *American Psychologist, 44,* 13–18.

Slavin, R. E. (1987). Grouping for instruction: Equity and effectiveness. *Equity and Excellence, 23,* 31–36.

__(1990). *Cooperative learning: Theory, research, and practice.* Englewood Cliffs, NJ: Prentice Hall.

__(1991). Synthesis of research on cooperative learning. *Educational Leadership, 48* (5), 71–82.

Slavin, R. E. (1988). Cooperative learning: A best evidence synthesis, Dr. R. E. Slavin (Ed.). *School and Classroom Organization.* Hillsdale, N.J.: Erlbaum.

Slavin, R. E., & Karweit, N. (1985). Effects of whole class, ability grouped, and individualized instruction on mathematics achievement. *American Educational Reseach Journal, 22,* 351–368.

Slavin, R. E., Karweit, N. L., & Wasik, B. A. (1994). *Preventing early school failure: Research on effective strategies.* Needham Heights, MA: Allyn & Bacon.

Sleeter, C.E. (1988). *Making choices for multicultural education: Five approaches to race, class, and gender.* Columbus, OH: Merrill.

Smith, D.J. (1997). Indigenous peoples' extended family relationships: A source for classroom structure. *McGill Journal of Education, 32(2),* 125-138.

Smith, G. B. (1986). Self-concept and the learning disabled child. *Journal of Reading, Writing, and Learning Disabilities International, 2* (3), 237–241.

Smith, J. (1991). What will the new SAT look like? An interview with Lawrence Hecht. *d'News: The Newsletter of Division D of the American Educational Research Association, 1* (2), 1–4.

Snider, V. E. (1990). What we know about learning styles from research in special education. *Educational Leadership, 48* (2), 53.

Snow, R. E., Corno, L., & Jackson, D. (1995). Individual differences in affective and conative functions. In D. C. Berliner (Ed.), *Handbook of educational psychology.* New York: Macmillan.

Snyder, L., Bates, E., & Bretherton, I. (1981). Content and context in early lexical development. *Journal of Child Language, 8,* 565–582.

Solomon, R., & Levine-Rasky, C. (1996). When principle meets practice: Teachers'

Soodak, L. C., & Podell, D. M. (1993). Teacher efficacy and student problems as factors in special education referral. *Journal of Special Education, 27* (1), 66–81.

Sorensen, M., & Krahn, H. (1996). Attitudes toward immigrants: A test of two theories. *The Alberta Journal of Educational Research, XLII(1),* 3-18.

Spence, J. T. (1984). Gender identity and its implications for concepts of masculinity and femininity. In T. B. Sonderegger (Ed.), *Nebraska Symposium on Motivation* (Vol. 32). Lincoln: University of Nebraska Press.

Spiro, R. J., Feltovich, P. J., Jacobson, M. J., & Coulson, R. L. (1991, May). Cognitive flexibility, constructivism, and hypertext: Random access instruction for advanced knowledge acquisition in ill-structured domains. *Educational Technology, 31,* 24–33.

Squires, D. A., Huitt, W. G., & Segars, J. K. (1983). *Effective schools and classrooms: A research-based perspective.* Alexandria, VA: Association for Supervision and Curriculum Development.

Stacy, K. (1992). Mathematical problem solving in groups: Are two heads better than one? *Journal of Mathematical Behavior, 11* (3), 261–275.

Stalikas, A., & Gavaki, E. (1995). The importance of ethnic identity: Self-esteem and academic achievement of second-generation Greeks in secondary school. *Canadian Journal of School Psychology, 11,* 1-9.

Stallings, J., & Krasavage, E. M. (1986). Program implementation and student achievement in a four-year Madeline Hunter follow-through project. *Elementary School Journal, 87* (2), 117–138.

Starko, A. J. (1995). *Creativity in the classroom: Schools of curious delight.* White Plains, NY: Longman.

Starrat, R. J. (1987). Moral education in the high school classroom. In K. Ryan & G. McLean (Eds.), *Character development in schools and beyond.* New York: Praeger.

Steinberg, L., Elman, J. D., & Mounts, N. S. (1989). Authoritative parenting, psychosocial maturity, and academic success among adolescents. *Child Development, 60,* 1424–1436.

Stenlund, K. V. (1995). Teacher perceptions across cultures: The impact of students on teacher enthusiasm and discouragement in a cross-cultural context. *The Alberta Journal of Education Research, XLI(2),* 145-161.

Stephan, W. G. (1985). Intergroup relations. In G. Lindzey & E. Aronson (Eds.). *The handbook of social psychology, Vol. 2.* (3rd ed.). New York: Random House.

Sternberg, R. J. (1986). *Intelligence applied: Understanding and increasing your own intellectual skills.* New York: Harcourt Brace Jovanovich.

__(1989). *The triarchic mind: A new theory of human intelligence.* New York: Penguin Books.

Sternberg, R.J. (1996). Myths, countermyths and truths about intelligence. *Educational Researcher, 25(2),* 11-16.

Sternberg, R.J. (1998) . Styles of thinking and learning. *Canadian Journal of School Psychology.* In press.

Stevens, R. J., Madden, N. A., Slavin, R. E., & Farnish, A. M. (1987). Cooperative integrated reading and composition: Two field experiments. *Reading Research Quarterly, 22,* 433–454.

Stevenson, H. W., & Lee, S. (1990). Contexts of achievement. *Monographs of the Society for Research in Child Development, 55* (1-2, Serial No. 221).

Stewart, M. J., & Corbin, C. B. (1988). Feedback dependence among low confidence preadolescent boys and girls. *Research Quarterly for Exercise and Sport, 59,* (2), 160–164.

Stiggins, R. J. (1991). Facing the challenges of a new era of educational assessment. *Applied Measurement in Education, 4* (4), 263–273.

__(1994). *Student-centered classroom assessment.* New York: Merrill-Macmillan.

Stiggins, R. J., Frisbie, D. A., & Griswold, P. A. (1989). Inside high school grading practices: Building a research agenda. *Educational Measurement: Issues and Practices, 8* (2), 5–14.

Stigler, J. W., Lee, S., & Stevenson, H. W. (1987). Mathematics classrooms in Japan, Taiwan, and the United States. *Child Development, 58,* 1272–1285.

Stipek, D. J. (1993). *Motivation to learn: From theory to practice* (2nd ed.). Needham Heights, MA: Allyn & Bacon.

Stipek, D. J., & McIver, D. (1989). Developmental change in children's assessment of intellectual competence. *Child Development, 60,* 531–538.

Stipek, D. J., Recchia, S., and McClintic, S. (1992). Self-evaluation in young children. *Monographs of the Society for Research in Child Development, 57* (1, Serial No. 226).

Strauss, C. C., Smith, K., Frame, C., & Forehand, R. (1985). Personal and interpersonal characteristics associated with childhood obesity. *Journal of Pediatric Psychology, 10,* 337–343.

Strauss, S. (1993). Theories of learning and development for academics and educators. *Educational Psychologist, 28* (3), 191–204.

Strunk, W., Jr., & White, E.B. (1979). *The elements of style* (3rd ed.). New York: Macmillan.

Stuart, J., & Rutherford, R. (1978). Medical student concentration during lectures. *Lancet, 2,* 514–516.

Sulzer, B., & Mayer, G. R. (1972). *Behavior modification procedures for school personnel.* New York: Holt, Rinehart & Winston.

Sulzer-Azaroff, B., & Mayer, G. R. (1986). *Achieving educational excellence through behavioral strategies.* New York: Holt, Rinehart & Winston.

Sumara, D.J.& Luce-Kapler, R. (1996). (Un)becoming a teacher: Negotiating identities while learning to teach. *Canadian Journal of Education,* 21(1), 65-83.

Suzuki, B. H. (1983). The education of Asian and Pacific Americans: An introductory overview. In D. Nakanishi & M. Hirano-Nakanishi (Eds.), *The education of Asian and Pacific Americans: Historical perspectives and prescriptions for the future.* Phoenix: Oryx Press.

Swain, M. (1984). A review of immersion education in Canada: Research and evaluatin studies. In P. Allen & M. Swain (Eds.), *Language issues and education policies: Exploring Canada's multilingual resources.* Oxford: Pergamon.

Swanson, H. L., O'Connor, J. E., & Cooney, J. B. (1990). An information processing analysis of expert and novice teachers' problem-solving. *American Educational Research Journal , 27,* (3), 533–556.

Talbert, J.E., & McLaughlin, M.W. (1993). Understanding teaching in context. In D. K. Cohen. M. W. Mclaughlin, & J. E. Talbert (Eds.), *Teaching for understanding: Challenges for policy and practice.* San Francisco: Jossey-Bass.

Tanner, J. (1978a). *Education and physical growth* (2nd ed.). London: Hadder & Stoughton.

__(1978b). *Fetus into man: Physical growth from conception to maturity.* Cambridge, MA: Harvard University Press.

Taylor, R. P. (Ed.). (1980). *The computer in the school: Tutor, tool, tutee.* New York: Teachers College Press.

Templin, M. C. (1957). Certain language skills in children: Their development and interrelationships. *University of Minnesota Institute of Child Welfare Monograph,* 26.

Terrace, H. (1963a). Discrimination learning with and without errors. *Journal of Experimental Analysis of Behavior, 6,* 1–27.

__(1963b). Errorless transfer of a discrimination across two continua. *Journal of Experimental Analysis of Behavior, 6,* 223–232.

The Alberta journal of Educational Research, XLII(3), 293-305.

Thorndike, E. L. (1913). *Educational psychology. Vol. II. The psychology of learning.* New York: Teachers College, Columbia University.

Tishman, S., Perkins, D., & Jay, E. (1995). *A thinking classroom: Learning and teaching in a culture of thinking.* Needham Heights, MA: Allyn & Bacon.

Tobias, S. (1982). When do instructional methods make a difference? *Educational Researcher, 11* (4), 4–10.

Tobin, K. G. (1987). The role of wait-time in higher cognitive level learning. *Review of Educational Research, 57,* 69–95.

__(1990). Changing metaphors and beliefs: A master switch for learning? *Theory into Practice, 29* (2) 122–127

Tobin, K. G., & Capie, W. (1982). Relationships between classroom process variables and middle-school science achievement. *Journal of Educational Psychology, 74,* 441–454.

Tobin, K. G., & Dawson, G. (1992). Constraints to curriculum reform: Teachers and the myth of schooling. *Educational Technology Research and Development, 40* (1), 81–92.

Triandis, H. C. (1986). Toward pluralism in education. G. K. Verma, K. Mallick, & C. Modgil (Eds.) In S. Modgil, *Multicultural education: The interminable debate,* London: Falmer.

Tucker, G.R. (1981). Social policy and second language teaching. In R.C. Gardner & R. Kalin (Eds.), *A Canadian social psychology of ethnic relations.* Toronto: Methuen.

Tucker, J. A. (1985). Curriculum-based assessment: An introduction. *Exceptional Children, 52,* 199–204.

Tuckman, B. W. (1988). *Testing for teachers* (2nd ed.). Orlando, FL: Harcourt Brace Jovanovich.

Tudge, J., & Rogoff, B. (1989). Peer influences on cognitive development: Piagetian and Vygotskian perspectives. In M. H. Bornstein & J. S. Bruner (Eds.), *Interaction in human development*. Hillsdale, NJ: Erlbaum.

Tulving, E. (1972). Episodic and semantic memory. In E. Tulving & W. Donaldson (Eds.), *Organization of memory*. New York: Academic Press.

Tyler, R. W. (1989). Educating children from minority families. *Educational Horizons, 67* (4), 114–118.

U.S. Department of Education. (1992). *Fourteenth annual report to Congress on the Individuals with Disabilities Act*. Washington, D.C.: U.S. Department of Education.

Unger, R.K., Draper, R.D., & Pendergrass, M.L. (1986). Personal epistemology and personal experience. *Journal of Social Issues, 42(2)*, 67-79.

Valero-Figueira, E. (1988). Hispanic children. *Teaching Exceptional Children, 20*, 47–49.

Vallerand, R.J., & Bissonnette, R. (1992). Intrinsic, extrinsic, and amotivational styles as predictors of behavior: A prospective study. *Journal of Personality, 60*, 599-620.

Vasquez, J. A. (1990). Teaching to the distinctive traits of minority students. *The Clearing House, 63*, 299–304.

Vasudev, J., & Hummel, R. C. (1987). Moral stage sequence and principled reasoning in an Indian sample. *Human Development, 30*, 105–118.

Veenman, S. (1984). Perceived problems of beginning teachers. *Review of Educational Research, 54* (2), 143–178.

Verner, C., & Dickinson, G. (1967). The lecture: An analysis and review of research. *Adult Education, 17* (2), 85–100.

Virgina Education Association & Appalachia Educational Laboratory (1992). *Alternative assessments in math and science: Moving toward a moving target*. Charleston, WV: Appalachian Educational Laboratory.

von Glasersfeld, E. (1988). *The construction of knowledge*. Salinas, CA: Intersystems Publications.

Vosniadou, S. (1988, April). *Knowledge restructuring and science instruction*. Paper presented at the Annual Meeting of the American Educational Research Association, New Orleans.

Vygotsky, L. S. (1962). *Thought and language*. Cambridge, MA: The MIT Press.

__(1978). *Mind in society*. Cambridge, MA: Harvard University Press.

__(1981). The genesis of higher mental functions. In J. V. Wertsch (Ed.), *The concept of activity in Soviet psychology*. Armonk, NY: Sharpe.

__(1987). *Thinking and speech*. New York: Plenum. (Originally published 1934).

Wadsworth, B. J. (1984). *Piaget's theory of cognitive development: An introduction for students of psychology and education* (3rd ed.). New York: Longman.

Waggoner, M., Chinn, C., Yi, H., and Anderson, R. C. (1993, April). *Reflective story discussions*. Paper presented at the Annual Meeting of the American Educational Research Association, Atlanta, GA.

Wahlstrom, M., & Danley, R.R. (1976). *Assessment of Student achievement*. Toronto: Ontario Ministry of Education.

Walker, L. J., DeVries, B., & Trevethan, S. D. (1987). Moral stages and moral orientations in real-life and hypothetical dilemmas. *Child Development, 58*, 842–858.

Walters, G. C., & Grusec, J. E. (1977). *Punishment*. San Francisco: Freeman.

Wang, M. C., Haertel, G. D., & Walberg, H. J. (1993). Toward a knowledge base of school learning. *Review of Educational Research, 63* (3), 249–294.

Wasik, B. A., & Karweit, N. L. (1994). Off to a good start: Effects of birth-to-three interventions on early school success. In R. E. Slavin, N. L. Karweit, & B. A. Wasik, *Preventing early school failure: Research on effective strategies*. Needham Heights, MA: Allyn & Bacon.

Watkins, D., & Astilla, E. (1984). The dimensionality, antecedents, and study method correlates of the causal attribution of Filipino children. *Journal of Social Psychology, 124* (2), 191–199.

Wechsler D. (1997). *Wechsler Adult Intelligence Scale - Third Edition*. San Antonio: the Psychological Corporation.

Wechsler, D. (1958). *The measurement and appraisal of adult intelligence* (4th ed.). Baltimore, MD: Williams & Wilkins.

Wechsler, D. (1991). *Wechsler Intelligence Scale for Children - Third Edition*. San Antonio: The Psychological Corporation.

Weiner, B. (1980a). *Human motivation*. New York: Holt, Rinehart & Winston.

__(1980b). The role of affect in rational (attributional) approaches to human motivation. *Educational Researcher, 9*, 4–11.

__(1986). *An attributional theory of motivation and emotion*. New York: Springer-Verlag.

__(1992). *Human motivation: Metaphors, theories and research*. Newbury Park, CA: Sage Publications.

Weiner, H. (1969). Controlling human fixed-interval's performance. *Journal of Experimental Analysis of Behavior, 12*, 349–373.

Weinstein, C. S., & Mignano, A. (1993). *Elementary classroom management: Lessons from research and practice*. New York: McGraw-Hill.

Weinstein, C. S., Woolfolk, A. E., Dittmeier, L., & Shanker, U. (1994). Protector or prison guard? Using metaphors and media to explore student teachers' thinking about classroom management. *Action in Teacher Education, 16* (1), 41–54.

West, C. K., Farmer, J. A., & Wolff, P. M. (1991). *Instructional design: Implications from cognitive science*. Englewood Cliffs, NJ: Prentice Hall.

Wheeler, R. (1977 April). Predisposition toward cooperation and competition: Cooperative and competitive classroom effects. Paper presented at the Annual Meeting of the American Psychological Association, San Francisco.

White, B. Y. (1993). TinkerTools: Causal models, conceptual change, and science education. *Cognition and Instruction, 10*, 1–100.

White, D.R., Mendelson, B.K., & Schlieker, E. (1995). Adolescent perceptions of self: Is apperance all that matters? In K. Covell.

Whitmore, J. R. (1986). Understanding a lack of motivation to excel. *Gifted Child Quarterly, 30,* 66–69.

Wiersma, W. (1995). *Research methods in education: An introduction* (6th ed.). Needham Heights, MA: Allyn & Bacon.

Wiggins, C. (1989). Teaching to the (authentic) test. *Educational Leadership, 46,* 1–47.

Wiggins, G. P. (1993). *Assessing student performance.* San Francisco: Jossey-Bass.

Wild, T.C., Enzle, M.E., & Hawkins, W.L. (1992). Effects of perceived extrinsic vs. intrinsic teacher motivation on student reactions to skill acquisition. *Personality and Social Psychology Bulletin, 18,* 245-251.

Wilgosh, L., Mulcahy, R., & Watters, B. (1986). Assessing intellectual performance of culturally different Inuit children with WISC-R. *Canadian Journal of Behavioral Sciene, 18,* 270-277.

Williams J. D., & Snipper, G. C. (1990). *Literary and bilingualism.* White Plains, NY: Longman.

Willig, A. C. (1985). A meta-analysis of selection studies on the effectiveness of bilingual education. *Review of Educational Research, 55,* 269–317.

Willoughby, T., Motz, M., & Wood, E. (1997). The impact of interest and strategy use on memory performance for child, adolescent, and adult learners. *The Alberta Journal of Education Research, XLIII(2/3),* 127-141.

Wilson, R.J. (1989). Evaluating student achievement in an Ontario high school. *Alberta Journal of Educational Research, 35,* 134-144.

Wilson, R.J. (1996). *Assessing Students in Classrooms and Schools.* Scarborough, ON: Allyn & Bacon Canada.

__(1990). Classroom processes in evaluating student achievement. *Alberta Journal of Educational Research, 36,* 4-17.

Wineburg, S. S. (1987). The self-fulfillment of the self-fulfilling prophecy: A critical appraisal. *Educational Researcher, 16,* 28–37.

Winzer, M. (1990). *Children with exceptionalities: A Canadian perspective* (2nd ed.). Scarborough, ON: Prentice Hall.

__(1995). *Educational Psychology in the Canadian Classroom* (2nd ed.). Scarborough, ON:Allyn & Bacon Canada.

Winzer, M. (1996). *Children with Exceptionalities in Canadian Classrooms (4th edition).* Scarborough, ON: Allyn & Bacon Canada.

Wittrock, M. C. (1974). Learning as a generative process. *Educational Psychologist, 11,* 87–95.

__(1990). Generative processes of comprehension. *Educational Psychologist, 24,* 345–376.

__(1991). Generative teaching and comprehension. *Elementary School Journal, 92,* 167–182.

Wittrock, M. C., Marks, C. B., & Doctorow, M. J. (1975). Reading as a generative process. *Journal of Educational Psychology, 67,* 484–489.

Woditsch, G. A. & Schmittroth, J. (1991). *The thoughful teacher's guide to thinking skills.* Hillsdale, NJ: Erlbaum.

Wolf, D. P. (1989). Portfolio assessment: Sampling student work. *Educational Leadership, 46* (4), 36–38.

Wolf, M. M., Giles, D. K., & Hall, V. R. (1968). Experiments with token reinforcement in a remedial classroom. *Behavioral Research and Therapy, 6,* 51–64.

Wolf, R. M. (1979). Achievement in the United States. In H. J. Walberg (Ed.), *Educational environments and effects: Evaluation, policy, and productivity.* Berkeley, CA: McCutchan.

Wolfgang, C. H. (1995). *Solving discipline problems: Methods and models for today's teachers* (3rd ed.). Needham Heights, MA: Allyn & Bacon.

Wolfgang, C. H., & Wolfgang, M. E. (1995). *Three Faces of Discipline for Early Childhood.* Needham Heights, MA: Allyn & Bacon.

Wollen, K. A., & Lowry, D. H. (1974). Conditions that determine effectiveness of picture-mediated paired-associated learning. *Journal of Experimental Psychology, 102,* 181–183.

Women's Educational Equity Program. (1983). *Fair play: Developing self-concept and decision-making skills in the middle school.* Newton, MA: Education Development Center.

Wong, K. K. (1994). Governance structure, resource allocation, and equity policy. *Review of Research in Education, 20,* 257–289.

Wood, B. S. (1981). *Children and communication: Verbal and nonverbal language development.* (2nd ed.). Englewood Cliffs, NJ: Prentice Hall.

Wood, D., Bruner, J., & Ross, S. (1976). The role of tutoring in problem solving. *British Journal of Psychology, 66,* 181–191.

Woolfolk, A. E. (1995). *Educational psychology* (6th ed.). Needham Heights, MA: Allyn & Bacon.

Woolfolk, A. E., & Hoy, W. K. (1990). Prospective teachers' sense of efficacy and beliefs about control. *Journal of Educational Psychology, 82,* 81–91.

Woolfolk, A. E., & McCune-Nicolich, L. (1984). *Educational psychology for teachers* (2nd ed.). Englewood Cliffs, NJ: Prentice Hall.

Worthen, B. R., & Spandel, V. (1991, February). Putting the standardized test debate in perspective. *Educational Leadership,* 65–69.

Wotherspoon, T. (1993). Families and labour reproduction. In P.S. Li & B.S. Bolaria (Eds.), *Contemporary sociology: Critical perspectives.* Toronto: Copp Clark Pitman.

Wynn, E. A. (1987). Students and schools. In K. Ryan & G. McLean (Eds.), *Character development in schools and beyond.* New York: Praeger.

Wynn, R. L., & Fletcher, C. (1987). Sex role development and early educational experiences. In D. B. Carter (Ed.), *Current conceptions of sex roles and sex typing.* New York: Praeger.

Yee, A. H. (1992). Asians as stereotypes and students: Misperceptions that persist. *Educational Psychology Review, 4,* 95–132.

Zerega, M. E., Haertel, G. D., Tsai, S., & Walberg, H. J. (1986). Late adolescent sex differences in science learning. *Science Education, 70* (4), 447–460.

Zessoules, R., Wolf, D., & Gardner, H. (1988). A better balance: Arts PROPEL as an alternative to discipline-based art education. In J. Burton, A. Lederman, and P. London (Eds.), *Beyond discipline-based art education.* North Dartmouth, MA:University Council on Art Education.

Ziegler, S. (1981). The effectiveness of cooperative learning teams for increasing cross-ethnic friendship: Additional evidence. *Human Organization, 40,* 264-268.

Ziegler, S., & Rosenstein-Manner, M. (1991). *Bullying at school: Toronto in an international context.* Toronto: Toronto Board of Education, Research Services.

Zirpoli, T.J. (1989). Child abuse and children with handicaps. *Remedial and Special Education, 7(2),* 39-48.Campbell, E. (1996). The tensions within: Diversity in a multi-everything secondary school. *The Alberta Journal of Educational Research, XLII(3),* 280-292.

GLOSSARY

absolute standard   A grading system in which scores are compared to a set performance standard.

accommodation   In Piaget's theory, a process of modifying existing cognitive structures or creating additional ones as a result of new experiences.

achievement motivation   A person's desire or tendency to overcome obstacles and to accomplish some difficult task through the exercise of power.

acronym   A word formed from the initial letters of a group of words (e.g., UNICEF).

acrostic   A sentence used as a memory cue for information to be remembered.

action zones   The areas in a classroom where a teacher directs most of his or her attention.

active learning   Students engaging in meaningful tasks in which they have ownership of content.

additive bilingualism   A form of bilingualism in which students have achieved complete literacy in two languages. Because of conceptual interdependence between languages, learning in one aids achievement in the other.

advance organizer   Information presented prior to instruction that assists in understanding new information by relating it to existing knowledge.

affective domain   Learning outcomes that relate to emotions, values, and attitudes, as classified by Krathwohl's taxonomy.

affordances   Opportunities offered a person by his or her environment.

anticipatory set   The first step in Hunter's approach to lesson delivery. This step establishes expectancies or a mind-set in students that anticipates the material to be covered.

applied behaviour analysis   The analysis of behaviour problems and the prescription of remedies.

ARCS model   A model teachers can use to identify and solve motivational problems in their classrooms. The ARCS model defines four categories of motivation that must exist for students to be motivated to learn: attention, relevance, confidence, and satisfaction.

arousal effects   Consequences of modelling that change an observer's physical and psychological reactions caused by the model's expressed emotions and actions.

assertive discipline   An approach to misbehaviour based on principles of applied behaviour analysis.

assessment   The process of gathering, analyzing, and interpreting information about students and their progress in school.

assimilation   In Piaget's theory, a process through which new experiences are incorporated into existing cognitive structures such as schemes.

assimilation   A view of diversity in which a hierarchy of values is assumed so that members of ethnic groups are expected to adopt and live by the values of the dominant culture.

at risk   Students whose characteristics or life experiences make them likely to fail in school or drop out.

attention   The process used to focus on one or more aspects of the environment to the exclusion of other aspects.

attitude   According to Gagné, a learned capability that influences a person's choice of personal action.

attribution theory   The explanations, reasons, or excuses students give for their own successes or failures in learning.

attribution training   Attempting to change the student's style of explaining his or her own learning successes or failures.

authentic activities   Instructional tasks that provide culturally and situationally relevant contexts for learning and development.

authentic assessment   Assessment of higher-order skills such as problem solving and critical thinking in real-life contexts through the use of projects, exhibitions, demonstrations, portfolios, observations, science fairs, peer- and self-assessments.

authentic task   An instructional task that is part of the world outside of school (e.g., comparison shopping) or part of the culture of a particular discipline (e.g., "exploiting extreme cases" in mathematics reasoning).

authoritative leadership   Authority established through the flexible implementation of standards and characterized by discussion with and explanation to followers.

automatic attention   The process of attention that occurs without effort.

automaticity   The point at which a mental operation can be executed without conscious effort.

autonomy   Independence. Autonomy versus shame and doubt marks Stage 2 of Erikson's theory of psychosocial development.

aversive   Undesirable.

behavioural approach   A school of thought in which learning is explained through observable aspects of the environment instead of mental or cognitive processes.

behavioural objectives   Specific statements of goals, which include the behaviour students should be able to perform as a result of instruction, the conditions of their performance, and the criteria used to judge attainment of the goals.

benchmarks   Standards against which evaluative judgments are made.

bias   The result of procedures or items used in assessment that unfairly discriminate among students.

bilingual education   Enriched learning whereby students gain a second language at no cost to their regular academic program or first language.

bilingualism   A term used to describe the ability to speak fluently in two different languages.

binary-choice items   Any selected response item that offers two optional answers from which to select.

Bloom's taxonomy   Bloom's classification of behaviour in the cognitive domain. From simplest to complex, it consists of knowledge, comprehension, application, analysis, synthesis, and evaluation.

central tendency   A score that is typical of a distribution of scores. Mode, median, and mean are three measures of central tendency.

chaining   Successively linking together discrete, simpler behaviours already known to the learner in order to establish complex behaviours.

classical conditioning   The process of bringing reflexes under control of the environment. Also known as Pavlovian and respondent conditioning.

classroom management   Actions taken by a teacher to facilitate student learning.

cognitive development   Changes in our capabilities as learners by which mental processes grow more complex and sophisticated.

cognitive domain   Learning outcomes that relate to memory, understanding, and reasoning.

cognitive modelling   An approach to instruction that combines demonstration of skill with verbalization of cognitive activity that accompanies the skill.

cognitive strategies   A learned capability that enables learners to organize and regulate their own internal processes.

collaborative leadership   Guidance through shared planning, decision making, and problem solving.

communication disorder   Speech (voice) and language (symbols) disorders.

compensatory education   Educational programs designed to combat the presumed effects of poverty on school performance.

competitive goal structure   A class management structure in which students must compete for rewards so that they view attainment of goals as possible only if other students do not attain them.

componential intelligence Part of Sternberg's theory of intelligence, referring to a person's ability to reason abstractly, process information, and determine the kind and sequence of operations required for a task or problem.

computer-assisted instruction (CAI)   Instruction delivered by a computer including tutorial, simulation, drill, and practice.

concrete concepts   Abstractions based on objects, events, people, and relations that can be observed.

concrete operations   Piaget's first stage of operational thought during which children develop skills of logical reasoning, but only about problems that are concrete.

conditioned reinforcer   A neutral object or event that acquires the power to reinforce behaviour as a result of being paired with one or more primary reinforcers, for example, money.

confidence bands   An interval around a particular score in which the true score probably lies.

construct   An idea devised by a theorist to explain observations and relationships between variables.

constructivist view of learning   A cognitive view of learning whereby learners are assumed to construct knowledge in the context of the activity of the culture and knowing cannot be separated from doing.

content integration   The degree to which teachers use content and examples in all subject areas that reflect both genders, diverse cultures, and different social classes.

contextual intelligence   Part of Sternberg's theory of intelligence, relating to one's ability to adapt, select, or shape one's environment to optimize one's opportunities.

contingencies of reinforcement   According to Skinner, learning principles based on the law of effect, the relationship between antecedent, response, and consequence.

continuous reinforcement   A schedule of reinforcement in which reinforcement is delivered after every correct response.

contract grading   Using an agreement that states what performances are required for a particular grade.

control theory   The view that students need to be empowered to control to meet their own needs and thus experience success in school.

conventional morality   Rules of conduct of older children (9 years–young adulthood) based on the conventions of society. This is Level 2 of Kohlberg's theory of moral reasoning.

cooperative goal structure   A class management structure in which rewards for performance are given to a group, not to individuals within the group. As a consequence, students view attainment of goals as possible only through cooperation with members of their group.

cooperative integrated reading and composition (CIRC)   Pairs of students from one homogeneous reading group join another pair from a different reading group to work cooperatively on comprehension and writing skills.

cooperative learning   An instructional strategy whereby students work in cooperative groups to achieve a common goal. Conditions that promote effective cooperative learning include positive interdependence among group members, face-to-face interaction, clearly perceived individual accountability to achieve the group's goals, frequent use of interpersonal skills, and regular group processing to improve the group's functioning.

criterion-referenced judgments   Assessment scores are compared to a set performance standard.

critical periods   each one of Erikson's eight stages of psychosocial development; each stage identifies the emergence of a part of an individual's personality.

critical thinking   Higher-level thinking used to analyze, synthesize, and evaluate.

cultural forces   Four teaching strategies used to help students acquire thinking skills: (1) providing models of the culture, (2) explaining important cultural knowledge, (3) providing interaction among students and other members of the cultural community, and (4) providing feedback on students' use of thinking skills.

cultural pluralism   A view of diversity that embraces cultural differences.

culture   A way of life in which people share a common language and similar values, religion, ideals, habits of thinking, artistic expressions, and patterns of social and interpersonal relations.

curiosity   An eager desire to know caused by stimuli that are novel, complex, or strange or that involve fantasy and ambiguity.

deficiency needs   According to Maslow's hierarchy of needs, the basic needs that humans require for physical and psychological well-being.

deficit model   The assumption that students who are members of ethnic minority groups are deficient in knowledge and skills required to contribute to the national culture.

defined concepts   Abstractions that cannot be observed in the environment but must be defined (e.g., liberty).

developmental crisis   According to Erikson, there is a conflict faced at each stage of psychological development. The way the crisis is resolved has a lasting effect on the person's self-concept and view of society in general.

developmentally appropriate instruction   Instruction that is child-centered and provides activities appropriate to the developmental level of the student.

dialect   A distinctive version or variation of a language in pronunciation, grammar, vocabulary, and usage.

difference model   The assumption that students from different cultural groups will have unique learning styles and therefore different learning needs.

direct instruction   A form of teacher-centered instruction in which goals are clear and the teacher controls the material and the pace.

direct reinforcement   Using direct consequences from the external environment to strengthen a desired behaviour.

disability   A diminished capacity to perform in a specific way.

discipline   The extent to which students are engaged in learning or other classroom-appropriate activities.

discovery learning   Bruner's approach to teaching, in which students are presented with specific examples and use these examples to form general principles. Discovery learning is inductive.

discrimination   Distinguishing between and responding differently to two or more stimuli.

discriminative stimulus   A stimulus that is present consistently when a response is reinforced and comes to act as a cue or signal for the response.

disinhibitory effects   Consequences of modelling that increase a behaviour already known but infrequently performed by the observer, by removing the inhibitions associated with that behaviour.

dispersion   An indication of how similar or different the scores in a distribution are from one another.

dominant bilingualism A form of bilingualism in which students are fully competent in their first language and nearly so in their second.

dual-code theory   The assumption of two systems of memory representation, one for verbal information and one for nonverbal, or imaginal, information.

educational psychology   The scientific study of the teaching–learning process.

elaborative rehearsal   A type of encoding that relates new information to information already in LTS.

emotional/behavioural disorders   A disorder in which people have difficulty controlling their feelings and behaviour.

enactive learning   Changes in thought or behaviour that are a function of environmental consequences experienced by the learner.

encoding   The process of converting a message from the environment to a cognitive code so that the information can be stored and later remembered.

enterprise schema   An overall learning context that integrates multiple instructional goals and communicates the purpose for learning these goals.

environmental enhancement effects   Consequences of modelling that direct an observer's attention to certain aspects or objects in the model's environment.

episodic memories   Memories associated with specific personal experiences, including the time and place they occurred.

equilibration   The self-regulating process in Piaget's theory through which people balance new experiences with present understanding.

ESL programs   Programs that teach English language skills to students with limited English proficiency.

essay items   Test items that require students to construct written responses of varying lengths.

ethnic group   The people who derive a sense of identity from their common national origin, religion, and, sometimes, physical characteristics.

ethnicity   A term used to describe the cultural characteristics of people who identify themselves with a particular ethnic group.

ethnocentrism   The assumption that one's own cultural ways are the right ways and universally appropriate to others.

evaluation   The process by which teachers make specific judgments by answering the questions "How good?" or "How well?" (e.g., How well have students understood this concept? How good is this instruction?).

exceptional learners   Learners who have special learning needs and who require special instruction.

experiential intelligence   Part of Sternberg's theory of intelligence, describing a person's capacity to deal with novel tasks or new ideas and to combine unrelated facts.

explanation   A clarification that provides a context or framework for a concept, event, or relationship.

extinction   Removing reinforcement that is maintaining a behaviour in order to weaken that behaviour.

extrinsic motivation   When learners work on tasks for external reasons, such as to please a parent or to avoid getting into trouble with the teacher.

fading   The gradual withdrawal of a discriminative stimulus while the behaviour continues to be reinforced.

foreclosure   According to Marcia, adolescents who simply accept the decisions made for them by others. These decisions are often made by their parents.

forethought   Anticipation of the future.

formal operations According to Piaget, the stage of development in which the abilities to reason abstractly and to coordinate a number of variables are acquired.

formative assessment   An assessment used to diagnose learning difficulties and to provide feedback to students to improve their learning.

full inclusion   The inclusion of all students in the regular classroom.

Gagné's events of instruction   According to Gagné, the external conditions required to support and facilitate the cognitive processes that occur during learning.

gender role stereotypes   Commonly held expectations about the roles of each sex.

generativity   A sense of concern for future generations, expressed through childbearing or concern about creating a better world. Generativity versus stagnation marks Stage 7 of Erikson's theory of psychosocial development.

gifted and talented   Students who are able to meet academic challenges better than the majority of their peers in any number of areas.

global education   An aim of multicultural programs that helps students to understand that all peoples living on earth have interconnected fates.

goal structure   A means by which teachers manage learning and evaluate and reward student performance.

grade equivalent score   A standardized test score that uses grade-level performances to place individuals.

growth needs   According to Maslow, the higher-level needs, the satisfaction of which enables human beings to grow psychologically.

growth spurt   A dramatic increase in height and weight that signals the onset of puberty.

guided practice   The sixth step in Hunter's approach to lesson delivery. This step begins the process of transfer.

handicap   A disadvantage imposed on an individual.

hidden curriculum   The tacit lessons and messages taught to students by the way teachers and schools operate.

Heritage language schools Programs designed to promote and preserve cultural identity by providing instruction in a heritage language other than French or English.

hierarchy of needs A theory proposed by Abraham Maslow in which human needs are arranged in a hierarchy from basic needs to self-actualization, or self-fulfillment.

higher-order rules Rules formed by combining two or more rules, thus allowing students to solve problems.

I-message A clear statement by a teacher that tells how he or she feels about misbehaviour but that does not lay blame on a student.

identity A sense of well-being, a feeling of knowing where one is going, and an inner assuredness of anticipated recognition from those who count. Identity versus role diffusion characterizes Stage 5 of Erikson's theory of psychosocial development.

identity achievement According to Marcia, adolescents who have made life-style decisions, although not in all areas.

identity diffusion To Marcia, adolescents who avoid thinking about life-style decisions and are unable to develop a clear sense of self.

identity statuses Different types of identity, as identified by Marcia.

independent practice Tasks that students complete independently either in the classroom or at home.

individual survival The first level of Gilligan's theory of moral reasoning, in which selfishness is identified as the primary concern.

individualistic goal structure A class management structure in which rewards are given on the basis of an individual's performance, unaffected by the performance of other students.

industry An eagerness to produce. Industry versus inferiority typifies Stage 4 of Erikson's theory of psychosocial development.

information-processing models Models of learning that rely on an analogy between the human mind and the computer to explain processing, storage, and retrieval of knowledge.

inhibitory effects Consequences of modelling that reinforce previously learned inhibitions.

initiative The quality of undertaking, planning, and attacking a new task. Initiative versus guilt characterizes Stage 3 of Erikson's theory of psychosocial development.

instruction According to Driscoll, the deliberate arrangement of learning conditions to promote the attainment of some intended goal.

instructional goals General statements of what students should be able to do as a consequence of instruction.

integration A view of diversity in which individual ethnic groups merge together to form a single, shared culture.

integrative model A view of moral development that combines cognition, affect, and behaviour; method of lesson presentation that combines inductive skills, deductive skills, and content in one model.

integrity A sense of understanding how one fits into one's culture and the acceptance that one's place is unique and unalterable. Integrity versus despair marks Stage 8 of Erikson's theory of psychosocial development.

intellectual skills According to Gagné, learned capabilities that enable learners to make discriminations, identify and classify concepts, and apply and generate rules; procedural knowledge.

intelligence A personal capacity to learn, often measured by one's ability to deal with abstractions and to solve problems.

intermittent reinforcement A schedule of reinforcement in which reinforcement is delivered on some, but not all, occasions.

intersubjectivity In Vygotsky's theory, the process in which learning partners negotiate a mutual understanding of the task and how to proceed with its solution.

interview sheet A means of recording a teacher's observations during a conference with the student, which generally consists of a list of questions to be asked of each student together with space for recording the student's responses.

intimacy The state of having a close psychological relationship with another person. Intimacy versus isolation is Stage 6 of Erikson's theory of psychosocial development.

intrinsic motivation When learners work on tasks for internal reasons, such as pleasure or enjoyment in the activity.

isolation Failure to establish a close psychological relationship with another person leads to this feeling of being alone. The negative outcome of Stage 6 of Erikson's theory of psychosocial development.

item analysis A procedure used to evaluate test items for the purpose of determining whether the item functions in the way the teacher intends it to.

knowledge base of teaching The source from which a theory of teaching can be reflectively constructed; that which is known from educational psychology and classroom practice.

knowledge construction process A process by which knowledge is socially and culturally constructed.

language immersion A form of bilingual education in which students study the second language intensively for extended periods of time.

law of effect Thorndike's law of learning, which states that any action producing a satisfying consequence will be repeated in a similar situation. An action followed by an unfavorable consequence is unlikely to be repeated.

learned helplessness A depressed state when a person feels that no matter what he or she does, it will have no influence on important life events.

learning Change in thought or behaviour that modifies a person's capabilities.

learning community A classroom environment built on ideals and values of kindness, fairness, and responsibility.

learning disability A generic term for disorders in cognitive processing that interfere with learning.

learning goal An aim of students who place primary emphasis on increasing competence.

learning outcomes According to Gagné, capabilities acquired by students resulting from the interaction of internal and external conditions of learning.

learning-oriented classrooms Classrooms in which the teacher values learning and facilitates, rather than directs, student activity.

lecturing A discourse given in class for the purpose of instruction.

limited English proficiency A phrase used to describe students whose first language is not English and who depend on their first language for communication and understanding.

logico-mathematical knowledge In Piaget's theory, knowledge that goes beyond physical experience and depends upon inventing or reorganizing patterns of ideas.

macroculture A larger shared culture representing core or dominant values of a society.

maintenance rehearsal   Rote memorization, which does not guarantee understanding.

mastery teaching   Refers to Madeline Hunter's seven-step lesson model.

matching items   Any test item consisting of two columns of words or phrases to be matched.

mean   The arithmetic average of a set of scores; one of the three measures of central tendency.

measurement   The process of describing a student's particular characteristics. Measurement answers the question, "How much?"

median   The central score of a set of scores; the score that divides the set of scores into two equal halves; one of the three measures of central tendency.

medium-level questions   Questions that guide a learner to new discoveries or to conceptual conflicts and inadequacies in his or her ways of thinking.

mental images   Cognitive representations of, for example, pictures, sounds, and smells.

mental model   A schema-based representation of experience, including perceptions of task demands and task performances.

mental retardation   Significantly subaverage intellectual functioning, usually present at birth, resulting in or associated with impairments in adaptive behaviour and manifested during the developmental period.

metacognition   Knowledge about thinking and the capability to monitor one's own cognitive processes, such as thinking, learning, and remembering.

metalinguistic awareness The ability to reflect on one's own knowledge of language.

metaphor   A way to represent and talk about experiences in terms of other, more familiar, or more commonly shared events that seem comparable.

microcultures   Groups within cultures that share particular values, knowledge, skills, symbols, and perspectives.

misbehaviour   According to Doyle, any behaviour, by one or more students, that competes with or threatens learning activities.

mnemonic device   A technique for remembering that connects new information with prior knowledge.

mode   The most frequently occurring score in a set of scores; one of the three measures of central tendency.

model   A person whose behaviour acts as a stimulus to learning, according to Bandura.

modelling   Learning by observing the behaviour of others.

moral judgments   Judgments about right or wrong.

morality of constraint   According to Piaget, a type of moral thinking made by children under ten years of age; rules come from some external authority and strictly define what is right and wrong.

morality of cooperation   According to Piaget, a type of moral thinking made by older children; rules provide general guidelines but should not be followed blindly without considering the context.

morality of nonviolence   The third level of Gilligan's theory of moral reasoning, in which there is a realization that it is wrong to serve oneself at the expense of others.

moratorium   According to Marcia, adolescents who have given thought to identity issues but have not reached any decisions.

motivation to learn   A disposition of learners that is characterized by their willingness to initiate learning activities, their contin-

ued involvement in a learning task, and their long-term commitment to learning.

motivation   The desire to produce modeled behaviour.

motor skills   According to Gagné, learned capabilities relating to movement or to muscles that induce movement, such as the ability to ride a bicycle or to operate a computer.

multiculturalism   A recognition that ethnic groups make up and contribute to a national culture while they maintain an individual identity.

multiple-choice items   Test items consisting of questions or incomplete sentences that are accompanied by three or more alternative responses, one of which is to be selected as the correct or best answer.

need for autonomy   The need to initiate and regulate our own actions; self-determination.

negative reinforcement   An aversive stimulus is removed or terminated following a desirable response in order to strengthen that response.

norm-referenced judgments   The performance of one student is compared against the performances of others.

normal curve   A mathematically defined function that approximates many educational phenomena.

objective tests   Paper-and-pencil tests made up of items, such as true/false and multiple-choice, that can be objectively scored (i.e., scored in exactly the same way no matter who or what is doing the scoring).

observational learning effects   Consequences of modelling that lead to the acquisition of cognitive and behavioural patterns that had no chance of occurring prior to modeling.

observer   The learner is an observer, according to Bandura.

on-task behaviour   Any time a student is engaged with an academic task.

operant behaviour   According to Skinner, behaviour that is not a simple reflex to a stimulus but an action that operates on the environment.

operant conditioning   According to Skinner, learning through responses and their consequences.

overlapping   A teacher's ability to deal with more than one issue at the same time.

pair shares   Short discussions between student dyads. Such discussions are usually interspersed with periods of lecture.

peer models   Models who are from the same social environment.

peg mnemonics   A strategy for memorization in which items of a list to be learned are associated with cue words and images.

perceived competence   An observer's evaluation of how expert a model is.

perceived similarity   An observer's perception of similarity between himself or herself and the model.

percentile rank   A standardized score that gives the test taker the percentage of people in the norm group above whom he or she has scored.

performance   Exhibiting a capability.

performance assessment   A demonstration of learning, or an exhibition of curriculum mastery that typically involves tasks focusing on students' use of knowledge and skills in a variety of realistic situations and contexts.

performance goal   An aim of students who place primary emphasis on gaining positive recognition from others and avoiding negative judgments.

phonology   The study of the sound system of a language and the structure of those sounds.

physical disability   Disorders of the skeleton, joints, and muscles, or health conditions that interfere with students' educational performances.

physical knowledge   In Piaget's theory, any knowledge about objects in the world that can be gained through experiencing their perceptual properties.

placement   A goal of assessment that determines what level of difficulty a student is capable of handling in instruction.

portfolio   A collection of evidence pertaining to students' developing knowledge and expertise, serving a particular assessment purpose.

positive reinforcement   The presentation of a satisfying stimulus, contingent on a response that results in strengthening the response.

postconventional morality   Rules of conduct of adults who recognize the societal need for mutual agreement and the application of consistent principles in making judgments. This is Level 3 of Kohlberg's theory of moral reasoning.

pragmatics   An area of language that refers to the effects of contexts on meaning and the ways to use language to create different contexts.

preconventional morality   Rules of conduct of children (birth–9 years) who do not yet understand the conventions of society. This is Level 1 of Kohlberg's theory of moral reasoning.

Premack principle   A special case of positive reinforcement in which a high-probability behaviour is used to reinforce a low-probability behaviour.

preoperational   According to Piaget, the stage at which children learn to mentally represent things.

primary reinforcer   Something that satisfies a basic biological need, such as food, water, or shelter.

prior knowledge   Knowledge that has already been acquired and stored in long-term memory.

problem solving   The activity of applying rules, knowledge, and cognitive strategies to move from the current situation, or initial state, to a desired outcome, or goal.

procedural knowledge   Prior knowledge that involves knowing how to do something.

procedures   Standards of behaviour that are specific to a particular classroom task or set of related tasks.

production   The act of producing modelled behaviour.

psychomotor domain   Learning outcomes that relate to skilled physical movements, as classified by Harrow's taxonomy.

psychosocial development   According to Erikson, the process whereby relationships with others influence one's search for his or her own identity.

puberty   The time of physical change during which individuals become sexually mature.

punishment   The presentation of an aversive stimulus immediately following a response in order to weaken the incidence of the response.

Pygmalion effect   The influence that a teacher's expectations may have on the behaviour of students. Also called the teacher expectancy effect and the self-fulfilling prophecy.

qualitative information   Information communicated through words.

quantitative information   Information communicated through numbers.

questioning   The act of asking questions as a tactic of instruction.

race   A socially constructed, complex, dynamic, and changing construction that is related to economic and political factors.

range   The difference between the highest and lowest scores in a set of scores.

rating scale   A measurement instrument used in observation-based assessment to make judgments about some continuing behaviour or performance.

readiness   A goal of assessment that shows whether students have the necessary prerequisite skills and knowledge to begin a unit of instruction.

reception learning   Ausubel's approach to teaching, in which students are presented with material in a complete, organized form and are shown how to move from broad ideas to more specific instances. Reception learning is deductive.

reciprocal determinism   In cognitive social theory, the three-way relationship that exists among personal factors, environment, and behaviour.

reciprocal questioning   A technique that uses question stems that students complete. The technique encourages critical thinking.

reciprocal teaching   A technique that begins with the teacher's questions designed to enhance metacognitive skills and that progresses to a gradual transfer of the control of questioning to the students, who work cooperatively.

reflective construction   Thinking critically about the principles and concepts of educational psychology and classroom practice in order to develop a theory of teaching.

reframing   Rethinking an event or problem in terms of metaphors in order to gain a new perspective.

reinforcement   The process by which the consequences of behaviour establish and maintain it.

relative standard   A grading system in which the performance of one student is compared against the performances of others.

reliability   A property of assessment that concerns the degree to which assessments are free of measurement errors.

response cost   A fine is exacted from an individual as punishment for misbehaviour.

response facilitation effects   Consequences of modelling that promote previously learned behaviour by introducing inducements to perform that behaviour.

retention   The capacity to remember modelled behaviour.

retrieval   The process that transfers information from LTS to STS in order to be used.

rhymes   Words that are identical to others in their terminal sound.

role diffusion   The negative outcome of Stage 5 of Erikson's theory of psychosocial development, whereby an adolescent is unable to develop a clear sense of self.

rubric   A scaled set of criteria clearly defining for the student and teacher the range of acceptable and unacceptable performance on a performance assessment.

rules   General standards of behaviour that are meant to apply across all classroom situations.

scaffolding   The process in Vygotsky's theory whereby a more advanced partner changes the degree and quality of support provided to the less skilled partner as he or she becomes more proficient.

schema   A mental structure for organizing information and representing knowledge. Any set of objects, experiences, or actions that is consistently classified forms a schema.

schemata   Theoretical knowledge structures that contain information, facts, principles, and the relationships among them.

schemes   In Piaget's theory, generalized ways of acting on the world that provide the basis for mental operations.

selection-type items   A test item format in which students select an answer from possible alternatives.

selective attention   The process of attention whereby the learner chooses to focus on a particular source of information from the environment.

selective perception   The process of selectively attending to important aspects or details in stimulus information in order to process them further.

self-actualization   Fulfilling one's personal potential.

self-concept   One's description of self in terms of roles and characteristics.

self-efficacy   A human being's judgment about his or her ability to deal effectively with tasks that need to be faced.

self-esteem   One's judgments about self and the feelings associated with those judgments.

self-reflection   The act of thinking about one's own experiences and reflecting on one's own thought processes.

self-regulation   The act of applying an internal set of standards and criteria to regulate one's own behaviour.

self-reinforcement   Using consequences that come from within to strengthen a desired behaviour.

self-sacrifice and social conformity   The second level of Gilligan's theory of moral reasoning, in which there is a realization that caring for others rather than just caring for oneself is good.

semantic memories   Memories of facts and general knowledge but not including the time and place they were learned.

semantics   The study of the meanings of words and sentences.

sensorimotor stage   The earliest stage in Piaget's theory of cognitive development, during which infants learn about their environment through their senses and motor actions.

sensory disorders   Disorders such as hearing and visual impairments.

shaping   The process of reinforcing responses that are successively closer to the ultimate desired behaviour.

short answer items   Supply-type items that include incomplete statements, such as fill-in-the-blanks or direct questions requiring a brief response.

short-term memory   The phase of processing at which a limited amount of information is stored for a limited time.

situated learning   Students engaging in problem solving of realistic or simulated problems that require the use of disciplinary knowledge and skills.

six dimensions of good thinking   Six aspects that characterize skill in thinking critically, which include a language of thinking, thinking dispositions, mental management, a strategic spirit, higher-order knowledge, and transfer.

small group discussion   Exchange of information and opinion among a small number of students.

social cognitive theory   A learning theory, originated by Bandura, that draws on both cognitive and behavioural perspectives. According to the theory, people learn by observing the behaviour of others in their social environment.

social-arbitrary knowledge   In Piaget's theory, knowledge gained solely by one's interactions with other people within one's cultural group.

socioeconomic status   Relative standing in society as measured by variables such as income, occupation, education, access to health coverage and community resources, and political power and prestige.

special education   Specially designed instruction and services to meet the needs of exceptional learners.

standard deviation   A statistic that expresses the variability in a distribution of scores.

standardized tests   Tests that are prepared to provide accurate and meaningful data on students' performances compared to others at their age or grade levels.

stanine   A standardized score from 1 to 9, each of which represents a range or band of raw scores.

story technique   A memorization technique that helps in recalling ordered information by combining the elements to be remembered in the correct order in a brief story.

student teams–achievement divisions (STAD)   A cooperative learning method that uses heterogeneous groups of four to five students. Rewards are given to teams whose members show the greatest improvement over their own past performance.

student-centred instruction   Instruction in which the student is the focus of learning activity.

students at risk   Students whose life circumstances make them more likely to fail in school

submersion   The "sink or swim" approach to teaching students from different cultures in which school programs do not take into account cultural and linguistic differences.

subtractive bilingualism   A form of bilingualism in which students, although conversationally competent in both languages, are not fully literate in either one; this has an adverse effect on achievement.

summative assessment   An assessment administered at the end of an instructional unit for the purpose of assigning a grade.

supply-type items   A test item format in which items ask students to generate an answer.

symbolize   To form mental representations of modelled events.

syntax   The grammatical arrangement of words in sentences.

systemic validity   A property of assessment in which assessment serves as an impetus for curriculum change.

T score   A standardized score that converts raw scores to a distribution with a mean of 50 and a standard deviation of 10.

table of specifications   Used for planning a test, a two-way chart or matrix that shows the content areas or objectives to be assessed along with the desired level of skill for each outcome.

teacher power   The authority that teachers have available to them to manage student behaviour; inversely, the extent to which students control their own behaviour.

teacher-centred instruction   Instruction in which the teacher is the focus of learning activity.

teaching   Action taken with the intent to facilitate learning

teaching efficacy   A teacher's belief that teaching, in general, will have an influence on students' learning.

teaching–learning process   The process of taking action to produce change in thought or behaviour and subsequent modification of capabilities.

team-assisted individualization(TAI)   A teaching tactic in which students work on programmed materials as members of a heterogeneous group. Rewards for completing the work accurately and quickly are given to the team as a whole.

teams-games-tournaments (TGT)   A cooperative learning method that uses heterogeneous groups of four to five students. Team members leave their teams to compete as individuals in homogeneous weekly tournaments. An individual's performance in the weekly tournament contributes to his or her team's score.

test   A formal procedure or an instrument used for measuring a sample of student performance.

test bias   An unfair disadvantage (less frequently an unfair advantage) that affects members of some subgroups because of some aspects of the test, the way the test is administered, or the way the result is interpreted.

test-wiseness   Using test characteristics and formats or the test situation to receive a higher score than expected if only subject matter knowledge was being measured.

theory of multiple intelligences   Howard Gardner's theory of seven distinct intelligences or talents.

theory of teaching   Description, explanations, and prediction of action staken with the intent to facilitate learning.

thinking dispositions   Mental habits, inclinations, or tendencies in thinking behaviour exhibited over time and across diverse thinking situations.

time-out   The practice of separating a disruptive student from the rest of his or her classmates in order to decrease the probability of the response that precedes it.

token economy   A behavioural program that allows students to earn objects for good behaviour. The objects can be redeemed for desirable goods or privileges.

transfer of learning   The application of knowledge acquired in one situation to other situations.

undermining effect   Consequence that an extrinsic reward can have on behaviour that is intrinsically motivated.

validity   A property of assessment concerning the extent to which interpretations of assessment results will be appropriate, meaningful, and useful.

verbal information   A learning outcome that enables learners to communicate about objects, events, or relations; declarative knowledge.

vicarious learning   Changes in thought or behaviour through observing the behaviour of others and the consequences of those behaviours.

vicarious reinforcement   Using consequences derived from viewing a model engaged in a desired behaviour to strengthen that behaviour.

wait-time I   The length of time between the teacher's question and the student's response.

wait-time II   The length of time between the student's response and the teacher's reaction to that response.

withitness   According to Kounin, the teacher's ability to observe all situations in the classroom and to deal effectively with misbehaviour.

work-oriented classrooms   Classrooms in which the teacher values production and is directive of student activity.

working memory   In some models, another term for STS because this is the stage at which a learner works on information from the environment.

Z score   A score given in standard deviation units. The mean of any normal distribution is assigned a Z score of 0. Scores above the mean are plus scores; scores below the mean are minus scores.

zone of proximal development (ZPD)   In Vygotsky's theory, the gap between actual and potential development—that is, between what a child can do unaided by an adult and what he or she can do under the guidance of an adult or in collaboration with more capable peers.

NAME INDEX

A

Achenbach, T.M., 157
Adams, R.S., 317
Agostino, V.R., 162
Alberto, P.A., 334
Algozzine, B., 61
Alladin, 99, 101, 127
Allemann-Brooks, J., 397
Allen, J.R., 162
Allington, R. L., 312
Allison, M., 82
Alschuler, A.S., 296
Alter, R. 75, 498
Ames, C., 293, 294
Ames, C.A., 274, 281, 293, 294, 295
Anastopoulos, 269
Anderman, E.M., 295
Anderson, 269
Anderson, C.M.B., 210
Anderson, J.R., 216, 378, 424
Anderson, L., 404
Anderson, L.M., 320, 397
Anderson, R.C., 13, 108, 225, 226
Andrews, 56, 165
Antes, R.L., 427, 491, 492
Arlin, M., 330
Arlin, P., 31
Armbruster, B.B., 217
Armstrong, T., 142, 143
Aronson, E., 285
Aschbacher, P.R., 464
Ashton, P.T., 289, 290
Assante, M.K., 116
Astilla, E., 286
Atkinson, J.W., 280
Atkinson, R.C., 204, 210, 222
Ausiker, A., 311
Asubel, D.P., 214, 368
Ayllon, T., 195
Azrin, N.H., 183, 195

B

Bachor, 438
Baer, D.M., 185
Bagley, W.C., 307
Bailey, S.M., 109
Bandura, A., 240-68, 283, 300, 320
Banks, C.A.M., 122
Banks, J.A., 98, 102, 104, 106, 116, 117, 122, 123, 124, 125, 126, 129, 156
Barenboin, C., 63
Barker, G.P., 285
Barnes, J., 67
Barnett, W.S., 165
Barnett-Foster, 431
Baron, J.B., 287, 421, 441, 443
Barone, W., 162
Bartley, 438
Bartz, W.H., 210
Baruth, L.G., 98, 99, 101, 106, 114, 123, 124, 129, 132

Bascia, 128
Bates, E., 49
Bateson, 435, 485
Baumrind, D., 313
Baxter, G.P., 127, 425
Beamer, 264
Beane, J.A., 62, 63, 65
Beaudry, J.S., 161
Becker, J.M., 122
Beery, R., 496
Behrenz, K., 74
Bell, K.J., 119
Bell, R., 83
Bell-Gredler, M.E., 209, 362
Bellon, E.C., 311
Bellon, J.J., 311
Bempechat, J., 77
Bennett, A., 37, 79
Berdine, 83
Berger, K.S., 49
Berk, L.E., 41, 54, 62, 67
Berliner, D.C., 12, 15, 41, 127, 326, 391, 397, 398
Berlyne, D.E., 291
Bernhard, J., 26
Berrueta-Clement, J.R., 165
Betsalel-Presser, R., 68
Berry, J.W., 100
Bhatt, G.S., 64
Bialystok, 102
Bibby, R.W., 103, 115, 116, 117
Biddle, B.J., 317
Bidwell, N., 83
Biffart, 410
Bigge, 81
Bishop, J.H., 501
Bissonnette, 275
Blackhurst, 83
Blakemore, 74
Blank, M.A., 311
Bligh, D.A., 389
Block, J., 77
Bloom, B.S., 223, 354, 355, 393
Boggiano, A.K., 62, 266
Bolton, I., 43
Book, C.L., 13
Borich, G.D., 426, 478, 479
Borko, H., 13, 14, 15
Borkowski, J.G., 353
Bowd, 421
Bower, G.H., 242
Bowman, B.T., 125
Boyle, M.H., 157, 269
Brabeck, M., 88
Bracey, G.W., 488
Brainerd, C.S., 28
Bransford, J.D., 147, 231
Bremmer, R., 74
Brenton, R., 124
Bretherton, I., 49
Brodkin., A.M., 80

Brody, J., 266
Brookhart, S.M., 13, 492, 494, 498, 501
Brophy, J.E., 308-26, 388, 389, 397
Brown, A.L., 232, 235, 401, 402,
Brown, I., 61
Brown, J.S., 232, 263, 353, 356
Brown, S., 401, 402, 412
Brubaker, N.,397
Bruffee, A., 403
Bruner, J.S., 27, 42, 50, 353, 366
Brutsaert, H., 77
Burke, J.C., 319
Bursuck, 377
Bushell, E., 195

C

Cable, G.W., 223
Cahen, L.S., 326, 397
Cain, K.M., 137
Callister, T.A., 488
Calvert, 483
Campione, J.C., 235
Cangelosi, J.S., 308
Canter, L., 337
Canter, M., 337
Capie, W., 396
Carey, L.M., 427, 464, 478
Carey, S., 49, 102, 499
Carlson, L.D., 118
Carlson, S.B., 429
Carr, 99, 128
Carter, K., 8, 11, 12, 15
Case, R., 45, 46
Casile, W.J., 498
Chance, P., 179
Charles, C.M., 319, 330, 331, 335, 339
Cherlin, D.L., 317
Chi, M., 226
Chilcoat, G., 389
Chinn, C., 108
Chittendon, E., 437
Chiu, L.H., 65
Church, J.A., 162
Clark, C., 371
Clark, E.V., 48, 49
Clark, H.H., 48, 49
Clark, J., 282, 393
Clarke, 403
Clay, M.M., 165
Clements, A.C., 205
Clements, B.S., 313, 316, 397
Clifford, 56
Clifton, R., 5, 405
Cobb, P., 202
Coburn, J., 407
Cochrane-Smith, 15, 18
Cohen, G., 232
Cohen, P.A., 400
Coladarci, T., 290
Colby, C., 87
Cole, E., 118, 484

Cole, M., 38, 40
Coleman, M.F., 80
Collins, A., 232, 263, 356, 421, 437, 439, 440, 441
Comeaux, M.A., 15
Comer, J.P., 127
Comfort, K.B., 433
Conte, R., 74, 165
Conway, M.A., 232
Cook, 378
Cookson, D., 484
Cooney, J.B., 11
Cooper, G., 217
Cooper, H.M., 326
Corbett, A.T., 219
Corbin, C.B., 77
Corno, L., 339, 398
Corson, 103
Coulson, R.L., 234
Coulter, D.L., 160
Covington, M., 496
Cox, P.D., 261
Craik, F.I.M., 210
Craven, R.G., 65
Cremo, E., 111
Crooks, T.J., 494
Csapo, M., 157
Cummins, J., 119, 120
Cunningham, C.E., 74
Cunningham, G.K., 4, 427, 487
Curwin, R.L., 309
Cushing, K., 12

D

Damon, W., 62, 64, 68
Danley, R.R.,, 425
Das, J.P., 55, 147, 148
Daum, J., 317
Dawson, G., 407
Debus, R., 65
DeCharms, R., 296-97
Deci, E.L., 281, 293, 297
Dei, 99, 112
DeCorte, E.,217
DeFord, D.E., 165
Delefes, P., 317
Delisle, J., 162
Derevensky, J., 79, 181
Derry, S.J., 352, 409
DeVries, B., 89
DeWin, L., 217
Dick, W. 353, 361, 372, 373, 456
Dickinson, G., 389
Dillon, J., 395
Dishaw, M.M., 326, 397
Ditricks, R., 260
Dittmeier, L., 308
Divecha, D.J., 137
Doctorow, M.J., 383
Dolan, L.J., 165
Downs, A.C., 77
Doyle, W., 233, 282, 311, 330, 331
Draper, R.D., 4
Driscoll, M.P., 30, 52, 53,, 211, 212, 217,

226, 263, 264, 298, 312, 348, 349, 352, 353, 372, 373, 398
Duell, O.K., 393, 394, 395
Duffy, G., 312, 389, 391, 397
Duffy, T.M., 232, 263
Duguid, P., 232, 263, 356
Duke, C.R., 13
Dupaul, 342
Dusek, J.B., 78
Dweck, C.S., 137, 281, 282, 285, 293
Dworet, D., 157

E

Eadie, 403
Eagly, A.H., 77
Earhard, 287
Ebel, R., 427, 449, 489
Eder, R.A., 62
Edwards, 408
Eggen, P., 112, 225
Elam, S.M., 74
Elawar, M.C., 398
Eller, B.F., 488
Elliott, E.S., 281, 397
Ellis, J.A., 232
Ellis, 158
Ellison, 269
Ellsworth, R., 393
Emmer, E., 311, 317, 319, 397
Emmer, E.T., 311, 313, 315, 316, 320, 321, 397
Engestrom, Y., 38, 40
Enzle, 287
Epstein, M.H., 160
Erickson, 114
Erickson, E., 68-72
Estes, T.H., 397
Evertson, C.M., 308-30, 397

F

Fagan, E.R., 61
Fagan, T.K., 61, 396
Fagot, B.I., 77
Farnish, A.M., 405
Feiman-Nemser, S., 6
Feldman, N.S., 62, 266
Feldman, R.D., 141, 147
Feldman, R.S., 230, 231
Felt, L., 105
Feltovich, P., 234
Feltovich, P.J., 226
Fenstermacher, G., 11
Fiedler, F.F., 313
Filby, N.N., 326, 397
Finders, M., 499, 500
Fishbaugh, 410
Fisher, C.W., 326, 397
Fishkin, J., 87
Fishman, B.J., 232, 263
Flavell, J.H., 44
Fleming, 322
Fletcher, C., 76
Flynn, M., 154
Foley, R., 160

Ford, B.A., 156
Ford, L., 62
Forgett-Giroux, 287
Forrest-Pressley, D.L., 47
Fox, L.H., 266
Frame, J., 484
Frederiksen, J.R., 421, 437
Freeman, D.J., 13, 494
French, F., 55
Frey, G., 92
Frideres, J., 100, 105
Friedl, A.E., 368
Friend, 377
Friesen, J.W., 103, 115, 116, 117, 120
Frieze, I., 285
Frisbie, D.A., 427, 449, 489, 490, 491, 494
Furlong, M., 409
Furst, E.J., 354
Fuson, K.C.,217
Futrell, M.K., 488

G

Gaa, J.P., 266
Gabor, T., 157
Gage, N.L., 11, 388, 391, 393, 399
Gagné, R.M.,, 217, 225,348, 349, 352, 353, 362, 365, 369, 394
Gallimore, R., 53
Gallup, A.M., 74
Gamble, 463
Garcia, J.E., 313
Gardner, H., 139, 140, 141, 147
Garlett, M.W., 75, 76
Gavaki, E., 64, 107
Geisert, P.G., 488
Gemmer, 269
Gettinger, M., 311
Gibbons, 340
Gilbert, 225
Giles, D.K., 195
Gilligan, C., 73, 88
Ginott, H., 332
Glaser, R., 217, 226, 464
Glaserfeld, 232
Glasser, W., 334, 343
Goin, M.T., 222
Goldenberg, C.N., 288
Goldman, S.R. 147
Gooch, 483
Good, T.L., 308-11, 313, 315, 320, 323, 326, 388, 389, 393, 397, 405
Goodlad, J., 313
Gordon, B., 160
Gordon, T., 331, 332, 333
Gorges, 397
Grabe, M., 223
Graham, S., 107, 116, 285
Grant, C.A., 122
Greenberg, 269
Greene, D., 293, 378
Greeno, J.G., 15
Greenough-Olsen, S.C., 27, 126, 421, 484
Greer, J.G., 297
Gresham, F., 268

Griffin, P., 40
Grigorenko, 150
Griswold, P.A., 494
Gronlund, N.E., 361, 418, 419, 425, 426, 427, 446
Grossman, H., 77, 108, 110, 266
Grossman, S., 77, 108, 110, 266
Gruber, H.E., 28
Grusec, J.E., 183
Guilford, J.P., 139
Gump, P., 330
Gunter, M.A., 397
Gupta, R., 78, 79
Gustafson, 225

H

Haertel, G.D., 109, 136
Haines, 410, 412
Hall, V.R., 195
Hallahan, D.P., 25, 79, 82, 157, 158, 161, 162, 166
Hambleton, R.K., 421, 443
Hanesian, H., 214, 368
Haney, W., 483
Hanna, G.S., 464
Hanson, A.R., 261
Harel, 232
Haring-Smith, T., 384, 403
Harper, 128
Harris, A., 269, 311
Harris, F.R., 185
Harrow, A.J., 355
Hart, D., 62, 64, 421, 435-38, 440, 441, 443, 456
Harter, S., 62, 65, 66, 67
Hartshorne, H., 90
Harsbrouck Schwab, J. 397
Hassler, D.M., 396
Hatch, T., 139, 140, 141
Havriluk, 408
Hawkins, 287
Hayes, L. 51
Heckhausen, H., 340
Hein, G.E., 441
Hemingway, 287
Henson, K.,389
Herbert, W., 287
Herman, J.L., 464
Hernstein, R.J., 137, 484
Hess, G.C., 61
Hetherington, E.M., 137
Heward, w.L., 156
Heyman, G.D., 137
Hiebert, F., 412
Hildebrand, D., 138, 149, 160
Hilgard, E.R., 242
Hill, K.T., 485, 486
Hill, W.H., 354
Hoge, R.D., 163
Hohn, R.L., 158
Holstein, B., 87, 88
Holubec, E., 401
Holz, W.C., 183
Homestead, E., 441

Honebein, P.C., 232, 263
Hopkins, B.R., 492, 498, 499
Hopkins, C.D., 427, 445, 491, 492, 498, 499
Houser, N., 223
Houston, J.P., 206, 219, 220
Howard, V., 139
Hoy, W., 289
Hoy, W.K., 290, 313
Huck, C.S., 165
Hughes, 409
Hull, 110
Huitt, W.G., 311
Huling-Austin, L., 4, 11
Hummel, R.C., 88
Hunt, D., 109
Hunt, E.B., 203
Hunter, B., 409, 434
Hunter, M., 387
Hunter, P., 463
Huston, A.C., 77
Hutton, 165
Hutchinson, 287, 377
Hwang, K., 88
Hysmith, C., 456

I

Inhelder, B., 29, 37
Iran-Najad, A., 205

J

Jackson, B., 317
Jackson, D., 340
Jacobs, E., 68
Jacobson, L., 287
Jacobson, M.J., 234
Jacoby, L.L., 210
Janda, 446
Janzen, B.L., 37, 154
Janzen, H.C., 428, 425, 485
Jarman, R., 147
Jay, E., 149, 356, 370, 384
Johnson, A., 388, 399
Johnson, C., 74
Johnson, D.W., 6, 92, 265, 293, 294, 388, 389, 398, 401, 402, 405, 490
Johnson, R.T., 111, 293, 294, 389, 398, 401, 405, 490
Jones, C., 156
Jones, L.S., 300, 311, 315, 323, 324, 326, 327, 328, 434
Jones, V.F., 311, 323, 324, 326, 327, 328, 401, 402, 496
Juliebo, 42
Jung, 164
Junker, L., 109

K

Kagan, S., 402
Kahle, J.B., 109
Kamman, 269
Kanevsky, L., 79
Karweit, N.L., 165, 405
Kauchak, D., 112

Kauffman, J.M., 25, 79, 82, 148, 149, 157, 158, 161, 162, 166, 225
Kaufmann, A.S., 488
Kearsley, G., 409
Keith, T.Z., 397
Keller, A., 62
Keller, J.M., 298
Kelly, I.W., 37, 154
Kelman, H.C., 323
Keniston, K., 87
Kennedy, M., 164
Kenny, R., 407
Kesner, R.P. 205
Kirby, J., 147, 148, 373
Klassen, 99, 128
Klauer, K.J., 361
Klein, C., 79
Klein, J.D., 226
Kloss, R.J., 395
Kneedler, P., 386
Knight, R.S., 13
Knowles, R.T. 90, 269
Koenig, D., 111,
Kohlberg, L., 85-88
Kohn, A., 179, 313, 337, 342
Kounin, J., 315, 323, 324, 325, 328, 330
Kourilsky, M., 383
Krasavage, E.M., 387, 388
Krathwohl, D.R., 354, 355, 467
Krechevsky, M., 141
Krywaniuk, L.W., 148, 149
Kubiszyn, T., 426, 478, 479
Kuhl, J., 340
Kukla, A., 285
Kulhavy, R.W., 209, 455
Kulik, C.C., 400
Kulik, J.A., 400
Kurtz, L., 79
Kusche, 269
Kutnick, P., 401

L

LaBerge, D., 224
Lajoie, S.P., 409
Lakoff, 6
Lamme, L.L., 456
Lampron, 269
Lan, K.S.K., 120
Landman, G.B., 285
Langlois, J.H., 77
Lashley, T.J., 308
Latham, G.P., 266
Latimer, V., 484
Lave, J., 232
LeBlanc, R., 140
Lebow, D., 196
Leckerman, R., 181
Leder, G.C., 288
Lee, S., 137, 396
LeFrancois, G.R., 48
Leggett, E.L., 281, 282
Leinhardt, G., 15, 213, 214, 232, 233, 235
Lemke, J.J., 55
Leont'ev, A.N., 40

Lepper, M.R., 293
Lesser, G.S., 299
Levin, B., 79
Levin, H.M., 136
Levin, J.R., 220, 222
Levine-Rasky, 98, 99, 128
Lewis, 410
Lewis, A.B., 217
Lewis, C., 499, 500
Lewis, J., 485
Li, A., 485
Lickona, T., 85, 90, 93, 279
Linden, 269
Lindsay, P.H. 213
Lipka, 62, 63, 65
Little, A., 286
Littlejohn, K., 27
Livingston, C., 13, 14, 15
Loadman, W.E., 13
Locke, E.A., 266
Lockman, 269
Lockwood, 88
Loebl, J.H., 62, 266
Loewen, 398
Loomer, 165
Lowry, D.H., 219
Luce-Kapler, R., 4
Luckasson, R., 160
Lum, D., 98
Lundberg, 264
Lunney, G.S., 77
Luria, A.R., 147
Lyman, 467
Lynch, D.J., 393
Lyons, C.A., 165
Lytle, 15
Lytton, H., 108

M

McAlpine, 104, 114
McCann, S.J.H., 420, 485
McCarrell, N.S., 231
McCarthy, H.D., 290
McCaslin, M., 308, 311, 313, 315
McClellan, 232
McClelland, D.C., 279, 280
McClelland, J.L., 205, 216
McClintic, S., 65
McCombs, B.L., 296, 298
McCormick, C.B., 220, 222
McCown, R.R., 498
McCutcheon, G., 371
McDaniel, E.A., 290
MacDonald, I.M., 157
McDougal, D., 420
McGee, 269
McGinn, 229
McGinnis, 441
McGivern, S., 222
McIntyre, D., 312, 412
Macionis, J.J., 105
McIver, D., 64
McKeachie, W.J., 389
MacKenzie, A.A., 216

MacKinnon, C.,87
MacKinnon, E., 47
McLaughlin, M.W., 309
McLean, 264, 278, 285
McLean. G.F., 90
McLean, J.E., 488
McLean, L.D., 424, 438
McLeish, J., 389
McWatters, 483
MacDonald, I.M., 157
Madaus, G., 483
Madsen, C.H., 334
Madsen, C.K., 334
Maehr, M.L., 295
Magee, L.J., 142
Mager, R., 360
Maguire, T., 104, 114, 494
Malden, 405
Male, 410, 412
Malicky, 42
Malkus, U., 141
Mancini, G., 484
Mandeville, G.K., 387
Maniet-Bellerman, P., 39, 168, 387
Manning, M.L., 99, 101, 106, 114, 123,
   124, 129, 132, 341
Mansbach, S.C., 499
Marcia, J.E., 70-73
Marfo, 56
Marks, C.B., 383
Marliave, R., 326, 397
Marsh, G.E., 205
Marsh, H.W., 61, 65, 67
Marshall, H.H., 62, 308, 310, 397, 398
Martin, G., 335
Martin, R., 227
Marx, R.W., 393
Marzano, R.J., 296, 298
Masia, B.B., 355
Maslow, A.H., 276-77
Massey, D., 420, 421, 485, 499
Mastropieri, M., 222
May, M.A., 90
Mayer, G.R., 182, 184
Meacham, J.A., 62
Meece, J.L., 109
Meichenbaum, D., 47, 261
Meier, S.E., 285
Meister, C., 402
Meloth, M.S., 391
Mendler, A.N., 309
Mendelson, B.K., 67
Merrill, M.D., 365
Meyer, 83
Michaelis, M., 195
Michaud, 287
Miller, A.G., 125
Miller, G.A., 209, 210
Miller, T.E., 13, 125
Mignano, 320, 330
Mira, M.P. 82
Misanchuk, 408
Miskel, C.G., 313
Mitchell, T., 266

Moallem, M., 372, 373
Monson, M.P., 441
Monson, R.J., 441
Moore, C.A., 393
Moore, J.E., 326
More, J., 111
Morgan, M., 293
Morris, C., 140
Moskal, R., 82
Motta, R.W., 79
Motz, 290
Mueller, H., 484
Mulcahy, R., 56, 484
Munby, H., 6, 8
Murphy, D.A., 353, 420
Murphy, E., 443
Murray, C.A., 137, 484
Myles, D.W., 287

N

Naglieri, J.A., 147, 148
Nagy, 431
Natriello, G., 493
Needels, M.C., 388
Nelson, R.W., 111, 112
Nesbitt, 269
Newman, D., 40
Nisbett, R.E., 293
Nielsen, 159
Nitko, A.J., 427, 447
Nock, D.A., 111, 112
Noonan, J.V., 488
Norman,. D.A., 42, 213, 220
Norris, M., 431
Novak, J.D., 214, 368
Nyberg, V., 420
Nye, R.D., 179, 197
Nyiti, R.M., 36
Nystul, M.S., 277

O

Obiakor, F.E., 61
O'Brien, M., 77
O'Connell, B., 49
O'Connor, J.E., 11
Oderkirk, J., 154
Offord, D.R., 157, 269
Okagaki, L., 137
Olweus, 83, 84
O'Loughlin, M., 232
Olson, L., 141
O'Neil, J., 487
Orland, M., 164
Orlansky, M.D., 156
Ormrod, J.E., 261
Oser, F.K., 168
O'Sullivan, J.T., 353
Ozier, 287

P

Paivio, A., 215
Palcic, R., 13
Palincsar, A.S., 401, 402
Papert, S., 232, 408

Parke, R.D., 137
Pascarella, E.T., 109
Pate, P.E., 441, 444
Patton, E.A., 160
Pavlov, I., 175
Pauls, 101, 110
Pear, J., 335
Peat, 56
Pelech, F., 120
Pelletier, L.G., 281, 298
Pendergrass, M.L., 4
Penner, J., 389
Perkins, D., 139, 149, 403
Perkins, D.N., 356, 370, 384
Peters, E.E., 222
Peters, R., 89
Peterson, D.R., 157
Peterson, L.R., 210
Peterson, M.J., 210
Peterson, P.L., 15, 371, 393
Peterson, S., 209
Pettifor, J., 89
Phillips, 110, 158
Piaget, J., 27, 28-37, 40, 84-85, 138
Pike, R., 62
Pilon, D., 280
Pine, J., 127, 425
Pinnegar, S., 12
Pinnell, G.S., 165
Piper, D., 100, 118, 119, 120
Podell, D.M., 290
Polloway, E.A., 160
Polyzoi, 401
Pool, 42
Popham, W.J., 421, 426, 427, 464, 484, 487
Postman, N., 3
Powers, 269
Prawatt, R.S., 398
Premack, D., 182
Pressley, M., 353
Price, K.R., 142
Price, S., 441

Q

Quay, H.C., 157
Quellmalz, E.S., 443, 444

R

Rachlin, H., 193
Racine, Y., 157, 269
Ramos-Ford, V., 141
Randhawa, B.S., 109, 227, 264, 434
Randolph, C.H., 308, 309, 310, 315
Rathberger, A.J., 157
Rathus, S.A., 48
Raugh, M.R., 222
Recchia, S., 65
Reese, H.W., 219
Reiser, R.A., 361, 372, 373, 456
Reiss, S.M., 160, 163
Renzulli, J.S., 162, 163
Reynolds, G.S., 185
Ribich, F., 162
Richard, 287

Rieber, L., 292, 408
Rivers, 387
Robert, L.J., 157, 405
Rogers, 447, 485
Robler, 408
Roblyer, 408
Robertson, 410, 412
Roehler, L.R., 391
Rogoff, B., 42
Romney, D.M., 108
Rose, L.C., 74
Rosenberg, M., 63
Rosenkrans, M.A., 260
Rosenshine, B.V., 323, 330, 386, 396, 402
Rosenstein-Manner, 83, 84
Rosenthal, R., 287
Rosenthal, T.L., 250
Ross, S., 42, 241
Roth, 229
Rotter, J., 284
Rowe, M.B., 395, 396
Rowell, 225
Rowley, K., 53
Royer, J.M., 223, 230, 231, 369
Rubin, L.J., 292
Ruble, D.N., 62, 266
Rumelhart, D.E., 213, 216
Russell, 6, 8
Rutherford, R., 389
Ryan, 90
Ryan, K., 90, 102
Ryan, R.M., 281
Ryder, 409
Rymer, 127

S

Saari, L.M., 266
Sabers, D., 12
Sacks, O.W., 161
Sadker, D., 109
Sanche, 410, 412
Saklofske, D.H., 5, 127, 138, 148, 158, 160, 203, 420, 425, 485
Salend, S.J., 168
Salmon, P., 83
Salomon, G., 369
Samuda, B., 485
Samuel, 98
Samuels, S.J., 224
Sappington, T.E., 277
Sarafino, E., 293
Sarvela, P.D., 488
Satzewich, V., 100, 101, 105
Saxe, G.B., 27
Scaldwell, W., 484
Schalock, R.L., 160
Schicke, M.C., 61
Schindler, 74
Schlieker, E., 67
Schmittroth, J., 384
Schneider, W., 224
Schoenfeld, A.H., 231, 232, 282
Schommer, M., 282
Schrage, 410

Schultz, 114
Schunk, D.H., 218, 243, 248, 250, 252, 260, 261, 262, 266, 268
Schwab, 397
Schwartz, N.H., 209
Schwean. V., 126, 127, 138, 148, 158, 420, 421
Schwebel, A.I., 317
Schweinhart, L.J., 165
Schwier, 408
Scott, L., 233
Scruggs, T.E., 222
Secord-Gilbert, M., 74
Segars, J.K., 311
Seligman, M.E.P., 285
Semb, G.B., 232
Senter, G.W., 319, 330, 331, 334
Seyfort, B., 484
Shanker, U., 308
Sharan, S., 125
Shatz, E., 164
Shavelson, R.J., 15, 127, 425
Shaw, K.N., 266
Shelton, 269
Shepard, L.A., 421
Shepherd-Look, D., 77
Sherman, G.P., 226
Shiffrin, R.M., 204, 210, 224
Shore, C., 49
Short, R.H., 420, 485
Sidorowicz, L.S., 77
Siegler, R.S., 28, 36, 37, 46
Silva, 269
Silver, E., 464
Simon, H.A., 210
Simon, S., 260
Simpson, G.E., 125
Simpson, R.L., 168
Skinner, B.F., 174-88, 335, 360, 402-405
Slavin, R.E., 54, 92, 125, 165
Sleeter, 122
Smith, G.B., 297
Smith, I.D., 67
Smith, K., 389
Snell, M.E., 160
Snipper, 102
Snow, R.E., 340
Snyder, L., 49
Solomon, 98, 99, 128
Soodak, L.C., 290
Sorensen, 98
Spandel, V., 474
Speckhart, L., 260
Spence, J.T., 260
Spiro, R.J. 234
Spitalnik, D.M., 160
Spreen, O., 484
Squires, D.A., 311
Stacy, K., 401
Stalikas, A., 64, 107
Stallings, J., 387, 388
Stanhope, N., 232
Stanovich, K., 203
Stanley, J.C., 427, 498, 499

Stark, J.A., 160
Starrat, R.J., 92
Staybrook, N.G., 393
Stein, P, 12
Stephan, W.G., 126
Sternberg, R.J., 137, 139, 144, 145, 147, 150
Stevens, R.J., 405
Stevenson, H.W., 137, 396
Stewart. M.J., 77
Stewin, L.L., 420, 485
Stiehm, E.R., 162
Stiggins, R.J., 419, 435, 464, 465, 494, 496, 497, 498, 502
Stigler, J.W., 396
Stipek, D., 64, 65
Stipek, D.J., 280
Stock, W.A., 455
Stoner, 342
Strunk, W., Jr., 352
Stuart, J., 389
Such, 483
Sulzer, B., 184
Sulzer-Azaroff, B., 182, 184 Sumara, D., 4
Swain, M., 119
Swanson, H.L., 11
Sweller, J., 217
Swoers, 269
Szabo, M., 396

T

Talbert, J.E., 3, 403
Tanner, J., 78
Taylor, R.P., 492
Templine, 49
Terrace, H., 186
Tharp, R., 53
Thomas, R., 125
Thomas, M., 401
Thorndike, E.L., 176
Tishman, S., 149, 150, 356, 370, 371, 384
Tobias, S., 213
Tobin, K.G., 6, 7, 293, 396, 407
Tollefson, N., 282
Tonks, R.G., 64
Trevethan, S.D., 89
Troutman, A.C., 334
Tsai, S., 109
Tsanos, A., 79
Tucker, G.R., 119
Tuckman, B.W., 354
Tudge, J., 42

Turner, 269
Tulving, E., 215
Tyler, J.S., 82
Tyler, R.W., 124

U

Ungerleider, C.S., 111-14
Unger, R.K., 4

V

Valent, E., 8
Vallerand, R.J., 275, 281, 298
Vasudev, J., 88
Vavrus, L.G., 391
Veenman, S., 308
Verner, C., 389
Vern Stenlund, 289
Verschaffel, L., 217
Voneche, J.J., 28
Vosniadou, S., 52
Vye, N.J., 147
Vygotsky, L.S., 27, 38-45

W

Wadsworth, B.J., 26, 28, 32
Waggoner, M., 108
Wahlstrom, M., 425
Walberg, H.J., 109, 136
Walker, L.J., 89
Waller, T.G., 47
Walters, G.C., 183
Walters, R., 241
Waltman, K.K., 489, 490, 491
Wang, M.C., 136
Wasik, B.A., 165
Watkins, D., 286
Watters, B., 484
Webb, R.B., 289, 290
Wechsler, D., 138-39
Weikart, D.P., 165
Weiner, B., 284, 285, 491
Weingartner, C., 13
Weinstein, C.S., 308, 320, 330
White, D.R., 68
White, E.B., 34, 352
White, R.T., 216
Whitemore, J.R., 163
Whordley, D., 13
Wideman, 403
Wiersma, W., 467
Wiggins, G.P.,418, 419, 421, 425, 435, 443, 456, 458

Wild, 287
Wilgosh, L., 484
Williams, 102, 269
Willoughby, 290
Wilson, J.R., 418, 425, 485
Wineburg, S.S., 288
Winne, P.H., 393
Winters, L., 464
Winzer, M., 154-57, 158, 160, 166, 420
Withered, C.E., 297
Wittrock, M.C., 383
Woditsch, G.A., 384
Wolf, D., 139, 142
Wolf, D.P., 440
Wolf, M.M., 185, 195
Wolf, R.M., 397
Wolfgang, C.H., 342, 343
Wolfgang, M.E., 317, 332, 342
Wollen, K.A., 219
Wong, 269
Wood, 290-91
Wood, B.S., 48
Wood, D., 42
Woodward, J., 100
Woolfolk, A.E., 196, 225, 280, 287, 289, 290, 308
Worsham, M.E., 313, 316, 397
Worthen, B.R., 474
Wotherspoon, T., 106
Wrobel, P., 195
Wynne, E.A., 92
Wynn, R.L., 76

Y

Yang, 447, 485
Yekovich, C.W., 394
Yekovich, F.R., 394
Yewchuk, C., 421
Yi, H., 108
Yinger, J.M., 125
Youssef, M., 368
Yuet Lin Lee, A., 231

Z

Zerega, M.E., 109
Zessoules, R., 142
Ziegler, S., 83, 84, 125
Zimmerman, B.J., 266
Zingle, H.W., 61

SUBJECT INDEX

A

Ability
accommodating differences in, 167–68
students' beliefs about, motivation and, 282–83
Aboriginal children, 120
communication styles, 114–15
learning styles, 152–53
Aboriginal People, 100
socio-economic status, 105
Absolute standards for grading, 489
Abstraction, knowledge construction and, 30
Abstract reasoning in formal operations stage, 36–37
Abuse, 82–83
sexual, 82
Academic performance. *See also* Student progress
assessing of. *See* Assessment
grading on basis of, 490–91
reinforcement to improve, specifying objectives for, 360–61
view of intelligence and, 137
Accommodation, cognitive development and, 29
Accountability, multicultural education for, 126–27, 131
Achievement, grading on basis of, 490–91
Achievement motivation, 279
Achievement-related behaviours, 423–24
Achievement tests, 473
Canadian Achievement Tests, 473
Canadian Test of Basic Skills, 473
Acquired Immune Deficiency Syndrome (AIDS), 162
Acquisition and performance phase as event of instruction, 362–65
Acronyms, 221
Action zones, 317
Active experience
constructing knowledge through, 30–31
development and, 26
Active learning, 232, 383
critical thinking and, 385–86
student-centred instruction for. *See* Cooperative learning
Adaptation
contextual intelligence and, 146–47
of mental constructs, 28–29
Additive approach to multicultural curricula, 122, 127–28
Additive bilingualism, 102
ADHD (Attention Deficit Hyperactivity Disorder), 74, 148, 158, 342
Adolescence
cognitive development during, 36–37
fears, 78
moral development during, 86

peer relationships during, 70–71
psychosocial development during, 73
puberty and, 71, 78
suicide, 79
Adulthood
cognitive development during, 36–37
moral development during, 86
psychosocial development during,
Advance organizers, 368, 369
Affective domain, 355
Krathwohl's taxonomy of learning outcomes for, 355
Affordances, 340
African-centred schools, 112
African origins, poverty among, 107
Alternative assessment, 435–44. *See also* Authentic assessment
Alternatives, multiple–choice items and, 429
Analogies, 223
Anticipatory set, 387
Anxiety, test, 485–87
Applied behaviour analysis approach to misbehaviour, 334–37, 353
contingency contracting and, 336–37
rules and, 334–35
token economies in, 335–36
Aptitude tests, 474
ARCS model, 298–300
attention in, 299
confidence in, 300
relevance in, 299–300
satisfaction in, 301–302
Arousal effects of modelling, 252
Artifacts in portfolios, 440
Arts PROPEL project, 142
Assertive discipline, 337–39
Assessment, 419–58
adapting for individual differences, 168–69
alternative. *See* Alternative assessment
application of, 454–59
creating a positive environment and, 458–59
effective feedback and, 454–55
modifying and improving instruction and, 456–57
student involvement in assessment and, 456
authentic. *See* Authentic assessment
bias and, 126, 447
anxiety and, 485–87
Canadian views, 419–21
classroom tests for. *See* Classroom tests
collaborative, 456
defintion of, 418–19
goals of, 422–24
of higher-level thinking, 357
in instructional planning, 357
interpreting results of, 467–72
quantitative and qualitative information and, 467–69

of standardized tests. *See* Standardized tests
summarizing quantitative information and, 469–72
item analysis and, 447–49
by peers, 456
performance, 441–44. *See also* Performance assessment
pitfalls in, 449–50
portfolio, 438–41. *See also* Portfolio assessments
Principles of Fair Practice, 450–54
questionnaires for, 456
reliability and, 446–47
standardized tests for. *See* Standardized tests
standards of, supporting teaching-learning process, 501–502
of student thinking, 50–52
validity, 446
views of, 419–21
Assimilation
cognitive development and, 28–29
education for, 115–16
Asthma, 163
Attention, 254
in ARCS model, 299
automatic, 207
gaining, 206–207, 209, 325–26
increasing, 44–45
maintaining, 326–27
encouraging student interaction and, 327
recognizing students and, 326–27
modelling and. *See* Modelling, attention and
selective, 206
Attention Deficit Hyperactivity Disorder (AHDH), 74, 148, 158, 342
Attestations in portfolios, 440
Attitudes as learning outcome, 353
Attributions
of causes for success and failure, 284–85
changing, in motivational training, 296–98
Attribution theory of motivation, 284
Attribution training, 296
Ausubel's reception learning, 368
Authentic activities to facilitate development, 53–54
Authentic assessment, 421, 435–37
observation-based, 437–38
performance, 441–44
portfolio, 438–41
Authentic communication in managing misbehaviour, 332
Authentic tasks, 233
Authoritative leadership, 314
Authority in classroom, 314–15
Automatic attention, 207
Automaticity, 46

encouraging thgough practice, 223
Autonomy, need for, 281
Autonomy versus shame and doubt stage of psychosocial development, 270
Aversive consequences, 180

B

Beginning the school year
  in elementary classrooms, 321
  in secondary classrooms, 322
Behaviour
  antecedents of, 177–78
  changing, 181–86
    determining reinforcers for, 191,
    evaluating progress and revising procedures for, 192–93
    goal setting and, 191
    implementing procedures and monitoring results and, 192
    selecting procedures for, 192
    strengthening desirable behaviours and, 181–82
    weakening undesirable behaviours and, 183–84
  maintaining, 186–90
    continuous reinforcement for, 186–88
    intermittent reinforcement for, 188–90
  on-task, 324
  reciprocal determinism and, 248–49
  reinforcement
    changing behaviours and, 181–86
    classical conditioning and, 175
    effective use of praise, 195–96
    enhancing teaching and learning using, 190–97
    increasing motivation with, 194
    managing by rules and, 193–95
    operant conditioning and, 175
    token economies for, 195
Behavioural approach, 174. *See also* Behaviour
Behavioural objectives, specifying, 360
Beliefs, motivation and. *See* Motivation
Benchmarks of student progress. *See* Student progress
Bias, test, 126, 448, 483–85
  anxiety and, 485–87
Bicultural education, 118–20
Bilingual education, 102–104, 118–20
Bilingualism, 102–104
Binary-choice items, 427, 428
Black Canadians, 100, 112
Blindness, 410
BNA (British North America Act), 102–103
Bloom's taxonomy of learning outcomes, 353
Bobo doll studies, 241
Bodily-kinesthetic intelligence, 141
Brain injury, 81–82
Bruner's discovery learning, 366–68
Bullying, 83–84

C

Canadian Achievement Test, 473
Canadian Test of Basic Skills, 473
Cancer, 163
Catch phrases for gaining attention, 325–26
Central tendency measures, 469–70
Cerebral palsy, 162
Chaining, 186
Charter of Rights and Freedoms (1982), 103
Child abuse, 82–83
Childhood
  early
    cognitive development during, 32–35
    gender roles during, 76–77
  middle
    cognitive development during, 35–36
    gender roles during, 76–77
    moral development during, 86
Classical conditioning, 175
Classroom(s)
  arrangement of, 316–19
    smooth transitions and, 330
  creating positive assessment environment in, 458–59
  cultural conflicts in. *See* cultural diversity
  culture-fair, 114
  elementary. *See* Elementary classrooms
  gender-fair, 109–110
  goal structures of, varying, 293
  inclusive, 166
  leadership and authority in, 314–15
  learning-oriented, 309, 315–23
  secondary, beginning school year in, 322
  work-oriented, 309
Classroom management, 307–15
  application of, 339–43
    accommodating cultural diversity and special needs, 341–42
    teacher power and, 342–43
    teaching self-responsibility and, 340–41
  defined, 311
  discipline contrasted with, 311
  metaphors for, 308–310
  processes and products of, 310–13
    instructing for learning and, 312–13
    managing for discipline and, 311–12
Classroom tests, 424–35
  planning, 425–26
  selection-type items for, 426, 427–32
    binary-choice, 427–29
    matching, 429
    multiple-choice, 429, 431–32
  supply-type items for, 432–35
    essay, 433–35
    short answer, 432–33
Cognition. *See also* Thinking; Thinking dispositions; Thinking skills

metacognition and, 217, 218
  viewpoints on, 202
Cognitive development, 25–58
  accommodating individual differences in, 50–56
  facilitation through learning, 43–44
  information-processing theory of, 44–47
  language development and, 47–50
  organization and adaptation of mental constructs and, 28–29
  Piaget's theory of, 31–37
  social basis for, 38–44
  through active experience, 30–31
  Vygotsky's theory of, 38–44
Cognitive development theory, 25
Cognitive domain, Bloom's taxonomy of learning outcomes for, 354
Cognitive modelling, 261
Cognitive rehearsal, 256–57
Cognitive strategies as learning outcome, 352
Collaborative leadership, 314
Collaborative learning, 402
Comfort, risks to, 81–83
Communication
  about student progress. *See* Student progress
  assertive discipline and, 337–39
  computers and, 409
Communication disorders, 159
Communication styles, cultural diversity and, 113–15
Communities of learning, 234–35, 315
Compensatory education
  for cultural diversity, 115–16
  for exceptional learners, 164
Competence, perceived of models, 260
Competitive goal structures, 294
Complexity of modelled actions, 255
Componential intelligence, 145–46
Comprehension as learning outcome, 354
Computer(s), 407–12
  cultures and communication and, 409
  instruction and, 407–408
  and students with special needs, 410, 412
  thinking and, 408–409
Computer-assisted instruction (CAI), 407
Computerized adaptive testing, 488–89
Concepts
  concrete, 350
  defined, 351
Concrete concepts, 350
Concrete experiences to facilitate development, 52–53
Concrete operations stage of cognitive development, 35–36
Conditional memory, 218
Conditioned reinforcers, 179
Conditioning. *See also* Behaviour, changing; Behaviour, maintaining; Reinforcement
  classical, 175

operant, 175
Conduct disorder, 157
Confidence bands, 479
Confidence in ARCS models, 300
Conflicts
    cultural. *See* Cultural diversity
    resolving without creating losers, 333
Confronting-contracting face, 343
Conservation tasks, 33, 36
Construct, 136
Constructivism, 230, 232, 235. *See also*
    Constructivist view of learning;
    Reflective construction
Constructivist view of learning, 232
    active learning and, 232
    authentic activity and situated learn-
        ing and, 232–34
    communities of learning and,
        234–35
Construct validity, 446
Content areas; thinking skills in, 356–57
Content validity, 446
Contextual intelligence, 146–47
Contingencies of reinforcement, 186
Contingency contracting for managing
    misbehaviour, 336–37
Continuous reinforcement, 186–88
Contract grading, 492
Contracting, contingency, for managing
    misbehaviour, 336–37
Contrasts for discovery learning, 366–67
Contributions approach to multicultural
    curricula, 122
Control theory approach to misbehav-
    iour, 333–34
Conventional morality, 86
Cooperative goal structures, 293
Cooperative groups. *See also* Cooperative
    learning
    to support social harmony, 125–26
Cooperative integrated reading and com-
    position (CIRC) approach, 405
Cooperative learning, 54, 124–25,
    402–407. *See also* Computers
    acceptance of disabilities and,
        167–68
    cooperative integrated reading and
        composition for, 405
    helping relations and, 92
    Student Teams-Achievement
        Divisions for, 403–404
    Team-Assisted Individualization for,
        405
    Teams-Games-Tournaments for,
        404–405
Coping models, 261
CoPlanner, 410–11
Covert rehearsal, 256
Criterion-referenced judgments, 464
    grading and. *See* Grading
Criterion validity, 446
Critical periods, 68
Critical thinking, 385. *See also* Thinking
    dispositions
Cultural context, development and, 27

Cultural diversity, 98–110
    beliefs and, impact on student moti-
        vation, 286
    classroom management for, 341–42
    conflicts in classroom and, 111–15
        communication styles and, 113–15
        learning styles and classroom organi-
            zation and, 111–12
        school versus home cultures and, 111
        techniques for creating culture–fair
            classrooms and, 114
    cultural awareness and
        multicultural education for, 123–24
        promoting acceptance of differences
            and, 117–18
    equity and multicultural education for,
        124–25
    exceptional ability and disability, 110
    gender and sexual identity and,
        107–109
    language and, 102–104
    multicultural education and. *See*
        Multicultural education
    parental involvement and, 499–501
    racial and ethnic identity and,
        99–101
    self-concepts and, 64–65
    socioeconomic status and, 104–107
    teacher acceptance of, 129
    teachers' knowledge of, 128–32
        accepting student diversity and, 129
        gender-fair education and, 109
        multicultural teaching strategies and,
            129–32
    views of intelligence and, 137
Cultural forces, 370
Cultural pluralism, 116–17
Culture.*See also* Culural diversity
    definition of, 98
Culture-based teaching of thinking skills,
    370–71
Culture-fair classrooms, 114
Curiosity
    arousing, 291
    as thinking disposition, 150
Curricula
    hidden, 111
    multicultural. *See* Multicultural
        education
Cystic fibrosis, 163

D

Deafness, 159–60
Decentration in concrete operations
    stage, 35–36
Decision making, participatory, 93
Deficiency needs, 277
Deficit model of multicultural education,
    116
Defined concepts, 351
Democratic classroom, 322–23
Development, 25–27
    cognitive. *See* Cognitive development
    developmental capabilities and, 25
    influences on, 26–27

language. *See* Language development
moral. *See* Moral development
psychosocial. *See* Psychosocial
    development
of self-concept. *See* self-concept
of self-esteem. *See* Psychosocial
    development
Developmental crises, 68
    significance for teachers, 73
Developmentally appropriate instruc-
    tions, 51–52
Developmental psychology, 25
Diabetes, 163
Diagnostic tests, 474
Dialects, 104
Dimensions of good thinking, 357
Direct instruction, 386
Direct reinforcement, 258
Disabled students, 80–82, 110
    adapting instruction for, 377
    child abuse and, 82–83
    computers and, 410–12
    cultural diversity and, 110
    definition of disability and, 155
    high-incidence disabilities and, 157,
        159
    including in classrooms, 166
    low-incidence disabilities and,
        159–62
Discipline. *See also* Applied behaviour
    analysis approach to misbehaviour
    assertive, 337–39
    classroom management contrasted
        with, 311
Discipline problems, 331–39
Discovery learning, 366
Discrimination, 349
    index of, 448–49
    as intellectual skill, 349
Discriminative stimulus, 177
Discussions, small-group, 399–400
Disequilibrium, 29
Disinhibitory effects, of modelling, 250
Dispersion of test scores, 470–72
Distractors, multiple-choice items and,
    429
Diversity. *See* Cultural diversity; Gender
    differences; Individual differences
Divorce, 79
Dominant bilingualism, 102
Double matching items, 429
Dual-code theory, 215

E

Early childhood. *See* Childhood, Early
Educational psychology, 15
Education, bilingual, 118–20
Effectors, 205
Effort, grading on basis of, 490–91
Egocentrism, 34
Elaborative rehearsal, 211
Elementary classrooms, 321
Emotional/behavioural disorder (E/BD),
    157
Empirical abstraction, 30–31

Enactive learning, 243
Encoding, 46, 209
  of information in short-term store, 209–12
    elaborative rehearsal and,. 211–12
    maintenance rehearsal and, 210–11
Enterprise schema as event of instruction, 365
Environment(s)
  acquiring tools to understand, 38–41
  assessment, positive, 458–59
  development and, 26–27
  in information-processing model, 204
  physical, of classroom, 316–19
    smooth transitions and, 330
  reciprocal determinism and, 248–49
Environmental enhancements, effects of modelling, 252
Epilepsy, 162
Episodic memory, 215
Equilibration, cognitive development and, 29
Erikson's theory of psychosocial development, 68–72
  stages of development and, 69–72
ESL Program, 119–20
Essay items, 433–34
Ethical issues. See Moral development
Ethnic groups, 99, 115
Ethnicity, 99
Ethnocentrism, 129
Evaluation, 419. See also Assessment
Exceptional learners. See also Disabled students; Gifted and talented students
  provisions for, 157, 163–66
Executive control, 205
Experiential intelligence, 146
Expert problem solving, 226–27
Expert teachers, 11–17
  differences between novice teachers and, 11–13
  reflective construction and, 15–17
  though processes of, 13–15
Explanation, 391
  in teaching-centred instruction, 391–93
Extended-response essays, 433–34
Extrinsic motivation, 279
Extinction, 183

F

Factory metaphor, 309–310
Fading, 186
Failure, attribution of causes for, 284–85
Fair Student Assessment Practices in Canada, 450–54
Far transfer, 370
Feedback
  effective, 454–55
  from peers, 497–98
French immersion programs, 119
Finger spelling, 160, 161
First Nations students, 110
Fixed interval reinforcement schedules, 188–89

Fixed ratio reinforcement schedules, 189
Foils, multiple-choice items and, 429
Foreclosure, 73
Forethought, social learning and, 246
Formal operations stage, 36–37
Formative assessments, 425
Full inclusion, 166. See also Inclusion

G

Gagné's events of instruction, 362
  acquisition and performance, 362–65
  enterprise schema, 365
  preparation phase, 362
  transfer of learning, 365
Gagné's taxonomy of learning outcomes. See Learning outcomes
Gardner's theory of multiple intelligences, 139–43
Gender differences, 107–109
  gender-fair classrooms and, 109
  in moral development, 88–90
Gender-fair classrooms, 109–110
Gender role stereotypes
  in elementary grades, 76–77
  techniques for encouraging gender equity and, 77
Generative model of learning, 383
Generativity versus stagnation stage, 71–72
Gifted and talented students, 162
  underachieving, 162–63
Gilligan's theory of gender-based morality, 88–90
Global education, 122
Goals
  of assessment, 422–24, 502
  instructional. See Instructional goals
  leadership, 314–15
  of students, 281–82
Goal setting
  in instructional planning, 372
  teaching, 265–66
Goal structures of classroom, 293
Grade equivalent scores, 478–79
Grading, 489–96
  of achievement versus effort, 490–91
  contract, 492
  of essay tests, 433–34
  grading systems and, 489–90
  pass/fail, 491–92
  research on, 493–96
Grammar, 48
Group assessment, 456
Groups. See Cooperative learning
Groupware, 410
Growth needs, 277
Growth spurt, 78
Guided practice, 387
Guilford's theory of intelligence, 139

H

Handicaps, 155
Harrow's taxonomy of learning outcomes, 355–56
Head injury, 80, 81
Health, risks to, 81

Hearing impairment, 162, 163
Helping relations, 92
Helplessness, learned, 285
Hemophilia, 163
Heritage language schools, 120
Hidden curriculum, 111, 126
Hierarchy of needs, 276
Higher-order knowledge, thinking and, 357
Higher-order rules, 352
High-road transfer, 370
Human activity systems, 40

I

Identity achievement, 73
Identity diffusion, 72
Identity statuses, 72–73
Identity vs. role diffusion, 70
Imagery, 219
  enhancing, 219
I-messages in managing misbehaviour, 332
Imitation in sensorimotor stage, 32–33
Immersion programs, 118–20
Inclusion, 160. See also Full inclusion; Classroom(s), inclusive
Independent practice, 396–98
Index of discrimination, 448–49
Index of item difficulty, 448, 449
Individual differences. See also Cultural diversity; Gender differences
  accepting, 167–68
  accommodating, instruction and, 167–68
  developmental, accommodating, assessing student thinking, for, 50–52
    authentic activities for, 53–54
    concrete experiences for, 52–53
    encouraging student interaction for, 54
    multiple sign systems for, 55
  enhancing teaching and learning and, 166–69
    accepting differences and, 167–68
    adapting instruction and, 168–69
    alternative assessments and, 169
    creating an inclusive classroom and, 168
  in intelligence, 136–49
Individualistic goal structures, 295
Individual survival, 88
Industry versus inferiority stage, 70
Infancy
  cognitive development during, 32–33
  moral development during, 86
Informal cooperative groups,
Information processing, facilitating, 203–13
  encoding information in short-term store and, 209–12
  retrieving information for long-term store and, 212–13
  transferring information in sensory register and, 206–209
Information-processing theory, 44–47
  increasing attention and, 44–45

knowledge acquisition and, 45–47
monitoring cognitive processes and, 47
Inhibitory effects of modelling, 250
Initiative versus guilt stage, 70
Inspiration, 409
Instruction, 312. *See also* Teaching
  accommodating student diversity and, 377–78
  adapting for individual differences, 167–68
  attention and. *See* Attention
  clear instructions for, 323–24
    precise directions and, 325
    student involvement and, 325
  computers and. *See* Computers
  direct, 386
  Gagné's events of. *See* Gagné's events of instruction
  for learning, 323–30
  modifying and improving, assessment and, 456–57
  pacing, 328
  programmed instruction and, 185
  revising, 375–77
  smooth transitions in, 330
  student-centred. *See* Student-centred instruction
  summarizing and, 328–29
  teacher-centred. *See* Questioning; Teacher-centred instruction
Instructional activities, 373
Instructional goals, 359
  deciding on, 359–60
  multiple, integrating, 365
Instructional materials
  acceptance of disabilities and, 167–68
  in instructional planning, 373
Instructional planning, 372
  adapting for special needs students, 377
  analyzing student characteristics and, 373
  assessments and, 373
  goal setting and, 372
  implementation and revision, 375–77
  instructional materials and, 373, 375
  objectives and 373
Integration, education for, 115–16
Integrative model of personal and interpersonal development, 90–93
Integrity versus despair, 72
Intellectual skills as learning outcome, 349
Intelligence, 136–49
  as construct, 136
  cultural views of, 137
  definition of, 136
  Gardner's theory of multiple, 139–43
  Guilford's theory of, 139
  measuring, 136–37
  Piaget's theory, 138
  Sternberg;s theory, 144–47
  Wechsler's theory, 138

Intelligence tests, 136
Interaction. *See* Social interaction
Interactive instructional technologies. *See* Computer(s)
Intermittent reinforcement, 188
  fixed interval schedules of, 188–89
  fixed ratio schedules of, 189
  variable interval schedules of, 189
  variable ratio schedules of, 190
Internalization, understanding environment and, 40–41
Internalizing, 158
Interpretation of test results, 467–72
Interpretive items, multiple-choice, 432
Intersubjectivity, 42
Intervention programs for exceptional learners, 165–66, 269
Interview sheets, 438
Intimacy versus isolation stage, 71
Intrinsic motivation, 274
Inuit students, 405–407
IQ scores, 136, 476–77
Irreversibility in preoperations stage, 34
Item analysis, 447–49

K

Kamehameha Elementary Education (Keep) Program, 53
Keyword mnemonics, 222
Knowledge
  acquiring, information processing theory of, 45–47
  higher-order thinking and, 357
  procedural, 319
  students' beliefs about, motivation and, 282–83
Knowledge acquisition components of componential intelligence, 145
Knowledge base of teaching, 15–16
Knowledge construction
  in multicultural education, 124
  through active experience, 30–31
Kohlberg's theory of moral development, 85–88
Krathwohl's taxonomy of learning outcomes, 355

L

Language
  cultural diversity and, 102–104
    bilingualism and, 102–104. *See also* Bilingual education
  dialects and, 104
  of thinking, 357
Language development, 47–50
  pragmatics and, 50
  semantics and, 49–50
  syntax and, 48–49
Language immersion, 118–19
Lateral transfer, 369
Law of effect, 176
Leadership and authority, 314–15
Learned helplessness, 285
Learning. *See also* Behaviour, changing; Conditioning; Reinforcement
  active. *See* Active learning

communities of, 315
constructivist view of. *See* Constructivist view of learning
cooperative. *See* Cooperative learning
definition of, 3
discovery, 366
enactive, 242
facilitation and development by, 43–44
generative model of, 383
learning how to learn, 202–203
metaphors for. *See* Metaphors
motivation. *See* Motivation
observational. *See* Modelling; Social learning
situated, 233
social. *See* Modelling; Social learning
transfer of. *See* Transfer of learning
vicarious, 244
Learning disabilities, 158
Learning goals, 281
Learning-oriented classrooms, 309, 315–23
Learning outcomes, 348
  accommodating student diversity and,
  Bloom's taxonomy of, 354
  determining and specifying, 357–61
    deciding on instructional goals and, 359–60
    specifying performance objectives and, 360–61
  facilitating, 361–71
    Ausubel's reception learning and, 368
    Bruner's discovery learning and, 366–68
    cultural approach to teaching thinking and, 370–71
    Gagné's events of instruction and, 362–65
    transfer of learning and, 365
  Gagné's taxonomy of, 348–54
    attitudes in, 353
    cognitive strategies in, 352–53
    intellectual skills in, 349–52
    motor skills in, 353–54
    verbal information in, 349
  Harrow's taxonomy of, 355–56
  instructional planning. *See* Instructional planning
  Krathwohl's taxonomy of, 355
  thinking in content areas and, 356–57
Learning styles,
  cultural conflicts and, 111–12
Lecturing, 388–90, 410
Lickona's model of personal and interpersonal development, 90–93
Linguistic intelligence, 139
Lipreading, 161
Logico-mathematical knowledge, 30–31
Long-term store (LTS), 205
Low-road transfers, 370
LSET program, 55

M

Macroculture, 98
Maintenance rehearsal, 210
Marcia's theory of identity statuses, 72–73
    foreclosure, 73
    identity achievement, 73
    identity diffusion, 72
    moratorium, 72–73
Maslow's hierarchy of needs, 276
Mastery models, 261
Mastery teaching, 387
Matching items, 429
Material tools, 39–40
Matrix items, 429
Maturation, development and, 26
Mean of distribution scores, 471
Measurement, 417. *See also* Assessment;
    Classroom tests; Standardized tests
Median of distribution of scores, 470
Mediation, 39
Medium-level questions, 50
Memor(ies)
conditional, 218
    enhancing, 219–23
      imagery and, 219
      metaphors and analogies for, 223
      mnemonic devices for, 220–22
      techniques for activating prior
        knowledge and, 213–14
    episodic, 215–16
    long-term. *See* Long-term store
      (LTS)
    procedural, 217
    semantic, 216–17
    short-term (working). *See* Encoding;
      Short-term store (STS)
Mental images, 215
Mental management, thinking and, 357
Mental models, 217
Mental retardation, 110, 159–60
Mentors, 8
Metacognition, 47, 217, 218
Metacomponents of componential intelli-
    gence, 145
Metalinguistic awareness, 102
Metaphors
    for classroom management, 308–310
    enhancing memory using, 223
    for teaching and learning, 6–10
      problem solving with, 7–10
Middle childhood. *See* Childhood,
    middle
Minimum competency testing, 487–88
Misbehaviour, 331–39. *See also* Discipline
    assertive discipline approach to,
      337–39
    control theory approach to, 333–34
    resolving conflicts without creating
      losers, 333
    self-correctional approach to, 331–33
Mnemonic devices, 211
    for encoding information, 209
    keyword, 222
    letter and sentence, 221

peg, 221
rhymes, 220
story, 222
Model(s), 240
    for discovery learning, 366
    influence on attention, 254–55
    peers as, 259
    selecting, 260–61
      diversity and 267
      perceived competence and, 260–61
      perceived similarity and, 260
Modelling, 250
    applications of
      cognitive modelling as instructional
        approach and, 261–63
      peer models and, 268
      selecting diverse models and, 267–68
      selecting effective models and,
        260–61
    arousal effects and, 252
    attention and, 254–56
      influence of models on, 254–55
      influence of observers on, 255–56
    cognitive, 240
    facilitative and environmental effects
      and, 251–52
    inhibitory and disinhibitory effects
      and, 250
    models for. *See* Models
    motivation and, 254
    observational learning effects and,
      252–53
    production and, 254, 257
    retention and, 254, 256–57
Mode of distribution of scores, 470
Moral development, 84–90
    theories of
      Gilligan, 88–90
      Kohlberg, 85–88
      Lickona, 90–93
      Piaget, 84–85
Moral flexibility, 85
Morality of constraint, 84
Morality of cooperation, 84
Morality of nonviolence, 88
Moral judgment, 84
Moral reflection, 92
Moral relativism, 85
Moratorium, 72–73
Motivation
    achievement, 279–80
    attribution of causes for success and
      failure, 284–85
    cultural values and, 286
    enhancing, 290–302
      ARCS model for, 298–301
      arousing curiosity, 291–93
      classroom goal structures, 293–95
      motivational training for, 296–98
      reinforcement for, 293
    internal/external sources of, 275
    intrinsic/extrinsic, 274
    to learn, 274
    learned helplessness and, 285–86
    modelling and, 254, 258

    needs and
      to achieve, 279–80
      for autonomy, 281
      Maslow's hierarchy of needs, 276
    perspectives on, 275–76
    students' beliefs and
      about knowledge and ability, 282–83
      cultural, impact of, 286
      in self-efficacy, 283
    students' goals and, 281–82
    teachers' beliefs and, 286–90
      about students, 286–87
      about teaching efficacy, 289–90
      Pygmalion effect and, 287–88
Motivational training, 296–98
    developing self-regulation in, 297–98
    setting goals and changing attribu-
      tions in, 296–97
Motor skills as learning outcome, 353
Multicultural education, 115–28
    bilingual, 118–20
    for cultural pluralism, 116–17
    curricula and school reform, 121–27
      accountability and, 126–27
      cultural awareness and, 123–24
      equity and, 124–25
      multiculturalism and, 117–28
      social harmony and, 125
    for integration and assimilation,
      115–16
    teaching strategies for, 129–32
Multiculturalism, 117–18. *See also*
    Cultural diversity
Multiple-choice items, 429, 431–32
Multiple classification in concrete opera-
    tions stage, 36

N

Narrative report, 498
Native Canadians, 108, 110
    children, 120
    communication, styles of, 114–15
    learning styles, 152–53
    poverty among, 107
Nature versus nurture, 26
Near transfer, 370
Negative reinforcement, 182
Nephritis, 163
Nephrosis, 163
Normal curve, 466
Normal distribution, 474–76
Norm-referenced judgments, 464

O

Objectives in instructional planning, 373
Objective tests, 421. *See also* Classroom
    tests; Standardized tests
Object permanence, 32
Observational learning. *See* Modelling;
    Social learning
Observation-based assessments, 437–38
Observers, 241
    influence on attention, 255–56
On-task behaviour, 324
Operant conditioning, 175

Operant behaviour, 175
Operating space, 45
Organization
    of mental constructs, 28–29
Outcomes of learning. *See* Learning outcomes
Overlapping in managing misbehaviour, 331
Overt rehearsal, 256

P

Pacing, 328
Pair shares, 390
Parental involvement, 74–76
Parent-teacher conferences, 498–99
PASS (Planning, Attention, Simultaneous Successive Processing), 147–49
Pass/fail grading, 491–92
PATHS curriculum, 269
Peer assessment, 456
Peer feedback, 497–98
Peer modelling, 268
Peer relationships, 78
Peg mnemonics, 221
Percentile rank, 476
Perceptual centration, 33
Performance. *See* Academic performance
Performance assessments, 441–44
Performance goals, 281
Personal factors, reciprocal determinism and, 248–49
Phonology, 48
Physical disabilities, 80, 162. *See also* Disabled students
Piaget's theory of cognitive development, 31–37
    knowledge construction and, 31–32
    stages of development and, 32–37
Piaget's theory of intelligence, 138
Piaget's theory of moral development, 84–85
Placement tests, 425
Plus-one matching, 88
Portfolio assessments, 438–41
Positive atmosphere, building, 320–21
Positive reinforcement, 181
Postconventional morality, 87
Poverty, 106–107
Pragmatics, 48, 50
Praise, effective use, of, 195–96
Preconventional morality, 86
Premack principle, 182
Premises, matching test items and, 429
Preoperations stage, 33–35
Preparation phase, 362
Prevention programs, 165–66
Primary reinforcers, 178
Prior knowledge, 213–18
Problem finding, 31, 353
Problem solving, 225–29, 353
    expert vs. novice, 226–27
    stage, 31
    strategic vs. tactical, 225

by teachers, metaphors for, 7–10
teaching, 227–29
    creating context for, 229
    identifying, defining and representing problems and, 227–28
    predicting candidate solutions and, 228
    reflecting on process, 229
    trying out and evaluating solutions, 228–29
Procedural knowledge, 217
Procedures, 319
Production(s)
    modelling, 254
    in portfolios, 440
Programmed instruction, 185
Project Spectrum, 141
Psychological tools, 39
Psychomotor domain, 355
Psychosocial development, 68
    developmental crises, 73
    Erikson's theory of, 68–72
    identity statuses (Marcia), 72–73
    and parental involvement, 74–76
Puberty, 78
Punishment, 183
Pygmalion effect, 287

Q

Qualitative information, 467, 468–69
Quantitative information, 467, 468–69
    summarizing, 469–72
Questioning, 393
    reaction and, 395–96
    reciprocal, 396
    solicitation and, 394–95
    structure and, 393–94
Questionnaires, assessment, 456

R

Race, 99. *See also* Cultural diversity
Racism, 101
Range of distribution scores, 472
Rating scales, 438
Reaction in questioning, 395–96
Readiness tests, 425
Reading Recovery Program, 165
Reasoning
    abstract, in formal operations stage, 36–37
    moral. *See* Moral development
Reception learning, 368
Receptors in information-processing model, 204–205
Reciprocal determinism, 248
    links between behaviour and environment and, 249
    links between personal factors and behaviour, 249
    links between personal factors and environment and, 249
Reciprocal questioning, 396
Reciprocal teaching, 401
Reconstructive retrieval, 213
Reflective construction, 15–17. *See also* Constructivist view of learning

Reflective abstraction, 30–31
Reframing, 8
Rehearsal
    elaborative, 211
    maintenance, 210
    retention of observational learning and, 256–57
Reinforcement, 174, 335–36. *See also* Conditioning
    antecedents of behaviour and, 177–78
    changing behaviour and.
        See Behaviour, changing
    contingencies of, 177
    continuous, 186–88
    intermittent, 188–90
    kinds of reinforcers and, 178–80
    maintaining behaviour and, 186–90.
        See also Behaviour, maintaining
    principles of, 180–81
    removal of, 183
Relationship-listening face, 343
Relative standards for grading, 490
Relevance
    in ARCS model, 299–300
    of modelled actions, 254–55
Reliability of assessments, 446–47
Report cards, 498
Reproductions in portfolios, 440
Research on grading, 493–96
Response(s), matching test items and, 429
Response cost, 184
Response facilitation effects of modelling, 251
Restricted–response essays, 433, 434
Retention
    facilitating, 256–57
    modelling and, 254, 256–57
Retrieval of information from long-term store, 212
Rheumatic fever, 163
Rhymes, 220
Role diffusion, 71
Role playing for summarizing, 328
Rubrics, 441
Rules, 319
    in applied behaviour analysis approach to misbehaviour, 334–35
    as intellectual skill, 351
Rules and consequences face, 343
Rules-ignore-praise (RIP) technique, 334–35
Rules-reward-punishment (RRP) technique, 335

S

Safety, risks to, 81–83
Salience of modelled actions, 254
Satisfaction in ARCS model, 301–302
Scaffolding, 42, 53
Schedules of reinforcement, 189–90
Schemas
    enterprise, as event of instruction, 365
    semantic memory and, 216

teachers' thought processes and, 13–15

Schemes, cognitive development and, 28

School. *See also* Classroom(s)
  culture of, conflict with home culture, 111

School reform, multicultural education and. *See* Multicultural education

School year, beginning. *See* Beginning the school year

Science 2000, 407

Science Vision, 407

Secondary classrooms, beginning school year in, 322

Security, risks to, 79–81

Selection-type items. See Classroom tests

Selective attention, 206

Selective perception, 207, 209

Self-actualization, 277

Self-concept
  development of, 61–65
    cultural diversity and, 64–65
  self-esteem compared with, 62

Self-efficacy, 246
  helping learners build a sense of, 263–65
  students' beliefs in motivation and, 283

Self-esteem. *See also* Psychosocial development
  development of, 65–67
    Lickona's theory of, 91–92
    self-concept compared with, 62

Self-fulfilling prophecies, 288

Self-reflection, social learning and, 246

Self-regulation skills, 246
  social learning and, 246
  teaching, 281, 297–98

Self-reinforcement, 179–80, 258

Self-responsibility, teaching, 340–41

Self-sacrifice and social conformity, 88

Semantic memory, 216

Semantics, 48, 49–50

Sensorimotor stage of cognitive development, 32–33

Sensory disorders, , 160–61

Sensory register, 205
  transferring information in, 206–209
    gaining attention and, 207–209
    perceiving information and, 207–209

Sex. *See* Gender entries

Sexual abuse, 82

Shaping, 147, 185

Short answer items, 432–33

Short-term store (STS), 205

Sickle-cell anemia, 163

Sign language, 161

Sign systems, multiple, 55

Similarity, perceived, of models, 260

Situated learning, 233

Situational context, development and, 27

Skeletal/muscular disabilities, 162

Small-group discussions, 399–400

Social action approach to multicultural

curricula, 123

Social-arbitrary knowledge, constructing, 31

Social cognitive theory, 240

Social harmony, multicultural education for, 125

Social interaction
  development and, 26–27
  among peers, encouraging, 68

Social learning, 240–70
  building of self-efficacy and, 263–65
  teaching goal-setting and self-regulation skills and, 265–66
  forethought, 246
  models and observers, 240–41
  performance vs., 241–43
  reciprocal determinism, 248
  self-regulation and self-reflection, 246–47
  symbolizing and, 245
  vicarious and enactive, 243–45

Social problems, 78–84
  risks to health and safety, 83–85
  risks to security and comfort, 81–83

Socioeconomic status, 104–107

Software. *See* Computers

Solicitation in questioning, 394–95

Spatial intelligence, 141

Special education, 166

Special needs students. *See* Disabled students; Gifted and talented students

Specific learning disabilities, 158–59

Speech reading, 160–61

Standard deviation of distribution of scores, 472

Standardized tests, 472–89
  anxiety and, 485–87
  computerized adaptive testing and, 488–89
  minimum competency testing and, 487–88
  normal distribution and, 474–76
  scores on, 476–79
    confidence and, 479
    grade equivalent scores, 478–79
    IQ scores, 476–77
    reading reports of, 482–83
    stanine scores, 477–78
    T scores, 477
    Z scores and percentile ranks, 476
  test bias and, 483–85
  types of, 472–74

Stanine scores, 477–78

Stem, multiple-choice items and, 396, 429

Stereotypes, 76
  gender role. *See* Gender-role stereo types

Sternberg's triarchic theory of intelligence, 144–47

Storage space, 45

Story techniques, 222

Strategic problem solving, 225

Strategic spirit, thinking and, 357

Structures in questioning, 393–94

Student(s)
  acceptance of diversity by, 167–68
  arousing curiosity of, 291
  changing behaviour of. See Reinforcement
  characteristics of, in instructional planning, 373
  developing sense of self-responsibility in, 340–41
  disabled. *See* Disabled students
  encouraging interaction of, 54, 327
  gifted and talented, 110, 162
  goals of, 281–82
  individual differences of. *See* Cultural diversity; Gender differences; individual differences
  involvement of. *See* Student involvement
  misbehaviour of. *See* Discipline; Misbehaviour
  motivation of. *See* Motivation
  random calling, 326
  recognizing, maintaining attention and, 326–27
  at risk, 79–83, 116
  provisions for, 163–66
  self-esteem of. *See* Psychosocial development; Self-esteem
  social problems of. *See* Social problems
  special needs. *See* Disabled students; Gifted and talented students
  underachieving, 162–63

Student-centred instruction, 386, 398–412
  computers in, 407–12
  cooperative learning, 402–407
  peer teaching and learning in, 400–402
  small-group discussions, 399–400

Student involvement
  in assessment, 456, 498
  instructions and, 325

Student progress, 463–503. *See also* Academic performance
  assessing of. *See* Assessment; Classroom tests; Standardized tests
  benchmarks of, 463–67
    criterion-referenced, 464–65. *See also* Grading
    norm-referenced, 465–67
  grading and. See grading
  reporting, 496–97
    involving parents from culturally and socially diverse backgrounds, 499–501
    involving students and parents and, 497–99

Student Teams-Achievement Divisions (STAD) method, 403

Submersion programs, 120

Subtractive bilingualism, 102, 120

Success for All program, 165

Suicide, 83

Summarizing, 328–29
Summative assessments, 425
Supply-type items. *See* Classroom tests
Symbolic representation, 33
Symbolizing, social learning and, 245
Symbol systems, multiple, 55
Syntax, 48–49
Systemic validity, 437
Systems approach to multicultural education, 127

T

Table of specifications, 426
Tabular items, 429
Tactical problem solving, 225
Talented students, 162
    underachieving, 162–63
TARGET learning goals, 295
Teacher(s)
    authority of, 314–15
    beliefs of, motivation and. *See* Motivation
    communication by. *See* Communication
    determination and specification of learning outcomes by. *See* Learning outcomes
    expert. *See* Expert teachers
    knowledge of cultural diversity. *See* Cultural diversity
    knowledge of individual differences. *See* Individual differences
    leadership and authority of, 314–15
    mentors for, 8
    as models, 268–69
    novice. *See* Novice teachers
    parent-teacher conferences and, 498–99
Teacher-centred instruction, 386
    explaining in, 391–93
    independent practice in, 387, 396–98
    lecturing in, 388–90
    questioning in, 393–96. *See also* Questioning
Teacher Effectiveness Training (TET), 331–32
Teacher expectancy effect, 288
Teacher power, classroom management and, 342
Teaching. *See also* Instruction
    defined, 3
    efficacy of, teachers' beliefs about, 289–90
    of goal-setting, 265–66
    knowledge base of, 15

mastery, 387
    metaphors for. *See* Metaphors, peer, 400–402
    of problem solving. *See* Problem solving
    reciprocal, 401
    scaffolding in, 42, 53
    of self-regulation skills, 265–66
    of self-responsibility, 340–41
    theory of. *See* Theory of teaching
Teaching-learning process, 3
Team-Assisted-Individualization (TAI) approach, 405
Teams-Games-Tournaments (TGT) method, 404
Telecommunications, 409
Telecomputing, 409
Test(s), 419
    classroom. *See* Classroom tests
    interpreting results of. *See* Assessment, interpreting results of
    objective, 421
    placement, 425
    readiness, 425
    scores on. *See* Assessment, interpreting results of
    standardized. *See* Standardized tests
    summative assessments, 425
Test anxiety, 485–87
Test bias, 483–85
    anxiety and, 485–87
Test-wiseness, 485
Textbooks
    in instructional planning, 373
    for multicultural education, 124
Theory of teaching, 4–6
    of authors, 17–20
    developing, 4–10
    metaphors for, 6–10
Thinking. *See also* Reasoning
    cultural approach to teaching, 370–71
Thinking dispositions, 149, 357
    active learning and, 384
    cultivating, 385
Thinking skills
    assessing, 50–52
    computers and 408–409
    in content areas, 356–57
    critical thinking and, 385
    dimensions of, 357
Time-out, 183–84
Token economies, 195
    for managing misbehaviour, 336–37

Transfer of learning, 365
    as event of instruction, 365
    low-road and high-road, 370
    near and far, 370
    thinking and, 357
    vertical and lateral, 369–70
Transformation approach to multicultural curricula, 123
Trust vs. mistrust stage of psychosocial development, 69–70
T scores, 477
Tuberculosis, 163

U

Underachieving students, 162–63
Undermining effect, 293

V

Validity of assessments, 446
Values. *See* Moral development
Variable interval reinforcement schedules, 189
Variable ratio reinforcement schedules, 190
Verbal information as learning outcome, 349
Verbal persuasion, 263
Vertical transfer, 369
Vicarious learning, 244
Vicarious reinforcement, 258
Virtual teams, 410
Visual impairment, 161
Vygotsky's theory of cognitive development, 38–44
    human activity systems, 40
    internalization, 40–41
    zone of proximal development, 41–42

W

Wait-time I and II, 327, 395
Wechsler's theory of intelligence, 138
Withitness, 331
Working memory, encoding information in, 209. *See also* Short-term store (STS)
Work-oriented classrooms, 309
World wide web, 410

Z

Zone of proximal development (ZPD), 41–42
    intersubjectivity and, 42
    scaffolding and, 42
Z scores, 476

PHOTO CREDITS